Richard G. Rogers · Eileen M. Crimmins
Editors

# International Handbook of Adult Mortality

*Editors*
Richard G. Rogers
University of Colorado, Boulder
Population Program
Institute of Behavioral Science
Campus Box 483
Boulder Colorado 80309-0483
USA
richard.rogers@colorado.edu

Eileen M. Crimmins
University of Southern California
Davis School of Gerontology
Andrus Gerontology Center
McClintock Ave. 3715
Los Angeles, California 90089-0191
USA
crimmin@usc.edu

ISSN 1877-9204
ISBN 978-90-481-9995-2        e-ISBN 978-90-481-9996-9
DOI 10.1007/978-90-481-9996-9
Springer Dordrecht Heidelberg London New York

Library of Congress Control Number: 2011921117

© Springer Science+Business Media B.V. 2011
No part of this work may be reproduced, stored in a retrieval system, or transmitted in any form or by any means, electronic, mechanical, photocopying, microfilming, recording or otherwise, without written permission from the Publisher, with the exception of any material supplied specifically for the purpose of being entered and executed on a computer system, for exclusive use by the purchaser of the work.

Printed on acid-free paper

Springer is part of Springer Science+Business Media (www.springer.com)

# Acknowledgments

We appreciate the wonderful support provided by numerous staff, graduate students, colleagues, and organizations.

We thank the Institute of Behavioral Science, including the Population Program, and the NICHD-funded University of Colorado Population Center (grant R21 HD51146) for administrative and computing support. CU-Boulder staff members Rajshree Shrestha, Steve Graham, Tom Dickenson, and Julie Na assembled chapters, generated graphics, and assisted with correspondence. We are especially grateful to the CU-Boulder Department of Sociology, which provided funding for editing, and to Nancy Mann, who expertly edited many of the chapters. CU-Boulder graduate students Bethany Everett, Justin Denney, and Rob Kemp read through, reformatted, and commented on preliminary drafts. We would also like to thank the NIA-supported USC/UCLA Center on Biodemography and Population Health (grant P30 AG17265) for administrative support. USC students Shieva Davaria and Lu Zhang helped with editing.

We acknowledge series editor Dudley Poston, who generously provided valuable advice and helpful suggestions, and Springer editor Evelien Bakker, who is a pleasure to work with. She provided gentle nudges to move the project forward, was quick to respond to our queries, and was always quite accommodating.

The volume benefited greatly from the outstanding contributions of the authors and co-authors, whose expertise and insight generated tremendous value that is likely to define the field of adult mortality for some time to come.

And we warmly thank our respective spouses (Cindy and Dick) and children (Mary [in memoriam], Molly, and Stacy; and Matt and Molly) for their encouragement, support, and unique and enlightening perspectives.

| | |
|---|---|
| Boulder, CO | Richard G. Rogers |
| Los Angeles, CA | Eileen M. Crimmins |

# Contents

1 **Introduction** ........... 1
Richard G. Rogers and Eileen M. Crimmins

**Part I    Temporal and Spatial Trends Associated with Mortality** ... 7

2 **Historical Trends in Mortality** ........... 9
France Meslé and Jacques Vallin

3 **Adult Mortality in Europe** ........... 49
Marc Luy, Christian Wegner, and Wolfgang Lutz

4 **Adult Mortality in the Former Soviet Union** ........... 83
Michael Murphy

5 **Adult Mortality in Latin America and the Caribbean** ........... 101
Alberto Palloni and Guido Pinto-Aguirre

6 **Adult Mortality in Asia** ........... 133
Zhongwei Zhao

7 **Adult Mortality in Africa** ........... 151
Georges Reniers, Bruno Masquelier, and Patrick Gerland

8 **Global Trends in AIDS Mortality** ........... 171
John P. Bongaarts, François Pelletier, and Patrick Gerland

**Part II    Sociodemographic, Economic, Behavioral, and Psychological Determinants of Mortality** ........... 185

9 **Early Life Conditions and Later Life Mortality** ........... 187
Jennifer Karas Montez and Mark D. Hayward

10 **Age Patterns in Adult Mortality** ........... 207
Jean-Marie Robine

11 **Hispanic Paradox in Adult Mortality in the United States** ........... 227
Kyriakos S. Markides and Karl Eschbach

12 **Educational Attainment and Adult Mortality** ........... 241
Robert A. Hummer and Joseph T. Lariscy

| | | |
|---|---|---|
| 13 | Work, Occupation, Income, and Mortality | 263 |
| | Patrick M. Krueger and Sarah A. Burgard | |
| 14 | Relationships Among Health Behaviors, Health, and Mortality | 289 |
| | Christine L. Himes | |
| 15 | Discrimination, Chronic Stress, and Mortality Among Black Americans: A Life Course Framework | 311 |
| | James S. Jackson, Darrell Hudson, Kiarri Kershaw, Briana Mezuk, Jane Rafferty, and Katherine Knight Tuttle | |
| 16 | Self-Rated Health and Subjective Survival Probabilities as Predictors of Mortality | 329 |
| | Marja Jylhä | |
| 17 | Religion and Adult Mortality: Group- and Individual-Level Perspectives | 345 |
| | Ellen L. Idler | |

**Part III  Biological Risk Factors** .................... 379

| | | |
|---|---|---|
| 18 | Links Between Biomarkers and Mortality | 381 |
| | Eileen M. Crimmins and Sarinnapha Vasunilashorn | |
| 19 | Genetic Factors and Adult Mortality | 399 |
| | Kaare Christensen and James W. Vaupel | |

**Part IV  Contextual Effects on Mortality** .................... 411

| | | |
|---|---|---|
| 20 | Neighborhood Effects on Mortality | 413 |
| | Arijit Nandi and Ichiro Kawachi | |
| 21 | Health and Mortality Consequences of the Physical Environment | 441 |
| | Christopher R. Browning, Eileen E.S. Bjornstrom, and Kathleen A. Cagney | |

**Part V  Classification of Causes of Death** .................... 465

| | | |
|---|---|---|
| 22 | Coding and Classifying Causes of Death: Trends and International Differences | 467 |
| | Robert N. Anderson | |
| 23 | Avoidable Mortality | 491 |
| | Hiram Beltrán-Sánchez | |

**Part VI  Mathematical and Modeling Approaches to Mortality** .... 509

| | | |
|---|---|---|
| 24 | Model Schedules of Mortality | 511 |
| | Patrick Heuveline and Samuel J. Clark | |
| 25 | Period Versus Cohort Life Expectancy | 533 |
| | Michel Guillot | |
| 26 | Healthy Life Expectancy | 551 |
| | Carol Jagger and Jean-Marie Robine | |

**Part VII  Government Policies Designed to Affect Mortality** . . . . . . . **569**

**27 Public Policies Intended to Influence Adult Mortality** . . . . . . . . . **571**
S. Jay Olshansky and Leonard Hayflick

**28 Mortality Affected by Health Care and Public Health Policy Interventions** . . . . . . . . . . . . . . . . . . . . . . . . . . . . . . . . . . . . . . **583**
Luc Bonneux

**Conclusion** . . . . . . . . . . . . . . . . . . . . . . . . . . . . . . . . . . . . . . . . . . **609**

**Index** . . . . . . . . . . . . . . . . . . . . . . . . . . . . . . . . . . . . . . . . . . . . . **613**

# Contributors

**Robert N. Anderson** Chief of the Mortality Statistics Branch, Division of Vital Statistics, National Center for Health Statistics, Centers for Disease Control and Prevention, Hyattsville, MD 20782, USA, rca7@cdc.gov

**Hiram Beltrán-Sánchez** Postdoctoral Fellow in the Andrus Gerontology Center, University of Southern California, Los Angeles, CA 90089, USA, beltrans@usc.edu

**Eileen E.S. Bjornstrom** Assistant Professor of Sociology, University of Missouri, Columbia, MO 65201, USA, bjornstrome@missouri.edu

**John P. Bongaarts** Vice President and Distinguished Scholar of the Population Council, New York, NY 10017, USA, jbongaarts@popcouncil.org

**Luc Bonneux** Netherlands Interdisciplinary Demographic Institute, The Hague, The Netherlands, bonneux@nidi.nl

**Christopher R. Browning** Professor of Sociology, The Ohio State University, Columbus, OH 43210, USA, browning.90@osu.edu

**Sarah A. Burgard** Assistant Professor of Sociology, Joint Assistant Professor of Epidemiology, Assistant Research Scientist, Population Studies Center, University of Michigan, Ann Arbor, MI 48109, USA, burgards@umich.edu

**Kathleen A. Cagney** Associate Professor in the Departments of Health Studies, Sociology, and Comparative Human Development, and Director of the Population Research Center, University of Chicago, Chicago, IL 60637, USA, kacagney@uchicago.edu

**Kaare Christensen** Director of The Danish Twin Registry and the Danish Aging Research Center, Institute of Public Health, University of Southern Denmark, Odense DK-5000, Denmark, kchristensen@health.sdu.dk

**Samuel J. Clark** Assistant Professor of Sociology, and a Research Affiliate of the Center for Studies in Demography and Ecology, University of Washington, Seattle, WA 98195, USA, work@samclark.net

**Eileen M. Crimmins** AARP Professor of Gerontology in the Davis School of Gerontology, University of Southern California, Los Angeles, CA 90089, USA, crimmin@usc.edu

**Karl Eschbach** Professor of Medicine, and Director of Population Research, Division of Geriatrics in Internal Medicine, University of Texas Medical Branch, Galveston, TX 77552, USA, kaeschba@utmb.edu

**Patrick Gerland** Population Affairs Officer, Population Policy Section, Population Division, United Nations, New York, NY 10017, USA, gerland@un.org

**Michel Guillot** Associate Professor of Sociology and the Population Studies Center, University of Pennsylvania, Philadelphia, PA 19104, USA, miguillo@sas.upenn.edu

**Leonard Hayflick** Professor of Anatomy, University of California, San Francisco, CA 94143, USA

**Mark D. Hayward** Professor of Sociology, and Director of the Population Research Center, University of Texas, Austin, TX 78712, USA, mhayward@prc.utexas.edu

**Patrick Heuveline** Professor of Sociology and a Research Affiliate of the California Center for Population Research, University of California, Los Angeles, CA 90077, USA, Heuveline@Soc.ucla.edu

**Christine L. Himes** Maxwell Professor of Sociology and Director of the Center for Policy Research, Syracuse University, Syracuse, NY 13244, USA, clhimes@syr.edu

**Darrell Hudson** Kellogg Health Scholar at the Center on Social Disparities in Health, Department of Family and Community Medicine, University of California, San Francisco, CA 94143, USA, HudsonD@fcm.usf.edu

**Robert A. Hummer** Professor of Sociology and Research Associate in the Population Research Center, University of Texas, Austin, TX 78712, USA, rhummer@prc.utexas.edu

**Ellen L. Idler** Professor of Sociology and Rollins School of Public Health, Emory University, Atlanta, GA, 30322, USA, eidler@emory.edu

**James S. Jackson** Director and Research Professor of the Institute for Social Research, and the Daniel Katz Distinguished University Professor of Psychology, Institute for Social Research, University of Michigan, Ann Arbor, MI 48109, USA, jamessj@umich.edu

**Carol Jagger** AXA Professor of Epidemiology of Ageing, Institute for Ageing and Health, Newcastle University, Newcastle upon Tyne, UK, carol.jagger@ncl.ac.uk

**Marja Jylhä** Professor of Gerontology, School of Health Sciences, University of Tampere, Tampere, Finland, Marja.Jylha@uta.fi

**Ichiro Kawachi** Chair of the Department of Society, Human Development, and Health, Harvard School of Public Health; Professor of Social Epidemiology, Harvard School of Public Health, Harvard University, Boston, MA 02115, USA, ikawachi@hsph.harvard.edu

**Kiarri Kershaw** Ph.D. student in the Center for Social Epidemiology and Population Health, Institute for Social Research, University of Michigan, Ann Arbor, MI 48109, USA, k-kershaw@northwestern.edu

**Patrick M. Krueger** Assistant Professor in the Department of Sociology and the Department of Health and Behavioral Sciences, University of Colorado-Denver, Denver, CO 80217, USA, Patrick.Krueger@ucdenver.edu

**Joseph T. Lariscy** Ph.D. student in the Department of Sociology and the Population Research Center, University of Texas, Austin, TX 78712, USA

**Wolfgang Lutz** Director of the Vienna Institute of Demography, Austrian Academy of Sciences, 1040 Vienna, Austria; Leader of the World Population Program, International Institute for Applied Systems Analysis, A-2361 Laxenburg, Austria; Professor at the WU–Vienna, University of Economics and Business, 1090 Vienna, Austria, wolfgang.lutz@oeaw.ac.at

**Marc Luy** Research Group Leader at the Vienna Institute of Demography, Austrian Academy of Sciences, Wohllebengasse 12-14, 1040 Vienna, Austria, mail@marcluy.eu

**Kyriakos S. Markides** Annie and John Gnitzinger Distinguished Professor of Aging Studies and Director of the Division of Sociomedical Sciences in Preventive Medicine and Community Health, University of Texas Medical Branch, Galveston, TX 77555-1156, USA, kmarkide@UTMB.edu

**Bruno Masquelier** Researcher at the Centre de Recherches en Démographie et Sociétés, Université Catholique de Louvain, Louvain, Belgium, Bruno.Masquelier@uclouvain.be

**France Meslé** Directrice de recherche at the Institut national d'études démographiques, Research Unit (Mortality, Health, Epidemiology), 133 Boulevard Davout, 75020 Paris, France, mesle@ined.fr

**Briana Mezuk** Assistant Professor in the Department of Epidemiology and Community Health, Virginia Commonwealth University, Richmond, VA 23250, USA, bmezuk@vcu.edu

**Jennifer Karas Montez** Ph.D. student in Department of Sociology and the Population Research Center, University of Texas, Austin, TX 78712, USA, jennkaras@prc.utexas.edu

**Michael Murphy** Professor of Demography, London School of Economics, 7512 London, UK, M.Murphy@lse.ac.uk

**Arijit Nandi** Assistant Professor in the Institute for Health and Social Policy & the Department of Epidemiology, Biostatistics, and Occupational Health, McGill University, Montreal, QC Canada, arijit.nandi@mcgill.ca

**S. Jay Olshansky** Professor in the School of Public Health, Division of Epidemiology and Biostatistics, School of Public Health, University of Illinois, Chicago, IL 60612, USA, sjayo@uic.edu

**Alberto Palloni** Professor of Sociology, Center for Demography and Ecology, University of Wisconsin, Madison, WI 53706, USA, palloni@ssc.wisc.edu

**François Pelletier** Chief of the Mortality Section, United Nations Population Division, New York, NY 10017, USA, pelletierf@un.org

**Guido Pinto-Aguirre** Social Scientist, Futures Group, Washington, DC 20006, USA, GPinto@futuresgroup.com

**Jane Rafferty** Research Associate in the School of Social Work and Institute for Social Research, University of Michigan, Ann Arbor, MI 48106, USA, jraffrty@umich.edu

**Georges Reniers** Assistant Professor of Sociology and Office of Population Research, Princeton University, Princeton, NJ 08544, USA, greniers@princeton.edu

**Jean-Marie Robine** Researcher at the Institut National de la Santé et de la Recherche Médicale, INSERM, Health & Demographie, Centre de Recherche en Cancérologie, Montpellier, France, robine@valdorel.fnclcc.fr

**Richard G. Rogers** Professor of Sociology and Director of the Population Program, Institute of Behavioral Science, University of Colorado, Boulder, CO 80309-0483, USA, richard.rogers@colorado.edu

**Katherine Knight Tuttle** Project Director of IPSOS Marketing, Cincinnati, Ohio, USA, kati.tuttle@gmail.com

**Jacques Vallin** Directeur de recherche at the Institut national d'études démographiques, Research Unit (Mortality, Health, Epidemiology), 133 Boulevard Davout, 75020 Paris, France, vallin@ined.fr

**Sarinnapha Vasunilashorn** Postdoctoral Fellow, Office of Population Research, Princeton University, 263 Wallace Hall, Princeton, NJ 08544, USA, svaunil@princeton.edu

**James W. Vaupel** Director of the Max Planck Institute for Demographic Research, Rostock D-18055, Germany, JWV@demogr.mpg.de

**Christian Wegner** Research Assistant at the Vienna Institute of Demography, Austrian Academy of Sciences, Wohllebengasse 12-14, 1040 Vienna, Austria, christian.wegner@oeaw.ac.at

**Zhongwei Zhao** Professor in the Australian Demographic and Social Research Institute, Australian National University, Canberra, Australia, zhongwei.zhao@anu.edu.au

# Chapter 1
# Introduction

Richard G. Rogers and Eileen M. Crimmins

Remarkable gains in life expectancy stand out as one of the most important accomplishments of the twentieth century. Individuals in more developed countries (MDCs) can expect to live longer now than ever before. What is perhaps more surprising is that life expectancy in some countries has not increased in recent years, and in some places, there have been declines. This is an exciting time for research on adult mortality because of unprecedented substantive, theoretical, methodological, data, and statistical developments and insights.

The study of mortality was once confined to demographers and epidemiologists examining age-, sex-, and sometimes race/ethnic-specific differences from vital registration systems. Now mortality analysis involves increasingly new and innovative data, models, and methods with researchers from multidisciplinary fields. Epidemiologists have clarified the importance of examining a wide range of behaviors to identify the health risks that lead to mortality. Psychologists and social psychologists have highlighted the influence of social networks and support, and psychological traits and attributes as buffers and risks for individual health. Economists have sharpened thinking about socioeconomic processes and health outcomes. The integration of medical and biological thinking has helped to reveal the pathways through which social, psychological, economic, and demographic variables work individually and in combination to affect mortality risk and also to point out the potential for intervention in this process.

Changes in mortality affect individuals and social institutions, including the age and sex structure of the population, family composition and structure, and labor-force participation and composition. Understanding the causes and consequences of mortality trends is crucial because they affect such factors as determining appropriate public health intervention; future spending for health care; social welfare spending, including Social Security; and allocating resources to basic and applied research.

This is an excellent time to synthesize the wealth of mortality information available, clearly articulate the central findings to-date, identify the most appropriate datasets and methods currently available, and illuminate the central research questions. Identifying these questions will indicate the appropriate research agenda through which we can contribute to further insight into mortality, which will ultimately result in additional increases in life expectancy.

Overall, many MDCs and less developed countries (LDCs) have experienced declines in mortality and increases in life expectancy over time. Over the long term this has been due, in part, to the epidemiologic transition, whereas causes of death change from a preponderance of deaths due to infectious and parasitic diseases to deaths due to chronic and degenerative diseases. Meslé and Vallin (Chapter 2) convincingly demonstrate that although over time there have been substantial life-expectancy gains for many countries—both MDCs and LDCs—we have started to observe some divergence in life expectancies, even in MDCs. Life expectancy has continued to increase in countries like Japan and France, while there has been some

R.G. Rogers (✉)
Department of Sociology and Population Program, IBS, University of Colorado, Boulder, CO 80309-0483, USA
e-mail: richard.rogers@colorado.edu

stagnation in countries like the United States and the Netherlands (Crimmins et al. 2010).

Mortality varies by region of the world, with substantial variations in Europe, the Former Soviet Union, Latin America and the Caribbean, Asia, and Africa (Chapters 3–7). But even within each of these regions, there are substantial differences. Luy, Wegner, and Lutz (Chapter 3) document the relatively favorable health situation in Western and Central Europe compared to Eastern Europe. Murphy (Chapter 4) shows that mortality rates in Russia, Ukraine, and the United States were similar in the mid-1960s, but that now, adult mortality in the former Soviet Union is similar to the level of 50 years ago, well below that of Western industrialized counties.

Palloni and Pinto-Aguirre (Chapter 5) highlight the heretofore data scarcity for examining mortality trends for Latin American and the Caribbean (LAC) countries. They have provided an important demographic service by presenting detailed historical and contemporary mortality trends by age and cause of death for LAC countries. They devise a useful classification of laggards and forerunners—including Argentina, Chile, Costa Rica, Cuba, Panama, and Uruguay, which enjoy exceptionally high and increasing life expectancies. For examples, female life expectancy at age five is 73.0 in Argentina (in 1996), 75.5 in Costa Rica (in 1992), and 74.0 in Panama (in 1995).

Previous conflicts, including world wars, have had devastating effects on countries and long-term effects on such demographic factors as the age and sex structure. But in many instances, short term wars have short-term mortality consequences, as illustrated for Cambodia, Rwanda, and Somalia (see Meslé and Vallin, Chapter 2). Moreover, some countries—including El Salvador, Guatemala, and Colombia—have experienced relatively high mortality, especially among males, due to external causes of death that were exacerbated by war and political and economic turmoil (Palloni and Pinto-Aguirre, Chapter 5).

As Zhao (Chapter 6) stresses, it is crucial to include detailed information and analysis about mortality trends in Asia; because the region is so populous, it has an enormous impact on the rest of the world. And Asian countries vary widely in life expectancy levels and trends, and in sex differences in life expectancy. For example, Asia may now include the two life-expectancy extremes, with the people of Afghanistan experiencing the lowest life expectancy in the world, at 44 years, and the Japanese experiencing the highest life expectancy ever achieved in the world, at 83 years.

There are many ready explanations for Japan's high life expectancy, including healthy diets, exercise, avoidance of the AIDS epidemic, health care aimed at prevention as well as treatment, ethnic homogeneity, a reverence for the elderly, modest income inequality, reasonably high average incomes, strong sense of family, relatively low unemployment, and nationalized health insurance. But there are also reasons to expect lower life expectancies, including stressful and demanding jobs, relatively low equality among women, increasing rates of unemployment, and high rates of some risky behaviors, particularly smoking.

Unfortunately, as Reniers, Masquelier, and Gerland (Chapter 7) articulate, one quarter of the countries around the world have experienced mortality reversals over the last two decades due to conflict, economic crises, problems with health care systems, and the deleterious effects of HIV/AIDS. In one decade, some southern African countries have eliminated gains that took 40 years to achieve. Military and political conflicts have contributed to increased mortality in many countries throughout the world, including Afghanistan, Angola, Chad, the Democratic Republic of Congo, El Salvador, Iraq, Liberia, Rwanda, Sierra Leone, and Somalia (Reniers, Masquelier, and Gerland, Chapter 7).

Many countries have experienced substantial mortality improvements due in part to improved treatment of such degenerative diseases as cancer and heart disease. But many countries are grappling with the tremendous effects of AIDS mortality. Two million individuals died of AIDS in 2007. And the number of AIDS deaths will continue into the future because of the large number of individuals—33 million—who are currently infected with HIV (Bongaarts, Pelletier, and Gerland, Chapter 8).

Understanding why some people live substantially longer than others and how this likelihood is related to one's social, economic, behavioral, psychological, and demographic characteristics has been a focus of significant research in recent years. Age has a powerful effect on mortality (Robine, Chapter 10), as does race/ethnicity (Markides and Eschbach, Chapter 11). In MDCs, the age of death has gotten older and older and there has been substantial increase in survival at even the oldest ages (Robine, Chapter 10). Racial differences in mortality are of interest in many countries because they suggest different life circumstances and treatment. The high mortality of the U.S. black population up to the oldest ages is well known. Jackson and co-authors (Chapter 15) suggest that the race crossover in mortality rates observed in old age is a product of life course differences in rates of mortality beginning at conception. On the other hand, the relatively low mortality of Hispanics in the United States is known as the "Hispanic Paradox" (Markides and Eschbach, Chapter 11).

Socioeconomic inequalities that result in early death represent perhaps the single greatest form of social disparity. And early life conditions can have substantial effects on mortality in later years (Montez and Hayward, Chapter 9). Detrimental early life conditions can affect overall mortality due to infectious diseases, heart disease, cerebrovascular disease, and some cancers. Early life conditions related to parental socioeconomic status (SES) include nutrition; social conditions; neighborhood environment; housing condition and structure; pathogen exposure; psychosocial stressors; hygiene; health behaviors; and family stress, conflict, abuse, and emotional support.

SES dynamics throughout the life course (e.g., bouts of underemployment and unemployment, poverty, and low occupational status) contribute to higher risk of death throughout adulthood. Hummer and Lariscy (Chapter 12) demonstrate that educational attainment has a special place in mortality research, and is considered a fundamental cause of health and longevity (Link & Phelan 1995; Phelan et al. 2004). Education contributes to better health and longer life through multiple avenues, including higher rates of employment, higher earnings, healthier behaviors, social psychological resources (for example, a greater sense of personal control), increased social networks, and reduced stress. Educational attainment shows a graded relationship between years of education and mortality. Further, even at advanced educational levels (for example, at 17 or more years), education reduces mortality risk.

Other central SES measures include work, occupation, and income (Krueger and Burgard, Chapter 13). There is a long-term relationship between income, wealth, and mortality that has persisted in MDCs since the end of the nineteenth century. Generally, the relations between work, occupation, income, and mortality are stronger for men than women, possibly because of men's longer historical ties and attachments to the labor force (Krueger and Burgard, Chapter 13). Individuals enjoy longer lives if they are employed rather than unemployed, and employed full rather than part time. Furthermore, compared to individuals with lower occupational scores, those with higher scores enjoy higher life expectancies. These relations persist for adults, both sexes, and all adult ages.

Individuals who eat nutritionally balanced diets in moderation, exercise, abstain from drug abuse, and avoid tobacco live longer lives that those who engage in one or more risky behaviors. Clustered risky behaviors—such as excessive consumption of alcohol and calorie-rich diets and sedentary lives—are generally worse than one isolated risky behavior that is buffered by other healthy behaviors. Risky behaviors are increasing in importance in their influence on mortality, in part because many environmental factors (including infectious diseases) are better controlled, especially in MDCs.

Cigarette smoking is the single-most preventable cause of death in the developed world and a major factor in LDCs (see Himes, Chapter 14). It is especially dangerous because it is addictive, accumulates over time, clusters with other risky behavior, places individuals "at risk of risks" (Link & Phelan 1995), and affects a large number of the body's organs. Smoking increases the risk of numerous causes of death, including heart disease, cerebrovascular disease, lower respiratory infections, chronic obstructive pulmonary disease, and numerous cancers, including cancer of the trachea, bronchus, and lung (see Himes, Chapter 14). Even though smoking prevalence rates have declined, and even with strong admonitions against smoking, people continue to smoke. And many subpopulations are especially prone to smoke, including adolescents and young adults, women, the homeless, the less educated, and the unemployed (Bonneux, Chapter 28).

Alcohol consumption and mortality display a J-shaped relationship, with light to moderate consumption showing lower risks of death than abstention or excessive consumption. Light to moderate consumption can reduce the risk of cardiovascular disease, the major cause of death. Heavy alcohol consumption is also related to increased risk of cardiovascular disease and to accidents, suicides, homicides, and some cancers (of the mouth, esophagus, stomach, colon, liver, and breast; Himes Chapter 14). Alcohol can have both immediate (through alcohol poisoning, accidents, and other external causes, including suicides and homicides) and long-term (through cirrhosis of the liver and chronic alcoholism) effects on mortality (see Guillot's Chapter 25). Russian mortality has been closely tied to alcohol consumption and policy, with relatively high consumption during Breshenev, declines during the anti-alcohol campaign of Gorbachev, and increases after Gorbachev and the relaxation or elimination of some of the previous anti-alcohol restrictions (Mesle and Vallin, Chapter 2). Intriguingly, education is directly related to alcohol consumption, but inversely related to other risky health behaviors (Himes, Chapter 14).

Exercise and diet contribute to fitness and low percentages of body fat. Physical activity contributes to longer lives through increased muscle mass, strength, endurance, and cardiovascular fitness. The Mediterranean diet, which includes high consumption of fruits and vegetables, as well as legumes, has been touted as healthy and can help to maintain a normal body mass. Obesity and overweight can be assessed through a variety of measures, including body mass index (BMI), waist circumference, and hip-to-waist ratios (Himes, Chapter 14). Obesity generally contributes to higher risks of disability, functional limitation, and mortality, although perhaps at extreme levels of obesity. Increasing rates of obesity in the United States and in other countries may thwart if not reverse future gains in life expectancy (Himes, Chapter 14). In addition to pursuing health behaviors, many researchers have explored multiple avenues to reduce mortality that theoretically could have been avoided through better medical care.

Adverse economic and social events, including chronic stress and discrimination, contribute to mortality (Jackson and colleagues, Chapter 15). Although health behaviors are often considered individual choices, there are structural impediments and constrains that can contribute to individuals' engagement in detrimental health behaviors as a way to cope, self-medicate, and capture brief moments of pleasure and enjoyment.

Individuals have a reasonably good sense of their overall health and likely longevity, as measured through self-rated health (SRH) and subjective survival probabilities (Jylhä, Chapter 16). Indeed, Jylhä shows that individuals can reflect on their own social support networks and health behaviors, and use interoceptive processes to assess their overall body, including their physical conditions, health conditions, feelings, and emotions. Such assessments may be difficult to fully convey to doctors and interviewers, but may be much easier to summarize into SRH measures.

Although risky behaviors are major mortality culprits, some behaviors promote good health and are linked to lower mortality. Idler (Chapter 17) provides a superb review of the research on religion and mortality. Religion can regulate and constrain risky behaviors such as tobacco consumption. Religion has been associated with lower rates of hypertension, diabetes, and cholesterol. Many religious groups, including the Amish, Seventh Day Adventists, Mormons, and Jews can expect higher survival than the general population because they engage in fewer risky behaviors. For example, Seventh Day Adventists and Mormons eschew overeating, caffeine, nicotine, and alcohol. Idler identifies an intriguing paradox: because of the U-shaped relationship between alcohol consumption and mortality, individuals of religious groups who champion abstention may miss the benefits of light to moderate drinking. Of course, these groups also avoid the hazards of heavy drinking. Religion not only regulates risky behavior but also provides social integration. Thus, individuals who are more tied to religion have a sense of belonging, community, and social support. Religion, a fundamental social institution, can provide support through multiple functions, including social, emotional, functional, financial, and instrumental support. Nevertheless, there may also be negative aspects to religion: it can ostracize individuals, impose severe sanctions, encourage practices that may conflict with medical care, restrict behavior, limit health-seeking behavior in favor of "bearing the burden," and create psychological distress.

There are a number of biological and physiological factors that affect mortality. Some of these indicate pathways through which the sociodemographic, economic, behavioral, and psychological factors discussed above get under the skin to affect mortality (Crimmins and Vasunilashorn, Chapter 18). We are only beginning to identify the role of specific genetic factors on mortality, but we do know that about a quarter of the variance in adult life span in contemporary Western populations can be explained by genetic factors, and that the influence is likely to be larger for exceptionally long survival and generally of little importance for early adult death (Christensen and Vaupel, Chapter 19).

There has been a renewed interest in the context in which people live and die, which has been reflected in studies of neighborhood effects and social capital. Moreover, it is now possible to link multiple datasets in unique ways, including linkages to the National Death Index. Thus, datasets that previously were not linked to mortality are becomingly increasingly useful for mortality research. Researchers are collecting innovative data, including information about such cultural factors as religious involvement, as well as longitudinal data and genetic information. Furthermore, many data collection efforts are being conducted throughout a number of MDCs and LDCs, which vastly increases the opportunities for international comparisons.

The physical environment, including the neighborhood, is an understudied but important area of mortality research. Such physical factors as housing (including vacant and substandard housing), retail outlets (including grocery and liquor stores), industry, transportation, and parks and recreational facilities can influence such individual factors as risky behaviors (including smoking and drug and alcohol abuse), emotional health (including stress, depression, energy, and hostility), and criminal acts (see Nandi and Kawachi, Chapter 20, and Browning, Bjornstrom and Cagney, Chapter 21). Furthermore, such natural hazards as floods, hurricanes, tornadoes, and fires can result in forced migration, infectious diseases, malnutrition, and limited water, which can further contribute to increased risk of disease, disability, and death. Chapter 20 focuses on the importance of conducing multilevel analyses that combine the effects of individual- and aggregate-level factors, and emphasizes the strong associations between neighborhood characteristics and mortality, but also makes clear the difficulty in determining causal relationships.

Results are driven in part by data. The United National Population Division (UN Population Division) and the World Health Organization (WHO) are two primary data sources for international mortality trends and comparisons. The UN and WHO data use different methods and therefore arrive at slightly different results, which mean that some results and conclusions are partly data driven. We should note that UN data have been made available to the authors of Chapters 7 and 8.

Over time, there have been increasing efforts to provide greater comparability in vital statistics information over time and space (see Anderson, Chapter 22).

Nevertheless, there may be slight differences across countries that affect international comparisons. For instance, differences in cause of death over time or space may be due in part to variations in the way causes of death are coded.

Avoidable mortality is a concept with theoretical appeal, although Beltran-Sanchez clarifies the difficulty in operationalizing this idea (Beltrán-Sánchez, Chapter 23). Nevertheless, avoidable mortality provides a potential approach to determining how well the medical system prevents untimely deaths, or deaths that could have been prevented with appropriate medical care.

Understanding the development of model schedules of mortality and their role in providing assessment of mortality where vital statistics are not well developed is important to mortality analysis in large parts of the world. Heuveline and Clark (Chapter 24) provide a good primer on a variety of approaches to developing model life tables. And they vividly underscore the importance of developing solid models through their examples of executions in Cambodia and the effects of HIV/AIDS on age-specific mortality from the Agincourt Study Population in South Africa.

Whereas life expectancy is one of the most important measures of mortality, it is informative to distinguish between period and cohort life expectancy, as well as tempo effects in mortality, a relatively new concept that may provide additional insight into changes in life expectancy over time and by country. Guillot (Chapter 25) adeptly shows that our understanding and interpretation of life-expectancy trends are predicated in part by the data and measures we employ.

Multistate models have been developed to incorporate indicators of morbidity as well as mortality into summary measures. These models show the implications of change and differences in life expectancy on population health (Jagger and Robine, Chapter 26). Hazards models, once uncommon, are now regularly used to show mortality differentials. And researchers are refining such models to examine time varying covariates, as well as life tables with covariates.

The last century has witnessed phenomenal public health improvements, including vaccinations, motor-vehicle and road safety, safer workplaces, control of infectious diseases, declines in deaths from coronary heart disease and stroke, safer foods, healthier mothers and babies, and recognition of tobacco use as a health hazard (Centers for Disease Control 1999). Advances in medicine have contributed to additional gains in life expectancy. Some of the most promising medical technologies either newly available or on the horizon include intraventricular cardioverter defibrillators, left ventricular assist devices, telomerase inhibitors, pacemakers to control arterial fibrillation, cancer vaccines, anti-angiogenesis, treatment of acute stroke, prevention of Alzheimer's disease, prevention of diabetes, and compounds that extend the life span (Goldman et al. 2005). Olshansky and Hayflick (Chapter 27) address the question of whether public policies are ready to promote life extension as well as disease avoidance and treatment.

Bonneux (Chapter 28) lends terrific insight into the effects of past health behaviors, advancements in public health, medical technology, and government policies on trends in life expectancies and overall and cause-specific mortality. The last several decades have ushered in new improvements in medical technology and health care, which can extend lives. The time from diagnosis to death and the stage of diagnosis of conditions are additional valuable indicators in understanding the process leading to death. How these stages of disease change over time and how they are affected by technological and medical developments is on great consequence.

Bonneux (Chapter 28) aids in our understanding of why ischemic heart disease is high among individuals in MDCs, but stroke is more common among Asians and individuals in rural Africa. He also discusses how MDCs have achieved substantial declines in coronary heart disease mortality through reductions in cholesterol and systolic blood pressure. Some of these reductions have come about through reductions in smoking, drug treatments, including antihypertensive drugs, cholesterol-lowering drugs, and statins (see Ford et al. 2007).

Knowledge about the detrimental effects of unhealthy behaviors is not new. German researchers in the Third Reich empirically demonstrated the risks of smoking many decades before the pernicious effects of smoking were widely known and accepted (Bonneux, Chapter 28). Thus, the Nazis mounted strong anti-smoking campaigns to ensure German health. The 1964 US Surgeon General's Report (U.S. Surgeon General's Advisory Committee on Smoking and Health 1964) is commonly considered the turning point of the medical literature on smoking, especially within the United States. Similar reports were published in other countries, including England. Nevertheless, the ill effects of smoking were selectively published in earlier periods, but were not given widespread credence (see Pearl 1938).

Thus, this volume documents trends and patterns in mortality over time and space. It also sets mortality within a historical, social, and demographic context. Enjoy the following chapters, which are chockfull of interesting and important tidbits of information.

# References

Centers for Disease Control. 1999. "Ten Great Public Health Achievements in the 20th Century." Office of Enterprise Communication, CDC, Atlanta, GA. *Morbidity and Mortality Weekly Report* (http://www.cdc.gov/media/tengpha.htm). A 2-page summary article is available at (http://www.cdc.gov/mmwr/preview/mmwrhtml/00056796.htm).

Crimmins, E.M., S.A. Preston, and B. Cohen (Eds.). 2010. *International Differences in Mortality at Older Ages: Dimensions and Sources*. The National Academies Press: Washington, DC.

Ford, E.S., U.A. Ajani, J.B. Croft, J.A. Critchley, D.R. Labarthe, T.E. Kottke, W.H. Giles, and S. Capewell. 2007. "Explaining the Decrease in U.S. Deaths from Coronary Disease, 1980–2000." *New England Journal of Medicine* 356(23):2388–98.

Goldman, D.P., B. Shang, J. Bhattacharya, A.M. Garber, M. Hurd, G.F. Youce, D.N. Lakdawalla, C. Panis, and P.G. Shekelle. 2005. "Consequences of Health Trends and Medical Innovation for the Future Elderly: When Demographic Trends Temper the Optimism of Biomedical Advances, How Will Tomorrow's Elderly Fare." *Health Affairs*. Web exclusive. September. Pages R5–R17.

Link, B.G. and J.C. Phelan. 1995. "Social Conditions as Fundamental Causes of Disease." *Journal of Health and Social Behavior* Extra Issue:80–94.

Pearl, R. 1938. "Tobacco Smoking and Longevity." *Science* 87:216–17.

Phelan, J.C., B.G. Link, A. Diez-Roux, I. Kawachi, and B. Levin. 2004. "'Fundamental Causes' of Social Inequalities in Mortality: A Test of the Theory." *Journal of Health and Social Behavior* 45(3):265–85.

U.S. Surgeon General's Advisory Committee on Smoking and Health. 1964. Smoking and Health: Report of the Advisory Committee to the Surgeon General of the Public Health Service. USGPO: Washington, DC.

# Part I
# Temporal and Spatial Trends Associated with Mortality

# Chapter 2

# Historical Trends in Mortality

France Meslé and Jacques Vallin

## Introduction

A large gap in health conditions has prevailed around the world for many decades. According to the United Nations estimates, in 2005–2010 life expectancy at birth ranged from less than 45 years in Afghanistan and Zimbabwe to more than 80 in Japan, Australia, and France (United Nations [UN] 2009). About the same gap existed in the 1950s (from 30 to 75 years); however, the distribution of population according to life expectancy at birth has changed markedly. Most of the world's population enjoys much more favorable health conditions than 50 years ago and most of the developing world has almost caught up to the developed world (Fig. 2.1). This results from a strong convergence between most "less developed countries" (LDCs) and most "more developed countries" (MDCs). However, the convergence is far from universal; among both groups of countries, some lag behind—among the LDCs, Sub-Saharan Africa, and among the MDCs, Eastern Europe (including Russia). In fact, not only is the diversity large around the world and increasing within both LDC and MDC groups, but not all national life expectancies have increased, as some have stagnated or even decreased. It is impossible to understand current diversity without revisiting the past to highlight the different trends in mortality by age and cause.

In the most advanced countries, life expectancy has progressed continuously for three centuries, but the reasons for this progress have changed markedly over time. Mainly driven by the decrease in infant and child mortality until World War II (WWII), it now depends exclusively on the decline in adult mortality at older and older ages, as is shown in the example of France (Fig. 2.2). This evolution has completely changed expectations about death. In the past, death frequently occurred at young ages and could occur at any time along the life cycle. Nowadays, most deaths are concentrated at very high ages and any premature death is considered unacceptable. Of course, such a change in the age structure of mortality is also related to fundamental changes in cause-of-death structure.

The first part of this chapter is devoted to an analysis of trends in life expectancy at birth across countries since the mid-eighteenth century. Successive divergence–convergence cycles can be identified that explain the diversity in current life expectancy. The second part focuses on mortality at different adult ages where trends may depend on varying factors.

## Trends in Life Expectancy at Birth

Figure 2.3 shows all available trends in national life expectancy. To improve readability, it separates MDCs (graph A) and LDCs (Graph B) because these sets of countries are quite different in both trends and data quality. On the left, trajectories in MDCs, relying on long historical series of high-quality data, show a period of divergence during the nineteenth century (from 1820 to about 1880), then a period of strong convergence during the first part of the twentieth century (from the 1880s to the 1960s), and finally a new period of divergence after the mid-1960s. For LDCs (right

F. Meslé (✉)
Institut national d'études démographiques, Research Unit (Mortality, Health, Epidemiology), 133 Boulevard Davout, 75020 Paris, France
e-mail: mesle@ined.fr

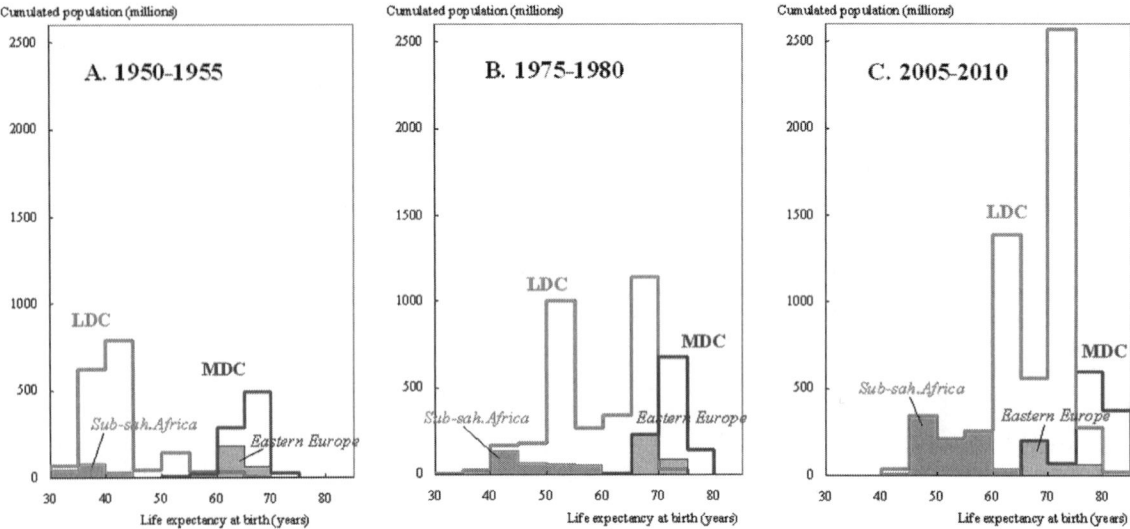

**Fig. 2.1** Cumulative country populations according to their level of life expectancy (both sexes) in 1950–1955, 1975–1980, and 2005–2010. For each period, countries are ranked according to their life expectancy (both sexes) by 5-year ranges and their populations are cumulated in each range. *Grey* and *black bold lines* show the population distribution of MDCs and LDCs separately by life expectancy while, in both groups of countries, *filled areas* show the specific cases of Sub-Saharan Africa (*light grey*) and Eastern Europe (*dark grey*). In 1950–1955 (**Graph A**), LDCs and MDCs formed two clearly separate and distant groups, while Sub-Saharan Africa and Eastern Europe were not isolated in the left part of each distribution; in 2005–2010 (**Graph C**), most LDCs' populations had caught up with those of MDCs, but Sub-Saharan Africa and Eastern Europe formed distinct subgroups with the lowest life expectancies of LDCs and MDCs respectively. Source: Meslé and Vallin (2002) updated

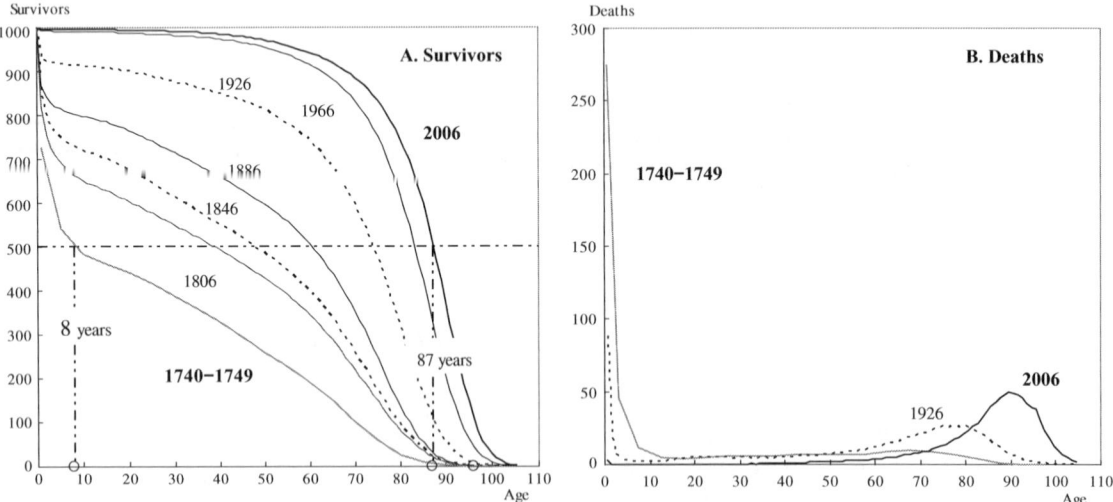

**Fig. 2.2** Change in the French female survival curve since 1750, and concentration of deaths at older ages. The two graphs differently represent secular change in the age structure of mortality. On the *left* (**Graph A**), survival curves show the decline by age in the survivors in a birth cohort. Over time, there are increases in the proportion surviving to a given age. In 1740–1749, almost 30% of the cohort died before age 1 and 50% before age 8. Thus, the curve fell very sharply at the youngest ages and then declined more progressively. In 2006, the proportion of survivors remained higher than 90% until age 70, with 50% still alive at age 87, and then dropped quite abruptly. The corresponding distributions of deaths by age (**Graph B**) displayed on the *right* show radical change: in the mid-eighteenth century, most deaths occurred at the youngest ages, while in 2006 they occurred around age 90. Source: Blayo (1975), Vallin and Meslé (2001a) updated

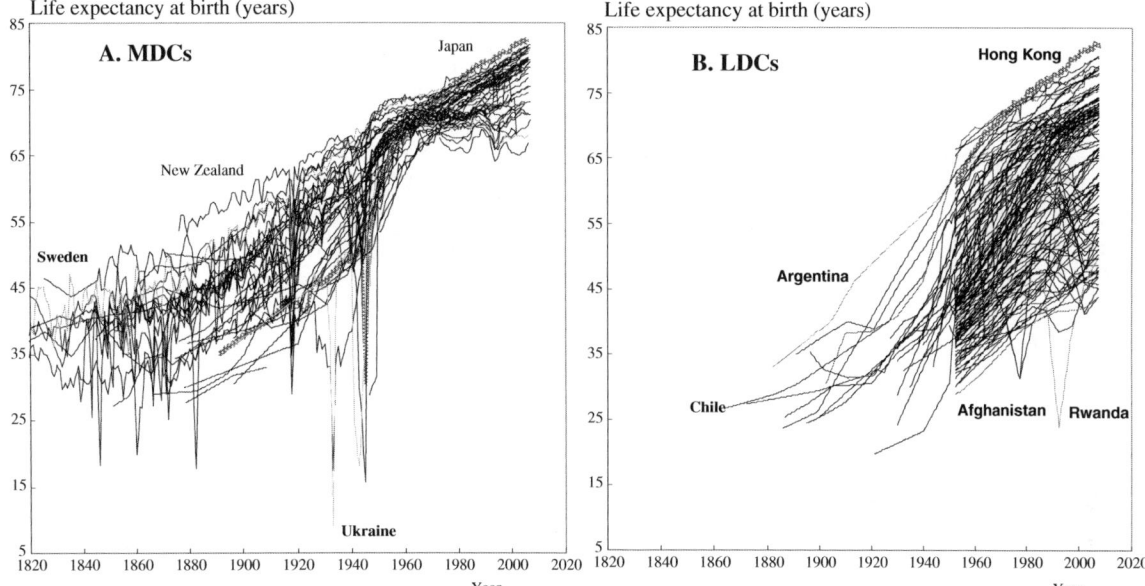

**Fig. 2.3** Historical trends in life expectancy (both sexes) of each country according to available data, since 1820. While each line corresponds to a national life-expectancy trajectory, the graphs are not drawn for readability of individual lines, but to display the observed diversity. Only a few *lines* are labelled to emphasize representative cases. Source: HMD, UN (2009); special database prepared for Vallin and Meslé (2009); various national statistical publications

graph) available data for the period before WWII are very rare. For the period since 1950, the graph relies on UN estimates systematically published for each country, the reliability of which is quite variable. The graph provides a valuable overview of the whole range of trajectories. Superimposing the two graphs would obscure the features of the MDC trajectories and would simply show a general process of divergence. Even shown separately, the LDC graph hides contradictory movements of divergence and convergence within this very heterogeneous group of countries.

Figure 2.4 provides a clearer view of the world range of diversity in historical change by showing the trajectories of both the best and the worst annual performers in life expectancy within MDCs and LDCs, respectively. Comparing the MDC best to the LDC worst performers gives the full world range. This clearly shows initial divergence, until the 1920s, and then a beginning of convergence. But comparing the best MDC performers to those of LDCs makes evident the radical convergence of the best LDCs' and MDCs' experiences, while, in contrast, the worst performers indicate a radical divergence, in spite of the recent negative trends among MDCs (due entirely to Eastern European countries).

In fact, the truth lies somewhere between the great complexity that makes Fig. 2.3 almost unreadable and the apparent simplicity of Fig. 2.4. Various authors have tried to theoretically categorize the different stages of health improvement. Abdel Omran's 1971 theory of "epidemiologic transition" was the first attempt to account for the extraordinary advances in healthcare made in industrialized countries since the eighteenth century. According to Omran, all societies experience three "ages" in the process of modernization: the "age of pestilence and famine," during which mortality is high and fluctuating, with an average life expectancy under 30 years; the "age of receding pandemics," during which life expectancy rises considerably, from under 30 to over 50; and the "age of degenerative and man-made diseases,"[1] during which the pace of the mortality decrease slackens, while the

---

[1] According to Omran (1971, 1983), man-made diseases include "diseases introduced by man such as radiation injuries, accidents, occupational hazards, carcinogens in the environment and in industry and food additives." In this chapter man-made diseases also include alcohol- and tobacco-related mortality, homicide, and suicide.

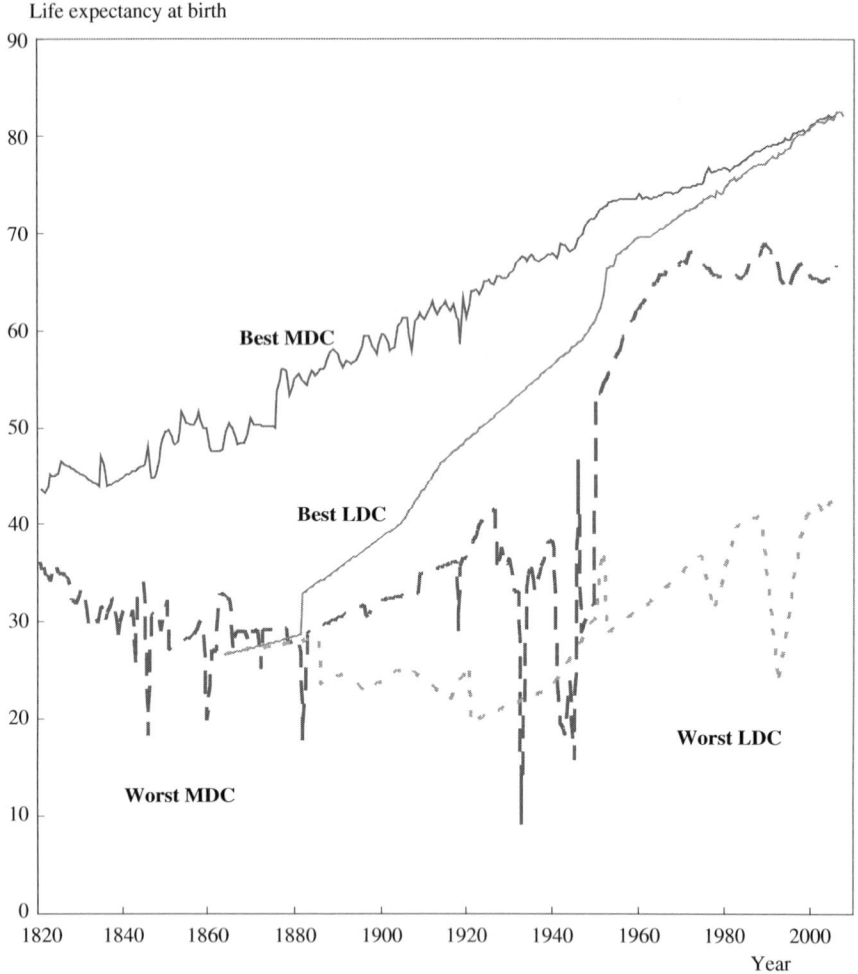

**Fig. 2.4** Trends in the highest and lowest life expectancy (both sexes) in either MDCs or LDCs, since 1820. The two upper series (*bold lines*) represent the highest life expectancy observed (among MDCs or among LDCs), during each calendar year. The two *dotted lines* represent the lowest ones. Each of the four lines includes performances from various countries, as was done for the first time by Oeppen and Vaupel (2002) for the highest life expectancy. Source: Special database prepared for Vallin and Meslé (2009)

disappearance of infectious diseases increases the visibility of degenerative diseases, and man-made diseases become more and more frequent. At the time Omran was developing his theory of epidemiologic transition, the most knowledgeable specialists, including UN experts, saw life expectancies as generally converging[2] toward a maximum age, with the most advanced countries appearing very close to it. According to the United Nations World Population Prospects, the point of convergence was 75 years (UN 1974). In point of fact, in the most advanced countries, the increase in life expectancy slowed during the 1960s and in some countries even halted, especially for men.

The cardiovascular revolution of the 1970s ushered in a new period of progress. Jay Olshansky and Brian Ault (1986), followed by Richard Rogers and Robert Hackenberg (1987), while not taking issue with the basic premises of epidemiologic transition theory, introduced the idea of a "fourth stage"[3] during which the maximum point of convergence of life expectancies would increase because of advances in the treatment of cardiovascular diseases. Olshansky and colleagues

---

[2] The idea of convergence is a general basis of the demographic transition theory, not only for life expectancy but also for fertility, and it is very commonly referred to in works related to the application of the theory. It has been discussed by various authors (see, for example, Coleman 2002).

[3] Olshansky and Ault: "A fourth stage of the epidemiologic transition." Rogers and Hackenberg refer to a "new" or "hybristic" stage.

(1990) set this new maximum at 85 years, the same as that chosen by the UN at the end of the 1980s for all countries (UN 1988). Today, however, the 85-year threshold is heavily criticized by a number of authors who believe that no such limit can be set (Barbi et al. 2003; Carey and Judge 2001; Vaupel 2001).

Furthermore, the epidemiologic transition theory, even as revised by Olshansky and other authors, seems to be challenged by dramatic exceptions to the general trend of increasing life expectancy observed since the 1960s. Not only have many countries (in particular eastern European countries) not experienced the cardiovascular revolution, but a number of others, especially in Africa, have not yet completed the second phase of epidemiologic transition and are now hard hit by the emergence of new epidemics, like AIDS, and the resurgence of older diseases (Caselli et al. 2002). Some authors have proposed adding a fifth age to the epidemiologic transition to accommodate AIDS: "the age of re-emergence of infectious and parasitic diseases" (Olshansky et al. 1998) or the "the age of aspired quality of life with paradoxical longevity and persistent inequities" according to Omran (1998). The latter even attempted to incorporate a future sixth age, "The age of health for all," which echoes the well-known WHO slogan (Omran 1998).

In our view, adding new stages to Omran's initial theory appears more and more artificial. The theory itself requires revision. Some authors have proposed a different approach. Two decades ago, Julio Frenk and colleagues (1991) proposed replacing the concept of epidemiologic transition with the wider one of "health transition," which had been suggested in the early 1970s by Lerner (1973). This would incorporate not only changes in epidemiologic patterns but also social and behavioral changes and the ways in which societies respond to health challenges. Frenk and colleagues attempted to combine various levels: "systemic," "societal," "institutional," and "individual." Their description, however, was purely theoretical without precise reference to facts, and it is difficult to see to what extent the theory fits reality.

Shiro Horiuchi (1999) linked the technological characteristics of societies and the main causes of death, associating hunting and gathering culture with violence, agriculture with infection, the industrial era with cardiovascular diseases, high-technology societies with cancers, and finally, the future with aging. This echoes the concept of *pathocenosis* established by Mirko Grmek (1969) to interpret important changes in remote human history. However, linking stages of societal development to health does not explain the diversity of patterns and changes observed within the last two centuries.

Vallin and Meslé (2004) attempted to summarize the historical process within a blueprint that might square with most of the observed trends in mortality. Arguably, each major improvement in health is likely to lead first to a divergence in mortality, as the most favored segments of the population benefit initially from the improvement. When the rest of the population gets access to the same benefits (through improved social conditions, behavioral changes, and health policies), a phase of convergence begins and can lead to homogenization until a new major advance occurs. The entire health transition process thus breaks down into successive stages, each including a specific divergence–convergence subprocess. Arguably, from the eighteenth century to the present, at least two and maybe three stages have occurred or are developing. Only the first one fits Omran's initial theory, and it was far from ended when the next two stages began, explaining the complexity of the whole story.

## First Divergence/Convergence: Pandemic Receding

For thousands of years, and notwithstanding exceptional dramatic crises at different times and places, human life expectancy probably never exceeded 30–35 years for very long periods until the mid-eighteenth century. This is not to say that the epidemiological profile was constant. On the contrary, historical studies highlighted the succession of *pathocenoses* that from the dawn of prehistory have been characterized by a specific epidemiological dynamic founded on specific pathological patterns (Biraben 1999; Grmek 1969; Vallin 2005). However, in mid-eighteenth century Europe, a new era began in which the switch from one pathocenose to the next one is also reflected by a critical and sustainable improvement in life expectancy. Within approximately two centuries, the epidemiological profile of European populations changed completely. Explaining this change is the main purpose of Omran's theory of the epidemiologic transition. At the end of this historical process, which can be put

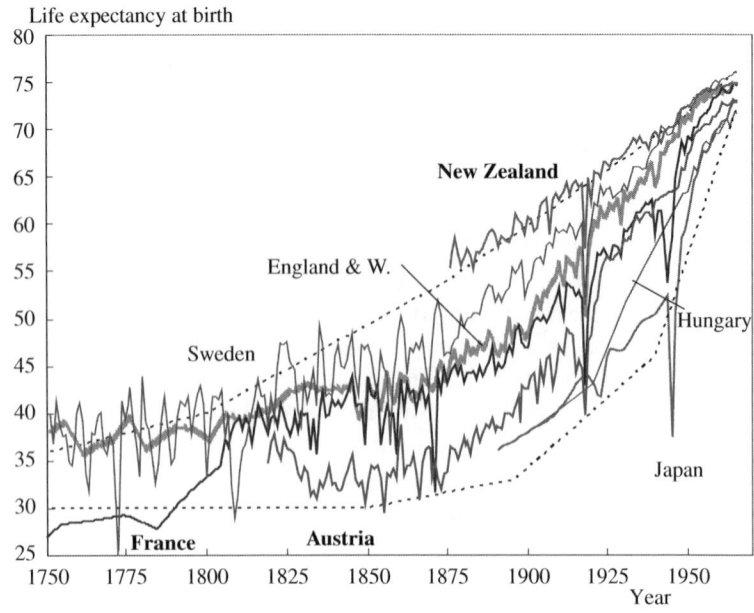

**Fig. 2.5** Long-term trends in female life expectancy for selected industrialized countries until the mid-1960s. The two *dotted lines* border an over-simplified range for real life expectancies of all industrialized countries. The range is enlarging during the divergence phase then narrowing during the convergence one. Source: Ediev and Giesser (2007), Vallin and Meslé (2004)

at around the mid-1960s, chronic diseases replaced infectious diseases as the main causes of death, while man-made diseases emerged as an additional factor in the global stagnation of life expectancy. However, just as the industrial revolution was born in Europe, so the pattern of epidemiologic transition was first seen in Europe before spreading over time to the rest of the world. Even now, not all countries have completed that process.

## The Successful MDC Story

Between the turn of the eighteenth century and the 1960s, the history of industrialized countries and especially European populations fits quite well with Omran's theory. During this period, life expectancy improved dramatically from its ancestral level of 30–35 years to about 70 years in the mid-1960s. It is well established that this was due almost exclusively to the near eradication of infectious mortality. The big historical epidemics were initially contained mainly by administrative rules preventing contamination (Biraben 1975). Then, major advances in agriculture and food distribution not only ended famine and starvation, still a concern up to the mid-eighteenth, and the beginning of the nineteenth century in some parts of Europe (Reinhard et al. 1968), but also reduced a large share of mortality that had been due to the synergic complex of malnutrition and infection (McKeown 1976). These improvements were reinforced in the nineteenth century by major investments in drinking water and sewerage systems. Finally, medical innovation, established with the Pasteur era, from immunization to antibiotics, combined with the establishment of social security systems, provided modern industrialized society with nearly total protection against major infectious causes of death.

But not all populations, even in Europe or other industrialized countries, benefited from this progress simultaneously. Figure 2.5 shows the available data on female life expectancy[4] for selected countries. While very few observed trajectories cover the entire two centuries, it is quite clear that fewer than a handful of countries pioneered early sustainable improvements in life expectancy. This improvement started in the latter half of the eighteenth century in France, England and Wales, and Sweden. Denmark and Norway, not included in Fig. 2.5 to make it easier to read, were also among the pioneers. In contrast, many European countries, especially in southern and eastern parts

---

[4] Because male trajectories are more affected by exceptional events like wars, it is preferable to use female trajectories to look at long-term trends.

of Europe, entered the trend much later. For example, continuous life-expectancy improvements did not begin in Austria before the end of the nineteenth century, and Fig. 2.5 suggests that the same applies to Hungary. This is also the case for most Mediterranean or eastern European countries not included in Fig. 2.5 for ease of interpretation (the onset came even later in Russia).

Among non-European industrialized countries, Fig. 2.5 shows two typical cases: New Zealand at the top and Japan at the bottom. New Zealand life tables include the "non-Maori" population only. In the mid-nineteenth century, most of this population consisted of immigrants from Europe, highly health-selected, with exceptionally high life expectancy (Vallin and Meslé 2009). Consequently, the highest value of the range shown by Fig. 2.5 for the mid-nineteenth century is probably somewhat exaggerated for a non-selected population. It is shown as an indication of the highest possible value; a more realistic highest value for that time is perhaps indicated by the Sweden trajectory, also shown in Fig. 2.5. At the bottom, Japanese life expectancy is unknown before the 1890s, but it was not until the Meiji era that Japan entered its phase of continuous increase in life expectancy. In sum, Fig. 2.5 clearly shows that, depending on their economic, social, and political contexts, industrialized countries began the trend at different times from the late eighteenth to the early twentieth century, but after this point the most recent arrivals advanced more rapidly than the pioneers. The aggregate progress made over the two centuries produced a first stage with major divergences, followed by a second in which all these countries dramatically converged toward the highest level of life expectancy permitted by the reduction in the burden of infectious mortality.

Intuitively, we added two dotted lines to Fig. 2.5 to try to represent the upper and lower limits between which life-expectancy improvements occurred in industrialized countries. Because very few points are available at the beginning, but also because of conflicting estimates for England and France, which could result from either real differences or methodological issues, it is difficult to estimate accurately the interval that characterized the pretransitional stage, but we contend that most female life expectancies probably ranged between 30 and 35 years. It is much clearer that in the mid-1960s, all countries were within a narrow range of less than 5 years, between 72 and 76. Contrast this to the turn of the nineteenth century, when these countries ranged between 33 and 60 years of life expectancy, a gap of approximately 27 years.

Considering the two contrasting periods of divergence, then convergence, Fig. 2.6 compares Sweden and Austria, two countries with long data series and very different timing of entering the era of

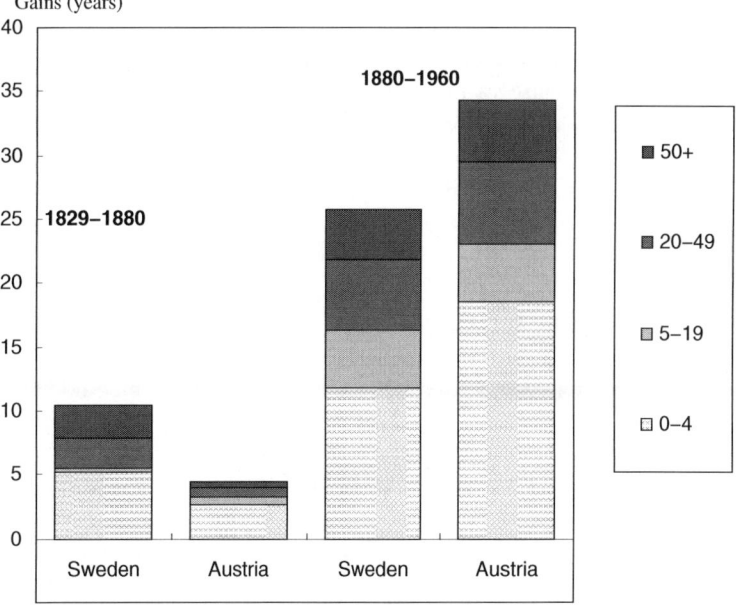

**Fig. 2.6** Contributions of decline in age-specific death rates to female life-expectancy increase in Sweden and Austria: 1829–1880 and 1880–1960. Each surface is proportional to the gains in life expectancy due to the fall in each age-specific mortality rate. Source: Authors' calculations based on HMD for Sweden, Ediev and Giesser (2007) for Austria

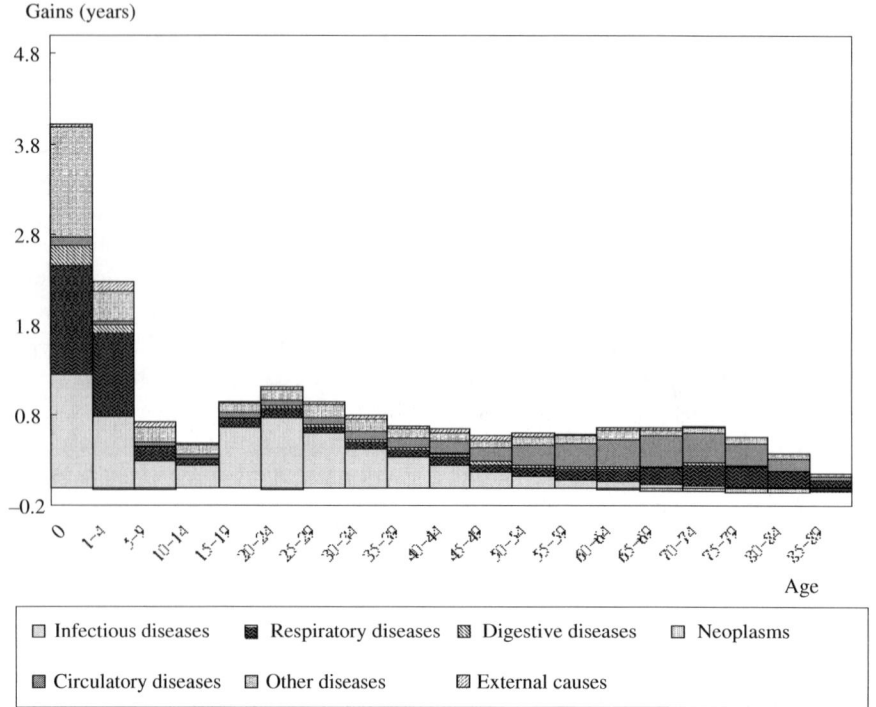

**Fig. 2.7** Contributions of decline in age- and cause-specific death rates to female life-expectancy increase in France, 1925–1960. Each surface is proportional to the change in life expectancy due to the change in mortality by one cause at one age-group. Positive changes (gains) in life expectancy are put above the 0 line, negative ones (losses) are under that line. Source: Vallin and Meslé (1988)

receding pandemics, to identify the roles played by age-specific mortality trends in the rise of female life expectancy.[5] From 1829[6] to 1880, Swedish life expectancy increased by more than 10 years while Austrian life expectancy progressed by less than 5. In both countries, most of the life-expectancy increase (50% in Sweden and 58% in Austria) came from reduction in infant and child mortality. During the second period (1880–1960) the jump in life expectancy was spectacular in both countries, but greater in Austria (+34 years) than in Sweden (+26 years), since, by the end, Austria caught up with Sweden. Again, and even more than in the previous period, progress was due primarily to the reduction of mortality at ages 0–4 complemented by a non-negligible effect of the fall of mortality at ages 5–19. In total, these two age groups were responsible for a life-expectancy increase of 16 years in Sweden and 23 years in Austria. In contrast, the reduction of mortality beyond age 50 resulted in less than 5 years of increased life expectancy in both countries.

Obviously, such reductions in age-specific mortality rates are the result of the successful fight against infectious diseases that had for so long dominated epidemiologic profiles of human populations. Unfortunately, long-term reliable series of death statistics by cause are lacking in most countries. The longest series of interest here is for France (Vallin and Meslé 1988), but it began only in 1925 and shows the causes of death responsible for change during the last part of the second period (1925–1960) (Fig. 2.7).

Both infectious diseases and respiratory diseases (also mostly infectious at that time) played important roles. The decline of infectious disease played a large part at all ages between 0 and about 50, while respiratory disease played an even more important role

---

[5] According to Andreev's (1982) method, which is equivalent to those proposed by others (Arriaga 1984; Pollard 1982; Pressat 1985).

[6] The year when Austrian historical data (Ediev and Giesser 2007) start to be reliable (available data start in 1819 but show an unrealistic decline of life expectancy until 1829).

at the very young ages (0–5) and at the older ages (50 and over). This confirms the prominence of the fight against infectious diseases even at the end of the first large movement of divergence–convergence among MDCs; it also introduces the next story of the cardiovascular revolution, for which France was in the vanguard (Meslé and Vallin 1988). Indeed, before 1960 the decline of circulatory diseases had begun and was already making an important contribution to the increase of French female life expectancy at ages 50 and over. But the infectious disease story was not over with the great success achieved in MDCs by the mid-1960s. It is still ongoing in LDCs.

## Expanding Diversity Among LDCs

Of course the completion of what Omran's theory refers to as the age of receding pandemics includes the spread to LDCs of the accomplishments in MDCs, as is shown by the strong convergence of life expectancy in a large number of LDCs toward that in MDCs after the mid-twentieth century (Figs. 2.3 and 2.4). But in other LDCs progress in life expectancy slowed markedly or even stopped.

### A Large Convergence

Figure 2.8 shows the life-expectancy trajectories of selected LDCs among those (the most numerous) that more or less converge to the values in MDCs.

Even though the timeframe of the data used does not provide the full picture for all countries, it appears very likely that in the late 1950s these countries experienced their maximal divergence in life expectancy.[7] With female life expectancies above 65 years, countries like Argentina and Puerto Rico were already at levels close to those of industrialized countries, while others like Afghanistan or Yemen were still at levels close to those of eighteenth-century Europe— around 30 years. Specifically, from the 1880s to the 1950s, a huge divergence was observed between the rapid progress of countries like Argentina, Chile, and Puerto Rico, and the stagnation of India, where life expectancy was as low as 25 years at the end of the nineteenth century. Then, in the following five decades, life-expectancy trajectories converged (with the exception of Afghanistan, which stopped progressing in the 1980s for quite specific reasons). It seems that Puerto Rico completed the first stage of the health transition when its life expectancy almost reached the Swedish level, provided here as a benchmark for the best MDCs, while the pace differential between Puerto Rico's and Yemen's trajectories gives a fairly clear picture of the convergence between the group of LDCs considered here, which are very likely completing Omran's epidemiologic transition.

Figure 2.8 also allows the comparison of LDC trajectories against two dotted lines that are repeated from Fig. 2.5, advanced by 60 years to make the lower one fit with the level of 30 years prevailing in 1900 in Puerto Rico, 1920 in Chile, 1945 in India, and about 1950 in Yemen. Two things are evident. First, the range of life expectancies at the stage of maximum divergence was greater for today's developing countries than for industrialized countries in the past; in the late 1950s, with a female life expectancy of 30 years, Afghanistan was 41 years lower than Puerto Rico (71), whereas the maximum gap for industrialized countries stood at 27 years. Second, the developing countries improved their life expectancy much more rapidly in recent decades than European countries did in earlier time periods. Within 55 years, Yemen gained 32 years of life expectancy, whereas the lower dotted line "predicts" a gain of 10 years. In the same time period, even a country like Chile, where female life expectancy was already over 50 years in the early 1950s, achieved very rapid additional gains for three or four additional decades. The data indicate that as early as the 1920s and 1930s in the most advanced LDCs, and especially after WWII, most LDCs made very rapid progress once they were able to take up European methods of infectious disease control and disseminate their benefit among their population. During this time, many LDCs completed most of Omran's epidemiologic transition.

As had been true for MDCs, the largest part of life-expectancy increase at this stage was due to the decline in infant and child mortality (as shown in Fig. 2.9 for females). But here too, countries started progressing at quite different dates. In Argentina, for example, the greatest part of life-expectancy gains was obtained between 1882 and 1947, while India made only small

---

[7] If we ignore the fact that Afghanistan stopped progressing in the 1980s for specific reasons that will be seen later.

**Fig. 2.8** Long-term trends in female life expectancy for selected developing countries. The two *dotted lines* border an over-simplified range for real life expectancies of all industrialized countries showed at Fig. 2.5, but advanced by 60 years to have the lower one fitting with the level of 30 years prevailing around 1900 in Puerto Rico, about 1920 in Chile, or about 1945 in India. They show the much faster progress in MDCs after beginning progress from the lowest levels observed in industrialized countries. India seems to start from an exceptionally low level, but it is because of the deterioration caused by colonization at the turn of the nineteenth century. In *light grey*, Sweden stands for a benchmark of the best levels currently achieved by MDCs. Source: After 1950: UN (2009); before 1950: Mari Bhat (1989) for India, Somoza (1971) for Argentina, UN (1968) for Puerto Rico, HLTD for Egypt, Arriaga (1968) and Munoz Pradas (1989) for Chile

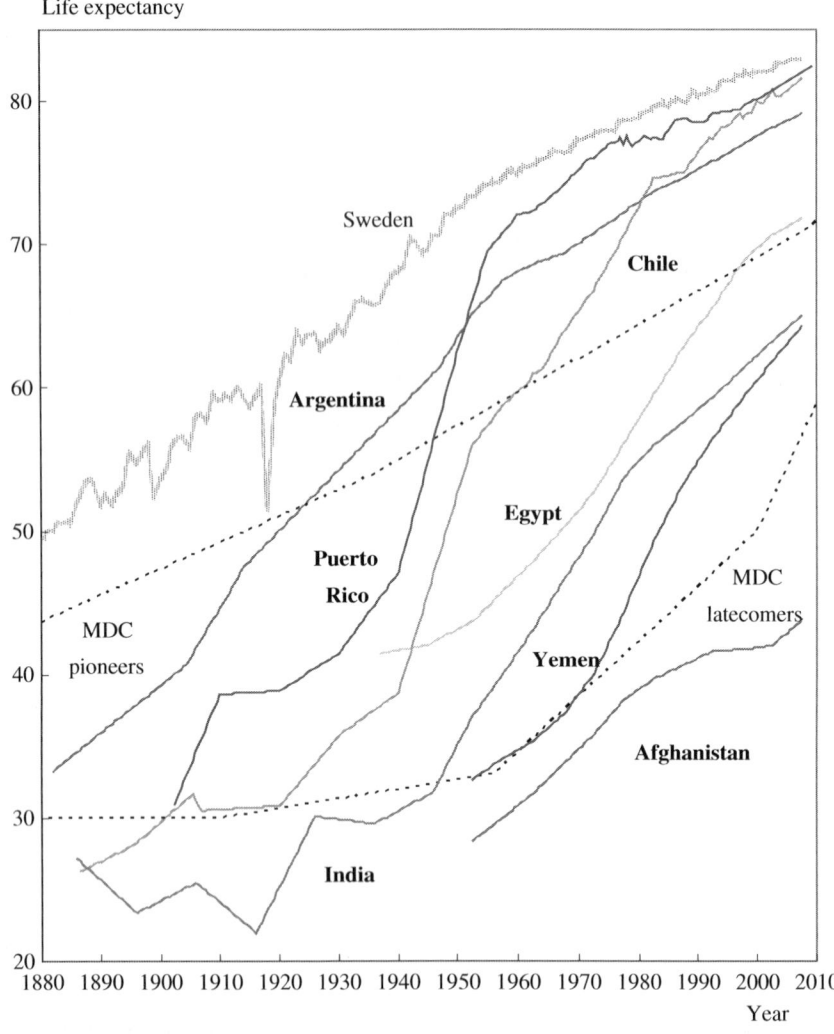

gains from 1886 to 1947. In India, these gains represented a recovery after the difficult years at the end of the nineteenth century rather than a real start of general progress. Among the 30 years gained by Argentina, 13 were due to reduction in under-5 mortality and 3 to reduction at ages 5–19. Mortality decline at young ages caused more than half of the total gain in life expectancy. The small Indian gains were also due to mortality decline at younger ages, but with almost no effect of mortality change under age 5.

In a second step, from about 1950 to 2007, the reverse situation occurred: Indian gains were much larger than Argentinean ones and they were much more related to the fall of mortality below age 20, with a huge impact of mortality decline at 0–4. Figure 2.9 also shows the age-specific components of life-expectancy increase in Afghanistan for that period. Gains were much less important than in India but, because of wars started in 1980, they actually represent results for a much shorter period. Finally, in all LDCs, up to the present, major progress in life expectancy has relied on the fall of infant and child mortality. This change is generally more recent in LDCs than in MDCs, but it started at varying times among LDCs, as it did for MDCs in the past. While Argentina started in the 1880s, India did so in the 1930s and Afghanistan in the 1950s. Unfortunately, no data allow the measurement of the role played by different causes of death, but nothing indicates that it is likely to be different from what was seen in the MDCs.

**Fig. 2.9** Contributions of the decline in age-specific death rates to female life-expectancy increase in Argentina, India, and Afghanistan, before and after WWII. Each surface is proportional to the gains in life expectancy due to the fall in each age-specific mortality rate. Source: Authors' calculations based on Somoza (1971) for Argentina; Mari Bhat (1989) for India; UN (2009) for Afghanistan

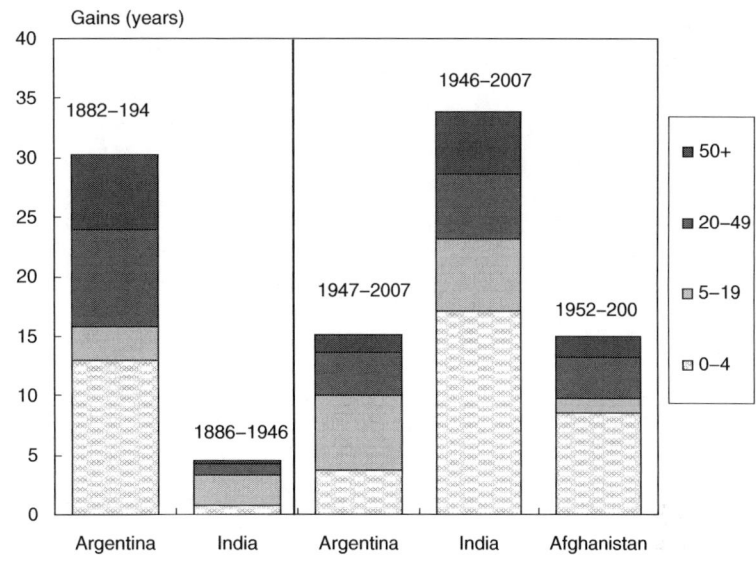

A Number of Obstacles

Another set of countries, mainly in Sub-Saharan Africa, seem to be exceptions to this globalization of the first stage of the health transition. In recent decades Sub-Saharan countries seem to have remained systematically outside the process of Omran's epidemiologic transition for a variety of reasons, including conflicts and other forms of political unrest. Although they can be significant, wars and conflicts usually have only a passing impact on life expectancy, which usually quickly resumes its long-term trend. This was the case in many European countries, especially with the two world wars. It is also the case for developing countries like Cambodia, Rwanda, and Somalia (as is shown in the fourth graph of Fig. 2.10). Such cases do not constitute real exceptions to the epidemiologic transition, since the Omran second age eliminates wars from the scheme.

Sub-Saharan Africa deserves more comment, as three different types of divergence have appeared. First, some countries progressed regularly over the last 50 years, but at a much slower pace than the LDCs shown in Fig. 2.8, where life expectancy progressed fast enough to catch up to MDCs. This is the case for Sudan, Mali, and Niger, here compared to Egypt (first graph of Fig. 2.10). In a second group, early progress was suddenly stopped. This group includes many Sub-Saharan countries, like Angola, Nigeria, and the Democratic Republic of Congo, that experienced the world economic crisis and structural adjustment programs in the 1980s (second graph of Fig. 2.10). Finally, a number of countries in southern and eastern Africa were severely affected by the AIDS epidemic. For example, within a period of 15 years, life expectancy fell by 10 years in Zambia, 12 in South Africa, and 20 in Zimbabwe (third graph of Fig. 2.10). Sub-Saharan countries most severely affected by AIDS were countries where life expectancy already had reached higher levels than in the rest of the region (53 years in Zambia, 64 in Zimbabwe, and 65 in South Africa). Their recent losses were due primarily to adult mortality increase, while their previous gains were the consequence of infant and child mortality decline.

To conclude, it is clear that the first stage of the health transition is progressing much more slowly in Sub-Saharan Africa than in most LDCs and has been retarded in the past three decades. The achievement of this first stage of transition is related not only to changes in epidemiologic patterns, but also to economic, social, and cultural development. In the case of Sub-Saharan Africa, three main obstacles opposed rapid progress in life expectancy. First, in the 1950s, the region was the world's least economically developed. When the world economic crisis arrived in the late 1970s, it was the only region where rapid demographic growth was still at its maximum, with very high levels of fertility, yet an already engaged mortality decline. The fragile economies of these countries were experiencing needs arising from population growth and

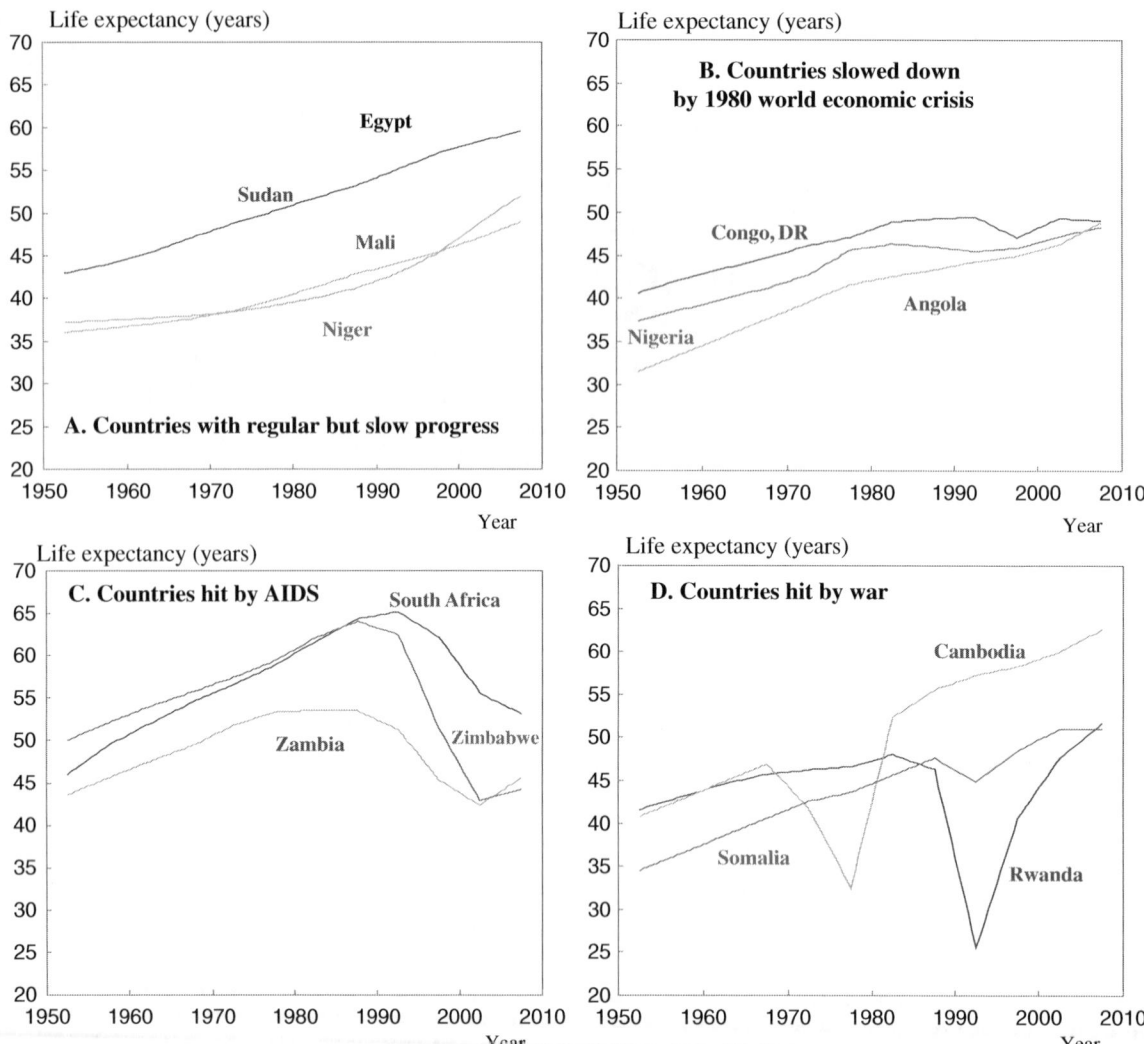

**Fig. 2.10** Different types of trends in Sub-Saharan Africa in female life expectancy. **Graph A** gives some examples of countries with regular but slow progresses as compared to faster Egyptian progress; **Graph B** gathers three examples of countries where initially slow progress was stopped by the 1980 world economic crisis and structural adjustment programs; **Graph C** shows three examples of countries where life-expectancy increase reversed drastically when AIDS spread; **Graph D** gathers three countries severely hit by genocide (Cambodia, Rwanda) or civil war (Somalia). Source: UN (2009)

structural adjustments that made it difficult to maintain their health services. Finally, when AIDS spread rapidly throughout the population because of exceptionally high heterosexual transmission, means of combating the epidemic were not feasible in the economic, social, and cultural context. Thus, for these countries the first cycle of divergence–convergence related to the fight against infectious diseases is still far from complete. Meanwhile, among industrialized countries, a second divergence–convergence cycle has been in process for several decades.

## The Second Wave of Divergence–Convergence: The Cardiovascular Revolution

It is now a matter of record that what Abdel Omran called "the age of degenerative and man-made diseases" was not the end of the story. Not only have most of the man-made diseases been under some control, with decreasing death rates since the end of the 1960s, but a new major step in life-expectancy improvement was begun with the successful fight against cardiovascular diseases. Arguably, however, it is not an appropriate interpretation to see that step as a fourth "age" of Omran's epidemiologic transition. Rather, it is an entirely new process of divergence–convergence based on a completely new approach to health, the success of which depends very much on society's current capacity to implement it. That new step, in fact, began with a dramatic divergence between countries in the two main social and political systems of the industrialized world: East and West.

## A New Phase of Divergence Among MDCs

In the industrialized world, the mid-1960s marked the start of a new divergence in life-expectancy changes (first graph of Fig. 2.3 above). On the one hand, after slowing down more or less during the 1960s, all western[8] countries reestablished rapid progress late in the decade. In contrast, eastern countries experienced a long period of stagnation or even deterioration. Figure 2.11 shows very clearly for males[9] the new divergence from a starting point in the mid-1960s, when all industrialized countries had converged to the same level of life expectancy (about 65 years).

The widest divergence is observed between Japan, which did not experience any slowdown and where the pace of progress has been especially rapid, and Russia, which has been facing the worst situation since the "end" of Omran's epidemiologic transition. From 1965 to 2005, male life expectancy increased from 68 to 79 years in Japan, but fell from 64 to 59 years in Russia. While the contrast was less stark between other countries, there was a clear divide between West and East, at least until the early 1990s. At that time, even between the closest countries in the two groups, the Czech Republic and the United States, there was more than a 4-year difference, while the two countries had been at similar levels in 1965.

That divergence continues today for countries of the former USSR, represented here by Russia and Ukraine, despite the wide fluctuations of the late 1980s and early 1990s, first upward with Gorbachev's anti-alcoholism campaign and then downward with the socioeconomic shock of an abrupt switch to a market economy (Meslé and Vallin 2003; Meslé et al. 1998; see also Chapter 4 by Murphy's, this volume). All other eastern European countries, however, embarked on a new phase of convergence in the last decade. At the very beginning of the 1990s the Czech Republic was the first of these countries to reestablish progress, followed soon after by Poland, Slovakia, and Hungary (which are not shown in Fig. 2.11). Even Romania and Bulgaria have entered this new stage more recently (Meslé 2004). Within the last 15 years, life-expectancy gains in the Czech Republic and Poland have outpaced those in Japan. For example, from 1990 to 2005, Czech male life expectancy increased by 5.2 years compared to Japan's 2.6 years. At that pace, the Czech Republic would reach the level of Japan in 2045 and Poland soon after. It is not clear that this will also be true for females. Indeed, during recent years, increase in Japanese male life expectancy seems to have slowed, while, as will be discussed later, Japanese females may already have embarked on a third stage of the health transition. For both sexes, the Czech Republic and Poland are actually catching up to life-expectancy levels in countries like the Netherlands, which provides an example of a country that is completing stage two of the health transition, but not yet entering stage three. From 1990 to 2005, its increase in female life expectancy was only 1.4 years compared to about 5 in the Czech Republic and Poland.

## The Role of Cardiovascular Mortality

Over and above the successful fight against man-made diseases that were described by Omran as a feature of the "third age" of his epidemiologic transition, the second stage of the health transition mainly relies on the reduction of cardiovascular diseases, classified by Omran among the difficult-to-reduce degenerative diseases. This applies equally to the divergence and convergence phases. A clearer picture of the dominant role of cardiovascular diseases can be gained by examining the contributions of age- and cause-specific mortality change to life-expectancy differentials between two dates[10] for selected countries.

---

[8] According to its economic system and performance, Japan is here considered as belonging to the western world.

[9] In this section, examples are given for males, for whom the contrast between eastern and western trends is much greater, but females follow the same process at the same time.

[10] According to Andreev's method (Andreev 1982).

**Fig. 2.11** Male life-expectancy trends in various industrial countries, 1965–2005. While life expectancy at birth went up almost linearly in Japan, France, and the United States, it went down in Russia and Ukraine. In-between, in the Czech Republic and Poland, it stagnated until the end of the 1980s, but resumed progress since the early 1990s. Source: Vallin and Meslé (2004) updated

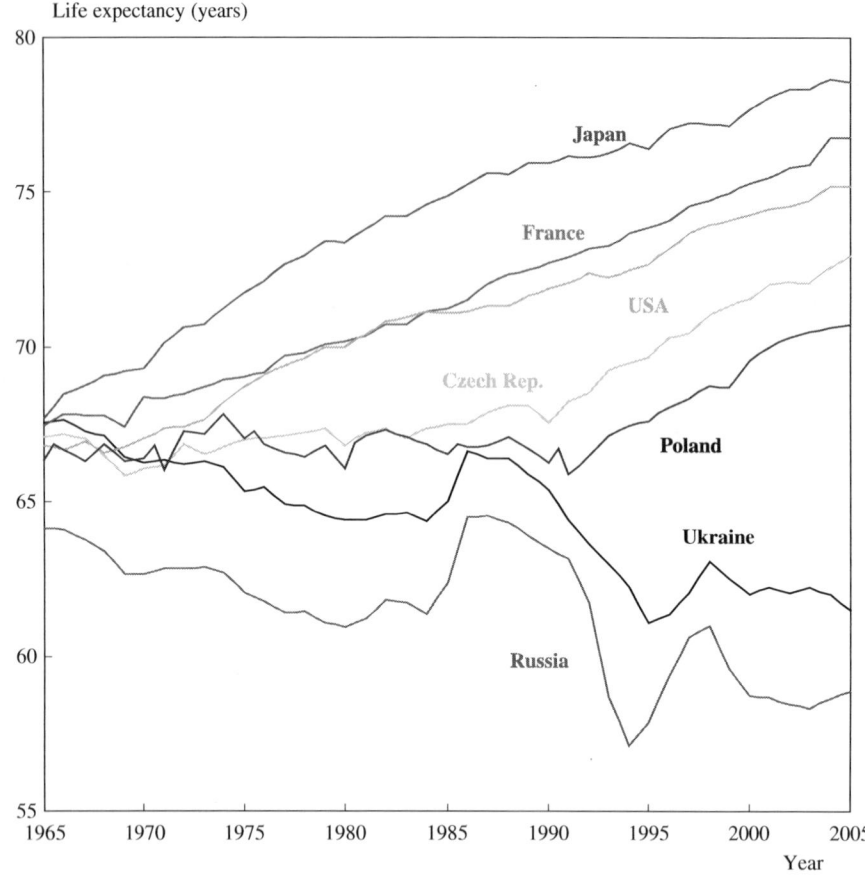

First, Fig. 2.12 compares the breakdown of life-expectancy change in France and Russia over the whole period 1965–2006. The only common feature between the two countries is the positive impact of the continuing decline in infant mortality, to which 1.5 year's life-expectancy gain in both countries can be credited, notwithstanding somewhat different cause-of-death attributions ("respiratory diseases" playing an important role in Russia but not in France, where "other diseases" dominate massively[11]). That aside, most of the remaining increase in life expectancy in France (7.9 years) stemmed from the decrease in cardiovascular mortality at adult ages, accounting for as much as 3.6 years. The other sources of gains at adult ages include the decline of "other diseases," "external causes," "respiratory diseases," and "digestive diseases." These groups of causes include "man-made diseases" like traffic accidents, liver cirrhosis, and alcoholism. During this period, therefore, France clearly benefited from the decline in those diseases that, according to Omran's theory, were the main feature of the "third age" of the epidemiologic transition, and consequently has more or less completed the second stage of the health transition. Advances were made at all adult ages over 35, but culminated between ages 60 and 70.

In Russia, by contrast, all these ages were affected by increasing cardiovascular mortality, which is estimated to have reduced life expectancy by 3.3 years. Another 2-year loss was caused at the same time by a sharp rise in "injury and poisoning" deaths, a category that, in Russia, includes alcoholism as well as road traffic accidents, suicides, and homicides. Russia therefore stands as a textbook example of a country that even now conforms to Omran's "third age." So acute is

---

[11] In fact at that age, most of the "other diseases" group corresponds to perinatal and congenital diseases.

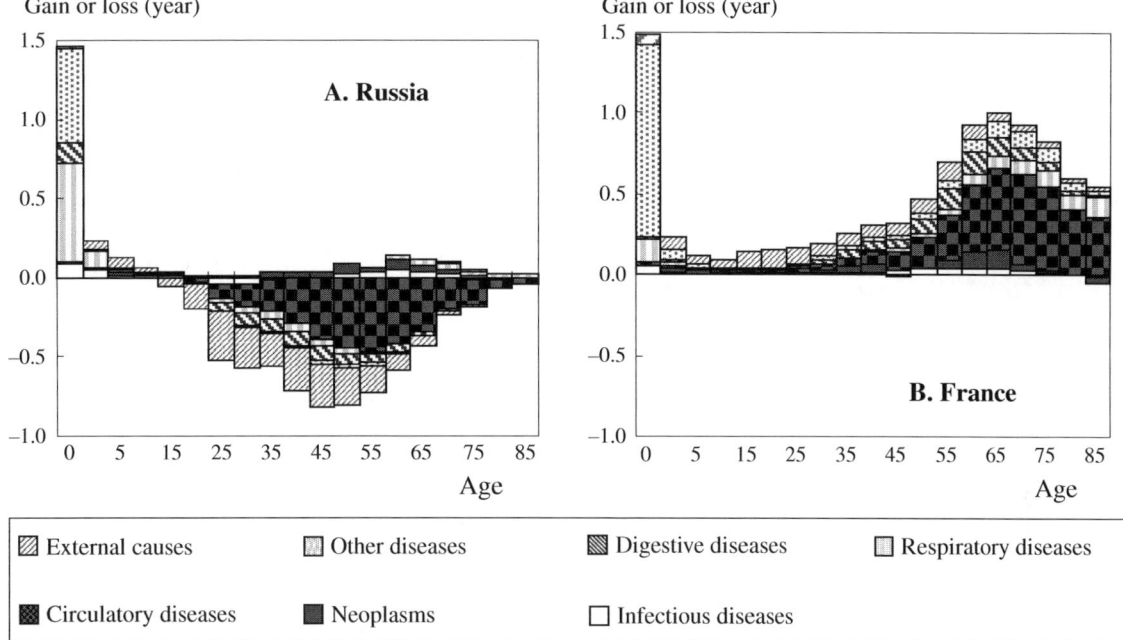

**Fig. 2.12** Contributions of age- and cause-specific death rate changes to male life-expectancy changes in Russia and France, 1965–2005. Each surface is proportional to the change in life expectancy due to the change in mortality by one cause at one age-group. Positive changes (gains) in life expectancy are put above the 0 line, negative ones (losses) are under that line.

Except for the youngest ages, almost symmetrical landscapes oppose Russia (**Graph A**) to France (**Graph B**). But Russian negative effects occurred at younger ages than French positive effects and they are much more related to external causes. Source: Vallin and Meslé (2004) updated

the pandemic of degenerative and man-made diseases that the decline in infectious diseases at young ages no longer compensates for its spread. The same trends are observed in other republics of the former USSR, like Ukraine (Meslé and Vallin 2003), Belarus (Grigoriev et al. 2010), and even the Baltic countries (Hertrich and Meslé 1999), at least until very recently.[12]

### The Beginning of Convergence in Cardiovascular Mortality

The same can no longer be said of central European countries. In Poland, taken here as an example, the negative trends reversed as early as 1991. During the period of deterioration, from 1965 to 1991, the Polish pattern of age and cause-of-death contribution to the decline of life expectancy was fairly similar to that of Russia (Fig. 2.13), with two noteworthy differences. One is that an even larger life-expectancy gain resulted from a dramatic fall in infant mortality (which, alone, would have produced a 2-year gain) and, even at adult ages, significant gains were due to the decline of infectious and respiratory mortality. During that time, Poland was actually moving toward completion of the first stage of its health transition. The other is that the impact of external causes was much less pronounced than in Russia, while that of cancer was more significant. However, years of life expectancy lost due to increasing cardiovascular mortality were fairly comparable. In fact, had the first stage of its health transition been completed before 1965, Poland would have lost almost the same number of years of life expectancy as Russia in that period of general divergence between East and West. By contrast, since 1991, gains in Polish life expectancy have been observed at all ages (second graph of Fig. 2.13). In fact, beyond the 0.6 year gained from the decline of infant mortality, most of the gains at other ages (3.7 years) are due to the decline of cardiovascular mortality (2.5 years).

---

[12] It seems increasingly likely that since the 1993–1994 socioeconomic crisis, the progress in the three Baltic countries has been more than reestablished (Meslé 2004).

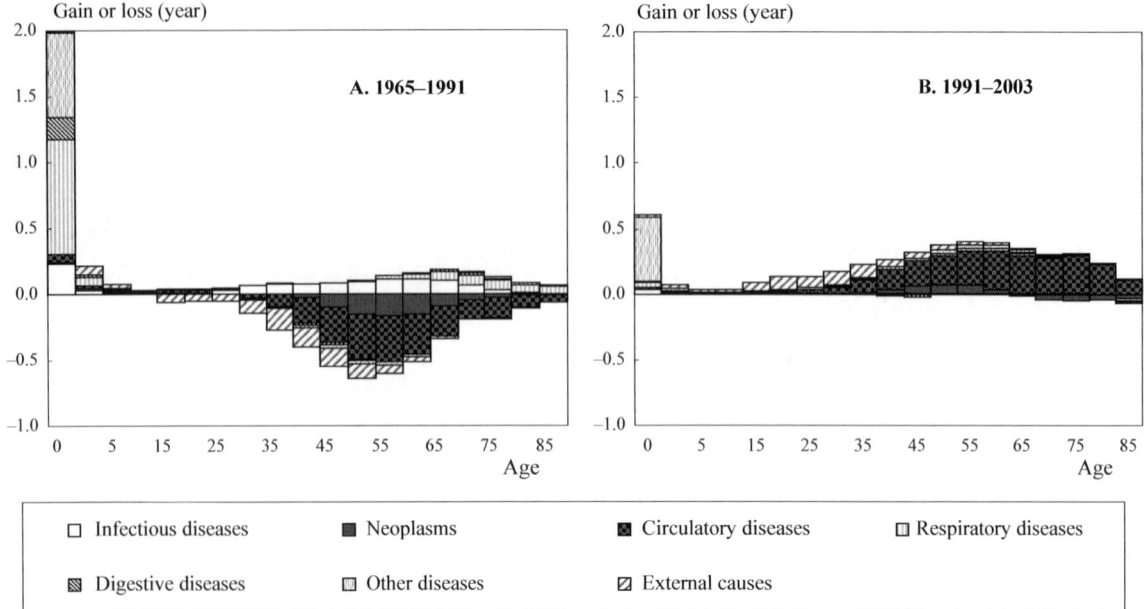

**Fig. 2.13** Contributions of age- and cause-specific death rate changes to male life expectancy changes in Poland, 1965–1991 and 1991–2003. Each surface is proportional to the change in life expectancy due to the change in mortality by one cause at one age-group. Positive changes (gains) in life expectancy are put above the 0 line, negative ones (losses) are under that line. Except for the youngest ages, almost symmetrical landscapes oppose the 1965–1991 period (**Graph A**) to the 1991–2003 one (**Graph B**). Source: Vallin and Meslé (2004) updated

What is seen here in the Polish case also is occurring in the other former communist Central European countries. Everywhere, the main cause of progress is the reduction of cardiovascular mortality, with some additional effect of the control of various man-made diseases (depending on the country).

This phenomenon of divergence–convergence between "western" and "eastern" countries is the best example of the occurrence of a second stage of the health transition based mainly on the trends in man-made and cardiovascular diseases. Initially, the divergence appears with the emergence of a new pathway, reestablishing progress in life expectancy after the population has gained almost all that could be expected from the fight against infectious diseases in the previous stage. Some countries, like Japan, followed by almost all western countries, were quick to maximize the benefits of new technologies, and perhaps even more, new means of prevention against cardiovascular diseases, while other countries, mainly in eastern Europe, failed to do so. It is very likely that the failure of the former communist countries was due largely to a double disadvantage. First, their economic difficulties held back the dissemination of costly new technologies, and, second, the highly centralized social system, well suited to fighting infectious diseases, worked to their disadvantage in getting individuals to take responsibility for their own health through behavioral and lifestyle changes. After the fall of the Berlin Wall, Central European countries were fast recovering the means to reverse their situation and to resume gains in life expectancy, while countries of the former USSR, like Russia or Ukraine, did not. The difference is probably related to the way these countries undertook reforms to turn to market economies.

## *A Third Wave?*

When we look more closely at the most recent trends in life expectancy for Western industrialized countries, the question arises: are they already engaged in a third stage of the health transition? For females in particular (right-hand chart, Fig. 2.14), a new divergence started after 1980. The process is less clear for men, but it is noteworthy that male life expectancy

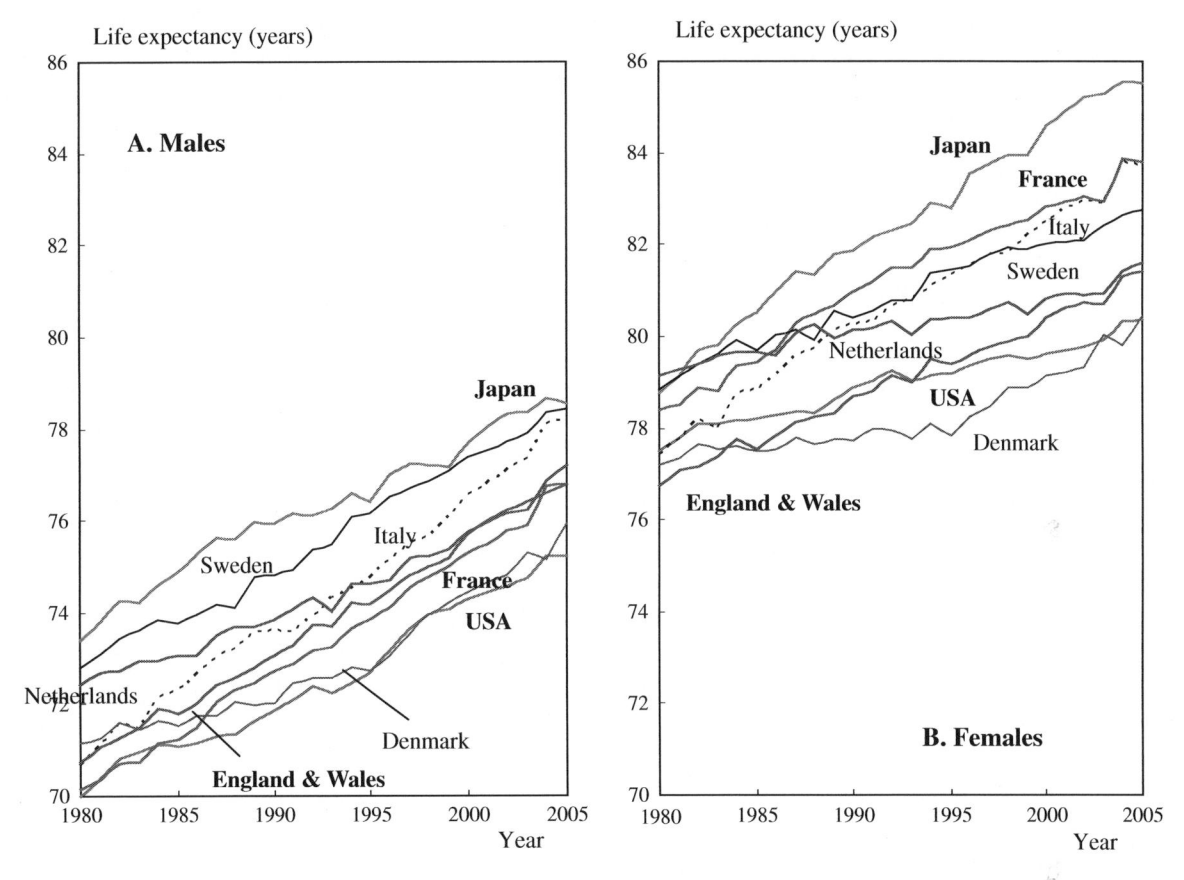

**Fig. 2.14** Trends in life expectancy at birth in the most advanced industrial countries, 1980–2005. The highest 2005 male life expectancy (Japan, **Graph A**) is still lower than the 1980 highest female one (**Graph B**). Source: Meslé and Vallin (2006) updated

is still consistently lower in 2005 than female life expectancy was in 1980. In Japan, for example, male life expectancy was 78.5 years in 2005; while female life expectancy was already 78.8 in 1980. It is even more marked in the United States, with 75.2 for males in 2000 against 77.4 for females in 1980.

Clearly, females are much further along the road in the health transition than males, and so more likely to enter a new stage first. At first glance, the female graph of Fig. 2.14 might seem to suggest a new stage starting with the very marked divergence between Denmark and countries like France and Japan. While progress slackens or even halts in the former from the 1980s, it continues at a sustained pace in France and Japan. From 1980 to 1995, female life expectancy gained only 0.7 year in Denmark (from 77.2 to 77.9) but as much as 3.5 years in France (78.4–81.9), and even 4 years in Japan (78.8–82.8). More recently, Denmark reestablished progress, gaining 2.6 years (to 80.5) in 10 years

while France gained 1.9 and Japan 2.7 years, which could be interpreted as the starting point of a new phase of convergence. Meanwhile, the Netherlands and the United States also entered a long period of slow improvement from the 1980s. Within 25 years, female life expectancy increased by only 3.4 years in the Netherlands and 2.9 in the United States, while it grew by 5.4 in France and 6.7 in Japan.

However, the case of Denmark is specific. Gains in female life expectancy might have been larger, had only cardiovascular diseases been involved, but that progress was completely obliterated by reverse trends in other causes of death like cancer, respiratory diseases, and digestive diseases, which are mainly smoking- and drinking-related and call into question Danish progress at ages around 50 and 60. In other words, notwithstanding progress against cardiovascular diseases, increases in life expectancy were slowed down by man-made diseases. In the same way, Danish male life-expectancy increase also slowed down. In short, Denmark was simply late completing the second stage of the health transition in man-made diseases (Vallin and Meslé 2004).

Quite different are the cases of the Netherlands and the United States, where life-expectancy increase slowed down because of lack of progress at older ages. The phenomenon appears very clearly when we compare recent trends in life expectancy at age 65 ($e_{65}$) in the Netherlands and the United States on one side, and France and Japan on the other (Fig. 2.15). After the convergence of the 1960s and 1970s that brought the four countries to the same level, a strong divergence started in the early 1980s, when progress in the United States and the Netherlands slowed while in France and Japan life expectancy at age 65 continued to increase rapidly. In 1984, the range for life expectancy at age 65 in the four countries was less than 0.2 years (between 18.6 and 18.8). In 2005, the difference was 2 years between the Netherlands (20) and France (22), and 3.2 years between the United States (19.9) and Japan (23.2). Thus, even when levels of life expectancy are very high, it is still possible for countries like France and Japan to continue making progress without any deceleration (Meslé and Vallin 2006).

Figure 2.16 displays the respective impact of cause- and age-specific mortality changes between 1984 and 2005 in each of the four countries. During this period, both the United States and the Netherlands gained less than 1.3 years in female life expectancy at age 65, whereas France gained 3.3 years and Japan gained 4.5 years. In every age group, French and Japanese gains are greater than those in the United States and the Netherlands, although they are closer at ages 65–69. At ages 90 and older, the United States fared worse than Japan and France, but the Netherlands did the worst, with no gain at the oldest ages. Interestingly, Japan was the only country that achieved notable gains at the oldest ages (95 and over). In France, and even more in Japan, gains are very impressive for most causes when compared to both the United States and the Netherlands, where smaller gains are offset by sizeable losses. But the differential impact of causes by age is even more remarkable.

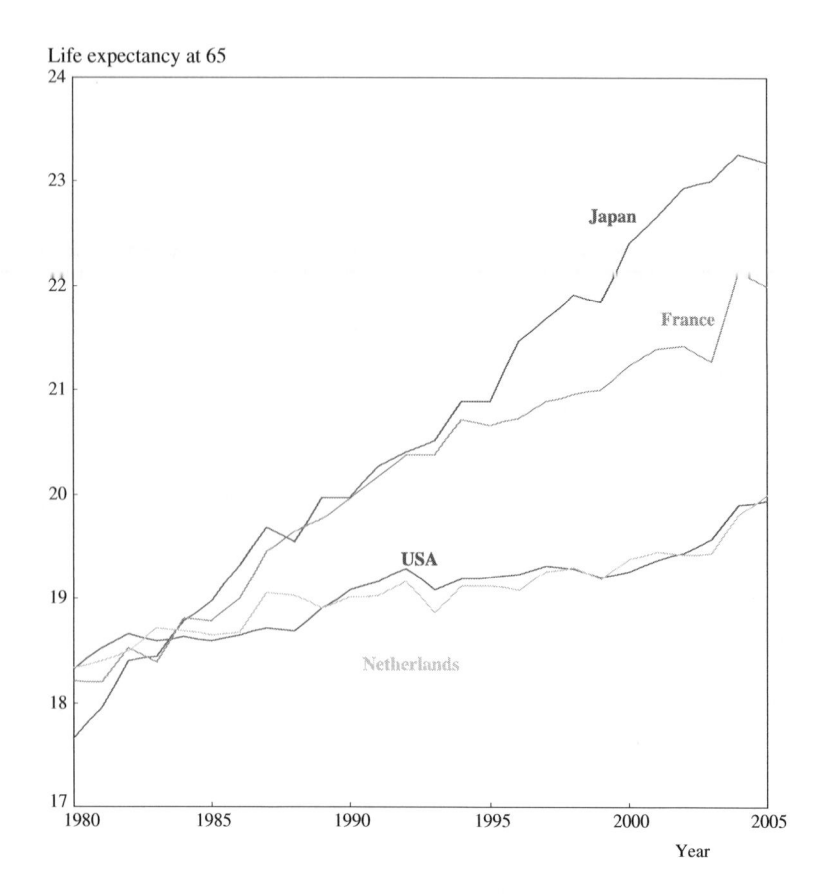

**Fig. 2.15** Trends in female life expectancy at age 65 in four advanced industrial countries, 1980–2005. Source: Meslé and Vallin (2006) updated

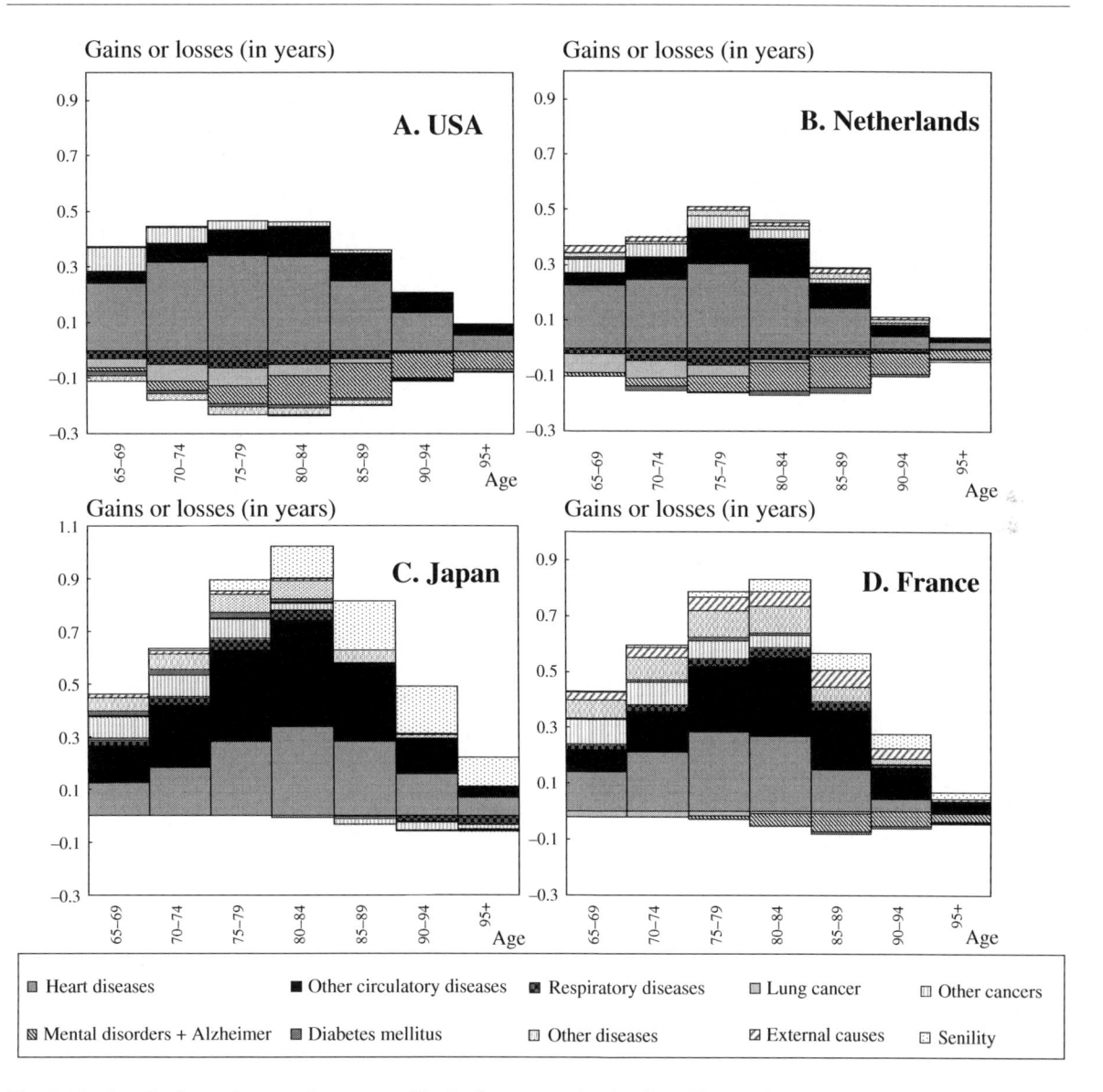

**Fig. 2.16** Contributions of age- and cause-specific death rate changes to change in female life expectancy at 65 in four advanced countries, 1984–2005. Each surface is proportional to the change in life expectancy due to the change in mortality by one cause at one age-group. Positive changes (gains) in life expectancy are put above the 0 line, negative ones (losses) are under that line. Three main contrasts oppose the United States and the Netherlands (**Graphs A** and **B**) to Japan and France (**Graphs C** and **D**): important negative impact of several causes, positive effects almost exclusively due to heart disease, smaller impact of mortality decline at the oldest ages. Source: Meslé and Vallin (2006) updated

In the four countries, the most important gains come from the reduction of circulatory diseases that increases $e_{65}$ by 1.7 years in the Netherlands, 2.2 years in both France and the United States, and 3 years in Japan; however, these gains are quite differently distributed by type of circulatory diseases. Cerebrovascular diseases account for the greatest part of progress in France and Japan, while this cause plays only a minor role in the United States and the Netherlands. On another hand, in the latter two countries, no other group of causes produces any substantial gain (only 0.2 year in the United States and 0.4 in the Netherlands in total), while other causes are responsible for 1.3 years in France and 1.4 in Japan.

The divergence between the two groups of countries is sharpened by the fact that many causes play a negative role in the United States and the Netherlands for all age groups. Only mental disorders at very old ages do so in France, and no cause does this in Japan. In total, mental diseases caused an $e_{65}$ loss of 1.1 year in the United States and 0.9 year in the Netherlands versus 0.3 in France and 0.0 in Japan.

Finally, the divergence is also driven by differentials in mortality trends by age: mortality decline above age 80 is responsible for about half of $e_{65}$ total gains in France and Japan, but only about one third in the United States and the Netherlands.

Even though cardiovascular mortality decrease continued in all four countries, it seems that France and Japan are already engaged in a new era of progress, relying on mortality decline at very old ages. This has not occurred in the United States and the Netherlands, where new causes of losses, like mental disorders, appear.

The increasing role of mental diseases could, however, be an indicator of the beginning of a new stage in the health transition (Meslé and Vallin 2006). The United States and the Netherlands might possibly be more affected than other countries by the threat of a "pandemic of mental disorders and disabilities" conjectured by some authors like Gruenberg (1978) and Kramer (1980), while France and Japan may already have reached a new age by fighting successfully against that emerging pandemic. Such success is not necessarily the result of a deliberate fight against specific mental disorders, but more probably due to greater general attention to the health of the elderly.[13] This would be consistent with the fact that Japan and France are also characterized by continuing progress in all other diseases, while in the United States and the Netherlands progress is limited to the field of heart disease. At this level of female life expectancy, further major improvement can no longer be based solely on the spread of recent techniques in the field of cardiovascular diseases.

Indeed, there is no definitive evidence for this interpretation, since cause-of-death structures vary considerably from country to country, because of both data coding and actual conditions. However, the consistency of the present findings for each set of two countries and the contrast between the two groups is impressive enough to accept it as a plausible hypothesis. Thus, whatever the reality regarding mental disorders, decrease in mortality rates above age 80 is much more important in France and Japan than in the United States or the Netherlands and that difference clearly points to the idea of a third stage of the health transition centered on the aging process, which gives rise to a new divergence rather similar to those already observed for infectious diseases at the beginning of the health transition, and then for cardiovascular diseases in the late 1960s and early 1970s (Vallin and Meslé 2004).

## Adult Mortality: Different Stories for Different Ages

Keeping in mind this general scheme for explaining historical trends and geographical patterns, let us examine the specific features of five adult age groups: youth (15–24), reproduction and working ages (25–44 and 45–64), retirement (65–79), and oldest-old (80 and above). Five countries serve as examples in the following analysis: France and Russia for Europe, Chile and the United States for the Americas, and Japan for Asia. We add one African country for the youngest age groups, alternatively Niger and Zimbabwe according to available data. Ideally, it would have been preferable to use a better representation of Asian and African diversity, but we needed countries with reliable historical information about mortality and causes of death. We also preferred using a small number of countries to make illustrations readable and to keep countries constant for comparisons across time and ages. As far as possible, for each age group we first examine historical trends in the probability of death for each sex, then analyze causes of death, with a special focus on the causes that are most important in shaping trends by age and sex.

---

[13] For example, through daily health care at home or in nursing homes, meal supply, and free access to drugs and other means to treat diseases that do not require hospitalization.

## Mortality Among Youth (15–24)

This first group represents the age of transition to adulthood. Because it is sensitive to infectious disease, it is the best illustration of the first stage of the health transition among adults. As Fig. 2.17 shows, the probability of death between ages 15 and 25 started to decline as early as the mid-nineteenth century in the most advanced countries like France and the United States, but much later in other industrialized countries like Japan as well as developing countries like Chile, and only quite recently in African countries like Niger.

This age group is also the most directly sensitive to wars, reflected in the high mortality peaks among males throughout the nineteenth century and the first half of the twentieth century. In France, for which annual series are available from the beginning of the nineteenth century (Vallin and Meslé 2001a), remarkable peaks appear around 1810 (Napoleonic wars), 1871 (Prussian war and Commune de Paris), 1914–1918 (WWI) and 1940 and 1944–1945 (WWII). In Russia, there is a very high peak caused by the terrible famine of 1933 among both sexes (unfortunately no annual estimates exist to show the impacts of WWI and WWII in this country). The impact of WWII is very clear in Japan at the end of the war in 1945. Both males and females were affected because most deaths were due to massive urban bombings, including atomic bombs on Hiroshima and Nagasaki. In France there were also special peaks in female mortality during these two centuries: in 1871 (civil victims of the Commune de Paris), 1918 (Spanish flu), and 1945 (Allied bombings).

After WWII, the mortality decrease at ages 15–24 accelerated sharply in countries where decline was already underway, and it extended to other countries mainly because of the dramatic fall of infectious diseases after the spread of antibiotics. Progress was particularly spectacular in Japan, which achieved the world's lowest mortality rates in the 1960s. By contrast, in France and the United States, male mortality increased for about 20 years from the mid-1950s, when traffic accidents became the major cause of death. Only after the mid-1970s was this new plague halted and mortality decrease resumed, though much less in the United States than in France. The same phenomenon occurred among females, but with only a period of stagnation instead of a mortality increase. The case of Russia was similar to that of France and the United States until the end of the 1970s, but diverged afterward. In recent decades, violent deaths in Russia have become more important and more linked to alcohol poisoning, suicides, and homicides than to traffic accidents. The large fluctuations in the age group have been

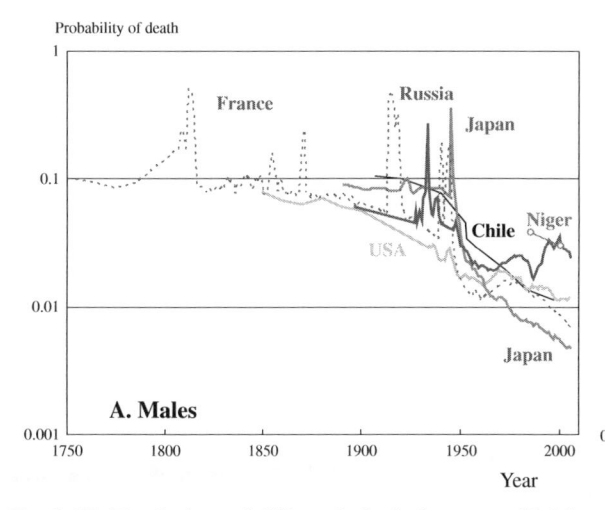

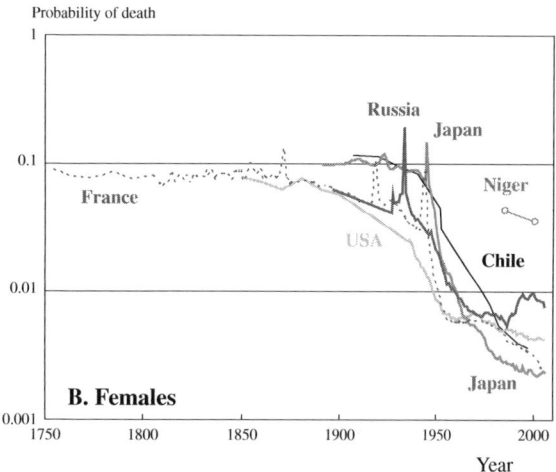

**Fig. 2.17** Trends in probability of death from age 15–25 in selected countries. Logged scale for probability of death. Sources: Vallin and Meslé (2001a) updated, for France; Arriaga (1968); Munoz Pradas (1989), and UN (2009) for Chile; special database prepared for Vallin and Meslé (2009) for Russia; HMD for Japan and the United States; Kourgueni et al. (1993) and INS (2007) for Niger

heavily affected by Gorbachev's anti-alcohol campaign and then the 1992–1993 socioeconomic crisis.

Although starting later, Chile, with regular mortality decline, caught up with France and the United States, but still had higher mortality than Japan in the early 2000s, while at the beginning of the 1950s its level of mortality had been similar to Japan's. For many other LDCs, especially in Africa, reliable data on adult mortality by age are very scarce. In Niger, taken here as an example of very poor countries not severely affected by AIDS, two Demographic and Health Surveys (DHS) provide evidence of mortality that is still very high and decreasing only slowly.

It is difficult to show precisely the importance of infectious diseases in the secular fall of mortality before the 1950s, when the WHO database begins its series. Figure 2.18 depicts only the end of the story, the time when Japan rapidly caught up to France and the United States while Chile took longer to do the same. The infectious mortality fall was so dramatic from the 1950s to the 1960s that changes that occurred afterward seem negligible. Nevertheless, a focus on the years 1980–2005 makes clear the big difference between Japan, which escaped the AIDS epidemic, and France and the United States. In the latter country, male mortality from infectious diseases at ages 15–25 was multiplied by four from 1980 to 1990, because of the impact of AIDS, and started to decline again after 1995 with the spread of AZT and tri-therapy.

Before WWII, cause-of-death data are scarcer and rarely comparable over time because of successive changes in classification of causes of death. Reconstruction of trends for France (Meslé and Vallin 1996; Vallin and Meslé 1988) provides an opportunity to see the prominent role of infectious diseases relative to external causes (left graph of Fig. 2.19). In France, mortality from external causes started increasing in the early 1950s, but total mortality still went down because of the very sharp decrease in infectious mortality. At the end of the 1950s, the impact of infectious diseases on total mortality became negligible, while the increase in external causes accelerated.

The right graph of Fig. 2.19 clarifies that traffic accidents were the main driver of the changes both upward (when road traffic increased markedly) and downward (when more efficient safety measures

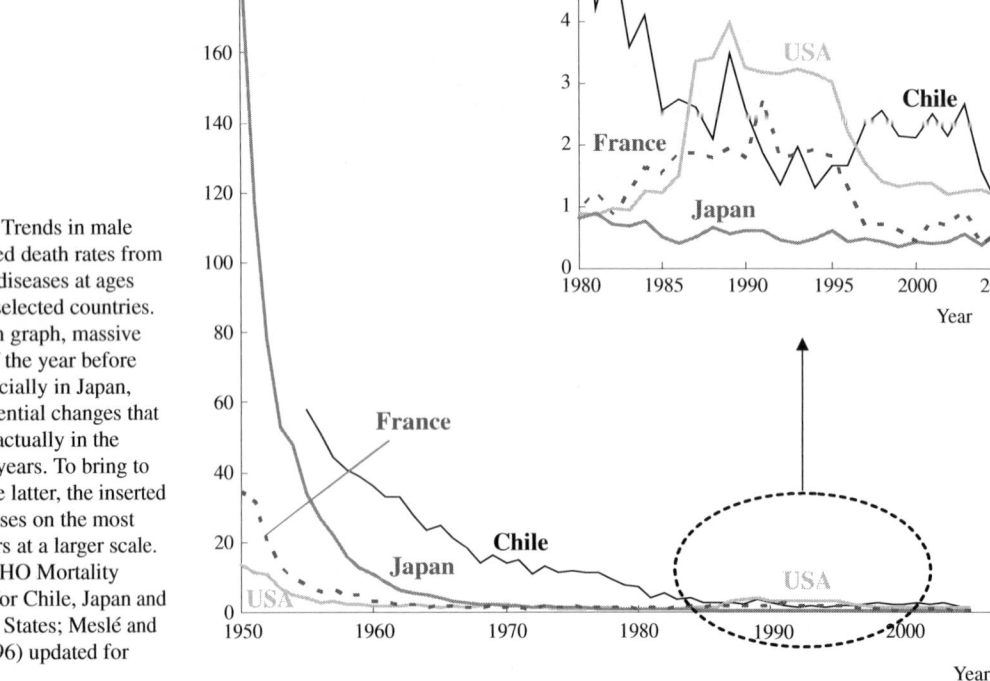

**Fig. 2.18** Trends in male standardized death rates from infectious diseases at ages 15–24, in selected countries. In the main graph, massive changes of the year before 1980, especially in Japan, hide differential changes that happened actually in the following years. To bring to the fore the latter, the inserted graph focuses on the most recent years at a larger scale. Source: WHO Mortality Database for Chile, Japan and the United States; Meslé and Vallin (1996) updated for France

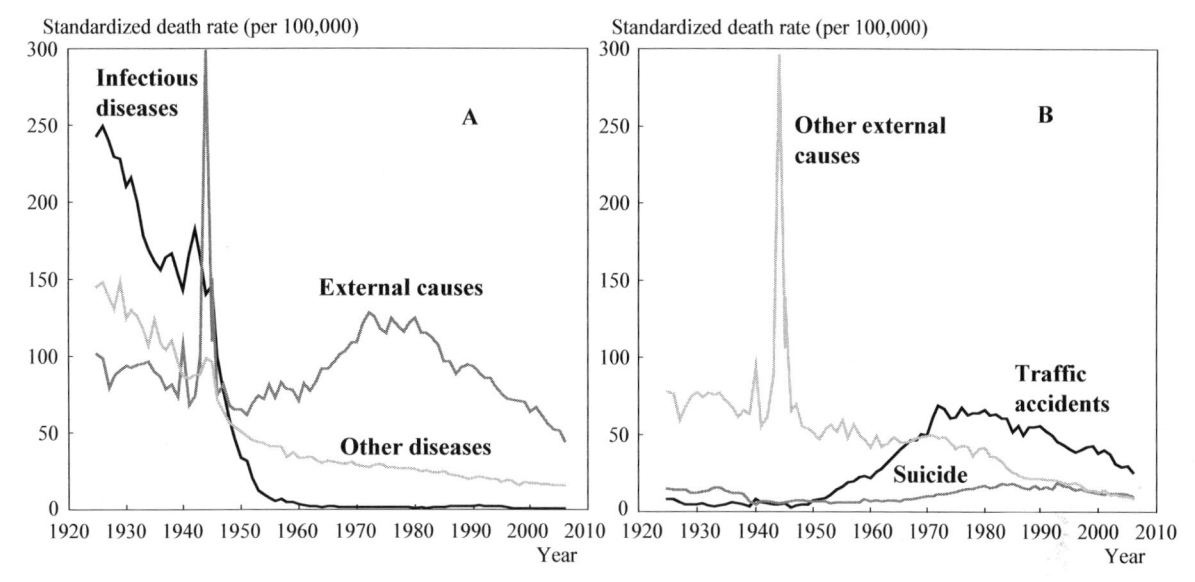

**Fig. 2.19** Trends in standardized death rates at ages 15–24 for selected groups of causes: France, males. **Graph A** compares trends in the two major groups of causes (infectious and external) as opposed to all the other causes; **Graph B** compares three main subgroups of external causes (suicide, traffic accidents, and other). Source: Meslé and Vallin (1996) updated

were implemented and the first oil shortage of the mid-1970s occurred (Vallin and Meslé 2001b)). The same trends were observed almost simultaneously in all industrialized countries.

While historical trends in young-adult mortality are a clear illustration of the prominent role of infectious diseases in the first stage of the health transition, they are also illustrative of the effect of man-made diseases in the second stage, but not of that of degenerative diseases, which do not affect these ages.

## Mortality Among Young Adults (25–44): Period of Reproduction and Production

The general shape of the trends in mortality at ages 25–44 is not radically different from that for the previous age group; the effects of violence and/or epidemics are similar. However, this age group is focused on reproductive activity among women and productive activity in both sexes. In countries like France and the United States and even Russia (in spite of less precise data) the decrease in total mortality started sooner and was much faster for females than for males after the end of the nineteenth century (Fig. 2.20). Pasteur's revolution and the spread of asepsis, reinforced in the 1930s by the arrival of sulfonamides, were decisive steps in the reduction of maternal mortality. More recently, in the Soviet world the working ages were most affected by the unfavorable mortality trends that started in the mid-1960s, and males were much more severely affected than females, as is shown here for Russia. In contrast to all other trajectories, Zimbabwe (here again assessed using scarce but valuable DHS findings) demonstrates the exceptional mortality explosion at this age resulting from the AIDS epidemic.

It is difficult to show directly the historical fall in maternal mortality from its beginning in developed countries in the absence of precise cause-of-death data for the past, but the phenomenon can be illustrated through the differences in the changes of female mortality compared to that of men across age groups, shown for France in Fig. 2.21. Age-specific mortality rates for successive periods after the mid-eighteenth century have been divided by those observed in 1938. The 1750–1759 curve shows clearly the burden of maternal mortality at ages 25–45 with the significant hump among females. The importance of male mortality changes at the same ages regularly decreased with age. The hump progressively decreased through the nineteenth century and the beginning of the twentieth century, until WWII. The phenomenon is still visible in 1920, although much smaller and restricted to younger ages, reflecting the drastic reduction of fertility. By contrast, from 1938

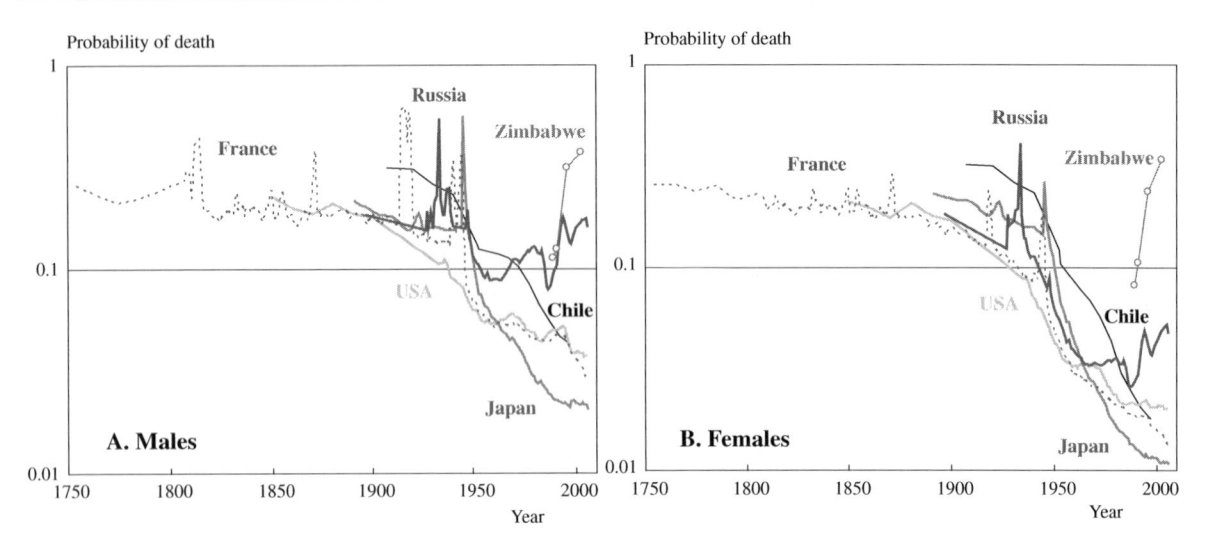

**Fig. 2.20** Trends in the probability of death from age 25–45 in selected countries. Logged scale for Probability of death. Sources: Vallin and Meslé (2001a) updated, for France; Munoz Pradas (1989); Arriaga (1968), and UN (2009) for Chile; special database prepared for Vallin and Meslé (2009) for Russia; HMD for Japan and the United States; CSO (1995, 2000); CSO and ORC Macro (2007) for Zimbabwe

to 1960, a time where maternal mortality was no longer a major public health problem, the pace of mortality decrease diminished with age for both sexes.

Much more recently this age group has been most severely affected by the AIDS epidemic. The case in eastern and southern Africa, here represented by mortality for males and females in Zimbabwe, is particularly impressive (Fig. 2.22). According to DHS surveys, in less than 15 years mortality at ages 35–39 was multiplied by more than 5 for both males and females.

In a more general approach, Fig. 2.23 displays trends in seven large groups of causes of death for males in five countries since 1950 (1955 for Chile, 1956 for Russia). Males are shown because male trends contrast more across countries. To clarify the

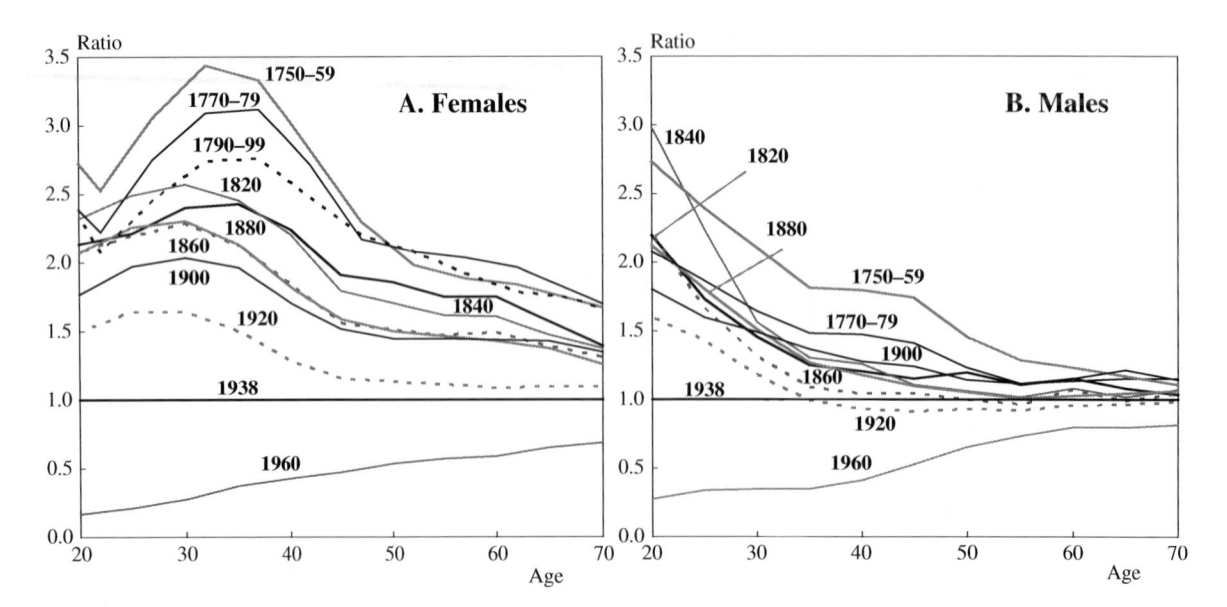

**Fig. 2.21** Ratio of 5-Year Age probabilities of death at selected periods to 1938 death probabilities: France. Source: Vallin and Meslé (2001a)

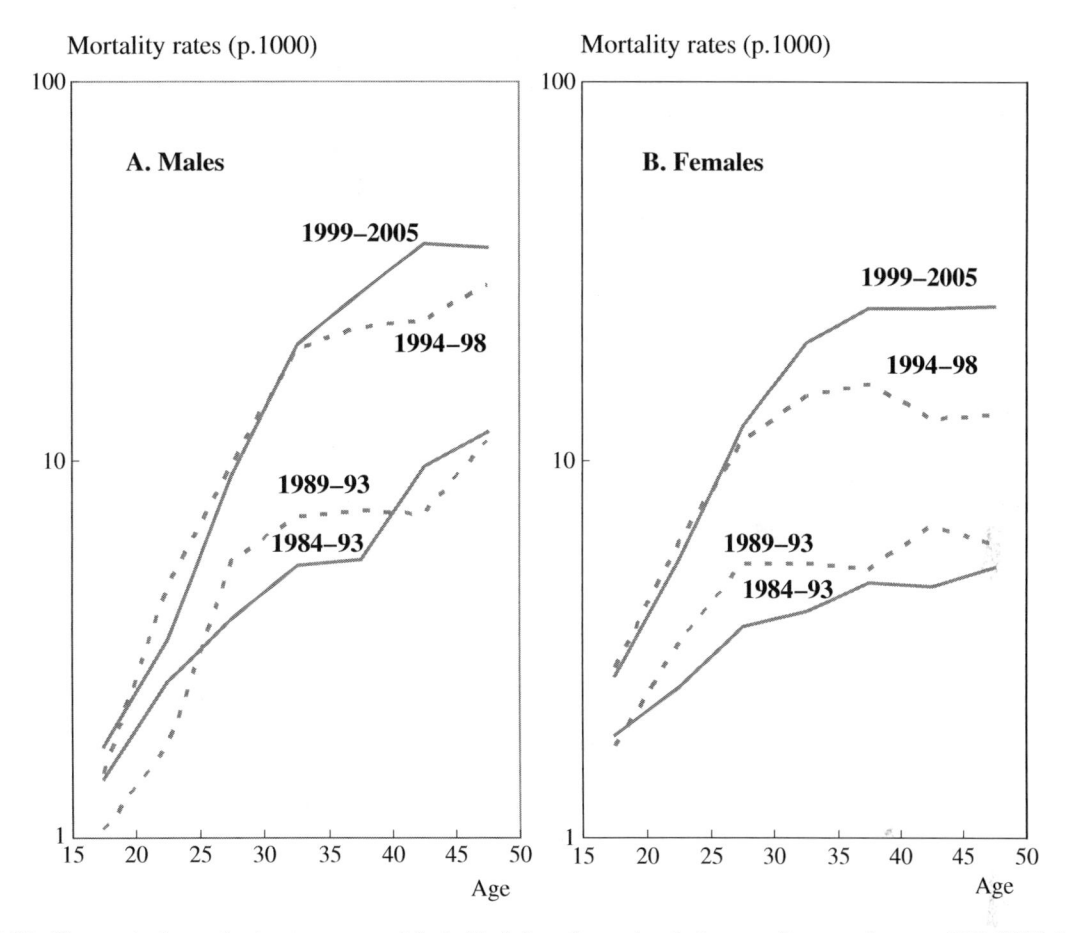

**Fig. 2.22** Changes in 5-year death rates among adults in Zimbabwe. Logged scale for mortality rates. Sources: CSO (1995, 2000), CSO and ORC Macro (2007)

comparison, the scale is the same for all countries. One generalization holds for all countries. Before the end of the 1950s, infectious diseases were no longer the main killer at these ages in all of these countries; instead, mortality was now dominated by external causes. Beyond that common feature, countries differed markedly from each other. First, mortality from external causes was more important in Chile (at least until the end of the 1980s) and Russia than in the United States, France, and Japan. In Chile, apart from the acute peak of 1973, related to the Pinochet coup, the progress made from the 1950s to the 1990s echoed that made several decades earlier by industrialized countries. In contrast, in Russia, from the 1950s to the early 1990s, the mortality curve for external causes closely followed changes in alcohol consumption: steady regular increase with the stagnating society of Brezhnev's era, then sudden decrease caused by Gorbachev's anti-alcohol campaign, and finally a new increase with the abandonment of anti-alcohol measures (Shkolnikov and Nemtsov 1997). A new peak was reached at the time of the socioeconomic crisis caused by the move to a market economy (Meslé et al. 1998), before the unfavorable long-term trends resumed in the second half of the 1990s. Recent economic improvement seemed to result in a favorable reversal of trends, but in 2006, the level of mortality from external causes at age 25–44 was four times higher in Russia than in the United States and almost eight times higher than in Japan.

Another difference is that the second most important group of causes varied across countries. In most of the period it was cancer in France, while it was digestive diseases in Chile, and circulatory diseases in the United States, Russia, and Japan. Trajectories of cardiovascular mortality were extremely different in these three countries. While Japan consistently had a very low level, hardly higher than that of cancers,

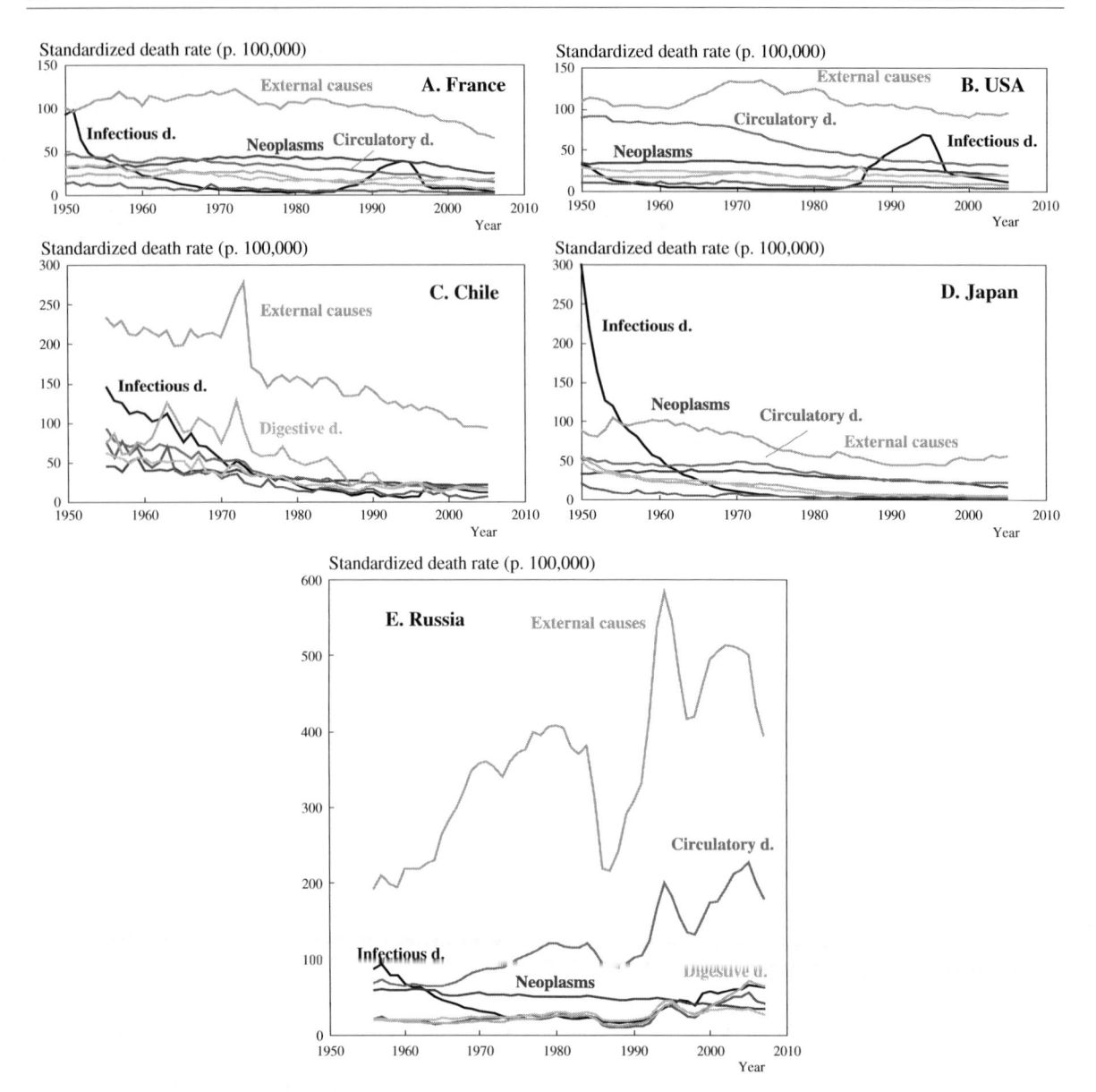

**Fig. 2.23** Trends in male standardized death rates for seven large groups of causes at ages 25–44: Five selected countries. The height of each graph varies to keep constant the ordinate scale. This brings to the fore the much larger variations observed in Russia (**Graph E**) both in time and according to cause, as compared to France (**Graph A**) or the United States (**Graph B**). In-between Chile (**Graph C**) and Japan (**Graph D**) show rather important ranges of changes in time but the highest levels of mortality observed in the 1950s stand much lower than the recent ones of Russia. Source: WHO Mortality Database for Chile, Japan, and the United States; Meslé and Vallin (1996) updated for France; Meslé et al. (1996, 2003) updated for Russia

mortality from cardiovascular disease was very high in the United States at the beginning of the 1950s, almost as high as for external causes, but it decreased rather rapidly in the 1970s, and has reached cancer levels in recent years. In contrast, in Russia, mortality from circulatory diseases increased rapidly (with large fluctuations linked to alcohol consumption), so that it is now ten times higher than in Japan. In Chile, digestive diseases were relatively important after the role of infectious diseases vanished, but their absolute level decreased as socioeconomic development increased, and finally reached the low level of industrialized countries. When we look simultaneously at Chilean trends in infectious diseases, digestive diseases, and external causes, it appears that this country was ending the first stage of the health transition as the industrialized countries had done some decades earlier, and at the same time was beginning a part of the second stage by controlling some effects of man-made diseases. In contrast, Russia under the communist regime was very successful in completing the first stage, but completely failed to enter the second stage, and was unable to stop the progression of man-made diseases and to avoid circulatory diseases.

Finally, some important remarks about infectious diseases. First, this group of causes was still the primary killer (far more important than any other) in Japan at the beginning of the 1950s. From an epidemiological point of view, Japan was still a "developing country" at this time, and the 1950s were clearly the moment when Japan made its spectacular entry into the MDCs. In Chile, infectious mortality, for which no comparable data are available before 1956, was probably as high as in Japan just after WWII, but it declined much more slowly, while the country's socioeconomic progress was not yet high enough for it to be classified among the MDCs by the UN. Infectious mortality at ages 25–44 also matters in countries like France and the United States, where its trajectory passed through a surprising hump during the 1990s. This is obviously the result of the AIDS epidemic. For a short time, in the United States, infectious disease mortality became the second major killer, not far from external causes and much higher than circulatory diseases.

Figure 2.24 provides more detail on external causes, which play so significant a role in the differences among the five countries. First, we can see that traffic accidents, though increasing quite markedly, are not the most important external cause in Russia. From the 1950s to the 1970s the extraordinary increase in suicide is the main factor of the external causes growth, while from the 1990s to the present it has been homicide: thus two different major types of violence characterize successively the communist time and the capitalist one.

Figure 2.24 also shows that trends in mortality from traffic accidents, which had increased dramatically in the 1960s, reversed completely in the mid-1970s in Chile as they did in the industrialized countries. This reversal occurred sooner in Japan, a country that enacted very strict road safety measures as early as the mid-1960s.

Suicide was generally less important in Chile than in France, Japan, and the United States. There is also an important contrast between the United States and France and Japan in homicide. At these ages, around the 1970s, this cause of death was higher in the United States than in all other countries, and it would still be highest there without the dramatic increase observed in Russia. Even though the relative gap between the United States and Japan or France has declined significantly since the 1970s, the homicide rate is still 25 times higher than in France and Japan today. The United States is a violent society.

## *Mortality Among Middle-Aged Adults (45–64)*

In the next age group, 45–64, the working environment still affects health, which also increasingly depends on the aging process. There are fewer historical peaks, and long-term trends are less confused. Three main features appear in Fig. 2.25, which depicts trends in the probabilities of death between ages 45 and 65 for the five countries under review. First, the long historical series available for France shows that (after a slight decline at the turn of the nineteenth century) male mortality remained almost constant (beyond annual fluctuations) from the 1820s until the mid-1940s, while female mortality seems to have started to decrease slowly after the end of the eighteenth century, and this decrease accelerated at the end of the nineteenth century. The United States followed the same route after the mid-nineteenth century. And during the phase of rapid reduction after WWII, mortality decline was much more rapid for females than for males in the two countries for about two decades. It was only in the most recent period (earlier in the United States than in France) that males progressed at the same pace as females, or even somewhat faster.

The second main feature is that Russian mortality, after having followed a comparable route (when not affected by exceptional mortality crises), started to diverge radically (as in the previous age groups), with an important increase after the mid-1960s for both sexes, but more pronounced for males.

The third characteristic is that mortality decline after WWII in Japan and after the mid-1970s in Chile was much faster than in both France and the United

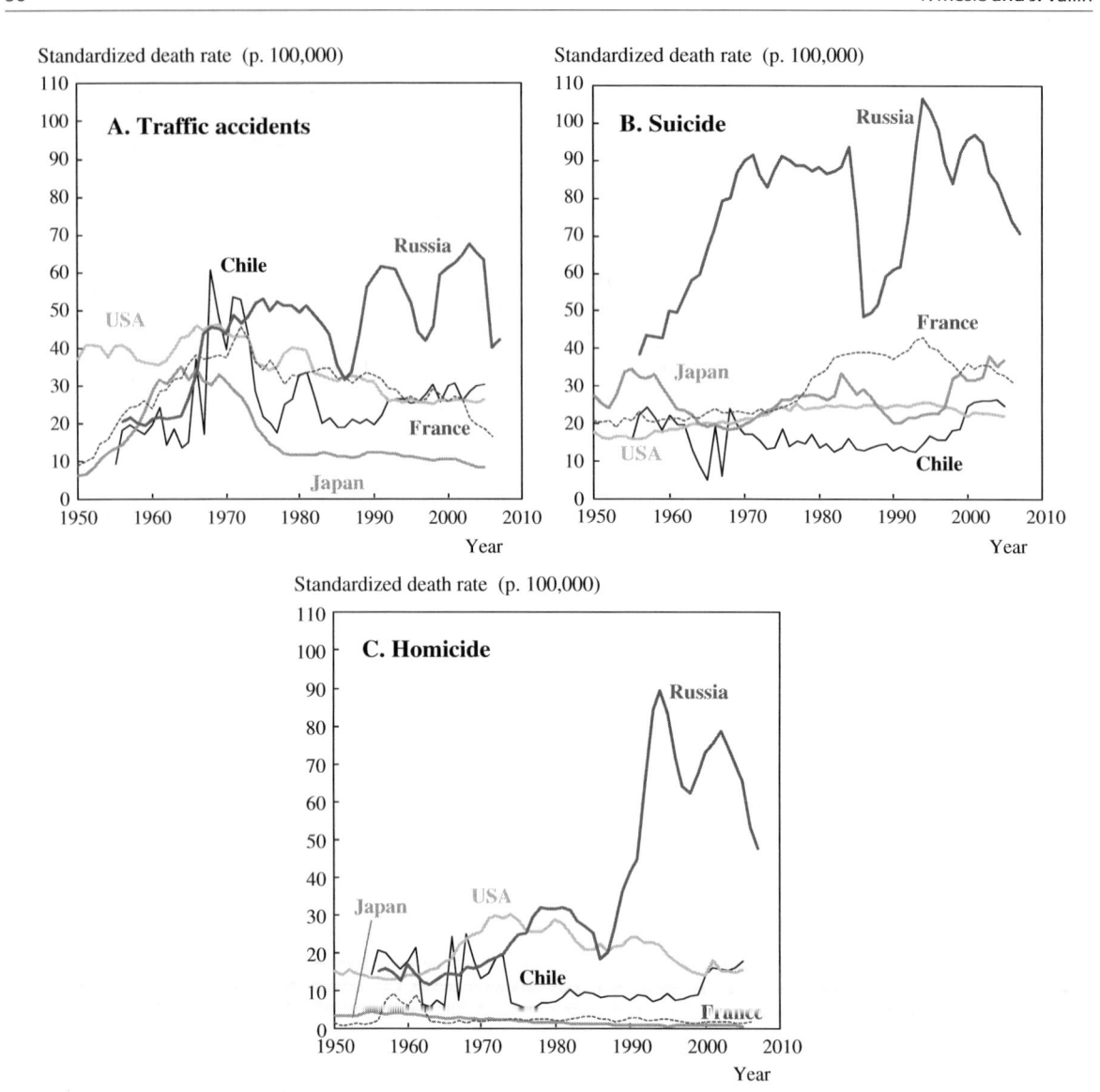

**Fig. 2.24** Trends in male standardized death rates by three external causes at ages 25–44: Five selected countries. Source: WHO Mortality Database for Chile, Japan and the Unites States; Meslé and Vallin (1996) updated for France; Meslé et al. (1996, 2003) updated for Russia

States. In that time, Japan caught up to all industrialized countries, and then surpassed them to become the international leader in very low mortality. Japanese mortality at ages 45–64 was the same as in France in the late 1940s for males and two decades later for females. Meanwhile, Chile reached the male levels in France and the United States (almost identical in past decades) in the 1990s. At that time, Chilean females also reached the US but not the French level, since French and US female mortality at this age have been diverging radically for about 25 years. This last fact could be pointed out here as a fourth main feature, but it will be even more obvious in the discussion of the older ages since it is strongly related to the aging process.

Focusing once again on male mortality trends since 1950, Fig. 2.26 shows clearly that in all five countries circulatory diseases and cancer have been the main mortality drivers at ages 45–64, while external causes continue to play an important and growing role in Russia. It also shows that these two groups of causes followed very different trajectories, with consequences

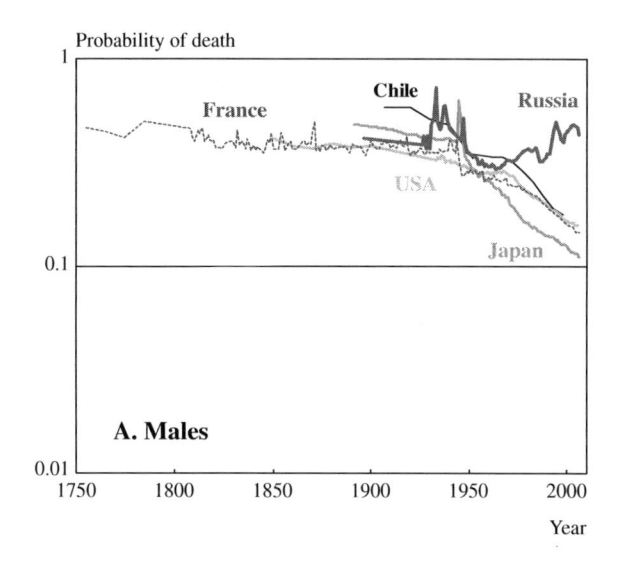

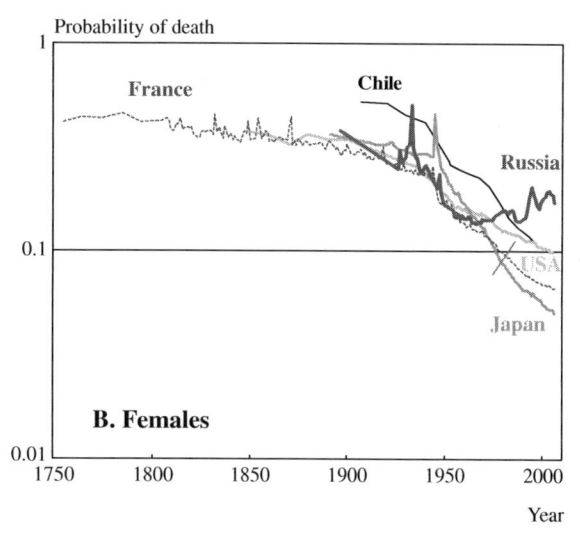

**Fig. 2.25** Trends in the probability of death from age 45 to 65 in selected countries. Logged scale for probability of death. Sources: Vallin and Meslé (2001a) updated, for France; Munoz Pradas (1989); Arriaga (1968) and UN (2009) for Chile; special database prepared for Vallin and Meslé (2009) for Russia; HMD for Japan and the United States

varying by country. In France, circulatory diseases, though at a lower level than in the four other countries, were still the most important cause of death. However, they declined very regularly and steadily to reach a level in 2006 that was a third of the level in 1950. Consequently, neoplasm mortality, which increased from 1950 to the mid-1980s, replaced circulatory diseases as the first cause of death. Today mortality from neoplasms is twice as high as that due to circulatory diseases.

In the United States, the same pattern of changes for these two main groups of causes produced a very different result because of the very high starting level of circulatory disease mortality. In spite of its dramatic fall, especially after the 1970s (the starting point of the so-called cardiovascular revolution), circulatory diseases have not yet been replaced by neoplasms as the leading cause of death. Indeed, there appears to be a convergence rather than a probable cross-over: both pathologies have very similar mortality rates that are decreasing at the same pace.

In Chile, circulatory disease mortality at ages 45–64 also declined from the beginning of the period. But starting from a much lower level, it is currently lower than in the United States, in spite of a slower pace of decrease. Since neoplasm mortality also declined regularly but even less rapidly, both mortality rates have been at the same level for the past 20 years.

As in the United States, these two groups of causes tie for first place, but both are at a lower level than in the United States. Japan, starting from a comparable level of circulatory disease mortality, experienced more rapid reductions than in Chile, while neoplasm mortality stagnated. Consequently, as in France, neoplasm mortality is the most important cause of death, almost twice as high as circulatory disease mortality. However, the gap between the two is much less than in France because cancer mortality is much lower while cardiovascular mortality is somewhat higher.

Finally, once again, Russia appears to be an atypical case. After the mid-1960s circulatory disease mortality increased markedly, from a rate of 530 per 100,000 in 1965 (lower than in the United States) to a rate of 1,500 per 100,000 in 2003, with large fluctuations strongly linked to alcohol consumption. It has subsequently started to decrease, but remains five times higher than in the United States and ten times higher than in France. Not only is cardiovascular mortality the most important cause of death, but it is far higher than cancer, which is also quite high relative to other countries and to external causes, which have more than doubled since 1950. The Russian pattern for both circulatory diseases and external causes is of the same nature as it was for the previous age group. For that reason, we prefer to focus here on the growing relative importance of neoplasms in the five countries.

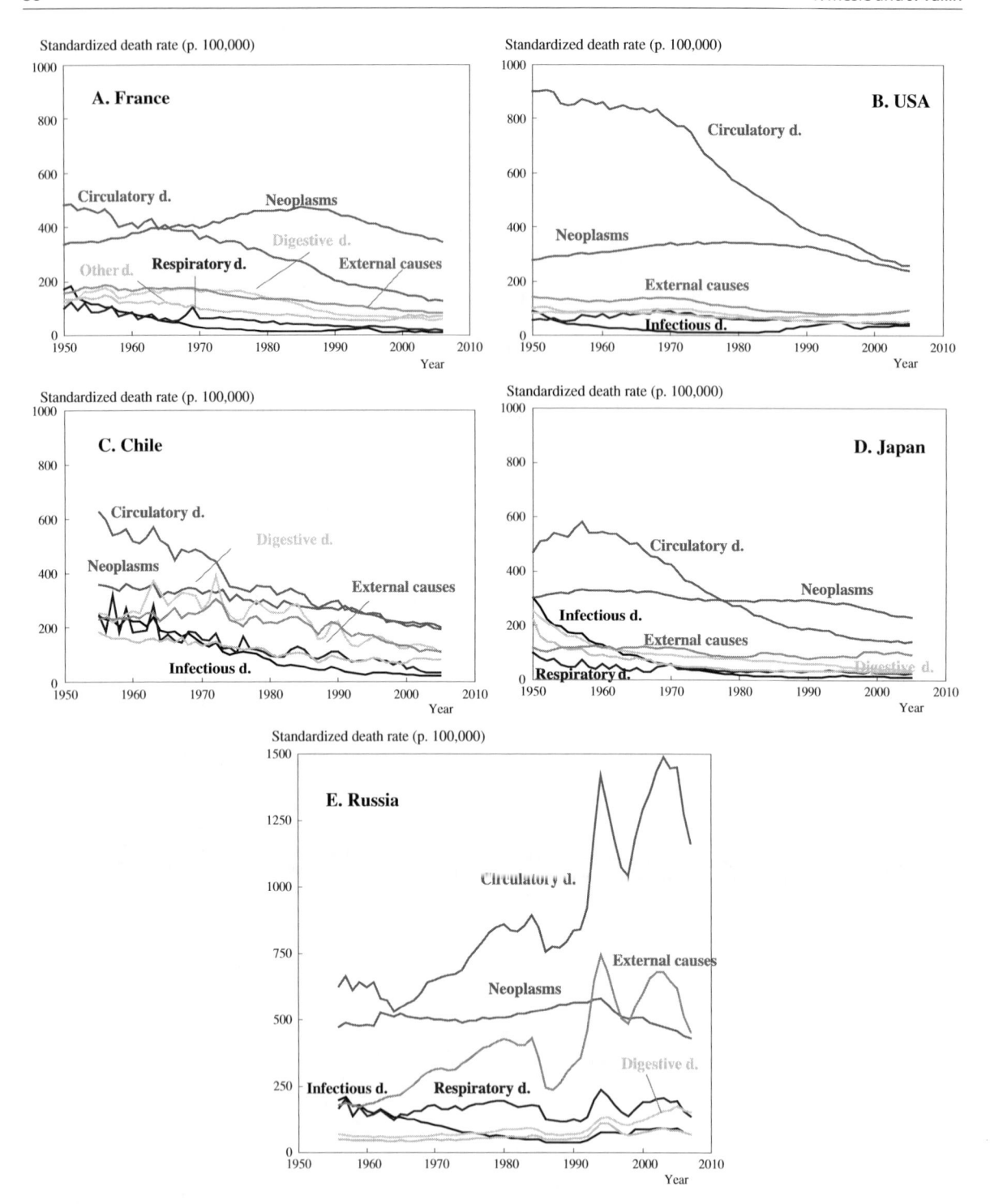

**Fig. 2.26** Trends in male standardized death rates by seven large groups of causes at ages 45–64: Five selected countries. The height of each graph varies to keep constant the ordinate scale. This brings to the fore the much larger variations observed in Russia (**Graph E**) both in time and according to cause, as compared to France (**Graph A**), the United States (**Graph B**), Chile (**Graph C**), and Japan (**Graph D**). Source: WHO Mortality Database for Chile, Japan and the United States; Meslé and Vallin (1996) updated for France; Meslé et al. (1996, 2003) updated for Russia

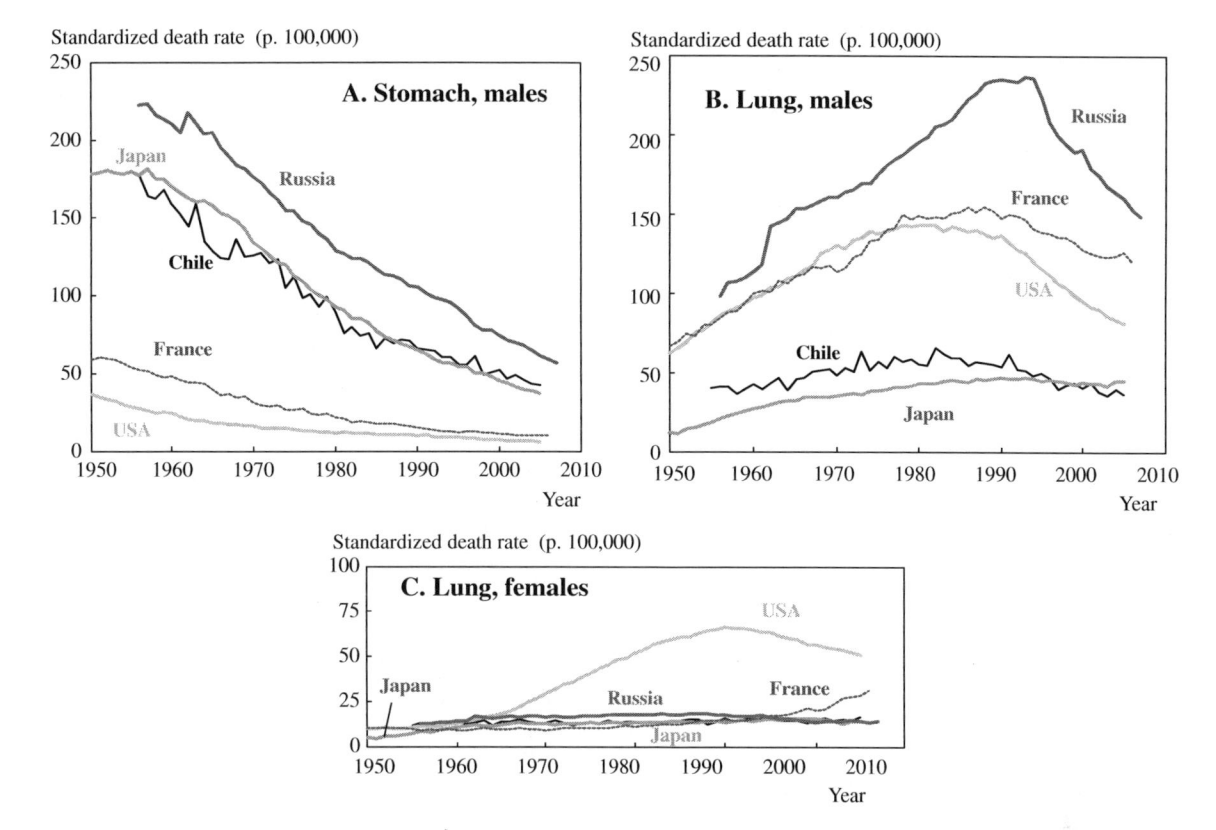

**Fig. 2.27** Trends in standardized death rates from stomach cancer (males) and lung cancer (males and females) at ages 45–64. Five selected countries. **Graphs A** and **B** compare mortality trends for two main sites of cancer in five countries for males. Graph **C** shows female mortality trends for only lung cancer. The height of each graph varies to keep constant the ordinate scale. This brings to the fore the much higher levels of lung cancer mortality among males than among females. Source: WHO Mortality Database for Chile, Japan and the United States; Meslé and Vallin (1996) updated for France; Meslé et al. (1996, 2003) updated for Russia

Figure 2.27 contrasts trends in stomach and lung cancers. Stomach cancer mortality decreased very rapidly and continuously in all five countries under review, from very different levels but at about the same pace. The result is exactly the same ranking and almost the same relative differences in 2006 as in 1950.[14] France and the United States have the lowest levels and Russia the highest. In-between, Japanese and Chilean trajectories are almost identical.

Conversely, until at least the 1980s, lung cancer mortality had a trend in the opposite direction, growing relatively fast in the five countries, but with an enormous difference in levels. Once again Russia had the highest mortality, but this time, France and the United States shared the second rank, while Chile and Japan were far below. However, after the 1980s in the United States and Chile, the early 1990s in France, and the late 1990s in Russia, lung cancer mortality stopped increasing and started to decrease rather dramatically in Russia and the United States, less rapidly in France and Chile, but not at all in Japan.

## Mortality in Old Age (65–79)

Ages 65–79 are the transition years from the adult ages to the elderly. It is even more obvious in this age group that major mortality reduction is quite recent.

---

[14] Figure 2.27, in arithmetic scale, seems to indicate that the pace of decline is much less in France and the United States than in Russia, Japan, and Chile. The arithmetic scale indicates absolute changes, not relative changes. In fact the much smaller absolute changes observed here in the first two countries correspond to relative changes as high as in the other three countries, in spite of their much larger absolute changes.

For males it began post-WWII; for females it started earlier, after about the 1920s. The much more rapid fall of mortality among females than among males is also more pronounced than for the previous age group (Fig. 2.28). Also more acute is the recent divergence since the 1980s between France and Japan and the United States. In contrast to the previous age group, the increase in male mortality after 1965 in Russia was less, and females suffered stagnation instead of an increase. These differences are rather typical of mortality changes specific to the elderly. Consequently, the emphasis on cause-of-death trends since the 1950s is particularly relevant, since nothing very important occurred before WWII. For this age group and the following, we will focus on cause-of-death trends among females for whom changes were quite impressive during this period.

Everywhere, the main causes of change were the trajectories of circulatory diseases, either downward in France, the United States, Chile, and Japan, or upward in Russia. In France, while mortality from circulatory diseases was the main killer for females, with rates three times higher than those for cancers in the 1950s, it is now second, far below cancers, which remained stable throughout the period (Fig. 2.29). In the United States and in Japan, the fall of cardiovascular mortality has been even more spectacular, but the starting point was much higher and the crossover with cancers is more recent and less pronounced. It occurred in the United States in 2005, in spite of a slight decrease in cancer mortality. It came a bit sooner in Japan in spite of a lower level of cancer. Once again, the case of Russia is dissimilar, since female mortality from circulatory diseases stagnated at a very high level until the end of the 1980s and even increased slightly during the 1990s.

Figure 2.30 displays the specific trajectories of the two main categories of circulatory diseases: heart diseases and cerebrovascular diseases (other circulatory diseases are rather marginal). Two main facts appear here. On one side, female heart disease mortality was always much higher in the United States than in France or Japan, even though it decreased quite rapidly. Furthermore, the pace of decrease was more rapid in France and Japan than in the United States. Consequently, while female US heart disease mortality was 1.6 times that of France in 1950, it is now 2.6 times higher.

On the other side, female cerebrovascular mortality started at a much higher level in Japan than in France and the United States, but Japan made such rapid progress (especially in the 1970s and 1980s) that its trajectory joins those of the other two countries. In 2006, it has exactly the same level as the United States, just a bit higher than France. The case of Russia is again quite the opposite, but with no important difference between heart diseases and cerebrovascular diseases.

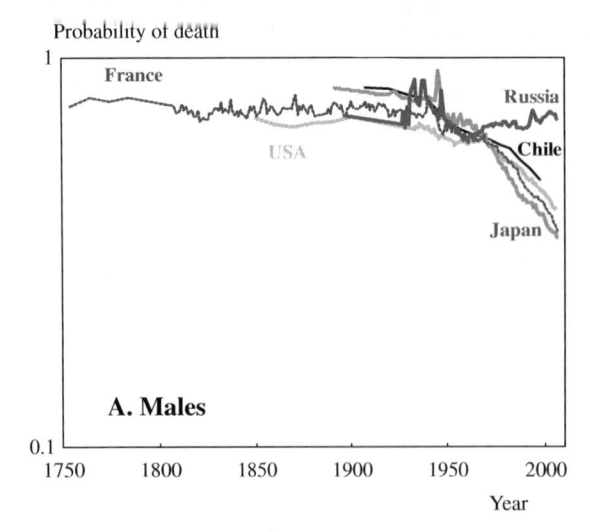

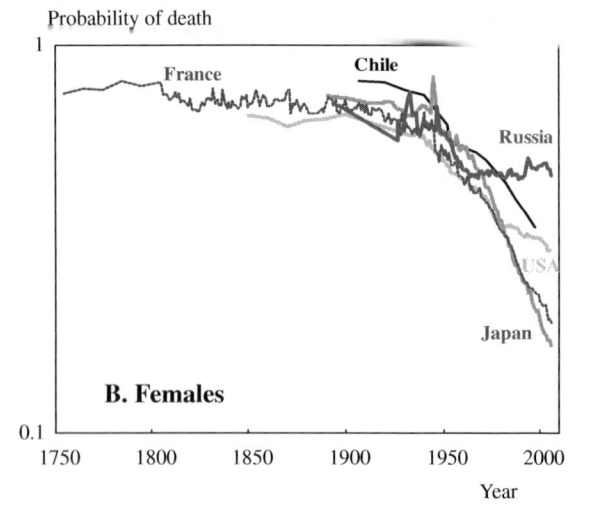

**Fig. 2.28** Trends in probability of death from ages 65 to 80 in selected countries. Sources: Vallin and Meslé (2001a) updated, for France; Arriaga (1968); Munoz Pradas (1989), and UN (2009) for Chile; special database prepared for Vallin and Meslé (2009) for Russia; HMD for Japan and the United States

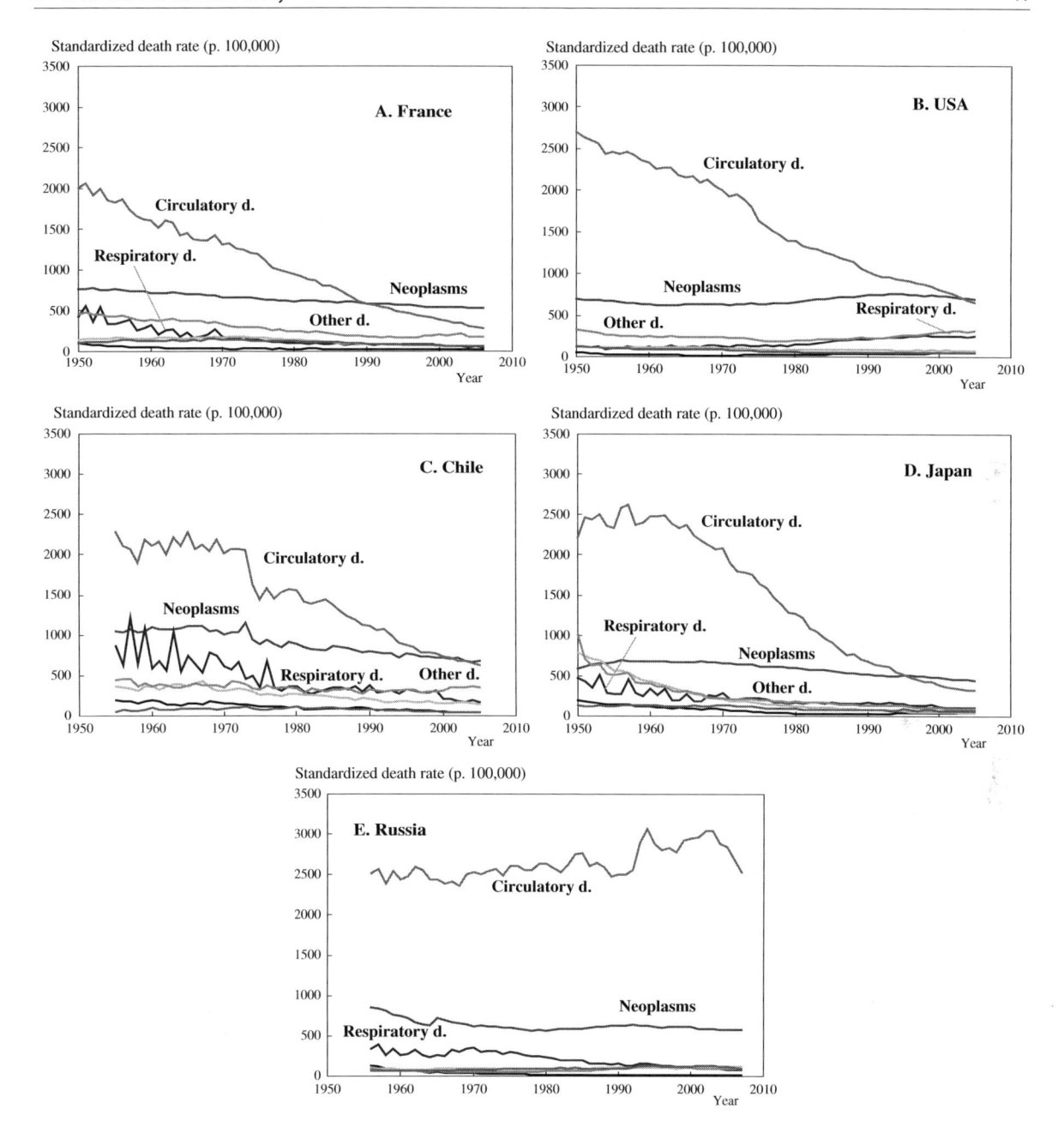

**Fig. 2.29** Trends in female standardized death rates from seven large groups of causes at ages 65–79: Five selected countries. The scale is kept constant to make levels comparable from country to country. Source: WHO Mortality Database for Chile, Japan and the United States; Meslé and Vallin (1996) updated for France; Meslé et al. (1996, 2003) updated for Russia

To highlight the causes of death that drive the recent divergence in total mortality between the United States and Japan and France, Fig. 2.31 displays graphs using the same scale for four larger categories of causes grouped according to the shape of their trajectories after 1980.

The important killer, circulatory diseases, is not the primary cause of the divergence. It explains an important part of the divergence between the United States and Japan, but much less of the divergence between the United States and France. At the other end of the scheme, external causes would act in the opposite

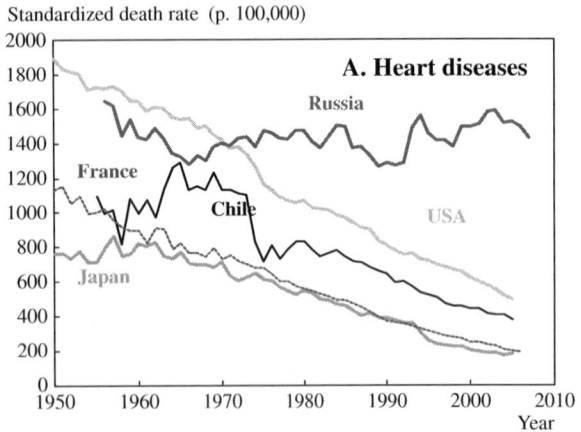

**Fig. 2.30** Trends in female standardized death rates from the two main groups of circulatory diseases at ages 65–79: Five selected countries. Source: WHO Mortality Database for Chile, Japan and the United States; Meslé and Vallin (1996) updated for France; Meslé et al. (1996, 2003) updated for Russia

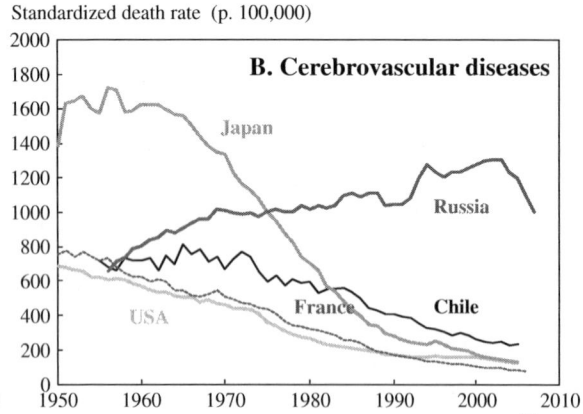

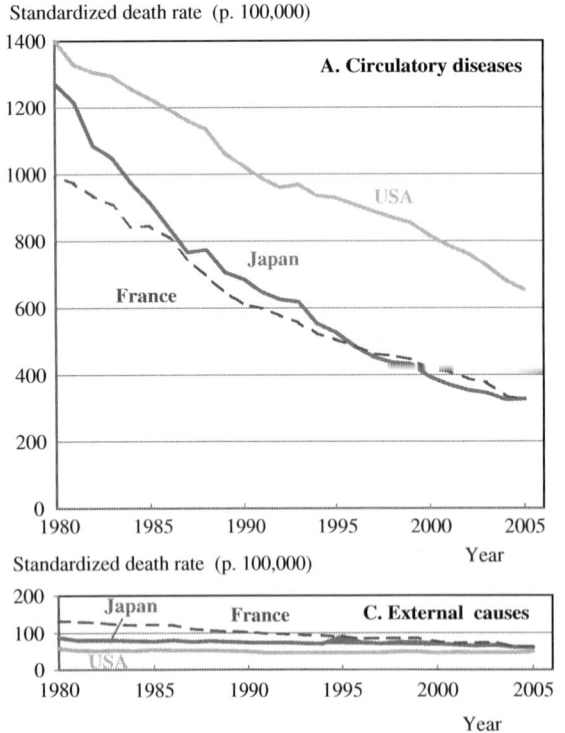

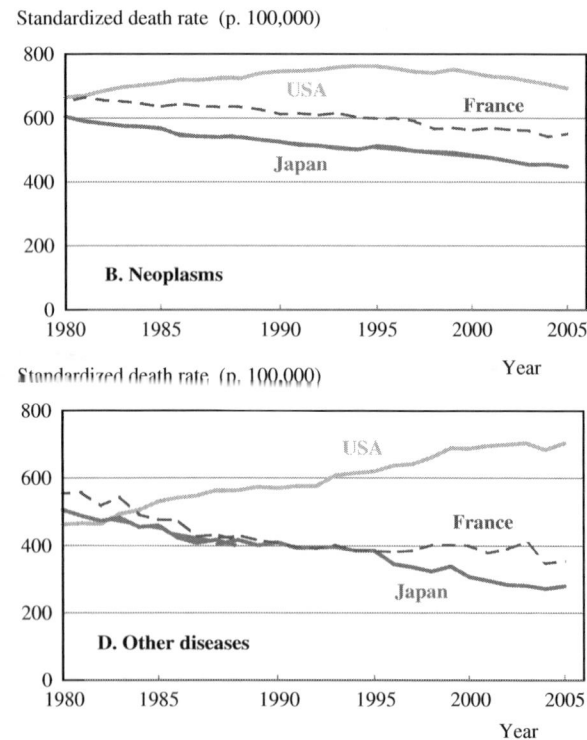

**Fig. 2.31** Recent trends in female standardized death rates by four groups of causes at ages 65–79 in the United States, France, and Japan. The height of each graph varies to keep constant the ordinate scale. This brings to the fore the much higher impact of circulatory diseases (**Graph A**) as compared to external causes (**Graph C**) while that of neoplasms (**Graph B**) and other diseases (**Graph D**) stand in-between. Source: WHO Mortality Database for Japan and the United States; Meslé and Vallin (1996) updated for France

direction (convergence), but their weight is negligible. Finally, the divergence process relies quite clearly on two different groups of causes: cancers and "other diseases." The cancer trajectory is largely driven by lung cancer and is strongly related to tobacco consumption. However, the diverging effect of that cause reached its maximum around 1995 and it then became a cause of convergence, echoing the reversal, some years before, of trends in US female tobacco consumption. In contrast, mortality from other diseases was a diverging factor throughout the period and was the most important one in the last decade. Among more specific diseases, almost all have a diverging influence: not only respiratory diseases (still partly linked to tobacco) but also infectious diseases, digestive diseases, and mental diseases and other diseases of the nervous system, to note only the most important ones. Thus, while the divergence is somewhat related to a less rapid decline of cardiovascular mortality in the United States, it is caused even more by the increase in mortality from a large number of less important causes that decreased in France and Japan. While the greater tobacco consumption of US females is a good candidate for explaining the first part of the divergence, the reversal of trends in cigarette consumption did not stop the divergence at all. The latter is probably more driven by general public health problems of the US female elderly that are better faced in France and Japan (Meslé and Vallin 2006).

## *Mortality at Very Old Ages (80 and Above)*

Mortality at very old ages is examined here only for three countries: France, Japan, and the United States. This is because the role that mortality at this age plays in life expectancy at birth is less in Chile and even more so in Russia, but also because measurement of mortality beyond age 80 requires great accuracy in data: countries must have birth registration of high quality for at least one century. Even for the United States, it is not clear if this requirement is fully fulfilled. The treatment of this last age group here also differs from that of the previous ones: because the probability of death after 80 is necessarily 100%, life expectancy at 80 is used to follow total mortality trajectories (Fig. 2.32).

It is even clearer than for the previous age group that progress began rather recently. While life expectancy at birth started to increase in most MDCs early in the nineteenth century, or even after the mid-eighteenth century, life expectancy at age 80 did not change at all until WWII for males in France. The starting point seems to have been earlier in the United States and in Japan as well, but in both cases, the data are not good enough to ensure that it is not simply an artifact. A starting point around 1930 is more reliable for French females. In any case, for the three countries, especially for females, the achievements of the most recent decades are spectacular. In particular, in Japan, life expectancy at 80 doubled within the last 30 years, from 5.7 years in 1976 to 11.3 in 2006. Here again, however, the US trajectory started to diverge strongly from the Japanese one, but more recently than for mortality at ages 65–79 (from about 1995, instead of 1980). The divergence with France seems less clear in Fig. 2.32, but it is due to the small peak of mortality in France caused by the heat wave of 2003. The reasons for that divergence are obviously the same as those mentioned above for ages 65–79.

Let us note here more generally the overwhelming role played by cardiovascular mortality fall in the progress achieved since 1950 (Fig. 2.33). At least up to the 1980s, this group of causes was far more important than others. In 1950, in France and Japan, mortality from cardiovascular diseases was more than double that of the second highest cause (respiratory diseases for France, and, at the same level, digestive diseases, respiratory diseases, and other diseases, for Japan). In the United States, the gap was even greater: eight times higher than the second killer, cancers. In spite of its rapid decline, especially after the 1970s, the relative position of cardiovascular mortality today is not radically different across the countries. In all three countries, circulatory disease mortality is now not far from twice as high as mortality from the second cause of death. The reason is that after about the 1980s the second major cause was either stagnating (like respiratory diseases in Japan) or increasing (like "other causes" in France and in the United States). Nevertheless, nowhere is the timing of a crossover easily predictable. In France and the United States it will depend a lot on trends in the "other diseases," which are quite uncertain, while in Japan, the last half-decade has been more or less characterized by a stabilization of cardiovascular mortality and the stagnation of all groups of causes.

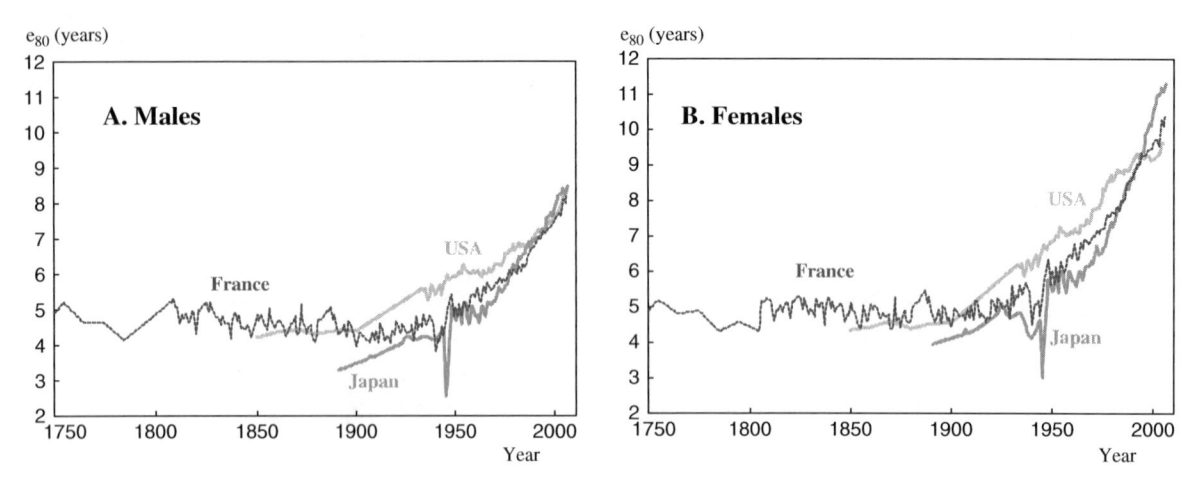

**Fig. 2.32** Trends in life expectancy at age 80 in France, Japan, and the United States. Sources: Vallin and Meslé (2001a) updated, for France; HMD for Japan and the United States

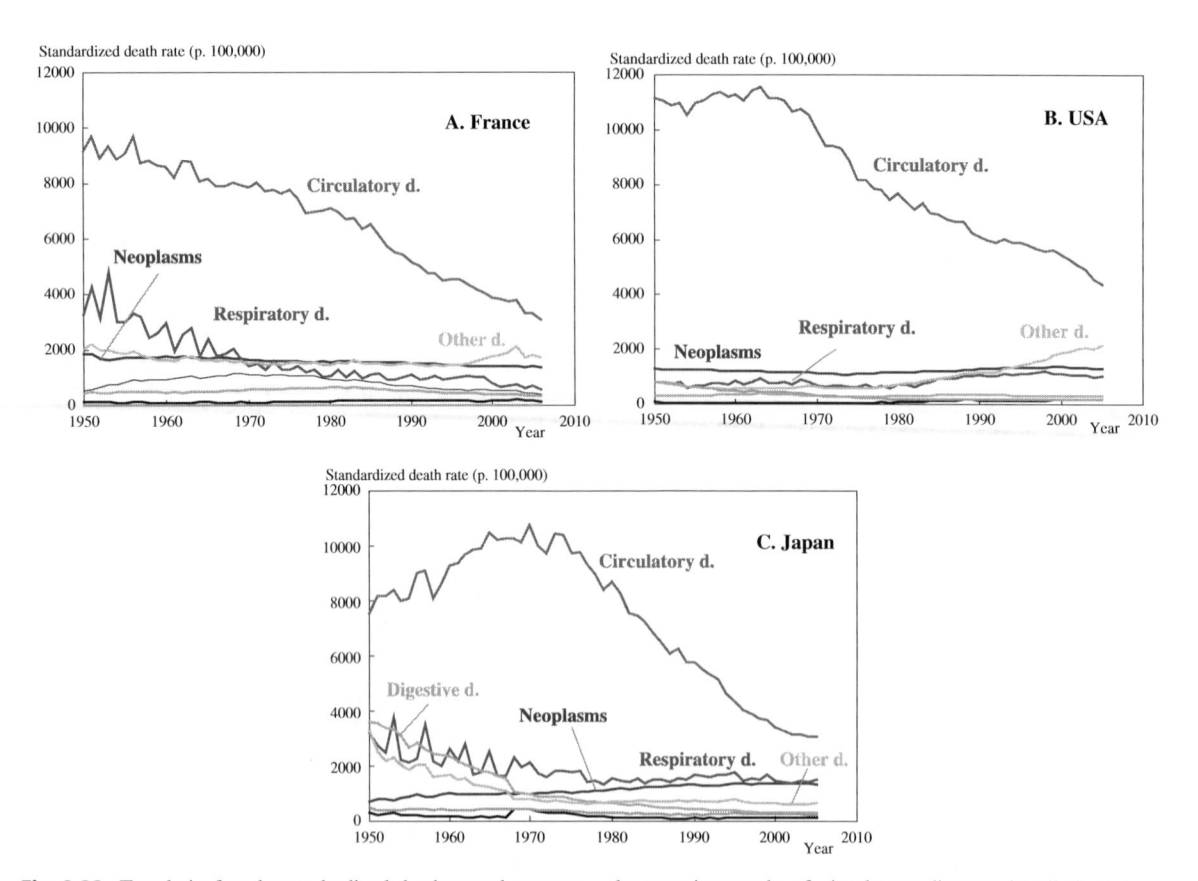

**Fig. 2.33** Trends in female standardized death rates by seven large groups of causes at ages 80 and over in France, Japan, and the United States. The scale is kept constant to make levels comparable from country to country. It brings to the fore the prominent role of circulatory diseases in all three countries, whatever the trends. Source: WHO Mortality Database for Japan and the United States; Meslé and Vallin (1996) updated for France

## Conclusion

During the first stage of the health transition (reduction of infectious diseases), infant and child mortality was the main driver of the increase in life expectancy at birth; change at adult ages became more important in the second stage (control of man-made diseases and the cardiovascular revolution). Most LDCs have still to achieve the first stage by fighting against infectious diseases mainly at young ages. Some of them, however, like Chile, are almost at the end of the second one. In those countries that are ending the second stage, differing adult ages were involved in it in differing ways and, more recently, oldest ages even became the field for a possible third stage (control of aging processes).

More precisely, the adult ages have exhibited heterogeneous mortality trends and have played different roles according to life-cycle phases. A main distinction can be made between young adult ages and older ones. Below age 45, once the major role of infectious diseases was reduced (in particular maternal mortality), adult mortality was most sensitive to the negative impact of societal changes that produce what Abdel Omran called man-made diseases (traffic and work accidents, suicide, homicide, tobacco consumption, and alcohol abuse). Males were much more affected than females by these causes. The younger adult age groups (15–24 and 25–44) benefited a lot from the control of man-made diseases in countries that were successful in the second stage of the health transition (Western Europe, Northern America, Japan, and most advanced LDCs), while they suffered significantly from the increase of these diseases in Central Europe and even more in the former Soviet Union.

Ages 45–64 were the great beneficiaries of the cardiovascular revolution. Once again the greatest progress from circulatory disease reduction was made by Western countries, while the former Soviet world suffered from its increase. At these ages, the success was so great that circulatory disease mortality is no longer the first cause of death in countries like France and Japan. In those two countries, cancer became the most important cause of death in this age group, even though its level today is not higher than in 1950. This is also true in the United States for females.

The oldest ages (over 65), and especially the very old ones, seem to be engaged in a new stage of mortality improvement, based on the control of many different causes of death specific to elderly people. This phase is rather obvious in countries like France and Japan but not yet in the United States. This new divergence probably paves the way for a third stage of the health transition. Taking in account the extreme diversity prevailing among LDCs, it is not impossible that some of the most advanced ones also enter such a third stage, before the lagging MDCs. Like Japan joined MDCs and entered the second stage, Chile, Mexico, Taiwan, or Korea are now close to be candidate for entering the third one.

## References

Andreev, E. 1982. "Метод компонент в анализе продолжительности жизни" [Method of Components for Life Expectancy Analysis] *Vestnik Statistiki* 3:42–47.

Arriaga, E.E. 1968. *New Life Tables for Latin American Populations in the Nineteenth and Twentieth Centuries.* Berkeley, CA, Institute of International Studies, University of California.

Arriaga, E.E. 1984. "Measuring and Explaining the Change in Life Expectancies." *Demography* 21(1):83–96.

Barbi, E., G. Caselli, and J. Vallin. 2003. "Trajectories of Extreme Survival in Heterogeneous Population." *Population-E* 58(1):43–66.

Bhat, P.N.M. 1989. "Mortality and Fertility in India, 1881–1961: A Reassessment." In T. Dyson *India's Historical Demography*, pp. 73–118. London, Curzon Press, 296p.

Biraben, J.-N. 1975. *Les hommes et la peste en France et dans les pays européens et méditerranéens. Tome I: la peste dans l'histoire.* Paris, Mouton, 459p.

Biraben, J.-N. 1999. "Les pathocénoses en Europe." In M. Grmek (coor.), *Histoire des maladies,* pp. 1–36. Paris, Association économie et santé. (Proceeding of the "Séminaire sur l'histoire des maladies", Courchevel, March 18–20, 1996).

Blayo, Y. 1975. "La mortalité en France de 1740 à 1829." *Population* 30 (special issue *Démographie historique*): 123–42.

Carey, J.R. and D.S. Judge. 2001. "Life Span Extension in Human is Self-Reinforcing: A General Theory of Longevity." *Population and Development Review* 27(3): 411–36.

Caselli, G., F. Meslé, and J. Vallin. 2002. "Epidemiologic Transition Theory Exceptions." *Genus* 58(1): 9–52.

Central Statistical Office (CSO) 1995. *Zimbabwe Demographic and Health Survey 1994.* Calverton, MD, Macro International Inc., 307p.

Central Statistical Office (CSO) 2000. *Zimbabwe Demographic and Health Survey 1999*. Calverton, MD, Macro International Inc., 289p.

Central Statistical Office [Zimbabwe] and Macro International Inc. 2007. *Zimbabwe Demographic and Health Survey 2005–06*. Calverton, MD, CSO and Macro International Inc., XXIV + 456p.

Coleman, D.A. 2002. "Populations of the Industrial World. A Convergent Demographic Community." *International Journal of Population Geography* 8:319–44.

Ediev, D. and R. Giesser. 2007. "Reconstruction of Historical Series of Life Tables and of Age-Sex Structures for the Austrian Population in the 19th and the First Half of the 20th Century." *Vienna Yearbook of Population Research* 7:327–55.

Frenk, J., J.L. Bobadilla, C. Stern, T. Frejka, and R. Lozano. 1991. "Elements for a Theory of the Health Transition." *Health Transition Review* 1(1):21–38.

Grigoriev, P., V.M. Shkolnikov, E.M. Andreev, D. Jasilionis, D.A. Jdanov, F. Meslé, and J. Vallin. 2010. "Possible Explanations of the Divergence in the Recent Mortality Trends Among Belarus Lithuania and Russia." *European Journal of Population* 26(3):245–274.

Grmek, M.D. 1969. "Préliminaires d'une étude historique des maladies." *Annales ESC* 24(6):1473–83.

Gruenberg, E.M. 1978. "Epidemiology of Senile Dementia." *Advances in Neurology* 19:437–57.

Hertrich, V. and F. Meslé. 1999. *The Health Crisis in the Baltic Countries: A Common and Varied Experience*. INED, 19p. (Paper presented at the European Population Conference, The Hague, August 30–September 3, 1999).

Horiuchi, S. 1999. "Epidemiological Transitions in Human History." In J. Chamie and R.L. Cliquet (eds.), *Health and Mortality Issues of Global Concern*. (Proceedings of the Symposium on Health an Mortality, Brussels, pp. 54–71, 19–22 November 1997). New York, NY, United Nations; CBGS, XV + 467p.

Human Life Table Database (HLTD). 2009. http://www.lifetable.de/. Consulted July 2009.

Human Mortality Database (HMD). 2009. http://www.mortality.org/. Consulted July 2009.

Institut national de la statistique (INS), Macro International Inc. 2007. *Enquête Démographique et de Santé et à Indicateurs Multiples du Niger 2006*. Calverton, MD, INS and Macro international Inc.

Kourguéni, I.A., B. Garba, and B. Barrère. 1993. "Enquête Démographique et de Santé Niger 1992." Niamey, Direction de la Statistique et des Comptes Nationaux, Direction Générale du Plan, Ministère des Finances et du Plan, Columbia, MD, Macro International Inc., XXIV + 296p.

Kramer, M. 1980. "The Rising Pandemic of Mental Disorders and Associated Chronic Diseases and Disabilities." *Acta Psychiatria Scandinavica* 62(suppl. 285):282–97.

Lerner, M. 1973. *Modernization and Health: A Model of the Health Transition*. San Francisco, CA, APHA. (Paper presented at the 1973 Annual Meeting of the "Reunión Anual de la American Public Health Association," San Francisco, CA, November 1973).

McKeown, T. 1976. *The Modern Rise of Population*. London, Edward Arnold, 169p.

Meslé, F. 2004. "Mortality in Central and Eastern Europe: Long-Term Trends and Recent Upturns." Demographic Research (Special Collection 2. Determinants of Diverging Trends in Mortality):46–70.

Meslé, F., V. Shkolnikov, V. Hertrich, and J. Vallin. 1996. *Tendances récentes de la mortalité par cause en Russie, 1965–1994*. Paris, INED, 140p. + 2 disquettes. (Données statistiques n°2).

Meslé, F. and J. Vallin. 1988. "Les composantes de la mortalité cardio-vasculaire en France depuis 1925: résultats d'une reconstitution historique." *Population* 43(2):391–425.

Meslé, F. and J. Vallin. 1996. "Reconstructing Long-Term Series of Causes of Death." *Historical Methods* 29(2):72–87.

Meslé, F. and J. Vallin. 1998. "L'évolution de la mortalité aux âges élevés en France depuis 1950." In J. Ankri, P. Bourdelais, F. Derriennic, M. Khlat, P. Mormiche, and C. Sermet (eds.), *La santé aux grands âges*, pp. 5–48. Paris, INED, 140p. (Les Cahiers de l'INED, n°147).

Meslé, F. and J. Vallin. 2002. "La mortalité dans le monde: tendances et perspectives". In J.-C. Chasteland and J.-C. Chesnais (eds.), *La population du monde: géants démographiques et défis internationaux*, pp. 527–46. Paris, INED, 768p. (Les Cahiers de l'INED, n°149, 2nd edition).

Meslé, F. and J. Vallin. 2003. *Mortalité et causes de décès en Ukraine au XX$^e$ siècle*. Paris, INED, 396p. + CD-Rom. (Cahier n°152, with contributions by V. Shkolnikov, S. Pyrozhkov, and S. Adamets).

Meslé, F. and J. Vallin. 2006. "Diverging Trends in Female Old-Age Mortality: The United States and the Netherlands versus France and Japan." *Population and Development Review* 32(1):123–45.

Meslé, F., J. Vallin, V. Hertrich, E. Andreev, and V. Shkolnikov. 2003. "Causes of Death in Russia: Assessing Trends since the 1950s." In I.E. Kotowska and J. Józwiak (eds.), *Population of Central and Eastern Europe. Challenges and Opportunities*, pp. 389–414. Warsaw, Statistical Publishing Establishment, 724p.

Meslé, F., J. Vallin, and V. Shkolnikov. 1998. "Reversal of Mortality Decline: The Case of Contemporary Russia." *World Health Statistics Quarterly/Rapport Trimestriel de Statistiques Sanitaires* 51(2–3–4):191–206. (Historical Epidemiology: Mortality Decline, and Old and New Transitions in Health, special issue edited. by O. Frank).

Muñoz, P.F. 1989. "La Estimación de la mortalidad chilena (1865–1940): Límites y posibilidades." *Latin American Population History* (15):2–9.

Oeppen, J. and J.W. Vaupel. 2002. "Broken Limits to Life Expectancy." *Science* 296(10):1029–31.

Olshansky, S.J. and A.B. Ault. 1986. "The Fourth Stage of the Epidemiologic Transition: The Age of Delayed Degenerative Diseases." *The Milbank Quarterly* 64(3):355–91.

Olshansky, S.J., B.A. Carnes, and C. Cassel. 1990. "In Search of Mathuselah: Estimating the Upper Limits to Human Longevity." *Science* 250:34–640.

Olshansky, S.J., B.A. Carnes, R.G. Rogers, and L. Smith. 1998. "Emerging Infectious Diseases: The Fifth Stage of the Epidemiologic Transition?" *World Health Statistics Quarterly* 51(2–3–4):207–17. (Historical Epidemiology:

Mortality Decline, and Old and New Transitions in Health, Special Issue edited by O. Frank).

Omran, A.R. 1971. "The Epidemiological Transition: A Theory of the Epidemiology of Population Change." *The Milbank Memorial Fund Quarterly* 49(4):509–38.

Omran, A.R. 1983. "The Epidemiologic Transition Theory. A Preliminary Update." *Journal of tropical Pediatrics* 29: 305–16.

Omran, A.R. 1998. "The Epidemiologic Transition Theory Revisited Thirty Years Later." *World Health Statistics Quarterly* 51(2–3–4):99–119. (Historical Epidemiology: Mortality Decline, and Old and New Transitions in Health, Special Issue edited by O. Frank).

Pollard, J.H. 1982. "The Expectation of Life and Its Relationship to Mortality." *Journal of the Institute of Actuaries* 109(part II, 442):225–40.

Pressat, R. 1985. "Contribution des écarts de mortalité par âge à la différence des vies moyennes." *Population* 40(4–5): 766–70.

Reinhard, M.R., A. Armengaud, and J. Dupâquier. 1968. *Histoire générale de la population mondiale*. Paris, Montchrestien, 708p.

Rogers, R.G. and R. Hackenberg. 1987. "Extending Epidemiologic Transition Theory." *Social Biology* 34:234–43.

Shkolnikov, V. and A. Nemtsov. 1997. "The Anti-Alcohol Campaign and Variations in Russian Mortality." In J.L. Bobadilla, C.A. Costello, and F. Mitchell (eds.), *Premature Death in the New Independent States*, pp. 239–61. Washington, DC, National Academy Press, 404p.

Somoza, J.L. 1971. *La mortalidad en la Argentina entre 1869 y 1960*. Buenos Aeres, Editorial del Instituto.

United Nations (UN). 1968. *Demographic Yearbook. Special Topic: Mortality Statistics 1967*. New York, NY, United Nations.

United Nations (UN). 1974. *Concise Report on the World Population Situation in 1970–1975 and Its Long-Range Implications*. New York, NY, United Nations, 77p. (Population Studies, n°56).

United Nations (UN). 1988. *World Demographic Estimates and Projections, 1950–2025*. New York, NY, United Nations, Department of International Economic and Social Affairs, 386p. (ST/ESA/Ser.R/79).

United Nations (UN). 2009. *World Population Prospects. The 2008 revision*. (http://esa.un.org/unpp).

Vallin, J. 2005. "Diseases, Deaths, and Life Expectancy." *Genus* 61(3–4):279–96. (Proceedings of the International Conference "Trends and Problems of the World Population in the XXI Century. 50 Years since Rome 1954," Rome, 26–28 May 2005).

Vallin, J. and F. Meslé. 1988. *Les causes de décès en France de 1925 à 1978*. Paris, INED, PUF, 608p. (Travaux et Documents, Cahier n°115 + 7 volumes of annexes).

Vallin, J. and F. Meslé. 2001a. *Tables de mortalité françaises pour les XIX$^e$ et XX$^e$ siècles et projections pour le XXI$^e$*. Paris, INED, 102p. + CD-rom. (Données statistiques, n°4-2001).

Vallin, J. and F. Meslé. 2001b. "Trends in Mortality in Europe since 1950: Age-, Sex- and Cause-Specific Mortality." In Council of Europe, *Trends in Mortality and Differential Mortality*, pp. 31–186. Strasbourg, Council of Europe Publishing, 334p. (Population Studies n°36).

Vallin, J. and F. Meslé. 2004. "Convergences and Divergences in Mortality. A New Approach to Health Transition." *Demographic Research* (Special Collection 2. Determinants of Diverging Trends in Mortality):12–43.

Vallin, J. and F. Meslé. 2009. "The Segmented Trend Line of Highest Life Expectancies." *Population and Development Review* 35(1):159–87.

Vaupel, J.W. 2001. "Demographic Insights into Longevity." *Population, An English Selection* 13(1): 245–60.

World Health Organization (WHO). 2009. Mortality Database. http://www.who.int/whosis/mort/download/en/index.html. Downloaded July 2009.

# Chapter 3
# Adult Mortality in Europe

Marc Luy, Christian Wegner, and Wolfgang Lutz

## Introduction

Europe has richer demographic data than other world regions both in terms of the populations and subpopulations covered and in terms of the time lengths for which these data are available. Many European countries have long had their current borders and have well-established statistical registers with comprehensive and detailed data on their populations. There are exceptions, however, in Central and Eastern Europe due both to more recent political changes and to less well-developed statistical systems.

For this chapter we defined Europe as comprising all the member countries of the Council of Europe. These include the 27 members of the European Union (EU-27)—Austria, Belgium, Bulgaria, Cyprus, Czech Republic, Denmark, Estonia, Finland, France, Germany, Greece, Hungary, Ireland, Italy, Latvia, Lithuania, Luxembourg, Malta, the Netherlands, Poland, Portugal, Romania, Sweden, Slovenia, Slovakia, Spain, and the United Kingdom (UK)—and the three EU candidate countries—Croatia, Turkey, and the former Yugoslav Republic of Macedonia—as well as Albania, Andorra, Armenia, Azerbaijan, Bosnia and Herzegovina, Georgia, Iceland, Liechtenstein, Moldova, Monaco, Montenegro, Norway, Russian Federation, San Marino, Serbia, Switzerland, and Ukraine. For completeness we also include Belarus, although it is currently not a member of the Council of Europe. For Germany, the eastern and the western part are listed separately, and for the UK, the distinctions among England and Wales, Scotland, and Northern Ireland are maintained. Serbia and Montenegro have been combined into one geographical unit. Hence, the following analysis and description of adult mortality trends in Europe comprises 50 countries in total.

For the presentation of adult mortality trends in Europe we examine life expectancy at age 15 separately for women and men throughout the chapter. The data on which the analyses are based were collected from different sources with the aim of reconstructing complete country-specific time series. Whenever possible, we used age-specific death rates for single years of age and single calendar years to construct life tables by means of standard demographic methodology. In some cases it was possible to get data on life expectancy directly only from data sources that did not provide age-specific mortality rates. In cases where multiple data sources were available for a given year, we chose the information in the following order of priority: the Human Mortality Database (www.mortality.org), the Human Life Table Database (www.lifetable.de), the Eurostat Population Database (http://epp.eurostat.ec.europa.eu/portal/page/portal/population/data/database), the World Health Organization (WHO) Mortality Database (http://www.who.int/healthinfo/morttables), and the database of the "length of life" project (www.lengthoflife.org). Data on causes of death stem exclusively from the WHO Database. Generally, statistics on adult mortality can be considered reliable in most European countries. According to the "technical report" section in *2006 UN World Population Prospects*, the direct calculation of sex- and

M. Luy (✉)
Vienna Institute of Demography, Austrian Academy of Sciences, Wohllebengasse 12-14,
1040 Vienna, Austria
e-mail: mail@marcluy.eu

age-specific death rates was possible for the majority of countries. Exceptions are Albania, Azerbaijan, Bosnia and Herzegovina, Estonia, Georgia, Lithuania, Macedonia, Moldova, and Ukraine, where some—mainly minor—adjustments in registered data for adult mortality were necessary, as well as Turkey, where model life tables were used to estimate the age pattern of adult mortality (see United Nations 2008).

We tried to trace the trends of adult mortality in Europe from 1950 to the present. For most countries we were able to get data for the whole period. However, for some countries the time series starts later, either because data are not available or because the country's current borders were constituted later than 1950. This is true for the former Yugoslavian countries and for countries from the former Soviet Union. For other countries we had data only for some specific calendar years within the period. These countries included Turkey, Monaco, and Andorra. In addition, the last year for which data are available varies from country to country. For most countries we have data until 2006 or 2007, but in some countries the latest estimate is earlier: 2004 (Albania), 2001 (Georgia), or 2000 (Bosnia and Herzegovina). We present the trends of adult mortality in Europe either in time series or for the three 5-year periods of 1961–1965, 1981–1985, and 2001–2005. The decision to present results for these three periods was based on the fact that data were available for most of the countries and that these periods approximately reflect the periods of changes in the basic trends in European adult mortality.

Our overview refers to units defined by the borders of national states. This is far from ideal for the observation of geographical variations in mortality. While each state has its own policies and some consistency in health regulations and behaviors, national borders can easily mask internal differentials within countries, as Caselli and Vallin (2006) have shown for Italy and the Baltic states. Heterogeneity is common within countries, and with finer territorial division, this heterogeneity could be observed. However, because of the large number of countries in Europe and the marked differences between them, further subdivision into smaller regional units is not possible for this general overview. More detailed regional mortality differences have been elaborated and are available for many European countries, for example, France (Caselli and Vallin 2006), Great Britain (Anson 1993; Dorling 1997), Italy (Barbi and Caselli 2003; Caselli and Vallin 2006; Caselli et al. 2003; Divino et al. 2009), Belgium (Anson 2003; Caselli and Egidi 1981; Van Oyen et al. 1996), Finland (Koskinen 1995; Saarela and Finnäs 2006), Germany (Luy and Caselli 2007; Paul 1992; Sommer 1998), the Netherlands (Spijker 2004), Switzerland (Kohli 2005), Russia (Vallin et al. 2005), the Czech Republic (Spijker 2004), and the Baltic states (Caselli and Vallin 2006), among others. Overviews of regional mortality differences for a larger number of European countries can be found in Van Poppel (1981), Shaw et al. (2000), Valkonen (2001), and Cayotte and Buchow (2009), as well as in several atlases of overall or cancer mortality in Europe (Boyle and Smans 2009; European Commission 2002, 2008; Smans et al. 1992; World Health Organization 1997; Zatonski et al. 1996).

Even using regional division based on national borders provides a challenging management task. Therefore, only the first two sections on trends in life expectancy at age 15 cover (essentially) all Council of Europe member states and Belarus. The sections on trends in age- and cause-specific mortality are limited to a selection of countries representing the European regions. Trends in overall and age-, sex-, and cause-specific mortality as well as in differential mortality in Europe have already been analyzed extensively on behalf of the European Council by Vallin et al. (2001). In this chapter we refer to this major overview of mortality trends in Europe, complemented by more recent data. We have also extended the analysis by illustrating mortality differences between European countries using recently developed mortality measures, including "length of life inequality" and "tempo-adjusted" life expectancy. Trends between the periods 1961–1965, 1981–1985, and 2001–2005 were decomposed by sex, age, and causes of the death using the method proposed by Andreev et al. (2002). The results for tempo-adjusted life expectancy at age 15 for the period 2001–2005 in the final section of this chapter were estimated using the method proposed by Bongaarts and Feeney (2002) and include only those 34 European countries for which the necessary data were available.

A number of the countries included in this overview achieved independent statehood very recently. This is true for Bosnia and Herzegovina, Croatia, Macedonia, Serbia and Montenegro, and Slovenia, all parts of the former Yugoslavia; it is also true for the Czech Republic and Slovakia as parts of the former Czechoslovakia, as well as Armenia, Azerbaijan, Estonia, Georgia, Latvia, Lithuania, Moldova, the

Russian Federation, and Ukraine as parts of the former Soviet Union. Mortality in periods before independence for these states is represented by the average mortality for their former country, as mortality statistics have not yet been reconstructed for today's borders.

## General Trends and Regional Disparities in Adult Mortality in Europe

During the second half of the twentieth century, trends in adult mortality became the driving force in changes of overall life expectancy in Europe. Before 1950 increases in life expectancy at birth were mainly due to reductions in infant and child mortality and mortality from infectious diseases. This reduction resulted from Pasteur's discoveries at the end of the nineteenth century, amplified by the spread of vaccines, the development of sulfonamide drugs between the two world wars, and the development of antibiotic treatment during World War II (for more details, see Cutler et al. 2006; Vallin and Meslé 2001). At the beginning of the 1960s, the benefits of further declines in infant mortality and infectious disease mortality were largely exhausted and the main causes of death became cardiovascular diseases and cancer. Since then, further progress in life expectancy at birth as well as at age 15 is mainly due to reductions in behavior-related causes of death (those resulting from smoking, alcohol abuse, and traffic accidents), cardiovascular diseases, and some forms of cancer at ages over 60 years (i.e., the second phase of the "health transition;" see Meslé and Vallin 2006). While these improvements have occurred in most Western European and, with a delay of approximately two decades, also in most Central European countries, the trend was quite different in the countries of Eastern Europe. In some of these countries, mortality related to certain social ills, such as alcoholism or violent deaths, has increased while health services have deteriorated. This led to an increase in mortality from causes of death that previously had been relatively well controlled (Meslé 1991, 2004; Meslé et al. 1998). As a consequence of these trends, current levels and past trends of adult mortality in Europe result in three country clusters: Western Europe, with the most favorable health situation; Eastern Europe, with the least favorable health conditions; and Central Europe, which falls between Eastern and Western Europe.

During the 1950s and 1960s, male life expectancy at age 15 remained more or less constant at the level reached shortly after WWII, or lower, in practically all European countries. But in the late 1960s and early 1970s trends began to differentiate along the lines described above. In the countries belonging to Western Europe life expectancy started to increase and has done so until the present, whereas among the former Communist states of Eastern and Central Europe it increased more slowly, remained constant, or started to decline. The latter include the countries of the Warsaw pact (Bulgaria, Czechoslovakia, the German Democratic Republic alias "East Germany", Hungary, Poland, Romania, and the USSR), along with Yugoslavia and Albania, which were not aligned with the Soviet Union after 1948 and 1960, respectively. Trends in Central and Eastern Europe changed during the mid-1980s. Since then, life expectancy has been increasing in practically all countries of Central Europe at rates parallel to or even stronger than the trends in Western Europe. On the other hand, the Eastern European populations experienced a marked increase and decrease of life expectancy linked to Gorbachev's anti-alcohol campaign and its subsequent failure. However, from today's perspective the two upward trends in the mid-1980s and mid-1990s seem merely short-term interruptions in an overall decline in life expectancy from the 1960s to the second half of the 1990s or the first years of the twenty-first century, as will be shown in more detail in the next section.

The upper panels of Figs. 3.1, 3.2, and 3.3 show maps of adult male life expectancy among European countries. Figure 3.1 displays the current life expectancy at age 15 for the years 2001–2005. The countries are grouped according to the level of life expectancy, classified in standard deviation units around the mean of all single values. The precise estimates of country-specific life expectancy at age 15 and the two-letter abbreviations for the countries can be found in Table 3.3 in the appendix to this chapter. The graph elucidates Europe's trisection of mortality, with the highest levels of life expectancy in the Western European countries. Among these, only Portugal and Scotland do not fall into the lowest mortality category, in which life expectancy at age 15 is higher than 60.44 years. The Eastern European countries belonging to the former Soviet Union—except

## A. Males

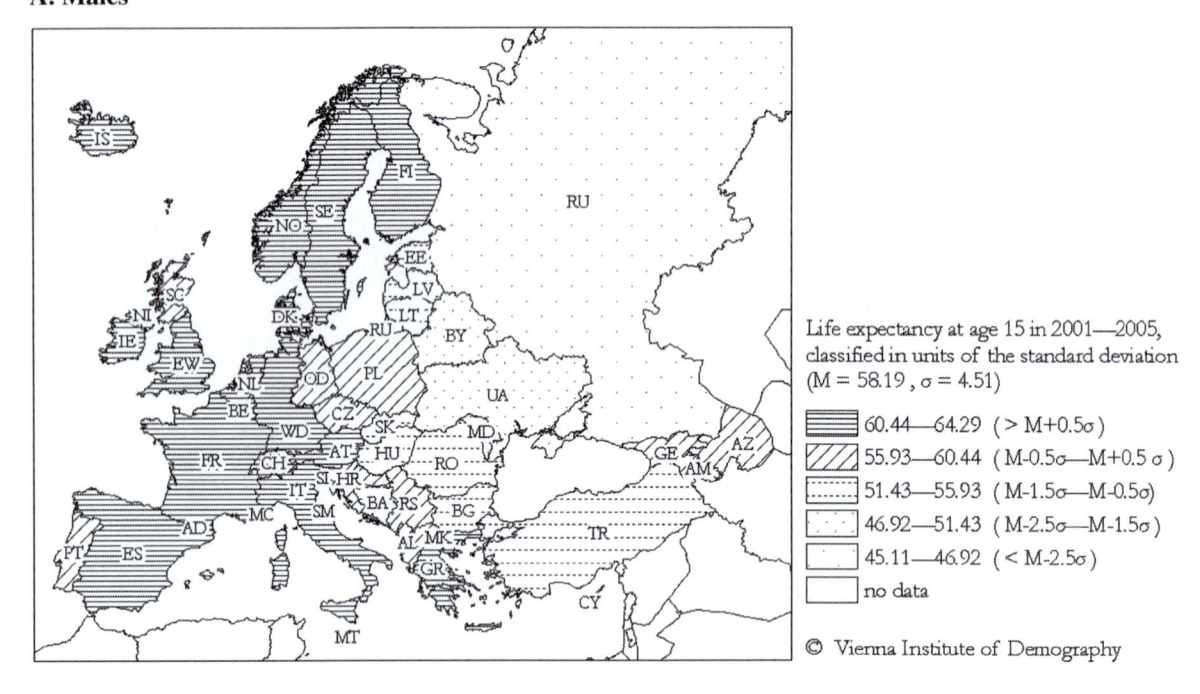

Life expectancy at age 15 in 2001—2005, classified in units of the standard deviation (M = 58.19, σ = 4.51)

- 60.44—64.29 ( > M+0.5σ )
- 55.93—60.44 ( M-0.5σ—M+0.5 σ )
- 51.43—55.93 ( M-1.5σ—M-0.5σ )
- 46.92—51.43 ( M-2.5σ—M-1.5σ )
- 45.11—46.92 ( < M-2.5σ )
- no data

© Vienna Institute of Demography

## B. Females

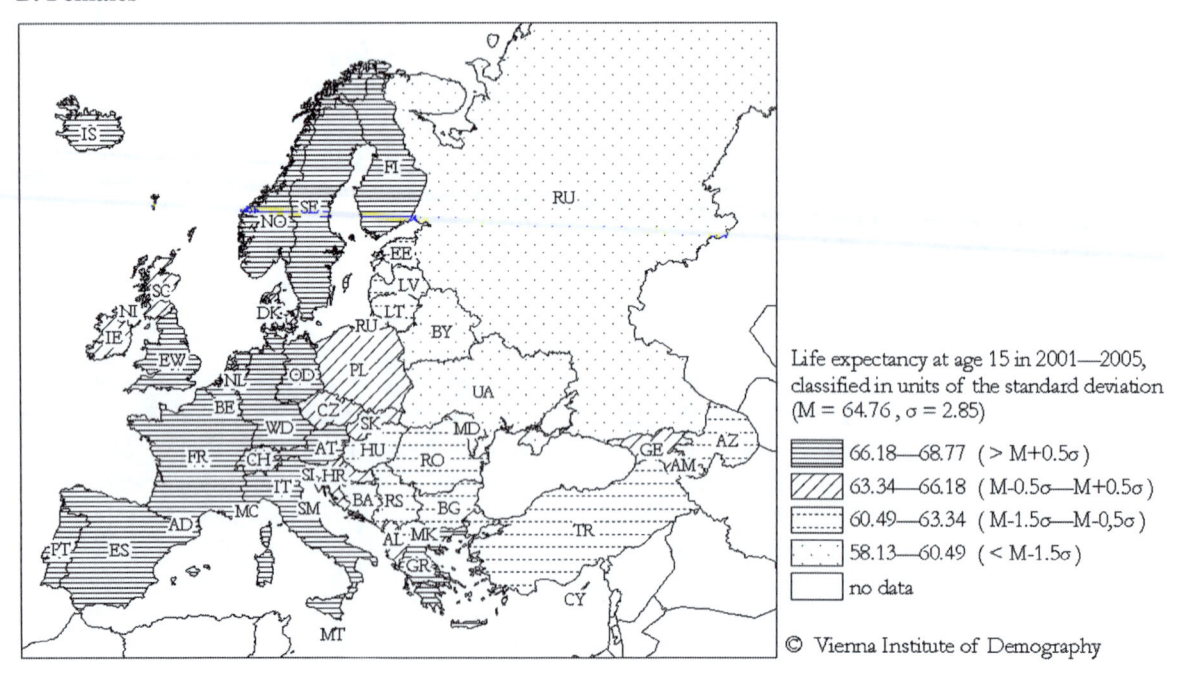

Life expectancy at age 15 in 2001—2005, classified in units of the standard deviation (M = 64.76, σ = 2.85)

- 66.18—68.77 ( > M+0.5σ )
- 63.34—66.18 ( M-0.5σ—M+0.5σ )
- 60.49—63.34 ( M-1.5σ—M-0,5σ )
- 58.13—60.49 ( < M-1.5σ )
- no data

© Vienna Institute of Demography

**Fig. 3.1** Life expectancy at age 15 by country in Europe, 2001–2005

## A. Males

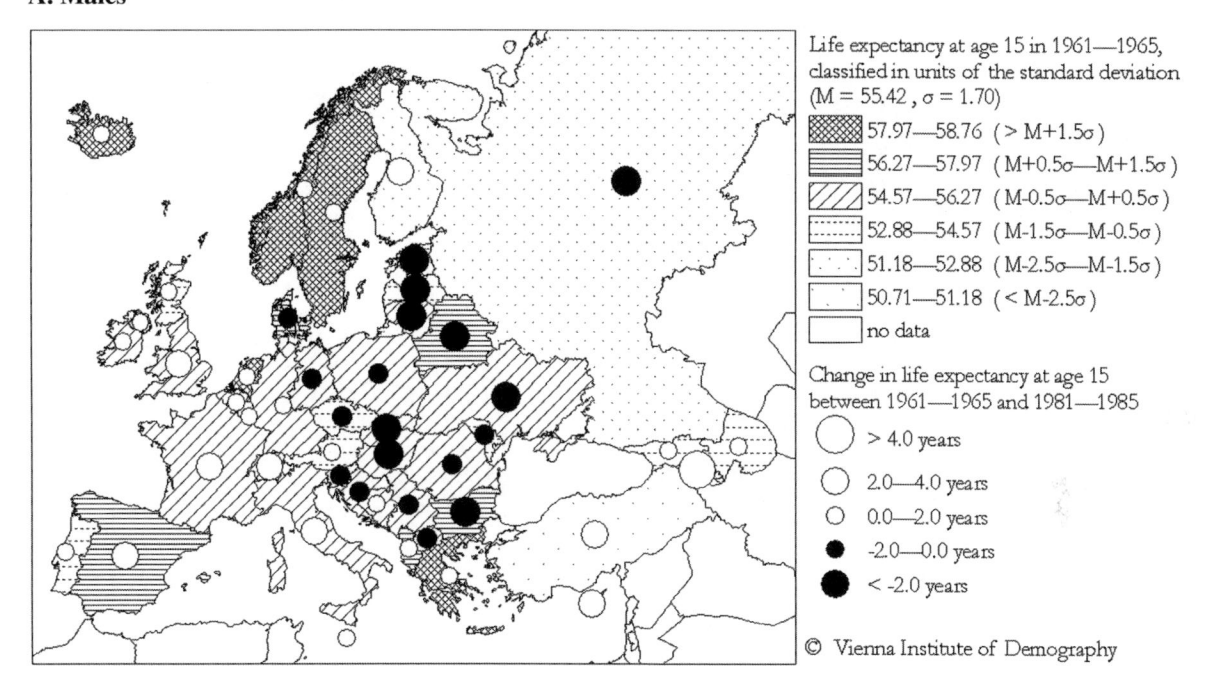

## B. Females

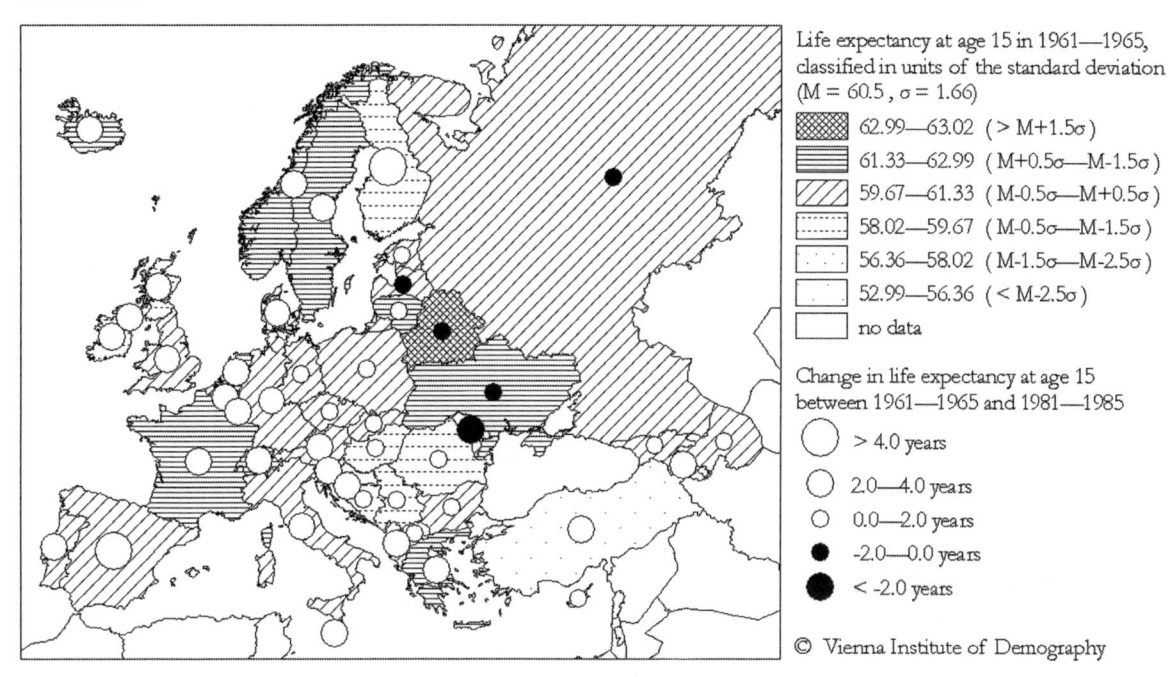

**Fig. 3.2** Life expectancy at age 15 by country in Europe in 1961–1965 and changes between 1961–1965 and 1981–1985

## A. Males

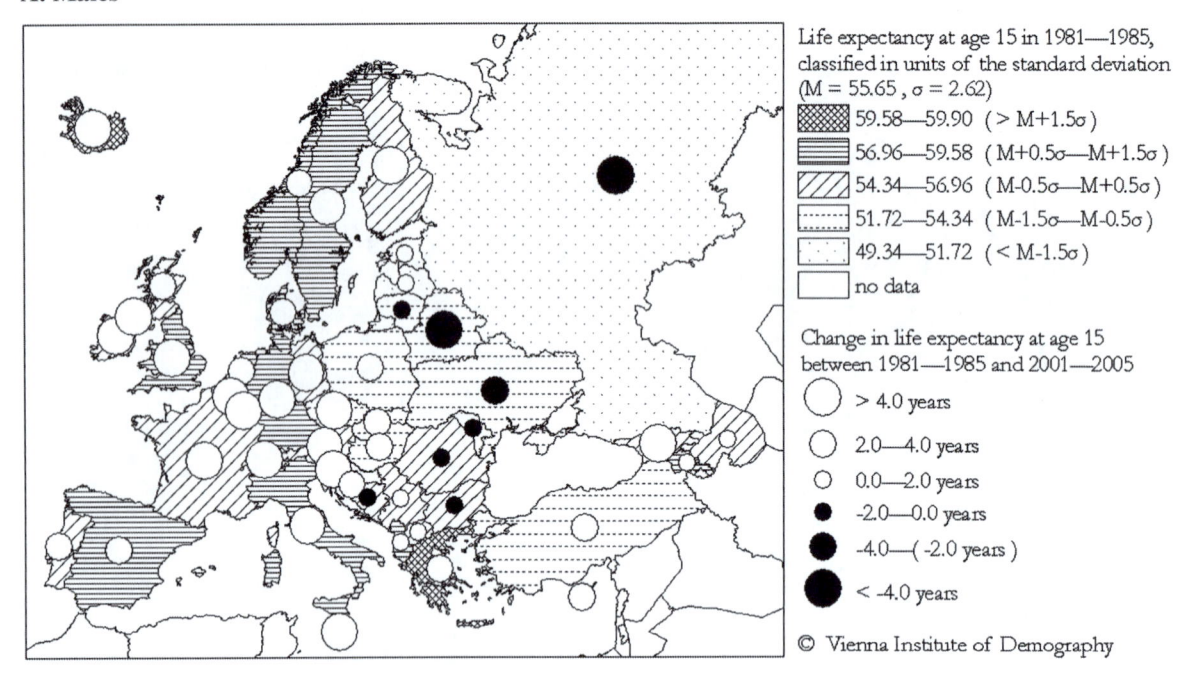

## B. Females

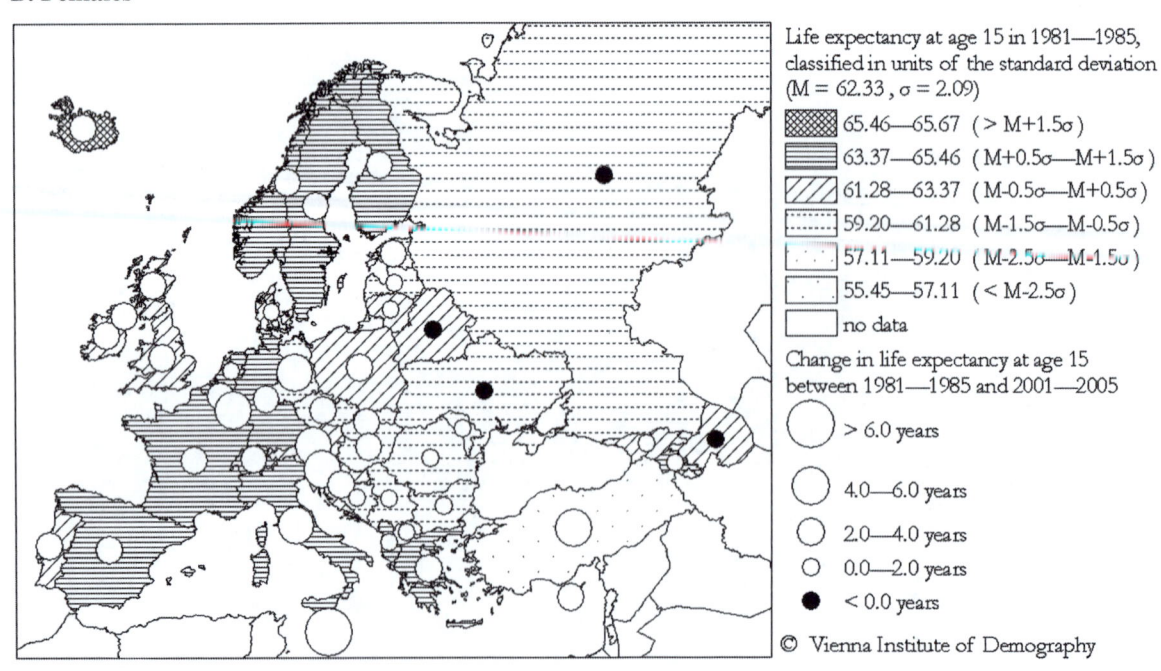

**Fig. 3.3** Male life expectancy at age 15 by country in Europe in 1981–1985 and changes between 1981–1985 and 2001–2005

the Caucasus countries Armenia, Azerbaijan, and Georgia—represent the other extreme, with the lowest life expectancy at age 15, ranging from 45.11 years in the Russian Federation to 51.91 years in Lithuania. These two regions of countries with highest and lowest male life expectancy are separated by a band of central Eastern European countries, former Yugoslavia, the eastern Mediterranean, and the Caucasus. Figure 3.1a gives the impression that the Baltic countries Estonia, Latvia, and Lithuania exhibit male mortality levels similar to those of some Central European countries like Bulgaria, Hungary, and Romania. However, the precise estimates reveal that life expectancy in the latter lies close to the upper border of the corresponding class, with 55.22, 54.22, and 54.62 years, respectively, whereas life expectancy in the Baltic states is between 51.51 and 51.91 years and thus lies close to the lower border (see Table 3.3). The seemingly better health conditions in the Caucasian republics Armenia, Azerbaijan, and Georgia must be viewed with caution because of the known underestimation of mortality there (see Caselli and Vallin 2006).

Figures 3.2a and 3.3a summarize the country-specific levels of life expectancy at age 15 for men in the periods 1961–1965 and 1981–1985 and illustrate the trends between 1961–1965 and 1981–1985 and between 1981–1985 and 2001–2005, respectively. Figure 3.2a shows that male life expectancy at age 15 did not have a clear geographical pattern of variation in the years 1961–1965. The highest levels occurred in the Nordic countries Denmark, Iceland, Norway, and Sweden as well as in the Netherlands and Greece; the lowest, in Finland, Russia, and Turkey. In the first half of the 1960s the populations of western and Communist societies did not divide by level of mortality. However, a separation clearly occurred after the changes in life expectancy between 1961–1965 and 1981–1985, as is graphically displayed by the circles in the center of each country in Fig. 3.2a. White circles reflect increasing life expectancy and black circles reflect decreasing life expectancy, while the size of the circles reflects the absolute amount of the changes. With the exception of Denmark, all Western European countries exhibited increasing life expectancy between the 1960s and the 1980s. On the other hand, all Communist countries, except Albania, experienced decreasing life expectancy. The other white circles in Central and Eastern Europe are difficult to interpret because we lack data for these regions using today's national borders—Serbia and Montenegro, Armenia, Azerbaijan, and Georgia are assigned to the prevailing life expectancies of Yugoslavia and the Soviet Union for one or both periods. Large improvements occurred among Turkish men. Note, however, that the underlying estimates of life expectancy are based on indirect estimates and refer to calendar years outside the two periods displayed (see Table 3.3 in the appendix).

Figure 3.3a reveals that European male mortality in the first half of the 1980s was characterized by a separation between Eastern and Western Europe, with the frontier between higher and lower life expectancy along the eastern borders of Finland, West Germany, Austria, and Italy. This subdivision of Europe into a western side with favorable and an eastern side with unfavorable health conditions became a dominant topic in European research on health and mortality (see, e.g., Bobak and Marmot 1996; Bobak et al. 2002; Meslé and Vallin 2002; Velkova et al. 1997; and the compilation of papers in Hertzman et al. 1996). The life expectancy of Finland and France already exceeded by more than 1 year that of several Central European countries—Bulgaria, East Germany, Romania, and Yugoslavia—that fall in the same life expectancy class in Fig. 3.3a (see Table 3.3 in the appendix). Inside the eastern half of Europe, Greece and Cyprus are exceptions in that they belonged to the western part of Europe both politically and by mortality level. The trends between 1981–1985 and 2001–2005 show that today's trisection arose during these years. Among the Eastern and Central European countries, the trends in life expectancy were more favorable among countries closer to Western Europe. Eastern Germany, the Czech Republic, and Slovenia exhibited the largest progress, with increases similar to those in most Western European countries, followed by Poland, Slovakia, Hungary, and Croatia. On the other hand, men from Russia, Lithuania, Belarus, Ukraine, Moldova, Bosnia and Herzegovina, Romania, and Bulgaria experienced further declines in life expectancy at age 15, the largest of more than 4 years in Russia and Belarus.

The trends among women differ from those among men, although they are described by basically the same trisection in levels and change in adult mortality. In Western European countries, female life expectancy rose from 1950 and only briefly stalled in some countries during the first half of the 1960s.

In most Central European countries, life expectancy was slightly lower than in Western European countries at the beginning of the 1950s, and the stall extended over the whole of the 1960s, in some countries even through the mid-1990s. Thus, since the 1970s, female life expectancy in Central European countries has been below the corresponding level for Western European women. Only Albania, Eastern Germany, and Slovenia could recently reach the lowest levels of Western European countries. On the other hand, women from Eastern Europe exhibited life expectancy as high as women from Western European countries until the early and mid-1970s. During most years of the 1960s, Belarus had the highest female life expectancy among all European countries. (Note, however, that the Human Mortality Database warns that for 1959–1969 Belarusian data is of poor quality and life expectancy may be overestimated.) During the 1980s and 1990s, however, Eastern European women showed trends of decreasing life expectancy similar to those for their male counterparts but less marked by fluctuations. In the most recent periods, the separation between Central and Eastern European countries is not as clear among women as among men, since the Baltic countries Estonia, Lithuania, and Latvia as well as Armenia have a higher life expectancy than some Central European countries like Serbia and Montenegro, Macedonia, Bulgaria, Hungary, and Romania. The latter countries either had the lowest life expectancy levels of all Europe until the 1980s (former Yugoslavia) or had stagnant life expectancy until the 1990s (Bulgaria, Hungary, Romania).

The basic patterns of these trends in female adult mortality in Europe are shown in the maps in the lower panels of Figs. 3.1, 3.2, and 3.3. Figure 3.1 shows that current levels of female life expectancy at age 15 in the period 2001–2005 are very similar to the situation among males (Fig. 3.1a). The main difference from men is that the absolute differentials across countries are smaller, as can be seen in the number of classes of life-expectancy levels in Figs. 3.1a, b and in the corresponding values in Table 3.4 in the appendix to this chapter. Sex differences in the regional pattern of life expectancy occur in eastern Germany, which already is integrated into the high-life-expectancy pattern of Western Europe among females, and Portugal, which, compared to the other countries, exhibits better health conditions among women than among men. Negative outliers Denmark, Ireland, and Northern Ireland exhibit unfavorable health conditions for women, as does Scotland, which has a similar unfavorable picture among both women and men.

Figure 3.2b reveals that in the period 1961–1965 the regional pattern of female adult mortality in Europe differed markedly from that among males. The map illustrates the unfavorable health situation in the southern part of Central Europe, especially Turkey. While the pattern of adult mortality levels in Western Europe is similar for both women and men, Lithuania, Ukraine, and particularly Belarus exhibited very favorable health conditions during the early 1960s. Whereas among men, almost all Central and Eastern European countries exhibited declines in life expectancy at age 15 between 1961–1965 and 1981–1985 (see Fig. 3.2a), only in Russia, Latvia, Belarus, and Ukraine did women experience similar negative trends, and they did so to a lesser extent than did men. (For Moldova no data were available for 1961–1965.) Among the other countries, the increases in life expectancy were smaller in Central Europe than in Western Europe. As a consequence, the separation in mortality levels between Western European countries and Central and Eastern European countries was clearer among women in the early 1980s (see Fig. 3.3b for women and Fig. 3.3a for men). The trends between the periods 1981–1985 and 2001–2005 show that most Central European countries, particularly eastern Germany and Slovenia and the Baltic countries, exhibited increases in female life expectancy comparable to or even larger than their Western European counterparts, whereas life expectancy at age 15 stagnated or further declined among women in other Eastern European countries. These trends led to the same trisection in current adult mortality levels in Europe among women and men (see Fig. 3.1a, b).

## Country-Specific Levels and Trends of Adult Mortality in Europe

The graphs presented in the previous section show that the levels and trends of adult mortality vary considerably inside the three main regions of Eastern, Western, and Central Europe. Figure 3.4 provides a detailed picture of the trends in life expectancy at age 15 for each country since 1950, excluding the states

3  Adult Mortality in Europe    57

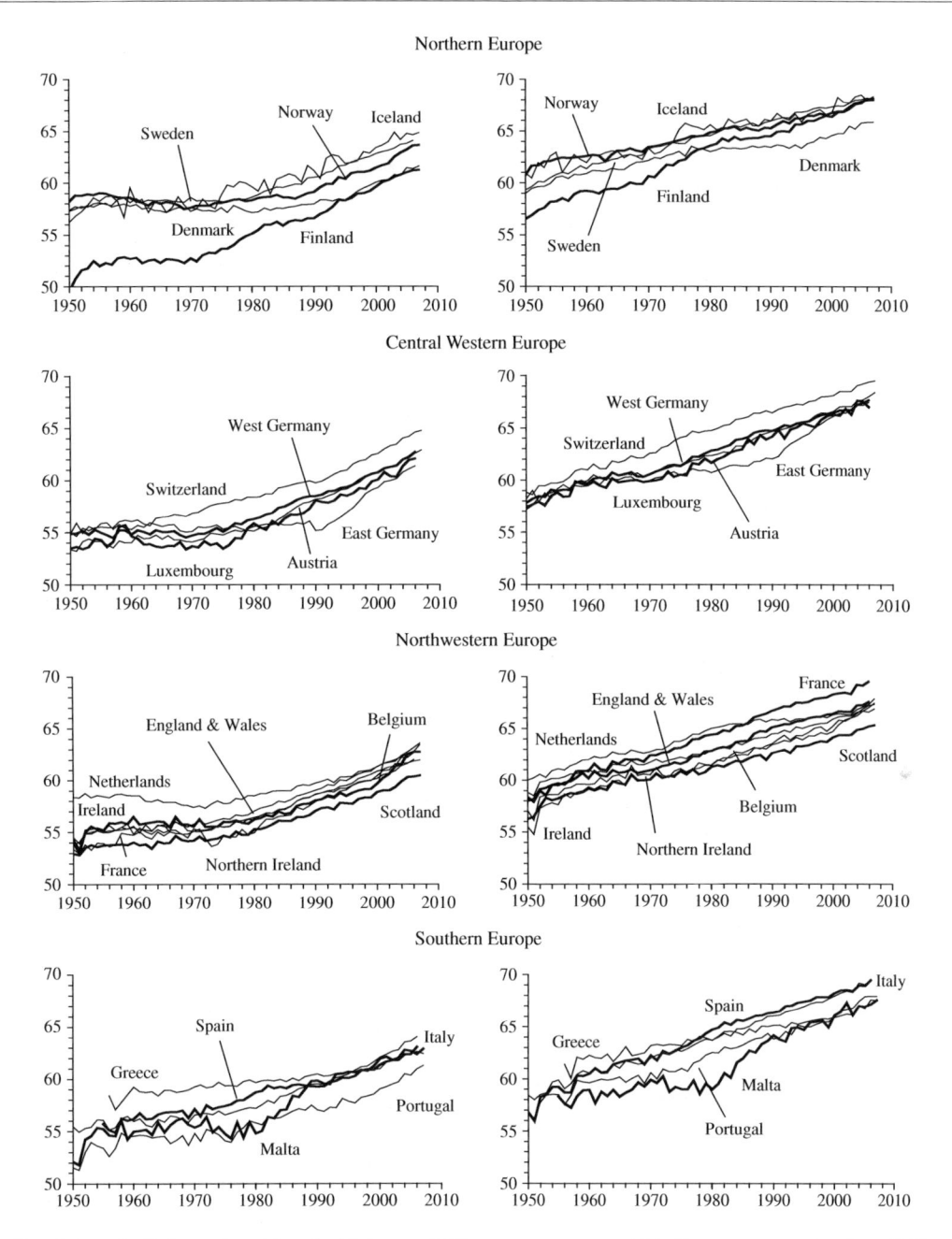

**Fig. 3.4** Trends in male (*left panel*) and female (*right panel*) life expectancy at age 15 in European countries since 1950

with fewer than 250,000 inhabitants in January 2008, i.e., Andorra, Liechtenstein, Monaco, and San Marino. (Data for these countries, even though of questionable reliability, are included in Tables 3.3 and 3.4 in the appendix.) To display and describe the country-specific trends in adult mortality, we grouped the countries geographically into the following eight regions of Europe (adopted from Vallin and Meslé 2001):

- Northern Europe: Denmark, Finland, Iceland, Norway, and Sweden;
- Central Western Europe: Austria, East (later eastern) Germany, West (later western) Germany, Luxembourg, and Switzerland;
- Northwestern Europe: Belgium, England and Wales, France, Ireland, the Netherlands, Northern Ireland, and Scotland;

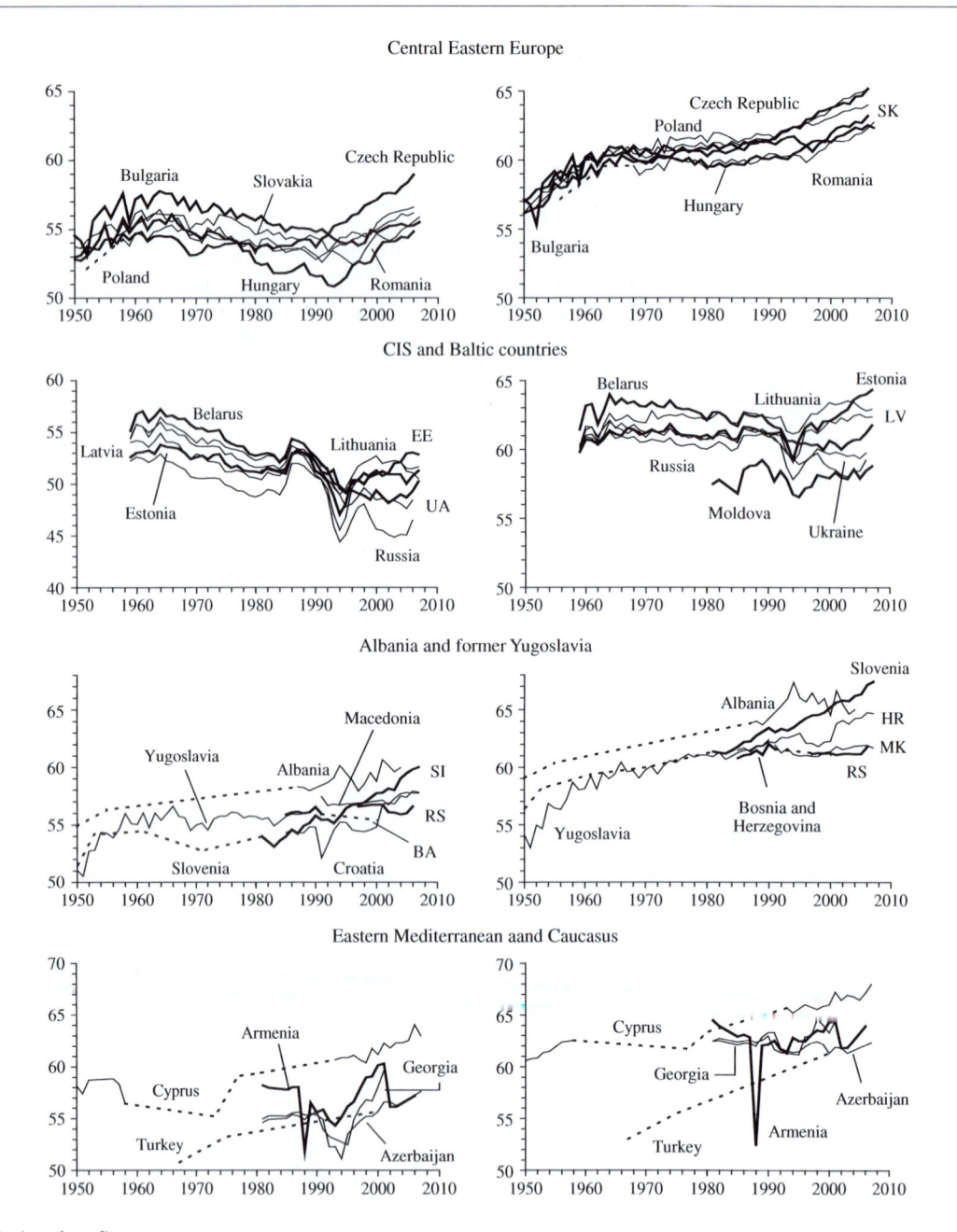

**Fig. 3.4** (continued)

- Southern Europe: Greece, Italy, Malta, Portugal, and Spain;
- Central Eastern Europe: Bulgaria, Czech Republic, Hungary, Poland, Romania, and Slovakia;
- European part of the Commonwealth of Independent States (CIS) and Baltic countries: Belarus, Estonia, Latvia, Lithuania, Moldova, Russia, and Ukraine;
- Albania and former Yugoslavia: Albania, Bosnia and Herzegovina, Croatia, Macedonia (TFYR), Serbia and Montenegro, Slovenia, and Yugoslavia;
- Eastern Mediterranean and Caucasus: Armenia, Azerbaijan, Cyprus, Georgia, and Turkey.

Interruptions in the availability of annual data are marked by dotted lines between the calendar years for which life expectancy at age 15 could be calculated or was available (Albania, Bosnia and Herzegovina, Cyprus, Poland, Slovenia, and Turkey). Figure 3.4 reveals that the country-specific variation of trends in life expectancy does not allow further geographical clustering of homogeneous mortality patterns than the basic separation between Eastern, Western, and Central Europe. The only exception is the region formed by the CIS and Baltic countries, where the trends appear to be almost perfectly parallel among both women and men, including the long-lasting mortality crises after 1960 and the fluctuations in the 1980s and 1990s (see also Chapter 4 by Murphy and Shkolnikov and Cornia 2000). The decline in life expectancy among the countries from the former Soviet Union between 1960 and 1985 was noted in the previous section. The extraordinary fluctuations in the succeeding decade were caused by the anti-alcohol campaign of Mikhail Gorbachev in 1985, which led to a sharp rise in life expectancy between 1985 and 1987. But the relaxation of the measures caused a very quick relapse in the late 1980s. This trend of decreasing life expectancy then continued under the shock of the break-up of the Soviet Union and the difficult transition to a market economy. In each of the CIS countries, the low point was reached in 1994 or 1995. Since then there has been a recovery in Belarus, Estonia, Latvia, and Moldova, whereas in Lithuania, Russia, and Ukraine life expectancy decreased again in the late 1990s and in the first years of the twenty-first century. Noticeable is the special case of Moldovan women, whose life expectancy is lower than that for women in the other countries of the former Soviet Union. On the other hand, Moldovan men show less excess mortality than most other men from the former Soviet Union. This, however, is not the result of a better position for the men but is rather due to an exceptionally unfavorable position for the women (Vallin and Meslé 2001).

Some of the countries from central Eastern Europe show a general trend similar to that of the CIS and Baltic countries, although without the marked fluctuations in the 1980s and 1990s. Among men, the Czech Republic stands apart because life expectancy at age 15 rose more than in the other countries after the early 1980s. Aside from the Czech Republic, the other countries show similar trends, with decreasing life expectancy during the 1960s, 1970s, and 1980s. However, the level of mortality varied, with Bulgaria having the highest and Hungary the lowest life expectancy. The increase in life expectancy started latest in Bulgaria, which has the second lowest life expectancy in Central Eastern Europe today. Among women, Poland and Slovakia show trends very similar to those in the Czech Republic. Since the early 1990s, Hungary and Romania, as well as Bulgaria, have fallen behind. Thus, the end of the Communist system has not solved the major health crises in all Central Eastern European countries, which may reflect variation in how the transition to a market economy takes place (see Vallin and Meslé 2001). Since around 1995, all Central Eastern European countries have shown similar trends of increasing life expectancy for both women and men.

The male populations from the former Communist Balkan states show the typical Central European trends in adult mortality until the beginning of the 1990s. From 1950 to 1960, life expectancy increased sharply and remained almost constant thereafter. While Albania seems to have a steady and slightly increasing life expectancy, the countries of former Yugoslavia show diverse trends beginning in the 1980s. In the most recent period Slovenia has experienced the most favorable changes in mortality and exhibited the highest life expectancy within this group, after having had the lowest life expectancy until the mid-1980s. On the other hand, Bosnia and Herzegovina seem to have the most unfavorable trend, with decreasing life expectancy, whereas Serbia and Montenegro, Macedonia, and Croatia are in between. The latter recovered recently after exhibiting the lowest life expectancy level until the year 2000. The situation among women is similar to that of men; however, the increases in life expectancy did not stall during the 1960s, 1970s, and 1980s for women, nor did their life expectancy in Slovenia and Croatia fall below the level in other countries.

In the eastern Mediterranean, the area with most data quality issues, Turkey has the lowest level of life expectancy but has also experienced rapid increase. Note, however, that information on Turkish life expectancy at age 15 was available for only three calendar years. Cyprus, on the other hand, shows very favorable mortality levels, comparable to those of Greece, which is assigned to Southern Europe. The Caucasus states exhibit very different mortality trends. Most marked is the tremendous fall of Armenian life expectancy in 1988, which was related to a strong earthquake in December of that year. The earthquake caused more than 25,000 deaths, leading life expectancy at age 15 to drop by more than 6 years among men and more than 10 years among women. Mortality trends in Azerbaijan and Georgia fluctuate like those in the CIS and Baltic countries, although more markedly among men than among women.

The Western European countries show more homogeneous trends, although significant differences in the level of life expectancy exist in each of the four sub-regions. Among the Nordic countries, Finland and Denmark clearly experience more unfavorable mortality trends, Finland until the mid-1970s and Denmark after this time. From 1950 to around 1975, Finnish women and men exhibited mortality levels closer to those of Russians than to those of their Scandinavian neighbors. Since then, life expectancy has increased in Finland at a pace similar to or even stronger than that of Sweden, Norway, and Iceland. Among women, the difference between Finland and these countries has vanished, whereas among males, Finland's life expectancy has been at the same level as Denmark's since the mid-1990s. Denmark's unfavorable mortality level as compared to the other countries of Northern Europe is especially apparent among females. This situation emerged between 1975 and 1995, when life expectancy in Denmark stalled while it increased in the other Nordic countries. Sweden and Iceland still are among the countries with the highest male life expectancy in Europe, but their advantage relative to the countries of Southern and Western Europe has decreased. This is because in the Nordic countries the stall observed elsewhere in the 1960s and early 1970s started earlier (in the mid-1950s) and ended later (at the end of the 1970s).

Among the Central Western European countries, Austria, Luxembourg, and West Germany have experienced the general Western European mortality trends since the middle of the twentieth century. The outliers here are Switzerland and East Germany, the former with higher life expectancy since the 1960s and the latter with lower life expectancy between the mid-1980s and 2000. Before unification, East German women and men exhibited mortality trends typical for most former Communist countries in Central Europe. Since 1990, however, life expectancy has increased in eastern Germany at the highest pace of all European countries among both women and men. Among women, eastern Germany reached the level of Austria, Luxembourg, and western Germany around 2005, and among men the differences shrank so that they are currently quite small. Since the mid-1960s Switzerland has retained an advantage relative to the other central Western European countries among both sexes, exhibiting life-expectancy levels comparable to Sweden and Iceland.

In Northwestern Europe, men from Belgium, Ireland, England and Wales, and Northern Ireland experienced the typical Western European trends in adult mortality. Only Northern Ireland fell a bit behind during the 1970s. Here, the outliers are the Netherlands and Scotland. During the 1950s, Dutch males had significantly higher life expectancy than all other Northwestern male populations. However, instead of stalling, their life expectancy at age 15 decreased somewhat during the 1960s, and since the 1970s has increased at a slower pace compared to the other countries. Thus, in terms of trends in adult mortality, the Netherlands appear to be closer to the Nordic countries. As a consequence of this trend, the Netherlands lost the role of leader among the Northwestern European countries in the second half of the 1990s. Scottish males have had the lowest life expectancy of all Northwestern European countries throughout the period examined, accompanied by French men during the first half of the 1950s and by men from Northern Ireland during the 1970s. Similarly, Scottish women show the lowest life expectancy of all female populations from Northwestern Europe. Women from the Netherlands lost their leading role in the 1980s; since then, French women have taken over as leaders in life expectancy, ranking now among the female populations with the highest life expectancy in Europe. For women from Ireland and Northern Ireland, the unfavorable health situation depicted in Fig. 3.1b in the previous section was due to low life-expectancy levels in the first years of the twenty-first century. Between 2003 and 2007, however, female life expectancy rose sharply in Ireland and Northern Ireland and reached the levels of England and Wales and the Netherlands.

Among Western European countries, those in Southern Europe showed the shortest stall in life expectancy during the 1960s. Greece exhibits mortality trends similar to those of the Netherlands, and Spain shows trends comparable to those of France. Greek women and men had the highest life expectancy in Southern Europe from the mid-1950s to the mid-1990s (men) respective mid-1970s (women) when they were overtaken by Italy and Spain, and also by Malta for men. Malta is an outlier among all Western European countries, since its life expectancy stalled until the early 1980s. On the other hand, during the 1980s, Maltese women experienced the highest increase in life expectancy among all European countries. Portugal is a negative outlier, exhibiting significantly lower life expectancy than the other Southern European countries for both sexes. Among women, however, Malta had a lower life expectancy than Portugal until the late 1980s, and has had a similar level of life expectancy in recent years. Today, Italian and Spanish women and Italian men are among the populations with the highest life expectancy in Europe.

## Trends in Age-Specific Adult Mortality in Europe

The trends in overall adult mortality in Europe are accompanied by general trends in age-specific mortality in Eastern, Western, and Central Europe. We chose three representative countries for the three European mortality regions: Italy for Western Europe, the Czech Republic for Central Europe, and Russia for Eastern Europe. Figures 3.5 and 3.6 relate, for each of these countries, age-specific death rates at ages 15–100 for 1981–1985 to values for 1961–1965, and for 2001–2005 to 1981–1985 (all values calculated as averages over the corresponding five calendar years). Among Italian men, mortality was reduced in each adult age group in both periods. But the age range of maximum relative improvement shifted from ages 25–45 for 1961–1965 to 1981–1985 (Fig. 3.5a) to ages 40–75 for 1981–1985 to 2001–2005 (Fig. 3.6a). In both cases the death rates were reduced up to 40%.

Among Italian women, the changes between the early 1960s and the early 1980s were similar (Fig. 3.5b), although the relative improvements were larger than among men at all ages. Between 1981–1985 and 2001–2005 the age-specific improvements in female mortality in Italy were more homogeneous, with reductions in death rates of 30–40% at most ages (Fig. 3.6b). Trends for Russian men were the opposite of those for Italian men, as mortality increased at almost all ages between 1961–1965 and 1981–1985 (Fig. 3.5a) as well as between 1981–1985 and 2001–2005 (Fig. 3.6b). Striking is the fact that the maximum increases of mortality occurred in the younger and middle adult ages, up to 60% in both periods. For women this is true only for the changes between the early 1980s and 2001–2005 (Fig. 3.6b). Between the early 1960s and 1981–1985, female mortality in Russia increased only at ages 50 and above, whereas mortality in the younger adult ages decreased (Fig. 3.5b). For both sexes the Czech Republic illustrates the shift from the Eastern European pattern of change between 1961–1965 and 1981–1985 (Fig. 3.5), to the Western European change pattern between 1981–1985 and 2001–2005 (Fig. 3.6). However, the changes between the early 1960s and the early 1980s were more favorable than in Russia. This holds especially for women, for whom mortality increased at only a few ages. At most ages mortality remained more or less unchanged. On the other hand, the improvements between 1981–1985 and 2001–2005 were similar to those in Italy. Among Czech men, the improvements between ages 40 and 75 were less marked than among men from Italy.

Most of the negative (and some of the positive) deviations from the typical regional patterns of mortality levels and trends described in the previous section can be explained—at least in part—by behavioral factors (data on these outliers are not shown here but can be found in Vallin and Meslé 2001). Danish men experienced improvements only at ages below 35, whereas almost no changes occurred at higher ages. Among Danish women, the situation is slightly more favorable, with mortality decreases among all adult ages between 1950 and the mid-1960s. Between 1965 and 1980, improvements occurred only at ages 65 and above, but even at these ages no further improvements occurred until the mid-1990s. It seems that it is no coincidence that mortality attributable to smoking is much higher among Danish women and men than in all other Scandinavian countries (see Peto et al. 2006). Portuguese and Greek men are among the few European male populations that show no recent decrease in lung cancer mortality (Didkowska et al. 2005). On the other hand, French women show large improvements in adult mortality over the whole period, as do Italian women. The largest gains relative to other low-mortality countries of Western

**A. Males**

**B. Females**

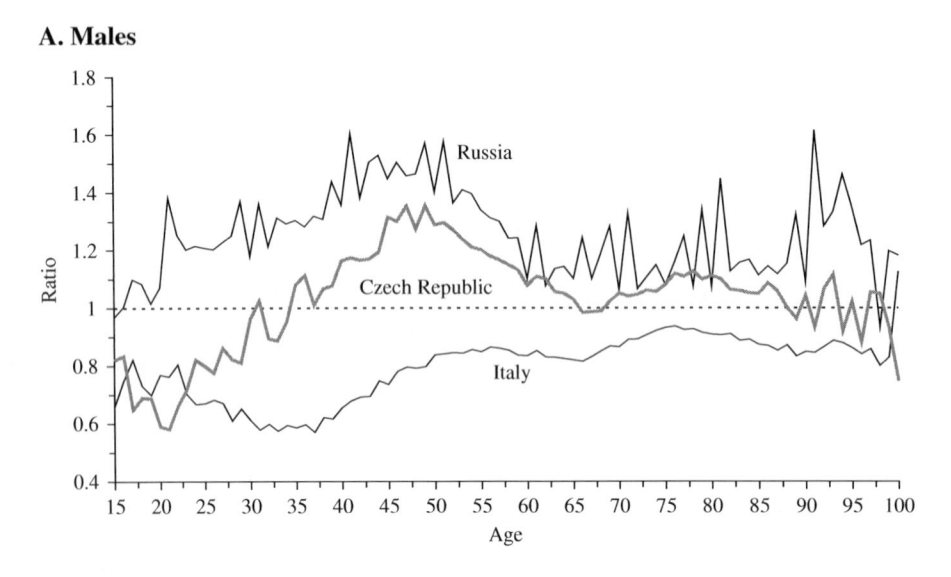

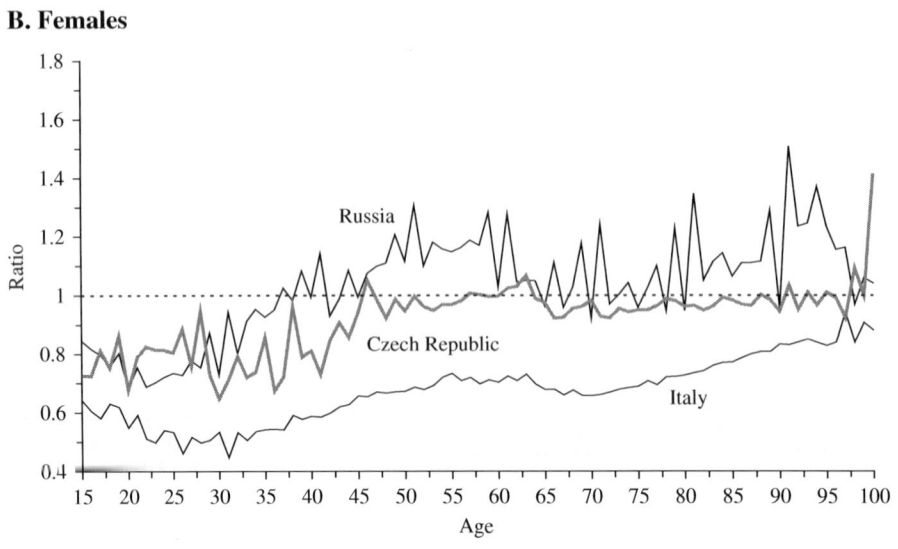

**Fig. 3.5** Ratios of death rates from ages 15 to 100 for 1981–1985 to the values for 1961–1965 in Italy, the Czech Republic, and the Russian Federation

Europe occurred in the higher adult ages. Compared to other Western European populations, smoking-related deaths are much lower among French women and began to contribute to overall mortality much later, as is also true for women from Switzerland, who have similar favorable health conditions. Mortality of French men was marked by a strong resistance to mortality decline at around age 20, especially between the early 1960s and the beginning of the 1980s. In 1980, as a result of road accidents, French men at age 20 had lost all the benefits gained from the decline in infectious diseases since the war. But also for French men in the middle adult age groups, progress was mixed. Among all EU-15 countries (EU member states until 2003), France has the highest percentage of heavy alcohol drinkers, and it is characterized by a high alcohol-related premature mortality (see Khlat and Darmon 2003). In fact, alcohol-related mortality is generally viewed as a significant determinant of adult mortality throughout Europe (Britton et al. 2003; Kuntsche et al. 2009; Ramstedt 2002; Rehm et al. 2009).

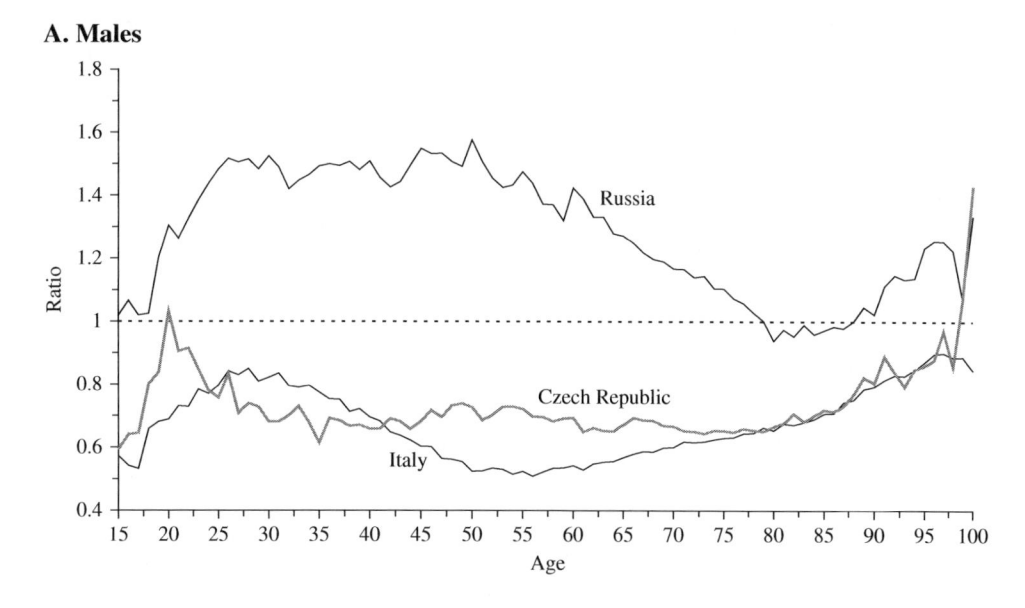

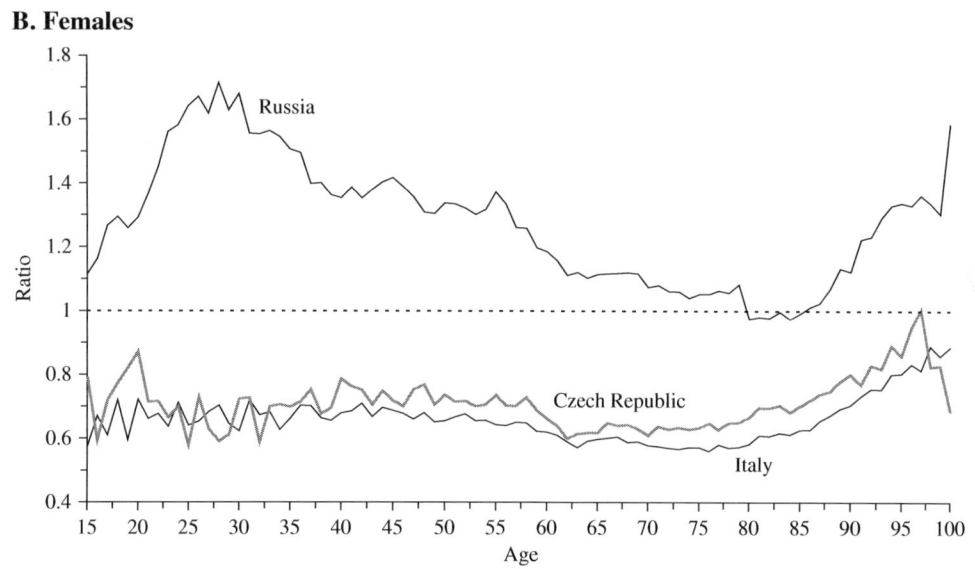

**Fig. 3.6** Ratios of death rates from ages 15–100 for 2001–2005 to the values for 1981–1985 in Italy, the Czech Republic, and the Russian Federation

## Length of Life Inequality

Recently, Smits and Monden (2009) suggested an indicator called "length of life inequality" (LLI) and applied it to most countries of the world using a new database (the "length of life database") of over 9,000 life tables covering over two centuries. The LLI is designed to measure the inequality in the age distribution of life table deaths after age 15 and thus provides an alternative look at the changing pattern of age-specific mortality trends. The basic idea behind the LLI is that when deaths are the more equally distributed within a population, the variance of ages at death around the average is lower, i.e., more people die at ages close to the average age at death and fewer deaths occur in older or younger ages (representing more or less privileged subpopulations, respectively). The LLI is derived by computing the Gini coefficient over the age distribution of life table deaths. Consequently, the higher the LLI values, the higher the inequality of adult length of life, or expressed differently, the more unevenly deaths are distributed over the range of ages. Generally, higher life expectancies are related to lower values of LLI, but there is also a wide variation of the LLI at specific levels of life expectancy and vice versa (see Smits and Monden 2009). We used the length of life database to analyze the trends in the LLI among Eastern, Western, and Central European countries from 1955 to 2005 or the most recent available year. The Western European countries for which the LLI was available are Andorra, Austria, Belgium, Cyprus, Denmark, England and

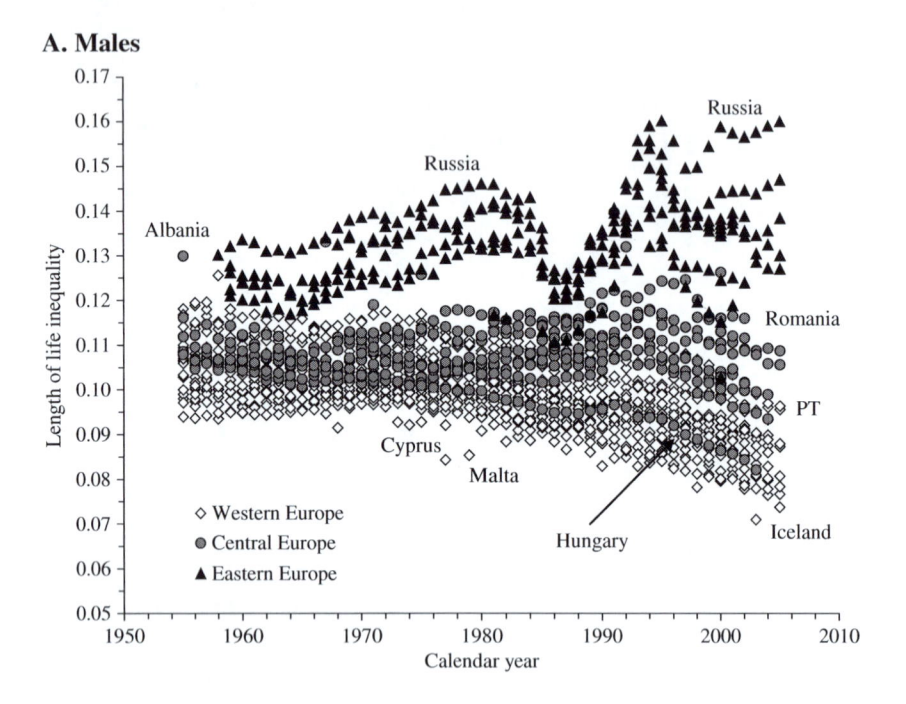

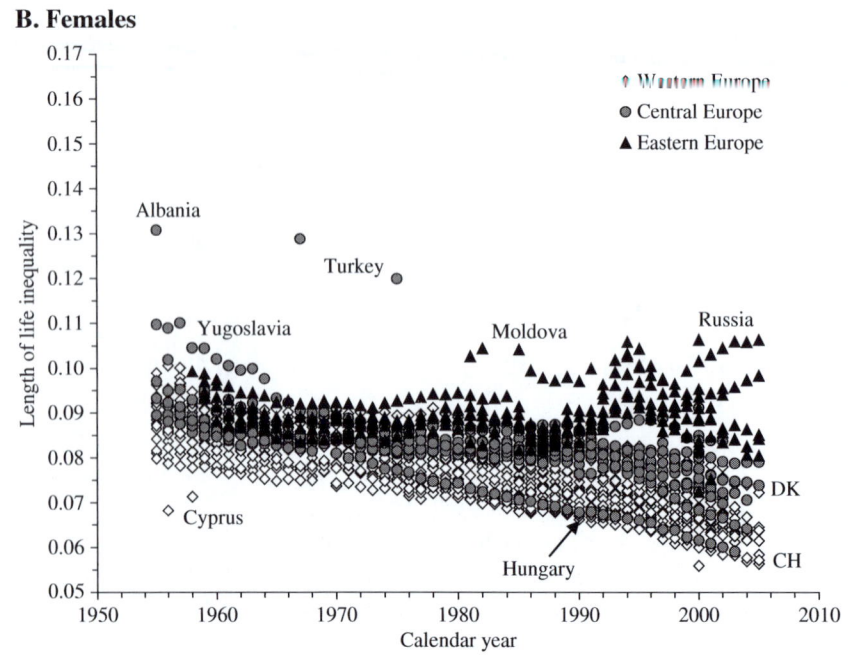

**Fig. 3.7** Length of life inequality (inequality across age groups) for adults (age 15+) of European populations, 1955–2005 (data: Smits and Monden 2009)

Wales, Finland, France, West Germany, unified Germany, Greece, Iceland, Ireland, Italy, Luxembourg, Malta, the Netherlands, Northern Ireland, Norway, Portugal, Scotland, Spain, Sweden, and Switzerland. The Central European countries include Albania, Bosnia and Herzegovina, Bulgaria, Croatia, Czech Republic, East Germany, Hungary, Poland, Romania, Serbia and Montenegro, Slovakia, Slovenia, Turkey, and Yugoslavia. Finally, Eastern Europe includes Armenia, Azerbaijan, Belarus, Estonia, Georgia, Latvia, Lithuania, Moldova, Russia, Ukraine, and the USSR.

Figure 3.7 shows the LLI for each available year and each country for men (Panel A) and women (Panel B) respectively, grouped into the basic mortality regions of Eastern Europe (black triangles), Western Europe (white diamonds), and Central Europe (grey circles). The maximum and minimum values as well as the outliers are designated by country. The graphs summarize the differences in trends in age-specific mortality accompanying trends in overall adult mortality. Among men, there is no clear difference between populations from Western and Central Europe until around 1980 (see Fig. 3.7a). In contrast, the male populations from Eastern European countries exhibit a considerably higher LLI because of the age pattern of mortality described above (see Figs. 3.5a and 3.6a). There seems to be an increasing trend over the whole period with short interruptions during the 1980s and 1990s, which coincide with the fluctuation in mortality of the populations from the former Soviet Union. The general LLI trend is similar among Central European men, but with a constant rather than increasing LLI level. Western European males, on the other hand, experience a reduction in the LLI beginning in the early 1980s. Furthermore, the differences in LLI between the Western European countries seem to decrease rather than to increase or remain constant. Thus, the trisection of overall adult mortality in Europe coincides with a trisection in the LLI: low levels and decreasing LLI in Western Europe, high levels and increasing LLI in Eastern Europe, and intermediate constant or moderately increasing LLI in Central Europe.

Basically, the same holds for the LLI trends among European women (Fig. 3.7b). But the differences in levels and trends are much smaller as compared to those for men. Above all, there is no difference in the initial level between women from Central and Eastern Europe. Both exhibit LLIs in the area of the upper levels of Western European women. Figure 3.7a and 3.7b reveal that, in general, those populations with the lowest life expectancy exhibit a higher LLI. A remarkable exception is Hungary, where both sexes simultaneously experience the lowest life-expectancy levels and the lowest LLI among all Central European countries. Among women, Hungary even shows one of the lowest LLIs of all of Europe. This indicates that the unfavorable health situation in Hungary is a consequence of a general trend; all ages are similarly affected by the health crises. In contrast, in most of Eastern and Central Europe the health crises produce specific determinants that affect selected age ranges.

## Trends in Cause-Specific Adult Mortality in Europe

To better understand the origins of the regional disparities in European adult mortality, one must examine causes of death. The period covered includes four revisions of the International Classification of Diseases (ICD), from the seventh (in the mid-1950s) to the tenth (since the 1990s). Different countries began using each revision at different dates. The changes from one revision to another create breaks in the cause-of-death statistics that can be significant for some causes. This makes it difficult to follow trends in some specific causes and even in major groupings. Furthermore, country-specific coding practices have severe impacts on the determination of causes of death. It is well known that cause of death statistics include a certain degree of uncertainty (e.g., Cameron and McGoogan 1981; Eisenblätter et al. 1981, 1994; Höhn and Pollard 1991; Meslé 2006; Modelmog et al. 1992; Wunsch 2006). Even the main cause-of-death groups can be significantly distorted by different definitions and ways of coding. For instance, according to official German cause-of-death statistics, 2 years after German unification (and 1 year after applying the western German coding rules in eastern Germany) the differences in cancer mortality between East and West Germany in favor of the East not only disappeared but reversed to excess cancer mortality in eastern Germany (see Luy 2004). Since the physiological nature of cancer rules out any very rapid change in cancer incidence or mortality, such a finding can be explained only by different coding practices. In West Germany the detailed coding of the "leading cause of death" was performed by specifically trained personnel at the Statistical Offices of the German States. In East Germany, doctors provided cause-of-death information that was directly entered into the official statistics (Brückner 1993). A final issue in international comparisons of causes of death results from the fact that the proportion of deaths of indeterminate cause varies greatly from one country to another.

The trends in cause-specific mortality in Europe have already been extensively analyzed and described by Vallin and Meslé (2001) for all European countries for the period 1950–1995, and with concentration on some Central and Eastern European countries by Boys et al. (1991), Shkolnikov et al. (1996a, b), and Meslé (2004). Since the decade between 1995 and 2005 did not exhibit major changes or new directions in age- and cause-specific mortality, we restrict this section mainly to a summary of the work of Vallin and Meslé (2001) and present only selected country-specific illustrations, including the most recent years up to 2005. First, we describe general trends in the main causes of death before connecting them directly to the specific changes in selected countries from Eastern, Western, and Central Europe. In most European countries, mortality due to infectious diseases and diseases of the respiratory system fell considerably after the middle of the twentieth century. This fall was especially marked and continuous in Southern Europe, the former Yugoslavia, and Central Eastern Europe. Exceptions include Switzerland, where infectious mortality rose in the 1990s owing to the effect of AIDS (Kohli 2005), and the Netherlands, where a similar increase in infectious mortality was probably due to the same cause (Vallin and Meslé 2001).

Within each of the eight subregions of Europe the cancer death rate has a consistent trend. In the Nordic and Central Western European countries, cancer mortality decreased almost through the whole second half of the twentieth century, whereas in Southern and Central Eastern Europe it increased. Among the Nordic countries Denmark stands out with a continuous rise in cancer mortality; in Central Eastern Europe, Bulgaria and Romania stand out with significantly lower cancer mortality than the other countries in the region. Northwestern Europe is in an intermediate position, with, for most countries, deterioration in the situation until the beginning of the 1980s, followed by marked improvement. Trends in cancer mortality can be summarized as follows: Western European countries, with a few exceptions, exhibited a decrease where cancer was initially high and an increase where it was initially lower. In Central and Eastern European countries, the trend has been upward in recent years. While cancer mortality has increased in Poland, Hungary, the Czech Republic, and Slovakia (especially before the split), in the Soviet Union it clearly increased only in the 1980s. Note, however, that cancer might have been underreported as cause of death in some countries at some times. Generally, it seems that the diagnosis of cancer is more accurate and socially more acceptable today than it was in the past, and some increases in cancer mortality may be partly due to more accurate assignment (Vallin and Meslé 2001).

Trends in circulatory diseases (mainly driven by cardiovascular diseases) show more regional disparities. In all Western European countries, circulatory mortality is decreasing, but there are substantial differences in both baseline levels and the rates of decline. Since circulatory diseases are the dominant causes of death, these disparities coincide with the differences in trends in life expectancy described above. By contrast, in all Central and Eastern European countries, the trends are generally unfavorable and quite similar among countries, at least within each of the regional subgroups. Central Europe is characterized by a slow but perceptible increase in circulatory mortality from the mid-1960s to the mid-1980s, after which the situation deteriorated further in Romania and Bulgaria, whereas it started to improve in the other countries. The countries of the former Soviet Union show a trend in circulatory mortality similar to the trend in overall mortality described above. Thus, circulatory—and above all cardiovascular—mortality seems to be not only the main vector in health crises in the Eastern European countries, but also the main cause of differences between Central Europe and the countries of the former Soviet Union.

External causes of death, including injury, poisoning, and other external causes, also show very marked differences in levels and trends. This category covers several causes of death, such as traffic accidents, suicide, and homicide, which are very strongly associated with social and individual behaviors and are dependent on social structures and changes in social factors. In the countries of the former Soviet Union and in some countries of Central Europe, most deaths due to alcohol abuse are classified as "alcohol poisoning" and thus fall into the "external causes" category, while in other countries many of these deaths are attributed to "acute alcoholism and alcoholic psychosis" in the "mental disorders" category or are registered as "alcoholic cirrhosis of the liver" and thus are part of the category "diseases of the digestive system" (see Vallin and Meslé 2001). In most of the Western European countries, mortality due to external causes increased or remained constant during the 1950s and 1960s. After the 1970s, the trend reversed to rapid decline, however, with important differences in level and timing. In the Nordic and Central Western European countries, the increase in the 1950s and 1960s was fairly modest, whereas the fall since 1970 has been considerable. The only exceptions are Finland and Denmark. Whereas the former showed a second increase in external-cause mortality at the end of the 1980s, the latter showed neither a rise during the 1950s and 1960s nor the typical decline thereafter. Among Southern European countries, Portugal stands out by having the highest level of external-cause mortality as well as by exhibiting a longer period of increasing external-cause mortality, lasting until the end of the 1970s. The other Western European countries have varying levels and trends, which do not directly reflect the levels and trends of overall mortality.

Trends in external-cause mortality among the former Communist countries are very different. In Central Eastern Europe, external causes of death increased until the early 1990s, and even later in Bulgaria and Romania. Only the former Czechoslovakia showed a pattern more similar to Western European countries, with mortality due to external causes plateauing in the early 1970s. In the countries of the former Soviet Union, the trend in external-cause mortality reflects the marked fluctuations during the 1980s due to Gorbachev's anti-alcohol campaign. The rise after the restrictions were relaxed in the second half of the 1980s was accelerated in the early 1990s with the economic and social crises that accompanied the problematic transition to a market economy. Since then, the situation has been improving. It is striking that the countries of the former Soviet Union despite their independence react very similarly to similar social events, with the same pattern of external-cause mortality trends over the whole period since 1950. In the Caucasus countries, this pattern is masked by the magnitude of temporary, event-related trends in specific countries, like the already mentioned earthquake in Armenia in 1988 and the Nagorno-Karabakh war in Armenia and Azerbaijan between 1992 and 1994. Similarly, the former Yugoslavian countries show the impact of the war of independence during the early 1990s in their mortality due to external causes.

We illustrate trends in age- and cause-specific adult mortality in Europe for more recent years and for selected countries by decomposing the changes in life expectancy at age 15 between 1981–1985 and 2001–2005 by 5-year age groups from 15–19 to 80–84 and 85+ into the contributions of broad cause-of-death categories: infectious diseases, malignant neoplasms (cancer), circulatory diseases, respiratory diseases, digestive diseases, external causes of death, and other medical causes. Figure 3.8 includes the results for Italian males (upper panel) and females (lower panel). Between 1981–1985 and 2001–2005 life expectancy at age 15 for Italian men rose by almost 5 years. Figure 3.8a shows how many years each age group contributed to this change. For instance, changes in mortality at ages 15–19 contributed 0.08 years and changes at ages 20–24 0.05 years to the total gain in life expectancy. The seven age groups between 50 and 84 contributed most to the total change in male life expectancy at age 15, i.e., almost 4 years; the seven age groups before age 50, together with the 85+ group, accounted for the remaining increase of about 1 year. The contribution of each age group is further subdivided by specific causes of death. Naturally, the impact of causes of death on overall adult mortality differs with age. Since in some cases cause-specific changes were unfavorable, some of the bars lie in the negative area, meaning that these specific causes resulted in a loss of life expectancy between 1981–1985 and 2001–2005. This is true in some younger adult ages for the category "other medical causes," and to a small extent for infectious diseases, and above age 80 (men) respective 85 (women) for malignant neoplasms.

Most of the bars are in the positive area, since life expectancy at age 15 for men increased between the two periods by almost 5 years. The graph shows that males gained some life expectancy from reductions in external-cause mortality at the youngest adult ages. During the 1980s and before, European men experienced excessive deaths at these young adult ages from traffic accidents. But in the other age groups as well, external causes contributed to the increase in life

**Fig. 3.8** Contribution of main groups of causes of death to the changes in life expectancy at age 15 between the periods 1981–1985 and 2001–2005 in Italy

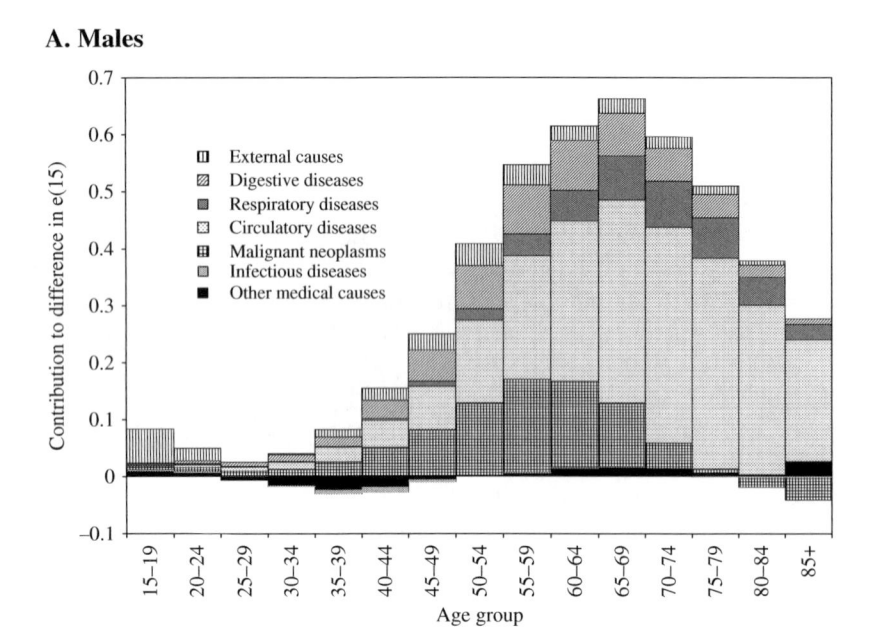

**A. Males**

**B. Females**

expectancy, about half a year over all age groups. Most of the increase in life expectancy was attributable to declines in deaths from circulatory diseases, cancer, and digestive diseases, accounting for approximately 2.5, 0.75, and 0.5 years, respectively. Figure 3.8b shows the same decomposition of causes of mortality trends for Italian women. Female life expectancy at age 15 rose by approximately 4 years between 1981–1985 and 2001–2005. Relative to men, the improvements were more concentrated at higher ages, but similarly dominated by reductions of mortality from circulatory diseases. The decrease of circulatory mortality contributed more than two-and-a-half years to the total increase of female life expectancy at age 15. Malignant neoplasms, digestive diseases, and external causes of death contributed around 0.4, 0.3, and 0.2 years, respectively.

Figure 3.9 displays the age- and cause-specific contributions to the changes in life expectancy at age 15 between 1981–1985 and 2001–2005 among

**Fig. 3.9** Contribution of main groups of causes of death to the changes in life expectancy at age 15 between the periods 1981–1985 and 2001–2005 in Russia

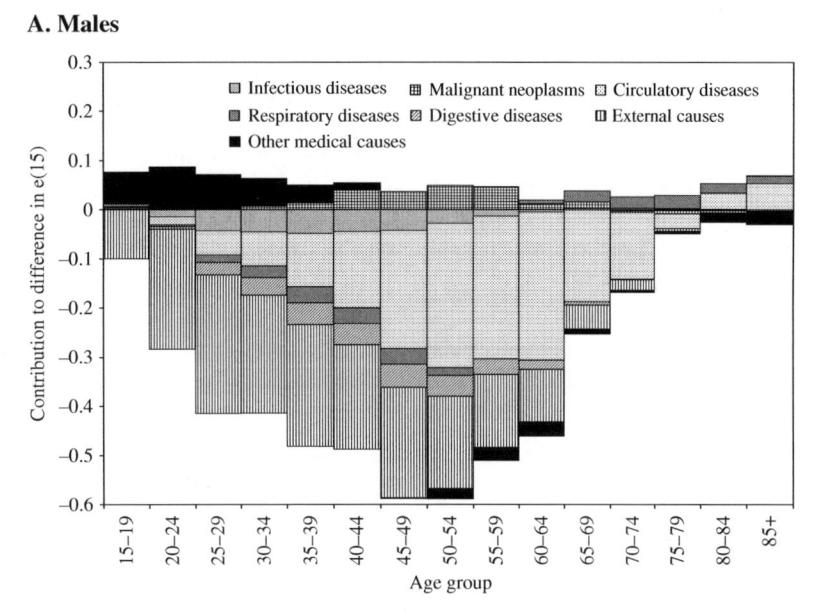

**A. Males**

**B. Females**

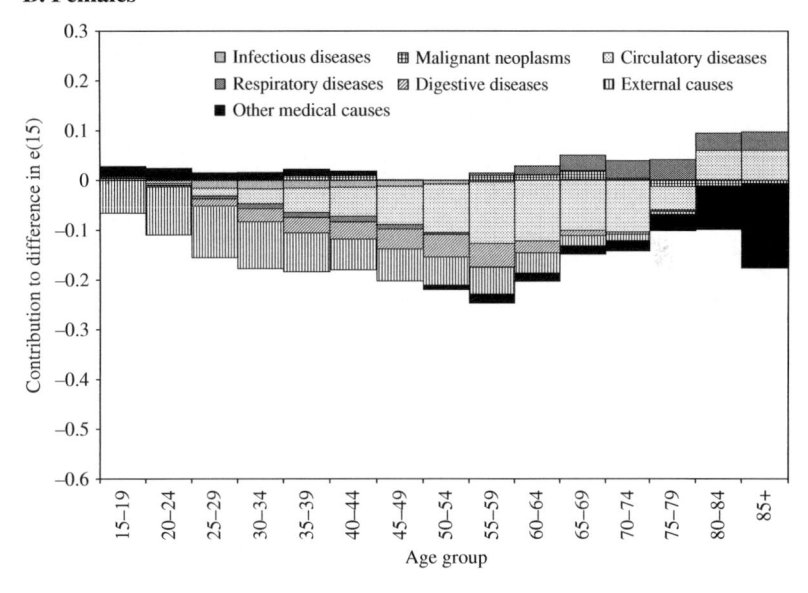

males (upper panel) and females (lower panel) of the Russian Federation. Here, life expectancy decreased by about 4 years among men and by about 2 years among women. The graph illustrates the significant role of external causes of death, which include most alcohol-attributable deaths but are dominated by accidents, which caused a decrease of approximately 2 years in life expectancy at age 15 among men and by three-quarters of a year among women. (The effect of alcohol-related deaths on overall mortality trends in Russia is also discussed in Chapter 4 and in Hinote et al. 2009, Moskalewicz et al. 2000, and Nicholson et al. 2005). More than half of the decrease in life expectancy among men and almost 40% among women was attributable to this cause-of-death category. But most other causes of death also contributed to the decrease in life expectancy: circulatory diseases, digestive diseases, and infectious diseases contributed about 1.8, 0.3, and 0.3 years, respectively, among men, and about 0.7, 0.3, and 0.1 years among women. Mortality due to respiratory diseases increased at younger adult ages but decreased at the older ages for both sexes, resulting in no contribution of this cause-of-death category to overall changes in life expectancy at age 15. The remainder category, "other medical causes," decreased at younger but increased at older adult ages. Only cancer mortality decreased in almost all age groups between 1981–1985 and 2001–2005 in the Russian Federation; however, decreases were much smaller than in Western European countries like Italy.

Finally, Fig. 3.10 illustrates the changes in mortality among Central European countries after 1961–1965 with the example of the former Czechoslovakia, for which causes of death were available for the whole time span. The figure shows the contributions of age and causes to life expectancy at age 15 for men between 1961–1965 and 1981–1985 in the upper panel, and between 1981–1985 and 2001–2005 in the lower panel. The interpretation of the data with regard to change between the early 1960s and early 1980s is limited by the fact that the causes of many deaths were undefined, and thus the category of "other medical causes" dominates. Nevertheless, explanations for the trends described above become apparent. Life expectancy at age 15 decreased among men from

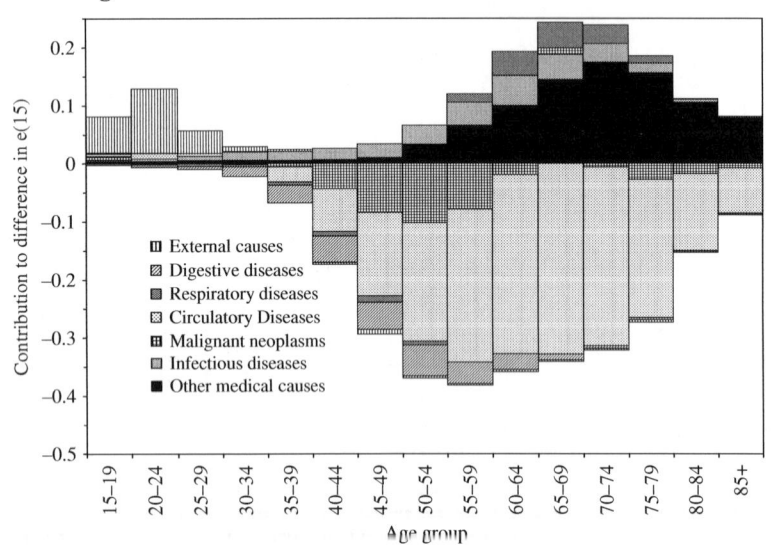

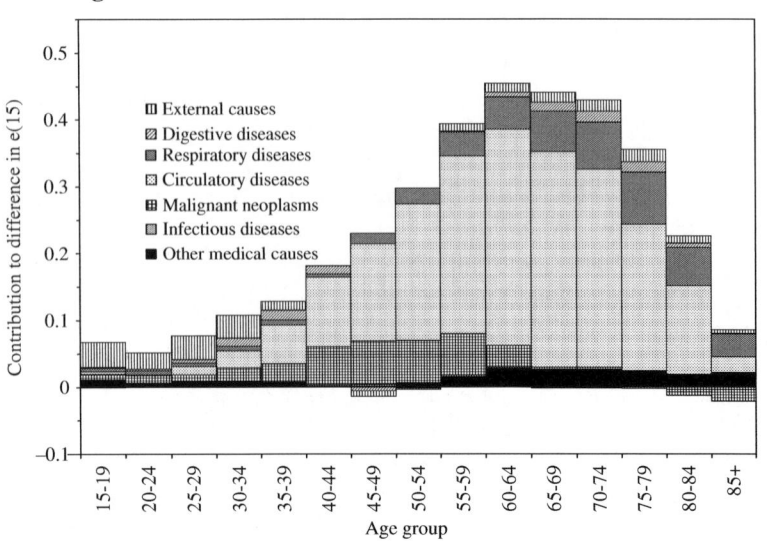

**Fig. 3.10** Contribution of main groups of causes of death to the changes in life expectancy at age 15 between the periods 1961–1965 and 1981–1985 and between 1981–1985 and 2001–2005 in the former Czechoslovakia, males

Czechoslovakia between 1961–1965 and 1981–1985 by 1.2 years, mainly because of increasing mortality from circulatory diseases, malignant neoplasms, and digestive diseases. During this time, this situation was typical of all countries of the former Soviet bloc, which failed in the fight against circulatory (mainly cardiovascular) diseases and did not succeed in preventing an increase in man-made diseases. The reduction in external causes of death in young adult ages prevented life expectancy from decreasing even further (see Fig. 3.10a). The same holds for infectious and respiratory diseases. Figure 3.10b shows the switch to the more Western European change pattern between the periods 1981–1985 and 2001–2005. The picture painted by the contributions of age- and cause-specific changes to the now increasing life expectancy among men in the former Czechoslovakia is very similar to that for Italian men in Fig. 3.8a. Life expectancy increased by about 3.5 years, mainly because of improvements at ages 50–84, which contributed 2.6 years. Among the causes of death, the largest contributions came from decreases in circulatory diseases, respiratory diseases, and cancer, which were responsible for increases in life expectancy of 2.1, 0.5, and 0.3 years, respectively.

## Tempo-Adjusted Life Expectancy in the Period 2001–2005

In the previous sections, we used conventional life table calculations. In a series of papers, Bongaarts and Feeney (2002, 2003, 2006) recently suggested using tempo-adjusted life expectancy for the analysis of period mortality, because conventional period life expectancy is affected by tempo effects. The term "tempo effect" describes a change of period rates in demographic events that results exclusively from a change of the average age at which the event occurs during the observation period. A tempo effect works in such a way that an increase of the average age at occurrence leads to a decrease in period rates, and a decrease of the average age leads to an increase in period rates. Since demographic period rates are often used to measure the quantum of the analyzed event during the observation period, Bongaarts and Feeney claim that tempo effects in this context have to be seen as undesirable distortions. This is true for all demographic measures derived from period rates, including life expectancy and the total fertility rate in fertility analysis, where adjustment for tempo has received broad acceptance in recent years. Although demographers do not yet agree whether conventional or tempo-adjusted life expectancy is the more appropriate measure for period mortality (see the collection of papers discussing this issue in Barbi et al. 2008), we provide tempo-adjusted life expectancy for European countries using the approach of Bongaarts and Feeney (2002). (See Luy and Wegner 2009 for a more detailed discussion of why tempo-adjusted life expectancy can be a more useful indicator for some purposes, e.g., a comparison of populations with different or diverging trends in mortality.)

Tempo adjustment for life expectancy means that in countries with rapid mortality improvements, which are supposedly exaggerated by the tempo effect, life-expectancy figures will be adjusted downward and for those, such as some Eastern European countries, with declines, figures will be adjusted upward. As appears below, these adjustments have significant impact on the description of trends over time and the ranking of countries by level of life expectancy. In the case of mortality differences between eastern and western Germany, it has been shown that the picture drawn by tempo-adjusted life expectancy better fits expected trends in changing mortality and self-reported health among eastern and western Germans than that painted by conventional life expectancy (see Luy 2006, 2008). Unfortunately, the estimation of tempo-adjusted life expectancy requires very detailed data on sex- and age-specific mortality trends that are not available for most countries. However, for the majority of European countries, the quality and quantity of the data are sufficient to estimate tempo-adjusted life expectancy.

We estimated tempo-adjusted life expectancy for 2001–2005 for the 34 European countries with sufficient mortality data. Tables 3.1 and 3.2 show the results for females and males, respectively. The first column presents the values for conventional life expectancy at age 15, labeled e(15); the second column provides the estimates for tempo-adjusted life expectancy, labeled e(15)*. The next column gives the difference between conventional and tempo-adjusted

**Table 3.1** Conventional life expectancy e(15) and tempo-adjusted life expectancy e(15)* at age 15 for 34 European countries, females 2001–2005

|  | e(15) | e(15)* | Difference | Rank e(15) | Rank e(15)* |
|---|---|---|---|---|---|
| Eastern Germany | 66.77 | 64.00 | 2.77 | 14 | 20 |
| Italy | 68.66 | 66.44 | 2.22 | 4 | 6 |
| Ireland | 66.16 | 64.07 | 2.09 | 18 | 18 |
| Austria | 67.30 | 65.23 | 2.07 | 8 | 13 |
| Slovenia | 65.97 | 64.03 | 1.94 | 20 | 19 |
| France | 68.75 | 66.83 | 1.92 | 2 | 2 |
| Western Germany | 67.03 | 65.16 | 1.87 | 11 | 14 |
| Spain | 68.67 | 66.81 | 1.86 | 3 | 3 |
| Finland | 67.25 | 65.39 | 1.86 | 9 | 11 |
| Portugal | 66.46 | 64.61 | 1.85 | 17 | 17 |
| Poland | 64.57 | 62.74 | 1.83 | 23 | 23 |
| England and Wales | 66.47 | 64.75 | 1.72 | 16 | 15 |
| Czech Republic | 64.31 | 62.60 | 1.71 | 24 | 24 |
| Switzerland | 68.77 | 67.09 | 1.68 | 1 | 1 |
| Belgium | 66.91 | 65.31 | 1.60 | 13 | 12 |
| Iceland | 68.17 | 66.58 | 1.59 | 5 | 4 |
| Scotland | 64.63 | 63.05 | 1.58 | 22 | 22 |
| Hungary | 62.57 | 61.01 | 1.56 | 28 | 31 |
| Greece | 67.06 | 65.54 | 1.52 | 10 | 10 |
| Northern Ireland | 66.13 | 64.62 | 1.51 | 19 | 16 |
| Estonia | 63.10 | 61.72 | 1.38 | 27 | 27 |
| Norway | 67.35 | 66.05 | 1.30 | 7 | 7 |
| Denmark | 65.22 | 63.96 | 1.26 | 21 | 21 |
| Sweden | 67.74 | 66.51 | 1.23 | 6 | 5 |
| Slovakia | 63.61 | 62.45 | 1.16 | 25 | 26 |
| Luxembourg | 66.93 | 65.80 | 1.13 | 12 | 8 |
| Romania | 61.61 | 60.58 | 1.03 | 31 | 32 |
| Russian Federation | 58.33 | 59.32 | −0.99 | 34 | 34 |
| Latvia | 62.26 | 61.34 | 0.92 | 29 | 28 |
| Netherlands | 66.56 | 65.71 | 0.85 | 15 | 9 |
| Bulgaria | 62.05 | 61.32 | 0.73 | 30 | 29 |
| Lithuania | 63.24 | 62.52 | 0.72 | 26 | 25 |
| Belarus | 60.45 | 61.10 | −0.65 | 32 | 30 |
| Ukraine | 59.59 | 60.10 | −0.51 | 33 | 33 |
| Maximum differences | 10.45 | 7.77 | – | – | – |
| Standard deviation | 2.72 | 2.17 | – | – | – |

Notes: Tempo-adjusted life expectancy was estimated by using the method proposed by Bongaarts and Feeney (2002), based on a series of sex- and age-specific death rates from 1960 to 2005 (exceptions: Greece 1961–2005, Romania 1968–2005, Slovenia 1983–2005); estimates for tempo-adjusted life expectancy assume no tempo effects below age 30; a dash (–) indicates that figures are not calculated.

life expectancy. In most cases this difference is positive, meaning that improvements of mortality conditions cause tempo effects that bias conventional life expectancy upward. However, there are some Eastern European countries, like Russia and Ukraine, where mortality increased during the last decades and thus tempo distortions caused the opposite effect. The last two columns contain the ranks of the countries according to conventional and tempo-adjusted life expectancy, respectively. Countries are ordered by the absolute size of tempo effects, i.e., by the difference between conventional and tempo-adjusted life expectancy, from the largest effect to the smallest.

**Table 3.2** Conventional life expectancy e(15) and tempo-adjusted life expectancy e(15)* at age 15 for 34 European countries, males 2001–2005

|  | e(15) | e(15)* | Difference | Rank e(15) | Rank e(15)* |
|---|---|---|---|---|---|
| Eastern Germany | 60.35 | 57.55 | 2.80 | 19 | 20 |
| Austria | 61.62 | 58.83 | 2.79 | 12 | 16 |
| Italy | 62.99 | 60.22 | 2.77 | 4 | 7 |
| Finland | 60.52 | 57.77 | 2.75 | 18 | 19 |
| Russian Federation | 45.11 | 47.74 | −2.63 | 34 | 34 |
| Ireland | 61.25 | 58.62 | 2.63 | 14 | 17 |
| England and Wales | 62.16 | 59.55 | 2.61 | 6 | 9 |
| Slovenia | 58.47 | 55.93 | 2.54 | 22 | 22 |
| France | 61.64 | 59.13 | 2.51 | 11 | 12 |
| Switzerland | 63.59 | 61.10 | 2.49 | 2 | 3 |
| Western Germany | 61.65 | 59.19 | 2.46 | 10 | 11 |
| Belarus | 48.63 | 51.04 | −2.41 | 32 | 31 |
| Northern Ireland | 61.38 | 59.11 | 2.27 | 13 | 13 |
| Norway | 62.42 | 60.25 | 2.17 | 5 | 6 |
| Czech Republic | 57.84 | 55.69 | 2.15 | 23 | 23 |
| Belgium | 61.03 | 58.89 | 2.14 | 15 | 15 |
| Scotland | 59.51 | 57.37 | 2.14 | 21 | 21 |
| Ukraine | 48.22 | 50.31 | −2.09 | 33 | 33 |
| Sweden | 63.38 | 61.34 | 2.04 | 3 | 2 |
| Portugal | 59.87 | 57.85 | 2.02 | 20 | 18 |
| Spain | 62.00 | 60.13 | 1.87 | 8 | 8 |
| Denmark | 60.69 | 58.95 | 1.74 | 17 | 14 |
| Netherlands | 62.01 | 60.29 | 1.72 | 7 | 5 |
| Poland | 56.19 | 54.57 | 1.62 | 24 | 25 |
| Luxembourg | 60.97 | 59.35 | 1.62 | 16 | 10 |
| Iceland | 64.29 | 62.77 | 1.52 | 1 | 1 |
| Greece | 61.99 | 60.65 | 1.34 | 9 | 4 |
| Hungary | 54.22 | 52.90 | 1.32 | 28 | 28 |
| Slovakia | 55.72 | 54.53 | 1.19 | 25 | 26 |
| Estonia | 51.79 | 51.07 | 0.72 | 30 | 30 |
| Latvia | 51.51 | 50.82 | 0.69 | 31 | 32 |
| Lithuania | 51.91 | 52.32 | −0.41 | 29 | 29 |
| Romania | 54.62 | 54.27 | 0.35 | 27 | 27 |
| Bulgaria | 55.22 | 55.02 | 0.20 | 26 | 24 |
| Maximum differences | 19.18 | 15.03 | – | – | – |
| Standard deviation | 4.91 | 3.71 | – | – | – |

Notes: Tempo-adjusted life expectancy was estimated by using the method proposed by Bongaarts and Feeney (2002), based on a series of sex- and age-specific death rates from 1960 to 2005 (exceptions: Greece 1961–2005, Romania 1968–2005, Slovenia 1983–2005); estimates for tempo-adjusted life expectancy assume no tempo effects below age 30; a dash (–) indicates that figures are not calculated.

Among females, the highest three rankings in life expectancy are not affected by tempo-adjustment. Switzerland has the highest life expectancy, followed by France and Spain (Table 3.1). Since tempo effects are higher in France and Spain than in Switzerland, the differences in tempo-adjusted life expectancy are around 0.2 years higher than the differences in conventional life expectancy. Italy ranks fourth in conventional life expectancy, but in tempo-adjusted life expectancy, Italy falls behind Iceland and Sweden. The countries with lowest female life expectancy remain those from Eastern and Central Europe, with some differences in the rankings between conventional and tempo-adjusted life expectancy (e.g.,

Hungary and Belarus). Only Denmark and Scotland, the Western European countries with the lowest female life expectancy, fall behind Slovenia, which has the highest life expectancy among the Central and Eastern European countries. This holds for conventional as well as for tempo-adjusted life expectancy. Conventional life expectancy for eastern German women increased sharply after unification; however, such rapid improvements in mortality conditions cause large tempo effects. In the case of eastern Germany, the tempo effect is the highest among all female populations in Europe. Consequently, in the tempo-adjusted ranking, eastern Germany falls six ranks compared to its rank using conventional life expectancy, and exhibits values close to those of Denmark and Slovenia. Thus, while eastern German females rank among the lower half of Western European countries according to conventional life expectancy, they can be found just above Central and Eastern European countries in tempo-adjusted life expectancy. This example indicates how the picture of life expectancy differentials can change after one accounts for tempo effects. According to the conventional calculation, eastern German women have a life expectancy 0.3 years higher than women from England and Wales, whereas the tempo-adjusted life expectancy of eastern German women is 0.75 years lower than the tempo-adjusted life expectancy for English and Welsh women. Besides Italy and eastern Germany, Ireland, Austria, western Germany, and Hungary are the "losers" in the ranking of tempo-adjusted life expectancy for females. The "winners" are the Netherlands (rising from rank 15 according to conventional life expectancy to rank 9 according to tempo-adjusted life expectancy), Luxembourg (rising from 12 to rank 8), and Northern Ireland (rising from 19 to rank 16).

Among males, the first place in life expectancy rankings remains unchanged, with Iceland showing the lowest mortality of all European countries (see Table 3.2). The difference between Iceland and the country with the second highest life expectancy increases once life expectancy is adjusted for tempo effects, from 0.70 years compared to Switzerland to 1.43 years compared to Sweden, which ranks second in tempo-adjusted life expectancies. Among males, too, the highest tempo effects occur in eastern Germany. Although their absolute extent is even slightly higher than among eastern German females, the relative effect in terms of lost places in the life expectancy ranking is minor, since eastern German males fall only from rank 19 according to conventional life expectancy, to rank 20 according to tempo-adjusted life expectancy. However, among males, there are also some cases where tempo adjustment provides a very different picture of mortality differentials. For instance, according to the conventional calculation, life expectancy of Italian males exceeds those of men from Greece by 1 year. After tempo adjustment, Greek males show an almost half-year higher life expectancy than Italian men. The effects of tempo adjustment on life-expectancy differences between Eastern European countries are also interesting. According to the conventional values, Latvia's life expectancy at age 15 exceeds that of Russia by 6.4 years. According to tempo-adjusted life expectancy, however, the differences are more than 3 years smaller. Among males, the "losers" in the ranking of life expectancy after tempo adjustment—falling three or more ranks—are Austria, Italy, Ireland, and England and Wales. The "winners" are Greece (rising from rank 9 according to conventional life expectancy to rank 4 according to tempo-adjusted life expectancy), Luxembourg (rising from 16 to rank 10), and Denmark (rising from 17 to rank 14).

Finally, Fig. 3.11 shows maps of the differences between conventional and tempo-adjusted life expectancy at age 15 in Europe for males (upper panel) and females (lower panel), respectively. It becomes apparent that the levels of tempo distortion exhibit basically the same trisection of Europe as does conventional life expectancy. This reflects the fact that during the last two to three decades, life expectancy increased most in Western Europe, whereas it decreased in Eastern Europe. In Central Europe life expectancy increased also, but the increase started later than in Western Europe. Thus, tempo-adjustment reduces life expectancy the most in the Western European populations and has the opposite effect in Eastern European populations. As a consequence, the absolute differences in life expectancy between countries decrease once they are adjusted for tempo effects. This is also demonstrated by the last two lines in Tables 3.1 and 3.2, which show the difference between the highest and lowest life expectancy and the standard deviation of the corresponding estimates for conventional and tempo-adjusted life expectancy.

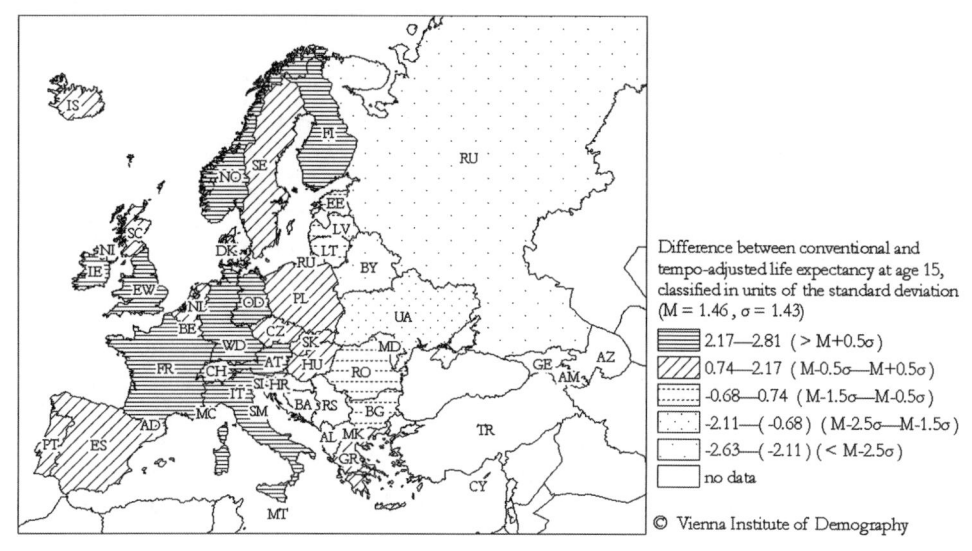

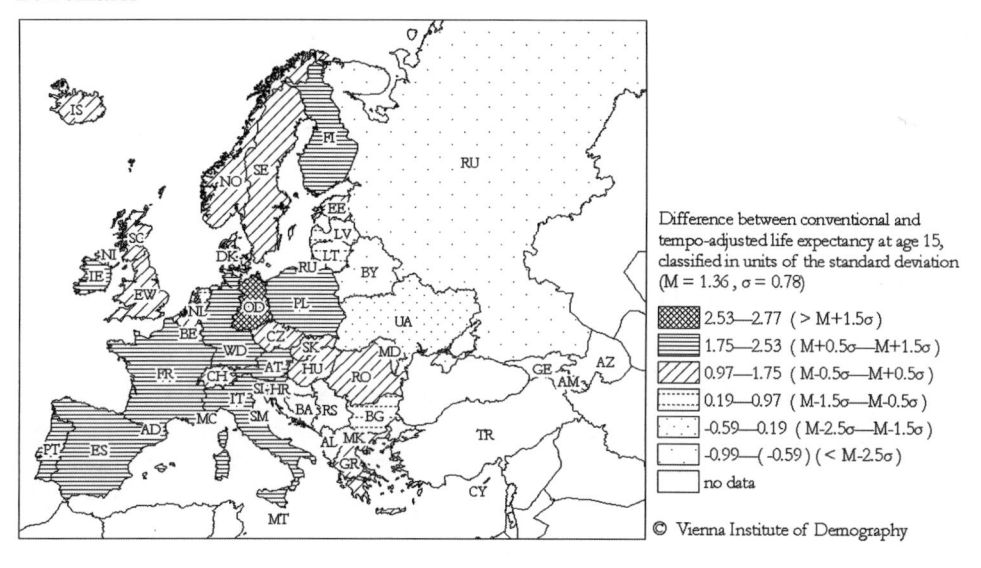

## A. Males

**Fig. 3.11** Difference between conventional and tempo-adjusted life expectancy at age 15 by country in Europe, 2001–2005

Compared to conventional life expectancy, the maximum differences decrease from 10.45 to 7.77 years among females and from 19.18 to 15.03 years among males, while standard deviations decrease from 2.72 to 2.17 among females and from 4.91 to 3.71 among males.

## Summary and Conclusions

This overview of adult mortality trends in Europe has shown that today's levels and trends over the last half-century were clustered geographically: Western

Europe with the most favorable health conditions, Eastern Europe with the least favorable, and Central Europe falling in between. Each of these regions shows internal variation in mortality levels, with the least variability among the Western European and the highest differences among the Eastern European countries. The trisection characterizes not only overall adult mortality but also, with a few exceptions, age- and cause-of-death-specific mortality as well as tempo-adjusted life expectancy.

Cause-specific trends of adult mortality in Europe can be characterized by the cardiovascular revolution in Western Europe and the health crises in Eastern Europe (Vallin and Meslé 2001). The large differences among men in length of life inequality show that there is still a significant potential for further reductions, even though Europe's populations exhibit some of the highest levels of life expectancy in the world.

The example of Europe shows that political systems can significantly affect health and mortality conditions. Once infectious diseases have been eliminated, overall progress in health depends on economic and social progress, public health regimes, and broader cultural changes that modify unhealthy behaviors and lifestyles (Caselli and Egidi 1981; Vallin and Meslé 2001). Such factors are powerful enough to create mortality gaps among countries experiencing different political and economic trends, and mortality convergence among countries belonging to the same sociocultural group with similar political histories (Caselli and Vallin 2006).

Future research on adult mortality in Europe needs to address several issues. It will be important to see when populations from Central Europe reach the levels of life expectancy in Western European countries, which countries are in the vanguard of increased life expectancy, and what factors are responsible for progress. Another important issue concerns future trends in Eastern Europe. Will the trend toward decreasing life expectancy continue, or will life expectancy start increasing toward the levels in other European regions? All of these issues might be addressed with the use of tempo-adjusted life expectancy to better elucidate the causes behind the observed trends, since tempo effects can distort the evaluation of period mortality conditions.

Although the quality of mortality data in Europe is quite good compared to that in other regions of the world, there are still countries where improvements in data quality are needed—mainly Eastern European countries, Albania, and Turkey, although some Western European countries have exhibited severe reductions in the quality of population data as well. For instance, Germany completed its last population censuses in 1981 (eastern Germany) and 1987 (western Germany), respectively. As a consequence, population figures for Germany become increasingly problematic, especially for mortality estimates in the highest age groups (see Jdanov et al. 2005).

The most important research questions regarding adult mortality in Europe concern the extent, trends, and determinants of mortality differentials by sex, region, education level, or occupation status, differentials that affect the financing of pension and health systems in Europe's aging societies. Many countries cannot estimate the extent and trend of such differentials because they lack sufficiently detailed statistical data. In the field of fertility research, similar constraints have led to the increasing use of survey data and methods of event history analysis to study topics that cannot be analyzed with official population statistics. For mortality, however, the potential of survey data is more limited. First, information about deaths cannot be gotten directly from the deceased individual. Second, direct analysis of mortality requires longitudinal data as well as long observation times and large sample sizes to provide a sufficient number of deaths; thus projects like SHARE ("Survey of Health, Ageing and Retirement in Europe," see http://www.share-project.org/) will be increasingly important. An alternative might be the use of adjusted indirect estimation techniques (see Luy 2009). Until now, indirect methods have been applied only rarely to analyze mortality in European populations. Examples include a study of mortality of Moroccans living in France (Courbage and Khlat 1996) and a series of papers on determinants of adult mortality in the Russian Federation (Bobak et al. 2002, 2003; Murphy et al. 2006; Nicholson et al. 2005). In sum, even in the European context, where data typically are rather high quality, much remains to be improved.

**Acknowledgments** The authors thank Karina Wibowo for her help in preparing the data, Angela Wiedemann for designing and producing the maps for this chapter, and the editors of this book for their suggestions and comments. This work was supported through grant P20649-G14 from the FWF Austrian Science Fund.

# Appendix

**Table 3.3** Male life expectancy at age 15 by country in Europe in the periods 1961–1965, 1981–1985, and 2001–2005

|  | 1961–1965 | ◀Diff.▶ | 1981–1985 | ◀Diff.▶ | 2001–2005 |
|---|---|---|---|---|---|
| Albania (AL) | 56.32[a] | +1.95 | 58.27[f] | +1.82 | 60.09[l] |
| Andorra (AD) | – | – | – | – | 62.69[m] |
| Armenia (AM) | – | – | 58.00[g] | +0.22 | 58.22[n] |
| Austria (AT) | 54.55 | +1.45 | 56.00 | +5.62 | 61.62 |
| Azerbaijan (AZ) | – | – | 54.86[g] | +1.64 | 56.50[l] |
| Belarus (BY) | 56.67 | −3.97 | 52.70 | −4.07 | 48.63 |
| Belgium (BE) | 55.08 | +1.83 | 56.91 | +4.12 | 61.03 |
| Bosnia and Herzegovina (BA) | – | – | 55.89[h] | −0.50 | 55.39[m] |
| Bulgaria (BG) | 57.36 | −2.02 | 55.34 | −0.12 | 55.22 |
| Croatia (HR) | – | – | 54.29[h] | +2.76 | 57.05 |
| Cyprus (CY) | 55.84[b] | +3.49 | 59.33[i] | +2.91 | 62.24 |
| Czech Republic (CZ) | 54.49 | −0.73 | 53.76 | +4.08 | 57.84 |
| Denmark (DK) | 57.55 | −0.11 | 57.44 | +3.25 | 60.69 |
| England and Wales (EW) | 55.38 | +2.25 | 57.63 | +4.53 | 62.16 |
| Estonia (EE) | 53.35 | −2.01 | 51.34 | +0.45 | 51.79 |
| Finland (FI) | 52.48 | +3.42 | 55.90 | +4.62 | 60.52 |
| France (FR) | 54.76 | +2.18 | 56.94 | +4.70 | 61.64 |
| Georgia (GE) | – | – | 55.17[g] | +4.48 | 59.65[o] |
| Germany, East (OD) | 55.71 | −0.08 | 55.63 | +4.72 | 60.35 |
| Germany, West (WD) | 55.08 | +1.89 | 56.97 | +4.68 | 61.65 |
| Greece (GR) | 58.76 | +1.10 | 59.86 | +2.13 | 61.99 |
| Hungary (HU) | 55.52 | −3.47 | 52.05 | +2.17 | 54.22 |
| Iceland (IS) | 57.97 | +1.93 | 59.90 | +4.39 | 64.29 |
| Ireland (IE) | 55.93 | +0.72 | 56.65 | +4.60 | 61.25 |
| Italy (IT) | 55.88 | +2.12 | 58.00 | +4.99 | 62.99 |
| Latvia (LV) | 54.15 | −3.23 | 50.92 | +0.59 | 51.51 |
| Liechtenstein (LI) | – | – | – | – | 62.51 |
| Lithuania (LT) | 55.56 | −3.08 | 52.48 | −0.57 | 51.91 |
| Luxembourg (LU) | 53.89 | +1.89 | 55.78 | +5.19 | 60.97 |
| Macedonia, TFYR (MK) | – | – | – | – | 57.31 |
| Malta (MT) | 55.14 | +1.23 | 56.37 | +5.91 | 62.28 |
| Moldova (MD) | – | – | 51.23[g] | −0.43 | 50.80 |
| Monaco (MC) | – | – | – | – | 62.87[p] |
| Netherlands (NL) | 58.10 | +0.77 | 58.87 | +3.14 | 62.01 |
| Northern Ireland (NI) | 55.44 | +0.82 | 56.26 | +5.12 | 61.38 |
| Norway (NO) | 58.08 | +0.56 | 58.64 | +3.78 | 62.42 |
| Poland (PL) | 54.77 | −0.85 | 53.92 | +2.27 | 56.19 |
| Portugal (PT) | 54.55 | +1.69 | 56.24 | +3.63 | 59.87 |
| Romania (RO) | 56.14[c] | −1.48 | 54.66 | −0.04 | 54.62 |
| Russian Federation (RU) | 52.44 | −3.10 | 49.34 | −4.23 | 45.11 |
| San Marino (SM) | – | – | – | – | 64.25[q] |
| Scotland (SC) | 53.82 | +1.92 | 55.74 | +3.77 | 59.51 |
| Serbia and Montenegro (RS) | – | – | – | – | 56.70[r] |
| Slovakia (SK) | 56.06 | −2.48 | 53.58 | +2.14 | 55.72 |
| Slovenia (SI) | 54.16[d] | −0.49 | 53.67[j] | +4.80 | 58.47 |

**Table 3.3** (continued)

|  | 1961–1965 | ◀Diff.▶ | 1981–1985 | ◀Diff.▶ | 2001–2005 |
|---|---|---|---|---|---|
| Spain (ES) | 56.53 | +2.61 | 59.14 | +2.86 | 62.00 |
| Sweden (SE) | 58.32 | +0.98 | 59.30 | +4.08 | 63.38 |
| Switzerland (CH) | 56.12 | +2.79 | 58.91 | +4.68 | 63.59 |
| Turkey (TR) | 50.71[e] | +2.55 | 53.26[k] | +2.44 | 55.70[m] |
| Ukraine (UA) | 55.42 | −3.69 | 51.73 | −3.51 | 48.22 |
| Yugoslavia, former | 55.63 | −0.24 | 55.39 | – | – |
| Total Europe (average) | 55.48 | +0.17 | 55.65 | +2.93 | 58.58 |
| Eastern Europe (average) | 54.60 | −1.82 | 52.78 | −0.55 | 52.23 |
| Central Europe (average) | 55.17 | −0.58 | 54.59 | +2.19 | 56.78 |
| Western Europe (average) | 55.88 | +1.70 | 57.58 | +4.41 | 61.99 |

Notes: [a]1955; [b]1958, 1973; [c]1963; [d]1960–1962; [e]1967; [f]1987; [g]1981–1982, 1985; [h]1985; [i]1980; [j]1980–1985; [k]1975; [l]2001–2004; [m]2000; [n]2001–2003, 2006; [o]2001; [p]2001, estimated from life expectancy at birth (Lopez et al. 2006) minus the difference between life expectancy at birth and life expectancy at age 15 in France of the year 2001; [q]2000, 2005; [r]2004–2005 (Serbia only); letters in brackets refer to the abbreviations in the figures; a dash (–) indicates that no data are available.

**Table 3.4** Female life expectancy at age 15 by country in Europe in the periods 1961–1965, 1981–1985, and 2001–2005

|  | 1961–1965 | ◀Diff.▶ | 1981–1985 | ◀Diff.▶ | 2001–2005 |
|---|---|---|---|---|---|
| Albania (AL) | 60.36[a] | +3.46 | 63.82[f] | +1.63 | 65.45[l] |
| Andorra (AD) | – | – | – | – | 69.25[m] |
| Armenia (AM) | – | – | 63.78[g] | +1.87 | 65.65[n] |
| Austria (AT) | 60.41 | +2.45 | 62.86 | +4.44 | 67.30 |
| Azerbaijan (AZ) | – | – | 62.35[g] | −0.69 | 61.66[l] |
| Belarus (BY) | 63.02 | −0.75 | 62.27 | −1.82 | 60.45 |
| Belgium (BE) | 60.65 | +2.74 | 63.39 | +3.52 | 66.91 |
| Bosnia and Herzegovina (BA) | – | – | 60.80[h] | +0.28 | 61.08[m] |
| Bulgaria (BG) | 60.43 | +0.46 | 60.89 | +1.16 | 62.05 |
| Croatia (HR) | – | – | 61.49[h] | +2.55 | 64.04 |
| Cyprus (CY) | 62.11[b] | +1.24 | 63.35[i] | +3.42 | 66.77 |
| Czech Republic (CZ) | 60.16 | +0.49 | 60.65 | +3.66 | 64.31 |
| Denmark (DK) | 61.23 | +2.07 | 63.30 | +1.92 | 65.22 |
| England and Wales (EW) | 61.08 | +2.24 | 63.32 | +3.15 | 66.47 |
| Estonia (EE) | 60.86 | +0.13 | 60.99 | +2.11 | 63.10 |
| Finland (FI) | 59.26 | +4.86 | 64.12 | +3.13 | 67.25 |
| France (FR) | 61.40 | +3.52 | 64.92 | +3.83 | 68.75 |
| Georgia (GE) | – | – | 62.54[g] | +1.94 | 64.48[o] |
| Germany, East (OD) | 59.99 | +1.27 | 61.26 | +5.51 | 66.77 |
| Germany, West (WD) | 60.33 | +3.10 | 63.43 | +3.60 | 67.03 |
| Greece (GR) | 62.08 | +2.30 | 64.38 | +2.68 | 67.06 |
| Hungary (HU) | 59.57 | +0.06 | 59.63 | +2.94 | 62.57 |
| Iceland (IS) | 62.89 | +2.78 | 65.67 | +2.50 | 68.17 |
| Ireland (IE) | 59.59 | +2.63 | 62.22 | +3.94 | 66.16 |
| Italy (IT) | 60.92 | +3.49 | 64.41 | +4.25 | 68.66 |
| Latvia (LV) | 61.23 | −0.33 | 60.90 | +1.36 | 62.26 |
| Liechtenstein (LI) | – | – | – | – | 70.31 |
| Lithuania (LT) | 61.74 | +0.48 | 62.22 | +1.02 | 63.24 |
| Luxembourg (LU) | 59.72 | +2.85 | 62.57 | +4.36 | 66.93 |
| Macedonia, TFYR (MK) | – | – | – | – | 61.46 |
| Malta (MT) | 58.42 | +2.33 | 60.75 | +6.01 | 66.76 |
| Moldova (MD) | – | – | 57.37[g] | +0.76 | 58.13 |
| Monaco (MC) | – | – | – | – | 69.78[p] |
| Netherlands (NL) | 62.42 | +2.92 | 65.34 | +1.22 | 66.56 |

**Table 3.4** (continued)

|  | 1961–1965 | ◄Diff.► | 1981–1985 | ◄Diff.► | 2001–2005 |
|---|---|---|---|---|---|
| Northern Ireland (NI) | 60.14 | +2.17 | 62.31 | +3.82 | 66.13 |
| Norway (NO) | 62.63 | +2.56 | 65.19 | +2.16 | 67.35 |
| Poland (PL) | 60.17 | +1.54 | 61.71 | +2.86 | 64.57 |
| Portugal (PT) | 59.98 | +2.97 | 62.95 | +3.51 | 66.46 |
| Romania (RO) | 59.55[c] | +0.36 | 59.91 | +1.70 | 61.61 |
| Russian Federation (RU) | 60.75 | −0.54 | 60.21 | −1.88 | 58.33 |
| San Marino (SM) | – | – | – | – | 70.44[q] |
| Scotland (SC) | 59.38 | +2.23 | 61.61 | +3.02 | 64.63 |
| Serbia and Montenegro (RS) | – | – | – | – | 61.56[r] |
| Slovakia (SK) | 60.37 | +0.82 | 61.19 | +2.42 | 63.61 |
| Slovenia (SI) | 58.14[d] | +3.30 | 61.44[j] | +4.53 | 65.97 |
| Spain (ES) | 61.07 | +4.25 | 65.32 | +3.35 | 68.67 |
| Sweden (SE) | 62.06 | +3.18 | 65.24 | +2.50 | 67.74 |
| Switzerland (CH) | 61.45 | +4.00 | 65.45 | +3.32 | 68.77 |
| Turkey (TR) | 52.99[e] | +2.46 | 55.45[k] | +5.83 | 61.28[m] |
| Ukraine (UA) | 61.54 | −0.73 | 60.81 | −1.22 | 59.59 |
| Yugoslavia, former | 59.05 | +1.98 | 61.03 | – | – |
| Total Europe (average) | 60.49 | +1.84 | 62.33 | +2.85 | 65.18 |
| Eastern Europe (average) | 61.52 | −0.18 | 61.34 | +0.35 | 61.69 |
| Central Europe (average) | 59.16 | +1.55 | 60.71 | +2.60 | 63.31 |
| Western Europe (average) | 60.87 | +2.86 | 63.73 | +3.79 | 67.52 |

Notes: [a]1955; [b]1958, 1977; [c]1963; [d]1960–1962; [e]1967; [f]1987; [g]1981–1982, 1985; [h]1985; [i]1980; [j]1980–1985; [k]1975; [l]2001–2004; [m]2000; [n]2001–2003, 2006; [o]2001; [p]2001, estimated from life expectancy at birth (Lopez et al. 2006) minus the difference between life expectancy at birth and life expectancy at age 15 in France of the year 2001; [q]1999–2000; [r]2004–2005 (Serbia only); letters in brackets refer to the abbreviations in the figures; a dash (–) indicates that no data are available.

# References

Andreev, E.M., V.M. Shkolnikov, and A.Z. Begun. 2002. "Algorithm for Decomposition of Differences Between Aggregate Demographic Measures and Its Application to Life Expectancies, Healthy Life Expectancies, Parity-Progression Ratios and Total Fertility Rates." *Demographic Research* 7:500–21.

Anson, J. 1993. "Regional Mortality Differences in Britain, 1931–87: A Two Dimensional Analysis." *Journal of Biosocial Science* 25:383–95.

Anson, J. 2003. "Sex Differences in Mortality at the Local Level: An Analysis of Belgian Municipalities." *European Journal of Population* 19:1–28.

Barbi, E., J. Bongaarts, and J.W. Vaupel. 2008. *How Long Do We Live? Demographic Models and Reflections on Tempo Effects.* Demographic Research Monographs, 5. Leipzig, Springer.

Barbi, E. and G. Caselli. 2003. "Selection Effects on Regional Mortality Differences in Survivorship in Italy." *Genus* 59:37–61.

Bobak, M. and M. Marmot. 1996. "East-West Mortality Divide and Its Potential Explanations: Proposed Research Agenda." *British Medical Journal* 312:421–25.

Bobak, M., M. Murphy, H. Pikhart, P. Martikainen, R. Rose, and M. Marmot. 2002. "Mortality Patterns in the Russian Federation: Indirect Technique Using Widowhood Data." *Bulletin of the World Health Organization* 80:876–81.

Bobak, M., M. Murphy, R. Rose, and M. Marmot. 2003. "Determinants of Adult Mortality in Russia. Estimates from Sibling Data." *Epidemiology* 14(5):603–11.

Bongaarts, J. and G. Feeney. 2002. "How Long Do We Live?" *Population and Development Review* 28:13–29.

Bongaarts, J. and G. Feeney. 2003. "Estimating Mean Lifetime." *Proceedings of the National Academy of Sciences* 100:13127–33.

Bongaarts, J. and G. Feeney. 2006. "The Quantum and Tempo of Life-Cycle Events." *Vienna Yearbook of Population Research* 2006:115–51.

Boyle, P. and M. Smans. 2009. *Atlas of Cancer Mortality in the European Union and the European Economic Area 1993–1997.* IARC Scientific Publication, 159. Geneva, World Health Organization.

Boys, R.J., D.P. Forster, and P. Józan. 1991. "Mortality From Causes Amenable and Non-Amenable to Medical Care: The Experience of Eastern Europe." *British Medical Journal* 303:879–83.

Britton, A., E. Nolte, I.R. White, M. Grønbæk, J. Powles, F. Cavallo, and K. McPherson. 2003. "A Comparison of the Alcohol-Attributable Mortality in Four European Countries." *European Journal of Epidemiology* 18:643–51.

Brückner, G. 1993. "Todesursachen 1990/91 im Vereinten Deutschland. Methodische Bemerkungen und Ergebnisse." *Wirtschaft und Statistik* 4:257–78.

Cameron, H.M. and E. McGoogan. 1981. "A Prospective Study of 1152 Hospital Autopsies. Part I: Inaccuracies in Death Certification." *Journal of Pathology* 133:273–83.

Caselli, G., L. Cerbara, F. Heins, and R.M. Lipsi. 2003. "What Impact Do Contextual Variables Have on the Changing Geography of Mortality in Italy?" *European Journal of Population* 19:339–73.

Caselli, G. and V. Egidi. 1981. "Géographie de la mortalité en Europe: Influence de l'environnement et de certains aspects du comportement." In International Union for the Scientific Study of Population ed., *International Population Conference, Manila 1981. Solicited Papers 2*, pp. 165–205. Liège: IUSSP.

Caselli, G. and J. Vallin. 2006. "Geographical Variations of Mortality." In G. Caselli, J. Vallin, and G. Wunsch (eds.), *Demography: Analysis and Synthesis*, Vol. 2, pp. 207–34. London, Academic Press.

Cayotte, E. and H. Buchow. 2009. *Who Dies of What in Europe Before the Age of 65*. Statistics in Focus, 67/2009. Luxembourg, Eurostat.

Courbage, Y. and M. Khlat. 1996. "Mortality and Causes of Death of Moroccans in France, 1979–91." *Population: An English Selection* 8:59–94.

Cutler, D., A. Deaton, and A. Lleras-Muney. 2006. "The Determinants of Mortality." *Journal of Economic Perspectives* 20:97–120.

Didkowska, J., M. Manczuk, A. McNeill, J. Powles, and W. Zatonski. 2005. "Lung Cancer Mortality at Ages 35–54 in the European Union: Ecological Study of Evolving Tobacco Epidemics." *British Medical Journal* 331:189–91.

Divino, F., V. Egidi, and M.A. Salvatore. 2009. "Geographical Mortality Patterns in Italy: A Bayesian Analysis." *Demographic Research* 20:435–66.

Dorling, D. 1997. *Death in Britain: How Local Mortality Rates Have Changed 1950–1990*. York, Joseph Rowntree Foundation.

Eisenblätter, D., H. Kant, and H. Heine. 1981. "Zur Entwicklung der Sterblichkeit an Herz-Kreislauf-Krankheiten in der DDR." *Deutsches Gesundheitswesen* 36(49): 2058–66.

Eisenblätter, D., G. Wolff, D. Michaelis, and M. Möhner. 1994. "Probleme unikausaler Todesursachenauswertung an Beispielen." In L. Heinemann and H. Sinnecker (eds.), *Epidemiologische Arbeitsmethoden*, pp. 354–68. New York, NY, Jena and Stuttgart: Gustav Fischer.

European Commission. 2002. *Health Statistics—Atlas on Mortality in the European Union*. Luxembourg, Office for Official Publications of the European Communities.

European Commission. 2008. *Health statistics—Atlas on Mortality in the European Union*. Luxembourg, Office for Official Publications of the European Communities.

Hertzman, C., S. Kelly, and M. Bobak. (Eds.). 1996. *East-West Life Expectancy Gap in Europe. Environmental and Non-Environmental Determinants*. Dordrecht, Kluwer.

Hinote, B.P., W.C. Cockerham, and P. Abbott. 2009. "The Specter of Post-Communism: Women and Alcohol in Eight Post-Soviet States." *Social Science and Medicine* 68: 1254–62.

Höhn, C. and J.H. Pollard. 1991. "Mortality in the Two Germanies in 1986 and Trends 1976–1986." *European Journal of Population* 7:1–28.

Human Mortality Database. University of California, Berkley, CA, and Max Planck Institute for Demographic Research (Germany). Available at: http://www.mortality.org/Public/CitationGuidelines.php (Accessed on July 31, 2009).

Jdanov, D.A., R.D. Scholz, and V.M. Shkolnikov. 2005. "Official Population Statistics and the Human Mortality Database Estimates of Populations Aged 80+ in Germany and Nine Other European Countries." *Demographic Research* 13(14):335–62.

Khlat, M. and M. Darmon. 2003. "Is There a Mediterranean Migrants Mortality Paradox in Europe?" *International Journal of Epidemiology* 32:1115–18.

Kohli, R. 2005. *Sterbetafeln für die Schweiz 1998/2003*. Neuchâtel, Office Fédéral de la Statistique (OFS).

Koskinen, S. 1995. *Origins of Regional Differences in Mortality from Ischaemic Heart Disease in Finland*. Helsinki, National Research and Development Centre for Welfare and Health.

Kuntsche, S., R.A. Knibbe, and G. Gmel. 2009. "Social Roles and Alcohol Consumption: A Study of 10 Industrialised Countries." *Social Science and Medicine* 68:1263–70.

Lopez, A.D., C.D. Mathers, M. Ezzati, D.T. Jamison, and C.J.L. Murray. 2006. *Global Burden of Disease and Risk Factors*. New York, Oxford University Press, World Bank.

Luy, M. 2004. "Mortality Differences Between Western and Eastern Germany Before and After Reunification. A Macro and Micro Level Analysis of Developments and Responsible Factors." *Genus* 60:99–141.

Luy, M. 2006. "Mortality Tempo-Adjustment: An Empirical Application." *Demographic Research* 15:561–90.

Luy, M. 2008. "Mortality Tempo-Adjustment: Theoretical Considerations and an Empirical Application." In E. Barbi, J. Bongaarts, and J.W. Vaupel. (eds.), *How Long Do We Live? Demographic Models and Reflections on Tempo Effects*, pp. 203–33. Leipzig, Springer.

Luy, M. 2009. *Estimating Mortality Differentials in Developed Populations from Survey Information on Maternal and Paternal Orphanhood*. European Demographic Research Papers, Vienna Institute of Demography, 2009-3. Vienna, Vienna Institute of Demography.

Luy, M. and G. Caselli. 2007. "The Impact of a Migration-Caused Selection Effect on Regional Mortality Differences in Italy and Germany." *Genus* 63:33–64.

Luy, M. and C. Wegner. 2009. "Conventional Versus Tempo-Adjusted Life Expectancy: Which is the More Appropriate Measure for Period Mortality?" *Genus* 65:1–28.

Meslé, F. 1991. "La Mortalité dans les Pays d'Europe de l'Est." *Population* 46(3):599–650.

Meslé, F. 2004. "Mortality in Central and Eastern Europe: Long-Term Trends and Recent Upturns." *Demographic Research* (Special Collection) 2:45–70.

Meslé, F. 2006. "Medical Causes of Death." In G. Caselli, J. Vallin, and G. Wunsch (eds.), *Demography: Analysis and Synthesis*, Vol. 2, pp. 29–44. London, Academic Press.

Meslé, F. and J. Vallin. 2002. "Mortality in Europe: The Divergence Between East and West." *Population-E* 57: 157–98.

Meslé, F. and J. Vallin. 2006. "Diverging Trends in Female Old-Age Mortality: The United States and the Netherlands Versus France and Japan." *Population and Development Review* 32:123–45.

Meslé, F., J. Vallin, and V. Shkolnikov. 1998. "Reversal of Mortality Decline: The Case of Contemporary Russia." *World Health Statistics Quarterly* 51:191–206.

Modelmog, D., S. Rahlenbeck, and D. Trichopoulos. 1992. "Accuracy of Death Certificates: A Population-Based, Complete-Coverage, One-Year Autopsy Study in East Germany." *Cancer Causes and Control* 3:541–46.

Moskalewicz, J., B. Wojtyniak, and D. Rabczenko. 2000. "Alcohol as a Cause of Mortality in Societies Undergoing Rapid Transition to Market Economy." In G.A. Cornia and R. Paniccià (eds.), *The Mortality Crisis in Transitional Economies*, pp. 83–104. Oxford, Oxford University Press.

Murphy, M., M. Bobak, A. Nicholson, R. Rose, and M. Marmot. 2006. "The Widening Gap in Mortality by Educational Level in the Russian Federation, 1980–2001." *American Journal of Public Health* 96(7):1293–99.

Nicholson, A., M. Bobak, M. Murphy, R. Rose, and M. Marmot. 2005. "Alcohol Consumption and Increased Mortality in Russian Men and Women: A Cohort Study Based on the Mortality of Relatives." *Bulletin of the World Health Organization* 83(11):812–19.

Paul, C. 1992. "Sterblichkeit im regionalen Vergleich. Allgemeine Sterbetafeln der elf alten Bundesländer." *Wirtschaft und Statistik* 2:82–87.

Peto, R., A.D. Lopez, J. Boreham, and M. Thun. 2006. *Mortality from Smoking in Developed Countries 1950–2000*, 2nd ed. Geneva, World Health Organization.

Ramstedt, M. 2002. "Alcohol-Related Mortality in 15 European Countries in the Postwar Period." *European Journal of Population* 18:307–23.

Rehm, J., C. Mathers, S. Popova, M. Thavorncharoensap, Y. Teerawattananon, and J. Patra. 2009. "Global Burden of Disease and Injury and Economic Cost Attributable to Alcohol Use and Alcohol-Use Disorders." *Lancet* 373(9682):2223–33.

Saarela, J. and F. Finnäs. 2006. "Regional Mortality Variation in Finland: A Study of Two Population Groups." *Genus* 62:169–211.

Shaw, M., S. Orford, N. Brimblecombe, and D. Dorling. 2000. "Widening Inequality in Mortality Between 160 Regions of 15 European Countries in the Early 1990s." *Social Science and Medicine* 50:1047–58.

Shkolnikov, V.M. and G.A. Cornia.. 2000. "Population Crisis and Rising Mortality in Transitional Russia." In G.A. Cornia and R. Paniccià (eds.), *The Mortality Crisis in Transitional Economies*, pp. 253–79. Oxford, Oxford University Press.

Shkolnikov, V., F. Meslé, and J. Vallin. 1996a. "Health Crisis in Russia. I. Recent Trends in Life Expectancy and Causes of Death from 1970–1993." *Population: An English Selection* 8:123–54.

Shkolnikov, V., F. Meslé, and J. Vallin. 1996b. "Health Crisis in Russia. II. Changes in Causes of Death: A Comparison with France and England and Wales (1970–1993)." *Population: An English Selection* 8:155–89.

Smans, M., C.S. Muir, and P. Boyle. 1992. *Atlas of Cancer Mortality in the European Economic Community*. IARC Scientific Publication, 107. Geneva, World Health Organization.

Smits, J. and C. Monden. 2009. "Length of Life Inequality Around the Globe." *Social Science and Medicine* 68: 1114–23.

Sommer, B. 1998. "Die Sterblichkeit in Deutschland im Regionalen und Europäischen Vergleich." *Wirtschaft und Statistik* 12:960–70.

Spijker, J. 2004. *Socioeconomic Determinants of Regional Mortality Differences in Europe*. Amsterdam, Dutch University Press.

United Nations. 2008. *World Population Prospects. The 2006 Revision. Volume 3: Analytical Report*. New York, United Nations Publication.

Valkonen, T. 2001. "Trends in Differential Mortality in European Countries." In J. Vallin, F. Meslé, and T. Valkonen (eds.), *Trends in Mortality and Differential Mortality*, pp. 185–321. Strasbourg, Council of Europe Publishing.

Vallin, J., E. Andreev, F. Meslé, and V. Shkolnikov. 2005. "Geographical Diversity of Cause-of-Death Patterns and Trends in Russia." *Demographic Research* 12: 323–80.

Vallin, J., F. Meslé, and T. Valkonen (eds.). 2001. *Trends in Mortality and Differential Mortality*. Population Studies, 36. Strasbourg, Council of Europe Publishing.

Vallin, J. and F. Meslé.. 2001. "Trends in Mortality in Europe Since 1950: Age-, Sex- and Cause-Specific Mortality." In J. Vallin, F. Meslé, and T. Valkonen (eds.), *Trends in Mortality and Differential Mortality*, pp. 31–184. Strasbourg, Council of Europe Publishing.

Van Oyen, H., J. Tafforeau, and M. Roelands. 1996. "Regional Inequalities in Health Expectancy in Belgium." *Social Science and Medicine* 43:1673–78.

Van Poppel, F.W.A. 1981. "Regional Mortality Differences in Western Europe: A Review of the Situation in the Seventies." *Social Science and Medicine* 15:341–52.

Velkova, A., J.H. Wolleswinkel-van den Bosch, and J.P. Mackenbach. 1997. "The East-West Life Expectancy Gap: Differences in Mortality From Conditions Amenable to Medical Intervention." *International Journal of Epidemiology* 26:75–84.

World Health Organization. 1997. *Atlas of Mortality in Europe. Subnational Patterns, 1980/1981 and 1990/1991*. WHO Regional Publications, European Series, 75. Geneva, World Health Organization.

Wunsch, G. 2006. "Dependence and Independence of Causes of Death." In G. Caselli, J. Vallin, and G. Wunsch (eds.), *Demography: Analysis and Synthesis*, Vol. 2, pp. 57–60. London, Academic Press.

Zatonski, W., M. Smans, J. Tyczynski, and P. Boyle. 1996. *Atlas of Cancer Mortality in Central Europe*. IARC Scientific Publication, 134. Geneva, World Health Organization.

# Chapter 4
# Adult Mortality in the Former Soviet Union

Michael Murphy

## Introduction

In recent decades the former Communist countries of Eastern Europe, and especially those from the former Soviet Union (FSU), have shown a very different trend in adult mortality from Western industrialized countries and Asia. Figure 4.1 shows the patterns of change in life expectancy at birth ($e_0$) from 1950 through 2000–2005 in the countries of the FSU together with values for Western Europe (according to the UN definition; see United Nations n.d.) in 2000–2005. While the improvements in life expectancy in the FSU in the first half of the period were substantial, there was little increase in the second half, and in some cases there were declines, especially in the Russian Federation (which accounts for half of the population of the FSU (see Table 4.1); the values for the USSR and Russia were close over the period). Meanwhile, in contrast, mortality improved not only in Western Europe, but in other parts of Europe and Asia as well. The Russian trend for male mortality was particularly poor, so that life expectancy at birth for males fell below that for Eastern Asia in the early 1970s and for females in about 1995. While in the second half of the twentieth century life expectancy at birth increased by about 30 years in East Asia and about 10 years in Western Europe (see also "Adult Mortality in Asia," Chapter 6; "Adult Mortality in Europe," Chapter 3; and United Nations n.d.), in the FSU, there has been a 40-year period with female mortality no better and male mortality actually worse at the end, with no obvious well-defined reason for this.

Figure 4.2 shows the differences in (period) life expectancy at age 20 and the probability of survival over the working age range from 20 to 65 years in the Russian Federation compared with a close neighbor, Sweden, in the period from 1959 to 2006, using data obtained from the Human Mortality Database (HMD n.d.). The Soviet Union ceased to exist after 1991, and detailed information for regions such as Western Europe is not available over such extended periods, so I compare Russia and Sweden to highlight some of the main differences between the FSU and Western Europe (comparable data for the 15 Western European EU member states before 2004 [EU-15] are available in more recent periods, and some comparisons with this group are made below). Apart from some stagnation for men in the early years, adult life expectancy increased steadily in Sweden. However, Russia exhibited very substantial fluctuations, especially from the mid-1980s, but with a generally declining trend, so that life expectancy for men at age 20 was much lower at the end than at the start point, i.e., 42 years in 2006, compared with 48 years in 1959.

The divergence in mortality experience over this period between Russia and Western countries has been much greater for men than for women, so that life expectancy at age 20 for Russian men in 2006 was 17 years less than for Swedish men, twice the 9 years' difference for women. In Western European countries the sex differential in adult life expectancy tended to increase until about 1990, largely reflecting men's initially heavier burden of mortality from circulatory system diseases, but more recently these differences have declined (World Health Organization Health for

---

M. Murphy (✉)
Professor of Demography, London School of Economics, 7512 London, UK
e-mail: M.Murphy@lse.ac.uk

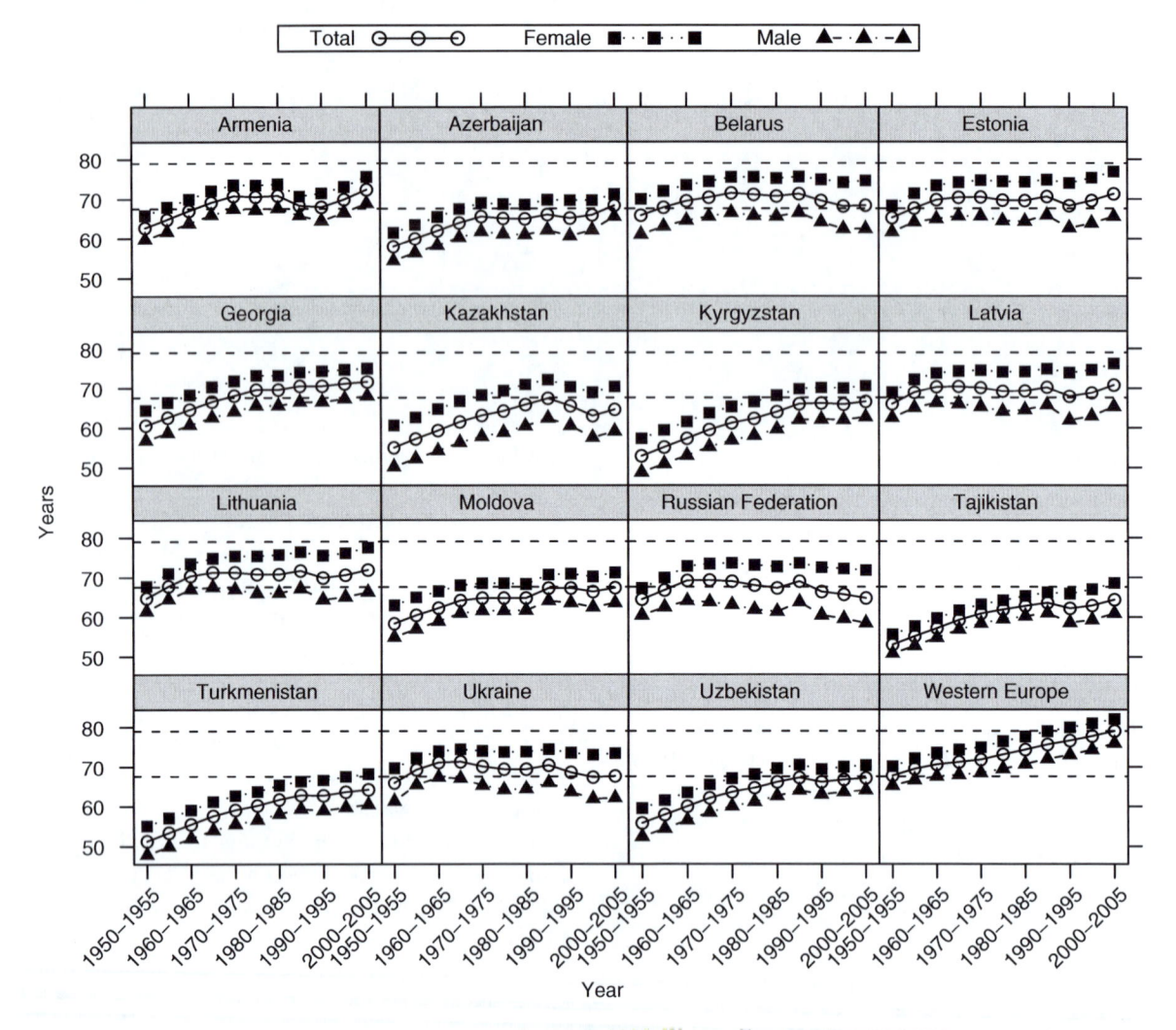

**Fig. 4.1** Life expectancy at birth by sex from 1950–1955 to 2000–2005. Western Europe values for both sexes in 1950–1955 and 2000–2005 shown as lower and upper dotted lines. Source: UN 2008 Revision

All database [WHO-HFA] n.d.). In contrast, the sex differential in Russia increased to 13 years in 2006, probably the largest difference in the world. If the mortality rates of 1994, the year that mortality reached its maximum, were to have held throughout their lifetime, six out of ten Russian men aged 20 would have died before age 65, and even at 2006 mortality rates over half would not survive, compared with fewer than one in eight in Sweden. Russian women fare much better, and even with 1994 mortality levels, three-quarters would survive through the working ages (compared with over 90% of Swedish women). Inevitably, considerable attention was given to the sharp mortality increase of the early 1990s, but this event should be set in a longer-term perspective.

## Historical Background

The FSU has had a turbulent history, which has led to three of the largest mortality crises in Europe in the past century. Citizens in their 90's would have been born before the establishment of the Soviet Union in 1922 following a civil war and famine, and alive after its collapse in 1991. The estimated number of excess deaths varies between authors and according to the precise definition of what constitutes an excess death, but in this period, there were an estimated two to three million excess deaths associated with the forced collectivization in the 1930s and the consequent famine of 1932–1934, which particularly affected Ukraine

**Table 4.1** Population of countries of the Former Soviet Union (FSU) in 2008

| Country | Mid-year 2008 population (millions) | Percent of FSU 2008 population |
|---|---|---|
| Armenia | 3.0 | 1.1 |
| Azerbaijan | 8.5 | 3.0 |
| Belarus | 9.6 | 3.4 |
| Estonia | 1.3 | 0.5 |
| Georgia | 4.4 | 1.5 |
| Kazakhstan | 15.5 | 5.5 |
| Kyrgyzstan | 5.4 | 1.9 |
| Latvia | 2.3 | 0.8 |
| Lithuania | 3.4 | 1.2 |
| Republic of Moldova | 3.6 | 1.3 |
| Russian Federation | 141.8 | 49.9 |
| Tajikistan | 6.8 | 2.4 |
| Turkmenistan | 5.0 | 1.8 |
| Ukraine | 45.9 | 16.1 |
| Uzbekistan | 27.8 | 9.8 |
| Former Soviet Union (FSU) | 284.2 | 100.0 |
| Commonwealth of independent states (CIS) | 277.3 | 97.5 |

Note: The Commonwealth of Independent States (CIS) includes as of early 2009 all countries of the FSU except the Baltic states of Estonia, Latvia, and Lithuania (although the precise nature of their role in the CIS varies among the constituent countries).
Source: WHO-HFA, available online at http://www.euro.who.int/hfadb

(Meslé and Vallin 2003; Wheatcroft 2009), where life expectancy at birth in 1933 was estimated as 7.3 years for males and 10.8 for females (Vallin et al. 2002, Table 3). World War II, referred to in the Soviet Union as the Great Patriotic War, led to an estimated 27 million deaths (Ellman and Maksudov 1994). Finally, and perhaps less visibly, a major mortality crisis, noted above, started to become apparent from the 1970s, but intensified after 1990 with the collapse of the Soviet Union. The estimated annual number of excess deaths

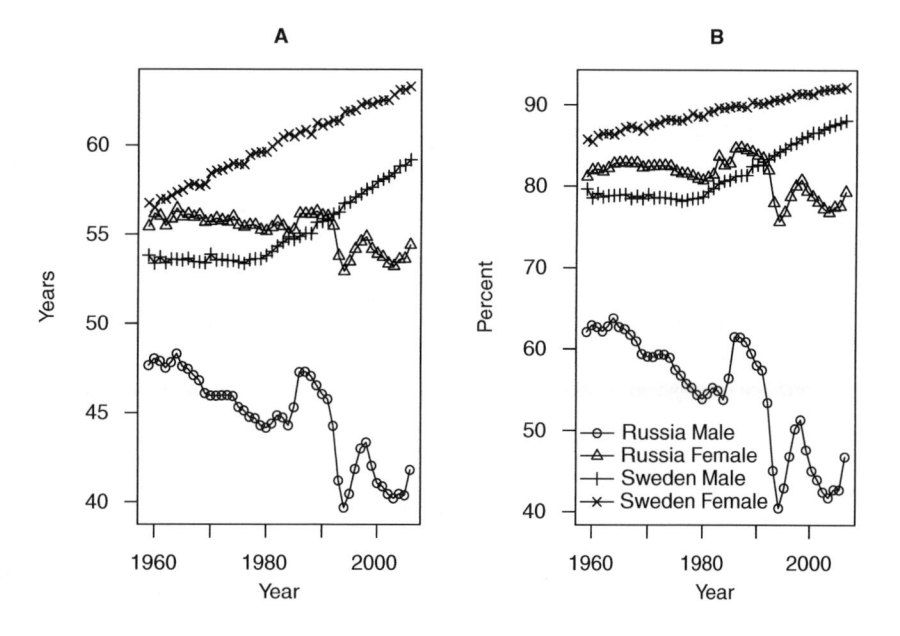

**Fig. 4.2** Life expectancy at age 20 ($e_{20}$) (**Panel a**) and probability of survival from age 20–65 ($_{45}p_{20}$) (**Panel b**). Source: Human Mortality Database

associated with the post-1990 crises depends on the method of calculation, but on any basis runs into several millions (e.g., Murphy et al. 2006 estimated the figure at about five million).

The USSR had been the world's largest country, accounting for about one sixth of the global landmass and bordering countries as diverse as Japan, Norway, and Iran. The USSR started to break up in the late 1980s, with protests and the election of nationalistic governments in the Baltic states of Estonia, Latvia, and Lithuania following a period of political strain after Yuri Andropov and Mikhail Gorbachev attempted to reform the existing system. The process of separation was fraught with difficulty both because it was not the preferred option for all parties and because the economy of the USSR was highly centralized. The population was ethnically heterogeneous, and internal population movements had placed substantial fractions of ethnic Russians in many of the republics of the USSR that were later to become fully independent states, a fact that has resulted in large-scale population redistribution and still unresolved territorial disputes (including armed conflict between Russia and Georgia in 2008) involving not only Russia, but also some of the other FSU states, particularly those in the Caucasus. At present (late 2010), there are 15 separate countries that formed part of the FSU, with the Russian Federation (or Russia) accounting for about half of the total population, the Ukraine 16%, and Uzbekistan 9%, and no other country accounting for more than 5% of the total (Table 4.1).

The demographic patterns, including adult mortality, differ among the main groupings: the predominantly Slavic group (Russia, Ukraine,[1] and Belarus, about 70% of the population of the FSU); the Baltic states (Estonia, Latvia, and Lithuania, about 2.5%), the Central Asian republics (Kazakhstan, Kyrgyzstan, Tajikistan, Turkmenistan, and Uzbekistan, about 20%), and the remaining states (mainly in the Caucasus—Armenia, Azerbaijan, and Georgia—together with the ethnically Romanian state of Moldova, 7% in total). Fertility is much higher in the Central Asian republics and particularly low in the Slavic and Baltic states, with the Caucasus states being intermediate in levels. About 40% of the population in Tajikistan and Turkmenistan is under age 15, compared with about 15% in the Slavic and Baltic states, which consequently have much higher proportions of older people and crude death rates (WHO-HFA n.d.). These trends continue to change the relative numbers of people in the constituent countries of the FSU, a change compounded as ethnic Russians relocate to the Russian Federation. There has been considerable international emigration outside the FSU as well, especially among the more skilled sectors of the labor force.

The quality of data and range of studies available for Russia, which are considerably greater than for most of the other countries of the FSU (data quality is discussed in more detail below)—together with the fact that Russia is the dominant country in size, population, economy, and political influence—mean that the great majority of mortality analyses for the FSU have concentrated on Russia. Information about other parts of the FSU is less systematic, and as the patterns diverge, it becomes increasingly less clear that they should continue to be analyzed as a single entity.

## Data Quality and Availability

The Russian Empire state statistical office was established in 1880, and censuses conducted in various years including 1897, 1926, 1937, and 1939 provided the basis for mortality analyses in earlier years (Goskomstat n.d.). In the early part of the twentieth century, there was a clear European east–west divide in mortality, with much higher mortality in the east than in the west (Caselli 1994). Given the closed and centralized nature of the Soviet government system, statistical information, including demographic information, was primarily regarded as the sole property of the state and data were not freely available, and there were parallel compilations of statistics for internal and external use (Anderson et al. 1994; Davies and Wheatcroft 2004). There were major problems with demographic data in the Soviet Union in the 1920s and 1930s. Regular publication of registration data on births and deaths ceased in 1927. Because registration data contradicted the political view that the population was increasing rapidly, the Statistical Office was closed in 1929 and the 1930 census was cancelled, and those responsible for data compilation suffered persecution

---

[1] The western Ukraine became part of the USSR only after World War II.

and even death (Wheatcroft 2009). The Soviet state at various periods had a strong interest in concealing, for example, the demographic consequences of the 1930s mortality crises arising from the forced collectivization of peasants and subsequent famine, or the worsening of mortality in the 1970s. However, the 1937 and 1939 censuses are regarded as being acceptably accurate for providing mortality estimates. The next census did not take place until 1959, after the death of Josef Stalin, who was apocryphally said to have stated that one death is a tragedy, a million deaths is a statistic.[2]

In 1938, life expectancy at birth in Russia was estimated at 40.4 years for males, similar to the value a century earlier in countries such as England and Wales (Charlton and Murphy 1997; Shkolnikov and Meslé 1996), and 46.7 years for women. Mortality improved substantially in the USSR after World War II (Table 4.2). By 1965, life expectancy in the Soviet Union was similar to that of the United States, 64.0 for men (USA 66.8) and 73.4 for women (USA 73.8). While Russia reported slightly lower life expectancy than the United States, values in Ukraine were higher, at 67.8 for men and 74.6 for women (HMD n.d.). Not only was Soviet mortality comparable to that of its main rival in the West in this period, it was also on a much more rapidly improving trajectory.

The two power blocs remained in competition (as typified by the emphasis given to the space race following the launch of the first Soviet sputnik in 1957), including an expensive arms race that the relatively poorer East was less well placed to engage in. The near-parity in mortality with Western countries reached around 1965 was not sustained, and in the following decades mortality trends in the Soviet Union and countries under its influence in Eastern Europe started to show a much less positive pattern, so that by the early part of the twenty-first century, the clear east–west divide in mortality in Europe of the early twentieth century had reappeared (WHO-HFA n.d.).

But publication of routine mortality statistics such as expectation of life at birth and the politically sensitive indicator of infant mortality (widely regarded as a key indicator of overall development) was suspended from the 1970s (Davis 2006). Such information was available internally (Anderson et al. 1994), but the facts became more widely known with publication of a book by Todd (1976), followed by a number of other studies (e.g., Anderson and Silver 1986; Davis and Feshbach 1980) that drew attention to the fact that since around 1965 mortality improvement appeared to have stagnated or regressed not only in the USSR, but in some other countries of Eastern Europe as well. A study by Dutton (1979) showed that the deterioration was due particularly to increases in male working-age mortality and gave considerable attention to misuse of alcohol as a likely cause.

Following the establishment of the Russian Federation, the production of demographic statistics became the responsibility of the State Statistics Commission (Goskomstat n.d.) and equivalent bodies in the other former republics of the USSR. While some countries, such as the Baltic states, had well-established systems and relatively peaceful transitions to statehood, this was not the case for most of the republics (Anderson and Silver 1997), and the World Health Organization (WHO) estimates that coverage of vital registration in the Central Asian republics is incomplete by up to 20%. In addition, conflict in areas such as the Caucasus makes estimation of population denominators also highly problematic. Nevertheless, mortality data are probably the most complete and comparable health indicators available (although the coding of causes of death contains some peculiarities, since the Russian Federation adopted only a subset of ICD-10 in 1999; Vishnevsky and Bobylev 2009), and some differences in patterns of overall mortality in FSU republics are apparent (Fig. 4.1). For about half of the states (and well over half of the population), life expectancy at birth (both sexes combined) was lower in 2000–2005 than it had been in Western Europe 50 years earlier. All republics showed rapid improvement in the earlier part of the period, but most then showed stagnation or even reversal from the mid-1980s. The Baltic states started from generally higher levels of life expectancy than the other states, and this group is the only one where the general trend of mortality has improved since about 1990 (although single-year data do show some fluctuations). The predominantly Slavic states

---

[2] Julia Solovyova (*Moscow Times*, October 28, 1997), in discussing Konstantin Dushenko's *Dictionary of Modern Quotations* (*Словарь современных цитат: 4300 ходячих цитат и выражений XX века, их источники, авторы, датировка*), stated that Russian historians have no record of this quotation (which probably originated from the 1956 novel *Der schwarze Obelisk* by Erich Maria Remarque): see http://bailey83221.livejournal.com/87856.html and http://en.wikipedia.org/wiki/Anecdotal_value

**Table 4.2** Life expectancy at birth in Russia and the United States, by sex, selected years 1896–2009

| Year | Males Russia | USA | Difference | Females Russia | USA | Difference |
|---|---|---|---|---|---|---|
| 1896 | 30.9 | 46.2 | 15.3 | 33.0 | 47.3 | 14.3 |
| 1926 | 39.3 | 55.5 | 16.2 | 44.8 | 58.0 | 13.2 |
| 1938 | 40.4 | 61.9 | 21.5 | 46.7 | 65.3 | 18.6 |
| 1958 | 61.9 | 66.8 | 4.9 | 69.2 | 73.2 | 4.0 |
| 1965 | 64.3 | 66.8 | 2.5 | 73.4 | 73.8 | 0.4 |
| 1970 | 63.0 | 67.1 | 4.1 | 73.4 | 74.7 | 1.3 |
| 1975 | 62.3 | 68.8 | 6.5 | 73.0 | 76.6 | 3.6 |
| 1980 | 61.5 | 70.0 | 8.5 | 73.1 | 77.4 | 4.3 |
| 1987 | 64.8 | 71.5 | 6.7 | 74.4 | 78.4 | 4.0 |
| 1990 | 63.8 | 71.8 | 8.0 | 74.3 | 78.8 | 4.5 |
| 1994 | 57.6 | 72.4 | 14.8 | 71.2 | 79.0 | 7.8 |
| 1998 | 61.3 | 73.8 | 12.5 | 72.9 | 79.5 | 6.6 |
| 2003 | 58.5 | 74.5 | 16.0 | 71.8 | 79.6 | 7.8 |
| 2004 | 58.9 | 74.9 | 16.0 | 72.3 | 79.9 | 7.6 |
| 2005 | 58.9 | 74.9 | 16.0 | 72.4 | 79.9 | 7.5 |
| 2006 | 60.4 | 75.1 | 14.7 | 73.2 | 80.2 | 7.0 |
| 2007 | 61.4 | 75.4 | 14.0 | 73.9 | 80.4 | 6.5 |
| 2008 | 61.8 | NA | NA | 74.2 | NA | NA |
| 2009 | 62.8 | NA | NA | 74.7 | NA | NA |

Sources: Russia 1896–1975, Table 4.1 in Shkolnikov and Meslé (1996) (further information given in that document).
Russia 1980–2006, WHO-HFA, available online at http://www.euro.who.int/hfadb
Russia 2007–2009, available online at http://www.gks.ru/free_doc/new_site/population/demo/demo26.xls
USA 1896–1938, Carter et al. (2006, Table Ab656–703). Expectation of life at birth all races: 1850–1998.
USA 1958–1970, National Center for Health Statistics (2007), Table 11. Life expectancy by age, race, and sex: Death-registration states, 1900–1902 to 1919–1921, and the United States, 1929–1931 to 2004.
USA 1970–2007, National Center for Health Statistics (2010), *National Vital Statistics Reports* 58(19), May 20, 2010, Table 8. Life expectancy at birth, race, and sex: the United States, 1940, 1950, 1960, 1970, and 1975–2007.

of Russia, Belarus, and Ukraine have about the same values as 50 years earlier and, to that extent, have had the poorest performance in mortality over the period. This was the case especially for sex differentials in mortality, which increased substantially in the Slavic and Baltic parts of the FSU, where they are now among the highest in the world. The other republics, in Central Asia and the Caucasus, started from a lower baseline in 1950, but now report levels similar to those of the Slavic republics, although the caveats about data quality should be noted.

Reported trends in adult mortality in many of the smaller FSU republics should be treated with caution; consequently, this chapter gives most attention to patterns of adult mortality in Russia, the largest and best documented of the FSU states (Anderson and Silver 1997; Chenet and Telishevska 2000; Vlassov 2000). More information about the Central Asian FSU Republics is included in "Adult Mortality in Asia," Chapter 6.

## Excess Mortality Associated with Recent Russian Mortality Patterns

While the trend for the past four decades was for Russian adult mortality to increase (Brainerd and Cutler 2005; Lutz et al. 1994; Shkolnikov et al. 2004), there were striking changes so that life expectancy improved sharply for a short period around 1985–1987, especially for men, to values similar to those of 1960, before two major crises occurred in the early 1990s and around 2000 (Fig. 4.2).

The sharp increase in mortality following the collapse of the Soviet Union in 1991 attracted considerable attention, although it was overlaid on a continuing mortality crisis. The fact that the increase was clearly concentrated among working-age adults was identified early (Bobak and Marmot 1996; DaVanzo and Farnsworth 1996; Shkolnikov and Meslé 1996). Relative to the high point of mortality improvement in 1987, age-standardized overall mortality had risen by just under one-half for males and one-quarter for females by 1994, but the values for children (under age 15) were actually lower in 1994 than in 1987 (Table 4.3). All other age groups showed increasing mortality, with the largest proportionate increases at ages 30–44, of 140% for men and 90% for women. For the latest date for which comparable data are available, 2006, values in all adult age groups were higher than in 1987, but childhood (including infant) mortality has continued to fall over the whole period. While care is needed in interpreting short series of data, there has been a substantial improvement in mortality between 2005 and 2009 (Table 4.2). Even so, values of life expectancy at birth for men were still lower in 2009 than in 1995, although values for women probably at their historical maximum (Table 4.2).

The progress of Russian adult mortality in the recent turbulent period may be assessed by comparing the observed values with those at key time points: 1964, when mortality in the USSR reached a value similar to that of the United States; 1984, just before the series of major societal transformations occurred; 1987, the high point of success in lowering mortality associated with Gorbachev's short-term anti-alcohol campaign (discussed later, White 1996); or with a continuation of the trend from the period 1959–1984, before the sharp rise and falls in life expectancy trend (Fig. 4.3). The estimate of the extent of the mortality crisis will depend on which choice is made.

Trends in age-specific Russian mortality over the period from 1980 to the early part of the twenty-first century may also be compared with those of the EU-15 Western European countries (Table 4.4). In 1980 age-standardized overall Russian mortality was about 50% higher than in the EU-15, but by 2006, while Russian male mortality had risen 9% and female mortality had risen 2%, in the EU both male and female mortality had fallen by over one third. In both areas childhood mortality fell substantially, rather more in the EU than in Russia. However, in Russia there were increases at adult ages, especially substantial at younger working ages, e.g., rates for men aged 15–44 were twice as high in 2006 as in 1987, and the increase in women's rates was only slightly less. The continuing relative increase of Russian adult mortality is striking, with the result that in 2006 male mortality at ages 30–44 was seven times higher than in the EU and female mortality over four times higher. Working-age

**Table 4.3** Age standardized mortality rates per 100,000 by age and sex, Russian Federation, selected years 1980–2006

|  | All ages | Age-group 0–14 | 15–29 | 30–44 | 45–59 | 60–74 | 75 and over |
|---|---|---|---|---|---|---|---|
| *Males* | | | | | | | |
| 1980 | 1,873 | *282* | 313 | 776 | 1,867 | 4,929 | 15,432 |
| 1984 | 1,880 | 264 | 289 | 743 | 1,900 | 5,009 | 15,594 |
| 1987 | 1,630 | 243 | 198 | 464 | 1,509 | 4,571 | 14,681 |
| 1994 | *2,382* | 233 | 389 | *1,116* | *2,831* | *6,177* | *17,684* |
| 1998 | 1,879 | 207 | 352 | 782 | 2,037 | 5,245 | 13,953 |
| 2003 | 2,306 | 166 | 381 | 1,061 | 2,702 | 6,132 | 17,258 |
| 2004 | 2,232 | 155 | 386 | 1,061 | 2,623 | 5,901 | 16,551 |
| 2005 | 2,227 | 147 | *392* | 1,082 | 2,624 | 5,861 | 16,418 |
| 2006 | 2,039 | 136 | 369 | 969 | 2,317 | 5,408 | 15,384 |
| *Females* | | | | | | | |
| 1980 | 959 | *204* | 79 | 212 | 658 | 2,300 | 11,140 |
| 1984 | 974 | 192 | 75 | 207 | 660 | 2,374 | 11,392 |
| 1987 | 899 | 170 | 61 | 150 | 553 | 2,269 | 10,849 |
| 1994 | *1,109* | 167 | 103 | 287 | *897* | *2,733* | 12,080 |
| 1998 | 962 | 151 | 101 | 209 | 676 | 2,392 | 11,047 |
| 2003 | 1,082 | 123 | 108 | 293 | 865 | 2,602 | *12,137* |
| 2004 | 1,039 | 114 | 108 | 295 | 836 | 2,499 | 11,554 |
| 2005 | 1,034 | 107 | *111* | *305* | 830 | 2,459 | 11,569 |
| 2006 | 977 | 101 | 103 | 276 | 746 | 2,304 | 11,244 |

Note: Largest value in group shown as italicized bold.
Source: WHO-HFA, available online at http://www.euro.who.int/hfadb

**Fig. 4.3** Russia and Sweden life expectancy at age 20 ($e_{20}$). Includes regression line for Russia fitted over period 1959–1984 and values for key years 1965, 1984 and 1987 (see text). Source: Human Mortality Database

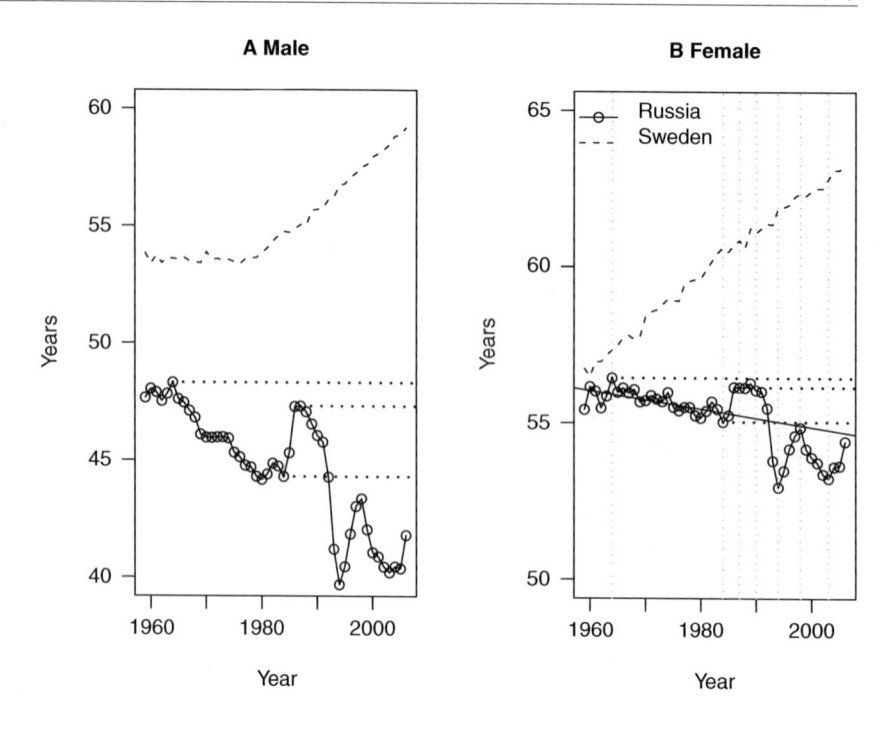

**Table 4.4** Ratio of age-standardized mortality rates (percent) by age and sex in Russian Federation to rates in EU-15, selected years 1980–2006

|  | All ages | Age-group 0–14 | 15–29 | 30–44 | 45–59 | 60–74 | 75 and over |
|---|---|---|---|---|---|---|---|
| *Males* | | | | | | | |
| 1980 | 162.1 | 209.7 | 281.6 | 381.4 | 219.7 | 154.1 | 121.8 |
| 1984 | 170.4 | 238.2 | 275.1 | 380.1 | 237.6 | 164.3 | 127.1 |
| 1987 | 154.2 | 241.1 | 191.8 | 241.0 | 199.3 | 156.9 | 124.4 |
| 1994 | 250.5 | 325.3 | 387.6 | 544.7 | 435.8 | 240.4 | 164.3 |
| 1998 | 209.8 | *347.3* | 396.7 | 448.4 | 339.2 | 221.1 | 132.7 |
| 2003 | 283.0 | 325.4 | 500.6 | 692.4 | 481.1 | 299.5 | 173.9 |
| 2004 | 289.6 | 319.6 | 534.6 | 726.3 | 485.7 | 304.1 | *177.3* |
| 2005 | *293.0* | 311.7 | *564.3* | *770.5* | *490.6* | *309.7* | 177.2 |
| 2006 | 277.6 | 294.6 | 552.9 | 706.4 | 441.5 | 295.7 | 172.8 |
| *Females* | | | | | | | |
| 1980 | 138.4 | 199.6 | 183.5 | 198.0 | 164.2 | 144.2 | 121.8 |
| 1984 | 149.3 | 226.4 | 190.3 | 206.9 | 176.0 | 157.8 | 130.4 |
| 1987 | 144.0 | 220.2 | 162.0 | 153.9 | 153.5 | 157.6 | 129.5 |
| 1994 | 198.1 | 296.7 | 294.5 | 308.4 | 280.1 | 217.2 | 158.4 |
| 1998 | 180.4 | *316.9* | 311.6 | 248.1 | 224.1 | 206.7 | 148.2 |
| 2003 | 214.0 | 295.8 | 387.0 | 387.1 | 300.5 | 254.3 | 165.8 |
| 2004 | 217.9 | 285.4 | 398.7 | 408.7 | 300.0 | 256.9 | 169.0 |
| 2005 | *219.5* | 280.2 | *434.4* | *433.4* | *300.9* | *258.1* | 170.0 |
| 2006 | 214.6 | 273.8 | 421.1 | 406.5 | 275.8 | 248.5 | *172.2* |

Note: Largest value in group shown as italicized bold.
Source: WHO-HFA, available online at http://www.euro.who.int/hfadb

mortality was the driver of overall mortality increase in Russia since 1987; the improvement in infant and child mortality actually mitigated the overall mortality increase, and mortality rates for older people remained relatively constant. Compared with 1994, the ratio of Russian to EU mortality was higher for every adult age group in 2005, and much higher at working ages (Table 4.4), even though 2005 was a period of relative social and economic stability compared with the previous two decades. The year 2005 rather than 1994 might be regarded as the time of worst adult mortality; for example, the difference between Russia and Sweden in life expectancy at age 20 and the probability of survival between ages 20 and 65 peaked in that year (Fig. 4.2).

Considerable attention was given to the unanticipated sharp mortality increase of the early 1990s, especially if compared with a year such as 1987, since there appeared to be no precedent for such an event in a developed country, nor any mechanism that would lead to such catastrophic mortality increase concentrated among working-age people in a society without major armed conflict, virulent pandemic, or mass starvation, none of which was present. However, changing patterns of cause of death suggest possible mechanisms (Dutton 1979).

## Causes of Death in the Former Soviet Union

In Russia in 2006, circulatory system diseases accounted for 57% of deaths at all ages, external causes (accidents and violence) for 13%, and cancers for 12%, with other causes accounting for the remaining 18%. This distribution is broadly similar to that in many developed countries, with adult deaths predominately due to noncommunicable rather than communicable diseases (Notzon et al. 2003). Mortality rates from most causes of death are higher in Russia than in the EU-15; of these three principal causes, cancer rates are higher than but broadly similar to those in other European countries, whereas both circulatory system disease and external causes of mortality are substantially higher. At working ages, circulatory system diseases account for about 40% of deaths, but external causes outnumber cancers substantially when both sexes are combined. While the distribution of deaths by cause did not change substantially in Russia between 1980 and 2006, the contrasts with Western Europe increased, with the ratio of Russian to EU-15 circulatory system death rates at ages 25–64 rising from a value of just over two to seven. Some of the more detailed causes show even more extreme patterns, with tuberculosis death rates in 2006 being over 100 times higher in Russia than in Western Europe for men and 60 times higher for women. Mortality rates from some external causes are much larger for Russian people of working age than for those in the EU-15; for example, 25 times higher for accidental poisoning (mostly associated with alcohol consumption) and 30 times higher for homicide, suggesting considerable potential for reducing "avoidable" mortality (Table 4.5, see also "Avoidable Mortality," Chapter 23).

## Explanations for the Observed Patterns

While the main trends of adult mortality in Russia are well established, there is less consensus about the explanations for them. Particular attention has been given to factors that might explain increases in the main causes of death among working-age men, especially circulatory system disease and external causes. While there were problems with pollution in Eastern Europe (Bobak and Marmot 1996), these did not appear large enough to account for the observed patterns, and explanations have tended to concentrate on three main areas:

1. individual risk factors such as smoking and diet, but in particular the role of alcohol abuse, especially in Russia (different patterns of alcohol consumption in other parts of the FSU, such as the mainly Muslim Central Asian republics, mean that such an explanation will not be as valid in all parts of the FSU);
2. macro-level factors such as changing standard of living or level of income inequality;
3. social stress arising from societal transformation in the FSU.

These areas clearly interact and potentially reinforce each other, and a number of possible explanations have been identified, including the following.

**Table 4.5** Distribution of Russian Federation selected age-standardized cause-specific death rates ages 25–64 (percent) and ratio of values to EU-15 in 1980 and 2006

|  | Age-standardized cause-specific rates ages 25–64 (percent of total) ||||  | Ratio to EU members before May 2004 ||||
|  | Males || Females || Males || Females ||
| Cause | 1980 | 2006 | 1980 | 2006 | 1980 | 2006 | 1980 | 2006 |
|---|---|---|---|---|---|---|---|---|
| Infectious and parasitic diseases | 3.0 | 3.8 | 1.5 | 2.4 | 6.6 | 7.9 | 2.5 | 4.2 |
| *Of which: Tuberculosis* | 2.7 | 3.3 | 0.9 | 1.8 | 10.7 | 114.3 | 4.4 | 61.6 |
| Neoplasms | 19.0 | 12.6 | 27.5 | 21.9 | 1.4 | 1.6 | 1.1 | 1.3 |
| Diseases of the circulatory system | 33.4 | 39.0 | 38.3 | 38.5 | 2.3 | 7.8 | 2.4 | 7.1 |
| *Of which: Ischemic heart disease* | 20.3 | 20.8 | 16.3 | 16.1 | 2.3 | 7.8 | 2.9 | 8.6 |
| Cerebrovascular diseases | 8.6 | 8.4 | 14.4 | 12.0 | 3.5 | 10.9 | 3.2 | 8.1 |
| Diseases of the respiratory system | 7.6 | 5.3 | 5.1 | 3.5 | 3.6 | 6.5 | 2.1 | 2.6 |
| *Of which: pneumonia* | 1.6 | 3.6 | 1.1 | 2.3 | 3.1 | 16.9 | 1.4 | 7.2 |
| Diseases of the digestive system | 3.9 | 6.1 | 4.0 | 8.9 | 1.1 | 3.7 | 0.9 | 4.1 |
| External causes of injury and poisoning | 27.5 | 26.1 | 17.0 | 17.0 | 5.0 | 8.7 | 3.2 | 6.2 |

Table 4.5 (continued)

| Cause | Age-standardized cause-specific rates ages 25–64 (percent of total) ||||| Ratio to EU members before May 2004 |||||
| | Males || Females || Males || Females ||
| | 1980 | 2006 | 1980 | 2006 | 1980 | 2006 | 1980 | 2006 |
| --- | --- | --- | --- | --- | --- | --- | --- | --- |
| Of which: accidents | 17.8 | – | 10.4 | – | 5.2 | – | 3.7 | – |
| Transport accidents | 3.7 | 2.9 | 2.1 | 2.4 | 2.1 | 3.7 | 1.4 | 4.2 |
| Accidental falls | 0.8 | 1.0 | 0.4 | 0.5 | 1.7 | 4.3 | 1.0 | 2.8 |
| Accidental drowning and submersion | 2.0 | 1.1 | 0.6 | 0.5 | 13.1 | 14.4 | 6.2 | 7.7 |
| Exposure to smoke, fire, and flames | 0.5 | 1.0 | 0.3 | 0.7 | 6.0 | 24.6 | 2.9 | 14.5 |
| Accidental poisoning | 7.0 | 5.6 | 4.7 | 4.0 | 48.2 | 28.0 | 30.0 | 20.7 |
| Suicide and intentional self-harm | 6.5 | 3.9 | 3.7 | 1.7 | 4.0 | 3.6 | 1.9 | 1.5 |
| Homicide and assault | 2.0 | 2.7 | 2.2 | 2.1 | 12.6 | 36.3 | 12.8 | 20.5 |
| Complications of pregnancy, childbirth, and puerperium | – | – | 0.4 | 0.1 | – | – | 6.9 | 3.8 |
| All causes age-standardized rate ages 25–64 (per 100,000 population) | 1,402 | 1,728 | 481 | 553 | 2.3 | 4.6 | 1.7 | 3.0 |

Note: Relative risks greater than 5 shown as bold.
Source: WHO-HFA, available online at http://www.euro.who.int/hfadb

## Artifact

There was no evidence of increases in communicable diseases large enough to produce the sharp and unanticipated changes in mortality after 1990 (see Table 4.3). But chronic conditions were assumed to arise from long-term accumulation of insult, and thus would not be expected to lead to such sharp increases, either. It was therefore suggested that these results might be due to error or inaccuracy in data collection or processing, including the possibility of underrecording of deaths in earlier periods (although much of this discussion centered around the different way of recording infant deaths in the Soviet Union, which yielded infant mortality levels about 22% lower than they would have been if the standard WHO definition of infant mortality had been used; Anderson and Silver 1986). However, the fact that recorded cancer deaths remained relatively constant, whereas deaths from causes such as cardiovascular disease and accidents and violence increased substantially, suggested that changing statistical coverage could not account for these findings, a point that was reinforced after detailed analyses of mortality statistics by both Russian and Western demographers (Leon et al. 1997). Therefore, the trends recorded by official statistics in Russia were real, and other explanations are required.

## Alcohol

The causes of the mortality crisis are complex and due to a range of distal historical, cultural, social, economic, and political factors. Alcohol is an important proximal cause. The roots of Russian drinking patterns are many centuries old (McKee 1999; Stickley et al. 2009) and are not the product of a particular political system. It is unclear whether alcohol is strongly implicated in the long-term increase in mortality, because suitable data for the period before 1990 do not exist, but consumption of alcohol increased in the postwar period (Dutton 1979; Treml 1997), with such harmful consequences that it had become a major concern to the Soviet government by the mid-1980s. The result was a wide-ranging anti-alcohol campaign initiated by Mikhail Gorbachev (White 1996); in the 2-year period 1985–1987, life expectancy increased 2 years. While the health benefits were clear-cut, the anti-alcohol campaign, like earlier sudden changes in alcohol availability (Stickley et al. 2009), was unsustainable: it was unpopular, and the government of the USSR obtained a substantial fraction of its revenues from taxes on officially produced alcohol, so the policy was reversed in 1987. After 1990 considerable attention was given to the role of alcohol in Russia, although the sharp increase in life expectancy, especially for men, that occurred simultaneously with the 1985–1987 anti-alcohol campaign had already provided evidence for the direct sensitivity of mortality to alcohol availability (no other plausible explanation has been advanced for these patterns).

The mechanisms whereby changes in alcohol availability led to almost instantaneous changes in cardiovascular mortality remained unclear, since alcohol abuse was mainly associated with long-term effects such as cirrhosis of the liver. Indeed, on balance alcohol consumption is often considered to reduce CVD: around this time, it was estimated that in the established market economies more male deaths were averted than were caused by alcohol consumption, although the averted deaths tended to occur at older ages (Murray and Lopez 1996, Fig. 6.4). However, in Russia, although per capita quantities of alcohol drunk were not particularly high compared with other countries such as France, binge drinking and heavy consumption of spirits led to much worse outcomes than did the moderate drinking patterns more common elsewhere (Bobak et al. 1999; Leon et al. 2007; McKee 1999). At the time, few studies had investigated the health outcomes for binge drinkers; but later it became apparent that alcohol not only contributed substantially to external causes of death, such as motor vehicle accidents, poisoning, homicide, and suicide, but also directly affected cardiovascular disease via arrhythmia (Britton and McKee 2000; Malyutina et al. 2002; Rehm et al. 2007). Indeed, cardiovascular disease mortality was substantially higher on the weekend and on Mondays than other days of the week because of the effects of binge drinking over the weekend (Chenet et al. 1998).

After the restrictions of the anti-alcohol campaign, the harmful effect of binge drinking was compounded by a substantial switch toward home-produced alcohol, which was often of unreliable quality (McKee 1999). Russia exhibits heavy consumption of home-produced spirits (samogen) and nonbeverage alcohol liquids, such as antifreeze and after-shave (Leon et al. 2007). In one Russian city such risky drinking accounted for about half of deaths among men aged 25–54, a figure confirmed in a later large-scale study of three Russian cities which found that 59% of deaths to men aged 15–54 were alcohol-related, as were 33% of those for women (Zaridze et al. 2009). The higher availability of low-quality alcohol in rural areas suggests that this is at least as great a problem there.

The lack of attention given to reducing the harmful effects of alcohol, apart from the short-term and ultimately unsuccessful attempt by Gorbachev, shows the difficulties in changing individual behavior, especially in a society whose institutional tolerance of alcohol was exemplified by the public behavior of the late Russian president Boris Yeltsin. It is likely that alcohol abuse was stimulated by societal transformation in the 1990s: large numbers of men lost employment and social prestige, and privatization of the former state-run alcohol industry led to increased marketing of alcohol. Poverty may have led to increased use of the most harmful types of nonbeverage alcohol. Alcohol abuse remains an important factor in the increase of adult mortality in recent decades (Zaridze et al. 2009).

## Smoking

Russia has one of the world's highest rates of smoking among men, 60% compared with 30% in typical Western countries; rates for women are about 15% (Bobak et al. 2006). But rates of lung cancer mortality are not particularly high by international standards and were actually falling from the early 1990s (Shkolnikov et al. 1999), largely because tobacco had been given high priority during the war but was relatively restricted immediately after it (Shkolnikov et al. 2004). However, in FSU countries smoking contributes to high levels of mortality, especially from cardiovascular disease, and, in the Russian Federation in particular, smoking contributes to the extreme sex differential in adult mortality given the differences in smoking patterns between the sexes. Present high levels of smoking are likely to result in higher mortality than would otherwise be the case in future years.

## Diet and Nutrition

About 60% of Russian adults have higher than recommended cholesterol levels, and about 20% are at high risk and in need of medical attention (Plavinski et al. 1999). The Russian diet is particularly deficient in micronutrients such as those obtained from vegetables (Shkolnikov et al. 2004), and its effects are compounded by lack of exercise. Russian nutrition is poor in both quantity and type of foods consumed (Popkin et al. 1997), although neither the risks of this diet nor the changing patterns of consumption fully explain Russian mortality over this period (Brainerd and Cutler 2005). Diets low in micronutrients and high in animal fats are likely to lead to poor outcomes when levels of cardiovascular disease are already high, and are likely to reinforce negative health trends.

## Health Services

Both the quality and the quantity of health care in the former USSR and its successor states have been identified as potential contributors to the mortality crisis. At the Alma Ata declaration and conference in 1970, the Soviet primary health care system had been strongly endorsed as a model for other countries to follow. This system was effective at ensuring high rates of coverage for vaccination, but received few resources and low priority compared to other parts of the economy. Access to advanced medicine and pharmaceuticals was limited, and the healthcare system tended to fall behind Western performance levels over time. In addition, the Soviet health system gave little emphasis to individual responsibility for health. However, the fact that mortality increases were so strongly concentrated among working-age people, especially men, the group who make least use of health services, suggested that deficiencies in those services could only have played a minor part in mortality trends over the past four decades.

## Stress and Living Conditions

Psychosocial problems in Russia were accentuated by the drastic changes in the economic transition. Reduction in the social safety net in the last 15 years and perceived lack of control before 1990 have been identified as contributors to the increase in Russian mortality over the period (Brainerd and Cutler 2005; Cornia 2003; Cornia and Paniccia 2000; Leon and Shkolnikov 1998). Increases in unemployment were associated with increased mortality (Stuckler et al.

2009). The increase in suicide suggested that stress was implicated in the mortality swings after 1990. The poorest groups in society were most affected by societal transformation, and they are the most likely to drink excessively and to consume nonbeverage alcohol. Also, general inequalities (which have an independent effect on mortality) increased. While the USSR had been a highly egalitarian state in terms of income distribution, socioeconomic differences in mortality by educational level were at least as large in pre-1990 Russia as in Western countries (Shkolnikov et al. 1998), and were stronger for men than for women. More recently, these differentials have increased substantially across a number of countries of the FSU (Shkolnikov et al. 2005). While adult mortality of those with tertiary education has decreased since 1990, mortality of those with secondary education has increased, and mortality among those with only primary level education has increased very sharply (Murphy et al. 2006).

Even though the Soviet economic system had substantial inefficiencies and relatively poor pay, the rapid transition from a system with stable employment and little or no unemployment or job insecurity, plus a high regard for people engaged in heavy manual labor, to a privatized system seriously worsened living conditions ("shock therapy") and contributed to the increase in mortality not only in the FSU but also in much of the former Communist bloc after 1990 (Stuckler et al. 2009). The preexisting tradition of binge drinking compounded the effect among the groups most affected, working-age men. The effect of this societal transformation was both longer and greater in the Slavic states of the FSU. A number of reasons may account for this: Russia not only lost its existing system but had no potential to gain autonomy as some of its client states did; the Russian transition was plagued with conflict between those who wanted to retain much of the old system and others who want to abolish it; and the transition was poorly managed, with breakdown of governance and a lack of support structures to replace the now-defunct state.

## Summary, Conclusions, and Implications

While the patterns of overall mortality in Russia are paralleled by those in the other Slavic and Baltic states, it is too simple to attribute them to a single cause. Over a long period of time, a series of factors have reinforced each other to shape the current outcome. Historically, Russia, like some other parts of northern Europe, has had patterns of binge drinking of spirits, but other countries in the region such as the Nordic countries did not show a similar increase in adult mortality. The series of economic and social shocks that occurred in a society that had provided the majority of its population with a stable and predictable existence, albeit at a level that fell increasingly below that of other industrialized nations, appears to have reduced the ability of the adult population to adjust to new crises. Discussion about whether societal transformation or alcohol was primarily responsible for the fluctuations after 1990 is unhelpful: they were both important and mutually reinforcing. Russia, in particular, had a damaging combination of factors, such as poor diet, low levels of exercise, hazardous drinking traditions, centralized but ineffective health care systems, and little emphasis on public health or responsibility of individuals for maintaining their own health, that led to mortality increases from the 1960s as the relatively easily achieved postwar benefits wore out. The subsequent changes from 1990 added a series of new problems: the new Russian Federation political system continued to give little attention to the health care system, and some risk factors increased, including higher levels of smoking, hazardous drinking, unemployment, poverty, and financial uncertainty (the 1998 banking crisis is often asserted to be the cause of the second mortality crisis about 2000). Social stress arising from the economic and physical shocks led to considerable loss of prestige among some occupations, compounding the problems for working-age men.

The long-term decline has been by far the most important driver of Russia's poor current adult mortality levels, and the crises since 1990 are relatively unimportant in comparison: indeed, if the trend of the period 1959–1984 were to be continued into the future, men's mortality in the early twenty-first century would actually lie above this trend line. Because the FSU trends are extreme and unique, it is difficult and perhaps impossible to definitively determine the relative importance of the responsible proximal and distal factors. It is likely that social upheavals that bore particularly on certain groups and sharp reductions in living standards contributed to the substantial increases in working-age adult mortality observed since 1990. But the longer-term combination of historical factors, such as alcohol consumption, poor diet, and low priority given to improving health, was responsible for the longer-term trend of the past four decades.

Mortality has been decreasing almost continuously in most parts of the world for many decades. However, adult mortality in Russia and some of its neighbors remains very high, with little evidence of sustained improvement 20 years after the former system collapsed, even in comparison with some countries in Eastern Europe with a similar experience: the Appendix to this chapter contains a number of relevant studies and sources of additional information. The optimistic assumption that political and economic change would automatically lead to Western European patterns has been dashed. It is clear that the underlying causes are multifactorial and of long standing. Mortality is only one indicator of poor health status in Russia (Andreev et al. 2003); addressing this crisis will require early interventions in a number of areas, such as improving diet and reducing consumption of tobacco and alcohol. The health system not only is underfunded in general (health expenditure accounted for 5.3% of GDP in 2006, about half of the proportion of Western European countries and about one ninth of the expenditure per capita of that in the United States, World Bank n.d.), but also gives low priority to public health measures. Poverty, compounded by a rapid increase in income inequality and population aging (the proportion of the Russian population aged 65 and over is projected to rise from 18 to 30% between 2010 and 2030, United Nations n.d.), remains a major social and health issue, especially in the neglected rural areas. The tombstone of Karl Marx, the intellectual father of Communism, bears the sentence "The philosophers have only interpreted the world in various ways; the point however is to change it." A similar point may be made with respect to improving future health status in the former Soviet Union, where priority will need to be given to implementing appropriate actions.

## Appendix: List of Additional Databases with Data on Mortality and Related Issues in FSU Countries

Information is available from national statistical offices, e.g., State Committee of the Russian Federation on Statistics: http://www.gks.ru/eng/default.asp.

Addresses for nation-specific sites are available online at http://www.who.int/whosis/database/national_sites/index.cfm

World Health Organization country page: http://www.who.int/countries/rus/en/

WHO Regional Office for Europe: http://www.euro.who.int/countryinformation, including

European health for all database (HFA-DB)

Mortality indicators by 67 causes of death, age, and sex (HFA-MDB)

European detailed mortality database (DMDB)

Country highlights on health, e.g., http://www.euro.who.int/countryinformation/CtryInfoRes?COUNTRY=RUS

US Census Bureau International Data Base (IDB): http://www.census.gov/ipc/www/idb/

UNICEF Innocenti Research Centre: http://www.unicef-irc.org/databases/transmonee/#TransMONEE

Electronic version of bulletin *Naselenie i obschestvo* (Population and Society)

Institute of Demography at the State University Higher School of Economic http://demoscope.ru/weekly/ includes statistics such as life expectancy at birth at http://demoscope.ru/weekly/app/app40e0e.php

CIA World Factbook for Russian Federation: https://www.cia.gov/library/publications/the-world-factbook/

## Additional Selected Publications with Data on Mortality and Related Issues in FSU Countries

### World Bank

Dying Too Young: Addressing Premature Mortality and Ill Health Due to Noncommunicable Diseases and Injuries in the Russian Federation. Available online at http://siteresources.worldbank.org/INTECA/Resources/DTY-Final.pdf

### UNDP

Vishnevsky, A. and S. Bobylev (eds.). 2009. "Human Development Report 2008 for the Russian Federation: Russia Facing Demographic

Challenges." Available online at http://hdr.undp.org/en/reports/nationalreports/europethecis/russia/NHDR_Russia_2008_Eng.pdf

## World Health Organization Regional Office for Europe

*The European Health Report 2005: Public Health Action for Healthier Children and Populations.* Available online at http://www.euro.who.int/ehr2005

"Highlights on Health in the Russian Federation 2005." Available online at http://www.euro.who.int/highlights

## European Observatory on Health Systems and Policies

Marc S., L. Rocco, M. McKee, S. Mazzuco, D. Urban, and A. Steinherr. "Economic Consequences of Noncommunicable Diseases and Injuries in the Russian Federation." Available online at http://www.euro.who.int/InformationSources/Publications/Catalogue/20070411_1

M. Suhrcke, S. Walters, S. Mazzuco, J. Pomerleau, M. McKee, and C.W. Haerpfer. "Socioeconomic Differences in Health, Health Behaviour and Access to Health Care in Armenia, Belarus, Georgia, Kazakhstan, Kyrgyzstan, the Republic of Moldova, the Russian Federation and Ukraine." Available online at http://www.euro.who.int/Document/E91873.pdf

## References

Anderson, B.A., K. Katus, and B.D. Silver. 1994. "Developments and Prospects for Population Statistics in Countries of the Former Soviet Union." *Population Index* 60:4–20.

Anderson, B.A. and B.D. Silver. 1986. "Infant Mortality in the Soviet Union: Regional Differences and Measurement Issues." *Population and Development Review* 12: 705–37.

Anderson, B.A. and B.D. Silver. 1997. "Issues of Data Quality in Assessing Mortality Trends and Levels in the New Independent States." In J.L. Bobadilla, C.A. Costello, and F. Mitchell (eds.), *Premature Death in the New Independent States*, pp. 120–55. Washington, DC, National Academy Press.

Andreev, E.M., M. McKee, and V.M. Shkolnikov. 2003. "Health Expectancy in the Russian Federation: A New Perspective on the Health Divide in Europe." *Bulletin of the World Health Organization* 81:778–87.

Bobak, M., A. Gilmore, M. McKee, R. Rose, and M. Marmot. 2006. "Changes in Smoking Prevalence in Russia, 1996–2004." *Tobacco Control* 15:131–35.

Bobak, M. and M. Marmot. 1996. "East-West Mortality Divide and Its Potential Explanations: Proposed Research Agenda." *British Medical Journal* 312:421–25.

Bobak, M., M. McKee, R. Rose, and M. Marmot. 1999. "Alcohol Consumption in a National Sample of the Russian Population." *Addiction* 94:857–66.

Brainerd, E. and D.M. Cutler. 2005. "Autopsy on an Empire: Understanding Mortality in Russia and the Former Soviet Union." *Journal of Economic Perspectives* 19:107–30.

Britton, A. and M. McKee. 2000. "The Relationship Between Alcohol and Cardiovascular Disease in Eastern Europe; Explaining the Paradox." *Journal of Epidemiology and Community Health* 54:328–32.

Carter, S.B., S.S. Gartner, M.R. Haines, A.L. Olmstead, R. Sutch, and G. Wright (eds.). 2006. *Historical Statistics of the United States, Volume One: Population*. New York, NY, Cambridge University Press.

Caselli, G. 1994. *Long Term Trends in European Mortality*. Studies on Medical and Population Subjects, 56. London, Office for Population Censuses and Surveys.

Charlton, J. and M. Murphy (eds.). 1997. *The Health of Adult Britain, 1841–1994*. London, Stationery Office.

Chenet, L., M. McKee, D. Leon, V. Shkolnikov, and S. Vassin. 1998. "Alcohol and Cardiovascular Mortality in Moscow: New Evidence of a Causal Association." *Journal of Epidemiology and Community Health* 52: 772–74.

Chenet, L. and M. Telishevska. 2000. "Epidemiology, Medical Demography and Data Quality Issues in the Former Soviet Union." *Journal of Epidemiology and Community Health* 54:722–23.

Cornia, G.A. 2003. "The Forgotten Crisis: Transition, Psychosocial Stress and Mortality Over the 1990s in the Former Soviet Block." In E. Ziglio, L. Levin, and E. Bath (eds.), *Investment for Health: A Discussion of the Role of Economic and Social Determinants of Population Health*. Copenhagen, WHO Regional Office for Europe.

Cornia, G.A. and R. Paniccia. 2000. *The Mortality Crisis in Transitional Economies*. Oxford, Oxford University Press.

DaVanzo, J. and G. Farnsworth (eds.). 1996. "Russia's Demographic 'Crisis.'" Available online at http://www.rand.org/pubs/conf_proceedings/CF124/index.html

Davies, R.W. and S.G. Wheatcroft. 2004. *The Years of Hunger: Soviet Agriculture, 1931–1933*. Basingstoke, Palgrave Macmillan.

Davis, C. 2006. "Commentary: The Health Crisis in the USSR: Reflections on the Nicholas Eberstadt 1981 Review of Rising Infant Mortality in the USSR in the 1970s." *International Journal of Epidemiology* 35:1400–5.

Davis, C. and M. Feshbach. 1980. *Rising Infant Mortality in the USSR in the 1970s*. US Bureau of the Census,

International Population Reports, Series P-95. Washington, DC, US Government Printing Office.
Dutton, J. Jr. 1979. "Changes in Soviet Mortality Patterns, 1959/1977." *Population and Development Review* 5: 267–91.
Ellman, M. and S. Maksudov. 1994. "Soviet Deaths in the Great Patriotic War: Comment." *Europe Asia Studies* 46:671–80.
Goskomstat. n.d. "History Russia's State Statistics 1802–1996." Available online at http://www.fsgs.ru/wps/portal/english/
Human Mortality Database (HMD). Available online at http://www.mortality.org/, accessed 7th October 2009.
Leon, D.A., L. Chenet, V.M. Shkolnikov, S. Zakharov, J. Shapiro, G. Rahmanova, S. Vassin, and M. McKee. 1997. "Huge Variation in Russian Mortality Rates 1984–1994: Artefact, Alcohol, or What?" *Lancet* 350:383–88.
Leon, D.A., L. Saburova, S. Tomkins, E. Andreev, N. Kiryanov, M. McKee, and V.M. Shkolnikov. 2007. "Hazardous Alcohol Drinking and Premature Mortality in Russia: A Population Based Case-Control Study." *Lancet* 369:2001–9.
Leon, D.A. and V.M. Shkolnikov. 1998. "Social Stress and the Russian Mortality Crisis." *Journal of the American Medical Association* 279:790–91.
Lutz, W., S. Scherbov, and A. Volkov (eds.). 1994. *Demographic Trends and Patterns in the Soviet Union Before 1991*. London, Routledge.
Malyutina, S., M. Bobak, S. Kurilovitch, V. Gafarov, G. Simonova, Y. Nikitin, and M. Marmot. 2002. "Relation Between Heavy and Binge Drinking and All-Cause and Cardiovascular Mortality in Novosibirsk, Russia: A Prospective Cohort Study." *Lancet* 360:1448–54.
McKee, M. 1999. "Alcohol in Russia." *Alcoholism* 34:824–29.
Meslé, F. and J. Vallin. 2003. *Mortalité et Causes de Décès en Ukraine au XXe Siècle*. Serie: Les Cahiers de l'INED, Cahier No 152. Paris, INED.
Murphy, M., M. Bobak, A. Nicholson, R. Rose, and M. Marmot. 2006. "The Widening Trend in Mortality by Educational Level in Russia, 1980–2001." *American Journal of Public Health* 96:1293–99.
Murray, C.J. and A.D. Lopez (eds.). 1996. *Global Burden of Disease: A Comprehensive Assessment of Mortality and Disability from Diseases, Injuries, and Risk Factors in 1990 and Projected to 2020*, Vol. 1. Harvard, MA, Harvard University Press.
National Center for Health Statistics. 2007. "United States Life Tables, 2004." *National Vital Statistics Reports* 56(9): 1–40.
National Center for Health Statistics. 2009. "Deaths: Final Data for 2006." *National Vital Statistics Reports*, 57(14):1–136.
Notzon, F.C., Y.M. Komarov, S.P. Ermakov, A.I. Savinykh, M.B. Hanson, and J. Albertorio. 2003. "Vital and Health Statistics: Russian Federation and United States, Selected Years 1985–2000 with an Overview of Russian Mortality in the 1990s." *Vital Health Statistics* 5(11):1–67.
Plavinski, S.L., S.I. Plavinskaya, V. Richter, F. Rassoul, W. Schilow, and A.N. Klimov. 1999. "The Total and HDL-Cholesterol Levels in Populations of St. Petersburg (Russia) and Leipzig (Germany)." *Nutrition, Metabolism, and Cardiovascular Diseases* 9:184–91.
Popkin, B., N. Zohoori, L. Kohlmeier, A. Baturin, A. Martinchik, and A. Deev. 1997. "Nutritional Risk Factors in the Former Soviet Union." In J.L. Bobadilla, C.A. Costello, and F. Mitchell (eds.), *Premature Death in the New Independent States*, pp. 314–34. Washington, DC, National Academy Press.
Rehm, J., U. Sulkowska, M. Manczuk, P. Boffetta, J. Powles, S. Popova, and W. Zatonski. 2007. "Alcohol Accounts for a High Proportion of Premature Mortality in Central and Eastern Europe." *International Journal of Epidemiology* 36:458–67.
Shkolnikov, V.M., E.M. Andreev, D. Jasilionis, M. Leinsalu, O.A. Antonova, and M. McKee. 2005. "The Changing Relation Between Education and Life Expectancy in Central and Eastern Europe in the 1990s." *Journal of Epidemiology and Community Health* 60:875–81.
Shkolnikov, V.M., E.M. Andreev, D.A. Leon, M. McKee, F. Meslé, and J. Vallin. 2004. "Mortality Reversal in Russia: The Story So Far." *Hygiea Internationalis* 4:29–80.
Shkolnikov, V.M., D.A. Leon, S. Adamets, E. Andreev, and A. Deev. 1998. "Educational Level and Adult Mortality in Russia: An Analysis of Routine Data 1979 to 1994." *Social Science and Medicine* 47(3):357–69.
Shkolnikov, V., M. McKee, D.A. Leon, and L. Chenet. 1999. "Why Is the Death Rate from Lung Cancer Falling in the Russian Federation?" *European Journal of Epidemiology* 15:203–6.
Shkolnikov, V.M. and F. Meslé. 1996. "Chapter 4. The Russian Epidemiological Crisis as Mirrored by Mortality Trends." In J. DaVanzo and G.Farnsworth (eds.), *Russia's Demographic 'Crisis'*, pp. 113–62. Available online at http://www.rand.org/pubs/conf_proceedings/CF124/index.html
Stickley, A., Y. Razvodovsky, and M. McKee. 2009. "Alcohol Mortality in Russia: A Historical Perspective." *Public Health* 123:20–26.
Stuckler, D., L. King, and M. McKee. 2009. "Mass Privatisation and the Post-Communist Mortality Crisis: A Cross-National Analysis." *Lancet* 373:399–407.
Todd, E. 1976. *La Chute Finale. Essai Sur La Décomposition De La Sphère Soviétique*. Paris, Robert Laffont.
Treml, V. 1997. "Soviet and Russian Statistics on Alcohol Consumption and Abuse." In J.L. Bobadilla, C.A. Costello, and F. Mitchell, *Premature Death in the New Independent States*, pp. 220–38. Washington, DC, National Academy Press.
United Nation. n.d. *World Population Prospects: The 2008 Revision Population Database*. Available online at http://esa.un.org/unpp/
Vallin, J., F. Meslé, S. Adamets, and S. Pyrozhkov. 2002. "A New Estimate of Ukrainian Population Losses During the Crises of the 1930s and 1940s." *Population Studies* 56: 249–64.
Vishnevsky, A. and S. Bobylev (eds.). 2009. *Human Development Report 2008 for the Russian Federation: Russia Facing Demographic Challenges*. Available online at http://hdr.undp.org/en/reports/nationalreports/europethecis/russia/NHDR_Russia_2008_Eng.pdf
Vlassov, V. 2000. "Is There Epidemiology in Russia?" *Journal of Epidemiology and Community Health* 54: 740–44.
Wheatcroft, S.G. 2009. "The First 35 Years of Soviet Living Standards: Secular Growth and Conjunctural Crises in a

Time of Famines." *Explorations in Economic History* 46: 24–52.

White, S. 1996. *Russia Goes Dry: Alcohol, State and Society*. Cambridge, Cambridge University Press.

World Bank. n.d. *World Development Indicators 2009*. Available online at http://web.worldbank.org/WBSITE/EXTERNAL/DATASTATISTICS/

World Health Organization Health for All Database (WHO-HFA). Available online at http://www.euro.who.int/hfadb

Zaridze, D., P. Brennan, J. Boreham, A. Boroda, R. Karpov, A. Lazarev, I. Konobeevskaya, V. Igitov, T. Terechova, P. Boffetta, and R. Peto. 2009. "Alcohol and Cause-Specific Mortality in Russia: A Retrospective Case-Control Study of 48,557 Adult Deaths." *Lancet* 373:2201–14.

# Chapter 5
# Adult Mortality in Latin America and the Caribbean

Alberto Palloni and Guido Pinto-Aguirre

## Introduction

This chapter reviews mortality trends during the twentieth century in selected countries of Latin America and the Caribbean (LAC). The chapter focuses only on female and male mortality patterns over age 5 during the period 1900–2000. For some countries, we reconstruct the trajectory from very high mortality prevailing at the beginning of the century to high levels of life expectancy attained by the year 2000. For others, we are able to estimate trajectories starting in 1950. Somewhat surprisingly, current levels of life expectancies in some of these countries are lower than those experienced in high-income countries.

The chapter is organized as follows: in "A Brief History of Mortality Statistics in LAC," we briefly summarize the nature of the relevant information for LAC countries. In "Estimation of Adult Mortality in LAC During 1900–2000," we identify problems and gaps in extant estimates of life expectancies and trends. In this section we summarize the procedures we apply to estimate adjusted life tables for intercensal periods. In all cases, we use only a combination of population censuses and vital statistics and ignore adult mortality estimates from indirect methods. The adjustments we implement are those designed to correct for completeness of census and death registration as well as for age misstatement in both sources. In "Evaluation of Estimates," we compare our estimates with alternative ones obtained using different methodologies, including those based on orphanhood, widowhood, and sibling survival as well as with those generated by a number of agencies using a mixture of adjustment procedures whose origin and nature are not always transparent. Our decision to forego estimation using well-established indirect methods, such as those based on orphanhood and sibling survival, stems from a desire to avoid assumptions about underlying age patterns of mortality which, *per force*, must be invoked to generate a complete life table above age 5 if any of these methods are applied. We invoke a similar rationale for excluding existing estimates of mortality for the period 1900–1950 for those countries with no existing vital statistics prior to 1950.

In "Mortality Trends," we summarize observed trends and attempt to indirectly identify the determinants responsible for the post-World War II gains in adult survival. In "The Contribution of Causes of Death," we estimate the contribution of major groups of causes of death to those survival gains; whereas in "The Determinants of Mortality Trends: 1950–2000," we estimate relations between life expectancy and macro determinants. We also assess the magnitude of gains accrued in the period 1950–2000 that are associated with shifts independent of improvements in measured covariates. The section "Mortality at Old Ages" examines patterns of mortality at older ages. Current theories of longevity and the assessment of the likely trajectory of future life expectancy have been informed by and based largely on what we know about mortality patterns in developed countries, those whose mortality transition began well before 1900. The contribution to this discourse from the experience of countries, whose mortality decline begins late, right

A. Palloni (✉)
Department of Sociology and Center for Demography and Ecology, University of Wisconsin, Madison, WI 53706, USA
e-mail: palloni@ssc.wisc.edu

before, or immediately after World War II, is scarce. This is an important lacuna, since the nature of mortality decline in these countries in general, and in LAC in particular, is sharply different from the mortality decline in more developed societies. The peculiarities of the mortality transition in LAC, including its highly compressed character and the evolution of a regime, where modern chronic conditions coexist with infectious diseases, may have important implications for the potential trajectory of life expectancy. The last section concludes.

## A Brief History of Mortality Statistics in LAC

Theories of mortality decline have been formulated, tested, and then reformulated mostly by exploring the characteristics of mortality changes in what are now high-income countries.[1] The most fundamental of these contributions by McKeown (1976) is entirely based on the experience of England and Wales. So, it is the expansion of McKeown's conjecture formulated by Fogel (2004). Similarly, mortality trends in France, Italy, and Spain (Caselli 2002; Schofield and Reher 2002; Vallin 2002), for example, have helped to refine the foundations of what could be considered a well-tested theory about the mechanisms that produce the transition from high- to low-mortality regimes. Nothing of the sort exists for low-income countries in general and Latin America in particular. Perhaps the first incursion into this unknown territory can be traced back to the work by Arriaga (1968) and by Arriaga and Davis (1969). Arriaga not only produced the first set of historical life tables for the majority of Latin American countries but, in collaboration with Davis, formulated a theory, albeit simple, about the conditions that explained the evolution of mortality up until 1970. But the seminal work by Arriaga was never followed up, challenged, modified, or updated, with one exception. This was the work by Stolnitz (1965) and especially by Preston who, in a series of classic papers, articulated a theory of mortality decline using statistics from a blend of low- and high-income countries (Preston 1976, 1987; Preston and Nelson 1974). This research, however, is not distinctly applied to Latin America but is an accounting of mortality decline in general. In addition, and with counted exceptions, this body of work is based on unadjusted statistics for the low-income countries included in the analyses.

During the period of 1970–2000, there was an explosion of new methods to estimate child and adult mortality using indirect techniques. Multiple estimates were produced for different countries largely for the period 1950–2000. But these efforts have three shortcomings. First, estimates were produced for the age group 0–5 or for adult mortality without generating entire life tables. Calculations of entire life tables were the result of stitching together the estimates for early childhood and adulthood, an operation that rested on assumptions about underlying age patterns of mortality. Second, the estimates were never assembled to generate a systematic account of the trajectory of mortality in the continent. Exceptionally, however, Centro Latinoamericano de Demografia (CELADE), the United Nations (UN), and Pan American Health Organization (PAHO) released adjusted estimates of mortality for almost all countries in Latin America for the period following 1950. These organizations employed a number of adjustments that rarely spelled out in detail the adjustment procedures. The exception was the work done in the late 1970s by the UN, which led to a redesign of models of mortality patterns (UN 1982). The data base used by the UN consisted of mortality statistics adjusted for completeness in the age segment 0–10 but rarely or never adjusted for adult mortality. Absent from this effort, however, was an attempt to explain the great intercountry heterogeneity. Third, with only one exception, the statistics available were never analyzed under the scope of an explicit theory of mortality decline, such as the one put forward by Arriaga and Davis (1969) or Preston (1976). This exception (Palloni and Wyrick 1981) fell short and did not fill the gaping vacuum of knowledge, since it focused on standardized death rates (total and by causes of deaths), and only some of these were known to be of sufficient accuracy, while a cloud of uncertainty covered all others. One finding from this work that deserves attention, because it partially confirms Preston's conjectures, is that the mortality decline that took place in LAC countries between 1950

---

[1] These theories are distinct from classificatory frameworks such as those proposed by Omran (1982) in that they explicitly seek identification of the ultimate causes of changes in mortality and morbidity regimes.

and 1980 was associated mostly with the implementation of public health policies and the application of new medical technology and much less so with improvements in standards of living. Furthermore, and echoing the work that had been done in the case of Ceylon—now Sri Lanka (Frederiksen 1970; Gray 1974)—Latin American countries whose mortality regime was heavily dominated by debilitating infectious diseases, such as malaria, benefited much more than expected from reduction of these diseases. Palloni and Wyrick proposed the idea that reduction or elimination of malaria in the period 1940–1960, following the massive application of dichloro-diphenyl-trichloroethane (DDT), led to improvements in immune function and nutritional status which, in turn, contributed to the decline of other infectious diseases even in the absence of additional interventions or improvements in the health care systems.

The last effort to produce a comprehensive review of adult mortality in Latin America is a volume edited by Timaeus and colleagues (1996). It consists of chapters devoted either to just one country, to an assessment of the quality of vital statistics, to a handful of diseases, or to an evaluation of estimates from indirect methods for a few countries with very poor vital statistics on adult mortality. The book lacks, and was not intended to produce, a consistent set of estimates for all countries covering a significantly long period of time, nor does it venture into the riskier territory of theory construction and falsification.

In this chapter, we attempt to move the discussion forward and generate adjusted estimates of mortality above age 5. We also engage directly in a discussion of the nature of forces that led to the sharp mortality decline in the region.

## Estimation of Adult Mortality in LAC During 1900–2000

### The State of Vital Statistics in the Region

Many countries of the LAC region have carried out censuses at regular intervals since 1900. And in most of them, the establishment of a vital statistics system has made possible the collection of information on births, deaths, and marriages since at least 1940 and from as early as 1900–1920 in only a handful of them. Andean and some Central American countries—suspected to have the highest levels of mortality—have yet to develop thorough vital statistics systems and only erratically carried out national censuses, though this has improved since 1970.

We concentrate exclusively on mortality above age 5 two reasons. First, this chapter mostly reviews and identifies trends in adult mortality that are usually quite distinct from trends in childhood mortality. Second, the adjustment of mortality estimates before age 5 must rely almost exclusively on sources other than vital statistics (that is, indirect methods), and requires special procedures to join them together with estimates of mortality above age 5 to arrive at a unique life table. Our aim was to rely exclusively on estimates derived from two sources, censuses and vital statistics, with no support from external assumptions regarding age patterns of mortality.

Armed with a series of censuses and intercensal vital statistics, it would be a routine matter to construct a series of life tables extending as far back as 1900–1920 for some countries or to 1950 for all of them, were it not for the fact that the mortality rates thus calculated are affected by three types of errors: completeness of death registration, completeness of census enumeration, and age misreporting.

### Completeness of Death Registration

The first type of error and the one to which demographers have devoted most of their attention is due to the fact that vital statistics are incomplete. In some countries, such as the Dominican Republic for example, the completeness of death registration was not higher than 60–70% as recently as 1990. In others, such as Mexico, vital statistics improved steadily over time to the point that unadjusted estimates of life expectancy are deceiving and may give the impression of an excessively slow upward trend. Finally, in other countries, such as Argentina, vital statistics have been virtually complete for many years, although their quality fluctuates from year to year and, more likely, from decade to decade.

### Completeness of Census Enumeration

The second difficulty is that completeness of census enumeration is highly variable and, in some cases, well below acceptable standards. Not all countries carry out post-enumeration surveys to calibrate censuses and pinpoint with some precision the amount of under (over) count. Furthermore, the naïve assumption that census coverage inevitably improves over time, which is roughly satisfied in the case of vital events, is not always realistic as census coverage can fluctuate sharply, following the vagaries of political transformations, economic crises, and the dynamics of internal population displacements.

## Age Misstatement

The two aforementioned problems can lead to estimated mortality rates that are too high, too low, or right on the mark. Thus, unless we have the means to estimate the completeness of death registration *relative* to census coverage, we will not be able to construct accurate life tables, let alone an accurate time series of life expectancy. A number of methods developed in the late 1970s had as a central objective the estimation of relative completeness of death enumeration (see, for examples, Bennet and Horiuchi 1981; Brass 1975; Hill 1987; Martin 1980; Preston 1983).

Most of these methods are flexible, do not rely on stifling assumptions about stability of the population or age patterns of mortality, and are simple to apply. Although it can be shown that these procedures produce satisfactory results when all assumptions on which they rest are approximately satisfied, none of them addresses the third difficulty we face when attempting to estimate mortality in a context with deficient statistics. This difficulty is that there appears to be a large amount of age misstatement both in censuses and deaths. By this we mean not just age heaping (or concentration around preferred digits), but a systematic propensity to over (under) state the true age.

Surprisingly enough, rising awareness about the potentially harmful effects of age misstatement on mortality estimates attracted widespread attention in the United States with the controversy about the so-called "mortality crossover," according to which the survival curves of US blacks tended to converge toward or even crossover that of whites. Some researchers attributed this to the role of unmeasured heterogeneity (Vaupel et al. 1979, whereas others argued that convergence and/or a crossover was an artifact of race differentials in age overstatement (Coale and Kisker 1990; Preston et al. 1996).

The idea that age overstatement could lead to misleading results was extended by Preston and colleagues to other developed countries (Condran et al. 1991) as well as to a handful of countries in Latin America (Dechter and Preston 1991; Grushka and Preston 1995) and to Puerto Rico (Rosenwaike and Preston 1984). In a nutshell, the main finding of this body of research is this: in most countries of the LAC region, there is a pronounced and systematic tendency to overstate ages both in census and death statistics, but much more so in the latter than the former. This tendency is particularly strong at older ages (above ages 45 or 50 and especially above age 60). The pattern is pervasive and affects all countries with available vital statistics (Dechter and Preston 1991; Grushka 1996; Grushka and Preston 1995). Furthermore, although there are empirical indications that age overstatement diminishes over time, the trend is by no means uniform, because it is confounded with the contribution of errors associated with coverage in censuses and vital statistics. Our own investigation suggests that, after adjusting for completeness of death registration and errors of census coverage, the levels and patterns of age overstatement experience noticeable amelioration over time.

The most important problem posed by a pattern whereby age overstatement of deaths dominates age overstatement in the population is that mortality rates will be systematically biased downward at older ages, with the resulting overestimation of life expectancy for the older population.[2] Furthermore, the age pattern of mortality will appear to be one where the level of mortality over age 60 is lower than expected, given the level of mortality prevailing in the age span 5–60. As

---

[2] Overstatement of ages in the population always leads to underestimates of the mortality rates provided that (a) the proportion overstating ages is invariant or increases with age and (b) the age distribution slopes downward as age increases. The effect of age overstatement of ages at death is not straightforward, since it depends on three factors: (a) the age-dependency of the proportion of deaths whose ages are overstated, (b) the magnitude of the downward slope of the age distribution at older ages, and (c) the magnitude of the upward slope of the force of mortality at older ages. In most countries of the regions, there are conditions that translate overstatement of ages at death into under (not over) estimation of mortality rates at older ages. If so, age overstatement of population and deaths will have offsetting effects and may actually lead to overstatement (not under) of mortality rates.

a consequence, the study of the relationship between early and late adult mortality and especially longevity and its progression over time can be severely compromised. The biases on estimates of life expectancy at age 5 are of lesser magnitude, since the proportion of years lived over age 60 or so is, as a norm, not high relative to the proportion lived over age 5. But as mortality improves, the proportion of years lived over 60 as a proportion of years lived over 5 tends to increase more rapidly than the proportion of years lived between 5 and 60. As a result, the persistence of patterns of age overstatement of deaths will lead to biases in estimates of life expectancy at age 5 that, *ceteris paribus*, will increase in magnitude as mortality improves. This, in turn, will lead to the misleading impression that the pace of gains is more rapid than it really is.

## Methods for the Adjustment of Observed Death Rates

In a companion paper (Palloni and Pinto 2004), we describe in detail the strategy to adjust observed intercensal death rates. What follows is a sketchy summary of the procedure.

We first estimate relative completeness of any two consecutive censuses using a procedures suggested by Brass (1975). As first intuited by Hill (2002), this estimate is remarkably robust to departures from stability and age misstatement. We then use this estimate to obtain corrected age-specific intercensal rates of population growth. These are then used as inputs for the method first proposed by Bennett and Horiuchi (1981) to estimate relative completeness of death registration under conditions of non-stability.[3] The final step consists of using estimates obtained from simulations of age misstatement to retrieve the level of net overstatement of both population and deaths once these are adjusted for completeness. The level of net overstatement is relative to a standard pattern of age over (under) statement, referred to as the "Costa Rican standard," for it was derived from the only empirical research that establishes a relation between "true" age and age declared in a census for a representative sample of a national population (Rosero and Brenes 2003). We assume that this observed pattern underlies both the age pattern of age misstatement of population censuses and the age pattern of misstatement of age at deaths in all countries of the region (Palloni and Pinto 2004).[4] Table 5.1 shows a list of countries and census years as well as intercensal deaths that were used in the estimation exercise.

Table 5.2 displays the adjusted values of life expectancy at ages 5 and 60 for males and females for all intercensal periods in the countries included in the data base.

## Evaluation of Estimates

To evaluate the quality of our estimates, we follow two strategies. The first contrasts our estimates of life expectancies at age 5 and 60 with alternative ones. The second examines the implied age patterns of the adjusted adult mortality estimates and searches for anomalies to reveal residual errors.

## Global Assessment: Alternative Estimates[5]

For the period 1950–2000, there are alternative estimates of life expectancy at age 5 and 60. For the period prior to 1950, there are a handful of estimates available to us. In the post-1950 period, the estimates of life expectancy at age 5 and 60 that we use in this chapter are always slightly higher (by not more than 5%) that those from CELADE. We suspect that this behavior is due to the fact that CELADE estimates may be constructed adjusting separately, rather than jointly as

---

[3] In a companion paper (Palloni and Pinto 2004), we justify the choice of Bennet-Horiuchi methods as the one producing minimum errors over a variety of simulated conditions.

[4] Note that we are not requiring that the level of age misstatement be the same as the Costa Rican but only the age pattern.

[5] To save space, we only provide a brief evaluation based on tables and figures that are available on request from the authors.

**Table 5.1** Countries and data sets used in the estimation exercise

| Countries | Census | Deaths | Countries | Census | Deaths |
|---|---|---|---|---|---|
| Argentina | 1947 | 1947–1960 | Guatemala | 1950 | 1950–1964 |
| | 1960 | 1960–1970 | | 1964 | 1964–1973 |
| | 1970 | 1970–1980 | | 1973 | 1973–1981 |
| | 1980 | 1980–1991 | | 1981 | 1981–1994 |
| | 1991 | 1991–2001 | | 1994 | 1994–2002 |
| | 2001 | | | 2002 | |
| Brazil | 1980 | 1980–1991 | Honduras | 1950 | 1950–1961 |
| | 1991 | 1991–2000 | | 1961 | 1961–1974 |
| | 2000 | | | 1974 | 1974–1988 |
| | | | | 1988 | |
| Chile | 1920 | 1920–1930 | Mexico | 1921 | 1921–1930 |
| | 1930 | 1930–1940 | | 1930 | 1930–1940 |
| | 1940 | 1940–1952 | | 1940 | 1940–1950 |
| | 1952 | 1952–1960 | | 1950 | 1950–1960 |
| | 1960 | 1960–1970 | | 1960 | 1960–1970 |
| | 1970 | 1970–1982 | | 1970 | 1970–1980 |
| | 1982 | 1982–1992 | | 1980 | 1980–1990 |
| | 1992 | 1992–2002 | | 1990 | 1990–2000 |
| | 2002 | | | 2000 | |
| Colombia | 1938 | 1938–1951 | Nicaragua | 1950 | 1950–1963 |
| | 1951 | 1951–1964 | | 1963 | 1963–1971 |
| | 1964 | 1964–1973 | | 1971 | 1971–1995 |
| | 1973 | 1973–1985 | | 1995 | |
| | 1985 | 1985–1993 | | | |
| | 1993 | 1993–2001 | | | |
| | 2001 | | | | |
| Costa Rica | 1927 | 1927–1950 | Panama | 1950 | 1950–1960 |
| | 1950 | 1950–1963 | | 1960 | 1960–1970 |
| | 1963 | 1963–1973 | | 1970 | 1970–1980 |
| | 1973 | 1973–1984 | | 1980 | 1980–1990 |
| | 1984 | 1984–2000 | | 1990 | 1990–2000 |
| | 2000 | | | 2000 | |
| Cuba | 1953 | 1953–1970 | Paraguay | 1950 | 1950–1962 |
| | 1970 | 1970–1981 | | 1962 | 1962–1972 |
| | 1981 | 1981–2002 | | 1972 | 1972–1982 |
| | 2002 | | | 1982 | 1982–1992 |
| | | | | 1992 | 1992–2002 |
| | | | | 2002 | |
| Dominican Republic | 1950 | 1950–1960 | Peru | 1961 | 1961–1972 |
| | 1960 | 1960–1970 | | 1972 | 1972–1981 |
| | 1970 | 1970–1981 | | 1981 | 1981–1993 |
| | 1981 | 1981–1993 | | 1993 | 1993–2005 |
| | 1993 | 1993–2002 | | 2005 | |
| | 2002 | | | | |
| Ecuador | 1950 | 1950–1962 | Uruguay | 1963 | 1963–1975 |
| | 1962 | 1962–1974 | | 1975 | 1975–1985 |
| | 1974 | 1974–1982 | | 1985 | 1985–1996 |
| | 1982 | 1982–1990 | | 1996 | 1996–2004 |
| | 1990 | 1990–2001 | | 2004 | |
| | 2001 | | | | |
| El Salvador | 1950 | 1950–1961 | Venezuela | 1950 | 1950–1961 |
| | 1961 | 1961–1971 | | 1961 | 1961–1971 |
| | 1971 | 1971–1992 | | 1971 | 1971–1981 |
| | 1992 | | | 1981 | 1981–1990 |
| | | | | 1990 | 1990–2001 |
| | | | | 2001 | |

Note: In all cases we used reported 5-year distributions, which were converted into single-year distributions by applying Sprague multipliers.
Source: United Nations Demographic Yearbooks.

**Table 5.2** Life expectation at ages 5 and 60, Latin America countries 1925–2000

|  |  | Males |  | Females |  |
|---|---|---|---|---|---|
| Countries | Years | E5 | E60 | E5 | E60 |
| **Forerunners** | | | | | |
| Argentina | 1953 | 60.9 | 14.4 | 65.8 | 17.7 |
| | 1965 | 62.4 | 15.0 | 69.1 | 19.3 |
| | 1975 | 63.7 | 15.8 | 70.2 | 19.9 |
| | 1985 | 64.8 | 16.2 | 71.7 | 20.7 |
| | 1996 | 66.3 | 17.2 | 73.0 | 21.6 |
| Chile | 1925 | 46.8 | 12.5 | 48.0 | 13.2 |
| | 1935 | 49.5 | 12.5 | 51.0 | 13.9 |
| | 1946 | 52.1 | 13.1 | 55.4 | 15.0 |
| | 1956 | 58.7 | 14.8 | 62.7 | 16.8 |
| | 1965 | 59.8 | 15.4 | 65.1 | 17.8 |
| | 1976 | 61.8 | 15.7 | 68.1 | 19.1 |
| | 1987 | 65.9 | 17.5 | 72.1 | 20.8 |
| | 1997 | 68.8 | 19.1 | 74.4 | 22.4 |
| Costa Rica | 1938 | 52.8 | 12.8 | 54.8 | 13.9 |
| | 1956 | 64.1 | 17.0 | 66.5 | 18.4 |
| | 1968 | 66.6 | 18.2 | 70.0 | 19.9 |
| | 1978 | 68.5 | 19.3 | 72.9 | 21.5 |
| | 1992 | 70.9 | 20.8 | 75.5 | 23.4 |
| Cuba | 1961 | 63.8 | 16.4 | 66.1 | 17.9 |
| | 1975 | 67.9 | 18.3 | 71.2 | 20.7 |
| | 1991 | 68.8 | 19.4 | 72.1 | 21.3 |
| Panama | 1955 | 60.6 | 15.7 | 61.8 | 17.3 |
| | 1965 | 64.1 | 16.9 | 65.8 | 18.4 |
| | 1975 | 66.1 | 18.1 | 68.9 | 19.8 |
| | 1985 | 67.9 | 19.1 | 72.3 | 21.5 |
| | 1995 | 69.0 | 20.2 | 74.0 | 22.9 |
| **Laggards** | | | | | |
| Brazil | 1985 | 61.5 | 15.8 | 68.1 | 18.5 |
| | 1995 | 63.0 | 17.0 | 70.2 | 20.3 |
| Colombia | 1944 | 52.9 | 13.9 | 55.8 | 15.1 |
| | 1957 | 59.2 | 15.8 | 61.5 | 16.7 |
| | 1968 | 61.0 | 15.2 | 64.7 | 17.5 |
| | 1979 | 62.9 | 16.7 | 68.2 | 19.0 |
| | 1989 | 63.8 | 18.4 | 70.2 | 19.9 |
| | 1999 | 64.7 | 19.3 | 72.1 | 21.2 |
| Dominican Republic | 1955 | 55.9 | 14.9 | 58.7 | 16.9 |
| | 1965 | 59.7 | 15.3 | 63.1 | 17.7 |
| | 1975 | 62.5 | 16.0 | 66.0 | 18.4 |
| | 1987 | 64.5 | 17.4 | 69.5 | 19.9 |
| | 1997 | 66.2 | 19.2 | 72.1 | 22.0 |
| Ecuador | 1956 | 56.1 | 15.8 | 57.2 | 16.5 |
| | 1968 | 60.9 | 16.7 | 62.7 | 17.7 |
| | 1978 | 63.7 | 18.2 | 67.3 | 19.7 |
| | 1986 | 65.5 | 18.7 | 69.4 | 20.2 |
| | 1995 | 67.2 | 21.0 | 71.4 | 22.1 |
| El Salvador | 1955 | 52.9 | 14.5 | 56.2 | 15.5 |
| | 1966 | 59.0 | 16.1 | 62.6 | 17.2 |
| | 1981 | 55.6 | 16.2 | 66.0 | 18.6 |

**Table 5.2** (continued)

| Countries | Years | Males E5 | Males E60 | Females E5 | Females E60 |
|---|---|---|---|---|---|
| Guatemala | 1957 | 51.7 | 14.0 | 52.8 | 14.4 |
|  | 1968 | 55.8 | 15.3 | 58.0 | 15.9 |
|  | 1977 | 57.6 | 16.2 | 61.3 | 17.0 |
|  | 1987 | 59.5 | 16.6 | 64.7 | 18.1 |
|  | 1998 | 62.0 | 18.8 | 68.1 | 19.9 |
| Honduras | 1955 | 51.4 | 15.3 | 54.0 | 16.1 |
|  | 1967 | 56.9 | 15.4 | 58.4 | 16.4 |
|  | 1981 | 61.4 | 17.1 | 65.0 | 17.9 |
| Mexico | 1925 | 43.8 | 12.9 | 46.7 | 12.9 |
|  | 1935 | 45.4 | 12.3 | 47.0 | 12.2 |
|  | 1945 | 50.8 | 13.8 | 53.9 | 14.4 |
|  | 1955 | 57.1 | 15.9 | 60.1 | 16.4 |
|  | 1965 | 60.5 | 16.9 | 63.8 | 17.7 |
|  | 1975 | 62.9 | 17.9 | 67.5 | 19.3 |
|  | 1985 | 64.1 | 18.4 | 70.5 | 20.6 |
|  | 1995 | 67.6 | 20.0 | 72.2 | 21.4 |
| Nicaragua | 1956 | 51.5 | 13.8 | 54.2 | 14.2 |
|  | 1967 | 56.2 | 15.0 | 59.4 | 15.6 |
|  | 1983 | 60.4 | 16.9 | 65.8 | 18.1 |
| Paraguay | 1956 | 62.4 | 16.3 | 66.1 | 19.0 |
|  | 1967 | 63.1 | 16.4 | 67.1 | 19.3 |
|  | 1977 | 64.2 | 16.6 | 68.2 | 19.4 |
|  | 1987 | 66.2 | 17.5 | 69.4 | 19.6 |
|  | 1997 | 67.0 | 18.5 | 70.9 | 20.6 |
| Peru | 1966 | 57.7 | 15.2 | 59.9 | 16.9 |
|  | 1976 | 61.9 | 16.6 | 65.4 | 18.8 |
|  | 1987 | 64.6 | 17.9 | 68.1 | 19.8 |
|  | 1999 | 66.0 | 18.4 | 70.5 | 20.7 |
| Uruguay | 1969 | 63.6 | 15.4 | 69.9 | 19.3 |
|  | 1980 | 64.8 | 16.1 | 71.1 | 20.1 |
|  | 1990 | 65.6 | 16.3 | 72.5 | 21.0 |
|  | 2000 | 66.5 | 17.2 | 73.9 | 22.3 |
| Venezuela | 1955 | 58.5 | 14.5 | 60.4 | 15.8 |
|  | 1966 | 61.4 | 15.3 | 65.0 | 17.2 |
|  | 1976 | 63.2 | 16.5 | 68.2 | 18.8 |
|  | 1985 | 65.2 | 17.6 | 71.0 | 20.5 |
|  | 1995 | 66.0 | 18.7 | 71.7 | 21.1 |

Source: Own estimates using data from U.N. Demographic Yearbooks.

we do here, for completeness of death registration and censuses. To test this, we performed a few experiments which suggest that CELADE's estimates may take into account only completeness of death registration, sometimes ignoring entirely census completeness (Jaspers and Orellana 1996). By and large, though, both sets of estimates are quite consistent with regard to trends.

For the pre-1960 period, we were able to contrast our estimates with those calculated by Arriaga (1968). Of a total of 62 possible comparisons, 16 are for the period before 1950 and involve Brazil, Chile, Colombia, Costa Rica, and Mexico. In all these cases, Arriaga's estimates are lower than ours by 0.5–4 years. Of the remaining contrasts, 24 pertain to the period 1950–1959, and in the bulk of these cases, Arriaga's estimates are either very close or slightly lower (not more than 5%) than ours. For the period 1960–1969 (22 contrasts), Arriaga's estimates are slightly higher than ours. This result for the most recent period is consistent with expectations: the backbone of Arriaga's method, the assumption of stability, is weaker after the year 1950 for some countries and after 1960 for all of them. A quasi-stable population induced by mortality decline will lead the observer who assumes stability to underestimate the force of mortality. Since our adjusted life expectancies do not depend on stability, they are not affected by mortality decline and we should expect them to be, *ceteris paribus*, lower than those derived from a procedure that assumes stability. It is more difficult to explain why Arriaga's estimates are lower than ours for the period when these populations were approximately stable, that is, before 1950. One possible explanation is that since our estimates depend on mortality statistics whereas those of Arriaga's depend only on population enumerations, the error associated with age exaggeration of deaths imparts a larger upward bias to our estimates of life expectancy than to those from Arriaga's. But if this is so for Brazil 1945–1950, Chile 1920–1945, Colombia 1940–1950, and Costa Rica 1930–1945, why this is not also the case for Mexico 1930–1950, or, for that matter, for any of the other countries with more deficient vital registration systems?

An important factor to consider is that whereas we adjust intercensal rates of increase for relative under (over) enumeration in population censuses, Arriaga does not. It is well known that errors in the observed rate of natural increase lead to sizeable biases in stable-based estimates (Coale and Demeny 1967), though the direction of these biases will depend on the nature of the under (over) count and should not always lead to overstated estimates of mortality.

Despite these caveats, we should not make too much of the observed discrepancies for two reasons. First, only in a few cases do they exceed 5%. The worst discrepancies are for Paraguay, a wretched case for which the stable population assumption is completely unrealistic, since the age distribution is severely distorted by wars that devastated the male population. Second, for periods when we cannot produce estimates due to lack of vital statistics, our estimates line up remarkably well with those produced by Arriaga for the earlier period. The consistency is so tight that simple linear backward extrapolations of our estimates yield values that are indistinguishable from those obtained by Arriaga, *precisely for the period when the assumption of stability was more reasonable*. In summary, the contrasts with Arriaga's estimates suggest that there are some irregularities in a few of our estimates perhaps attributable to age misstatement, but also that there is an overall consistency in the estimation of trends.

## *Local Assessments: Age Patterns*

An important innovation of our estimates is that they include adjustments for age overstatement, a flaw known to be pervasive in Latin American's vital statistics and censuses. To check the outcome of these adjustments, we calculate "expected values" for life expectancy at age 60 implied by our estimates of life expectancy at age 5 using all four Coale-Demeny model mortality patterns. We know that age overstatement is more likely to occur at ages over 45 or 50 (Dechter and Preston 1991) and that this should impart an upward bias to life expectancies above those ages, but particularly at ages over 60. If age overstatement swamps our estimates, the expected life expectancy at age 60 from Coale-Demeny life tables with equivalent life expectancy at age 5 should be always lower than our estimates *regardless* of model pattern. This is not the case. Indeed, as shown in Fig. 5.1, the values implied by the North model lead to a quasi normal dispersion of deviations centered at 0, as it should be if there is no systematic deviation from the pattern. Instead, the deviations associated with the remaining models are almost always centered at values well over 0. Why should the North model lead to a "better" fit of adult patterns of mortality?

One explanation is related to the nature of the morbidity and mortality regimes that underlie the Coale-Demeny North model life table. This model is based on mortality in Northern European countries, most of which experienced high endemicity of respiratory tuberculosis (TB) before the beginning of the twentieth century (Coale and Demeny 1966). Thus, life expectancy at age 5 should be lower relative to life expectancy at older ages in the North model when compared to other model mortality patterns due to the presence of selection, because high prevalence of active TB inflates mortality levels for younger adults relative to that of older adults. Is this consistent with the experience of the LAC region? Although TB was endemic in some of these countries, and levels of mortality due to TB around 1950–1960 remained quite high, we find only a weak relationship between the

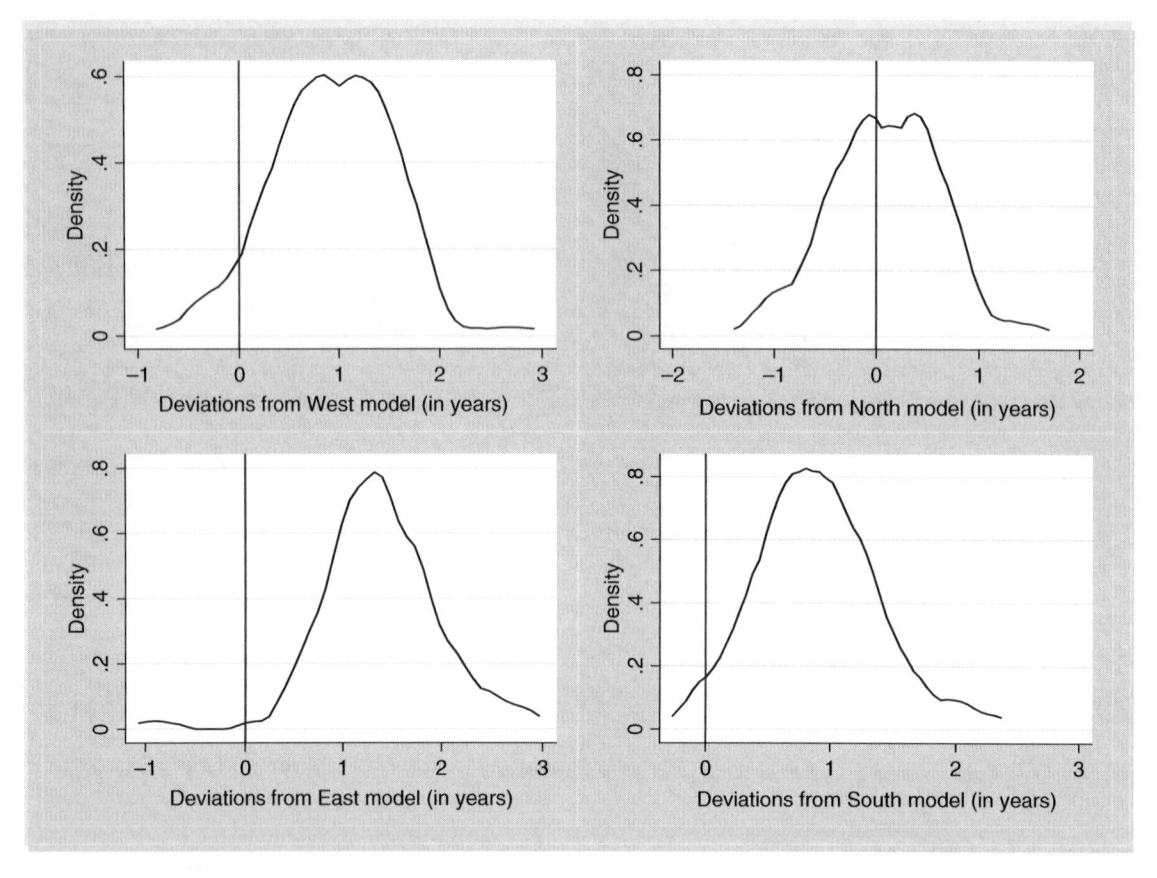

**Fig. 5.1** Differences between observed and expected life expectancies at age 5, for West, North, East, and South Models, LAC countries, 1925–2000

magnitude of deviations associated with all four sets of deviations and lagged mortality rates due to TB in all age groups.[6]

A second feature of interest is that the absolute magnitude of deviations between observed and expected life expectancy at age 60 increases gradually over time. This is inconsistent with the explanation invoking prevalence of respiratory TB, as this would lead one to expect that deviations should *decrease over time*, apace with the dissolution of a mortality regime with high endemicity of respiratory TB. Overall, we conclude that one cannot impute the observed agreement with the North model and the pattern of deviations from the other models to the influence of respiratory TB.

It is indeed possible that our adjusted mortality rates may still be contaminated by age overstatement that *mimics the effects that past levels of respiratory TB would impart on the age pattern of mortality*. That is, the similarity between LAC adult mortality patterns and those in the North model could be an artifact of age overstatement. But this interpretation is also unsupported by the data. Evidence for severe age overstatement decreases sharply and steadily over time, as shown by the systematic convergence to unity of the age-specific ratio of expected to observed deaths. As an illustration, Table 5.3 displays these ratios for two countries. Ratios for other country-intercensal periods

---

[6] We used mortality rates due to TB for age groups 0–19, 20–39, 40–59, and 60+ with lags of 5 and 10 years. Rates were averaged over 5 and then over 10 years prior to the time for which we had the measure of model pattern deviation. We used pooled estimators of effects and in no case did we obtain a positive and significant effect of mortality rates due to TB and magnitude of the deviations. On the assumption that the observed deviation could be due to age overstatement and mortality rates due to TB, we also estimated a fixed effect model (that assumes that effects of age overstatement are invariant over time). But the expected patterns did not materialize.

**Table 5.3** Ratio of enumerated to expected population in Chile and Uruguay

| Age groups | 1930–1940 | 1940–1952 | 1960–1970 | 1982–1992 | 1992–2002 | 1963–1975 | 1975–1985 | 1985–1996 | 1996–2004 |
|---|---|---|---|---|---|---|---|---|---|
| | | | Chile | | | | Uruguay | | |
| Males | | | | | | | | | |
| 40+ | 1.749 | 1.639 | 1.398 | 1.437 | 1.412 | 1.379 | 1.336 | 1.310 | 1.264 |
| 45+ | 1.104 | 1.006 | 0.994 | 1.049 | 1.025 | 0.993 | 1.009 | 1.017 | 0.993 |
| 50+ | 1.188 | 1.100 | 1.027 | 1.067 | 1.047 | 0.999 | 1.029 | 1.033 | 1.008 |
| 55+ | 1.311 | 1.141 | 1.078 | 1.099 | 1.070 | 1.026 | 1.052 | 1.052 | 1.014 |
| 60+ | 1.468 | 1.268 | 1.073 | 1.105 | 1.070 | 1.052 | 1.077 | 1.075 | 1.027 |
| 65+ | 3.505 | 2.320 | 1.200 | 1.160 | 1.108 | 1.145 | 1.151 | 1.160 | 1.037 |
| 70+ | (–) | (–) | 1.488 | 1.319 | 1.175 | 1.295 | 1.205 | 1.313 | 1.084 |
| Females | | | | | | | | | |
| 40+ | 1.632 | 1.538 | 1.336 | 1.359 | 1.332 | 1.315 | 1.295 | 1.241 | 1.210 |
| 45+ | 1.096 | 1.030 | 0.986 | 1.037 | 1.010 | 1.000 | 1.026 | 1.013 | 0.992 |
| 50+ | 1.212 | 1.123 | 1.023 | 1.058 | 1.032 | 1.020 | 1.051 | 1.026 | 1.004 |
| 55+ | 1.344 | 1.213 | 1.062 | 1.081 | 1.049 | 1.046 | 1.086 | 1.040 | 1.006 |
| 60+ | 1.577 | 1.394 | 1.065 | 1.110 | 1.054 | 1.090 | 1.115 | 1.069 | 1.018 |
| 65+ | 7.325 | 4.450 | 1.254 | 1.199 | 1.108 | 1.230 | 1.227 | 1.147 | 1.020 |
| 70+ | (–) | (–) | 1.639 | 1.438 | 1.201 | 1.545 | 1.394 | 1.288 | 1.069 |

Note: In parenthesis are negative values.
Source: Own estimates using data from UN Demographic Yearbooks.

show similar patterns. A decrease in the value of the indicator in Table 5.3 signals certain decrease in the severity of age overstatement. But this improvement over time is incompatible with the foregoing interpretation that attributes over time increases of deviations from model patterns to age overstatement. We cannot have it both ways: either the deviations from model patterns increase over time due to increased severity of age overstatement, in which case the indicator in Table 5.3 should have a behavior opposite to the observed one, or the indicator in Table 5.3 reflects a true decrease in age overstatement, in which case the increased deviations from model patterns must be unrelated to age overstatement and instead may reveal a peculiarity of old-age mortality in the region.

An alternative test is to contrast the age pattern of adjusted old-age mortality in countries of the region with those obtained for developed countries. To do this, we estimate models of the following form:

$$\ln\left(\frac{Mx}{1-Mx}\right) = \alpha + \beta\varphi(x)$$

where $\varphi(x)$ is the logit transform of a standard set of mortality rates estimated by Himes et al. (1994). Systematic overstatement of ages at death must lead to two outcomes. The first is a downward bias (away from unity) in the estimate of $\beta$. The second is an exaggeration of the absolute value of $\alpha$.[7] Estimates of $\beta$ systematically below 1 and relatively high negative values of $\alpha$ are consistent with the conjecture about age overstatement. Table 5.4 displays the estimates of both parameters for the populations included in our analyses. A glance at the table reveals an important feature: estimates of $\beta$ are systematically below one but much less so in the past than in recent years. This is consistent with the conjecture of gradual improvements in declaration of ages at death. The behavior of the parameter $\alpha$ is, as it should be, a bit more erratic as it reflects both the push of changes in levels of mortality and the impact of age overstatement, both of which will lead to increments in its absolute magnitude. With some exceptions, the estimated (absolute) values of $\alpha$ increase regularly over time. An important feature is that countries reputed to have the best quality vital statistics (Argentina, Chile, Costa Rica, Cuba, Panama, and Uruguay) all yield estimates of $\beta$ that are close to 1, particularly in the most recent periods.

---

[7] If $\alpha$ is held constant, sub-estimation of $Mx$ produced by age overstatement should lead to *overestimates* of $\beta$. However, when both parameters are free to vary, the best linear fit is always achieved at the expense of a more negative value of $\alpha$ and an estimate of $\beta$ that is smaller than one.

**Table 5.4** Estimated coefficient of the regression between the logit of old-age mortality rates in LAC countries and European mortality standard, 1925–2000

|  |  | Males |  | Females |  |
|---|---|---|---|---|---|
| Countries | Years | α | β | α | β |
| **Forerunners** | | | | | |
| Argentina | 1953 | −0.061 | 0.874 | −0.132 | 0.860 |
|  | 1965 | −0.156 | 0.880 | −0.169 | 0.911 |
|  | 1975 | −0.287 | 0.870 | −0.219 | 0.921 |
|  | 1985 | −0.199 | 0.911 | −0.233 | 0.947 |
|  | 1996 | −0.311 | 0.922 | −0.442 | 0.924 |
| Chile | 1925 | −0.240 | 0.712 | −0.136 | 0.684 |
|  | 1935 | −0.264 | 0.713 | −0.128 | 0.711 |
|  | 1946 | −0.380 | 0.713 | −0.235 | 0.729 |
|  | 1956 | −0.518 | 0.746 | −0.302 | 0.776 |
|  | 1965 | −0.689 | 0.709 | −0.388 | 0.782 |
|  | 1976 | −0.521 | 0.781 | −0.361 | 0.840 |
|  | 1987 | −0.413 | 0.889 | −0.285 | 0.930 |
|  | 1997 | −0.436 | 0.955 | −0.409 | 0.955 |
| Costa Rica | 1938 | −0.320 | 0.727 | 0.008 | 0.756 |
|  | 1956 | −0.815 | 0.844 | −0.662 | 0.817 |
|  | 1968 | −0.412 | 0.927 | −0.311 | 0.894 |
|  | 1978 | −0.593 | 0.915 | −0.401 | 0.925 |
|  | 1992 | −0.641 | 0.954 | −0.492 | 0.961 |
| Cuba | 1961 | −0.193 | 0.930 | −0.158 | 0.865 |
|  | 1975 | −0.295 | 0.986 | −0.442 | 0.893 |
|  | 1991 | −0.440 | 0.961 | −0.365 | 0.918 |
| Panama | 1955 | −0.422 | 0.823 | −0.483 | 0.744 |
|  | 1965 | −0.266 | 0.920 | −0.343 | 0.826 |
|  | 1975 | −0.425 | 0.918 | −0.392 | 0.861 |
|  | 1985 | −0.454 | 0.948 | −0.385 | 0.922 |
|  | 1995 | −0.570 | 0.951 | −0.478 | 0.936 |
| **Laggards** | | | | | |
| Brazil | 1985 | −0.280 | 0.852 | −0.063 | 0.904 |
|  | 1995 | −0.557 | 0.817 | −0.433 | 0.862 |
| Colombia | 1944 | −0.485 | 0.717 | −0.408 | 0.692 |
|  | 1957 | −0.550 | 0.779 | −0.561 | 0.752 |
|  | 1968 | −0.379 | 0.835 | −0.142 | 0.794 |
|  | 1979 | −0.400 | 0.869 | −0.553 | 0.825 |
|  | 1989 | −0.576 | 0.872 | −0.317 | 0.885 |
|  | 1999 | −0.654 | 0.884 | −0.398 | 0.912 |
| Dominican | 1955 | −0.690 | 0.695 | −0.609 | 0.688 |
| Republic | 1965 | −0.467 | 0.799 | −0.611 | 0.726 |
|  | 1975 | −0.432 | 0.846 | −0.584 | 0.764 |
|  | 1987 | −0.546 | 0.866 | −0.500 | 0.850 |
|  | 1997 | −0.849 | 0.816 | −0.790 | 0.817 |
| Ecuador | 1956 | −0.670 | 0.760 | −0.415 | 0.730 |
|  | 1968 | −0.460 | 0.841 | −0.332 | 0.803 |
|  | 1978 | −0.773 | 0.801 | −0.574 | 0.811 |
|  | 1986 | −0.725 | 0.840 | −0.511 | 0.850 |
|  | 1995 | −1.050 | 0.775 | −0.817 | 0.795 |
| El Salvador | 1955 | −0.551 | 0.713 | −0.523 | 0.667 |
|  | 1966 | −0.646 | 0.755 | −0.512 | 0.729 |
|  | 1981 | −0.814 | 0.685 | −0.520 | 0.773 |

**Table 5.4** (continued)

| Countries | Years | Males α | Males β | Females α | Females β |
|---|---|---|---|---|---|
| Guatemala | 1957 | −0.584 | 0.687 | −0.229 | 0.682 |
| | 1968 | −0.635 | 0.722 | −0.333 | 0.741 |
| | 1977 | −0.708 | 0.731 | −0.313 | 0.782 |
| | 1987 | −0.705 | 0.749 | −0.346 | 0.806 |
| | 1998 | −1.016 | 0.718 | −0.589 | 0.796 |
| Honduras | 1955 | −1.031 | 0.599 | −0.898 | 0.582 |
| | 1967 | −0.419 | 0.801 | −0.219 | 0.753 |
| | 1981 | −0.582 | 0.830 | −0.321 | 0.824 |
| Mexico | 1925 | −0.681 | 0.590 | −0.145 | 0.661 |
| | 1935 | −0.418 | 0.655 | 0.194 | 0.728 |
| | 1945 | −0.526 | 0.691 | −0.149 | 0.731 |
| | 1955 | −0.748 | 0.705 | −0.352 | 0.748 |
| | 1965 | −0.785 | 0.735 | −0.432 | 0.773 |
| | 1975 | −1.016 | 0.709 | −0.653 | 0.774 |
| | 1985 | −0.850 | 0.769 | −0.563 | 0.835 |
| | 1995 | −0.950 | 0.799 | −0.586 | 0.855 |
| Nicaragua | 1956 | −0.547 | 0.694 | −0.532 | 0.635 |
| | 1967 | −0.843 | 0.663 | −0.905 | 0.592 |
| | 1983 | −0.775 | 0.745 | −0.578 | 0.749 |
| Paraguay | 1956 | −0.199 | 0.911 | −0.576 | 0.783 |
| | 1967 | −0.021 | 0.967 | −0.152 | 0.890 |
| | 1977 | −0.227 | 0.925 | −0.253 | 0.881 |
| | 1987 | −0.292 | 0.942 | −0.292 | 0.891 |
| | 1997 | −0.504 | 0.906 | −0.509 | 0.858 |
| Peru | 1966 | −0.657 | 0.722 | −0.510 | 0.723 |
| | 1976 | −0.584 | 0.803 | −0.550 | 0.783 |
| | 1987 | −0.549 | 0.861 | −0.512 | 0.826 |
| | 1999 | −0.533 | 0.894 | −0.534 | 0.857 |
| Uruguay | 1969 | −0.123 | 0.910 | −0.104 | 0.935 |
| | 1980 | −0.258 | 0.891 | −0.228 | 0.928 |
| | 1990 | −0.128 | 0.949 | −0.269 | 0.954 |
| | 2000 | −0.330 | 0.922 | −0.591 | 0.905 |
| Venezuela | 1955 | −0.351 | 0.789 | −0.316 | 0.738 |
| | 1966 | −0.427 | 0.808 | −0.388 | 0.775 |
| | 1976 | −0.574 | 0.804 | −0.454 | 0.809 |
| | 1985 | −0.616 | 0.833 | −0.525 | 0.848 |
| | 1995 | −0.707 | 0.842 | −0.533 | 0.863 |

Note: α is the constant and β the slope of the logistic model.

While this test shows that the behavior of our estimates of adult life expectancies is consistent with an interpretation invoking distortions due to overstatement of ages at death, it does not prove the case, much in the same way as the test based on the Coale-Demeny mortality patterns could not: true peculiarities of old-age mortality in the region could produce exactly the observed pattern.

In summary, evaluation of the quality of age adjustments of mortality rates is not unequivocal but instead sends painfully mixed signals. First, our estimates of life expectancy at age 5 line up fairly well with alternative estimates, and there are no strong signals that the adjustments result in systematic biases. Second, the estimated age patterns of mortality reveal evidence of peculiarities and one of the alternative explanations, but not the only one, is age at death overstatement. The evidence from model patterns is contradictory. On the one hand, findings from comparisons with Coale-Demeny mortality models are inconsistent with a view that singles out age overstatement as an important factor. On the other hand, evidence from comparisons with a modern standard of mortality at old ages behaves as we would expect if the adjusted estimates continue to contain effects of systematic age overstatement.

## Mortality Trends

Gains in life expectancy at age 5 during a period of time, say ($t$, $t+n$), are a function of the initial level of mortality associated with causes of death that contribute the most to mortality at time $t$ and that, simultaneously, are potentially more vulnerable to the effects of new infrastructure (water and sewage), diffusion of knowledge, adoption of new behaviors and public health interventions, improvements in standards of living and nutrition, and medical technology. Infrastructure refers to large undertakings designed to supply clean water and safe disposal of sewage. They require large investments and almost always depend on interventions by a central state. Diffusion of knowledge refers to new ideas that influence beneficial behavior, such as personal hygiene, that minimizes exposure to disease. As plentiful empirical evidence in Western Europe (McKeown 1976) and North America (Preston and Haines 1991) shows, the role of these factors is influential particularly at the beginning of the secular mortality change. Adoption of deleterious behaviors, such as diet, sedentary lifestyles, and smoking, become important brakes of mortality decline but only after the initial phase of the transition toward lower mortality. Due to lack of information, we can only speculate on their influence on illnesses such as diabetes, heart disease, and neoplasms. Improvements of standards of living and nutrition refer to average levels of per family income and supply of sources of calories (as opposed to nutritional status),[8] respectively. Finally, medical technology refers to resources generated by improved medical knowledge that are deployed to reduce exposure to disease (vector eradication campaigns), increase resistance (antibiotics and vaccines), and improve recovery (new medications and treatments).

Increases in life expectancy after 1950 were in all likelihood fueled by the widespread diffusion of medical technology, even though other determinants continued to play a role in most countries. The bulk of mortality improvements over age 5 associated with the diffusion of medical technology throughout the region must have taken place after 1950, since prior to that period, direct medical interventions on a massive scale were rare in most countries. The widespread diffusion of antibiotics, sulfas, and vaccines that made a significant dent on the prevalence of infectious diseases was not feasible before 1950 for two reasons. First, because generalized application of these innovations in more developed countries took well over 30 years and was not firmly established until the period around World War II. Second, because their implementation requires institutional strength and complexity which, with some exceptions, was not in place in LAC until much later, during the post-World War II period.

Increases in life expectancy that took place prior to 1950 are more reasonably attributed to one of two determinants. The first is deployment of public health measures, including large-scale infrastructure (water purification systems, piped water, sewage processing and disposal), foreign-funded campaigns to eradicate vector-borne diseases (mainly malaria, dengue, yellow fever), and sanitation techniques to prevent exposure in households and among individuals. The second determinant is increases in standards of living and improvements in nutrition.

The two determinants identified above reinforce each other and produce synergisms that prevent a clearcut attribution of effects to each one of them separately. For example, eradication of malaria through DDT spraying reduces exposure and has spillover effects by reinforcing individual immune function, thus promoting increased resistance to other infectious diseases. Similarly, reduction of incidence of diarrhea and other wasting intestinal conditions, a result of water purification, sewage treatment, and shifts in individual behavior, boost nutritional status, even in the absence of direct increases in nutrient intake. In turn, improved nutritional status strengthens individuals' resistance and recovery.

In what follows, we summarize the trajectory of gains in life expectancy at age 5 during the period 1950–2000 and, whenever possible, attempt to identify the determinants that played the most important role. To facilitate description, we divide our observations

---

[8] See Preston (1976) and Fogel and Costa (1997).

as follows: we classify as "forerunners" (Argentina, Chile, Costa Rica, Cuba, Panama, and Uruguay) countries that by 1950 had already attained levels of life expectancy at age 5 of 58.7 years among females and 56.6 years among males. These values correspond to life expectancies at age 5 attained by Norway around 1900, that is, after mortality had been declining for 50 or more years in *the absence of advances of medical technology*. Thus, the level attained around 1900 in Norway could only be associated with public health or better standards of living or a combination of the two. The remaining countries are classified as "laggards."

Figure 5.2 displays the values of life expectancies at age 5 (E5) for females by group of countries. Two lines are drawn at values of E5 for Norway during 1900 and 2005.[9] The estimated difference in E5 between the two groups of countries around 1950 was close to 4 years, but by the year 2000 it was reduced to no more than 2 years. The reduction in the difference between the two groups is explained by the fact that after 1950, the laggard group experiences the beneficial effects of medical technology, public health, and better standards of living simultaneously, whereas the forerunners had already succeeded in controlling an important fraction of infectious diseases before 1950. Thus, the diffusion effects of medical technology among the forerunners should have been more muted and contributed somewhat less to gains in life expectancy.[10]

Gains in life expectancy at age 5 during a period of time, say $(t, t+n)$, are a function of the initial level of mortality associated with causes of death that contribute the most to mortality at time $t$ and that, simultaneously, are potentially more vulnerable to the effects of new infrastructure (water and sewage), diffusion of knowledge and public health interventions,

improvements in standards of living and nutrition, and medical technology. We use McKeown's (1976) classification of diseases (waterborne, vector-borne, and airborne) to identify the relation between their initial levels and subsequent gains in life expectancy at age 5. We predict the relative rate of change in life expectancy at age 5 during a period, say $(t, t+k)$ as a function of lagged values of the log of the mortality rates for each of the groups of causes mentioned above. To attenuate the influence of fluctuations, we construct the average rate over the first 5 years prior to the beginning of the period (between $t–4$ and $t$) and then the average value over the second past 5 years (between $t–5$ and $t–9$). We will refer to these as the first and second lag, respectively. We should expect that relative changes in life expectancy at age 5 during the period $(t, t+k)$ should be responsive to changes in the determinants identified above. Since we do not have information on these changes, we use as a proxy the levels of mortality caused by illnesses that could be improved (more or less) by the unmeasured interventions. Thus, for example, in a country with high prevalence of malaria, an intervention designed to eradicate the vector will result in a sizeable change in life expectancy. If the intervention is inefficient or inexistent, it should have no effect on changes in life expectancy, regardless of how high the mortality level due to malaria may be. If instead mortality rates due to malaria are low, the interventions should have no effects regardless of how effective it might be. The expected relations are as follows:

| Intervention | | | | |
|---|---|---|---|---|
| Disease group | Eradication | Infrastructure (other public health) | Medical | Behavioral |
| Vector-borne | + | – | – | – |
| Waterborne | – | + | + | + |
| Airborne | – | – | + | + |

where "+" signifies that the intervention has strong impact, whereas "–" signifies that the intervention has weak impact. As an illustration, assume that vector-borne diseases weigh heavily on life expectancy at age 5 at time $t$ and that effective interventions are in place also at time $t$. We would then expect that the estimated effects of mortality rates due to vector-borne diseases (with pertinent lags) on the relative change in life expectancy at age 5 during the period $(t, t+k)$ will be

---

[9] It will not go unnoticed that the trends in both groups of countries are almost linear, with a slight but noticeable decreased slope in the last 10 years among forerunners. The same applies to trends of life expectancy at age 60 (see Part VIII). These regularities, combined with the fact that the rate of decline in infant and child mortality has decreased in the last 10 years, imply that the trajectory of life expectancy cannot be linear but rather must follow a quadratic form. This goes against inferences made by Oppen and Vaupel (2002) from a pooled sample of life expectancies using a mixture of countries with wildly heterogeneous mortality regimes.

[10] The graph for males is omitted since it leads to the same conclusions.

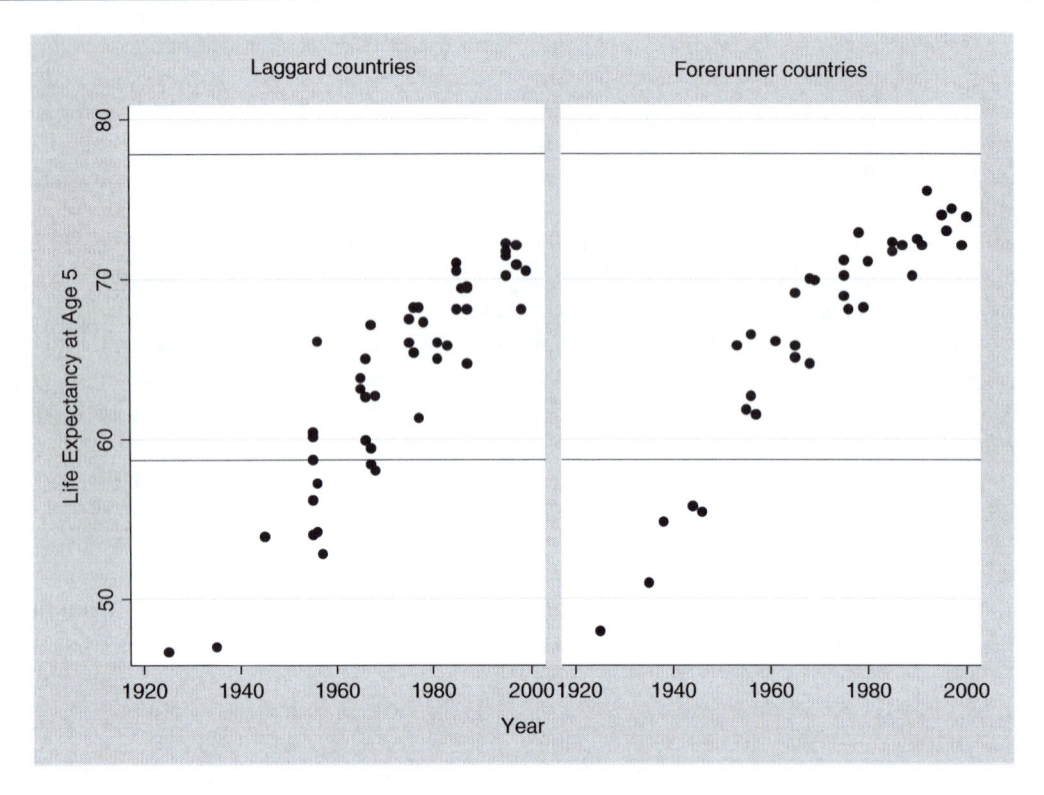

**Fig. 5.2** Female life expectancies at age 5 by Group of LAC Countries, 1925–2000

high and significant. Instead, if a group of causes exert little influence on life expectancy at age 5 and/or there are no efficient interventions in place, the relations will be weak.

Table 5.5 displays estimated regression coefficients using the first lag for the mortality rates and the absolute change in life expectancy between two successive intercensal periods.[11] The results are presented separately for each of the two groups of countries (laggards and forerunners). Vector-borne and waterborne diseases play the most important role for countries in the laggard group. Indeed, the effects of vector-borne mortality rates on the absolute change in life expectancies over two intercensal periods are substantial and statistically significant. Thus, for example, a 1% change in the magnitude of the initial level of mortality due to vector-borne diseases brings about a gain in life expectancy of about 0.023 per year. A similar change in waterborne diseases entails gains that are twice as large, 0.044 per year. Among forerunners, the heavy lifting is done by airborne diseases, as neither vector-borne nor waterborne diseases play an important role. A 1% increase in the initial levels of mortality due to airborne diseases potentiates life expectancy gains of the order of 0.044 per year.

These results are in agreement with expectations. First, with one or two exceptions (Cuba and Panama), vector-borne diseases were more prevalent among laggards and played no significant role in sculpting the mortality patterns among forerunners. Second, although eradication campaigns in Cuba and Panama began early in the century, most other countries experienced the benefits of vector eradication later in the century, mainly after World War II. Third, waterborne diseases were highly prevalent throughout LAC, but the large infrastructure required to contain them was in place before 1950 only among forerunners, not among laggards. This suggests that after 1950, they should

---

[11] Estimates in the table are from pooled sample. Fixed effects models yield somewhat different values for the estimates but lead to the same conclusions and are not presented here. The addition of lag 2 (10 years) does not improve model fit and was ignored.

**Table 5.5** Estimated coefficients of the regression between absolute change in life expectancy and lagged causes of death in LAC countries, 1950–2005

| Causes of deaths | All countries | Laggards countries | Forerunners countries |
|---|---|---|---|
| Vector-borne | 0.155* | 0.023* | 0.007 |
|  | (0.006) | (0.009) | (0.008) |
| Waterborne | 0.022 | 0.045* | 0.004 |
|  | (0.013) | (0.017) | (0.020) |
| Airborne | 0.020 | −0.004 | 0.044 |
|  | (0.022) | (0.027) | (0.038) |
| Intercept | 0.167 | 0.221 | 0.096 |
|  | (0.071) | (0.090) | (0.120) |
| Adj R-squared | 0.541 | 0.590 | 0.474 |
| N | 37 | 24 | 13 |

Note: The independent variables are the natural logarithm of the causes of death. (standard errors are in parentheses)
*$p < 0.05$.

have played a major role among the latter not the former. The data bear this out. Finally, airborne diseases (streptococcus pneumonia, respiratory TB, measles) are highly responsive to vaccination campaigns that were probably more efficiently implemented among forerunners and increasingly so during the post-World War II period. This is reflected in the stronger influence of airborne diseases on the absolute changes in life expectancies.

## The Contribution of Causes of Death

In this section, we summarize the contribution of groups of causes of deaths to gains in life expectancy between 1950 and 2000.

### Trends in Mortality by Causes of Death

Trends by causes of death in Latin American countries reflect advances in medical technology, improvement in health care systems, and changes in lifestyles and living conditions of their populations. As suggested by the "epidemiological transition" framework (Omran 1982), we find a sudden shift in the profile of deaths by causes and age groups from one dominated by communicable diseases to one swamped by chronic and degenerative diseases. However, in contrast to Omran's framework, we will also observe that in some countries, chronic diseases coexist with still prevalent infectious diseases.

Figure 5.3 a–f display time trends of leading groups of causes of death, namely, neoplasms, circulatory diseases, diabetes, infectious diseases, accidents and violence, and ill-defined causes in 18 Latin American countries. On average, these groups of causes account for nearly 70% of all deaths in the period under examination, from 1950 to 2005.

Figure 5.3a reveals mostly upward trends for neoplasms. There are some irregularities in the middle of the period but, by and large, the rates move up particularly during the last 10 years of the period examined. This increase in mortality due to neoplasms is universal: it applies to both genders and to forerunners as much as laggards, though there is important heterogeneity in the rates of acceleration.

Figure 5.3b shows evidence of large heterogeneity in trends of circulatory diseases, and there are only faintly discernible patterns. Among forerunners, mortality rates due to circulatory diseases tend to drop or to stay steady after the middle of the period (circa 1960–1970), whereas the majority of laggards experience increases from the beginning or from the middle of the period under examination. The drop among forerunners mirrors the experience of more developed countries where death rates due to circulatory diseases have come down substantially. The experience of laggards appears to follow the trajectory of countries that started the epidemiological transition more recently.

Figure 5.3c is perhaps the most telling. It shows an almost universal and sometimes sharp increase in mortality rates due to diabetes. Cuba, Costa Rica, and Uruguay are the only countries where the impact of diabetes remains steady, behaves somewhat erratically around fixed levels, or declines slightly. The sharp increase elsewhere is a hallmark of these countries, where the obesity epidemic has progressed swiftly, independently of the past history of mortality decline. An important similarity is that death rates

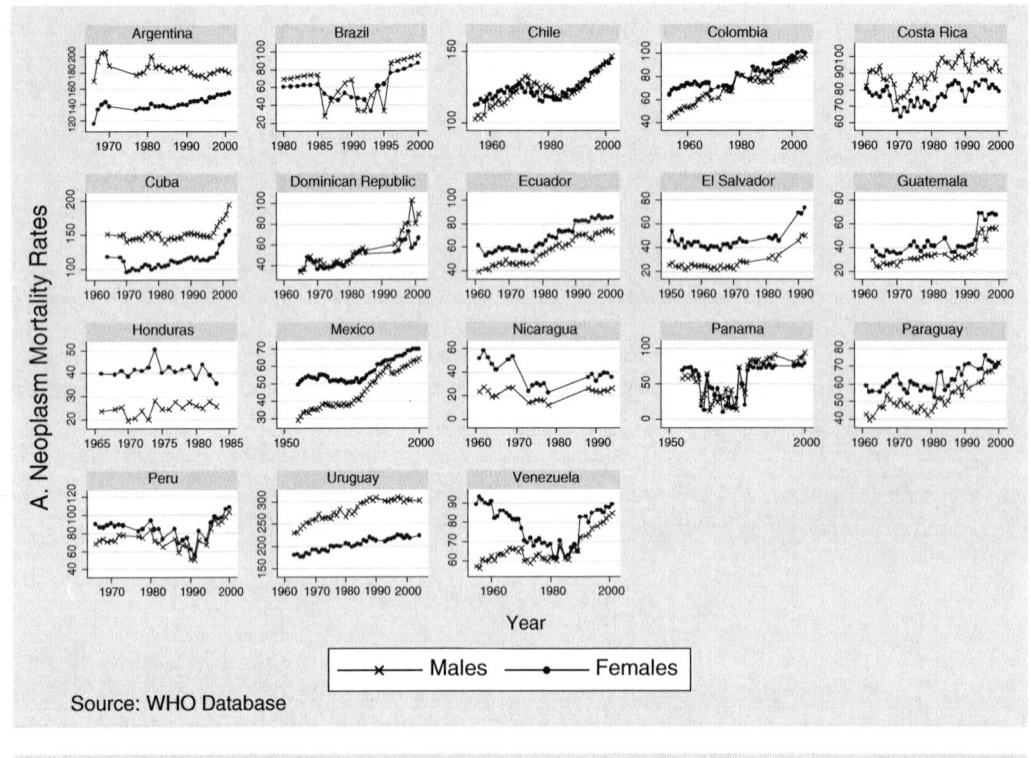

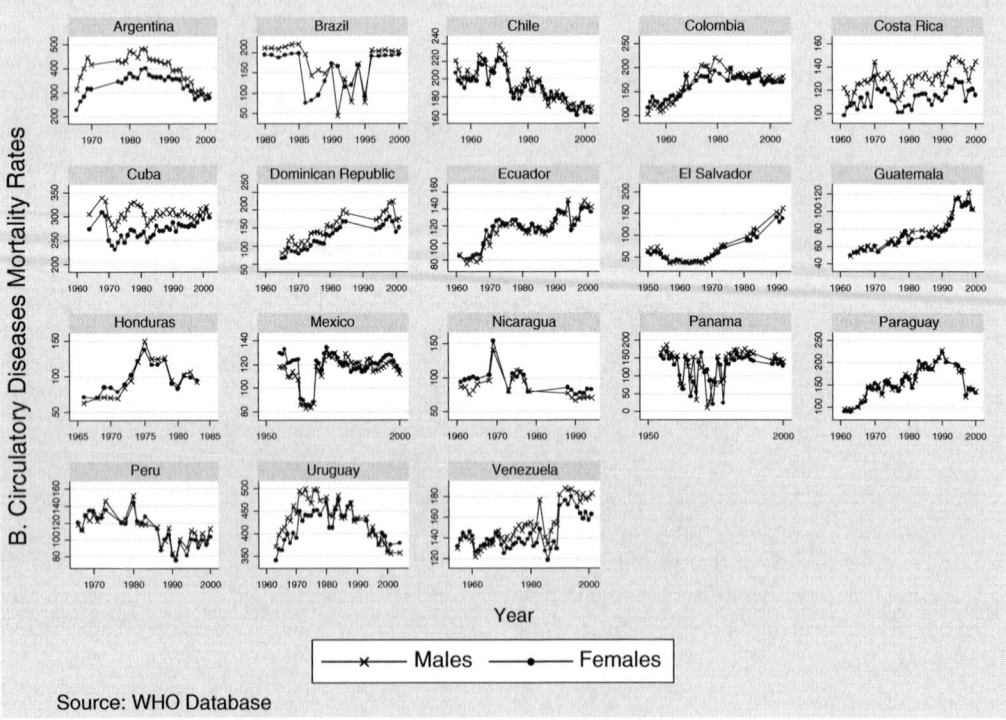

**Fig. 5.3** Mortality rates (per 100,000 persons) for leading causes of death in LAC countries, 1950–2000

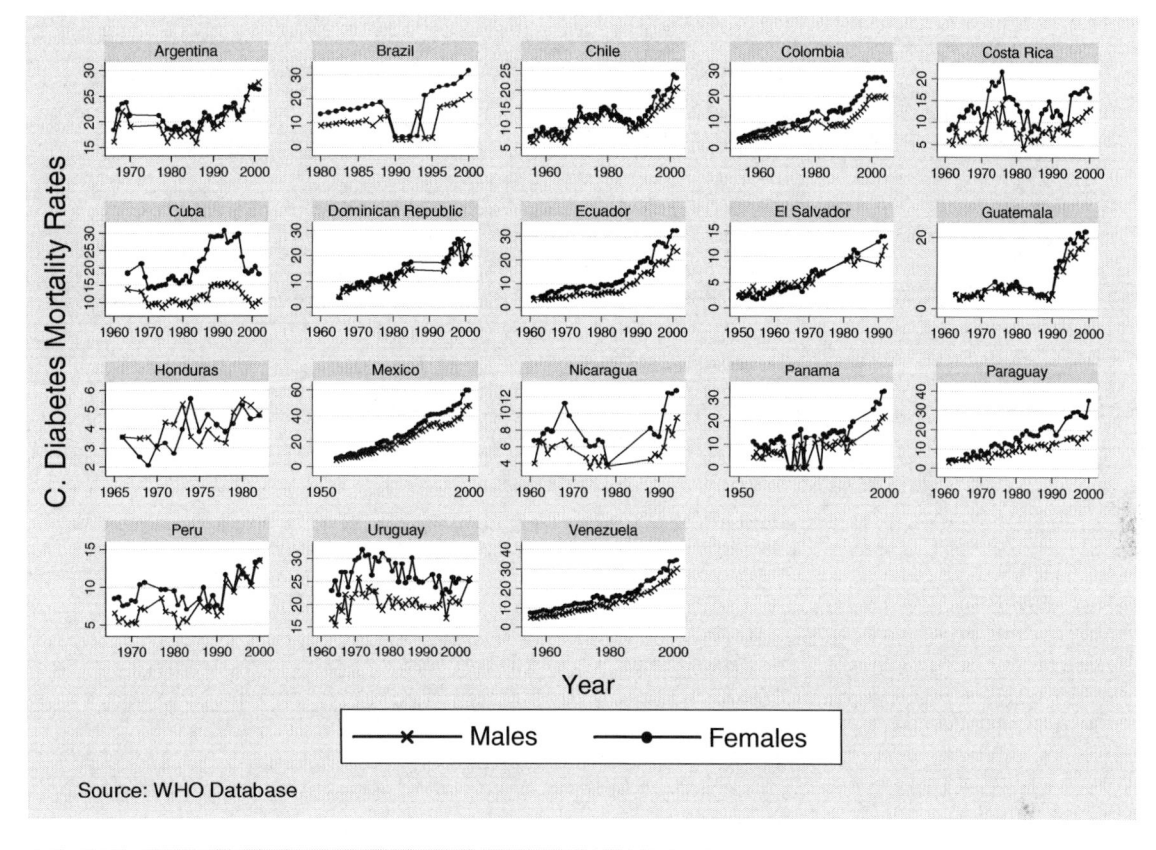

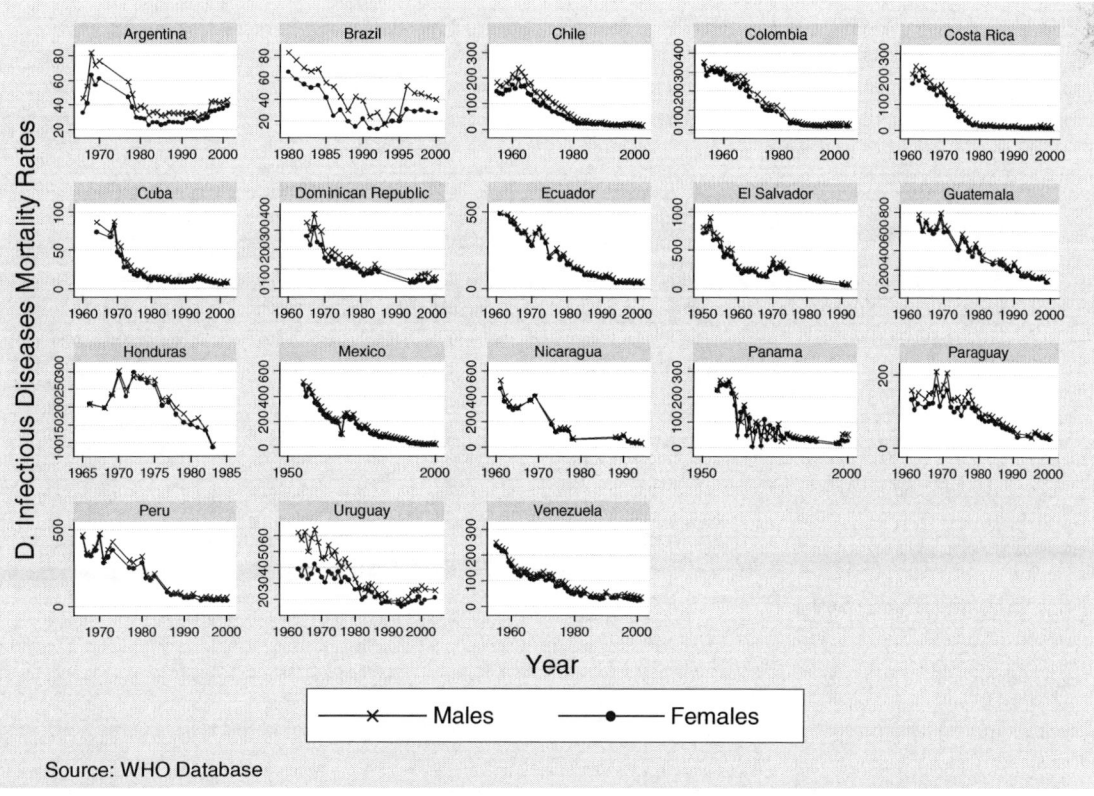

5 Adult Mortality in Latin America and the Caribbean

**Fig. 5.3** (continued)

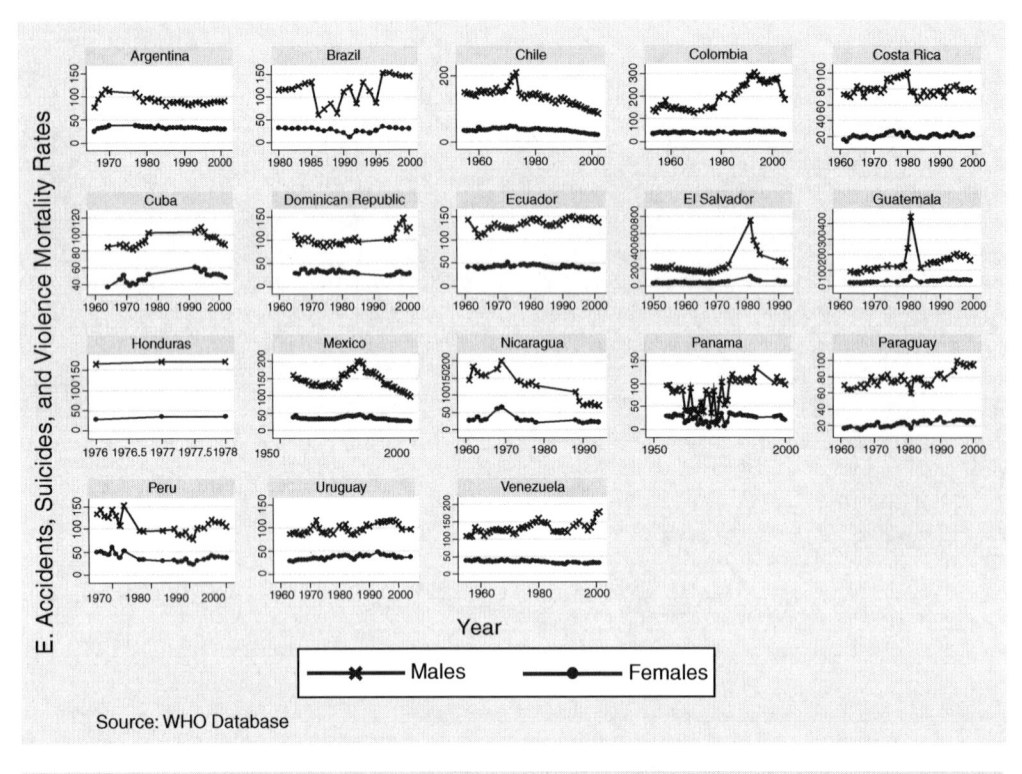

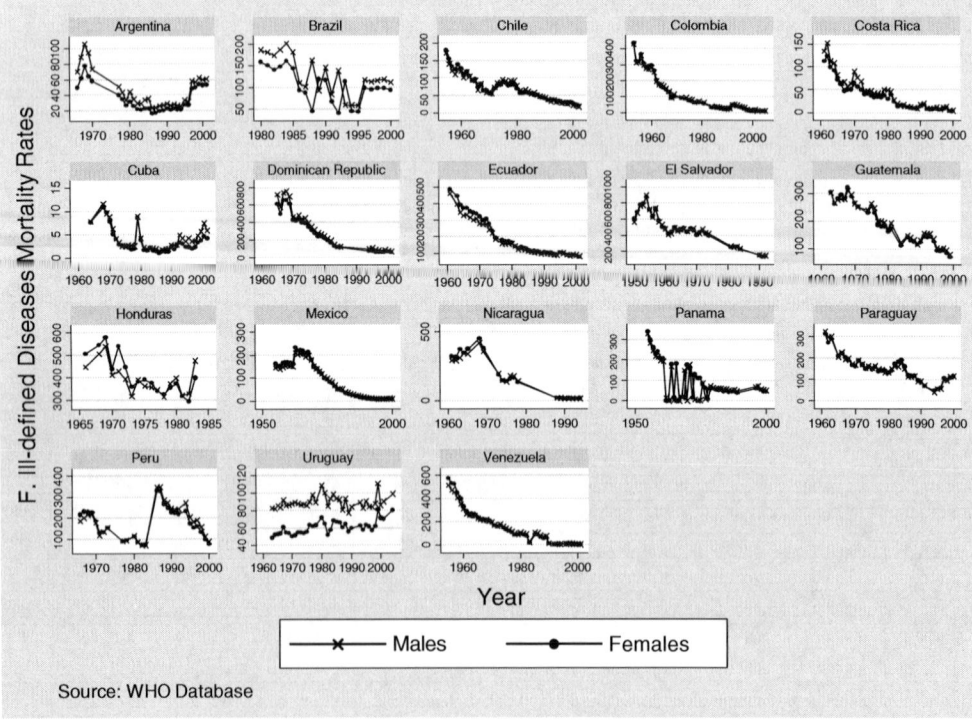

**Fig. 5.3** (continued)

due to diabetes do not show the stark gender contrast observed in mortality due to cancer or circulatory diseases.

Figure 5.3d shows an unsurprising and universal precipitous decline in infectious diseases. In some cases, there are small short-run increases, perhaps reflecting the impact of economic crises (Palloni and Noronha 2010). This is particularly the case in Argentina and Brazil, two of the countries that experienced massive economic contractions and sharp increases of poverty after the middle of the 1990s.

As illustrated in Fig. 5.3e, and as happens in most high-income countries, there is a marked excess of male death rates due to accidents, suicides, and violence. There are no clearly identifiable time trends, only spikes of significance in countries that experience war and protracted political upheavals (El Salvador, Guatemala, and Colombia).

Finally, mortality rates due to ill-defined causes (including those classified as senility) displayed in Fig. 5.3 f drop significantly in all countries as a result of increases in the proportion of properly certified deaths. The magnitude of the rates and the slope of the downward trends are much flatter in countries that have a long tradition of virtually complete death coverage, most of which pertain to the group of forerunners.[12]

## Contributions of Causes of Deaths to Increases in Life Expectancies

Figure 5.4 a–b display the contribution of number of years gained (lost) of life expectancy at age 5 during the period 1950–2000 associated with each group of causes. Figure 5.4a is for forerunners whereas Fig. 5.4b corresponds to laggards. These calculations were carried out using a decomposition method suggested by Pollard (1983) and Arriaga (1984).

With the exception of diabetes, which leads to losses of life expectancies of the order of 0.5 for both males and females, changes in all other groups of causes of deaths tend to increase life expectancy at age 5 among forerunners. The single-most important contributor is the group of causes associated with circulatory diseases that contributes with average gains between 1 and 2 years among males and between 1.8 and 3 years among females. Lower contributions are associated with neoplasms and infectious diseases.

The contrast with countries in the laggard group could not be starker. Among these, the single-most important contributor to life expectancy gains are reductions in infectious diseases, which led to gains of between 0.5 and 5 years of life. The only commonality between forerunners and laggards is found in the perverse role of diabetes, since also among laggards this disease leads to losses in life expectancy of about 0.5 years.

Finally, Table 5.6 displays estimates of the contributions made by mortality reductions in broad age groups and by groups of causes within the two groups of countries. These figures show that among forerunners, the reduction in mortality during the period is mostly attributable to adult ages (over 20), whereas among laggards, the largest contributions are associated with ages between 5 and 20 and with infectious diseases. The figures for diabetes reveal that despite the generalized upward trend, it is mostly among individuals in the oldest age group that the disease has a significant impact.

## The Determinants of Mortality Trends: 1950–2000

What were the forces behind the rapid change in mortality during the period 1950–2000? In a previous section, we conjectured that forerunners, well into the transition at the beginning of the period under study, experience early improvements that were mostly rooted in increases of standards of living and nutritional status as well as in the creation of massive infrastructure for water and sewage that reduced exposure to waterborne diseases particularly. These

---

[12] If the category "ill-defined" had a distribution of cause of deaths proportional to the observed one, none of the inferences drawn before would change. There is no evidence to suggest that the observed distribution is unlike that of "ill-defined causes" and even less reason to assume that deaths categorized as ill-defined are attributable to causes that are difficult to diagnose. It is more likely that the ill-defined causes are composed disproportionately of deaths associated with mortality among the poorest segments of the population, namely, infectious diseases.

**Fig. 5.4** Contributions of changes in life expectancies at age 5, 1950–2000 **a.** Forerunner countries, **b** Laggard countries (Note: the dots are outliers that are beyond the 75th/25th percentiles)

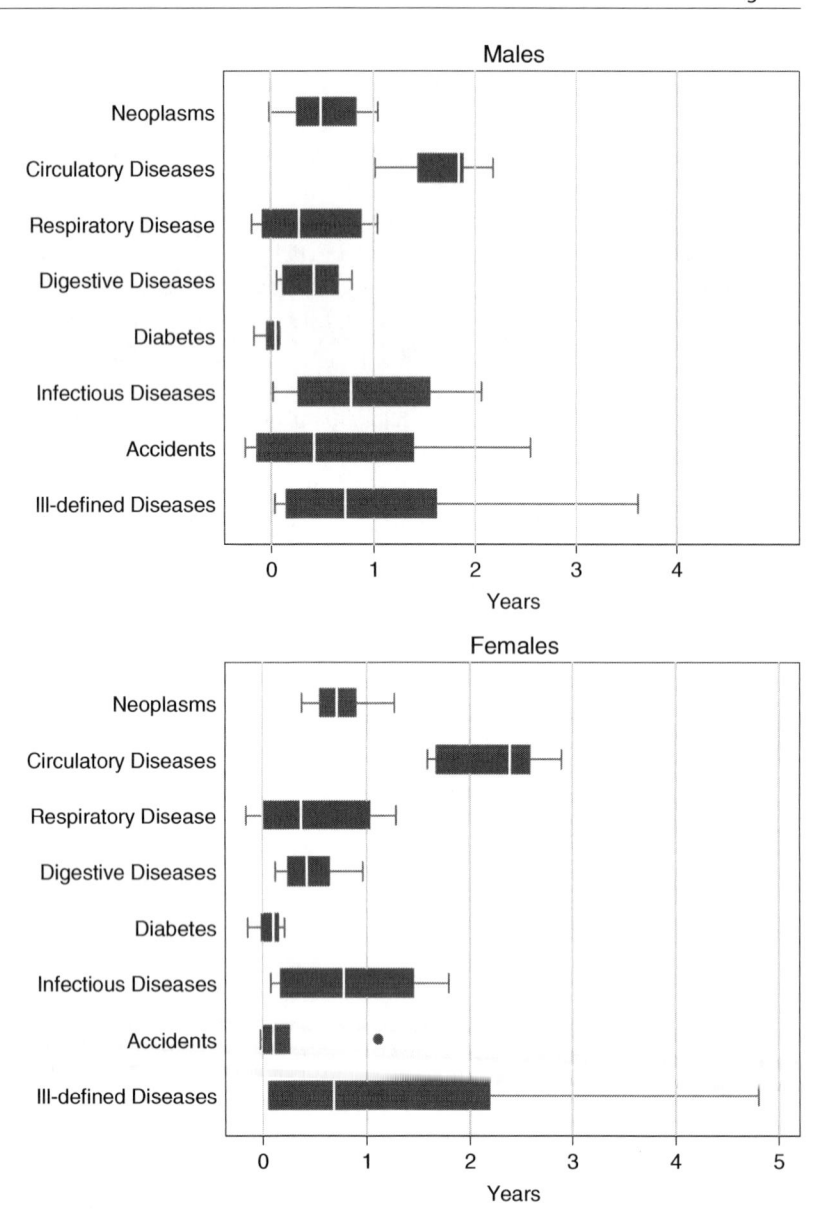

changes took place before 1950, perhaps beginning immediately before and after World War I, and were associated with incipient industrialization, large flows of foreign capital, and an active export sector and export-based social class that secured access not just to solid reserves in foreign currency but also constituted a portal for the dissemination of new ideas about minimization of exposure. Furthermore, in two of these countries (Cuba and Panama), early eradication campaigns played an important direct and indirect role. Forerunners benefited during the post-World War II period from the diffusion of modern medical technology, but the spillover effects that these might have had otherwise should be lower, since standards of living had already inched upward and exposure to waterborne diseases had been reduced considerably.

This storyline does not fit laggard countries well. Mortality reductions in this group were most likely originated in vector eradication financed by foreign countries that were heavily invested in export sectors and, especially, in the importation

**Fig. 5.4** (continued)

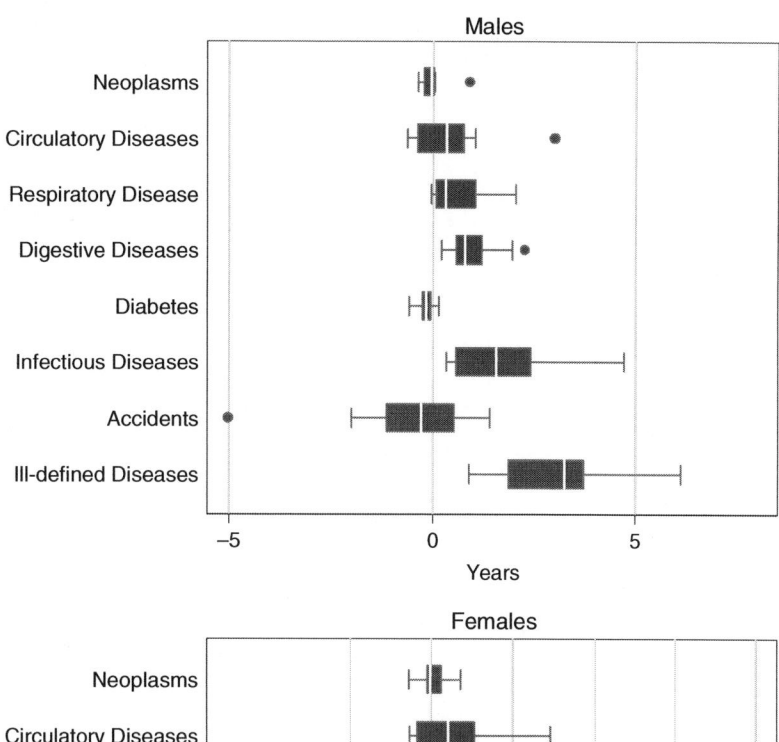

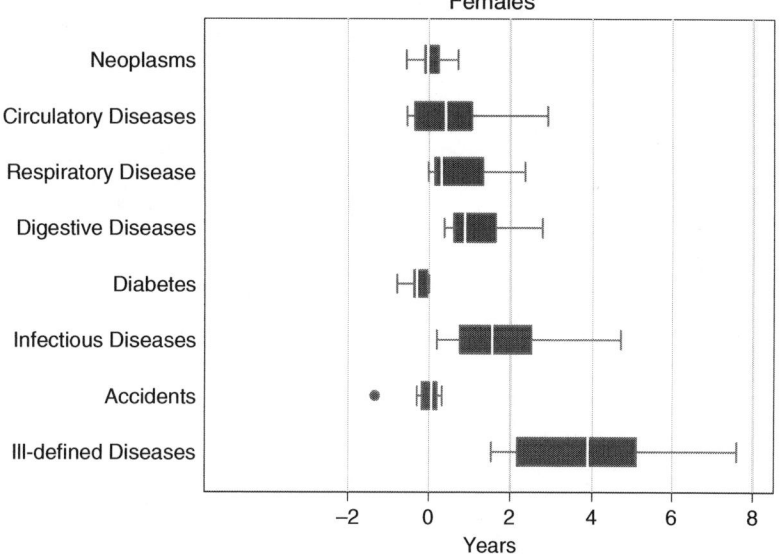

of medical technology. The role of better standards of living and improved infrastructure is probably secondary.

To test these conjectures, we follow closely the ideas put forward by Preston (1976, 1980) and Palloni and Wyrick (1981). We first estimate the relation between life expectancy at age 5 and various indicators of standards of living: Gross Domestic Product (GDP), proxies for infrastructure (proportion of households with potable water and electricity; proportion of population living in urban areas) and, finally, the proportion literate among the adult population. The relation is estimated for two periods, the years before 1970 and those after 1970. Unlike previous research, we use three different models to assess the relation between the variables of interest.

The first is a logistic model for country $i$ and year $t$ of the form:

$$E5_{it} = \frac{\alpha_t}{1 + \exp(\beta Z_{it})} \qquad (1)$$

$\alpha_t$ is a free parameter reflecting the maximum value of E5, $\boldsymbol{\beta}$ is a vector of parameters, including a constant, and $\mathbf{Z}_{it}$ a vector of covariates for country $i$ and year $t$, including a column of ones. No error term is specified.

Table 5.6 Contributions of changes in life expectancy at age 5, LAC countries, 1950–2005

| Causes | Forerunners | | | | | Laggards | | | | |
|---|---|---|---|---|---|---|---|---|---|---|
| | Total | 5–19 | 20–39 | 40–59 | 60+ | Total | 5–19 | 20–39 | 40–59 | 60+ |
| **Males** | | | | | | | | | | |
| Neoplasms | 0.514 | 0.024 | 0.073 | 0.237 | 0.180 | −0.039 | −0.015 | 0.007 | 0.048 | −0.080 |
| Circulatory | 1.698 | 0.048 | 0.119 | 0.516 | 1.015 | 0.362 | 0.023 | 0.071 | 0.138 | 0.130 |
| Respiratory | 0.368 | 0.098 | 0.094 | 0.131 | 0.045 | 0.605 | 0.162 | 0.134 | 0.172 | 0.136 |
| Digestive | 0.409 | 0.046 | 0.097 | 0.143 | 0.124 | 0.954 | 0.231 | 0.177 | 0.242 | 0.303 |
| Diabetes | 0.008 | 0.003 | 0.010 | 0.009 | −0.014 | −0.169 | 0.000 | −0.007 | −0.066 | −0.096 |
| Infections | 0.910 | 0.147 | 0.228 | 0.316 | 0.219 | 1.776 | 0.531 | 0.413 | 0.471 | 0.360 |
| Accidents | 0.729 | 0.162 | 0.349 | 0.173 | 0.045 | −0.563 | −0.093 | −0.318 | −0.120 | −0.032 |
| Ill-defined | 1.142 | 0.161 | 0.196 | 0.313 | 0.472 | 3.176 | 0.443 | 0.525 | 0.820 | 1.388 |
| **Females** | | | | | | | | | | |
| Neoplasms | 0.750 | 0.024 | 0.071 | 0.305 | 0.350 | 0.039 | −0.015 | 0.035 | 0.075 | −0.056 |
| Circulatory | 2.251 | 0.057 | 0.190 | 0.506 | 1.499 | 0.523 | 0.026 | 0.135 | 0.140 | 0.222 |
| Respiratory | 0.483 | 0.119 | 0.112 | 0.112 | 0.140 | 0.730 | 0.187 | 0.187 | 0.160 | 0.197 |
| Digestive | 0.469 | 0.045 | 0.105 | 0.164 | 0.155 | 1.184 | 0.243 | 0.250 | 0.306 | 0.385 |
| Diabetes | 0.067 | 0.006 | 0.004 | 0.017 | 0.040 | −0.278 | −0.002 | −0.008 | −0.080 | −0.188 |
| Infections | 0.840 | 0.165 | 0.296 | 0.221 | 0.158 | 1.859 | 0.575 | 0.500 | 0.400 | 0.384 |
| Accidents | 0.257 | 0.086 | 0.096 | 0.033 | 0.042 | −0.064 | −0.012 | −0.050 | −0.008 | 0.007 |
| Ill-defined | 1.411 | 0.167 | 0.320 | 0.292 | 0.633 | 3.958 | 0.502 | 0.759 | 1.004 | 1.693 |

Note: Figures represent unweighted average of age- and cause-specific mortality rates.

The second specification is a double log model for the pooled sample in each period. It has the following form

$$\ln E5_{it} = \varphi Z^*_{it} + \varepsilon_{it} \qquad (2)$$

where $\varphi$ is a vector of elasticities of E5 relative to a vector of covariates $Z^*_{it}$ (in log form) and $\varepsilon_{it}$ is a normally distributed error term independent of the covariate vector.

The third model is the fixed effects version of model (2) and takes the following form:

$$\ln E5_{it} = \lambda_i + \theta Z^*_{it} + \delta_{it} \qquad (3)$$

where $\lambda_i$ is a country-specific fixed effect and $\delta_{it}$ are independent, normally distributed variates (with mean 0 and variance 1). All three models are estimated separately for the pooled years 1950–1969 and 1970+. Since we only use data for intercensal intervals (rather than year-to-year observations), each country is at most represented twice in each pooled period.

## The Nature of the Variables

While the analysis carried out initially by Preston (1976) placed heavy emphasis on the role of income, the later versions of his model were more fully specified and included a number of covariates, among them literacy (Preston 1987). Similarly, the analysis by Palloni and Wyrick (1981) relies on a model that places more emphasis on a specification with variables that reflect different dimensions of the process. The formulation that we follow here has a simple rationale. A measure of income (real GDP) is a proxy for general standards of living, though it probably leaves much to be desired on that front as much as it does regarding nutritional status. GDP is not the best measure of material wealth, general standards of living, or nutritional status. But it is the only one we have at our disposal. The most important interventions to reduce exposure to infectious diseases are vector eradication campaigns and large infrastructure to supply clean water and safe sewage disposal. We use proportion of households served by piped water and with electricity to proxy for the magnitude and reach of infrastructure and complement these with a measure of urbanization. Instead of using the mortality level associated with vector-borne illnesses at the outset of the period as a proxy for the potential for vector eradication campaigns, we leave it unspecified, as part of the error term in the equations. We attempt *ex-post* to account for its role.

The variable literacy deserves special consideration. There is a fair amount of research indicating that education is the best predictor of fertility and mortality both at the individual and aggregate levels. What is less known and still the object of controversy is exactly what the nature of the relation is. At a very aggregate level, the connection between literacy and mortality is probably minimally related to individual levels of ability to obtain, process, and react to information. It is more plausible that literacy level, as in the case of the analysis of fertility, is a good proxy of institutional complexity, social integration, and the existence of flows from large institutions to individuals. This much was intuited by Caldwell (1976) in his classic treatment of the relation between massive schooling and fertility decline. Something similar could be at work with mortality. As we show later, literacy is as close to a perfect predictor for life expectancy at age 5 as we can possibly aspire to.[13]

## The Nature of the Models

The logistic model is defective. Though originally suggested by Preston for the very broad cross section of countries he studied, it is under-identified in our sample since the observations we have do not allow estimation of the inflection point of the logistic curve. The result is that the parameter estimates reflect only the upward bending part of the logistic curve. Although the fit of this model is very good, the interpretation of parameters is not as clear cut as would be true had we been able (perhaps with more observations) to identify the point of inflection of the logistic curve.

---

[13] The effect of education we are posing here is broader than and distinct from the effect usually identified in the literature that is reflected in the association between individual level of education and mortality. What we have in mind is that the aggregate level of education (in this case literacy) represents not just the average individual effects, but an added and more important influence of the strength of social institutions.

The pooled log model replicates closely the reformulated Preston model (Preston 1987) and the one suggested by Palloni and Wyrick after a search in the Box-Cox space of transforms. Both the logistic and the pooled log model are vulnerable to an important threat: the estimates will be inconsistent if the error is correlated with some of the covariates. We know for sure that we are omitting a variable reflecting eradication campaigns and another proxying for magnitudes of the flows of medical technology (in the form of vaccination or effective use of antibiotics). These factors are likely to be related to one of the variables included in the model. The solution is to estimate a fixed effects model where the effect of the country-specific unmeasured factor is removed.

## Results

Estimation of effects is carried out in a pool of observations corresponding to the period before 1970 and in another one containing observations for the period after 1970. The rationale behind this partition is that during the earlier period, wealth should have played the most important role, whereas later (unmeasured) interventions and medical innovations should play a more important role.

After estimating alternative specifications, we settled on one that ignored the variables for electricity, water, and urbanization, since they contribute trivially to the explained variance in all three models. We settled on a specification that included GDP and literacy. The astonishing part of our results is that literacy is not only properly signed everywhere but also predicts almost perfectly the dependent variables, regardless of the role played by GDP. Furthermore, the estimated elasticity of life expectancy relative to literacy varies across models within a very small range (0.15–0.31) and the effects are highly significant regardless of model specification. Table 5.7 displays the main results. Several features of the estimates are worth noting. First, the logistic model fits extremely well ($R^2 = 0.99$) in both periods. The effects of literacy are properly signed and highly significant. In contrast, the direction of the effect of GDP is opposite to the expected, though statistically insignificant. Second, the pooled log model also fits very well in both periods, though is clearly less powerful than the logistic if one judges by the $R^2$. Again, the effects of literacy are powerful and bear the proper sign, whereas the effects of GDP are trivial, incorrectly signed, and statistically insignificant.

The fact that the estimated effects of GDP bear the wrong sign and are statistically insignificant is suspicious. Admittedly, it could be explained partly by invoking measurement error and partly by arguing that mean income without a measure of inequality reveals very little. An alternative explanation is that there are unmeasured factors affecting life expectancy at age 5 that are themselves related to GDP. Figure 5.5 suggests potential representation of the (unobserved) relations. Now suppose that flows (and their effects) of medical technology as well as vector eradication campaigns are positively related to life expectancy ($\gamma > 0$), but that the relation between GDP and the unmeasured traits is negative ($\beta < 0$). The total (estimated) effect of GDP is $\alpha + \beta^*\gamma$ and $\alpha > 0$. It follows that our estimates will be biased downward and may have a negative sign. Why would $\beta$ be negative? There are at least two powerful reasons to suspect that this will be so. First, import of medical technology may have occurred selectively and flows of vaccines, antibiotics, and the like may have disproportionally targeted low-income countries. The same applies to interventions involving vector eradication campaigns. Second, both interventions should have been more effective in low-income countries, since it is there where the pool of potentially troublesome communicable diseases is more densely populated.

The estimates from the fixed effects model are consistent with our interpretation. First, note that the estimated effects of literacy are again powerful and statistically significant in both periods and, for the latest period, larger than in the other two models. However, the effects of GDP are properly signed and, in the earliest but not in the latest period, strong and statistically significant. This suggests that at least during the earliest period, country wealth played a role that complemented that of institutional factors proxied by literacy.

## Decomposition of Effects

The next step is to decompose the gains in life expectancy at age 5 into two components. The first is associated with changes in literacy and GDP

**Table 5.7** Estimated coefficients of the regression between life expectancy at age 5 and socioeconomic determinants, LAC countries, 1950–2005

| Type of specification and period | Intercept | Gross domestic product (GDP) | Literacy | Adj R-squared | N |
|---|---|---|---|---|---|
| Logistic before 1970 | 138.221 | 0.007 | −0.365* | 0.999 | 31 |
|  | (5.229) | (0.007) | (0.031) |  |  |
| Logistic after 1970 | 147.348 | 0.008** | −0.424* | 0.999 | 45 |
|  | (3.249) | (0.004) | (0.032) |  |  |
| Linear before 1970 | 4.236 | −0.003 | 0.206* | 0.813 | 31 |
|  | (0.042) | (0.004) | (0.020) |  |  |
| Linear after 1970 | 4.302 | −0.004** | 0.233* | 0.795 | 45 |
|  | (0.023) | (0.002) | (0.019) |  |  |
| Fixed effects before 1970 | 3.561 | 0.072** | 0.155** | 0.328 | 31 |
|  | (0.275) | (0.028) | (0.070) |  |  |
| Fixed effects after 1970 | 4.130 | 0.015 | 0.313* | 0.625 | 45 |
|  | (0.123) | (0.011) | (0.057) |  |  |

Note: The dependent variable is the logarithm of life expectancy at age 5 in linear and fixed effect models. The independent variables are the natural logarithm of the GDP and literacy. (standard errors are in parentheses)
*$p < 0.10$, **$p < 0.05$.

**Fig. 5.5** Relations between a measure of wealth (GDP), life expectancy at age 5 and unmeasured conditions

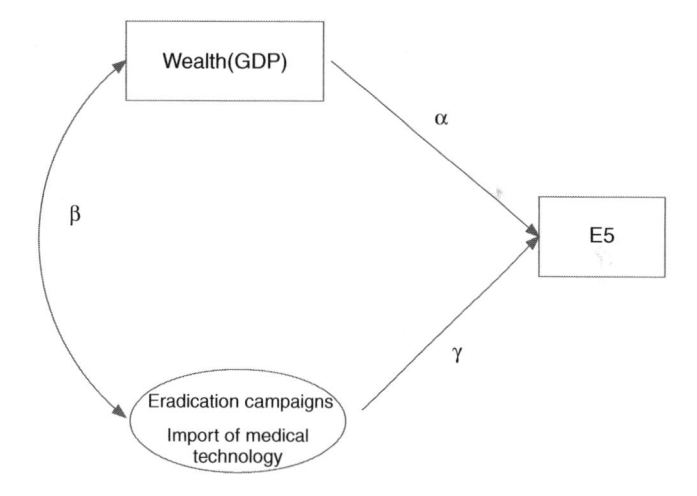

across the two periods. The second is associated with changes in the relation between the variables and must be attributed to the role played by unmeasured factors among which we include vector eradication campaigns, diffusion of medical technology, and unmeasured effects of infrastructure. To do this, we need to settle on a model. To increase comparability with results obtained by Palloni and Wyrick (1981) and by Preston (1980), we settled on the logistic model. None of the inferences we draw from the decomposition exercise are different if we had instead used any of the other two models.

The first application of the previous estimates is to decompose the gains in life expectancy at age 5 between the two periods for each country. Figure 5.6 displays the estimated proportion of the total change that is attributable to changes in the variables and changes in the parameters. Among laggards, more than 60% of the changes in life expectancy at age 5 are attributable to changes in the values of parameters. Instead among forerunners and with the exception of Paraguay, the bulk of gains are associated with changes in literacy. There is a clear shift in the relation that favors laggard countries. This shift should be attributed to unmeasured conditions that have either a strong (among laggards) or a weak (forerunners) influence. Two factors can account for such a shift. The first is interventions to eradicate vector-borne diseases.

**Fig. 5.6** Estimated percentage of the total change in life expectancies at age 5 attributable to changes in variables and parameters, LAC countries, 1925–2000

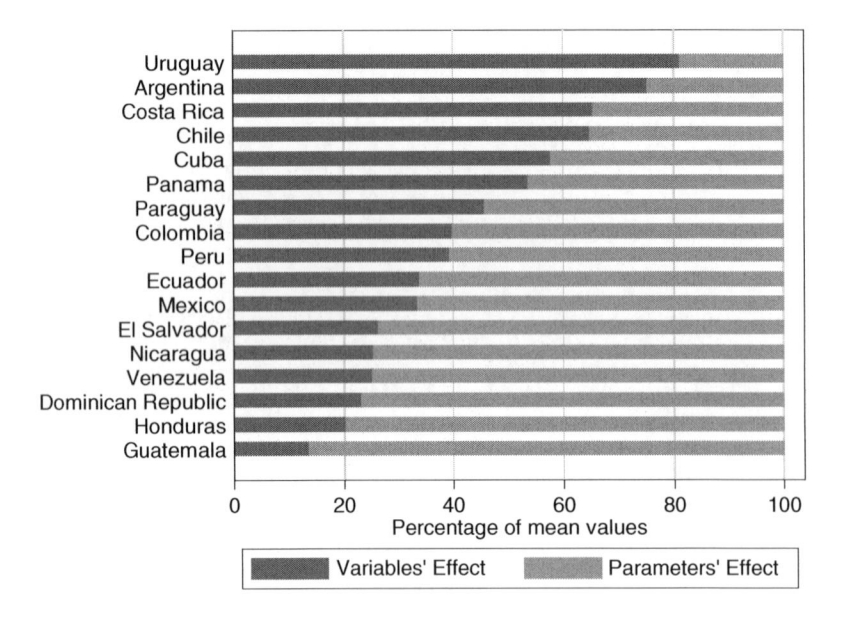

Rapid elimination of malaria, for example, is likely to have a multiplying effect, since it not only leads to gains associated with deaths due to malaria, but it also affects the average resistance of the population to other infectious diseases by boosting the immune function. Secondary gains will be obtained as increased resistance to other infectious diseases improves nutritional status.

The second factor is the diffusion of medical technology, particularly antibiotics and vaccinations. These surely had important effects in all countries, but their impact must have been large in those before 1950 had made only minor inroads in survival gains. If these two factors are indeed responsible for the shift, we should see an association between the fraction of gains in life expectancy at age 5 and proxies for the potential gains associated with the aforementioned factors. Table 5.8 displays estimates of the regression coefficients of the log of the proportion of gains in life expectancy at age 5 associated with changes in parameters and variables and the log of deaths rates due to water, vector, and airborne diseases as of the beginning of the period. As expected, both vector-borne and waterborne diseases are positively related to the log of the fraction of gains attributable to shifts in the relations, but only the coefficient of waterborne diseases is marginally significant. The opposite is true for airborne diseases: they are positively related to the fraction of gains attributable to changes in the variables and negatively related to the fraction of gains attributable to changes in parameters. Although these estimates are based on few cases, they suggest that the conjectures we put forward at the outset are not contradicted by the observed relations.

In summary, gains in life expectancy at age 5 during the period 1950–2000 are tracked tightly by increases in literacy, not by changes in measures of wealth or indicators of infrastructure. This relation is intriguing but not unknown to demographers studying fertility, as there too the association is very tight. Rather than attributing to literacy effects related to mechanisms involving access to and use of information only, it is preferable to deploy a broader interpretation, suggesting that this indicator is a proxy for social integration and, most important, for the ability of central governments to allocate resources to the population at large. These flows may imply a number of advantages, including learning and information, access to health care, and to resources such as clean water supply, adequate housing and, more generally, to environments that reduce exposure to infectious diseases. Yet, literacy cannot proxy for all of the factors that explain changes over time. Indeed, our analysis suggests that the relation shifted in the period 1950–2000, and that countries experienced gains in life expectancy even if levels of literacy remained unchanged. All laggards benefited greatly from this shift. Among forerunners, the relative gains associated with the shift are of marginal importance. We interpret this as an indication that the shift was produced by changes induced by

**Table 5.8** Estimated coefficients of the regression between the proportion of gains in life expectancy at age 5 and cause of death, LAC countries, 1950–2005

| Causes of Deaths | Gains associated to changes in parameters | Gains associated to changes in variables |
|---|---|---|
| Vector-borne | 0.045 | −0.026 |
| | (0.036) | (0.055) |
| Waterborne | 0.232* | −0.346* |
| | (0.123) | (0.191) |
| Airborne | −0.189* | 0.256 |
| | (0.101) | (0.156) |
| Intercept | −0.658* | −0.857 |
| | (0.371) | (0.573) |
| Adj R-squared | 0.446 | 0.275 |
| N | 16 | 16 |

Note: Dependent and independent variables are expressed as natural logarithm. Rates of mortality are considered for the total population. (standard errors are in parentheses)
*$p < 0.10$.

two factors that are omitted in our models: vector eradication campaigns and the diffusion of medical innovations, particularly those that control exposure and increase resistance to waterborne diseases. Indeed, there is a tangible though not strong relation between the magnitude of gains associated with the shift of the relation and the magnitude of death rates due to illnesses that could be attenuated by these two factors.

## Mortality at Old Ages

In this last section, we make a brief incursion into an important territory, that of progression of longevity. For this purpose, we focus on mortality over age 60, and the best indicator we have available is life expectancy at age 60. Figure 5.7 displays the values of female life expectancy at age 60 for laggards and forerunners. In this case, we only draw one horizontal line at the top of the graph at around 24.8, the life expectancy at age 60 among females in Norway circa 2005. At the outset, the differences between the two groups of countries are of the order of 2 years and, like the case of life expectancy at age 5, there is some convergence, though a gap still remains at the end of the period. Importantly, and unlike the case for life expectancy at age 5, life expectancy at age 60 among forerunners grows linearly and there is a hint of a slowdown of improvements by the end of the period of reference.

The trajectory of mortality at old ages is astonishing. Gains per year are of the order of 0.13 in both groups of countries. If one assumes that the force of mortality at older ages has been decreasing at a constant and age-invariant rate during the period, the observed yearly gains in life expectancy at age 60 imply an average reduction per year of about 0.045. This is four times as high as the rate of reduction in the yearly force of mortality experienced by developed countries after 1960 (Kannisto et al. 1994) though, admittedly these are progressing from higher levels of life expectancy at age 60. But even conceding that point, the march toward longevity occurs at a very accelerated pace.

To what extent are these gains an artifact of age overstatement? As pointed out before, age overstatement is particularly serious at older age and, despite our best efforts, some residual errors may remain. But these should affect the level of life expectancy at age 60, not the trends. Or put in another way, if there is residual age overstatement, and if we also observe a marked tendency toward better age declaration over time, the observed trend must underestimate the speed of change in the force of mortality. Thus, it is very likely that the rate of gains in survival over age 60 that we estimate here is a lower bound.

An entirely different matter is whether the rhythm of gains observed in the past can be sustained for long. We argue elsewhere that there are ominous signs pointing to the possibility of rapid deceleration of gains as a result of the nature of mortality decline and the consequent composition by frailty of cohorts

**Fig. 5.7** Female life expectancies at age 60 by group of LAC countries, 1925–2000

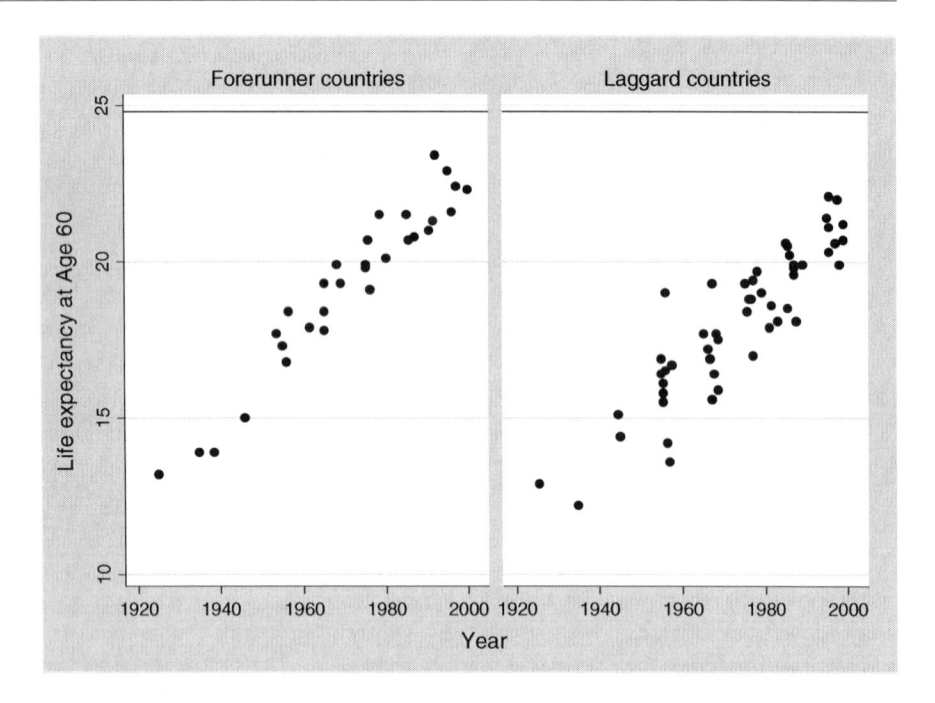

who will become 60 and over during the next 30 years (Palloni and Noronha 2010; Palloni and Pinto 2004). But this is not all. In fact, Fig. 5.7 shows signs of a slowdown among forerunners at least. Indeed, among forerunners, the rate of increase per year in life expectancy at age 60 has dropped from 0.14 in the period before 1980 to 0.09 after that period. Laggards, on the other hand, experienced lower rates of gains in before 1980 (0.12) but it increased after 1980. Thus, among countries that have attained higher levels of life expectancy at age 60, there are clear signs of deceleration.

## Conclusions

Although the inferences contained in this chapter are not inconsistent with a body of research done in the past, they introduce more precision and allow a more nuanced interpretation of the mechanisms that were at play in the rapid decrease of mortality in the LAC region. First, we work with a body of data that avoids strong assumptions about model mortality patterns. Mortality rates have been adjusted for completeness of death registration, census enumeration, and age misstatement. If any errors remain, they are likely to be of trifling magnitude and cannot constitute a stumbling block against our inferences.

Second, the evidence we marshal here indicates that adult mortality (over age 5) was reduced at unprecedented speed beginning before 1940 in selected countries and after 1950 for most of them. The levels attained as of the end of the twentieth century are close to those in a handful of developed countries. For others, a gap remains. This gap, however, is closing rapidly. Of particular importance is the rapid decrease in mortality over age 60 and the gains in longevity that this implies. The fact that Costa Rica and Cuba experience levels of life expectancy at age 60 similar to or even above those in some developed countries may be startling but cannot be attributed to faulty data. The progress during the period 1950–2000 has been fast but appears to be slowing down and may run into important obstacles in the years to come.

Third, for the most part, mortality trends by causes have progressed according to expectations, though there are singularities that stand out. Thus, infectious diseases have plummeted and circulatory diseases have ceased to be as dominant as they were early in the period. The most important peculiarity is the rapid increase in diabetes.

Fourth, the analysis of determinants confirms the broad outlines but not the detail of Preston's original conjectures. They also replicate the findings previously uncovered by Palloni and Wyrick in LAC made with a much-less refined data base. Wealth, as measured by GDP, plays an important role early on the process, but a much more modest one in the latter part of the period under study. Instead, literacy is always a potent driver of changes, perhaps reflecting the effects of institutional changes unrelated to country wealth that are required to alter the exposure and resistance to diseases.

Fifth, decomposition of gains over the period 1950–2000 shows that countries who are forerunners in the mortality decline took advantage of structural changes (as reflected in GDP and literacy), as these explain the bulk of gains in life expectancy at age 5. Instead, countries whose mortality decline starts late in the period showcase the important role of selected interventions and of the diffusion of medical technology, neither of which we are able to measure directly. More than 60% of these countries' gains are associated with these two unmeasured factors and the rest with improvements in institutional contexts and standards of living. This estimate is much smaller among forerunners. Our analysis thus illustrates the payoffs of examining shifts in the relation between mortality and its determinants separately by groups of countries with very heterogeneous experiences.

What remains undone is a more thorough analysis of gender differentials which, at least under some conditions, may provide clues about underlying determinants. Similarly, the extension of the analysis to the period 1900–1950 for a larger number of countries is sorely needed to complete the description of mortality trajectories. This will also help us to identify and assess the role of standards of living, nutritional status, and of early interventions embedded in the creation of large infrastructure as these must have undoubtedly contributed to diminish exposure to infectious diseases well before medical technologies and massive eradication campaigns sealed once and for all the transition to very low mortality levels.

**Acknowledgment** This research was supported by National Institute on Aging grants R37 AG025216, R03 AG15673, and R01 AG18016. Research work for University of Wisconsin-Madison researchers is supported by core grants to the Center for Demography and Ecology, University of Wisconsin (R24 HD47873) and to the Center for Demography of Health and Aging, University of Wisconsin (P30 AG017266).

## References

Arriaga, E. 1968. *New Life Tables for Latin American Populations in the Nineteenth and Twentieth Centuries*, Population Monograph Series No. 3. Berkeley, CA, University of California.

Arriaga, E. 1984. "Measuring and Explaining the Change in Life Expectancies." *Demography* 21(1):83–96.

Arriaga, E. and K. Davis. 1969. "The Pattern of Mortality Change in Latin America." *Demography* 6(3):223–42.

Bennett, N.G. and S. Horiuchi. 1981. "Estimating the Completeness of Death Registration in a Closed Population." *Population Index* 47(2):207–21.

Brass, W. 1975. *Methods for Estimating Fertility and Mortality from Limited and Defective Data.* Chapel Hill, NC, Laboratories for Population Statistics, Carolina Population Center.

CELADE. 2001. "America Latina: Tablas de Mortalidad. 1950–2005." *Boletin Demografico*, No. 67. Santiago de Chile, CEPAL.

Caldwell, J.C. 1976. "Toward a Restatement of Demographic Transition Theory." *Population and Development Review* 2(3–4):321–66.

Caselli, G. 2002. "Health Transition and Cause-Specific Mortality." In R. Schofield, D. Reher, and A. Bideau, *The Decline of Mortality in Europe*, pp. 68–96. IUSSP, Oxford, England, Clarendon Press.

Coale, A.J. and P. Demeny. 1966. *Regional Models Life Tables and Stable Populations.* Princeton, NJ, Academic Press.

Coale, A.J. and P. Demeny. 1967. *Manual IV. Methods of Estimating Basic Demographic Measures from Incomplete Data.* New York, NY, United Nations.

Coale, A.J. and E.E. Kisker. 1990. "Defects in Data on Old Age Mortality in the United States: New Procedures for Calculating Mortality Schedules and Life Tables at the Highest Ages." *Asian and Pacific Population Forum* 4(1):1–31.

Condran, G.A., C. Himes, and S.H. Preston. 1991. "Old-Age Mortality Patterns in Low Mortality Countries: An Evaluation of Population and Death Data at Advanced Ages, 1950 to the Present." *Population Bulletin of the United Nations* 30:23–60.

Dechter, A. and S.H. Preston. 1991. "Age Misreporting and Its Effects on Adult Mortality Estimates in Latin America." *Population Bulletin of the United Nations* 31/32:1–16.

Fogel, R.W. 2004. *The Escape from Hunger and Premature Death, 1700–2100. Europe, America and the Third World.* Cambridge, England, Cambridge University Press.

Fogel, R.W. and D.L. Costa 1997. "A Theory of Technophysio-Evolution with Some Implications for Forecasting Population, Health Care Costs and Pension Costs." *Demography* 34(1):49–66.

Frederiksen, H. 1970. "Malaria Eradication and the Fall of Mortality: A Note." *Population Studies* 24(1):111–13.

Gray, R.H. 1974. "The Decline of Mortality in Ceylon and the Demographic Effects of Malaria Control." *Population Studies* 28(2):205–29.

Grushka, C.O. 1996. *Adult and Old Age Mortality in Latin America: Evaluation, Adjustment and a Debate over a Distinct Pattern*. Ph.D. thesis, Philadelphia, PA, University of Pennsylvania.

Grushka, C.O. and S.H. Preston. 1995. *Latin America Adult Mortality with Special Attention to Advanced Ages*. Philadelphia, PA, University of Pennsylvania/Population Studies Center.

Hill, K. 1987. "Estimating Census and Death Registration Completeness." *Asian and Pacific Population Forum* 1(3):8, 23–13, 24.

Hill, K. 2002. *Methods for Measuring Adult Mortality in Developing Countries: A Comparative Review*. Baltimore, MD, John Hopkins University.

Himes, C.L., S.H. Preston, and G.A. Condran. 1994. "A Relational Model of Mortality at Older Ages in Low Mortality Countries." *Population Studies* 48:240–91.

Jaspers, D. and H. Orellana. 1996. "Evaluation of Vital Statistics for Study of Causes of Death." In I.M. Timaeus, J. Chackiel, and L. Rusickapp (eds.), *Adult Mortality in Latin America*, pp. 45–68. Oxford, England, Clarendon Press.

Kannisto, V., J. Lauritsen, A. Roger Thatcher, and J. Vaupel. 1994. "Reductions in Mortality at Advanced Ages: Several Decades of Evidence from 27 Countries." *Population and Development Review* 20(4):793–810.

Martin, L. 1980. "A Modification for Use in Destabilized Populations of Brass's Techniques for Estimating Completeness of Death Registration." *Population Studies* 34(2):381–95.

McKeown, T. 1976. *The Modern Rise of Population*. London, England, Edward Arnold.

Oeppen, J. and J.W. Vaupel 2002. "Broken Limits to Life Expectancies." *Science* 296:1029–930.

Omran, A.R. 1982. "Epidemiologic Transition." In *International Encyclopedia of Population*, pp. 172–83. New York, NY, The Free Press.

Palloni, A. and K. Noronha. 2010. *Future Trajectories of Healthy Life Expectancy in Latin America and the Caribbean*. Dallas, TX, Paper presented at the Population Association of America Meeting.

Palloni, A. and G. Pinto. 2004. *One Hundred Years of Mortality in Latin American and the Caribbean: The Fragile Path from Hunger to Longevity*. Boston, MA, Paper presented at the Population Association of America Meeting.

Palloni, A. and R. Wyrick. 1981. "Mortality Decline in Latin America: Changes in the Structures of Causes of Deaths, 1950–1975." *Social Biology* 28(3–4):187–216.

Pollard, J.H. 1983. "On the Decomposition of Changes in Expectation of Life and Differentials in Life Expectancy." *Demography* 25:265–76.

Preston, S.H. 1976. *Mortality Patterns in National Populations: With Special Reference to Recorded Causes of Death*. New York, NY, Academic Press.

Preston, S.H. 1980. "Causes and consequences of mortality declines in less developed countries during the 20th century". In R. Easterlin (ed.) *Population and Economic Change in Developing Countries*. Chicago, University of Chicago Press.

Preston, S.H. 1983. "An Integrated System for Demographic Estimation from Two Age Distributions." *Demography* 20(2):213–26.

Preston, S.H. 1987. "Causes and Consequences of Mortality Declines in Less Developed Countries during the Twentieth Century." In R. Easterlin (ed.), *Population and Economic Change in Developing Countries*, pp. 289–360. National Bureau of Economic Research, Chicago, IL, The University of Chicago Press.

Preston, S.H., I. Elo, I. Rosenwaike, and M. Hill. 1996. "African-American Mortality at Older Ages: Results of a Matching Study." *Demography* 33(2):193–209.

Preston, S.H. and M. Haines 1991. *Fatal Years*. Princeton, NJ, Princeton University Press.

Preston, S.H. and V.E. Nelson. 1974. "Structure and Change in Causes of Death: An International Summary." *Population Studies* 28(1):19–51.

Rosenwaike, I. and S.H. Preston. 1984. "Age Overstatement and Puerto Rican Longevity." *Human Biology* 56(3): 503–25.

Rosero-Bixby, L. and G. Brenes. 2003. *Informe de Evaluacion de la Validez de las Estadisticas Vitales y el Censo, y los Parametros para Corregirla*, Reporte Tecnico, Centro Centroamericano de Poblacion. San Jose Costa Rica, Universidad de Costa Rica.

Schofield, R. and D. Reher. 2002. "The Decline of Mortality in Europe." In R. Schofield, D. Reher, and A. Bideau (eds.), *The Decline of Mortality in Europe*, pp. 1–17. IUSSP, Oxford, England, Clarendon Press.

Stolnitz, G. 1965. "Recent Mortality Trends in Latin America, Asia and Africa: Review and Re-interpretation." *Population Studies* 19(2):117–38.

Timaeus, I.M., J. Chackiel, and L. Rusicka (eds.). 1996. *Adult Mortality in Latin America*. Oxford, England, Clarendon Press.

United Nations [UN]. 1982. *Model Life Tables for Developing Countries*. New York, NY, Department of International Economic and Social Affairs.

Vallin, J. 2002. "Mortality in Europe from 1720 to 1914: Long-term Trends and Changes in Patterns by Age and Sex." In R. Schofield, D. Reher, and A. Bideau (eds.), *The Decline of Mortality in Europe*, pp. 38–67. IUSSP, Oxford, England, Clarendon Press.

Vaupel, J., K. Manton, and E. Stallard. 1979. "The Impact of Heterogeneity in Individual Frailty on the Dynamics of Mortality." *Demography* 16(3):439–54.

# Chapter 6
# Adult Mortality in Asia

Zhongwei Zhao

## Introduction

Asia, the largest and most populous continent in the world, has experienced a rapid demographic transition since the end of World War II. According to a recent estimate by the United Nations Population Division (UN Population Division 2009), between 1950–1955 and 2005–2010 life expectancy at birth in Asia has increased from 41 to 69 years and the total fertility rate has fallen from 5.7 to 2.4 children per woman. Largely driven by these changes, Asia's population size has nearly tripled. More than four billion people, accounting for 60% of the world total, now live in some 50 countries and areas in Asia (UN Population Division 2009).

Asia is the most diverse continent in many respects. People in Asia live in hugely varied natural environments, and many populations have a distinctive history, cultural tradition, and religion. Many Asian countries have radically different political and social systems, and have pursued different routes to development in recent history. Partly for these reasons, many Asian populations are now at very different stages of the demographic transition, with remarkably different demographic characteristics.

Asia has two of the world's most populated countries, China and India, which between them have 2.5 billion people, but some small countries such as Maldives or Brunei Darussalam have populations of fewer than half a million. Singapore, among all Asian countries, has the highest population density, with more than 7,000 persons/km$^2$, but in Mongolia, only 2 persons live in an area of the same size. Japan has long completed the classic demographic transition, and its population, with one of the oldest age structures in the world, has already started to decline. But countries like Yemen are still in the early stage of the demographic transition, with a very young age structure and a high rate of population growth. Marked mortality differentials are also found in Asia. The Japanese now enjoy the highest life expectancy ever achieved by a national population, close to 83 years, but at current mortality, people in Afghanistan can expect to survive for less than 44 years, the lowest life expectancy in the world (UN Population Division 2009).

The great disparities summarized above make the discussion of adult mortality in Asia both interesting and challenging. The challenge is further exacerbated by the lack of detailed and reliable mortality data, especially for the older ages. Because of this constraint, this chapter concentrates on mortality of people aged 15–59, and old-age mortality is addressed only briefly. For the same reason, the discussion focuses on mortality changes, sex differentials in survival, and causes of death in Asia's national populations in recent years, although mortality declines in subnational populations or over a longer period are mentioned in some sections of the chapter.

Following this introduction, the second section of the chapter examines the availability of mortality data in Asian countries and its impact on the study of adult mortality. Subsequent sections discuss changes in adult mortality, gender differences in survival, and major causes of death in Asia, respectively. The last section of the chapter summarizes a number of lessons

Z. Zhao (✉)
Australian Demographic and Social Research Institute,
Australian National University, Canberra, Australia
e-mail: zhongwei.zhao@anu.edu.au

learned from the mortality transition in Asia and major challenges that the Asian population faces in further improving health and mortality.

## Mortality Data Collection in Asia

Four major data sources are commonly used in the study of mortality. The first is death records made through nationwide vital registration. These records can provide detailed information on all deaths in the population over a long period and are widely regarded as the best data source for mortality study (Murray et al., 1992). The second is death records gathered through censuses or nationwide health or mortality surveys. These data also provide important information about mortality in a population, but they tend to be collected for a short period, generally 1 year. They are also less adequate for the investigation of cohort mortality, because the census is usually conducted only every 5 or 10 years in most countries. The third major source is death records obtained through various kinds of sample surveys or registration systems (including hospital registration) established in parts of the country, either randomly or nonrandomly. These records often are of better quality than those collected from the whole population, but are subject to sampling errors or selective biases when they are used to estimate mortality in the national population. The last source comprises death records found in family genealogies, parish registers, or other kinds of registration, which have been increasingly used in the study of mortality in the past (Zhao 2008).

The collection of mortality data is less satisfactory in Asia than in Europe, North America, South America, and major countries in Oceania. Out of some 50 countries and areas in the region, life tables constructed continuously for a period of over a 100 years are available for only Japan and Taiwan, and for the latter, mortality data gathered in recent decades have not been reported by the World Health Organization (WHO) or the UN Population Division for political reasons. In most countries and areas, mortality data covering a large part of the population and with high or moderate quality simply did not exist until the mid- or even late-twentieth century.

As the UN Department of International Economic and Social Affairs (1982a) noted, around 1950 only a few countries and territories in Asia had "complete" vital registration (i.e., with 90% or more of all deaths recorded). This situation did not change significantly in the next 25 years; in 1975, the number of countries and territories having such "complete" registration remained small. Except for Japan, the countries and territories that did—such as Singapore, Hong Kong, and Sri Lanka—were arguably atypical, were small, and accounted for an insignificant share of Asia's population (UN Department of International Economic and Social Affairs 1982a). In the last quarter of the twentieth century, countries with nationwide vital registration increased notably in Asia, but they were still a minority, and records collected through such registration were available for only a short period in many of these countries (Lopez et al., 2000).

Some Asian countries and territories collect mortality data through population censuses or nationwide mortality or health surveys. But before 1980, mortality data obtained through these methods, those of good quality in particular, were also limited. This was a major reason why only 36 life tables (18 for each sex) were selected from 11 Asian populations and used in the construction of the United Nations *Model Life Tables for Developing Countries* in the early 1980s (UN Department of International Economic and Social Affairs 1982b). Since then, the role of censuses in collecting mortality data has increased, but in comparison with Europe, North America, and major countries in Oceania, Asia is still far behind in the systematic gathering of national mortality data.

Facing the urgent need to monitor health and mortality and the difficulty of gathering health and mortality data for the whole population, Asian countries have made great efforts to collect the required data through specially designed sample surveys or various kinds of registration systems in randomly or nonrandomly selected areas. Examples include the Demographic and Health Surveys conducted in many countries, vital registration in the Matlab district of Bangladesh, and the Disease Surveillance Points system in China. Death records obtained through these activities have already become a major data source for mortality study in Asia.

Mortality data collected from most Asian populations, just like those gathered elsewhere, are often affected by under-registration and other reporting problems. The impact of such problems sometimes is so severe that an adjustment or estimation must be made before any meaningful conclusion about mortality in the population can be drawn. Many mortality statistics, especially some of those published by the WHO and the UN Population Division, are in fact estimated rather than computed directly from available data. This is particularly the case for mortality statistics for earlier time periods or for older people.

In producing detailed mortality estimates for most Asian populations, both the WHO and the UN Population Division have made great efforts to evaluate and adjust available mortality data. While their results arguably represent the best mortality estimates that one could have, they may have some limitations. These estimates may be affected by sampling errors or selective biases when they are made on the basis of mortality data collected from a subnational rather than national population, especially if the subnational population is not selected randomly. These estimated results may also be affected by the assumptions used (e.g., assumptions about the age pattern of mortality in the population) when they are derived from incomplete data (e.g., death rates of limited age groups). Uncertainties arising from such limitations are often related positively to the seriousness of the registration problems in the population. They could have considerable implications when these estimates are used to study changes in age patterns of mortality or survivorship at old ages.

Because of the constraints imposed by data availability and the issues summarized above, the following discussion concentrates on recent mortality changes in the population aged 15–59, gender differences, and major causes of death. The decision to examine mortality at these ages rather than in the 20–59 year age group, as in some other chapters of this book, is largely due to the fact that for many Asian populations, mortality statistics computed for the 20–59 age group are not available in early years. To maintain internal consistency in the data used, I base the discussion primarily on mortality estimates made by the WHO, although in a number of places I also cite estimates published by the UN Population Division, especially those for years before 1990.

It is worth noting that while mortality statistics for 2007 provided by the WHO and those for 2005–2010 provided by the UN Population Division are largely consistent, with fairly small differences in recorded or estimated life expectancies at birth, there are noticeable discrepancies in their estimated adult mortality for the following countries: Armenia, the Democratic People's Republic of Korea, Indonesia, Iraq, the Lao People's Democratic Republic, Lebanon, Maldives, Myanmar, Nepal, Oman, Pakistan, Qatar, Saudi Arabia, the Syrian Arab Republic, and Viet Nam. Adult (both male and female) mortality estimated for these countries by the WHO is more than 20% higher than that estimated by the UN Population Division, with only two exceptions. For Maldives and Qatar, adult mortality reported by the WHO is more than 20% lower than that released by the UN Population Division.[1] These differences may be related to the fact that mortality statistics provided by the WHO are only for a single year while those obtained from the UN Population Division are for a period of 5 years, but they could also arise from differences between the two organizations in the procedures and data used in making these estimates. These differences and their potential implications should be kept in mind by anyone using these estimated results or considering some of the suggestions made in this chapter.

## Changes in Adult Mortality in Asia Since 1950

Asia witnessed an extraordinary mortality decline in the last 60 years: life expectancy at birth increased by 28 years from 1950–1955 to 2005–2010. This improvement is far greater than that recorded in any other continent or in the world population as a whole, where the life expectancy rose by 21 years from 47 to 68 years (and this change would be smaller if Asia were excluded). During this remarkable transition, two major changes took place in Asia. First, because of the reduction in infant and child mortality, the chance of surviving to adulthood greatly increased, and those who could live to age 15 rose from some 70% to nearly 95%. Second, mortality in the adult population also fell significantly, and people who have entered adulthood now live much longer than before.

---

[1] Detailed adult mortality data used in this comparison have been provided by the WHO and the UN Population Division. The relative difference between the two sets of adult mortality is computed using $({}_{45}q_{15}^{WHO,2007} - {}_{45}q_{15}^{UN,2005-10}) \div {}_{45}q_{15}^{WHO,2007}$.

If we accept the estimate made by the UN Population Division, then in the first half of the 1950s, life expectancy at age 15 ($e_{15}$) was probably around 40 years for the Asian population as a whole. At this mortality level, around 50% of those who reached age 15 were expected to die between age 15 and 59. It would be more useful if adult mortality differentials between countries or regions were also examined, but this is not possible because of the lack of data collected at national or subnational levels.

A noticeable decline in adult mortality was observed in many Asian countries during the 1950s and 1960s. According to the data published by the UN Population Division and other researchers, life expectancy at age 15 reached 45 years or higher in Bangladesh, China, India, Japan, and Pakistan by the early 1970s. Indonesia was the only country with more than 50 million people where life expectancy at age 15 did not reach this level. Improvement was particularly notable in Japan and some other populations. By the early 1970s, male life expectancy at age 15 had reached 55 years or higher in Hong Kong, Iran, Israel, Japan, Kuwait, and Sri Lanka. Female life expectancy at the same age was close to or higher than 60 years in Hong Kong, Israel, Japan, Kuwait, and Singapore (UN Department of International Economic and Social Affairs 1982a: 132; UN Population Division 2007; Zhao and Kinfu 2005).

Adult and old-age mortality declined further in Asia between the early 1970s and 1990. As Table 6.1 shows, in the early 1970s life expectancies at age 15 ranged from 39.8 to 57.0 years for males and from 42.0 to 61.9 years for females among the listed populations. By 1990, life expectancies at this age had increased notably in most of these populations, ranging from 49.7 to 61.7 years for males and from 49.6 to 67.6 years for females. In three of the listed populations, Iran, Lebanon, and Sri Lanka, however, male life expectancy at age 15 declined over this period, likely because of wars during the 1980s.

Because of improvement in collecting mortality data, detailed mortality estimates for Asian populations, especially those produced by the WHO and the UN Population Division, have increasingly become available since the second half of the 1980s. These data allow a closer examination of changes, variations, and sex differentials in adult mortality in Asia. Table 6.2 presents probabilities of dying between age 15 and 59 ($_{45}q_{15}$) in Asian populations by sex in 1990 and 2007. Percentage changes, computed using $Percentage\ of\ change = (_{45}q_{15}^{2007} - {}_{45}q_{15}^{1990}) \div {}_{45}q_{15}^{1990}$, are also shown.

According to the statistics published by the WHO, many countries and areas experienced at least a 25% reduction in adult mortality in both male and female populations over the period 1990–2007. These populations can be broadly divided into two groups. One group consists of Brunei Darussalam, Cyprus, Hong Kong, Kuwait, the Republic of Korea, Singapore, and the United Arab Emirates. All of these populations, except for the Republic of Korea, are small, have experienced rapid development in recent decades, and enjoy considerable wealth. Their life expectancy was already high in 1990 and has improved further since. Bahrain, Israel, Japan, and Qatar in many respects are similar to these populations, although their mortality decline has been somewhat slower. The second group consists of populations that in 1990 had notably lower levels of socioeconomic development and only moderate life expectancies. Populations in this group include China, the Islamic Republic of Iran, Jordan, Lebanon, Maldives, Sri Lanka, the Syrian Arab Republic, and Turkey. Timor-Leste has also witnessed a marked improvement in adult survival, but its mortality level was and still is much higher than in this group of countries.

In contrast to those listed above, the following populations showed a slow decline, no notable changes, or even an increase in adult mortality over the period 1990–2007: Afghanistan, Cambodia, the Democratic People's Republic of Korea, Iraq, Kazakhstan, Kyrgyzstan, Mongolia, Myanmar, Thailand, Turkmenistan, and Uzbekistan. Many of these populations have recently experienced wars, social unrest, famines, restructuring after the collapse of the former USSR, or the spread of AIDS, which at least partly contributed to their poor performance in lowering adult mortality in recent years. For the Democratic People's Republic of Korea, the seemingly unchanged adult mortality shown in Table 6.2 is partly a result of the lack of accurate data.[2]

---

[2] There are clear differences between mortality estimates for the Democratic People's Republic of Korea made by the WHO and the UN Population Division. According to the WHO, life expectancies were 64.5 for males and 68.4 for females in 1990,

**Table 6.1** Changes in life expectancies at age 15 in selected Asian populations, 1970–1990

| Populations | Male c1970 | Male 1990 | Female c1970 | Female 1990 |
|---|---|---|---|---|
| Bangladesh | 46.3 | 50.8 | 46.1 | 49.6 |
| China | 54.0 | 55.8 | 56.4 | 58.6 |
| China, Hong Kong SAR | 54.6 | 60.3 | 61.9 | 65.9 |
| India | 49.1 | 50.3 | 47.6 | 52.0 |
| Indonesia | 39.8 | 51.6 | 42.0 | 52.9 |
| Iran (Islamic Republic of) | 54.8 | 51.4 | 56.2 | 55.5 |
| Israel | 57.0 | 60.9 | 60.1 | 64.3 |
| Japan | 56.0 | 61.7 | 61.1 | 67.6 |
| Jordan | 48.2 | 53.6 | 50.1 | 57.9 |
| Kuwait | 55.4 | 59.0 | 59.5 | 61.4 |
| Lebanon | 54.0 | 51.3 | 57.6 | 56.7 |
| Malaysia | 54.0 | 55.1 | 58.6 | 59.7 |
| Myanmar | 49.3 | 49.7 | 52.7 | 53.8 |
| Pakistan | 47.1 | 52.4 | 46.2 | 53.9 |
| Philippines | 51.8 | 52.4 | 56.4 | 57.7 |
| Republic of Korea | 48.3 | 53.6 | 55.5 | 61.9 |
| Singapore | 53.1 | 58.4 | 59.1 | 63.1 |
| Sri Lanka | 54.8 | 51.2 | 57.5 | 59.9 |
| Syrian Arab Republic | 51.8 | 53.3 | 55.0 | 57.0 |
| Taiwan | 54.0 | 57.3 | 58.6 | 62.5 |
| Thailand | 51.6 | 52.9 | 56.2 | 58.8 |
| Turkey | 53.2 | 54.5 | 55.4 | 58.3 |

Sources: UN (1982a), WHO (2009a), UN (2007), HMD; http://sowf.moi.gov.tw/stat/english/elife/5th-f.htm; and http://www.censtatd.gov.hk/products_and_services/products/individual_statistical_tables/index.jsp

There are still marked regional variations in adult mortality across Asia today. The lowest adult mortality is recorded in eastern Asia, followed by western Asia and southeastern Asia. South-central Asia has the highest adult mortality. The ten Asian populations with the lowest adult (male and female combined) mortality are Brunei Darussalam, Cyprus, Hong Kong, Israel, Japan, Kuwait, Qatar, the Republic of Korea, Singapore, and the United Arab Emirates. All of them are world or regional economic powers, or small and wealthy countries. In these populations, where standards of living and levels of health care are generally high, the probability of dying between ages 15 and 59 is lower or considerably lower than 0.10.

On the other end of the spectrum, the ten Asian populations with the highest adult mortality are Afghanistan, Bangladesh, Cambodia, Iraq, Kazakhstan, the Lao People's Democratic Republic, Mongolia, Myanmar, Nepal, and Turkmenistan. For these populations the probability of dying between ages 15 and 59 ranges from 0.25 to 0.49, markedly higher than the average for all of Asia. Most of these countries have low levels of socioeconomic development and standards of living. Many of them have recently experienced no decline, or even some increase, in adult mortality. Other Asian countries and territories spread between the two extreme groups, with their probabilities of dying at adult ages ranging between 0.10 and 0.25.

Old-age mortality also shows great variations in Asia. At age 60, for example, life expectancies are only 12.9 and 14.5 years for male and female populations in Afghanistan, but they are almost doubled in Japan, where men and women at the same age can expect to

---

and 64.4 for males and 68.4 for females in 2007 (WHO 2009a). According to the latest estimates made by the UN Population Division, life expectancies were 66.1 for males and 73.6 for females in 1990–1995, and 65.1 for males and 69.3 for females in 2005–2010 (UN Population Division 2009).

**Table 6.2** Changes in adult mortality in Asia, 1990–2007

| Populations | q15 males 1990 | q15 males 2007 | Percentage of change | q15 females 1990 | q15 females 2007 | Percentage of change |
|---|---|---|---|---|---|---|
| Afghanistan | 0.501 | 0.524 | 4.6 | 0.447 | 0.448 | 0.2 |
| Armenia | 0.280 | 0.242 | −13.6 | 0.135 | 0.102 | −24.6 |
| Azerbaijan | 0.285 | 0.219 | −23.2 | 0.165 | 0.137 | −17.3 |
| Bahrain | 0.106 | 0.116 | 9.9 | 0.107 | 0.083 | −22.1 |
| Bangladesh | 0.306 | 0.251 | −17.9 | 0.333 | 0.258 | −22.5 |
| Bhutan | 0.345 | 0.265 | −23.1 | 0.266 | 0.194 | −26.9 |
| Brunei Darussalam | 0.151 | 0.108 | −28.4 | 0.112 | 0.080 | −28.1 |
| Cambodia | 0.317 | 0.313 | −1.2 | 0.231 | 0.213 | −7.9 |
| China | 0.193 | 0.142 | −26.5 | 0.148 | 0.085 | −42.5 |
| China, Hong Kong SAR | 0.121 | 0.077 | −36.2 | 0.060 | 0.038 | −37.6 |
| Cyprus | 0.110 | 0.083 | −24.9 | 0.061 | 0.044 | −28.6 |
| Dem. People's Republic of Korea | 0.232 | 0.233 | 0.6 | 0.166 | 0.166 | 0.0 |
| Georgia | 0.242 | 0.219 | −9.5 | 0.110 | 0.085 | −22.8 |
| India | 0.306 | 0.250 | −18.2 | 0.257 | 0.177 | −31.2 |
| Indonesia | 0.286 | 0.229 | −19.9 | 0.266 | 0.188 | −29.1 |
| Iran (Islamic Republic of) | 0.291 | 0.161 | −44.6 | 0.208 | 0.100 | −51.8 |
| Iraq | 0.253 | 0.386 | 52.9 | 0.171 | 0.180 | 5.6 |
| Israel | 0.107 | 0.086 | −20.2 | 0.071 | 0.048 | −32.6 |
| Japan | 0.109 | 0.088 | −18.7 | 0.053 | 0.044 | −18.0 |
| Jordan | 0.241 | 0.181 | −24.7 | 0.166 | 0.117 | −29.5 |
| Kazakhstan | 0.318 | 0.427 | 34.3 | 0.150 | 0.185 | 23.2 |
| Kuwait | 0.112 | 0.071 | −37.0 | 0.084 | 0.049 | −41.7 |
| Kyrgyzstan | 0.290 | 0.320 | 10.0 | 0.156 | 0.166 | 6.7 |
| Lao People's Dem. Republic | 0.386 | 0.320 | −17.0 | 0.354 | 0.291 | −17.7 |
| Lebanon | 0.291 | 0.198 | −32.1 | 0.193 | 0.133 | −31.3 |
| Malaysia | 0.209 | 0.184 | −12.1 | 0.129 | 0.098 | −23.5 |
| Maldives | 0.287 | 0.110 | −61.7 | 0.341 | 0.079 | −76.9 |
| Mongolia | 0.263 | 0.401 | 52.3 | 0.196 | 0.192 | −1.8 |
| Myanmar | 0.331 | 0.366 | 10.6 | 0.238 | 0.266 | 11.9 |
| Nepal | 0.352 | 0.285 | −19.0 | 0.350 | 0.276 | −21.0 |
| Oman | 0.202 | 0.161 | −20.1 | 0.131 | 0.091 | −30.5 |
| Pakistan | 0.265 | 0.216 | −18.5 | 0.235 | 0.192 | −18.5 |
| Philippines | 0.282 | 0.231 | −17.9 | 0.167 | 0.121 | −27.5 |
| Qatar | 0.094 | 0.077 | −18.2 | 0.082 | 0.054 | −33.7 |
| Republic of Korea | 0.237 | 0.114 | −51.9 | 0.102 | 0.047 | −54.0 |
| Saudi Arabia | 0.222 | 0.192 | −13.4 | 0.148 | 0.116 | −21.3 |
| Singapore | 0.152 | 0.081 | −46.8 | 0.093 | 0.047 | −49.0 |
| Sri Lanka | 0.368 | 0.213 | −42.1 | 0.159 | 0.095 | −40.1 |
| Syrian Arab Republic | 0.248 | 0.181 | −27.2 | 0.187 | 0.121 | −35.3 |
| Taiwan | 0.179 | 0.148 | −17.6 | 0.090 | 0.062 | −31.2 |
| Tajikistan | 0.217 | 0.188 | −13.2 | 0.180 | 0.163 | −9.4 |
| Thailand | 0.259 | 0.282 | 9.0 | 0.147 | 0.141 | −4.1 |

**Table 6.2** (continued)

| Populations | $q_{15}$ males 1990 | $q_{15}$ males 2007 | Percentage of change | $q_{15}$ females 1990 | $q_{15}$ females 2007 | Percentage of change |
|---|---|---|---|---|---|---|
| Timor-Leste | 0.413 | 0.287 | −30.5 | 0.293 | 0.200 | −31.7 |
| Turkey | 0.216 | 0.150 | −30.5 | 0.147 | 0.086 | −41.5 |
| Turkmenistan | 0.301 | 0.372 | 23.6 | 0.192 | 0.210 | 9.1 |
| United Arab Emirates | 0.140 | 0.081 | −42.1 | 0.111 | 0.060 | −45.6 |
| Uzbekistan | 0.250 | 0.226 | −9.6 | 0.144 | 0.141 | −1.9 |
| Viet Nam | 0.236 | 0.193 | −18.1 | 0.168 | 0.113 | −32.7 |
| Yemen | 0.312 | 0.258 | −17.2 | 0.248 | 0.187 | −24.8 |

Sources: WHO (2009a); http://sowf.moi.gov.tw/stat/english/elife/te965210.ht; and http://www.censtatd.gov.hk/products_and_services/products/individual_statistical_tables/index.jsp

live for 22.7 and 28.2 years, respectively. A very strong positive relationship between adult and old-age mortality has been found in many Asian countries. Generally, populations with a relatively low adult mortality also have relatively low old-age mortality, and vice versa, so that many of the conclusions drawn above about adult mortality could also be applied to old-age mortality in Asia. Nonetheless, there are exceptions. There are eight female populations where the probabilities of dying between ages 15 and 59 are all very low, ranging from 0.04 to 0.06. Of these, in Cyprus, Israel, Japan, the Republic of Korea, and Singapore, female life expectancies at age 60 have reached 23.6, 24.5, 28.2, 24.7, and 25.4 years; but in Kuwait, Qatar, and the United Arab Emirates they have achieved only 21.3, 17.9, and 22.5 years, respectively. Although the difference between Japan and Qatar in the probability that an adult woman will die before age 60 is only 0.01, the gap between them in her life expectancy at age 60 is more than 10 years. In contrast, the gaps in male life expectancy at age 60 among populations with very low adult mortality are relatively small.

## Sex Differentials in Adult Mortality in Asia

Sex differentials in mortality are affected by the biological and genetic makeup of males and females, and the differences in their exposure to the risks of morbidity and mortality (Waldron 1983). This exposure is often related to different roles played by males and females in productive activities and human reproduction, their different status in the family and society, and their different risky behaviors (Bhatia 1983; Hetzel 1983; Kamel 1983; Verbrugge 1983). For these reasons, notable mortality differences are frequently found between males and females, and such differences also vary greatly across populations and over time (Lopez 1983).

In the late 1970s and early 1980s, a number of researchers and the UN Population Division examined sex differentials in mortality in some Asian populations on the basis of available mortality data. Their investigations revealed that in contrast to most developing countries studied, in India in 1970–1972, Iran in 1973–1976, Sri Lanka from the late 1940s to the early 1960s, and the Matlab district of Bangladesh in 1974–1976, male mortality was either lower than or very close to female mortality. In these populations, higher mortality was recorded in the female population aged from 1 to 44 (starting from age 0 in India and Iran) than for males. In contrast, in some populations in Eastern and Southeastern Asia (Hong Kong from the early 1960s to the mid-1970s, the Republic of Korea in 1971–1975, Singapore in 1969–1971, and Taiwan in 1960 and earlier), female mortality was much lower than male mortality, especially at age 45 and above (Goldman 1980; UN Department of International Economic and Social Affairs 1982b; UN Population Division 1983). Goldman suggested that "large sex differences in death rates" at older ages were found "only in Far Eastern populations," and this was a major characteristic of the so-called Far Eastern mortality pattern (Goldman 1980: 17; 2003). My recent study has shown that while a high sex ratio in adult and old-age mortality was indeed observed in some Asian populations at the time, the Far Eastern mortality pattern is not region-specific. Changes in sex differentials in mortality are closely related to the stage of mortality transition or the level of mortality, in addition to other factors (Zhao 2003, 2004). This suggestion has been supported by recent changes in sex differentials in mortality in Asia and other parts of the world.

Sex differentials in mortality showed notable changes in the 1970s and 1980s in many Asian populations where available data allow these changes to be examined. In general, mortality decline has been faster among females than males. The number of countries and areas with higher female than male mortality has decreased greatly. In many populations (e.g., Japan, the Republic of Korea, Singapore, and Taiwan) where female mortality was already lower than male mortality in the early 1970s, the gap between male and female life expectancies has further widened (UN Population Division 2009; Zhao and Kinfu 2005). One of the major factors contributing to this change is the increase in sex differentials in mortality among people aged 15–59.

Table 6.3 shows sex ratios of adult mortality for Asian populations in 1990 and 2007, which are calculated using the *Sex ratio of adult mortality* $= {}_{45}q_{15}^m \div {}_{45}q_{15}^f$. According to the statistics provided by the WHO, sex ratios of adult mortality have not changed or have decreased slightly over this period in the following countries: Azerbaijan, Brunei Darussalam, Japan, Lebanon, Myanmar, Pakistan, Sri Lanka, Tajikistan, and Uzbekistan. However, in more than 80% of Asian populations, sex ratios of adult mortality have further increased. Changes of this kind are particularly noticeable in Bahrain, China, Iraq, Maldives, Mongolia, Qatar, Taiwan, and Viet Nam, where the relative increase in the sex ratio of adult mortality is greater than 20%. These changes conform to a general pattern that mortality differentials between males and females tend to increase in the process, especially in the early stages, of mortality decline.

Table 6.4 lists Asian populations by their life expectancies and sex ratios of adult mortality. According to the data presented in this table, sex differentials of adult mortality in Asia in the early twenty-first century show the following patterns. While there are exceptions, higher sex ratios (1.75 and above) of adult mortality are largely found in two groups of countries or areas according to the estimates made by the WHO. The first includes Japan, the Republic of Korea, Hong Kong, Israel, Cyprus, and Taiwan (Singapore can also be listed in this group if the figure published by the UN Population Division is used).[3] All these populations have very low overall mortality—similar to that observed in most developed countries worldwide, where life expectancy at birth is around 76 years and the sex ratio of adult mortality is 2.3, according to the estimates made by the UN Population Division in 2006.[4]

The second group of countries with sex ratios of adult mortality of the same magnitude consists of five former members of the Union of Soviet Socialist Republics, Armenia, Georgia, Kazakhstan, Kyrgyzstan, and Turkmenistan, plus Mongolia. These countries generally have a life expectancy of less than 70 years. Their mortality patterns share some common characteristics with those of other former Soviet Republics and Eastern European countries (Holzer and Mijakowska 1983). According to the estimates made by the UN Population Division in 2006, in Eastern Europe, the life expectancy at birth was about 68 years and the sex ratio of adult mortality was 2.8. In Russia and the European members of the former Union of Soviet Socialist Republics life expectancies ranged from 64 to 72 years and sex ratios of adult mortality were even higher than the average for Eastern Europe, between 2.9 and 3.3 in the period 2000–2005 (UN Population Division 2007). This is a remarkable feature of the adult mortality found in these populations.

In contrast to those listed in the first group, countries and areas with a relatively low sex ratio of adult mortality are generally those with high-mortality risks. This group consists of Afghanistan, Bangladesh, the Lao People's Democratic Republic, Nepal, and Pakistan. In these countries and areas, life expectancies at birth

---

[3] The data for Taiwan are reported by the Taiwanese government.

[4] In this and the following two paragraphs, I use life expectancies at birth and sex ratios of adult mortality that are computed from mortality estimates for 2000–2005 made by the UN Population Division as an approximation to compare with mortality statistics for 2007 calculated from the data obtained from the WHO, because detailed adult mortality estimates for 2005–2010 are not available. The statistics for developed countries, Eastern European countries, and least developed countries are published by the UN Population Division, and the WHO has a different way of grouping its member countries. According to the latest estimate made by the UN Population Division, life expectancy at birth is around 77 years in more developed regions in the world (UN Population Division 2009).

**Table 6.3** Sex ratios of adult mortality in Asia, 1990 and 2007

| Populations | 1990 | 2007 | Populations | 1990 | 2007 |
|---|---|---|---|---|---|
| Afghanistan | 1.12 | 1.17 | Malaysia | 1.63 | 1.87 |
| Armenia | 2.07 | 2.37 | Maldives | 0.84 | 1.40 |
| Azerbaijan | 1.73 | 1.60 | Mongolia | 1.35 | 2.09 |
| Bahrain | 0.99 | 1.39 | Myanmar | 1.39 | 1.37 |
| Bangladesh | 0.92 | 0.97 | Nepal | 1.01 | 1.03 |
| Bhutan | 1.30 | 1.37 | Oman | 1.54 | 1.77 |
| Brunei Darussalam | 1.35 | 1.35 | Pakistan | 1.13 | 1.13 |
| Cambodia | 1.37 | 1.47 | Philippines | 1.68 | 1.90 |
| China | 1.30 | 1.67 | Qatar | 1.15 | 1.42 |
| China (Hong Kong SAR) | 2.02 | 2.03 | Republic of Korea | 2.33 | 2.44 |
| Cyprus | 1.80 | 1.89 | Saudi Arabia | 1.51 | 1.66 |
| Dem. People's Republic of Korea | 1.40 | 1.40 | Singapore | 1.64 | 1.71 |
| Georgia | 2.21 | 2.59 | Sri Lanka | 2.32 | 2.24 |
| India | 1.19 | 1.42 | Syrian Arab Republic | 1.32 | 1.49 |
| Indonesia | 1.08 | 1.22 | Taiwan | 1.99 | 2.39 |
| Iran (Islamic Republic of) | 1.40 | 1.61 | Tajikistan | 1.21 | 1.16 |
| Iraq | 1.48 | 2.15 | Thailand | 1.75 | 1.99 |
| Israel | 1.52 | 1.80 | Timor-Leste | 1.41 | 1.43 |
| Japan | 2.04 | 2.02 | Turkey | 1.47 | 1.75 |
| Jordan | 1.45 | 1.55 | Turkmenistan | 1.56 | 1.77 |
| Kazakhstan | 2.12 | 2.31 | United Arab Emirates | 1.26 | 1.34 |
| Kuwait | 1.34 | 1.45 | Uzbekistan | 1.74 | 1.60 |
| Kyrgyzstan | 1.86 | 1.92 | Viet Nam | 1.40 | 1.71 |
| Lao People's Democratic Republic | 1.09 | 1.10 | Yemen | 1.26 | 1.38 |
| Lebanon | 1.51 | 1.49 | | | |

Sources: WHO (2009a); http://sowf.moi.gov.tw/stat/english/elife/te965210.ht; and http://www.censtatd.gov.hk/products_and_services/products/individual_statistical_tables/index.jsp

range from 41.5 to 63.6 years, or 15–41 years lower than those recorded in the populations listed in the first group. Patterns of sex differentials of mortality in these countries are similar to those indicated by mortality estimates made by the UN Population Division in 2006 for the least developed countries in the world, where the life expectancy at birth was 53 years and the sex ratio of adult mortality was 1.14 in 2000–2005 (UN Population Division 2007). Although sex ratios of adult mortality are slightly higher in Bhutan, Cambodia, India, Myanmar, Timor-Leste, and Yemen, they are very similar to those of the five countries listed above and can be classified into the same group.

In other Asian countries and territories, sex ratios of adult mortality largely fall between the two extremes described above. These results further confirm that the increase in sex differentials of mortality is closely related to the mortality decline. In populations currently having a low or relatively low life expectancy, the sex ratio of adult mortality is likely to increase. This will further widen the gap between male and female life expectancies in these countries. Nonetheless, it is notable that among countries and areas that have reached similar life expectancies, many Arabic populations tend to have a lower sex ratio of adult mortality than their eastern and southeastern Asian counterparts. For example, life expectancies in Bahrain, Kuwait, Qatar, and the United Arab Emirates (and also Brunei Darussalam) are very close to those achieved in Hong Kong, Japan, the Republic of Korea, and Taiwan, but their sex ratios of adult mortality are considerably lower, as Table 6.4 shows.

Sex differentials of mortality among people aged 60 and over are broadly similar to those identified among people aged 15–59. Populations where females have a much lower mortality than males in adult ages are

**Table 6.4** Distribution of Asian populations by life expectancy at birth and sex ratio of adult mortality, 2007

| Life expectancy | Adult mortality ratio ≤1.24 | 1.25–1.49 | 1.50–1.74 | 1.75–1.99 | 2.00+ |
|---|---|---|---|---|---|
| <60 | Afghanistan | Myanmar | | | |
| 60.0–64.9 | Bangladesh<br>Lao People's Democratic Republic<br>Nepal<br>Pakistan | Bhutan<br>Cambodia<br>India<br>Timor-Leste<br>Yemen | | Turkmenistan | Iraq<br>Kazakhstan<br>Mongolia |
| 65.0–69.9 | Indonesia<br>Tajikistan | Dem. People's Republic of Korea | Azerbaijan<br>Uzbekistan | Kyrgyzstan | Armenia |
| 70.0–74.9 | | Lebanon<br>Maldives<br>Syrian Arab Republic | China<br>Iran (Islamic Republic of)<br>Jordan<br>Saudi Arabia<br>Viet Nam | Malaysia<br>Oman<br>Philippines<br>Thailand<br>Turkey | Georgia<br>Sri Lanka |
| 75.0 + | | Bahrain<br>Brunei Darussalam<br>Kuwait<br>Qatar<br>United Arab Emirates | Singapore | Cyprus<br>Israel | Japan<br>Republic of Korea<br>Taiwan<br>Hong Kong |

Sources: WHO (2009a); http://sowf.moi.gov.tw/stat/english/elife/te965210.ht; and http://www.censtatd.gov.hk/products_and_services/products/individual_statistical_tables/index.jsp

usually the populations where females have a considerably higher chance of surviving to very old ages than their male counterparts. A notable division is again observed in the populations where life expectancies at birth reach 75 years or higher. In Hong Kong, Japan, the Republic of Korea, Singapore, and Taiwan, ratios of male to female life expectancies at age 60 vary between 0.80 and 0.86. They are very similar to those found in western, southern, and northern Europe, where this ratio ranges from 0.82 to 0.84.[5] But in Bahrain, Brunei Darussalam, Kuwait, Qatar, and the United Arab Emirates, ratios of male to female life expectancies at age 60 are higher, ranging from 0.90 to 1.13.

## Major Causes of Death in Asia

Variations in levels and age patterns of mortality and their sex differentials are closely related to causes of death. Knowledge about these causes plays an important role in developing and implementing interventions to improve population health and reduce mortality (Murray et al., 1992). In his classic work on the epidemiological transition, Omran correctly pointed out that during this transition the impact of infectious and parasitic diseases, which greatly affected population health in the pretransition society, declines gradually. As a result, cardiovascular diseases and cancers become the major killers and mortality falls progressively (Omran 1971). Changes in causes of death and their variations across Asia provide additional evidence for the epidemiological transition theory and shed further light on recent mortality decline in the continent.

Collecting data on causes of death is even more difficult than recording the number of deceased people and often needs to be carried out by qualified medical professionals. For this reason, data on causes of

---

[5] The ratios for the Asian populations are derived from data provided by the WHO, and those for the three European regions are computed using the estimates made by the UN Population Division in 2006. Even if the UN estimates are used to compute the ratios for the Asian populations, the conclusion persists.

death collected from a large population over a long period were difficult to find in the past. In a book dedicated to the discussion of adult mortality and published in the early 1990s (Feachem et al., 1992), only seven Asian populations were listed as having complete recent vital registration data classified according to causes of death.

Since then, the WHO has made further efforts to collect and estimate cause-specific mortality data for its member countries. One of its latest endeavors is the recent update on causes of death and burden of diseases for 2004, but these data have two limitations. First, they do not provide detailed information by age groups, and can be used to examine major causes of death only in a whole country rather than in its adult population. This prevents us from establishing direct links among causes of death, adult mortality, and its sex differentials. Second, for a large number of countries, the cause-specific death rates are estimated from incomplete registration data, which could lead to considerable uncertainties about their reliability. Despite such limitations, these data can highlight some major changes in adult mortality and their variations in Asia at the beginning of the twenty-first century.

Available evidence shows that death from infectious diseases was high in many Asian populations in the past, and marked changes in the causal structure of deaths have taken place in the last half century (Abeykoon 2005; Choe and Chen 2005; Kim 2005; Murray et al., 1992; Nagaraj et al., 2008; Ruzicka and Hansluwka 1982; Zhao and Kinfu 2005). As a general trend, deaths caused by infectious diseases have fallen drastically in many countries, leading to a great reduction in overall mortality. As the epidemiological transition theory predicts, cardiovascular diseases, cancers, and other noncommunicable diseases have increasingly become the major health threat. Remarkable progress has been made in treating cardiovascular diseases and other degenerative diseases in recent decades. Because of this success, a number of Asian populations now share among the highest life expectancies ever recorded in the world. The epidemiological transition is not linear, however. In some other populations, some of the old infectious diseases have resurfaced. This together with the spread of new diseases such as AIDS and other health threats has greatly hampered further improvement in population health. Disparities in the causal structure of mortality in contemporary Asia remain very large.

Asia's populations can be broadly divided into three groups, reflecting patterns of major causes of death according to the data recently made available by the WHO (2009b). The first group consists of Japan, Bahrain, Brunei Darussalam, China, Cyprus, Georgia, Israel, Kuwait, Oman, Qatar, the Republic of Korea, Singapore, the Syrian Arab Republic, and the United Arab Emirates. In these countries, standardized mortality rates are all lower than 8.0 per thousand and those for deaths caused by communicable, maternal, perinatal, and nutritional conditions are lower than 1.0 per thousand. The contribution of these deaths to the standardized mortality rates ranges from 3.6 to 17.6%. Standardized mortality rates for noncommunicable diseases are also low (6.8 per thousand or lower) in these populations, though their contribution to overall mortality is relatively high, reaching 76.4% or higher. Standardized mortality rates for injuries are 0.7 per thousand or lower. Their contribution to total mortality accounts for less than 12.0%. It can be said that these countries and territories have led the epidemiological transition in Asia, and some of these countries have long been in what Olshansky and Ault (1986) identified as "the age of delayed degenerative diseases." (Table 6.5).

The second group consists of Afghanistan, Bangladesh, Cambodia, India, Indonesia, Iraq, Kazakhstan, Kyrgyzstan, the Lao People's Republic, Maldives, Myanmar, Nepal, Pakistan, Sri Lanka, Tajikistan, Turkmenistan, and Yemen. These countries all have a standardized mortality rate that is higher than 12.0 per thousand. The reasons for their high mortality vary, however. In Afghanistan, Bangladesh, Cambodia, India, the Lao People's Republic, Myanmar, Nepal, and Pakistan, standardized mortality rates for communicable, maternal, perinatal, and nutritional conditions are still higher than 3.8 per thousand. These countries seem to be still in the late stage of the classic epidemiological transition, where communicable, maternal, perinatal, and nutritional conditions still contribute more than 31.0% to total mortality. In 2005 maternal mortality ratios in these populations were still very high, all above 300 maternal deaths per 100,000 live births. In Afghanistan, Bangladesh, Cambodia, the Lao People's Republic, and Nepal, the ratios ranged from 540 to 1,800 maternal deaths per 100,000 live births—135 to 450 times higher than the lowest level (4 maternal deaths per 100,000 births) recorded in Asia. Bhutan

**Table 6.5** Standardized mortality rates (/1,000) in Asia, 2004

| Populations | All causes | Type 1 | Type 2 | Type 3 |
|---|---|---|---|---|
| Afghanistan | 23.67 | 9.61 | 13.09 | 0.97 |
| Armenia | 11.83 | 0.75 | 10.64 | 0.44 |
| Azerbaijan | 10.55 | 1.73 | 8.56 | 0.27 |
| Bahrain | 7.77 | 0.62 | 6.78 | 0.37 |
| Bangladesh | 12.43 | 4.13 | 7.30 | 1.00 |
| Bhutan | 11.83 | 3.76 | 7.08 | 0.99 |
| Brunei Darussalam | 5.40 | 0.37 | 4.73 | 0.29 |
| Cambodia | 15.65 | 6.60 | 8.32 | 0.73 |
| China | 7.86 | 0.86 | 6.27 | 0.73 |
| Cyprus | 4.73 | 0.35 | 4.12 | 0.27 |
| Democratic People's Republic of Korea | 10.22 | 3.17 | 6.43 | 0.62 |
| Georgia | 6.72 | 0.98 | 5.54 | 0.20 |
| India | 12.07 | 3.77 | 7.14 | 1.16 |
| Indonesia | 11.95 | 2.72 | 6.91 | 2.33 |
| Iran (Islamic Republic of) | 8.74 | 0.92 | 6.87 | 0.95 |
| Iraq | 18.58 | 3.55 | 10.18 | 4.86 |
| Israel | 4.23 | 0.26 | 3.68 | 0.29 |
| Japan | 3.62 | 0.39 | 2.84 | 0.39 |
| Jordan | 8.48 | 0.78 | 7.12 | 0.59 |
| Kazakhstan | 14.65 | 1.69 | 11.45 | 1.52 |
| Kuwait | 5.38 | 0.53 | 4.54 | 0.32 |
| Kyrgyzstan | 12.67 | 1.60 | 10.12 | 0.95 |
| Lao People's Democratic Republic | 14.02 | 4.45 | 8.28 | 1.30 |
| Lebanon | 8.86 | 0.80 | 7.15 | 0.91 |
| Malaysia | 8.37 | 1.61 | 6.23 | 0.53 |
| Maldives | 12.78 | 1.60 | 9.53 | 1.65 |
| Mongolia | 11.62 | 1.52 | 9.24 | 0.86 |
| Myanmar | 13.83 | 5.13 | 7.75 | 0.96 |
| Nepal | 13.52 | 4.63 | 7.69 | 1.19 |
| Oman | 7.29 | 0.26 | 6.64 | 0.39 |
| Pakistan | 12.11 | 4.03 | 7.17 | 0.91 |
| Philippines | 9.65 | 2.85 | 6.20 | 0.60 |
| Qatar | 6.09 | 0.61 | 5.13 | 0.35 |
| Republic of Korea | 5.69 | 0.32 | 4.70 | 0.67 |
| Saudi Arabia | 8.52 | 0.98 | 6.78 | 0.76 |
| Singapore | 4.52 | 0.79 | 3.45 | 0.27 |
| Sri Lanka | 12.52 | 1.13 | 6.81 | 4.58 |
| Syrian Arab Republic | 7.91 | 0.66 | 6.79 | 0.46 |
| Tajikistan | 12.27 | 3.10 | 8.84 | 0.34 |
| Thailand | 8.32 | 2.25 | 5.16 | 0.92 |
| Timor-Leste | 11.67 | 4.21 | 6.63 | 0.83 |
| Turkey | 8.21 | 0.82 | 7.01 | 0.39 |
| Turkmenistan | 14.24 | 2.53 | 11.00 | 0.71 |
| United Arab Emirates | 5.27 | 0.80 | 4.10 | 0.37 |
| Uzbekistan | 10.94 | 1.64 | 8.80 | 0.49 |
| Viet Nam | 8.44 | 1.70 | 6.11 | 0.64 |
| Yemen | 13.65 | 3.14 | 9.41 | 1.10 |

Source: WHO (2009b).
Notes: (1) Data for Hong Kong and Taiwan are not available. (2) Type 1: Communicable, maternal, perinatal, and nutritional conditions; Type 2: Noncommunicable diseases; and Type 3: Injuries.

**Table 6.6** Adult mortality rates (/1,000) by major causes of death in selected WHO regions, 2004

| | Male | | | | Female | | | |
|---|---|---|---|---|---|---|---|---|
| Region | All causes | Type 1 | Type 2 | Type 3 | All causes | Type 1 | Type 2 | Type 3 |
| World | 5.01 | 1.25 | 2.41 | 1.35 | 3.44 | 1.22 | 1.67 | 0.55 |
| EMR (B) | 2.90 | 0.21 | 1.67 | 1.03 | 1.78 | 0.24 | 1.22 | 0.32 |
| EMR (D) | 6.10 | 1.21 | 3.08 | 1.80 | 3.94 | 1.40 | 1.93 | 0.61 |
| EUR (B) | 4.02 | 0.27 | 2.96 | 0.79 | 1.97 | 0.15 | 1.64 | 0.18 |
| SEAR (B) | 5.92 | 1.56 | 2.35 | 2.01 | 4.72 | 1.14 | 1.98 | 1.60 |
| SEAR (D) | 5.36 | 1.52 | 2.50 | 1.33 | 4.15 | 1.38 | 1.94 | 0.83 |
| WPR (A) | 2.21 | 0.09 | 1.50 | 0.62 | 1.11 | 0.04 | 0.88 | 0.19 |
| WPR (B) | 3.29 | 0.45 | 1.96 | 0.89 | 1.98 | 0.22 | 1.29 | 0.46 |

Source: WHO, Deaths: WHO subregions, at http://www.who.int/healthinfo/global_burden_disease/estimates_regional/en/index.html.

Notes: (1) Type 1: Communicable, maternal, perinatal, and nutritional conditions; Type 2: Noncommunicable diseases; and Type 3: Injuries. (2) EMR B: Bahrain, Iran (Islamic Republic of), Jordan, Kuwait, Lebanon, Libyan Arab Jamahiriya, Oman, Qatar, Saudi Arabia, Syrian Arab Republic, Tunisia, and United Arab Emirates. EMR D: Afghanistan, Djibouti, Egypt, Iraq, Morocco, Pakistan, Somalia, Sudan, and Yemen. EUR B: Albania, Armenia, Azerbaijan, Bosnia and Herzegovina, Bulgaria, Georgia, and Kyrgyzstan, Poland, Romania, Serbia and Montenegro, Slovakia, Tajikistan, the former Yugoslav Republic of Macedonia, Turkey, Turkmenistan, and Uzbekistan. SEAR B: Indonesia, Sri Lanka, and Thailand. SEAR D: Bangladesh, Bhutan, Democratic People's Republic of Korea, India, Maldives, Myanmar, Nepal, and Timor-Leste. WPR A: Australia, Brunei Darussalam, Japan, New Zealand, and Singapore. WPR B: Cambodia, China, Cook Islands, Fiji, Kiribati, Lao People's Democratic Republic, Malaysia, Marshall Islands, Micronesia (Federated States of), Mongolia, Nauru, Niue, Palau, Papua New Guinea, Philippines, Republic of Korea, Samoa, Solomon Islands, Tonga, Tuvalu, Vanuatu, and Viet Nam.

and Timor-Leste can also be classified into this group, although their overall mortality is marginally lower.

In contrast, in Kazakhstan, Kyrgyzstan, Maldives, Tajikistan, Turkmenistan, and Yemen (and to some extent in Afghanistan and Iraq), the standardized mortality rate of deaths caused by communicable, maternal, perinatal, and nutritional conditions is relatively low, and their high overall mortality is largely driven by the relatively high standardized mortality rate for noncommunicable diseases, which are all higher than 8.8 per thousand. Mortality caused by these diseases in all these countries, except Afghanistan and Iraq, accounts for more than 69.0% of the overall mortality. Armenia, Mongolia, and Uzbekistan also have a high standardized mortality for noncommunicable diseases and can be classified into this group, although their standardized mortality rates for all deaths are slightly lower. Another noticeable characteristic in the causal structure of deaths in many high-mortality countries is the large proportion of people who died from road traffic accidents, AIDS, wars, and violence. For example, Sri Lanka and Iraq have extremely high standardized mortality rates for injuries (more than 4.5 per thousand), a result of war. These and other types of avoidable deaths will be further discussed in the next section.

Standardized death rates in other populations fall between the above two groups, ranging from 8.2 to 11.8 per thousand. In most of these populations, standardized mortality rates computed for communicable, maternal, perinatal, and nutritional conditions, noncommunicable diseases, and injuries are also at levels intermediate within Asia.

While there is no detailed data to compute adult mortality by causes of death for every Asian country, this can be done for some regions using data provided by the WHO. These results, which are shown in Table 6.6, are limited by the fact that they are calculated according to the WHO regional classifications, and some of these regional groups include non-Asian countries.[6] The results, therefore, can only approximate the causal structure of deaths among Asian populations in the listed regions, which are noted underneath the table.

Mortality statistics shown in Table 6.6 confirm the major conclusions drawn earlier. There are noticeable sex differentials in adult mortality, with male to

---

[6] Further information about the WHO's classifications of regional groups can be found on its website and in many of its publications.

female mortality ratios ranging from 1.3 to 2.0 in the selected regions. Among these regions, high adult mortality is observed in the WHO Eastern Mediterranean Region Group D and the WHO Southeast Asia Region Groups B and D, where mortality rates for all three broad categories of deaths are high for both male and female populations. These regions include the following Asian countries: Afghanistan, Bangladesh, Bhutan, the Democratic People's Republic of Korea, India, Indonesia, Iraq, Maldives, Myanmar, Nepal, Pakistan, Sri Lanka, Thailand, Timor-Leste, and Yemen. In contrast, adult mortality rates are markedly lower in the WHO Eastern Mediterranean Region Group B and WHO Western Pacific Region Groups A and B. The Eastern Mediterranean Region Group B consists mainly of oil-rich Arab countries in the Middle East. The Western Pacific Region is largely dominated by China and Japan, although Malaysia, the Philippines, the Republic of Korea, Viet Nam, and some other Asian countries are also clustered into this group. In the WHO European Region Group B, where seven former members of the Union of Soviet Socialist Republics and Turkey are found, the mortality rate due to noncommunicable diseases is rather high, in male populations in particular, although death rates from communicable, maternal, perinatal, and nutritional conditions and injuries are relatively low. These observations provide further evidence for the conclusions drawn earlier.

## Asian Mortality Transition: Some Lessons and Challenges

Many Asian countries have made significant progress in improving population health and lowering mortality. Their successful experiences not only provide further support to the theories of demographic and epidemiological transition, but also offer new lessons and insights that have greatly enriched our knowledge of these changes.

Asia's mortality decline and its variations further confirm the close link between the level of socioeconomic development and that of mortality. Because a low level of development often results in a low standard of living, unsanitary environment, poor nutrition, and inadequate health facilities, all of which directly affect population health, countries with an underdeveloped economy generally exhibit high mortality. It is due to this close link that promoting sustainable development and fighting poverty are overwhelmingly regarded as the most important strategies in improving population health and mortality. Sometimes, however, the level of development, especially when it is measured at the national level and exclusively in terms of the outcome of production or income, such as GDP or per capita GDP, may not give an accurate indication of health and mortality in the population, because the relationship between them is frequently affected by other factors. Indeed, relatively low mortality was achieved in a number of Asian populations when their economic development level was still rather low. This made a considerable contribution to the mortality decline in the world.

In the 1970s and 1980s, a positive correlation between per capita GDP and life expectancy was widely observed. Many countries had a life expectancy of less than 60 years even when their per capita GDP reached more than US $6,000. Differing from this general pattern, China, Sri Lanka, Kerala in India, Costa Rica, and some other populations achieved life expectancies of 66 years or higher even though their per capita GDP was still very low—in the three Asian populations, below US $320. According to Caldwell (1986), this impressive success, which was regarded as showing the route to low mortality in poor countries, was attributable to relatively egalitarian economic and social policies, including an emphasis on providing basic health to all or most people, the promotion of education, and a comparatively high degree of female autonomy. It is interesting to note, however, that the survival advantage observed in China and Sri Lanka has largely disappeared in recent years. Viet Nam is perhaps the only notable exception where a comparatively high life expectancy has been reached while the level of per capita GDP is still relatively low.[7] This seems to suggest that the relationship between mortality level and per capita GDP has become stronger than before.

While economic development is widely seen as the major driver of improvement in standards of living, nutritional intake, living and working environments,

---

[7] The comparison was made on the basis of mortality data provided by the WHO (2009) and the World Development Indicator Database constructed by the World Bank (2008).

and availability of and access to medical care, which in turn contribute to the reduction in mortality, various other factors determine whether such benefits reach all subpopulation groups. These factors include certain social practices and traditions, distribution of wealth in the population, gender differences in roles and statuses in society or family, and people's health knowledge and risk-preventing behavior. This is another area where Asia's experiences can considerably enrich our knowledge about the mortality transition.

The evidence provided in this chapter has shown that as far as sex differentials in mortality are concerned, there is a notable divide between some Asian populations. In many of the former Republics of the Soviet Union and a few countries that share some characteristics with them, a marked female survival advantage has been observed. In contrast, a comparatively low sex ratio in mortality (as shown in Table 6.4) has been found in some South Asian and Western Asian populations. The notable male mortality disadvantage in the first group is partly attributable to certain risky behaviors such as alcohol abuse and smoking that have been widespread in their male populations. The comparatively small female survival advantage in the second group, at least in some countries, is likely to be related to the relatively low status and lack of autonomy of women, as Caldwell (1986) suggested. These conclusions are largely consistent with and are supported by those drawn from other studies (Bhatia 1983; Caldwell 1986; Holzer and Mijakowska 1983; Chapter 4 by Murphy, this volume). Another possible factor contributing to the small sex difference in adult and old-age mortality in some of these countries may be the relatively low prevalence of smoking in their male populations.

Asia has great potential for further improving population health and reducing mortality. According to the medium variant of the latest population projection made by the UN Population Division, life expectancy in Asia will increase from its current 69 to 77 years by 2050 (UN Population Division 2009). During this process, there will be further changes in the causal structure of deaths. Adult mortality will continue to fall. Sex differentials in mortality will widen in many countries. Although mortality improvement will take place widely in Asian populations, great discrepancies in their mortality levels, gender differences, and age patterns of overall and cause-specific mortality will remain.

Asian populations face enormous challenges in achieving the UN projected outcomes in improving population health and lowering mortality. These challenges are clearly indicated by the significant gap in health situation and survivorship between a large number of Asian countries and developed countries worldwide. In many of these Asian countries, mortality attributable to communicable, maternal, perinatal, and nutritional conditions is still high. Many of them still suffer greatly from certain infectious diseases that were common in the past, their reemergence, or the spread of new infectious diseases. Their life expectancies are 15–40 years lower than those achieved in many developed countries. These populations are still working toward what had been accomplished by developed countries half a century or even a century ago. One of the best examples is the level of maternal mortality. According to the WHO, in high-income countries worldwide in 2005, the maternal mortality ratio was less than 10 per 100,000 live births, but there were still 14 Asian countries where maternal mortality ratios were higher than 300 per 100,000 live births, with many women dying from childbearing-related causes (WHO et al., 2007). If these countries could greatly reduce their maternal mortality by the year 2015, as recommended by the Millennium Development Goals, their female adult mortality rates would be markedly lower.

After the completion of the classic epidemiological transition as described by Omran, major causes of death have been replaced by noncommunicable diseases, such as cardiovascular diseases and cancers, in most Asian populations. There are great variations across countries in age-standardized mortality rates for noncommunicable diseases, however, as Table 6.5 shows. In Japan, Singapore, and Israel, these death rates have already fallen below 4 per thousand, but the rates in many other countries are significantly higher. In contrast to fighting traditional infectious diseases, which could be achieved through immunization and vaccination, public health campaigns, or other relatively easily implemented health programs, lowering mortality caused by cancers, cardiovascular, and other degenerative diseases usually requires more expensive medicine, sophisticated medical technology, and long-term or even lifetime treatment. Combating these diseases is often costly and needs to be supported by adequate health facilities and health care systems. From this point of view, fighting major noncommunicable diseases is a more challenging task that most

Asian countries, just like many other parts of the world, will face in the twenty-first century.

Another major challenge facing many Asian populations is reducing avoidable mortality. It is worth noting that, accompanying the epidemiological transition, there are substantial changes in major health risk factors and strategies of risk prevention. When mortality was high, effective intervention was usually concentrated on reducing poverty, eradicating unsanitary living conditions, improving availability of and access to health services (though often very basic), and implementing immunization and vaccination programs. But when mortality fell to moderate levels, promoting individual awareness about achieving a healthy lifestyle became increasingly important (Devasahayam 2005). The discussion of causes of death presented earlier has shown that in Asia many deaths are behavior-related and therefore could be prevented with sufficient public and individual effort. This is clearly demonstrated by the following examples.

First, smoking is a major health threat in Asia, where a large number of people die each year from smoking-related diseases. According to the latest estimates made by the WHO, more than half of adult males are smokers in many Asian countries, including Armenia (55%), China (60%), the Democratic People's Republic of Korea (59%), Georgia (57%), Indonesia (66%), Jordan (63%), the Lao People's Democratic Republic (65%), Malaysia (54%), the Republic of Korea (53%), and Turkey (52%). In countries like Bangladesh, Japan, the Philippines, and Viet Nam, proportions of smokers among adult males are higher than 40% (WHO 2008b). Although it has been well established that smoking is a major risk factor for certain types of cancers and cardiovascular diseases, it remains a serious health problem in these countries. For this reason, their death rates for certain diseases, lung cancers for example, are likely to increase in the near future.

Second, mortality caused by injuries, traffic-accident-related injuries in particular, remains relatively high in many Asian countries. In Iran, Iraq, Lebanon, Mongolia, and Yemen, standardized mortality rates for deaths caused by traffic accidents alone reached more than 0.4 per thousand (WHO 2009b). A reduction of 50% in traffic-accident-related deaths will make a considerable contribution to mortality decline in these countries.

Third, population health is threatened by the spread of HIV/AIDS in some Asian countries. According to the WHO, prevalence rates of HIV among people aged 15 years and over were more than 1.0 per thousand people in nearly 20 Asian populations in 2005. In Cambodia, Myanmar, and Thailand, the prevalence rates were particularly high, at 14.68, 9.82, and 11.44 per 1,000 people, respectively. The cause-specific mortality rates for HIV/AIDS in Cambodia, Myanmar, and Thailand reached 1.14, 0.73, and 0.33 per 1,000 people in the same year (WHO 2008a). As the latest UNAIDS publication reports, the epidemic in these three countries has shown a slight decline in recent years, but in some other countries such as Pakistan, Viet Nam, and Indonesia, the estimated number of people living with HIV increased markedly between 2000 and 2005. The total number of people living with HIV has reached five million in Asia (UNAIDS 2008). A significant reduction in these behavior-related deaths would make a major contribution toward improving population health and survival, especially adult mortality, but this will require great efforts made jointly by both the government and all members in the society.

**Acknowledgment** The author would like to thank the WHO and the UN Population Division for providing detailed mortality data for this chapter, Pfizer and University of Cambridge for providing partial support to this research and Mie Inoue, Yohannes Kinfu, François Pelletier, and Jiaying Zhao for their help and support.

## References

Abeykoon, A.T.P.L. 2005. "Maternal and Adult Mortality in Sri Lanka." In Social Development Division, the United Nations Economic and Social Commission for Asia and the Pacific (ESCAP) (eds.) *Emerging Issues of Health and Mortality in the Asian and Pacific Region*, pp. 97–108. Asian Population Studies Series No. 163. New York, NY, United Nations.

Bhatia, S. 1983. "Traditional Practices Affecting Female Health and Survival: Evidence from Countries of South Asia." In A.D. Lopez and L.T. Ruzicka (eds.), *Sex Differentials in Mortality*, pp. 165–77. Canberra, Australian National University Press.

Caldwell, J. 1986. "Routes to Low Mortality in Poor Countries." *Population and Development Review* 12(2):171–219.

Choe, M.K. and J. Chen. 2005. "Health Transition in Asia: Implications for Research and Health Policy." In Social Development Division, the United Nations Economic and Social Commission for Asia and the Pacific (ESCAP) (eds.) *Emerging Issues of Health and Mortality in the Asian and*

*Pacific Region*, pp. 37–57. Asian Population Studies Series No. 163. New York, NY, United Nations.

Devasahayam, T.W. 2005. "Health and Mortality: Situations and Challenges in Asia and the Pacific." In Social Development Division, the United Nations Economic and Social Commission for Asia and the Pacific (ESCAP) (eds.) *Emerging Issues of Health and Mortality in the Asian and Pacific Region*, pp. 11–35. Asian Population Studies Series No. 163. New York, NY, United Nations.

Feachem, R.G.A., T. Kjellstrom, C.J.L. Murray, M. Over, and M.A. Phillips. 1992. *The Health of Adults in the Developing World*. Oxford, Oxford University Press.

Goldman, N. 1980. "Far Eastern Patterns of Mortality." *Population Studies* 34:5–19.

Goldman, N. 2003. "A Reply to 'On the Far Eastern Pattern of Mortality' by Zhongwei Zhao." *Population Studies* 57(3):367–70.

Hetzel, B.S. 1983. "Lifestyle Factors in Sex Differentials in Mortality in Developed Countries." In A.D. Lopez and L.T. Ruzicka(eds.), *Sex Differentials in Mortality*, pp. 247–77. Canberra, Australian National University Press.

Holzer, J.Z. and J. Mijakowska. 1983. "Differential Mortality of the Sexes in the Socialist Societies of East Europe." In A.D. Lopez and L.T. Ruzicka (eds.), *Sex Differentials in Mortality*, pp. 121–39. Canberra, Australian National University Press.

Kamel, N.M. 1983. "Determinants and Patterns of Female Mortality Associated with Women's Reproductive Role." In A.D. Lopez and L.T. Ruzicka(eds.), *Sex Differentials in Mortality*, pp. 179–91. Canberra, Australian National University Press.

Kim, T.H. 2005. "Changes in Age-Sex Mortality Patterns and Causes of Death in the Republic of Korea." *Asia-Pacific Population Journal* 20(2):97–111.

Lopez, A. 1983. "The Sex Mortality Differential in Developed Countries." In A.D. Lopez and L.T. Ruzicka (eds.), *Sex Differentials in Mortality*, pp. 53–120. Canberra, Australian National University Press.

Lopez, A.D., J. Salomon, O. Ahmad, C.J.L. Murray, and D. Mafat. 2000. *Life Tables for 191 Countries: Data, Methods and Results*. GPE Discussion Paper No. 9. Geneva, World Health Organization.

Murray, C.J.L., G. Yang, and X. Qiao. 1992. "Adult Mortality: Levels, Patterns, and Causes." In R.G.A. Feachen, T. Kjellstrom, C.J.L. Murray, M. Over, and M.A. Phillips (eds.), *The Health of Adults in the Developing World*, pp 23–111. Oxford, Oxford University Press.

Nagaraj, S., N. Tey, C. Ng, B. Balakrishnan, and N. Sah. 2008. "Ethnic Dimensions of Gender Differentials in Mortality in Malaysia." *Journal of Population Research* 25:183–205.

Olshansky, S.J. and B. Ault. 1986. "The Fourth Stage of the Epidemiologic Transition: The Age of Delayed Degenerative Diseases." *Milbank Quarterly* 64(3):355–91.

Omran, A.R. 1971. "The Epidemiologic Transition." *Milbank Quarterly* 49(4):509–38.

Ruzicka, L.T. and H. Hansluwka. 1982. "Mortality Transition in South and East Asia: Technology Confronts Poverty." *Population and Development Review* 8:567–88.

UNAIDS. 2008. *Report on the Global AIDS Epidemic*. Available online at http://www.unaids.org/en/Knowledge Centre/HIVData/GlobalReport/2008/2008_Global_report.asp. Retrieved 22 July 2009.

United Nations Department of International Economic and Social Affairs. 1982a. *Levels and Trends of Mortality Since 1950*. New York, NY, United Nations.

United Nations Department of International Economic and Social Affairs. 1982b. *Model Life Tables for Developing Countries*. New York, NY, United Nations.

United Nations Population Division. 1983. "Patterns of Sex Differentials in Mortality in Less Developed Countries." In A.D. Lopez and L.T. Ruzicka (eds.), *Sex Differentials in Mortality: Trends, Determinants and Consequences*, pp. 7–32. Canberra, Department of Demography, Australian National University.

United Nations Population Division. 2007. *World Population Prospects: The 2006 Revision, Detailed Mortality Statistics for Member States*, provided to the author by UN Population Division.

United Nations Population Division. 2009. *World Population Prospects: The 2008 Revision Population Database*. Available online at http://esa.un.org/unpp/index.asp?panel=1. Retrieved July 29, 2009.

Verbrugge, L.M. 1983. "The Social Roles of the Sexes and Their Relative Health and Mortality." In A.D. Lopez and L.T. Ruzicka (eds.), *Sex Differentials in Mortality: Trends, Determinants and Consequences*, pp. 221–45. Canberra, Department of Demography, Australian National University.

Waldron, I. 1983. "The Role of Genetic and Biological Factors in Sex Differentials in Mortality." In A.D. Lopez and L.T. Ruzicka (eds.), *Sex Differentials in Mortality: Trends, Determinants and Consequences*, pp. 141–64. Canberra, Department of Demography, Australian National University.

WHO, UNICEF, UNFPA, and the World Bank. 2007. *Maternal Mortality in 2005: Estimates Developed by WHO, UNICEF, UNFPA, and the World Bank*. Geneva, WHO.

World Bank. 2008. *World Development Indicators Database*. Washington, DC, World Bank. Available online at http://unstats.un.org/unsd/demographic/products/socind/inc.eco.htm. Retrieved July 2009.

World Health Organization (WHO). 2008a. *The Global Burden of Disease: 2004 Update*. Geneva, WHO. Available online at http://www.who.int/healthinfo/global_burden_disease/2004_report_update/en/index.html. Retrieved July 2009.

World Health Organization (WHO). 2008b. *WHO Report on the Global Tobacco Epidemic: The MPOWER Package*. Geneva, WHO.

World Health Organization (WHO). 2009a. *Life Tables for WHO Member States for 1990, 2000 and 2007*, provided to the author by the WHO.

World Health Organization (WHO). 2009b. *Estimated Total Deaths by Cause and WHO Member State*, provided to the author by the WHO.

World Health Organisation (WHO). 2010. WHO subregions, at http://www.who.int/healthinfo/global_burden_disease/estimates_regional/en/index.html. Retrieved October 2010.

Zhao, Z. 2003. "On the Far Eastern Pattern of Mortality." *Population Studies* 57(2):131–47.

Zhao, Z. 2004. "The Far Eastern Pattern of Mortality Is Not a Unique Regional Mortality Model: A Reply to Noreen Goldman." *Population Studies* 58(1):121–24.

Zhao, Z. 2008. "Historical Demography." In Y. Zeng (ed.), *Demography, in Encyclopedia of Life Support Systems (EOLSS)*. Oxford, UK, Eolss Publishers. Available online at http://www.eolss.net. Retrieved July 2009. Developed Under the Auspices of the UNESCO.

Zhao, Z. and Y. Kinfu. 2005. "Mortality Transition in East Asia." *Asian Population Studies* 1(1):3–30.

# Chapter 7
# Adult Mortality in Africa

Georges Reniers, Bruno Masquelier, and Patrick Gerland

## Introduction

In the 1960s and 1970s, it was common for observers to speculate about a global convergence in mortality patterns (Omran 1971; Stolnitz 1965; UN 1975). The optimism was based on the diffusion of medical knowledge and technologies in the post-World War II period, which facilitated faster improvements in the life expectancy of developing countries compared to the eighteenth- and nineteenth-century mortality transitions in Western Europe (Davis 1956; Omran 1971). Meanwhile, the optimism about anticipated trajectories of mortality around the world has been replaced by more uncertainty, and more cautious—in some instances pessimistic—assessments of mortality patterns and speculations about future trends (Moser et al. 2005; Sen and Bonita 2000; Wilson 2001). The changing tone in the literature is led by observations of mortality reversals in a wide range of populations and for a variety of reasons: over the last two decades, about one out of four countries in the world experienced a mortality crisis and decreasing life expectancy due to conflict (e.g., Rwanda, Angola, Sierra Leone, Liberia, Iraq, Somalia), economic crises and the failure of health systems (e.g., Russia, Kazakhstan, Belarus, Ukraine, Democratic People's Republic of Korea, Zimbabwe), and, most importantly, because of the mortality impact of the HIV/AIDS epidemic (UN 2009). The idea of a global convergence in mortality patterns is also challenged by unabated gains in life expectancy in many of the industrialized countries since the 1970s (Vallin and Meslé 2004), and persistent health inequalities within countries.

African countries often contribute in conspicuous ways to the growing global inequality in mortality levels and life expectancies, but a thorough analysis is constrained by the lack of reliable and exhaustive vital events data for the region. The paucity of vital statistics is problematic for estimating adult mortality in particular because information on infant and child mortality is—in principle—easily elicited from the mothers. In this chapter, we present a review of all-cause adult mortality estimates based on sibling survival data from the Demographic and Health Surveys (DHS), and complement these with estimates from United Nations (UN) agencies. In some countries, adult health has drastically deteriorated since the 1980s, leading to an increasing heterogeneity in adult mortality levels. More hopeful are the first indications of a decline in adult mortality in some of the countries that are hardest hit by the HIV/AIDS epidemic. Sparse information on causes of death suggests, however, that the extremely high adult mortality levels in some of the southeastern African countries are not the sole result of the HIV/AIDS epidemic, but due to the triple burden of infectious and chronic diseases, as well as external injuries (Box 7.2). Before presenting these results in greater detail, we discuss some of the existing approaches for estimating adult mortality in African populations and the methodological challenges involved (see also Box 7.1).

G. Reniers (✉)
Department of Sociology and Office of Population Research, Princeton University, Princeton, NJ 08544, USA
e-mail: greniers@princeton.edu

## Approaches for Estimating Adult Mortality

A review of adult mortality trends in Africa inevitably induces controversies about data sources and methods of estimation, and these intensified following the resurgence of epidemics, HIV/AIDS in particular. Because of a lack of reliable data for estimating adult mortality, a common practice has been to derive adult mortality indices for populations in developing countries from childhood mortality estimates and model mortality schedules. Even though it was well understood that the construction of model life tables hardly relied on empirical data from populations to which they were applied, it was deemed to produce satisfactory results for most purposes. The estimation of maternal mortality rates serves as an illustrative exception. HIV/AIDS, however, drastically changed the age structure of mortality, and, therefore, the relationship between childhood and adult mortality implied in these model age patterns of mortality. In addition, the HIV/AIDS epidemic complicates the task of estimating child mortality itself (Hallett 2010). The limitations of this childhood mortality-matching methodology in populations with generalized HIV/AIDS epidemics thus invigorated the search for alternatives. This section presents a cursory overview of some of the direct and indirect approaches for estimating adult mortality that have been developed or that received more attention since the advent of HIV/AIDS. Other—in some instances—more comprehensive discussions are presented elsewhere (Bradshaw and Timaeus 2006; Brass 1996; Gakidou et al. 2004; Hill 2003; Hill et al. 2005, 2007; Timæus 1991b; UN 1983, 2002).

The crux of all difficulties in estimating adult mortality in most African countries is the absence of an accurate vital registration system. Apart from the northern African countries, only Mauritius, Cape Verde, Réunion, and South Africa have consistently provided nationally representative vital statistics over the last few decades (Table 7.1). Furthermore, the quality of vital registration in developing countries has not changed much in the last few decennia (Cleland 1996; Mahapatra et al. 2007; Mathers et al. 2005; Setel et al. 2007). Despite these shortcomings, vital events registration has proven useful for documenting the severe mortality impact of HIV/AIDS in South Africa and Zimbabwe (Dorrington et al. 2001; Feeney 2001). Parish registers and burial surveillance, data sources reminiscent of those used in historical mortality studies in Europe, have been used in South Africa, Namibia, and Ethiopia (Katzenellenbogen et al. 1993; Notkola et al. 2000; Reniers et al. 2009), but these remain localized endeavors that are unlikely to be reproduced on a large scale. Sample vital registration systems, which restrict the registration of vital events to a nationally representative selection of population clusters, have been used with some success in India and China only (Bhat 2002; Cleland 1996; Hill et al. 2007; Setel et al. 2005).

**Table 7.1** Number of African countries with data for estimating mortality, by type of information and period ($n = 54$)

| Type of information collected | 1950–1959 | 1960–1969 | 1970–1979 | 1980–1989 | 1990–1999 | 2000 and later |
|---|---|---|---|---|---|---|
| Infant and child mortality | | | | | | |
| – Children ever born and children surviving only | 5 | 20 | 27 | 33 | 37 | 39 |
| – Maternity histories | – | – | 10 | 20 | 35 | 38 |
| Adult mortality | | | | | | |
| – Household deaths | 5 | 14 | 20 | 22 | 20 | 20 |
| – Maternal orphanhood[a] | – | 5 | 13 | 26 | 18 | 13 |
| – Paternal orphanhood[a] | – | 5 | 13 | 20 | 15 | 13 |
| – Survival of siblings | – | – | – | – | 23 | 32 |
| – Widowhood | – | – | 6 | 5 | – | 1 |
| – Vital registration | 11 | 15 | 14 | 10 | 13 | 11 |

Source: (UN 2007).

Notes: In some countries, the same information has been collected on multiple occasions. In the case of household deaths, for example, this question has been asked at least once for 40 of the 54 countries.

[a]Some surveys (e.g., DHS) collect data on maternal and paternal survival for youngsters under the age of 18. These are not included in the table.

In populations with reasonable coverage of vital registration, population censuses provide the denominator for calculating death rates. An obvious disadvantage of this approach is that the events of interest and the exposure time are obtained through different data-generating systems, and these are not necessarily characterized by the same coverage. In these situations, a variety of death distribution methods (e.g., growth balance, synthetic extinct generations, or a combination of both) can be used to evaluate the completeness of death registration and enumerated census populations, and to adjust mortality estimates in case of reporting or coverage deficiencies (Bennett and Horiuchi 1984; Hill 1987; Hill et al. 2005, 2009; Preston et al. 1980; Timæus 1991b).

Where vital registration data are lacking, censuses can also provide direct estimates of adult mortality via the inclusion of questions about the number of household deaths in the past calendar year or another reference period. More than 40 countries have included these questions in one or more of their censuses or surveys (Table 7.1), and even though the same death distribution methods can be used for evaluating data quality and correcting mortality estimates, the results can be variable and characterized by considerable uncertainty due to extensive underreporting of deaths (Hill et al. 2009; Timæus 1991b). Murray and colleagues (2010) therefore suggest that the corrected estimates produced by death distribution methods need to be evaluated alongside other estimates of adult mortality.

In countries with multiple censuses, intercensal survival methods can be used to derive adult mortality estimates from successive census counts (UN 1983, 2002). Besides potential problems with intercensal migrations, age distributions often suffer from age heaping, age exaggeration, and variation in census coverage rates, and these undermine the accuracy of the ensuing estimates (Pison 1995).

Population censuses and surveys have proven to be a more useful source of child mortality estimates based on the Brass questions of children ever born alive and children surviving. The Brass estimation approach was one of the first of a family of methods commonly referred to as *indirect estimation* techniques. Brass and his students later developed a set of related methods based on the survival status of parents (i.e., the orphanhood method), spouses (i.e., the widowhood method), and siblings (e.g., the sisterhood method) (Brass and Hill 1973; Graham et al. 1989; Hill and Trussell 1977; Timæus 1991a; Timæus et al. 2001). All these methods depart from the idea that mortality estimates can be derived from the survival status of a relative, as long as exposure time can be assessed via the age of the respondent. Calculations typically make use of the proportion of living mothers, sisters, or spouses at the time of the survey. In the maternal orphanhood method, for example, the proportion with mothers who are alive is closely related to the life table probability of surviving for a number of years equal to the age of the respondent and starting from the mean age at childbearing at the time of the respondent's birth. Because these estimates pertain to a mortality regime of the past, part of the difficulty consisted of developing schemes for dating those estimates (e.g., Brass and Bamgboye 1981; Palloni and Heligman 1985; Zlotnik and Hill 1981).

Much of the progress in estimating mortality in the majority of African countries thus rested on the development of more sophisticated methods for data that are not suitable for calculating conventional events-exposure type rates. The alternative has been to collect better and more comprehensive data on smaller and thus more manageable geographic units. Sample vital registration systems are an example, but more common in Africa are the Demographic Surveillance Sites (DSS). Over 20 such sites exist in Africa (many are part of the INDEPTH Network), and they typically cover a population ranging from 50,000 to 200,000 (INDEPTH Network 2002). The methodology used for the surveillance varies, but usually consists of regular (e.g., trimestrial, semestrial, or annual) household visits by an enumerator to record all vital events. In recent years, the registration of a death in the household is often followed by a verbal autopsy interview with a close relative or caretaker of the deceased (Soleman et al. 2006). Routine verbal autopsy collection in most DSS sites has contributed to a better understanding of the cause-of-death structure in African populations (see Box 7.2). Often-cited weaknesses of the DSS for adult mortality estimates are the modest size of the enumerated population and their non-representativeness. The latter may result from the fact that some sites have been selected for their particular epidemiological profile. In addition, nearly all DSS sites are in rural settings, and that limits our understanding of mortality patterns in urban areas (exceptions are the DSS in Bissau, Dar es Salaam, Ouagadougou, and Nairobi).

None of the data sources or approaches discussed above have been formally embraced by international organizations for producing time series of adult mortality because they do not usually produce estimates for all African countries, and because of the challenges involved in (1) reconciling differences between estimates from different sources and methods for each country (see Box 7.1), (2) reconstructing internally consistent national time series (e.g., avoiding implausible sex crossovers by age and over time), and (3) ensuring that levels and trends by country are coherent with key relationships (e.g., between $_5q_0$ and $_{45}q_{15}$, between $_{45}q_{15}$ and $e_{60}$) inferred from trustworthy demographic datasets (e.g., DSS, Human Mortality Database) and model life tables.

### Box 7.1 Reconciling Adult Mortality Estimates

Mortality estimation for African populations is not only hindered by the lack of data. In settings where multiple data sources exist, the estimates are often discrepant. In this short exposition, we demonstrate that the reconciliation of these estimates is complex, an exercise that is often complicated by simultaneous changes in mortality patterns and the quality of the data that are available for estimating those trends.

Figure 7.1 depicts female adult mortality estimates for Zimbabwe derived from (adjusted) vital registration data, (adjusted) household deaths, indirect maternal orphanhood estimates from census and DHS data, as well as data from a longitudinal population-based survey in Manicaland. These are compared with estimates from the United Nations Population Division (UNPD) and the sibling survival estimates reported in Table 7.3. Most of these estimates correspond relatively well, both in terms of the mortality level and in terms of the trends. If anything, the slope of the trend in $_{45}q_{15}$ based on the sibling survival data is not as steep as the one suggested by reported household deaths or the UNPD estimate, and they tend to diverge more toward the end of the estimation period. The

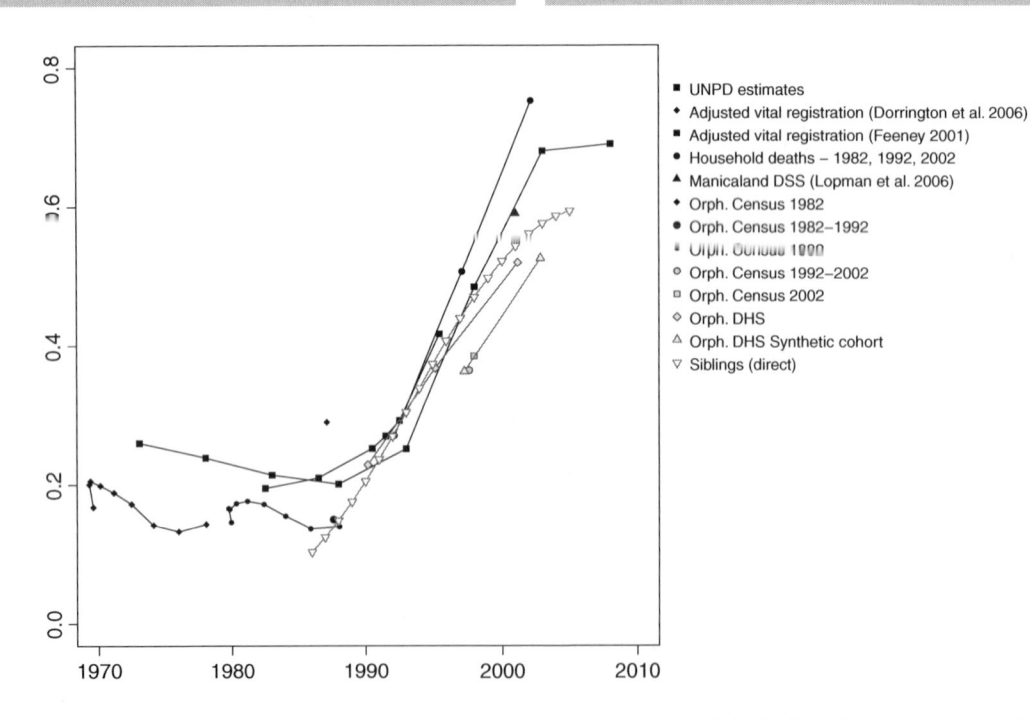

**Fig. 7.1** Zimbabwe: female 45q15 by estimation method and data source. Notes: Sibling survival and UNPD estimates are those reported in Fig. 7.7. Estimates based on vital registration data come from Feeney (2001) and Dorrington et al. (2006), adjusted household deaths from Dorrington et al. (2006), indirect maternal orphanhood estimates from census and DHS data are based on our own calculations. The small area data from the Manicaland DSS come from Lopman et al. (2006)

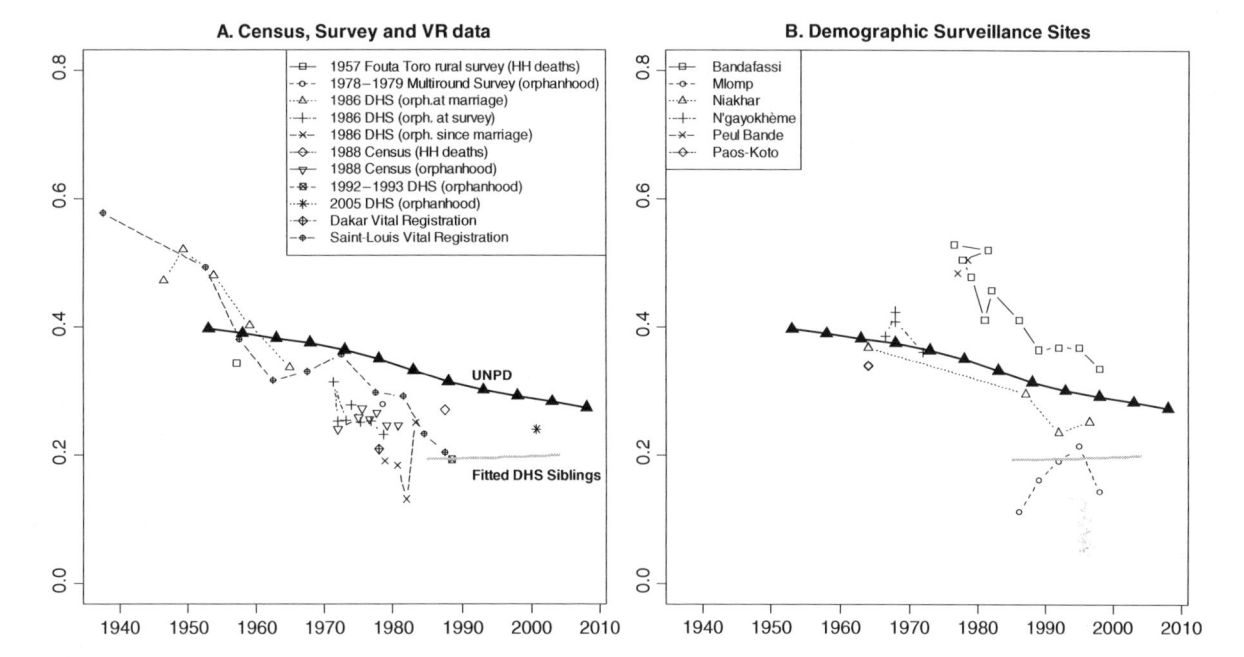

**Fig. 7.2** Senegal: female 45q15 by estimation method and data source. Notes: Sibling survival and UNPD estimates are those reported in Fig. 7.7. Household deaths are based on estimates from ORSTOM, INSEE, and INED (1967) and Pison (1995). Indirect maternal orphanhood estimates from census and DHS data come from Cantrelle et al. (1986), Pison (1995), Timæus (1991c, 1999), and own calculations. Estimates based on vital registration data for urban centers come from Diop (1990) the Direction de la Statistique (Senegal 1981), Waltisperger and Rabetsitonta (1988). Small area data for the Bandafassi, Mlomp, Niakhar, N'gayokhème, Peul Bande, and Paos-Koto DSS have been retrieved from the INDEPTH Network (2002), Pison et al. (1982, 1995, 1993, 1985), Condé (1980), Waltisperger and Rabetsitonta (1988), Garenne (1981), and Cantrelle et al. (1986)

situation for Senegal is more complex (Fig. 7.2). In addition to the UNPD and sibling survival estimates, we present in these plots estimates based on reports of household deaths, indirect maternal orphanhood reports from census and DHS data, vital registration data for a few urban centers (left panel) as well as small area data from various DSS (right panel). Put together, these estimates suggest a decline in adult female mortality in the second half of the twentieth century. Apart from that, however, the discrepancies between various sources and estimates are somewhat larger than is the case for Zimbabwe. This is true for the level of mortality, and in the case of the sibling survival estimates, also for the suggested trend. Even though there are only a few data points covering the most recent period, the sibling survival estimates appear rather low. Whereas the sibling survival estimates of $_{45}q_{15}$ are of a magnitude comparable to indirect estimates based on the orphanhood method applied to DHS data, they are considerably lower than estimates based on reports of deaths in the household (1988 census) and indirect estimates based on maternal orphanhood reports (2005 DHS). The UNPD estimates, derived from a $_5q_0$ estimate matched to the Timæus Sahelian age pattern of mortality ("Notes on a Series of Life Table Estimates of Mortality in the Countries of the Sub-Saharan Africa Region." Unpublished manuscript prepared for the WHO) using a Brass relational logit model is substantially higher than siblings survival mortality estimates and consistent with the overall level and trend provided by six rural DSS. A plausible yet unconfirmed explanation for the relatively large discrepancy between estimates based on the survivorship of siblings and those from other sources is that the greater complexity of family structures in western African populations (in part due to the higher incidence of polygyny) produces greater underreporting of dead siblings, parents, and others.

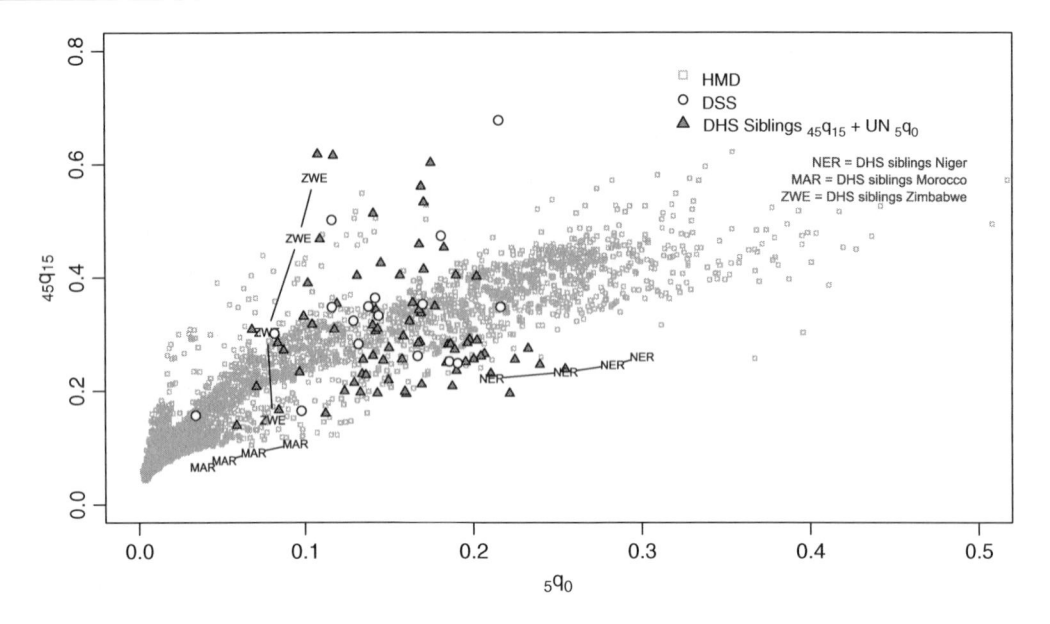

**Fig. 7.3** Comparison of female $_5q_0$ and $_{45}q_{15}$ relationship between data sources. Notes: HMD (2009), Indepth Network (2004), and DHS sibling survival data (own estimates), matched with $_5q_0$ from UNPD estimates for the years 1988, 1993, 1998, and 2003 (UN 2009). Each country often contributes more than one data point

The case of Senegal illustrates that distilling the most reliable path of adult mortality from a variety of estimates can be complex; the challenge is not just one of resolving the regional heterogeneity in the accuracy of estimates from different sources.

A comparison with the historical record provides the first indications of another lurking problem in mortality estimation, namely, the temporal variation in the quality of data inputs. In Fig. 7.3 we plot female $_5q_0$ against $_{45}q_{15}$ for all life tables included in the Human Mortality Database (HMD), estimates from 17 African DSS, and the direct sibling survival estimates reported in Fig. 7.7 (UNPD data are used for $_5q_0$). We have singled out the sibling survival estimates for a number of countries that we discuss below. The HMD contains only life tables that are of presumed good quality. It contains 4,084 life tables spanning the period from 1757 to 2007 for 40 countries or subpopulations. They are plotted as a background cloud of observations representing the historical experience in the age structure of mortality. Unfortunately, none of these life tables pertain to African populations.

The first observation to be made from the plot is that some countries (e.g., Zimbabwe) contribute data points with a much higher ratio of adult over child mortality than has been recorded in the HMD. Given the disproportionate impact of HIV/AIDS on adult mortality in these countries, this is to be expected. The second observation from Fig. 7.3 is that the sibling survival data for Niger and Morocco and a few other countries produce consistently lower estimates of the ratio of adult to child mortality than observed in the HMD. None of the DSS estimates are suggestive of a comparably low ratio, and that suggests that sibling survival estimates of adult mortality are too low. We cannot exclude, however, that the DSS underestimate both adult and child mortality, but that is not as likely. Importantly, the underreporting of adult mortality in the sibling survival reports does not seem to be a phenomenon that only characterizes western and northern African countries. It also characterizes the earlier data points from the countries that are now severely affected by the HIV/AIDS epidemic (e.g., Zimbabwe). For the more recent period, the downward bias in sibling survival data is obfuscated by the large impact of HIV/AIDS on adult mortality, and no longer visible in Fig. 7.3. This observation leads to two different hypotheses about the nature

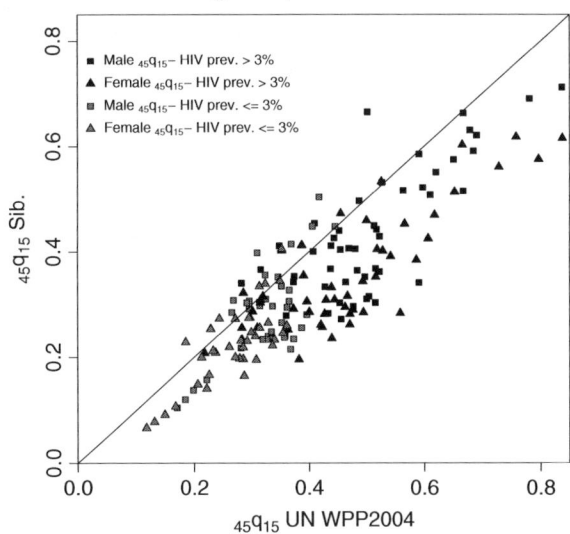

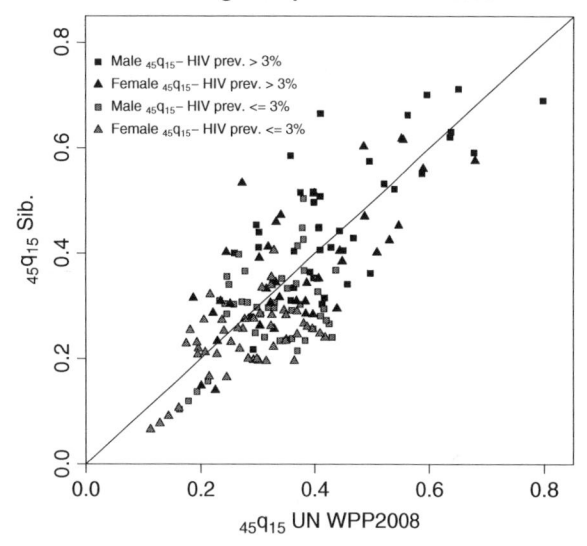

**Fig. 7.4** Sibling survival estimates of adult mortality compared with subsequent revisions of UNPD's World Population Prospects. Notes: For each country, sex and source, estimates are plotted for 1988, 1993, 1998 and 2003. The sibling survival estimates are computed by the authors and are the same in both plots. The UNPD estimates come from the World Population Prospects (UN 2005, 2009)

and sources of bias in mortality estimates that we explore further by means of a comparison of the sibling survival estimates with subsequent revisions of the UNPD's World Population Prospects (Fig. 7.4). In interpreting these plots, one needs to keep in mind that the UNPD uses UNAIDS HIV prevalence data as standard inputs for generating its mortality estimates (see Bongaarts, Pelletier, and Gerland, Chapter 7), and that UNAIDS estimates have been subject to a considerable downward adjustment following the publication of results from an increasing number of DHS that included an HIV testing component (Ghys et al. 2008).

Sibling survival estimates of adult mortality are generally lower than UNPD estimates presented in the 2004 revision of the World Population Prospects, and that observation holds irrespective of the HIV prevalence of the population in question (Fig. 7.4, left panel). The—possible—downward bias in sibling survival estimates is also visible in comparison with the 2008 revision of the World Population Prospects, but this time only for countries with low HIV prevalence. For high prevalence countries, the estimates from both sources are, on average, about equal (Fig. 7.4, right panel). More than one explanation can be formulated for this temporal difference in the degree with which the estimates from both sources line up. One hypothesis is that the 2008 revision of the UNAIDS HIV prevalence estimates are more accurate than the earlier versions, and that there is indeed regional variation in the quality of sibling survival data with more reliable estimates for eastern and southern Africa (coincidentally also those countries that are hardest hit by the HIV/AIDS epidemic). An alternative explanation is that the sibling survival estimates underestimate adult mortality irrespective of the region, but that a downward bias also characterizes the adult mortality estimates from the 2008 World Population Prospects for countries with large HIV/AIDS epidemics. One possible reason for that is systematic downward bias in HIV prevalence estimates published by UNAIDS for countries with severe epidemics (Reniers and Eaton 2009). New and, hopefully, better data will assist us in parsing out which of these scenarios is the most plausible.

**Table 7.2** Input data and methodology for background[a] adult mortality estimates by the United Nations Agencies (Africa, $n = 55$)

| Input | UNPD 1990 | UNPD 2008 | Input | WHO 2007 |
|---|---|---|---|---|
| Life table (adjusted or not) from vital registration or censuses | 15 | 7 | Life table (adjusted or not) from vital registration | 3 |
| $_5q_0$, $_{45}q_{15}$ and relational Brass logit life table system | – | 7 | $_5q_0$, $_{45}q_{15}$ and modified Brass logit life table system with global standard | 5 |
| $_5q_0$ only and model life table | 20 | 41 | $_5q_0$ and modified logit with global standard | 43 |
| Not available[b] | 20 | – | Not Available | 4 |
| Total | 55 | 55 | Total | 55 |

Sources: United Nations Population Division (UN 1991, 2009) and the World Health Organization (WHO 2008b).
[a]Background adult mortality excludes AIDS mortality.
[b]No technical notes were published to explain the data sources or methods that were used to compute the estimates.

The UNPD and the World Health Organization (WHO) thus continue to derive adult mortality estimates for the majority of African countries from child mortality indices and a set of model life tables (or, in the case of the WHO, an extension of the Brass logit life table system (Murray et al. 2003) (Table 7.2)). The UNPD uses a multistep estimation protocol in countries where adult HIV prevalence exceeds 1%. For these populations, background mortality (i.e., the mortality pattern net of AIDS) is still routinely derived from child mortality and model age patterns, and AIDS mortality is subsequently added as an extra cause to obtain the overall mortality estimates from all causes combined (UN 2010). The estimation of AIDS-specific mortality combines an epidemiological and multistate model to simulate the dynamics of the HIV/AIDS epidemic, its diffusion through subpopulations, and its demographic impact by age, sex, and duration since infection (Stover et al. 2008). In a similar vein, the WHO adds a UNAIDS estimate of the number of adult AIDS deaths to its estimates of background mortality. The estimates that ensue are usually contrasted with those from other sources (including direct sibling survival estimates) and for other countries in the same region. If deemed necessary, the analyst may adjust the UN estimates to reconcile discrepancies. As a result, the estimates of the UN agencies are not entirely independent of the estimates from other sources. As more and better empirical data for a country become available, estimates for earlier periods are sometimes retroactively adjusted.

This chapter presents adult mortality estimates from the UN agencies and compares those with direct estimates from sibling survival data collected as part of the maternal mortality modules in many DHS. As the number of surveys is accumulating, this data source has become an increasingly viable resource for timely and comparable adult mortality data in countries with weak vital registration systems. The sibling survival estimates are not free of bias, however, and the section below discusses our estimation methodology and highlights some of the potential flaws therein (see also Box 7.1). A separate section presents the distribution of causes of death based on verbal autopsy data from a few DSS (Box 7.2).

### Box 7.2 Causes of Death

An understanding of the causes of deaths in adults can be obtained from the DSS sites that are scattered over eastern, western, and southern Africa. In most DSSs, verbal autopsy interviews are routinely conducted with caregivers and relatives of deceased residents, and the reported signs and symptoms are subsequently used to ascertain the most likely cause of death. The assignment of causes of death is usually done by local physicians, but there has been considerable experimentation with various automation procedures for standardizing and accelerating that task (Soleman et al. 2006). In Fig. 7.5, the cause-specific mortality fractions obtained from verbal autopsies are used in conjunction with all-cause death rates (ages 15 and above) to produce cause-specific death rates by broad

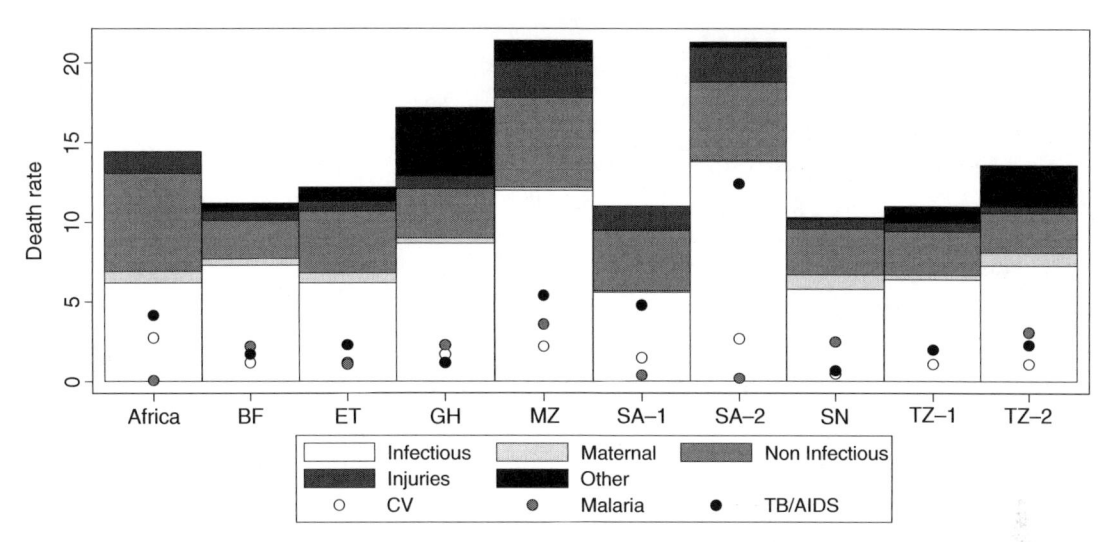

**Fig. 7.5** Cause-specific mortality rates (per 1,000 person-years) in adults of 15 years and above (both sexes) in nine African DSS sites and Africa as a whole (1999–2003). Notes: BF: Burkina Faso (Nouna), ET: Ethiopia (Butajira), GH: Ghana (Navrongo), MZ: Mozambique (Manhica), SA-1: South Africa (Agincourt), SA-2: South Africa (ACDIS-Kwazulu Natal), SN: Senegal (Niakhar), TZ-1: Tanzania (Ifakara), TZ-2: Tanzania (Rufiji). Sources: Data for the DSS sites are adapted from Adjuik et al. (2006). Data for Africa as a whole come from the Global Burden of Disease study (WHO 2008a)

disease group. We also present estimates for a few specific causes of death that are of particular interest. The rates are standardized using an INDEPTH model age distribution. The fraction of deaths with unclassifiable diagnoses varies by site and depends on the protocol that was used for assigning causes of death (see Adjuik et al. (2006)). For comparative purposes, estimates are included from the Global Burden of Disease study for Africa as a whole (WHO 2008a).

In all sites, infectious diseases still constitute the main mortality threat in adults. This is in large part due to tuberculosis and AIDS mortality (here combined), but in some of the DSS sites, malaria is a more immediate cause of concern (e.g., Navrongo (GH), Niakhar (SN), and Rufiji (TZ)). In Manhica (MZ), both HIV and malaria account for a substantial fraction of adult mortality. More striking perhaps is that the high burden of mortality in southern African populations is not the sole result of the heavy toll that HIV is taking in these populations. In the Mozambican and South African DSS, the mortality rates are relatively high for all-cause-of-death groups (infectious, non-infectious, as well as injuries).

The Agincourt DSS stands out as an exception, but its population has a more rural character with presumably lower HIV prevalence rates than in northern Kwazulu Natal, where the ACDIS DSS site is located. The burden of chronic diseases in southern Africa is high and has been increasing in recent years (Mayosi et al. 2009; Tollman et al. 2008). In Fig. 7.5, that is evidenced by the relatively high mortality levels due to cardiovascular problems. Contributing to this phenomenon are the relatively high prevalence of hypertension and stroke, the persistence of pre-transitional diseases (e.g., rheumatic fever and idiopathic cardiomyopathies), and the emergence of obesity and diabetes. Ischemic heart disease is uncommon in the black population (Mayosi et al. 2009). The heavy burden of non-communicable diseases has also been reported for other African populations, in some instances accompanied by assertions that age-standardized rates are higher than those in established market economies (Duthé and Pison 2008; Unwin et al. 2001). Despite high fertility levels, the African population is expected to age considerably over the next few decades. For example, the population above age 25 is expected to increase from 39 to 57% between 2010 and 2050 (UN 2010), and the increasing burden of chronic diseases will be a straightforward implication of that demographic trend. Additionally, dietary and lifestyle changes could contribute to the increasing importance of non-communicable diseases.

The southern African DSS sites also confirm the region's notoriety for violent deaths. In South Africa as a whole, the injury death rate is nearly twice the global average (Seedat et al. 2009). In sum, the relatively high adult mortality levels in southern Africa are the result of the triple burden of resurgent or persistent infections, the diseases of "modernity," and high death rates from external injuries. It is quite plausible that the prevalence of non-communicable diseases is on the rise in other African populations as well. They may have better prospects, however, to avoid an AIDS epidemic of the magnitude known in the east and southeast, and hopefully also to avoid the level mortality from external causes currently observed in South Africa.

## Sibling Survival Data as a Source of Direct Mortality Estimates

Starting with the Sudanese survey in 1990, sibling survival histories have been collected from female respondents (ages 15–49) as part of a maternal mortality module in over 50 African DHS (Table 7.1). In about one fifth of these surveys, questions about sibling survival are also included in the male questionnaire. In a standardized set of questions, respondents are asked to list all siblings born to the same mother by birth order, and then to provide information about their gender, survival status, and current age, or age at death and years since death. Such data provide an opportunity to estimate rates directly because both events and exposure time are known. When successive DHS are available for one country, they can be pooled together, which allows for the estimation of longer-term trends and to model recall bias (see below).

Despite their widespread availability, sibling histories remain underutilized. Many researchers remain skeptical about the quality of the data. This skepticism is primarily due to underreporting of deaths, especially when the reference period stretches over more than a few years (Gakidou et al. 2004; Timæus and Jasseh 2004). Analysis of bias for the period 1989–1995 suggests that there is evidence of omissions by older respondents in particular (Gakidou et al. 2004; Stanton et al. 2000). Worth noting is that recall problems will only affect the estimates if the omitted siblings survived to age 15.

Aside from underreporting, sibling history data suffer from three structural limitations (Trussell and Rodriguez 1990). First, groups of siblings (also referred to as *sibships*) with high mortality will be underrepresented because no information is available for sibships without a surviving member. Second, low mortality sibships are overrepresented because the experience of the respondent's siblings is counted multiple times when more than one sibling might be interviewed (as is the case in the DHS surveys). Third, the respondents themselves are not counted in the denominator, which produces upward bias in the mortality estimates. Even though each of these sources of bias are potentially worrisome for the analyst, Trussell and Rodriguez (1990) have shown mathematically that these limitations neutralize each other, provided that there is no association between mortality and sibship size. Whereas such an assumption would be clearly violated in childhood, it is less problematic in adulthood.

Gakidou and King (2006) developed a weighting scheme to correct for the underrepresentation of sibships with high mortality. The logic is to give less weight to sibships where many siblings survived, by computing family-level weights of the form B/S, where B is the number of siblings at the start of the observation period and S is the number of surviving siblings at the time of the survey (respondents are counted as well). A weighted average of the proportion of dead siblings reported by each survivor, using B/S as weights, will give the true proportion for sibships with at least one survivor. When applied to individual-level data files, this weight takes the form 1/S. Further adjustments need to be made because families without survivors are not represented.

This weighting scheme is a promising approach to correct for the mortality selection bias in sibling survival data. In a recent analysis of the DHS, Obermeyer and colleagues (2010) have used a similar weighting scheme and obtain adult mortality estimates that are considerably higher than those computed without weighting. Unfortunately, their weights include siblings who died in childhood (and include brothers, whereas they only use data from female respondents). They also use weights of the form B/S with individual data, and that is likely to inflate mortality rates in settings where fertility and mortality are correlated. In sum, we consider the debate about the adjustment of estimates from sibling survival data unresolved, and with the understanding that this may lead to lower bound estimates, we present unweighted data only. We also reiterate that we do not correct for sibships without survivors.

The basis for the estimation approach used here has been developed by Timæus and Jasseh (2004). We extend their estimates for all standard African DHS with sibling survival histories available on May 1, 2010. We disregard the DHS for the Sudan (1990) because the dataset is not standardized, the DHS for Nigeria (1999) because the data are presumably not of very good quality (Timæus and Jasseh 2004), and the DHS for Sierra Leone (2008) because the survival status is unknown for as much as 9% of all siblings. Our study thus covers 56 surveys from 30 different African countries. Each available dataset with a sibling survival module has first been reshaped into a person-years file. All surveys—including those for males if the relevant questions were asked—are merged for a given country. The mean date of the last survey is used as the most recent cutoff point for calculating exposure. Data related to siblings whose gender or survival status is unknown are discarded, as well as data for periods prior to nine completed years before the survey. This last restriction on the dataset is imposed because estimates for earlier points in time may suffer from excessive recall bias (time-reference problems and underreporting), and the estimates tend to become erratic because the data get sparser as we go back farther in time (e.g., because the age range of the respondents in the DHS is restricted to 15–49 for women, and 15–54 or 15–59 for men, relatively few respondents will have brothers and sisters older than 50 more than 10 years prior to the survey). To discard the peak of the genocide, the recall period was reduced to 6 years for the 2000 Rwanda DHS (Timæus and Jasseh 2004). Data for the 56 surveys sum to 101,000 deaths and 16,600,000 person-years of exposure for siblings aged 15–60, and for the period ranging from 1983 to 2006. DHS survey weights were used.

As noted by Timæus and Jasseh (2004), sample sizes are too small to allow for the direct calculation of age-specific rates for each country. We therefore fit a quasi-Poisson regression model to the observed deaths with exposure time as an offset parameter. The main features of that model are discussed below, and we refer to their article for a more detailed description of the estimation methodology. The overall mortality level and sex differences therein are allowed to vary by country. Both follow a log-linear trend with a country-specific rate of increase. A standard mortality pattern is introduced in the model to smooth non-AIDS mortality, which implies that death rates are linked to this standard with a relational two-parameter model. We use the General Pattern of the United Nations life tables for developing countries (UN 1982), but a different choice does not produce substantial differences in the estimates. The background age pattern of mortality is specific to each country, but is not assumed to be time-dependent. An exception is made, however, for countries that are severely affected by the HIV/AIDS epidemic: 4 years after HIV prevalence reaches 1%, it is assumed that AIDS deaths start increasing, and the age pattern of mortality is allowed to change along with the duration of the epidemic. Whereas Timæus and Jasseh (2004) let it vary in a similar way across all the countries of their sample, we assume a regional age pattern of mortality increase. A quadratic term is added for countries with a stalling or decreasing HIV prevalence to accommodate possible declines in adult mortality. The HIV prevalence figures used for this application as well as those cited in this chapter come from UNAIDS (2008).

In 16 out of the 30 countries of our sample, reference periods for successive surveys overlap and it is thus possible to assess how the completeness of death reporting changes as we go back farther in time (Obermeyer et al. 2010; Timæus and Jasseh 2004). In other words, estimated death rates for *distant* periods of *recent* surveys can be compared with those obtained for *recent* periods of *earlier* surveys to get an estimate of the relative underreporting of deaths in the more-distant past. The time prior to the survey is coded in blocks of 3 years, overlapping periods for all surveys are pooled together, and the model described above is fitted for each sex separately. Coefficients indicate that (1) deaths are progressively underreported for reference periods that are located further back in time, and (2) that the underreporting is significantly stronger for reports on brothers than for sisters. Compared to the 3 years immediately prior to the survey, the fitted age-specific death rates for females (sisters) are 83% lower 6–9 years prior to the survey. The relative underreporting is not significant for the period 3–6 years before the survey, but this could be the result of a digit preference for 5 (respondents are asked how many years have passed since the death of their sibling). For males (brothers), there is significant underreporting as soon as 3–6 years before the survey (91%), and past that point, completeness of death reporting drops to approximately 75%. Because of this rapid decline in the completeness of death reporting, unadjusted estimates are likely to exaggerate the rate of recent mortality increases. We thus present adjusted estimates for all countries and assume the sex-specific pattern of underreporting described above.

We present our results in terms of synthetic or period probabilities of survival between ages 15 and 60 ($_{45}q_{15}$). In other words, this version of $_{45}q_{15}$ does not necessarily reflect the lived experience of a real cohort, but is a summary measure of the mortality regime for a snapshot in time. Compared to other indices of adult mortality that include the elderly (e.g., $e_{15}$), $_{45}q_{15}$ is not as susceptible to age misreporting.

## Trends in Adult Mortality

Long-term trends in adult mortality starting from the 1950s are displayed in Fig. 7.6. These estimates come from the 2008 revision of the UNPD's World Population Prospects (UN 2009). Most African countries experienced a decline in adult mortality between the 1950s and mid to late 1980s. The pace of the

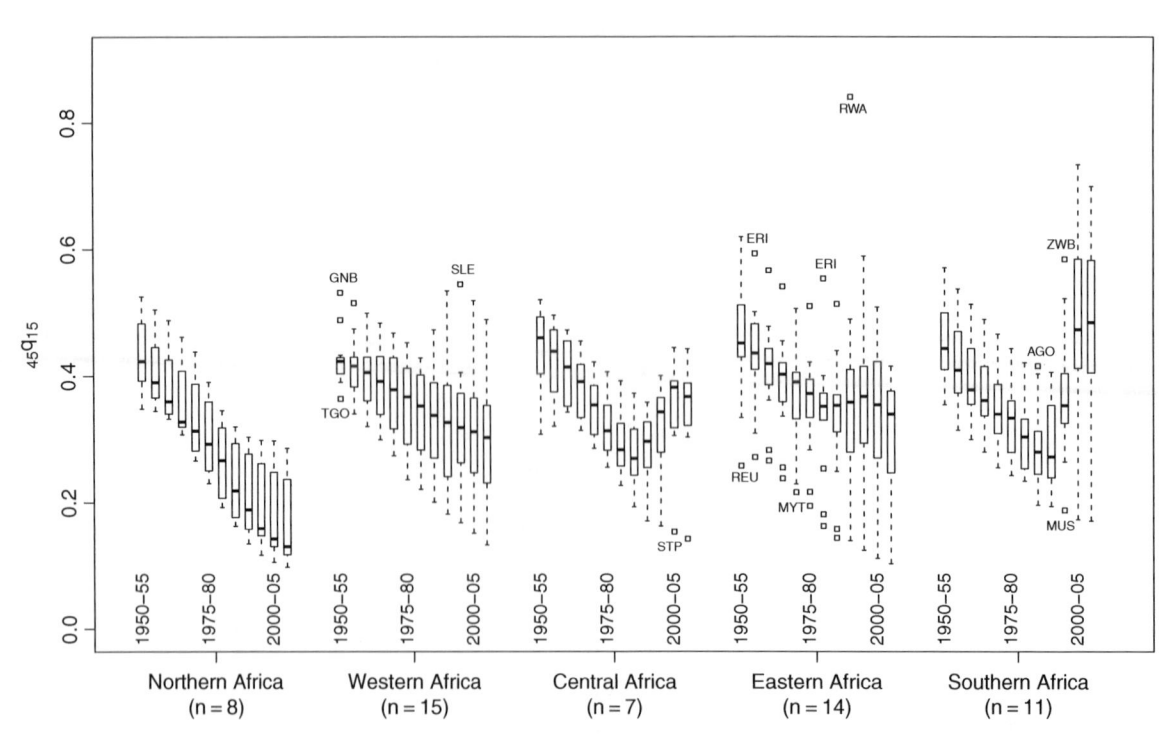

**Fig. 7.6** Long-term trends in $_{45}q_{15}$ by region (*box plots*, both sexes combined, 1950–2010). Notes: Northern Africa includes Algeria, Egypt, Libyan Arab Jamahiriya, Mauritania, Morocco, Sudan, Tunisia, and the Western Sahara; Western Africa includes Benin, Burkina-Faso, Cape Verde, Côte d'Ivoire, Gambia, Ghana, Guinea, Guinea Bissau (GNB), Liberia, Mali, Niger, Nigeria, Senegal, Sierra Leone (SLE), and Togo (TGO); Central Africa includes Cameroon, Central African Republic, Chad, Congo, Equatorial Guinea, Gabon, and Sao Tome and Principe (STP); Eastern Africa includes Burundi, Comoros, Democratic Republic of Congo, Djibouti, Eritrea (ERI), Ethiopia, Kenya, Madagascar, Mayotte (MYT), Reunion (REU), Rwanda (RWA), Seychelles, Somalia, United Republic of Tanzania, and Uganda; Southern Africa includes Angola (AGO), Botswana, Lesotho, Malawi, Mauritius (MUS), Mozambique, Namibia, South Africa, Swaziland, Zambia, and Zimbabwe (ZWB). Source: United Nations Population Division (UN 2009) includes previously unpublished data for the period prior to 1980 for countries with generalized HIV/AIDS epidemics, and prior to 1995 for all other countries and regions

decline was faster in the north, center, and south than in the other two regions, and is very much in line with the trajectories in south-east and south-central Asia (not shown). A 20%-point improvement in the probability of surviving from age 15 to 60 was not uncommon. The attentive reader will realize, however, that these trends in the distribution of mortality estimates by region will conceal short-term fluctuations or even temporary reversals in country-specific mortality trends.

Northern African countries are the success story on the continent: they have witnessed a sustained adult mortality decline since the 1950s with rates that are now comparable to those in southern and central America. Mortality levels are declining in western Africa as well, but that decline is by no means as steep as in northern Africa. In the other regions, the first signs of the mortality impact of HIV/AIDS become visible in the early 1990s. These were the precursor for one of the most drastic reversals in adult mortality that have been documented to date: in southern Africa in particular, the mortality gains made during the previous four decades have been wiped out in less than 10 years. In eastern Africa, adult mortality levels have already peaked, and seem to be declining again. The increasing heterogeneity in adult mortality levels in some regions testifies to the unequal impact that HIV/AIDS has had. In central Africa, the mortality reversal is the result of the combined effects of rising HIV prevalence levels (e.g., Cameroon) and civil strife (e.g., Democratic Republic of Congo and Chad). Internal conflicts have been an important determinant of adult mortality in Rwanda, Angola, Liberia, Somalia, and Sierra Leone as well.

In Fig. 7.7 and Table 7.3, the focus shifts to the last two–three decades for which sibling survival estimates of mortality can be produced. Figure 7.7 contains

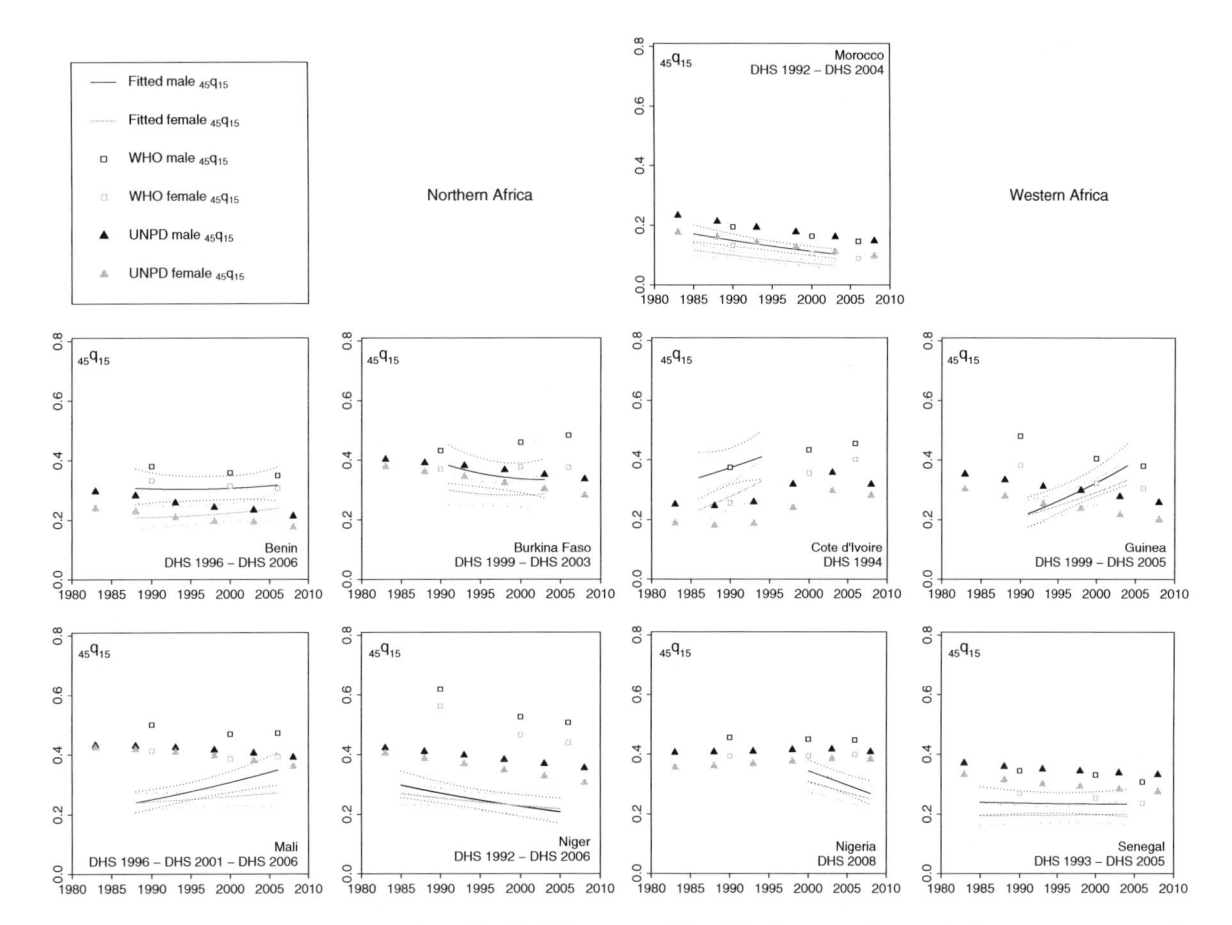

**Fig. 7.7** Trends in $_{45}q_{15}$ by country and sex for 30 African countries. Notes: Sibling survival estimates have been produced with inputs from the Demographic and Health Surveys. 95%-confidence intervals are computed using a quasi-Poisson model which increases the standard errors to account for overdispersion. The other estimates are extracted from official publications of the UN-agencies (UN 2009; WHO 2008b)

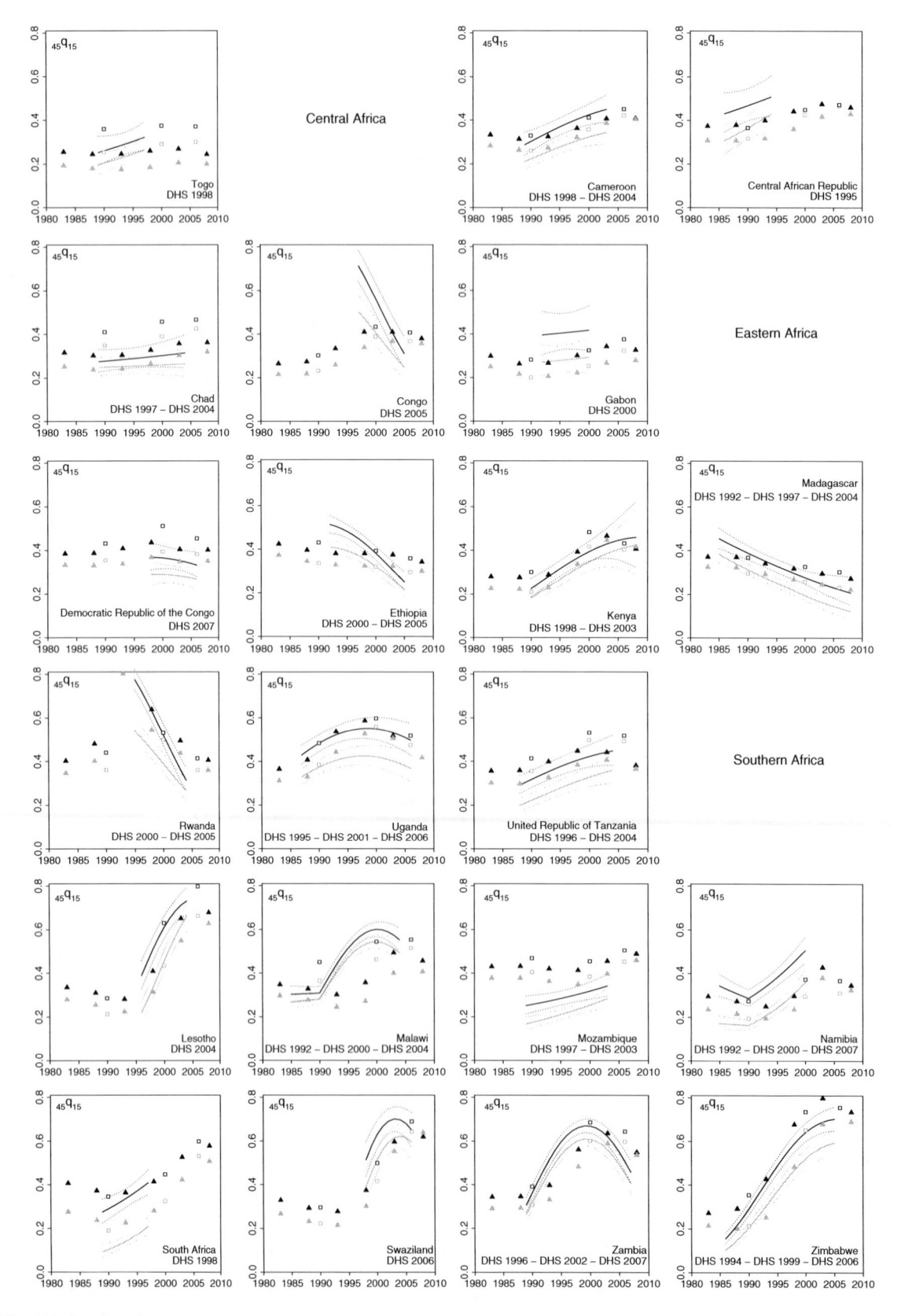

**Fig. 7.7** (continued)

**Table 7.3** Estimates in $_{45}q_{15}$ by country and sex derived from sibling histories (Africa, 1990–2005)

| | Females | | | | Males | | | |
|---|---|---|---|---|---|---|---|---|
| | 1990 | 1995 | 2000 | 2005 | 1990 | 1995 | 2000 | 2005 |
| Northern Africa | | | | | | | | |
| Morocco | 0.100 | 0.085 | 0.073 | – | 0.149 | 0.130 | 0.113 | – |
| Western Africa | | | | | | | | |
| Benin | 0.209 | 0.214 | 0.223 | 0.236 | 0.305 | 0.303 | 0.307 | 0.315 |
| Burkina Faso | – | 0.286 | 0.282 | – | – | 0.355 | 0.338 | – |
| Cote d'Ivoire | 0.277 | – | – | – | 0.373 | – | – | – |
| Guinea | – | 0.247 | 0.292 | – | – | 0.262 | 0.324 | – |
| Mali | 0.241 | 0.250 | 0.259 | 0.270 | 0.250 | 0.277 | 0.308 | 0.342 |
| Nigeria | 0.254 | 0.240 | 0.228 | 0.218 | 0.271 | 0.247 | 0.227 | 0.208 |
| Nigeria | – | – | 0.304 | 0.271 | – | – | 0.343 | 0.297 |
| Senegal | 0.195 | 0.196 | 0.198 | – | 0.236 | 0.235 | 0.234 | – |
| Togo | 0.205 | 0.246 | – | – | 0.260 | 0.303 | – | – |
| Central Africa | | | | | | | | |
| Cameroon | 0.223 | 0.277 | 0.322 | – | 0.302 | 0.370 | 0.426 | – |
| CAR | 0.367 | – | – | – | 0.478 | – | – | – |
| Chad | 0.248 | 0.253 | 0.258 | – | 0.276 | 0.289 | 0.303 | – |
| Congo | – | – | 0.405 | 0.249 | – | – | 0.563 | 0.312 |
| Gabon | – | 0.277 | 0.291 | – | – | 0.402 | 0.418 | – |
| Eastern Africa | | | | | | | | |
| DR Congo | – | – | 0.289 | 0.274 | – | – | 0.365 | 0.340 |
| Ethiopia | – | 0.391 | 0.322 | 0.220 | – | 0.480 | 0.382 | 0.251 |
| Kenya | 0.182 | 0.268 | 0.347 | – | 0.223 | 0.316 | 0.397 | – |
| Madagascar | 0.318 | 0.250 | 0.191 | – | 0.394 | 0.329 | 0.276 | – |
| Rwanda | – | 0.538 | 0.391 | – | – | 0.775 | 0.523 | – |
| Uganda | 0.371 | 0.418 | 0.422 | 0.382 | 0.481 | 0.539 | 0.550 | 0.512 |
| Tanzania | 0.221 | 0.278 | 0.329 | – | 0.316 | 0.376 | 0.424 | – |
| Southern Africa | | | | | | | | |
| Lesotho | – | – | 0.455 | – | – | – | 0.610 | – |
| Malawi | 0.281 | 0.470 | 0.544 | – | 0.309 | 0.515 | 0.602 | – |
| Mozambique | 0.174 | 0.210 | 0.254 | – | 0.257 | 0.285 | 0.319 | – |
| Namibia | 0.163 | 0.244 | 0.360 | – | 0.287 | 0.383 | 0.508 | – |
| South Africa | 0.103 | 0.171 | – | – | 0.286 | 0.369 | – | – |
| Swaziland | – | – | 0.514 | 0.615 | – | – | 0.631 | 0.681 |
| Zambia | 0.314 | 0.536 | 0.608 | 0.494 | 0.361 | 0.596 | 0.669 | 0.552 |
| Zimbabwe | 0.205 | 0.373 | 0.522 | 0.594 | 0.291 | 0.491 | 0.643 | 0.705 |

Notes: Sibling survival estimates have been produced with inputs from the Demographic and Health Surveys. See Fig. 7.7 for a list of surveys included.

country-specific estimates of $_{45}q_{15}$ by sex derived from sibling survival data, plotted along with estimates from the UNPD and the WHO. In Table 7.3 we present direct sibling survival estimates for 1990, 1995, 2000, and 2005.

Overall, DHS sibling histories yield estimates that are lower than those from the UNPD (or the WHO), especially in countries that have not been severely affected by the HIV epidemic. The discrepancy in sibling survival and UN-based estimates are particularly large for some of the Sahelian countries (Senegal, Mali, and Niger). Pinning down the reasons for this is difficult. On one hand, underreporting of sibling deaths might be more severe for some western African countries because of the greater complexity in family structures, and that could lead to downward bias in the sibling survival estimates. On the other hand, the Sahelian populations are notorious for their relatively high levels of mortality between the ages 1 and 5 (Hill and Amouzou 2006; Timæus 1993) and because that age pattern of mortality does not fit any of the classical model life tables particularly well, the child mortality-matching procedure may lead to overestimates of adult mortality. In recent revisions of the World Population Prospects, however, that additional complication has been addressed by using a model age schedule of mortality for the Sahel that was developed by Timæus ("Notes on a Series of Life Table Estimates of Mortality in the Countries of the Sub-Saharan Africa Region." Unpublished manuscript prepared for the WHO). A third possible explanation is that the sibling survival data produce low estimates of adult mortality for countries across the continent, but that the bias is obscured for high HIV prevalence populations because the UN estimates for these countries are also characterized by downward bias (see Box 7.2).

The WHO estimates are comparable to those from the UNPD, but in a number of western African countries, they are considerably higher. This observation contrasts with a comparison of earlier versions of estimates from both agencies, which suggested that the WHO estimates were higher for high HIV prevalence countries in particular (Bradshaw and Timaeus 2006). Setting aside differences in the level of the estimates by source, the mortality trends that they highlight are often reasonably consistent.

Morocco is the only northern African country with DHS sibling survival data. In terms of the estimated trends, all sources suggest a slow but steady decline in adult mortality throughout the 1980s and 1990s. Morocco's adult mortality level was comparable to that of South Africa (females), and Zimbabwe (both sexes) in the 1980s. By the turn of the century, however, it is by far the country in Fig. 7.7 with the most favorable adult mortality regime.

Sibling survival data for western Africa are generally suggestive of stagnant or even increasing adult mortality levels. While systematic bias in estimates from sibling data is plausible (e.g., differences in the quality of subsequent DHS surveys for the same country may corrupt the estimated trend based on pooled sibling survival data), the stagnation or deterioration of adult health regimes in populations that are not seriously affected by the HIV/AIDS epidemic (e.g., Mali, Benin, and Guinea) is not reflected in the UNPD or WHO estimates, and deserves further inquiry. Because of a significant HIV/AIDS epidemic that attained a maximum HIV prevalence of 6.3% in 1998, the level of adult mortality has risen sharply in Côte d'Ivoire in the late 1980s and early 1990s, reaching 0.33 for women and 0.41 for men in 1994.

In central Africa, the increasing adult mortality levels in Cameroon are probably related to an HIV/AIDS epidemic of comparable proportions to the one in Côte d'Ivoire. In Chad, adult health is deteriorating even in the absence of a serious HIV/AIDS epidemic, and that is possibly related to the political instability and ethnic rivalry that has characterized the country throughout the 1990s and beyond. In that case, the trend based on sibling survival data is corroborated by estimates from the UNPD and the WHO. The estimated trends in adult mortality for the Central African Republic, the Congo, and Gabon are based on one DHS only, and should be considered tentative.

The same applies to the estimates for the Democratic Republic of Congo in eastern Africa. The adult mortality trends in Rwanda reflect the postgenocide mortality decline, and a decrease in AIDS mortality. The Rwandan HIV/AIDS epidemic reached a maximum prevalence of 7.1% in 1993, and a declining adult mortality in the late 1990s would be the logical epidemiological implication of that. In other eastern African countries such as Kenya, Tanzania, and Uganda, AIDS mortality contributed to a significant increase in adult mortality throughout most of the 1990s. As one of the earliest African countries with a generalized epidemic capable of keeping its HIV prevalence rates in check, Uganda is also one of the first countries where adult mortality trends reversed: according to the sibling histories, in 1998 the $_{45}q_{15}$ reached a level of 0.55 for men and 0.42 for women, and modest declines have been registered ever since. Madagascar is the only eastern African country shown here with a relatively steady decline in mortality. Madagascar has not known a generalized HIV/AIDS epidemic. The high levels of adult mortality in Ethiopia in the 1980s and 1990s are probably the result of a combination of recurrent droughts and local famines, civil strife, and a border conflict with Eritrea that ended in 2000. On a national scale, adult HIV prevalence never exceeded 3%.

Southern African countries experienced the most severe HIV/AIDS epidemics. Starting in the early 1990s, increases in adult mortality levels outpaced those on the rest of the continent. In some countries, such as Malawi and Zambia, adult mortality is again declining, but the peak occurred at much higher levels than in, for example, Uganda. In Zambia, $_{45}q_{15}$ reached a maximum at 0.67 and 0.61 for men and women, respectively. Our estimates suggest that this occurred in 2000, and that is well before the widespread availability of antiretrovirals. In Zimbabwe, adult mortality levels are still on the rise, despite falling HIV prevalence rates. In addition, it is unlikely that the extremely high levels of adult mortality ($_{45}q_{15}$ in 2005 is 0.70 for men and 0.59 for women) are the consequence of the HIV/AIDS epidemic only (see also Box 7.2). Mortality levels in Mozambique are generally lower than in the other southern African countries, but the impact of recent increases in HIV prevalence have yet to be felt.

A careful evaluation of the sibling survival estimates in Fig. 7.7 and Table 7.3 also suggests that $_{45}q_{15}$ in countries with severe HIV/AIDS epidemics (e.g., Uganda and Zimbabwe) increased faster for men than for women in the early stages of the epidemic. In reading that result, one should keep in mind that AIDS mortality affects women at younger ages than men, and because of the young age structure of African populations, the sex differential in the absolute number of deaths may be smaller.

## Discussion

Reliable vital events estimates for many African countries will remain elusive for the foreseeable future, and controversies over data collection approaches and estimation methods are unlikely to fade. Resolving any of these controversies falls beyond the scope of this chapter. Instead, we juxtaposed estimates based on sibling survival data extracted from the DHS and estimates from the UN agencies. At first glance, there appears to exist a puzzling regional heterogeneity in the quality of direct mortality estimates from sibling survival data, but the discrepancy in the estimates between sources is as likely to be the result of systematic downward bias in adult mortality estimates from the UN agencies for countries with severe HIV/AIDS epidemics (see Box 7.1). Overall, sibling survival data seem to produce lower bound estimates of adult mortality, but despite their potential flaws, they capture the most important trends in adult mortality and correctly locate them in time. They do, in other words, present an important empirical counterpoint to model-based estimates, and deserve a place in the methodological machinery for monitoring adult health and mortality in resource-poor settings.

Substantively, the information conveyed by the levels and trends in adult mortality reveals a mixture of success and failure. With the exception of northern Africa, adult mortality declines have been modest, and in some populations, drastic mortality reversals have been observed because of the HIV/AIDS epidemic. In some eastern and southeastern African countries, mortality is again declining. For Uganda, the textbook example of a country where HIV prevalence rates were contained relatively early, this is expected, but we also witness recent adult mortality declines in a few of the southeastern African countries (e.g., Malawi and Zambia). If real, this implies that the renewed mortality declines occurred before the widespread availability of antiretroviral therapy, and that we should expect further declines in adult mortality following the expansion of these antiretroviral therapy programs (and in the absence of drug resistance).

In a few countries, war and civil unrest have led to temporary but substantial mortality crises, and it remains questionable whether our methods and data sources are capable of accurately documenting the true magnitude of these conflicts (e.g., Obermeyer et al. 2008; Reed and Keely 2001). Even in populations that are not severely affected by the HIV/AIDS epidemic or conflict, adult mortality declines have been modest in recent years. In some western African countries, the sibling survival data even suggest that mortality in adulthood has been increasing (e.g., Mali and Guinea). While this could be an artifact of the data, mortality reversals driven by an increase in chronic diseases cannot be excluded. The increasing burden of chronic diseases has been documented for populations with reasonably good data on age- and cause-specific adult mortality (e.g., South Africa). For most populations the available adult mortality data are not very refined, however, and often limited to synthetic summary measures of the kind that we presented in this chapter. For countries with generalized HIV/AIDS epidemics, these summary measures are dominated by the large mortality impact of HIV/AIDS, and do not shed light on trends in other causes of death. Reversals in what is sometimes referred to as *background mortality* would be a serious public health concern, but such strong claims require the support from independent and high quality data sources.

**Acknowledgments and Disclaimer** The authors are grateful to Rob Dorrington, Francois Pelletier, and the volume's editors for helpful discussions and insightful comments, and all other staff members of the Population Division who worked on the 2008 Revision of the World Population Prospects: Gerhard K. Heilig, Kirill Andreev, Taeke Gjaltema, Vladimira Kantorova, Pablo Lattes, and Nan Li. The authors also thank Mie Inoue for clarifications about the WHO estimation methodology. The views and opinions expressed in this paper are those of the authors and do not necessarily represent those of the United Nations. This chapter has not been formally edited or cleared by the United Nations.

# References

Adjuik, M., T. Smith, S. Clark, J. Todd, A. Garrib, Y. Kinfu, K. Kahn, M. Mola, A. Ashraf, H. Masanja, K. Adazu, J. Sacarlal, N. Alam, A. Marra, A. Gbangou, E. Mwageni, and F. Binka. 2006. "Cause-Specific Mortality Rates in Sub-Saharan Africa and Bangladesh." *Bulletin of the World Health Organization* 84(3):181–88.

Bennett, N.G. and S. Horiuchi. 1984. "Mortality Estimation from Registered Deaths in Less Developed Countries." *Demography* 21(2):217–33.

Bhat, P.N.M. 2002. "Completeness of India S Sample Registration System: An Assessment Using the General Growth Balance Method." *Population Studies* 56(2):119–34.

Bradshaw, D. and I. Timaeus. 2006. "Levels and Trends of Adult Mortality." In D.T. Jamison, R.D. Feachem, M.W. Makgoba, E.R. Bos, F.K. Baingana, K.J. Hofman, and K.O. Rogo (eds.), *Disease and Mortality in Sub-Saharan Africa* (2nd ed.). Washington, DC, The World Bank.

Brass, W. 1996. "Demographic Data Analysis in Less Developed Countries: 1946–1996." *Population Studies* 50(3):451–67.

Brass, W. and E. Bamgboye. 1981. *The Time Location of Reports of Survivorship: Estimates for Maternal and Paternal Orphanhood and the Ever-Widowed*. London, London School of Hygiene and Tropical Medicine, CPS Working Paper.

Brass, W. and K. Hill. 1973. *Estimating Adult Mortality from Orphanhood*. Presented at International Population Conference, Liège.

Cantrelle, P., I.L. Diop, M. Garenne, M. Gueye, and A. Sadio. 1986. "The Profile of Mortality and Its Determinants in Senegal, 1960–1980." In United Nation (ed.), *Determinants of Mortality Change and Differentials in Developing Countries: The Five-Country Case Study Project*, pp. 86–116. Department of International Economic and Social Affairs. Population Division and World Health Organization. Division of Health Statistics. New York, NY, United Nations.

Cleland, J. 1996. "Demographic Data Collection in Less Developed Countries 1946–1996." *Population Studies* 50(3):433–50.

Condé, J. 1980. *La Mortalité Dans Les Pays En Développement—Mortality in Developing Countries*. Paris, New York, NY, Centre de développement de l'Organisation de cooperation et de développement économiques; Division de la population des Nations-Unies.

Davis, K. 1956. "The Amazing Decline of Mortality in Underdeveloped Areas." *The American Economic Review* 46(2):305–18.

Diop, I.L. 1990. *Étude De La Mortalité À Saint-Louis Du Sénégal À Partir Des Données D'état Civil*. University Paris I-Panthéon-Sorbonne.

Dorrington, R., D. Bourne, D. Bradshaw, R. Laubscher, and I.M. Timæus. 2001. *The Impact of HIV/AIDS on Adult Mortality in South Africa*. Cape Town, Medical Research Council.

Dorrington, R., I. Timaeus, and S. Gregson. 2006. *Adult Mortality in Southern Africa Using Deaths Reported by Households: Some Methodological Issues and Results*. Presented at Population Association of America Annual Meeting, March 30–April 1, Los Angeles, CA.

Duthé, G. and G. Pison. 2008. "Adult Mortality in a Rural Area of Senegal: Non-Communicable Diseases Have a Large Impact in Mlomp." *Demographic Research* 19(37):1419–48.

Feeney, G. 2001. "The Impact of HIV/AIDS on Adult Mortality in Zimbabwe." *Population and Development Review* 27(4):771–80.

Gakidou, E., M. Hogan, and A.D. Lopez. 2004. "Adult Mortality: Time for a Reappraisal." *International Journal of Epidemiology* 33(4):710–17.

Gakidou, E. and G. King. 2006. "Death by Survey: Estimating Adult Mortality without Selection Bias from Sibling Survival Data." *Demography* 43(3):569–85.

Garenne, M. 1981. "Age Patterns of Mortality in West Africa." In P.S. Center (ed.), *Working Paper*. Philadelphia, PA, University of Pennsylvania.

Ghys, P.D., N. Walker, W. McFarland, R. Miller, and G.P. Garnett. 2008. "Improved Data, Methods and Tools for the 2007 HIV and AIDS Estimates and Projections." *Sex Transm Infect* 84(Suppl 1):i1–i4.

Graham, W. W. Brass, and R.W. Snow. 1989. "Estimating Maternal Mortality: The Sisterhood Method." *Studies in Family Planning* 20(3):125–35.

HMD. 2009. *Human Mortality Database*. Berkeley and Rostock, University of California and Max Planck Institute for Demographic Research, http://www.mortality.org/. Accessed November 9, 2009

Hallett, T.B. 2010. "Measuring and Correcting Biased Child Mortality Statistics in Countries with Generalized Epidemics of HIV Infection." *WHO Bulletin* 88(10):761–8.

Hill, K. 1987. "Estimating Census and Death Registration Completeness." *Asian Pacific Population Forum* 1(3):8–13, 23–24.

Hill, K. 2003. *Adult Mortality in the Developing World: What We Know and How We Know It*. Presented at Training Workshop on HIV/AIDS and Adult Mortality in Developing Countries, United Nations, Department of Economic and Social Affairs, 8–13 September, New York, NY.

Hill, K. and A. Amouzou. 2006. "Trends in Child Mortality, 1960–2000." In D.T. Jamison, R.D. Feachem, M.W. Makgoba, E.R. Bos, F.K. Baingana, K.J. Hofman, and K.O. Rogo (eds.), *Disease and Mortality in Sub-Saharan Africa*, (2nd ed.). Washington, DC, The World Bank.

Hill, K., Y. Choi, and I. Timaeus. 2005. "Unconventional Approaches to Mortality Estimation." *Demographic Research* 13:281–300.

Hill, K., A.D. Lopez, K. Shibuya, and P. Jha. 2007. "Interim Measures for Meeting Needs for Health Sector Data: Births, Deaths, and Causes of Death." *Lancet* 370(9600):1726–35.

Hill, K. and J. Trussell. 1977. "Further Developments in Indirect Mortality Estimation." *Population Studies* 31(2):313–34.

Hill, K., D. You, and Y. Choi. 2009. "Death Distribution Methods for Estimating Adult Mortality." *Demographic Research* 21(9):235–54.

INDEPTH Network. 2004. *Indepth Model Life Tables for Sub-Saharan Africa*. Aldershot, Aldershot Ashgate Pub Ltd.

Katzenellenbogen, J., D. Yach, and R.E. Dorrington. 1993. "Mortality in a Rural South African Mission, 1837–1909: An Historical Cohort Study Using Church Records." *International Journal Epidemiology* 22(6):965–75.

Lopman, B.A., R. Barnabas, T.B. Hallett, C. Nyamukapa, C. Mundandi, P. Mushati, G.P. Garnett, and S. Gregson. 2006. "Assessing Adult Mortality in HIV-1-Afflicted Zimbabwe (1998–2003)." *Bull World Health Organ* 84(3): 189–97.

Mahapatra, P., K. Shibuya, A.D. Lopez, F. Coullare, F.C. Notzon, C. Rao, and S. Szreter. 2007. "Civil Registration Systems and Vital Statistics: Successes and Missed Opportunities." *Lancet* 370(9599):1653–63

Mathers, C.D., D.M. Fat, M. Inoue, C. Rao, and A.D. Lopez. 2005. "Counting the Dead and What They Died from: An Assessment of the Global Status of Cause of Death Data." *Bulletin of the World Health Organization* 83(3):171–77.

Mayosi, B.M., A.J. Flisher, U.G. Lalloo, F. Sitas, S.M. Tollman, and D. Bradshaw. 2009. "The Burden of Non-Communicable Diseases in South Africa." *Lancet* 374(9693):934–47.

Moser, K., V. Shkolnikov, and D.A. Leon. 2005. "World Mortality 1950–2000: Divergence Replaces Convergence from the Late 1980s." *Bulletin of the World Health Organization* 83(3):202–9.

Murray, C.J.L., B.D. Ferguson, A.D. Lopez, M. Guillot, J.A. Salomon, and O. Ahmad. 2003. "Modified Logit Life Table System: Principles, Empirical Validation, and Application." *Population Studies* 57(2):165–82.

Murray, C.J.L., J.K. Rajaratnam, J. Marcus, T. Laakso, and A.D. Lopez. 2010. "What Can We Conclude from Death Registration? Improved Methods for Evaluating Completeness." *PLoS Med* 7(4):e1000262.

INDEPTH Network. 2002. *Population and Health in Developing Countries. Population, Health, and Survival at Indepth Sites*, Volume 1. Ottawa, Canada, International Development Research Centre.

Notkola, V., I.M. Timaeus, and H. Siiskonen. 2000. "Mortality Transition in the Ovamboland Region of Namibia, 1930–1990." *Population Studies* 54(2):153–67.

ORSTOM, INSEE, and INED. 1967. *Afrique Noire, Madagascar, Comores Texte—Démographie Comparée*. Paris, I.N.S.E.E.

Obermeyer, Z., C.J. Murray, and E. Gakidou. 2008. "Fifty Years of Violent War Deaths from Vietnam to Bosnia: Analysis of Data from the World Health Survey Programme." *BMJ* 336(7659):1482–86.

Obermeyer, Z., J.K. Rajaratnam, C.H. Park, E. Gakidou, M.C. Hogan, A.D. Lopez, and C.J. Murray. 2010. "Measuring Adult Mortality Using Sibling Survival: A New Analytical Method and New Results for 44 Countries, 1974–2006." *PLoS Med* 7(4):e1000260.

Omran, A.R. 1971. "The Epidemiologic Transition. A Theory of the Epidemiology of Population Change." *Milbank Memorial Fund Quarterly* 49(4):509–38.

Palloni, A. and L. Heligman. 1985. "Re-Estimation of Structural Parameters to Obtain Estimates of Mortality in Developing Countries." *Population Bulletin of the United Nations* 18: 10–33.

Pison, G. 1982. *Dynamique D'une Population Traditionnelle: Démographie, Apparentement Et Mariage Dans Une Population D'effectif Limité: Les Peul Bandé (Sénégal Oriental)*. Paris, Presses Universitaires de France.

Pison, G. 1995. *Population Dynamics of Senegal*. Washington, DC, National Academy Press.

Pison, G. and A. Desgrees du Loû. 1993. "Bandafassi (Sénégal) – Niveaux Et Tendances Démographiques. 1971–1991." Paris, Institut National d'Etudes Démographiques. *Dossiers et Recherches* nr. 40.

Pison, G. and A. Langaney. 1985. "The Level and Age Pattern of Mortality in Bandafassi (Eastern Senegal): Results from a Small-Scale and Intensive Multi-Round Survey." *Population Studies* 39(3):387–405.

Preston, S., A.J. Coale, J. Trussell, and M. Weinstein. 1980. "Estimating the Completeness of Reporting of Adult Deaths in Populations That Are Approximately Stable." *Population Index* 46(2):179–202.

Reed, H. and C.B. Keely. 2001. *Forced Migration and Mortality*. Washington, DC, National Academy Press.

Reniers, G., T. Araya, G. Davey, N. Nagelkerke, Y. Berhane, R. Coutinho, and E.J. Sanders. 2009. "Steep Declines in Population-Level Aids Mortality Following the Introduction of Antiretroviral Therapy in Addis Ababa, Ethiopia." *AIDS* 23(4):511–18.

Reniers, G. and J. Eaton. 2009. "Refusal Bias in HIV Prevalence Estimates from Nationally Representative Seroprevalence Surveys." *AIDS* 23(5):621–29.

Seedat, M., A. Van Niekerk, R. Jewkes, S. Suffla, and K. Ratele. 2009. "Violence and Injuries in South Africa: Prioritising an Agenda for Prevention." *Lancet* 374(9694): 1011–22.

Sen, K. and R. Bonita. 2000. "Global Health Status: Two Steps Forward, One Step Back." *Lancet* 356(9229): 577–82.

D.S. Senegal. 1981. *Analyse Des Donnees De L'état Civil De La Region Du Cap-Vert (1978)*. Dakar, Direction de la Statistique.

Setel, P.W., S.B. Macfarlane, S. Szreter, L. Mikkelsen, P. Jha, S. Stout, and C. Abouzahr. 2007. "A Scandal of Invisibility: Making Everyone Count by Counting Everyone." *Lancet* 370(9598):1569–77.

Setel, P.W., O. Sankoh, C. Rao, V.A. Velkoff, C. Mathers, Y. Gonghuan, Y. Hemed, P. Jha, and A.D. Lopez. 2005. "Sample Registration of Vital Events with Verbal Autopsy: A Renewed Commitment to Measuring and Monitoring Vital Statistics." *Bulletin of the World Health Organization* 83(8):611–17.

Soleman, N., D. Chandramohan, and K. Shibuya. 2006. "Verbal Autopsy: Current Practices and Challenges." *Bulletin of the World Health Organization* 84(3):239–45.

Stanton, C., N. Abderrahim, and K. Hill. 2000. "An Assessment of DHS Maternal Mortality Indicators." *Studies in Family Planning* 31(2):111–23.

Stolnitz, G.J. 1965. "Recent Mortality Trends in Latin America, Asia and Africa: Review and Re-Interpretation." *Population Studies* 19(2):117–38.

Stover, J., P. Johnson, B. Zaba, M. Zwahlen, F. Dabis, and R.E. Ekpini. 2008. "The Spectrum Projection Package: Improvements in Estimating Mortality, Art Needs, PMTCT Impact and Uncertainty Bounds." *Sexually Transmitted Infections* 84(Suppl 1):i24–i30.

Timæus, I.M. 1991a. "Estimation of Mortality from Orphanhood in Adulthood." *Demography* 28(2):213–27.

Timæus, I.M. 1991b. "Measurement of Adult Mortality in Less Developed Countries: A Comparative Review." *Population Index* 57(4):552–68.

Timæus, I.M. 1991c. *New Estimates of Adult Mortality from DHS Data on the Timing of Orphanhood Relative to Marriage*. Presented at Demographic and Health Surveys World Conference, August 5–7, 1991, Washington, DC.

Timæus, I.M. 1993. "Adult Mortality." In K.A. Foote, K.H. Hill, and L.G. Martin (eds.), *Demographic Change in Sub-Saharan Africa*, pp. 218–55. Washington, DC, National Academy Press.

Timæus, I.M. 1999. *Adult Mortality in Africa in the Era of Aids*. Presented at 3rd African Population Conference: The African Population in the Twenty-first Century.

Timæus, I.M. and M. Jasseh. 2004. "Adult Mortality in Sub-Saharan Africa: Evidence from Demographic and Health Surveys." *Demography* 41(4):757–72.

Timæus, I.M., B. Zaba, and M. Ali. 2001. "Estimation of Adult Mortality from Data on Adult Siblings." In B. Zaba and J. Blacker (eds.), *Brass Tacks: Essays in Medical Demography. A Tribute to the Memory of Professor William Brass*, pp. 43–66. London, England, Athlone Press.

Tollman, S.M., K. Kahn, B. Sartorius, M.A. Collinson, S.J. Clark, and M.L. Garenne. 2008. "Implications of Mortality Transition for Primary Health Care in Rural South Africa: A Population-Based Surveillance Study." *Lancet* 372(9642):893–901.

Trussell, J. and G. Rodriguez. 1990. "A Note on the Sisterhood Estimator of Maternal Mortality." *Studies in Family Planning* 21(6):344–46.

UN. 1975. *World Population Prospects as Assessed in 1973*. New York, NY, United Nations, Department of Economic and Social Affairs.

UN. 1982. *Model Life Tables for Developing Countries*. New York, NY, United Nations, Department of International Economic and Social Affairs.

UN. 1983. *Manual X: Indirect Techniques for Demographic Estimation*. New York, NY, United Nations Population Division, Department of international Economic and Social Affairs.

UN. 1991. *World Population Prospects: The 1990 Revision*. New York, NY, United Nations Population Division, Department of Economic and Social Affairs.

UN. 2002. *Methods for Estimating Adult Mortality*. New York, NY, United Nations Population Division, Department of Economic and Social Affairs.

UN. 2005. *World Population Prospects: The 2004 Revision (CD-Rom Edition)*. New York, NY, United Nations Population Division, Department of Economic and Social Affairs.

UN. 2007. *World Mortality Report 2007 (CD-Rom Edition)*. New York, NY, United Nations Population Division, Department of Economic and Social Affairs.

UN. 2009. *World Population Prospects: The 2008 Revision (CD-Rom Edition)*. New York, NY, United Nations Population Division, Department of Economic and Social Affairs.

UN. 2010. "World Population Prospects: The 2008 Revision. Highlights." New York, NY, United Nations, Department of Economic and Social Affairs, Population Division.

UNAIDS. 2008. *Report on the Global Aids Epidemic*. Geneva, Joint United Nations Programme on HIV/AIDS, http://data.unaids.org/pub/GlobalReport/2008/20080813_gr08_prev1549_1990_2007_en.xls. Accessed 9 November 2009.

Unwin, N., P. Setel, S. Rashid, F. Mugusi, J.C. Mbanya, H. Kitange, L. Hayes, R. Edwards, T. Aspray, and K.G. Alberti. 2001. "Noncommunicable Diseases in Sub-Saharan Africa: Where Do They Feature in the Health Research Agenda?" *Bulletin of the World Health Organization* 79(10):947–53.

Vallin, J. and F. Meslé. 2004. "Convergences and Divergences in Mortality. A New Approach to Health Transition." *Demographic Research* S2(2):9–43.

WHO. 2008a. *The Global Burden of Disease: 2004 Update*. Geneva, World Health Organization.

WHO. 2008b. *Life Tables for Who Member States for 1990, 2000 and 2006: Indicator Definitions and Metadata of Life Expectancy at Birth*. http://www.who.int/whosis/indicators/2007LEX0/en/index.html. Accessed 16 November 2009 [see also the 2007 World Health Report].

Waltisperger, D. and T. Rabetsitonta. 1988. *Un Bilan De Trente Ans De Mesures Directes De La Mortalite Adulte En Afrique*. Presented at African Population Conference – Congres Africain de population, Dakar, Senegal.

Wilson, C. 2001. "On the Scale of Global Demographic Convergence, 1950–2000." *Population and Development Review* 27(1):155–71.

Zlotnik, H. and K. Hill. 1981. "The Use of Hypothetical Cohorts in Estimating Demographic Parameters under Conditions of Changing Fertility and Mortality." *Demography* 18(1):103–22.

# Chapter 8
# Global Trends in AIDS Mortality

John P. Bongaarts, François Pelletier, and Patrick Gerland

## Introduction

The global HIV/AIDS[1] pandemic is one of the deadliest epidemics of modern times. In 2007, a total of 2.0 million men, women, and children died of AIDS worldwide. The death toll will remain high in the future because 33 million individuals are currently infected and about 2.7 million new HIV infections occur each year (UNAIDS 2008). Most of these currently and newly infected individuals are likely to die of AIDS eventually, despite the increasing availability of antiretroviral treatment (ART).

Although the HIV virus has reached all corners of the globe, the sizes of epidemics vary widely among countries (UNAIDS 2008). In 2007, HIV prevalence (measured as the percent of adults aged 15–49 who are currently infected) in world regions outside Sub-Saharan Africa averaged a fraction of 1%. In contrast, prevalence in Sub-Saharan Africa was 5.0%—an order of magnitude larger than in the rest of the world (see Fig. 8.1). Even larger differences in epidemics exist within Sub-Saharan Africa, where prevalence levels range from less than 1% in a few countries in Western Africa to above 15% in parts of Eastern and Southern Africa. Worldwide, approximately 0.8% of adults are infected with HIV.

This huge variation in epidemic sizes is partly explained by the fact that HIV is not a particularly infectious agent in heterosexual relationships, which is the dominant mode of transmission in many countries. On average, in low-income countries the risk of transmission per act between an infected man or woman and his or her uninfected heterosexual partner is about 3–4 per 1,000 in the absence of commercial sex exposure (Boily et al. 2009). This low transmission risk prevents large epidemics in most populations. The exceptions are populations in which a substantial proportion of the population engages in high-risk sexual behavior (i.e., frequent change of partners and multiple concurrent partners), especially if—as in Southern Africa—male circumcision is limited, the use of condoms is low, and additional risk factors such as other sexually transmitted infections (STIs) and genital ulcers are present (Bongaarts et al. 2008; Caldwell 2000; Halperin and Epstein 2004, 2007; Powers et al. 2008; Shapiro 2002).

This chapter begins with a summary of data sources and then reviews the evolution of the epidemic over time. This is followed by a summary of the dynamics of HIV infection and mortality from AIDS. The second part of the chapter describes past trends and future projections in AIDS mortality indicators, including numbers of AIDS deaths, the proportion of all deaths that are due to AIDS, and life expectancy.

## Data

Estimates of HIV prevalence and incidence and AIDS mortality from 1980 to 2007 and projections from 2008 to 2030 were calculated for 58 countries by

---

J.P. Bongaarts (✉)
Population Council, New York, NY 10017, USA
e-mail: jbongaarts@popcouncil.org

The views and opinions expressed in this chapter are those of the authors and do not necessarily reflect those of the United Nations.

[1] HIV is the Human Immunodeficiency Virus responsible for the Acquired Immune Deficiency Syndrome (AIDS), which left untreated results in premature death.

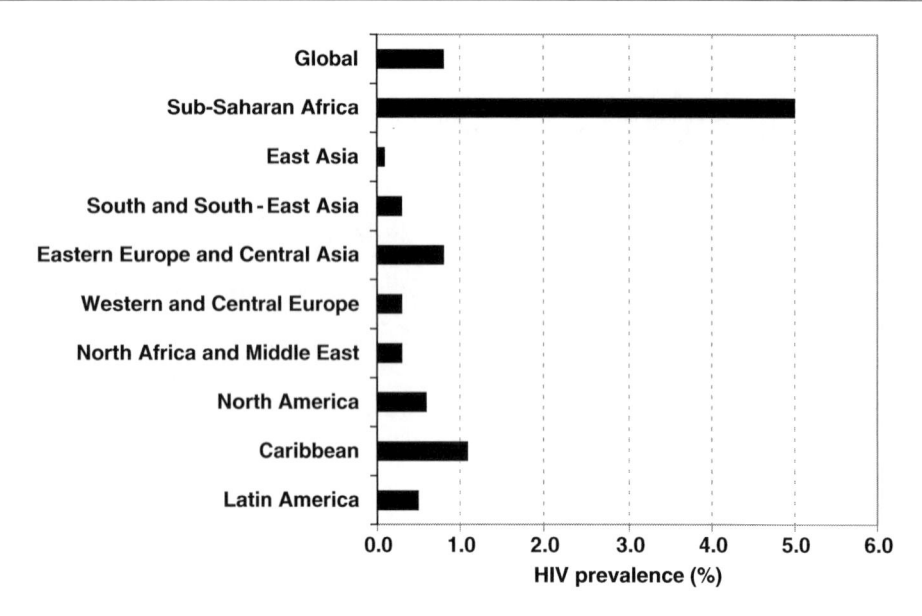

**Fig. 8.1** HIV prevalence in 2007 among adults aged 15–49. Source: UNAIDS (2008)

the United Nations Population Division as part of the preparation of the *2008 Revision* of *World Population Prospects* (United Nations et al. 2009a). The starting points for these calculations are estimates of country-specific HIV prevalence for selected years provided by UNAIDS (2008). Annual estimates and projections of prevalence are obtained by refitting UNAIDS estimates and extrapolating them using a model developed by the UNAIDS Reference Group on Estimates, Modeling, and Projections (Brown et al. 2008; Ghys et al. 2008; UNAIDS Reference Group 2002) that was adopted and customized by the Population Division for its own needs. Further details on the projection methodology and assumptions are provided by the United Nations (2006, 2009b). Once trends in HIV prevalence are established, the model calculates HIV incidence as well as deaths attributable to AIDS. These estimates and projections are made for the same set of 58 countries, which includes all countries with HIV prevalence above 1% as well as very populous countries with lower prevalence (China, India, the United States, the Russian Federation, and Brazil). For those 58 countries, which accounted for 93.2% of all AIDS deaths in 2007, information by age for different indicators and events, including deaths, is available by calendar year.

To obtain global estimates of AIDS deaths at the world and regional levels, estimates for all other countries for the period 1980–2007 produced by UNAIDS (2008)[2] were used and added to the estimates for the 58 countries. The projection of AIDS deaths at aggregated levels for the period 2008–2030 is based mainly on the 58 country-specific projections and assumes that the proportion of AIDS deaths that occurred in those countries in 2007 at the world level (that is 93.2%) remains constant in the future (a similar assumption is made at the regional level, though the proportion of AIDS deaths varies by region). Consequently, the projected numbers of AIDS deaths presented worldwide are based on the 58 countries adjusted by a factor of 1.073 to account for AIDS deaths in other countries.

## The Evolution of the Epidemic

HIV prevalence levels from 1975 to 2030 are plotted in Fig. 8.2, Panel a for selected non-African countries and in Panel b for selected African countries. The vertical line in this and other figures separates estimates up to 2007 and projections from 2008 onward. The epidemics in Sub-Saharan African countries in Panel b

---

[2] For some countries and for specific periods, estimates extracted from Spectrum files were also used. For consistency purposes, slight prorating adjustments were also made when deemed necessary.

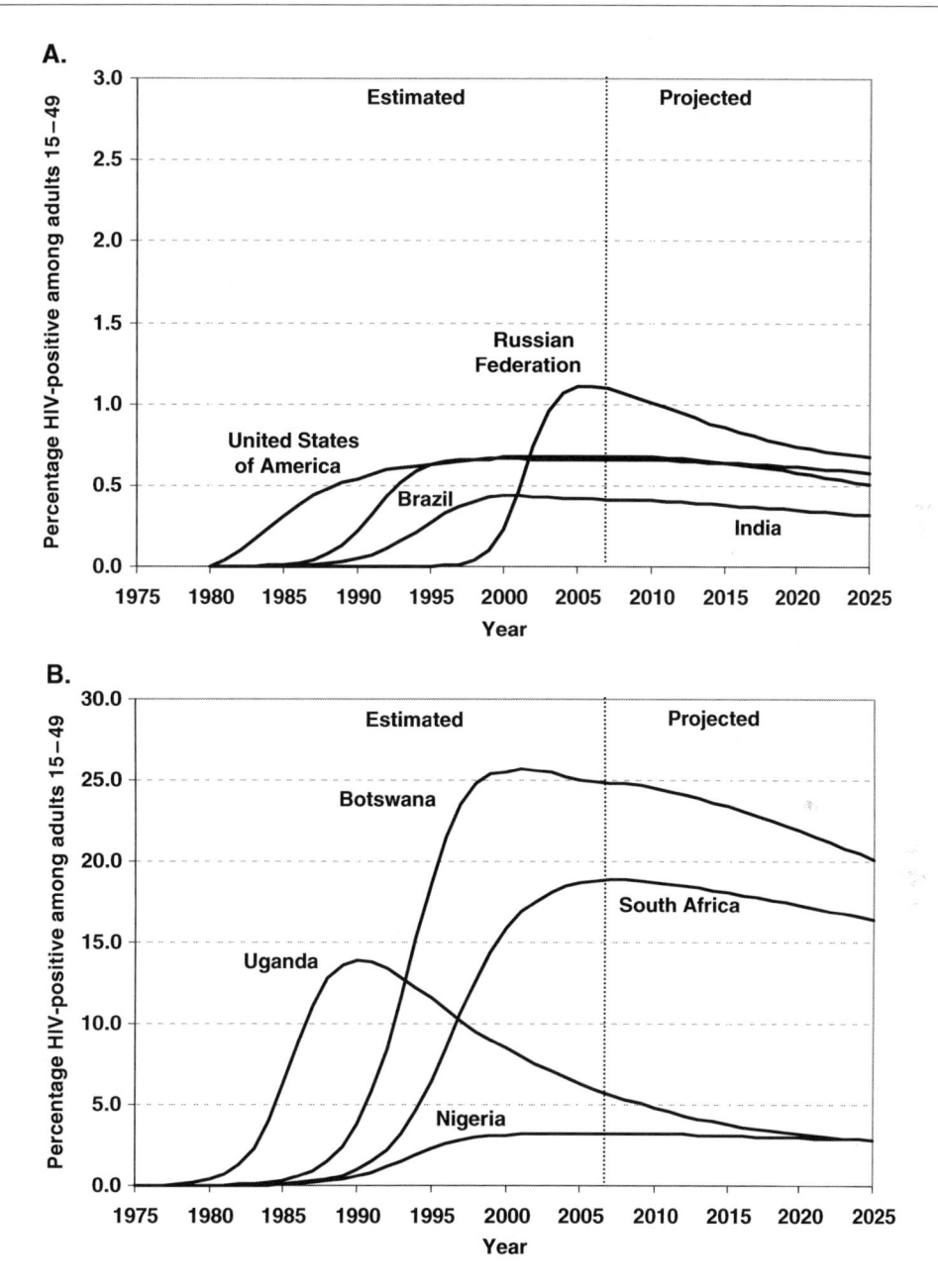

**Fig. 8.2** Estimated and projected prevalence of HIV, 1975–2025. Selected non-African countries. Selected African countries. Source: United Nations et al. (2009a) (special tabulations)

are all larger than those in countries in other continents in Panel a (note the difference in scales on the vertical axes of these figures). Epidemics also started at different times—for example, the ones in the United States and Uganda started relatively early and the ones in the Russian Federation and South Africa relatively late. Despite these differences, the general shapes of the prevalence patterns are broadly similar. Epidemics initially spread slowly, are followed by a period of rapid expansion, and end with a plateau. In a number of countries, a significant decline started before 2007. Nearly all epidemics reached their plateau in the 1990s or the early 2000s.

The appearance of recent plateaus is one of the epidemic's most interesting and important features. A stable or declining infection level implies that the virus is present in a proportion of the population yet is not spreading any further. There are several explanations for such an unexpected development (Bongaarts et al. 2008; Potts et al. 2008; Shelton et al. 2006).

First, high-risk behavior has declined in a number of countries, in part because of prevention programs that encourage abstinence, sexual fidelity, and condom use and that discourage needle-sharing. For example, in Uganda, following a vigorous campaign that started in the late 1980s, HIV prevalence declined by about half. There is strong evidence that behavioral change contributed to this decline, and both men and women have reported a reduction in sex with non-regular partners and a rise in condom use (Stoneburner and Low-Beer 2004). Declines in high-risk behavior and infection rates have also occurred in Kenya, Malawi, Thailand, and Zimbabwe (UNAIDS 2006, 2007, 2008).

A second explanation for the decline in HIV prevalence is that epidemics have reached their natural limits. Every population consists of a heterogeneous mixture of subgroups with widely varying infection risks. Sex workers and their clients, needle-sharing intravenous drug users (IDUs), and homosexual men are at relatively high risk, while men and women living in monogamous unions or without sexual partners are at low risk. At the onset of an epidemic, the virus quickly invades the highest-risk groups, but then encounters resistance when the pools of high-risk and most-susceptible individuals are infected or die out[3]. The epidemic reaches a plateau when the virus has achieved maximum penetration of the vulnerable subgroups. This point seems to have been reached in most countries by the early 2000s. In the United States and Europe, for example, parts of the homosexual and IDU groups are at relatively high risk of infection, but infection risks are much lower for the vast majority of heterosexuals. As a result, HIV prevalence among heterosexuals in these regions is a fraction of 1%. In contrast, Southern African populations have relatively large high-risk groups of sex workers and their partners, and the virus spreads more readily among the general population through diffuse networks of multiple and concurrent sexual partners (Halperin and Epstein 2004, 2007). The overall size of a country's epidemic depends on the sizes of the different risk groups and their behaviors (i.e., frequency of partner change, condom use), physiological characteristics (e.g., male circumcision), and the prevalence of other STIs.

A third contributing factor is that the initial wave of infections in the epidemic leads about a decade later to a wave of AIDS deaths (in the absence of ART). These deaths remove infected individuals from the population (and from the numerator of the HIV prevalence rate), thus contributing to plateaus or declines in prevalence levels.

It is not possible to quantify precisely the roles of any of the factors outlined above. Behavioral change is likely to have occurred in countries where HIV prevalence is declining, but epidemics can also reach a plateau without significant behavioral change when the epidemic runs its natural course.

## The Dynamics of HIV Infections and AIDS Deaths

The preceding analysis relied on HIV prevalence rates to assess epidemic trends. HIV prevalence is the most widely available indicator of epidemic size and it is readily interpreted. But prevalence is a lagging indicator of HIV infections. The numerator of the HIV prevalence rate consists of all currently infected adults (15–49), regardless of the time when they became infected. Because in the absence of ART individuals survive about a decade after infection, the estimated prevalence in a given year is determined by the number of infections that occurred in the past decade or earlier. The HIV incidence rate (i.e., the annual rate of new infections among adults aged 15–49) is therefore a better indicator to track epidemic trends. The total infected population at a point in time is the net result of past additions to the infected population through new infections and subtraction through deaths. The incidence rate measures the rate of new additions to the pool of infected individuals.

Figure 8.3 presents estimates of incidence rates (solid lines) for Botswana and Uganda, two countries with large epidemics. As mentioned before, HIV incidence typically rises rapidly in the initial years of the epidemic, followed by a peak and then a large but

---

[3] Assuming the presence of proper screening of blood supply and organ donors from high-risk groups to prevent non-sexual transmission to the general population through medical procedures.

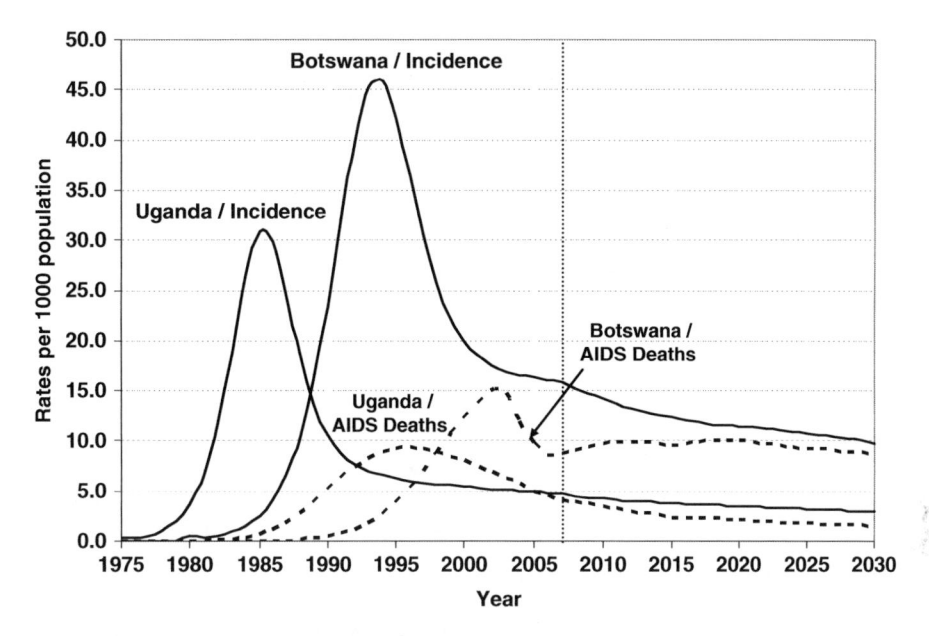

**Fig. 8.3** HIV incidence rate in population 15–49 (per 1,000) and AIDS death rates in ages 15–59 (per 1,000), Uganda and Botswana, 1975–2030. Source: United Nations (2009a) (special tabulations)

slower decline. As expected, the peaks in incidence in Botswana (46 per 1,000 per year) and Uganda (31 per 1,000 per year) are more than an order of magnitude higher than the peaks in countries in other continents. The timing of the peaks in incidence also varies significantly. The first occurred in the United States and in Uganda in the mid-1980s. The ongoing declines in incidence in most countries are caused by the same factors noted above for prevalence trends: saturation of high-risk groups and changes in high-risk behavior. But there is an additional third factor: a decline in the average infectiousness of infected individuals because fewer are in the acute post-infection stage and because of higher levels of ART. Note that the

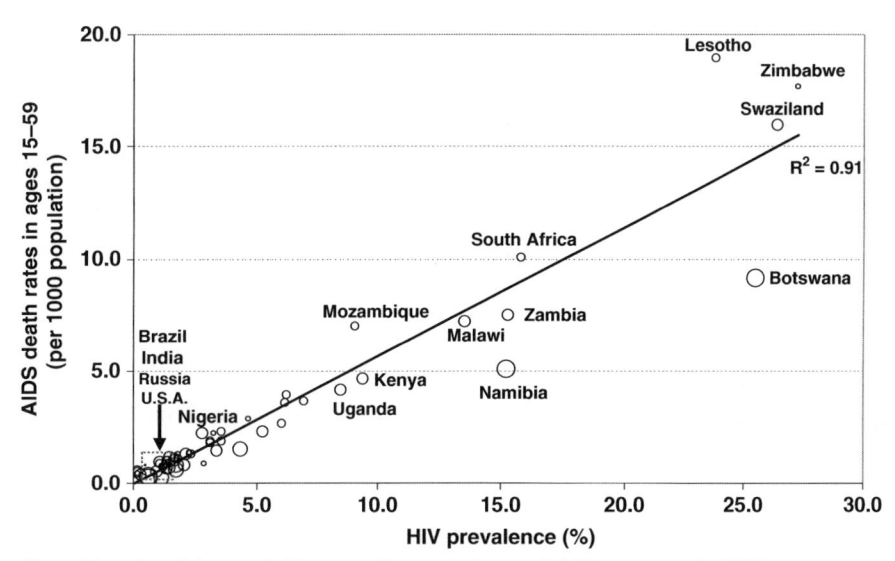

Note: The size of the symbol is proportionate to the adult ART coverage in 2007

**Fig. 8.4** AIDS death rates in ages 15–59 during 2005–2010 by HIV prevalence levels among adults aged 15–49 in 2000. Source: United Nations et al. (2009a) (special tabulations)

peaks in incidence seen in Fig. 8.3 occurred several years before the peaks in prevalence shown in Fig. 8.2, Panel b.

In the absence of treatment, HIV disease runs its natural course, which means that in infected people the infection is followed by a period of years in which few symptoms are present before the onset of AIDS and then death. The distribution of the survival interval from infection to death has a mean of 11 years for males, 12 years for females, and a rather large variance. Some individuals die shortly after infection, about half die within the first 11 years, and one in four survive more than 15 years even without treatment.

Figure 8.3 includes the estimated and projected trends in death rates because of AIDS (AIDS deaths per 1,000 population aged 15–59 as dashed lines). Note that the peaks in the death rates occur about a decade after the peaks in the incidence rates. The peaks in death rates are also lower in magnitude than the corresponding peaks in incidence rates because survival times between infection and death because of AIDS vary substantially among individuals, and because treatment reduces death rates. The trajectory of the AIDS death rate in Botswana shows a sudden decline between 2003 and 2006. This decline is largely attributable to a very rapid increase in the availability and use of ART during and shortly before this period.

As expected, the AIDS death rate of a country depends on the size of the HIV epidemic. Figure 8.4 plots the AIDS death rate in 2005–2010 by HIV prevalence in 2000 for 58 countries. The correlation is high ($R^2 = 0.91$), but still below one. Countries with high levels of ART (e.g., Botswana and Namibia) tend to have lower than expected death rates for a given level of prevalence because treatment suppresses the disease.

## Trends in AIDS Mortality

The UN projection model provides detailed country-level estimates of AIDS deaths and mortality rates by age and sex from 1980 to 2030 for the 58 countries for which the demographic impact of the HIV/AIDS epidemic was estimated and projected explicitly. To simplify the presentation below, only selected findings for both sexes combined are presented. Except for Fig. 8.5, which encompasses global estimates, all other findings are based on the estimates and projections provided by the United Nations Population Division.

## *AIDS Deaths*

Panel a of Fig. 8.5 plots the estimated and projected global number of AIDS deaths from 1980 to 2030. This number rose from near 0 in 1980 to 2.1 million in 2007, with a peak at 2.2 million in 2005. The estimate for 2007 is virtually the same as that provided by UNAIDS (2.0 million with a range of 1.8–2.3 million). The projection indicates only a slight rise in the global number of AIDS deaths, reaching a maximum value of 2.36 million in 2030. A notable feature of the global projection is the modest fluctuations in the future number of AIDS deaths. The initial decline in AIDS deaths starting around 2006 is partly related to the ongoing intensive global effort to provide ART to increasing proportions of AIDS patients. However, AIDS deaths subsequently rise again because of the postponement of deaths related to treatment and the occurrence of new infections; a changing population size and age distribution may also contribute to these fluctuations.

The noticeable inflection point in 2015 and the subsequent increase in the number of AIDS deaths are also partly related to assumptions made with respect to the future treatment coverage levels. The proportion of the HIV-positive adult population receiving treatment in each country is consistent with estimates prepared by the World Health Organization (WHO/UNAIDS/UNICEF 2008), which averaged 36% in 2007 among the 58 countries, with country levels ranging from 8 to 99%. The projected coverage levels for the treatment of adults are expected to increase substantially and reach on average 64% for the 58 affected countries, with country levels ranging from 40 to 99% by 2015. However, coverage levels are then assumed to remain constant until 2030 at the level reached in each country in 2015. The assumptions made for treatment coverage levels as well as for other parameters in modeling the demographic impact of the 58 countries most affected by the HIV/AIDS epidemic

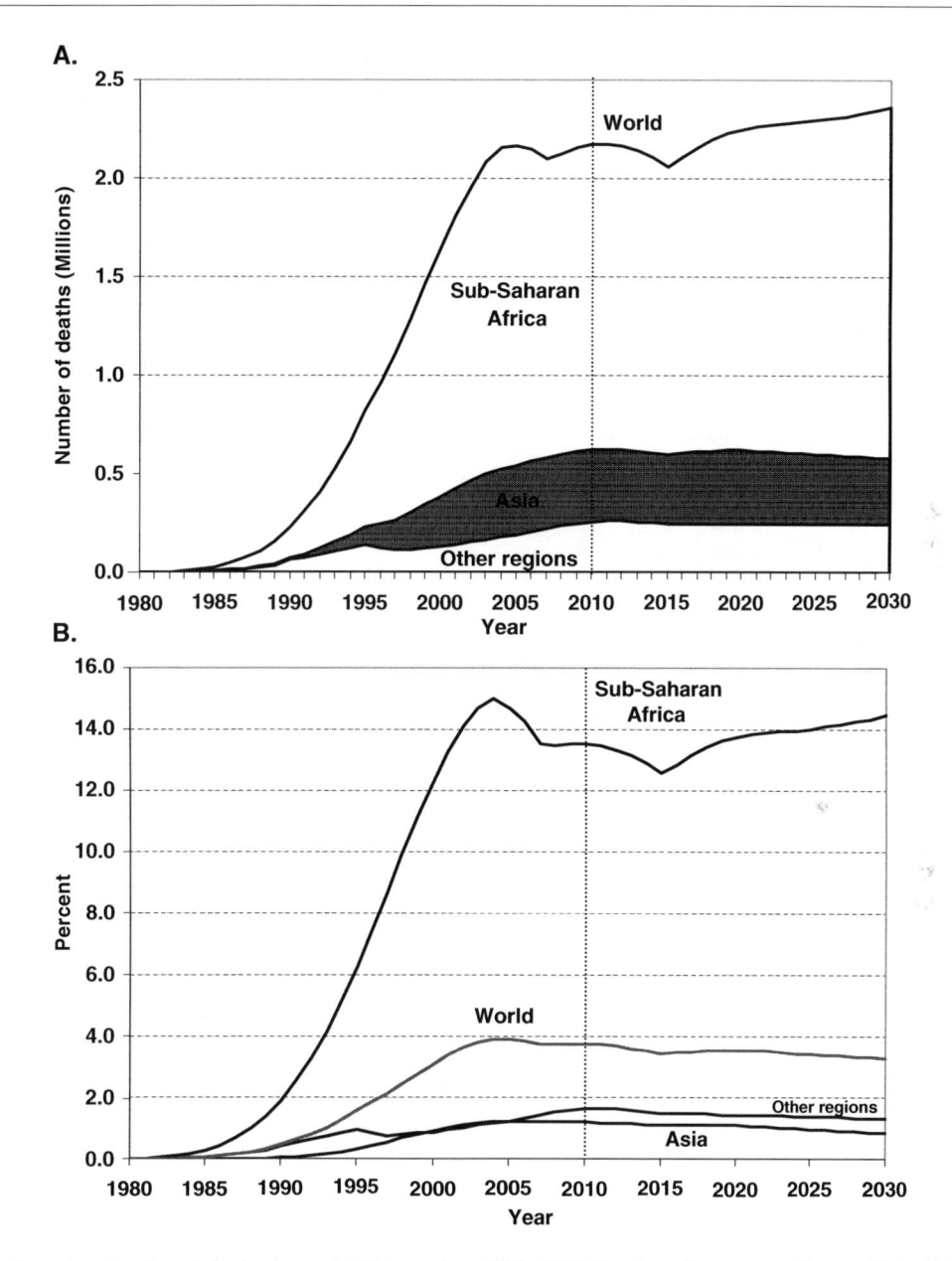

**Fig. 8.5** Estimated and projected deaths due to AIDS by region, 1980–2030. Numbers. Percentages. Source: United Nations et al. (2009a) (special tabulations and authors calculations)

have major bearing on the projected number of AIDS deaths at the world and regional levels.

The number of AIDS deaths varies widely by region, with the largest number in Sub-Saharan Africa (see Panel a, Fig. 8.5). In 2007 an estimated 1.5 million AIDS deaths occurred in Sub-Saharan Africa, which represent 72% of the global total. In the rest of the world, which contains nearly 9 out of 10 of the world's people, the number of AIDS deaths is estimated at 0.6 million (mostly in Asia).

Panel b of Fig. 8.5 plots the proportion of all deaths that are attributable to AIDS for the world, as well as for Sub-Saharan Africa and Asia. For the world as a whole, this proportion peaked in 2004 at 3.9%. As expected, the proportion is much higher in Sub-Saharan Africa (15% in 2004) than in the rest of the world (1.2% in Asia and 1.1% in other regions). The global proportion is expected to decline modestly to 3.3% by 2030.

## AIDS Deaths by Age

AIDS deaths are concentrated among young adults and children. The reason for the large impact of the epidemic among young adults is that sexual intercourse is the dominant mode of HIV transmission. The secondary mode of transmission, from infected mother to infant around the time of birth, leads to substantial infection levels among infants, particularly in countries where fertility is high and treatment of pregnant women is lacking.

In 2007 an estimated 86% of AIDS deaths occurred among adults aged 15–59 in the 58 countries included in the UN projections (see Fig. 8.6, Panel a). In contrast, only 14% of AIDS deaths occurred in age group 0–14 and 0.4% in age group 60 and over. By 2030 only a slight change in the proportion of AIDS deaths at ages 15–59 (to 91%) is expected, but the proportions under age 15 and over age 60 are expected to decline and rise, respectively. Three factors are responsible for

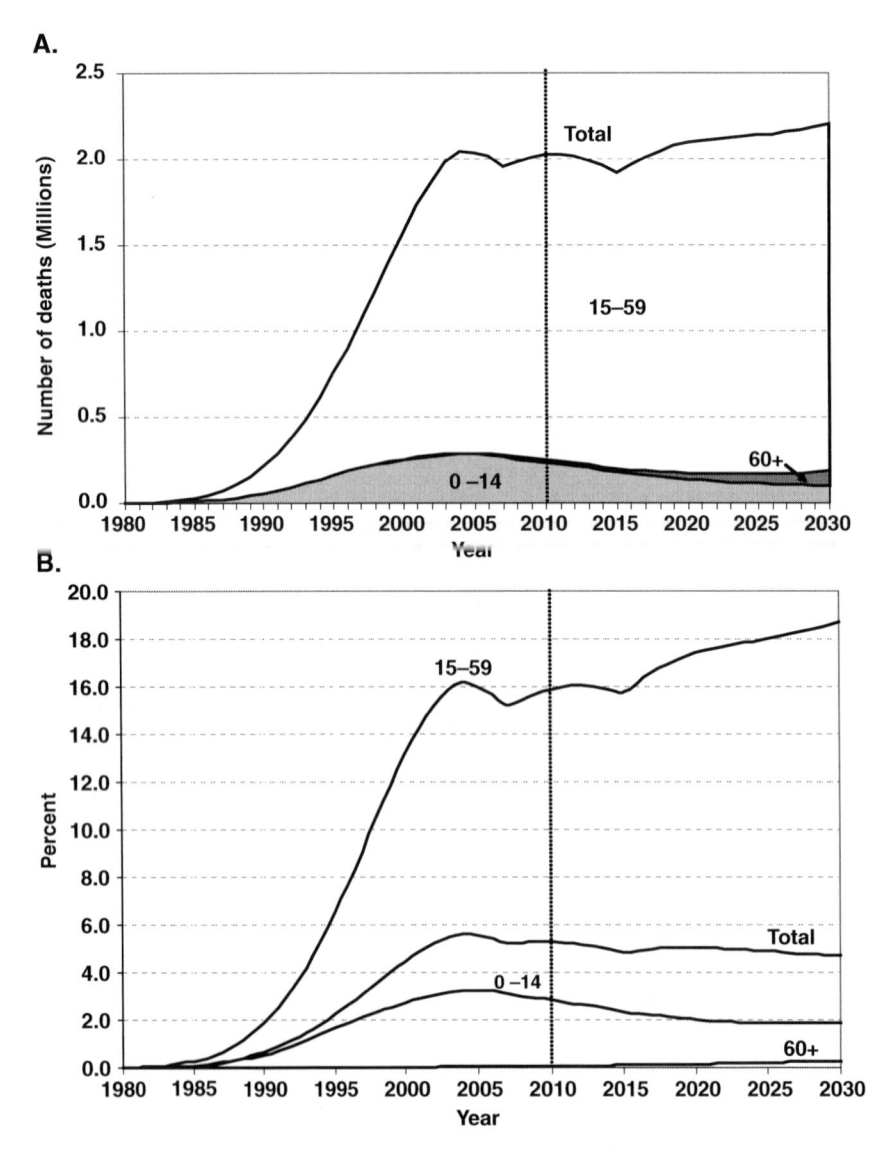

**Fig. 8.6** Estimated and projected deaths due to AIDS by broad age group, 58 countries, 1980–2030. Numbers. Percentages. Source: United Nations et al. (2009a) (special tabulation)

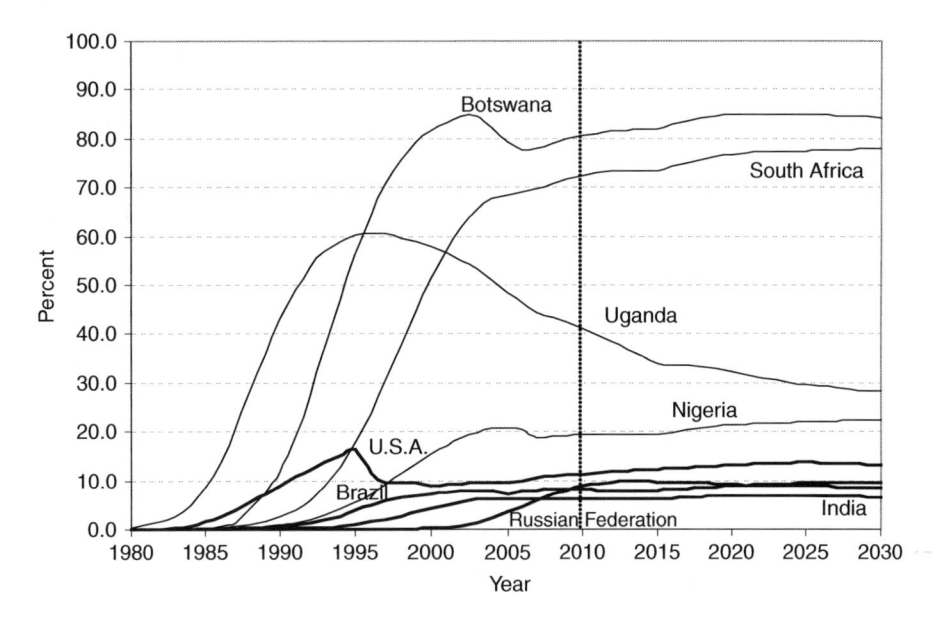

**Fig. 8.7** Percentage of deaths due to AIDS in age group 15–59, selected countries, 1980–2030. Source: United Nations et al. (2009a) (special tabulations)

the projected decline in the proportion under age 15: a rise in prevention of mother-to-child transmission of HIV (PMTCT), expanded access to ART treatment of pregnant mothers and infected children, and a decline in fertility.

The proportion of all deaths due to AIDS is much higher among adults aged 15–59 than in other age groups. As shown in Fig. 8.6, Panel b, this proportion reached 5.6% for all ages combined in 2004, but equaled 16% in age group 15–59, and just 3.2% for age group 0–14. This finding is explained by the concentration of AIDS deaths among young adults, combined with the fact that death rates from other causes are very low in this age group.

As shown in Fig. 8.7, the proportion of deaths due to AIDS among adults aged 15–59 has reached very high levels in a few countries in Sub-Saharan Africa (e.g., 85% in Botswana in 2003 and 61% in Uganda in 1996). These two countries have very large epidemics, and by African standards they have a relatively high quality of healthcare, so that their death rates from other causes are relatively low. In contrast, in many countries outside Sub-Saharan Africa, the proportion of deaths attributable to AIDS is typically well below 10%.

The projections to 2030 suggest that the proportion of AIDS deaths at ages 15–59 will remain approximately at current levels for the 58 countries combined (see Fig. 8.6, Panel b). The same is true in many individual countries, as shown in Fig. 8.7. The exceptions to this general trend are countries with relatively rapid declines in HIV incidence, which are expected to see future declines in proportions of deaths due to AIDS (e.g., in Uganda).

## Life Expectancy at Age 15

Life expectancy at age 15 (denoted $e_{15}$) is a widely used and easily interpretable indicator of adult mortality; it represents the average number of additional years that individuals reaching their 15th birthday expect to live. The epidemic's impact on this indicator can be assessed by comparing the "AIDS" and "No-AIDS" scenarios prepared by the United Nations Population Division as part of its *2008 Revision* of *World Population Prospects* (United Nations et al. 2009a). The AIDS scenario incorporates the impact of the HIV/AIDS epidemic since its inception in the 1980s. In the No-AIDS scenario, the mortality rates of uninfected individuals are applied to the entire population, leading to a hypothetical scenario of what the mortality in each country would have been in the absence of AIDS.

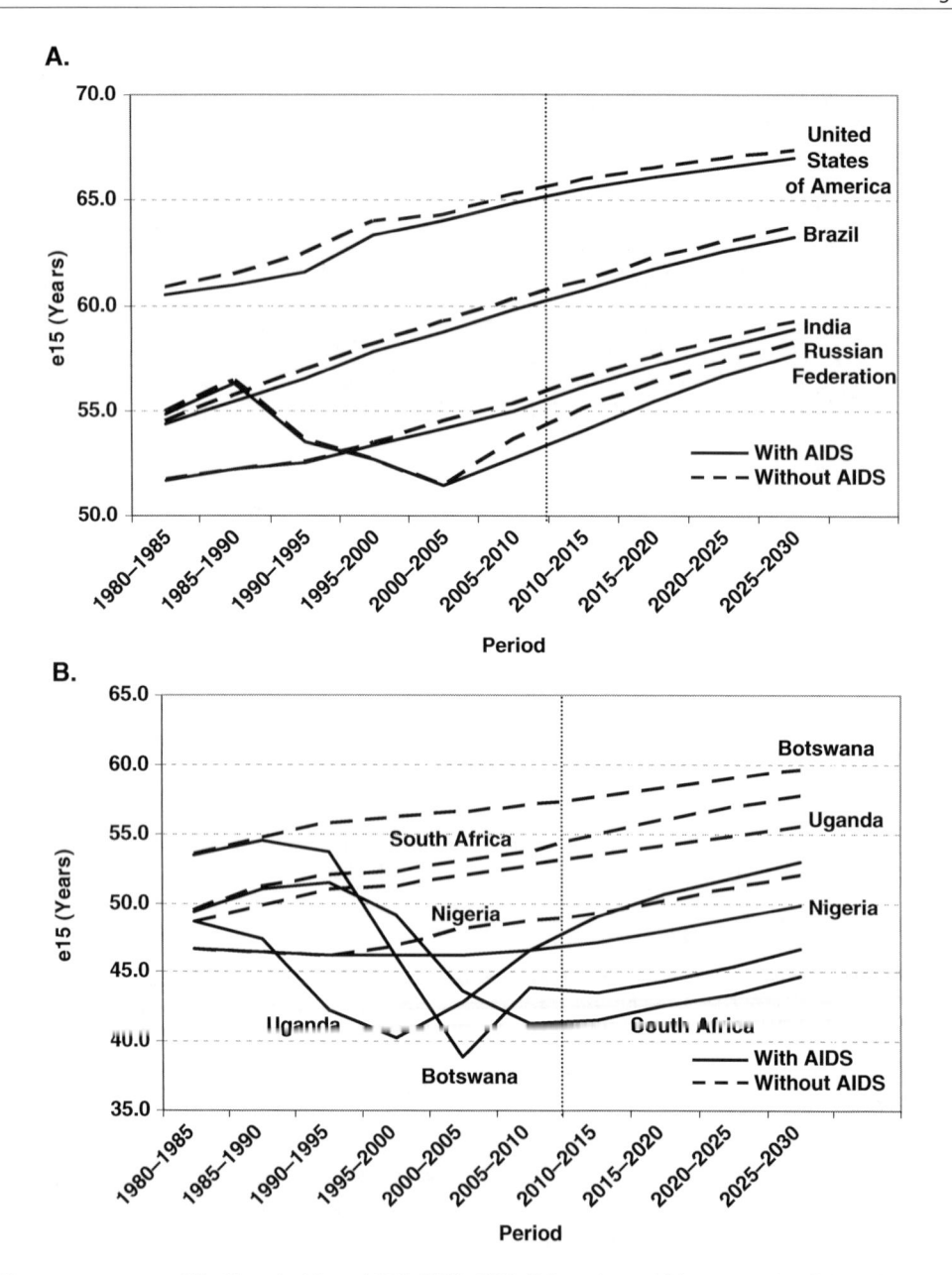

**Fig. 8.8** Life expectancy at age 15 with and without AIDS, 1980–2030. Selected non-African countries. Selected African countries. Source: United Nations et al. (2009a)

Estimates of $e_{15}$ from 1980 to 2007 and projections from 2008 to 2030 are plotted in Fig. 8.8 for selected non-African (Panel a) and African countries (Panel b). The net reduction in $e_{15}$ caused by the epidemic (i.e., the difference between the No-AIDS and AIDS scenarios) is plotted in Fig. 8.9. According to these results, the epidemic's impact on $e_{15}$ in the non-African countries has been relatively modest—around 1 year or less in 2005–2010 (the large decline in $e_{15}$ in the Russian Federation between the late 1980s and the early 2000s is unrelated to the HIV/AIDS epidemic). In contrast, a much larger impact is evident in African countries. For example, in Botswana in 2000–2005 the epidemic reduced $e_{15}$ by 17.8 years, from 56.6 in the No-AIDS scenario to 38.9 years in the AIDS scenario. As previously noted, the modest rebound in

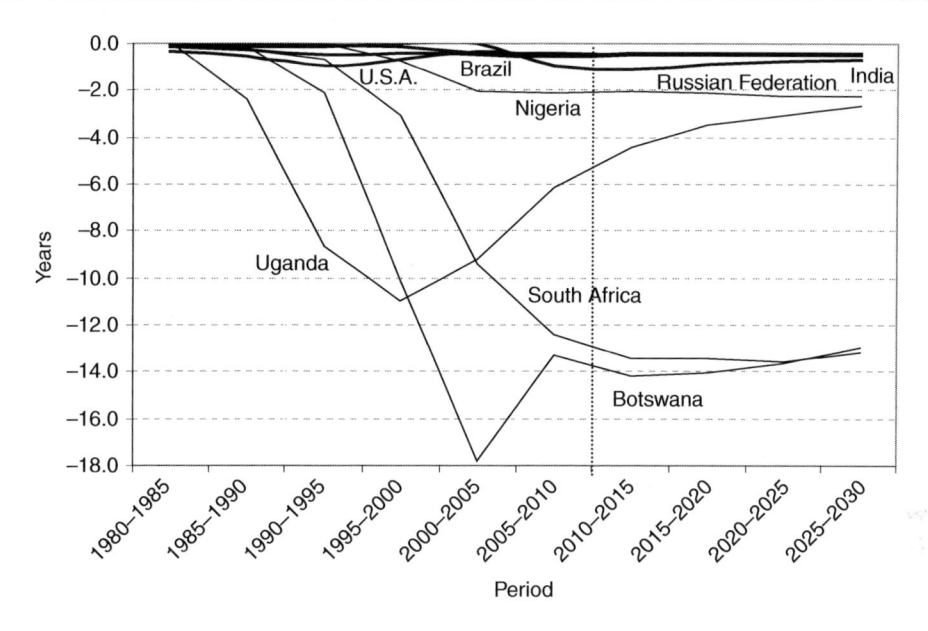

**Fig. 8.9** Change in life expectancy at age 15 due to AIDS, selected countries, 1980–2030. Source: United Nations et al. (2009a)

**Fig. 8.10** Absolute difference in $e_{15}$ levels, AIDS versus No-AIDS scenarios, 2005–2010 by HIV prevalence among adults aged 15–49 in 2000. Source: United Nations et al. (2009a) (special tabulations)

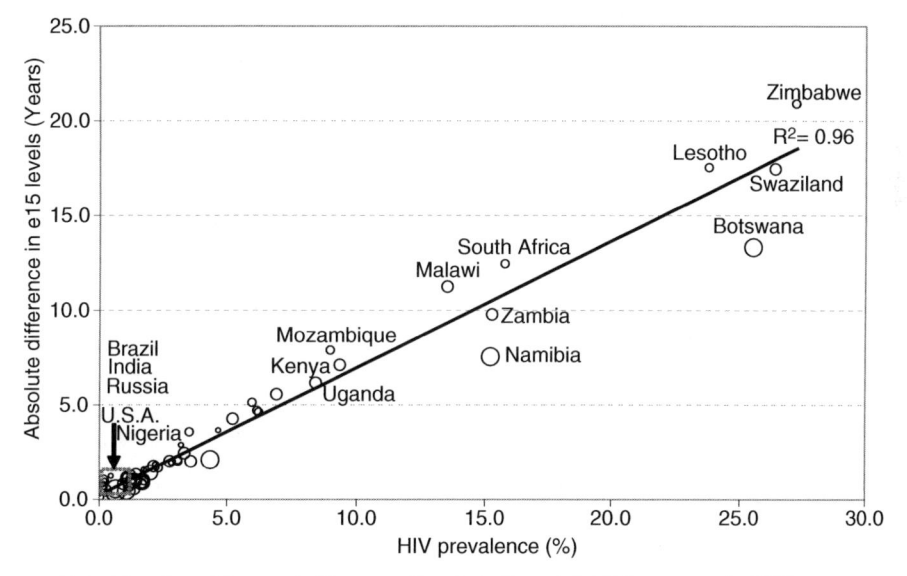

Note: The size of the symbol is proportionate to the adult ART coverage in 2007

$e_{15}$ in recent years in Botswana is due to the wider availability and use of ART.

As was the case for the AIDS death rate, a country's reduction in $e_{15}$ caused by AIDS mortality varies directly with the size of the HIV epidemic. Figure 8.10 plots the decline in $e_{15}$ in 2005–2010 by HIV prevalence in 2000 for all 58 countries. The small proportion of the variance not explained by the regression ($R^2 = 0.96$) is largely due to the mortality-reducing effect of ART in countries with high ART coverage (e.g., Botswana and Namibia).

## Conclusion

Based on our estimates, a cumulative total of 24 million people have died from AIDS between 1980 and 2007, and by 2030 this cumulative total is projected to reach 75 million. This pandemic is one of the most serious epidemics of modern times, and the eventual death toll will substantially exceed the toll from the 1918 influenza epidemic. In 2004, HIV/AIDS was the sixth leading cause of death at the world level and the fourth leading cause in low-income countries, after lower respiratory infections, ischemic heart disease, and diarrheal diseases (WHO 2008).

Despite these grim statistics and the exceedingly rapid spread of this new disease during the 1980s and 1990s, the epidemic has reached a major turning point in recent years as the incidence of new infections peaked and began to decline. Several factors were responsible for this turnaround, including a reduction in high-risk behavior, the natural limits of the epidemic, and a decline in the infectiousness of people living with HIV. The peak in new infections is followed by a peak in death rates about a decade later because of the long average interval between infection and the onset of AIDS. Our estimates indicate that the global number of new HIV infections peaked in the mid-1990s and the number of AIDS deaths peaked at 2.16 million in 2005. Worldwide, the proportion of all deaths that are caused by AIDS reached 3.9% in 2004. This proportion varies widely from a high of 15% in Sub-Saharan Africa to around 1% in Asia and other regions. In the future, the number of AIDS deaths and the proportion of deaths due to AIDS are projected to remain approximately at their current levels. Modest fluctuations may occur partly because of the rapidly spreading availability of treatment, which initially delays deaths, pushing them to later years. Fluctuations also arise because of the assumptions made with respect to future coverage levels of treatment. The size and age composition of the population are also partly responsible for the projected trends in the number of AIDS deaths.

The AIDS epidemic's impact on life expectancy at age 15 is less than a year in much of the world outside Africa but has amounted to over 10 years in Southern Africa. Projections indicate that life expectancies with AIDS will increase for nearly all countries from their current depressed levels. The impact of AIDS on $e_{15}$ is expected to remain approximately at current levels until 2030 except in a few countries (e.g., Uganda and Zimbabwe) where the epidemic is declining substantially.

These projections depend on the assumptions underlying them and further interventions—in particular, prevention efforts—could reduce the number of AIDS deaths to lower levels. Uncertainty regarding the accuracy of the estimates of past trends in HIV prevalence, incidence, and AIDS deaths, as well as an incomplete understanding of the dynamics of the epidemic and its behavioral and biological determinants, makes any projections tentative. The difficulty of predicting future trends in behavior, prevention efforts, and affordable access to treatment must also be considered. Further research on these issues is essential to improve the accuracy of medium-term projections.

**Acknowledgment** The authors are grateful to Mr. Thomas Buettner, Assistant Director of the Population Division, for kindly updating the Population Division's AIDS program and designing queries that enabled the production of special tabulations, which were used in this study; the authors would also like to thank all other staff members of the Population Division who worked on the *2008 Revision* of *World Population Prospects*: Mr. Gerhard Heilig, Mr. Kirill Andreev, Mr. Taeke Gjaltema, Ms. Vladimira Kantorova, Mr. Pablo Lattes, and Mr. Nan Li. The authors also wish to thank Ms. Hania Zlotnik, Director of the Population Division, for her insightful comments.

## References

Boily, M.C., R.F. Baggaley, L. Wang, B. Masse, R. White, R. Hayes, and M. Alary. 2009. "Heterosexual Risk of HIV-1 Infection Per Sexual Act: Systematic Review and Meta-analysis of Observational Studies." *The Lancet Infectious Diseases* 9(2):118–29.

Bongaarts, J., T. Buettner, G. Heilig, and F. Pelletier. 2008. "Has the AIDS Epidemic Peaked?" *Population and Development Review* 34(2):199–224.

Brown, T., J.A. Salomon, L. Alkema, A.E. Raftery, and E. Gouws. 2008. "Progress and Challenges in Modelling Country-Level HIV/AIDS Epidemics: The UNAIDS Estimation and Projection Package 2007." *Sexually Transmitted Infections*, 84(Suppl 1):i5–i10. doi:10.1136/sti.2008.030437. http://sti.bmj.com/cgi/content/full/84/Suppl_1/i5

Caldwell, J.C. 2000. "Rethinking the African AIDS Epidemic." *Population and Development Review* 26(1):117–35.

Ghys, P.D., N. Walker, W. McFarland, R. Miller, and G.P. Garnett. 2008. "Improved Data, Methods and Tools for the 2007 HIV and AIDS Estimates and Projections." *Sexually Transmitted Infections* 84(Supp 1):i1–i4. doi:10.1136/sti.2008.032573. http://sti.bmj.com/cgi/content/full/84/Suppl_1/i1

Halperin, D.T. and H. Epstein. 2004. "Concurrent Sexual Partnerships Help to Explain Africa's High HIV Prevalence: Implications for Prevention." *The Lancet* 364(9428):4–6.

Halperin, D.T. and H. Epstein. 2007. "Why is HIV Prevalence So Severe in Southern Africa?" *The Southern African Journal of HIV Medicine* (March) 8(1):19–24.

Potts, M., D.T. Halperin, D. Kirby, A. Swidler, E. Marseille, J.D. Klausner, N. Hearst, R.G. Wamai, J.G. Kahn, and J. Walsh. 2008. "Reassessing HIV Prevention." *Science* 320(5877):749–50.

Powers, K.A., C. Poole, A.E. Pettifor, and M.S. Cohen. 2008. "Rethinking the Heterosexual Infectivity of HIV-1: A Systematic Review and Meta-Analysis." *The Lancet Infectious Diseases* 8(9):553–63.

Shapiro, R. 2002. "Drawing Lines in the Sand: The Boundaries of the HIV Pandemic in Perspective." *Social Science and Medicine* 55:107–10.

Shelton, J.D., D.T. Halperin, and D. Wilson. 2006. "Has Global HIV Incidence Peaked?" *Lancet* 367(9517):1120–21.

Stoneburner, R.L. and D. Low-Beer. 2004. "Population-Level HIV Declines and Behavioral Risk Avoidance in Uganda." *Science* 304:714–18 (30 April).

UNAIDS Reference Group on Estimates, Modelling, and Projections. 2002. "Improved Methods and Assumptions for Estimation of the HIV/AIDS Epidemic and its Impact: Recommendations of the UNAIDS Reference Group on Estimates, Modeling and Projections." *AIDS* 16: W1–W14.

UNAIDS. 2006. *Report on the Global AIDS Epidemic*. Joint United Nations Programme on HIV/AIDS. Geneva, UNAIDS.

UNAIDS. 2007. *AIDS Epidemic Update: December 2007*. Joint United Nations Programme on HIV/AIDS (UNAIDS) and World Health Organization (WHO). Geneva, UNAIDS.

UNAIDS. 2008. *2008 Report on the Global AIDS Epidemic*. Joint United Nations Programme on HIV/AIDS (UNAIDS) and World Health Organization (WHO). Geneva, UNAIDS. See online tables: "Adult (15–49) HIV Prevalence Percent by Country, 1990–2007 (with 95% Confidence Intervals)"; and "AIDS Deaths in Adults and Children by Country, 1990–2007". http://data.unaids.org/pub/GlobalReport/2008/080813_gr08_prev1549_1990_2007_en.xls. http://data.unaids.org/pub/GlobalReport/2008/080818_gr08_deaths_1990_2007_en.xls

United Nations, Department of Economic and Social Affairs, Population Division. 2006. *World Population Prospects: The 2004 Revision*, vol. 3, *Analytical Report* (United Nations Publication, Sales No. E.05.XIII.7).

United Nations, Department of Economic and Social Affairs, Population Division. 2009a. *World Population Prospects: The 2008 Revision, CD-ROM Edition—Extended Dataset in Excel and ASCII formats*. United Nations Publication, ST/ESA/SER.A/283; Special Tabulations Were Prepared for this Study.

United Nations, Department of Economic and Social Affairs, Population Division. 2009b. *Assumptions Underlying the Results of the 2008 Revision of World Population Prospects*. http://esa.un.org/unpp/index.asp?panel=4

WHO/UNAIDS/UNICEF. 2008. *Towards Universal Access: Scaling Up Priority HIV/AIDS Interventions in the Health Sector*. Progress Report 2008. Geneva, WHO, June 2008, http://www.who.int/entity/hiv/pub/towards_universal_access_report_2008.pdf

World Health Organization. 2008. *The Global Burden of Disease: 2004 Update*. Geneva, WHO, http://www.who.int/healthinfo/global_burden_disease/GBD_report_2004update_part2.pdf

# Part II
# Sociodemographic, Economic, Behavioral, and Psychological Determinants of Mortality

# Chapter 9
# Early Life Conditions and Later Life Mortality

Jennifer Karas Montez and Mark D. Hayward

## Introduction

The preponderance of research on adult mortality over the past several decades emphasizes the impact of relatively proximate social and behavioral factors in adulthood. Mortality's associations with job conditions, income, wealth, education, smoking, obesity, and marriage, for example, are well documented even if the mechanisms are not completely well characterized (Davey Smith et al. 1998b; Lillard and Waite 1995; Marmot and Shipley 1996; Preston and Taubman 1994; Rogers et al. 2000). Researchers have also become increasingly sensitive to the mortality effects of social and behavioral factors at different points in adulthood. For example, research on occupational careers and mortality points to cumulative effects of occupational conditions both early and later in the career (Cambois 2004; Moore and Hayward 1990; Pavalko et al. 1993).

With the growing interest in the effects of exposure to social conditions over the adult life course, it is not surprising that researchers have also begun to attend to the ways in which early life conditions influence adult mortality. And, in fact, this has become one of the liveliest areas of research on adult mortality. How strong is the association between early life conditions and adult mortality? Which early life conditions matter the most? How do early life conditions combine with adult conditions to influence mortality? What are the social and biological pathways through which early life conditions influence adult mortality? These general questions have shaped the development of research in this area.

Here, we review the development of the theoretical ideas and empirical evidence on this topic. Our discussion begins with a historical overview of the growth of research examining the association between early life conditions and adult mortality. What were the types of studies and key findings that have shaped current understanding of the association? We then discuss the two major conceptual frameworks, which we call *biological imprint* and *social pathways* frameworks, and weigh the evidence for these frameworks. Because the evidence appears highly contingent on the types of childhood exposure, we review the associations and mechanisms linking types of childhood social exposures (socioeconomic and family conditions) and physical exposures (infectious disease and nutrition) with adult mortality. We then illustrate empirically how childhood exposures are associated with adult mortality through the biological imprint and social pathways mechanisms, drawing on the Health and Retirement Study. This analysis points to key conceptual and analytical challenges facing researchers that will likely motivate new longitudinal studies, measures, and analyses. We end the chapter by noting the importance of historical conditions in contextualizing the associations and mechanisms that link early life conditions with adult mortality.

## History of the Idea that Early Life Conditions Shape Adult Mortality Risks

The idea that early life conditions shape later life mortality risks is not new. As early as the 1600s, public

J.K. Montez (✉)
Department of Sociology and Population Research Center,
University of Texas, Austin, TX 78712, USA
e-mail: jennkaras@prc.utexas.edu

health advocates began implicating childhood conditions, particularly nutrition, as factors shaping adult health and vitality (Bengtsson and Mineau 2009). By the early twentieth century, researchers in public health and epidemiology, as well as government officials and private-sector actuaries, were reporting nontrivial associations between childhood conditions and adult mortality (Kuh and Davey Smith 1993). Initial evidence was based largely on birth cohort and ecological mortality differentials. More recently, the availability of individual-level data from prospective studies has reinvigorated interest in the association. That said, the notion that childhood conditions are associated with adult mortality, net of adult circumstances, has not gone uncontested. Nor has the idea consistently remained in the forefront of scholarly thinking about the origins of adult mortality. The following section briefly reviews the development of the idea over the twentieth century.

Birth cohort studies provided some of the first empirical evidence linking childhood mortality risks with later life mortality risks. For instance, studies of the secular mortality decline in England and Wales uncovered patterns that suggested that childhood mortality experiences act as an anchor for mortality experiences in adulthood (Derrick 1927; Kermack et al. 1934). These scholars claimed that the secular decline could be better understood by examining the decline across successive years of birth cohorts rather than the conventional years of death. Indeed, Derrick (1927: 144–45) wrote that "nearly the whole of the temporal change [in mortality from 1846 to 1923] is due to an entirely independent 'generation' influence, each generation being endowed with a vitality peculiarly its own, which persistently manifests itself throughout the succeeding stages of its existence." While some scholars remained unconvinced that childhood conditions were such potent determinants, others accepted the notion but disagreed about the causal mechanisms (see Derrick 1927; Kermack et al. 1934).

As promising as these studies were, around World War II, attention in many disciplines shifted from childhood to adulthood conditions as major risk factors for adult mortality (Bengtsson and Mineau 2009; Kuh and Davey Smith 1993). The shift occurred for several reasons. First, the mortality regularities reported earlier in England and Wales were now less apparent as childhood mortality continued to decline without a commensurate decline in old-age mortality. Moreover, the rise in lung cancer and ischemic heart disease in industrialized countries, combined with emerging evidence that smoking was a major contributor to lung cancer etiology, shifted the focus from the effect of childhood conditions on all-cause mortality in later life to the effect of adult risk factors on cause-specific mortality (Kuh and Davey Smith 1993).

During the 1970s, there was a resurgence of interest in the role of childhood conditions in the etiology of adult mortality (Lynch and Davey Smith 2005). However, this wave of research was based largely on ecological data, focused on cause-specific mortality, and used area-based infant mortality rates as a proxy for early life conditions, such as nutrition, poverty, and pathogen exposure. For example, using county-level mortality data from Norway, Forsdahl (1977) discovered that counties that experienced high infant mortality rates also experienced high mortality rates when those cohorts were middle-aged adults. The strength of the association was strongest for arteriosclerotic heart disease for men and women, and lung cancer and cerebrovascular disease for men, leading Forsdahl to speculate that undernutrition in childhood may cause permanent biological damage or susceptibility to high-fat diets in adulthood. These findings were replicated using state-level data from the United States (Buck and Simpson 1982). Later ecological studies in England and Wales expanded the emerging hypotheses by suggesting that the causal processes may start earlier than was previously thought, that is, in utero (Barker 2007; Barker and Osmond 1989; Barker et al. 1989). For instance, Barker and colleagues examined the spatial correlations of neonatal and postneonatal mortality with subsequent adult mortality from specific causes. The positive association was particularly pronounced between neonatal mortality and adult mortality from cardiovascular diseases, leading them to hypothesize that the intrauterine environment is a crucial factor because neonatal mortality is strongly linked to low birthweight.

Taken together, the birth cohort and ecological studies offered compelling evidence that childhood conditions leave an indelible imprint on later life mortality risks. But numerous uncertainties remained. First, it was unclear whether the association was causal. It was conceivable that the association was due simply to the fact that children raised in adverse socioeconomic conditions tend to experience similar conditions as adults, and the adult environment may be the salient factor

(Gillman and Rich-Edwards 2000). It also remained unclear whether childhood conditions played a larger role than adulthood conditions, and which biological, behavioral, and/or psychosocial pathways explained the association.

As individual-level, prospective data became available in the 1980s and 1990s, studies confirmed many of the patterns and hypotheses derived from cohort and ecological data. These studies also expanded our understanding of the association in a number of ways. They identified specific childhood factors associated with adult mortality, including prenatal and postnatal nutrition, exposure to infectious diseases and environmental pathogens, socioeconomic environment, and family environment. They also demonstrated that several childhood factors influence adult mortality risks net of adult conditions. Finally, more recent studies support the idea that the relative contributions of childhood and adult circumstances depend on the specific health condition (Davey Smith et al. 1998a; Lawlor et al. 2006) and age of death (Su 2009).

## Theoretical Frameworks

One of the most powerful conceptual frameworks accounting for the links between early life conditions and later life mortality risks was developed by Preston and colleagues (Preston et al. 1998). Their framework is a two-dimensional typology showing that the association between childhood and adulthood mortality risks can be direct or indirect on one dimension, and it can exhibit a positive or negative correlation on the other. For example, a direct and positive association indicates that survivors of pernicious childhood environments carry a lifelong vulnerability to adverse adult circumstances, or simply to natural aging processes. This association, termed "scarring," is consistent with the cohort pattern of the historical mortality decline (Crimmins and Finch 2006). On the other hand, a direct and negative association indicates that survivors carry a lifelong immunity from the types of diseases they survived in childhood. This association, termed "immunity," is consistent with the hygiene hypothesis, which posits that a lack of pathogenic challenges in childhood permanently compromises immune function (Strachan 2000). Alternatively, an indirect and positive association, labeled "correlated environments," suggests that adverse (salutary) circumstances in childhood elevate (reduce) adult mortality because individuals tend to experience similar health-damaging (enhancing) circumstances throughout the life course. Findings from Preston et al. (1998) supported this scenario. Finally, an indirect and negative association, termed "selection," implies that inherently robust individuals survive adverse childhood environments, and thus carry a survival advantage throughout their lifetimes.

## The Biological Imprint Framework

Scholars tend to conceptualize the four scenarios described above as falling within two broad frameworks. One framework encompasses the scarring and immunity scenarios. It is referred to by many names including critical period, latency, biological programming, biological imprint, biological embedding, or in specific cases, the fetal origins hypothesis. It asserts that certain experiences, or "exposures," in early life permanently and irreversibly alter the structure and/or function of organs, tissues, and systems (Barker 1997; Ben-Shlomo and Kuh 2002). It further claims that exposures in adulthood may temporarily moderate the baseline level of structure and function, but they cannot erase the body's "memory" of early exposures. For example, *prenatal* nutrition influences the number of pancreatic β-cells that create and release insulin (Van Assche and Aerts 1979), while *infant* nutrition influences the baseline number of ovarian follicles in women (Hardy and Kuh 2002), and ambient temperatures during the first 3 years of life determine the lifelong number of functioning sweat glands (Diamond 1991). As these examples illustrate, this framework is generally concerned with exposures that occur in utero or in early childhood, developmentally active periods when humans exhibit a high degree of phenotypic plasticity.

Phenotypic plasticity is an important concept within this framework and in life history theory more generally. It is "the ability of a single genotype to produce more than one alternative form of morphology, physiological state, and/or behavior in response to environmental conditions" (West-Eberhard 1989: 249). Life history theory posits that conditions in utero provide clues to the fetus about the postnatal environment.

From these clues, the fetus allocates resources such as nutrition across three areas—growth, maintenance, and reproduction—to optimize its survival chances in the postnatal world (McDade 2005; Worthman and Kuzara 2005). However, when resources are limited, allocating resources to one area leaves fewer resources for others. For example, a fetus may respond to malnutrition by diverting resources away from less critical metabolic systems toward those more critical for short-term survival such as the brain (Barker 1997). While this optimizes survival chances in a nutritionally poor postnatal world, it may create a biological vulnerability to a nutritionally abundant one. Resource allocation continues during childhood. For instance, infectious disease exposure in early life diverts resources away from growth and toward maintenance—in this case, immune function activation (see McDade 2005). Indeed, the well-documented relation of infectious disease burden and undernutrition in childhood to adult height is one manifestation of this resource tradeoff (Fogel 2004). Life history theory also asserts that when prenatal and postnatal environments are similar, phenotypic plasticity is advantageous, particularly from an evolutionary perspective (Worthman and Kuzara 2005). Thus, biological imprinting is not the categorically pathological process that it is often depicted to be. As McDade (2005: 92) states, "the early origins of disease and the early origins of developmental plasticity can be seen as merely two sides of the same coin."

Another important concept within this framework is the distinction between critical and sensitive periods, which identify the appropriate time frames for capturing exposures. Ben-Schlomo and Kuh (2002: 288) define a critical period as a "limited time window in which an exposure can have adverse or protective effects on development and subsequent disease outcome," and a sensitive period as a "period when an exposure has a stronger effect on development and hence disease risk than it would at other times." While critical periods typically concern biological subsystems, sensitive periods generally concern behavioral development.

## The Pathway Framework

The pathway framework is similar to the correlated environments scenario described by Preston et al. (1998). In contrast to the imprint framework, it does not view childhood conditions as directly and permanently leaving a biological imprint on adult mortality risks. Instead, it views these conditions as having an *indirect* influence because they set in motion lifelong trajectories of health-related advantages or disadvantages, and it is the temporally proximate adult conditions that influence mortality risks (e.g., Lundberg 1993). For instance, this framework posits that childhood poverty elevates later life mortality risks because children raised in economically adverse environments tend to experience similar environments throughout life (e.g., Blau and Duncan 1967; Palloni et al. 2009). In contrast, the imprint framework would assert that characteristics of poor childhood environments, such as undernutrition and pathogen exposure, cause permanent biological damage, which elevates adult mortality risks. According to the pathway framework, health-related exposures occur and accumulate over the life course. They can accumulate as random and unrelated events, or more commonly, in chains or clusters (Ben-Shlomo and Kuh 2002). For example, not only are adults with low education more likely to experience economic hardship, they are also more likely to smoke, drink heavily, avoid physical exercise, and report fewer and lower-quality social supports (Ross and Wu 1995). Moreover, exposures can accumulate additively or interactively, although this issue has been understudied. The few studies that have tested whether childhood and adulthood socioeconomic conditions accumulate additively or interactively for all-cause mortality risks generally support an additive relationship (Hayward and Gorman 2004; Kuh et al. 2002a). However, a study of premature mortality in Norway found a significant interaction between housing characteristics in childhood and adult income: adults who suffered poor conditions in both periods had markedly higher risks for all-cause and cardiovascular mortality among both men and women, for accidental and violent deaths among men, and for psychiatric mortality among women (Claussen et al. 2003). The relatively small number of adults who experience significant intra-generational social mobility within most longitudinal studies hinders empirically finding an interaction between childhood and adult socioeconomic conditions.

A well-known concept from sociology and labor economics, "health selection," is closely linked to the pathway framework. In the present context, health selection refers to the potential for good (poor) health status in early life to increase the chance of achieving a higher (lower) socioeconomic status (SES) in adulthood, which, in turn, reduces (elevates) mortality (Palloni 2006). The notion of health selection does not dismiss the possibility that early health status has a direct, biological effect on mortality risks. Instead, it stresses that at least part of the association between early and later life health operates indirectly through cognitive and noncognitive traits (e.g., height) that derive from early health status and are rewarded in the labor market. Indeed, a study of British males estimated that 10–12% of the association between adult social class (measured by occupation) and self-reported health at 41–42 years of age was attributable to early health selection into those social classes (Palloni et al. 2009).

## Biological Imprint, or Pathway, or Both?

Scholars often evaluate the imprint and pathway frameworks as competing hypotheses within a given study. A common approach is to first confirm a statistical association between a childhood condition (e.g., birthweight) and adult mortality risks, and then determine whether adjusting for adult conditions (e.g., education, health behaviors) mediates the association. If the association is unaffected, this is considered evidence for the imprint hypothesis. If it is largely eliminated, this is taken as evidence for the pathway hypothesis.

However, some scholars have expressed concerns about pitting the frameworks against each other as mutually exclusive and exhaustive explanations (Ben-Shlomo and Davey Smith 1991; Lundberg 1993; Lynch and Davey Smith 2005). Ben-Shlomo and Davey Smith (1991: 533) state that "it is unhelpful to consider an either/or model, which would exclude the possible interaction and cumulative effect of factors acting early and later in life." Another consideration is that the relative importance of earlier versus later life exposures will vary by cause of death because of unique etiologies (Davey Smith et al. 1997, 1998a; Lawlor et al. 2006). For example, a study of Scottish males found that childhood socioeconomic conditions exhibited a strong influence on the risks of death from stomach cancer and stroke that was unaltered by adjusting for adult SES (an imprint process); part of their influence on deaths from coronary heart disease (CHD) and respiratory diseases was mediated by adult status (a cumulative process); most of their association with lung cancer deaths was mediated by adult circumstances (a pathway process); and they showed no bivariate association with deaths from accidents and violence (Davey Smith et al. 1998a). In addition, childhood conditions may be more crucial for certain types of cancer. Swedish adults raised in manual social classes had higher mortality rates from stomach, liver, pancreatic, and lung cancers, but not from colon, breast, brain, or lymphatic cancers, or from melanoma or leukemia (Lawlor et al. 2006).

Thus, a third framework has emerged that integrates imprint and pathway processes. The cumulative framework claims that some childhood exposures leave a biological imprint while others set in motion health-related trajectories, and that adult exposures add to, exacerbate, or ameliorate earlier exposures (Ben-Shlomo and Kuh 2002; Halfon and Hochstein 2002; Power and Hertzman 1997). This framework also allows for biological interactions between imprint and pathway processes. Some exposures in adulthood, for example, may have a more pronounced effect on adults who are biologically vulnerable because of earlier exposures. For instance, having a low household income or a manual occupation in adulthood elevated the risk of CHD more for men who were thin at birth than for those who were not (Barker et al. 2001). Conversely, early childhood exposures that minimize biological vulnerabilities may ward off the effects of later life health risks (Luo and Waite 2005).

The three frameworks are depicted in Fig. 9.1. The dotted line shown within the imprint process indicates that adult circumstances may be able to compensate temporarily for compromised structure of organs and tissues (e.g., muscle hypertrophy via exercise), but the structural damage is irreversible and will inevitably cause health to deteriorate earlier and/or faster than in adults without structural damage. For instance, while both childhood and adult circumstances influence the age of onset of functional limitations, only childhood socioeconomic environment and health influence the rate of decline after onset (Haas 2008). This process is in contrast to the similarly positioned solid line within the cumulative framework, which indicates that some circumstances can fully ameliorate earlier exposures.

```
(a) Imprint      [Early life exposures]     [Adulthood exposures]     [Adult Mortality Risks]

(b) Pathway      [Early life exposures] → [Adulthood exposures] → [Adult Mortality Risks]

(c) Cumulative   [Early life exposures] → [Adulthood exposures] → [Adult Mortality Risks]
```

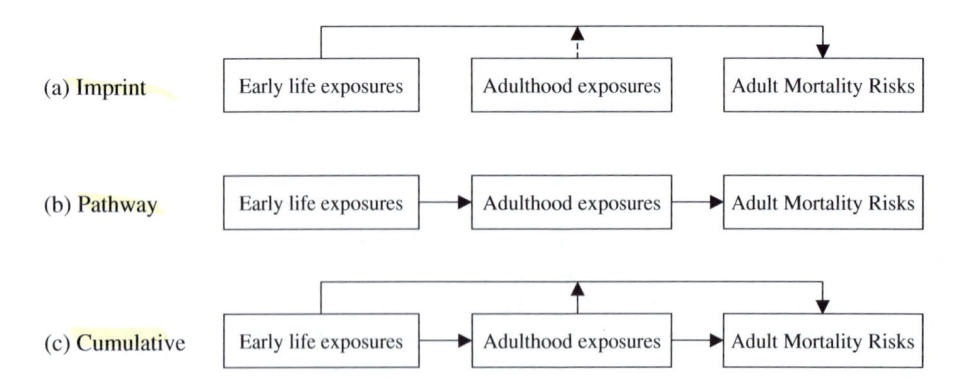

**Fig. 9.1** Three frameworks linking early life conditions with adult mortality risks adapted from Berkman 2009

## Social Exposures in Childhood and Adulthood Mortality Risks

Childhood conditions that shape adult mortality risks can be generally classified as either social or physical exposures. Key social exposures include socioeconomic conditions and the family environment, while key physical exposures include nutrition and infectious diseases. Other social and physical exposures exist; however, these four have captured scientific attention. Each type of exposure can influence adulthood mortality risks through imprint and pathway processes. This section briefly summarizes key literature that has documented these associations, although the review is admittedly modest. A crude diagram of the associations discussed below is provided in Fig. 9.2. In the figure, solid lines indicate biological imprint processes, while dotted lines indicate pathway processes that link childhood exposures with subsequent adult mortality. In reality, the associations are certainly more complex and the distinctions between processes somewhat blurred.

## Socioeconomic Environment as an Imprint Process

One of the most widely studied childhood exposures is the socioeconomic environment, perhaps because it may be the best single indicator of a collection of related exposures, such as nutrition, health behaviors, psychosocial stressors, hygiene, pathogen exposure, housing structure, and neighborhood context.

The association between childhood socioeconomic conditions and adult mortality risks, net of adult conditions, is widespread and substantial. It has been documented in numerous countries including Norway (Claussen et al. 2003), Sweden (Lawlor et al. 2006; Peck 1994), Finland (Notkola et al. 1985; Pensola and Martikainen 2003), South Korea (Khang and Kim 2005), Scotland (Davey Smith et al. 1997), the United States (e.g., Turrell et al. 2007), and England (e.g., Kuh et al. 2002a). The association is also quite strong. For example, the risk of death among working-age British adults was roughly twice as high among those who were raised in the lowest socioeconomic group as it was among those from the highest group, irrespective of adult social class (Kuh et al. 2002a).

The notion that childhood socioeconomic conditions exert an imprint on adult mortality risks is supported by studies which find that their effect persists after researchers adjust for adult circumstances. Childhood socioeconomic conditions are particularly influential on the risk of death from cardiovascular disease and stomach cancer (Beebe-Dimmer et al. 2004; Claussen et al. 2003; Davey Smith et al. 1998a). Childhood socioeconomic conditions may be more crucial for certain cardiovascular disease subtypes, such as stroke, while adult conditions may be more crucial for others, such as CHD (Galobardes et al. 2006).

Most studies that focus on childhood socioeconomic exposures do not investigate which causal mechanisms (e.g., nutrition, pathogens, stress) underlie the association. However, the fact that the link is more pronounced among certain causes of death offers some clues. For instance, the strong link with stomach

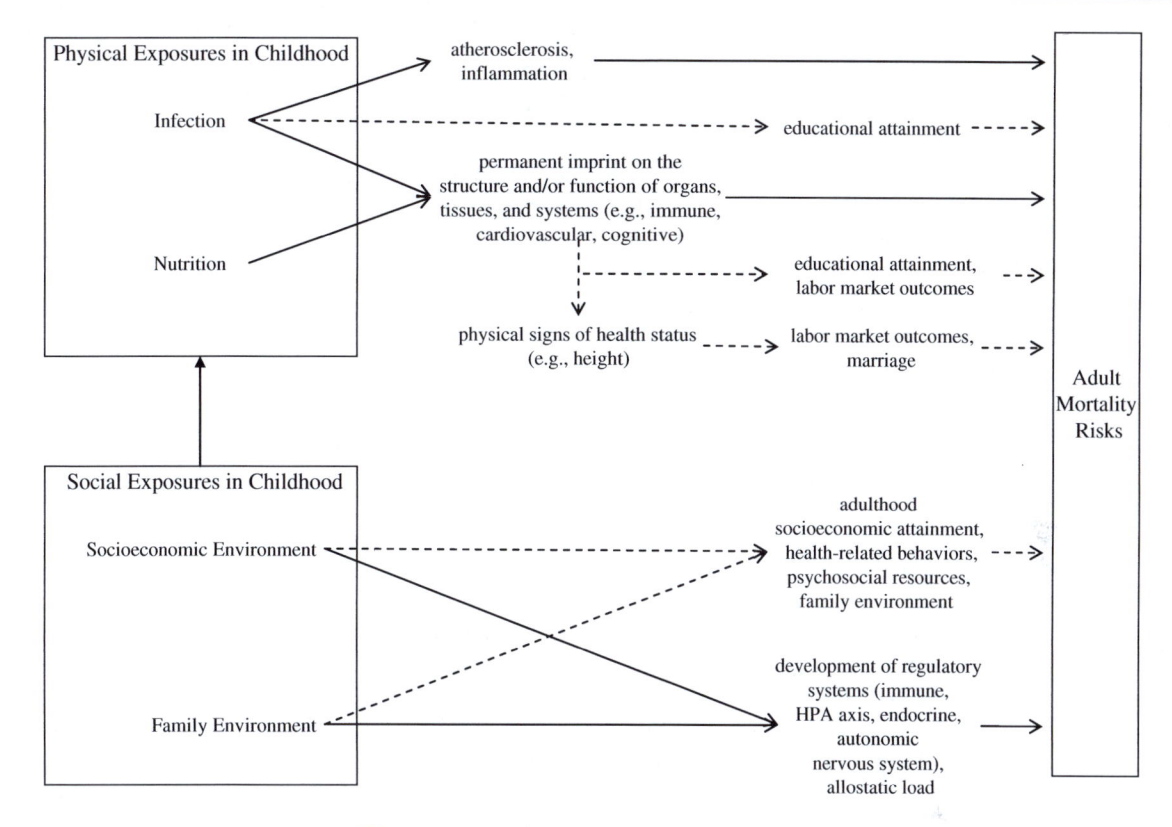

# 9 Early Life Conditions and Later Life Mortality

**Fig. 9.2** Key imprint and pathway linkages between early life exposures and adult mortality risks

cancer suggests that crowded and unsanitary childhood environments may be to blame because they elevate the risk of exposure to *Helicobacter pylori*, a precursor to stomach cancer. The link with cardiovascular disease likely has multiple intervening mechanisms, including inadequate nutrition (Barker et al. 1989) and compromised immune function development. For instance, susceptibility to upper respiratory infection among adults is linked in a dose–response relationship with the number of childhood years in which their parents owned their home (Cohen et al. 2004), and parental education and family income exhibit an inverse gradient with biomarkers of infectious disease burden among US children (Dowd et al. 2009). Another potential mechanism is prenatal exposure to nicotine. In many industrialized countries today, smoking is more common among low socioeconomic groups. Mother's smoking during pregnancy predicts low educational attainment and worse health among adult offspring, net of birthweight (see Case et al. 2005).

## Socioeconomic Environment as a Pathway Process

The intergenerational transmission of educational attainment, income, and occupational status remains strong in many regions of the world (Palloni 2006; Palloni et al. 2009). Thus, childhood SES can influence adult mortality risks simply by placing people into similar adult statuses, and it may be the temporally proximate adult status that is important. Indeed, the inverse association between adult SES and mortality risks has been consistently documented around the world (see, for example, Chapter 12 by Hummer and Lariscy, this volume). As an example of pathway processes, a study of US men found that many childhood socioeconomic conditions (e.g., father's occupation, parental nativity) were significant predictors of adult mortality risks (Hayward and Gorman 2004). However, with the exception of parental nativity, their influence operated through adult education, income, wealth, occupation, and health behaviors. Childhood SES may also operate through adult conditions for mortality from lung cancer (Davey Smith et al. 1998a), heart attack risk for men (Hamil-Luker and O'Rand 2007), and depression, CHD, and chronic bronchitis (Marmot et al. 2001). Yet it is rare that childhood socioeconomic conditions operate entirely through adult pathway mechanisms. It is more commonly reported that a fraction of the association operates in this manner. For instance, part of the association with the risk of death from CHD and respiratory diseases operates through adult socioeconomic attainment (Davey Smith et al. 1998a).

In addition to setting the stage for adulthood SES, childhood status shapes adult mortality risks through its influence on a range of behavioral and psychosocial characteristics. Lifestyle and psychosocial characteristics are often engrained when children are socialized for certain behaviors or proclivities. For example, childhood SES predicts a host of adult behaviors including smoking, drinking, diet, and physical activity (Lynch et al. 1997); psychosocial characteristics, such as the degree of hopelessness and cynical hostility (Lynch et al. 1997); and risk taking, deferred gratification, and a sense of personal control (Elo and Preston 1992). All of these factors can, in turn, influence later life mortality risks.

## Family Environment as an Imprint Process

Early development of psychosocial resources and regulatory systems, such as the immune, metabolic, and autonomic nervous systems, and the hypothalamic-pituitary-adrenal (HPA) axis, is molded by the family environment. Environments characterized by stability, emotional support, and cognitive stimulation provide a solid foundation for adult health, while those characterized by dissension, distress, and disruption can have deleterious consequences. A recent review concluded that three characteristics of the family environment have direct and indirect long-term consequences for health and mortality risks: conflict, anger, violence, and abuse; lack of warmth, cohesiveness, and emotional support; and a parenting style that is either controlling and dominating or uninvolved and unstructured (Taylor et al. 1997). With respect to direct mechanisms, prolonged exposure to psychosocial stressors such as these chronically overworks regulatory systems, keeping them in a constant state of stimulation without the ability to promptly turn on or off in response to a stressor (McEwen 1998). These chronic exposures can then permanently alter the "set point" and functioning of regulatory systems. The resulting wear and tear on the brain and body, termed allostatic load, facilitates a host of adult health problems, including hypertension, diabetes, atherosclerosis, inflammatory and autoimmune disorders, immunosuppression, and neuronal atrophy (see McEwen 1998).

Family disruption (e.g., divorce, death) is a significant source of emotional and financial distress in childhood. Because adults who experienced parental divorce in childhood have an increased risk of poor psychosocial health (Crosnoe and Elder Jr. 2004; Kuh et al. 2002b) and mortality (Preston et al. 1998; Schwartz et al. 1995), net of adult circumstances, they also may be at greater risk of long-run adverse health and mortality outcomes. Exposure to abuse or household dysfunction in childhood increases the risk of ischemic heart disease, cancer, chronic lung disease, skeletal fractures, and liver disease in adulthood, net of adult education (Felitti et al. 1998). Parent–child affection may also have long-term impacts on health. For instance, experimental studies with rat pups found that those who received no maternal attention secreted more glucocorticoids in response to stress at all ages and had higher basal glucocorticoids at older ages, which accelerated hippocampal neuron loss and aging-related cognitive deficits (Meaney et al. 1988). Even prenatal exposure to the mother's physiological responses to psychosocial stressors can permanently alter the structure and function of the child's HPA axis, which has in turn been linked with cognitive deficits, altered immune function, and behavioral problems (see Worthman and Kuzara 2005).

## Family Environment as a Pathway Process

The childhood family environment can *indirectly* influence adult health and mortality risks through multiple mechanisms. Environments characterized by dissension within the family home, family disruption, or a lack of emotional support from parents can disrupt the development of psychosocial resources, create chronic stress that strains immune function and increases susceptibility to illness, increase the likelihood of maladaptive health behaviors and coping mechanisms, impair emotion regulation and social competence, and increase the risk of experiencing family disruption in the children's own adult lives—all of which elevate the risk of poor health and mortality in adulthood (Taylor et al. 1997).

A handful of studies support the hypothesis that family dissension, disruption, and divorce elevate adult health and mortality risks through pathway processes (Felitti et al. 1998; Lundberg 1993; Schwartz et al. 1995). For instance, life expectancy among US adults who experienced parental divorce before age 21 was 4.5 years less than among those who did not (Schwartz et al. 1995). The authors speculated that the causal pathways include unhealthy behaviors, stress and coping mechanisms, and few social supports in adulthood. Exposure to abuse or household dysfunction in childhood increases the likelihood of behavioral risk factors in adulthood, including smoking, alcoholism, drug use, physical inactivity, and obesity (Felitti et al. 1998). In addition, a lack of emotional support from parents during childhood increases the risk of poor physical and mental health in adulthood by disrupting development of psychosocial resources, including personal control beliefs, self-esteem, and healthy social relationships, which in turn have negative health consequences (Shaw et al. 2004). Chronic exposure to psychosocial stressors in the childhood home also taxes the immune system and increases the frequency of illnesses, such as respiratory tract infections among children (Drummond and Hewson-Bower 1997). To the extent that this translates into missed school days and impaired academic performance, childhood stressors can ultimately affect mortality by disrupting socioeconomic achievement. Finally, divorce within the childhood family can indirectly increase adult mortality risks because the children of divorce are more likely to divorce as adults which, in turn, elevates the risk of mortality.

## Physical Exposures in Childhood and Adulthood Mortality Risks

### Nutrition as an Imprint Process

For decades, David Barker and colleagues have advanced the hypothesis that undernutrition in utero and in infancy permanently alters the structure and function of organs, tissues, and systems, predisposing the individual to morbidity and mortality from cardiovascular and metabolic conditions in adulthood (Barker 1997, 2007; Barker et al. 1989; Hales and Barker 1992). They hypothesize that a fetus or infant adapts to undernutrition through quantitative responses, such as slowing the rate of cell division of organs and tissues that are undergoing critical periods of development, and qualitative responses, such as modifying the cells themselves so that they function abnormally. They claim that the resulting "thrifty phenotype" has an elevated risk of cardiovascular and metabolic conditions in a nutritionally abundant postnatal environment (Hales and Barker 1992). Fogel (2004) has also argued that changes in early life nutrition have influenced secular trends toward increased stature, robustness, and longevity of humans over the past three centuries.

A large body of empirical work supports the hypothesized link between early nutrition and adult morbidity and mortality. Low birthweight—a marker of inadequate prenatal nutrition—is associated with the risk of impaired glucose tolerance, type 2 diabetes, hypertension, stroke, and CHD in adulthood (Barker 1997). It also increases the risk of poor educational attainment, net of parental characteristics, and may thus signal permanent cognitive damage caused by nutritional deficiencies (Black et al. 2007; Conley and Bennett 2000). Some scholars have raised the possibility that the relationship between birthweight and adult health is spurious because it may actually be due to environmental or genetic influences. However, mortality risks associated with low birthweight appear independent of childhood socioeconomic circumstances (Osler et al. 2003). In addition, a study of Norwegian twins discounted a purely genetic explanation by documenting that the lower birthweight twin had worse short-term outcomes for APGAR scores and infant mortality risks, and worse long-term outcomes for educational attainment, earnings, height, body-mass-index, and IQ (Black et al. 2007). Genetics may play some role, however, because parents who were low birthweight infants are more likely to have a low birthweight child, net of other family factors, sparking an intergenerational cycle of disadvantage (Conley and Bennett 2000). Postnatal nutrition is also important. For example, a study of Finnish men found that the link between childhood SES and adult mortality risks from CHD was better explained by adult height—a marker of early nutrition—and smoking than by adult SES, cholesterol levels, or blood pressure (Notkola et al. 1985).

Early malnutrition can also impair multiple aspects of immune system function (see McDade 2005). For example, a study in the Philippines found that prenatal undernutrition reduced antibody responsiveness to vaccinations among adolescents who reported poor current nutrition (McDade et al. 2001a), and it reduced thymopoietin production (McDade et al. 2001b). It is less clear whether immune deficiencies caused by early malnutrition persist in adulthood, although experimental research with rats found that prenatal malnutrition caused deficiencies that persisted through third-generation offspring, despite nutritionally adequate postnatal diets (Beach et al. 1982).

## Nutrition as a Pathway Process

Early nutrition can also *indirectly* influence adult mortality through at least three pathways, including height, cognitive endowment, and behaviors. However, the importance of these pathways is contingent on social, cultural, and economic contexts. For example, height may increase access to health-enhancing resources, such as marriage and employment, only within contexts where it is a perceived marker of socially desirable attributes, including strength, attractiveness, social esteem, leadership, and intelligence (see Judge and Cable 2004).

It is well established that early nutrition and height are positively correlated (e.g., Fogel 2004), although genetic influences and childhood disease exposures also matter. Height may indirectly shape mortality risks through marriage prospects, because adults who exhibit physical characteristics associated with good health such as tall stature are more likely to marry than those who appear in poor health (Fu and Goldman 1996; Murray 2000). Marriage, in turn, reduces mortality risks through economic and psychosocial resources and healthier lifestyles (Hu and Goldman 1990; Murray 2000; Ross et al. 1990). Another pathway through which height may indirectly shape mortality risks is labor market achievement. Height is positively related to earnings, even after researchers control for weight, age, and intelligence (Judge and Cable 2004).

Early nutrition may also indirectly shape adult mortality risks through its influence on cognitive development and function. Indeed, low birthweight is associated with poor cognitive performance in late childhood (Palloni 2006) and lower educational attainment (Case et al. 2005), net of parental and household characteristics. Stunting is also associated with lower scores on intelligence tests in late childhood (Berckman et al. 2002). Even irregularities in childhood meal patterns may have implications (see Bellisle 2004). Impaired cognitive development may, in turn, elevate mortality risks through lower educational attainment, at least for men (Hemmingsson et al. 2006; Kuh et al. 2004). The indirect pathway between early nutrition, cognitive function, and mortality is particularly salient in industrialized countries, where cognitive ability and higher education are essential for acquiring resources such as good jobs, high incomes, and good health care.

Early nutrition may also indirectly influence adult mortality through behavioral mechanisms that ultimately impede educational attainment and the health-enhancing resources education provides. For example, severe iron deficiency in infancy predicts poor cognitive function and behavioral problems, such as anxiousness, depression, and attention problems, net of parental and household factors (Lozoff et al. 2000). Behavioral problems may in turn impede educational attainment. For instance, British males who scored high on behavioral maladjustment at age 10 achieved lower education as adults (Palloni 2006).

## Infectious Diseases as an Imprint Process

Childhood exposure to pathogens, such as infectious diseases, bacteria, and environmental toxins, may leave a biological imprint that shapes adult mortality risks. However, researchers disagree about whether pathogen exposure decreases or increases adult mortality risks. One school of thought asserts that childhood exposure reduces adult mortality risks because pathogenic challenges in early life promote regulation of inflammatory responses and immune function (Strachan 2000). For example, allergic diseases are less prevalent among adults from large families, suggesting that frequent exposure to infection in childhood teaches the immune system to respond appropriately to pathogens (Strachan 2000). Evidence from the Philippines shows that exposure to pathogens in infancy is associated with enhanced immune function in adolescence (McDade et al. 2001a).

In contrast, a second school of thought asserts that chronic exposure to infectious pathogens in childhood elevates adult mortality risks. Chronic exposure may damage organs and cause lifelong inflammation, which then promotes atherosclerosis and death due to heart disease (Crimmins and Finch 2006). In fact, the secular decline in old-age mortality risks across birth cohorts exhibits a much stronger correlation with early life mortality risks (which were largely due to infectious diseases) than with mid-life mortality risks; and the concomitant increase in height suggests that reductions in infectious disease burden freed up resources for growth that were previously spent on immune responses (Crimmins and Finch 2006). Similarly, Buck and Simpson (1982) reported that exposure to diarrhea-inducing infections during the first 2 years of life was associated with higher mortality rates from arteriosclerotic heart disease among US adults. Moreover, US adults who experienced a major infectious illness in childhood were 2.5, 1.7, 4.9, and 1.8 times more likely to report cancer, cardiovascular conditions, lung conditions, or arthritis in adulthood, respectively (Blackwell et al. 2001). Both schools of thought provide compelling evidence. Reconciliation may require greater attention to contextual circumstances (e.g., average levels of nutrition or industrialization in a region) and to the timing of effects over the life course, and recognition that there may be an optimal infection challenge in childhood, so that too little challenge promotes an unregulated immune system while too much promotes inflammation and atherosclerosis.

### *Infectious Diseases as a Pathway Process*

Infectious disease exposure in early childhood can also *indirectly* mold adult mortality risks through several mechanisms, including school absenteeism, impaired academic performance, and short stature. Children 5–17 years of age lose an average of three school days per year to infectious diseases (Adams et al. 1996). Among college students, upper respiratory infections result in missed classes and poor academic performance (Nichol et al. 2005). Serious illness in childhood (Kuh et al. 2004) and infectious disease exposure in childhood (Berckman et al. 2002) also predict lower cognitive ability in late childhood through permanent damage to cognitive systems (an imprint process) and/or school absenteeism (a pathway process).

Another indirect pathway by which infection can shape adult mortality risks is through its effect on height. Infectious disease exposure, particularly when chronic, can result in short stature because the body diverts resources such as nutrition away from growth toward expensive immune responses (McDade 2005). The height-related consequences of the resource trade-off may be more severe during critical periods of growth and/or when resources are scarce. For example, a study of 2- to 4-year-olds in Bolivia found that children in low-pathogen environments grew 2.35 cm during a 3-month period compared with just 1.97 cm of growth among children in high-pathogen environments (McDade et al. 2003). A relationship between infectious disease burden and height has also been reported among children in the United States (Dowd et al. 2009). Shortened stature may then indirectly shape mortality risks because height is positively associated with marriage and employment prospects and the social and economic resources they confer. See "Nutrition as a Pathway Process" for further explanation.

## Association of Childhood and Adult Conditions with the Risk of Death Among Older US Adults

This section illustrates the ideas described above by documenting the mortality risks associated with certain childhood and adulthood conditions among US adults 50 years of age and older. We first show the bivariate associations between theoretically important childhood conditions and the risk of death in adulthood. We then expand the statistical models to assess the contributions of imprint and/or pathway mechanisms in explaining these associations. Although clearly not an exhaustive or causal analysis, our results highlight the involvement of both pathway and imprinting mechanisms in linking early life conditions and adult mortality.

The statistical models are based on the 1998–2006 waves of the Health and Retirement Study (HRS), when questions about childhood conditions were asked of the full sample. Well-known to American social scientists, the HRS is a longitudinal survey representative of US adults over age 50. The survey currently contains a national sample of persons born before 1947, with younger birth cohorts scheduled for inclusion in upcoming survey waves. We take advantage of the large sample size to examine the childhood–mortality associations separately for the major race/ethnic groups: non-Hispanic whites, non-Hispanic blacks, and Hispanic respondents. We excluded a few respondents (fewer than 1%) who did not provide information on educational attainment or their height, which are the two potentially mediating adulthood conditions of interest in this analysis. Because of sample size limitations, we included Hispanic adults only as a single group even though this group includes people with differing countries of birth, years lived in the United States, and so on. Nonetheless, our results offer a glimpse into how childhood conditions might shape mortality risks differently for this important demographic group.

Our outcome of interest is the risk of death from any cause. HRS respondents are asked about several important dimensions of their childhood environment and experiences before age 16. Respondents were asked whether their childhood health was excellent, very good, good, fair, or poor. We collapsed this measure into a dichotomous indicator of fair/poor (hereafter poor) health, because our analyses showed a marked increase in mortality risks for those reporting poor childhood health, and because respondents who report poor health are likely to have experienced an infectious or autoimmune condition in childhood (Haas 2008). We incorporated several dichotomous indicators of childhood SES, including whether the respondents thought that their childhood family was poor; whether their father had a blue-collar occupation; whether they ever moved for financial reasons; and two indicators for whether each parent had less than 8 years of education. In some cases, respondents did not know their parents' education level or their father's occupation. We assigned these respondents to the low-education and blue-collar categories, respectively, because they were similar on other economic and health variables (see, e.g., Luo and Waite 2005). Unfortunately, the HRS does not inquire about childhood family structure. However, we extracted some information about family disruption from responses to the question, "Before age 16, was there a time of several months or more when your father had no job?" This allows us to compare adults who stated that they never lived with their father or their father was not alive with those who had a father in the home. Finally, we included two adult conditions often posited as important mediating mechanisms: educational attainment (less than high school, high school, and more than high school as the omitted reference) and height measured in race–gender-specific quartiles.

We estimated the risk of death associated with each childhood and adult condition from logistic regression models. The models were based on a person-year data structure in which each respondent was represented by an observation for the survey year and each subsequent year until his or her year of death or the end of the 2006 follow-up period if the respondent survived. We first estimated bivariate models using age and a single childhood or adult condition to show the "zero-order" associations. We then estimated multivariate models that included age and all childhood and adult conditions to illustrate whether childhood conditions operate via imprint and/or pathway mechanisms. All models were stratified by gender–race/ethnicity and weighted to account for the HRS sample design. Although the stratification strategy clearly reduces statistical power, we chose this approach to enhance the level of detailed information given the exploratory nature of our analysis.

## Results

Table 9.1 shows the distribution of childhood and adulthood conditions for each race–gender group. For illustrative purposes we retain the categories for missing parental education and occupation in this table only. The table highlights numerous race/ethnic disparities in childhood and adulthood conditions. Non-Hispanic white adults tend to report better childhood health, more favorable childhood socioeconomic conditions for all indicators, and higher educational attainment in adulthood than non-Hispanic blacks and Hispanics, illustrating the health advantages that they garner across the entire life course. Comparisons between black and Hispanic adults are mixed. While

**Table 9.1** Distribution of select childhood and adulthood conditions by gender and race/ethnicity among adults 50 years and older in the Health and Retirement Study 1998–2006

| Childhood and adult conditions | Non-Hispanic white Men | Non-Hispanic white Women | Non-Hispanic black Men | Non-Hispanic black Women | Hispanic Men | Hispanic Women |
|---|---|---|---|---|---|---|
| *Self-reported childhood health* | | | | | | |
| Excellent | 0.551 | 0.536 | 0.509 | 0.465 | 0.435 | 0.403 |
| Very good or good | 0.402 | 0.401 | 0.430 | 0.448 | 0.486 | 0.488 |
| Fair or poor | 0.048 | 0.063 | 0.062 | 0.087 | 0.079 | 0.108 |
| *Mother's education* | | | | | | |
| 8 years or more | 0.772 | 0.747 | 0.534 | 0.520 | 0.266 | 0.266 |
| Less than 8 years | 0.139 | 0.173 | 0.264 | 0.304 | 0.573 | 0.591 |
| Missing | 0.089 | 0.080 | 0.202 | 0.176 | 0.161 | 0.143 |
| *Father's education* | | | | | | |
| 8 years or more | 0.685 | 0.665 | 0.358 | 0.361 | 0.235 | 0.264 |
| Less than 8 years | 0.188 | 0.210 | 0.321 | 0.325 | 0.516 | 0.497 |
| Missing | 0.128 | 0.126 | 0.321 | 0.315 | 0.249 | 0.238 |
| *Perceived childhood economic status* | | | | | | |
| Pretty well off financially | 0.077 | 0.076 | 0.047 | 0.044 | 0.071 | 0.078 |
| Average | 0.646 | 0.676 | 0.512 | 0.554 | 0.486 | 0.517 |
| Poor | 0.277 | 0.247 | 0.441 | 0.402 | 0.442 | 0.405 |
| Ever moved due to financial reasons | 0.168 | 0.159 | 0.218 | 0.170 | 0.258 | 0.192 |
| *Father's occupation* | | | | | | |
| White collar | 0.224 | 0.233 | 0.052 | 0.055 | 0.100 | 0.124 |
| Blue collar | 0.474 | 0.505 | 0.466 | 0.490 | 0.446 | 0.446 |
| Missing occupation | 0.301 | 0.262 | 0.482 | 0.454 | 0.455 | 0.430 |
| Father never present in household | 0.054 | 0.059 | 0.183 | 0.204 | 0.113 | 0.140 |
| Adulthood height (meters) | 1.781 | 1.629 | 1.775 | 1.634 | 1.716 | 1.583 |
| *Adulthood educational attainment* | | | | | | |
| More than high school | 0.523 | 0.441 | 0.331 | 0.344 | 0.281 | 0.226 |
| High school | 0.300 | 0.381 | 0.262 | 0.296 | 0.177 | 0.196 |
| Less than high school | 0.177 | 0.179 | 0.407 | 0.360 | 0.542 | 0.579 |
| N | 8,191 | 10,462 | 1,380 | 2,165 | 914 | 1,229 |

black adults tend to report better childhood health and higher parental education (53% of black men report that their mother had at least 8 years of education versus 27% of Hispanic men), they are somewhat less likely to consider their childhood family "pretty well off financially" and more likely to have a father who never lived in the household (18% for black men versus 11% for Hispanic men).

Table 9.2 shows odds ratios that indicate the age-adjusted risk of death for each childhood and adulthood condition individually. The results clearly illustrate elevated mortality risks among adults who experienced poor childhood health across most gender and race/ethnic groups. For example, the odds of death among non-Hispanic white women who experienced poor childhood health are 1.386 times greater than among those who did not. Being raised in unfavorable socioeconomic conditions also elevates the risk of death, particularly among white adults with low-educated or blue-collar fathers. The mortality advantage for black men who reported poor childhood economic status is curious and difficult to interpret. Although we performed no formal statistical tests of interactions and the sample sizes for the minority groups are relatively small, the results in the table suggest that there is not always uniformity in how childhood "risks" are associated with adult mortality across the gender/race-ethnic groups.

For adult conditions, Table 9.2 shows little association between height and mortality risks, with the

**Table 9.2** Bivariate odds ratios of death for each childhood and adulthood condition by Gender and Race/Ethnicity among adults 50 years and older in the Health and Retirement Study 1998–2006

|  | Non-Hispanic white | | Non-Hispanic black | | Hispanic | |
|---|---|---|---|---|---|---|
|  | Men | Women | Men | Women | Men | Women |
| *Childhood conditions* | | | | | | |
| Self-reported fair or poor childhood health | 1.074 | 1.386*** | 1.526** | 1.721*** | 1.577* | 1.034 |
| Mother had less than 8 years of education | 1.101* | 1.061 | 1.007 | 1.180 | 1.098 | 0.852 |
| Father had less than 8 years of education | 1.189*** | 1.126*** | 0.954 | 1.128 | 1.009 | 1.508* |
| Perceived poor economic status in childhood | 1.070 | 1.105* | 0.757*** | 1.078 | 0.842 | 0.959 |
| Ever moved due to financial reasons | 0.960 | 1.058 | 1.276* | 0.817 | 0.999 | 0.862 |
| Father had blue collar occupation | 1.142** | 1.117* | 0.792 | 0.944 | 1.074 | 1.183 |
| *Adulthood conditions* | | | | | | |
| Height (using quartiles) | 1.020 | 1.039** | 0.955 | 1.002 | 0.991 | 0.966 |
| *Educational attainment (more than high school)* | | | | | | |
| High school | 1.237*** | 1.110* | 1.001 | 1.175 | 0.943 | 0.426** |
| Less than high school | 1.340*** | 1.356*** | 1.144 | 1.458*** | 1.134 | 0.913 |
| Number of deaths | 1,866 | 1,995 | 366 | 425 | 165 | 158 |

$*p < 0.10$; $**p < 0.05$; $**p < 0.01$ (two-tailed tests).

Notes: All models control for age and are weighted to account for the HRS sample design. We do not report the odds ratios for never having lived with one's father because the question was not designed to capture this information. We report the distribution of responses for this variable in Table 9.1 for illustrative purposes only.

exception of white women, for whom ancillary analyses revealed that the excess risk is confined to women in the top quartile of the height distribution. The general lack of association between height and mortality risks is consistent with other US studies (e.g., Blackwell et al. 2001) and with the notion that height may not be a good indicator of childhood conditions in regions with abundant nutrition and low infectious disease burden. As we expected, educational attainment is inversely related to adult mortality risks, particularly for white adults and black women. Educational differences in mortality risks among Hispanic adults are much smaller, likely because of heterogeneity within the sample and because education brings smaller financial and health behavioral gains to Hispanics. Note also the much smaller number of deaths for Hispanic men and women.

We now examine whether the childhood conditions measured in the HRS influence adult mortality risks through imprint and/or pathway mechanisms. To that end, Table 9.3 contains a series of multivariate logistic regression models that begin with the complete set of childhood conditions in Model 1, then add adult height in Model 2, and add educational attainment in Model 3. We focus on non-Hispanic white adults simply because we have an adequate number of deaths for the analysis. For males, Model 1 shows that when all childhood variables are jointly modeled, only having a father with low education continues to elevate adult mortality risks beyond the other conditions, although it is worth noting that having a father with a blue-collar occupation elevates mortality risks at the $\alpha = 0.15$ level. Adding height in Model 2 does not attenuate any of the childhood odds ratios, suggesting that height is not a pathway through which these childhood conditions operated for these men. Adding educational attainment in Model 3 attenuates the effect of father's education (evidence of a pathway mechanism), although the latter remains statistically significant (evidence of a permanent biological imprint).

As for men, Model 1 for women shows that having a father with low education increases the risk of death, and part of this effect operates through educational attainment as in Model 3. Unlike men, however,

**Table 9.3** Multivariate odds ratios of death for childhood and adulthood conditions by gender among non-Hispanic white adults 50 years and older in the Health and Retirement Study 1998–2006

|  | Non-Hispanic white men ||| Non-Hispanic white women |||
|---|---|---|---|---|---|---|
|  | Model 1 | Model 2 | Model 3 | Model 1 | Model 2 | Model 3 |
| *Childhood conditions* | | | | | | |
| Self-reported fair or poor childhood health | 1.047 | 1.048 | 1.035 | 1.360*** | 1.352*** | 1.327*** |
| Mother had less than 8 years of education | 0.980 | 0.982 | 0.948 | 0.973 | 0.979 | 0.926 |
| Father had less than 8 years of education | 1.177*** | 1.177*** | 1.150** | 1.108* | 1.113* | 1.081 |
| Perceived poor economic status in childhood | 1.040 | 1.041 | 1.024 | 1.057 | 1.059 | 1.037 |
| Ever moved due to financial reasons | 0.931 | 0.930 | 0.932 | 1.027 | 1.026 | 1.030 |
| Father had blue-collar occupation | 1.094 | 1.096 | 1.028 | 1.076 | 1.073 | 1.021 |
| *Adulthood conditions* | | | | | | |
| Height (using quartiles) |  | 1.024 | 1.013 |  | 1.041** | 1.043** |
| *Educational attainment (more than high school)* | | | | | | |
| High school |  |  | 1.214*** |  |  | 1.102 |
| Less than high school |  |  | 1.298*** |  |  | 1.333*** |
| –2LL | 1,4550 | 1,4549 | 1,4532 | 1,5975 | 1,5791 | 1,5772 |
| Number of deaths | 1,886 | 1,886 | 1,886 | 1,995 | 1,995 | 1,995 |

*$p < 0.10$; **$p < 0.05$; ***$p < 0.01$ (two-tailed tests).
Notes: All models control for age and are weighted to account for the HRS sample design.

women who reported poor childhood health had significantly increased mortality. A small portion of this effect was explained by adult height (evidence of a biological imprint mechanism), but a larger portion was explained by adulthood educational attainment (evidence of a pathway mechanism). It is unclear whether gender differences in the effect of childhood health reported here are real and replicable (most studies combine men and women), whether they are an artifact of gender differences in biological frailty (men who experienced poor childhood health may not have survived long enough to be included in the initial HRS sampling frame), or whether these cohorts of white men simply had more adulthood opportunities to compensate for poor childhood health than white women.

Taken together, the analyses demonstrate that childhood conditions have an enduring influence on all-cause mortality risks through both imprint and pathway processes. The bivariate relationships show that experiencing poor health and adverse socioeconomic conditions in childhood elevated mortality risks to various degrees across our race–gender groups. The multivariate analyses among non-Hispanic white adults further reveal that these adverse conditions operated partly through low adulthood educational attainment, while remaining in part independently significant. Comparisons across gender and race/ethnic groups indicate that childhood conditions may influence adult mortality risks differently across demographic subgroups. These results clearly warrant greater attention to gender and race/ethnic differences in future studies. Our analyses are not without limitations, however. One is that the HRS does not collect much information on childhood conditions. Information on prenatal conditions such as birthweight, postnatal conditions such as growth trajectories, and childhood family structure and stress would provide a more complete picture. Another limitation is the left censoring of our data. Only adults who survived to middle age could be included in the HRS sampling frame. Ideally, analyses of this type derive from prospective data that commence at birth to avoid any systematic biases that arise from premature mortality.

# Challenges and Directions for Future Research

## Key Conceptual and Analytical Challenges

Life-course research presents unique conceptual and analytical challenges because it requires information on numerous social and physical exposures spanning multiple time points across the life course that are biologically, socially, and psychologically relevant. One challenge is selecting the appropriate window of time for capturing the manifestation of the adult health or mortality outcome of interest. Indeed, emerging evidence reveals that the effect of certain childhood conditions on adult mortality risks is contingent on the adult age range studied (e.g., Su 2009). For example, the influence of childhood socioeconomic indicators on women's mortality risks was stronger for women who died before age 76 than for those who died afterward (Beebe-Dimmer et al. 2004). Furthermore, the period of manifestation may vary by gender. A study of US adults found that childhood SES exhibited a stronger association with women's mortality risks among young adults, a stronger association with men's risks for middle-aged adults, and no gender difference among older adults (Turrell et al. 2007). In fact, age- and gender-dependent associations should be expected, considering the interactions of social and biological exposures across the life course, as well as specific latency periods for various chronic diseases. Note that these types of associations are difficult to examine in studies such as the HRS, given the age-based selection criterion for inclusion. A related issue concerns the appropriate time frame to measure childhood exposures: any given exposure may have different consequences for long-term health, depending on whether it occurs during a critical or sensitive developmental period.

Because the influence of childhood socioeconomic indicators on adult health, and the degree to which each is mediated by adult education and income, varies by indicator and health outcome (Luo and Waite 2005), researchers should also carefully select indicators of SES that are etiologically relevant for the outcomes of interest. Specific socioeconomic indicators operate through different social–biological pathways to affect health. To illustrate, a study of British males found that father's education and occupation influenced son's health in middle age through its effects on his educational attainment (a pathway mechanism), while mother's education and occupation influenced son's health through its effect on his health in early life (an imprint mechanism) (Case et al. 2005). Our analysis above also illustrated the sensitivity of the associations to the SES indicator as well as gender and race/ethnicity. In addition, the strength of the associations may be influenced by how data on childhood conditions were collected. Historical records such census data and school records tend to correlate more strongly with adult mortality risks than do retrospective measures, perhaps because of recall error (Galobardes et al. 2006; Kauhanen et al. 2006). Also problematic is how to measure adult SES for women. Status measures that integrate husband's information tend to provide a stronger relationship with health and mortality risks than do measures based on wives' status alone (Beebe-Dimmer et al. 2004; Montez et al. 2009). This issue has important implications for life-course research because underestimating the effect of adult women's SES can lead to overestimating the effect of childhood SES for women compared with men.

Another consideration is the cause of death structure of the region studied. Industrialized countries might show stronger associations with adulthood conditions, while less economically developed countries might show stronger associations with childhood circumstances, and these factors should be considered when comparing results across regions and even between cohorts within a region. For instance, South Korea exhibits very low mortality from CHD, which has both childhood and adulthood antecedents, but high mortality from conditions such as stroke and stomach cancer that have particularly strong links to childhood circumstances. This might explain why childhood circumstances explained substantially more of the all-cause mortality differentials in South Korea than did adulthood risk factors (Khang and Kim 2005).

## Directions for Future Research

Even though research has generated abundant evidence that adult mortality risks are influenced by childhood circumstances, we clearly lack a firm understanding of the precise causal mechanisms and the contexts that moderate their influence. Thus, future research should move beyond documenting the association to disentangle the biological, social, and psychological mechanisms that underlie it. This will require careful consideration of the conceptual and analytical challenges outlined above, as well as collaboration among social scientists, epidemiologists, and biologists. New and innovative data sources are also needed. Prospective studies that follow adults from birth and collect biological, anthropometric, and social data at multiple points across the life course are the "gold standard," but they are also rare. Commencing studies of this kind today would undoubtedly benefit researchers 50 years from now. Shorter term gains could be made by linking administrative data such as birthweight, APGAR scores, school health records, and school disciplinary records with existing data from longitudinal or cross-sectional surveys. This alternative approach would be immensely informative at a fraction of the cost and time involved in prospective birth cohort studies.

## Conclusions

Life-course research makes clear that the timing and sequencing of events throughout life, and the mechanisms in play that influence these events, are affected by historical conditions—technologies, schooling opportunities, nutritional abundance, environmental pathogens, the nature of work environments, health care, opportunities for social mobility, and so on. Obviously, these conditions change over time and influence a population's life-course experience. American children born in the early part of the twentieth century had no vaccines, were exposed to a greater array of infectious pathogens, had higher rates of malnutrition, frequently lived in noxious urban environments, lived in larger families, and had fewer socioeconomic resources than children born in the middle and later parts of the century. Similarly, early birth cohorts experienced very different adulthoods than subsequent cohorts—the majority did not graduate from high school, they were more likely to work in jobs requiring physical labor and highly routine activities, they were more likely to smoke, and medical technologies were less available and efficacious in dealing with the major chronic killers.

Much of what is known about biological imprinting and pathways affecting adult mortality, and the social and physical exposures involved, is almost certainly a consequence of historical context. In birth cohorts since the introduction of vaccines, for example, it will probably be increasingly difficult to detect a biological imprinting effect of childhood infectious disease. But the growing prevalence of childhood autoimmune conditions and obesity may allow for the emergence of new biological imprinting and pathway mechanisms heretofore relatively rare and difficult to document at the population level. Comparing populations across countries or extrapolating from one population to others is equally tied to differences in historical context. Some populations may be subjected to pernicious epidemiological environments early in life, with only a minority of people experiencing adulthoods offering health advantages. This could potentially elevate the importance of early life biological imprinting and dampen the influence of pathway mechanisms, compared to populations growing up in less pernicious circumstances and more favorable adult conditions. While historical and cross-national comparisons may be challenging, these comparisons may also offer a unique opportunity to understand how different processes come into play under varying sociohistorical conditions.

The role of historical context brings us back to a basic point made by a growing number of researchers (Ben-Shlomo and Davey Smith 1991; Ben-Shlomo and Kuh 2002; Halfon and Hochstein 2002; Power and Hertzman 1997). A cumulative framework is essential to understanding how biological imprinting and pathway mechanisms combine to influence adult health and mortality. Such a framework must allow for the fact that some childhood exposures leave a biological imprint while others set in motion a cascade of health-related trajectories, and that adult exposures may add to, exaggerate, or even ameliorate earlier exposures. Furthermore, researchers should articulate this framework within the sociohistorical context of the population(s) under study. On one hand, researchers will likely find themselves in the quagmire of reconciling disparate findings across studies from different populations and historical periods. On the other hand, the growing number of studies for different birth cohorts and countries may offer a tremendous opportunity for investigating how large-scale social changes are shaping the fundamental ways in which early conditions shape a population's life chances.

# References

Adams, P.F., G.E. Hendershot, and M.A. Marano. 1996. "Current Estimates from the National Health Interview Survey, 1996." *Vital Health Statistics* 10(200):1–211.

Barker, D.J.P. 1997. "Maternal Nutrition, Fetal Nutrition, and Disease in Later Life." *Nutrition* 13(9):807–13.

Barker, D.J.P. 2007. "The Origins of the Developmental Origins Theory." *Journal of Internal Medicine* 261:412–17.

Barker, D.J.P., T.J. Forsen, A. Uutela, C. Osmond, and J.G. Erikkson. 2001. "Size at Birth and Resilience to Effects of Poor Living Conditions in Adult Life: Longitudinal Study." *British Medical Journal* 323:1–5.

Barker, D.J.P. and C. Osmond. 1989. "Infant Mortality, Childhood Nutrition and Ischaemic Heart Disease in England and Wales." *Lancet* 1:1077–81.

Barker, D.J.P., C. Osmond, and C.M. Law. 1989. "The Intrauterine and Early Postnatal Origins of Cardiovascular Disease and Chronic Bronchitis." *Journal of Epidemiology and Community Health* 43:237–40.

Beach, R.S., M.E. Gershwin, and L.S. Hurley. 1982. "Gestational Zinc Deprivation in Mice: Persistence of Immunodeficiency for Three Generations." *Science* 218(4571):469–71.

Beebe-Dimmer, J., J.W. Lynch, G. Turrell, S. Lustgarten, T. Raghunathan, and G.A. Kaplan. 2004. "Childhood and Adult Socioeconomic Conditions and 31-Year Mortality Risk in Women." *American Journal of Epidemiology* 159(5):481–90.

Bellisle, F. 2004. "Effects of Diet on Behavior and Cognition in Children." *British Journal of Nutrition* 92(Suppl 2):S227–S32.

Ben-Shlomo, Y. and G. Davey Smith. 1991. "Deprivation in Infancy or in Adult Life: Which Is More Important for Mortality Risk?" *Lancet* 337(8740):530–34.

Ben-Shlomo, Y. and D. Kuh. 2002. "A Life Course Approach to Chronic Disease Epidemiology: Conceptual Models, Empirical Challenges and Interdisciplinary Perspectives." *International Epidemiological Association* 31:285–93.

Bengtsson, T. and G.P. Mineau. 2009. "Early-Life Effects on Socio-Economic Performance and Mortality in Later Life: A Full Life-Course Approach Using Contemporary and Historical Sources." *Social Science and Medicine* 68(9):1561–64.

Berckman, D.S., A.G. Lescano, R.H. Gilman, S.L. Lopez, and M.M. Black. 2002. "Effects of Stunting, Diarrhoeal Disease, and Parasitic Infection During Infancy on Cognition in Late Childhood: A Follow-up Study." *Lancet* 359:564–71.

Berkman, L.F. 2009. "Social Epidemiology: Social Determinants of Health in the United States: Are We Losing Ground?" *Annual Review of Public Health* 30:27–41.

Black, S.E., P.J. Devereux, and K.G. Salvanes. 2007. "From the Cradle to the Labor Market? The Effect of Birth Weight on Adult Outcomes." *Quarterly Journal of Economics* 122(1):409–39.

Blackwell, D.L., M.D. Hayward, and E.M. Crimmins. 2001. "Does Childhood Health Affect Chronic Morbidity in Later Life?" *Social Science and Medicine* 52:1269–84.

Blau, P.M. and O.D. Duncan. 1967. *The American Occupational Structure*. New York, NY, Free Press.

Buck, C. and H. Simpson. 1982. "Infant Diarrhoea and Subsequent Mortality from Heart Disease and Cancer." *Journal of Epidemiology and Community Health* 36:27–30.

Cambois, E. 2004. "Careers and Mortality in France: Evidence on How Far Occupational Mobility Predicts Differentiated Risks." *Social Science and Medicine* 58(12):2545–58.

Case, A., A. Fertig, and C. Paxson. 2005. "The Lasting Impact of Childhood Health and Circumstance." *Journal of Health Economics* 24:365–89.

Claussen, B., G. Davey Smith, and D. Thelle. 2003. "Impact of Childhood and Adulthood Socioeconomic Position on Cause Specific Mortality: The Oslo Mortality Study." *Journal of Epidemiology and Community Health* 57:40–45.

Cohen, S., W.J. Doyle, R.B. Turner, C.M. Apler, and D.P. Skoner. 2004. "Childhood Socioeconomic Status and Host Resistance to Infectious Illness in Adulthood." *Psychosomatic Medicine* 66:553–58.

Conley, D. and N.G. Bennett. 2000. "Is Biology Destiny? Birth Weight and Life Chances." *American Sociological Review* 65:458–67.

Crimmins, E.M. and C.E. Finch. 2006. "Infection, Inflammation, Height, and Longevity." *Proceedings of the National Academy of Sciences* 103(2):498–503.

Crosnoe, R. and G.H. Elder Jr. 2004. "From Childhood to the Later Years: Pathways of Human Development." *Research on Aging* 26(6):623–54.

Davey Smith, G., C. Hart, D. Blane, C. Gillis, and V. Hawthorne. 1997. "Lifetime Socioeconomic Position and Mortality: Prospective Observational Study." *British Medical Journal* 314(7080):547–52.

Davey Smith, G., C. Hart, D. Blane, and D. Hole. 1998a. "Adverse Socioeconomic Conditions in Childhood and Cause Specific Adult Mortality: Prospective Observational Study." *British Medical Journal* 316:1631–35.

Davey Smith, G., C. Hart, D. Hole, P. MacKinnon, C. Gillis, G. Watt, D. Blane, and V. Hawthorne. 1998b. "Education and Occupational Social Class: Which Is the More Important Indicator of Mortality Risk?" *Journal of Epidemiology and Community Health* 52(3):153–60.

Derrick, V.P.A. 1927. "Observations on (1) Errors on Age on the Population Statistics of England and Wales and (2) the Changes in Mortality Indicated by the National Records." *Journal of the Institute of Actuaries* 58:117–59.

Diamond, J. 1991. "Pearl Harbor and the Emperor's Physiologists." *Natural History* 100(12):2–7.

Dowd, J.B., A. Zajacova, and A. Aiello. 2009. "Early Origins of Health Disparities: Burden of Infection, Health, and Socioeconomic Status in U.S. Children." *Social Science and Medicine* 68:699–707.

Drummond, P.D. and B. Hewson-Bower. 1997. "Increased Psychosocial Stress and Decreased Mucosal Immunity in Children With Recurrent Upper Respiratory Tract Infections." *Journal of Psychosomatic Research* 43(3):271–78.

Elo, I.T. and S.H. Preston. 1992. "Effects of Early-Life Conditions on Adult Mortality: A Review." *Population Index* 58(2):186–212.

Felitti, V.J., R.F. Anda, D. Nordenberg, D.F. Williamson, A.M. Spitz, V. Edwards, M.P. Koss, and J.S. Marks. 1998. "Relationship of Childhood Abuse and Household Dysfunction to Many of the Leading Causes of Death in

Adults: The Adverse Childhood Experiences (ACE) Study." *American Journal of Preventive Medicine* 14(4):245–58.

Fogel, R.W. 2004. *The Escape from Hunger and Premature Death, 1700–2100: Europe, America, and the Third World.* New York, NY, Cambridge University Press.

Forsdahl, A. 1977. "Are Poor Living Conditions in Childhood and Adolescence an Important Risk Factor for Arteriosclerotic Heart Disease?" *British Journal of Preventive and Social Medicine* 31:91–95.

Fu, H. and N. Goldman. 1996. "Incorporating Health into Models of Marriage Choice: Demographic and Sociological Perspectives." *Journal of Marriage and the Family* 58(3):740–58.

Galobardes, B., G. Davey Smith, and J.W. Lynch. 2006. "Systematic Review of the Influence of Childhood Socioeconomic Circumstances on Risk for Cardiovascular Disease in Adulthood." *Annals of Epidemiology* 16:91–104.

Gillman, M.W. and J.W. Rich-Edwards. 2000. "The Fetal Origins of Adult Disease: From Sceptic to Convert." *Paediatric and Perinatal Epidemiology* 14(3):192.

Haas, S. 2008. "Trajectories of Functional Health: The 'Long Arm' of Childhood Health and Socioeconomic Factors." *Social Science and Medicine* 66:849–61.

Hales, C.N. and D.J.P. Barker. 1992. "Type 2 (Non-Insulin-Dependent) Diabetes Mellitus: The Thrifty Phenotype Hypothesis." *Diabetologia* 35(7):595–601.

Halfon, N. and M. Hochstein. 2002. "Life Course Health Development: An Integrated Framework for Developing Health, Policy, and Research." *Milbank Quarterly* 80(3):433–79.

Hamil-Luker, J. and A.M. O'Rand. 2007. "Gender Differences in the Link Between Childhood Socioeconomic Conditions and Heart Attack Risk in Adulthood." *Demography* 41(1):137–58.

Hardy, R. and D. Kuh. 2002. "Does Early Growth Influence Timing of the Menopause? Evidence from a British Birth Cohort." *Human Reproduction* 17(9):2474–79.

Hayward, M.D. and B.K. Gorman. 2004. "The Long Arm of Childhood: The Influence of Early-Life Social Conditions on Men's Mortality." *Demography* 41(1):87–107.

Hemmingsson, T., B. Melin, P. Allebeck, and I. Lundberg. 2006. "The Association Between Cognitive Ability Measured at Ages 18–20 and Mortality During 30 Years of Follow-up—A Prospective Observational Study Among Swedish Males Born 1949–51." *International Journal of Epidemiology* 35(3):665–70.

Hu, Y. and N. Goldman. 1990. "Mortality Differentials by Marital Status: An International Comparison." *Demography* 27(2):233–50.

Judge, T.A. and D.M. Cable. 2004. "The Effect of Physical Height on Workplace Success and Income: Preliminary Test of a Theoretical Model." *Journal of Applied Psychology* 89(3):428–41.

Kauhanen, L., H.-M. Lakka, J.W. Lynch, and J. Kauhanen. 2006. "Social Disadvantage in Childhood and Risk of All-cause Death and Cardiovascular Disease in Later Life: A Comparison of Historical and Retrospective Childhood Information." *International Journal of Epidemiology* 35:962–68.

Kermack, W.O., A.G. McKendrick, and P.L. McKinley. 1934. "Death Rates in Great Britain and Sweden: Some General Regularities and Their Significance." *Lancet* 226:698–703.

Khang, Y.-H. and H.R. Kim. 2005. "Explaining Socioeconomic Inequality in Mortality Among South Koreans: An Examination of Multiple Pathways in a Nationally Representative Longitudinal Study." *International Journal of Epidemiology* 34:630–37.

Kuh, D. and G. Davey Smith. 1993. "When Is Mortality Risk Determined? Historical Insights into a Current Debate." *Social History of Medicine* 6(1):101–23.

Kuh, D., R. Hardy, C. Langenberg, M. Richards, and M.E.J. Wadsworth. 2002a. "Mortality in Adults Aged 26–54 Years Related to Socioeconomic Conditions in Childhood and Adulthood: Post War Birth Cohort Study." *British Medical Journal* 325(7372):1076–80.

Kuh, D., R. Hardy, B. Rodgers, and M.E.J. Wadsworth. 2002b. "Lifetime Risk Factors for Women's Psychological Distress in Midlife." *Social Science and Medicine* 55:1957–73.

Kuh, D., M. Richards, R. Hardy, S. Butterworth, and M.E.J. Wadsworth. 2004. "Childhood Cognitive Ability and Deaths Up Until Middle Age: A Post-war Birth Cohort Study." *International Journal of Epidemiology* 33(2):408–13.

Lawlor, D.A., J.A.C. Sterne, P. Tynelius, G. Davey Smith, and F. Rasmussen. 2006. "Association of Childhood Socioeconomic Position with Cause-specific Mortality in a Prospective Record Linkage Study of 1,839,384 Individuals." *American Journal of Epidemiology* 164(9):907–15.

Lillard, L.A. and L.J. Waite. 1995. "Til Death Do Us Part: Marital Disruption and Mortality." *American Journal of Sociology* 100:1131–56.

Lozoff, B., E. Jimenez, J. Hagen, E. Mollen, and A.W. Wolf. 2000. "Poorer Behavioral and Developmental Outcome More Than 10 Years After Treatment for Iron Deficiency in Infancy." *Pediatrics* 105(4):e51.

Lundberg, O. 1993. "The Impact of Childhood Living Conditions on Illness and Mortality in Adulthood." *Social Science and Medicine* 36(8):1047–52.

Luo, Y. and L.J. Waite. 2005. "The Impact of Childhood and Adult SES on Physical, Mental, and Cognitive Well-Being in Later Life." *Journal of Gerontology* 60B(2):S93–S101.

Lynch, J. and G. Davey Smith. 2005. "A Life Course Approach to Chronic Disease Epidemiology." *Annual Review of Public Health* 26:1–35.

Lynch, J.W., G.A. Kaplan, and J.T. Salonen. 1997. "Why Do Poor People Behave Poorly? Variation in Adult Health Behaviours and Psychosocial Characteristics by Stages of the Socioeconomic Lifecourse." *Social Science and Medicine* 44(6):809–19.

Marmot, M.G. and M.J. Shipley. 1996. "Do Socioeconomic Differences in Mortality Persist After Retirement? 25 Year Follow Up of Civil Servants from the First Whitehall Study." *British Medical Journal* 313(7066):1177–80.

Marmot, M., M. Shipley, E. Brunner, and H. Hemingway. 2001. "Relative Contribution of Early Life and Adult Socioeconomic Factors to Adult Morbidity in the Whitehall II Study." *Journal of Epidemiology and Community Health* 55(5):301–7.

McDade, T.W. 2005. "Life History, Maintenance, and the Early Origins of Immune Function." *American Journal of Human Biology* 17:81–94.

McDade, T.W., M.A. Beck, C. Kuzawa, and L.S. Adair. 2001a. "Prenatal Undernutrition, Postnatal Environments, and Antibody Response to Vaccination in Adolescence." *American Journal of Clinical Nutrition* 74(4):543–48.

McDade, T.W., M.A. Beck, C.W. Kuzawa, and L.S. Adair. 2001b. "Prenatal Undernutrition and Postnatal Growth Are Associated with Adolescent Thymic Function." *Journal of Nutrition* 131(4):1225–31.

McDade, T.W., W.R. Leonard, J. Burhop, V. Reyes-Garcia, V. Vadez, T. Huanca, and R.A. Godoy. 2003. "Acculturation, C-Reactive Protein, and Child Growth in Lowland Bolivia." *American Journal of Human Biology* 15:273–74.

McEwen, B.S. 1998. "Stress, Adaptation, and Disease: Allostasis and Allostatic Load." *Annals of the New York Academy of Sciences* 840:33–44.

Meaney, M.J., D.H. Aitken, C.V. Berkel, S. Bhatnagar, and R.M. Sapolsky. 1988. "Effect of Neonatal Handling on Age-Related Impairments Associated with the Hippocampus." *Science* 239(4841):766–68.

Montez, J.K., M.D. Hayward, D.C. Brown, and R.A. Hummer. 2009. "Why Is the Educational Gradient in Mortality Steeper for Men?" *Journal of Gerontology: Social Sciences* 64:S625–S34.

Moore, D.E. and M.D. Hayward. 1990. "Occupational Careers and Mortality of Elderly Men." *Demography* 27:31–53.

Murray, J.E. 2000. "Marital Protection and Marital Selection: Evidence from a Historical-Prospective Sample of American Men." *Demography* 37(4):511–21.

Nichol, K.L., S. D'Heilly, and E. Ehlinger. 2005. "Colds and Influenza-Like Illnesses in University Students: Impact on Health, Academic and Work Performance, and Health Care Use." *Clinical Infectious Diseases* 40(9):1263–70.

Notkola, V., S. Punsar, M.J. Karvonen, and J. Haapakoski. 1985. "Socio-Economic Conditions in Childhood and Mortality and Morbidity Caused by Coronary Heart Disease in Adulthood in Rural Finland." *Social Science and Medicine* 21(5):517–23.

Osler, M., A.-M.N. Anderson, P. Due, R. Lund, M.T. Damsgaard, and B.E. Holstein. 2003. "Socioeconomic Position in Early Life, Birth Weight, Childhood Cognitive Function, and Adult Mortality. A Longitudinal Study of Danish Men Born in 1953." *Journal of Epidemiology and Community Health* 57:681–86.

Palloni, A. 2006. "Reproducing Inequalities: Luck, Wallets, and the Enduring Effects of Childhood Health." *Demography* 43(4):587–615.

Palloni, A., C. Milesi, R.G. White, and A. Turner. 2009. "Early Childhood Health, Reproduction of Economic Inequalities and the Persistence of Health and Mortality Differentials." *Social Science and Medicine* 68(9):1574–82.

Pavalko, E.K., G.H. Elder Jr., and E.C. Clipp. 1993. "Worklives and Longevity: Insights from a Life Course Perspective." *Journal of Health and Social Behavior* 34(4):363–80.

Peck, M.N. 1994. "The Importance of Childhood Socio-Economic Group for Adult Health." *Social Science and Medicine* 39(4):553–62.

Pensola, T.H. and P. Martikainen. 2003. "Effect of Living Conditions in the Parental Home and Youth Paths on the Social Class Differences in Mortality Among Women." *Scandinavian Journal of Public Health* 31(6):428–38.

Power, C. and C. Hertzman. 1997. "Social and Biological Pathways Linking Early Life and Adult Disease." *British Medical Bulletin* 53(1):210–21.

Preston, S.H., M.E. Hill, and G.L. Drevenstedt. 1998. "Childhood Conditions That Predict Survival to Advanced Ages Among African-Americans." *Social Science and Medicine* 47(9):1231–46.

Preston, S.H. and P. Taubman. 1994. "Socioeconomic Differences in Adult Mortality and Health Status." In L.G. Martin and S.H. Preston (eds.), *Demography of Aging*, pp. 279–318. Washington, DC, National Academy Press.

Rogers, R.G., R.A. Hummer, and C.B. Nam. 2000. *Living and Dying in the USA*. New York, NY, Academic Press.

Ross, C.E., J. Mirowsky, and K. Goldsteen. 1990. "The Impact of the Family on Health: The Decade in Review." *Journal of Marriage and the Family* 52(4):1059–78.

Ross, C.E. and C.-L. Wu. 1995. "The Links Between Education and Health." *American Sociological Review* 60:719–45.

Schwartz, J.E., H.S. Friedman, J.S. Tucker, C. Tomlinson-Keasey, D.L. Wingard, and M.H. Criqui. 1995. "Sociodemographic and Psychosocial Factors in Childhood as Predictors of Adult Mortality." *American Journal of Public Health* 85(9):1237–45.

Shaw, B.A., N. Krause, L.M. Chatters, C.M. Connell, and B. Ingersoll-Dayton. 2004. "Emotional Support from Parents Early in Life, Aging, and Health." *Psychology and Aging* 19(1):4–12.

Strachan, D.P. 2000. "Family Size, Infection and Atopy: The First Decade of the 'Hygiene Hypothesis.'" *Thorax* 55(Suppl1):S2–S10.

Su, D. 2009. "Risk Exposure in Early Life and Mortality at Older Ages." *Population and Development Review* 35(2):275–95.

Taylor, S.E., R.L. Repetti, and T. Seeman. 1997. "Health Psychology: What Is an Unhealthy Environment and How Does It Get Under the Skin?" *Annual Review of Psychology* 48(1):411–47.

Turrell, G., J.W. Lynch, C. Leite, T. Raghunathan, and G.A. Kaplan. 2007. "Socioeconomic Disadvantage in Childhood and Across the Life Course and All-Cause Mortality and Physical Function in Adulthood: Evidence from the Alameda County Study." *Journal of Epidemiology and Community Health* 61:723–30.

Van Assche, F.A. and L. Aerts. 1979. "The Fetal Endocrine Pancreas." *Contributions to Gynecology and Obstetrics* 5:44–57.

West-Eberhard, M.J. 1989. "Phenotypic Plasticity and the Origins of Diversity." *Annual Review of Ecology and Systematics* 20:249–78.

Worthman, C.M. and J. Kuzara. 2005. "Life History and the Early Origins of Health Differentials." *American Journal of Human Biology* 17:95–112.

# Chapter 10
# Age Patterns in Adult Mortality

Jean-Marie Robine

## Introduction

This chapter gives us the opportunity to revisit some of the work of the founding fathers of demographic science. While modern life tables usually begin with probabilities of death, $_nq_x$, the first life tables made in London during the seventeenth century began with counts from the *Bills of Mortality*. The first life tables were based on a very small amount of data, leading Edmund Halley (1656–1742) to conclude that the relationship between age and mortality described by his predecessors (Halley 1693) "has been only done by imaginary Valuation". Indeed, John Graunt (1620–1674) had no real information on ages of deaths when he published the first life table (1662). The age at death of 1,495 individuals for whom life annuities were subscribed by the Government of the United Provinces (The Netherlands) from 1586 to 1590, compiled by Johannes Hudde (1628–1704) on the occasion of his collaboration with Johan De Witt (1625–1672) in 1671, provides the only available dataset on mortality by age before 1693, when Halley published data compiled by Caspar Neumann (1648–1715) on 6,193 registered births and 5,869 deaths by age occurring from 1687 to 1691 in Breslau, the capital of Silesia (Halley 1693). From this material, some of the major figures of modern science hypothesized the first age patterns of adult mortality and deduced the associated life tables, i.e. the corresponding survivors. This approach led to the publication of the work of Wilhelm Lexis (1837–1914) on usual longevity that two centuries later gave a realistic description of the age pattern of adult mortality for the first time (Lexis 1878). However, during the nineteenth century and the first part of the twentieth century, infant mortality was the main public health issue and life expectancy at birth (i.e. the mean life duration), summarizing the mortality experience of the whole population, the most useful indicator.

The current emergence of the oldest old people, nonagenarians and centenarians, has raised issues about the ability of life expectancy at birth to provide a good indication of the duration of an ordinary life. Indeed, a new focus on the age pattern of adult mortality has disclosed that an increase in the adult modal age at death of several years has occurred over time. This silent revolution in adult longevity has been missed by standard demographic indicators. Whether the increase in the modal lifespan is accompanied by a homogenization of the individual adult life durations (the compression of mortality hypothesis) or not (the shifting mortality hypothesis) is an important issue for the future.

When they started working on the age patterns of mortality, the first "demographers" had neither the words nor the concepts or the statistical models necessary to analyse mortality data. This chapter shows how having data without concepts or vice versa leads to a deadlock. It took at least two centuries from the work of Graunt (1662) to gather all the necessary elements before Lexis provided a realistic description of the age pattern of adult mortality (1878).

This chapter covers these different topics in four sections. The first section summarizes the historical developments from the first hypothesized age patterns

---

J.-M. Robine (✉)
Institut National de la Santé et de la Recherche Médicale,
French Institute of Health and Medical Research, INSERM,
Health & Démographie, Centre de Recherche en Cancérologie,
Montpellier, France
e-mail: robine@valdorel.fnclcc.fr

of adult mortality to the Lexis' distribution of ages at death. The second section describes the adult longevity revolution which paralleled the demographic transitions. The third section focuses on the emergence of the oldest old population, nonagenarians and centenarians. The final section deals with directions for future research. These topics led us to focus more on developed countries, especially European countries where population science emerged during the eighteenth century, and on females who are at the forefront of the longevity revolution.

## Historical Development

When Aristotle (384 BC–322 BC) gathered information on various biometric quantities, such as the duration of gestation, the size of a litter, and the length of life, he did not provide information about the length of life for humans. For other species, he wrote "the peacock lives about twenty-five years", "most horses live eighteen or twenty years" (Aristotle, The History of Animal). Francis Bacon (1561–1626) maintained the looseness and the ambiguity of this wording in his manuscript *Length and Shortness of Life in Living Creatures* (1670) as did the Count de Buffon (1707–1788) in his *Natural History* (1749). Buffon did not give any value for the duration of life for men in his *Table on Fertility Ratios of Animals*, published in 1776, but he did provide several indications in his *History* (Robine et al. 2009a).[1] When he writes "the man who does not die of accidental diseases lives around ninety or a hundred years", it is clear that he was not talking of a mean expectation of life. Though this notion is still not well-established by the mid-eighteenth century when Buffon specifies, "Man, as we know, dies at any age, and although in general we can say that its life is longer than the life of almost all animals, we cannot deny it is also more uncertain and variable." The notions of frequency distribution and most frequent values were not established before the nineteenth century (Quetelet 1835, 1871).

[1] We know the table of Buffon mainly through the version of William Smellie (1740–1795), who placed it in the central part of his *Philosophy of Natural History* (1790) Charles Elliot, Edinburgh, 1790. First Edition.

The terminology used by European authors to describe human longevity during the seventeenth and eighteenth centuries – common, usual or ordinary term and/or lifetime – seems to refer to maximum longevity, the modern biological lifespan. However, it is not incompatible with a few exceptional super long-living individuals, such as the famous Thomas Parr (1483–1635). Given this background, how do we interpret the oft-quoted biblical *threescore and ten*: as a mean, modal value or maximum? Comparing the duration of contemporary life to the long duration of the lives of the Patriarchs, Thomas Browne (1605–1682) hesitated between "threescore, fourscore, or an hundred years" (Browne 1646). Indeed, the initial confusion introduced by Aristotle about the length of life – or how long a species would live – was not clarified until 1878, when Lexis provided estimates of usual longevity. Within this muddled context, some of the major figures of modern science hypothesized the first age patterns of adult mortality.

## *The Number of Deaths Diminishes with Age*

John Graunt was clear that the number of deaths should decrease with age in proportion to the number of people. However, in his famous treatise on mortality, the *Natural and Political Observations on the Bills of Mortality* (1662), there is very little information on ages at death. Indeed, while the bills provided Graunt with a wealth of information on causes of death, on gender of decedents and on the seasonality of mortality, the bills contain virtually no information on ages at death. Thus, Graunt notes *In the matter of* Infants *I would desire but to know, what* Searchers *mean by* Infants, *as whether Children that cannot speak, as the word* Infans *seems to signifie, or Children under two or three years old...* (Chapter II, 8) and about elderly people *Onely the question is, what number of Years the* Searchers *call* Aged, *which I conceive must be the same, that* David *calls so, viz. 70. For no man can be die properly of Age, who is much less...* (Chapter II, 18). However, from this meagre data, Graunt extracted two essential pieces of information – the level of infant and child mortality and the proportion of people surviving to age 76.

**Fig. 10.1** Reproduction of the survival curve drawn by Christiaan Huygens in 1669 with the survival series estimates by John Graunt in 1662. Source: Huygens (1669)

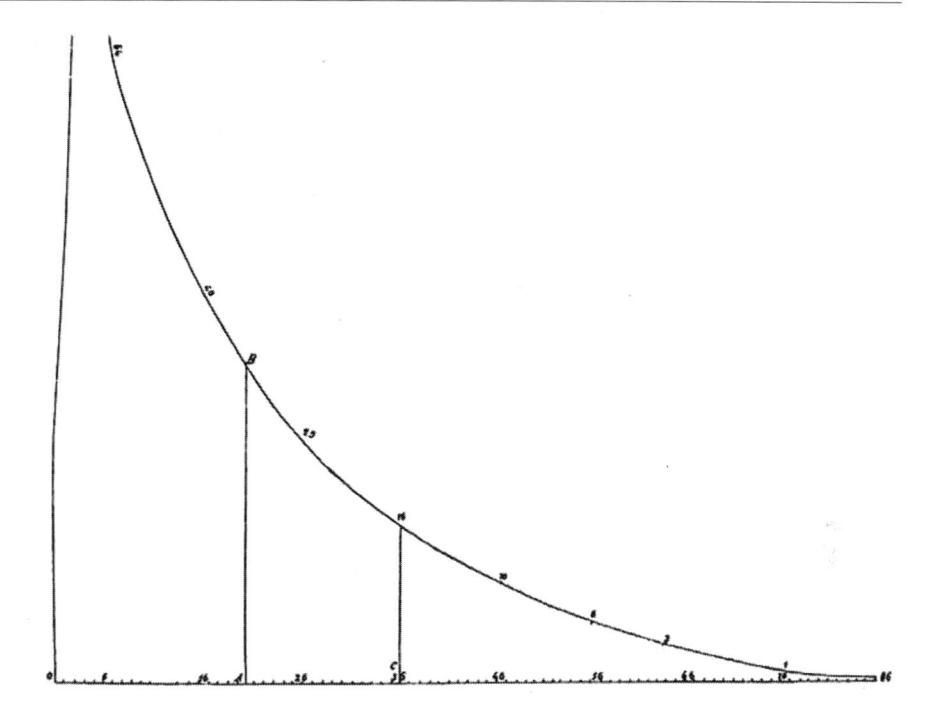

His famous table of survivors by age is built with only this information: "Where as we have found, that of 100 quick Conceptions about 36 of them die before they be 6 years old, and that perhaps but one surviveth 76, we, having seven Decads between 6 and 76, we sought six mean proportional numbers between 64, the remainer, living at 6 years, and the one, which survives 76..." (Graunt 1662). He inferred from this line of reasoning a decreasing series of numbers of death by 10-year age group as well as a series of survivors by age (6, 16, 26...). Graunt does not compute anything that resembles a mortality rate, as he was only looking for the proportion and the number of males aged from 16 to 56 years who can be soldiers. The implicit hypothesis of Graunt, i.e., that the number of deaths declines with age in proportion to the number of survivors, is that the level of mortality is constant from the 6th birthday onwards and possibly from birth (Le Bras 2000).

In their private correspondence on life expectancy (mean life duration) and probable or likely life (the modern median life) based on the Graunt's table, Christiaan (1629–1695), Lodewijk (1631–1699) Huygens did not call into question this hypothesis (Rohrbasser and Véron 1999). On the contrary, they seemed to accept it as evidenced by the great survival curve drawn by Christiaan and annexed to his letter dated November 21, 1669 (Fig. 10.1).

## The Number of Deaths Remains Constant with Age

In contrast, Gottfried Wilhelm Leibniz (1646–1716) and Abraham de Moivre (1667–1754) independently developed the hypothesis that the number of deaths by single year of age remained constant from birth to the end of the lifespan. Of course, this hypothesis leads to a dramatic increase in the mortality rate by age. The work of Leibniz is poorly known, as several manuscripts were published long after his death.[2] The most important, the *Essay*, is dated circa 1680. In *Loss- und Leibrenten* (1680), Leibniz wrote that his hypothesis of a constant number of deaths by age is drawn from an observation made by Hudde in Amsterdam (Rohrbasser and Véron 1998).

---

[2] The exact contribution of Leibniz in the Breslaw's data collection is still unknown (Le Bras 2003; Reed 1942).

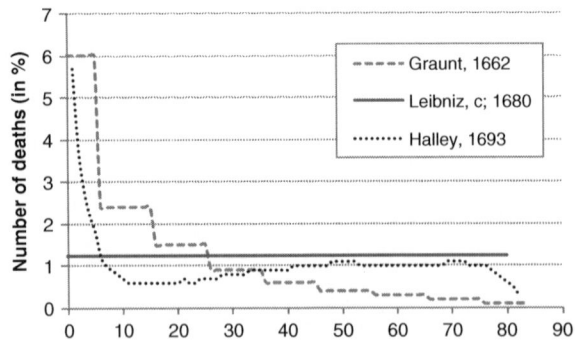

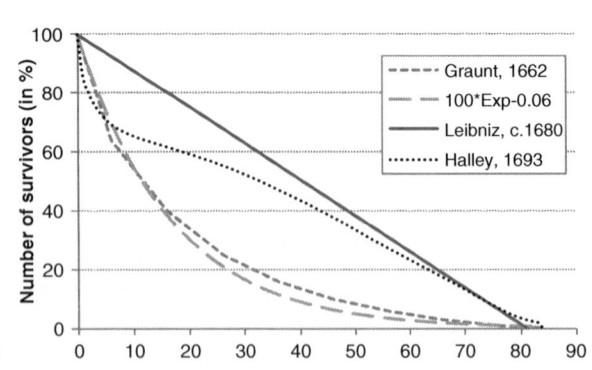

**Fig. 10.2** Alternative hypothetical distributions of the number of deaths by age (*left*) and alternative hypothetical survival curves by age (*right*). According to John Graunt (1662) and Gottfried Wilhelm Leibniz (c. 1680) with the empirical data gathered by Caspar Neumann in Breslaw between 1687 and 1691, and published by Halley (1693)

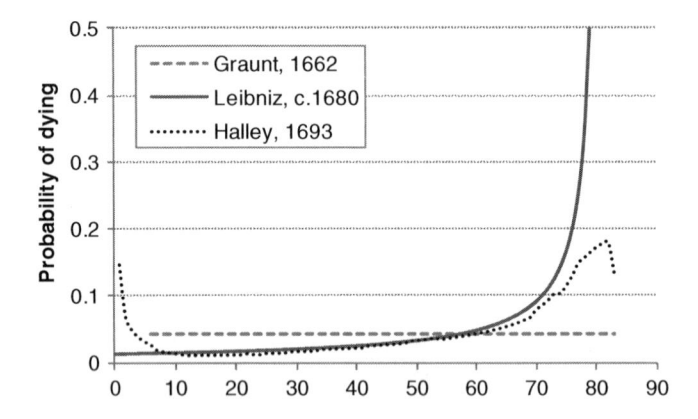

**Fig. 10.3** Alternative mortality trajectory by age deduced from the hypotheses on the distribution of the number of deaths by age according to John Graunt (1662) and Gottfried Wilhelm Leibniz (c. 1680), with the empirical trajectory deduced from the data gathered by Caspar Neumann in Breslaw between 1687 and 1691, and published by Halley (1693)

The work of de Moivre is better known. He explained himself in his Treatise of Annuities on Lives (1725), "…2 or 3 Years after the Publication of the first Edition of my Doctrine of Chances [1718], I took the Subject into Consideration; and consulting Dr. Halley's Table of Observations, I found that the decrements of Life, for considerable Intervals of Time, were in Arithmetic Progression" (Moivre 1756).

Figures 10.2 and 10.3 summarize the two alternative hypotheses with the first series of empirical data published by Halley.[3] On the left panel of Fig. 10.2, the three distributions of the age of deaths that were the entry point for this initial demographic reasoning are shown, and on the right panel the associated survival curves which were seen by Graunt and Leibniz as a consequence of the distribution of the number of deaths by age. Halley did not look at the survival curve, rather focusing on the distribution of deaths by age. Figure 10.3 displays the associated mortality trajectory by age, which was overlooked by Graunt and Halley. Only Leibniz paid attention to the associated mortality trajectory and provided clear explanations for his computed mean duration of life.

## Lexis's Distribution of the Ages at Death

From this point, little progress was made until Lexis published his work on usual longevity in 1878. While even more data became gradually available throughout the eighteenth century, the publication of the [*Treatise of*] *Annuities Upon* [*on*] *Lives* of Moivre, in five editions from 1725 to 1756, consolidated the idea that the distribution of the number of deaths by age is constant. In his last edition (1756), Moivre claimed his

---

[3] We kept track of the data assembled by Johannes Hudde thanks to Christian Huygens to whom Hudde sent his data in August 1671 and that Huygens used under the name of *Tableau de mortalité dressé par J. Hudde*. Johan De Witt and Johannes Hudde are possibly the first ones to understand that mortality increases with age.

**Table 10.1** Slow accumulation of mortality datasets by age over the eighteenth century, after the publication of the *Natural and Political Observations* of John Graunt (1662)

| Data collection | Data | Published by | Claimed representativeness | Year of publication | References |
|---|---|---|---|---|---|
| Hudde (1628–1704) | Annuities, United Netherlands, 1586–1590 | De Witt | Annuitants | 1671 | Correspondence of Christiaan Huygens (1895) |
| Neumann (1648–1715) | Bills of mortality, Beslaw, 1687–1691 | Halley | Universal | 1693 | Halley (1693) |
| King (1648–1712) | Lichfield, 1695 | | | | Laslett (1973) |
| Struyck (1687–1769) | Annuitants | Struyck | Annuitants | 1740 | Struyck (1740) |
| Kersseboom (circa 1690–1771) | | Kersseboom | Universal | 1742 | Kersseboom (1742) |
| Deparcieux (1703–1768) | Tontines (annuities), 1689 and 1696 | Deparcieux | Annuitants | 1746 | Deparcieux (1746) |
| Hogdson | Bills of mortality, London | | City of London | 1747 | Gaeta and Fontana (1776) |
| Dupré de Saint-Maur (1695–1774) | Statistics on death for 3 main parishes in Paris and 12 rural parishes | Buffon | Universal | 1749 | Buffon (1749) |
| Smart, revised by Simpson (1710–1761) | Possibly, bills of mortality, City of London, 1728–1737 | Morris | City of London | 1751 | Morris (1751) |
| Morris (1710–1779) | Bills of mortality, City of London, 1728–1750 | Morris | City of London | 1751 | Morris (1751) |
| Struyck (1687–1769) | Statistics on deaths, Geneva, 1741 | Struyck | Local | 1753 | Struyck (1753) |
| Struyck (1687–1769) | Statistics on deaths, Middelbourg, Zelande, 1752 | Struyck | Local | 1753 | Struyck (1753) |
| Wargentin (1717–1783) | Statistics on the death in Sweden, 1754–1756 | Deparcieux | Universal | 1760 | Deparcieux (1760) |
| Süssmilch (1707–1767) | Several kingdoms and provinces | Süssmilch | Universal | 1765 | Süssmilch (1765) |

proposal to be applied to other tables of observations. During the eighteenth century, Johann-Peter Süssmilch (1707–1767), Nicolas Struyck (1687–1769), Antoine Deparcieux (1703–1768), Richard Price (1723–1791), Gregorio Fontana (1735–1803)[4] and Jean-Baptiste Moheau (1745–1794) gathered and thoroughly examined the tables published by their predecessors as Moivre did (Moheau 1778). This approach had many advantages: spreading data across Europe, increasing scientific exchange between the authors and strengthening the discussion. But the fame of Halley and the reputation of Moivre caused the authors of the eighteenth century to ignore some of the implications of their data.

However, analysis of existing data allowed the terminology to be readdressed. Thus, Süssmilch questions in 1741 the idea that 90 years can be seen as the ordinary term of life. He uses arguments similar to those Michel de Montaigne (1533–1592) used two centuries before him in 1595, the common term cannot be exceptional.[5] But like Montaigne, he is unable to

---

[4] His translation of *Treatise* of Moivre in collaboration with Roberto Gaeta is accompanied by an almost complete bibliography of previous work on mortality.

[5] « *Ne nous flattons pas de ces beaux mots: on doit à l'aventure appeler plus tôt naturel, ce qui est général, commun, et universel. Mourir de vieillesse, c'est une mort rare, singulière et extraordinaire, et d'autant moins naturelle que les autres: c'est la dernière et extrême sorte de mourir: plus elle est éloignée de nous, d'autant est elle moins espérable: c'est bien la borne,*

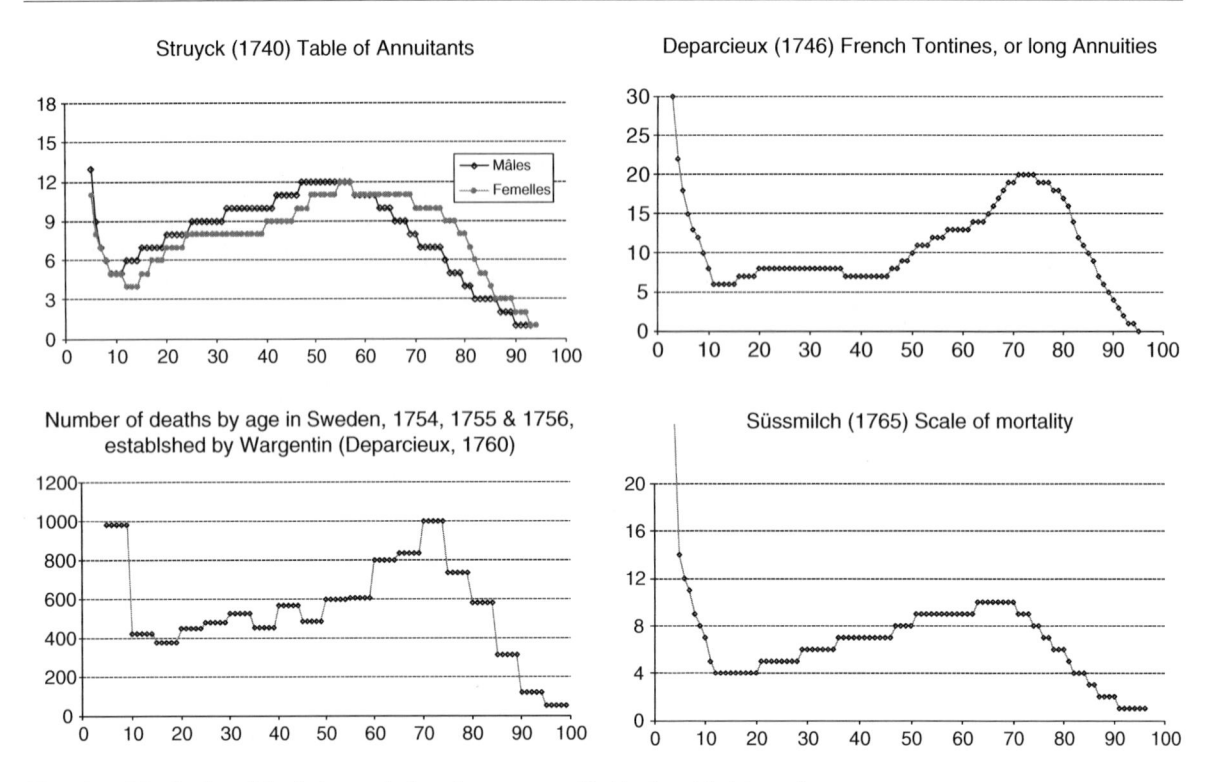

**Fig. 10.4** Distribution of deaths by age in four datasets assembled in the mid-eighteenth century

provide the right concept. Reading the authors of the eighteenth century, we sense an inability to describe adult mortality. For instance, in 1746, Deparcieux clearly distinguishes the median life duration (highest age reached by half of the newborns) from the mean life duration. He proposed calling the latter the common life, missing his opportunity to discover the notion of modal values.[6] Süssmilch may be the one who approached better than Halley[7] the modern idea of statistical distribution when he wrote "Until the 20th year, the number of deaths decreases for increasing right after to the 50th and 60th year; from the 70th year it decreases again until nobody remains to die" (Süssmilch 1741). In 1765, when he published his scale of mortality, he had at his disposal all the datasets accumulated through the eighteenth century, but he did not see the modal values present in his data (see Fig. 10.4).

During the nineteenth century, the mean life duration (i.e. the life expectancy at birth) progressively becomes the most important indicator of the length of life, summarizing the mortality experience of the whole population, even if it cannot be seen as a good indicator of the duration of an ordinary life. Indeed, a correct description of the distribution of deaths by age was not provided until Lexis gave his famous lecture

---

*au delà de laquelle nous n'irons pas, et que la loy de nature a prescrit, pour n'être point outrepassée: mais c'est un sien rare privilège de nous faire durer jusques là »* Montaigne (1595).

[6] « *J'ai dit, page 56 [Essai 1 de 1746], que j'entends par vie moyenne ou commune, le nombre d'années qu'ont encore à vivre, les uns portant les autres, un nombre de personnes d'un même âge, & non le temps au bout duquel il sera mort la moitié des personnes auxquelles appartient la vie moyenne, comme l'ont cru quelques personnes.* » Deparcieux (1746).

[7] Halley wrote in 1693 "From this Table it is evident, that from the Age of 9 to about 25 there does not die above 6 per Annum of each Age, which is much about one per Cent... From 25 to 50 there seem to die from 7 to 8 and 9 per Annum of each age; and after that to 70, they growing more crasie, though the number be much diminished, yet the Mortality encreases, and there are found to die 10 or 11 of each Age per Annum: From thence the number of the Living being grown very small, they gradually decline till there be none left to die; as may be seen at one View in the Table."

**Fig. 10.5** Lexis's normal life duration. Source: Lexis (1878)

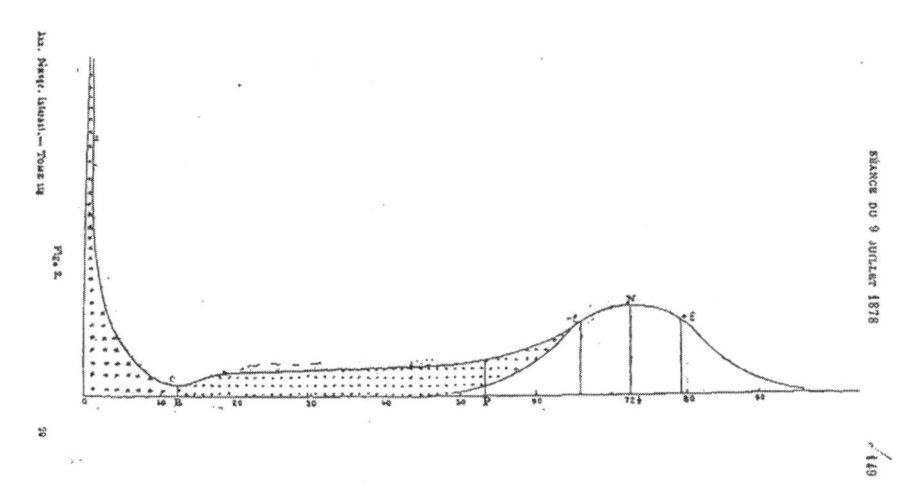

on the common length of life in Paris in 1878. Lexis extends to the duration of life "the outstanding work of Quetelet [who] have told us this interesting fact that individuals belonging to a nationality [i.e. a population] are more or less accurate copies of a model in fixed proportions, and that individual differences from the model, taken in large numbers, are grouped around the mean, according to the well-known law of accidental errors." To determine the typical duration, "that popular opinion believes vaguely be seventy to eighty years", Lexis puts aside premature mortality. Thus, he observes that "in every generation assumed large enough, a certain group will perform in average the normal lifetime with differences conform to the formula called by Quetelet the binomial law." Applied to France, his method shows a concentration of deaths around a centre of density fixed at 72.5 years for men and 72 for women, "representing the normal life" (see Fig. 10.5).

Jacques Bertillon (1851–1922) immediately welcomed this conceptual and methodological advance "[Lexis] established a maximum probability of death in the years immediately following birth, then another up to 72–73 years. Indeed, our results lose much of their precision, when we confuse probabilities so much different as we do by calculating the length of the average life [i.e., life expectancy at birth]. In France it is 40 years or so, though this is just an age when death occurs most rarely" (Bertillon 1878).[8]

Karl Pearson (1857–1936) was also working on the age patterns in mortality. He can be credited with the introduction of the modern term of mode: "We may term that occurrence, which happens not necessarily a majority of times, but more frequently than any other the 'mode'." From that point, the distribution of deaths by age is described with modern statistical terminology. But all authors, from Graunt (1662) to Pearson (1897), assume that ordinary life is unchanged since the time of David. They do not even speak about the possibility of change over time (Buffon 1749; Derham 1726; Maynwaring 1670; Süssmilch 1765).

## The Adult Longevity Revolution

Figure 10.6 displays changes over time in the adult modal age at death (M) for females (upper panel) and males (lower panel) in four European countries from the first year where official vital statistics by age became available in each country through the year 2000. The most frequent age at death (M) for females was 72 years in France in 1816, 76 years in Denmark in 1835, and 68 years in Switzerland in 1876 when national statistics became available in these countries. It was already in the same age range in Sweden in 1751 when vital statistics by age became available at a country level for the first time (see Fig. 10.6). These four observations suggest that going back in the past in Europe it is difficult to find values below 70 years for the modal age at death, implying a kind of floor level for this indicator of the most typical adult longevity. "Threescore years and ten" seems to be a starting point

---

[8] The same type of arguments had been used by Christiaan Huygens in the epistolary discussion he had with his brother about the concepts of average life and probable life.

Upper panel: Females

Lower panel: Males

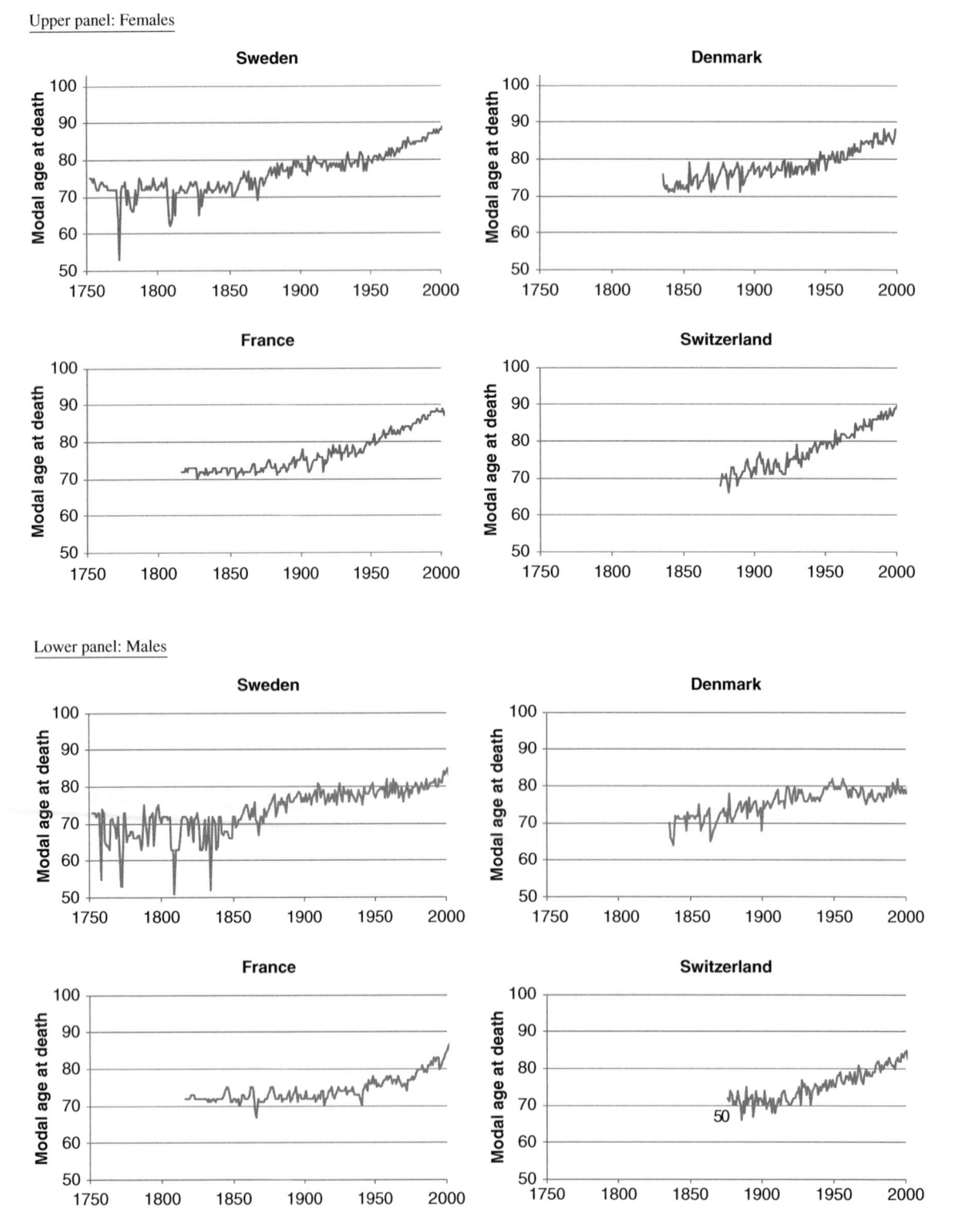

**Fig. 10.6** Increase in the modal length of life (M) in four countries since 1751. Source of data: Period life tables, human mortality database (HMD)

for all series. See lower panel for the corresponding male values.

In Sweden for more than a century, between 1751 and 1875, M fluctuates around 72 years for females, with few values below 70 years and only two values above 75 years, in 1860 and 1863. Then, in about 25 years, the female adult modal age at death increases and reaches the vicinity of 80 years circa 1900, where it stagnates with little fluctuation until 1950. Since that time, M for females regularly increases in Sweden to approach 90 years in 2000. Denmark has larger fluctuations but similar changes over time. Before 1850, M fluctuates a little above 70 years. During the second part of the nineteenth century, it reaches a little below 80, where it stagnates until 1950. Since that time, M for females increases regularly as in Sweden.

In France for 75 years, between 1816 and 1890, M for females is around 72 years with little fluctuation. Then, the female adult modal age at death increases and fluctuates below 80 years for the 30 years from 1920 to 1950; it eventually reaches 80 years, 50 years after Sweden has reached this value. Since that time, M for females regularly increases in France, approaching 90 years in 2000 as in the two other countries. In Switzerland, M for females is still in the vicinity of 70 years in 1876, when the national series starts. Aside

Upper panel: Females

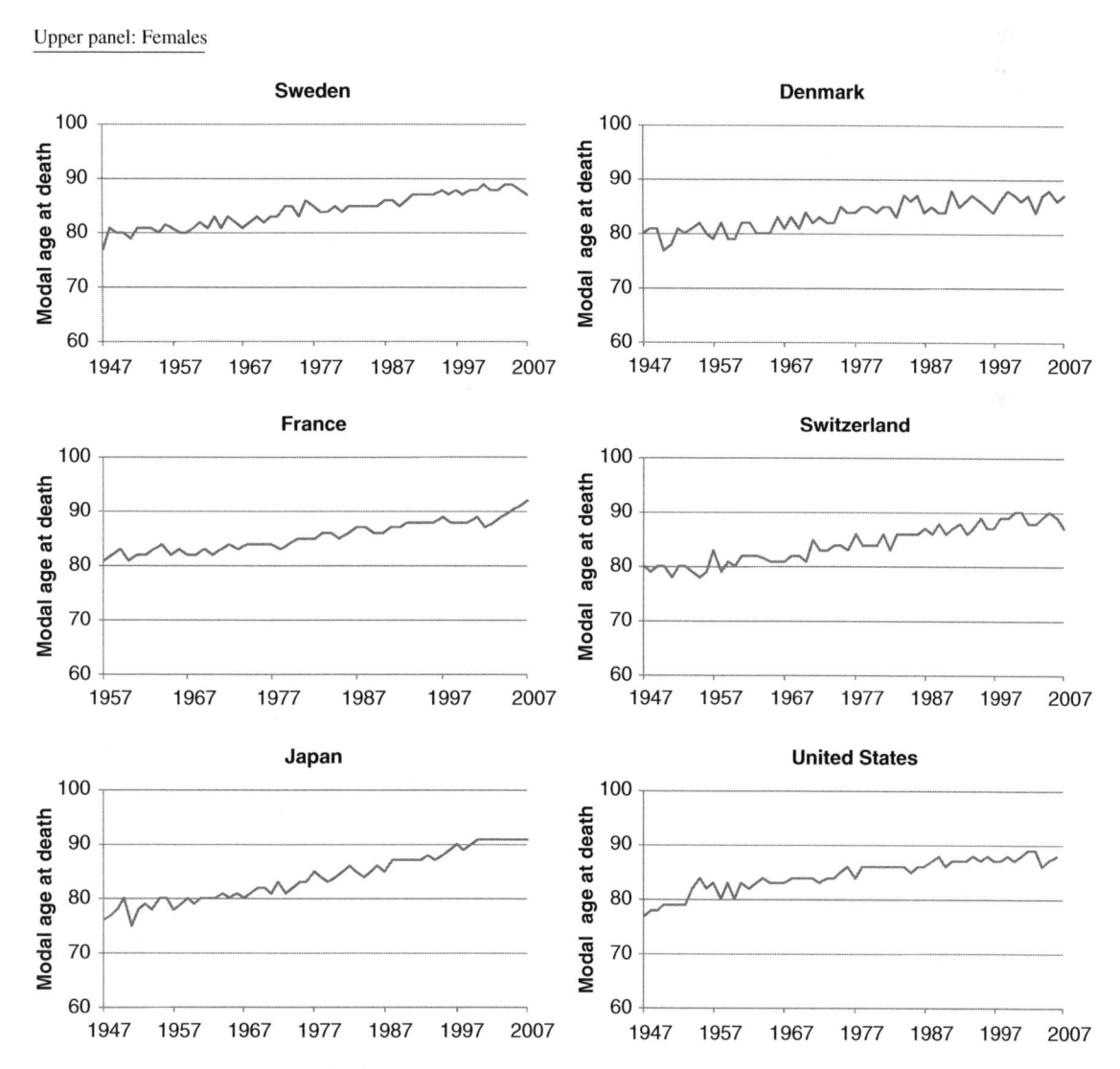

**Fig. 10.7** Increase in the modal length of life (M) in six countries since 1947. Source of data: Period life tables, human mortality database (HMD)

Lower panel: Males

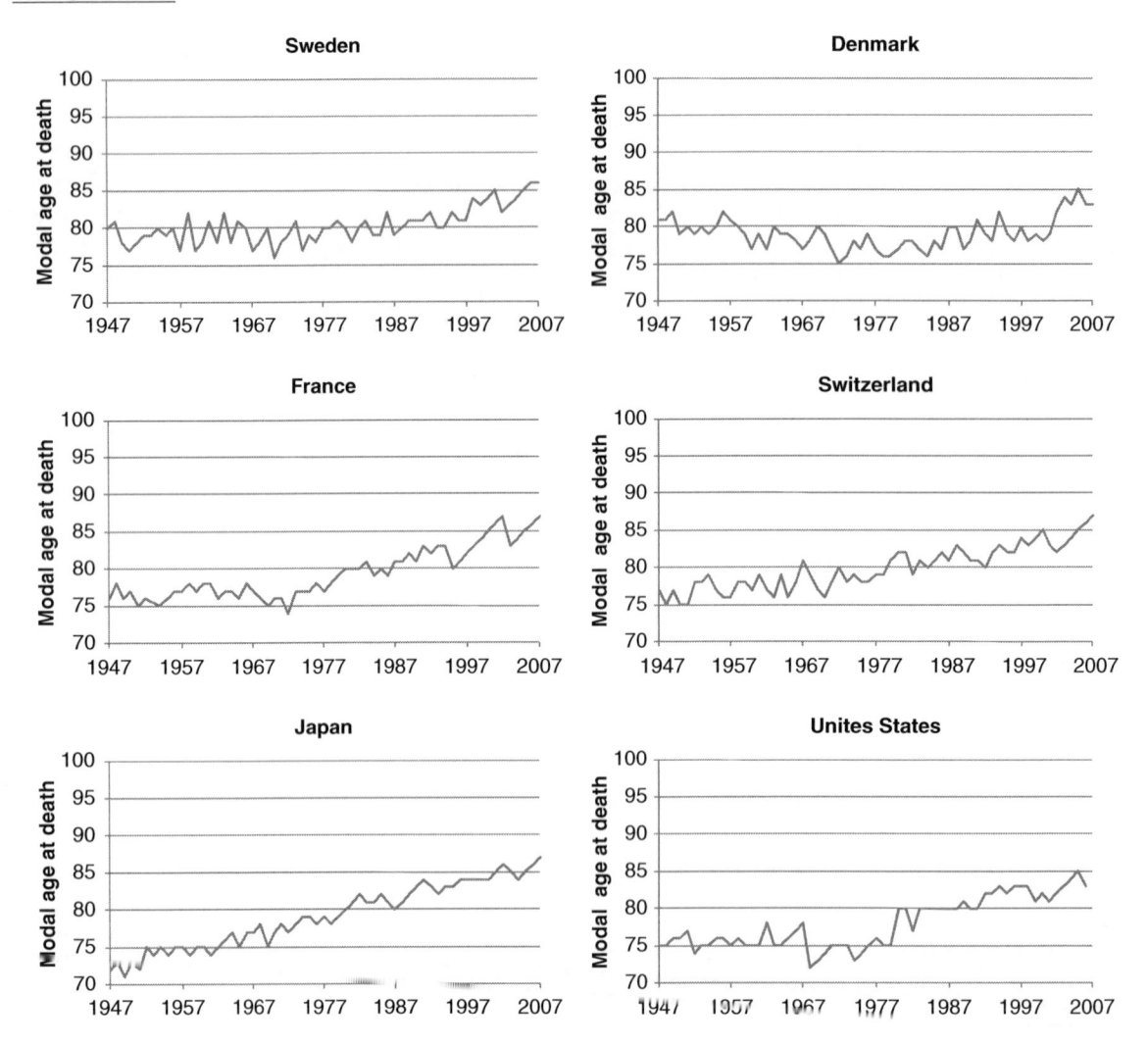

**Fig. 10.7** (continued)

from fluctuations, it increases more regularly than in the three other countries during the last part of the nineteenth century and the first part of the twentieth century and reaches the value of 80 during the Second World War. The adult female modal age at death remains in the vicinity of 80 years in Switzerland until 1950, and since that time M for female regularly has increased, attaining the value of 90 years in 2000.

In sum, these four European countries display the same pattern of change over time after 1950. They seem to share the same earlier female M values, possibly between 72 and 73 years. However, they differ in the timing and in the pattern of change, leading them from the earlier M values to the values that they share in 1950 (circa 80 years). These differences are due to the different timing in the demographic changes in these countries during the nineteenth century. It is a new facet of the first demographic transition. The lower panel of Fig. 10.6 displays the corresponding changes over time for males. Interestingly, males in these four countries present different patterns of change over time in the adult modal age at death, with patterns in the Nordic countries, Sweden and Denmark, different from France and Switzerland.

Figure 10.7 details the changes that occurred since 1947 for females (upper panel) and males (lower panel) respectively, adding Japan and the United States to the four European countries presented above. For females (upper panel), with the notable exception of France, where the adult modal age at death is still increasing in the first years of the twenty-first century reaching the value of 92 years in 2007, the selected countries display a similar pattern of increase in M over the last 60 years. In 1947, right after the Second World War, modal values for females are quite close, spanning from 76 (Japan) and 77 years (Sweden and the United States) to 80 years (Denmark, France and Switzerland). They regularly increase until the end of the twentieth century, reaching a maximum of 88 years in 1999 in Denmark, of 89 years in 2001 in Sweden and in 2002 in the United States, of 90 years in Switzerland and of 91 years in Japan in 2000. After these dates, 1999 in Denmark, 2000 in Japan and Switzerland, 2001 in Sweden and 2002 in the United States, the modal values stagnate near their previous maximum values, i.e. from 88 years in Denmark to 91 years in Japan.

For males (lower panel), with the notable exception of Denmark, where the adult modal age at death only increased by 2 years over the period, and to a lesser extent Sweden with an increase of 6 years only, M strongly increased between 1947 and 2007. In most countries, male M values stagnated at their 1947 level for several years before increasing. Only Japan displays a steady increase from 1947 (72 years) to 2007 (87 years). In 1947, male M values range from 72 in Japan to 81 years in Denmark (75 years in the United States, 76 years in France, 77 years in Switzerland and 80 years in Sweden). Increase in male M values starts in Switzerland in the early 1970s, in France in the late 1970s, in the United States in the early 1980s, in Sweden in the late 1990s and in Denmark not until the 2000s. Indeed, in Denmark M tends to decrease from 1947 to the early 1970s then stagnates at a low level until the 1980s before returning to the 1947 level in the 1990s.

Males and females do not seem to be in synchrony in this longevity revolution in low-mortality countries, which quietly brought typical adult longevity from 72 to 73 years in the mid-eighteenth century, to values today (2007)[9] of between 83 and 87 years for males and 5 years higher, between 88 and 92 years for females.

---

[9] Except for the United States of America, where the last year available when this chapter was written was 2006.

## Emergence of the Oldest Old Population

According to the Lexis hypothesis that adult lifespans are normally distributed when premature mortality is disregarded, an increase in the adult modal age at death means that the whole distribution of adult deaths should move to higher ages (i.e. to the right). This is illustrated in Fig. 10.8 with empirical data from Japan, France, Sweden and Denmark for females covering the period 1947–2007, which distributes by age the 100,000 life table deaths at 20 year intervals. In France, until the life table of 1907 (not shown in Fig. 10.8), less than 2% of females die at age 90 or above, 2% in 1927, 6% in 1947, 12% in 1967, 23% in 1987 and 39% in 2007. This dramatic increase in the number of deaths occurring at age 90 and above illustrates the emergence of the oldest old resulting from changes in the mortality conditions.

On the whole, Fig. 10.8 illustrates three different patterns of change over the last 60 years. In France and Sweden, the increase in the modal age at death is accompanied by an increase in the number of people dying at the modal age; in other words, the distribution is more concentrated. In both cases, close to 5% of females die at the modal age in 2007. In contrast, in Denmark there is little change in the number of people dying at the modal age, about 4% of females for the whole period 1947–2007. In Japan, the number of people dying at the modal age clearly increases from 1947 to 1987, from 2.5 to 4.6% of females, but this concentration does not continue to increase to 2007, remaining at 4.6%.

These different patterns affect the pace of increase in the number of oldest old people across countries as we will see with more detail below in the sections devoted to the number of nonagenarians and centenarians. In this chapter, the terms nonagenarians and centenarians refer to the groups of people between 90 and 99 years of age and 100 years of age and over, respectively. However, in a few specified instances, centenarians correspond to the single age of 100 years. In France and in Sweden, the concentration of deaths at the modal age limits the increase in the number of nonagenarians and centenarians associated with the large increase in the modal age at death (a 12-year increase over the 60-year period in both countries). In Denmark, the relative lack of a concentration of deaths during the period can compensate for the relatively

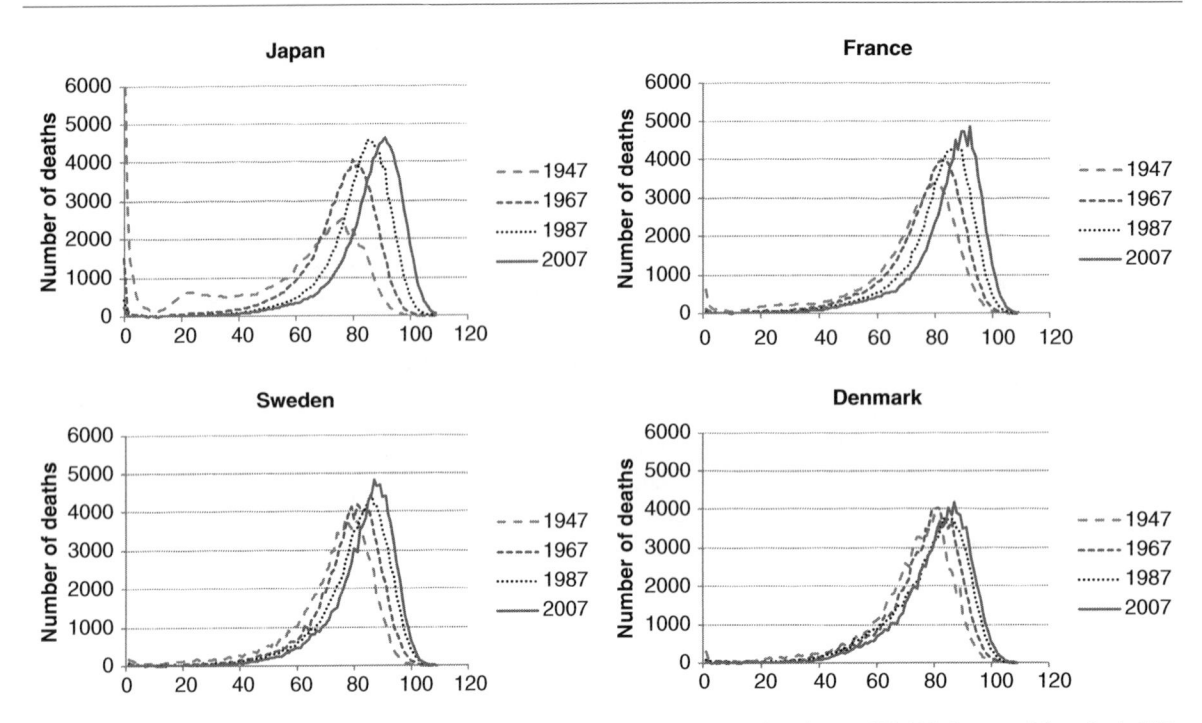

**Fig. 10.8** Change in the distribution of deaths by age in four countries since 1947, females per 100,000. Source of data: Period life tables, human mortality database (HMD)

weak increase in the modal age at death (an 8-year increase over the 60-year period) and lead to a significant increase in the number of nonagenarians and centenarians. In Japan, where the modal age at death increased by 15 years over the period, the same mechanism may multiply the increase in the number of nonagenarians and centenarians.

Lexis and his contemporary colleagues understood the centre of density (Lexis 1878), i.e. the maximum probability of death (Bertillon 1878) or the mode (Pearson 1897) as a constant characteristic of human longevity. In 1939, Major Greenwood (1880–1949) and Joseph O. Irwin (1898–1982) suggested that the adult mode increased over time, but the increase in M was not clearly demonstrated until the work of Väinö Kannisto (1916–2002), published in 2001. Kannisto also showed that the increase in the modal age at death is accompanied by a reduction in the dispersion of ages at death occurring after the modal age. These observations allowed him to formulate the hypothesis that there is an "invisible wall" against which mortality would gradually compress as the modal age increases (Kannisto 2001).

But more recent research following the thread of Kannisto's work suggests that the dramatic increase in the modal age at death in the low-mortality countries after the 1950s may no longer be accompanied by a reduction in the dispersion of ages at death beyond this mode (Cheung and Robine 2007). This scenario, called "shifting mortality", was described by John Bongaarts in 2005. These two current assumptions, "compression" and "shifting mortality", correspond exactly to the two scenarios devised by the Marquis de Condorcet (1743–1794) in 1793: "Indeed the average length of life that must continually increase as we plunge into the future may receive increases according to a law such that this duration approaches continually a limited extent without ever being able to reach it, or according to a law such that the same term may acquire in the immensity of the centuries an ever greater extent than any specific amount assigned as limit." This text is dated October 4, 1793.[10] As an aside, its publication in 1795 sparked the ire of Thomas Malthus (1766–1834) and led him to write his famous *Essay on the Principles of Population*, published in 1798.

---

[10] Condorcet was arrested March 27, 1794, and found dead in his cell the next day.

## The Number of Centenarians

The most spectacular consequence of this silent adult longevity revolution, occurring when almost everybody was looking at infant and/or young adult premature mortality, is the explosion of the number of centenarians. This phenomenon is illustrated in Fig. 10.9 for 14 European countries taken together and Japan. In both settings, the number of centenarians is extremely low in the middle of the twentieth century. For instance, in 1963, when the Japanese Ministry of Health and Welfare started to publish an annual *List of Centenarians*, the total number of centenarians is as low as 154. By 2009, Japan enumerates more than 40,000 centenarians. In 1946, the 14 European countries having available centenarian figures at this date have 1,333 individuals aged 100 or over. By 2006, the same 14 countries have more than 43,000 centenarians. While in both cases, the pattern of change over time is exponential growth as represented in Fig. 10.9, it is clear that the number of centenarians is increasing much faster in Japan than in Europe.

This dramatic increase in the number of centenarians contradicts most writings from the second part of the twentieth century, at least until the 1990s. In the tradition of Buffon researchers stated that there were no more centenarians than in the past as far back as when *Homo sapiens* appeared; only a few individuals could live for 100 years and thus achieve the maximum potential longevity of the *species* (Cutler 1985; Hayflick 1996; Walford 1985). This was one of fundamental arguments put forward by James Fries in 1980 to support his theory of *compression of morbidity*.

While many books have been written on centenarians and almost all classical authors wrote at least some thoughts on the topic, many just copied older documents and opinions and/or completed centenarian lists without questioning the quality of the information. Very few questioned the data quality; Abraham de Moivre was an early exception (Laslett 1999; Thoms 1873). However, modern and thorough studies of available statistics in Denmark (Jeune 1995), France (Robine and Saito 2009) and Japan (Robine et al. 2003) have disclosed an identical pattern of change over time in the number of centenarians to that illustrated for France in Fig. 10.10.

In these three countries when vital statistics by age, including death counts and population estimates, first became available, they recorded a significant number of centenarians. But they also revealed, beyond fluctuations due to small numbers, a decreasing trend over time. In France and in Denmark, where the process spanned over two centuries, we can identify three periods. During the first period which lasted until the 1870s in France, the number of centenarians reported in the national statistical series decreases. During the second period, which lasts until the 1950s, the number of centenarians remains extremely low. According to Bernard Jeune, during this period, centenarians are rare but not exceptional people. Eventually, during the third period, which started in the 1950s in Denmark and France and in the 1960s in Japan, the numbers

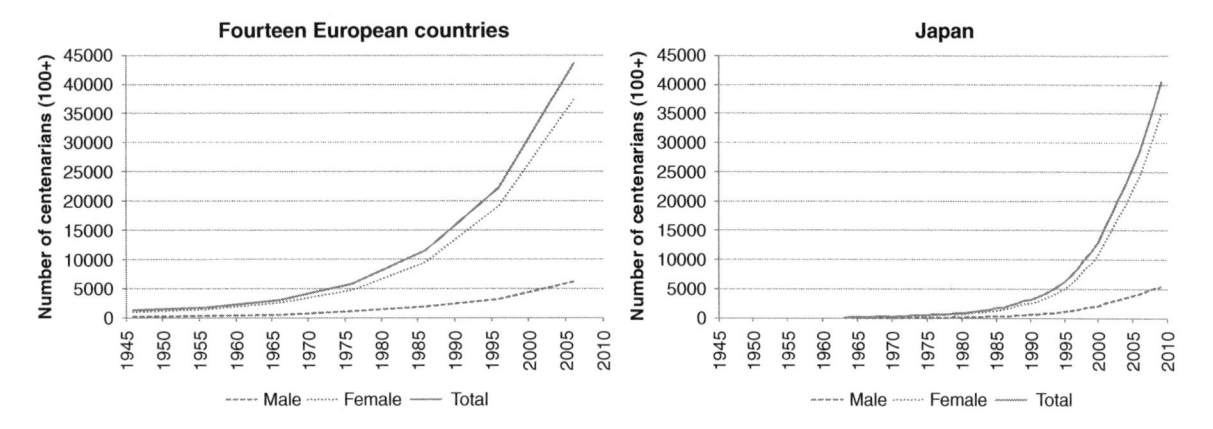

**Fig. 10.9** Increase in the number of centenarians (100+) in 14 European countries since 1946 and in Japan since 1963, by sex. Source of data: Robine and Saito (2009)

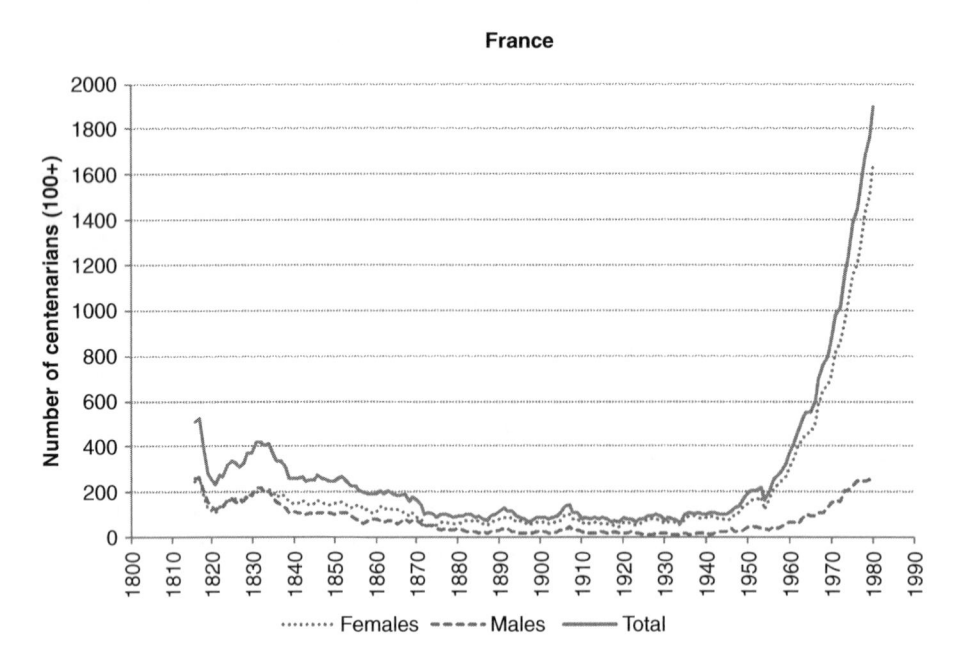

**Fig. 10.10** Increase in the number of centenarians (100+) in France since 1816, by sex. Source of data: Robine and Saito (2009)

start increasing and centenarians are no longer rare. In Japan, where vital statistics became available only in 1899, the first and third periods nearly overlap, leaving little time for a second period with a low reported number of centenarians, but the general pattern is the same (Robine et al. 2003).

The modern interpretation of these patterns is that when statistical series begin, the quality of the data is quite poor, especially for historical data and for extreme values. Then, with the development of the data series, or of the statistical capacity in general for historical series, the quality of the data improves, progressively eliminating erroneous cases. Bernard Jeune concludes that centenarians were exceptional during the nineteenth century, rare during the first half of the twentieth century, and are becoming more and more frequent since the Second World War (Jeune 1995), leading to the current emergence of the supercentenarians, defined as people who have reached their 110th birthday (Maier et al. 2010). The second major feature illustrated in Fig. 10.9 is that most centenarians are women, but beyond the difference of numbers, the pace of increase over time is quite similar for both sexes.

Table 10.2 gathers data for the European countries for which we have data for 2006 (27 countries in total) and Japan. This table summarizes both the main features of centenarians in 2006 and the main differences between Europe and Japan. First, the centenarian (100+) sex-ratios are quite similar in the two regions, 5.9 females for one male in Japan and 6 for one on average in Europe. Second, the pace of increase in centenarians is much faster in Japan than in Europe; the number of centenarians was only multiplied by 2 in Europe between 1996 and 2006, while it was multiplied by 4.2 in Japan. Robine and Caselli (2005) developed the centenarian rate (CR), which indicates the chance of a person aged 60 years becoming a centenarian 40 years later. Third, the chance for a Japanese person aged 60 years in 1966 to have celebrated his/her 100th birthday in 2006 was three times higher than the corresponding chance for a European person. Indeed, 158 out of 10,000 Japanese people aged 60 years in 1966 became centenarians in 2006 versus only 55 out of 10,000 on average in Europe.

Table 10.3 and Fig. 10.11 detail some of these figures for European countries. They disclose an unexpected range of values for the centenarian sex-ratios, ranging from 19.2 females for one male in Luxemburg to 0.9 female for one male in Lithuania. While small population numbers can possibly explain the ratio observed in Luxemburg, local explanations including data quality should be sought for the low ratio observed in Lithuania. Extreme values should always be carefully checked before being used. The pace of

**Table 10.2** Total number of centenarians in Japan and in 27 European countries in 2006 and various centenarian indicators, by sex

| Country | Males | Females | Total | Sex-ratio | Males | Females | Total |
|---|---|---|---|---|---|---|---|
| | Number of people aged 100 years and more | | | | 10 year increase | | |
| Japan | 3,906 | 23,236 | 27,142 | 5.9 | 3.0 | 4.5 | 4.2 |
| European countries | 8,228 | 49,078 | 57,306 | 6.0 | 2.0 | 2.0 | 2.0 |
| | Number of people aged 100 years | | | | Centenarian rate (CR)[a] | | |
| Japan | 1,644 | 9,181 | 10,826 | 5.6 | 49.3 | 259.4 | 157.5 |
| European countries | 3,823 | 20,675 | 24,499 | 5.4 | 18.5 | 86.5 | 55.0 |

[a]Slovenia excluded
Source of data: Robine and Saito (2009)

increase between 1996 and 2006 is more homogenous among the European countries, tending to be faster in Mediterranean countries and slower in Nordic countries.

Figure 10.11 displays the CR for the 26 European countries with the requisite data. The values indicate the chance of a woman who was aged 60 years in 1966 celebrating her 100th birthday in 2006, according to her country of residency. This chance varied from a low of 16.7 per 10,000 in Bulgaria to a high of 156.5 per 10,000 in France, which is about ten times larger. This range indicates the significant European

**Table 10.3** Number of centenarians (100+) in 27 European countries in 2006, sex-ratio and 10-year increase since 1996

| Country | Males | Females | Total | Sex-ratio | Males | Females | Total |
|---|---|---|---|---|---|---|---|
| | Number of centenarians (100+) by January 1, 2006 | | | | 10-Year increase | | |
| France | 1,532 | 10,941 | 12,473 | 7.1 | 2.3 | 2.0 | 2.0 |
| Italy | 1,385 | 7,765 | 9,150 | 5.6 | 2.2 | 2.5 | 2.4 |
| Germany | 1,033 | 7,806 | 8,839 | 7.6 | 1.8 | 2.1 | 2.1 |
| England & Wales | 946 | 7,079 | 8,025 | 7.5 | 1.9 | 1.6 | 1.6 |
| Spain | 1,139 | 4,688 | 5,827 | 4.1 | 2.2 | 2.2 | 2.2 |
| Poland | 420 | 1,544 | 1,963 | 3.7 | 1.9 | 2.0 | 2.0 |
| Netherlands | 195 | 1,203 | 1,398 | 6.2 | 1.0 | 1.6 | 1.5 |
| Sweden | 194 | 1,115 | 1,309 | 5.7 | 1.4 | 1.7 | 1.7 |
| Belgium | 126 | 1,159 | 1,285 | 9.2 | 1.3 | 1.9 | 1.8 |
| Switzerland | 155 | 821 | 977 | 5.3 | 1.9 | 1.9 | 1.9 |
| Portugal | 139 | 731 | 870 | 5.3 | 1.9 | 2.1 | 2.1 |
| Austria | 112 | 666 | 778 | 6.0 | 2.5 | 2.2 | 2.2 |
| Denmark | 99 | 581 | 680 | 5.9 | 1.3 | 1.7 | 1.6 |
| Scotland | 60 | 575 | 635 | 9.6 | 1.6 | 1.6 | 1.6 |
| Norway | 96 | 446 | 542 | 4.6 | 1.1 | 1.4 | 1.3 |
| Lithuania | 243 | 212 | 454 | 0.9 | 3.1 | 0.7 | 1.2 |
| Hungary | 95 | 330 | 424 | 3.5 | 2.9 | 2.0 | 2.2 |
| Finland | 50 | 295 | 345 | 5.9 | 1.7 | 1.6 | 1.6 |
| Czech Rep | 47 | 270 | 317 | 5.7 | 2.2 | 2.0 | 2.0 |
| Ireland | 38 | 223 | 262 | 5.8 | 1.5 | 2.0 | 1.6 |
| Bulgaria | 43 | 163 | 206 | 3.8 | 1.1 | 1.3 | 1.2 |
| Latvia | 22 | 157 | 179 | 7.2 | 1.7 | 1.4 | 1.4 |
| Slovakia | 28 | 117 | 145 | 4.2 | 3.2 | 2.0 | 2.1 |
| Slovenia | 14 | 76 | 90 | 5.2 | 3.6 | 3.3 | 3.3 |
| Estonia | 7 | 72 | 79 | 10.7 | 1.9 | 2.5 | 2.4 |
| Iceland | 9 | 24 | 33 | 2.7 | 1.3 | 1.2 | 1.2 |
| Luxemburg | 1 | 19 | 20 | 19.2 | 0.5 | 1.3 | 1.2 |
| All countries | 8,228 | 49,078 | 57,306 | 6.0 | 2.0 | 2.0 | 2.0 |

Source of data: Robine and Saito (2009)

**Fig. 10.11** Female Centenarian rate (CR) in 26 European countries in 2006, by sex. Source of data: Robine and Saito (2009)

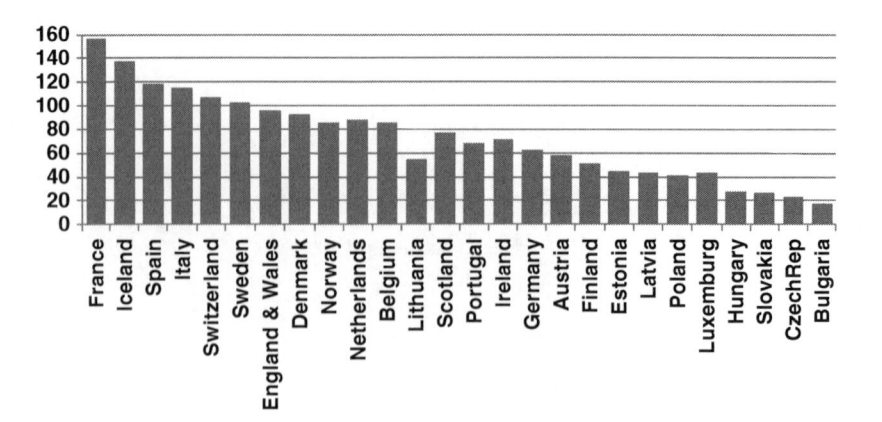

heterogeneity in old-age mortality. As expected, traditional Mediterranean and Nordic long-lived countries cluster on the left of the figure while Eastern European countries cluster on the right.

## Nonagenarians

The last section focused on centenarians (100 years or 100+), but a review of Fig. 10.8 helps to understand that similar results would have been discussed if the focus had been on people aged 90, 95, or 105 years. While the media have noted the increase in the number of centenarians because of the symbolic meaning of the figure "100" and the custom of official celebrations for centenarians' birthdays, the increase in the numbers at all ages 90 and above remains almost unrecognized. The increase in the number of centenarians is only the tip of the iceberg of the silent adult longevity revolution.

## Directions for Future Research

This chapter detailing age patterns in adult mortality has uncovered gaps in our knowledge. For instance, we do not know what the typical adult length of life was before the mid-eighteenth century. We do not know how far we can generalize Swedish observations to other European countries. Some studies suggest that even if the distribution of ages at death was quite flat, a small heaping about a mode can already be observed for the citizens of ancient Greece (Finch 2009, personal communication) as well as for contemporaneous hunter-gatherers (Gurven and Kaplan 2007). These observations, combined with a modern look at the data gathered during the eighteenth century (see Fig. 10.4), suggest that when mortality conditions are good enough to allow a typical length of life to emerge, the mode is located in the age range 70–75. This, however, needs better documentation with data from the past as well as contemporary data from countries and regions at different stages of economic development.

The increase in nonagenarians and centenarians is a new phenomenon and it is proceeding at a different pace across countries. While the gap between Japan and Europe is large, there is significant heterogeneity within Europe. The uncertainty about current figures at regional and global levels is considerable. We have no idea of the number of nonagenarians and centenarians in the vast majority of the countries of the world, especially in less-developed countries.

Future research should give priority to the following four topics:

- Improving data quality and expanding data collection
- Estimating modal values of age at death
- Assessing dispersions around the mode
- Understanding the mortality dynamics leading to the observed changes.

Improving data quality is the basic requirement if we want to extend our study of human longevity across countries. This requires more research on age validation, especially in countries where population or

# 10 Age Patterns in Adult Mortality

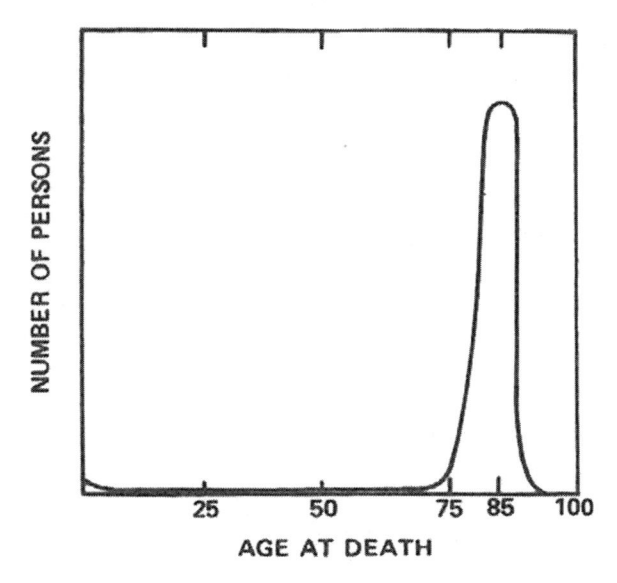

**Fig. 10.12** Mortality according to age, in the absence of premature death (Fries 1980). Source: Fries (1980), Copyright C 1980 Massachusetts Medical Society. All rights reserved

vital registration is quite recent or where migration is high.

Beginning with his initial work on the mode of the distribution of ages at death, Karl Pearson (1902) highlighted that relative to the reliability of life expectancy at birth or the median age at death, the modal age at death displays more fluctuations making its correct assessment crucial. More parametric or non-parametric work on the determination of the modal values would be welcome.

Figure 10.12 illustrates the most interesting proposal associated with the theory of compression of morbidity presented by James Fries in 1980. According to Fries, after elimination of all premature mortality, natural deaths should be normally distributed, as in the Lexis' model, around a mean value of 85 years with a standard deviation of ±4 years. His prediction of 85 years for the mean life duration was much too low, but what about his prediction for the standard deviation? His proposal implied that no one can become a centenarian as almost nobody can exceed four standard deviations from the mean in a normal distribution (i.e. 85 years + (4 × 4 years) = 101 years), excepting exceptional people and in extraordinarily large populations.

Empirical observations suggest that the distribution of adult ages at death tends to be more concentrated when the modal age at death increases. This tendency is illustrated in Fig. 10.13 with data coming from the almost 5,000 life tables gathered in the Human Mortality Database by the year 2006 beginning with the life tables by sex for Sweden in 1751 (Robine et al. 2008). The relationship is not linear and the figure suggests that the standard deviation may approach a

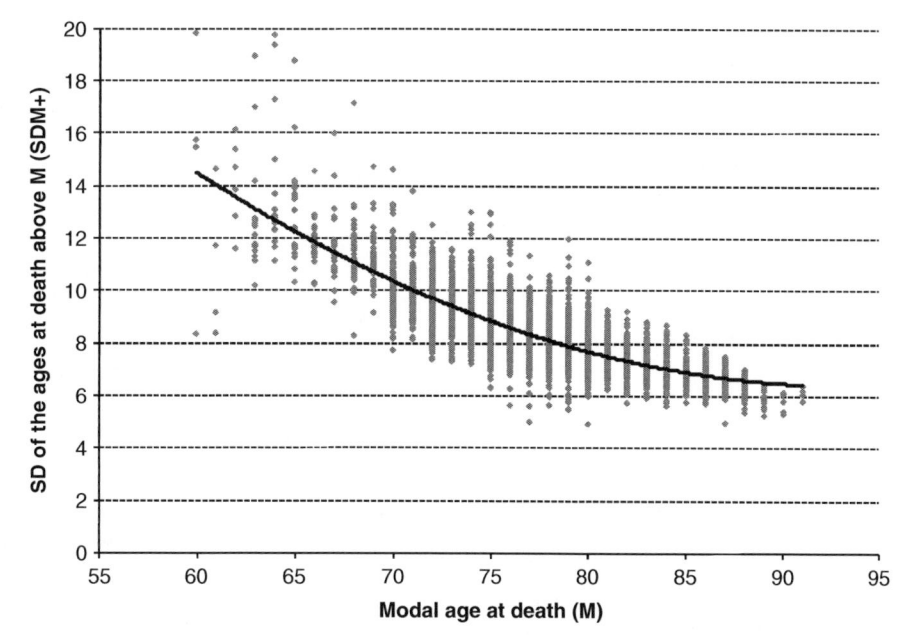

**Fig. 10.13** Correlation between the modal age at death (M) and the standard deviation of the ages at death occurring above M, observed in the 4,981 life tables gathered in the human mortality database (HMD) in 2006. Source of data: Period life tables, human mortality database (HMD)

floor level in the vicinity of 6 years when the modal age at death goes over the age of 90 years. This slowdown in the decrease in the standard deviation when M is increasing will strongly impact the pace of increase in the number of nonagenarians and centenarians. It is the main reason why the number of centenarians multiplied by 4 in Japan between 1996 and 2006 when Europe only experienced a doubling of this population over the same period (Cheung and Robine 2007).

Small changes in the standard deviation of adult ages at death may have dramatic impact on the number and on the ages of the oldest old. More research is needed on indicators of the shape of the distribution and on the dispersion/concentration of deaths. In addition, research on possible changes over time, including simulation and "what if" scenarios would be useful.

Eventually, understanding the mortality dynamics leading to the observed changes in the modal age at death as well as in the dispersion of individual life durations around the central value is the ultimate goal for future research. Work expanding this approach to cause of death or introducing health determinants and risk factors would be welcome. A number of researchers are already providing additional results in these new demographic domains (Canudas-Romo 2008; Cheung et al. 2005, 2009; Cheung et al. 2008; Ouellette and Bourbeau 2009; Thatcher et al. 2010).

## Conclusion

Knowledge on adult longevity was extremely limited before the publication of the work by Wilhelm Lexis (1878). In the late nineteenth century, high infant mortality was the main public health issue, and life expectancy at birth, which averaged all individual life durations into one unique value, provided a reliable and valid indication of the level of high early life mortality. Life expectancy was soon considered the best index of the lifespan (Dublin 1923) and remains today the most popular longevity indicator (Population Reference Bureau 2009).

Like his predecessors, Lexis considered that adult longevity was constant over time. Major Greenwood and Joseph Irwin were the first scholars challenging this idea in 1939. But again, it was probably too early; we had to wait until the work of Kannisto in 2001 to have clearly demonstrated that an increase in the modal lifespan occurred over time. Subsequent work disclosed a silent adult longevity revolution. In a first phase, which accompanied the first demographic transition, the adult modal age at death increased from an initial value, slightly above 70 years, to about 80 years. In a second phase, which started soon after the Second World War in the developed countries, the adult modal age at death steadily increased until the end of the twentieth century, reaching values approaching 90 years for females. The latest observations for the years 2000–2007 in the countries most advanced in the longevity revolution suggest a running out of steam in the increase in the female modal values. Is this the end of the longevity revolution or is it merely a pause before the modal age at death resumes again its course to higher ages, leading the whole distribution rightward. Only time will tell.

## References

Aristotle. 350 B.C.E. *The History of Animal: Traduced by D'Arcy Wentworth Thompson.* Available online at http://classics.mit.edu/Aristotle/history_anim.html

Bacon, F. 1670. *Sylva Sylvarum, or, Natural History in Ten Centuries. Whereunto is Newly Added, the History Natural and Experimental of Life and Death, or of the Prolongation of Life.* Published after the Authors Death by William Rawley, Doctor in Divinity, One of his Majesties Chaplains, 9th ed. London, Printed by J.R. for William Lee.

Bertillon, J. 1878. "[Discussion of Lexis' paper: Sur la Durée Normale de la Vie Humaine et sur la Théorie de la Stabilité des Rapports Statistiques]." *Annales de Démographie Internationale* 2(6–7):460–61.

Bongaarts, J. 2005. "Long-Range Trends in Adult Mortality: Models and Projection Methods." *Demography* 42(1):23–49.

Browne, T. 1646. *Pseudodoxia Epidemica or, Enquiries into Very many Received Tenets, and commonly Presumed Truths*, 3rd ed., 1658. London, Nath. Ekins. Available online at http://books.google.fr/books?id=kSjH4tiEhGUC&dq=Pseudodoxia+Epidemica+or,+Enquiries+into+Very+many+Received+Tenets,+and+commonly+Presumed+Truths&printsec=frontcover&source=bn&hl=fr&ei=W5FyS53qLIi14Qbjy4nYCQ&sa=X&oi=book_result&ct=result&resnum=4&ved=0CBYQ6AEwAw#v=twopage&q=&f=false

Buffon, G.-L.L. (1749). "De la Vieillesse et de la Mort." In *Histoire naturelle*, Vol. 2, pp. 557–89. Paris, Imprimerie Royale.

Buffon, G.-L.L. (1776). "Des Mulets. Histoire Naturelle." In *Histoire naturelle,* Vol. 3(Supplément), pp. 1–38. Paris, Imprimerie Royale.

Canudas-Romo, V. 2008. "The Modal Age at Death and the Shifting Mortality Hypothesis." *Demographic Research*

19(3):1179–1204. Available online at http://www.demographic-research.org/volumes/vol19/30/19-30.pdf

Cheung, S.L.K. and J.-M. Robine. 2007. "Increase in Common Longevity and the Compression of Mortality: The Case of Japan." *Population Studies* 61(1):85–97.

Cheung, S.L.K., J.-M. Robine, and G. Caselli 2008. "The Use of Cohort and Period Data to Analyze Change in Normal Longevity in Low Mortality Countries." *Genus* LXIV(1–2):101–29.

Cheung, S.L.K., J.-M. Robine, F. Paccaud, and A. Marazzi. 2009. "Dissecting the Compression of Mortality in Switzerland, 1876–2005." *Demographic Research.* 21(19): 569–98. Available online at http://www.demographic-research.org/volumes/vol21/19/21-19.pdf

Cheung, S.L.K., J.-M. Robine, J.C.E. Tu, and G. Caselli. 2005. "Three Dimensions of the Survival Curve: Horizontalization, Verticalization, and Longevity Extension." *Demography* 42(2):243–58.

Condorcet, M.J.A.N. de Caritat. ([1795] 2004). "Dixième Epoque." In J.-P. Schandeler and P. Crépel (eds.), *Tableau Historique des Progrès de l'Esprit Humain: Projets, Esquisse, Fragments et Notes (1772–1794)*, pp. 429–59. Paris, Institut National d'Etudes Démographiques.

Cutler, R.G. 1985."Biology of Aging and Longevity." *Gerontologica Biomedica Acta* 1:35–61.

de Moivre, A. 1756. "The Doctrine of Chances: Or, a Method of Calculating the Probabilities of Event in Play." The 3rd ed., Fuller, Clearer, and More Correct than the Former. London: Printed for A. Millar, in the Strand. MDCCLVI – It includes: A Treatise of Annuities on Lives. Preface to the 2nd ed.

Deparcieux, A. 1746. *Essai sur les Probabilités de la Durée de la Vie Humaine (1746) Addition à l'essai (1760) 2003*. Paris, Institut National d'Etudes Démographiques.

Derham, W. 1726. *Théologie Physique ou Démonstration de l'Existence et des Attributs de Dieu, tirées des Oeuvres de la Création. Accompagnée d'un grand nombre de Remarques et d'Observations Curieuses. Traduite de l'Anglois.* Rotterdam, Jean-Daniel Beman. Trad. J. Lufneu [Physico-Theology or, a Demonstration of the Being and Attributes of God, from His Works of Creation].

Dublin, L.I. 1923. "The Possibility of Extending Human Life." *Metron* 3(2):175–97.

Fries, J.F. 1980."Aging, Natural Death, and the Compression of Morbidity." *New England Journal of Medicine* 303: 130–35.

Gaeta, R. and G. Fontana (1776). "Discours Préliminaire en Préface de la Traduction Italienne de La Dottrina degli Azzardi applicata ai Problemi della Probabilità della Vita, delle Pensioni Vitalizie, Reversioni, Tontine, ec. d'Abraham de Moivre." In dir. T. Martin, Arithmétique politique dans le France du XVIII siècle 200. Paris, Institut National d'Etudes Démographiques.

Graunt, J. 1662. *Natural and Political Observations Mentioned in a Following Index and Made upon the Bills of Mortality.* London, T. Raycroft.

Greenwood, M. and J.O. Irwin. 1939."The Biostatistics of Senility." *Human Biology* 11:1–23.

Gurven, M. and H. Kaplan. 2007. "Longevity among Hunter-Gatherers: A Cross-cultural Examination." *Population and Development Review* 33(2):321–65.

Halley, E. 1693. "An Estimate of the Degrees of Mortality of Mankind, Drawn from Curious Tables of the Births and Funerals at the City of Breslaw." *Philosophical Transactions of the Royal Society of London* XVII(196): 576–610.

Hayflick, L. 1996. *How and Why We Age?* New York, Ballantine Books.

Hudde, J. 1671. "Letter to Christiaan Huigens" In la Société Hollandaise des Sciences (ed.), *OEuvres complètes de Christiaan Huygens*, Vol. 7 [Correspondance, 1670–1675, letter # 1839, August 18, 1671], pp. 95–98. La Haye: M. Nijhoff. Available online at http://mathdoc.emath.fr/cgi-bin/linum?aun=001649.

Human Mortality Database. 2010. Available-online at http://www.mortality.org/. Accessed on February 14, 2010.

Huygens, C. 1669. "Letter to Ludewijk Huigens" In la Société Hollandaise des Sciences (ed.), *OEuvres complètes de Christiaan Huygens*, Vol. 6 [Correspondance, 1666–1669, letter # 1776, November 21, 1669], pp. 524–32. La Haye: M. Nijhof. Available online at http://mathdoc.emath.fr/cgi-bin/linum?aun=001649

Jeune, B. 1995. "In Search of the First Centenarians." In B. Jeune and J.W. Vaupel(eds.), *Exceptional Longevity: From Prehistory to the Present*, pp. 11–24. Odense, University Press.

Kannisto, V. 2001. "Mode and Dispersion of the Length of Life." *Population* 13(1):159–71.

Kersseboom, W. 1742. "Deuxième Traité. Vérification de l'Essai." In *Essais d'Arithmétique Politique 1970*, pp. 41–96. Paris, Institut National d'Etudes Démographiqes.

Laslett, P. 1973. *The Earliest Classics*. John Graunt, *Natural and Political Observations made upon the Bills of Mortality* (1662). Gregory King, *Natural and Political Observations and Conclusions upon the State and Condition of England* (1696). London, Gregg International.

Laslett, P. (1999) "The Bewildering History of the History of Longevity." In B. Jeune and J.W. Vaupel (eds.), *Validation of Exceptional Longevity*, pp. 23–40. Odense, University Press.

Le Bras, H. 2000. *Naissance de la Mortalité.* Paris, Gallimard/Le Seuil.

Le Bras, H. 2003."Les Politiques de l'Age." *L'Homme* 167–168:25–48.

Leibniz, G.W. (1680) "Essay de quelques Raisonnement Nouveaux sur la Vie Humaine et sur le Nombre des Hommes." In J.M. Rohrbasser and J. Véron (eds.), *Leibniz et les Raisonnements sur la Vie Humaine 2001*, pp. 105–23. Paris, Institut National d'Etudes Démographiques.

Lexis, W. 1878. "Sur la Durée Normale de la Vie Humaine et sur la Théorie de la Stabilité des Rapports Statistiques." *Annales de Démographie Internationale* 2(5):447–60.

Maier, H., J. Gampe, B. Jeune, J.-M. Robine, and J.W. Vaupel (eds.). 2010. *Supercentenarians.* Berlin Heidelberg, Springer.

Malthus, T.R. 1798. *An Essay on the Principle of Population.* Oxford World's Classics reprint.

Maynwaring, E.. 1670. *Vita sana et longa, the preservation of health and prolongation of life.* See Haycock, D.B. (2006) *"A Thing Ridiculous"? Chemical Medicine and the Prolongation of Human Life in Seventeenth-Century England.* Working papers on the Nature of Evidence:

How Well Do 'Facts' Travel? N°10/06 http://www.lse.ac.uk/collections/economicHistory/

Moheau, J.B. 1778. *Recherches et Considérations sur la population de la France, 1994*. Paris, Institut National d'Etudes Démographiques. Réédition annotée par E. Vilquin.

Montaigne, M.de. 1595. "De l'Aage." *Livre 1, Chapitre LVII in Essais 1854*. Paris, Firmin Didot Frères. Available-online at http://www.voltaire-integral.com/gallica/Montaigne.html

Morris, C. 1751. *Observations of the Past Growth and Present State of the City of London*. London, s.n.

Ouellette, N. and R. Bourbeau. 2009. "Changes in Age-at-Death Distribution in Low-Mortality Countries: A Nonparametric Approach" 162(#110). In *XXVI International Population Conference, Marrakech, Book of abstracts*. Paris, IUSSP.

Pearson, K. 1897. *The Chances of Death*, Vol. 2. London, Edward Arnold.

Pearson, K. 1902. "On the Modal Value of an Organ or Character." *Biometrika* 1(2):260–61.

Population Reference Bureau. 2009. *World Population Data Sheet* (released on August 12). Available-online at http://www.prb.org

Quetelet, A. 1835. *Sur l'Homme et le Développement de ses Facultés, Essai d'une Physique Sociale*. London, Bossange & Co.

Quetelet, A. 1871. *Anthropométrie ou Mesure des différentes Facultés de l'Homme*. Brussels, Muquardt.

Reed, L.J. 1942. *Introduction to Degrees of Mortality of Mankind by Edmund Halley*. Baltimore, MD, The Johns Hopkins Press.

Robine, J.-M. and G. Caselli 2005. "An Unprecedented Increase in the Number of Centenarians." *Genus* LXI(1, Special issue: Increasing Longevity: Causes, Trends, and Prospects, Ed by S. Horiuchi and J.-M. Robine):57–82.

Robine, J.-M., S.L.K. Cheung, S. Horiuchi, and A.R. Thatcher. 2008. "Is There a Limit to the Compression of Mortality?" In *2008 Living to 100 and Beyond Monograph*. Orlando, USA, Society of Actuaries. Available-online at http://www.soa.org/library/monographs/retirement-systems/living-to-100-and-beyond/2008/january/mono-li08-03-cheung.pdf

Robine J.-M., H.C. Petersen, B. Jeune (2009a). "Buffon et la Longévité des Espèces." In M.O. Bernez (ed.), *L'héritage de Buffon*, pp. 257–72. Dijon, Editions Universitaires.

Robine, J.-M. and Y. Saito. 2009."The Number of Centenarians in Europe." *European Papers on the New Welfare, the Counter-Ageing Society; Steps Towards the European Welfare* 13:47–62.

Robine, J.-M., Y. Saito, and C. Jagger 2003. "The Emergence of Extremely Old People: The Case of Japan." *Experimental Gerontology* 38:735–39.

Robine, J.-M., Y. Saito, and C. Jagger 2009. "The Relationship between Longevity and Healthy Life Expectancy." *Quality in Ageing* 10(2):5–14.

Rohrbasser, J.-M. and J. Véron 1998. "Leibniz et la Mortalité: Mesure des « Apparences » et Calcul de la Vie Moyenne." *Population* 53(1–2):29–44.

Rohrbasser, J.-M. and J. Véron 1999. "Les Frères Huygens et le « calcul des Aages »: l'Argument du Pari Equitable." *Population* 54(6):993–1012.

Struyck, N. 1740. "Hypothèse sur l'Etat de l'Espèce Humaine [Inleideing tot de algemeene geografie, beneevens eenige sterrekundige en andere verhandelingen]." In *Les Œuvres de Nicolas Struyck (1667–1769)*, 1912, Traduites du hollandais par J.A. Vollgraff., pp. 165–249. Amsterdam, s.n.

Struyck, N. 1753. "Découvertes plus Détaillées concernant l'état du Genre Humain, basées sur des Expériences. [Vervolg van de beschrijving der staartsterren, en nadere ontdekkingen omtrent den staat van het menschelijk geslagt, uit ondervindingen opgemaakt, beneevens eenige sterrekundige, aardrijkskundige en andere aanmerkingen.]" In *Les Œuvres de Nicolas Struyck (1667–1769)*, 1912, Traduites du hollandais par J.A. Vollgraff., pp. 250–410. Amsterdam, sn.

Süssmilch, J.P. 1741. *L'ordre Divin 1998*, Traduit et annoté par J.M. Rohrbasser JM. Paris, Institut National d'Etudes Démographiques.

Süssmilch, J.P. 1765. *L'ordre Divin 1979*, 3ème ed. Translated by J. Hecht. Paris, Institut National d'Etudes Démographiques.

Thatcher, A.R., S.L.K. Cheung, S. Horiuchi, and J.-M. Robine. 2010. "The Compression of Deaths above the Mode." *Demographic Research* 22(Article 17):505–38. Available from: http://www.demographic-research.org/Volumes/Vol22/17/

Thoms, W.J. 1873. *Human Longevity*. London, John Murray.

Walford, R. 1985. *Maximum Life Span*. New York, WW Norton & Company.

# Chapter 11
# Hispanic Paradox in Adult Mortality in the United States

Kyriakos S. Markides and Karl Eschbach

This chapter provides an update to our earlier review on the Hispanic paradox in adult mortality (Markides and Eschbach 2005). We focus primarily on manuscripts published beginning in 2005. As in our earlier review, we concentrate on mortality at adult and older ages. When relevant, however, we will draw on recent literature examining other outcomes, such as disability, health behaviors, medical conditions, and mental health. While there is a rather extensive relevant literature on infant mortality and low birth weight, that literature is not brought into the discussion, given our objectives, with one exception: the paper by Hummer et al. (2007) on infant mortality is discussed because of its importance to the overall debate in the Hispanic mortality literature.

This review devotes greater attention to the influence of the community context on Hispanic mortality. Because high neighborhood Hispanic concentration appears to be protective of the health of Hispanics, we believe that it plays a role in helping explain the mortality paradox. Below we provide some historical background to the Hispanic Paradox literature followed by a review of recent relevant literature. Our conclusion suggests another "new" paradox also alluded to by us, as well as by others (e.g., Sudano and Baker 2006), namely, that Hispanics as a whole have lower mortality rates but higher disability rates, and generally poorer health than older non-Hispanic whites. This other apparent paradox is discussed in the context of recent evidence in trends in the prevalence of poor health and disability in the general United States population, similar trends in other Western countries, as well as trends in the health of older Mexican Americans using data from the Hispanic Established Population for the Epidemiological Study of the Elderly (EPESE), an ongoing longitudinal study in the Southwestern United States. Since much of what appears to be a mortality advantage among Hispanics (specifically Mexican Americans) can be explained by selective migration, we question the tendency in the literature to speak of an "Immigrant Paradox" since it is widely accepted, and for good reasons, that immigrants to Western societies are selected for good health.

## Background to the Hispanic Paradox Through 2004

The first paper to use the term "epidemiologic paradox" to describe the health of Hispanics appeared almost 25 years ago (Markides and Coreil 1986). It focused on the health of Hispanics in the Southwestern United States who were mostly Mexican Americans. The epidemiologic paradox basically stated that the health status of Hispanics in the Southwestern United States was comparable to the health status of non-Hispanic whites and was considerably better than the health status of African Americans with whom they were more similar socioeconomically. This conclusion was based on reviews of evidence on several health indicators, including infant mortality, overall life expectancy, and mortality from cardiovascular diseases and most major cancers. Hispanics were

K.S. Markides (✉)
Division of Sociomedical Sciences, Preventive Medicine and Community Health, University of Texas Medical Branch, Galveston, TX 77555-1156, USA
e-mail: kmarkide@UTMB.edu

clearly disadvantaged vis-à-vis the general population on other health indicators, such as diabetes and infectious and parasitic diseases (see also, Hayes-Bautista 1992; Vega and Amaro 1994).

As we previously argued (Markides and Eschbach 2005), the existence of a paradox at the time was not based on superior health profiles, but on what appeared to be similar health profiles of Hispanics and non-Hispanic whites. Similarity in health profiles was still paradoxical, given wide disparities in socioeconomic status (SES) and living conditions between the two populations. Similar mortality profiles were evident in data from both Texas (Sullivan et al. 1984) and California (California Center for Health Statistics 1984) and were primarily due to relatively low death rates of Hispanics from major causes of death, especially among men. Explanations offered at the time focused on certain cultural practices, strong families, and selective migration (Markides and Coreil 1986).

It was not long before the evidence began suggesting a mortality advantage among Mexican Americans and among other Hispanic populations, and the epidemiologic paradox began to be commonly referred to as the "Hispanic Paradox" or the "Latino Paradox" (Abraido-Lanza et al. 1999; Franzini et al. 2001; Palloni and Morenoff 2001). Franzini et al. (2001) conducted a comprehensive review over a 20-year period and concluded that the paradox was most apparent in mortality and especially in infancy and in old age. The authors concluded that the reasons behind the paradox remained largely unknown and that there was reason to believe that part of the paradox may result from selective immigration of healthy immigrants and selective return migration to the country of origin by old people in poor health, a phenomenon referred to as "salmon bias." Abraido-Lanza et al. (1999) found that a salmon bias accounted for some but not all the Hispanic mortality advantage.

Because of problems inherent in the official mortality statistics using vital statistics and population enumeration data, namely, misclassification of ethnicity on death certificates, investigators have employed national community surveys linked to the National Death Index because they avoid the misclassification problems, since ethnicity is established up front at the time of the interview. Such studies have tended to find a smaller Hispanic mortality advantage but an advantage nevertheless (e.g., Hummer et al. 2004). Palloni and Arias (2004) used the National Health Interview Survey (NHIS) data and found little support for the data quality, cultural factors, and healthy migrant hypotheses in explaining the Mexican-American mortality advantage. At the same time, they found evidence in support of the selective out-migration or salmon bias hypothesis, which is consistent with the mortality advantage observed in old age among foreign-born Mexican Americans. They also note that the same effect for other Hispanics for whom return migration to their countries of origin was less likely because of their remoteness. They note that the mortality advantage was limited to Mexican Americans and "Other Hispanics" and did not pertain to Cubans or Puerto Ricans.

We previously argued (Markides and Eschbach 2005) that these conclusions were limited by the unknown provenance of "Other Hispanics" as well as by the limitations of the NHIS sample, something also acknowledged by Palloni and Arias (2004). We suggested that using more recent expanded National Longitudinal Mortality Study (NLMS) data would be able to address some of these limitations and would give us a better idea regarding the viability of the salmon bias hypothesis. Furthermore, we noted another approach to estimating mortality rates for older people using data from the Social Security Administration's Master Beneficiary Record and the NUDIMENT file. Using these data, Elo et al. (2004) found a smaller Hispanic mortality advantage than found using vital statistics. The presumed superiority of these data rests on more complete follow-up than is the case with NHIS-MCD and the NLMS.

Thus, the majority of the evidence through 2004 continued to support a Hispanic mortality advantage, at least among Mexican Americans. At the same time, there was one major challenge to the Hispanic Paradox, namely, the Palloni and Arias (2004) analysis which suggested that health selective return migration may explain the mortality advantage of older Mexican Americans. Since our previous review, the literature has continued its attention to the Hispanic Paradox and a number of studies have generated insightful analyses. We review these below.

## Recent Evidence

Our previous review included a table giving age-specific death rates by gender for African Americans, non-Hispanic whites, and Hispanics for the United

States in (2000). These data, which were revised by Anderson and Arias (2003) to adjust for misclassification of Hispanic ethnicity on death certificates, showed a Hispanic mortality advantage for both genders. The overall age-adjusted ratio for Hispanic men relative to non-Hispanic white men was 0.79. Among women, the corresponding figure was 0.76. By contrast, mortality rates for African Americans were higher than rates for non-Hispanic whites at all ages except at ages 85 and over, suggesting a persisting racial mortality crossover (Manton and Stallard 1997; Markides and Black 1995).

Table 11.1 updates the above mortality rates with 2006 data. The table clearly shows a similar picture to that from the 2000 data. The age-standardized rate ratio for Hispanic men relative to non-Hispanic white men was 0.73. The corresponding figure for women was 0.71. Again, African-American death rates were higher than non-Hispanic white death rates at every age except 85 and over, suggesting the continued existence of a racial crossover. The Hispanic advantage among males was present at all ages beginning at age 25–29 and was only slightly higher at older ages. Among females, the advantage began at age 15–19 and was relatively similar at all ages. Thus, unlike the 2000 rates, 2006 rates do not show a marked increase in the mortality advantage at older ages among men. Arias et al. (2008) have recently shown that the adjustment for death certificate misclassification did not significantly affect mortality advantages of Hispanics relative to non-Hispanic whites.

## Adjusting for Misclassification of Ethnicity on Death Certificates

Arias et al. (2010) recently undertook the examination of whether Hispanic origin misclassification of ethnicity or death certificates can explain the Hispanic mortality advantage in another analysis that used the National Longitudinal Mortality Study, which links Current Population Survey data to death certificates for the years 1979–1998. They found that Hispanic origin reporting on death certificates is quite good, with only around 5% higher net Hispanic origin ascertainment on survey records compared to death certificates. Thus, correction for death certificate misclassification had only a small effect on death rates among Hispanics, with the Hispanic age-adjusted death rate increasing from 79 to 83% of the non-Hispanic white age-adjusted rate. Recently released life tables with appropriate corrections for missclassification of ethnicity on death certificates as well as age misstatement at ages 80 and over suggest the existence of a 2.5 year life expectancy advantage of Hispanics over non-Hispanic Whites (Arias 2010).

We previously reviewed the manuscript by Elo et al. (2004), which linked vital registration mortality data at older ages for the years 1989–1991 to population denominators taken from the 1990 census. This analysis applied corrections for a presumed 7% under-ascertainment of Hispanic ethnicity on death certificates (Rosenberg et al. 1999) and for ethnic differences in Census undercount. A Hispanic advantage was estimated for both men and women, which was consistent with other analyses using different data sets. Elo et al. (2004) use of Social Security and Medicare records included data where ethnicity of the population and mortality data came from the same source, thus avoiding inconsistencies found in the vital statistics method.

Eschbach and his research team (2006) examined the influence of ascertainment of Hispanic ethnicity in California and found under-ascertainment is lower among the foreign-born than among the US-born. After appropriate adjustments for foreign-born deaths, foreign-born Hispanics exhibited a significant mortality advantage of 25–30% compared to non-Hispanic whites. US-born Hispanics had only a slight advantage over non-Hispanic whites, which could be explained by misclassification of ethnicity on death certificates. These findings reinforce the conclusion that the Hispanic Paradox of lower mortality than is the case among non-Hispanic whites is primarily an immigrant phenomenon.

## The Salmon Bias Hypothesis Revisited

Turra and Elo (2008) more recently used data from the Master Beneficiary Record and NUDIMENT data files of the Social Security Administration to provide as yet the most rigorous test of whether "Salmon Bias," or return migration of older sick Hispanics to their countries of origin, can explain the Hispanic mortality advantage (see Abraido-Lanza et al. 1999; Palloni and Arias 2004). They obtained results that were consistent with the salmon bias hypothesis in that foreign-born primary Social Security beneficiaries living abroad

**Table 11.1** Age-specific and age-standardized death rates per 100,000 persons for Hispanics, non-Hispanic whites, and non-Hispanic blacks, 2006

| Age | Hispanic | Non-Hispanic white | Non-Hispanic black | Rate ratio Hispanic: non-Hispanic white |
|---|---|---|---|---|
| *Male* | | | | |
| Under 1 year | 640.7 | 621.9 | 1,453.3 | 1.03 |
| 1–4 years | 28.8 | 26.7 | 48.2 | 1.08 |
| 5–9 years | 13.5 | 14.2 | 23.7 | 0.95 |
| 10–14 years | 19.3 | 18.0 | 27.6 | 1.07 |
| 15–19 years | 98.0 | 79.0 | 134.7 | 1.24 |
| 20–24 years | 141.4 | 136.5 | 223.0 | 1.04 |
| 25–29 years | 111.7 | 137.2 | 253.7 | 0.81 |
| 30–34 years | 113.9 | 145.2 | 279.9 | 0.78 |
| 35–39 years | 142.4 | 183.0 | 336.8 | 0.78 |
| 40–44 years | 215.6 | 278.0 | 471.1 | 0.78 |
| 45–49 years | 326.7 | 417.1 | 732.9 | 0.78 |
| 50–54 years | 507.1 | 621.0 | 1,199.1 | 0.82 |
| 55–59 years | 718.7 | 869.7 | 1,662.0 | 0.83 |
| 60–64 years | 1,030.0 | 1,327.5 | 2,355.8 | 0.78 |
| 65–69 years | 1,553.4 | 2,000.1 | 3,190.8 | 0.78 |
| 70–74 years | 2,393.6 | 3,100.3 | 4,451.9 | 0.77 |
| 75–79 years | 3,720.7 | 4,983.5 | 6,441.8 | 0.75 |
| 80–84 years | 5,719.9 | 8,103.3 | 9,165.9 | 0.71 |
| 85 years and over | 9,435.5 | 14,841.1 | 13,403.1 | 0.64 |
| Age standardized | 675.6 | 922.8 | 1,241.0 | 0.73 |
| *Female* | | | | |
| Under 1 year | 538.3 | 503.7 | 1,220.1 | 1.07 |
| 1–4 years | 24.0 | 23.2 | 40.3 | 1.03 |
| 5–9 years | 10.1 | 11.7 | 17.3 | 0.86 |
| 10–14 years | 13.7 | 11.9 | 18.4 | 1.15 |
| 15–19 years | 30.5 | 38.1 | 38.2 | 0.80 |
| 20–24 years | 40.0 | 47.6 | 68.6 | 0.84 |
| 25–29 years | 38.7 | 55.3 | 93.5 | 0.70 |
| 30–34 years | 47.7 | 70.2 | 130.9 | 0.68 |
| 35–39 years | 69.0 | 103.7 | 196.5 | 0.67 |
| 40–44 years | 107.0 | 165.1 | 308.4 | 0.65 |
| 45–49 years | 177.0 | 246.7 | 467.0 | 0.72 |
| 50–54 years | 263.9 | 356.7 | 673.7 | 0.74 |
| 55–59 years | 389.3 | 528.4 | 929.8 | 0.74 |
| 60–64 years | 622.4 | 851.6 | 1,348.2 | 0.73 |
| 65–69 years | 957.8 | 1,306.2 | 1,911.3 | 0.73 |
| 70–74 years | 1,554.8 | 2,107.8 | 2,732.5 | 0.74 |
| 75–79 years | 2,569.3 | 3,400.4 | 4,118.7 | 0.76 |
| 80–84 years | 4,178.9 | 5,718.8 | 6,438.9 | 0.73 |
| 85 years and over | 8,803.5 | 13,150.7 | 12,350.5 | 0.67 |
| Age standardized | 468.6 | 660.0 | 828.4 | 0.71 |

Source: Heron et al. (2009).

had higher mortality rates than foreign-born beneficiaries living in the United States. They also found that a significant number of Hispanic men and women living abroad returned to the United States when their health declined and thus had high mortality rates. The authors suggest that the effect of the salmon bias on death rates is partially offset by the high mortality of Hispanic emigrants returning to the United States.

They conclude that while a salmon bias exists, it is too small in magnitude to explain the Hispanic mortality advantage.

A rather different test of the salmon bias hypothesis was recently made by Hummer et al. (2007) who used data from the US birth and infant death cohort files from 1995 to 2000 to compute age-specific infant mortality rates for infants born in the United States to Mexican-origin women by nativity and in comparison to rates for US-born non-Hispanic white women. The very large sample enabled the computation of stable infant death rates for the first hour of life, first day, and first week. They found that the rates for infants born to Mexican immigrant women were around 10% lower than those for infants born to non-Hispanic white US-born women. Mortality rates of infants born to US-born Mexican-origin women were similar to those of non-Hispanic women and were considerably lower than those for infants born to non-Hispanic black women. Hummer and colleagues concluded that the favorable rates so early in life for Mexican-born women were unlikely to be the result of out-migration of Mexican-origin women and infants.

## The SES Gradient

Turra and Goldman (2007) followed suggestions from the literature on the Hispanic Paradox and examined whether socioeconomic gradients in mortality differed between Hispanics and other groups. They employed data from the 1989 to 1994 waves of the National Health Interview Survey (NHIS) linked to mortality data from the National Death Index (NDI) through 1997. As expected, differences in mortality by education were smaller for Hispanic groups than from non-Hispanic whites. Also, as predicted from the literature (e.g., Markides and Eschbach 2005), a Hispanic mortality advantage was not present at younger ages. A Hispanic mortality advantage was observed in middle age and was largest in old age. The mortality advantage was greater among foreign-born Hispanics than among the native-born, again, especially so in old age. The mortality advantage was most notable among "Other Hispanics" (other than those of Mexican, Cuban, or Puerto Rican origin). In fact, Puerto Ricans had higher mortality rates than non-Hispanic whites, especially at the younger and middle years. The authors underscore an important pattern that has not received much attention in the literature: "The Hispanic mortality advantage pertains primarily to persons of lower SES" (Turra and Elo 2007: S187). This was the case in middle and old age. Hispanics with higher education or income had similar or higher mortality rates than non-Hispanic whites.

Goldman et al. (2006) investigated socioeconomic gradients in health behaviors and health outcomes for the Mexican-origin population compared to non-Hispanic whites. They used data from three studies: the Los Angeles Family and Neighborhood Survey, the Fragile Families and Well Being Study, and the NHIS. They found evidence of an absence of significant educational differentials for a number of health-related variables among adults but also among adolescents and infants in the Mexican-origin population compared to non-Hispanic whites. The absence of such differentials was especially notable in the Mexican immigrant population. The authors suggested alternative explanations, including different SES gradients in Mexico (e.g., higher SES has been associated with more smoking, alcohol consumption, and consumption of high calorie foods), healthy immigrant selection, and negative changes in health behaviors associated with acculturation and assimilation. The above two studies, as well as others, raise questions about the meaning of low education, low income, and low SES in general in the Mexican-origin population, especially among immigrants. We return to this issue in the discussion and conclusion section.

## Mortality at Younger Ages

Eschbach et al. (2007) investigated mortality differences among Hispanics by nativity using Texas and California vital registration data from 1999 to 2001 linked to 2000 US Census population data. They focused on ages 15–44, where little attention has been paid and where consistent Hispanic advantages have not always been found. In addition, causes of death at younger ages may have a different etiology than at older ages where cardiovascular disease and cancer account for most deaths. The results presented by 5-year age groups revealed that for most age groups, mortality rates were lower among foreign-born Hispanics than among non-Hispanic whites. On the other hand, US-born Hispanic men had higher mortality rates than non-Hispanic white men.

Similarly, while a mortality advantage was observed for foreign-born Hispanic women, US-born Hispanic women had similar mortality profiles as non-Hispanic white women.

Further analyses focused on cause-of-death patterns. US-born Hispanic men had a slight advantage in mortality from unintentional accidents and injuries over foreign-born Hispanic men. US-born Hispanic men had higher mortality rates from all other causes of death. Substance abuse and circulatory diseases accounted for the largest share of the mortality difference. Further examination revealed that homicide and alcohol-related mortality was higher among Hispanic immigrant men than non-Hispanic white men. These disadvantages were offset by substantially lower rates from suicide and substance abuse (other than alcohol) among Hispanic immigrant men than among non-Hispanic white men. US-born Hispanic men had higher mortality rates than non-Hispanic white men for both social and behavioral causes as well as chronic diseases. Approximately 78% of the mortality disadvantages were attributed to substance abuse, HIV and other sexually transmitted diseases, alcohol-related causes, and homicide. As with men, death rates of foreign-born Hispanic women were lower than those of US-born Hispanic women as well as those of non-Hispanic white women. These advantages were primarily attributable to social and behavioral causes but also to mortality from major cancers and circulatory diseases. US-born Hispanic women in comparison to non-Hispanic white women had higher death rates from homicide, HIV, and infectious and parasitic diseases. They had lower rates from suicide, substance abuse, and unintentional accidents. As with men, no differences were observed with respect to chronic disease mortality. Thus, the Hispanic Paradox is primarily an immigrant phenomenon among both men and women at younger ages.

One implication of the findings reported in this chapter is that evaluation of net mortality differentials between Hispanics and non-Hispanics should be sensitive to the mix of causes of death that create them. For example, data from the 1980s and 1990s from both vital registration and NDI-linkage reported higher rather than lower Hispanic mortality at younger ages. However, between the period from 1990 to 1993 and 2004 to 2006, homicide mortality rates for adults aged 25–44 dropped by more than 50% for non-Hispanic whites and by nearly 2/3rds for Hispanics in Texas.

While Hispanics remain disadvantaged from this cause of death compared to non-Hispanic whites, homicide has become a considerably smaller influence on group differences. Motor vehicle accident mortality dropped substantially for younger Hispanics over this period in Texas, so that younger Texas Hispanics now report lower rather than higher motor vehicle mortality than non-Hispanic whites in the same state. A corollary implication is that studies based on National Death Index linkage may be challenged with respect to their ability to be responsive to period changes in mortality, because they cumulate patterns of death over time, with limited sample size in any period.

Our previous paper reported and discussed several studies that have used data from a file that linked NHIS survey records to the NDI (Markides and Eschbach 2005). Palloni and Arias (2004) provided the most thorough analysis. Recently, an enlarged public-use file was issued that included more years of survey records (1986 through 2000) and more years of mortality follow up (through 2002). A recent study used the new and expanded file, and corroborated previously reported findings of lower mortality among Hispanics relative to non-Hispanic whites (Borrell and Crawford 2009). As in previously reported research with earlier releases of the same data set, most of the advantage occurs in old age with inconsistent findings among younger people where higher mortality rates were observed at age 25–44 than among non-Hispanic whites, regardless of nativity and age. Also as in previous work, Puerto Ricans appear to have higher death rates than other Hispanic groups. The report did not clarify the relationship of the new data release to the versions used in previously published studies, so it is unclear to what extent the reported findings are independent of those reported from previous releases of the same data. Models reported were either crude—though stratified in broad age bands—or fully adjusted for a large number of covariates, so that it is difficult to assess the degree of concordance of the reported hazard rate ratios with previously reported studies.

The immigrant mortality advantage is not confined to Hispanics. In fact, there appears to be an overall immigrant mortality advantage that may have increased in recent years. Singh and Hiatt (2006) estimated that immigrants had a life expectancy that was 2.3 years longer than that of the US-born in 1979–1981 (76.2 vs. 73.9 years). This immigrant advantage increased to 3.4 years in 1999–2001 (80.0 vs.

76.6) and was evident for cardiovascular diseases, major cancers, diabetes, respiratory diseases, suicide, and unintentional injuries. They conclude that these trends are due in part to growing heterogeneity of the immigrant population, continuing advantages in behavioral characteristics, and migration selectivity. Among men, Asian/Pacific Islander immigrants had the highest life expectancy at birth in 1999–2001 (80.7 years) followed by Hispanic immigrants (79.0 years) and non-Hispanic white immigrants and black immigrants (both at 75.6 years). Among women, US-born Asian/Pacific Islanders had the highest life expectancy (85.0) followed by Asian/Pacific Islander immigrants (85.0) and Hispanic immigrants (84.1). For each ethnic origin, there was an immigrant advantage, except for Asian/Pacific Islanders, which may reflect compositional differences between the native-born and immigrants, especially in old age where most deaths occur. In an analysis of disability rates using 2000 Census data, we noted an immigrant disadvantage among older Asian Americans who were increasingly of Filipino and Vietnamese origins compared to the native-born, a substantial percentage of whom were of Japanese origin (Markides et al. 2007). Singh and Hiatt (2006) found that the largest nativity differences were observed among blacks and Hispanics and in both genders. They conclude that health selectivity as well as behavioral advantages such as lower smoking, obesity, and chronic disease prevalence account for much of the immigrant mortality advantage.

## Hispanic Neighborhoods

In our work on older Mexican Americans using data from the Hispanic EPESE, we found lower all-cause mortality in high Hispanic density census tracts (Eschbach et al. 2004). We concluded that cultural factors may have contributed to the lower mortality in terms of protective support systems available to older Mexican Americans. Similar findings were obtained by LeClere et al. (1997) and Palloni and Arias (2004) using National Health Interview Survey-Multiple Cause of Death (NHIS-MCD) data. The latter used county-level data and concluded that the effect was too weak to account for a mortality advantage of Hispanics relative to non-Hispanic whites. Our previous review suggested that the literature had not identified specific cultural mechanisms that might account for lower mortality (Markides and Eschbach 2005).

We might add that in the above analysis (Eschbach et al. 2004), we also found that high Hispanic ethnic concentration was associated with lower prevalence of stroke, cancer, and hip fracture, all three of which are major contributors to mortality. Other analyses using Hispanic EPESE data found similar results with respect to depressive symptoms (Ostir et al. 2004) and with respect to self-rated health (Patel et al. 2003).

A question raised was whether the above findings on the positive influence of Hispanic concentration were unique to older Mexican Americans. Eschbach et al. (2005) used Surveillance, Epidemiology, and End Results (SEER) program data and US Census Bureau data to examine a potential protective influence of Hispanic concentration on cancer incidence at all ages. They found that the incidence of breast, colorectal, and lung carcinoma decreased with increasing percentage of Hispanics in the census tract. More recently, Reyes-Ortiz and colleagues (2010) found similar findings with respect to cancer mortality. Both studies concluded that the greater assimilation of Hispanics of all ages into ethnically heterogeneous neighborhoods is likely to increase their cancer incidence and mortality in the future. A possible mechanism responsible for this association is changing health behaviors with greater residential assimilation into the larger society.

Reyes-Ortiz et al. (2009) used data from the Third National Health and Nutrition Examination Survey (NHANES) from 1988 to 1994 to more directly assess the association of Hispanic neighborhood concentration and one possible mechanism through which advantages in health and mortality might operate: consumption of foods and nutrients by Mexican Americans. They found somewhat mixed results: higher percentage of Mexican Americans in the census tract was associated with lower consumption of fruits, carrots, spinach/greens, and broccoli, and with lower levels of serum Se, Vitamin C, a-carotene, lycopene, and folate. At the same time, Mexican-American concentration was associated with great consumption of other foods, such as tomatoes, legumes, and corn products that may confer some advantages.

Another analysis of data from NHANES III examined the association of neighborhood SES on fruit and vegetable consumption among non-Hispanic whites, blacks, and Mexican Americans. A notable finding was that the positive association of neighborhood SES and fruit and vegetable consumption was significantly greater among non-Hispanic whites than among blacks and Mexican Americans (Dubawitz et al. 2008), suggesting that non-Hispanic whites are better able to take advantage of the availability of fruits and vegetables in more affluent neighborhoods.

Lee and Ferraro (2007) report an analysis of effects of ethnic isolation for Mexican Americans and Puerto Ricans on two measures of physical health: an index measure of six acute physical symptoms and self-reported limitations of instrumental activities of daily living. The data used are from the Midlife Development in the United States (MIDUS) Chicago sample. Survey cases are linked to 1990 Census data for neighborhood clusters of residence as defined by the Project on Human Development in Chicago Neighborhoods. For Puerto Ricans, increased ethnic isolation is associated with significantly poorer outcomes on both measures. For Mexican Americans, by contrast, a mixed effect is reported. The main effect of ethnic isolation is associated with lower reported disability and physical symptoms that is not statistically significant, given the sample size. However, a cross-level interaction with immigrant generation indicates significant reductions of both measures for generations after the immigrant generation. Lee and Ferraro (2007) suggest that ethnic isolation facilitates additional social support and access to health care, but that only second and subsequent generations living in these environments are positioned to take advantage of these assets. As in Eschbach et al.'s papers using data from the Hispanic EPESE, the study lacks direct evidence as to mechanism, because the reported findings pertain only to cross-sectional associations with census measures of ethnic composition.

A question that has arisen in the literature is whether it is Hispanic concentration in the neighborhood that affords protection or whether it is the proportion of immigrants. Osypuk et al. (2009) recently attempted to delineate the influence of "immigrant enclaves" on the health of Hispanics and Chinese Americans using data from the Multi-Ethnic Study of Atherosclerosis (MESA). They suggested that there are various mechanisms through which neighborhood characteristics such as immigrant composition can influence health outcomes over and above individual characteristics. For example, immigrant enclaves' social networks and social control mechanisms may promote healthy behaviors (see Portes and Rumbaut 2006), and ethnic enclaves may insulate immigrants from discriminatory exposures. Other structural factors may include access to healthy ethnic food, but also may include the deleterious effects of poverty and unsafe living environments. Hispanic participants in the MESA were recruited from Los Angeles, New York, and St. Paul. Chinese-American participants were recruited from Los Angeles and Chicago. Participants were aged 45–84 at baseline in 2000. After adjusting for individual characteristics and neighborhood poverty, census tract proportion of immigrants was associated with a lower consumption of high-fat foods among Hispanics and Chinese Americans. In contrast, among Hispanics, immigrant concentration was associated with lower levels of physical activity. Subjects residing in heavily immigrant neighborhoods reported greater availability of healthy food but also poorer walkability, recreational exercise resources, safety, lower social cohesion, and lower civic engagement. The authors concluded that some aspects of ethnic enclaves might be beneficial to health while others may not.

The above studies provide at best mixed evidence that high Hispanic concentration in neighborhoods confers advantages in health behaviors that might lead to better health and lower mortality among Mexican Americans. No studies have been reported that corroborate Eschbach et al.'s finding of lower all-cause mortality in high-density Hispanic census tracts, raising questions about whether the effect is specific to that sample. Certainly, as Palloni and Arias (2004) concluded, there is no evidence of a beneficial effect of ethnic co-residence of sufficient strength to support attributing a significant portion of the reduced mortality of Hispanics to cultural characteristics associated with residence in barrio neighborhoods. We will return to other possible protective mechanisms later on in the discussion and conclusion section.

## Biological Risk Profiles

Crimmins et al. (2007) reviewed the literature on the Hispanic Paradox and noted, as have we and others, that the majority of the evidence has identified a Hispanic advantage principally in mortality especially among immigrants. They undertook analysis that went beyond mortality statistics and self-reported data to examine whether evidence of a Hispanic Paradox is present in biological risk factors for poor health, such as blood pressure, blood glucose, and cholesterol. They employed data from the NHANES for 1999–2002 on adults aged 40 and over to compare blood pressure and metabolic and inflammatory risk profiles for non-Hispanic whites, blacks, US-born Hispanics, foreign-born Hispanics, and Hispanics of Mexican origin.

Their results showed that the risk profiles for Hispanics were more favorable than those for blacks, but less favorable than those for non-Hispanic whites. After adjusting for SES, the differences between foreign-born Hispanics and non-Hispanic whites became non-significant. However, US-born Mexican Americans continued to have worse biological risk profiles than did non-Hispanic whites or Mexican immigrants. They conclude that such results question the notion of a Hispanic Paradox in biological risk profiles. At the same time, the similar Mexican immigrant and non-Hispanic white profiles was consistent with a migration selection hypothesis and to some extent with differences in certain health behaviors. They also conclude that biological measures are more amenable to interventions and help researchers avoid pitfalls of self-report as well as of mortality data.

Finch et al. (2009) recently added to the Mexican immigrant health literature by examining an index of cumulative biological risk using NHANES III data. They found that recent immigrants were the most advantaged on this and other measures, followed by long-term immigrants, and subsequently by US-born Mexican Americans, who appear to have the poorest health. Such findings based on biological measures add new information to reports based on such measures as mortality and self-reports of health, and corroborate the healthy immigrant advantage found in numerous studies (see, for examples, Abraido-Lanza et al. 2005; Akresh and Frank 2008; Bates et al. 2008; Cho et al. 2004; Jerant et al. 2008; Lara et al. 2005; Vega et al. 2009). The same relationship has been observed with respect to mental health. For example, Escobar et al. (2000) reviewed five large studies which suggested that immigrants from Mexico have better mental health than US-born Mexican Americans. Explanations offered were similar to those found in the physical health literature, namely, migration selection and strong family support.

## Migration Data from Mexico

While the majority of the data relevant to the Hispanic Paradox dialogue are based on data collected in the United States, there are now a few analyses that have examined data from Mexico. Crimmins et al. (2005), in addition to using data from the NHANES for 1999–2002, employed data from the baseline of the Mexican Health and Aging Study (MHAS) collected in 2001 to examine objective indicators of health selection of migrants to the United States from Mexico as well as return migrants from the United States back to Mexico. They found that Mexican immigrants to the United States are selected for higher education and for greater height, which suggests better childhood nutrition and health. At the same time, return migrants to Mexico are shorter than migrants who stay in the United States, suggesting the possible existence of a salmon bias. In addition, return migrants had similar self-reported health as people of the same age in Mexico but were less likely to report hypertension. The authors conclude that their data support the role of health selection in the Hispanic Paradox for Mexican Americans living in the United States.

Additional analyses of MHAS data by Wong and Palloni (2009) question the extent to which a significant salmon bias is reflected in return migration from the United States to Mexico. Specially, while there is a considerable return migration to Mexico, the data show that the vast majority of return migrants are younger. MHAS and other data such as from the Hispanic EPESE suggest that very few older Mexican Americans return to Mexico in their older years, primarily because their children live in the United States (Markides et al. 2010).

Another valuable resource that is enabling additional insights into the Hispanic Paradox is the Mexican Family Life Survey. Rubalcava et al. (2008) examined the health of immigrants to the United States between the 2002 and the 2005 surveys. They employed data on 6,446 respondents aged 15–29 in 2002, some of whom moved to the United States during the next 3 years, to find that health significantly predicted migration among females and rural males. But the associations were weak, with considerable variation in the estimates between males and females, and urban and rural dwellers. Health measures included such objective measures as height, weight, and blood pressure, in addition to self-reported measures. At this point, however, these results are limited by the small number of migrants: 113 rural men, 87 urban men, 90 rural women, and 55 urban women. Another issue is the youth of the sample, when a significant prevalence of health problems is unlikely to occur.

## Convergence to Native Levels in the United States, Canada, and Australia

We saw earlier that health migrant selection is not unique to Mexican Americans and other Hispanics (Singh and Hiatt 2006). Other analyses with US data on immigrant health corroborate the findings on Hispanic populations and question whether the Paradox is unique to Hispanics and whether the Hispanic Paradox is a paradox at all. Antecol and Bedard (2006) examined whether and how time in the United States leads to a convergence in the health of immigrants to American health status levels. They used data from the 1989 to 1996 NHIS and focused on obesity, a key mechanism for convergence often discussed in the literature but rarely tested directly. They found that immigrants enter the United States with average Body Mass Index (BMI) rates that are lower than those of native-born Americans. They found that female immigrants converge to native BMI rates within 10 years, while men close approximately one third of the gap within 15 years, suggesting that the immigrant health advantage dissipates with time since immigration, especially among women (see earlier analyses by House et al. 1990; Stephen et al. 1994).

The immigrant health advantage and subsequent convergence to native levels has also been observed in the two other major immigrant destinations: Canada (Chen et al. 1996) and Australia (Donovan et al. 1992). Markides (2001) provides additional discussion of these and other studies.

There is more recent evidence from both Canada and Australia of the presence of a "healthy immigrant" effect and subsequent convergence to native levels. For Canada, McDonald and Kennedy (2004) used multiple cross-sections of the National Population Health Survey (NPHS), which showed that immigrants, especially recent immigrants, are less likely than the native-born to have ever been smokers. This was especially the case for non-European-origin immigrants. At the same time, non-European-origin immigrants were less physically active, which has also been found for Hispanic immigrants to the United States (see earlier). It was also found that health levels of immigrants tend to converge to Canadian-born levels within approximately 10 years, a pattern also present in the United States as discussed earlier (Antecol and Bedard 2006). The data showed that a healthy immigrant effect is present in both men and women and for the incidence of chronic conditions. McDonald and Kennedy (2004) found that convergence to native levels over time reflects actual convergence in physical health rather than convergence in screening and diagnosis of existing health problems.

Recent data from Australia corroborate the above findings from Canada as well as those for the United States discussed earlier. Biddle et al. (2007) used data on immigrants to Australia aged 20–64, which showed that immigrants have better health than the Australian-born. Immigrants from non-English-speaking Europe and from non-European countries had better health upon arrival than those from English-speaking countries, such as the United Kingdom and Canada. They also found that within 10–20 years, the health of immigrants converges to the health of native-born Australians.

## Discussion and Conclusion

We have updated our previous review (Markides and Eschbach 2005) with more recent evidence relevant to the ongoing dialog regarding the Hispanic Paradox in adult mortality. Immigrant health selection, most relevant to the Mexican-origin population of a mortality or health advantage, remains the most viable explanation. We also argued that the Hispanic/Mexican-origin advantage is not unique to the Hispanic population in the United States in that it is present among most immigrants to the United States as well as immigrants, especially those from non-Western-origins, to Canada and Australia, the two other traditionally major destinations of immigrants. Moreover, we noted that the evidence from all three countries suggests the existence of convergence to native levels within 10–20 years of arrival.

Since our previous review (Markides and Eschbach 2005), there have been two major analyses relevant to the "salmon bias" or return migration of unhealthy Hispanics to the countries of origin. Turra and Elo (2008) found that indeed there is evidence of a salmon bias among Medicare beneficiaries, but the bias is too small to explain the Hispanic mortality advantage. In a rather different test of the salmon bias hypothesis, Hummer et al. (2007) found mortality advantages in infant deaths born to Mexican-born mothers in the United States in the first few hours or days of life, a time of highly unlikely migration of mothers and infants back to Mexico. There are also data from the MHAS, which suggest that very few older Mexican immigrants to the United States return to Mexico in old age (Wong and Palloni 2009), most likely because their children live in the United States (Markides et al. 2010).

So if there is a mortality advantage of Hispanics, especially in their older years, the search for mechanisms must continue. We suggested that one area of fruitful inquiry is communities of high Hispanic concentrations, which might confer some health advantages. Advantages appear to be mostly confined to immigrants, which raise questions regarding specific mechanisms. Limited available evidence does not support that advantages are due to dietary practices or health behaviors overall, at least not to the point of explaining health or mortality advantages over and above immigrant health selection. There are suggestions of cultural supports that alleviate stress in immigrant communities, but direct tests are lacking.

With respect to mortality and health of Hispanics, and more specifically those of Mexican origin, the literature suggests a much weaker socioeconomic gradient among Hispanics in both mortality (Turra and Goldman 2007) and general health (Goldman et al. 2006). These and earlier findings suggest that the meaning of low education, social class, occupational status, and overall SES among Mexican and other Hispanic immigrants must be scrutinized. As originally conceived, the Hispanic Epidemiologic Paradox suggested that the health of Hispanics was similar (or closer to) the health of non-Hispanic whites despite their disadvantaged SES, and superior to the health of African Americans with whom they shared similar SES and living conditions in general (Markides and Coreil 1986). All this evidence raises questions about whether low social class and SES are less detrimental among Mexican-origin individuals than they are among African Americans or even non-Hispanic whites. Poor Mexican immigrants appear to be more socially engaged than other low-income groups. Most are employed, some with multiple jobs, many send remittances to family members in Mexico, and may benefit from such engagement despite living in substandard and unsafe environments. Low income and SES likely have different meanings for African Americans and non-Hispanic whites, the latter often drifting to lower SES and poverty because of psychosocial and environmental forces. Certainly, more inquiry into the above ideas and speculation is warranted.

Finally, there appears to be substantial evidence that the health of Hispanic and other immigrants convergences to that of the native-born in the United States. The same appears to take place in Canada and Australia, the two other traditional immigrant destinations. More attention to this recurring pattern is likely to lead to valuable information relevant to needed research, as well as health policy interventions to stem the apparent decline in the health of immigrants in the host countries. Clearly, Mexican immigrants arrive in the United States relatively healthy, and by the time they become old, they experience high rates of disability for a number of reasons alluded to earlier, including a lifetime of substandard medical care (Markides et al. 2009). We have described this as another "epidemiologic paradox" (Markides and Eschbach 2005; see also Sudano and Baker 2006), because the mortality advantage is the highest in old age.

The above evidence begs the question whether the Hispanic Paradox is a paradox at all, given that similar mortality and health advantages are present in other immigrant populations and in other traditionally immigrant destinations. With increasing globalization and increasing immigration from non-Western origins to more developed societies, it is paramount that more attention be paid to how these trends influence public health outcomes in both Western and non-Western countries where immigrants are likely to continue to flock and non-Western countries where most immigrants originate.

# References

Abraido-Lanza, A., M.T. Chao, and K.R. Florez. 2005. "Do Health Behaviors Decline With Greater Acculturation? Implications for the Latino Mortality Paradox." *Social Science and Medicine* 61:1243–55.

Abraido-Lanza, A.F., B.P. Dohrenwend, D.S. Ng-Mak, and J.B. Turner. 1999. "The Latino Mortality Paradox: A Test of the 'Salmon Bias' and Healthy Migrant Hypotheses." *American Journal of Public Health* 89:1534–48.

Akresh, I.R. and R. Frank. 2008. "Health Selection Among Immigrants." *American Journal of Public Health* 98:2058–64.

Anderson, R.N. and E. Arias. 2003. "The Effect of Revised Populations on Mortality Statistics for the United States, 2000." *National Vital Statistics Reports* 51(9):1–24.

Antecol, H. and K. Bedard. 2006. "Unhealthy Assimilation: Why Do Immigrants Converge to American Health Status Levels?" *Demography* 43:337–60.

Arias, E. 2010. United States Life Tables by Hispanic Origin. National Center for Health Statistics. Vital and Health Statistics, 2(152).

Arias, E., K. Eschbach, W.S. Schauman, E.L. Bachlund, and Sorlie, P.D. 2010. "Is the Hispanic Mortality Advantage a Data Artifact?" *American Journal of Public Health*, 100:171–77.

Arias, E., W.S. Schauman, K. Eschbach, P.D. Sorie, and E. Backlund. 2008. "The Validity of Race and Hispanic Origin Reporting on Death Certificates in the United States. National Center for Health Statistics." *Vital Health Statistics* 2(148):1–23.

Bates, L.M., D. Acevedo-Garcia, M. Alegria, and N. Krieger. 2008. "Immigration and Generational Trends in Body Mass Index and Obesity in the United States: Results of the National Latino and Asian American Survey, 2002–2003." *American Journal of Public Health* 98:70–77.

Biddle, N., S. Kennedy, and J.T. McDonald 2007. "Health Assimilation Patterns amongst Australian Immigrants." *The Economic Record* 83:16–30.

Borrell, L.N. and N.D. Crawford. 2009. "All-Cause Mortality among Hispanics in the United States: Exploring Heterogeneity by Nativity Status, Country of Origin, and Race in the National Health Interview Survey-Linked Mortality Files." *Annals of Epidemiology* 19:336–43.

California Center for Health Statistics. 1984. "Health Status of Californians by Race/Ethnicity, 1970 and 1980." *Data Matters*, No. 84-02085, State of California Health and Welfare Agency, Sacramento.

Chen, J., E. Ng, and R. Wilkins. 1996. "The Health of Canada's Immigrants in 1994–95." *Health Reports* 7(4):33–45.

Cho, Y., W.P. Frisbie, and R.G. Rogers. 2004. "Nativity, Duration of Residence, and the Health of Hispanic Adults in the United States." *International Migration Review* 38:184–211.

Crimmins, E.M., J.K. Kim, D.W. Alley, A. Karlamanga, and T. Seeman. 2007. "Hispanic Paradox in Biological Risk Profiles." *American Journal of Public Health* 97:1305–10.

Crimmins, E.M., B.J. Soldo, J.K. Kim, and D.E. Alley. 2005. "Using Anthropometric Indicators for Mexicans in the United States and Mexico to Understand the Selection of Migrants and the 'Hispanic Paradox'." *Social Biology* 52:164–77.

Donovan, J.M., E. Espainget, C. Merton, and M. van Ommeren (eds.). 1992. "A Health Profile." *Immigrants in Australia Australian Institute of Health and Welfare, Ethnic Health Series* (1), Canberra, Australia, AGPS.

Dubowitz, T., M. Heron, C.E. Bird, N. Lurie, B.K. Finch, R. Basurdo-Davila, L. Hale, and J.J. Escaru. 2008. "Neighborhood Socioeconomic Status and Fruit and Vegetable Intake among Whites, Blacks, and Mexican Americans in the United States." *American Journal of Clinical Nutrition* 87:1883–91.

Elo, I.T., C.M. Turra, B. Kestenbaum, and R.F. Ferguson. 2004. "Mortality Among Elderly Hispanics in the United States: Past Evidence and New Results." *Demography* 41:109–28.

Eschbach, K., Y.F. Kuo, and J.S. Goodwin. 2006. "Ascertainment of Hispanic Ethnicity on California Death Certificates: Implications for the Explanation of the Hispanic Mortality Advantage." *American Journal of Public Health* 96:2209–15.

Eschbach, K., J.D. Mahnken, and J.S. Goodwin 2005. "Neighborhood Concentration and Incidence of Cancer Among Hispanics in the United States." *Cancer* 103:1036–44.

Eschbach, K.S., G.V. Ostir, K.V. Patel, K.S. Markides, and J.S. Goodwin. 2004. "Neighborhood Context and Mortality Among Older Mexican Americans: Is There a Barrio Advantage?" *American Journal of Public Health* 94(10):1807–12.

Eschbach, K., J.P. Stimpson, Y.F. Kuo, and J.S. Goodwin. 2007. "Mortality of Foreign-Born and US-Born Hispanic Adults at Younger Ages: A Re-Examination of Recent Patterns." *American Journal of Public Health* 97:1297–304.

Escobar, J.I., C.H. Nervi, and M.A. Gara. 2000. "Immigration and Mental Health: Mexican Americans in the United States." *Harvard Review of Psychiatry* 8(2):64–72.

Finch, B.K., D.P. Do, R. Frank, and T. Seeman 2009. "Could 'Acculturation' Effects be Explained by Latent Health Disadvantage Among Mexican Immigrants?" *International Migration Review* 43(3):471–95.

Franzini, L., J.C. Ribble, and A.M. Keddie. 2001. "Understanding the Hispanic Paradox." *Ethnicity and Disease* 11:496–518.

Goldman, N., R.T. Kimbro, C.M. Turra, and A.R. Pebley. 2006. "Another Hispanic Paradox: Differences in Socioeconomic Gradients in Health Between White and Mexican-Origin Populations." *American Journal of Public Health* 96(12):2186–93.

Hayes-Bautista, D. 1992. "Latino Health Indicators and the Underclass Model: From Paradox to New Policy Models." In A. Furino (ed.), *Health Policy and the Hispanic*, pp. 32–47. Boulder, CO, Westview Press.

Heron, M.P., D.L. Hoyert, S.L. Murphy, J.Q. Xu, K.D. Kochanek, and B. Tejada-Vera. 2009. "Deaths: Final Data for 2006." *National Vital Statistics Reports* 57(14). Hyattsville, MD, National Center for Health Statistics.

House, J.S., R.C. Kessler, A.R. Herzog, R.P. Mero, A.M. Kinney, and M.J. Breslow. 1990. "Age, Socioeconomic Status and Health." *The Milbank Quarterly* 68:383–411.

Hummer, R.A., M.R. Benjamins, and R.G. Rogers. 2004. "Racial and Ethnic Disparities in Health and Mortality among the US Elderly Population." In R.A. Bulatao and N.B. Anderson (eds.), *Understanding Racial and Ethnic Differences in Health in Late Life: A Research Agenda*, pp. 53–94. Washington, DC, National Academy Press.

Hummer, R.A., D.A. Powers, S.G. Pullum, G.L. Grossman, and W.P. Frisbie. 2007. "Paradox Found Again: Infant Mortality Among the Mexican-Origin Population in the United States." *Demography* 44:441–58.

Jerant, A., R. Arellanes, and P. Franks. 2008. "Health Status among US Hispanics: Ethnic Variation, Nativity, and Language Moderation." *Medical Care* 46:709–17.

Lara, M., C. Gamboa, M.I. Kahramanian, L.S. Morales, and D. Hayes-Bautista. 2005. "Acculturation and Latino Health in the United States: A Review of the Literature and its Sociopolitical Context." *Annual Review of Public Health* 26:367–97.

LeClere, F.B., R.G. Rogers, and K.D. Peters. 1997. "Ethnicity and Mortality in the United States: Individual and Community Correlates." *Social Forces* 76(1):169–98.

Lee, M.A. and K.F. Ferraro. 2007. "Neighborhood Residential Segregation and Physical Health among Hispanic Americans: Good, Bad, or Benign?" *Journal of Health Social Behavior* 48:131–48.

Manton, K.G. and E. Stallard. 1997. "Health and Disability Differences Among Racial and Ethnic Groups." In L.G. Martin and B.J. Soldo (eds.), *Racial and Ethnic Differences in the Health of Older Americans*, pp. 43–104. Washington, DC, National Academy Press.

Markides, K.S. 2001. "Migration and Health." In P. Baltes and N.J. Smelser (eds.), *International Encyclopedia of the Social and Behavioral Sciences*, pp. 9799–803. New York, Elsevier.

Markides, K.S. and S.A. Black. 1995. "Race, Ethnicity, and Ageing: The Impact of Inequality." In R.H. Binstock and L.K. George (eds.), *Handbook of Aging and the Social Sciences*, pp. 137–73. San Diego, CA, Academic Press.

Markides, K.S. and J. Coreil. 1986. "The Health of Southwestern Hispanics: An Epidemiologic Paradox." *Public Health Reports* 101:253–65.

Markides, K.S. and K. Eschbach. 2005. "Aging, Migration, and Mortality: Current Status of Research on the Hispanic Paradox." *Journals of Gerontology: Psychological and Social Sciences* 60B:68–72.

Markides, K.S., K. Eschbach, L.A. Ray, and M.K. Peek. 2007. "Census Disability Rates among Older People by Race/Ethnicity and Type of Hispanic Origin." In J.L. Angel and K.W. Whitfield (eds.), *The Health of Aging Hispanics: The Mexican Origin Population*. New York, Springer.

Markides, K.S., J. Salinas, and K. Sheffield Winter 2009. "The Health of Older Immigrants." *Generations* 32:46–52.

Markides, K.S., J. Salinas and R. Wong. 2010. "Ageing and Health among Hispanic/Latinos in the Americas." In W.D. Dannefer and C. Philips (eds.), *Handbook of Social Gerontology*. London, Sage Publications.

McDonald, J.T. and S. Kennedy. 2004. "Insights into the 'Healthy Immigrant effect': Health Status and Health Service Use of Immigrants to Canada." *Social Science and Medicine* 59:1613–27.

Ostir, G.V., K. Eschbach, K.S. Markides, and J.S. Goodwin. 2004. "Neighborhood Composition and Depressive Symptoms Among Older Mexican Americans." *Journal of Epidemiology and Community Health* 57: 987–92.

Osypuk, T.L., A.V. Diez Roux, C. Hadley, and N. Kandula 2009. "Are Immigrant Enclaves Healthy Places to Live? The Multi-Ethnic Study of Atherosclerosis." *Social Science and Medicine* 69:110–20.

Palloni, A. and E. Arias. 2004. "Paradox Lost: Explaining the Hispanic Adult Mortality Advantage." *Demography* 41:385–415.

Palloni, A. and J. Morenoff. 2001. "Interpreting the Paradoxical in the Hispanic Paradox: Demographic and Epidemiological Approaches." In A. Weinstein, A. Hermalin, and M.A. Soto (eds.), *Population Health and Aging: Strengthening the Dialogue between Epidemiology and Demography*, pp. 140–74. New York, Academy of Sciences.

Patel, K.V., K. Eschbach, L. Rudkin, M.K. Peek, and K.S. Markides. 2003. "Neighborhood Context and Self-Rated Health in Older Mexican Americans." *Annals of Epidemiology* 13:620–28.

Portes, A. and R.G. Rumbaut. 2006. *Immigrant America: A Portrait*. Berkeley, CA, University of California Press.

Reyes-Ortiz, C., H. Ju, K. Eschbach, Y.F. Kuo, and J.S. Goodwin. 2009. "Neighborhood Ethnic Composition and Diet among Mexican Americans." *Public Health Nutrition* 12:2293–301.

Reyes-Ortiz, C.A., Zhang, D., Stimpson, J., Eschback, K., Goodwin, J.S. 2010. Disparities in cancer survival among Hispanics as a function of neighborhood ethnic composition. Unpublished manuscript, University of North Texas Health Science Center, Fort North, Texas.

Rosenberg, H.M, Maurer, J.D., Sorlie, P.D., Johnson, N.J., MacDorman, M.F., Hoyert, D.L. 1999. Quality of death rates by race and Hispanic origin: A summary of current research. *Vital and Health Statistics*, 2,128.

Rubalcava, L.N., G.M. Teruel, D. Thomas, and N. Goldman. 2008. "The Healthy Migrant Effect: New Findings from the Mexican Family Life Survey." *American Journal of Public Health* 998:78–83.

Singh, G.K. and R.A. Hiatt. 2006. "Trends and Disparities in Socioeconomic and Behavioral Characteristics, Life Expectancy, and Cause-Specific Mortality of Native-Born and Foreign-Born Populations in the United States, 1979–2003." *International Journal of Epidemiology* 35:903–19.

Stephen, E.H., K. Foote, G.E. Hendershot, and C.A. Schoenborn. 1994. "Health of the Foreign-born Population: United States, 1989–90." *Advance Data Vital and Health Statistics* 241(14):1–12.

Sudano, J.J. and D.W. Baker. 2006. "Explaining U.S. Racial/Ethnic Disparities in Health Declines and Mortality in Late Middle Age: The Role of Socioeconomic Status, Healthy Behaviors, and Health Insurance." *Social Science and Medicine* 62: 909–22.

Sullivan, T.A., F.P. Gillespie, M. Hout, and R.G. Rogers. 1984. "Alternative Estimates of Mexican American Mortality in Texas, 1980." *Social Science Quarterly* 65: 609–17.

Turra, C.M. and I. Elo. 2007. Socioeconomic Differences in mortality among U.S Adults: Insights into the Hispanic

Paradox. *Journal of Gerontology Social Sciences*, 52B:S184–S192.

Turra, C.M. and I.T. Elo. 2008. "The Impact of Salmon Bias on the Hispanic Mortality Advantage. New Evidence from Social Security Data." *Population Research and Policy Review* 27:515–30.

Turra, C.M. and N. Goldman. 2007. "Socioeconomic Differences in Mortality among US Adults: Insights in the Hispanic Paradox." *Journal of Gerontology: Social Sciences* 62B:S184–S92.

Vega, W.A. and H.L. Amaro. 1994. "Latino Outlook: Good Health, Uncertain Prognosis." *Annual Review of Public Health* 15:39–67.

Vega, W.A., M.A. Rodriquez, and E. Gruskin. 2009. "Health Disparities in the Latino Population." *Epidemiologic Reviews* 31:99–112.

Wong, R. and A. Palloni. 2009. "Aging in Mexico and Latin America." In P. Uhlenberg (ed.), *International Handbook of Population Aging*, pp. 231–52. New York, Spring Publications.

# Chapter 12
# Educational Attainment and Adult Mortality

Robert A. Hummer and Joseph T. Lariscy

## Introduction

Throughout the twentieth century, adult mortality rates in the United States and in all high-income countries exhibited impressive declines. The latter half of the twentieth century was characterized by well-documented differences in adult mortality rates across categories of educational attainment (Elo and Preston 1996; Kitagawa and Hauser 1973; Lauderdale 2001; Rogers et al. 2000), a social fact that now garners much greater concern and research attention than perhaps ever before. Clearly, socioeconomic mortality differentials—including those by educational attainment—stand at the heart of the public health agenda of the United States. This was not always the case. Indeed, education was added to the US Standard Certificate of Death only in 1989; before then, researchers had little readily available data to examine socioeconomic differentials in mortality (Moss and Krieger 1995). Theoretical and empirical understanding of socioeconomic mortality differentials was also hampered by a relative lack of academic interest. Demographic and epidemiologic studies in the 1950s through the 1970s largely downplayed socioeconomic health and mortality differences because of more pressing interest in other topics (Krieger et al. 1993). Because of growing awareness of and concern over social inequalities since that time, as well as substantial improvements in available data and computing power, a new generation of studies in social demography and social epidemiology has focused on the link between socioeconomic and survival inequalities (Hoffmann 2008; Hummer et al. 1998). Moreover, because life itself is such a treasured resource, it stands to reason that wide socioeconomic differences in mortality signal critical inequalities in the way that social structure works to differentiate the life chances of individuals. Thus, the topic of educational differences in adult mortality is not only one of immense scientific and public policy interest, but also one related to issues of opportunity, equity, and fairness within societies.

Beyond the radical improvements in human survival across the twentieth century and the growing recognition of wide educational differences in adult mortality, there were phenomenal changes in education itself that need to be considered to elucidate the link between educational attainment and adult mortality. The distribution, content, and importance of education have changed in fundamental ways over time. Younger individuals tend to have higher levels of education, have been exposed to more sophisticated content than ever before, and have more at stake on their education than individuals in previous cohorts. In terms of distribution, data from the United States illustrate that a higher percentage of individuals graduate from high school and college now than ever before. The percentage of US persons aged 25 and older who were high-school graduates was 41 in 1960, 52 in 1970, 66 in 1980, 78 in 1990, and 84 in 2005–2007 (US Census Bureau 2009). These percentages reflect the steadily increasing levels of education across birth cohorts in the United States. Recent high-school graduates have been exposed to more ideas about health promotion and disease prevention than graduates from decades ago. Students learn about the hazards of smoking, the importance

R.A. Hummer (✉)
Department of Sociology and Population Research Center,
University of Texas, Austin, TX 78712, USA
e-mail: rhummer@prc.utexas.edu

of diet and exercise, the risk of sexually transmitted diseases, and the prevention of air-, water-, and food-borne diseases (Lynch 2003). Moreover, recent cohorts of people with higher levels of education are taught to deal with such day-to-day complexities as navigating new forms of communication, interacting effectively in the health care setting, and working with people in different cultures and countries. These dramatic educational changes affect not only their ability to navigate an increasingly fluid and global labor market, but also their health and, ultimately, their length of life.

With these immense mortality and educational changes in mind, the overall aim of this chapter is to review current knowledge on adult mortality differences by educational attainment. We focus largely on the United States because that is where our expertise is greatest, and because the enormous size of this literature makes it impossible to provide in-depth international coverage in a single chapter. Moreover, reducing educational differences in mortality is a key goal for *Healthy People 2010* and will likely be one for *Healthy People 2020* when its goals, objectives, and action plans are released sometime in 2010 (U.S. Department of Health and Human Services [DHHS] 2008); thus, it is clear that this is a pressing area of scientific and policy concern in the United States.

This chapter first presents a conceptual framework for understanding educational differences in adult mortality. Second, we document the basic patterns of association between educational attainment and adult mortality using contemporary data from the United States. Third, we give substantial attention to how the education–mortality relationship varies by age, gender, and race/ethnicity, and over time. Although this review and our empirical examples focus primarily on the United States, we then briefly discuss this relationship in an international context. Finally, we discuss policy and future research issues in this area of study.

## Conceptual Framework

### Measuring Education

Educational attainment, the focus of this chapter, is one of the principal components of socioeconomic status (SES), the others being occupation, income, and wealth (see, for example, Chapter 13 by Krueger and Burgard, 2011, this volume). There are several very important reasons for using educational attainment as the key indicator of SES when studying socioeconomic differentials in adult mortality (Preston and Taubman 1994). First, educational attainment is most often completed relatively early in adult life and usually remains constant throughout adulthood. In contrast, occupational status, income level, and the accumulation of wealth may vary in considerable ways throughout the life course and, at least in part, respond to health fluctuations (Smith 2004). Second, it follows that educational attainment may be more relevant than other measures of SES for individuals who have retired, are currently unemployed, or are out of the labor force. Third, survey and census respondents, as well as informants on death certificates, are more likely to report educational attainment (and with reasonable accuracy) than to report other socioeconomic indicators, particularly income and wealth. Thus, using educational attainment rather than income or wealth tends to prevent exclusion of individuals from study populations because of missing or imprecise data. Fourth, the use of educational attainment rather than income, occupational status, or wealth may make international comparisons more relevant because of the commonalities in educational systems across national contexts (Valkonen 1993). Finally, educational attainment typically precedes occupational status, income, and the accumulation of wealth in both the life course and the causal sense. Thus, we advocate using educational attainment as the most fundamental indicator of SES in studies of adult mortality, though we acknowledge that the choice of indicator must be made with substantial thought and attention to the purpose of the study at hand (Braveman et al. 2005).

Most studies focusing on educational attainment and adult mortality measure educational attainment using a single indicator of years of completed schooling. Such an indicator is used either in a continuous fashion with values ranging from 0 to 17 or so (e.g., Zajacova 2006) or in a set of categories that demarcate important cut-points (e.g., 0–11, 12, 13–15, and 16 or more years) in the distribution of degrees that are usually awarded after a certain number of years of attained education (e.g., Rogers et al. 2000). Backlund et al. (1999) specifically tested whether a continuous or categorical specification of years of education best captured the functional form of the relationship between educational attainment and working-aged adult mortality risk in the United States. They found that educational attainment was best specified in a trichotomous categorization (less than a high-school diploma, a high-school diploma but no college degree, or a college degree or more) rather than as a continuous predictor of mortality risk. At the same time, another recent paper using US data shows that both a continuous measure of educational attainment and a six-category scheme yield valuable insights that are obscured when only one or the other specification is used (Zajacova and Hummer 2009; also see Elo and Preston 1996). Clearly, researchers should continue to examine the functional form of the education–mortality relationship, most specifically to best determine where in the educational distribution mortality risks are highest and lowest and especially as this relationship changes across time and varies across place.

It is also the case that a single measure of educational attainment based on years of completed schooling misses out on capturing the full extent to which education, in a broader sense, is related to adult mortality risks. One potential line of research is to examine actual degrees awarded, rather than (or, preferably, in addition to) years of schooling. Rogers et al. (2010), for example, show that US adults who have completed some college but without any postsecondary degrees have a 6% lower mortality risk than do high-school diploma holders across a 5-year follow-up period, while persons with an associate of arts degree have an 18% lower mortality risk than do those with a high-school diploma. Measures of the content of educational attainment—quality of education received, courses taken, skills learned, and mastery of the subject matter—are almost never available in population-based data sets that are large enough to analyze mortality risks. Given such a crucial data limitation, we probably know much less about the relationship between education and adult mortality risk than the large array of previous studies might suggest. Much more work that considers a variety of education indicators and subsequent mortality risks is needed.

Beyond individual-level measures of education, some research has examined the influences of a broader set of educational context measures—such as the educational levels of families and neighborhoods—on the mortality risks of individual adults. For example, studies by Jaffe et al. (2005) and Brown et al. (2009) have shown that, among married couples, a spouse's level of education importantly influences individual mortality risk, even after accounting for the individual's own level of education. Similarly, Huie et al. (2002) showed that, net of a range of individual-level factors that include individuals' own educational attainment, a lower level of education within neighborhoods is associated with higher mortality risks. Such work provides evidence that the relationship between educational attainment and adult mortality risk is best conceptualized in a manner that not only takes into account the individual educational characteristics of adults, but their broader educational contexts as well.

## Conceptualizing the Association Between Educational Attainment and Adult Mortality

No matter what schemes they use to measure educational attainment, most studies implicitly or explicitly conceptualize that a higher level of educational attainment is associated with lower mortality risk because education helps individuals develop a very useful set of flexible resources that shape health over the life course and, ultimately, how and when individuals die. A higher level of educational attainment helps individuals acquire better and more stable employment, increase earning power, develop effective agency, attain a greater sense of personal control over their lives, and develop beneficial social connections. These resources can help more educated people earn and accumulate more money, work in stable and creative jobs, live a healthier lifestyle, live in a safer environment, and experience less stress and more social support than less-educated people (Mirowsky and Ross 2003). This conceptualization emphasizes that education provides resources well beyond increased income. In a broad sense, education helps individuals to learn by improving reading comprehension, increasing writing skills, enabling learners to better follow important instructions, teaching abstract reasoning skills, creating a future-oriented way of thinking, and facilitating effective and efficient problem solving. Compared to less-educated individuals, highly educated individuals are also more likely to exercise, abstain from tobacco use, maintain a healthy body weight, and incorporate new health knowledge into their lives. In short, "education enables people to coalesce health-producing behaviors into a coherent lifestyle that improves health" (Mirowsky and Ross 2003: 52). These positive influences of education persist throughout the life course, long after the formal completion of schooling.

The strength and consistency of the inverse relationship between educational attainment and mortality risk over time, across different places, and among individuals in different demographic groups suggests that education is a "fundamental cause" of health and mortality (Link and Phelan 1995; Phelan et al. 2004). That is, the mechanisms by which education works to influence mortality risks—discussed above—are broad and varied, and can and do change over time. As a result, while the mechanisms that link educational attainment to mortality risk may vary across contexts, the flexible resources that are shaped by educational attainment help to make educational differences in adult mortality very resistant to change. In the section on policy implications below, we comment on the immense challenge that this fundamental cause perspective poses to program and policy initiatives that aim to close education–mortality gaps.

The discussion thus far strongly suggests that educational attainment works in a causal fashion to influence adult mortality risk. And indeed, a growing and creative econometric literature demonstrates that a substantial portion of the association between educational attainment and adult health and mortality risk does seem to be due to the causal influences of higher levels of schooling (Chandola et al. 2008; Glied and Lleras-Muney 2008; Lleras-Muney 2005; Smith 2004). Nevertheless, a primary concern of social and epidemiologic scientists who examine the relationship between educational attainment and mortality risk is the possibility of spuriousness. That is, there could be a set of factors—often unobserved by researchers—that influence both educational attainment and adult mortality risk that are the actual causes of this statistical relationship. For example, persons who experience poor health during childhood and adolescence, who have lower levels of intelligence, and/or whose parents were not highly educated may complete fewer years of schooling and die earlier than their counterparts, thus creating a statistical association between educational attainment and mortality risk that is actually caused by those other underlying factors (Batty and Deary 2005; Gottfredson 2004; Hoffmann 2008; Palloni 2006). Recent research that has begun to take into account some of these underlying factors—such as intelligence scores and childhood health and socioeconomic conditions—generally finds that the relationship between educational attainment and mortality risk is modestly weaker than without such controls, but still strong (Hayward and Gorman 2004; Link et al. 2008; but also see Batty et al. 2006). Clearly, this line of research remains important, perhaps most so because answers to critical policy questions will rely on a better understanding of the true causal impacts of educational attainment than most observational studies to date have been able to demonstrate.

## *Mechanisms Relating Educational Attainment to Adult Mortality Risk*

The above section emphasizes that educational attainment is linked to adult mortality risk because it helps individuals acquire and use a set of flexible resources that improve health and lessen age-specific risks of death throughout the life course. Here, we highlight four sets of mechanisms (or mediating factors) through which educational attainment is thought to influence health and mortality risk: socioeconomic attainment, health behaviors, social psychological resources, and access to and utilization of health care (Hoffmann 2008; Mirowsky and Ross 2003; Rogers et al. 2000; Williams 1990). These mechanisms most likely do not operate with equal strength across demographic groups (age, gender, race/ethnicity), across time, or across places.

*Socioeconomic Attainment.* A substantial portion of the beneficial association between educational attainment and adult mortality risk is due to the increased income that individuals with higher levels of education tend to earn. Income is an immediately available economic resource that can pay for nutritious food, high-quality housing in a safe neighborhood, health insurance premiums, medical bills, and health club memberships, as well as be saved for future needs (Smeeding and Weinberg 2001). Not only does higher education enable individuals to earn more, but it may also improve spending choices. That is, even among individuals who have identical income levels, more educated individuals may be better able to navigate through bureaucracies to obtain the most for their money—for example, by finding the lowest interest rates and closing costs on a mortgage, making use of appropriate saving and investment strategies, or effectively budgeting their income to meet their needs (Mirowsky and Ross 1998; Schnittker 2004). In turn, higher family income is associated with lower mortality risk among adults of all ages, women and men, and majority and minority populations (Krueger et al. 2003; Pappas et al. 1993; Sorlie et al. 1995).

In addition to income, higher levels of education may also work partly through employment and occupational status to decrease the risk of mortality. Education provides the skills to navigate through tedious or difficult instructions required by some jobs and even job applications. Frequently, workers need to have a certain level of education to qualify for a job or a promotion. More educated individuals may find employment in higher status professions, have more control over their own work and the work of others, be more valuable to a company, be better able to achieve work-related agendas, be viewed with greater esteem by their peers, and gain protection against the risks of job loss even during layoffs. In turn, regular employment, high status occupations, and creatively oriented jobs are associated with better health and lower adult mortality risks (Marmot 2004; Mirowsky and Ross 2007; Rogers et al. 2000; Sorlie et al. 1995).

*Health Behavior.* A second prominent mechanism that links educational attainment to mortality risk is health behavior. Relative to persons with less education, those with more education are more likely to exercise, refrain from heavy alcohol consumption, quit smoking or avoid smoking altogether, maintain a healthy weight, and eat more nutritious meals. Among all sociodemographic characteristics, education is the only one that correlates positively and consistently with health-enhancing behaviors (Mirowsky and Ross 1998: 419). Most important, educational attainment influences the risk of adult mortality because less-educated individuals are more likely to initiate smoking, less likely to seek out and follow antismoking advice, and less likely to quit (Rogers et al. 2005). Individuals with lower education tend to confront more immediate concerns than quitting smoking, and may smoke as a way to cope with stressful living conditions (Lawlor et al. 2003). And smoking, of course, is a leading cause of preventable mortality, associated with increased risks of mortality from a host of causes, including cardiovascular diseases, various cancers, and respiratory diseases.

In comparing mortality risks across US educational attainment groups over a 7.5-year period, Lantz et al. (1998) found that the odds ratio of mortality for the lowest to the highest education group decreased by 14% with controls for smoking, alcohol use, sedentary lifestyle, and relative body weight (also see Feldman et al. 1989). However, the strength of these behavioral mechanisms, particularly smoking, may be increasing among more recent birth cohorts because cigarette smoking in the United States has become increasingly concentrated among individuals with low levels of schooling (Meara et al. 2008). For example, Denney et al. (2010) show that smoking may account for up to 44% of the education–mortality association among working-aged US men.

*Social Psychological Resources.* Social psychological resources are another plausible mechanism through which higher levels of education improve health and reduce mortality (Williams 1990). Unfortunately, relatively few studies in this area use data sets that can tap into the wide array of social and psychological resources that are important for mortality risk. Research suggests that education is perhaps most important for increasing effective agency and developing a heightened sense of personal control (Mirowsky and Ross 1998). Increased agency and personal control help individuals to believe that they can effectively alter their surroundings and therefore to seek health-related information and adopt a lifestyle that enhances their health trajectories and length of life.

Additionally, more highly educated individuals may have access to other highly educated individuals—coworkers, religious leaders, friends, and neighbors—who can provide advice in times of need, reinforce healthy lifestyles, and intervene effectively and directly in a crisis. Recent research, for example, finds that marital status affects educational differences in adult mortality: educational differences are particularly wide among unmarried US men and narrower among married individuals (Montez et al. 2009). Persons with more education may also encounter fewer non-health stressors—such as marital and family problems, conflicts with friends and neighbors, legal hassles, and on-the-job troubles—that impair health and increase mortality risks (House et al. 1988; Lantz et al. 2005). Further, education may help individuals ease the impact of stressful life events such as illness and grief.

*Access to and Utilization of Health Care.* Some research attention has been given to the possibility that access to and utilization of health care is a mechanism linking educational attainment to mortality risk, although the consensus to date suggests that health care most likely plays only a minor mediating role (Hoffmann 2008). This may particularly be the case after accounting for the increased income associated with higher levels of education. In the United States, the implementation of Medicare in 1966 significantly improved access to health care for the elderly and reduced overall old-age mortality (Drevenstedt 2001); however, the program apparently did little to reduce socioeconomic differences in old-age mortality (Preston and Elo 1995; Preston and Taubman 1994). This was consistent with earlier findings regarding the implementation of the British National Health Service in 1946 (Pamuk 1985).

It may be that highly educated individuals are more likely than the less educated to use and successfully navigate the medical system, by seeking care from the most skilled and knowledgeable practitioners, complying with treatment regimens, and learning and retaining crucial medical information during health care visits and hospitalizations. For instance, highly educated persons adhere better to treatments for diabetes and HIV than their less-educated counterparts, resulting in improved self-rated health among HIV patients and a slower decline in self-rated health among diabetics (Goldman and Smith 2002). Relatively few population-based studies have examined such possibilities, however, particularly in relation to mortality.

## Educational Attainment and US Adult Mortality: Patterns of Relative Risk

In this section, we use US public use data from the National Health Interview Survey-Linked Mortality File (NHIS-LMF; see Lochner et al. 2008) to produce current estimates of relative educational differentials in mortality. In a subsequent section, we supplement our analyses by focusing on findings from other recent studies using different data sets that examine absolute differences in mortality (in the form of life expectancy estimates) across educational attainment groups.

The NHIS is a multistage probability cross-sectional sample of the US noninstitutionalized adult population that is conducted each year by the National Center for Health Statistics (NCHS). Here we use aggregated data from years 1986 through 2000. The NHIS respondents from 1986 to 2000 are matched by NCHS to 1986–2002 death records in the National Death Index (NDI). A probabilistic algorithm is used to determine whether NHIS respondents match a death record in the NDI during this follow-up period. We chose the NHIS-LMF dataset for this because it is current and nationally representative of the noninstitutionalized US population, contains critical measures of sociodemographic characteristics related to educational attainment and adult mortality risk, has a high response rate, has an excellent record of matching to subsequent death records, and contains underlying cause of death information for respondents who died.

Because most adults complete their education by early adulthood, our analysis includes respondents 25 years old and older. We further restrict our sample to those who report that they are non-Hispanic white, non-Hispanic black, and Hispanic because sample sizes for other racial/ethnic groups are small. Moreover, we exclude a small number of individuals who did not report a value for educational attainment. Thus, our analytic sample contains 831,820 adult respondents aged 25 and over who were interviewed between 1986 and 2000, among whom 104,238 were determined to have died at some point during the follow-up period. We use Cox proportional hazard models to estimate the association between educational attainment and the risk of adult mortality across the follow-up period (Allison 1984). Our tables depict results from the models in the form of hazard ratios, with persons who have 12 years of education (or a completed high-school degree) serving as the reference category of educational attainment in all models. Thus, in each model hazard ratios above one indicate a higher risk of mortality for a particular education category compared to persons with 12 years of education, while hazard ratios below one indicate a lower risk. Analyses were performed in SUDAAN 10.0 to account for the complex NHIS survey design (Research Triangle Institute 2008).

Educational attainment is measured here in six categories (as in Zajacova and Hummer 2009): less than 9, 9–11, 12, 13–15, 16, and 17 or more years. While some studies select different cut-points and credential thresholds, these categories assure a distribution that allows for detailed documentation of mortality differentials. The categories were selected to roughly represent individuals with a primary school education or less (less than 9 years), some high school (9–11 years), a high-school diploma or its equivalent (12 years), some college (13–15 years), a bachelor's degree (16 years), and graduate school or professional education (17 or more years). Age, sex, and race/ethnicity are included as controls in the most general models (Tables 12.1 and 12.2); subsequently, we stratify our models by age, sex, and race/ethnicity to show educational differences in adult mortality within demographic subgroups (Tables 12.3, 12.4, and 12.5).

We first document educational differences in all-cause mortality among US adults aged 25–84 in Table 12.1. Because the relationship between educational attainment and adult mortality varies across causes of death, we next present results for underlying causes of death in Table 12.2. The underlying causes that we specify include heart disease, stroke, diabetes, lung cancer, all other cancers, respiratory diseases, external causes, and a residual category. We then present the education–mortality association for specific demographic subgroups by age, gender, and race/ethnicity in Tables 12.3, 12.4, and 12.5; this detailed subgroup examination focuses on all-cause mortality rather than on cause-specific mortality because of the relatively small number of deaths within some age-sex-race/ethnic strata of the data set.

## Educational Attainment and Mortality Risk Among US Adults Aged 25–84

Table 12.1 shows that, in accord with the results of many previous studies, individuals with less education are more likely to die during the follow-up period than individuals with more education, net of age, sex, and race/ethnicity. Because persons with 0–8 years and 9–11 years of schooling have similar mortality risks, many previous studies have tended to group these categories together (e.g., Backlund et al. 1999). Among US adults aged 25–84, individuals with eight or fewer years of education are 21% more likely to die during the follow-up period than are individuals with 12 years of education. Interestingly, persons with 9–11 years of schooling exhibit an even larger difference, of 24%. This suggests that the relationship between educational attainment and adult mortality risk may not be strictly linear, at least for the (nearly) entire age range of adults of both sexes. The results in Table 12.1 also clearly show that adults with more than 12 years of education exhibit increasingly lower risks of death across the follow-up period than do individuals with 12 years of education. And the mortality benefits of education do not top off at 16 years: people with 17 or more years of schooling are 33% less likely to die during the follow-up period than are those with 12 years, in comparison to a 25% lower mortality risk among those with 16 years. There is a substantial difference (not specifically shown in the table) between individuals with 17 or more years of education and those with either 0–8 or 9–11 years; persons in these two lowest educational categories are about 1.8 times as likely to die in the follow-up period as are those in the 17 and over category (for comparable results, see Rogers et al. 2000).

The magnitude of educational differences in mortality varies by specific cause of death (Kitagawa and Hauser 1973; Phelan et al. 2004; Rogers et al. 2000), and eliminating those differences may depend on understanding why. Education generally exhibits a strong, inverse association with circulatory disease mortality, the leading cause of death in the United

**Table 12.1** Hazard ratios for the association between educational attainment and US adult mortality, 1986–2002

| Educational attainment | |
|---|---|
| 8 or fewer years | 1.21*** |
| 9–11 years | 1.24*** |
| 12 years | Ref. |
| 13–15 years | 0.93*** |
| 16 years | 0.75*** |
| 17 or more years | 0.67*** |
| Age (25–84, continuous) | 1.09*** |
| Sex (male=1) | 1.60*** |
| Race/ethnicity | |
| Hispanic | 0.94** |
| Non-Hispanic black | 1.26*** |
| Non-Hispanic white | Ref. |
| Observations | 831,820 |
| Deaths | 104,238 |
| –2*Log-likelihood | 748,730.3 |

Source: National Center for Health Statistics (2005).
*$p < 0.10$; **$p < 0.05$; ***$p < 0.001$

**Table 12.2** Hazard ratios for the association between educational attainment and US cause-specific adult mortality, 1986–2002

|  | Heart disease | Stroke | Diabetes | Lung cancer | All other cancers | Respiratory | External | Other causes |
|---|---|---|---|---|---|---|---|---|
| Educational attainment | | | | | | | | |
| 8 or fewer years | 1.32*** | 1.13** | 1.30*** | 1.23*** | 1.01 | 1.25*** | 1.33*** | 1.16*** |
| 9–11 years | 1.28*** | 1.13** | 1.39*** | 1.40*** | 1.08** | 1.30*** | 1.30*** | 1.24*** |
| 12 years | Ref. | Ref. | Ref. | Ref. | Ref. | Ref. | Ref. | Ref. |
| 13–15 years | 0.91*** | 0.92* | 0.87** | 0.87** | 0.94** | 0.90** | 0.92 | 0.97 |
| 16 years | 0.76*** | 0.79*** | 0.58*** | 0.61*** | 0.85*** | 0.61*** | 0.63*** | 0.77*** |
| 17 or more years | 0.68*** | 0.76*** | 0.54*** | 0.51*** | 0.76*** | 0.55*** | 0.58*** | 0.68*** |
| Age (25–84, continuous) | 1.11*** | 1.12*** | 1.08*** | 1.07*** | 1.08*** | 1.11*** | 1.02*** | 1.08*** |
| Sex (male=1) | 1.79*** | 1.19*** | 1.25*** | 2.21*** | 1.40*** | 1.77*** | 2.36*** | 1.41*** |
| Race/ethnicity | | | | | | | | |
| Hispanic | 0.84*** | 1.02 | 1.97*** | 0.54*** | 0.96 | 0.71*** | 1.16** | 1.11** |
| Non-Hispanic black | 1.26*** | 1.33*** | 2.02*** | 1.12** | 1.25*** | 0.77*** | 1.12* | 1.55*** |
| Non-Hispanic white | Ref. | Ref. | Ref. | Ref. | Ref. | Ref. | Ref. | Ref. |
| Deaths | 32,830 | 6,749 | 3,221 | 8,705 | 20,399 | 9,490 | 4,525 | 18,319 |
| –2*Log-likelihood | 281,248.5 | 73,298.7 | 40,862.9 | 99,161.9 | 207,287.4 | 100,562.8 | 59,896.1 | 184,884.7 |

Source: National Center for Health Statistics (2005).
*$p < 0.10$; **$p < 0.05$; ***$p < 0.001$.

**Table 12.3** Hazard ratios for the association between educational attainment and US adult mortality, stratified by age and sex, 1986–2002

|  | Female | | | Male | | |
|---|---|---|---|---|---|---|
|  | 25–44 years | 45–64 years | 65–84 years | 25–44 years | 45–64 years | 65–84 years |
| Educational attainment | | | | | | |
| 8 or fewer years | 1.66*** | 1.43*** | 1.12*** | 1.60*** | 1.48*** | 1.14*** |
| 9–11 years | 1.81*** | 1.40*** | 1.13*** | 1.50*** | 1.33*** | 1.13*** |
| 12 years | Ref. | Ref. | Ref. | Ref. | Ref. | Ref. |
| 13–15 years | 0.91* | 0.93** | 0.94** | 0.87** | 0.98 | 0.91*** |
| 16 years | 0.64*** | 0.77*** | 0.84*** | 0.55*** | 0.72*** | 0.80*** |
| 17 or more years | 0.60*** | 0.63*** | 0.82*** | 0.52*** | 0.59*** | 0.76*** |
| Age (25–84, continuous) | 1.09*** | 1.08*** | 1.09*** | 1.08*** | 1.09*** | 1.09*** |
| Race/ethnicity | | | | | | |
| Hispanic | 1.43*** | 0.86*** | 0.79*** | 1.31*** | 0.84*** | 0.80*** |
| Non-Hispanic black | 1.74*** | 1.39*** | 1.11*** | 1.88*** | 1.32*** | 1.05** |
| Non-Hispanic white | Ref. | Ref. | Ref. | Ref. | Ref. | Ref. |
| Observations | 217,467 | 139,785 | 88,098 | 195,621 | 126,049 | 64,800 |
| Deaths | 4,479 | 13,255 | 32,632 | 6,239 | 17,254 | 30,379 |
| –2*Log-likelihood | 49,368.8 | 116,427.8 | 208,082.7 | 65,016.5 | 139,045.1 | 174,249.3 |

Source: National Center for Health Statistics (2005).
*$p < 0.10$; **$p < 0.05$; ***$p < 0.001$.

States. Cancer mortality, the second leading cause of death, exhibits a weaker association with education than do other causes of death (Rogers et al. 1996). Low education is linked to higher odds of respiratory disease mortality (Rogers 1992), and perhaps increasingly so as cigarette smoking becomes more concentrated among individuals with low education. Diabetes mortality has also been linked to low education (Zhang et al. 1991). Higher mortality from external causes (homicide, suicide, accidents) is also due in part to low levels of education (Rogers et al. 2000). Similarly, Phelan et al. (2004) find that the education–mortality gradient is strongest for those causes of death that they classify as most preventable. Most recently, deaths from circulatory disease and cancer were shown to have contributed most profoundly to rising relative educational differentials in mortality through the 1980s and 1990s (Meara et al. 2008).

**Table 12.4** Hazard ratios for the association between educational attainment and US adult mortality for females, stratified by age and race/ethnicity, 1986–2002

|  | Hispanic | | | Non-Hispanic black | | | Non-Hispanic white | | |
|---|---|---|---|---|---|---|---|---|---|
|  | 25–44 years | 45–64 years | 65–84 years | 25–44 years | 45–64 years | 65–84 years | 25–44 years | 45–64 years | 65–84 years |
| Educational attainment | | | | | | | | | |
| 8 or fewer years | 1.51** | 1.32** | 1.31** | 1.62** | 1.19** | 1.13** | 1.85*** | 1.52*** | 1.11*** |
| 9–11 years | 1.45** | 1.07 | 1.30 | 1.63*** | 1.21** | 1.11 | 1.99*** | 1.46*** | 1.13*** |
| 12 years | Ref. | Ref. | Ref. | Ref. | Ref. | Ref. | Ref. | Ref. | Ref. |
| 13–15 years | 1.04 | 0.97 | 0.89 | 0.99 | 0.89 | 0.99 | 0.87** | 0.93** | 0.93** |
| 16 years | 0.56* | 0.61** | 1.28 | 0.71** | 0.67** | 0.95 | 0.64*** | 0.79*** | 0.82*** |
| 17 or more years | 0.59 | 0.60 | 1.33 | 0.27*** | 0.62*** | 0.98 | 0.65*** | 0.64*** | 0.80*** |
| Age (25–84, continuous) | 1.06*** | 1.08*** | 1.09*** | 1.09*** | 1.07*** | 1.07*** | 1.09*** | 1.09*** | 1.10*** |
| Observations | 27,927 | 12,637 | 4,767 | 33,832 | 20,388 | 10,415 | 155,708 | 106,760 | 72,916 |
| Deaths | 686 | 877 | 1,187 | 1,131 | 2,712 | 4,172 | 2,662 | 9,666 | 27,273 |
| –2*Log-likelihood | 7,932.7 | 8,908.9 | 8,466.7 | 11,066.2 | 21,902.7 | 26,231.9 | 31,352.9 | 86,549.0 | 173,155.5 |

Source: National Center for Health Statistics (2005).
*$p<0.10$; **$p<0.05$; ***$p<0.001$.

**Table 12.5** Hazard ratios for the association between educational attainment and US adult mortality for males, stratified by age and race/ethnicity, 1986–2002

|  | Hispanic | | | Non-Hispanic black | | | Non-Hispanic white | | |
|---|---|---|---|---|---|---|---|---|---|
|  | 25–44 years | 45–64 years | 65–84 years | 25–44 years | 45–64 years | 65–84 years | 25–44 years | 45–64 years | 65–84 years |
| Educational attainment | | | | | | | | | |
| 8 or fewer years | 1.48*** | 1.24** | 1.03 | 1.51** | 1.32*** | 1.16** | 1.71*** | 1.57*** | 1.15*** |
| 9–11 years | 1.29** | 1.25 | 1.23 | 1.35** | 1.26*** | 1.06 | 1.61*** | 1.33*** | 1.14*** |
| 12 years | Ref. | Ref. | Ref. | Ref. | Ref. | Ref. | Ref. | Ref. | Ref. |
| 13–15 years | 0.73** | 1.12 | 1.10 | 0.89 | 0.83* | 1.00 | 0.88** | 0.99 | 0.90*** |
| 16 years | 0.83 | 0.70** | 0.71 | 0.57*** | 0.80 | 0.78 | 0.54*** | 0.72*** | 0.80*** |
| 17 or more years | 0.61** | 0.53** | 1.08 | 0.43*** | 0.63** | 0.79 | 0.53*** | 0.59*** | 0.75*** |
| Age (25–84, continuous) | 1.06*** | 1.07*** | 1.07*** | 1.08*** | 1.07*** | 1.07*** | 1.08*** | 1.09*** | 1.09*** |
| Observations | 25,589 | 10,822 | 3,484 | 23,355 | 14,786 | 6,813 | 146,677 | 100,441 | 54,503 |
| Deaths | 893 | 1,087 | 1,160 | 1,307 | 2,849 | 3,471 | 4,039 | 13,318 | 25,748 |
| −2*Log-likelihood | 9,750.5 | 10,253.3 | 7,696.3 | 12,044.3 | 21,196.8 | 19,220.3 | 43,843.5 | 108,194.2 | 147,118.2 |

Source: National Center for Health Statistics (2005).
*p<0.10; **p<0.05; ***p<0.001.

Our analysis by cause of death is depicted in Table 12.2. As is true for overall mortality, there are substantial differences in mortality risk by educational attainment, with the most highly educated persons exhibiting the lowest risk for each underlying cause, net of age, sex, and race/ethnicity. For example, US adults with 17 or more years of education are 49% less likely to die of lung cancer during the follow-up period than are those with 12 years. While the relative mortality risk advantages for the most educated are smallest for the cause categories of stroke and all other cancers, even for these causes people with 17 or more years of education still have a 24% lower risk of mortality than do those with 12 years. People with 8 or fewer years of education do not differ very much from those with 9–11 years in mortality from most causes of death; both of these less-educated groups tend to have cause-specific mortality risks around 13–33% higher than do people with 12 years of education. Again, the educational differences in other cancer-related mortality are the narrowest, while the less educated exhibit especially heightened mortality risk for heart disease, lung cancer, diabetes, respiratory diseases, and external cause mortality. Future work in this area should examine these cause-specific mortality differentials by educational attainment specific to age, sex, and race/ethnicity. Indeed, our next section examines such subgroup differences in overall mortality risk by educational attainment, and illustrates that patterns for the entire population differ to some degree from those for these demographic groups.

## Educational Attainment and US Adult Mortality: Differences by Age and Sex

The association between educational attainment and mortality risk does not operate the same way for all population subgroups. For example, analyses invariably show that educational disparities in mortality are narrower at older than at younger adult ages. This finding is consistent with an age-as-leveler hypothesis (Beckett 2000). In contrast, the cumulative advantage hypothesis posits that, unlike the effects of other social and behavioral factors that may fade with increasing age, the benefits of education for health and mortality risk accumulate over the life course, through at least age 75 (Lynch 2003; Ross and Wu 1995). Crimmins (2005), for example, used both mortality and health data to show that mortality selection is the most likely reason for narrower educational differences in mortality observed among the elderly in cross-sectional studies; cumulative advantages operate over the life course but are not easily observed in old-age mortality patterns because of the effects of mortality selection. We do not aim to untangle the age-as-leveler and cumulative advantage hypotheses here; we merely note that there remains considerable debate on this issue.

Furthermore, studies suggest that educational differences in adult mortality vary by sex, although not dramatically. Interestingly, some previous US studies using data from the 1960s and 1970s suggested a stronger education–mortality relationship among women than among men (Feldman et al. 1989; Kitagawa and Hauser 1973). In contrast, more recent studies have found that the relationship between educational attainment and mortality risk may be somewhat stronger for men (Backlund et al. 1999; Pappas et al. 1993). Still others have found no gender differences in the educational gradient of adult mortality risk (Elo and Preston 1996; Zajacova 2006). Most recently, Zajacova and Hummer (2009) specifically examined these relationships and found substantial similarity in the education–mortality association between women and men, but with some exceptions. Most notably, they found a steeper educational gradient at high levels of schooling for white men than for white women, indicating somewhat more substantial benefits at the highest levels of education for men than for women.

Table 12.3 uses the same NHIS-LMF data as above, but this time shows relative differences in overall mortality risk by educational attainment separately both by sex and by three adult age groups. These six separate models each control for individual years of age within the broader age range and for race/ethnicity. Two sets of important patterns, one by age and one by sex, are evident. Relative educational differences in mortality are the widest at ages 25–44, second widest at ages 45–64, and narrowest at ages 65–84 for each sex. While the educational mortality differences at ages 65–84 appear smaller, and *are* smaller in a relative sense, than those seen among younger adults, it is important to remember that overall death rates are far higher in this age range. Thus, for example, the relative differences at ages 65–84 for women—in comparison with women with 12 years of schooling, 12% higher mortality among the least educated and 18% lower mortality among the most educated—continue to be extremely meaningful because of the concentration of deaths within this age range. Indeed, the work of Huisman et al. (2005), which focused on educational differences in adult mortality among 11 European countries, showed that absolute mortality differentials by education were actually wider among elderly individuals (80–89) than among young adults, even with smaller relative mortality differentials among the elderly. We also show here that, among the youngest age group (25–44), relative differences for both men and women are extremely wide. Both men and women with 9–11 years of schooling, for example, exhibit about three times the mortality risks of their most highly educated gender-specific counterparts (specific comparisons not shown).

Gender differences in the education–mortality relationship are not particularly striking, for the most part, with a couple of exceptions. For adults aged 65–84, there are no real differences. Among the two younger age groups, the relative advantages for men at the highest two levels of education (16 and 17 or more years) appear to be modestly stronger than the relative advantages for women. This is consistent with recent findings discussed above (Zajacova and Hummer 2009).

## *Educational Attainment and US Adult Mortality: Differences by Race/Ethnicity*

With immigration generating increasingly diverse populations in many countries, health and mortality researchers must consider race/ethnicity in their analyses. Most work on education and mortality in the United States does not consider whether educational differences in adult mortality vary for Hispanic subgroups or non-Hispanic blacks in comparison to non-Hispanic whites. There is substantial reason to think, however, that educational differences in mortality may be narrower for racial and ethnic minority groups than for non-Hispanic whites. It is well known that compared to whites, members of racial and ethnic minority groups tend to live in areas that have lower-performing schools, attend less prestigious colleges and universities, and face discrimination in the labor market—all of which would devalue their educational achievements, particularly at the highest levels (Conley 1999; Massey and Denton 1993; Tienda and Mitchell 2005). Accordingly, several recent studies have shown a substantially weaker educational gradient in US adult mortality for Hispanics than for whites (Lin et al. 2003; McKinnon and Hummer 2007; Turra and Goldman 2007).

Tables 12.4 and 12.5 expand upon Table 12.3 by showing estimates of relative educational differences in US adult mortality for Hispanics, non-Hispanic blacks, and non-Hispanic whites, stratified by age group for women (Table 12.4) and men (Table 12.5). For women (Table 12.4), two patterns emerge. First, among the younger age groups, there are relatively higher mortality risks among less-educated non-Hispanic whites than among non-Hispanic blacks or Hispanics. Put another way, the relative penalties for low-educated white women seem to be greater than among low-educated black and Hispanic women. Second, while the highly educated among the oldest age group of non-Hispanic black and Hispanic women do not exhibit lower mortality than do their high-school-educated counterparts, highly educated women in the two younger age categories of *all* race/ethnic groups exhibit substantially lower mortality risks than their high-school-educated counterparts. While the effects of mortality selection surely help to mute educational differences in old-age mortality (Crimmins 2005), it is clear from these data that educational attainment seriously differentiates the mortality prospects of young adult (25–44) and middle-aged (45–64) women for each of these groups in ways that are not seen among the oldest minority group women.

For men, Table 12.5 shows nine mortality risk models that are stratified within age group and race/ethnic group, with 12 years of educational attainment serving as the reference category for each age- and race/ethnic-specific model. The patterns exhibited for men are very similar to those of women: (1) educational attainment differences in mortality are pronounced for each of the three race/ethnic groups among the younger adult age groups, while it is only among non-Hispanic whites that there are wide differences among older (65–84) adults; and (2) heightened mortality risk among less-educated younger adults, compared to each group's reference category of high-school-educated adults, seems to be particularly prominent among non-Hispanic white men. Together, the age-related patterns for both women and men suggest that educational attainment may be becoming more and more important for differentiating mortality risks among younger cohorts of all racial/ethnic groups in the United States (Lauderdale 2001).

## Life Expectancy Differences by Educational Attainment

An important question in this and any subset of the mortality differentials literature involves the extent to which relative mortality differences—as shown and discussed above—translate into variations in life expectancy (a measure of absolute mortality differences) across groups. Preston and Taubman (1994) provide a very useful and important distinction between mortality differentials in a relative and an absolute sense. If, for example, relative mortality differentials between two groups are large (e.g., a risk ratio of two) but both of the mortality rates are very low, then life-expectancy differences between the two groups will be modest. If, on the other hand, the same ratio holds for two groups with high mortality rates, life expectancy differences between the two groups will be much larger. Because life expectancy figures and, hence, life expectancy differentials are calculated using mortality rates rather than ratios, they provide a very useful indicator of the extent to which mortality differences between groups result in meaningful disparities in the estimated length of life for those groups.

Table 12.6 shows data abstracted from three recent studies that have calculated educational differences in US life expectancy at age 25 ($e_{25}$). Panel A, taken from a study by Molla et al. (2004), uses official US mortality data to generate $e_{25}$ estimates across three educational groups: 0–8, 9–12, and 13 or more years. Official US mortality data, based on numerator mortality counts from death certificates and denominator estimates from census population data, are quite useful because they cover the complete population. An important limitation, however, is that death certificate information is collected from informants and, as a result, data on educational attainment tend to be overstated (Christensen and Johnson 1995; Molla et al. 2004). The 1998 $e_{25}$ estimates from Molla et al. (2004) shown here are grouped in an educational categorization scheme (0–8, 9–12, 13 or more years) that is both unconventional and not particularly useful for understanding the potential impacts that degree attainment has on adult mortality. That being said, the differentials shown in Panel A of Table 12.6 are wide. US women with 13 or more years of education had an $e_{25}$ estimate of 57.8 years, compared to 52.9 among women with 0–8 years of education; this is roughly a 5-year difference. The differential is even larger for men: 54.6 for men with 13+ years compared to 47.0 for men with 0–8 years, or a 7.6-year difference. These data clearly indicate that education differences in US adult mortality rates result in substantial life expectancy differences across educational attainment groups.

Panels B and C of Table 12.6 show $e_{25}$ estimates from Lin et al. (2003) and Meara et al. (2008), respectively. Both research groups use data from the National Longitudinal Mortality Study (NLMS): the Lin et al. estimates come from the 1979–1989 NLMS while the Meara et al. estimates are based on the 1991–1998 NLMS. Like the NHIS-LMF data that we used above, the NLMS consists of survey-based data (multiple years of the US Current Population Survey) linked to follow-up mortality information for those who died from the National Death Index. Thus it shares an important strength with the NHIS-LMF: education data are reported by either the individuals in the survey or a proxy household respondent. One downside of both the NHIS-LMF and the NLMS, however, is that they initially exclude institutionalized individuals, that is, persons who reside in nursing homes, on military bases, or in prison. As a result, life expectancy estimates from both the NHIS-LMF and NLMS should be, and are, slightly higher than those from official data because some high-risk individuals are not included in these survey-based data sets (Hummer et al. 2009).

The estimates from both Panels B and C, though, correspond fairly well with those from the official data in Panel A. Keep in mind as well that the three panels of Table 12.6 categorize educational attainment somewhat differently because of the different ways that education data were collected and/or the specific aims of each of these studies. Both Panels B and C show that life-expectancy differences by education tend to be somewhat larger among men than among women; further, Panel B shows that life expectancy differences between the most and least educated black women and men are wider than those between the most and least educated white women and men. Even though Hispanics are now the largest racial/ethnic minority group in the United States, only Lin et al. (2003) have estimated educational differences in life expectancy

Table 12.6 Three recent estimates of educational differences in US life expectancy at age 25

| Panel A | 0–8 years | 9–12 years | 13+ years |
|---|---|---|---|
| All US females | 52.9 | 53.6 | 57.8 |
| All US males | 47.0 | 47.5 | 54.6 |

Source: Molla et al. (2004), using official US mortality data from 1998

| Panel B | <12 years | 12 years | 13+ years |
|---|---|---|---|
| Non-Hispanic black females | 50.2 | 53.6 | 56.1 |
| Non-Hispanic white females | 55.1 | 55.1 | 57.9 |
| Non-Hispanic black males | 43.5 | 46.5 | 50.2 |
| Non-Hispanic white males | 47.2 | 50.2 | 52.6 |

Source: Lin et al. (2003), using data from the National Longitudinal Mortality Study, 1979–1989

| Panel C | < 13 years | 13+ years |
|---|---|---|
| White females | 55.7 | 58.1 |
| White males | 49.6 | 54.0 |

Source: Meara et al. (2008) using data from the National Longitudinal Mortality Study 1991–1998

among Hispanics, and even they did not show life expectancy estimates for Hispanics with 13 or more years of education because of the relatively small number of Hispanic deaths with which they had to work. Future work in this area, then, should focus on both broadening the educational attainment categories that are used and the population subgroups specified; both of these enhancements pose significant challenges because some of the age/sex/race/education cells used to calculate mortality rates become quite sparse among relatively small population subgroups.

## Changes in Educational Differences in Mortality over Time

There is a growing literature that examines changes in educational differences in US adult mortality since the classic Kitagawa and Hauser (1973) study (which used data from 1960). In an initial set of studies, most analysts found that educational differences in mortality widened between 1960 and 1985–1990, owing to steeper mortality declines experienced by the more highly educated over that period, particularly among men (Duleep 1989, 1998; Feldman et al. 1989; Lauderdale 2001; Pappas et al. 1993; Preston and Elo 1995). Between 1970 and 1990, for example, the gap in life expectancy for white men at age 30 between those with 0–8 years of education and those with 13 or more years grew from 4.1 to 6.7 years (Crimmins and Saito 2001). With more and more of a premium being placed on educational credentials in the US labor force, there is ample reason to hypothesize that educational differences in mortality have continued to widen between the mid-1980s to late 1980s and the present, as persons with the highest levels reap the greatest rewards while persons with low levels of education are increasingly isolated in low-wage, less-rewarding, and unstable jobs.

Emerging evidence is indeed showing even wider educational differentials in US adult mortality than existed just 20 or so years ago (Jemal et al. 2008; Meara et al. 2008; Montez et al. forthcoming). This is in direct contrast to one of the two current overall US health goals, which aimed to eliminate health disparities across population subgroups by 2010 (US DHHS 2000). Although all three recent studies in this area arrive at the same general conclusion, there are also some differences to note based on the data sets used, specific age groups examined, and measures of educational attainment employed. Both Meara et al. and Montez et al., for example, reported that the widening was more pronounced among women than men, while Jemal et al. reported more pronounced widening among men. Both Jemal et al. and Montez et al. found no particular pattern of widening among blacks (although they did not find any narrowing gaps either), while Meara et al. did report a widening of educational differences among blacks. Finally, Montez et al. showed that the widening between 1990 and 2000 was largely evident among younger cohorts of US adults, among whom the most highly educated have experienced the steepest mortality declines. Despite their particular differences, all of these most recent studies find that relative educational differences in US adult mortality have probably increased in recent decades, and this unanimity points to the need both to continue to monitor such disparities and to work on program and policy initiatives to help reduce the relatively high risk of mortality among the least educated segments of society.

## International Comparisons

International comparisons of mortality differences by educational level can tell us to what extent socioeconomic inequality results in unequal life chances in different contexts. Such international comparisons are difficult, though. Valkonen (1993) outlines a number of data and analytic issues that hamper the comparison of educational differences in adult mortality across national contexts. Studies that link census records or surveys to death certificates through personal identification numbers—such as those we reported above in the main analytic portion of this chapter—provide the strongest evidence of mortality differences by education. But such high-quality data are available in only a few nations. Other nations must estimate death rates from separate data sources; for example, the numerator of a death rate may need to be taken from death records while the denominator will come from census data. Countries without nationally representative data on education and adult mortality often rely on data that are representative of a major metropolitan area. For example, Huisman et al. (2005) use data from Turin, Italy, and Barcelona and Madrid, Spain, to estimate educational differences in adult mortality within those two countries.

Analytic concerns highlighted by Valkonen (1993) include differences in study design across nations, differences in the timing of studies or length of follow-up periods, and coverage of specific subgroups (e.g., by age) for the nations being compared. The skewness of educational distributions may present difficulties in estimating educational differences in mortality. For example, if a large majority of a population obtains a relatively uniform level of schooling, there may not be enough variation in levels of education to estimate educational differences in mortality. Despite these data and analytic concerns, however, more and more studies are making useful comparisons of educational mortality differences across national contexts, as both levels of education and educational inequality increase within countries and data bases that can be used for this purpose proliferate. Nevertheless, most comparisons in this area of study to date have been based on data from Europe and the United States. While most early comparative studies examined only the working-aged population (e.g., 25–64 or 35–64) and often only men, more recent studies have covered broader age ranges and both genders, and have focused on cause-specific as well as overall mortality (Huisman et al. 2004, 2005).

For all countries studied, death rates are higher for less-educated individuals than for more educated ones. This pattern has been established in comparative work examining Scandinavian nations (Denmark, Finland, Norway, and Sweden); western and southern European countries (Austria, Belgium, Bulgaria, the Czech Republic, England and Wales, France, Italy, Hungary, the Netherlands, Spain, and Switzerland); several countries of the former Soviet Union (Estonia, Lithuania, and Russia); and countries in North America (Canada and the United States) (Elo and Preston 1996; Elo et al. 2006; Huisman et al. 2004, 2005; Kalediene and Petrauskiene 2005; Kohler et al. 2008; Kunst and Mackenbach 1994; Mackenbach et al. 1999; Regidor et al. 2003; Roos et al. 2004; Sholnikov et al. 1998). Evidence supporting educational differences in adult mortality certainly exists for additional nations; this list is simply intended to show that educational differences in adult mortality are ubiquitous across the high-income countries that have been examined to date.

Early comparative work in this area found that absolute differences in mortality by education for men appeared to be approximately the same for all countries examined; that is, for every year of education attained, death rates diminished by about 8% (Valkonen 1989). Kunst and Mackenbach (1994) later found that the United States, France, and Italy were characterized by larger educational differences in adult mortality than the Netherlands, Sweden, Denmark, Norway, England and Wales, and Finland; however, the wider disparities in the United States and France were largely explained by greater educational inequality within those countries in comparison to the others. That is, effect sizes of the education–mortality relationship were quite similar in all countries.

Using data from the 1990s, Huisman et al. (2005) more recently showed quite similar patterns in educational inequalities across eight western European populations—Finland, Norway, England and Wales, Belgium, Austria, Switzerland, Italy, and Spain. At the same time, they documented substantial differences in the contribution of specific causes of death to these disparities in different contexts. For example, cardiovascular diseases contribute more strongly to educational differences in mortality in northern European nations than in southern European nations, while cancers and other causes tend to contribute more strongly in the southern European countries. Around the same time, Huisman et al. (2004) examined age patterns of the education–mortality relationship among a somewhat broader set of 11 European nations. They showed that in most of the countries relative educational differences in adult mortality tended to be narrower among older age groups, but persisted all the way through the 80–89 age group. Our findings for US white adults presented above similarly showed persistent educational disparities in adult mortality through at least age 84. Interestingly, Huisman et al. (2004) also showed that absolute differences in mortality rates between the most and least educated groups were largest among the older age group (80–89) of adults in most of these countries, although relative educational differences tended to be widest among the younger age groups (e.g., 50–59).

Finally, another recent set of studies comparing the United States with Finland (Elo et al. 2006) and with Bulgaria and Finland (Kohler et al. 2008) revealed larger educational disparities in mortality for US women than for women in Bulgaria and Finland, but the largest educational differences in mortality were found for Finnish men. In general, most comparative studies using recent data have found somewhat larger educational disparities in adult mortality among men than among women, particularly among working-aged adults (Elo et al. 2006; Koskinen and Martelin 1994; Mackenbach et al. 1999; Mustard and Etches 2003; Zajacova and Hummer 2009). Again, it is important to note that in spite of the particular differences across causes of death by gender and to some degree age in all of these international comparisons, overall educational differences in mortality have been shown to be consistently wide and have shown little if any signs of closure for any of the populations studied.

## Policy Implications

If education so powerfully and ubiquitously enhances health-promoting resources, can mortality disparities by educational attainment be reduced or eliminated? This is not an easy question to answer because, if anything, educational disparities in adult mortality risks have widened over the past several decades, even with substantial research and governmental attention devoted to this issue. But it is also the case that the health policy agenda, at least in the United States, is rarely devoted to influencing the basic socioeconomic factors that so powerfully underlie health and mortality patterns of national populations. Such thinking can, however, change. Recent work by Schoeni et al. (2008), for example, emphasizes the potentially powerful influences that social policy can have on population health and urges researchers and policymakers to give more thought to *treating social policy as health policy*. More specifically, Cutler and Lleras-Muney (2008), in a chapter within the Schoeni et al. (2008) volume, estimate that the health benefits of increases in educational attainment may be even greater than the well-documented lifelong financial benefits of educational attainment.

Thus, one possible and very straightforward way to reduce educational differentials in adult mortality would be to shift more and more people out of the lower portions of the educational distribution into more advanced educational categories, as was clearly the case across birth cohorts for most of the twentieth century in the United States (Montez et al. forthcoming). At present, 16% of US adults aged 25 and over do not have a high-school diploma; among the narrower adult age range of 25–34, the figure is not much lower, at 14% (US Census Bureau 2009). Another 30% of US adults have a high-school diploma or its equivalent, but nothing further; moreover, in no adult 10-year age category do college graduates make up even 30% of the US population (U.S. Census Bureau 2009). These figures illustrate that there is very substantial room for improvement within the US educational distribution, even within recent birth cohorts. And such substantial improvements in composition could help lead to progress in health and reductions in mortality over time if the effects of education on health and mortality are at all causal, as seems to be at least partially the case (Chandola et al. 2008; Glied and

Lleras-Muney 2008; Lleras-Muney 2005; Mirowsky and Ross 2003; Smith 2004). While compositional change in educational attainment would, in and of itself, have no impact on relative educational disparities in mortality, it would clearly expose fewer and fewer people to the heightened health and mortality risks that persons with low educational attainment face. Moreover, more highly educated individuals not only live longer lives on average than less-educated individuals, but also live a greater proportion of their lives in good health than do less-educated persons (Crimmins and Saito 2001).

A second policy angle to reduce educational disparities in mortality involves the attempt to influence the hazardous "downstream" mechanisms that are associated with low levels of educational attainment. This is arguably a more difficult and expensive angle than cohort-by-cohort improvements in basic levels of education, and may do little to alter the social structure on which such inequalities in outcomes are based (Link 2008; Link and Phelan 1995). Nevertheless, for the millions and millions of adults who have already completed their educational careers, this may be the only option available. Denney et al. (2010) have recently shown that cigarette smoking may account for more than 40% of the mortality gap between the most and least educated groups of young adults in the United States. Thus, continued efforts to curb cigarette smoking—through policies such as increased taxation on tobacco products, advertising restrictions on tobacco products, and smoking bans in nightclubs, restaurants, and workplaces—will improve health and decrease mortality not only among the population as a whole, but especially so among the less-educated portion of the population. Similarly, policy efforts to make health insurance more accessible to adults who are not covered by employer plans have potential not only to improve the health of the nation as a whole, but to have a particular impact on the least educated segment of society.

## Future Research Directions

Educational differences in adult mortality are omnipresent and wide, and may even be increasing in some contexts. Over the next decade or more, it will be important for researchers to continue to monitor trends in the education–mortality relationship, particularly given major governmental initiatives that aim to close socioeconomic disparities in health and mortality. Are education–mortality gaps narrowing or widening? What are the trends when both relative disparities and absolute disparities are considered? Are there widening or narrowing gaps among specific subgroups of the population defined by birth cohort, gender, and race/ethnicity? Are there widening or narrowing gaps for specific causes of death that help indicate pathways by which these educational differences are changing? And if there are changes in the disparities, is one educational attainment group making faster gains than another, or is mortality lessening in one educational group while actually increasing in another? Social demographers and epidemiologists should continue to carefully monitor these large-scale patterns and trends to best inform policymakers. In addition, the changing educational composition of populations needs to be taken into account. For example, in the United States and many other countries, it will no longer be adequate to consider 13 or more years as the highest category of educational attainment when more and more individuals are pursuing college and advanced degrees.

While a huge literature in the United States and Europe has documented education and mortality patterns and trends over the last several decades, and such monitoring should definitely continue, we actually may know less in this area than we seem to, because of the relative scarcity of high-quality educational data in most mortality data sets. On the whole, this leaves us with excellent knowledge of the basic patterns of educational attainment and adult mortality, but with much less specific knowledge regarding just what it is about educational attainment that ends up relating so strongly to how long people live. As new demographic and health surveys are designed, researchers should think carefully about the education questions that are being asked and, if at all possible, probe more deeply into the educational attainment process beyond years of completed schooling. Moreover, innovative data linkages should be explored. For example, individuals in demographic and health surveys may be linked with their high school and postsecondary educational transcripts to allow for a much better sense of what schools they attended, what courses they took while in school, what majors they pursued, what grades they earned, what specific degrees they acquired, and more. Surveyed individuals can also be linked to the records of other household members in the survey or to neighborhood-based census data to better tap into the educational contexts in which individuals are living. Appending such transcript, household, and neighborhood data to ongoing demographic and health surveys will allow researchers a much greater opportunity to understand the context in which individuals are schooled and allow for a much deeper understanding of educational attainment and adult mortality patterns than has so far been the case.

Important questions regarding whether or not (and to what degree) educational attainment causally influences mortality risks across the life course are also critically important for scientific and policy-related reasons and in need of much additional study. Such investigations should aim to use data sets and measures that better tap into the precursors of educational attainment as well as the subsequent health and mortality patterns. Most studies in this area to date examine educational attainment differences in adult mortality either by looking at age-specific mortality rate differences across educational attainment groups or through regression analyses of educational attainment and mortality risk that control for basic demographic factors like age, sex, and race/ethnicity. These are very informative approaches, but at the same time, cannot speak to the actual causal influences of educational attainment on mortality risk. More comprehensive methodological approaches are needed to take account of the family background, early life, health, and genetic factors that influence the educational trajectories of individuals as well as their length of life. Data requirements for such a true life-course approach to the issue are stringent, but this is probably the most important aspect of future study in this area if we are to truly understand the extent to which educational attainment operates as a causal mechanism to influence the mortality prospects of individuals.

**Acknowledgments** This chapter was supported by an Eunice Kennedy Shriver National Institute of Child Health and Human Development (NICHD) research grant (1 R01 HD053696) and by an NICHD infrastructure grant (5 R24 HD042849) awarded to the Population Research Center at the University of Texas at Austin. We thank Anna Zajacova and the editors of this handbook, Richard Rogers and Eileen Crimmins, for very helpful comments and edits.

# References

Allison, P.D. 1984. *Event History Analysis: Regression for Longitudinal Event Data*. Beverly Hills, CA, Sage.

Backlund, E., P.D. Sorlie, and N.J. Johnson. 1999. "A Comparison of the Relationships of Education and Income with Mortality: The National Longitudinal Mortality Study." *Social Science and Medicine* 49:1373–84.

Batty, G.D. and I.J. Deary. 2005. "Education and Mortality: A Role for Intelligence?" *Journal of Epidemiology and Community Health* 59:809–10.

Batty, G.D., G. Der, S. Macintyre, and I.J. Deary. 2006. "Does IQ Explain Socioeconomic Inequalities in Health? Evidence from a Population Based Cohort Study in the West of Scotland." *British Medical Journal* 332:1–5.

Beckett, M. 2000. "Converging Health Inequalities in Later Life: An Artifact or Mortality Selection?" *Journal of Health and Social Behavior* 41:106–19.

Braveman, P.A., C. Cubbin, S. Egerter, S. Chideya, K.S. Marchi, M. Metzler, and S. Posner. 2005. "Socioeconomic Status in Health Research: One Size Does Not Fit All." *Journal of the American Medical Association* 294:2879–88.

Brown, D.C., M.D. Hayward, and R.A. Hummer. 2009. "Spousal Education and Mortality in the NHIS-LMF." Paper presented at the annual meeting of the Southern Demographic Association, Galveston, TX.

Chandola, T., P. Clarke, J.N. Morris, and D. Blane. 2008. "Pathways Between Education and Health: A Causal Modeling Approach." *Journal of the Royal Statistical Society: Series A (Statistics in Society)* 169(2):337–59.

Christensen, B.A. and N.E. Johnson. 1995. "Educational Inequality in Adult Mortality: An Assessment with Death Certificate Data From Michigan." *Demography* 32(2):215–29.

Conley, D. 1999. *Being Black, Living in the Red: Race, Wealth, and Social Policy in America*. Los Angeles, CA, University of California Press.

Crimmins, E.M. 2005. "Socioeconomic Differentials in Mortality and Health at the Older Ages." *Genus* LXI(1):163–77.

Crimmins, E.M. and Y. Saito. 2001. "Trends in Healthy Life Expectancy in the United States, 1970–1990: Gender, Racial, and Educational Differences." *Social Science & Medicine* 52:1629–41.

Cutler, D.M. and A. Lleras-Muney 2008. "Education and Health: Evaluating Theories and Evidence." In R.F. Schoeni, J.S. House, G.A. Kaplan, and H. Pollack (eds.), *Making Americans Healthier: Social and Economic Policy as Health Policy*, pp. 29–60. New York, NY, Russell Sage Foundation.

Denney, J.T., R.G. Rogers, R.A. Hummer, and F.C. Pampel 2010. "Education Inequality in Mortality: The Age and Gender Specific Mediating Effects of Cigarette Smoking." *Social Science Research* 29:662–673.

Drevenstedt, G.L. 2001. "Mortality Patterns in the United States Since 1960: Essays on Migrant Mortality, the Impact of Medicare, and Demographic Consequences of Cause-specific Mortality Change." *ProQuest*, Paper AAI3003622. Available online at http://repository.upenn.edu/dissertations/AAI3003622

Duleep, H.O. 1989. "Measuring Socioeconomic Mortality Differentials Over Time." *Demography* 26:345–51.

Duleep, H.O. 1998. "Has the U.S. Mortality Differential by Socioeconomic Status Increased Over Time?" *American Journal of Public Health* 88(7):1125.

Elo, I.T., P. Martikainen, and K.P. Smith. 2006. "Socioeconomic Differentials in Mortality in Finland and the United States: The Role of Education and Income." *European Journal of Population* 22:179–203.

Elo, I.T. and S.H. Preston. 1996. "Educational Differentials in Mortality: United States, 1979–85." *Social Science and Medicine* 42:47–57.

Feldman, J.J., D.M. Makuc, J.C. Kleinman, and J. Cornoni-Huntley. 1989. "National Trends in Educational Differentials in Mortality." *American Journal of Epidemiology* 129:919–33.

Glied, S. and A. Lleras-Muney. 2008. "Technological Innovation and Inequality in Health." *Demography* 45(3):741–61.

Goldman, D.P. and J.P. Smith. 2002. "Can Patient Self-Management Help Explain the SES Health Gradient?" *Proceedings of the National Academy of Sciences of the United States of America* 99(16):10929–34.

Gottfredson, L. 2004. "Intelligence: Is It the Epidemiologists' Elusive 'Fundamental Cause' of Social Class Inequalities in Health?" *Journal of Social and Personality Psychology* 86:174–99.

Hayward, M.D. and B.K. Gorman. 2004. "The Long Arm of Childhood: The Influence of Early-Life Social Conditions on Men's Mortality." *Demography* 41(1):87–108.

Hoffmann, R. 2008. *Socioeconomic Differences in Old Age Mortality*. New York, NY, Springer.

House, J.S., K.R. Landis, and D. Umberson. 1988. "Social Relationships and Health." *Science* 241:540–45.

Huie, S.A.B., R.A. Hummer, and R.G. Rogers. 2002. "Individual and Contextual Risks of Death Among Race and Ethnic Groups in the United States." *Journal of Health and Social Behavior* 43(3):359–81.

Huisman, M., A.E. Kunst, O. Anderson, M. Bopp, J.K. Borgan, C. Borrell, G. Costa, P. Deboosere, G. Desplanques, A. Donkin, S. Gadeyne, C. Minder, E. Regidor, T. Spadea, T. Valkonen, and J.P. Mackenbach. 2004. "Socioeconomic Inequalities in Mortality Among Elderly People in 11 European Populations." *Journal of Epidemiology and Community Health* 58:468–75.

Huisman, M., A.E. Kunst, M. Bopp, J. Borgan, C. Borrell, G. Costa, P. Deboosere, S. Gadeyne, M. Glickman, C. Marinacci, C. Minder, E. Regidor, T. Valkonen, and J.P. Mackenbach. 2005. "Educational Inequalities in Cause-Specific Mortality in Middle-Aged and Older Men and Women in Eight Western European Populations." *Lancet* 365:493–500.

Hummer, R.A., R.G. Rogers, and I.W. Eberstein. 1998. "Sociodemographic Differentials in Adult Mortality: A Review of Analytic Approaches." *Population and Development Review* 24(3):553–78.

Hummer, R.A., R.G. Rogers, R. Masters, and J. Saint Onge 2009. "Mortality Patterns in Late Life." In P. Uhlenberg (ed.), *International Handbook of Population Aging*, pp. 521–42. New York, NY, Springer.

Jaffe, D.H., Z. Eisenbach, Y.D. Neumark, and O. Manor. 2005. "Does One's Own and One's Spouse's Education Affect Overall and Cause-Specific Mortality in the Elderly?" *International Journal of Epidemiology* 34:1409–16.

Jemal, A., E. Ward, R.N. Anderson, T. Murray, and M.J. Thun 2008. "Widening of Socioeconomic Inequalities in U.S. Death Rates, 1993–2001." *PLoS ONE* 3(5):e2181. doi:10.1371/journal.pone.0002181.

Kalediene, R. and J. Petrauskiene. 2005. "Inequalities in Mortality by Education and Socio-Economic Transition in Lithuania: Equal Opportunities?" *Public Health* 119(9):808–15.

Kitagawa, E.M. and P.M. Hauser. 1973. *Differential Mortality in the United States: A Study in Socioeconomic Epidemiology*. Cambridge, MA, Harvard University Press.

Kohler, I.V., P. Martikainen, K.P. Smith, and I.T. Elo. 2008. "Educational Differences in All-Cause Mortality by Marital Status: Evidence from Bulgaria, Finland, and the United States." *Demographic Research* 19:2011–42.

Koskinen, S. and T. Martelin. 1994. "Why Are Socioeconomic Mortality Differences Smaller Among Women Than Among Men?" *Social Science and Medicine* 38(10):1385–96.

Krieger, N., D. Rowley, A. Herman, B. Avery, and M. Phillips. 1993. "Racism, Sexism, and Social Class: Implications for Studies of Health, Disease, and Well-Being." *American Journal of Preventative Medicine* 9:82–122.

Krueger, P.M., R.G. Rogers, R.A. Hummer, S.A. Bond Huie, and F. LeClere. 2003. "Socioeconomic Status and Age: The Effect of Income Sources and Portfolios on Adult Mortality in the United States." *Sociological Forum* 18(3):465–82.

Krueger, P.M. and S.A. Burgard. 2011. "Work, Occupation, Income, and Mortality." In R.G. Rogers and E.M. Crimmins (eds.), *International Handbook of Adult Mortality*. New York, NY, Springer.

Kunst, A.E. and J.P. Mackenbach. 1994. "The Size of Mortality Differences Associated with Educational Level in Nine Industrialized Countries." *American Journal of Public Health* 84(6):932–37.

Lantz, P.M., J.S. House, J.M. Lepkowski, D.R. Williams, R.P. Mero, and J. Chen. 1998. "Socioeconomic Factors, Health Behaviors, and Mortality." *Journal of the American Medical Association* 279(21):1703–8.

Lantz, P.M., J.S. House, R.P. Mero, and D.R. Williams. 2005. "Stress, Life Events, and Socioeconomic Disparities in Health: Results from the Americans' Changing Lives Study." *Journal of Health and Social Behavior* 46:274–89.

Lauderdale, D.S. 2001. "Education and Survival: Birth Cohort, Period, and Age Effects." *Demography* 38:551–61.

Lawlor, D.A., S. Frankel, M. Shaw, S. Ebrahim, and G.D. Smith 2003. "Smoking and Ill Health: Does Lay Epidemiology Explain the Failure of Smoking Cessation Programs Among Deprived Populations?" *American Journal of Public Health* 93(2):266–70.

Lin, C.C., E. Rogot, N.J. Johnson, P.D. Sorlie, and E. Arias. 2003. "A Further Study of Life Expectancy by Socioeconomic Factors in the National Longitudinal Mortality Study." *Ethnicity and Disease* 13:240–47.

Link, B.G. 2008. "Epidemiological Sociology and the Social Shaping of Population Health." *Journal of Health and Social Behavior* 49:367–84.

Link, B.G. and J. Phelan 1995. "Social Conditions as Fundamental Causes of Disease." *Journal of Health and Social Behavior* 35(extra issue):80–94.

Link, B.G., J.C. Phelan, R. Miech, and E.L. Westin. 2008. "The Resources that Matter: Fundamental Social Causes of Health Disparities and the Challenge of Intelligence." *Journal of Health and Social Behavior* 49(1):72–91.

Lleras-Muney, A. 2005. "The Relationship Between Education and Adult Mortality in the United States." *Demography* 38(4):551–61.

Lochner, K., R.A. Hummer, S. Bartee, G. Wheatcroft, and C. Cox. 2008. "The Public-Use National Health Interview Survey Linked Mortality Files: Methods of Re-identification Risk Avoidance and Comparative Analysis." *American Journal of Epidemiology* 168:336–44.

Lynch, S.M. 2003. "Cohort and Life-Course Patterns in the Education-Health Relationship." *Demography* 40: 309–31.

Mackenbach, J.P., A.E. Kunst, F. Groenhof, J. Borgan, G. Costa, F. Faggiano, P. Jozan, M. Leinsalu, P. Martikainen, J. Rychtarikova, and T. Valkonen. 1999. "Socioeconomic Inequalities in Mortality Among Women and Men: An International Study." *American Journal of Public Health* 89(12):1800–6.

Marmot, M.G. 2004. *The Status Syndrome: How Social Standing Affects Our Health and Longevity*. New York, NY, Henry Holt and Company.

Massey, D.S. and N.A. Denton 1993. *American Apartheid: Segregation and the Making of the Underclass*. Cambridge, Harvard University Press.

McKinnon, S.A. and R.A. Hummer 2007. "Education and Mortality Risk Among Hispanic Adults in the United States." In J.L. Angel and K.E. Whitfield (eds.), *The Health of Aging Hispanics: The Mexican-Origin Population*. New York, NY, Springer.

Meara, E.R., S. Richards, and D.M. Cutler. 2008. "The Gap Gets Bigger: Changes in Mortality and Life Expectancy, by Education, 1981–2000." *Health Affairs* 27:350–60.

Mirowsky, J. and C.E. Ross. 1998. "Education, Personal Control, Lifestyle and Health: A Human Capital Hypothesis." *Research on Aging* 20(4):415–49.

Mirowsky, J. and C.E. Ross. 2003. *Education, Social Status, and Health*. New York, NY, Aldine de Gruyter.

Mirowsky, J. and C.E. Ross. 2007. "Creative Work and Health." *Journal of Health and Social Behavior* 48:385–403.

Molla, M.T., J.H. Madans, and D.K. Wagener. 2004. "Differentials in Adult Mortality and Activity Limitation by Years of Education in the United States at the End of the 1990s." *Population and Development Review* 30:625–46.

Montez, J.K., M.D. Hayward, D.C. Brown, and R.A. Hummer. 2009. "Why Is the Educational Gradient of Mortality Steeper for Men?" *Journal of Gerontology: Social Sciences* 64B:625–34.

Montez, J.K., R.A. Hummer, M.D. Hayward, H. Woo, and R.G. Rogers. Forthcoming. "Trends in the Educational Gradient of U.S. Adult Mortality from 1986 through 2006 by Race, Gender, and Age Group." *Research on Aging*.

Moss, N. and N. Krieger. 1995. "Measuring Social Inequalities in Health: Report on the Conference of the National Institutes of Health." *Public Health Reports* 110:302–5.

Mustard, C.A. and J. Etches. 2003. "Gender Differences in Socioeconomic Inequality in Mortality." *Journal of Epidemiology and Community Health* 57(12): 974–80.

National Center for Health Statistics. 2005. "The 1986–2000 National Health Interview Survey Linked Mortality Files: Matching Methodology." Hyattsville, MD, National Center for Health Statistics, Office of Analysis and Epidemiology.

Palloni, A. 2006. "Reproducing Inequalities: Luck, Wallet, and the Enduring Effects of Childhood Health." *Demography* 43:587–615.

Pamuk, E.R. 1985. "Social Class Inequality in Mortality from 1921 to 1972 in England and Wales." *Population Studies* 39:17–31.

Pappas, G., S. Queen, W. Hadden, and G. Fisher. 1993. "The Increasing Disparity in Mortality Between Socioeconomic Groups in the United States, 1960 and 1986." *New England Journal of Medicine* 329:103–9.

Phelan, J.C., B.G. Link, A. Diez-Roux, I. Kawachi, and B. Levin. 2004. "'Fundamental Causes' of Social Inequalities in Mortality: A Test of the Theory." *Journal of Health and Social Behavior* 45:265–85.

Preston, S.H. and I.T. Elo. 1995. "Are Educational Differentials in Adult Mortality Increasing in the United States?" *Journal of Aging and Health* 7:476–96.

Preston, S.H. and P. Taubman. 1994. "Socioeconomic Differences in Adult Mortality and Health Status", Chapter 8. In L.G. Martin and S.H. Preston (eds.), *Demography of Aging*, pp. 279–318. Washington, DC, National Academy Press.

Regidor, E., M.E. Calle, P. Navarro, and V. Domínguez. 2003. "The Size of Educational Differences in Mortality from Specific Causes of Death in Men and Women." *European Journal of Epidemiology* 18:395–400.

Research Triangle Institute. 2008. *SUDAAN Language Manual, Release 10.0*. Research Triangle Park, NC, Research Triangle Institute.

Rogers, R.G. 1992. "Living and Dying in the USA: Sociodemographic Determinants of Death Among Blacks and Whites." *Demography* 29(2):287–303.

Rogers, R.G., B.G. Everett, A. Zajacova, and R.A. Hummer 2010. "Educational Degrees and Adult Mortality Risk in the United States." *Biodemography and Social Biology* 56(1):80–99.

Rogers, R.G., R.A. Hummer, and P. Krueger 2005. "Adult Mortality." In D. Poston and M. Micklin (eds.), *Handbook of Population*, pp. 169–206. New York, NY, Kluwer/Plenum Academic Publishers.

Rogers, R.G., R.A. Hummer, and C.B. Nam. 2000. *Living and Dying in the USA: Behavioral, Health, and Social Differentials of Adult Mortality*. San Diego, CA, Academic Press.

Rogers, R., R. Hummer, C. Nam, and K. Peters. 1996. "Demographic, Socioeconomic, and Behavioral Factors Affecting Ethnic Mortality by Cause." *Social Forces* 74:1419–38.

Roos, L.L., J. Magoon, S. Gupta, D. Chateau, and P.J. Veugelers. 2004. "Socioeconomic Determinants of Mortality in Two Canadian Provinces: Multilevel Modeling and Neighborhood Context." *Social Science & Medicine* 59(7): 1435–47.

Ross, C.E. and C. Wu. 1995. "The Links Between Education and Health." *American Sociological Review* 60:719–45.

Schnittker, J. 2004. "Education and the Changing Shape of the Income Gradient in Health." *Journal of Health and Social Behavior* 45:286–305.

Schoeni, R.F., J.S. House, G.A. Kaplan, and H. Pollack 2008. *Making Americans Healthier: Social and Economic Policy as Health Policy*. New York, NY, Russell Sage Foundation.

Sholnikov, V.M., D.A. Leon, S. Adamets, E. Andreev, and A. Deev. 1998. "Educational Level and Adult Mortality in Russia: An Analysis of Routine Data 1979 to 1994." *Social Science & Medicine* 47(3):357–69.

Smeeding, T.M. and D.H. Weinberg. 2001. "Toward a Uniform Definition of Household Income." *Review of Income and Wealth* 47:1–24.

Smith, J.P. 2004. "Unraveling the SES-Health Connection." *Population and Development Review* 30:108–32.

Sorlie, P.D., E. Backlund, and J.B. Keler. 1995. "U.S. Mortality by Economic, Demographic, and Social Characteristics: The National Longitudinal Mortality Study." *American Journal of Public Health* 85:949–56.

Tienda, M. and F. Mitchell (eds.). 2005. *Multiple Origins, Uncertain Destinations: Hispanics and the American Future*. Washington, DC, National Academies Press.

Turra, C. and N. Goldman 2007. "Socioeconomic Differences in Mortality Among U.S. Adults: Insights Into the Hispanic Paradox." *Journal of Gerontology: Social Sciences* 62B(3):S184–S92.

U.S. Census Bureau. 2009. "Educational Attainment." 2005–2007 American Community Survey, Table S1501. Available online at http:factfinder.census.gov. Retrieved July 9, 2009.

U.S. Department of Health and Human Services [DHHS]. 2000. *Healthy People 2010: Understanding and Improving Health*. Washington, DC, U.S. Government Printing Office.

U.S. Department of Health and Human Services [DHHS]. 2008. *Healthy People 2020: The Road Ahead*. Washington, DC, U.S. Government Printing Office.

Valkonen, T. 1989. "Adult Mortality and Level of Education: A Comparison of Six Countries." In J. Fox (ed.), *Health Inequalities in European Countries*. Aldershot, England, Gower.

Valkonen, T. 1993. "Problems in the Measurement and International Comparisons of Socio-economic Differences in Mortality." *Social Science & Medicine* 36(4):409–18.

Williams, D.R. 1990. "Socioeconomic Differentials in Health: A Review and Redirection." *Social Psychology Quarterly* 53:81–99.

Zajacova, A. 2006. "Education, Gender, and Mortality: Does Schooling Have the Same Effect on Mortality for Men and Women in the US?" *Social Science & Medicine* 63:2176–90.

Zajacova, A. and R.A. Hummer. 2009. "Gender Differences in Education Effects on All-Cause Mortality for White and Black Adults in the United States." *Social Science and Medicine* 69:529–37.

Zhang, J., K. Markides, and D. Lee. 1991. "Health Status of Diabetic Mexican Americans: Results From the Hispanic HANES." *Ethnicity and Disease* 1:273–79.

# Chapter 13
# Work, Occupation, Income, and Mortality

Patrick M. Krueger and Sarah A. Burgard

Work is a key indicator of the productive capacity of populations, and many individuals work for a majority of their adult lives. Classical sociological thought has emphasized the importance of work for integrating individuals into the broader social order and fostering mutual dependence among those who specialize in different occupations (Durkheim 1933), allowing workers to express their creativity through their productive efforts (Marx 1957), or offering individuals the promise of insight into their destination in the afterlife (Weber 1958). Work is central to the stratification of society because it facilitates social interactions with co-workers, customers, and other business contacts, sorts workers into occupational statuses, exposes employees to specific working conditions, and provides earnings (Friedmann and Havighurst 1954; Hauser and Warren 1997; Kasl and Jones 2000). Earnings, in turn, may be converted into other material resources, including savings, housing, and other forms of wealth, and occupational status is considered so fundamental for individuals and society that it is often used as the primary indicator of a person's social status. Given the importance of work in society, it seems intuitive that it would be linked to the distribution of other valued outcomes, such as long and healthy lives. Importantly, not all jobs promote health, and some are outright dangerous. Some estimates suggest that there were up to 1.3 million work-related fatalities in the world in 1990, primarily from work-related accidents or exposure to noxious agents (Driscoll et al. 2005; Murray and Lopez 1996; Takala 1999). Thus, our chapter is devoted to understanding the relationship between mortality and work, occupation, income, and related material resources.

Our chapter is comprised of four substantive sections. The first section engages with a persistent concern of researchers: is employment, occupation, or material resources causally related to mortality? This is a topic of theoretical importance to researchers who attempt to untangle the reciprocal relationships between health and different measures of socioeconomic status (SES) over the life course and by gender. Researchers have also devised numerous methodological strategies in an attempt to determine the circumstances under which work, occupation, and material resources are most clearly linked to health and subsequent mortality outcomes, and to understand the direction and magnitude of these associations. The reciprocal relationship between various indicators of SES and health and mortality outcomes is a theme that we touch on throughout all sections of our chapter, but given the centrality of causal concerns in contemporary research, we devote a section to this specifically.

The second section focuses on individual and family dimensions of work, occupation, and material resources and their connections to mortality in more-developed countries (MDCs). Throughout this and other sections of the chapter, we will emphasize the theoretical distinctions among work, occupation, and material resources (Duncan et al. 2002; Galobardes et al. 2006), and their connections to mortality. Education is closely tied to work opportunities, occupational mobility, and income and wealth, and also has independent relationships with mortality, as

P.M. Krueger (✉)
Department of Sociology and the Department of Health and Behavioral Sciences, University of Colorado-Denver, Denver, CO 80217, USA
e-mail: Patrick.Krueger@ucdenver.edu

described in Chapter 12 of this volume. We present empirical findings that illustrate and support the key substantive issues, rather than providing an exhaustive literature review.

The third section focuses on the relationships between individual and family dimensions of work, occupation, and material resources, and adult mortality in less-developed countries (LDCs). Some theoretical and methodological concerns are similar for MDCs and LDCs, but the social and economic contexts of LDCs have important implications for the relationships among work, material resources, and mortality. For example, LDCs often have more limited public-health infrastructures than MDCs, so life-saving medical care may be unavailable for purchase regardless of the economic resources available. Further, the character of work in LDCs may be very different from work in MDCs in ways that can impact mortality: there are fewer legal protections for workers, less regulation to ensure safe work environments, and the most common occupations may include subsistence farming or, more recently, jobs in manufacturing, which confer different risks for health and survival than the service sector and administrative jobs that are more common in MDCs.

Throughout the first three sections, we frequently return to the importance of gender and life course for shaping the relationship between mortality and work, occupations, and material resources. Gender is important because it structures participation in the labor force, the occupations held, and the remuneration received. In some societies, or in some historical periods, men may spend more of their lives in the formal workforce, and women's disproportionate efforts in caring for the home or other family members, or their participation in part-time work may be undercounted (Buvinic et al. 2002; Sullivan 2006). For example, between 1940 and 2007 the percent of US women who worked outside the home (or "for pay") steadily increased from 28% to about 59%, although women remain more likely than men to take time out of the labor force to care for children or ailing parents (Smith and Bachu 1999; U.S. Census Bureau 2007). Perhaps as a result of their weaker attachment to the labor force, the relationship between various socioeconomic characteristics and health or mortality are weaker for women than for men (Macintyre and Hunt 1997).

With regard to the life course, both men and women often transition into and out of the labor force multiple times as they complete or return to school, experience spells of unemployment or disability, take time to care for children or other family members, or retire one or more times (Pavalko and Smith 1999). Each of those transitions, the time that individuals spend in each state, and the trajectories workers experience within their careers can have important implications for mortality (Hayward et al. 1989; Pavalko et al. 1993).

The fourth section turns to research on the relationships between societal patterns of work, income, and material resources and mortality, often within a comparative or historical framework. Inequality and cycles of unemployment and economic growth can leave their mark not only on the survival of individuals, but also on the mortality experiences of populations. This section also describes some of the implications of globalization for mortality, especially the movement of low skill, low wage, and unsafe jobs from MDCs to LDCs.

Due to the limitations of extant data, prior research has often examined health outcomes other than mortality, but that are associated with survival (e.g., morbidity, mental health, medical conditions, and self-rated health). Mortality is unique in that it marks the irreversible exit from a population and reflects the culmination of a lifetime of work, occupational, and material conditions. Our discussion focuses on the theoretical connections between work, occupations, and income and various health and mortality outcomes, and where possible, we emphasize studies that specifically examine mortality. We draw on theory and research from demography, sociology, economics, social epidemiology, and occupational epidemiology.

## Empirical Relationships: Work, Occupations, Income, and Mortality Among US Adults

Before we discuss major findings from the empirical literature, we present some numbers to provide a sense of the magnitude of the relationships among employment status, occupational status, material resources, and overall mortality. For most of this exercise, we use data from the 1990 Family Resources Supplement to the National Health Interview Survey (NHIS), linked to prospective mortality in the National Death Index through 2002 (National Center for Health Statistics

1992, 2007). Gompertz proportional hazard models estimated the risk of death between the respondent's age at interview and their age of death or their age at the end of the follow-up period in 2002 (Korn et al. 1997). Gompertz models capture the exponentially increasing risk of death as adult's age. The models also adjust for race/ethnicity, sex, foreign-born status, marital status, and education. We include each employment status, occupational status, and income variable separately, rather than simultaneously, to provide a sense of the gross relationship between each measure and prospective mortality in a nationally representative sample of adults aged 18 and older. We also present models that are stratified by sex and broad age groups at baseline. Our models are not designed to test the theoretical frameworks described below, but instead highlight many of the measures that are commonly used and their relationships with mortality.

## Employment Status

Table 13.1 presents the results for three sets of employment status variables. In the first column, the first set of variables shows that compared to those who are employed at the time of survey, those who are unemployed have 35% higher risks of death, and those who are not in the labor force and not looking for work have 60% higher risks of death over the follow-up period. The next set of variables distinguishes among those who usually work full-time (35 or more hours per week) and those who usually work part-time (1 and 34 h/week). Compared to those who work full-time, adults who work part-time have 30% higher risks of death, those who are unemployed have 52% higher risks of death, and those who are not in the labor force have 72% higher risks of death over the follow-up period. The third set of variables finds no difference in the risk of death between those who are employed at a job and those who are self-employed.

The next two columns estimate these relationships separately by gender and show that working part-time, being unemployed, or not participating in the labor force is associated with higher risks of death for males than for females, potentially because it is more common for males to serve as the primary breadwinners in families and select out of the labor force only if their health is quite poor, whereas women have weaker attachments to the labor force. The final three columns show that the relationship between employment status and mortality weakens after age 65. However, even adults aged 65 or older have increased risks of death if they are not in the labor force, potentially because they are in poor health and are unable to work.

## Occupational Status

Table 13.2 presents the relationship between occupational status and mortality. We examine six different occupational status indices (discussed in more detail in the following sections). The indices include the Hauser

**Table 13.1** Gompertz proportional hazard ratios for the relationship between employment status and overall mortality, US adults aged 18 and older, 1990–2002[a,b]

|  | All adults | Males | Females | Aged 18–44 | Aged 45–64 | Aged 65+ |
|---|---|---|---|---|---|---|
| Employed | Ref. | Ref. | Ref. | Ref. | Ref. | Ref. |
| Unemployed | 1.35*** | 1.51*** | 1.05 | 1.40 | 1.30* | 1.11 |
| Not in the labor force | 1.60*** | 1.66*** | 1.50*** | 1.82*** | 1.85*** | 1.33*** |
| Employed full-time | Ref. | Ref. | Ref. | Ref. | Ref. | Ref. |
| Employed part-time | 1.30*** | 1.35*** | 1.23* | 1.26*** | 1.41*** | 1.09 |
| Unemployed | 1.52*** | 1.71*** | 1.18 | 1.52** | 1.61*** | 0.90 |
| Not in the labor force | 1.72*** | 1.78*** | 1.62*** | 1.92*** | 1.96*** | 1.38*** |
| Employed at a job | Ref. | Ref. | Ref. | Ref. | Ref. | Ref. |
| Self-employed | 0.96 | 0.99 | 0.88* | 0.97 | 0.86 | 1.01 |
| Unemployed | 1.42*** | 1.61*** | 1.08 | 1.46* | 1.47*** | 0.86 |
| Not in the labor force | 1.56*** | 1.63*** | 1.46*** | 1.83*** | 1.78*** | 1.32*** |

Note: $*p<0.05$; $**p<0.01$; $***p<0.001$ (two-tailed tests).
[a]Data come from the 1990 Family Resources Supplement to the National Health Interview Survey, and the linked mortality files.
[b]Each set of employment status variables comes from a separate model. All models also adjust for age, sex, race/ethnicity, foreign-born status, marital status, and education.

**Table 13.2** Gompertz proportional hazard ratios for the relationship between standardized occupation scores and overall mortality, US adults aged 18 and Older, 1990–2002[a,b]

|  | All adults | Males | Females | Aged 18–44 | Aged 45–64 | Aged 65+ |
|---|---|---|---|---|---|---|
| Hauser-Warren socioeconomic index | 0.90*** | 0.87*** | 0.96* | 0.85*** | 0.95*** | 0.98 |
| Not in the labor force | 1.62*** | 1.65*** | 1.56*** | 1.86*** | 1.86*** | 1.36*** |
| Siegel prestige score | 0.89*** | 0.88*** | 0.92** | 0.85*** | 0.92*** | 0.99 |
| Not in the labor force | 1.63*** | 1.66*** | 1.57*** | 1.85*** | 1.88*** | 1.36*** |
| Nakao and Treas prestige score | 0.89*** | 0.87*** | 0.93** | 0.85*** | 0.93*** | 0.98 |
| Not in the labor force | 1.63*** | 1.67*** | 1.57*** | 1.85*** | 1.88*** | 1.36*** |
| Nam–Powers–Boyd occupational status score | 0.89*** | 0.85*** | 0.95* | 0.83*** | 0.93*** | 1.00 |
| Not in the labor force | 1.63*** | 1.65*** | 1.58*** | 1.88*** | 1.88*** | 1.36*** |
| Occupation earnings score | 0.90*** | 0.87*** | 0.96 | 0.86*** | 0.91*** | 1.03 |
| Not in the labor force | 1.62*** | 1.62*** | 1.58*** | 1.84*** | 1.87*** | 1.35*** |
| Occupation education score | 0.90*** | 0.88*** | 0.95*** | 0.83*** | 0.98*** | 0.97 |
| Not in the labor force | 1.63*** | 1.67*** | 1.56*** | 1.87*** | 1.87*** | 1.36*** |

Note: *$p<0.05$; **$p<0.01$; ***$p<0.001$ (two-tailed tests).
[a]Data come from the 1990 Family Resources Supplement to the National Health Interview Survey, and the linked mortality files.
[b]Each occupational status variable comes from a separate model. All models also adjust for age, sex, race/ethnicity, foreign-born status, marital status, and education.

and Warren (1997) socioeconomic index, the Siegel (1971) prestige score, the Nakao and Treas (1994) prestige score, the Nam–Powers–Boyd occupational status score (Nam and Boyd 2004), an occupational earnings score that indicates the percentage of workers who are in occupations that have lower median incomes than those in the respondent's own occupation, and an occupational education score that indicates the percentage of people in the occupational category who had completed one or more years of college. Except for the Hauser and Warren socioeconomic index, all of the scores were calculated by staff at the Integrated Public Use Microdata Series (Ruggles et al. 2009), and were then merged into the NHIS based on the three-digit 1990 Census Occupational Codes. Those who are not in the labor force do not report an occupation. Thus, we standardize the occupational status indices to have a mean of 0 and a standard deviation of 1, and code those who are not in the labor force as 0. Then we include a dummy variable to indicate those individuals who are not in the labor force.

The first column of Table 13.2 shows that a one standard deviation increase in any of the occupational status indices we examine is associated with a 10–11% lower risk of death over the follow-up period. The next two columns show that the inverse association between the occupational status scores and overall mortality is generally stronger for men than for women. The final three columns show that the inverse relationships among the occupational status scores and mortality are strongest among those aged 18–44 at baseline, and weaken with age until none of the scores are significantly associated with mortality among adults aged 65 and older at baseline. Although prior research emphasizes differences in the measurement and conceptual purpose of each index (Mutchler and Poston 1983; Nam 2000), our (quite simple) models show that each has a similar relationship with mortality. Future work could more systematically explore whether different dimensions of occupational status or prestige confer different survival advantages.

Given important differences among occupations in working conditions and their links with specific causes of death, Table 13.3 presents the relationship between selected causes of death and some major occupational groups and specific occupations, based on data from the US National Occupational Mortality Surveillance (NOMS) System (National Institute for Occupational Safety and Health 2009). The NOMS System uses data from death certificates that include occupation and industry information from 28 states that have participated in the project for two or more years from 1984 through 1998. The NOMS database does not provide information on length of employment or estimates of workplace exposures, but it includes information on numerous recent deaths and has broad geographic

# 13 Work, Occupation, Income, and Mortality

**Table 13.3** Proportionate mortality ratios (PMR) for white males (M) and females (F) aged 15 and older for selected usual occupations, 1984–1998[a,b]

| | Cancers of the trachea, bronchus and lung M | Cancers of the trachea, bronchus and lung F | Heart disease M | Heart disease F | Chronic obstructive pulmonary disease (COPD) M | Chronic obstructive pulmonary disease (COPD) F | Pneumoconioses and lung diseases due to external agent M | Pneumoconioses and lung diseases due to external agent F | External causes of injury and poisoning M | External causes of injury and poisoning F |
|---|---|---|---|---|---|---|---|---|---|---|
| Executive, administrative, and managerial | 97* | 131* | 99* | 89* | 82* | 110* | 71* | 94 | 89* | 104* |
| Business managers | 100 | 130* | 99* | 90* | 81* | 109* | 70* | 91 | 92* | 106* |
| Professional specialty | 76* | 91* | 97* | 92* | 68* | 90* | 70* | 97 | 93* | 114* |
| Teachers | 63* | 76* | 98* | 92* | 57* | 74* | 69* | 101 | 93* | 111* |
| Technical, sales, and admin. support | 95* | 113* | 101* | 93* | 87* | 106* | 72* | 97 | 91* | 103* |
| Admin. support, incl. clerical | 95* | 111* | 102* | 91* | 90* | 108* | 76* | 101 | 82* | 99* |
| Service occupations | 101 | 113* | 102* | 101* | 103* | 108* | 81* | 94* | 92* | 108* |
| Janitors and cleaners | 105* | 109* | 102* | 110* | 107* | 86* | 93 | – | 99 | 111* |
| Farming, forestry, and fishing | 82* | 92* | 103* | 99 | 102* | 96 | 68* | – | 127* | 141* |
| Farm workers | 79* | 111 | 96* | 98 | 135* | – | 72* | – | 131* | 161* |
| Precision production, craft, and repair | 113* | 116* | 98* | 99* | 110* | 104 | 161* | 101 | 108* | 110* |
| Extractive occupations | 112* | – | 97* | 102 | 134* | – | 973* | – | 110* | 173* |
| Operators, fabricators, and laborers | 108* | 104* | 101* | 103* | 114* | 98* | 96* | 102 | 105* | 105* |
| Truck drivers | 118* | 118 | 101* | 95 | 125* | 122 | 75* | – | 106* | 157* |
| Homemakers | 73* | 92* | 103 | 103* | 86* | 98* | – | 98* | 72* | 94* |

Notes: * $p < 0.05$ (two-tailed tests).
[a] Data come from the National Occupational Mortality Surveillance System.
[b] The PMR indicates whether the age-standardized proportion of deaths from a specific cause of death for a particular occupation or industry appears to be higher (above 100) or lower (below 100) than the expected proportion for a particular occupation or industry. PMRs not calculated for cells with small numbers of deaths.

coverage. The proportionate mortality ratios (PMRs) indicate whether the age-standardized proportion of deaths from a specific cause of death for a particular occupation is higher (i.e., PMR > 100) or lower (i.e., PMR < 100) than expected. For example, deaths from cancers of the trachea, bronchus, and lung are significantly lower than expected among males in executive, administrative, and managerial occupations overall, but are not different from the expected levels for business managers.

Table 13.3 shows several noteworthy patterns. First, men in white collar positions generally have lower than expected mortality from most of these causes, with the exception of higher than expected mortality from heart diseases among men in technical, sales, and administrative support occupations. By contrast, women in executive, administrative, and managerial occupations, and in technical, sales, and administrative support occupations have higher than expected mortality from lung and related cancers and COPD—causes affected by smoking, which may have been more common among higher-status women who were dying over the period considered here.

Second, while external causes of death due to injury and poisoning are inexplicably higher than expected for women in many occupations, for women and men they are particularly high in farming, forestry, and fishing occupations and in blue collar occupations like extractive work (e.g., mining) and in jobs that involve a high risk of traffic accidents (e.g., truck drivers). Third, there are remarkably strong associations between extractive occupations and deaths from pneumoconioses and lung diseases like silicosis (PMR = 973), due to the external agents that are frequently inhaled in mining work.

## Income and Material Resources

Table 13.4 returns to the NHIS data and presents results for overall mortality and material resources. Individual and family income are the sum of the income from sources including jobs, self-employment, social security/railroad retirement, retirement accounts, interest bearing accounts, dividends, and other sources. Income from self-employment or dividends can be negative if individuals take a loss at their businesses or on their investments. Thus, we code our income variables for analysis by bottom-coding individual and family income to ensure that there are no negative values, dividing by $10,000, and taking the natural log. We also include a dichotomous variable to indicate whether individuals (or any family members, in the case of family income) reported negative income values from self-employment or dividends. Although persistent income losses may be disadvantageous, short-term losses may be less problematic if the ownership of a business or investments is associated with reduced mortality.

The first column of Table 13.4 shows that each $10,000 increase in logged individual income is associated with 3% lower risk of mortality over the follow-up period. Individuals who have any negative income have 38% lower risk of death than those without negative income. Family income has a similar inverse

**Table 13.4** Gompertz proportional hazard ratios for the relationship between individual and family income and income portfolios, and overall mortality, US adults aged 18 and older, 1990–2002[a,b]

|  | All adults | Males | Females | Aged 18–44 | Aged 45–64 | Aged 65+ |
|---|---|---|---|---|---|---|
| Individual income, divided by $10,000, logged | 0.97*** | 0.96*** | 0.98*** | 0.97*** | 0.96*** | 0.99* |
| Any negative individual income | 0.62*** | 0.65* | 0.50 | 0.63* | 0.48 | 1.08 |
| Family income, divided by $10,000, logged | 0.97*** | 0.96*** | 0.97*** | 0.96*** | 0.97** | 0.99 |
| Any negative family income | 0.94 | 0.78*** | 1.21 | 0.65 | 0.96 | 1.26*** |
| Family income equivalence, divided by $10,000, logged | 0.97*** | 0.96*** | 0.97*** | 0.96*** | 0.96** | 0.98 |
| Any negative family income | 0.94 | 0.77*** | 1.20 | 0.65 | 0.96 | 1.26*** |
| Individual income portfolio | 0.87*** | 0.86*** | 0.89*** | 0.70*** | 0.74*** | 0.94*** |
| Family income portfolio | 0.90*** | 0.89*** | 0.90*** | 0.74*** | 0.76*** | 0.95*** |

Notes: *p < 0.05; **p < 0.01; ***p < 0.001 (two-tailed tests).
[a]Data come from the 1990 Family Resources Supplement to the National Health Interview Survey, and the linked mortality files.
[b]Each income or income portfolio variable comes from a separate model. All models also adjust for age, sex, race/ethnicity, foreign-born status, marital status, and education.

relationship with the risk of death. We also examine a family income equivalence measure that adjusts the family income variable for the purchasing power of different size families, as described by Van der Gaag and Smolensky (1982), and again find an inverse relationship between family income and mortality.

The income portfolios capture the income diversification of individuals or households (Krueger et al. 2003). The individual income portfolio is the sum of the number of income sources an individual has received from jobs, self-employment, social security/railroad retirement, other pensions, interest, dividends, and other income. The family income portfolio includes the number of sources of income from all family members, divided by the number of family members. The individual income portfolio indicates that each additional source of income is associated with 13% lower risks of death over the follow-up period. The family income portfolio shows that each additional source of income per family member is associated with a 10% lower risk of death over the follow-up period. The next two columns show that the relationships between each measure and mortality are modestly weaker for women than for men. The final three columns show that the relationship between material resources and mortality weakens with age.

## Causal, Reciprocal, and Spurious Relationships

### Theoretical Concerns

Nearly all research that examines relationships between overall or cause-specific mortality and employment or work conditions, occupational exposures or prestige, or income and material resources grapples with the difficulty of establishing causal connections among those variables in the population of interest. Education is unique among the commonly used indicators of SES, as is described in Chapter 12. Because education is usually determined early in life before the onset of age-related poor health and does not change with age, it has a more clearly established causal effect on mortality, although the mechanisms that link education to mortality are incompletely understood (Link 2008; Lleras-Muney 2005; Mirowsky and Ross 2003). By contrast, work, occupation, and material resources may change multiple times over the life course, and are likely to be more sensitive to the influence of underlying (and potentially unobserved) health conditions (Kitagawa and Hauser 1973; Smith 1999).

There are clear theoretical reasons to suspect a causal connection leading from better work conditions, higher-status occupations, and higher incomes to longer lives. Indeed, this is the primary focus of this chapter, so we will not belabor the point here. Nevertheless, individuals with higher incomes can afford to live in safer housing in safer neighborhoods, purchase more nutritious foods or access to gyms or other recreational facilities, and buy better healthcare; high-quality jobs may be safe, interesting, and relatively free of stress; and higher-status occupations can offer greater prestige that one can use to command resources that promote health. All of these factors could plausibly lead to better health and longer lives.

In contrast, although mortality is the last event that individuals will ever experience, placing it clearly after a lifetime of exposure to work and material conditions, it remains possible that those who are sickly or disabled may be less able to work, more likely to lose their jobs or to move into lower status occupations if they are working, less likely to earn high incomes, and ultimately, more likely to die (Smith 1999). For example, the inverse association between household wealth and the risk of death among older adults (Bond Huie et al. 2003) could be explained by the need for sickly individuals to spend down their assets to qualify for long-term care through the Medicaid program (Smith 1999). Haas (2006) has demonstrated that poor health in early life is associated with reduced earnings in later life.

What remains most likely, however, is that there are reciprocal relationships between health and work, income, and occupation (Mulatu and Schooler 2002; Mullahy and Robert 2008), and that the predominant direction of that relationship (i.e., from health to SES, or from SES to health) varies over the life course and across social circumstances. At younger ages, relatively few adults are too disabled to work, and instead, those who are not working are often attending school, at home caring for young children, or, less frequently, participating in underground economies that may offer greater rewards than the formal labor market

(Subramanian and Kawachi 2003). In mid- and late-life, however, early life conditions may begin to exact their toll on the ability of individuals to maintain fully active lives, which may result in greater disability, lower incomes, and increased risks of death (Haas 2006; Hayward and Gorman 2004; also see Chapter 9). Further, over the life course, individuals may experience bouts of illness that reduce their socioeconomic position, and some individuals may be better able to recover their health and socioeconomic standing than others.

The role of gender in selection into the labor force, certain occupations, and earning at the highest levels changes over time and varies across birth cohorts. In prior decades in MDCs, when relatively fewer women worked outside the household, women who did hold full-time jobs outside of the home in high-status occupations were a very select group. More recently and in most parts of the world, women are commonly spending part or all of their adult lives in the paid-labor force, although they remain more likely than men to leave the labor force to care for children or elderly dependents (Buvinic et al. 2002; Heymann et al. 2003). Little research has systematically examined how changes in the employment of women across cohorts might shape the relationship between work, occupation, material resources, and health and mortality outcomes among women, men, and their families.

Finally, an alternate hypothesis warrants mention. Work, occupation, and material resources may have spurious relationships with mortality outcomes in some circumstances. For example, unobserved genetic or environmental factors that are associated with employment or occupational status attainment (Guo 2006; Nielsen 2006) may also account for differential mortality by employment or occupational status. Importantly, the unobserved factors need not be genetic. Cultural capital—or the underlying tastes and preferences that convey a person's status (Bourdieu 1984, 1986)—may shape educational and occupational prospects, as well as health behaviors that have established connections to mortality (Pampel 2006; Stempel 2005). Although cultural capital theories are commonly linked to education, Bourdieu's (1984) emphasis on the cultivation of cultural capital within families suggests that interventions that target increases in educational attainment (e.g., mandatory schooling laws) may do little to shape the underlying tastes for high-status work or healthy behaviors.

## Methodological Concerns

There are multiple strategies for attempting to address causal concerns. First, researchers can try to find socioeconomic measures that are less sensitive to individuals' bouts of poor health. For example, family income or one-time income transfers from family members may be less sensitive to personal health than individual earnings (Kitagawa and Hauser 1973). However, this approach can be problematic if unhealthy individuals (e.g., smokers) tend to live together, resulting in poor health and lower earnings among all family members, or if families nonrandomly provide transfers or bequests based on the health of recipients (McGarry and Schoeni 1995). Second, some researchers use instrumental variables or fixed-effects methods, or attempt to find natural experiments to exploit plausibly exogenous variation in socioeconomic resources that result from policies or plant closings, to account for the impact of unobserved factors on the relationship between socioeconomic indicators and mortality (Glied and Lleras-Muney 2008; Krueger et al. 2004; Strully 2009).

Third, some researchers attempt to directly model reciprocal relationships between health and work, occupation, and material resources. Moore and Hayward (1990) focus on changes in occupation and find that the least healthy individuals appear to leave physically demanding occupations like farming that they hold through midlife and move into clerical positions in later life. The mixing of career clerks with those who moved from farming to clerical work in later life inflates the mortality rate for clerical occupations, and deflates the rate for farmers. Finally, researchers can make stronger causal claims when they identify causal pathways—such as from shift work, to sleep loss, to accident mortality, or from work-related crystalline silica exposure to silicosis mortality. But the biological, behavioral, and psychosocial links between many social factors and specific causes of death are seldom observed in the available data.

The remaining sections of the chapter emphasize the theoretical reasons and empirical support for the influence of work, occupation, and material resources on health and mortality outcomes. Throughout the chapter we will note where the reciprocal relationships between SES and health or mortality outcomes are most apparent, or indicate where there is scant firm evidence to support causal connections in either direction.

## Individual and Family Level: More-Developed Countries (MDCs)

### *Work and Employment*

In industrialized societies, work, or employment, is often defined as effort that is spent in the paid-labor force in exchange for wages or a salary. Of course, Sullivan (2006) points out that this definition of "work" is imprecise. Not all work is done for pay in the near term (e.g., farmers may only accrue earnings if they have a successful crop that sells for a profit at the end of the growing season), yields financial remuneration, and takes place outside the home (e.g., housework or carework). In LDCs, much work can be informal and inconsistent. Because a detailed examination of informal economies and household production are beyond the scope of this chapter (but see Becker 1981; Sullivan 2006), we will focus our attention on participation in the paid-labor force. This generally includes people who are employed and those who are unemployed but looking for work, while others are classified as not in the labor force and not looking for work because they are retired, attending school, homemakers, or disabled. Research has documented higher mortality among those who are unemployed or not in the labor force but who are of working age, compared to working-aged adults who are employed (Rogers et al. 2000; Sorlie and Rogot 1990), potentially due to the benefits of work itself, or because the least healthy individuals may be most likely to be unemployed or to exit the labor force.

Mortality risk and health also vary considerably among those who are employed, and several bodies of research seek to identify the mechanisms that link work conditions to mortality. The "job strain model" focuses on the survival consequences of workplace demands and the ability of workers to meet those demands: Fig. 13.1 shows the hypothesized relationships (adopted from Karasek 1979; see also Theorell 2000). Jobs that place high demands on workers, but that offer workers little control over their work conditions and limited ability to meet those demands tend to be associated with higher risks of death, especially from cardiovascular disease (Johnson et al. 1996; Kivimäki et al. 2002) and suicide (Tsutsumi et al. 2007). But not all research has confirmed the impact of job strain (the combination of high demands and

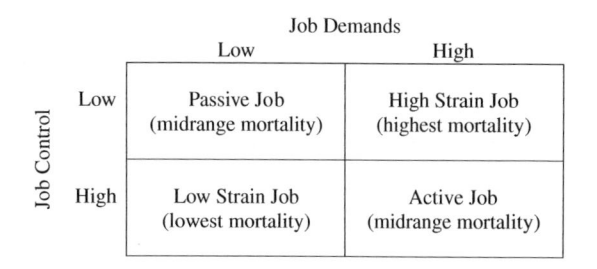

|  | | Job Demands | |
|---|---|---|---|
|  | | Low | High |
| **Job Control** | Low | Passive Job (midrange mortality) | High Strain Job (highest mortality) |
|  | High | Low Strain Job (lowest mortality) | Active Job (midrange mortality) |

**Fig. 13.1** Job-strain model and the hypothesized impact on mortality. Source: Adopted from Karasek (1979: 288)

low control) on coronary heart disease or mortality (de Lange et al. 2003; Eaker et al. 2004), and some find that "passive" jobs marked by low demands and low control may be linked to excess mortality (Amick et al. 2002). Further, some research finds that social support in the workplace is directly associated with improved cardiovascular health or buffers workers from the harm of high job strain (Kawakami et al. 2000), but others find no effect of work-related social support on mortality (Astrand et al. 1989). Ambiguous findings in the job strain literature may result from differences across studies in control variables or the time between measuring job conditions and assessing mortality (Theorell 2000).

The "effort-reward imbalance (ERI) model" provides another common perspective for examining the health and mortality consequences of the fit between workers and their jobs. The ERI model characterizes jobs on two dimensions: effort and reward (Siegrist 1996; van Vegchel et al. 2005). The effort dimension indicates the job-related obligations required of the employee. The reward dimension captures money, esteem, job security, and other opportunities that are conferred to the employee through the job. In addition to the characteristics of the job itself, workers who exhibit "overcommitment" will be less likely than others to leave jobs that are marked by an imbalance between efforts and rewards due to their intrinsic need for approval and esteem, in combination with high levels of ambition (Siegrist 1996; van Vegchel et al. 2005). The theory predicts that workers who exhibit overcommitment and who work in jobs that require high effort but that offer few rewards should have increased levels of stress; higher levels of smoking, drinking, and other behaviors that are often undertaken in response to stress; and thus, increased risks of death. Empirical studies have generally found that the effort-reward imbalance is associated with worse self-rated health, higher levels of smoking and alcohol consumption, and a greater incidence of cardiovascular disease incidence and mortality (Bosma et al. 1998; Kivimäki et al. 2002; van Vegchel et al. 2005), although the model typically fits better for men than for women (Niedhammer et al. 2004). Research on the importance of overcommitment, however, is less often studied and the extant results are inconclusive (van Vegchel et al. 2005).

Other research has examined how different types of employment contracts may lead to variations in mortality among employed people. "Standard" employment contracts imply full-time work, typically on a fixed schedule, with the expectation of continued employment, and at the employer's place of business under the employer's direction (Kalleberg 2000). In contrast, nonstandard work encompasses alternate employment relationships that may include on-call work and day labor, temporary-help agency employment, employment with contract companies or independent contracting, other self-employment, and part-time employment in otherwise "conventional" jobs (Kalleberg et al. 2000).

Some researchers have hypothesized that nonstandard employment contracts are linked to increased adult mortality because such jobs often lack access to health insurance coverage, retirement benefits, and unemployment insurance coverage in the United States, they provide less on-the-job training and managerial oversight of occupational safety and health, and they involve employment insecurity (Price and Burgard 2008; Quinlan et al. 2001). For example, self-employed individuals may have worse health than those who are employed by others because self-employment can be fraught with uncertainty due to market fluctuations and the risk of losing personal assets (Jamal 2007; Lewin-Epstein and Yuchtman-Yaar 1991). Because self-employed workers may have to rely on their own savings and cannot count on employer contributions to pension programs, self-employed workers tend to work longer, retire later, and die more quickly after they retire (Hayward and Grady 1990).

There is tremendous variety among nonstandard contracts and in their health consequences across occupations, industries, and societies. Some studies have found no difference in the health of nonstandard workers and their counterparts with standard contracts, possibly because of different labor policies across employment sectors, or differential selection of persons into nonstandard contracts based on their age, gender, preferences for terms of employment, and baseline health (Artazcoz et al. 2005; Virtanen et al. 2006). In contrast, the risk of traumatic and fatal occupational injuries was higher among temporary workers in Spain than among their standard contract counterparts (Benavides et al. 2006), and temporary workers in Finland had higher all-cause mortality and higher mortality from alcohol-related causes and from smoking-related cancers than their standard contract counterparts (Kivimaki et al. 2003).

Work schedules are also associated with health outcomes that are closely linked to mortality. Working late, long, or rotating shifts is associated with shorter sleep durations and higher rates of automobile and workplace accidents among truck drivers and medical workers (Lockley et al. 2004; Pack et al. 2006), and increased risk of myocardial infarction (Liu and Tanaka 2002). Epidemiological research has also linked late-night work and prolonged exposure to light at night to hormonal changes that result in increased risks of breast cancer (Davis et al. 2001; Schernhammer et al. 2001), a leading cause of cancer mortality among women. Overtime hours have been associated with poorer perceived health, more work-related injuries and illnesses, and even increased mortality for US workers (Caruso et al. 2004). In post-industrial economies, however, overtime work is increasingly performed by highly educated professionals, so future research is needed to understand if and how they are affected by longer work hours in the context of generally healthy working conditions.

Importantly, employment transitions can have implications for health. Involuntary job loss has been linked to downturns in physical and mental health (Burgard et al. 2007) and can increase stress due to the loss of an important social role and reduced income. The increased stress associated with unemployment can, in turn, lead to higher levels of smoking, excess drinking, and increases in biomarkers (e.g., inflammation, cholesterol) that indicate worse cardiovascular health (Dooley et al. 1996). Further, job loss can mean the loss of healthcare coverage and decreased access to preventive healthcare services in the United States, where insurance coverage is frequently tied to an employer. Even individuals who lose their jobs but are quickly re-employed have a greater incidence of medical conditions than those who are continuously employed (Strully 2009).

Transitions into and out of, or within the labor force can have important implications for health over the life course. Intuitively, job loss or a lack of employment could impact mortality differently depending on whether an individual has just completed a college degree and not yet started a new career and become self-sufficient, is middle aged and has a family to support, or is near retirement and has been working for years in a physically demanding occupation (Kasl and Jones 2000). Spending more time in the labor force is generally associated with better health (Pavalko and Smith 1999), but men who move through a series of unrelated jobs, or who make progress early in their career but were not promoted later in their careers, have increased risks of death compared to men who work in the same job over time or who are promoted throughout their careers (Pavalko et al. 1993). Participation in the labor force is also associated with better health among women, and having children or spending time doing housework does not appear to greatly diminish those benefits (Pavalko and Smith 1999; Schnittker 2007).

## *Occupations and Occupational Status*

Research on occupations or occupational status and mortality typically focuses either on work-related exposures and harmful environments, or on social status aspects of occupation. A substantial body of research examines the connections between particular occupations or occupational exposures and specific health outcomes. Work that entails exposure to toxic chemicals, the use of unsafe machinery or work environments, or that requires intense physical effort may be associated with increased risks of mortality. For example, exposure to fine particles of crystalline silica when mining, working with stone, or sandblasting can increase the risk of silicosis-related mortality (Bang et al. 2008), and asbestos exposure can increase the risk of lung cancer (Yano et al. 2001). Some occupations are physically demanding and lead to increased rates of disability and mortality. Longer exposures to more physically demanding occupations are associated with increased risks of mortality, regardless of the most recent occupation held (Moore and Hayward 1990). Nonetheless, not all work-related physical activity is harmful to health. Some physically strenuous work may promote cardiovascular health and reduce the risk of cardiovascular disease mortality (Morris et al. 1966; Paffenbarger and Hale 1975). Declining levels of physical activity in the workplace in recent decades are a major contributor to the total declines in physical activity among US adults (Brownson et al. 2005), and sedentary lifestyles are associated with greater risks of morbidity and mortality.

A second line of research conceptualizes occupation as an indicator of SES or prestige. Because adults in industrialized societies typically spend long hours in the labor force and derive central aspects of their identities from their work, occupational status is often considered a key indicator of an individual's status in society. Indeed, those who work in higher-status occupations as indicated by standard occupational indices or military or government rank live longer than those in lower status positions (Marmot 2004; Rogers et al. 2000; Seltzer and Jablon 1977). Adjusting for income and education reduces but does not eliminate the impact of occupational status on mortality in the United States (Rogers et al. 2000), although that association is less persistent for other health outcomes in more homogeneous samples (Miech and Hauser 2001).

Marmot (2004) focuses on the status dimensions of occupation in the Whitehall study of British civil servants. Because all British civil servants have access to high-quality healthcare and other social benefits, and because an occupational status gradient in mortality persists even among the Whitehall respondents, all of whom have fairly high levels of income, Marmot argues that status itself drives the relationship between occupational class and mortality. Specifically, he suggests that individuals compare themselves unfavorably to others in higher-status positions, which leads to higher levels of stress and higher levels of drinking and smoking in response to that stress (see also Wilkinson 2006).

Marmot's (2004) findings are consistent with research on the importance of subjectively reported social status on health and mortality outcomes even after adjusting for objective indicators of SES (Adler et al. 2000). But it remains possible that unmeasured material resources, perhaps from earlier in life, may drive both current occupational status, perceptions of status relative to others, and health and mortality outcomes (MacLeod et al. 2005). Some researchers have focused on mortality within very specific and high-status occupations. For example, Major League baseball players can expect to live longer than those in the general US population (Saint Onge et al. 2008), although their survival advantage may come from the selection of only the healthiest individuals into baseball careers (Saint Onge et al. 2007). Similarly, boosts in prestige—such when actors and actresses win an Academy Award—are associated with increased survival (Redelmeier and Singh 2001), although errors in statistical analysis might account for those results (Sylvestre et al. 2006). In sum, the causal effect of occupational prestige on mortality remains ambiguous.

Occupational status also has important implications for the retirement process and subsequent mortality. Men typically retire from the labor force multiple times, and men who work in occupations that are marked by low status, low earnings, and few opportunities for advancement tend to spend more years working after they initially retire, and spend a greater share of their working lives in post-retirement jobs (Hayward et al. 1988). Further, workers in physically demanding jobs with little intellectual complexity are more likely to become disabled and to retire, and to die sooner after retiring than workers in higher-status occupations (Hayward et al. 1989). Prior research typically finds that retirement may not lead to worse health in general, but poor health may often precipitate retirement (Kasl and Jones 2000).

While evidence suggests a link between occupation and survival, it can be difficult to measure and operationalize occupational status for several reasons. Occupation can change over the life course, making it difficult to compare studies using occupation in early life at the beginning of the career to studies that use occupation in later life that is closer to retirement. Additionally, occupational status may be more variable among younger workers who have not yet established themselves in a single career, and among older workers who may have retired from their primary occupation but who continue to work in new fields (Moore and Hayward 1990). Characterizing an individual's occupation can be especially difficult for women, who tend to move in and out of the labor force more frequently than men to care for children or elderly parents (Kitagawa and Hauser 1973; Martikainen 1995; Pavalko and Smith 1999), although this sex difference is becoming less pronounced in recent cohorts (Schnittker 2007).

There is no single standard method for measuring occupational status, nor is there a consensus about whether the various indices have similar relationships with mortality. Various occupational status indices have been devised, each with a different focus: the Duncan (1961) socioeconomic index of all occupations links information about average education and income of incumbents to an indicator of prestige; the Nam–Powers–Boyd (2004) occupational status scale emphasizes occupation-specific differences in earnings and education; and Siegel's (1971) occupational prestige scores are derived solely from prestige-based survey items (see Miller and Salkind 2002; Nam 2000). Jencks et al. (1988) raise numerous criticisms of standard occupational status indices that fail to account for the substantial heterogeneity within occupations, and instead devise an index of job desirability that incorporates both pecuniary (e.g., earnings) and nonpecuniary (e.g., work hours, job stability, whether individuals get dirty at work, frequency of supervision, and repetitive tasks) aspects of jobs. Gender differences may be greater for measures of occupational status than of occupational prestige (Mutchler and Poston 1983). Indeed, Hauser and Warren (1997) note the difficulty of creating occupational status indices that are adequate for both men and women, and that capture something more than education within and across generations.

In terms of mortality, we are aware of no studies that compare these indices in terms of their impact on overall or cause-specific mortality, nor that theorize why some scales should be more important than others for predicting mortality. Some research has documented links between mortality and single measures of occupational status; Rogers et al. (2000) find that Nam–Powers–Boyd occupational status scores are inversely associated with the risk of death. Our simple models in Table 13.2 show that the indices have similar associations with mortality, but future research that examines these relationships more systematically would offer greater insight into the most salient dimensions of occupational status for survival.

Finally, there are limitations associated with both self-reported and objective data on occupation-specific or workplace stress, insecurity, exposure to noise, injuries, fatalities, and exposures to noxious substances (Jencks et al. 1988; Theorell 2000). Objective reports from employers of the number of workplace injuries or temporary workers, or expert raters' observations of working conditions in specific occupations are costly to collect and quickly become outdated because working conditions can change quickly over time. Self-reports are more sensitive to workers' actual experiences because conditions vary considerably even within the same occupation, and because workers also have different levels of coping resources, social support, and sense of control. But self-reports are vulnerable to bias if some workers are pessimistic and report negatively about both their job characteristics and their wellbeing, creating a spurious association between the two. Objective data avoid this problem of spurious association, but provide only a rough estimate of conditions that may be important for mortality and that are experienced by the many different workers in a given occupation.

## *Income and Related Material Resources*

Work provides earnings that are a major component of household income and that contribute to other material resources, including retirement accounts, savings, and home ownership. We distinguish between material resources that are fluid and that are available to spend immediately (e.g., earnings), and accumulated material resources that may be more difficult to liquidate but that may nevertheless promote longevity (e.g., housing, retirement accounts, financial assets).

Fluid resources like earnings can be used immediately to promote health and reduce the risk of death by paying for medications and medical care, aiding smoking cessation efforts, or purchasing more nutritious foods and gym memberships. Higher levels of income are generally associated with lower risks of death, although that relationship is weaker at higher levels of income than at lower levels (Rogers et al. 2000). Income from a variety of sources (self-employment, jobs, interest, dividends) each promote longer lives, but income from jobs and self-employment are especially important for reducing mortality among working-aged adults (Krueger et al. 2003; McDonough et al. 1999). Although income from self-employment may be more volatile than income from jobs, the amount of income from each source has the same inverse relationship with the risk of death (Krueger et al. 2003). But not all income is associated with lower risks of death. McDonough et al. (1999) find that women have lower risks of death when their husbands have high earnings, although men have increased risks of death when their wives have high earnings, potentially because sickly men rely on the higher earnings of their wives, or because high earning wives may violate traditional gender roles.

Some research suggests that access to Medicare and social security may weaken the link between income and mortality at the older ages by providing access to medical care and diminishing income inequality among older adults (House et al. 1990). But others find that the equalizing forces of the social security program on income at the oldest ages are modest compared to the immense disparities in the accrual of private pensions and asset income over the life course (Crystal and Shea 1990). Although the relationship between income and mortality weakens with age, adults who are 75 years or older who receive income from multiple sources have lower risks of death than those with fewer income sources, even after adjusting for the total amount of income received, because their income may be more stable if any single source should falter (Krueger et al. 2003). Moreover, recent research suggests that the selective mortality of adults with low levels of education and earnings before they reach the oldest ages may partially account for the smaller socioeconomic gradient in mortality at the oldest ages (Dupre 2007).

Wealth, or accumulated material resources, has important implications for mortality. Home ownership is a primary source of wealth for many US families (Oliver and Shapiro 1997), with a smaller share of households holding stocks, bonds, mutual funds, and personal retirement accounts. Wealth is particularly important when viewed in a life course framework because it tends to accumulate with age, and as such, is a stronger predictor of mortality outcomes among older adults than is income, which often declines as older adults exit the labor force (Bond Huie et al. 2003).

Historical research from the eighteenth and nineteenth centuries in England suggests, however, that wealth was not associated with mortality in that era, possibly because excess food consumption, tobacco use, and sedentary lifestyles were more common among the aristocracy, merchants, and professionals, than among the laborers (Razzell and Spence 2006). By 1865 in Providence Rhode Island, however, a clear mortality gradient was apparent; individuals who paid taxes (because they had higher incomes) had lower mortality rates than those who did not pay taxes (Chapin 1924). Thus, the income and wealth gradient in mortality may have appeared only at the end of the nineteenth century. Other research focuses on why the inverse relationship between material resources and mortality may continue to increase in contemporary societies (Glied and Lleras-Muney 2008; Phelan et al. 2004).

In contrast to holding wealth, being in poverty suggests severe material deprivation. Although a small but not insubstantial share of the US population may be in poverty at any given time, up to 30% of household heads in the Panel Study of Income Dynamics experienced some form of poverty between 1967 and 1982, and about 11% were in poverty throughout that period (McDonough et al. 2005). Compared to men, women are more likely to live in poverty because they are more likely to be the unmarried heads of households with dependent children, to have lower levels of education (at least among older cohorts of women), and to earn lower incomes. Being in poverty is associated with increased risks of death among both men and women (Zick and Smith 1991). Although the risk of death increases with the number of spells of poverty, the first time that individuals move into poverty is especially harmful, perhaps because individuals may be able to adapt to repeated spells or longer durations of poverty (Oh 2001). There is some evidence that redistributive policies that target individuals in economic need can promote survival. Compared to those who are estimated to be eligible but who did not participate in the Food Stamp program, those who participate in the program have significantly lower risks of death after adjusting for unobserved factors, possibly because the program ensures adequate nutrition and allows the family to allocate monetary resources to other areas that promote health (Krueger et al. 2004).

## Individual and Family Level: Less-Developed Countries (LDCs)

### Work and Employment

More than 80% of workers live in the developing world, and while they face some of the same mortality risks related to employment, occupation, and income as individuals in MDCs, their work circumstances are also unique (Rosenstock et al. 2005). Although there is considerable variation across societies and regions, LDCs often have a substantial share of their workforce—70% or more in some cases—engaged in the agricultural sector (World Bank 2003). Further, many adults in LDCs are engaged in informal work that occurs in households or on the streets and that is completely unregulated for occupational health and safety risks. The close integration of subsistence agriculture and informal home-based production into the household context blurs the separation between work and home that is more apparent in MDCs, and can make it difficult to identify injuries and deaths that are specifically work-related (Driscoll et al. 2005; Rosenstock et al. 2005). Further, work-related exposures, whether due to pesticides used for farming or to lead used to make batteries in home workshops, can directly impact the health and mortality of both the worker and other family members (Rosenstock et al. 2005).

Vulnerable social groups are often more likely to work in the informal economy (Giuffrida et al. 2002) and with nonstandard contracts (Kalleberg et al. 2000), but the situation is perhaps even more evident in LDCs than in MDCs. Child labor is rare but still exists in MDCs; 96% of child laborers live in LDCs, with up to one in three children under the age of 15 working in some regions of the world (Facchini et al. 2003). Children routinely do dangerous work that exposes them to serious injury and hazardous chemicals. For example, children work in charcoal production in Brazil and manufacture fireworks in Guatemala and Columbia (Giuffrida et al. 2002; Salazar 1998). Adverse conditions may be particularly damaging to the health of children who are still undergoing physical development, and can add to the cumulative burden of workplace dangers they face over the life course. Women are more likely than men to work in the low-paying informal economy, where they are often overlooked by labor unions or public-health services (Buvinic et al. 2002; Toyota 2006), and they experience dangerous occupational exposures during pregnancy and ergonomic challenges when using production equipment that was designed for male workers (Loewenson 2001). Internal and international migrants who work in LDCs and even MDCs are often relegated to low-paying and risky work in the informal economy (Toyota 2006).

Formal investment in occupational health and safety (OHS) is lower and enforcement of regulations to protect workers or compensate them for workplace accidents or illness covers a smaller share of the population in LDCs than in wealthier nations. OHS regulations are typically not very stringent or only apply to certain types of employers in many countries that are still undergoing industrialization (Giuffrida et al. 2002; Yu et al. 1999), and the large informal sector is largely unregulated. For example, a study of auto body shops in Sonora, Mexico, found outdated equipment and technology for mitigating exposure to hazardous chemicals, and little awareness of environmental and occupational health and safety (Velazquez et al. 2008). Small businesses that employ only a handful of workers are plentiful in developing countries, and they are less able to invest in the OHS infrastructure than larger businesses that can spread the costs over larger numbers of workers (Giuffrida et al. 2002). Many business owners have limited capital to invest in improving conditions for workers or for the residents in surrounding communities that may also be affected by toxic emissions.

Governments in poorer countries have limited data collection systems in place to evaluate work-related injuries or mortality, few resources to enforce any existing health and safety regulations, and few scientists or bureaucrats to influence decision-makers (Nuwayhid 2004). Further, many individuals who retire from paid work in LDCs cannot expect the same pension benefits or income and health support programs that many MDCs provide, because LDCs often lack the financial resources, motivation, or infrastructure to offer these benefits (Willmore 2006), and because large fractions of the population work in the informal economy and do not pay into social security or pension programs (van Ginneken 1999).

## *Occupations*

Workers in lower-income societies are exposed to both the "classic" dangerous occupational exposures, resulting in outcomes including accidental injuries and fatalities, and exposure to silicosis and lead poisoning, but increasingly they also face risks that are prevalent in higher income countries, such as high job strain (Rosenstock et al. 2005). The globalization of production means that may dangerous occupations and working conditions are moving from MDCs to LDCs, where workers will accept lower wages and where OHS regulations are weaker (Loewenson 2001). In LDCs, for example, workers in export processing zones may have workplaces characterized by high levels of machine-related accidents, dust, noise, and exposure to toxic chemicals (Denman et al. 2003). These workplaces also enforce unrealistic production quotas, productivity incentives, and unregulated overtime, resulting in jobs that place high demands on workers who have little ability to control their circumstances (International Labour Organization 1988).

Certain occupations in LDCs have been the target of extensive study. In African nations with high rates of HIV/AIDS, truck drivers show very high rates of infection with the disease because they are highly mobile and spend a great deal of time away from their families and communities. These working conditions and the wide availability of commercial sex workers along major transport routes mean that they are much more likely than those in other occupations to engage in high-risk sexual encounters and to contract sexually transmitted infections, including HIV/AIDS (Ramjee and Gouws 2002). Similarly, men who migrate long distances to work in mining centers in Southern Africa have high rates of contracting HIV/AIDS due to long spells spent away from family, residence in single-sex hostels, and the ready availability of commercial sex workers (Lurie et al. 2003). Those male workers, their spouses, and the sex workers the men visit have increased risk of HIV/AIDS infection and mortality in these contexts.

The high level of exposure to pesticides and the resulting morbidity and mortality among agricultural workers in LDCs has also been studied extensively. Some estimates suggest that 99% of all deaths from acute pesticide poisoning occur in LDCs, even though those countries use only 20% of the world's pesticides (Christiani and Wang 2003). The meaning of pesticide-related deaths may be unclear because they can result from work-related exposure, accidental exposure in the home if improperly stored, or intentional ingestion in suicide attempts (Litchfield 2005). Agricultural workers also have high rates of injuries that are related to their work.

## *Income, Remittances, and Material Resources*

On the one hand, individuals in LDCs may be well poised to convert relatively low levels of material resources into survival gains, because many causes of death in LDCs result from the deprivation of basic resources. Incremental increases in income can facilitate the purchase of additional calories and nutrients that will greatly improve even adult health and survival. On the other hand, the scant availability of basic medical, occupational safety and health, and social-welfare infrastructure means that individuals in LDCs may be less able to convert their income into survival than adults in MDCs. Weaker social safety nets, a poorer public-health infrastructure, few medical facilities, and underfinanced or inexistent pension or healthcare programs may leave families responsible for the care of sick and elderly adults. Because formal safety nets are lacking, parents may invest their earnings and wealth in the education and employment prospects of their children as a method for ensuring their own health and material wellbeing in later life.

Although adult children in LDCs sometimes migrate for school or marriage, they most often migrate within the country or internationally to find better paying jobs (Knodel and Saengtienchai 2007). Consistent with the idea that migration decisions are made with the interests of all family members in mind (Massey 1990), adults whose children migrate intra- or internationally for work typically have improved survival compared to adults whose children did not migrate, even after adjusting for baseline health and the propensity to have migrant children (Kuhn 2006; Kuhn et al. 2011). This effect is strongest when focusing on migrant sons in countries where sons and their wives are expected to provide the primary source of support for parents. Part of the salubrious effect of having migrant children is mediated by the higher education and greater earning potential of migrant children, which suggests that children's remittances may be important for parents' health (Kuhn 2006; Zimmer et al. 2007).

Nevertheless, it is often difficult to measure income in communities where many households are engaged in subsistence agriculture or home-based production, where remittances and earnings may be irregular, or where the ownership of durable goods rather than cash reserves may be more important indicators of economic wellbeing. Indeed, it is difficult to identify the impact of children's remittances on parents' mortality in many surveys, given that children who migrate for work may only sporadically send money to their parents, but they may buy them gifts, like cellular phones, property, and automobiles, and only make large-cash transfers when parents have acute healthcare needs (Knodel and Saengtienchai 2007; Kuhn 2006). Other researchers have collected information on expenditures on basic necessities, such as food and housing, and have created asset indices of ownership of durable goods. For example, Filmer and Pritchett (2001) developed an asset index based on ownership of consumer durables (e.g., radio, bicycle) and housing characteristics (e.g., presence of piped water in the home). However, ownership of assets may confer different survival benefits than the availability of income, depending on the families' abilities to convert those assets into health.

## *Measurement Issues in Less-Developed Countries*

Data quality is especially problematic in LDCs. Due to gaps in vital statistics records and errors in recording information about the cause of death, it can be difficult to ascertain who died and why. In any country, there are two kinds of occupational mortality: acute accidents or outcomes that are linked to immediate work conditions, and mortality from diseases that have a long-latency period and that are more difficult to establish as specifically caused by work or a particular occupation (Driscoll et al. 2005). In both MDCs and LDCs, it is difficult to assess the impact of work on diseases or causes of death that have long-latency periods, and this is even more difficult in LDCs that lack adequate record keeping systems on employment, occupational exposures, and overall and cause-specific mortality. Moreover, workplace injuries and accident-related mortality may be undercounted in LDCs where there are few regulatory agencies that ensure the accurate reporting of work-related deaths (Concha-Barrientos et al. 2005).

An illustrative example is the underreporting of fatal and nonfatal accidents involving pesticides in LDCs. Estimates suggest that only 10–20% of pesticide-related exposures are reported appropriately, and that only 5% of fatal cases are appropriately reported (London and Bailie 2001). Underreporting of occupational fatalities in agricultural work and in rural areas more generally may be particularly severe. A study of the Western Cape region of South Africa found that occupational fatalities in rural areas were underreported by 85% (Schierhout et al. 1997). Large farm owners in South Africa exercise a great deal of control over their workers who are isolated from transportation and information because they live and work on the farms. Under these conditions, and because it is up to the farm owner to be informed about regulations and to report fatalities, many agriculture-related deaths are missed. Further, workers' deaths and injuries in construction and manufacturing industries in rapidly industrializing areas of China may be substantial but are routinely underreported, especially for those working in the growing private sector rather than in state owned enterprises (Yu et al. 1999).

## Aggregate and Comparative Research

### Global Labor Relationships and Mortality

The job characteristics that shape the mortality experiences of a population change as economies transition from predominantly agricultural to industrial and post-industrial modes of production. The relative importance of physical and environmental hazards at work declines as fewer individuals hold agricultural and manufacturing jobs, while the importance of psychosocial stressors rises as the dominance of the service sector grows. Wealthier countries that transition toward service-based economies often "export" physically and environmentally hazardous jobs to nations with fewer regulations and more workers willing to perform these jobs for relatively low pay. The global competition for manufacturing means that employers may cut wages and LDCs may enact weak OHS standards in an effort to attract jobs, which may result in stressful and unsafe working conditions (Denman et al. 2003). Increasing globalization also means that psychosocial stressors, notably perceived job insecurity, may rise for workers in wealthier countries. This is true even for higher-status workers, whose job security falls as technological innovation and the push for enhanced flexibility and competitiveness lead to organizational restructuring and layoffs (Cappelli et al. 1997). Even in the United States, where unemployment is often much lower than in other MDCs, both low- and high-status workers lose their jobs relatively often, even if many subsequently become re-employed quickly (Strully 2009).

The consequences of social inequalities in the distribution of "good" jobs and material resources are also heavily influenced by societal contexts. Many western European nations provide relatively generous social safety nets and have high levels of unionization, providing protection for workers from across the social spectrum. The United States provides fewer institutionalized supports for workers, especially those in "bad" jobs. Low- and middle-income countries generally have even less support available for workers in risky occupations, or for those working informally or in subsistence agriculture. Indeed, a weaker public-health infrastructure and limited access to adequate nutrition can exacerbate the harms of the more dangerous jobs that are more common in many LDCs.

### Macroeconomic Growth and Unemployment

A society's level of economic development—or the growth of their economy—has also been linked to longer lives, although the importance of economic growth may have been more important in pre-industrial and industrializing societies than in contemporary MDCs (Preston 1976; Sen 2001). Adequate material resources in a population can be used to improve sanitation and the public-health infrastructure, eradicate or ameliorate the harmful effects of parasites and infectious diseases, and improve the human capital of the population through education (Cutler and Lleras-Muney 2008; Cutler and Miller 2005). Indeed, Omran's (1971) description of the epidemiologic transition from high- to low-mortality regimes in western societies specifically invoked the importance of economic development, given that the advent of modern antibiotics and immunizations, and large-scale improvements in water treatment, occurred after the most dramatic declines in mortality already took place.

In MDCs more recently, however, the connection between economic growth and mortality is less clear. A series of papers by Brenner suggested that macroeconomic recessions lead to increased mortality, especially for vulnerable populations (Brenner 1971, 1979). Long-term economic growth may promote survival by reducing poverty, allowing greater investments in medical or workplace technologies that directly aim to improve health, and fostering stronger social support programs such as social security and Medicare (Brenner 2005). Thus, Brenner (2005) suggests that long-term economic growth and low levels of unemployment should promote longevity, although he notes that in the short-term, economic growth may result in companies investing in new technologies which may foster workplace competition, require employees to learn new skills, and increase stress-related mortality.

In contrast, although there is clear evidence that unemployment is harmful for individuals who have lost their jobs, some research at the aggregate level suggests that unemployment rates are inversely associated with mortality at least for some causes of death and in countries with social-welfare programs that buffer individuals from the immediate harms of unemployment. Adult mortality from traffic accidents, coronary heart disease, and cirrhosis appears counter-cyclical and increases when the economy improves (Granados 2008; Ruhm 2007).

Various mechanisms might account for the inverse relationship between unemployment rates and some causes of death. For example, people may have more time for sleep and exercise if they are unemployed or have reduced hours, and they may reduce unhealthy behaviors such as consuming alcohol and other substances because they have less income. Even individuals who are employed may be less willing to undertake unhealthy behaviors that may lead to job loss in an uncertain economic climate (Catalano et al. 1993). But Ruhm (2007) discounts the importance of health behaviors, especially given that mortality declines as much among those who are aged 65 or older (and who already have time for exercise and sleep), as among working-aged adults. He posits that a sluggish economy may impact the mortality of adults of all ages by reducing air pollution and traffic congestion, or fostering social support as younger family members spend less time working. Further, and somewhat inexplicably, some evidence suggests that fewer individuals receive medical treatments including coronary artery bypass grafting or coronary angiography when the economy is strong (Ruhm 2007). In contrast, deaths from other causes, including suicide, diabetes, and hypertension are pro-cyclical and increase as the economy declines (Granados 2008; Kammerling and O'Connor 1993).

Another factor that may weaken the link between economic growth and mortality includes the widespread availability and affordability of cigarettes and calorie dense but nutritionally poor foods. So-called "diseases of affluence," including obesity, diabetes, high cholesterol, hypertension, and heart disease may increase with economic growth, especially in low- and middle-income countries (Brandt 2007; Ezzati et al. 2005). The economic development that accompanied major declines in fertility and mortality, also leads to increases in nutrition. But MDCs, and more recently, LDCs have become increasingly reliant on processed foods that have relatively high levels of fat and sugar, and that facilitate the rise of obesity (Cutler et al. 2003; Popkin 1993). Similarly, the global diffusion of cigarette smoking—spurred by growing affluence around the world—has contributed to increasing levels of heart disease and lung cancer (Brandt 2007; Pampel 2007). These increases in obesity and smoking are particularly harmful in LDCs where there are few resources to treat chronic diseases and where individuals may simultaneously remain at an elevated risk of infectious diseases.

## *Income Inequality*

Some researchers have examined the relationships between economic inequality within populations and individual or aggregate mortality experiences (Lynch et al. 2004; Ross et al. 2000; Wilkinson 1997; Wilkinson and Pickett 2006). At least some research finds that among countries at comparable levels of development, more inequitable nations have higher mortality, regardless of the measure of inequality used in the analyses (Kawachi and Kennedy 1997). Thus, the question arises about why the inequality of a population would matter for longevity, even after adjusting for individual socioeconomic factors or the level of economic development, and even in populations where even the poorest should have access to basic material and social resources, such as healthcare or a reasonable government safety net.

Three mechanisms have been posited that link economic inequality to population health and mortality outcomes. First, economic inequality might undermine the development or maintenance of social capital, as indicated by trust among citizens, norms of reciprocity, and strong civic organizations (Kawachi et al. 1997). Not only might those factors directly influence health (Kawachi and Berkman 2000), but they may make it harder to achieve effective political solutions to problems associated with population health and wellbeing. Second and concomitantly, economic inequality may undermine support for the development of human capital through high-quality public education, a strong social safety net, affordable access to healthcare, and an equitable distribution of public resources (Lynch et al. 2000). The immensely different resources of high- and low-status individuals in very inequitable societies can make it hard for policy makers to achieve a consensus about the benefits of social programs that are supported by taxes on the most wealthy but primarily benefit the least wealthy (Kawachi and Kennedy 1999). Third, inequality may lead to increased mortality due to the psychosocial stress experienced by low-status individuals. In highly unequal societies, low-status individuals may make social comparisons—whether in terms of ownership of high-status items, access to the most elite institutions, or opportunities for success—in which they always appear to be failing. In turn, adverse social comparisons can lead to a sense of relative deprivation, increased levels of psychosocial stress, worse health behaviors such as drinking and smoking as individuals seek to cope with that stress, and, ultimately, increased mortality (Wilkinson 2006).

Evidence for the relationship between economic inequality and mortality, however, is somewhat mixed. Although some studies find that income inequality and mortality or other adverse health indicators are positively associated, others have found null or even inverse relationships (Deaton and Paxson 2001; Mansyur et al. 2008; Subramanian and Kawachi 2004; Wilkinson and Pickett 2006). Wilkinson and Pickett (2006) suggest that many of the null or inverse relationships emerged in data from the 1980s and 1990s when there were rapid increases in both inequality and longevity in many countries, a finding that is consistent with results from Deaton and Paxson (2001). However, in subsequent research, Deaton and Paxson (2004) show that changes in mortality poorly track changes in income inequality, which undermines a clear connection between income inequality and mortality in their data. Rather, they suggest that declines in mortality appear to be driven by technological advances—a finding supported by others (Glied and Lleras-Muney 2008). Interestingly, some research documents that the inverse association between personal income and mortality is stronger as the level of income inequality in a population increases (Mansyur et al. 2008), possibly because high incomes in unequal societies lead to favorable social comparisons (Deaton and Paxson 2001).

## Conclusion and Future Directions

Work, occupation, and material resources are clearly important for survival in both MDCs and LDCs, although their relationships with mortality are not always straightforward. Some jobs and occupations promote long and healthy lives, whereas others expose workers to dangerous and stressful conditions. Further, there are important differences across countries—such as the availability of public safety nets and OHS regulations—that shape the relationship between work and mortality. Based on the wealth of important research findings that we describe above, we have identified several areas that future work might explore.

First, much research in MDCs focuses solely on the work, occupation, and income of an individual, without providing sophisticated insight into how decisions about work and the allocation of income are shaped by family members in ways that might impact health and mortality. Marriage and family relationships have persistent relationships with mortality, but the complex relationships among family, work or income, and mortality are under-theorized and understudied. A few notable exceptions focus on gender differences in the impact of spousal earnings or time in the labor force on personal health or mortality (McDonough et al. 1999; Stolzenberg 2001), but many questions remain. Research from LDCs has more directly focused on the nexus of work, family, and health. Perhaps because of the lack of social and healthcare safety nets, families in LDCs might play a more central role in determining who should attend school or migrate for work, to maximize the wellbeing of all family members (Kuhn 2006).

Second, comparative research could more directly examine the global flows of both work and workers, and their implications for mortality. The movement of relatively low-skill migrants from LDCs into MDCs for low-paying jobs that cannot be outsourced (e.g., agriculture, construction), and the flow of highly skilled immigrants (e.g., doctors) from LDCs into MDCs for improved opportunities might have important implications for the spread of infectious diseases (Tatem et al. 2006), the stress associated with job uncertainty as outsourcing increases (Strully 2009), and the dearth of physicians who can provide adequate healthcare in LDCs (Ahmad 2005). The global flow of both workers and jobs might be particularly acute for workers at certain stages of their life course or by gender. Indeed, men are more likely than women to migrate internationally for work, where they may have fewer workplace protections than native-born workers. Further, older workers in MDCs may be in jobs that are more likely to be outsourced (e.g., manufacturing) and may be less able to find new jobs and to benefit from additional education. Research that considers the increasingly global economy may reveal important patterns in the impact of moving jobs and workers on mortality in both the sending and receiving countries.

Third, our chapter draws together research from demography, sociology, social epidemiology, and occupational epidemiology. The distinct orientations of each body of research are clear. Occupational epidemiology emphasizes the relationship between workplace exposures to noxious agents and social stressors to clinical health and mortality outcomes, such as mortality from silicosis and myocardial infarction. In contrast, the sociological and demographic research more often focuses on life course and gender issues in the progression through jobs or occupations, emphasizes the importance of status rather than occupational exposures, and examines overall mortality. Future research in each field might benefit by recognizing the strengths of research in other areas to more clearly understand the mechanisms that link work, occupations, and material resources to overall and cause-specific mortality.

Finally, future research should continue to collect more extensive and accurate data. Data limitations are especially pressing in LDCs where the quality of vital statistics data may be questionable and where data about workplace exposures and stressors may be particularly difficult to collect given that many individuals work in informal or unregulated jobs. In both MDCs and LDCs, extensive data collection efforts are required to establish the workplace fatalities that occur after long-latency periods. Further, there are limited data that link work and occupation to mortality through specific psychosocial, behavioral, and biological pathways, especially in low-income countries.

Our chapter also highlights the many ways that policy might impact the relationship between work, occupation, income, and mortality. For example, policies and interventions could target workplaces and their owners by designing laws and encouraging the implementation of technologies that limit exposure to noxious agents, reduce the need for repetitive motions and heavy lifting, and provide training to workers and managers to facilitate stress-free environments. Alternately, social policies could target the population more holistically, without focusing narrowly on the circumstances of employment. Redistributive policies, such government mandated healthcare, social security, and income redistribution may directly impact the mortality of all individuals, regardless of whether they are employed for pay, thereby having a greater impact on population health (Link and Phelan 2005). Nevertheless, work, occupation, and material resources are central features in the broader stratification of society, and it seems likely that they will continue to be linked to life chances, including survival.

**Acknowledgment** We would like to acknowledge helpful suggestions from Benjamin Amick, Barbara Anderson, Eileen Crimmins, George Delclos, and Richard Rogers, research assistance from Patricia Chen, and core funding for administrative support from the University of Colorado-Boulder, Population Program (NICHD R21 HD51146), and the University of Michigan Population Studies Center (NICHD R24 HD041028 and NIA P30 AG012846-14).

## References

Adler, N.E., E.S. Epel, G. Castellazzo, and J.R. Ickovics. 2000. "Relationship of Subjective and Objective Social Status with Psychological and Physiological Functioning: Preliminary Data in Healthy White Women." *Health Psychology* 19: 586–92.

Ahmad, O.B. 2005. "Managing Medical Migration from Poor Countries." *British Medical Journal* 331:43–45.

Amick, B.C., P. McDonough, H. Chang, W.H. Rogers, C.F. Pieper, and G. Duncan. 2002. "Relationship between All-Cause Mortality and Cumulative Working Life Course Psychosocial and Physical Exposures in the United States Labor Market from 1968 to 1992." *Psychosomatic Medicine* 64:370–81.

Artazcoz, L., J. Benach, C. Borrell, and I. Cortes. 2005. "Social Inequalities in the Impact of Flexible Employment on Different Domains of Psychosocial Health." *Journal of Epidemiology and Community Health* 59:761–67.

Astrand, N.E., B.S. Hanson, and S.O. Isacsson. 1989. "Job Demands, Job Decision Latidutde, Job Support, and Social Network Factors as Predictors of Mortality in a Swedish Pulp and Paper Company." *British Journal of Industrial Medicine* 46:334–40.

Bang, K.M., M.D. Attfield, J.M. Wood, and G. Syamlal. 2008. "National Trends in Silicosis Mortality in the United States, 1981–2004." *American Journal of Industrial Medicine* 51:633–39.

Becker, G.S. 1981. *A Treatise on the Family*. Boston, MA, Harvard University Press.

Benavides, F.G., J. Benach, C. Muntaner, G.L. Delclos, N. Catot, and M. Amable. 2006. "Associations between Temporary Employment and Occupational Injury: What Are the Mechanisms?" *Occupational and Environmental Medicine* 63:416–21.

Bond Huie, S.A., P.M. Krueger, R.G. Rogers, and R.A. Hummer. 2003. "Wealth, Race, and Mortality." *Social Science Quarterly* 84:667–84.

Bosma, H., R. Peter, J. Siegrist, and M. Marmot. 1998. "Two Alternative Job Stress Models and the Risk of Coronary Heart Disease." *American Journal of Public Health* 88: 68–74.

Bourdieu, P. 1984. *Distinction: A Social Critique of the Judgment of Taste*. Cambridge, MA, Harvard University Press.

Bourdieu, P. 1986. "The Forms of Capital." In J.G. Richardson. (ed.), *Handbook of Theory and Research for the Sociology of Education*, pp. 241–58. New York, NY, Greenwood Press.

Brandt, A. 2007. *The Cigarette Century: The Rise, Fall, and Deadly Persistence of the Product That Defined America*. New York, NY, Basic Books.

Brenner, M.H. 1971. "Economic Changes and Heart Disease Mortality." *American Journal of Public Health* 61:606–11.

Brenner, M.H. 1979. "Unemployment, Economic Growth, and Mortality." *Lancet* 318:672.

Brenner, M.H. 2005. "Comentary: Economic Growth Is the Basis of Mortality Rate Decline in the 20th Century—Experience of the United States 1901–2000." *International Journal of Epidemiology* 34:1214–21.

Brownson, R.C., T.K. Boehmer, and D.A. Like. 2005. "Declining Rates of Physical Activity in the United States: What Are the Contributors?" *Annual Review of Public Health* 26:421–43.

Burgard, S.A., J.E. Brand, and J.S. House. 2007. "Toward a Better Estimation of the Effect of Job Loss on Health." *Journal of Health and Social Behavior* 48:369–84.

Buvinic, M., A. Giuffrida, and A. Glassman. 2002. "Gender Inequality in Work, Health, and Income." In J. Heymann (ed.), *Global Inequalities at Work: Work's Impact on the Health of Indivdiauls, Families, and Societies*, pp. 188–221. New York, NY, Oxford University Press.

Cappelli, P., L. Bassi, H. Katz, P. Knoke, P. Osterman, and M. Useem. 1997. *Change at Work*. New York, NY, Oxford University Press.

Caruso, C., E. Hitchcock, R. Dick, J. Russo, and J. Schmit. 2004. *Overtime and Extended Work Shifts: Recent Findings on Illnesses, Injuries, and Health Behaviors (No. 2004-143)*. Cincinnati, OH, National Institute of Occupational Safety and Health.

Catalano, R., D. Dooley, G. Wilson, and R. Hough. 1993. "Job Loss and Alcohol Abuse: A Test Using Data from the Epidemiologic Catchement Area Project." *Journal of Health and Social Behavior* 34:215–25.

Chapin, C.V. 1924. "Deaths Among Taxpayers and Non-Taxpayers, Income Tax, Providence, 1865." *American Journal of Public Health* 14:647–51.

Christiani, D.C. and X.-R. Wang. 2003. "Impact of Chemical and Physical Exposures on Workers' Health." In J. Heymann (ed.), *Global Inequalities at Work: Work's Impact on the Health of Individuals, Families, and Societies*, pp. 15–30. New York, NY, Oxford University Press.

Concha-Barrientos, M., D.I. Nelson, M. Fingerhut, T. Driscoll, and J. Leigh. 2005. "The Global Burden Due to Occupational Injury." *American Journal of Industrial Medicine* 48:470–81.

Crystal, S. and D. Shea. 1990. "Cumulative Advantage, Cumulative Disadvantage, and Inequality Among Elderly People." *Gerontologist* 30:21–31.

Cutler, D.M., E.L. Glaeser, and J.M. Shapiro. 2003. "Why Have Americans Become More Obese?" *The Journal of Economic Perspectives* 17:93–118.

Cutler, D.M. and A. Lleras-Muney. 2008. "Education and Health: Evaluating Theories and Evidence." In R.F. Schoeni, J.S. House, G.A. Kaplan, and H. Pollack. (eds.), *Making Americans Healthier: Social and Economic Policy as Health Policy*. New York, NY, Russell Sage Foundation.

Cutler, D.M. and G. Miller. 2005. "The Role of Public Health Improvements in Health Advances: The Twentieth-Century United States." *Demography* 42:1–22.

Davis, S., D.K. Mirick, and R.G. Stevens. 2001. "Night Shift Work, Light at Night, and Risk of Breast Cancer." *Journal of the National Cancer Institute* 93:1557–62.

Deaton, A. and C. Paxson. 2001. "Mortality, Education, Income, and Inequality Among American Cohorts." In D.A. Wise (ed.), *Themes in the Economics of Aging*, pp. 129–70. Chicago, IL: University of Chicago Press.

Deaton, A. and C. Paxson. 2004. "Mortality, Income, and Income Inequality over Time in Britain and the United States." In D.A. Wise (ed.), *Perspectives on the Economics of Aging*, pp. 247–86. Chicago, IL, University of Chicago Press.

de Lange, A.H., T.W. Taris, M.A.J. Kompier, I.L.D. Houtman, and P.M. Bongers. 2003. "The Very Best of the Millennium: Longitudinal Research and the Deamnd-Control-(Support) Model." *Journal of Occupational Health Psychology* 8: 282–305.

Denman, C.A., L. Cedillo, and S.D. Harlow. 2003. "Work and Health in Export Industries at National Borders." In J. Heymann. (ed.), *Global Inequalities at Work: Work's Impact on the Health of Individuals, Families, and Societies*, pp. 247–77. New York, NY, Oxford University Press.

Dooley, D., J. Fielding, and L. Levi. 1996. "Health and Unemployment." *Annual Review of Public Health* 17: 449–65.

Driscoll, T., J. Takala, K. Steenland, C. Corvalan, and M. Fingerhut. 2005. "Review of Estimates of the Global Burden of Injury and Illness Due to Occupational Exposures." *American Journal of Industrial Medicine* 48:491–502.

Duncan, O.D. 1961. "A Socioeconomic Index for All Occupations." In A.J. Reiss (ed.), *Occupations and Social Status*, pp. 109–38. New York, NY, Free Press.

Duncan, G.J., M.C. Daly, P. McDonough, and D.R. Williams. 2002. "Optimal Indicators of Socioeconomic Status for Health Research." *American Journal of Public Health* 92:1151–57.

Dupre, M.E. 2007. "Educational Differences in Age-Related Patterns of Disease: Reconsidering the Cumulative

Disadvantage and Age-as-Leveler Hypotheses." *Journal of Health and Social Behavior* 48:1–15.

Durkheim, É. 1933. *The Division of Labor in Society*. New York, NY, Free Press.

Eaker, E.D., L.M. Sullivan, M. Kelly-Hayes, R.B. D'Agostino, and E.J. Benjamin. 2004. "Does Job Strain Increase the Risk for Coronary Heart Disease or Death in Men and Women? The Framingham Offspring Study." *American Journal of Epidemiology* 159:950–58.

Ezzati, M., S. Vander Hoorn, C.M.M. Lawes, R. Leach, W.P.T. James, A.D. Lopez, A. Rodgers, and C.J.L. Murray. 2005. "Rethinking the "Diseases of Affluence" Paradigm: Global Patterns of Nutritional Risks in Relation to Economic Development." *PLoS Medicine* 2:404–12.

Facchini, L.A., A. Fassa, M. Dall'agnol, M. de Fátima Maia, and D.C. Christiani. 2003. "Individuals at Risk: The Case of Child Labor." In J. Heymann. (ed.), *Global Inequalities at Work: Work's Impact on the Health of Individuals, Families, and Societies*, pp. 52–71. New York, NY, Oxford University Press.

Filmer, D. and L.H. Pritchett. 2001. "Estimating Wealth Effects without Expenditure Data-or Tears: An Application to Educational Enrollments in States of India." *Demography* 38:115–32.

Friedmann, E.A. and R.J. Havighurst. 1954. *The Meaning of Work and Retirement*. Chicago, IL, University of Chicago Press.

Galobardes, B., M. Shaw, D.A. Lawlor, G.D. Smith, and J. Lynch. 2006. "Indicators of Socioeconomic Position." In J.M. Oakes and J.S. Kaufman. (eds.), *Methods in Social Epidemiology*, pp. 47–85. San Francisco, CA: Jossey Bass.

Giuffrida, A., R.F. Iunes, and W.D. Savedoff. 2002. "Occupational Risks in Latin America and the Caribbean: Economic and Health Dimensions." *Health Policy and Planning* 17:235–46.

Glied, S. and A. Lleras-Muney. 2008. "Technological Innovation and Inequality in Health." *Demography* 45:741–61.

Granados, J.A.T. 2008. "Macroeconomic Fluctuations and Mortality in Postwar Japan." *Demography* 45;323–43.

Guo, G. 2006. "The Linking of Sociology and Biology." *Social Forces* 85:145–49.

Haas, S.A. 2006. "Health Selection and the Process of Social Stratification: The Effect of Childhood Health on Socioeconomic Attainment." *Journal of Health and Social Behavior* 47:339–54.

Hauser, R.M. and J.R. Warren. 1997. "Socioeconomic Indices for Occupations: A Review, Update, and Critique." *Sociological Methodology* 27:177–298.

Hayward, M.D. and B.K. Gorman. 2004. "The Long Arm of Childhood: The Influence of Early-Life Social Conditions on Men's Mortality." *Demography* 41:87–107.

Hayward, M.D. and W.R. Grady. 1990. "Work and Retirement Among a Cohort of Older Men in the United States, 1966–1983." *Demography* 27:337–56.

Hayward, M.D., W.R. Grady, M.A. Hardy, and D. Sommers. 1989. "Occupational Influences on Retirement, Disability, and Death." *Demography* 26:393–409.

Hayward, M.D., W.R. Grady, and S.D. McLaughlin. 1988. "Changes in the Retirement Process Among Older Men in the United States: 1972–1980." *Demography* 25: 371–86.

Heymann, J., A. Fischer, and M. Engelman. 2003. "Labor Conditions and the Health of Children, Elderly, and Disabled Family Members." In J. Heymann. (ed.), *Global Inequalities at Work: Work's Impact on the Health of Individuals, Families, and Societies*, pp. 75–104. New York, NY, Oxford University Press.

House, J.S., R.C. Kessler, A.R. Herzog, R.P. Mero, A.M. Kinney, and M.J. Breslow. 1990. "Age, Socioeconomic Status, and Health." *The Milbank Quarterly* 68:383–411.

International Labour Organization. 1988. *Economic and Social Effects of Multinational Enterprises in Export Processing Zones*. Geneva, International Labour Organization.

Jamal, M. 2007. "Short Communication: Burnout and Self Employment: A Cross-Cultural Empirical Study." *Stress and Health* 23:249–56.

Jencks, C., L. Perman, and L. Rainwater. 1988. "What Is a Good Job? A New Measure of Labor-Market Success." *American Journal of Sociology* 93:1322–57.

Johnson, J.V., W. Stewart, E.M. Hall, P. Fredlund, and T. Theorell. 1996. "Long-Term Psychosocial Work Environment and Cardiovascular Mortality Among Swedish Men." *American Journal of Public Health* 86:324–31.

Kalleberg, A.L. 2000. "Nonstandard Employment Relations: Part-Time, Temporary and Contract Work." *Annual Review of Sociology* 26:341–65.

Kalleberg, A.L., B.F. Reskin, and K. Hudson. 2000. "Bad Jobs in America: Standard and Nonstandard Employment Relations and Job Quality in the United States." *American Sociological Review* 65:256–78.

Kammerling, R.M. and S. O'Connor. 1993. "Unemployment Rate as Predictor of Rate of Psychiatric Admission." *British Medical Journal* 307:1536–39.

Karasek, R.A. 1979. "Job Demands, Job Decision Latitude, and Mental Strain: Implications for Job Redesign." *Administrative Science Quarterly* 24:285–308.

Kasl, S.V. and B.A. Jones. 2000. "The Impact of Job Loss and Retirement on Health." In L.F. Berkman and I. Kawachi (eds.), *Social Epidemiology*, pp. 119–36. New York, NY, Oxford University.

Kawachi, I. and L.F. Berkman. 2000. "Social Cohesion, Social Capital, and Health." In L.F. Berkman and I. Kawachi (eds.), *Social Epidemiology*, pp. 174–90. New York, NY, Oxford University Press.

Kawachi, I. and B.P. Kennedy. 1997. "The Relationship between Income Inequality to Mortality: Does the Choice of Indicator Matter?" *Social Science and Medicine* 45:1121–27.

Kawachi, I. and B.P. Kennedy. 1999. "Income Inequality and Health: Pathways and Mechanisms." *Health Services Research* 34:215–27.

Kawachi, I., B.P. Kennedy, K.A. Lochner, and D. Prothrow-Stith. 1997. "Social Capital, Income Inequality, and Mortality." *American Journal of Public Health* 87:1491–98.

Kawakami, N., K. Akachi, H. Shimizu, T. Haratani, F. Kobayashi, M. Ishizaki, T. Hayashi, O. Fujita, Y. Aizawa, S. Miyazaki, H. Hiro, S. Hashimoto, and S. Araki. 2000. "Job Strain, Social Support in the Workplace, and Haemoglobin A1c in Japanese Men." *Occupational and Environmental Medicine* 57:805–9.

Kitagawa, E.M. and P.M. Hauser. 1973. *Differential Mortality in the United States: A Study in Socioeconomic Epidemiology*. Cambridge, MA, Harvard University Press.

Kivimaki, M., J. Vahtera, M. Virtanen, M. Elovainio, J. Pentti, and J.E. Ferrie. 2003. "Temporary Employment and Risk of Overall and Cause-Specific Mortality." *American Journal of Epidemiology* 158:663–68.

Kivimäki, M., P. Leino-Arjas, R. Luukkonen, H. Riihimäki, J. Vahtera, and J. Kirjonen. 2002. "Work Stress and Risk of Cardiovascular Mortality: Prospective Cohort Study of Industrial Empoyees." *British Medical Journal* 325:857–61.

Knodel, J. and C. Saengtienchai. 2007. "Rural Parents with Urban Children: Social and Economic Implications of Migration for the Rural Elderly in Thailand." *Population, Space and Place* 13:193–210.

Korn, E.L., B.I. Graubard, and D. Midthune. 1997. "Time-to-Event Analysis of Longitudinal Follow-up of a Survey: Choice of the Time-Scale." *American Journal of Epidemiology* 145:72–80.

Krueger, P.M., R.G. Rogers, R.A. Hummer, F.B. LeClere, and S.A. Bond Huie. 2003. "Socioeconomic Status and Age: The Effect of Income Sources and Portfolios on Adult Mortality in the United States." *Sociological Forum* 18:465–82.

Krueger, P.M., R.G. Rogers, C. Ridao-Cano, and R.A. Hummer. 2004. "To Help or to Harm? Food Stamp Receipt and Mortality Risk Prior to the 1996 Welfare Reform Act." *Social Forces* 82:1573–99.

Kuhn, R.S. 2006. "A Longitudinal Analysis of Health and Mortality in a Migrant-Sending Region of Bangladesh." In S. Jatrana, M. Toyota, and B.S.A. Yeoh (ed.), *Migration and Health in Asia*, pp. 177–208. New York, NY, Routledge.

Kuhn, R.S., B.G. Everett, and R. Silvey. 2011. "The Effects of Children's Migration on Elderly Kin's Health: A Counterfactual Approach." *Demography* 48:forthcoming.

Lewin-Epstein, N. and E. Yuchtman-Yaar. 1991. "Health Risks of Self-Employment." *Work and Occupations* 18:291–312.

Link, B.G. 2008. "Epidemiological Sociology and the Social Shaping of Population Health." *Journal of Health and Social Behavior* 49:367–84.

Link, B.G. and J. Phelan. 2005. "Fundamental Sources of Health Inequities." In D. Mechanic, L.B. Rogut, D.C. Colby, and J.R. Knickman (eds.), *Policy Challenges in Modern Health Care*, pp. 71–84. Piscataway, NJ, Rutgers University.

Litchfield, M.H. 2005. "Estimates of Acute Pesticide Poisoning in Agricultural Workers in Less Developed Countries." *Toxicological Reviews* 24:271–78.

Liu, Y. and H. Tanaka. 2002. "Overtime Work, Insufficient Sleep, and Risk of Non-Fatal Acute Myocardial Infarction in Japanese Men." *Occupational and Environmental Medicine* 59:447–51.

Lleras-Muney, A. 2005. "The Relationship between Education and Adult Mortality in the United States." *Review of Economic Studies* 72:189–221.

Lockley, S.W., J.W. Cronin, E.E. Evans, B.E. Cade, C.J. Lee, C.P. Landrigan, J.M. Rothschild, J.T. Katz, C.M. Lilly, P.H. Stone, D. Aeschbach, and C.A. Czeisler. 2004. "Effect of Reducing Intern's Weekly Work Hours on Sleep and Attentional Failures." *New England Journal of Medicine* 351:1829–37.

Loewenson, R. 2001. "Globalization and Occupational Health: A Perspective from Southern Africa." *Bulletin of the World Health Organization* 79:863–68.

London, L. and R. Bailie. 2001. "Challenges for Improving Surveillance for Pesticide Poisoning: Policy Implications for Developing Countries." *International Journal of Epidemiology* 30:564–70.

Lurie, M.N., B.G. Williams, K. Zuma, D. Mkaya-Mwamburi, G.P. Garnett, A.W. Sturm, M.D. Sweat, J. Gittelsohn, and S.S. Abdool Karim. 2003. "The Impact of Migration on HIV-1 Transmission in South Africa: A Study of Migrant and Nonmigrant Men and Their Partners." *Sexually Transmitted Diseases* 30:149–56.

Lynch, J., S. Harper, G.A. Kaplan, and G.D. Smith. 2004. "Associations between Income Inequality and Mortality Among U.S. States: The Importance of Time Period and Source of Income Data." *American Journal of Public Health* 95:1424–30.

Lynch, J.W., G.D. Smith, G.A. Kaplan, and J.S. House. 2000. "Income Inequality and Mortality: Importance to Health of Individual Income, Psychosocial Environment, or Material Conditions." *British Medical Journal* 320:1200–4.

MacLeod, J., G. Davey Smith, C. Metcalf, and C. Hart. 2005. "Is Subjective Social Status a More Important Determinant of Health than Objective Social Status? Evidence from a Prospective Observational Study of Scottish Men." *Social Science and Medicine* 61:1916–29.

Macintyre, S. and K. Hunt. 1997. "Socio-Economic Position, Gender, and Health: How Do They Interact?" *Journal of Health Psychology* 2:315–34.

Mansyur, C., B. Amick, R.B. Harrist, and L. Franzini. 2008. "Social Capital, Income Inequality, and Self-Rated Health in 45 Countries." *Social Science and Medicine* 66:43–56.

Marmot, M.G. 2004. *The Status Syndrome: How Social Standing Affects Our Health and Longevity*. New York, NY: Henry Holt and Co.

Martikainen, P. 1995. "Mortality and Socio-Economic Status Among Finnish Women." *Population Studies* 49:71–90.

Marx, K. 1957. *Capital*. New York, NY, Dutton.

Massey, D.S. 1990. "Social Structure, Household Strategies, and the Cumulative Causation of Migration." *Population Index* 56:3–26.

McDonough, P., A. Sacker, and R.D. Wiggins. 2005. "Time on My Side? Life Course Trajectories of Poverty and Health." *Social Science and Medicine* 61:1795–808.

McDonough, P., D.R. Williams, J.S. House, and G.J. Duncan. 1999. "Gender and the Socioeconomic Gradient in Mortality." *Journal of Health and Social Behavior* 40:17–30.

McGarry, K. and R.F. Schoeni. 1995. "Transfer Behavior in the Health and Retirement Study: Measurement and the Redistribution of Resources within the Family." *Journal of Human Resources* 30:184–226.

Miech, R.A. and R.M. Hauser. 2001. "Socioeconomic Status and Health at Midlife: A Comparison of Educational Attainment with Occupation-Based Indicators." *Annals of Epidemiology* 11:75–84.

Miller, D.C. and N.J. Salkind. 2002. *Handbook of Research Design and Social Measurement* (6th ed.) Thousand Oaks, CA, Sage Publications.

Mirowsky, J. and C.E. Ross. 2003. *Education, Social Status, and Health*. Hawthorne, NY, Aldine De Gruyter.

Moore, D.E. and M.D. Hayward. 1990. "Occupational Careers and Mortality of Elderly Men." *Demography* 27:31–53.

Morris, J.N., A. Kagan, D.C. Pattison, M.J. Gardner, and P.A.B. Raffle. 1966. "Incidence and Prediction of Ischaemic Heart-Disease in London Busmen." *Lancet* 288:553–59.

Mulatu, M.S. and C. Schooler. 2002. "Causal Connections between SES and Health: Reciprocal Effects and Mediating Mechanisms." *Journal of Health and Social Behavior* 43: 22–41.

Mullahy, J. and S.A. Robert. 2008. *No Time to Lose? Time Constraints and Physical Activity*. National Bureau of Economic Research Working Paper 14513.

Murray, C.J.L. and A.D. Lopez. 1996. "Quantifying the Burden of Disease and Injury Attributable to Ten Major Risk Factors." In C.J.L. Murray and A.D. Lopez (eds.), *The Global Burden of Disease*, pp. 295–324. Cambridge, MA, Harvard University Press.

Mutchler, J.E. and D.L. Poston. 1983. "Do Females Necessarily Have the Same Occupational Status Scores as Males? A Conceptual and Empirical Examination of the Duncan Socioeconomic Status Index and Nam-Powers Occupational Status Scores." *Social Science Research* 12:353–62.

Nakao, K. and J. Treas. 1994. "Updating Occupational Prestige and Socioeconomic Scores: How the New Measures Measure Up." *Sociological Methodology* 24:1–72.

Nam, C.B. 2000. *Comparison of Three Occupational Scales*. Center for Demography and Population Health Working Paper, Florida State University.

Nam, C.B. and M. Boyd. 2004. "Occupational Status in 2000: Over a Century of Census-Based Measurement." *Population Research and Policy Review* 23:327–58.

National Center for Health Statistics. 1992. *1990 Family Resources Supplement to the National Health Interview Survey*. Hyattsville, MD, US Department of Health and Human Services.

National Center for Health Statistics. 2007. *National Health Interview Survey, Multiple Cause of Death Public Use Data File: 1986–2002 Survey Years*. Hyattsville, MD, US Department of Health and Human Services.

National Institute for Occupational Safety and Health. 2009. "National Occupational Mortality Surveillance System." Centers for Disease Control, http://www.cdc.gov/niosh/topics/surveillance/NOMS/default.html

Niedhammer, I., M.L. Tek, D. Starke, and J. Siegrist 2004. "Effort-Reward Imbalance Model and Self-Reported Health: Cross-Sectional and Prospective Findings from the Gazel Cohort." *Social Science and Medicine* 58: 1531–41.

Nielsen, F. 2006. "Achievement and Ascription in Educational Attainment: Genetic and Environmental Influences on Adolescent Schooling." *Social Forces* 85:193–216.

Nuwayhid, I.A. 2004. "Occupational Health Research in Developing Countries: A Partner for Social Justice." *American Journal of Public Health* 94:1916–21.

Oh, H.J. 2001. "An Exploration of the Influence of Household Poverty Spells on Mortality Risk." *Journal of Marriage and Family* 63:224–34.

Oliver, M.L. and T.M. Shapiro. 1997. *Black Wealth/White Wealth: A New Perspective on Racial Inequality*. New York, NY, Routledge.

Omran, A.R. 1971. "The Epidemiologic Transition: A Theory of the Epidemiology of Population Change." *Milbank Quarterly* 49:509–38.

Pack, A.I., G. Maislin, B. Staley, F.M. Pack, W.C. Rogers, C.F.P. George, and D.F. Dinges. 2006. "Impaired Performance in Commercial Drivers: Role of Sleep Apnea and Short Sleep Duration." *American Journal of Respiratory and Critical Care Medicine* 174:446–54.

Paffenbarger, R.S. and W.E. Hale. 1975. "Work Activity and Coronary Heart Mortality." *New England Journal of Medicine* 292:545–50.

Pampel, F.C. 2006. "Socioeconomic Distinction, Cultural Tastes, and Cigarette Smoking." *Social Science Quarterly* 87:19–35.

Pampel, F.C. 2007. "National Income, Inequality, and Global Batterns of Cigarette Use." *Social Forces* 86:455–66.

Pavalko, E.K., G.H. Elder, and E.C. Clipp. 1993. "Worklives and Longevity: Insights from a Life Course Perspective." *Journal of Health and Social Behavior* 34:363–80.

Pavalko, E.K. and B. Smith. 1999. "The Rhythm of Work: Health Effects of Women's Work Dynamics." *Social Forces* 77:1141–62.

Phelan, J., B.G. Link, A.V. Diez-Rouz, I. Kawachi, and B. ILevin. 2004. "'Fundamental Causes' of Social Inequalities in Mortality: A Test of the Theory." *Journal of Health and Social Behavior* 45:265–85.

Popkin, B.M. 1993. "Nutritional Patterns and Transitions." *Population and Development Review* 19:138–57.

Preston, S.H. 1976. *Mortality Patterns in National Populations*. New York, NY, Academic Press.

Price, R.H. and S.A. Burgard. 2008. "The New Employment Contract and Worker Health in the United States." In R.F. Schoeni, J.S. House, G.A. Kaplan, and H. Pollack. (eds.), *Social and Economic Policy as Health Policy: Rethinking America's Approach to Improving Health*, pp. 201–27. New York, NY, Russell Sage.

Quinlan, M., C. Mayhew, and P. Bohle. 2001. "The Global Expansion of Precarious Employment, Work Disorganization, and Consequences for Occupational Health: A Review of Recent Research." *International Journal of Health Services* 31:335–414.

Ramjee, G. and E. Gouws. 2002. "Prevalence of HIV Among Truck Drivers Visiting Sex Workers in Kwazulu-Natal, South Africa." *Sexually Transmitted Diseases* 29: 44–49.

Razzell, P. and C. Spence. 2006. "The Hazards of Wealth: Adult Mortality in Pre-Twentieth Century England." *Social History of Medicine* 19:381–405.

Redelmeier, D.A. and S.M. Singh. 2001. "Survival in Academy Award-Winning Actors and Actresses." *Annals of Internal Medicine* 134:955–62.

Rogers, R.G., R.A. Hummer, and C. Nam. 2000. *Living and Dying in the USA: Behavioral, Health, and Social Differentials of Adult Mortality*. New York, NY, Academic.

Rosenstock, L., M.R. Cullen, and M. Fingerhut. 2005. "Advancing Worker Health and Safety in the Developing World." *Journal of Occupational and Environmental Medicine* 47:132–36.

Ross, N.A., M.C. Wolfson, J.R. Dunn, J.M. Berthelot, G.A. Kaplan, and J.W. Lynch. 2000. "Relation between Income Inequality and Mortality in Canada and in the United States: Cross Sectional Assessment Using Census Data and Vital Statistics." *British Medical Journal* 320:898–902.

Ruggles, S., M. Sobek, T. Alexander, C.A. Fitch, R. Geoeken, P.K. Hall, M. King, and C. Ronnander. 2009. *Integrated Public Use Microdata Series: Version 4.0 [Machine-Readable Database]*. Minneapolis, MN, Minnesota Population Center.

Ruhm, C.J. 2007. "A Healthy Economy Can Break Your Heart." *Demography* 44:829–48.

Saint Onge, J.M., R.G. Rogers, and P.M. Krueger. 2007. "Historical Trends in Height, Weight, and Body Mass in the US: Data from Baseball Players, 1869–1983." *Economics and Human Biology* 6:482–88.

Saint Onge, J.M., R.G. Rogers, and P.M. Krueger. 2008. "Major League Baseball Players' Life Expectancies." *Social Science Quarterly* 89:818–30.

Salazar, M.C. 1998. "Child Work and Education in Latin America." In M.C. Salazar and W.A. Glasinovich. (eds.), *Child Work and Education: Five Case Studies from Latin America*, pp. 1–19. Brookfield, VT, Ashgate.

Schernhammer, E.S., F. Laden, F.E. Speizer, W.C. Willett, D.J. Hunter, I. Kawachi, and G.A. Colditz. 2001. "Rotating Night Shifts and Risk of Breast Cancer in Women Participating in the Nurses' Health Study." *Journal of the National Cancer Institute* 93:1563–68.

Schierhout, G.H., A. Midgley, and J.E. Myers. 1997. "Occupational Fatality under-Reporting in Rural Areas of the Western Cape Province, South Africa." *Safety Science* 25:113–22.

Schnittker, J. 2007. "Working More and Feeling Better: Women's Health, Employment, and Family Life, 1974–2004." *American Sociological Review* 72: 221–38.

Seltzer, C.C. and S. Jablon. 1977. "Army Rank and Subsequent Mortality by Cause: 23 Year Follow-Up." *American Journal of Epidemiology* 105:559–66.

Sen, A. 2001. "Economic Progress and Health." In D. Leon and G. Walt. (eds.), *Poverty, Inequality, and Health: An International Perspective*, pp. 333–45. Oxford, Oxford University Press.

Siegel, P.M. 1971. *Prestige in the American Occupational Structure*. Unpublished doctoral dissertation, University of Chicago.

Siegrist, J. 1996. "Adverse Health Effects of High-Effort/Low Reward Conditions." *Journal of Occupational Health Psychology* 1:27–41.

Smith, J.P. 1999. "Healthy Bodies and Thick Wallets: The Dual Relation between Health and Economic Status." *Journal of Economic Perspectives* 13:145–66.

Smith, K.E. and A. Bachu. 1999. *Women's Labor Force Attachment Patterns and Maternity Leave: A Review of the Literature*. U.S. Bureau of the Census: Population Division Working Paper 32.

Sorlie, P.D. and E. Rogot. 1990. "Mortality by Employment Status in the National Logitudinal Mortality Study." *American Journal of Epidemiology* 132:983–92.

Stempel, C. 2005. "Adult Participation in Sports as Cultural Capital: A Test of Bourdieu's Theory of the Field of Sports." *International Review for the Sociology of Sport* 40: 411–32.

Stolzenberg, R.M. 2001. "It's About Time and Gender: Spousal Employment and Health." *American Journal of Sociology* 107:61–100.

Strully, K.W. 2009. "Job Loss and Health in the U.S. Labor Market." *Demography* 46:221–46.

Subramanian, S.V. and I. Kawachi. 2003. "Wage Poverty, Earned Income Inequality, and Health." In J. Heymann. (ed.), *Global Inequalities at Work: Work's Impact on the Health of Individuals, Families, and Societies*, pp. 165–87. New York, NY, Oxford University Press.

Subramanian, S.V. and I. Kawachi. 2004. "Income Inequality and Health: What Have We Learned So Far?" *Epidemiologic Reviews* 26:78–91.

Sullivan, T.A. 2006. "Labor Force." In D.L. Poston and M. Micklin. (eds.), *Handbook of Population*, pp. 209–25. New York, NY, Springer.

Sylvestre, M.P., E. Huszti, and J.A. Hanley. 2006. "Do Oscar Winners Live Longer Than Less Successful Peers? A Reanalysis of the Evidence." *Annals of Internal Medicine* 145:361–63.

Takala, J. 1999. "Global Estimates of Fatal Occupational Accidents." *Epidemiology* 10:640–46.

Tatem, A.J., D.J. Rogers, and S.I. Hay. 2006. "Global Transport Networks and Infectious Disease Spread." *Advances in Parasitology* 62:293–343.

Theorell, T. 2000. "Working Conditions and Health." In L.F. Berkman and I. Kawachi. (eds.), *Social Epidemiology*, pp. 95–117. New York, NY, Oxford University Press.

Toyota, M. 2006. "Health Concerns of 'Invisible' Cross-Border Domestic Maids in Thailand." *Asian Population Studies* 2:19–36.

Tsutsumi, A., K. Kayaba, T. Ojima, S. Ishikawa, and N. Kawakami. 2007. "Low Control at Work and the Risk of Suicide in Japanese Men: A Prospective Cohort Study." *Psychotherapy and Psychosomatics* 76:177–85.

U.S. Census Bureau. 2007. *Statistical Abstract of the United States: 2008*. Washington, DC, US Census Bureau.

Van der Gaag, J. and E. Smolensky. 1982. "True Household Equivalence Scales and Characteristics of the Poor in the United States." *Review of Income and Wealth* 28:17–28.

van Ginneken, W. 1999. *Social Security for the Excluded Majority: Case Studies of Developing Countries*.Geneva, International Labour Office.

van Vegchel, N., J. de Jonge, H. Bosma, and W. Schaufeli. 2005. "Reviewing the Effort-Reward Imbalance Model: Drawing up the Balance of 45 Empirical Studies." *Social Science and Medicine* 60:1117–31.

Velazquez, L., D. Bello, N. Munguia, A. Zavala, A. Marin, and R. Moure-Eraso. 2008. "A Survey of Environmental and Occupational Work Practices in the Automotive Refinishing Industry of a Developing Country: Sonora, Mexico." *International Journal of Occupational and Environmental Health* 14:104–11.

Virtanen, P., A. Saloniemi, J. Vahtera, M. Kivimaaki, M. Virtanen, and M. Koskenvuo. 2006. "The Working Conditions and Health of Non-permanent Employees: Are There Differences between Private and Public Labour Markets?" *Economic and Industrial Democracy* 27: 39–65.

Weber, M. 1958. *The Protestant Ethic and the Spirit of Capitalism*. London, Unwin Paperbacks.

Wilkinson, R.G. 1997. "Socioeconomic Determinants of Health: Health Inequalities: Relative or Absolute Material Standards?" *British Medical Journal* 314:591–94.

Wilkinson, R.G. 2006. "Health, Hierarchy, and Social Anxiety." *Annals of the New York Academy of Sciences* 896:48–63.

Wilkinson, R.G. and K.E. Pickett. 2006. "Income Inequality and Population Health: A Review and Explanation of the Evidence." *Social Science and Medicine* 62:1768–82.

Willmore, L. 2006. "Universal Pensions for Developing Countries." *World Development* 35:24–51.

World Bank. 2003. *World Development Indicators.* Washington, DC, The World Bank.

Yano, E., S.M. Wang, X.R. Wang, M.Z. Wang, and Y.J. Lan. 2001. "Cancer Mortality Among Workers Exposed to Amphibole-Free Chrysotile Asbestors." *American Journal of Epidemiology* 154:538–43.

Yu, T.S.I., Y.M. Liu, J.L. Zhou, and T.W. Wong. 1999. "Occupational Injuries in Shunde City—A Country Undergoing Rapid Economic Change in Southern China." *Accident Analysis & Prevention* 31: 313–17.

Zick, C.D. and K.R. Smith. 1991. "Marital Transitions, Poverty, and Gender Differences in Mortality." *Journal of Marriage and Family* 53:327–36.

Zimmer, Z., L.G. Martin, M.B. Ofstedal, and Y.-L. Chuang. 2007. "Education of Adult Children and Mortality of Their Elderly Parents in Taiwan." *Demography* 44: 289–305.

# Chapter 14
# Relationships Among Health Behaviors, Health, and Mortality

Christine L. Himes

## Introduction

Individual and population measures of health reflect a variety of underlying factors, including genetics, disease environments, behaviors, and health-care factors. Individuals are at risk of disease because of their genetic predispositions, the disease environment in which they live, and the individual behaviors in which they engage. The medical care system can alleviate those risks, but once basic housing, sanitation, and public-health interventions have been established, the most cost-effective way of intervening in the disease process is through the adoption of personal healthy lifestyle behaviors. Three lifestyle characteristics—tobacco use, poor diet and physical inactivity, and alcohol consumption—account for nearly 40% of deaths in the United States (Mokdad et al. 2004). Understanding the patterns of these health behaviors and the ways in which they influence health is critical to advancing health and longevity.

Health behaviors can be examined at both individual and population levels. Research focused on individual factors explores the molecular and cellular effects of tobacco, alcohol, or specific nutrients on the body. The interest lies in the biological mechanisms through which particular behaviors interact with genetic predispositions to create disease. Other research at the individual level focuses on the socioeconomic or behavioral correlates of health and health behaviors. For instance, a considerable body of research has examined the changes in health behaviors that accompany changes in marital status (Hu and Goldman 1990; Liu and Umberson 2008; Waite and Gallagher 2000). Additional research has focused on the effects of education, occupation, and income on health (Adler and Rehkopf 2008; Mirowsky and Ross 2003; Warren and Hernandez 2007). Again, health behaviors are often viewed as intervening variables, in this case linking socioeconomic status (SES) to disease; some researchers have argued that those with more education have better information about the value of healthy behaviors and greater resources to act on that information (Cutler and Lleras-Muney 2006; Goldman and Smith 2002; Lahelma et al. 2004).

A focus on population-level characteristics, such as cultural differences in diet, exercise, and lifestyle, shifts away from entirely individual-based explanations for disease patterns. Instead, at the population level, patterns of behavior are examined for their correlation with the prevalence of a particular disease within a country or subpopulation. Countries in which the diet is high in fatty fish, for instance, have been found to exhibit lower prevalence of coronary heart disease (Stone 1996). This correlation at the population level can then be examined at the individual level to determine the mechanisms through which that particular diet may affect the onset of disease (Kris-Etherton et al. 2002). Early work on population-level behaviors focused on mortality as the endpoint. Preston's (1976) study of national mortality patterns focused on differences between countries in the structure of causes of death. In earlier work, Preston (1970) focused on the role of smoking patterns in explaining mortality differentials. In the field of epidemiology, Keys et al. (1980) led path-breaking investigations on the prevalence of

C.L. Himes (✉)
Department of Sociology and Center for Policy Research,
Syracuse University, Syracuse, NY 13244, USA
e-mail: clhimes@syr.edu

heart attacks and strokes in seven countries in an effort to identify the elements of lifestyle and diet associated with differential incidence.

Both individual and population approaches contribute to our understanding of the role of health behaviors in affecting health. In his seminal work on public-health measures, Rose (2008) describes this interrelationship. As he notes, some population characteristics, such as mean cholesterol levels, are aggregations of individual characteristics. Other population characteristics, such as herd immunity, are properties of the society from which an individual may benefit. Further, societies exist not just as collections of individuals, but have their own distinctive characteristics, many that influence health. Behavioral activities such as eating, drinking, and exercising are socially conditioned. These characteristics are not evenly distributed among those in the population, partly as a result of wider social forces that determine access to resources and information. There is increasing evidence that addressing the societal determinants of disease is important for further reductions in disease prevalence and improvements in mortality (Adler and Rehkopf 2008; Murray et al. 2006; Rose 2008; Stafford and Marmot 2003).

The three leading causes of death in high-income countries are heart disease, cancer, and stroke. For all three, health behaviors may be as significant as genetic disposition for risk. A recent report by the World Health Organization (WHO 2008) estimates that 80% of premature deaths worldwide could be eliminated by regular exercise, refraining from tobacco use, and the consumption of a healthy diet. This chapter examines tobacco use, diet and nutrition, physical activity, obesity, and alcohol consumption. For each, I examine individual-level explanations for that behavior's effects on health, as well as population-level prevalence data.

## Measurement Issues

The measurement of both health and health behaviors is fraught with pitfalls. Most studies must rely on the self-reports of individuals. With respect to health behaviors, self-reports tend to suffer from two general types of errors. First, people may report answers that they feel are socially acceptable—that is, they may underreport stigmatized behaviors and over-report socially desirable ones. Second, people may remember events inaccurately. Despite these potential sources of error, researchers have concluded that self-reports of health behaviors generally provide accurate data (Babor et al. 2000; Patrick et al. 1994). In some cases, however, bias differs by sex and age. Kuczmarski et al. (2001) find that self-reports of height and weight are more accurate for younger adults than for those aged 60 and older. At the other end of the spectrum, Brener et al. (2003) find that adolescents are not very sensitive about behaviors related to physical activity, but are sensitive to those involving tobacco use. Men tend to over-report their height and women underreport their weight (Rogers et al. 2003). Both social desirability bias and recall error can be ameliorated to some extent by survey techniques (Warnecke et al. 1997). Confidential or anonymous surveys tend to yield greater validity. Limiting the time frame in which recall is required, and using specific terms, such as "in the last year" or "often," also help to reduce error.

Other measurement and classification issues arise in cross-cultural and cross-ethnic comparisons. For instance, because of the reliance in the United States on the Medicare system for particular coding of disease conditions, the United States continues to use ICD-9 codes for morbidity reports and ICD-10 codes for mortality (National Center for Health Statistics [NCHS] 2009). This creates some problems with cross-national comparisons, although the effect is seen at very fine levels of analysis. In addition, some cultural differences exist in the naming of diseases and the interpretation of questions. For instance, African-Americans may refer to diabetes as "sugar" and to hypertension as "high blood" (Stevens et al. 1994). Some measures of health status, such as Katz's index of limitations in activities of daily living (ADLs), have been shown to be consistent within an ethnic group, but less valid in comparisons across ethnicities (Reijneveld et al. 2007). A gender bias may also be present in some measures, such as those that ask about the ability to perform household tasks which are linked to traditional gender roles, like cooking or housework (Allen et al. 1993). Such cultural differences need to be considered when measures are compared across cultures or ethnicities (Ramirez et al. 2005; Warnecke et al. 1997).

Further confusion stems from the use of similar terms to describe particular disease conditions. In referring to a variety of sources, this chapter retains the disease term used in the original research, rather than attempting to standardize terminology. The term "heart disease" encompasses a wide range of underlying conditions including diseases of the heart muscle (cardiomyopathy) or valves (stenosis), the circulatory system (coronary artery disease), or the function of the heart (arrhythmias). The terms cardiovascular disease (CVD), coronary heart disease (CHD), and coronary artery disease (CAD) usually refer broadly to the underlying atherosclerotic process—the "hardening" of the arteries, although the usage of these terms is often imprecise and their relative popularity varies over time. The term CVD is more often associated with the broad spectrum of conditions relating to the heart and blood vessels, including CAD and stroke (http://www.who.int/mediacentre/factsheets/fs317/en/). Currently, the National Heart, Lung, and Blood Institute refers to CHD and CAD as interchangeable terms describing the most common type of heart disease in the United States in which plaque accumulates in the coronary arteries (http://www.nhlbi.nih.gov/health/dci/Diseases/Cad/CAD_WhatIs.html). Ischemic heart disease refers to damage to the heart muscle from inadequate oxygen. Cerebrovascular disease defines a group of conditions that affect the blood supply to the brain, but most commonly refers to stroke, in which blood flow to the brain is interrupted either through an ischemic stroke (due to a blockage in the blood vessels) or a hemorrhagic stroke (due to a broken blood vessel). Hypertension refers to consistently high blood pressure. Current guidelines in the United States specify that blood pressure readings that exceed 140 mm Hg systolic or 90 mm Hg diastolic define hypertension.

The known risk factors for CHD include high serum level of low-density lipoprotein (LDL) cholesterol, low serum level of high-density lipoprotein (HDL) cholesterol, a family history of CHD, hypertension, diabetes mellitus, cigarette smoking, advancing age, and obesity (Castelli 1996; Hennekens 1998). There is a positive linear relationship between serum total cholesterol and LDL cholesterol concentrations and risk of CHD or mortality from CHD (Jousilahti et al. 1998; Neaton and Wentworth 1992; Stamler et al. 1986). A low concentration of HDL cholesterol is positively correlated with risk of CHD, independently of other risk factors (Austin et al. 2000). The particular effects of measurement will be discussed further as each health behavior is examined.

## Tobacco Use

Tobacco use is a serious global public-health concern. The use of tobacco is a risk factor for at least six of the eight leading causes of death worldwide: ischemic heart disease, cerebrovascular disease, lower respiratory infections, chronic obstructive pulmonary disease, tuberculosis, and trachea, bronchus, and lung cancers. Smoking is the primary causal factor for at least 30% of all cancer deaths, for nearly 80% of deaths from chronic obstructive pulmonary disease, and for early cardiovascular disease and deaths from this cause (Centers for Disease Control 2004). Although the smoker's own health is most directly affected, secondhand smoke exposes millions more to the harmful effects. The use of "smokeless" tobacco products, like chewing tobacco and snuff, also increases serious health problems and mortality. The WHO (2008) estimates that worldwide more than 5 million deaths a year can be attributed to tobacco use, and that number could rise to 8 million by the year 2030.

Lung cancer was the first disease to be causally linked to tobacco, and it exhibits the strongest health relationship between tobacco use and cancer; between 80 and 90% of lung cancer deaths are attributable to tobacco use (CDC 2004). Tobacco contains over 60 known carcinogens, chemicals including polyaromatic hydrocarbons and nitrosamines (CDC 2004). These and other carcinogens cause genetic changes in lung cells that lead to the development of lung cancer. The increased use of filtered cigarettes and cigarettes with lower tar and nicotine content (lower yield) may reduce the amount of carcinogens ingested, but has not clearly reduced the incidence of lung cancer (Institute of Medicine 2001). Smokers may increase the number of cigarettes smoked or inhale more deeply with filtered cigarettes, thereby negating the benefits of lower yield.

The risk of developing lung cancer varies with the number of cigarettes smoked and the duration of smoking (CDC 2004). The longer an individual smokes and the more cigarettes smoked, the greater the likelihood that lung cancer will develop. The deleterious effects remain even after a smoker quits smoking, although the relative risks do decline, especially over time and for specific diseases. In one estimate, the cumulative risk of developing lung cancer by age 75 was 16% among those still smoking, versus 10% for those who had quit at age 60 (Peto et al. 2000). The benefits of smoking cessation on mortality vary based on the presence of disease conditions (Nam et al. 1994). Recent quitters often include those who have stopped smoking due to health problems, muting the decline in mortality within 1–3 years of smoking cessation. Among those who are "healthy" at the time of smoking cessation, mortality rates begin to approach those of non-smokers 10–15 years after quitting. The mortality rates of former smokers remain higher than those of non-smokers, but substantially lower than those who continue smoking (CDC 1990).

Smoking is also associated with the development of chronic respiratory diseases. The US surgeon general has consistently reported a relationship between smoking and chronic obstructive pulmonary disease (COPD; CDC 1964, 1984, 2004). Smoking is responsible for 90% of COPD cases in the United States (CDC 2004). COPD is composed primarily of two diseases, emphysema and chronic bronchitis, both of which create obstructions in the movement of air through the airways and out of the lungs (National Heart, Lung, and Blood Institute 2009). Chronic bronchitis involves inflammation and swelling of the lining of the airways, narrowing and obstructing them. The inflammation also stimulates production of mucus, which can further obstruct the airways. Emphysema results from damage to the walls between air sacs (alveoli) in the lungs. This damage reduces the ability of the lung to expand and contract, and both reduces the amount of air taken in with each breath and increases the energy required to take a breath. As a result, in both conditions, individuals develop chronic coughs, shortness of breath, and increased susceptibility to acute respiratory infections.

COPD is especially important to consider given the long periods of disability associated with it. The progressive loss of lung function can lead to severe shortness of breath, restriction of activity, and the inability to work or carry out daily activities. Evidence from the US National Health and Nutrition Examination Survey (NHANES) indicates that those with obstructive lung disease are less likely to be able to walk one-quarter of a mile or to lift 10 pounds and are more likely to need help with daily activities (Mannino et al. 2003). Other research indicates that COPD affects all muscle groups and is associated with a broad array of functional limitations (Eisner et al. 2008). In addition, COPD is associated with high rates of medical care utilization, including office-based physician visits and hospitalizations (Sullivan et al. 2000). In fact, those suffering from COPD are more likely to be hospitalized and to have longer hospital stays than those with lung cancer (Au et al. 2006).

In considering trends in the development of pulmonary diseases, we must acknowledge the effects of tobacco smoke inhalation and early uptake of smoking among children and adolescents. There is substantial evidence that secondhand smoke can affect lung development in utero, infancy, and childhood (CDC 2004). In addition, among smokers and those exposed to smoke, lung function grows more slowly during childhood and adolescence, ceases to grow prematurely, and begins to decline in late adolescence and early adulthood. The 2006 surgeon general's report (CDC 2006a) concluded that secondhand smoke exposure from parental smoking contributes to lower respiratory illnesses in infants and children, and that the greatest effect comes from smoking by the mother.

Cigarette smoking is considered the single most preventable cause of premature death in the United States, and 20% of deaths in the United States are attributable to cigarette smoking (CDC 2009). The direct health-care costs of smoking are immense. Direct medical costs for the detection and treatment of smoking-related illnesses, and for patient care, account for 6–8% of all annual expenditures for health care in the United States (Warner et al. 1999). Combining the direct medical costs with the loss in productivity associated with illness results in an estimated $158 billion cost for the period 1995–1999 (CDC 2002). Some researchers have argued, however, that long-term health-care costs might increase if there were no smokers. While smokers have higher medical costs, they also have higher mortality rates, meaning that their lifetime health-care costs may be lower than those of non-smokers who have considerably longer life expectancy (Barendregt et al. 1997). The inclusion of lost productivity due to early mortality, however, may negate these lifetime health-care savings, particularly if smoking cessation occurs early in life (Rasmussen et al. 2005).

Cigarette smoking rates in the United States have dropped significantly since the mid-1960s, when about 42% of adults were current cigarette smokers, compared to 20% today (CDC 2008). However, this decline has slowed in recent years. In the most recent year of data, 2007, a slight decline has been observed after 3 years of virtually no change. Now, 19.8% of American adults report being current smokers. Smoking rates are higher among those with less education and lower incomes, as well as among American-Indian populations (CDC 2008). Based on data for teenagers enrolled in school, cigarette smoking among adolescents declined dramatically during 1997–2002, but has stalled since then. In 2006, 25.6% of high-school students reported current use of any tobacco product, with cigarettes (19.7%) being the most common type of tobacco used. This compares to an estimated 36% of teens who reported current smoking in 1997 (CDC 2006b).

Figure 14.1 provides a global perspective on tobacco use using select countries from the WHO statistical database. In all countries examined, tobacco use is higher among men than among women. However, the extent of this disparity varies widely. In Asia, represented by China, Indonesia, India, and Japan, male smoking prevalence is many times more than that recorded for women. A similar pattern is observed in Russia where male smoking prevalence is particularly high (70%), although female smoking is also relatively high (26%). Many of those same countries exhibit the highest smoking rates for men overall. The smallest gender differentials in these select countries are seen in the United Kingdom and United States. Smoking prevalence in Europe is slightly higher than that observed in Australia and the United States.

Smoking prevalence rates in the WHO European region are estimated at 28.6% overall, 40% among men, and 18% among women (WHO 2007). These averages mask important differences, however, among countries. For instance, male smoking prevalence is less than 15% in Sweden but exceeds 40% in Austria, and in Sweden and Iceland female smoking rates exceed those of males (WHO 2007). Also, smoking rates in western European countries have stabilized or declined in recent years, but the trends are less clear in eastern European countries, especially among women. Among all European youth there appears to be a slight downward trend in the smoking rates of boys and a slight uptick in the smoking rates of girls (WHO 2007). Lifetime tobacco use is most common in the

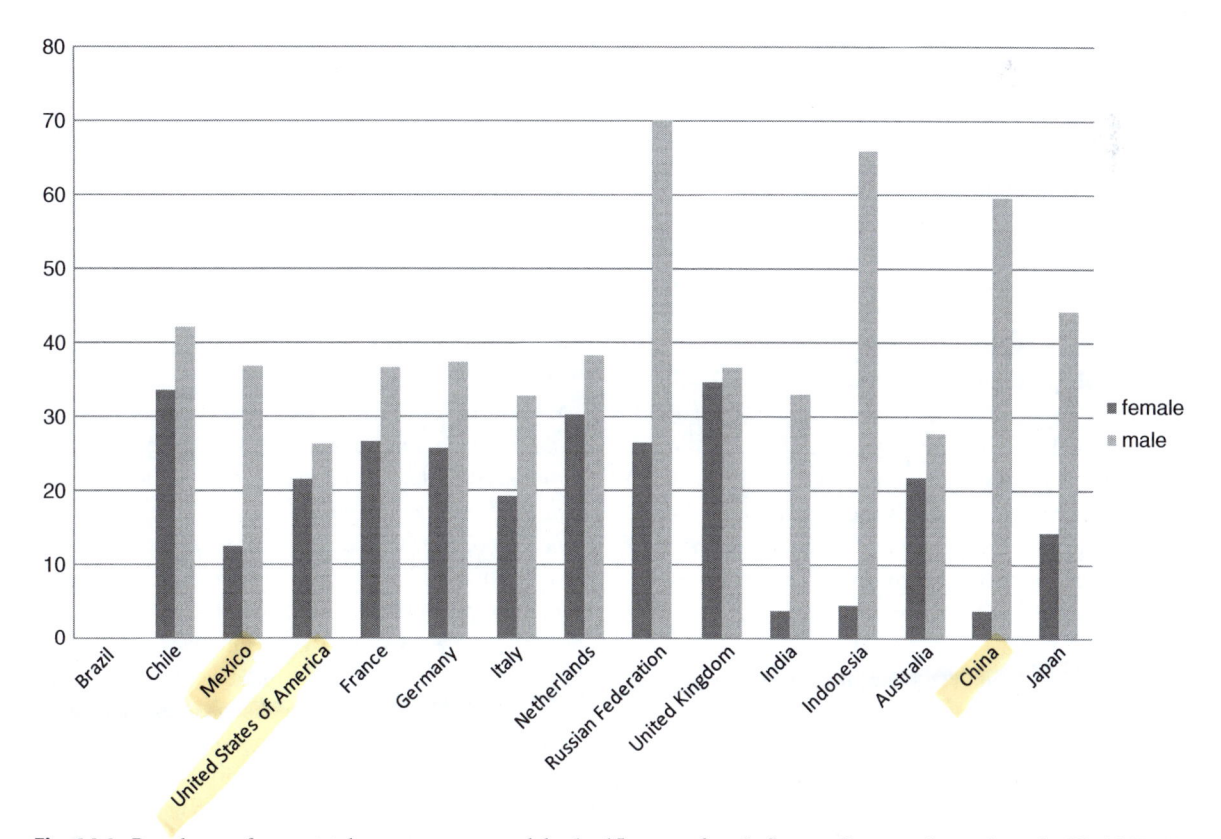

**Fig. 14.1** Prevalence of current tobacco use among adults (≥ 15 years of age). Source: Data are drawn from the World Health Organization Statistical Information System (WHOSIS). World Health Organization. Retrieved August 22, 2009

United States and Europe, with the lowest prevalence in Africa (Degenhardt et al. 2008). But while smoking rates have stabilized or declined in the United States and western Europe, smoking rates are rising in many less-developed countries, particularly in Asia (WHO 2002).

In nearly all countries, men are more likely to smoke than women, although the gap has been narrowing as women increase their rates of smoking. In fact, recent evidence suggests that in a few western European countries (Denmark and Germany) more young women (aged 14–19) than young men smoke (WHO 2003). The historically narrowing gender difference in tobacco use can be seen today in increased death rates from lung cancer among older women. Throughout Europe and North America, women took up smoking later than men (Pampel 2002). As a result, the health effects for women have lagged behind those for men. The smoking behavior of women is responsible, in part, for the narrowing of the sex differential in mortality between men and women during the 1990s. In each year of the last two decades, more women have died from lung cancer than from breast cancer (American Cancer Society 2006). However, the general decline in smoking may lead to an increase in life expectancy as deaths from tobacco-related causes decline (Preston and Wang 2006).

Smoking rates are closely tied to SES at both the individual and the country level. In the latest European study, those countries with the lowest gross national product (GNP) per capita had higher male-smoking rates and higher death rates due to smoking than did countries with higher per capita GNP (WHO 2004a). In general, poor and less-educated people are more likely to smoke than rich or better-educated ones. Those with the highest rates of smoking are the unemployed (54%) and manual workers (51%); the overall population rate is 34%. This socioeconomic differential has increased with time, so that now 60–65% of male smokers are concentrated in lower socioeconomic classes, compared to 35–40% in the 1970s (WHO 2007).

Given the clear evidence that tobacco use is related to adverse health outcomes, the WHO formulated its first treaty around tobacco control, the WHO Framework Convention on Tobacco Control (http://www.who.int/fctc/en/index.html). The treaty, which now has 168 signatories, emphasizes the need to reduce both demand and supply. The WHO advocates a strong educational program, assistance for smoking cessation programs, and the regulation and control of tobacco production and marketing.

The extent of the tobacco problem can be seen by examining the case of China. In recent years China has experienced a rapid increase in the prevalence of tobacco use. Although national-level statistics are scarce, estimates from a variety of studies have found prevalence rates for men ranging from 50 to 67% (Ma et al. 2004). In the same studies, prevalence rates for women ranged from less than 1 to 14%. Some regions of China, though, have remarkably low rates of smoking. For example, in the Ningxia province, inhabited by Chinese Muslims, fewer than 10% of adults smoke (Weng et al. 1987). There are great difficulties, however, in comparing these statistics across time and region given the different sampling strategies and measurement methods (Johnson et al. 2006).

Smoking constitutes a huge economic burden on Chinese society, through increased health-care costs as well as through household consumption patterns. One estimate is that smoking costs China $5 billion every year (Sung et al. 2006). About one-third of this estimate ($1.7 billion) is for the direct health-care costs associated with smoking and accounts for over 3% of all Chinese health-care expenditures in 2000. At the household level, spending on tobacco crowds out spending on basic needs (Wang et al. 2006), as well as investments in human and economic capital through education, medical care, and farming equipment and supplies. One estimate is that Chinese smokers spend 17% of household income on cigarettes (Gong et al. 1995).

While the health-care costs of smoking are great, China has become economically dependent upon the tobacco industry. China is the world's largest tobacco consumer and producer. The state controlled tobacco industry has been a vital component of economic growth in the country. Tobacco sales and taxes accounted for approximately 7.6% of China's total revenue and some provincial governments receive more than 50% of their revenues from tobacco sales (Wright and Katz 2007). Recently, taxes on cigarettes were raised from 6 to 11% (to a total tax rate of 36–56% per pack), to both raise revenues and curb smoking (China Daily 2009). The heavy dependence upon the economy on tobacco is likely to make efforts to curb smoking difficult.

Clearly, although the health problems associated with tobacco use are well-documented, and smoking rates in some parts of the world are falling, the increased prevalence of tobacco use in Asia and Africa is likely to have a negative effect on future health and health-care costs.

## Nutrition and Diet

Poor diet and a sedentary lifestyle contribute significantly to the two million or so annual deaths in the United States (Flegal et al. 2005; Mokdad et al. 2004). Specific diseases and conditions linked to poor diet include cardiovascular disease (CVD), hypertension, dyslipidemia (elevated cholesterol levels), type 2 diabetes, overweight and obesity, osteoporosis, constipation, diverticular disease, iron-deficiency anemia, oral disease, and malnutrition (U.S. Department of Health and Human Services and U.S. Department of Agriculture 2005). A diet rich in fruits, vegetables, whole grains, and fish reduces the incidence of cardiovascular and neoplastic diseases (Willett 2006). This section focuses on the role of diet and nutrition in health. The following section addresses physical activity. Finally, I discuss the special role of overweight and obesity, consequences of both diet and activity level.

The role of diet in influencing health has been recognized for many years. The great strides in human longevity achieved over the past several centuries are due, in large measure, to improved nutritional status and food safety (CDC 1999). Although there are pockets of malnutrition, a diet with adequate nutritional variety is generally available in developed countries. As a result, the focus of recent nutritional research has been on the role of individual food items and nutrients. However, there are inherent difficulties in studying the relationship between diet and health: individuals are notoriously poor at reporting food intake, it is difficult to control for confounding factors, and individual foods and nutrients are rarely eaten in isolation from other items (Sofi et al. 2008).

Given the general availability of adequate food supplies, dietary recommendations in developed countries focus on the quality rather than the quantity of the food consumed, emphasizing nutrient-rich diets, encouraging consumption of fruits, vegetables, and whole grains, and discouraging the over-consumption of fats, particularly saturated fats. The importance of population and cultural differences in developing dietary guidelines is highlighted in the process undertaken by the European Union's European Food Safety Authority (EFSA). In scientific discussions, the idea of developing a guideline for all of Europe, similar to that in the United States, was abandoned (European Food Safety Authority 2008). Instead, the group is developing dietary reference values that can be used by member nations in the development of country-specific recommendations and public-health policies. Each of the elements of a "healthy diet" has been linked to a reduction in risk of particular diseases. The following section reviews some of these relationships.

## *Fat*

Fats are essential to the human body. They supply energy and essential fatty acids, and carry certain fat-soluble vitamins such as vitamins A, D, E, and K, and carotenoids. In addition, fats serve a key regulatory role in numerous biological functions. Dietary fat is found in foods derived from both plants and animals. Despite its vital role, dietary fat, through its relationship to blood triglyceride and cholesterol levels, is associated with disease. The effects of dietary fat on health depend upon the amount and type of fats consumed.

The current dietary recommendation for Americans is that fat should comprise 20–35% of daily calories (DHHS and USDA 2005). Dietary fat can be divided into three categories: saturated fats, unsaturated fats, and trans fats. Saturated fats are found in dairy products and meats, particularly beef, and in tropical oils, and often appear in processed and fried foods. Diets high in saturated fats are associated with increased risk for heart disease (Mensink and Katan 1992; Posner et al. 1995). Unsaturated fats are found in nuts, vegetable oils, and fish. Some fish contain high levels of omega 3 fatty acids, which have been shown to reduce the risks of cardiovascular disease (Yokoyama et al. 2007).

Trans fats, found almost exclusively in processed foods (cookies, crackers, breads), are not essential and provide no known benefit to human health. Most trans fats are formed by hydrogenating liquid vegetable oils to convert them into solid fats with good qualities for baking and a long shelf life. The use of trans fats in processed foods increased substantially after 1985, as did CHD in the United States and elsewhere (Booyens et al. 1988). Trans fats increase LDL cholesterol, the type associated with increased risk of atherosclerosis, and also reduce HDL cholesterol, the type associated with lower risks of heart disease.

## *Fruits and Vegetables*

There is considerable evidence that a diet high in fruits and vegetables is related to better health and a decreased risk of chronic diseases associated with high mortality (Bazzano et al. 2002; Cerhan et al. 2004; DHHS and USDA 2005; Fung et al. 2001; Joshipura et al. 1999). Diets including fruits and vegetables, particularly green leafy vegetables and vitamin C-rich foods have been shown to prevent cardiovascular disease through the combination of vitamins, antioxidants, phytochemicals, and fiber found in these foods (Joshipura et al. 2001). In addition, a diet high in fruits and vegetables, with their low calorie-to-volume ratio, helps maintain a healthy weight. The consumption of fruits and vegetables in the United States falls far below the standards set in the US Healthy People 2010 objectives. In the most recent data collected, just over 32% of Americans consumed at least two daily servings of fruit, compared to the Healthy People 2010 objective of 75%, and only 27% of Americans ate vegetables three or more times a day, compared to the objective of 50% (CDC 2007).

One specific area that has garnered increased attention is the role of antioxidants in the prevention of chronic disease and aging. Antioxidants, which include beta carotene, vitamins C and E, and selenium, can prevent or repair damage to cells (American Dietetic Association 2009). Antioxidants act by "neutralizing" free radicals in the body. Inadequate antioxidant levels may lead to oxidative stress and damage to cells, and damaged cells undergo more free radical reactions than healthy ones. This process of oxidative stress and cell damage is thought to be one of the main mechanisms of aging (Finkel and Holbrook 2000) and contributes to tissue damage in rheumatoid arthritis, inflammatory bowel disease, and Parkinson's disease (Halliwell 1996). The evidence for the role of antioxidants in preventing cardiovascular disease is mixed. Early epidemiological studies reported that these micronutrients might lower CVD risk (Osganian et al. 2003; Tribble 1999). Antioxidants may inhibit the oxidative process in the artery walls, which contributes to the formation of atherosclerotic plaque. Despite this evidence, controlled clinical trials examining the effect of antioxidant supplementation have not found a similar effect (Kris-Etherton et al. 2004). Further, a meta-analysis of studies relating antioxidant supplement use to mortality found, that in some cases, antioxidant supplement use actually was related to increased mortality rates (Bjelakovic et al. 2007).

## *Carbohydrates*

Carbohydrates are found in many foods. The liver breaks carbohydrates down into their component sugar molecules, which are then used by the body for energy. Foods high in carbohydrates include breads, pastas, beans, potatoes, bran, rice, and cereals. Carbohydrates come in three main forms: sugars, fibers, and starches. Starch and dietary fiber are considered complex carbohydrates, whereas sugars are considered simple carbohydrates. Sources of starch include beans, grains, potatoes, peas, and corn. Sugars may be found in fruits, vegetables, and milk products. Dietary fiber is found in fruits, vegetables, and grains. Divided into two categories, soluble and insoluble, fiber provides three main benefits to the body. First, it contributes to weight control by adding bulk to the diet, making a person feel full faster, and regulating the body's use of sugars, helping to keep hunger and blood sugar in check. Second, fiber aids in digestion. Finally, soluble fiber binds to fatty substances in the intestines and carries them out as waste, thus lowering LDL, or "bad" cholesterol.

These beneficial effects translate into high-fiber consumption being clearly associated with lower risks for CVD and both cardiovascular and all-cause mortality (Timm and Slavin 2008; Van Horn 1997). With respect to CVD, the addition of fiber to the diet is usually accompanied by a reduction in dietary fat that reduces blood cholesterol levels. As is mentioned above, fiber itself also affects CVD risk by decreasing the absorption of cholesterol. Finally, fiber also may affect the body's metabolism of fatty acids. Despite clear evidence that increased fiber reduces risks for CVD, the effects of a high-fiber diet on cancer are less clear. Early evidence suggested a link between increased fiber intake and lower rates of colorectal cancer (Kaaks and Riboli 1995; Steinmetz and Potter 1996). But this result has not been found in more recent studies (Park et al. 2005). Among women, high-fiber diets do seem to be associated with lower risks of breast cancer (Baghurst and Rohan 1994), although this association may be weak (Adebamowo et al. 2005).

## Special Diets

The examination of individual nutrients and their impact on disease puts the focus on individuals and individual-level risk factors; however, other studies have attempted to look not at individual consumption of specific food or nutrient items, but at population-level differences in broad diet patterns. For the individual, dietary behavior is a result of age, gender, health status, genetic make-up, SES, knowledge, skills, and attitudes. At the population level, diet is determined in part by the availability of foods and their cost, and is also influenced by culture, education, marketing, and advertising.

There is considerable difference in dietary patterns around the world. The variation in diets among developed countries has led to a focus on the qualities of those diets that may enhance longevity. The DHHS and USDA regularly review the scientific literature regarding nutrition and health and issue general population guidelines. The latest guidelines, *Dietary Guidelines for Americans 2005* (DHHS and USDA 2005), recommend that Americans "Consume a variety of nutrient-dense foods and beverages within and among the basic food groups while choosing foods that limit the intake of saturated and transfats, cholesterol, added sugars, salt, and alcohol." The report emphasizes that nutrient needs should be met primarily through foods, as opposed to dietary supplements. To meet these goals, the report urges adherence to either the USDA food guide (in the past this was represented by the "food pyramid") or the dietary approaches to stop hypertension (DASH) eating plan.

One area receiving considerable attention is the "Mediterranean diet." Although diet in the Mediterranean area varies considerably, generally it involves high consumption of fruits, vegetables, bread and other cereals, potatoes, beans, nuts, and seeds; the use of olive oil as a main fat source; low to moderate consumption of dairy products, fish and poultry, with little red meat; low egg consumption; and low to moderate wine consumption (Kris-Etherton et al. 2001). This diet meets many of the specific nutritional recommendations discussed earlier—it is low in saturated fat, and high in fruits, vegetables, and nonmeat sources of protein. Interest in this dietary pattern emerged from the seminal Seven Countries Study (Keys 1966), which identified national differences in the prevalence of CVD and its risk factors.

Several studies have attempted to quantify the advantage of such a diet. A meta-analysis of studies examining the effect of the Mediterranean diet found that it decreased overall mortality and significantly reduced the risk of mortality from cardiovascular disease and neoplasms (Sofi et al. 2008). The Lyon Diet Heart Study was one attempt to test the effectiveness of a Mediterranean-style diet on cardiovascular disease. Subjects in the experiment had suffered a first myocardial infarction. The experimental group was instructed to adopt a Mediterranean-style diet; the control group received no special dietary advice. After nearly 4 years of follow-up, subjects following the Mediterranean diet had a 50–70% lower risk of recurrent heart disease (Kris-Etherton et al. 2001).

In sum, both general diet and individual nutrients affect health and risk for disease. Adherence to a diet low in fats and high in fruits, vegetables, and whole grains has been consistently found to be associated with better health and lower mortality at the individual and population level.

## Physical Activity

Regular physical activity has been shown to reduce mortality from many chronic diseases. People who are physically active live longer than those who are not (DHHS 2008; Sherman et al. 1994). Early studies in the United States have linked a sedentary lifestyle to 23% of deaths from chronic diseases (Hahn et al. 1998). A review of 73 studies conducted in developed countries around the world concludes that active men and women have about a 30% lower risk of death during the follow-up period than do inactive ones (DHHS 2008). More physically active people have lower rates of cardiovascular disease, type 2 diabetes, and some types of cancer. In addition, physical fitness and activity can contribute to improved balance, which can reduce the risk of falling, and higher bone density, which can reduce the risk of fractures (Nelson et al. 1994).

In pure terms, physical activity is any bodily movement, whether in leisure or in work activities. But physical activity frequently is categorized by the context in which it is performed, as work, leisure, household, and self-care activities. The term "exercise" implies planned and structured movement for the purpose of increasing physical fitness. Surveys commonly ask respondents for reports of activity frequency (number of days per week), intensity (light, moderate, or vigorous), and duration (minutes of activity). Exercise intensity is measured clinically by the metabolic energy expenditure (MET) of the activity compared to sitting quietly. Examples of moderate activity are walking (less than 3 mph), gardening, ballroom dancing, and tennis doubles. Vigorous activity includes jogging or running, jumping rope, bicycling more than 10 mph, and swimming laps (http://www.cdc.gov/physicalactivity/everyone/measuring/index.html).

Although the inverse relationship between physical activity and all-cause mortality extends into older ages, levels of physical activity and measures of physical fitness (muscle mass, strength, oxygen consumption) tend to decline with age. Data from the National Health Interview Survey indicate that 62% of American adults engage in some regular leisure time physical activity, defined as any physical activity lasting at least 10 min without any specific time reference. This prevalence declines steadily with age, to about 55% of Americans age 65–74 and 40% of Americans age 75 and older (NCHS 2006). At all ages, the rates are higher for men than for women. Engaging in "regular physical activity," defined as light-moderate activity at least five times a week for 30 min or vigorous activity at least three times a week for 20 min, is less common. Only 31% of all adults report that they engage in regular physical activity. Although older adults are less active, research has shown that even at very advanced ages increased physical activity can provide health benefits (Mazzeo et al. 1998).

The Eurobarometer provides similar evidence for member states in the European Union. In the latest survey, 2002, 43% of respondents reported engaging in vigorous physical activity in the past 7 days and 60% reported engaging in moderate activity in the same time period (European Opinion Research Group 2003). Among the oldest respondents, those age 65 and older, the prevalence of activity declines; only 20% of the elderly report engaging in vigorous activity and 44% in moderate activity. Men in the EU are more likely than women to be physically active and more likely to engage in both vigorous and moderate activity. Within the EU 15 (Austria, Belgium, Denmark, Finland, France, Germany, Greece, Ireland, Italy, Luxembourg, the Netherlands, Portugal, Spain, Sweden, and the United Kingdom), the highest levels of activity are found in the Netherlands, Germany, Luxembourg, and Finland; the lowest, in Ireland, Italy, and Spain.

Widespread epidemiological evidence links an active lifestyle to reduced risks of the major causes of death: cardiovascular disease, hypertension, and some types of cancer (Albanes et al. 1989; DHHS 2008; Thompson et al. 2003). But the mechanisms linking increased physical activity to improved cardiovascular health are still being investigated. A great deal of research has focused on the structure of blood vessels. Endothelial cells, which line the insides of blood vessels and the heart, move blood through the circulatory system and help to control blood pressure. Exercise appears to improve endothelial function, and therefore improve blood flow and reduce hypertension. In addition, exercise appears to improve microcirculation, the movement of blood through small blood vessels (Gielen et al. 2001). Increased physical activity can also improve cardiac output (the volume of blood ejected from the heart) and increase the ability of muscles to extract and use oxygen from the blood (DHHS 2008). Finally, exercise improves muscle and joint health, and may thereby reduce the risks of osteoporosis and arthritis.

At the population level, most research has focused on the relationship between activity level and cardiovascular disease. There appears to be a direct effect of physical activity on the development of symptomatic disease, and also an effect of physical activity on modifying other risk factors related to the development of cardiovascular disease, such as hypertension, high cholesterol, and impaired glucose tolerance (Thompson et al. 2003). The amount of activity needed to create positive results is relatively small. People at highest risk are those who are least active and spend much of their day in activities that consume low amounts of energy (Manson et al. 1999; Paffenberger et al. 1993). Men and women who perform small amounts of moderate-intensity activity, such as 60 min/week of walking at a brisk pace, have fewer CVD events. But the greatest benefit is seen among those men and women performing 150 or more minutes per week of that type of moderate-intensity physical activity (DHHS 2008).

Exercise and physical activity play a clear role in preventing and treating type 2 diabetes (Weinstein et al. 2004). Meta-analysis of several studies shows that exercise significantly improves glycemic control and reduces visceral adipose tissue and plasma triglycerides (Thomas et al. 2006). These benefits seem to stem from both increased oxygen consumption through aerobic exercises and increased strength and muscle mass from endurance exercises (Barnard et al. 1994). In addition, exercise helps to maintain a healthy weight, which reduces the risk of complications from diabetes.

## Obesity

Body fat, or adipose tissue, is a normal and necessary part of the human body. Fat stores energy that can be used in response to metabolic demands; therefore, the optimal amount of body fat needed by an individual should reflect the environmental situations he or she faces. Obesity, an excess of body fat, results from an increased size and in extreme cases an increased number of fat cells. At the most basic level, obesity results from an imbalance between energy intake and energy expenditure. This imbalance may result from excess caloric intake, decreased physical activity, or metabolic disorders, individually or in combination (National Institutes of Health 1998). Increases in caloric intake combined with decreases in physical activity have resulted in high rates of obesity in the populations of the developed world.

The most widely used measure of obesity is the body mass index (BMI), calculated as weight for height squared (kg/m$^2$). Other measures of adiposity, such as skinfold thickness, waist-to-hip ratio, and direct measures of adiposity through bioelectrical impedance, bone density (DEXA) scan, or hydrostatic weighing provide more accurate measures of body composition, but require special equipment and training. In the first federal guidelines on the evaluation and treatment of obesity (NIH 1998), the National Heart, Lung, and Blood Institute (NHLBI) adopted definitions of overweight as a BMI of 25–29.9 kg/m$^2$, and obesity as a BMI of 30 kg/m$^2$ or greater. Within the category of obesity, further distinctions are made between class I obesity, BMI of 30 up to 35; class II obesity, BMI of 35 up to 40; and class III obesity, BMI 40 or above. These guidelines are consistent with those adopted by the WHO (2000) and used in international studies.

Because of its ease of collection (primarily from self-reports), BMI has become the standard measure of obesity. However, the limitations of this measure are well-known. The distribution of body fat—in particular, abdominal obesity, as measured by waist circumference or waist-to-hip ratio—has repeatedly been shown to be a more important predictor of health than BMI alone (Pischon et al. 2008). Men have on average twice as much abdominal fat as pre-menopausal women (Lemieux et al. 1993). The EPIC (European Prospective Investigation into Cancer and Nutrition) study found that both waist circumference and waist-to-hip ratio were associated with mortality, even after adjusting for BMI (Pischon et al. 2008). In particular, abdominal adiposity was more important at lower BMI levels. This finding may help explain why a linear relationship between BMI and mortality has not been found across the range of BMI values. In the same study, the effect of obesity on mortality appeared to be stronger among younger men than among older men, although a similar relationship was not observed for women.

Results from the 2003–2004 NHANES, using measured heights and weights, indicate that an estimated 66% of American adults are either overweight or obese (Ogden et al. 2006). The prevalence of obesity at all ages has increased dramatically in the United States over the last four decades. Between 1960 and 2000, the proportion of adult men who were overweight rose from 50 to 70%; the proportion of women, from 40 to over 60% (Flegal et al. 2002). In the past several years the trend has changed somewhat. Between 2000 and 2004 the percentage of men who were obese rose from 27.5 to 31.1%, but the proportion of women who were obese showed no significant increase, remaining stable at about 33% (Ogden et al. 2006).

In cross-sectional studies, peak values of BMI are observed in the age range 50–59 in both men and women, with gradual declines in BMI after age 60 (Flegal et al. 1998; Hedley et al. 2004; Ogden et al. 2006). However, premature mortality of the obese may influence these cross-sectional relationships. In a 10-year follow-up study, individuals under age 55 exhibited a greater tendency to gain weight, with the magnitude of increase decreasing with age (Williamson 1993). However, individuals over age 55 tended to lose weight, with an increasing magnitude of weight loss with age. Rates of overweight and obesity in longitudinal studies generally increase with age until age 75, when there is a small drop (Ferraro et al. 2003; Flegal et al. 1998; Must and Strauss 1999).

Men are more likely than women to be overweight, but women are more likely to be obese, especially with BMIs greater than 35 (Hedley et al. 2004). Overweight and obesity rates for women vary starkly by race and ethnicity in the United States, but such differences are not as apparent for men (Flegal et al. 1998; Hedley et al. 2004). Black and Hispanic women are much more likely to be overweight and obese than white women. According to the NCHS analysis of NHANES data (Hedley et al. 2004), 77.5% of black women are overweight, compared to 71.4% of Mexican-American women, and 57% of white women. The prevalence of obesity is similarly skewed, with the rates for black, Mexican-American, and white women at 49.6%, 38.9%, and 31.3%, respectively. In fact, over 10% of middle-aged black women have BMIs greater than 40 (Flegal et al. 1998).

Social class appears to be related to body size in complex ways, with studies showing socioeconomic characteristics to be both a cause and an effect of body size. Most evidence points to a causal relationship between socioeconomic characteristics, poor health behaviors (poor diet, lack of exercise), and being overweight (Goldblatt et al. 1965; Stunkard and Sorenson 1993). However, studies of young adults have lent support to the notion that being overweight leads to lower educational attainment and income through discrimination and lower self-esteem (Gortmaker et al. 1993).

Figure 14.2 provides a global perspective on the prevalence of obesity among adults. Of the 11 selected countries from the WHO database for which there is information, overall obesity prevalence is highest in the United Kingdom and United States. Although women usually have higher rates of obesity prevalence than men, this difference is particularly strong in Chile and Mexico which have high rates of obesity among women (25 and 28%, respectively) compared to men (19%). In only one country, Germany, do men have higher rates of obesity than women. Obesity prevalence rates are very low in Asia, where less than 5% of the population is obese, compared to over 30% in the United States and over 20% in the UK.

Overweight and obesity are significant risk factors for diabetes, high blood pressure, high cholesterol, CHD, arthritis, and certain types of cancer (Mokdad et al. 2004; Paul and Townsend 1995; Villareal et al. 2005; Wolf and Colditz 1998). These effects are found across the life course, beginning in childhood and persisting into later life (Calle et al. 1999; Ferraro et al. 2003; Gregg et al. 2005; Koplan et al. 2005; Whitmer et al. 2005). Most generally, obesity has been shown to be related to an overall decline in health-related quality of life (Ford et al. 2001).

The effects of obesity on mortality are less definitive. Although researchers agree there is some effect, the overall magnitude and age gradient are less clear (Flegal et al. 2005; Fontaine et al. 2003; Olshansky et al. 2005). Early estimates using a meta-analysis of published studies claimed that about 400,000 deaths in the United States were attributable to excess weight caused by poor diet and physical inactivity (Mokdad et al. 2004). Using different methodology, Flegal et al. (2005) estimated that the number of deaths attributable to excess weight to be closer to 112,000. The risk is highest for those who have been overweight for longer periods of time and decreases if one does not become overweight or obese until after age 50 (Flegal et al. 2005; Paul and Townsend 1995; Stevens et al. 1998).

The effects of obesity on mortality vary by age. Adults under the age of 50 show the clearest association between obesity and increased mortality (Stevens et al. 1998; Thorpe and Ferraro 2004). In longitudinal analyses, obesity in middle adulthood (ages 30–49) has been shown to lead to an approximately 6-year lesser life expectancy than for normal-weight individuals (Peeters et al. 2003). Among the elderly, the BMI associated with the lowest mortality appears to increase compared to younger age groups (Heiat et al. 2001). The effect of obesity on mortality may be changing over time as well. The introduction of better drugs for treating high cholesterol and hypertension appear to be reducing the disease risks of the obese, at least with respect to cardiovascular disease (Gregg

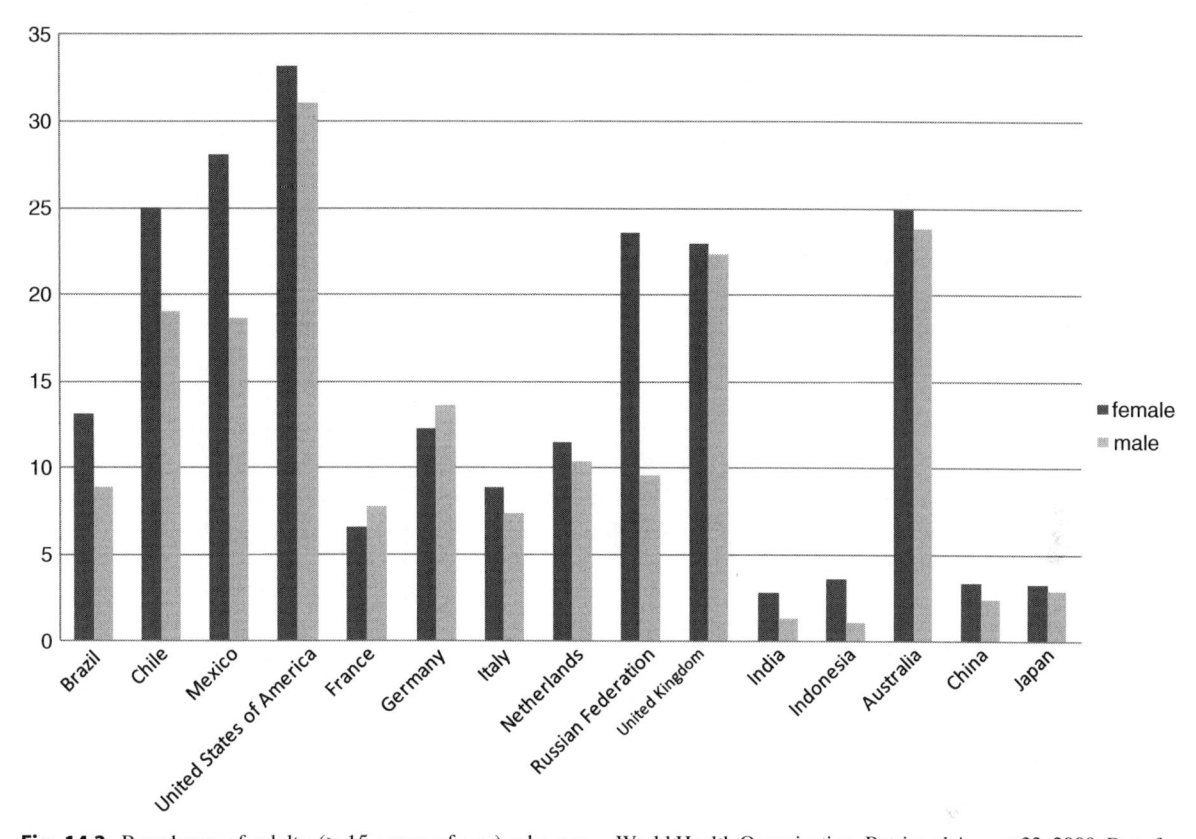

**Fig. 14.2** Prevalence of adults (≥ 15 years of age) who are obese (BMI ≥ 30.0), Source: Data are drawn from the World Health Organization Statistical Information System (WHOSIS). World Health Organization. Retrieved August 22, 2009. Data for France, the Netherlands, the Russian Federation, and Austrialia (https://apps.who.int/infobase)

et al. 2005). Although opinions differ, the long-term impact of these interventions on mortality rates and life expectancy may counteract the increased risks associated with obesity, at least at BMI levels below 35.0 (Olshansky et al. 2005; Preston 2005; Reuser et al. 2008).

## Alcohol Consumption

Unraveling the effects of alcohol on health can be difficult. The excess consumption of alcohol contributes to a range of health problems, chronic conditions, and mortality. However, many studies have documented a health benefit from moderate consumption of particular types of alcohol. This section reviews the evidence that links moderate alcohol consumption to improved health, focuses on the health consequences of excess alcohol consumption, and looks at the population effects of excess alcohol consumption, using Russia as a case study.

Some of the ambiguity in study results stems from the difficulty of measuring alcohol consumption and the variation in measurements used across studies. Under the Dietary Guidelines for Americans, moderate drinking is considered as the consumption of up to one drink per day for women and two drinks per day for men (DHHS and USDA 2005). One drink is defined as 12 oz of regular beer, 5 oz of wine (12% alcohol), or 1.5 oz of 80 proof distilled spirits. Each of these contains approximately 12 g of alcohol. International research uses this measurement of grams of alcohol, with "one drink" being considered as approximately 13 g of alcohol, although in England the standard measure of a drink is 8 g of alcohol and in Japan it is 19.75 g (Kloner and Rezkalla 2007). Most studies rely on self-reports, and respondents have a tendency to underreport consumption (Greenfield and Kerr 2008).

In addition, self-reports often ask for daily or weekly frequency of consumption, which may make irregular heavy drinking (sometimes called "binge drinking," the infrequent consumption of several alcoholic drinks in 1 day) difficult to detect. In some surveys it can be difficult to differentiate between heavy daily drinking and binge drinking.

As I mentioned earlier in discussing the Mediterranean diet, the moderate consumption of alcohol, particularly red wine, has been associated with better health. Two recent meta-analyses show that the relationship between alcohol consumption and mortality is J-shaped, with the lowest mortality occurring at 6 g of alcohol per day, about one-half a drink a day (Di Castelnuovo et al. 2006; Gmel et al. 2003). The "protective" effect was present for men who consumed up to 4 drinks per day, but the effects diminished for women after only 2 drinks. Other studies have found this effect to be stronger for wine consumption versus beer or spirits (Gronbaek et al. 2000), although epidemiological support for the advantage of red wine over other types of alcohol is weak (Mukamal et al. 2003).

The beneficial effects of alcohol appear to operate mainly through decreasing the risk of cardiovascular disease (Comargo et al. 1997; Goldberg et al. 1994; Kloner and Rezkalla 2007). The inverse association between light-to-moderate alcohol consumption and CHD morbidity and mortality is independent of age, sex, smoking habits, and BMI, but the mechanisms for this protective effect are unclear (National Institute on Alcohol Abuse and Alcoholism 2003). About one-half of the decreased risk of cardiovascular disease can be attributed to increased HDL cholesterol levels. Other biological mechanisms include decreased LDL oxidation, decreased platelet aggregation and blood clotting, and decreased inflammation (National Institute on Alcohol Abuse and Alcoholism 2003).

Although there is evidence for some health benefits from light or moderate drinking, the evidence for the detrimental effects of excessive drinking on health and mortality is clearer. Excessive alcohol consumption is considered the third leading lifestyle-related cause of death in the United States (Mokdad et al. 2004). In 2000, there were approximately 85,000 alcohol-attributable deaths in the United States if only current drinkers are considered, 140,000 if past drinkers are also considered.

Less than one-half of the world's population uses alcohol, and alcohol use is higher among men than women (WHO 2004b). There are wide regional variations in alcohol consumption. In Europe, approximately 77% of men and 59% of women are current drinkers. These prevalence rates are slightly higher than those observed in the United States; approximately 61% of adult Americans are current drinkers (NCHS 2006), 68% of men and 55% of women. The part of the world with the highest overall consumption level, in terms of consumption per drinker per day, is eastern Europe and central Asia (WHO 2004b).

Figure 14.3 provides a global perspective on the level of annual alcohol consumption among adults. Country-level alcohol consumption data is presented as liters of alcohol consumed per capita per year (population 15 and older). One liter of alcohol is approximately 800 g, 60 drinks. Annual per capita consumption is highest in Europe, with Germany, France, and the United Kingdom showing the highest levels. In the United States the average per capita consumption is about 8.5 l annually, more than one drink a day. Alcohol consumption levels are very low in India and Indonesia. Brazil and China have moderate levels of per capita consumption. Of course, these numbers mask important age, gender, and drinking style differences not captured by the WHO data.

The age pattern of drinking in the US is typical for developed countries; current drinking rates are highest among adults aged 25–44, and decline steadily after age 45 (NCHS 2006). Unlike other risky health behaviors, alcohol consumption is directly related to education. This gradient is more pronounced among women; 36% of women with less than a high-school degree report themselves as current drinkers, compared to 56% of men with a similar level of education. In comparison, over 70% of men and women with graduate degrees are current drinkers (NCHS 2006).

Excessive alcohol consumption is both a direct and an indirect cause of morbidity and mortality. Certain conditions are completely attributable to alcohol use, including alcoholic cirrhosis of the liver and alcohol poisoning. Other deaths are attributed to alcohol if they occur at a specific blood alcohol concentration, such as motor vehicle accidents, drownings, and suicide. While light-to-moderate drinking may protect against cardiovascular disease, heavy drinking, whether regular or infrequent (binge drinking), is associated with higher risks of CVD. Heavy drinking appears to

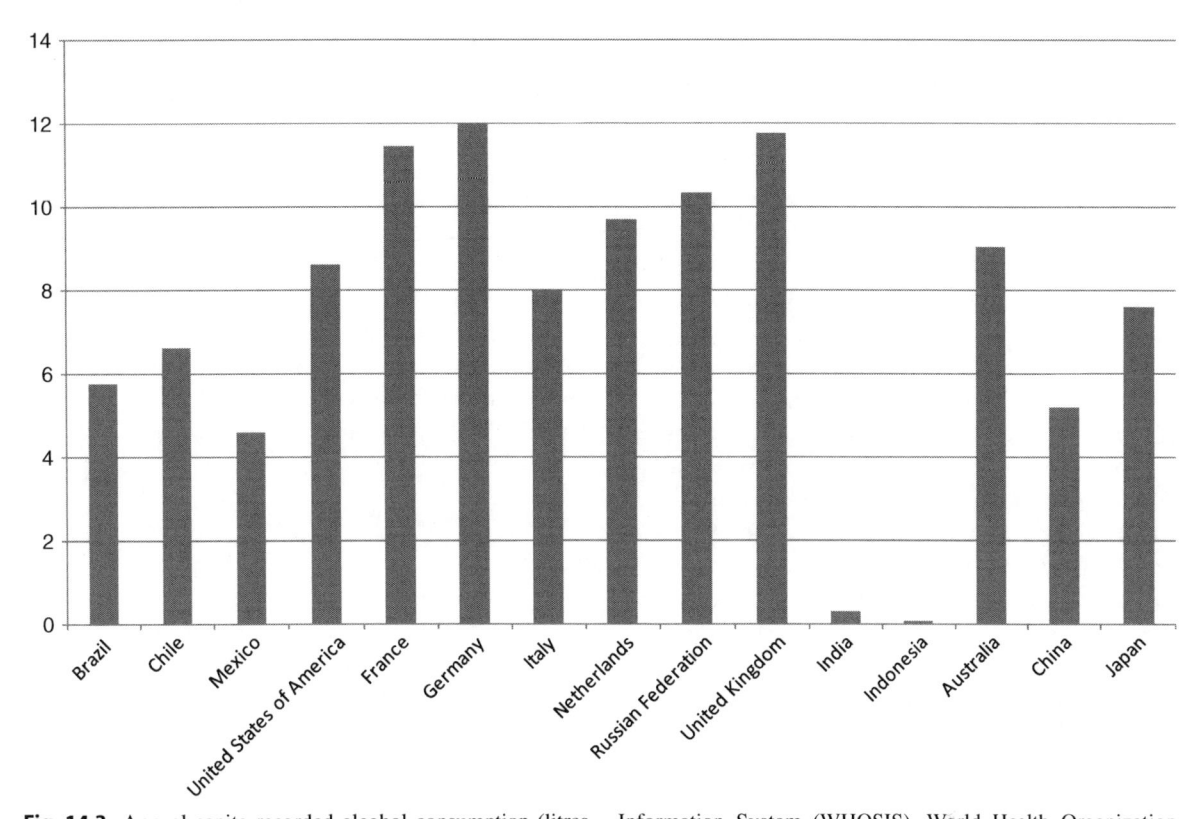

**Fig. 14.3** Annual capita recorded alcohol consumption (litres of pure alcohol) among adults (≥ 15 years). Source: Data are drawn from the World Health Organization Statistical Information System (WHOSIS). World Health Organization. Retrieved August 22, 2009

increase the likelihood of sudden cardiac arrest and stroke due to increased clotting and increased risk of ventricular fibrillation (Rehm et al. 2003). Alcohol consumption is associated with the development of some types of cancers—in particular, cancers of the mouth, esophagus, stomach, colon, liver, and breast (Bagnardi et al. 2001).

The effects of excessive alcohol consumption on population measures of health can be seen most dramatically in eastern Europe. As noted above, the WHO data mask many important differences in alcohol consumption by age, gender, and drinking style. One of the highest rates of alcohol use is currently found in Russia and countries of the former Soviet bloc. In one study of Russian health behaviors, over 43% of men reported binge drinking (Perlman and Bobak 2008). A recent study in the Ukraine found that nearly 39% of men were heavy alcohol users (Webb et al. 2005), and among Czech men, 59% reported consuming more than 40 g of alcohol daily (Rehm et al. 2007). The prevalence of heavy alcohol use among women is much lower; in Russia, 9% of women report binge drinking (Perlman and Bobak 2008), and 8.5% of Ukrainian women (Webb et al. 2005) and 7% of Czech women (Rehm et al. 2007) were considered heavy drinkers.

These patterns of heavy male drinking have been linked to the mortality increase observed in these areas during the 1980s and 1990s. In Russia, between 1989 and 1994 life expectancy at birth decreased by 6.5 years for men and 3.5 years for women (Cockerham 2000). Alcohol may not have been the only factor contributing to this decline, since it was accompanied by stressful socioeconomic conditions and other lifestyle and medical system changes, but one estimate attributes as many as 32% of all deaths in 1984 directly or indirectly to alcohol (Nemtsov 2002). These deaths include direct alcohol poisoning, alcohol psychoses, and alcohol liver cirrhoses. Alcohol use may also contribute heavily to deaths from motor vehicle accidents, injuries, and violence. Most importantly, heavy alcohol use is linked to increased cardiovascular disease.

In response to this mortality increase, Mikhail Gorbachev instituted an anti-alcohol campaign in the period 1984–1987 that significantly reduced alcohol consumption. While this change briefly improved life expectancy for men, the downward trend resumed when the campaign ended in 1988 because of widespread unpopularity (Cockerham 2000). After 1995, there was a short period of mortality improvement, lasting until about 1998, when Russian male life expectancy reached a high of 61.3 years. However, the downward trend reappeared briefly, and male life expectancy in Russia is now estimated to be 59 years. These recent changes again can be attributed to broad economic and societal crises that contribute to increased alcohol consumption (Zaridze et al. 2009) See also "Adult Mortality in the Former Soviet Union", Chapter 4.

Light-to-moderate alcohol use may have health benefits, but heavy drinking is clearly associated with increased mortality risks. The increased use of alcohol in times of economic uncertainty is associated with dramatic short- and long-term increases in mortality. As an acute effect on health, alcohol increases the risks of injury, violence, and accidents. As a chronic problem, heavy alcohol use is associated with an increased risk of mortality from liver cirrhosis, CHD, stroke, and pancreatitis (Corrao et al. 2004; Thun et al. 1997).

## Conclusions

Health in adulthood is the result of genetic predispositions, childhood experiences, and the environment. Medical care may reduce these risks; however, lifestyle factors play a tremendous role in the development of most chronic diseases. In developed countries, tobacco, high blood pressure, alcohol, high cholesterol, and high BMI are the leading causes of loss of healthy life and death (Ezzati et al. 2002; Mokdad et al. 2004). Understanding the relationship between health behaviors and the development of disease is crucial for projecting future health and care needs of the population.

The mechanisms underlying the relationships between health behaviors and health that operate at the individual level are generally well-understood. Epidemiologic evidence bears out many of these relationships at the population level. While these relationships are well-known, changing individual behavior in response to this information has been difficult. Smoking rates have dropped in developed countries, but continue to rise in less-developed regions of the world. Alcohol consumption, particularly among men, is dangerously high in some regions. Despite the widespread attention to the obesity "epidemic" in the United States, there is little evidence for improvements in diet or levels of physical activity. While medical treatments are likely to continue to advance, improvements in the health risk profile of the population, particularly with respect to diet and exercise, are likely to yield the greatest future health gains.

## Future Research Directions

Three avenues of future research are suggested by this summary. First, behavioral changes are likely to play an important role in determining the future health of the population. But such changes can be difficult to realize on an individual or population level. Research is needed on how to facilitate positive behavioral changes on a broad level. Such research could take the form of the study of individual-level interventions or state or national policy changes. For example, how effective is tax policy for regulating behavior? There are examples of effective public-health campaigns, for instance, the use of seat belts.

Second, while this chapter examined these factors in isolation, they are often found in combination—tobacco use and alcohol consumption may appear together, for instance, and either may be associated with poor nutrition. Future research needs to continue to look at risk profiles, combinations of health behaviors, and the trade-offs associated with different risk factors. One study that examined the combination of risk factors in the United States concludes that while the health behavior profile of the population improved between the early 1970s and the early 2000s, the increasing rates of obesity may start to counter the reductions seen in other risky behaviors (Cutler et al. 2009; see also Olshansky et al. 2005). Sturm (2002) concludes that obesity has a greater effect on medical problems and costs than either smoking or problem drinking.

Finally, much of the recent improvement in healthy life in the United States and other developed countries has been attributed to declines in smoking and the improved medical treatment of hypertension and high cholesterol (Cutler et al. 2009). The precise role of pharmaceuticals, early detection, and surgical intervention in health improvements is not fully understood. A better understanding of the role of medical care in the treatment and prevention of disease must complement our understanding of the behavioral factors critical for future health and mortality levels.

## References

Adebamowo, C.A., F.B. Hu, E. Cho, D. Spiegelman, M.D. Holmes, and W.C. Willett. 2005. "Dietary Patterns and the Risk of Breast Cancer." *Annals of Epidemiology* 15:789–95.

Adler, N.E. and D.H. Rehkopf. 2008. "U.S. Disparities in Health: Descriptions, Causes, and Mechanisms." *Annual Review of Public Health* 29:235–52.

Albanes, D., A. Blair, P.R. Taylor. 1989. "Physical Activity and Risk of Cancer in the NHANES I Population." *American Journal of Public Health* 79:744–50.

Allen, S.M., V. Mor, V. Raveis, and P. Houts. 1993. "Measurement of Need for Assistance with Daily Activities: Quantifying the Influence of Gender Roles." *Journal of Gerontology* 48:S204–S11.

American Cancer Society. 2006. *Cancer Facts and Figures, 2006*. Atlanta, American Cancer Society.

American Dietetic Association. 2009. *Lycopene: An Antioxidant for Good Health*. Available online at http://www.eatright.org/cps/rde/xchg/ada/hs.xsl/nutrition_5328_ENU_HTML.htm

Au, D.H., E.M. Udris, S.D. Fihn, M.B. McDowell, and J.R. Curtis. 2006. "Differences in Health Care Utilization at the End of Life Among Patients With Chronic Obstructive Pulmonary Disease and Patients With Lung Cancer." *Archives of Internal Medicine* 166:326–31.

Austin, M.A., B.L. Rodriguez, B. McKnight, M.J. McNeely, K.L. Edwards, J.D. Curb, and D.S. Sharp. 2000. "Low-density Lipoprotein Particle Size, Triglycerides, and High-density Lipoprotein Cholesterol as Risk Factors for Coronary Heart Disease in Older Japanese-American Men." *American Journal of Cardiology* 86:412–16.

Babor, T.F., K. Steinberg, R. Anton, and F. Del Bocca. 2000. "Talk Is Cheap: Measuring Drinking Outcomes in Clinical Trials." *Journal of Studies on Alcohol* 61(1):55–63.

Baghurst, P.A. and T.E. Rohan. 1994. "High-Fiber Diets and Reduced Risk of Breast Cancer." *International Journal of Cancer* 56:173–76.

Bagnardi, V., M. Blangiardo, C. La Vecchia, and G. Corrao. 2001. "A Meta-Analysis of Alcohol Drinking and Cancer Risk." *British Journal of Cancer* 85:1700–5.

Barendregt, J.J., L. Bonneux, P.J. van der Maas. 1997. "The Health Care Costs of Smoking." *New England Journal of Medicine* 337:1052–57.

Barnard, R.J., T. Jung, S.B. Inkeles. 1994. "Diet and Exercise in the Treatment of NIDDM-The Need for Early Emphasis." *Diabetes Care* 17:1469–72.

Bazzano, L.A., J. He, L.G. Ogden, C.M. Loria, S. Vupputuri, L. Myers, P.K. Whelton. 2002. "Fruit and Vegetable Intake and Risk of Cardiovascular Disease in US Adults: The First National Health and Nutrition Examination Survey Epidemiologic Follow-up Study." *American Journal of Clinical Nutrition* 76:93–99.

Bjelakovic, G., D. Nikolova, L.L. Gluud, et al. 2007. "Antioxidants May Increase Mortality." *Journal of the American Medical Association* 297:842–57.

Booyens, J., C.C. Louwrens, and I.E. Katzeff. 1988. "The Role of Unnatural Dietary Trans and Cis Unsaturated Fatty Acids in the Epidemiology of Coronary Heart Disease." *Medical Hypotheses* 25:175–82.

Brener, N.D., J.O. Billy, and W.R. Grady. 2003. "Assessment of Factors Affecting the Validity of Self-reported Health-risk Behavior Among Adolescents: Evidence from the Scientific Literature." *Journal of Adolescent Health* 33:436–57.

Calle, E.E., M.J. Thun, J.M. Petrelli, C. Rodriguez, and C.W. Heath. 1999. "Body Mass Index and Mortality in a Prospective Cohort of U.S. Adults." *New England Journal of Medicine* 341:1097–105.

Camargo, C.A., M.J. Stampfer, R.J. Glynn, F. Grodstein, J.M. Gaziano, J.E. Manson, J.E. Buring, and C.H. Hennekens. 1997. "Moderate Alcohol Consumption and Risk for Angina Pectoris or Myocardial Infarction in U.S. Male Physicians." *Annals of Internal Medicine* 126:372–75.

Castelli, W.P. 1996. "Redefining CHD Risk Assessment. The Role of New Cardiovascular Risk Factors." *Cardiovascular Risk Factors* 6:181–85.

Centers for Disease Control. 1964. *Smoking and Health: Report of the Advisory Committee to the Surgeon General of the Public Health Service*. Atlanta, US Department of Health and Human Services.

Centers for Disease Control. 1984. *The Health Consequences of Smoking: Chronic Obstructive Lung Disease*. A Report of the Surgeon General. Atlanta, US Department of Health and Human Services. Available online at http://profiles.nlm.nih.gov/NN/B/C/C/S/_/nnbccs.pdf

Centers for Disease Control. 1990. *The Health Benefits of Smoking Cessation*. A Report of the Surgeon General. Atlanta, US Department of Health and Human Services. Available online at http://profiles.nlm.nih.gov/NN/B/B/C/T/_/nnbbct.pdf

Centers for Disease Control. 1999. "Ten Great Public Health Achievements in the 20th Century." *Morbidity and Mortality Weekly Report* 48:1–3.

Centers for Disease Control. 2002. "Annual Smoking-Attributable Mortality, Years of Potential Life Lost, and Economic Costs—United States, 1995–1999." *MMWR Weekly* 51:300–3.

Centers for Disease Control. 2004. *The Health Consequences of Smoking: A Report of the Surgeon General*. Atlanta, US Department of Health and Human Services. Available online at http://www.Centers for Disease Control.gov/tobacco/data_statistics/sgr/sgr_2004/index.htm

Centers for Disease Control. 2006a. *The Health Consequences of Involuntary Exposure to Tobacco Smoke: A Report of the Surgeon General*. Atlanta, US Department of Health and Human Services. Available online at http://www.surgeongeneral.gov/library/secondhandsmoke/report/

Centers for Disease Control. 2006b. *2006 National Youth Tobacco Survey and Key Prevalence Indicators*. Atlanta, US Department of Health and Human Services. Available online at http://www.cdc.gov/tobacco/data_statistics/surveys/nyts/pdfs/indicators.pdf

Centers for Disease Control. 2007. "Fruit and Vegetable Consumption Among Adults—United States, 2005." *Morbidity and Mortality Weekly Report* 56:213–17.

Centers for Disease Control. 2008. "Cigarette Smoking Among Adults—United States, 2007." *Morbidity and Mortality Weekly Report* 57:1221–26.

Centers for Disease Control. 2009. http://www.cdc.gov/tobacco/data_statistics/fact_sheets/health_effects/cig_smoking_mort.htm

Cerhan, J.R., J.D. Potter, J.M.E. Gilmore, C.A. Janney, L.H. Kushi, D. Lazovich, K.E. Anderson, T.A. Sellers, K.E. Folsum. 2004. "Adherence to the AICR Cancer Prevention Recommendations and Subsequent Morbidity and Mortality in the Iowa Women's Health Study Cohort." *Cancer Epidemiology, Biomarkers and Prevention* 13:1114–20.

China Daily. 2009. *To Raise Revenue China Turns to Tobacco Tax*. June 20, http://www.chinadaily.com.cn/china/2009-06/20/content_8305592.htm

Cockerham, W.C. 2000. "Health Lifestyles in Russia." *Social Science and Medicine* 51:1313–24.

Corrao, G., V. Bagnardi, A. Zambon, and C. LaVecchia. 2004. "A Meta-Analysis of Alcohol Consumption and the Risk of 15 Diseases." *Preventive Medicine* 38:613–19.

Cutler, D.M, E. Glaeser, and A.B. Rosen. 2009. "Is the United States Population Behaving Healthier?" In J.R. Brown, J. Liebman, and D. Wise (eds.), *Social Security Policy in a Changing Environment*. USA, National Bureau of Economic Research.

Cutler, D.M. and A. Lleras-Muney. 2006. *Education and Health: Evaluating Theories and Evidence*. NBER Working Paper 12352. Cambridge, MA, NBER.

Degenhardt, L., W.T. Chiu, N. Sampson, R.C. Kessler, J.C. Anthony, M. Angermeyer, R. Bruffaerts, G. de Girolamo, O. Gureje, Y.Q. Huang, A. Karam, S. Kostyuchenko, J.P. Lepine, M.E.M. Mora, Y. Neumark, J.H. Ormel, A. Pinto-Meza, J. Posada-Villa, D.J. Stein, T. Takeshima, and J.E. Wells. 2008. "Toward a Global View of Alcohol, Tobacco, Cannabis, and Cocaine Use: Findings from the WHO World Mental Health Surveys." *PLoS Medicine* 5:1053–67.

Di Castelnuovo, A., S. Costanzo, V. Bagnardi, M.B. Donati, L. Iacoviello, and G. de Gaetano. 2006. "Alcohol Dosing and Total Mortality in Men and Women." *Archives of Internal Medicine* 166:2437–45.

Eisner, M.D., P.D. Blanc, E.H. Yelin, S. Sidney, P.P. Katz, L. Ackerson, P. Lathon, I. Tolstykh, T. Omachi, N. Byl, and C. Irribarren. 2008. "COPD as a Systemic Disease: Impact on Physical Functional Limitations." *American Journal of Medicine* 121:789–96.

European Food Safety Authority. 2008. "Food Based Dietary Guidelines, Draft." *EFSA Journal*. Available online at http://www.efsa.europa.eu/cs/BlobServer/DocumentSet/nda_op_fbdg_draft_en_released_for_consultation.pdf?ssbinary=true

European Opinion Research Group. 2003. *Physical Activity*. Brussels, European Commission. Available online at http://ec.europa.eu/health/ph_determinants/life_style/nutrition/documents/ebs_183_6_en.pdf

Ezzati, M., A.D. Lopez, A. Rodgers, S. Vander Hoorn, and C.J.L. Murray. 2002. "Selected Major Risk Factors and Global and Regional Burden of Disease." *The Lancet* 360:1347–60.

Ferraro, K.F., R.J. Thorpe, Jr., and J.A. Wilkinson 2003. "The Life Course of Obesity: Does Childhood Overweight Matter?" *Journal of Gerontology: Social Sciences* 58b: S110–S19.

Finkel, T. and N.J. Holbrook. 2000. "Oxidants, Oxidative Stress and the Biology of Aging." *Nature* 408:239–47.

Flegal, K.M., M.D. Carroll, R.J. Kuczmarski, and C.L. Johnson. 1998. "Overweight and Obesity in the United States: Prevalence and Trends, 1960–1994." *International Journal of Obesity and Related Metabolic Disorders* 22:39–47.

Flegal, K.M., M.D. Carroll, C.L. Ogden, and C.L. Johnson. 2002. "Prevalence and Trends in Obesity Among US Adults, 1999–2000." *JAMA* 288:1723–27.

Flegal, K.M., B.I. Graubard, D.F. Williamson, and M.H. Gail. 2005. "Excess Deaths Associated With Underweight, Overweight, and Obesity." *JAMA* 293:1861–67.

Fontaine, K.R., D.T. Redden, C. Wang, A.O. Westfall, and D.B. Allison. 2003. "Years of Life Lost to Obesity." *JAMA* 289:187–93.

Ford, E.S., D.G. Moriarty, M.M. Zack, A.H. Mokdad, and D.P. Chapman. 2001. "Self-Reported Body Mass Index and Health Related Quality of Life: Findings from the Behavioral Risk Factor Surveillance System." *Obesity Research* 9: 21–31.

Fung, T.T., W.C. Willett, M.J. Stampfer, J.E. Manson, F.B. Hu. 2001. "Dietary Patterns and the Risk of Coronary Heart Disease in Women." *Archives of Internal Medicine* 161:1857–62.

Gielen, S., G. Schuler, and R. Hambrecht. 2001. "Exercise Training in Coronary Artery Disease and Coronary Vasomotion." *Circulation* 103:E.

Gmel, G., E. Gutjahr, and J. Rehm. 2003. "How Stable Is the Risk Curve Between Alcohol and All-cause Mortality and What Factors Influence the Shape? A Precision-Weighted Hierarchical Meta-analysis." *European Journal of Epidemiology* 18:631–42.

Goldberg, R.J., C.M. Burchfiel, D.M. Reed, G. Wergowske, and D. Chiu. 1994. "A Prospective Study of the Health Effects of Alcohol Consumption in Middle-aged and Elderly Men: The Honolulu Heart Program." *Circulation* 89: 651–59.

Goldblatt, P.B., M.E. Moore, and A.J. Stunkard. 1965. "Social Factors in Obesity." *JAMA* 152:1039–42.

Goldman, D.P. and J.P. Smith. 2002. "Can Patient Self-management Explain the SES Health Gradient?" *Proceedings of the National Academy of Science* 99: 10929–34.

Gong, Y.L., J.P. Koplan, W. Feng, C.H. Cheng, P. Zheng, and J.R. Harris. 1995. "Cigarette Smoking in China: Prevalence, Characteristics, and Attitudes in Minhang District." *Journal of the American Medical Association* 74:1232–34.

Gortmaker, S.L., A. Must, J.M. Perrin, A.M. Sobol, and W.H. Dietz. 1993. "Social and Economic Consequences of Overweight in Adolescence and Young Adulthood." *New England Journal of Medicine* 329:1008–12.

Greenfield, T.K. and W.C. Kerr. 2008. "Alcohol Measurement Methodology in Epidemiology: Recent Advances and Opportunities." *Addiction* 103:1082–99.

Gregg, E.W., Y.L.J. Cheng, B.L. Cadwell, G. Imperatore, D.E. Williams, K.M. Flegal, K.M.V. Narayan, and D.F. Williamson. 2005. "Secular Trends in Cardiovascular

Disease Risk Factors According to Body Mass Index in U.S. Adults." *JAMA* 293:1868–74.

Gronbaek, M., U. Becker, D. Johansen, A.Gottschau, P. Schnorr, H.O. Hein, G. Jensen, and T.I.A. Sorensen. 2000. "Type of Alcohol Consumed and Mortality from All Causes, Coronary Heart Disease, and Cancer." *Annals of Internal Medicine* 133:411–19.

Hahn, R.A., S.M. Teuesch, R.B. Rothenberg, and J.S. Marks. 1998. "Excess Deaths from Nine Chronic Diseases in the United States, 1986." *JAMA* 264:2554–59.

Halliwell, B. 1996. "Free Radicals, Proteins and DNA: Oxidative Damage Versus Redox Regulation." *Biochemical Society Transactions* 24:1023–27.

Hedley, A.A., C.L. Ogden, C.L. Johnson, M.D. Carroll, L.R. Curtin, and K.M. Flegal. 2004. "Prevalence of Overweight and Obesity Among US Children, Adolescents, and Adults, 1999–2002." *JAMA* 291:2847–50.

Heiat, A., V. Vaccarino, and H.M. Krumholz. 2001. "An Evidence Based Assessment of Federal Guidelines for Overweight and Obesity as They Apply to Elderly Persons." *Archives of Internal Medicine* 161:1194–203.

Hennekens, C.H. 1998. "Increasing Burden of Cardiovascular Disease—Current Knowledge and Future Directions for Research on Risk Factors." *Circulation* 97:1995.

Hu, Y. and N. Goldman. 1990. "Mortality Differentials by Marital Status: An International Comparison." *Demography* 27:233–50.

Institute of Medicine. 2001. *Clearing the Smoke: Assessing the Science Base for Tobacco Harm Reduction*. Washington, DC, National Academy Press

Johnson, C.A., P.H. Palmer, C.P. Chou, Z.C. Pang, D.J. Zhou, L.J. Dong, H.Q. Xiang, P.J. Pang, H.J. Xu, J. Wang, X.L. Fu, Q. Guo, P. Sun, H.Y. Ma, P.E. Gallaher, B. Xie, L.M. Lee, T.R. Fang, and J.B. Under. 2006. "Tobacco Use Among Youth and Adults in Mainland China: The China Seven Cities Study." *Public Health* 120:1156–69.

Joshipura, K.J., A. Ascherio, J.E. Manson, M.J. Stampfer, E.B. Rimm, F.E. Speizer, C.H. Hennekens, D. Spiegelman, and W.C. Willett. 1999. "Fruit and Vegetable Intake in Relation to Risk of Ischemic Stroke." *Journal of the American Medical Association* 282:1233–39.

Joshipura, K.J., F.B. Hu, J.E. Manson, M.J. Stampfer, E.B. Rimm, F.E. Speizer, G. Colditz, A. Ascherio, B. Rosner, D. Spiegelman, and W.C. Willett. 2001. "The Effect of Fruit and Vegetable Intake on Risk for Coronary Heart Disease." *Annals of Internal Medicine* 134:1106–14.

Jousilahti, P., E. Vartianinen, J. Pekkanen, J. Tuomilehto, J. Sundvall, and P. Puska. 1998. "Serum Cholesterol Distribution and Coronary Heart Disease Risk—Observations and Predictions Among Middle-aged Population in Eastern Finland." *Circulation* 97:1087–94.

Kaaks, R. and E. Riboli. 1995. "Colorectal Cancer and Intake of Dietary Fibre: A Summary of the Epidemiological Evidence." *European Journal of Clinical Nutrition* 49: S10–S17.

Keys, A. 1966. "Epidemiological Studies Related to Coronary Heart Disease: Characteristics of Men Aged 40–59 in Seven Countries." *Acta Medica Scandinavica Supplement* 460:1–392.

Keys, A., C. Aravanis, H. Blackburn, R. Buzina, et al. 1980. *Seven Countries. A Multivariate Analysis of Death and Coronary Heart Disease*. Cambridge, MA, Harvard University Press.

Kloner, R.A. and S.H. Rezkalla. 2007. "To Drink or Not to Drink? That Is the Question." *Circulation* 116:1306–17.

Koplan, J.P., C.T. Liverman, V.L. Kraak (eds.). 2005. *Preventing Childhood Obesity: Health in the Balance*. Washington, DC, National Academy Press.

Kris-Etherton, P.M., R.H. Eckel, B.V. Howard, S. St. Jeor, and T.L. Bazzarre 2001. "Lyon Diet Heart Study: Benefits of a Mediterranean-Style, National Cholesterol Education Program/American Heart Association Step 1 Dietary Pattern on Cardiovascular Disease." *Circulation* 103:1823–25.

Kris-Etherton, P.M., W.S. Harris, and L.J. Appel. 2002. "Fish Consumption, Fish Oil, Omega-3 Fatty Acids, and Cardiovascular Disease." *Circulation* 106:2747–57.

Kris-Etherton, P.M., A.H. Lichtenstein, B.V. Howard, D. Steinberg, and J.L. Witztum. 2004. "Antioxidant Vitamin Supplements and Cardiovascular Disease." *Circulation* 110:637–41.

Kuczmarski, M.F, R.J. Kuczmarski, and M. Najjer. 2001. "Effects of Age on Validity of Self-Reported Height, Weight, and Body Mass Index: Findings from the Third National Health and Nutrition Examination Survey, 1988–1994." *Journal of the American Dietetic Association* 101:28–34.

Lahelma, E., P. Martikainen, M. Laaksonen, and A. Aittomaki. 2004. "Pathways Between Socioeconomic Determinants of Health." *Journal of Epidemiology and Community Health* 58:327–32.

Lemieux, S., D. Prudhomme, C. Bouchard, A. Tremblay, and J.P. Despres. 1993. "Sex Differences in the Relation of Visceral Adipose Tissue Accumulation to Total Body Fatness." *American Journal of Clinical Nutrition* 58: 463–67.

Liu, H. and D.J. Umberson. 2008. "The Times They Are a Changin': Marital Status and Health Differentials from 1972 to 2003." *Journal of Health and Social Behavior* 49:239–53.

Ma, G.X., Y. Lan, M.I. Toubbeh, and C. Zhai. 2004. "Tobacco Use in China: Prevalence, Consequences, and Control." *Californian Journal of Health Promotion* 2:107–19.

Mannino, D.M., E.S. Ford, and S.C. Redd. 2003. "Obstructive and Restrictive Lung Disease and Functional Limitation: Data from the Third National Health and Nutrition Examination." *Journal of Internal Medicine* 254:540–47.

Manson, J.E., F.B. Hu, J.W. Rich-Edwards, G.A. Colditz, M.J. Stampfer, W.C. Willett, F.E. Speizer, C.H. Hennekens. 1999. "A Prospective Study of Walking as Compared with Vigorous Exercise in the Prevention of Coronary Heart Disease in Women." *New England Journal of Medicine* 341:650–58.

Mazzeo R.S., P. Cavanaugh, W.J. Evans, M. Fiatarone, J. Hagberg, E. McAuley, J. Startzell. 1998. "Exercise and Physical Activity for Older Adults." *Medicine and Science in Sports and Exercise* 30:992–1008.

Mensink, R.P. and M.B. Katan. 1992. "Effect of Dietary Fatty-Acids on Serum-lipids and Lipoproteins—A Metaanalysis of 27 Trials." *Arteriosclerosis and Thrombosis* 12:911–19.

Mirowsky, J. and C.E. Ross. 2003. *Education, Social Status and Health*. New York: Aldine De Gruyter.

Mokdad, A.H., J.S. Marks, D.F. Stroup, and J.L. Gerberding. 2004. "Actual Causes of Death in the United States, 2000." *JAMA* 291:1238–45.

Mukamal, K.J., K.M. Conigrave, M.A. Mittleman, C.A.J. Camargo, M.J. Stampfer, W.C. Willett, and E.B. Rimm. 2003. "Roles of Drinking Pattern and Type of Alcohol Consumed in Coronary Heart Disease in Men." *New England Journal of Medicine* 348:109–18.

Murray, C.L., S.C. Kulkarni, C. Michaud, N. Tomijima, M.T. Bulzacchelli, T.J. Iandiorio, M. Ezzat. 2006. "Eight Americas: Investigating Mortality Disparities across Races, Counties, and Race-Counties in the United States." *PLoS Medicine* 3:e260. doi:10.1371/journal.pmed. 0030260.

Must, A. and R.S. Strauss. 1999. "Risks and Consequences of Childhood and Adolescent Obesity." *International Journal of Obesity* 23:s2–s11.

Nam, C.B, R.A. Hummer, and R.G. Rogers. 1994. "Underlying and Multiple Causes of Death Related to Smoking." *Population Research and Policy Review* 13:305–25.

National Center for Health Statistics. 2006. *Health Behaviors of Adults: United States, 2002–04*. Vital and Health Statistics, Series 10, Number 230. Washington, DC, U.S. Government Printing Office.

National Center for Health Statistics. 2009. *About the International Classification of Diseases, Tenth Revision, Clinical Modification*. Available online at http://www.cdc.gov/nchs/about/otheract/icd9/abticd10.htm

National Heart, Lung and Blood Institute. 2009. http://www.nhlbi.nih.gov/health/dci/Diseases/Copd/Copd_WhatIs.html

National Institute on Alcohol Abuse and Alcoholism. 2003. *State of the Science Report on the Effects of Moderate Drinking*. http://pubs.niaaa.nih.gov/publications/ModerateDrinking-03.htm

National Institutes of Health. 1998. *Clinical Guidelines on the Identification, Evaluation and Treatment of Overweight and Obesity in Adults*. Bethesda, MD: National Institutes of Health

Neaton, J.D. and D. Wentworth. 1992. "Serum-cholesterol, Blood Pressure, Cigarette Smoking, and Death from Coronary Heart Disease—Overall Findings and Differences by Age for 316,099 White Men." *Archives of Internal Medicine* 152:56–64.

Nelson, M.E., M.A. Fiatarone, C.M. Morganti, I. Trice, R.A. Greenberg, W.J. Evans. 1994. "Effects of High-Intensity Strength Training on Multiple Risk Factors for Osteoporotic Fractures-A Randomized Controlled Trial." *JAMA* 272:1909–14.

Nemtsov, A.V. 2002. "Alcohol-related Human Losses in Russia in the 1980s and 1990s." *Addiction* 97:1413–25.

Ogden, C.L., M.D. Carroll, L.R. Curtin, M.A. McDowell, C.J. Tabak, and K.M. Flegal. 2006. "Prevalence of Overweight and Obesity in the United States, 1999–2004." *JAMA* 295:1549–55.

Olshansky, S.J., D.J. Passaro, R.C. Hershow, J. Layden, B.A. Carnes, J. Brody, L. Hayflick, R.N. Butler, D.B. Allison, and D.S. Ludwig. 2005. "A Potential Decline in Life Expectancy in the United States in the 21st Century." *New England Journal of Medicine* 352:1138–45.

Osganian, S.K., M.J. Stampfer, E. Rimm, D. Spiegelman, J.E. Manson, and W.C. Willett. 2003. "Dietary Carotenoids and Risk of Coronary Artery Disease in Women." *American Journal of Clinical Nutrition* 77:1390–99.

Paffenberger, R.S., R.T. Hyde, A.L. Wing, I.M. Lee, D.L. Jung, J.B. Kampert. 1993. "The Association of Changes in Physical Activity Level and Other Lifestyle Characteristics with Mortality among Men." *New England Journal of Medicine* 328:538–45.

Pampel, F.C. 2002. "Cigarette Use and the Narrowing Sex Differential in Mortality." *Population and Development Review* 28:77–104.

Park, Y., D.J. Hunter, D. Spiegelman, L. Bergkvist, F. Berrino, P.A. van den Brandt, J.E. Buring, G.A. Colditz, J.L. Freudenheim, C.S. Fuchs, E. Giovannucci, R.A. Goldbohm, S. Graham, L. Harnack, A.M. Hartman, D.R. Jacobs, I. Kato, V. Krogh, M.F. Leitzmann, M.L. McCullough, A.B. Miller, P. Pietinen, T.E. Rohan, A. Schatzkin, W.C. Willett, A. Wolk, A. Zeleniuch-Jacquotte, S.M.M. Zhang, and S.A. Smith-Warner. 2005. "Dietary Fiber Intake and Risk of Colorectal Cancer: A Pooled Analysis of Prospective Cohort Studies." *JAMA* 294:2849–57.

Patrick, D.L., A. Cheadle, D.C. Thompson, P. Diehr, T. Koepsell, and S. Kinne. 1994. "The Validity of Self-reported Smoking: A Review and Meta-analysis." *American Journal of Public Health* 84(7):1086–93.

Paul, R.J. and J.B. Townsend. 1995. "Shape Up or Ship Out? Employment Discrimination Against the Overweight." *Employee Responsibilities and Rights Journal* 8(2):133–45.

Peeters, A., J.J. Barendregt, F. Willekens, J.P. Mackenback, A.A. Mamun, and L. Bonneux. 2003. "Obesity in Adulthood and Its Consequences for Life Expectancy: A Life-table Analysis." *Annals of Internal Medicine* 138:24–32.

Perlman, F. and M. Bobak. 2008. "Socioeconomic and Behavioral Determinants of Mortality in Posttransition Russia: A Prospective Population Study." *Annals of Epidemiology* 18:92–100.

Peto, R., S. Darby, H. Deo, P. Silcocks, E. Whitley, and R. Doll. 2000. "Smoking, Smoking Cessation, and Lung Cancer in the UK Since 1950: Combination of National Statistics With Two Case-control Studies." *British Medical Journal* 321:323–29.

Pischon T., H. Boeing, K. Hoffmann, et al. 2008. "General and Abdominal Adiposity and Risk of Death in Europe." *New England Journal of Medicine* 359(2105):20.

Posner, B.M., N.M. Franz, P.A. Quatromoni, et al. 1995. "Secular Trends in Diet and Risk-Factors for Cardiovascular Disease—The Framingham Study." *Journal of the American Dietetic Association* 95:171–79.

Preston, S.H. 1970. *Older Male Mortality and Cigarette Smoking: A Demographic Analysis*. Berkeley, Population Monograph #7. Institute of International Studies, University of California.

Preston, S.H. 1976. *Mortality Patterns in National Populations*. New York, NY: Academic Press.

Preston, S.H. 2005. "Obesity and Longevity—Reply." *New England Journal of Medicine* 352:2556–57.

Preston, S.H. and H.D. Wang. 2006. "Sex Mortality Differences in the United States: The Role of Cohort Smoking Patterns." *Demography* 43:631–46.

Ramirez, M., M.E. Ford, A.L. Stewart, and J.A. Teresi. 2005. "Measurement Issues in Health Disparities Research." *Health Services Research* 40:1640–56.

Rasmussen, S.R., E. Prescott, T.I.A. Sorensen, J. Sogaard. 2005. "The Total Lifetime Health Cost Savings of Smoking Cessation to Society." *European Journal of Public Health* 15:601–06.

Rehm, J., C.T. Sempos, and M. Trevisan. 2003. "Average Volume of Alcohol Consumption, Patterns of Drinking and Risk of Coronary Heart Disease—A Review." *Journal of Cardiovascular Risk* 10:15–20.

Rehm, J., U. Sulkowska, M. Manczuk, P. Boffetta, J. Powles, S. Popova, and W. Zatonski. 2007. "Alcohol Accounts for a High Proportion of Premature Mortality in Central and Eastern Europe." *International Journal of Epidemiology* 36:458–67.

Reijneveld, S.A., J. Spijker, and H. Kijkshoorn. 2007. "Katz' ADL Index Assessed Functional Performance of Turkish, Moroccan, and Dutch Elderly." *Journal of Clinical Epidemiology* 60:382–88.

Reuser, M., L. Bonneux, and F. Willekens. 2008. "The Burden of Mortality of Obesity at Middle and Old Age is Small. A Life Table Analysis of the US Health and Retirement Survey." *European Journal of Epidemiology* 23: 601–07.

Rogers, R.G., R.A. Hummer, and P.M. Krueger. 2003. "The Effects of Obesity and Overall, Circulatory-Disease and Diabetes Specific Mortality." *Journal of Biosocial Science* 35:107–29.

Rose, G. 2008. *Rose's Strategy of Preventive Medicine*. New York: Oxford University Press.

Sherman, S.E., R.B. D'Agostino, J.L. Cobb, and W.B. Kannel. 1994. "Physical Activity and Mortality in Women in the Framingham Heart Study." *American Heart Journal* 128:879–84.

Sofi, F., F. Cesari, A. Rosanna, G.F. Gensini, and A. Casini. 2008. "Adherence to Mediterranean Diet and Health Status: Meta-Analysis." *British Medical Journal* 337:a1344.

Stafford, M. and M. Marmot. 2003. "Neighborhood Deprivation and Health: Does it Affect Us All Equally?" *International Journal of Epidemiology* 32:357–66.

Stamler, J., D. Wentworth, and J.D. Neaton. 1986. "Is Relationship Between Serum Cholesterol and Risk of Premature Death From Coronary Heart Disease Continuous and Graded? Findings in 356,222 Primary Screenees of the Multiple Risk Factor Intervention Trial (MRFIT)." *JAMA* 256:2823–28.

Steinmetz, K.A. and J.D. Potter. 1996. "Vegetables, Fruit, and Cancer Prevention: A Review." *Journal of the American Dietetic Association* 96:1027–39.

Stevens, J., J.W. Cai, E.R. Pamuk, D.F. Williamson, M.J. Thun, and J.L. Wood. 1998. "The Effect of Age on the Association Between Body-mass Index and Mortality." *New England Journal of Medicine* 338:1–7.

Stevens, J.S., K. Kumanyika, and J.E. Keil. 1994. "Attitudes Towards Body Size and Dieting: Differences Between Elderly Black and White Women." *American Journal of Public Health* 84:1322–25.

Stone, N.J. 1996. "Fish Consumption, Fish Oil, Lipids, and Coronary Heart Disease." *Circulation* 94:2337–40.

Stunkard, A.J. and T.I.A. Sorenson. 1993. "Obesity and Socioeconomic Status—A Complex Relationship." *New England Journal of Medicine* 329:1036–37.

Sturm, R. 2002. "The Effects of Obesity, Smoking and Drinking on Medical Problems and Costs." *Health Affairs* 21: 245–53.

Sullivan, S.D., S.D. Ramsey, and T.A. Lee. 2000. "The Economic Burden of COPD." *Chest* 117(2):5S–9S.

Sung, H.Y., L. Wang, S. Jin, T.W. Hu, and Y. Jiang. 2006. "Economic Burden of Smoking in China, 2000." *Tobacco Control* 15:I5–I11.

Thomas, D.R., E.J. Elliott, and G.A. Naughton. 2006. "Exercise for Type 2 Diabetes Mellitus." *Cochrane Database of Systematic Reviews* 3:CD002968.

Thompson, P.D., D. Buchner, I.L. Pina, G.J. Balady, M.A. Williams, B.H. Marcus, K. Berra, S.N. Blair, F. Costa, B. Franklin, G.F. Fletcher, N.F. Gordon, R.R. Pate, B.L. Rodriguez, A.K. Yancey, N.K. Wenger. 2003. "Exercise and Physical Activity in the Prevention and Treatment of Atherosclerotic Cardiovascular Disease: A Statement from the Council on Clinical Cardiology." *Circulation* 107: 3109–16.

Thorpe, R. and K. Ferraro. 2004. "Aging, Obesity, and Mortality: Misplaced Concern about Obese Older People?" *Research on Aging* 26:108–29.

Thun, M.J., R. Peto, A.D. Lopez, et al. 1997. "Alcohol Consumption and Mortality Among Middle-Aged and Elderly U.S. Adults." *New England Journal of Medicine* 337:1705–14.

Timm, D.A. and J.L. Slavin. 2008. "Dietary Fiber and the Relationship to Chronic Diseases." *American Journal of Lifestyle Medicine* 2:233–40.

Tribble, D.L. 1999. "Antioxidant Consumption and Risk of Coronary Heart Disease: Emphasis on Vitamin C, Vitamin E, and Beta-carotene—A Statement for Healthcare Professionals from the American Heart Association." *Circulation* 99:591–95.

U.S. Department of Health and Human Services and U.S. Department of Agriculture. 2005. *Dietary Guidelines for Americans, 2005* (6th ed.), Washington, DC, U.S. Government Printing Office.

U.S. Department of Health and Human Services. 2008. *Physical Activity Guidelines Advisory Committee Report*. Washington, DC: U.S. Government Printing Office.

Van Horn, L. 1997. "Fiber, Lipids, and Coronary Heart Disease." *Circulation* 95:2701–4.

Villareal, D.T., C.M. Apovian, R.F. Kushner, and S. Klein. 2005. "Obesity in Older Adults: Technical Review and Position Statement of the American Society for Nutrition and NAASO, the Obesity Society." *American Journal of Clinical Nutrition* 82:923–34.

Waite, L. and M. Gallagher. 2000. *The Case for Marriage: Why Married People Are Happier, Healthier, and Better Off Financially*. New York, NY: Doubleday.

Wang, H., J.L. Sindelar, and S.H. Busch. 2006. "The Impact of Tobacco Expenditure on Household Consumption Patterns in Rural China." *Social Science and Medicine* 62:1414–26.

Warnecke, R.B., T.P. Johnson, N. Chavez, S. Sudman, D.P. ORourke, L. Lacey, and J. Horm. 1997. "Improving Question Wording in Surveys of Culturally Diverse Populations." *Annals of Epidemiology* 7:334–42.

Warner, K.E., T.A. Hodgson, and C.E. Carroll. 1999. "Medical Costs of Smoking in the United States: Estimates, Their Validity, and Their Implications." *Tobacco Control* 8: 290–300.

Warren, J.R. and E.M. Hernandez. 2007. "Did Socioeconomic Inequalities in Morbidity and Mortality Change in the United States Over the Course of the Twentieth Century?" *Journal of Health and Social Behavior* 48(4):335–51.

Webb, C.P.M, E.J. Bromet, S. Gluzman, N.L. Tintle, J.E. Schwartz, S. Kostyuchenko, and J.M. Havenaar. 2005. "Epidemiology of Heavy Alcohol Use in Ukraine: Findings from the World Mental Health Survey." *Alcohol and Alcoholism* 40:327–35.

Weinstein, A.R., H.D. Sesso, I.M. Lee, N.R. Cook, J.E. Manson, J.E. Buring, and J.M. Gaziano. 2004. "Relationship of Physical Activity vs. Body Mass Index with Type 2 Diabetes in Women." *JAMA* 292:1188–94.

Weng, X.Z., Z.G. Hong, and D.Y. Chen. 1987. "Smoking Prevalence in Chinese Aged 15 and Above." *Chinese Medical Journal* 100:886–92.

Whitmer, R.A., E.P. Gunderson, E. Barrett-Connor, C.P. Quesenberry, Jr., and K. Yaffe. 2005. "Obesity in Middle Age and Future Risk of Dementia: A 27 Year Longitudinal Population Based Study." *British Medical Journal* 330:1360–62.

Willett, W.C. 2006. "The Mediterranean Diet: Science and Practice." *Public Health Nutrition* 9:105–10.

Williamson, D.F. 1993. "Descriptive Epidemiology of Body Weight and Weight Change in U.S. Adults." *Annals of Internal Medicine* 119:646–49.

Wolf, A.M. and G.A. Colditz. 1998. "Current Estimates of the Economic Cost of Obesity in the United States." *Obesity Research* 6:97–106.

World Health Organization. 2000. *Obesity: Preventing and Managing the Global Epidemic*. Geneva, World Health Organization.

World Health Organization. 2002. *Tobacco Atlas*. Geneva: World Health Organization.

World Health Organization. 2003. *Gender, Health and Tobacco*. Geneva: World Health Organization.

World Health Organization. 2004a. *World No Tobacco Day 2004. European Region Fact Sheet. Tobacco and Poverty*. Copenhagen, World Health Organization Regional Office for Europe, World Health Organization.

World Health Organization. 2004b. *Global Status Report on Alcohol, 2004*. Geneva: World Health Organization.

World Health Organization. 2007. *The European Tobacco Control Report, 2007*. Copenhagen: World Health Organization.

World Health Organization. 2008. *The Global Burden of Disease: 2004 Update*. Geneva, World Health Organization.

Wright, A.A. and I.T. Katz. 2007. "Tobacco Tightrope—Balancing Disease Prevention and Economic Development in China." *New England Journal of Medicine* 356:1493–96.

Yokoyama, M., H. Origasa, M. Matsuzaki, Y. Matsuzawa, Y. Saito, Y. Ishikawa, S. Oikawa, S, Sasaki, H. Hishida, H. Itakura, T. Kita, A. Kitabatake, N. Nakaya, T. Sakata, K. Shimada, and K. Shirato. 2007. "Effects of Eicosapentaenoic Acid on Major Coronary Events in Hypercholesterolaemic Patients (JELIS): A Randomised Open-label, Blinded Endpoint Analysis." *The Lancet* 369:1090–98.

Zaridze, D., D. Maximovitch, A. Lazarev, V. Igitov, A. Boroda, J. Boreham, P. Boyle, R. Peto, and P. Boffetta. 2009. "Alcohol Poisoning Is a Main Determinant of Recent Mortality Trends in Russia: Evidence From a Detailed Analysis of Mortality Statistics and Autopsies." *International Journal of Epidemiology* 38:143–53.

# Chapter 15

# Discrimination, Chronic Stress, and Mortality Among Black Americans: A Life Course Framework

James S. Jackson, Darrell Hudson, Kiarri Kershaw, Briana Mezuk, Jane Rafferty, and Katherine Knight Tuttle

## Introduction

We use a life course framework to analyze lifetime patterns of mortality among black Americans. Using this framework directs attention to specific questions regarding the potential causes of racial group differentials in mortality, and we hope moves the field toward more comprehensive and testable explanations. The work on aging, the life course, and health has long highlighted the racial crossover effect in late-life mortality (e.g., Johnson 2000). While there are heated debates about the causes of this racial crossover in the United States (e.g., Johnson 2000; Preston et al. 1996), demographers have noted its existence in both cross-sectional population-level data, and in longitudinal panel studies (Johnson 2000). Gibson (Gibson 1991, 1994; Gibson and Jackson 1987) speculated that the racial crossover is based upon a series of mortality sweeps beginning in the black population in midlife, thereby leaving a hardier group of blacks in very older ages whose probability of survival in comparison to whites' reverses and becomes more favorable.

This chapter explores an even more radical suggestion that the racial group crossover in mortality rates in old age is a product of life course differences in rates of mortality beginning at conception. Succinctly, we propose that black American children in the post-infant mortality period may be on average hardier than comparable non-Hispanic white children. Rates of mortality are consistently higher prior to childhood for blacks, but in childhood, adolescence, and early adulthood, the black–white mortality gap narrows considerably. This narrowing trend reverses at midlife and until very old age favors non-Hispanic whites. We suggest that the major culprit of these observed differences is chronic stress, and the wear and tear on organs and organ systems (Geronimus 1996; McEwen 1998). We believe that because of a combination of poorer pre- and post-natal care, and more severe intrauterine sources of damage, that a mortality sweep occurs in pre-childhood resulting in constitutionally weaker blacks dying, leaving a constitutionally stronger set of organisms than non-Hispanic whites in childhood. During childhood, adolescence, and young adulthood, however, chronic stress due to both mundane sources and discrimination takes a major toll on the black population, resulting in earlier chronic disease and wearing of organ systems, and the observed rise in premature death rates. This proposed life course mortality framework is consistent with the observed epidemiological data over the life course and differential mortality outcomes in the black and white populations.

Following from a life course framework, consideration must be given to the ebb and flow of mortality patterns from conception to death; and any comprehensive explanation must include the interaction of factors, such as living conditions and stressors, and the processes underlying racial group differentials in mortality sweeps of the populations. There is a wealth of work on mortality patterns: taken in isolation, a number of causal mechanisms, such as stress and low socioeconomic status (SES), are adequate in explaining pieces of the empirical phenomenon, but insufficient to account for the complete empirical patterns. In

J.S. Jackson (✉)
Institute for Social Research, and Department of Psychology, University of Michigan, Ann Arbor, MI 48106, USA
e-mail: jamessj@umich.edu

this chapter we first present evidence of the shifting mortality patterns between blacks and whites across the life course. Second, we explore research addressing early life stages of the phenomenon and conditions that contribute to the race differentials in prenatal, birth, and infant mortality outcomes, what we believe is the "launching" point of the shifting pattern of racial mortality ratios over the life course. Third, we briefly discuss research-documenting evidence of race differences in stress over the mid-period of the life course; this helps to account for the increasing racial gap in mortality patterns favoring whites. Fourth, we discuss the evidence of the racial crossover of mortality patterns in late life, a phenomenon that we believe is only the end product of successive race differentials in mortality sweeps over the life course that begins at conception.

## Documenting the Shifting Pattern of Mortality Rates

Figures 15.1, 15.2, 15.3, 15.4, and 15.5 present evidence of shifting black–white differences in mortality rates. Figure 15.1 shows the changing ratio of black–white mortality rates during the first year of life in the United States during the period 2003–2005. Figures 15.2 and 15.3 demonstrate, for males and females, an ebb and flow of the all-cause mortality rates for the period 2003–2006, and arguing against a historical period explanation, for the period 1979–1984. For both men and women and in both time periods we observe the following: blacks die at twice the rate as whites up to the first year of life, then the black–white gap narrows during childhood and adolescence; the black–white ratio increases during the middle of the life course, and then late in life the gap narrows, ultimately favoring blacks. A similar pattern is found when examining black–white differences in mortality rates for stress implicated endocrine, nutritional, and metabolic diseases in the same time periods. Overall, the gap is generally even higher during middle age (see Figs. 15.4 and 15.5). Since the patterns are similar across the two time periods, this suggests that the ebb and flow pattern is not a particular cohort or historical time period effect.

## Gestation and Early Life Mortality Crossover

African-Americans are at greater risk for a myriad of chronic, debilitating conditions than whites; and population health indicators, including overall mortality rates and infant mortality rates, indicate systematic

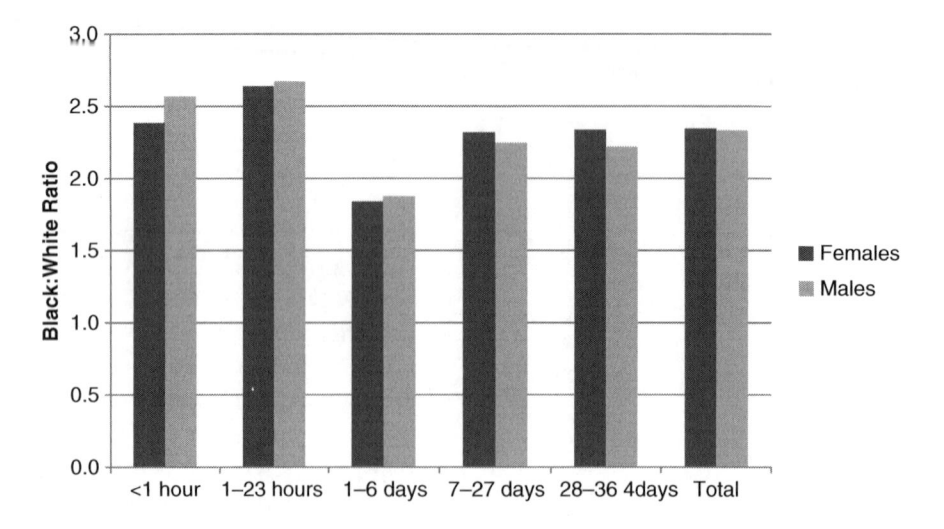

**Fig. 15.1** Black:white ratios of linked birth/infant mortality rates 2003–2005. Source: United States Department of Health and Human Services (US DHHS), Centers for Disease Control and Prevention (CDC), National Center for Health Statistics (NCHS), Division of Vital Statistics (DVS), Linked Birth/Infant Death Records 2003–2005 on CDC WONDER On-line Database

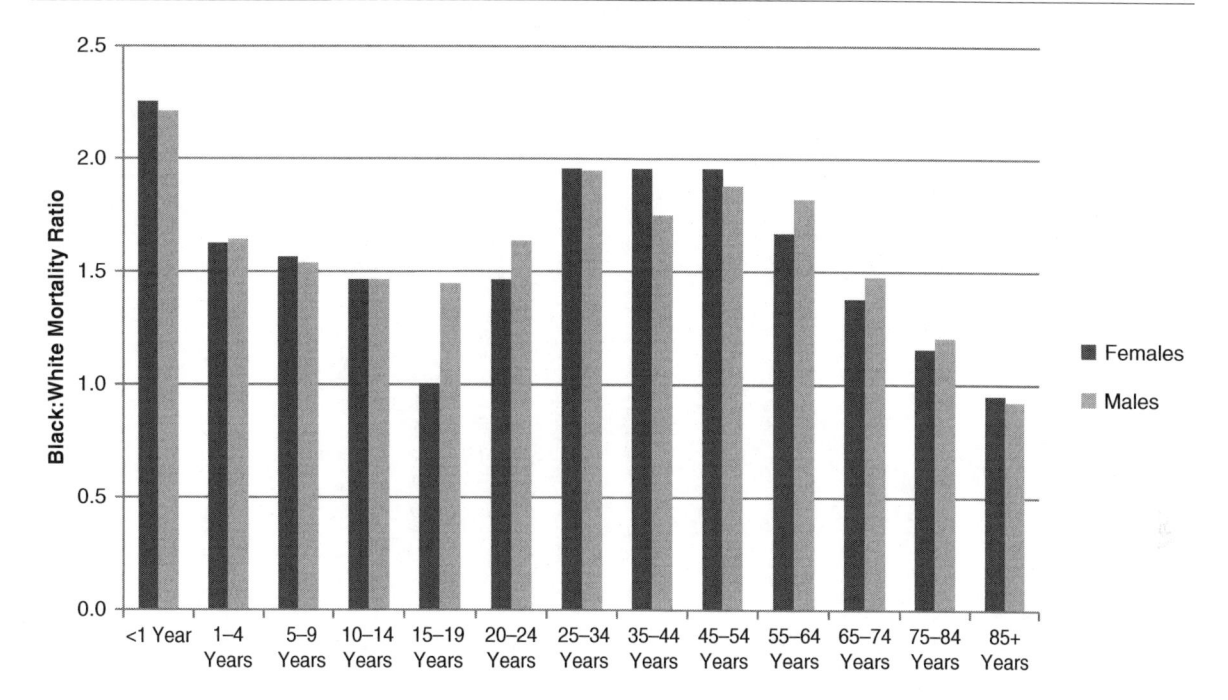

**Fig. 15.2** Black:white ratio of all-cause mortality rates between 2003 and 2006 for males and females. Source: Centers for Disease Control and Prevention, National Center for Health Statistics. Compressed Mortality File 1999–2004. CDC WONDER On-line Database, compiled from Compressed Mortality File CMF 1999–2004, Series 20, No. 2J, 2007

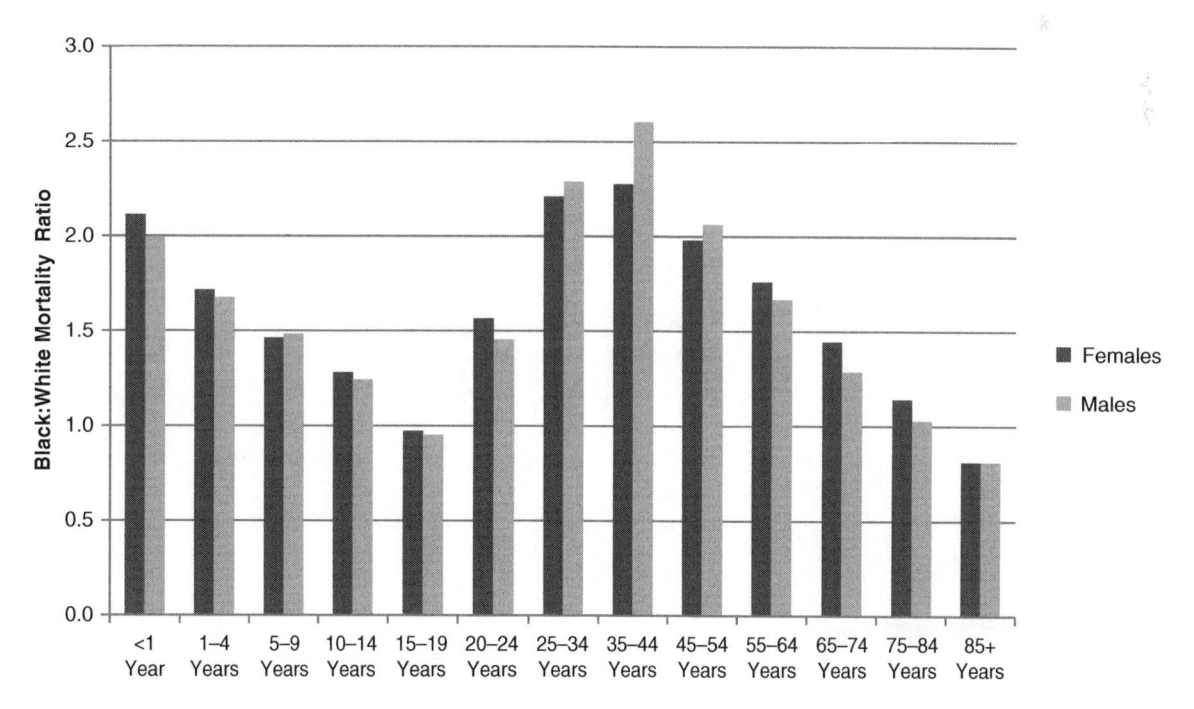

**Fig. 15.3** Black:white ratio of all-cause mortality rates between 1979 and 1984 for males and females. Source: Centers for Disease Control and Prevention, National Center for Health Statistics. Compressed Mortality File 1999–2004. CDC WONDER On-line Database, compiled from Compressed Mortality File CMF 1999–2004, Series 20, No. 2J, 2007

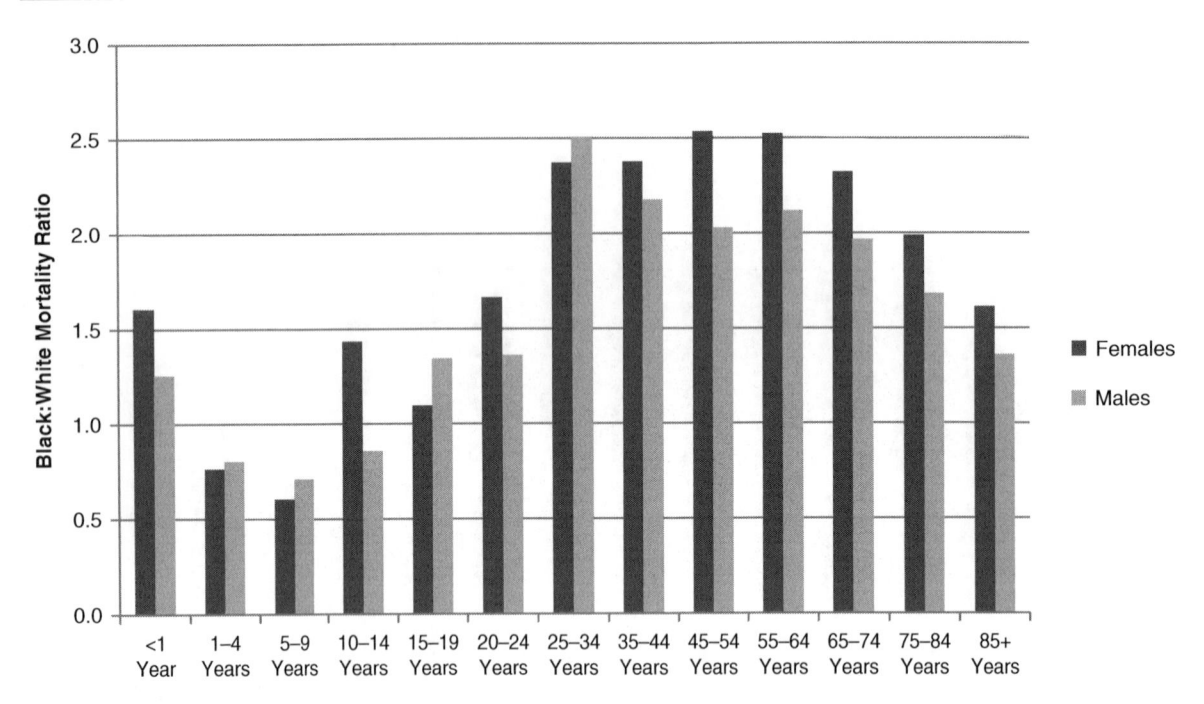

**Fig. 15.4** Black:white ratio of endocrine, nutritional, and metabolic diseases mortality rates between 2003 and 2006 for males and females. Source: Centers for Disease Control and Prevention, National Center for Health Statistics. Compressed Mortality File 1999–2004. CDC WONDER On-line Database, compiled from Compressed Mortality File CMF 1999–2004, Series 20, No. 2J, 2007

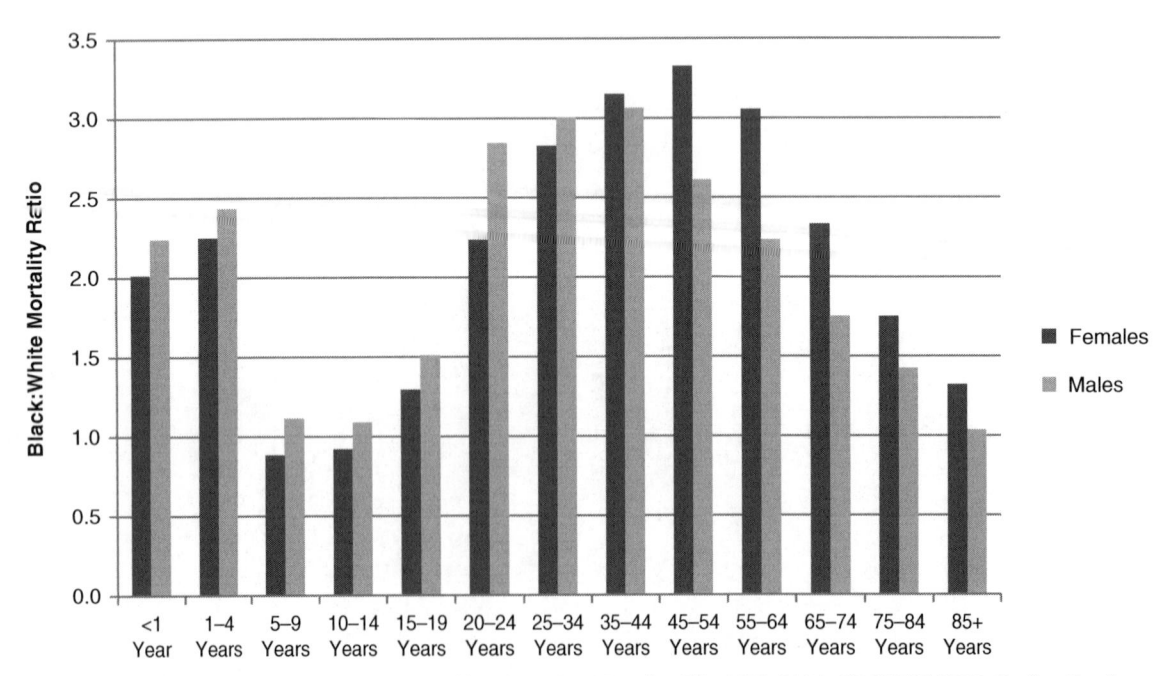

**Fig. 15.5** Black:white ratio of endocrine, nutritional, and metabolic diseases mortality rates between 1979 and 1984 for males and females. Source: Centers for Disease Control and Prevention, National Center for Health Statistics. Compressed Mortality File 1999–2004. CDC WONDER On-line Database, compiled from Compressed Mortality File CMF 1999–2004, Series 20, No. 2J, 2007

inequalities in health between African-Americans and whites in the United States (Geronimus et al. 2001; Kaufman et al. 1997; LaVeist 2002). Early life socioeconomic conditions can play a role in the development of morbidity and mortality in adult life. For instance, Warner and Hayward (2006) find that for African-American men, early life socioeconomic conditions and family structure, particularly the lack of biological parents in the household, are associated with increased rates of adult mortality (Warner and Hayward 2006). Even after accounting for the effects of SES during adulthood, African-Americans still bear a disproportionate amount of morbidity and mortality (Geronimus et al. 2001; Williams 2003). Increasingly, researchers have highlighted the importance of applying a life course perspective to understanding the link between SES and health, noting that the origins of pathology that emerge during adulthood often develop during early life and even in the intrauterine environment (Barker 1997; Hertzman and Power 2003).

Of all racial and ethnic groups in the United States, African-Americans experience the highest rates of low birth weight, preterm birth, and infant mortality. The African-American infant mortality rate of 13.63 deaths per 1,000 live births is about twice the national average of 6.89 (MacDorman and Mathews 2008). Additionally, African-American babies are between two and three times more likely to be low weight at birth (<2,500 g at birth) and are more likely to be born preterm (defined as less than 37 weeks of gestation) (MacDorman and Mathews 2008). Not only are low birth weight and preterm birth are major risk factors for infant death, but also these factors have been linked to morbidities that arise during adulthood. The underlying mechanisms that explain these black–white disparities in infant mortality, low birth weight, and preterm birth are thought to be firmly rooted in systematic race-based discrimination (e.g., Geronimus and Thompson 2004; Williams and Collins 1995; Williams 2005). A number of theoretical orientations have been advanced to explain how the confluence of structural or institutional-level discrimination, manifest in socioeconomic, environmental, and political inequalities, as well as direct personal experiences of discrimination lead to the disproportionate levels of low birth weight, preterm births, and infant mortality that affect African-Americans.

There are substantial social and economic inequalities in the United States largely determined by racial group membership that negatively affect African Americans. For instance, Shapiro (2004) finds that the net worth of typical white families is $81,000 compared to $8,000 for the typical African-American family, showing that African-American families possess only ten cents for every dollar of wealth held by white families (Shapiro 2004). Socioeconomic disparities between African-Americans and whites are historically rooted in unfair governmental policies and social practices (Katznelson 2005). Additionally, African-Americans experience varied forms of racial discrimination, ranging from interpersonal to institutional, that limit their ability and potential to accumulate socioeconomic resources and pose direct threats to their mental and physical health (David and Selina 2009). For instance, African-Americans do not receive the same financial compensation as their white counterparts, even controlling for education and experience, and their occupational trajectories are often truncated compared to whites (Geronimus et al. 1996; Wilson 1996). Additionally, the experience of racial discrimination has been identified as a significant stressor that African-Americans must contend with, one that has negative effects upon mental and physical health (e.g., Kessler et al. 1999).

Racial residential segregation has been highlighted as a key structural mechanism in which racial group inequalities are allowed to persist (Williams 1999; Williams and Collins 1995). Importantly, African-Americans remain the most highly segregated ethnic group in the United States (Charles et al. 2004), subsequently influencing the quality of the environments in which African-Americans reside. African-Americans' residences contain a much larger proportion of homes composed of older, poorer stock, and they live in neighborhoods with substantially reduced access to equitable services (LaVeist 2002; Williams and Collins 1995). Additionally, housing value, the primary sources of wealth for most Americans, are largely determined by the racial composition of neighborhoods.

Socioeconomic inequalities could not only increase the rates of low birth weight, preterm births, and infant mortality among African-American women, but could also affect the health of individuals over the life course. One prominent theoretical framework advanced in the literature to illustrate the connection between poor socioeconomic and environmental conditions and the intrauterine environment is the fetal origins hypothesis. Posited by Barker, this hypothesis asserts that exposures during gestation have permanent effects on the fetus. Specifically, it predicts that individuals who are exposed to unfavorable intrauterine environments during certain stages of fetal development, particularly due to undernourishment, are at greater risk of infant and adult mortality (Barker 1997; Barker et al. 1989). A number of studies have demonstrated that the nature of, and experiences in, the intrauterine environment have profound influences upon adult health and diseases, such as diabetes (Barker 2003), hypertension (Barker et al. 1989), and cardiovascular disease (Barker 1997, 1999). Barker has shown that there are associations between birth weight and increased heart rate and blood pressure and notes the relationship between height and cardiovascular mortality observed in various studies (Barker et al. 1989). Barker posits that low birth weight and smaller overall size of infants is due to decreased amounts of available nutrients in the intrauterine environment.

Barker (1995) finds that under-nutrition during critical periods of fetal development are related to restricted intrauterine growth. This under-nutrition leads to abnormal placental growth, fetal insulin resistance, low birth weight, and increased rates of hypertension and diabetes (Barker 1995). It is possible that slowed intrauterine growth could lead to postnatal growth that is accompanied by increases in blood pressure. As a result of a more deprived intrauterine environment, individuals are born at lower weights and have smaller frames during adulthood. More specifically, shorter height is associated with increased rates of mortality due to cardiovascular disease. Recent work suggests an even more fine-tuned understanding: distinguishing between measurements of the minor and major axes of the placenta suggests that there is a differential relationship between placental diameter and later hypertension among men and women (Eriksson et al. 2010).

Komlos (2009, 2010) has found that the height of black women has been declining in birth cohorts that have recently reached adulthood, compared to white men and women as well as black men. He noted that a substantial disparity in height between black and white women's height despite the fact that, on average, black women in the 20–39 age range weigh 9.5 kg (21.0 lb) more than their white counterparts. Considering the simultaneous decline in height and increase in weight, Komlos suggest that future cohorts of black women are at risk for negative health consequences (Komlos 2009, 2010).

Barker finds that there is significant geographic variation associated with lower birth weight in studies in the United Kingdom. Furthermore, Barker suggests that these exposures are manifest in organ systems, and later in the development of morbidities, such as cardiovascular disease. As discussed earlier, African-Americans are more likely to live in poorer areas and to be exposed to greater social and environmental hazards in their neighborhoods, contributing to higher rates of low birth weight and infant mortality. Nonetheless, there is substantial criticism of the fetal origins hypothesis and more research is needed to evaluate how, and processes by which, stress and deprivation could negatively affect the intrauterine environment. Although African-Americans may be more likely to be low weight at birth, there is not enough known about the process to definitely say that persons of low birth weight will be smaller during adulthood. For instance, although Asian-Americans have the lowest rates of low birth weight and infant mortality, they are usually shorter and weigh less than African-Americans and whites (Ruffing et al. 2006). Additionally, there are other factors that may play a more important role in explaining poor birth outcomes and infant mortality among African-Americans.

For example, African-American women face substantial stressors related to SES, including perceptions of neighborhood safety, erratic work schedules, lower quality housing, and job strain (Mullings and Wali 2001). The multiplicative effect of care giving along with occupational stress, experiences of discrimination, as well as addressing the financial needs of maintaining their households is likely to play a role in the accelerated deterioration of the health of African-American women over time (Geronimus 1996; Newman 1999). The weathering hypothesis, proposed by Arline Geronimus, suggests that African-American women have greater rates of infant mortality due to the experience and accumulation of various psychosocial stressors, particularly socioeconomic disadvantage, throughout the life course. The weathering hypothesis suggests that African-Americans experience early health deterioration as a result of the cumulative effects of chronic exposure to social or economic adversity and political marginalization (Geronimus and Thompson 2004). Weathering is also described as the notion that health is worsened due to the manifestations of living in a society that devalues certain groups of people (Geronimus 2001). It is also possible that black women experience premature and accelerated health deterioration because of the accumulation of material hardships, exposure to environmental hazards, stress from leadership roles, frustration with structural level, racial inequalities (Geronimus et al. 2006), and pressure to adopt unhealthy behaviors, such as smoking and unhealthy eating (Jackson and Knight 2006).

According to the weathering hypothesis, it is important to consider social, economic, and political inequalities because their stressful effects interact with age. Thus, maternal age, a key risk factor for infant mortality, needs to be interpreted differently across racial groups (Geronimus 2003; Geronimus et al. 1999). More precisely, African-American women are thought to experience accelerated aging due to weathering; thus, African-Americans are more likely to have low birth weight and preterm infants as well as a higher overall infant mortality rates. Support for the weathering hypothesis has been found in a number of studies showing increased rates of infant mortality for African-American women associated with increased age, even when adjusting for the effects of SES (Colen et al. 2006; Geronimus 1996). In 1989, using a sample of black and white female Michigan residents aged 15–44, Geronimus and her colleagues ( 2006) found that there were increased odds of having low and very low birth weight infants among black women beyond the age of 15. This association was not observed among white women. They suggested that risk factors associated with poor birth outcomes may increase with age more rapidly for blacks in comparison to whites.

Conventional wisdom suggests that improvements in SES would eliminate racial differences in rates of infant mortality. However, several papers have offered evidence showing that infant mortality is not affected by SES among African-Americans. Alternatively, Colen et al. (2006) show that African-American women with higher levels of SES have greater rates of infant mortality. In the analysis of data drawn from the National Longitudinal Survey of Youth, Colen et al. (2006) did not find a significant relationship between adult SES and low birth weight. Potential explanations include the fact that despite increases in SES over the life course and into adulthood, many African-American women spent considerable amounts of their childhoods in poverty. This finding also lends support to the notion that early life exposures have effects upon African-Americans throughout the life course, even their fertility patterns. For instance, many blacks grow up in poverty during childhood and are faced with numerous stressful events throughout their lives. The weathering framework asserts that the health of blacks who have reached higher SES can still be negatively affected due to the time they have spent in poverty during childhood and adolescence. Additionally, weathering may still occur for high-achieving blacks who still have to negotiate challenges across multiple contexts.

Is the intrauterine exposure that African-Americans experience the reason behind greater rates of morbidity and mortality for African-Americans over the life course? Or does this evidence suggest that psychosocial stressors make it more difficult for African-Americans to have healthy babies, but after the weakest organisms die the remaining African-American infants are actually healthier? Considering the elevated level of infant mortality, relative to whites and other racial and ethnic minority groups, it is possible that African-Americans who survive to 1 year of age are somehow more highly selected. In other words, do the weakest African-Americans die in utero and soon after birth before the end of the first year, leaving a group selected for stronger and healthier African-American children? However, due to the environmental exposures and social stressors African-Americans are subjected to beginning early and sustained over the life course, it is possible through weathering or some similar process that hardy individuals lose their resilience, and are selected for advantage over time, to an initially less positively selected for white population that is advantaged in the environment.

## Stressors and Stress Effects over the Life Course

This section discusses the evidence that socially patterned stressors are associated with poor health over the life course. Using data from the Baltimore Epidemiologic Catchment Area (ECA) study, a population-based longitudinal study of mental and physical health to speculate about how such stressors may explain the excess mortality risk of black Americans. As noted earlier, in the United

States blacks continue to be overrepresented in low socioeconomic strata, whether indicated by occupational prestige, income, wealth, or educational attainment, relative to whites (LaVeist 2005). For example, in 2007 nearly three times as many black families were living in poverty as whites (32.2% vs. 11.5%, respectively; Kaiser Family Foundation). Disadvantaged SES is associated with worse health outcomes than more advantaged SES, although the specific mechanisms linking low SES to poor health are not well-specified. Several researchers have suggested that the persistent and, in some cases, qualitatively unique social stressors that characterize low SES, may be one way by which environmental factors translate into morbidity and mortality (Baum et al. 1999, 1999; Geronimus et al. 2006). How these experiences are related to cardiovascular and metabolic disorders is not yet fully understood, although there is growing evidence that such exposures may have influences on both health behaviors, such as smoking and dietary intake, and physiology, including the immune system and the hypothalamic pituitary adrenal (HPA) axis (Jackson et al. 2010). There is growing evidence that social stressors influence physiology in numerous ways, including over activation of the sympathetic nervous system (SNS), changes in immune function, and stimulation of HPA axis accompanied by desensitization of the negative feedback loops that regulate this system, as well as alterations in gene expression (Crimmins et al. 2009; Miller et al. 2008, 2009). These stressors and the associated physiologic responses may over time influence risk for chronic health conditions, including asthma, diabetes, hypertension, cardiovascular disease, and some types of cancer (McEwen 1998; Seeman et al. 1994; Taylor et al. 2006).

## Differential Exposure to Stress

Exposure to and protection from stressful life circumstances during childhood vary by poverty status, cultural background, and racial group membership (Menard et al. 2004), and some stressors (e.g., parental absence due to incarceration) are systematically experienced more frequently by black children (Wildman 2009). Even within the same urban community blacks are more likely to experience traumatic events (e.g., being assaulted, witness trauma to others, have to cope with unexpected deaths) than white residents, particularly in early adulthood (Breslau et al. 1998). In the Baltimore ECA Study, whites and blacks reported experiencing similar numbers of negative life events (e.g., divorce, job loss, widowhood, death of a/another loved one) (2.67 and 2.77 events on average, respectively), but the distribution of these events varies significantly by age group (Fig. 15.6a). When the "expectedness" of the events is accounted for (based on the notion that unexpected events would be more disruptive than if those same events had been anticipated) the differences between whites and blacks is even more striking (Fig. 15.6b). Events that were "completely unexpected" were given a weight of five, those that were somewhat expected were assigned a weight between four and two (indicating "not very sure," "fairly sure," and "quite sure," respectively), and events that were highly expected ("absolutely sure") were given a weight of one. This excess exposure to negative life events early in the life course, during times of peak-resource accumulation (e.g., educational attainment, occupational status, wealth, social capital) has detrimental effects on health in later life for blacks.

Negative life events are a crude measure of life stress, and some researchers have argued that other characteristics of the social environment, such as daily hassles, contextual restraints, or exposure to extreme, traumatic events are more pertinent to understanding the influence of stress on disparities in health (Myers 2009; Wheaton 1999). In the Baltimore ECA, whites and blacks are equally likely to report having ever experienced a traumatic event (e.g., violent assault, natural disaster, or rape), but the quality and type of the traumatic events differs significantly, with blacks being significantly more likely to witness the assault or violent death of another person than whites (Fig. 15.7), providing an unfortunate parallel to the excessive burden of homicide among blacks in the United States (Williams and Jackson 2005). Overall, these results indicate that there is substantial heterogeneity in the experience of social stressors even within a defined environmental context (e.g., the Baltimore metropolitan area), and that failure to account for the differential patterning of social stress over the life course by racial groups will lead to an underestimation of the influence of environmental context on health outcomes for blacks.

Blacks are also more likely to experience unique stressors due to their socially disadvantaged status,

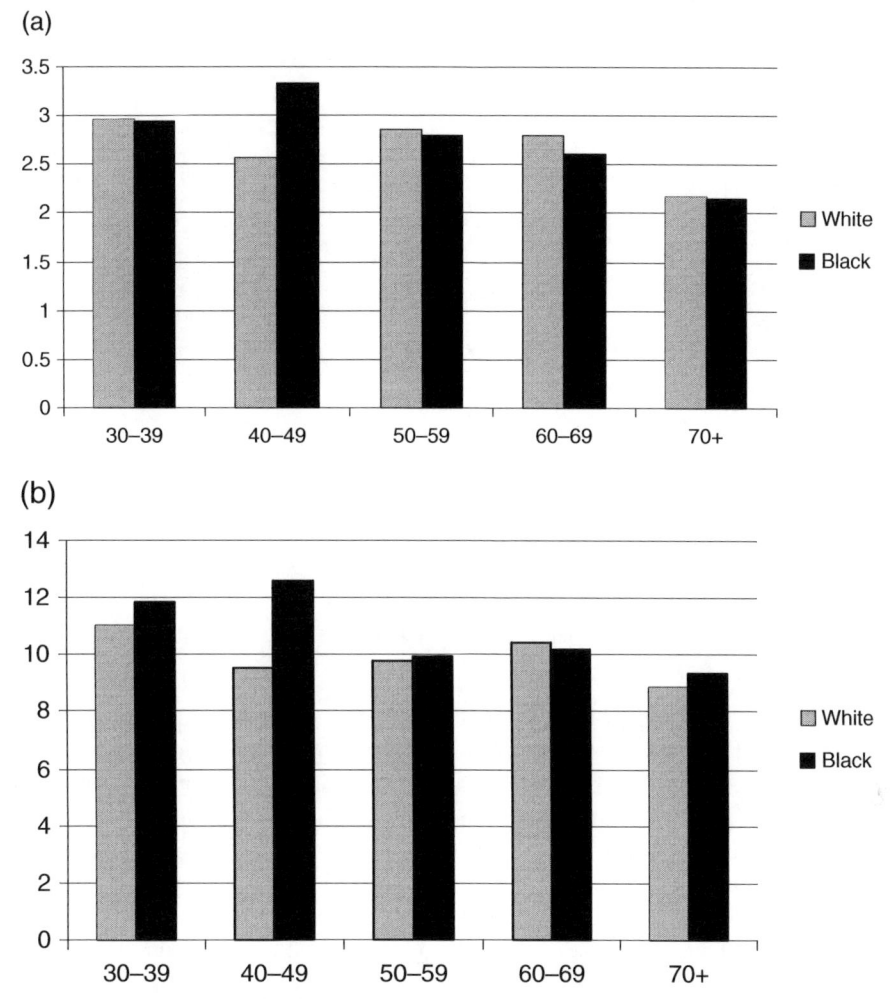

**Fig. 15.6** Number of negative life events by age and race: Baltimore ECA 1993/6 follow-up. Panel a: Unweighted. Panel b: Weighted by expectedness. Note: Negative life events include such as divorce, death of a loved one, widowhood, and job loss, from 1981 to 1993. Source: Baltimore ECA 1993/6 (for description of data collection see, Badawi et al. 1999)

such as discrimination in obtaining housing, the workplace, and social encounters (Williams and Jackson 2005) and residential segregation (Landrine and Corral 2009). Residential segregation is one example of a contextual factor that influences the racial disparities in morbidity and mortality. Residential segregation has been linked to exposure to numerous types of social and physical stressors, including witnessing and experiencing violence, drug use, ambient air pollution, and neighborhood deterioration. Residential segregation is also associated with numerous factors that influence health behaviors, including proximity to liquor stores and advertisements for tobacco products (Landrine and Corral 2009). In residential areas where whites and blacks truly "share the same space" and have similar socioeconomic characteristics (which are extraordinarily uncommon places in the United States), the black–white difference for conditions that disproportionately affect blacks, such as type 2 diabetes and hypertension, is almost entirely absent (LaVeist et al. 2009; Thorpe et al. 2008). This suggests that the environmental context, including stressors and the ways that individual behavior is influenced by stressors and constraints, substantially contribute to the poor-health status of blacks in the United States.

## Stress and Coping

Broadly, the psychological stress response involves a series of processes, including cognitive appraisal (which is particularly important in uncertain or

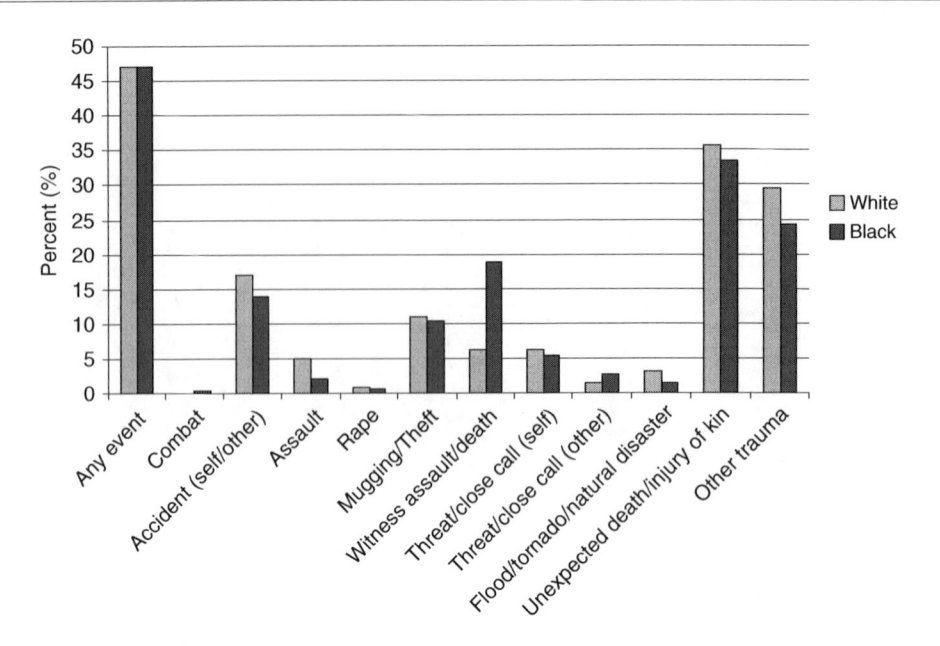

**Fig. 15.7** Percent of adults who experienced a traumatic event in the Baltimore ECA: 1993/6 follow-up

ambiguous threat situations) and coping (Lazarus and Folkman 1984). In addition, the ways that individuals cope with these stressors are constrained by their physical environment, culture, and social norms (Gibson 1977), and there is evidence that these constrictions encourage coping behaviors that are damaging to health (e.g., smoking, dietary intake high in simple carbohydrates and fat, excessive alcohol intake) (Jackson and Knight 2006; Krueger and Chang 2008; Winkleby et al. 1999). In the Baltimore ECA, those who reported experiencing a traumatic event were asked how long it took them to adjust to the changes caused by the event. As shown by Fig. 15.8, blacks were significantly more likely to report that they had still not adjusted to the repercussions of the event than whites. This may be due to qualitative differences in the types of events experienced (Fig. 15.7), or may reflect differences in availability of coping resources between the groups.

## Stress and Health

In addition to the psychological stress coping response, there is a physiologic coping response which involves the activation, mobilization, and gradual return to basal state via inhibition (often through negative feedback loops) of numerous neuroendocrine systems. These systems are adaptive for acute stress (e.g., stunting of the immune response, a result of activation of the hypothalamic–pituitary–adrenal axis, is appropriate for responding to a situation that requires a quick mobilization of energy, such as running from danger). However, the prolonged activation of these stress-response systems, or reduced sensitivity to respond appropriately to stress, has been hypothesized to result in a host of physical and mental health problems, including depression, cardiovascular disease, diabetes, and premature mortality (McEwen and Seeman 1999, Sapolsky 1999).

The relationship between stress and health is not limited to contemporaneous exposures. Stressful events early in the life course, such as poverty during childhood or unemployment in young adulthood, can have lasting effects on health in later life. For example, a history of unemployment is associated with elevated C-reactive protein, a risk factor for cardiovascular disease and diabetes, 10 years after the event (Janicki-Deverts et al. 2008). Childhood poverty has been associated with risk of developing diabetes and cardiovascular disease in middle and later adulthood, even after accounting for current SES (Loucks et al. 2009). Factors such as parental education and family environment during childhood have also been related to psychological well-being and blood pressure in adulthood

**Fig. 15.8** Recovery from traumatic events by race in the Baltimore ECA study: 1993/6 follow-up. Source: Baltimore ECA 1993/6 (for description of data collection see, Badawi et al. 1999)

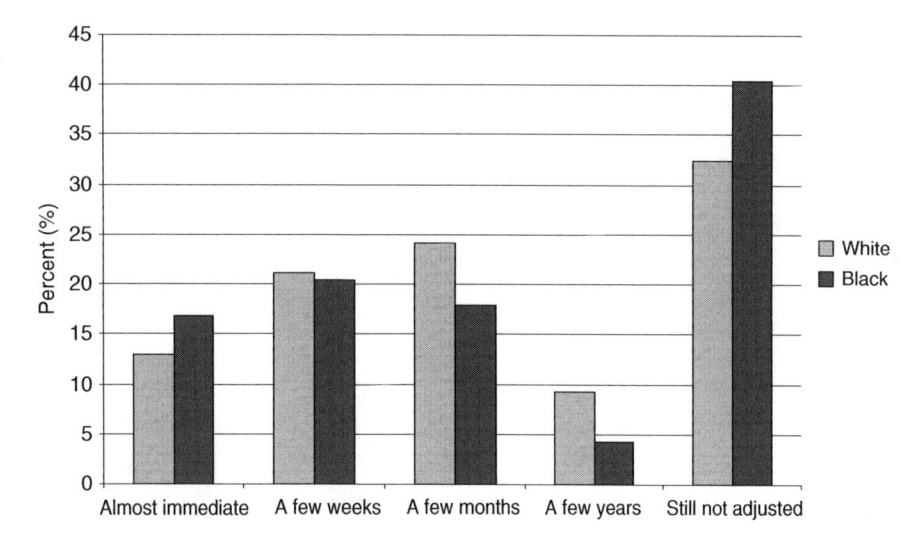

among blacks (Lehman et al. 2009). These relationships are important factors in the white–black mortality gap, since blacks are substantially overrepresented in poor households in the United States. Stressors that are more common among blacks relative to whites, such as experiences of discrimination and exposure to trauma (Barnes et al. 2004; Breslau et al. 1998), have been associated with a host of mental and physical health outcomes, including mortality (Barnes et al. 2008). The association between perceived discrimination and health outcomes also extends to health-care settings, where it has been associated with preventive health behaviors (i.e., willingness to participate in cancer screenings) (Crawley et al. 2008).

As noted earlier, Geronimous and others have hypothesized that the physiologic consequences of these stressors (and their associated coping strategies) accumulate over the life course, eventuating in a sort of "weathering" on the body that results in both increased burden and *earlier onset* of chronic conditions and reduced life expectancy (Geronimus et al. 2006). Consistent with this hypothesis, in the Baltimore ECA blacks have earlier age of onset of two health conditions common among older adults, diabetes and arthritis, as well as the normal age-related change of menopause (Fig. 15.9). The degree to which these conditions reflect accumulated stress-related physiologic (e.g., stunting of gonadal hormones, weight gain, centralized deposition of body fat) and behavioral (e.g., eating habits, cigarette smoking, physical inactivity) changes may explain this apparent "premature aging" of black adults relative to whites. Disparities in socioeconomic resources have also been identified as a major potential source of differences in burden of chronic health conditions (Hayward et al. 2000).

In sum, blacks in the United States experience greater burdens of negative life events early in the life course and are also subject to qualitatively unique exposures due to their socially disadvantaged status (e.g., discrimination, residential segregation, witnessing violence). This differential exposure to stress begins early and accumulates over time, eventuating in both increased overall burden and earlier onset of leading causes of death, including cardiovascular disease and type 2 diabetes.

## Exploring the Mortality Crossover

A long-running focus of investigation within discussions of mortality rates is the existence of a mortality crossover. A mortality crossover refers to a pattern in which the mortality rates for a socially disadvantaged group are higher during early periods of the life course but then converge and ultimately fall below the rates of a more socially advantaged group. This phenomenon has been documented in numerous geographical settings examining a range of groups, including Muslims compared to individuals of European ancestry in Algeria, Maoris compared to individuals of European ancestry in New Zealand, and

**Fig. 15.9** Age of onset of diabetes, arthritis, and menopause in the Baltimore ECA study: 1993/6 follow-up. Source: Baltimore ECA 1993/6 (for description of data collection see, Badawi et al. 1999)

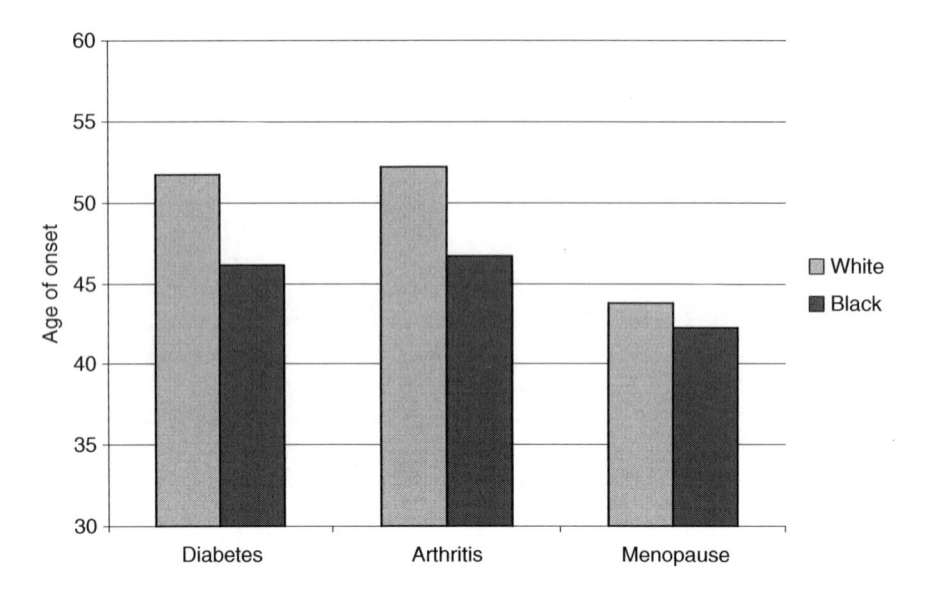

native-born versus foreign-born residents in Canada and the United States (Nam 1995; Nam et al. 1978; Spiegelman 1948; Swallen 1997; Trovato 1993). Of particular interest in this chapter is the mortality crossover between non-Hispanic blacks and whites in the United States, with mortality rates favoring whites at younger ages and a reverse pattern at older ages (Clark and Gibson 1997; Hummer et al. 2004, 2009; Johnson 2000). In the US context, the pattern has been the center of a continuing debate regarding simultaneously the validity of the phenomenon and an explanation of the pattern. One perspective contends that the phenomenon reflects inaccurate data; in contrast, another perspective asserts that the crossover is real and reflects a variation in experience and selection effects.

Among the skeptics of the idea of a racial group crossover in mortality rates a starting premise is the argument that there is systematic misreporting of age, and hence the crossover is merely an artifact (Coale and Kisker 1986; Elo and Preston 1994; Preston et al. 1996). Misreporting can occur in both the numerator (e.g., death certificates) and the denominator (e.g., census questionnaire).

Preston and colleagues have done extensive assessment of data related to blacks' mortality statistics, including vital records, census records, and Social Security Administration records. Analyses using techniques such as intercensal cohort comparisons and extinct generation estimates suggest that death rates may be inaccurate among age cohorts in the 50-plus range. For example, intercensal cohort comparisons represent a ratio of actual to expected population; these calculations are based on comparing populations in a subsequent enumerated census with the expected population based on extracting known deaths (based on vital statistics) occurring between two census collections. Preston calculated such ratios among black females and black males. Among both groups, the intercensal cohort comparisons in 5-year-age cohorts between 65 and 80 are above 1.0. One explanation is that there is a tendency to overestimate one's age on census assessments.

Extending the investigation, Preston et al. (1996) linked death certificates to census questionnaires and Social Security Administration (SSA) records, as a means of evaluating the accuracy and consistency of mortality indicators. They collected a sample of 5,262 death certificates for blacks dying in 1985. Of this sample, they were able to match just over half of these death certificates to the respective census questionnaire in the years 1900, 1910, or 1920 and to their record in the Death Master File within the SSA. Their analytical strategy included assessing consistency of age across these sources and then imputing a revised age at death where there was inconsistency. They evaluated whether the age at death was synchronous across all three sources, and if so no imputation is needed; if the age at death based on the census questionnaire was younger, this age was then imputed; if there was a match on age based on the SSA records and the death certificate, then this age was taken to be accurate; and finally, if none of the ages matched, the age based on the SSA records was imputed for those born after 1900 (according to the SSA records) and for others the age based on census records was taken to be accurate. Recalculating mortality rates among blacks based on this revised subsample and comparing these mortality rates with those among whites in 1985 suggests that there was no mortality crossover.

A key criticism of Preston and colleagues' work is the fact that they did not perform the same imputation methods among whites. There have been a number of studies that have continued investigation of the accuracy of mortality estimates using alternative methods and sources. In contrast to Preston, these authors suggest the validity of a racial crossover in mortality rates. Kestenbaum (1992) analyzed data collected as part of Medicare Part B that is part of the SSA's master beneficiary record along with data from the Numident file which includes data from applications for Social Security numbers. Medicare Part B is insurance available to US citizens aged 65 and above; Part B has a methodological advantage since nonpayment of the required monthly fee leads to additional record keeping and data gathering regarding termination of coverage. Kestenbaum created a data register based on Medicare Part B records, the Numident file, as well as cross-checking efforts. His analytic procedures included using the date of birth from the Numident file if it was later than the date reported in the Medicare records; he relied on the Numident date of death if there was no date reported in the Medicare records or if a later date of death was reported. The results from these data suggest a racial crossover in mortality rates at age 87 for men and 88 for women.

Using the extinct cohort method, Manton and Stallard (1997) found a racial group crossover among both men and women at age 81. This method is motivated by the assumption that death certificates provide more accurate data than that reported in the census. In brief, this strategy involves summing deaths among the oldest cohorts backward as a means of ascertaining population estimates based solely on mortality data.

Hummer and colleagues (2004, 2009) present mortality rates for 1999; the calculations are based on data collected by the National Center for Health Statistics (NCHS) (Hoyert et al. 2001). Specifically, the numerator in the NCHS estimates represents data from the US vital statistics and the denominator represents estimates from the census. For both men and women, these data suggest that mortality rates for non-Hispanic blacks are substantially higher than non-Hispanic whites between the ages of 65 and 79; the rates begin to converge within the 80–84 age cohort, and there is evidence of a crossover of the rates among the 85-plus cohort.

Additional research using the NCHS data paired with the National Health Interview Survey and the National Death Index represents further support for a racial crossover (Eberstein et al. 2008) at the age of 85-plus. These researchers pushed the investigation and assessed the crossover by cause of death. Findings suggest a crossover among individuals dying of cardiovascular disease, cerebrovascular diseases, and influenza and pneumonia.

As opposed to using a mix of census, vital statistics, or insurance records, another category of analysis involves the use of data collected in prospective studies. By their very nature, longitudinal panel studies allow researchers to gather baseline information and follow a study population until a death is observed. It is true that errors can be made in reporting age at the baseline interview; however, it is generally agreed that there is less misreporting of age at younger ages. Findings from a number of prospective studies, including the Piedmont Health Survey of the Elderly in North Carolina (Land et al. 1994) and the Evans County (Georgia) Heart Study (Wing et al. 1985), demonstrate a crossover in mortality rates among both men and women. Rates were calculated for various sex and functional ability subgroups; depending on the specific subclassification, the crossover was observed between the ages of 73 and 85.

Although paralleling some findings discussed above, it is instructive to point to a competing explanation of the racial group crossover. The starting assumption is that the crossover in mortality rates represents differential experience over the life course (Clark and Gibson 1997; Johnson 2000; Liu and Witten 1995). Therefore, more stressful and adverse environments lead to earlier onset of chronic diseases. The long-term result is that there may be "mortality sweeps" early in the life course and those among a social disadvantaged group who survive are heartier; this overall phenomenon helps to account for the observed mortality crossover later in the life course.

Johnson (2000) explored this hypothesis using two waves of data from the Survey on Asset and Health Dynamics Among the Oldest Old (AHEAD). AHEAD is a national probability sample of community dwelling individuals born in or before 1923; wave I was conducted in late-1993 and early-1994 and wave II was administered in late-1995 and early-1996. Johnson's focus was assessing the presence and timing of race crossovers among three estimates: comorbidity of critical health conditions, functional disabilities, and mortality. A guiding hypothesis was that a comparative analysis of the crossovers would suggest that the age of the crossover in comorbidity of health conditions occurs at the youngest age, followed by a crossover in functional disunities, and finally, a crossover in mortality rates. Uncovering such a sequencing of crossovers would broaden our understanding of racial group crossover in mortality rates and help substantiate a perspective centering on differential experience across the life cycle.

Taken as a whole, Johnson's analyses provide partial support for a life course account. Using wave I data, Johnson found a racial group crossover in the number of critical health conditions that are potentially fatal (e.g., lung disease, cancer, stroke) occurring at age 76, with the higher number of conditions shifting from blacks to whites. Analyses incorporating the wave I–II panel respondents, predicting mortality at wave II, points to the existence of a race crossover at age 81. The timing of the age of the crossover in comorbid conditions versus mortality is consistent with the life course explanation. However, finding a crossover in the number of disabilities (using the advanced activities of daily living checklist, which includes difficulty in eating, driving, and making phone calls) at age 86 is inconsistent with this explanation.

## Conclusions

It is well-established that middle-aged blacks have a higher prevalence of several chronic diseases compared with whites (Hajjar and Kotchen 2003; Mokdad et al. 2001; Norris and Nissenson 2008; Pathak and Sloan 2009); a few studies have suggested that disease prevalence increases with age more rapidly among younger blacks than whites of the same age. A study of black–white differences in age trajectories in hypertension found that blacks had higher hypertension prevalence at almost every age group studied and that the predicted increase in hypertension with age was steeper among blacks compared to whites (Geronimus et al. 2007). A study of black–white differences in age trajectories of functional health found similar results (Kim and Miech 2009); independent of baseline status, they found that blacks had an increased rate of decline in functional health with increasing age.

The "weathering" hypothesis attributes this uneven deterioration in physical health seen in blacks versus whites to the cumulative impact of repeated exposure to social and economic adversity and marginalization (Geronimus 1992). According to this theory, chronic exposure to stressors such as negative major life events, discrimination, and daily hassles may explain why blacks in middle age show the morbidity and mortality profiles typical of much older whites. Another possible, similar explanation for these black–white differences in morbidity and mortality among middle-aged adults is allostatic load (Geronimus et al. 2006; McEwen and Seeman 1999; McEwen and Stellar 1993). Allostasis is the process in which physiologic systems are altered in response to external forces to achieve homeostasis, or physiological balance. Allostatic load is the cost of chronically stimulating these physiologic pathways in response to repeated exposure to stressful conditions. Allostatic load is conceptualized as the physiological response to chronic stress as measured by biomarkers that are released in response to stress (e.g., norepinephrine) and those that result from the release of stress-related biomarkers (e.g., systolic and diastolic blood pressure levels).

Taking a life course approach leads to the recognition of the complex ebb and flow of black–white differences in mortality patterns. As noted in the Introduction, uterine and infant mortality is significantly higher among African-Americans compared to non-Hispanic whites, resulting, we believe, in the selection of a hardier group of black children compared with white children, and, as shown earlier, a reduction in racial group disparities in all-cause, and especially specific stress implicated, mortality during earlier life periods. However, early in life, repeated and sustained exposure to chronically stressful conditions associated with concentrated disadvantage and group marginalization experiences lead to increased black–white mortality disparities throughout middle and early old-age. These disparities contributing to early adult mortality differentials persist until late life, with disparities diminishing until eventually mortality rates become higher for whites than blacks.

Although provocative, we believe that this life course hypothesis comports well with the observed racial differences in mortality from conception until death. The routine use of age-adjusted death rates to study differences in black and white populations has obscured this theoretically interesting life course phenomenon. We believe that greater research attention is needed on how the life course, chronic stress exposure, and population selection may affect the understanding of racial group differences in disease and mortality in adulthood in the United States. Similar studies are needed in other countries where significant social group differences in resources and stress exposures may exist. Long-term cohort birth studies should be examined that permit explorations of intra- and inter-individual group differences in morbidity and mortality. Finally, more work on disaggregating causes of death could be an important source of information regarding the SES and physiological pathways affecting mortality among differently advantaged social groups. Finally, we believe if we are to fully understand the patterning of late-life mortality differentials among population groups, then theoretical frameworks addressing distal causes related to intrauterine, early childhood, and early adult environmental, social, and discriminatory experiences must be explored.

## References

Badawi, M.A., W.W. Eaton, J. Myllyluoma, L.G. Weimer, and J.J. Gallo. 1999. "Psychopathology and Attrition in the Baltimore ECA 15-Year Follow-up 1981–1996." *Social Psychiatry and Psychiatric Epidemiology* 34:91–98.

Barker, D.J.P. 1995. "Fetal Origins of Coronary Heart Disease." *British Medical Journal* 311:171–74.

Barker, D.J.P. 1997. "Fetal Nutrition and Cardiovascular Disease in Later Life." *British Medical Bulletin* 53(1):96–108.

Barker, D.J.P. 1999. "Early Growth and Cardiovascular Disease." *Archives of Disease in Childhood* 80:305.

Barker, D.J.P. 2003. "The Developmental Origins of Adult Disease." *European Journal of Epidemiology* 18:733–36.

Barker, D.J.P., C. Osmond, J. Golding, D. Kuh, and M.E.J. Wadsworth. 1989. "Growth in Utero, Blood Pressure in Childhood and Adult Life, and Mortality from Cardiovascular Disease." *British Medical Journal* 298(4):564–67.

Barnes, L.L., D.L. Mendes, C.F. Wilson, R.S. Bienias, J.L. Bennett, and D.A. Evans. 2004. "Racial Differences in Perceived Discrimination in a Community Population of Older Blacks and Whites." *Journal of Health and Aging* 16:315–37.

Barnes, L.L., C.F. de Leon, T.T. Lewis, J.L. Bienias, R.S. Wilson, and D.A. Evans. 2008. "Perceived Discrimination and Mortality in a Population-based Study of Older Adults." *American Journal of Public Health* 98: 1241–1247.

Baum, A., J.P. Garofalo, and A.M. Yali. 1999. "Socioeconomic Status and Chronic Stress. Does Stress Account for SES Effects on Health?" *Annals of the New York Academy of Medicine* 896:131–44.

Breslau, N., R.C. Kessler, H.D. Chilcoat, L.R. Schultz, G.C. Davis, and P. Andreski. 1998. "Trauma and Posttraumatic Stress Disorder in the Community: The 1996 Detroit Area Survey of Trauma." *Archives of General Psychiatry* 55:626–32.

Charles, C.Z., G. Dinwiddie, and D.S. Massey. 2004. "The Continuing Consequences of Segregation: Family Stress and College Academic Performance." *Social Science Quarterly* 85(5):1353–73.

Clark, D.O. and R.C. Gibson. 1997. "Race, Age, Chronic Disease, and Disability." In K.S. Markides and M.R. Miranda (eds.), *Minorities, Aging, and Health 1997*, pp. 107–260. Thousands Oaks, CA, Sage.

Coale, A.J. and E.E. Kisker. 1986. "Mortality Crossovers: Reality or Bad Data?" *Population Studies: American Journal of Demography* 40(3):389.

Colen, C.G., A.T. Geronimus, J. Bound, and S.A. Bound. 2006. "Maternal Upward Socioeconomic Mobility and Black-White Disparities in Infant Birthweight." *American Journal of Public Health* 96(11):2032–39.

Crawley, L.M., D.K. Ahn, and M.A. Winkleby. 2008. "Perceived Medical Discrimination and Cancer Screening Behaviors of Racial and Ethnic Minority Adults." *Cancer Epidemiology Biomarkers Prevention* 17:1937–44.

Crimmins, E.M., J.K. Kim, and T.E. Seeman. 2009. "Poverty and Biological Risk: The Earlier 'Aging' of the Poor." *Journal of Gerontology: Medical Sciences* 64A:286–292.

David, R.W. and A.M. Selina. 2009. "Discrimination and Racial Disparities in Health: Evidence and Needed Research." *Journal of Behavioral Medicine* 32(1):20.

Eberstein, I.W., C.B. Nam, and K.M. Heyman. 2008. "Causes of Death and Mortality Crossovers by Race." *Biodemography and Social Biology* 54:214–28.

Elo, I.T. and S.H. Preston. 1994. "Estimating African-American Mortality from Inaccurate Data." *Demography* 31(3): 427–58.

Eriksson, J.G., E. Kajantie, C. Osmond, K. Thornburg, and D. Barker. 2010."Boys Live Dangerously in the Womb." *American Journal of Human Biology* 22:330–35.

Geronimus, A.T. 1992. "The Weathering Hypothesis and the Health of African-American Women and Infants: Evidence and Speculations." *Ethnicity and Disease* 2: 207–21.

Geronimus, A.T. 1996. "Black/White Differences in the Relationship of Maternal Age to Birthweight: A Population-Based Test of the Weathering Hypothesis." *Social Science and Medicine* 42(4):589–97.

Geronimus, A.T. 2001. "Understanding and Eliminating Racial Inequalities in Women's Health in the United States: The Role of the Weathering Conceptual Framework." *Journal of the American Medical Women's Association* 56(4): 133–36.

Geronimus, A.T. 2003. "Damned If You Do: Culture, Identity, Privilege, and Teenage Childbearing in the United States." *Social Science and Medicine* 57(5):881–93.

Geronimus, A.T., J. Bound, D. Keene, and M. Hicken. 2007. "Black-White Differences in Age Trajectories of Hypertension Prevalence Among Adult Women and Men, 1999–2002." *Ethnicity and Disease* 17:40–48.

Geronimus, A.T., J. Bound, and T.A. Waidman. 1999. "Health Inequality and Population Variation in Fertility-Timing." *Social Science and Medicine* 49(12):1623–36.

Geronimus, A.T., J. Bound, T.A. Waidman, C.G. Colen, and D. Steffick. 2001. "Inequality in Life Expectancy, Functional Status, and Active Life Expectancy Across Selected Black and White Populations in the United States." *Demography* 38(2):227–51.

Geronimus, A.T., J. Bound, T.A. Waidman, M.M. Hillemeier, and P.B. Burns. 1996. "Excess Mortality Among Blacks and Whites in the United States." *The New England Journal of Medicine* 335(21):1552–58.

Geronimus, A.T., M. Hicken, D. Keene, and J. Bound. 2006. "Weathering and Age Patterns of Allostatic Load Score Among Blacks and Whites in the United States." *American Journal of Public Health* 96:826–33.

Geronimus, A.T. and J.P. Thompson. 2004. "To Denigrate, Ignore, or Disrupt: Racial Inequality in Health and the Iimpact of a Policy-Induced Breakdown of African American Communities." *Du Bois Review* 1(2):247–79.

Gibson, J.J. 1977. "The Theory of Affordances." In R. Shaw and J. Bransford (eds.), *Perceiving, Acting and Knowing*, pp. 67–82. Hillsdale, NJ, Lawrence Erlbaum Associates.

Gibson, R.C. 1991. "Age-by Race Differences in the Health and Functioning of Elderly Persons." *Journal of Aging and Health* 3:335–51.

Gibson, R.C. 1994. "The Age-by-Race Gap in Health and Mortality in the Older Population: A Social Science Research Agenda." *The Gerontologist* 34:454–62.

Gibson, R.C. and J.S. Jackson. 1987. "The Health, Physical Functioning, and Informal Supports of the Black Elderly." *Milbank Quarterly* 65(Supplement 2):421–54.

Hajjar, I. and Kotchen, T.A. 2003. "Trends in Prevalence, Awareness, Treatment, and Control of Hypertension in the United States, 1988–2000." *Journal of the American Medical Association* 290(2):199–206.

Hayward, M.D., E.M. Crimmins, T. Miles, and Y. Yang. 2000. "The Significance of Socioeconomic Status in Explaining the Race Gap in Chronic Health Conditions." *American Sociological Review* 65:910–20.

Hertzman, C. and C. Power. 2003. "Health and Human Development: Understandings from Life Course Research." *Developmental Neuropsychology* 24(2–3): 719–44.

Hoyert, D.L., E. Arias, B.L. Smith, S.L. Murphy, and K.D. Kochanek. 2001. "Deaths: Final data for 1999." *National Vital Statistics Reports*, 49(8).

Hummer, R., M. Benjamins, and R. Rogers. 2004. "Race/Ethnic Disparities in Health and Mortality among the Elderly: A Documentation and Examination of Social Factors." In N. Anderson, R. Bulatao, and B. Cohen. (eds.), *Critical Perspectives on Racial and Ethnic Differences in Health in Late Life 2004*, pp. 53–94. Washington, DC, National Research Council.

Hummer, R., R. Rogers, R. Masters, and J. Saint Onge. 2009. "Mortality Patterns in Late Life." In P. Uhlenberg (ed.), *International Handbook of Population Aging*, pp. 521–42. New York, NY, Springer.

Jackson, J.S. and K.M. Knight. 2006. "Race and Self-Regulatory Behaviors: The Role of the Stress Response and HPA Axis in Physical and Mental Health Disparities." In L.L. Carstensen and K.W. Schaie. (eds.), *Social Structure, Aging and Self-Regulation in the Elderly*, pp. 189–207. New York, NY, Springer.

Jackson, J.S., K.M. Knight, and J.A. Rafferty. 2010. "Race and Unhealthy Behaviors: Chronic Stress, the HPA Axis, and Physical and Mental Health Disparities Over the Life Course." *American Journal of Public Health* 100:933–39.

Janicki-Deverts, D., S. Cohen, K.A. Matthews, and M.R. Cullen. 2008. "History of Unemployment Predicts Future Elevations in C-Reactive Protein Among Male Participants in the Coronary Artery Risk Development in Young Adults (CARDIA) Study." *Annals of Behavioral Medicine* 36: 176–85.

Johnson, N.E. 2000. "The Racial Crossover in Comorbidity, Disability, and Mortality." *Demography* 37(3):267–83.

Kaiser Family Foundation. 2007. *Poverty Rate by Race/Ethnicity, U.S. 2007*. Available at http://statehealthfacts.kff.org.Retrieved10/1/2009.

Katznelson, I. 2005. *When Affirmative Action was White: An Untold Story of Racial Inequality in Twentieth Century America*. New York, NY, W.W. Norton & Co.

Kaufman, J.S., R.S. Cooper, and D.L. McGee. 1997. "Socioeconomic Status and Health in Blacks and Whites: The Problem of Residual Confounding and the Resiliency of Race." *Epidemiology* 8(6):621–28.

Kessler, R., K. Mickelson, and D.R. Williams. 1999. "The Prevalence, Distribution, and Mental Health Correlates of Perceived Discrimination in the United States." *Journal of Health and Social Behavior* 40:208–30.

Kestenbaum, B. 1992. "A Description of the Extreme Aged Population Based on Improved Medicare Enrollment Data." *Demography* 29(4):565–80.

Kim, J. and R. Miech. 2009. "The Black-White Difference in Age Trajectories of Functional Health Over the Life Course." *Social Science and Medicine* 68: 717–25.

Komlos, J. 2009. *Recent Trends in Health by Gender and Ethnicity in the US in Relation to Levels of Income*. NBER Working Paper w14635.

Komlos, J. 2010. "The Recent Decline in the Height of African-American Women." *Economics and Human Biology* 8(1):58–66.

Krueger, P.M. and V.W. Chang. 2008. "Being Poor and Coping with Stress: Health Behaviors and the Risk of Death." *American Journal of Public Health* 98:889–92.

Land, K.C., J.M. Guralnik, and D.G. Blazer. 1994. "Estimating Increment-Decrement Life Tables with Multiple Covariates from Panel Data: The Case of Active Life Expectancy." *Demography* 31(2):297–319.

Landrine, H. and I. Corral. 2009. "Separate and Unequal: Residential Segregation and Black Health Disparities." *Ethnicity and Disease* 19:179–84.

Laveist, T.A. 2002. *Race, Ethnicity, and Health*. San Francisco, CA, Jossey Bass.

LaVeist, T.A. 2005. "Disentangling Race and Socioeconomic Status: A Key to Understanding Health Inequalities." *Journal of Urban Health* 82:iii26–iii34.

Laveist, T.A., R.J. Thorpe, J.E. Galarraga, K.M. Bower, and T.L. Gary-Webb. 2009. "Environmental and Socio-Economic Factors as Contributors to Racial Disparities in Diabetes Prevalence." *Journal of General Internal Medicine*. doi:10.1007/s11606-009-1085-87.

Lazarus, R.S. and S. Folkman. 1984. *Stress, Appraisal and Coping*. New York, NY, Springer.

Lehman, B.J., S.E. Taylor, C.I. Kiefe, and T.E. Seeman. 2009. "Relationship of Early Life Stress and Psychological Functioning to Blood Pressure in the CARDIA Study." *Health Psychology* 28:338–46.

Liu, X. and M. Witten. 1995. "A Biologically Based Explanation for Mortality Crossover in Human Populations." *Gerontologist* 35(5):609–15.

Loucks, E.B., J.W. Lynch, L. Pilote, R. Fuhrer, N.D. Almeida, H. Richard, G. Agha, J.M. Murabito, and E.J. Benjamin. 2009. "Life Course Socioeconomic Position and Incidence of Coronary Heart Disease: The Framingham Offspring Study." *American Journal of Epidemiology* 169(7):829–36.

MacDorman, M.F. and T.J. Mathews. 2008. *Recent Trends in Infant Mortality in the United States*. Hyattville, MD, National Center for Health Statistics.

Manton, K.G. and E. Stallard. 1997. "Health and Disability Differences Among Racial and Ethnic Groups." In L.G. Martin and B.J. Soldo (eds.), *Racial and Ethnic Differences in the Health of Older Americans*, pp. 43–105. Washington, DC, National Academy Press.

McEwen, B.S. and E. Stellar. 1993. "Stress and the Individual: Mechanisms Leading to Disease." *Arch Intern Med* 153(18):2093–2101.

McEwen, B.S. 1998. "Stress, Adaptation, and Disease. Allostasis and Allostatic Load." *Annals of the New York Academy of Sciences* 840:33–44.

McEwen, B.S. and T.E. Seeman. 1999. "Protective and Damaging Effects of Mediators of Stress. Elaborating and Testing the Concepts of Allostasis and Allostatic Load." *Annals of the New York Academy of Medicine* 896:30–47.

Menard, C.B., K.J. Bandeen-Roche, and H.D. Chilcoat. 2004. "Epidemiology of Multiple Traumatic Childhood Events: Child Abuse, Parental Psychopathology, and Other Family-Level Stressors." *Social Psychiatry and Psychiatric Epidemiology* 39:857–65.

Miller, G., E. Chen, A.K. Fok, H. Walker, A. Lim, E.F. Nicholls, S.W. Cole, and M.S. Kobor. 2009. "Low Early-Life Social Class Leaves a Biological Residue Manifested by Decreased Glucocorticoid and Increased Proinflammatory Signaling." *Proceedings of the National Academy of Sciences* 106:14716–21.

Miller, G.E., E. Chen, J. Sze, T. Marin, J.M. Arevalo, R. Doll, R. Ma, and S.W. Cole. 2008. "A Functional Genomic Fingerprint of Chronic Stress in Humans: Blunted Glucocorticoid and Increased NF-kappaB Signaling." *Biological Psychiatry* 64:266–72.

Mokdad, A.H., B.A. Bowman, E.S. Ford, F. Vinicor, J.S. Marks, and J.P. Koplan. 2001. "The Continuing Epidemics of Obesity and Diabetes in the United States." *Journal of the American Medical Association* 286(10):1195–200.

Mullings, L. and A. Wali. 2001. *Stress and Resiliencr: The Social Context of Reproduction in Central Harlem*. New York, NY, Plenium Publishers.

Myers, H.F. 2009. "Ethnicity- and Socio-Economic Status-Related Stresses in Context: An Integrative Review and Conceptual Model." *Journal of Behavioral Medicine* 32: 9–19.

Nam, C.B. 1995. "Another Look at Mortality Crossovers." *Social Biology* 42(1–2):133–42.

Nam, C.B., N.L. Weatherby, and K.A. Ockay. 1978. "Causes of Death Which Contribute to the Mortality Crossover Effect." *Social Biology* 25(4):306–14.

Newman, K. 1999. *No Shame in My Game: The Working Poor in Inner City New York*. New York, NY, Russell Sage Foundation.

Norris, K. and A.R. Nissenson. 2008. "Race, Gender, and Socioeconomic Disparities in CKD in the United States." *Journal of the American Society of Nephrology* 19(7): 1261–70.

Pathak, E.B. and M.A. Sloan. 2009. "Recent Racial/ethnic Disparities in Stroke Hospitalizations and Outcomes for Young Adults in Florida, 2001–2006." *Neuroepidemiology* 32(4):302–11.

Preston, S.H., L.T. Elo, I. Rosenwaike, and M. Hill. 1996. "African-American Mortality at Older Ages: Results of a Matching Study." *Demography* 33(2):193–209.

Ruffing, J., F. Cosman, M. Zion, S. Tendy, P. Garrett, R. Lindsay, and J.W. Nieves. 2006. "Determinants of Bone Mass and Bone Size in a Large Cohort of Physically Active Young Adult Men." *Nutrition and Metabolis* 3(1):14.

Sapolsky, R.M. 1999. "Glucocorticoids, Stress, and Their Adverse Neurological Effects: Relevance to Aging." *Experimental Gerontology* 34:721–32.

Seeman, T.E., L.F. Berkman, D. Blazer, and J. Rowe. 1994. "Social Ties and Support and Neuroendocrine Function: The MacArthur Studies of Successful Aging." *Annals of Behavioral Medicine* 16:95–106.

Shapiro, T.M. 2004. *The Hidden Cost of Being African American: How Wealth Perpetuates Inequality*. New York, NY, Oxford University Press.

Spiegelman, M. 1948. "The Longevity of Jews in Canada," 1940–1942. *Population Studies* 2(3):292–304.

Swallen, K.C. 1997. *Cross-National Comparisons of Mortality Differentials: Immigrants to the U.S. and Stayers in Common Countries of Origins*. Presented at the Annual Meetings of the Population Association of America, March 28, Washington, DC.

Taylor, S.E., B.J. Lehman, C.I. Kiefe, and T.E. Seeman. 2006. "Relationship of Early Life Stress and Psychological Functioning to Adult C-reactive Protein in the Coronary Artery Risk Development in Young Adults Study." *Biological Psychiatry* 60:819–24.

Thorpe, R.J., D.T. Brandon, and T.A. LaVeist. 2008. "Social Context as an Explanation for Race Disparities in Hypertension: Findings from the Exploring Health Disparities in Integrated Communities (EHDIC) Study." *Social Science and Medicine* 67(10):1604–11.

Trovato, F. 1993. *Differential Mortality Between Immigrants and the Canadian-Born, 1985–1987: General and Cause-Specific.* Presented at the 22nd General Conference of the International Union for the Scientific Study of Population, August 24–September 1, Montreal.

Warner, D.G. and M.D. Hayward. 2006. "Early-Life Origins of the Race Gap in Men's Mortality." *Journal of Health and Social Behavior* 47:209–26.

Wheaton, B. 1999. "Social Stress." In C.S. Aneshensel and J.C. Phelan (eds.), *Handbook of the Sociology of Mental Health*, pp. 227–300. New York, NY, Springer Publishers.

Wildman, C. 2009. "Parental Imprisonment, the Prison Boom, and the Concentration of Childhood Disadvantage." *Demography* 46:265–80.

Williams, D.R. 1999. Race, Socioeconomic Status, and Health: The Added Effects of Racism and Discrimination." *Annals of the New York Academy of Science* 896:173–88.

Williams, D.R. 2003. "The Health of Men: Structured Inequalities and Opportunities." *American Journal of Public Health* 93(5):724–31.

Williams, D.R. and C. Collins. 1995. "US Socioeconomic and Racial Differences in Health: Patterns and Explanations." *Annual Review of Sociology* 21:349–86.

Williams, D.R. 2005. "The Health of U.S. Racial and Ethnic Populations." *Journal of Gerontology* 60B:53–62.

Williams, D.R. and P.B. Jackson. 2005. "Social Sources of Racial Disparities in Health." *Health Affair* 24:325–34.

Wilson, W.J. 1996. *When Work Disappears: The World of the New Urban Poor*. New York, NY, Knopf.

Wing, S., K.G. Manton, E. Stallard, C.G. Hames, and H.A. Tryoler. 1985. "The Black/White Mortality Crossover: Investigation in a Community-Based Study." *Journal of Gerontology* 40(1):78–84.

Winkleby, M.A., C. Cubbin, D.K. Ahn, and H.C. Kraemer. 1999. "Pathways by Which SES and Ethnicity Influence Cardiovascular Disease Risk Factors." *Annals of the New York Academy of Medicine* 896:191–209.

# Chapter 16
# Self-Rated Health and Subjective Survival Probabilities as Predictors of Mortality

Marja Jylhä

## Introduction

Self-rated health and subjective probability of survival (or self-rated life expectancy) are two simple, subjective indicators that are both strongly associated with mortality. For five decades, self-rated health has been one of the indicators most frequently employed in health research and social science, but still it is unclear how a subjective opinion given without any explicit criteria can predict the strongest biological event, death. Self-rated life expectancy is a measure used mostly in economic research, and only during recent decades. Focusing mainly on self-rated health, this chapter discusses three main questions: (1) what do we mean by saying that these indicators "predict" mortality? (2) what do people know about their health that creates such a strong association between these two measures and death? and (3) what should a researcher take into account when using these measures in empirical studies?

The starting point is to acknowledge that both self-rated health and self-rated life expectancy originate in an active cognitive process, and better understanding of this process helps clarify their relations to mortality. Next, I discuss the behavior of self-rated health—the more widely used and better understood of these two measures—as a variable used in research and its comparability across population groups. The final part of the chapter reviews the characteristics and use of self-rated life expectancy and compares them with those of self-rated health.

## Self-Rated Health and Mortality

Self-rated health (or self-perceived health, or self-assessed health) is derived from a single question that asks the respondent to evaluate her or his health status on a four- or five-category scale, usually ranging from excellent to poor (Jylhä 2009). The question has two main forms, one without a specified reference and one asking the respondent to compare his or her health to that of others at the same age ("How would you assess your health status in comparison with other people of your age that you know? Is it better, the same, or worse?"). The most commonly used, noncomparative form of the question usually refers to "your health at present."

In sociological research, self-rated health has a long history (Maddox 1962; Suchmann et al. 1958). Credit for identifying its association with mortality is usually given to Mossey and Shapiro (1982). In fact, as early as 1963 Heyman and Jeffers and in 1970 Pfeiffer observed in small samples that older people who rated their health as "good" survived longer than those who rated their health as "poor." In 1976, in the Midtown Manhattan Restudy, Eleanor Singer and colleagues followed a population sample of 1,600 persons aged 20–59 years at baseline for 20 years. The study focused on mental health, but included demographic information and information on several health conditions and symptoms. Among the variables included, aside from sex and age, self-rated health was the most powerful predictor of death.

M. Jylhä (✉)
Department of Gerontology, School of Health Sciences,
University of Tampere, Tampere, Finland
e-mail: Marja.Jylha@uta.fi

The study of Jana Mossey and Evelyn Shapiro (1982: 800) was the first with an explicit purpose "to test the hypothesis that self-rated health is a predictor of mortality independent of 'objective health status.'" This paper provided a model for numerous studies in the years to follow. In a population sample of 3,128 persons aged 65 and over in the Manitoba Longitudinal Study, self-rated health at baseline was defined by using an age-referential question: "For your age would you say, in general, your health is excellent, good, fair, poor, or bad?" In a model where age, sex, area of residence, income, life satisfaction, and "objective health," based on physician's reports and self-reports of diagnoses, were included, self-rated health showed a significant graded association with mortality. The risk of death was almost three times higher for those with "poor" than for those with "excellent" health, and it was higher than the risk of "poor" compared to "excellent" "objective" health. A year later, in the Human Population Laboratory Survey, George Kaplan and Terry Camacho (1983) obtained very similar results among people with a wide age range, from 16 years to the oldest old.

Since then, the association of self-rated health with mortality has been confirmed in at least 100 population studies (Benyamini and Idler 1999; DeSalvo et al. 2005; Idler and Benyamini 1997; Jylhä 2009). These studies expand and refine the results of early studies, but the basic findings remain unchanged: self-rated health, adjusted for age, shows a graded association with mortality. It predicts mortality not only in middle-aged and older populations, but also in both nonagenarians (Nybo et al. 2003) and young people (Larsson et al. 2002). The result has been repeated in very different cultural environments, such as China (Yu et al. 1998), Indonesia (Frankenberg and Jones 2004), Israel (Ben-Ezra and Shmotkin 2006), and Japan (Ishizaki et al. 2006), in addition to the United States, Canada, and several European countries, for example, Denmark (Nielsen et al. 2008), Finland and Italy (Jylhä et al. 1998), and Germany (Heidrich et al. 2002); in a population with very few health problems (Schoenfeld et al. 1994); and in different patient groups, such as people with HIV (Dzekedzeke et al. 2008), with coronary artery disease (Bosworth et al. 1999), and with advanced cancer (Shadbolt et al. 2002), and even in people with mild to moderate cognitive decline (Walker et al. 2004). Self-rated health seems to be a constant and universal predictor of mortality, significant in very different population groups, and it identifies people at an increased risk of death as well as do multi-item indicators of health status, such as the widely used 36-item short-form health survey (SF-36) or the Seattle index of comorbidity (DeSalvo et al. 2005).

## The Process of Evaluation

As there is no operational definition of "health," there are no explicit criteria on which to base the self-assessment. In everyday life, our answers to a friend's question about our health tend to be complex and multidimensional, "Well, at my age, you know ... I have this heart problem as you know and sometimes my legs hurt, but nothing bigger. ..." For self-rated health, however, the individual is asked to describe health as a single option on a one-dimensional scale.

For analytic purposes, the cognitive process of evaluation can be divided into different stages (see Fig. 16.1). The process and the frameworks of evaluation are discussed in more detail in Jylhä (2009). First, the person has to recognize the meaning of the word "health." In contrast to specific negative health conditions, such as diagnosed diseases, "health" has no operational definition to guide the respondent. Instead, people have considerable freedom in choosing the information on which to base their answers. This does not mean that the information used is random or arbitrary; instead, the choices are guided by our shared cultural understanding of the issues that belong to the realm of "health." The information used in the evaluations varies by type and source. Information on medical diagnoses usually comes from a physician or contact with the health care system. Functional status and disability can be observed directly in everyday life by the person and by people around him or her, and indirectly through medication, sick leaves, or disability retirement. Various symptoms and sensations, such as pain, dizziness, and fatigue are directly available only to the person him- or herself. In numerous studies, these three types of health information—formal medical diagnoses, observations of functional status, and subjective sensations—have been found to be associated with self-rated health; they are also the most important components of health that people mention when they are directly asked about the basis for their self-ratings in qualitative studies (Idler et al. 1999; Simon et al. 2005; Van Dalen et al. 1994).

In their self-assessments, people also take into account the severity of the conditions, their timelines, and their potential consequences (Leventhal et al. 1999). The factors that are considered as relevant components of "my health" are historically and culturally conditional, and likely to vary with cultural changes. One example is provided by health behaviors. For older generations, health behavior seems to be considered among factors that influence their health, but recent studies suggest that younger generations often consider their positive or negative health behaviors as direct components of their health (Chen et al. 2007). It may well be that in the future people will also include information about their genetic constitution as a component in their self-ratings (Jylhä 2009).

Different cultural, situational, and individual factors play roles in the process of evaluation; together they are here called "contextual frameworks of evaluation" (Fig. 16.1). Not only does the understanding of what constitutes "health" vary, at least to some extent, but the frameworks also modify the way in which different components of health are taken into account in self-ratings. As no formal criteria are available, an obvious yardstick is a reference group: either people known to

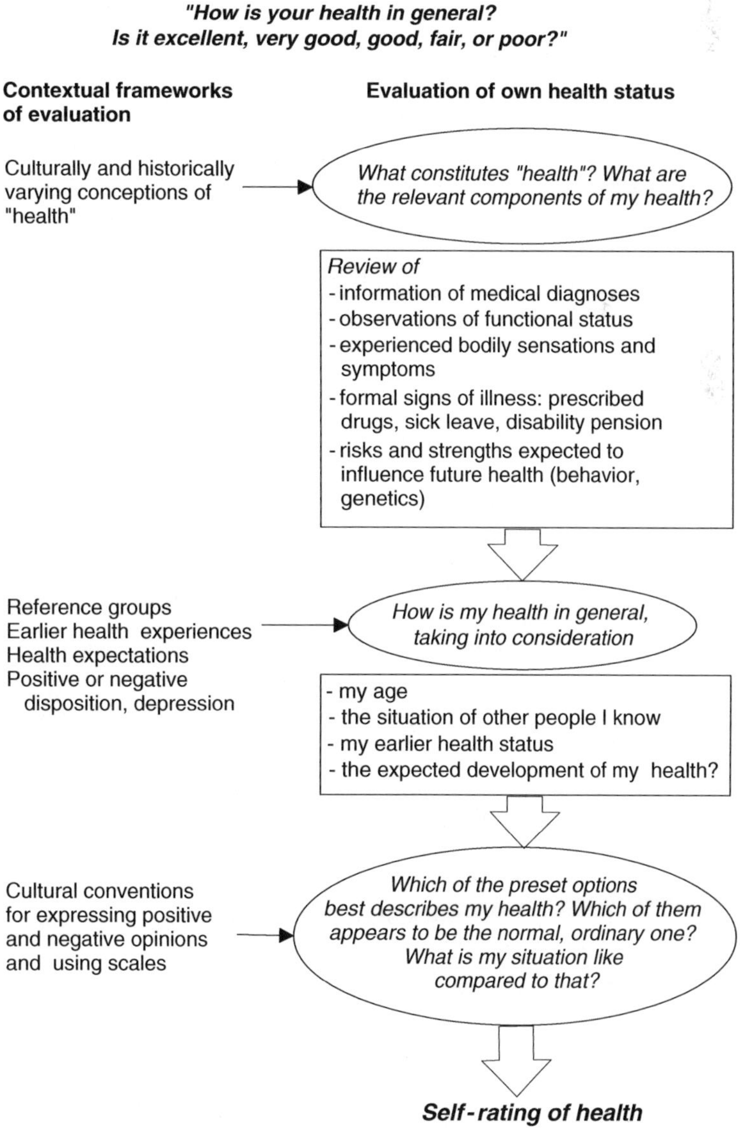

**Fig. 16.1** The process of health evaluation. This figure was first published in *Social Science and Medicine* (Jylhä 2009)

the individual, or general images or stereotypes, such as people of the same age, or people in the respondent's neighborhood (Festinger 1954; Merton 1957). In old age, some health problems are often considered normal and do not necessarily lead to negative health assessments. Someone suffering from depression or having a pessimistic disposition is likely to see his or her health in a more negative way than someone else with a more optimistic disposition (Jylhä 2009; Mora et al. 2008).

Finally, the individual has to make a choice among the preset categories from, say, excellent to poor, or from very good to bad. Qualitative analyses show that this can be a difficult task; often a complex process of reasoning is needed to fit the multidimensional phenomenon into the preset scale (Jylhä 1994).

The model described above is meant to be an analytic tool rather than a realistic picture of the evaluation experience. In processing their assessments, people usually do not separate different stages, nor do they deliberately select, decide, or weigh the descriptors of health for their evaluations, or explicitly relate these descriptors to their individual situations. To a large extent, the assessment is likely to happen intuitively and without much conscious reasoning. Still, there are good reasons to believe that these cognitive processes, more or less consciously, are involved in the process (Jylhä 2009).

## Why and How Does Self-Rated Health Predict Mortality?

If the model of evaluation described above is valid and self-rated health describes, with some precision, the state of the human organism, it is no wonder that people who rate their health as good survive longer than those who rate their heath as poor. But how are we to understand the repeated findings that the association between self-rated health and mortality in statistical models often persists, although weaker, after researchers control for a wide variety of clinical, objectively measured indicators of health and illness? Probably the most comprehensive health information used together with self-rated health was available in the Cardiovascular Health Study (Fried et al. 1998). In this study, self-rated health showed a strong graded association with mortality; good (RR 1.77), fair (RR 3.27), and poor (RR 7.52) self-rated health were all associated with a higher probability of death than was excellent self-rated health. When congestive heart failure, blood pressure, use of diuretics, posterior tibial artery blood pressure, albumin, creatinine, forced vital capacity, abnormal ejection fraction, aortic stenosis, major ECG abnormality, maximum stenosis of internal carotid artery, digit symbol test, instrumental activities of daily living, socioeconomic characteristics, and lifestyle factors were controlled—all significant independent predictors of mortality in the Cox proportional hazards model—mortality was still significantly higher for those with poor than those with excellent self-rated health (RR 1.91).

Because of such findings, self-rated health is considered "an independent predictor of mortality." It may be useful to specify what we mean by this. Death is a biological event, and its proximal causes must involve failures in the regulation of vital physiological processes. Distal predictors of mortality, such as social class, assume roles in a causal chain that, through differences in the probability and severity of pathological conditions, produces differences in the likelihood of vital dysregulations and, consequently, in length of life. Through which pathways, then, could self-rated health contribute to the likelihood of dying?

There are three main lines of explanation. The first possibility is that self-rated health is a better measure of physical health status than many other health indicators. Second, self-rated health may be a measure of psychological traits and dispositions, such as optimism and pessimism, that can influence the length of life. Third, self-ratings of health may reflect something else, such as health behaviors, that in turn may affect the probabilities of survival. Studies show that emotions, such as happiness, and optimistic or pessimistic disposition do predict mortality (Giltay et al. 2004; Peterson et al. 1988). This effect, however, is not independent of the biological state of the body, but operates through the direct and indirect influences of emotions and disposition on physiological state and health (Steptoe et al. 2005). Good health behaviors and optimism predict longer survival because they are beneficial to one's health. In fact, there is no good evidence to support the second and third explanations (Giltay et al. 2004; Manderbacka et al. 1999). Most researchers now believe in the first type of explanation that self-rated health may predict mortality because it "is a very inclusive measure of health reflecting health aspects relevant to survival which are not covered by other health indicators" (Mackenbach et al. 2002: 1162; Idler and Benyamini 1997). This conclusion does not deny the role of psychological disposition and health behaviors in the process of health evaluation, discussed earlier in this chapter. However, it does argue that self-rated health is associated with mortality, first of all, because it is a good measure of physical health status. Self-rated health does not influence the proximity of death but reflects the factors that do. Therefore, the description of self-rated health as "an independent predictor of mortality" refers not to a genuine causal role in the biological chain of events leading to death but to a role in a statistical model.

Building on earlier work on the theme (Idler and Benyamini 1997; Idler et al. 2004; Kaplan and Camacho 1983; Mackenbach et al. 2002), I have suggested two complementary rather than mutually exclusive pathways to explain the superior inclusiveness of self-rating, one referring to research methodology, and the other to human biology. First, the number of health variables that can be included in any empirical study is always limited. Even the best of studies rarely, if ever, cover all the diseases and conditions experienced by the entire study group. Nor do the measures of functioning cover the whole variety of functional states among study subjects. The severity, consequences, and prognosis of conditions are almost never included among the study variables. But people can take all this into account in their self-ratings. Therefore, one reason for the "independent" association between self-rated health and mortality may be that the self-ratings simply reflect the variance of health status among the study subjects better than the "objective" measures included. This does not mean that they reflect only those dimensions of health that are relevant to the likelihood of mortality; on the contrary, both quantitative and qualitative studies show that self-ratings take into account all aspects of health, both severe and less severe. What is important is that self-rated health is more inclusive than other, more specific indicators. In fact, it is fair to say that self-rated health is able to predict mortality better because the question is nonspecific, not in spite of that fact.

Second, individuals have access to information about their organism that no other person has, that is, their bodily sensations, feelings, symptoms, and emotions. The possible importance of this pathway has been proposed by researchers from the very beginning of the research on self-rated health and mortality. Mossey and Shapiro (1982) referred to "a prescient understanding of subtle biological and physiological change" through which self-rated health could be interpreted as "a finely tuned indicator of physiological well-being." Kaplan and Camacho (1983: 302) wrote, "The data point to still another possibility more consistent with the concept of general susceptibility. Although the pathways by which such generalized effects operate are unclear, recent work in the field of psychoneuroimmunology is suggestive. This evidence demonstrates the considerable interaction between nervous, endocrine, and immunologic systems and the existence of psychosocial influences on these interactions. It seems possible that individuals may be able to access information about the state of these systems and that such information can be utilized in arriving at judgments of perceived health." Since then, several others have considered the possibility that various bodily sensations about which it may even be difficult to verbalize may contribute to self-assessments and thus to the association of self-rated health and mortality (Idler and Kasl 1991; Unden et al. 2007).

Today, researchers in neurobiology, neuroendocrinology, immunology, and cognitive neuroscience are increasingly interested in the pathways of afferent information that convey messages from the organism to the brain, informing about the internal state of the body (Cameron 2001; Craig 2003; Dantzer 2001). Not all the information reaches consciousness; in fact, most of it participates in the regulation and adaptation of physiological functions at lower levels of the central nervous system. To some extent, however, the biological messages are perceived by individuals as sensations, feelings, and emotions. "Interoception" refers to the sense that reflects the physiological condition of the entire body, the "afferent information that arises from anywhere and everywhere within the body—the skin and all that is underneath the skin" (Cameron 2001: 97).

An especially interesting new line of research deals with conscious representations of humoral, biochemical bodily processes, particularly those belonging to immunological defense. It is now known that a family of proteins called cytokines is involved in different inflammatory processes that in turn have a major role not only in infectious conditions, but also in many chronic conditions such as cardiovascular disease, Alzheimer's disease, diabetes, and cancer. The level of many cytokines is elevated with aging. Increasing evidence indicates that inflammatory processes and certain cytokines are associated with symptoms such as tiredness, impaired sleep, depressive mood, general malaise, and poor appetite (Danzer et al. 2008; Miller et al. 2008). These symptoms are common in acute infections but may also appear without any diagnosed disease, reflecting subclinical dysregulation of the organism. For instance, chronic unexplained fatigue is now understood largely as a result of immune dysregulation (Klimas and Koneru 2007).

We do not know to what extent the processes described above really are involved with self-rated health. Yet, the research available justifies the hypothesis that interoceptive processes constitute one pathway through which information about bodily states is conveyed and included in self-rated health, a hypothesis suggested by Asser Stenback as early as 1964. We do know that symptoms such as chronic pain (Mantyselka et al. 2003) and fatigue (Molarius and Janson 2002) are important components of self-rated health, and there is also evidence on its association with inflammatory markers, such as interleukin-1β, tumor necrosis factor alpha (TNF-α) (Lekander et al. 2004; Unden et al. 2007), and interleukin-6 (Janszky et al. 2005). In one study, a graded association was observed between poor self-rated health and lower hemoglobin, higher white cell count, and lower albumin, even for values that are not considered pathological (Jylhä et al. 2006). These analyses adjusted for several clinically verified conditions and other health indicators. The respondents were unlikely to be aware of the values measured from the blood, or their clinical interpretation. Therefore, it is unlikely that they had taken these values deliberately into account in their self-ratings. It is possible that the values represent the unmeasured severity of various health conditions of which the participants were aware. However, it is also possible that even bodily irregularities too minor to be defined as medical conditions or conceptualized as illness can be sensed, interpreted as messages about one's health status, and incorporated into self-rated health, and thus contribute to its association with mortality (Jylhä 2009).

To summarize, the most plausible explanation for the "independent" statistical association of self-rated health with mortality seems to be its capacity to capture the different dimensions of health status more exhaustively than other health indicators used in research studies. Probably, global self-ratings are superior partly because empirical studies are necessarily constrained in the range and number of health variables they can include, and partly because the individual can employ, more or less consciously, subtle and even nonconceptualized sensations of his or her bodily status in self-ratings of health. The latter is still more a hypothesis than a conclusion based on firm empirical evidence.

## Is Self-Rated Health a Measure of "True Health?"

To a large extent, researchers analyzing the association of self-rated health with mortality have aimed to validate it as a general indicator of health. In the previous section, I suggested pathways through which an individual has access to information that may explain why self-rated health is able to predict future mortality better than many other health indicators. Does this imply that self-rated health should be considered as a valid measure of "true health" (Quesnel-Vallee 2007)?

For quantitative empirical research, "health" is a problematic concept. Unlike medical diagnoses or functional states, "health" has no operational definition. Both in research and in clinical practice, it is used as a generic term that is empirically approached by various indicators, such as medical diagnoses or laboratory values. Our common cultural understanding says that "health" has to do with survival, functioning, and well-being, but there is no standard rule or equation for how to integrate all these dimensions into one single global indicator of "health" (Jylhä 2009). Therefore, discussion of whether self-rated health measures "real" or "true" health may not be very useful. Instead, for the purpose of empirical studies, it is important to know how far self-rated health reflects major health conditions or significant pathological processes, how sensitive it is to differences and changes in them, and whether these associations are comparable between different population groups.

The relation of self-rated health to mortality or to any objectively verified health condition is highly dependent on the information available to the person at the time of self-rating; if people do not have a clue about their diseases, whether in the form of diagnoses, symptoms, or even indefinite sensations, they cannot take them into account. Idler et al. (2004) showed that among people with cardiovascular disease, self-rated health was a significant "independent" predictor of mortality only in the subgroup of people who knew about their diagnosis or had symptoms; in those who were unaware of the disease, the association was not significant. The association also seems to vary according to the cause of death, being stronger for causes such as infectious disease, diabetes, or heart disease that are likely to be known or cause symptoms at the time of self-rating than for external causes such as violence or accidents (Benjamins et al. 2004; Dowd and Zajacova 2007). Also, the strength of the association varies by the length of the follow-up. Although diverse findings exist (Deeg and Kriegsman 2003), there is rather convincing evidence that self-rated health is a stronger predictor of death over shorter periods than over longer ones (Benyamini et al. 2003; Singh-Manoux et al. 2007; Vuorisalmi et al. 2005), which is understandable as the self-rating would not reflect changes in health during the follow-up.

The pioneers, Suchmann et al. (1958), in their analysis of the validity of health questionnaires, emphasized the need to specify the purpose of a measure before validity can be determined. They concluded, "self-ratings of health measure something different than physician's ratings—what we have called 'perceived' or 'subjective' health as opposed to 'actual' or 'objective' health—but ... depending upon one's hypothesis such a self-rating may or may not be valid" (232). Given our present knowledge, it may be justified to believe that self-rated health is a valid but not a specific indicator of those objective dimensions of health status that are related to the probability of death, and its value as such an indicator is largely dependent on the coverage and accuracy of the health information that the respondent is able to incorporate into the rating.

## Is Self-Rated Health Comparable Across Population Groups?

When self-rated health is used as a proxy for objectively verified clinical health measures, as an estimator of future mortality, or to examine differences in health status between populations, comparability is an essential question. Basically, comparability can refer to different things. We may ask whether self-rated health reflects various clinical conditions or states of the organism in the same way; whether mortality in different population groups is similar at similar levels of self-rated health; or whether the relative risks of mortality in those reporting poor health compared to those reporting excellent health are similar across population groups.

It seems clear that the association of self-rated health with mortality is a rather universal finding in all populations for which results are available. However, studies show that there are *relative* differences between the population groups: self-rated health seems to be a stronger predictor of mortality in younger than in older groups, and in the young-old than in the old-old (Benyamini et al. 2003; Franks et al. 2003); in men than in women (Deeg and Kriegsman 2003; Dowd and Zajacova 2007; Huisman et al. 2007; Spiers et al. 2003); in higher than in lower socioeconomic groups (Dowd and Zajacova 2007; Huisman et al. 2007); and, when ethnic groups are compared in the United States, for whites than for other groups (Lee et al. 2007).

Age is a major element in the evaluation framework and perhaps the most important modifier of self-rated health. It is likely that because different aspects of health are relevant to different age groups, the bases of their self-ratings differ. Young people who assess their health against the age-specific expectation of good health may interpret information about their own health differently from older people who expect to have some degree of health problems. It seems that old people are likelier than younger ones to base their assessments on social and temporal comparisons with age peers (Cheng et al. 2007; Idler et al. 2004; Suls et al. 1991). These comparisons not only with specific people, but also with deceased members of one's own birth cohort, or with negative stereotypes of old age, are likely to lead to a lower aspiration level for "good" health (Tornstam 1975). Recent studies (Heller et al. 2009) show that self-rated health of older people with higher baseline morbidity is less sensitive to new incident morbidity than are self-ratings of younger people with fewer earlier health problems. As a result, the behavior of the age variable in statistical analyses is paradoxical. Both cross-sectional age group comparisons and longitudinal studies show that global self-rated health does not decrease as much with higher age as chronic disease and disability increase (Jylhä et al. 2001; Liang et al. 2005). At a given level of measured health conditions, older people usually assess their health more positively than younger people

(Ferraro 1980; Hoeymans et al. 1997), and controlling for other health indicators in multivariate analyses usually leads to a negative correlation between age and poor self-rated health (Cockerham et al. 1983; Ishizaki et al. 2009; Jylhä et al. 2001; Mulsant et al. 1997).

Therefore, it is only logical that similar self-ratings do not translate into similar rates of mortality across age groups, but at each level of self-rated health, mortality is higher for older age groups (Helweg-Larsen et al. 2003; Wannamethee and Shaper 1991). In a Danish study (Helweg-Larsen et al. 2003), among those who rated their health as very good, the mortality rate in 13 years was 8% among 45–55-year olds but 78% among those aged 78 years and older; among those who rated their health poor it was 29% and 95%, respectively. Few studies give relative risks of death for different age groups, but in a Swedish study with more than 170,000 men and women aged 16 and over, the crude relative risks of mortality for poor health compared to good health varied from 10.3 in the age group 25–34 to 1.7 among those aged 85 or older (Burstrom and Fredlund 2001). In a US study, the risk decreased from 5.9 in those aged 50–69 to 2.0 in those aged 80 or older in the white population, and from 3.7 to 1.9 in the black population, respectively (Lee et al. 2007). The lower relative risks at older ages are probably influenced by a higher baseline mortality in the older groups and the fact that older people are more likely than younger ones to experience new severe health events after the self-rating.

The latter findings also demonstrate the differences between ethnic groups and cultures. The few available comparative studies indicate differences between countries in the strength of the association of self-rated health with mortality (Appels et al. 1996; Jylhä et al. 1998), although the associations of self-rated health with other health indicators were largely similar. The differences likely arise from several sources: from different levels of medical information available to the respondents, from different evaluation frameworks that modify the ways in which various health factors are interpreted and taken into account, and, finally, from culturally conditioned ways of using the preset response scales, including the choice of options at either extreme of the scale. Linguistic factors, particularly the different connotations of the preset options, play a role here: in standard translations to Spanish and Russian, the middle option "fair" or "average" seems to describe normal health, while in many other countries "good" seems to be considered as an anchor point for evaluations (Bzostek et al. 2007; Palosuo et al. 1998).

A major question is whether self-perceptions of health reflect physical health status in a fundamentally different way in poor areas in developing countries than in affluent western societies. In his influential contribution, Amartaya Sen (2002) compared life expectancy and self-reported morbidity between two states in India and in the United States. The finding that prevalence of self-reported morbidity was lowest in Bihari where the life expectancy was lowest, and highest in the United States where the life expectancy was highest, led Sen to warn against relying on self-perceptions of health in assessing health care or medical strategies. In areas with heavy disease burden, poor medical services, and poor awareness of ill health among the population, self-perceptions may be "extremely misleading" (Sen 2002: 861). The findings concerned self-reported morbidity, but are relevant also for self-rated health. In their more recent between-state comparisons using Indian data, however, Subramanian et al. (2009) showed that longer life expectancy was associated with lower reported morbidity. They also found that poor self-rated health had a graded association with lower levels of education. Therefore, in their opinion, self-rated health is a valid health measure also in developing countries. Findings about its association with mortality in low-income countries are almost nonexistent—with the exception of Frankenberg and Jones (2004) in Indonesia, who demonstrated an association similar to that in other countries—and no direct comparisons are available between low- and high-income countries.

The results concerning the role of gender in associations between self-rated health and mortality vary by study sample and design (Deeg and Kriegsman 2003; Idler 2003). Most but not all findings imply a stronger, although not substantially stronger, age-adjusted association for men than for women (Deeg and Kriegsman 2003; Idler 2003; Jylhä et al. 1998; Singh-Manoux et al. 2007). Self-rated health seems to be a stronger predictor of mortality in higher than in lower socioeconomic groups (Burstrom and Fredlund 2001; Huisman et al. 2007; McFadden et al. 2009), yet the results usually are of the same magnitude. In all, even if self-rated health predicts mortality in all age groups, in both genders, in all socioeconomic groups in the high-income countries, and in different cultural environments, it is not clear that it would serve as a surrogate for clinically measured indicators of physical health or predict subsequent mortality in a comparable way across these groups. Particularly, it seems evident that self-rated health does not measure physical health or mortality in the same way at different ends of the age range, or in very different cultural environments.

## The Use of Different Question Versions in Empirical Research

The exact wording and response options of questions about self-rated health vary. The basic division is between the global, nonreferential question and the question asking the respondent to compare his or her health with that of others of the same age. For the global version, the scale most widely used in the United States includes options from excellent through very good, good, and fair to poor. The options recommended by the WHO (1996) and the EURO-REVES 2 group (Robine and Jagger 2003), and widely used in Europe, include very good, good, fair, bad, and very bad. One version, used, for example, in the study "The Elderly in Eleven Countries" (Heikkinen et al. 1983; Jylhä et al. 1998) uses the options very good, fairly good, average, fairly poor, and poor. The levels and distributions of these different versions are not directly comparable, but they represent parallel assessment of the same phenomenon and show basically concordant answers (Jürges, Avedano, and Mackenbach 2008).

Multiple studies have compared the global and the age-referential, comparative question in relation to mortality. To some extent, the results vary according to the study sample, age, and model and covariates used. In some studies, both non-adjusted and age-adjusted comparative measures had shown a stronger association than the global measure, at least in older populations (Grand et al. 1990; Heidrich et al. 2002; Manderbacka et al. 2003; Vuorisalmi et al. 2005), but there are also opposite findings, and, in general, the differences are likely to be not substantively important. Because of the great sensitivity to age of the comparative measure, studies have recommended the global question over the age-referential measure for use in comparative studies and in clinical settings (Baron-Epel et al. 2004; Vuorisalmi et al. 2005).

Another methodological discussion concerns the use of one baseline measure versus time-dependent measures or measures of change in self-rated health. It is understandable that at least during a long follow-up period, health status may change and baseline self-ratings may no longer reflect current status. The best predictors of mortality therefore would seem to include both the level and the direction of the trajectory in self-rated health (Han et al. 2005). A few studies also found that direct questions on change in self-rated health may be more sensitive to change in physical health than calculated change in global self-rated health between two time points (Benitez-Silva and Ni 2008; Leinonen et al. 1998). Wang and Satariano (2007) demonstrated that the value of self-rating as a predictor of mortality is increased if, in addition to current health, the respondents also evaluate their future health status. Not many studies, however, include repeated measures and alternative indicators. The contribution of the studies that compare different versions of the question is mainly methodological, demonstrating the behavior of the variable. For practical use, self-rated health is a valuable indicator because it works as a single baseline measure.

In comparative studies, it is also important to be aware of the different meanings of crude, unadjusted values of self-rated health and values that are adjusted for other available indicators. Differences between two population groups in self-rated health adjusted for other medical and health indicators may reflect differences in knowledge about these dimensions of health, or group-specific evaluation frameworks and response styles. They can hardly be considered as measures of health status. Therefore, if self-rated health is used as a general measure of physical health status, crude or age-adjusted values may be preferred.

## Subjective Probability of Survival as a Predictor of Mortality

Subjective probability of survival, also called subjective life expectancy or self-rated life expectancy, is derived from respondents' estimates of either the length of their whole lives or the number of remaining years. At least three different questions have been used in empirical studies. First, respondents have been asked to estimate their chances of living to a given age

(Guiso et al. 2005; Hurd and McGarry 1995). Second, they have been asked a direct question, "To what age do you expect to live?" (Mirowsky 1999). Third, they have been asked how likely it is, on a four-level scale from very likely to very unlikely, that they will live another 10 years (van Doorn and Kasl 1998). These indicators have gained currency mainly in economic attempts to understand and predict individual behavior. The baseline hypothesis is that, when making decisions about investments, housing, or retirement, people take into account not only their current life situation, but also their expected future situation, most importantly their expected remaining years of life (Hurd and McGarry 2002). When the measure is used to predict behaviors such as saving or retirement decisions, it is the expectation itself that is important, not its ability to predict the actual survival, and the measure may be considered valid even if it does not predict correctly the real mortality experience. In this chapter, however, the subjective survival probability is discussed in relation to observed survival and mortality.

Up to now, only a few large-scale health studies have data on subjective probabilities of survival. In the US Health and Retirement Study (HRS) this information has been collected every 2 years since the baseline interview in 1992. In Europe, the question has recently been adopted by two major surveys, the English Longitudinal Study of Ageing (ELSA) and the Survey of Health, Ageing and Retirement in Europe (SHARE) (Delavande and Rohwedder 2009; Guiso et al. 2005). To a large extent, although not entirely, our present knowledge about the behavior of the variable comes from analyses in the HRS data.

Several studies have found that subjective life expectancy parallels the actuarial estimates in official life tables (Benitez-Silva and Ni 2008; Hurd and McGarry 1995, 2002; Mirowsky 1999; Perozek 2008; Siegel et al. 2002). Compared to the life tables, men in the HRS tended to overestimate and women to underestimate the probability of living to 75 (Hurd and McGarry 1995). In the SHARE, subjective and actuarial survival probabilities were compared for people aged 50 or older in 10 European countries. In men, subjective and actuarial survival probabilities corresponded very well until the age of 60; after that the subjective survival exceeded the actuarial figures. In women, the actuarial survivals were higher than the subjective until the age of 75; after that, as for men, subjective survival figures were higher (Guiso et al. 2005). Life tables, however, reflect present mortality and do not take into account potential changes during the lifetime of the population. Interestingly, Perozek (2008) found that subjective life expectancies in men and women foreshadowed revisions to actual cohort life tables between 1992 and 2004, implying the narrowing of the gender gap.

At least in middle-aged and older people, subjective survival probabilities predict observed mortality (Hurd and McGarry 2002; Siegel et al. 2002; Smith et al. 2001; van Doorn and Kasl 1998). In the SHARE, subjective survival probabilities were higher for those who survived about 2 years than for those who died during this time, and this was true also when the comparisons were made separately for the five self-rated health categories (Winter 2008). In the HRS, the subjective probability of living to age 75 stayed as an independent predictor of 2-year mortality in a model where several chronic conditions, smoking, body mass index (BMI), education, and demographic variables were included, and even when self-rated health was included (for relations of subjective probability of survival and self-rated health see below) (Hurd and McGarry 2002).

Several indicators known to predict lower mortality have been found to be associated with higher subjective survival probabilities, such as female gender, higher social class and higher education, being a non-smoker, having no limiting illness (Hurd and McGarry 1995; Popham and Mitchell 2007), and having a higher grip strength (Hurd, Rohwedder, and Winter 2005, cited in Delavande and Rohwedder 2009). Delavande and Rohwedder (2009) found that in each of the ten European countries analyzed in the SHARE Wave 1, the subjective probability of survival was higher for respondents with higher wealth and higher education, although the strength of the association varied. The subjective probability of survival is also associated with the age of death of the respondents' parents (Hamermesh and Hamermesh 1983; Hurd and McGarry 1995).

Hurd and McGarry (2002) analyzed longitudinal changes in the subjective survival probability of participants aged 46–64 years in the HRS. In 2 years, approximately two-thirds of respondents changed their assessment of their survival probabilities, more often for the worse: out of those who participated in both waves, four out of ten gave a lower probability in the second wave. Those with chronic conditions that appeared between the waves, and particularly those with a newly diagnosed cancer, were more likely to decrease their probability estimates. Also in the HRS data, Benitez-Silva and Ni (2008) found that newly diagnosed stroke and changed ADL mobility worsened estimates of survival probability between two waves. Curiously, newly diagnosed diabetes and newly diagnosed high blood pressure were associated with a positive change in self-rated life expectancy, possibly because the illnesses now were being treated.

## Subjective Probablity of Survival and Self-Rated Health

Subjective probability of survival shows a strong correlation with self-rated health, and with time people tend to change their assessments of both indicators in the same direction (Hurd and McGarry 1995). This is no surprise, as health is a major factor people are likely to consider when asked about their future life expectancy, and the two variables share most of their statistical determinants. One analysis indicates that when parallel changes of these two indicators are examined, change in subjective survival probability correlates more strongly with the measure that directly asks respondents to assess change in their health than with the calculated change in global self-ratings of health between two points of time (Benitez-Silva and Ni 2008).

Yet, empirical findings show important differences between the two measures. While people with incident cancer changed both their self-rated health and subjective survival probability for the worse, those with incident arthritis decreased only their health ratings, not their estimated survival probabilities (Hurd and McGarry 2002). In one study, smoking had a stronger impact on subjective survival probability than on self-rated health, whereas the General Health Questionnaire (GHQ12) showed a stronger association with self-rated health (Popham and Mitchell 2007). In adults aged 25–64 years, older people gave poorer health assessments than younger ones, but had equally long subjective estimates of total life expectancy (Popham and Mitchell 2007). In a longitudinal analysis, parents' death during the follow-up time at the age of 75 or younger was associated with decrease in subjective probability of survival but had no association with change in self-rated health (Hurd and McGarry 2002). In most studies available, subjective probability of survival and self-rated health both maintain their independent associations with mortality when introduced into the model simultaneously and together with several health and socioeconomic measures (Hurd and McGarry 2002; Siegel et al. 2002; van Doorn and Kasl 1998).

The parallel and combined analyses of subjective probability of survival and self-rated health help clarify the shared and specific characteristics of both measures. These analyses imply that to the respondents, health status and survival are not identical concepts, and the data on which the two assessments are based are not identical either. A clear difference is that the question on health refers to the present situation, while the one on survival invites people to forecast the future. From the respondents' perspective, the meaning of survival until a certain age or living another 10–20 years is clear, although the data to estimate the probability understandably are lacking; for self-rated health, multiple pieces of valid information are available, and the problem is rather how to construct a generic estimate of "health" by using this information. People's judgments about future life expectancies seem to be based on present health status, expected changes in health, and the various risk factors that may influence future health, as well as on knowledge of the actuarial life expectancy of their birth cohort and the age their parents reached. Self-rated health, again, reflects mainly the multiple dimensions of present health status, including those that are not life-threatening, such as arthritis. Both assessments require selection of relevant information and judgment about its relative importance. It is likely that contextual evaluation frameworks, including optimistic or pessimistic dispositions and cultural conventions, that are known to modify self-rated health also modify subjective survival probabilities.

To summarize, subjective probability of survival is a direct, although subjective, indicator of the probability of mortality, while self-rated health is an indicator of health status, and only indirectly related to mortality. Researchers interested in mortality may find subjective life expectancy to be their first choice. There are, however, a few methodological questions that deserve consideration when using this variable in an empirical study. In contrast to self-rated health, information on the behavior of self-rated life expectancy as a study variable is scarce and up to now comes from only a few data sets and mainly from English-speaking high-income countries; the first analyses of the SHARE data provide a European diversity, but there still is not data from other parts of the world than Europe and the United States. Therefore, the role of cultural context in the evaluation is poorly understood. The follow-up studies all cover less than 5 years, and very little information is available on the possible age differences in the ways people estimate their length of life. A few studies suggest that self-rated life expectancy may be a good predictor of mortality specifically in old age (Siegel et al. 2002; van Doorn and Kasl 1998). However, the question about the remaining years, or the time of death, is likely to be more sensitive in a situation where one cannot expect many more years than among younger people for whom death is only a distant possibility. This sensitivity may be the reason why the willingness to answer the question decreases with older age (Mirowsky 1999; Siegel et al. 2002).

## Future Research

Self-rated health and subjective probability of survival both are subjective assessments that predict mortality: self-rated health indirectly, because it reflects physical health status, and subjective probability of survival directly, as a respondent's evaluation about his or her remaining years of life. The indicators share the important characteristic that they are not standardized and no formal criteria are available for individuals to use in their assessments. Research evidence on both measures indicates that individuals have a considerable ability to identify and consider factors that affect the length of their lives.

The challenges for future research are partly shared, partly different for these two measures. It is well-established that self-rated health shows a constant and universal association with mortality in very diverse populations, in different cultures, and in different age groups. Much less is known about the behavior of subjective survival probability. For both measures, future research should shed light first on the cognitive processes of subjective evaluations, and second on the different types of information people are using as a basis of their evaluations.

The most important aspects of health and well-being that people take into account in the self-ratings of health are reasonably well-known already. Still, it is essential to know not only what these aspects are, but also how they are used in the evaluations. Qualitative studies focusing on people's own accounts and explanations could help understand the processes of negotiating, reasoning, and reflecting through which people reach a conclusion that their health is "fairly poor" or "good," and, thus, demonstrate any differences in the evaluation frameworks between population groups (Jylhä 2009).

The potential importance of different bodily sensations in self-rated health has been discussed earlier in this chapter. I suggested that through various symptoms, ailments, and feelings, people incorporate into their self-ratings important biological information that is not necessarily represented as diagnosed health conditions, and this may partly explain the association of self-rated health with mortality. In future research, two approaches would contribute to better understanding of the role of these sensations. First, information on the association of objectively measured biological and physiological parameters with self-rated health is needed to clarify the biological basis underlying subjective health status. Here, secondary analyses in already existing population studies would be appropriate. Second, we need to know how people experience and verbalize often diffuse and variable bodily sensations. Qualitative analysis inviting people to describe and explain these sensations and how they are interpreted in relation to health status would give us access to unique subjective information used in self-ratings (Jylhä 2009).

As health apparently is one major component of subjective survival probabilities, analysis of self-rated health also sheds light on self-rated life expectancy. For the latter, however, not all health information is relevant, and, on the other hand, information that does not directly concern one's own health status may be important. To investigate the validity and comparability of subjective survival probability, researchers could apply the same basic strategies as for self-rated health: statistical analyses of associated factors in large-population data sets, and qualitative analyses of the factors people themselves say they have taken into account in their evaluations. The factors external to the respondent her- or himself are perhaps of particular interest here; how do people reason about actuarial life expectancies or the ages of their parents when forecasting their own life expectancy? Like self-rated health, self-rated life expectancy is also likely to be modified by the contextual framework of evaluation. Studies from different cultural environments and different age groups are needed to predict whether, in the future, self-ratings of life expectancy will constitute as useful a variable in population studies as self-rated health.

## References

Appels, A., H. Bosma, V. Grabauskas, A. Gostautas, and F. Sturmans. 1996. "Self-Rated Health and Mortality in a Lithuanian and a Dutch Population." *Social Science and Medicine* 42(5):681–89.

Baron-Epel, O., G. Shemy, and S. Carmel. 2004. "Prediction of Survival: A Comparison Between Two Subjective Health Measures in an Elderly Population." *Social Science and Medicine* 58(10):2035–43.

Ben-Ezra, M. and D. Shmotkin. 2006. "Predictors of Mortality in the Old-Old in Israel: The Cross-Sectional and Longitudinal Aging Study." *Journal of the American Geriatrics Society* 54(6):906–11.

Benitez-Silva, H. and H. Ni. 2008. "Health Status and Health Dynamics in an Empirical Model of Expected Longevity." *Journal of Health Economics* 27:564–84.

Benjamins, M.R., R.A. Hummer, I.W. Eberstein, and C.B. Nam. 2004. "Self-Reported Health and Adult Mortality Risk: An Analysis of Cause-Specific Mortality." *Social Science and Medicine* 59(6):1297–306.

Benyamini, Y., T. Blumstein, A. Lusky, and B. Modan. 2003. "Gender Differences in the Self-Rated Health-Mortality Association: Is It Poor Self-Rated Health That Predicts Mortality or Excellent Self-Rated Health that Predicts Survival?" *The Gerontologist* 43:397–405.

Benyamini, Y. and E.L. Idler. 1999. "Community Studies Reporting Association Between Self-Rated Health and Mortality: Additional Studies, 1995 to 1998." *Research on Aging* 21:392–401.

Bosworth, H.B., I.C. Siegler, B.H. Brummett, J.C. Barefoot, R.B. Williams, N.E. Clapp-Channing, and D.B. Mark. 1999. "The Association Between Self-Rated Health and Mortality in a Well-Characterized Sample of Coronary Artery Disease Patients." *Medical Care* 37(12):1226–36.

Burstrom, B. and P. Fredlund. 2001. "Self Rated Health: Is It As Good a Predictor of Subsequent Mortality Among Adults in Lower As Well As in Higher Social Classes?" *Journal of Epidemiology and Community Health* 55(11):836–40.

Bzostek, S., N. Goldman, and A. Pebley. 2007. "Why Do Hispanics in the USA Report Poor Health?" *Social Science and Medicine* 65(5):990–1003.

Cameron, O.G. 2001. "Interoception: The Inside Story – A Model for Psychosomatic Processes." *Psychosomatic Medicine* 63(5):697–710.

Chen, H., P. Cohen, and S. Kasen. 2007. "Cohort Differences in Self-Rated Health: Evidence from a Three-Decade, Community-Based, Longitudinal Study of Women." *American Journal of Epidemiology* 166(4):439–46.

Cheng, S., H. Fung, and A. Chan. 2007. "Maintaining Self-Rated Health Through Social Comparison in Old Age." *Journals of Gerontology Series B: Psychological Sciences and Social Sciences* 62(5):P277–P85.

Cockerham, W.C., K. Sharp, and J.A. Wilcox. 1983. "Ageing and Perceived Health Status." *Journal of Gerontology* 38(3):349–55.

Craig, A.D. 2003. "Interoception: The Sense of the Physiological Condition of the Body." *Current Opinion in Neurobiology* 13(4):500–5.

Dantzer, R. 2001. "Cytokine-Induced Sickness Behavior: Where Do We Stand?" *Brain Behavior and Immunity* 15(1):7–24.

Danzer, R., J.C. O'Connor, G.G. Freund, R.W. Johnson, and K.W. Kelley. 2008. "From Inflammation to Sickness and Depression: When the Immune System Subjugates the Brain." *Nature Reviews Neuroscience* 9(1):46–57.

Deeg, D.J.H. and D.M.W. Kriegsman. 2003. "Concepts of Self-Rated Health: Specifying the Gender Difference in Mortality Risk." *Gerontologist* 43(3):376–86.

Delavande, A. and S. Rohwedder. 2009. *Differential Survival in Europe and the United States: Estimates Based on Subjective Probablitities of Survival.* Working Report 614, RAND Corporation.

DeSalvo, K.B., V.S. Fan, M.B. McDonell, and S.D. Fihn. 2005. "Predicting Mortality and Healthcare Utilization with a Single Question." *Health Research and Educational Trust* 40(4):1234–46.

Dowd, J.B. and A. Zajacova. 2007. "Does the Predictive Power of Self-Rated Health for Subsequent Mortality Risk Vary by Socioeconomic Status in the US?" *International Journal of Epidemiology* 36(6):1214–21.

Dzekedzeke, K., S. Siziya, and K. Fylkesnes. 2008. "The Impact of HIV Infection on Adult Mortality in Some Communities in Zambia: A Cohort Study." *Tropical Medicine and International Health* 13(2):152–61.

Ferraro, K. 1980. "Self-Ratings of Health Among the Old and the Old-Old." *Journal of Health and Social Behavior* 21:377–83.

Festinger, L. 1954. "A Theory of Social Comparison Processes." *Human Relations* 7:117–40.

Frankenberg, E. and N.R. Jones. 2004. "Self-Rated Health and Mortality: Does the Relationship Extend to a Low Income Setting?" *Journal of Health and Social Behavior* 45(4):441–52.

Franks, P., M.R. Gold, and K. Fiscella. 2003. "Sociodemographics, Self-Rated Health, and Mortality in the U.S." *Social Science and Medicine* 56(12):2505–14.

Fried, L.P., R.A. Kronmal, A.B. Newman, D.E. Bild, M.B. Mittelmark, J.F. Polak, J.A. Robbins, and J.M. Gardin. 1998. "Risk Factors for 5-Year Mortality in Older Adults: The Cardiovascular Health Study." *Journal of the American Medical Association* 279(8):585–92.

Giltay, E.J., J.M. Geleijnse, F.G. Zitman, T.S. Hoekstra, and E.G. Schouten. 2004. "Dispositional Optimism and All-Cause and Cardiovascular Mortality in a Prospective Cohort of Elderly Dutch Men and Women." *Archives of General Psychiatry* 61(11):1126–35.

Grand, A., P. Grosclaude, H. Bocquet, J. Pous, and J.L. Albarede. 1990. "Disability, Psychosocial Factors and

Mortality Among the Elderly in a Rural French Population." *Journal of Clinical Epidemiology* 43(8):773–82.

Guiso, L., A.Tiseno, and J.Winter. 2005. "Expectations." In A. Börsch-Supan, A. Brugiavini, H. Jürges, J. Mackenbach, J. Siegrist, and G. Weber (eds.), *Health, Aging, and Retirement in Europe*, pp. 332–38. Mannheim, Mannheim Research Institute for the Economics of Aging.

Hamermesh, D.S. and F.W. Hamesmesh. 1983. "Does perceptions of life expectancy reflect health knowledge?" *American Journal of Public Health* 73(8):911–14.

Han, B., C. Phillips, L. Ferrucci, K. Bandeen-Roche, M. Jylhä, J. Kasper, and J.M. Guralnik. 2005. "Change in Self-Rated Health and Mortality Among Community-Dwelling Disabled Older Women." *The Gerontologist* 45(2):216–21.

Heidrich, J., A.D. Liese, H. Lowel, and U. Keil. 2002. "Self-Rated Health and Its Relation to All-Cause and Cardiovascular Mortality in Southern Germany: Results From the MONICA Augsburg Cohort Study 1984–1995." *Annals of Epidemiology* 12(5):338–45.

Heikkinen, E., E. Waters, and Z. Brzezinski (eds.). 1983. *The Elderly in Eleven Countries: A Sociomedical Survey*. Copenhagen, World Health Organization, Regional Office for Europe.

Heller, D.A., F.M. Ahern, K.E. Pringle, and T.V. Brown. 2009. "Among Older Adults, the Responsiveness of Self-Rated Health Changes in Charlson Comorbidity Was Moderated by Age and Baseline Comorbidity." *Journal of Clinical Epidemiology* 62(2):177–87.

Helweg-Larsen, M., M. Kjoller, and H. Thoning. 2003. "Do Age and Social Relations Moderate the Relationship Between Self-Rated Health and Mortality Among Adult Danes?" *Social Science and Medicine* 57(7):1237–47.

Heyman, D.K. and C.C. Jeffers. 1963. "Effect of Time Lapse on Consistency of Self-Health and Medical Evaluations of Elderly Persons." *Journal of Gerontology* 18(2):160–64.

Hoeymans, N., E.J.M. Feskens, D. Kromhout, and G.A.M. Van Den Bos. 1997. "Ageing and the Relationship Between Functional Status and Self-Rated Health in Elderly Men." *Social Science and Medicine* 45(10):1527–36.

Huisman, M., F. van Lenthe, and J. Mackenbach. 2007. "The Predictive Ability of Self-Assessed Health for Mortality in Different Educational Groups." *International Journal of Epidemiology* 36(6):1207–13.

Hurd, M.D. and K. McGarry. 1995. "Evaluation of the Subjective Probabilities of Survival in the Health and Retirement Study." *Journal of Human Resources* 30:S268–S92.

Hurd, M.D. and K. McGarry. 2002. "The Predictive Validity of Subjective Probabilities of Survival." *Economic Journal* 112(482):966–85.

Idler, E. 2003. "Discussion: Gender Differences in Self-Rated Health, in Mortality, and in the Relationship Between the Two." *The Gerontologist* 43(3):372–75.

Idler, E.L. and Y. Benyamini. 1997. "Self-Rated Health and Mortality: A Review of Twenty-Seven Community Studies." *Journal of Health and Social Behavior* 38(1):21–37.

Idler, E.L., S.V. Hudson, and H. Leventhal. 1999. "The Meanings of Self-Ratings of Health: A Qualitative and Quantitative Approach." *Research on Aging* 21(3):458–76.

Idler, E.L. and S. Kasl. 1991. "Health Perceptions and Survival: Do Global Evaluations of Health Status Really Predict Mortality?" *Journal of Gerontology* 46(2):S55–S65.

Idler, E., H. Leventhal, J. McLaughlin, and E. Leventhal. 2004. "In Sickness but Not in Health: Self-Ratings, Identity, and Mortality." *Journal of Health Social Behavior* 45(3):336–56.

Ishizaki, T., I. Kai, and Y. Imanaka. 2006. "Self-Rated Health and Social Role as Predictors for 6-Year Total Mortality Among a Non-Disabled Older Japanese Population." *Archives of Gerontology and Geriatrics* 42(1):91–99.

Ishizaki, T., H. Yoshida, T. Suzuki, and H. Shibata. 2009. "The Association Between Self-Rated Health Status and Increasing Age Among Older Japanese Living in a Rural Community Over a 6-Year Period: A Longitudinal Data Analysis." *Gerontology* 55(3):344–52.

Janszky, I., M. Lekander, M. Blom, A. Georgiades, and S. Ahnve. 2005. "Self-Rated Health and Vital Exhaustion, but Not Depression, Is Related to Inflammation in Women with Coronary Heart Disease." *Brain Behavior and Immunity* 19(6):555–63.

Jürges, H., M. Avendano, and J.P. Mackenbach. 2008. "Are different measures of self-rated health comparable? An assessment in Five European Countries." *European Journal of Epidemiology* 23:772–81.

Jylhä, M. 1994. "Self-Rated Health Revisited: Exploring Survey Interview Episodes with Elderly Respondents." *Social Science and Medicine* 39(7):983–90.

Jylhä, M. 2009. "What Is Self-Rated Health and Why Does It Predict Mortality? Towards a Unified Conceptual Model." *Social Science and Medicine* 69:307–16.

Jylhä, M., J.M. Guralnik, J. Balfour, and L.F. Fried. 2001. "Walking Difficulty, Walking Speed, and Age as Determinants of Self-Rated Health: The Womens' Health and Aging Study." *Journals of Gerontology Series A: Biological Sciences and Medical Sciences* 56A(10):M609–M17.

Jylhä, M., J.M. Guralnik, L. Ferrucci, J. Jokela, and E. Heikkinen. 1998. "Is Self-Rated Health Comparable Across Cultures and Genders?" *Journals of Gerontology Series B: Psychological Sciences and Social Sciences* 53(3):S144–S52.

Jylhä, M., S. Volpato, and J.A. Guralnik. 2006. "Self-Rated Health Showed a Graded Association with Frequently Used Biomarkers in a Large Population Sample." *Journal of Clinical Epidemiology* 59(5):465–71.

Kaplan, G.A. and T. Camacho. 1983. "Perceived Health and Mortality: A Nine-Year Follow-Up of the Human Population Laboratory Cohort." *American Journal of Epidemiology* 117:292–304.

Klimas, N.G. and A.O. Koneru. 2007. "Chronic Fatigue Syndrome: Inflammation, Immune Function, and Neuroendocrine Interactions." *Current Rheumatology Reports* 9(6):482–87.

Larsson, D., T. Hemmingsson, P. Allebeck, and I. Lundberg. 2002. "Self-Rated Health and Mortality Among Young Men: What Is the Relation and How May It Be Explained?" *Scandinavian Journal of Public Health* 30(4):259–66.

Lee, S.J., S.Y. Moody-Ayers, C.S. Landefeld, L.C. Walter, K. Lindquist, M.R. Segal, and K.E. Covinsky. 2007. "The

Relationship Between Self-Rated Health and Mortality in Older Black and White Americans." *Journal of the American Geriatrics Society* 55(10):1624–29.

Leinonen, R., E. Heikkinen, and M. Jylhä. 1998. "Self-Rated Health and Self-Assessed Change in Health in Elderly Men and Women: A Five-Year Longitudinal Study." *Social Science and Medicine* 46(4–5):591–97.

Lekander, M., S. Elofsson, I.M. Neve, L.O. Hansson, and A.L. Unden. 2004. "Self-Rated Health Is Related to Levels of Circulating Cytokines." *Psychosomatic Medicine* 66(4):559–63.

Leventhal, H., E.L. Idler, and E. Leventhal. 1999. "The Impact of Chronic Illness on the Self System." In R.J. Contrada and R.D. Ashmore (eds.), *Self, Social Identity, and Physical Health*, pp. 185–208. New York, NY, Oxford University Press.

Liang, J., B.A. Shaw, N. Krause, J.M. Bennett, E. Kobayashi, T. Fukaya, and Y. Sugihara. 2005. "How Does Self-Assessed Health Change with Age? A Study of Older Adults in Japan." *Journals of Gerontology Series B: Psychological Sciences and Social Sciences* 60(4):S224–S32.

Mackenbach, J.P., J.G. Simon, C.W. Looman, and I.M. Joung. 2002. "Self-Assessed Health and Mortality: Could Psychosocial Factors Explain the Association?" *International Journal of Epidemiology* 31(6):1162–68.

Maddox, G. 1962. "Some Correlates of Differences in Self-Assessment of Health Among the Elderly." *Journal of Gerontology* 17:180–85.

Manderbacka, K., I. Kareholt, P. Martikainen, and O. Lundberg. 2003. "The Effect of Point of Reference on the Association Between Self-Rated Health and Mortality." *Social Science and Medicine* 56(7):1447–52.

Manderbacka, K., O. Lundberg, and P. Martikainen. 1999. "Do Risk Factors and Health Behaviors Contribute to Self-Ratings of Health?" *Social Science and Medicine* 48(12):1713–20.

Mantyselka, P.T., J.H. Turunen, R.S. Ahonen, and E.A. Kumpusalo. 2003. "Chronic Pain and Poor Self-Rated Health." *Journal of the American Medical Association* 290(18):2435–42.

McFadden, E., R. Luben, S. Bingham, N. Wareham, A. Kinmonth, and K. Khaw. 2009. "Self-Rated Health Does Not Explain the Socioeconomic Differential in Mortality: A Prospective Study in the EPIC-Norfolk Cohort." *Journal of Epidemiology and Community Health* 63(4):329–31.

Merton, R.K. 1957. *Social Theory and Social Structure*. Glencoe, IL, The Free Press.

Miller, A.H., S. Ancoli-Israel, J.E. Bower, L. Capuron, and M.R. Irwin. 2008. "Neuroendocrine-Immune Mechanisms of Behavioral Comorbidities in Patients with Cancer." *Journal of Clinical Oncology* 26(6):971–82.

Mirowsky, J. 1999. "Subjective Life Expectancy in the US: Correspondence to Actuarial Estimates by Age, Sex and Race." *Social Science and Medicine* 49(7):967–79.

Molarius, A. and S. Janson. 2002. "Self-Rated Health, Chronic Diseases, and Symptoms Among Middle-Aged and Elderly Men and Women." *Journal of Clinical Epidemiology* 55(4):364–70.

Mora, P.A., M.D. DiBonaventura, E. Idler, E.A. Leventhal, and H. Leventhal. 2008. "Psychological Factors Influencing Self-Assessments of Health: Toward an Understanding of the Mechanisms Underlying How People Rate Their Own Health." *Annals of Behavioral Medicine* 36(3):292–303.

Mossey, J.M. and E. Shapiro. 1982. "Self-Rated Health: A Predictor of Mortality Among the Elderly." *American Journal of Public Health* 72(8):800–8.

Mulsant, B.H., M. Ganguli, and E.C. Seaberg. 1997. "The Relationship Between Self-Rated Health and Depressive Symptoms in an Epidemiological Sample of Community-Dwelling Older Adults." *Journal of the American Geriatrics Society* 45(8):954–58.

Nielsen, A.B., V. Siersma, L.C. Hiort, T. Drivsholm, S. Kreiner, and H. Hollnagel. 2008. "Self-Rated General Health Among 40-year-old Danes and Its Association with All-Cause Mortality at 10-, 20-, and 29 years' Follow-Up." *Scandinavian Journal of Public Health* 36(1):3–11.

Nybo, H., H.C. Petersen, D. Gaist, B. Jeune, K. Andersen, M. McGue, J.W. Vaupel, and K. Christensen. 2003. "Predictors of Mortality in 2,249 Nonagenarians: The Danish 1905 Cohort Survey." *Journal of the American Geriatrics Society* 51(10):1365–73.

Palosuo, H., A. Uutela, I. Zhuravleva, and N. Lakomova. 1998. "Social Patterning of Ill Health in Helsinki and Moscow: Results From a Comparative Survey in 1991." *Social Science and Medicine* 46(9):1121–36.

Perozek, M. 2008. "Using Subjective Expectations to Forecast Longevity: Do Survey Respondents Know Something We Don't Know?" *Demography* 45(1):95–113.

Peterson, C., M.E.P. Seligman, and G.E. Vaillant. 1988. "Pessimistic Explanatory Style Is a Risk Factor for Physical Illness: A Thirty-Five-Year Longitudinal Study." *Journal of Personality and Social Psychology* 55(1):23–27.

Pfeiffer, E. 1970. "Survival in Old Age." *Journal of the American Geriatric Association* 18(4):273–85.

Popham, F. and R. Mitchell. 2007. "Self-Rated Life Expectancy and Lifetime Socioeconomic Position: Cross-Sectional Analysis of the British Household Panel Survey." *International Journal of Epidemiology* 36(1):58–65.

Quesnel-Vallee, A. 2007. "Self-Rated Health: Caught in the Crossfire of the Quest for 'True' Health?" *International Journal of Epidemiology* 36(6):1161–64.

Robine, J.M., C. Jagger, and Euro-REVES Group. 2003. "Creating a Coherent Set of Indicators to Monitor Health Across Europe – The Euro-REVES 2 Project." *European Journal of Public Health* 13:6–14.

Schoenfeld, D.E., L.C. Malmrose, D.G. Blazer, D.T. Gold, and T.E. Seeman. 1994. "Self-Rated Health and Mortality in the High-Functioning Elderly: A Closer Look at Healthy Individuals: MacArthur Field Study of Successful Aging." *Journal of Gerontology: Medical Sciences* 49(1):109–15.

Sen, A. 2002. "Health: Perception Versus Observation – Self Reported Morbidity Has Severe Limitations and Can Be Extremely Misleading." *British Medical Journal* 324(7342):860–61.

Shadbolt, B., J. Barresi, and P. Craft. 2002. "Self-Rated Health as a Predictor of Survival Among Patients With Advanced Cancer." *Journal of Clinical Oncology: Official Journal of the American Society of Clinical Oncology* 20(10):2514–19.

Siegel, M., E.H. Bradley, and S.K. Kasl. 2002. "Self-Rated Life Expectancy as a Predictor of Mortality: Evidence From the HRS and AHEAD Surveys." *Gerontology* 49:265–71.

Simon, J.G., J.B. De Boer, I.M.A. Joung, H. Bosma, and J.P. Mackenbach. 2005. "How Is Your Health in General? A Qualitative Study on Self-Assessed Health." *European Journal of Public Health* 15(2):200–08.

Singer, E., R. Garfinkel, S.M. Cohen, and L. Srole. 1976. "Mortality and Health: Evidence From the Midtown Manhattan Restudy." *Social Science and Medicine* 10(11–12):517–25.

Singh-Manoux, A., A. Gueguen, P. Martikainen, J. Ferrie, M. Marmot, and M. Shipley. 2007. "Self-Rated Health and Mortality: Short and Long-Term Associations in the Whitehall II Study." *Psychosomatic Medicine* 69(2):138–43.

Smith V.K., D.H. Taylor, and F.A. Sloan. 2001. "Longevity Expectations and Death: Can People Predict Their Own Demise?" *American Economic Review* 91(4):1126–34.

Spiers, N., C. Jagger, M. Clarke, and A. Arthur. 2003. "Are Gender Differences in the Relationship Between Self-Rated Health and Mortality Enduring? Results From Three Birth Cohorts in Melton Mowbray, United Kingdom." *Gerontologist* 43(3):406–11.

Stenback, A. 1964. "Physical Health and Physical Disease as Objective Facts and Subjective Experiences." *Archives of General Psychiatry* 11:290–301.

Steptoe, A., J. Wardle, and M. Marmot. 2005. "Positive Affect and Health-Related Neuroendocrine, Cardiovascular, and Inflammatory Processes." *Proceedings of the National Academy of Sciences of the United States of America* 102(18):6508–12.

Subramanian, S.V., M.A. Subramanyam, S. Selvaraj, and I. Kawachi. 2009. "Are Self-Reports of Health and Morbidities in Developing Countries Misleading? Evidence from India." *Social Science and Medicine* 68(2):260–65.

Suchmann, E.A., B.S. Phillips, and G.F. Streib. 1958. "Analysis of the Validity of Health Questionnaires." *Social Forces* 36:223–32.

Suls, J., C.A. Marco, and S. Tobin. 1991. "The Role of Temporal Comparison, Social-Comparison, and Direct Appraisal in the Elderlys' Self-Evaluations of Health." *Journal of Applied Social Psychology* 21(14):1125–44.

Tornstam, L. 1975. "Health and Self-Perception." *The Gerontologist* 15(3):264–70.

Unden, A., A. Andreasson, S. Elofsson, K. Brismar, L. Mathsson, J. Ronnelid, and M. Lekander. 2007. "Inflammatory Cytokines, Behavior and Age as Determinants of Self-Rated Health in Women." *Clinical Science* 112(5–6):363–73.

van Dalen, H., A. Williams, and C. Gudex. 1994. "Lay People's Evaluations of Health: Are There Differences Between Subgroups?" *Journal of Epidemiology and Community Health* 48:248–53.

van Doorn, C. and S.V. Kasl. 1998. "Can Parental Longevity and Self-Rated Life Expectancy Predict Mortality Among Older Persons? Results From an Australian Cohort." *Journals of Gerontology Series B: Psychological Sciences and Social Sciences* 53(1):S28–S34.

Vuorisalmi, M., T. Lintonen, and M. Jylhä. 2005. "Global Self-Rated Health Data from a Longitudinal Study Predicted Mortality Better Than Comparative Self-Rated Health in Old Age." *Journal of Clinical Epidemiology* 58(7):680–87.

Walker, J.D., C.J. Maxwell, D.B. Hogan, and E.M. Ebly. 2004. "Does Self-Rated Health Predict Survival in Older Persons with Cognitive Impairment?" *Journal of the American Geriatrics Society* 52(11):1895–900.

Wang, C. and W.A. Satariano. 2007. "Self-Rated Current and Future Health Independently Predict Subsequent Mortality in an Aging Population." *Journals of Gerontology Series A: Biological Sciences and Medical Sciences* 62(12):1428–34.

Wannamethee, G. and A.G. Shaper. 1991. "Self-Assessment of Health-Status and Mortality in Middle-Aged British Men." *International Journal of Epidemiology* 20(1):239–45.

Winter, J. 2008. "Expectations and Attitudes." In A. Börsch-Supan, A. Brugiavini, H. Jürges, A. Kapteyn, J. Mackenbach, J. Siegrist, and G. Weber.(eds.), *First Results from the Survey of Health, Ageing and Retirement in Europe 2004–2007*, pp. 306–11. Mannheim, Mannheim Research Institute for the Economics of Aging.

World Health Organization, Statistics Netherlands. 1996. *Health Interview Surveys: Towards International Harmonization of Methods and Instruments*. Copenhagen, WHO Office for Europe.

Yu, E.S., Y.M. Kean, D.J. Slymen, W.T. Liu, M. Zhang, and R. Katzman. 1998. "Self-Perceived Health and 5-Year Mortality Risks Among the Elderly in Shanghai, China." *American Journal of Epidemiology* 147(9):880–90.

# Chapter 17
# Religion and Adult Mortality: Group- and Individual-Level Perspectives

Ellen L. Idler

The modern scientific study of religion as a risk factor for mortality has an interesting history dating to a series of observational studies of what were called "natural experiments" published from the 1960s to 1980s (reviewed in Fraser 1986): comparisons of the mortality rates of specific religious groups with those of larger general populations. This early work has been overshadowed by more recent individual-level research on religion as a risk factor in all-cause mortality that has been the subject of recent reviews by McCullough et al. (2000), Koenig et al. (2001), Sloan and Bagiella (2001), and Powell et al. (2003). Powell et al. (2003), for example, conclude in their review of these individual-level studies that "... there is a strong, consistent, prospective and often graded reduction in risk of mortality in church/service attenders" (36). This chapter reviews the existing group- and individual-level studies that analyze the relationship between some indicator of religion, and all-cause and cause-specific mortality. Reviewing both types of studies is useful not only because of continuing high interest in understanding behavioral and social risk factors for survival, particularly in middle age and late life, but also because of the increasing interest in multilevel approaches to the analysis of social factors in health.

Because so many of the primary risk factors for mortality involve behaviors—smoking, exercise, nutrition—effective social influences on relevant behaviors are important to identify. Psychosocial health research in general, and research on religion and health specifically, has often tended to focus on the positive social support and stress-reducing coping functions of social groups, particularly during stressful life events (Krause 2001). The many studies of individuals coping with crises such as serious illness, bereavement, or unemployment, bring to light the myriad ways in which social groups provide help to individuals; these are the inclusive, friendly, helping-hand functions of social groups that Durkheim (1898 [1951]) would have called the "integrating" functions, those that reduce the alienation or estrangement of individuals from society.

Less attention in recent health research has been given to other important functions of social groups—the "regulating" functions that reduce normlessness or *anomie*, the twin threat of the modern world (along with alienation) responsible for the increase in suicide in western Europe that so concerned Durkheim (1951). Social groups (and religious groups were important exemplars for Durkheim) reduce *anomie* by providing rules for behavior and then ensuring that individuals follow the rules; they constrain and control behavior, and they may not always do this in the most friendly way. The reduction of normlessness implies that the laws, rules, or practices of the social group are imposed on individuals, and that discipline of some kind will occur if they are not adhered to. The society imposing these rules is an external, constraining social force that limits the desires of individuals ("... a thirst for novelties, unfamiliar pleasures, nameless sensations ..." 1951: 256) that Durkheim thought were insatiable and that needed to be controlled if individuals were to live together in a social order. In other words, the natural desires of individuals for material wealth, pleasure,

E.L. Idler (✉)
Department of Sociology and Rollins School of Public Health, Emory University, Atlanta, GA, 30322, USA
e-mail: eidler@emory.edu

status, and other "goods" cannot ever be satisfied, they can only be disciplined and controlled.

An application of the latter approach to understanding the impact of psychosocial influences in health is Umberson (1987), who showed the important health consequences of the regulating, constraining, social control functions of families. With data from a US adult national sample, Umberson demonstrated that married persons and parents had consistently better health practices with respect to drinking problems, substance use, and risk-taking, and she argues that "the family relationship of marriage and parenting may provide external regulation and facilitate self-regulation of health behaviors which can affect health" (1987: 306). Later studies have shown that unmarried persons are more likely than married persons to report multiple unhealthy behaviors (Laaksonen et al. 2003). Waite and Lehrer (2003) argue that religion and marriage ("... both clearly on everyone's short list of 'most important institutions' ...") function in similar ways in benefiting health: they provide social support and integration and they regulate healthy lifestyles. Religion and marriage reinforce each other by affecting joint activities, enhancing and maintaining social networks and contacts, and reinforcing common beliefs and values (Waite and Lehrer 2003: 255). Both religion and marriage are highly effective social control mechanisms, to which individuals make serious, frequently permanent commitments, and for which they almost always sacrifice some measure of self-interest for a greater good.

This chapter reviews the available literature on religion and mortality to assess the existence and strength of the association between them, and to describe evidence of the mechanism(s) of association, with particular attention to the social control of unhealthy behaviors as a fundamental reason for the beneficial effect of religion on mortality outcomes. The purpose is not to dispute the importance of the more frequently studied integrative functions of religion and spirituality in providing social support, intimacy, and emotional closeness. It is simply to draw more attention to the importance of religion's role in improving health-risk profiles through the establishment and effective enforcement of norms. Evidence for this perspective will be found if we see differences in behavior-dependent mortality risks between religious groups/individuals when compared with the general population, and if adjustment for those differences appears to account for some, most, or all of the effect of religion on all-cause and cause-specific mortality.

## Methods

Studies were identified for the review by searching Medline for the combination of terms (mortality, religio-); by identifying studies in the reviews of religion and all-cause mortality cited above as well as two earlier, excellent reviews by Jarvis and Northcott (1987) and Levin and Vanderpool (1987); and by following citations from the studies found. Only studies of population-based, representative samples in English language publications were included; that is, I excluded the very large number of clinical, patient-based samples. Where there were multiple published analyses of a single data set, the study with the longest follow-up and/or the analysis of data from the full sample was used. Related analyses of these data sets are noted in footnotes at the bottom of the tables. The identified studies fell naturally into two quite different groups. The first set (group-level, presented in Table 17.1) comprises studies of specific religious groups whose distinctive lifestyles set them apart from population norms on one or more known risk factors for all-cause or cause-specific mortality. Comparisons between the number of deaths in the religious group and the regional or national population from which it came are made, primarily using standardized mortality ratios (SMRs). The SMR compares the observed deaths in the religious group to the number it would be expected to have if its population were age-adjusted to the comparison population; SMRs less than 1.0 represent a lower risk, SMRs more than 1.0 indicate excess risk (in some studies the SMR is multiplied by 100). An SMR of 0.50 (or 50), for example, represents a mortality rate that is half that of the comparison population. SMRs are usually reported in the article with 95% confidence intervals or $p$ values for statistical significance (Newell 1988), and I include that information.

The second set of studies (individual level, presented in Table 17.2) focuses on measures of religiousness as a characteristic of individuals; most often the behavioral indicator of attendance at religious services is used (while the individual's specific religious affiliation, the focus of Table 17.1, is ignored). These

**Table 17.1** Results of studies comparing all-cause and cause-specific mortality of specific religious groups to state, US, or other country general population

| Study | Data period | Religious group population | Reference population | Cause of death | SMR Males | SMR Females | Authors' attributed causal mechanism |
|---|---|---|---|---|---|---|---|
| *Amish* | | | | | | | |
| Hamman et al. (1981) | 1960–1975 15 years | US Amish in Ohio, Indiana, and Pennsylvania counties Ages 40–69, 70+ N = 896 deaths | Non-Amish neighbors in Ohio, Indiana, and Pennsylvania counties Ages 40–69, 70+ N = 52,800 deaths | All causes ICD-8 000-999 ICD-7 001-999 Ages 40–69 Ages 70+ Circulatory system ICD-8 390-458 ICD-7 400-468 | 0.61*** 0.88* | 0.98 1.19** | "The different patterns for Amish males and females for several causes, including neoplasms, cardiovascular diseases and external trauma may indicate important differences in the exposure to hazardous environmental agents." (p. 859) |
| | | | 1970 US whites Ages 40–69 | Ages 40–69 Ages 70+ All causes ICD-8 000-999 ICD-7 001-999 Circulatory system ICD-8 390-458 ICD-7 400-468 | 0.65*** 0.97 0.55*** 0.63*** | 0.89 1.34*** 0.96 0.95 | |
| *Seventh-Day Adventists* | | | | | | | |
| Phillips et al. (1978)[a] | 1960–1965 5 years | California Seventh-Day Adventists (SDA) Ages 35+ N = 24,044 | California population Ages 35+ | Coronary heart disease[e] Age 35–64 Age 65+ | 0.26[c] 0.51[c] | 0.34[c] 0.48[c] | "The low CHD risk in SDAs is due either to some component of the SDA lifestyle or to selective factors.... It is likely that a large portion of the reduced risk of CHD deaths in SDAs can be attributed to their lack of smoking." (pp. S193–94) |

**Table 17.1** (continued)

| Study | Data period | Religious group population | Reference population | Cause of death | SMR (standardized mortality ratios) for religious groups reference = 1.0 (or other statistical test as specified) Males | SMR Females | Authors' attributed causal mechanism |
|---|---|---|---|---|---|---|---|
| Phillips et al. (1980) | 1960–1976 16 years | California Seventh-Day Adventists (SDA) Ages 35+ whites $N = 30,665$ | California American Cancer Society Study (non-SDA) Ages 35+ whites $N = 112,726$ | All causes | 0.66** | 0.88** | "Among males, the clear relationship between the Health Habit Index and risk of fatal…, coronary heart disease, 'other circulatory disease,' and nonmalignant-noncirculatory disease strongly suggests that one or more of the typical SDA lifestyle are protective for these diseases." (p. 310) |
|  |  |  |  | Coronary heart disease[e] | 0.66** | 0.98 |  |
|  |  |  |  | Cerebrovascular disease[e] | 0.72** | 0.82** |  |
|  |  |  |  | Other circulatory disease[e] | 0.64** | 0.92 |  |
| Berkel and de Waard (1983) | 1968–1977 9 years | Netherlands Seventh-Day Adventists $N = 3,217$; 522 deaths | Dutch population | All causes |  | 0.45** | "We therefore conclude that because of their unique lifestyle (non-smoking, more appropriate diet) the mortality pattern of SDAs in the Netherlands differs significantly from that of the total Dutch population." (p. 459) |
|  |  |  |  | Cardiovascular diseases ICD-8 390-458 |  | 0.41** |  |
|  |  |  |  | Ischemic heart diseases ICD-8 410-414 |  | 0.43** |  |
|  |  |  |  | Cerebrovascular diseases ICD-8 430-438 |  | 0.54** |  |
|  |  |  |  | Neoplasms ICD-9 140-209 |  | 0.50** |  |

Table 17.1 (continued)

| Study | Data period | Religious group population | Reference population | Cause of death | SMR Males | SMR Females | Authors' attributed causal mechanism |
|---|---|---|---|---|---|---|---|
| Jedrychowski et al. (1985) | 1972–1983 10 years | Polish Seventh-Day Adventists (SDA) N = 86 males; 11 deaths N = 150 females; 24 deaths | Polish urban population | All causes Age 30–39 SDA Non-SDA Age 80–89 SDA Non-SDA | Survival probability 0.985 0.925 0.464 0.039 | Survival probability 1.000 0.959 0.358 0.129 | "The results obtained are not really unexpected, since abstinence from smoking and alcoholic drinks is in fact observed by all or, at least, most of the church members." (pp. 51–52) |
| Fønnebø (1992) | 1962–1986 24 years | Norwegian Seventh-Day Adventists (SDA) N = 2,476 males; 815 deaths, 4,697 females; 1,661 deaths | European population | All causes Cardiovascular diseases ICD-9 390-459, 798.1 Age at entry to SDA < 19 Age at entry to SDA 19–34 Age at entry to SDA 35+ | 0.82*** 0.44 0.76 0.87[d] | 0.95 0.52 0.79 1.02[d] | "Establishing a healthy lifestyle in childhood and early teenage seems to be of substantial importance for later cardiovascular death risk.... Converting after the age of 35 seems, however, to be associated with a much smaller benefit in mortality." (p. 165) |

*Mormons (Latter-Day Saints)*

| Study | Data period | Religious group population | Reference population | Cause of death | Males | Females | Authors' attributed causal mechanism |
|---|---|---|---|---|---|---|---|
| Enstrom (1975) | 1950, 1960, 1970 | Utah Mormons California Mormons | Utah non-Mormons California non-Mormons | All causes 1970 Utah Mormon Non-Mormon 1960 Mormon Non-Mormon 1950 Mormon Non-Mormon 1970 California Mormon Non-Mormon 1960 Mormon Non-Mormon 1950 Mormon Non-Mormon | Crude mortality rate per 1,000 6.0 8.4 6.0 8.4 6.4 9.0 4.5 8.4 4.6 8.7 5.5 9.3 | | "It remains to be determined exactly what components of Mormon lifestyle, including the 'Word of Wisdom' are related to their low mortality rates. Several possible factors are: low consumption of tobacco, alcohol, coffee, tea, soft drinks, and drugs; certain dietary habits; general health practices, including exercise and proper sleep and weight; various social and psychological aspects connected with the nature of their religion; and other environmental effects." (p. 840) |

**Table 17.1** (continued)

| Study | Data period | Religious group population | Reference population | Cause of death | SMR Males | SMR Females | Authors' attributed causal mechanism |
|---|---|---|---|---|---|---|---|
| Lyon et al. (1978) | 1969–1971 2 years | Utah Mormons Ages 30+ N = 3,782 cardiovascular disease deaths | US whites | Rheumatic heart disease | 1.55** | 1.51** | "The favorable cardiovascular mortality in Utah is primarily due to the more favorable experience for IHD enjoyed by the Mormon portion of the population and is partly explained by lower consumption of cigarettes." (p. 365) |
| | | | | ICDA-8 390-398 Hypertensive heart disease | 0.57** | 0.73* | |
| | | | | ICDA-8 400-404 Ischemic heart disease | 0.64** | 0.65** | |
| | | | | ICDA-8 410-413 Acute ischemic heart disease[e] | 0.71** | 0.60** | |
| | | | | Chronic ischemic heart disease[e] | 0.54** | 0.70** | |
| Jarvis (1977) | 1967–1975 8 years | Alberta, Canada Mormons N = 1,120 deaths | Alberta, Canada population | All causes | 0.76 | 0.90 | "… more research is needed to ascertain the effects of the use of meat, coffee, tea, and other dietary elements as well as the possible effects of athletic fitness programs, family solidarity, extensive social participation, and stress-reducing religious ideology." (p. 301) |
| | | | | Circulatory disease[e] | 0.72** | 0.93 | |
| | | | | Ischemic heart disease[e] | 0.62** | 0.71** | |
| | | | | Cerebrovascular disease[e] | 0.71** | 1.03 | |
| Enstrom (1980) | California 1968–1975 7 years Utah 1970, 1975 2 years | California Mormons N = 6,460 male deaths N = 6,109 female deaths Utah active Mormon males 1970 884 deaths 1975 972 deaths | 1970 US whites | California Mormons Smoking-related cancer[e] | 58[c] | 80[c] | "… California Mormons, particularly active Mormon males, are a low-risk population, with cancer mortality patterns not clearly explained by their smoking habits. This population is excellent for epidemiologic investigation because it appears to be demographically and socioeconomically similar to the general white population, and yet has several distinct health-related characteristics that could be related to its low risk of cancer." (p.1082) |
| | | | | Non-smoking-related cancer[e] | 74[c] | 83[c] | |
| | | | | Utah active Mormon males Smoking-related cancer[e] | 19[c] | (No females) | |
| | | | | Non-smoking-related cancer[e] | 68[c] | | |

Table 17.1 (continued)

| Study | Data period | Religious group population | Reference population | Cause of death | SMR (standardized mortality ratios) for religious groups reference = 1.0 (or other statistical test as specified) Males | Females | Authors' attributed causal mechanism |
|---|---|---|---|---|---|---|---|
| Enstrom (1989) | 1980–1987 7 years | California Mormon High Priest cohort Ages 25–99 N = 5,231 Mormon high priests; 406 deaths, 4613 wives; 206 deaths | US whites | All causes | 0.47[c] | 0.66[c] | "... the overall SMRs for the high priest cohort appear to be reasonably well explained by the fact that the cohort consists of white nonsmokers who attend church weekly." (p. 1812) |
| | | | | Cardiovascular diseases ICD-9 390-459 | 0.52[c] | 0.64[c] | |
| Enstrom and Breslow (2008) | 1980–2004 24 years | California Mormon High Priest cohort Ages 25–99 N = 5,223 Mormon high priests; 1,897 deaths, 4,592 wives; 1,123 deaths | National Health Interview Survey Cancer Risk Factor Supplement 1988–1997 Ages 25–99 N = 15,872 whites 1997 deaths | All causes, entire cohort | 0.54[c] | 0.61[c] | "The death rates observed among these active California Mormons were largely explained by four basic lifestyle characteristics associated with long-term 'regularity of life'." (p. 135) |
| | | | | Optimum subgroup (Never smoker & 12+ education and married and weekly attender) | 0.45[c] | 0.55[c] | |
| | | | | Optimum subgroup, plus moderate BMI & physical activity and 7–8 h sleep | 0.40[c] | 0.47[c] | |

JEWS

| Study | Data period | Religious group population | Reference population | Cause of death | Average annual age-adjusted death rate Males | Average annual age-adjusted death rate Females | Authors' attributed causal mechanism |
|---|---|---|---|---|---|---|---|
| Herman and Enterline (1970) | 1953–1967 14 years | Jewish residents of Pittsburgh, PA in 40 census tracts Ages 45+ N = 13,240 115 lung cancer deaths | Non-Jewish residents of Pittsburgh, PA in 40 census tracts N = 39,122 572 lung cancer deaths | Lung cancer, International Statistical Classification (ISC) Nos. 162–163 | | | "... the low lung cancer death rate among Jewish males might be due to their low rate of cigarette smoking ... cigarette smoking may not be the reason for the high death rate of the Jewish females relative to other females." (p. 363) |
| | | | | Jews | 92.5/100,000 | 41.8/100,000 | |
| | | | | Non-Jews | 148.6/100,000 | 21.7/100,000 | |

**Table 17.1** (continued)

| Study | Data period | Religious group population | Reference population | Cause of death | SMR (standardized mortality ratios) for religious groups reference = 1.0 (or other statistical test as specified) Males | Females | Authors' attributed causal mechanism |
|---|---|---|---|---|---|---|---|
| Friedlander et al. (1995) | 1972 and 1983 | Israeli population, in 65 standard census units | Census units compared by income, education, ethnicity, religious party voting, proximity to health care, marital status, industrial jobs, women in labor force | Religion as predictor of life expectancy at age 65<br><br>1983<br>1972 | Regression coefficient<br><br>4.606***<br>ns | Regression coefficient<br><br>4.078***<br>ns | "Frequent visits to the synagogue for various religious activities, work with communal mutual aid organizations, and other voluntary activities may be assumed to provide purpose and moral strength at old age, which may contribute to higher life expectancies." (p. 74) |
| Kark et al. (1996) | 1970–1985 15 years | 11 Israeli religious Kibbutzim members aged 35+<br>$N = 924$ men; 853 women; 69 deaths | 11 Israeli secular Kibbutzim members aged 35+, matched to religious kibbutzim on: location, hospital used, size, date of founding<br>$N = 1072$ men; 1051 women; 199 deaths | All causes<br><br><br><br>Coronary heart disease<br>ICD-9 410-414<br>All circulatory conditions<br>ICD-9 390-459 | Age-adjusted rate ratio (compares secular to religious)<br>1.76 (1.26,2.46)<br>2.4 (1.3,4.42)<br>1.88 (1.14,3.1) | Age-adjusted rate ratio (compares secular to religious)<br>2.72 (1.6,4.62)<br>1.31 (0.54,3.18)<br>1.73 (0.77,3.89) | "Differences in the more traditional risk factors such as diet, smoking, obesity, alcohol intake, exercise, and exposure to accidents might play a role.... A cogent explanation for the salutary effect of living on a religious kibbutz would need to relate to a pervasive protectivity evident for all main causes of death.... A major possibility is that such a social environment induces less stress, enhances host resistance, and promotes overall well-being and a positive health status." (p. 345) |

# 17 Religion and Adult Mortality

**Table 17.1** (continued)

| Study | Data period | Religious group population | Reference population | Cause of death | SMR Males | SMR Females | Authors' attributed causal mechanism |
|---|---|---|---|---|---|---|---|
| *Clergy/Religious Orders* | | | | | | | |
| Taylor et al. (1959) | 1870–1954 84 years | Three New York and Massachusetts women's religious orders, birth cohorts 1870–1909 N = 2,637; 773 deaths | Massachusetts females born 1870–1909 | All causes<br><br>Religious orders Massachusetts Diseases of cardiovascular and renal systems ICD-6<br>Religious orders Massachusetts Cancer deaths all sites[e]<br>Religious orders Massachusetts | No males in population | Deaths per 1,000<br>698.4<br>694.4<br><br><br>268.3<br>337.4<br><br>122.4<br>117.7 | "These results agree in general with other studies and with United States mortality rates for single and married women." (p. 1221) |
| King et al. (1975) | 1951–1960 9 years | US United Presbyterian clergy N = 9,160; 1,932 deaths US Missouri Synod Lutheran clergy N = 4,689; 625 deaths | 1955 US white males | All causes Diseases of cardiovascular and renal systems ICD-7 330-334, 400-468, 592-594 | 0.72[f]<br><br><br>0.75[f] | Few women in population | "... the influence of the clerical life-style in general is often cited as an important factor. Selectivity could be another contributing element: those who are healthier may be more likely to enter into or complete the college and seminary training required." (p. 252) |

**Table 17.1** (continued)

| Study | Data period | Religious group population | Reference population | Cause of death | SMR Males | SMR Females | Authors' attributed causal mechanism |
|---|---|---|---|---|---|---|---|
| King and Locke (1980) | 1950–1960 10 years | US Protestant clergymen $N = 28,134$; 5,207 deaths | 1955 US white males Ages 20+ | All causes | 72 (70–74) | Few women in population | "… Protestant clergymen constitute a population at low risk of developing most diseases and cancers at various sites that may be partly a reflection of their being predominantly from the upper classes." (p. 1121) |
| | | | | Cardiovascular-renal diseases ICD-7 330-334, 400-468, 592-594 | 74 (71–77) | | |
| | | | | Malignant neoplasms ICD-7 140-205 | 63 (58–68) | | |
| Locke and King (1980) | 1950–1959 10 years | American Baptist convention clergy $N = 3,446$; 654 deaths | 1955 US white males Ages 20+ | All causes | 69 (64–75) | No women in population | "… some of the relatively unfavorable health effects stemming from the ascribed status of Baptist ministers, based on 'father's occupation,' would have been attenuated by other positive influences associated with the achieved educational status of these clergymen." (p. 589) |
| | | | | Cardiovascular-renal diseases ICD7 330-334; 400-468; 592-594 | 76 (69–83) | | |
| | | | | Malignant neoplasms ICD7 140-205 | 62 (50–76) | | |
| Ogata et al. (1984) | 1955–1978 23 years | Japanese Zen Buddhist priests $N = 4,352$; 1,396 deaths | Japanese males Ages 20+ | All-cause mortality | 0.82*** | No women in population | "Finally, their reputable moderate attitude in all the aspects of daily life and their mental stableness, both of which could be cultivated by practicing self control under the daily discipline of Zen, … such mental state is believed to exert an over all beneficial effect on their health." (p. 165) |
| | | | | Cerebrovascular diseases ICD-8 430-438 | 0.78*** | | |
| | | | | Heart diseases ICD-8 410-414, 420-429 | 0.93 | | |
| | | | | Hypertensive diseases ICD-8 400-404 | 0.50*** | | |

**Table 17.1** (continued)

| Study | Data period | Religious group population | Reference population | Cause of death | SMR Males (Regression coefficient) | Females | Authors' attributed causal mechanism |
|---|---|---|---|---|---|---|---|
| *Geographic Concentration* | | | | | | | |
| Dwyer et al. (1990) | 1968–1980 13 years | US County concentrations of Conservative Protestants, Moderate Protestants, Liberal Protestants, Catholics, Jews, Mormons N = 3,063 counties | US County concentrations of noncommunicants | Cancer deaths[e] 1968–70 | | | "In general, counties with high concentrations of conservative Protestants, moderate Protestants, or Mormons have the lowest cancer mortality rates. Conversely, counties with greater proportions of liberal Protestants, Catholic, and Jewish communicants have higher cancer mortality rates. The overall consistency of this interpretation suggests that a conservative-versus-liberal dichotomy may represent this relationship effectively in future research. ...Religion may have structural properties that transcend individual health behavior choices and influence the social context in which people make lifestyle decisions that affect those behaviors." (p. 197) |
| | | | | Conservative Protestants | −0.002** | | |
| | | | | Moderate Protestants | −0.005** | | |
| | | | | Liberal Protestants | 0.003 | | |
| | | | | Catholic | −0.007 | | |
| | | | | Jewish | 0.154** | | |
| | | | | Mormon | −0.004** | | |
| | | | | Cancer deaths[e] 1971–75 | | | |
| | | | | Conservative Protestants | −0.009 | | |
| | | | | Moderate Protestants | −0.002* | | |
| | | | | Liberal Protestants | 0.006** | | |
| | | | | Catholic | −0.005 | | |

**Table 17.1** (continued)

| Study | Data period | Religious group population | Reference population | Cause of death | SMR Males | SMR Females | Authors' attributed causal mechanism |
|---|---|---|---|---|---|---|---|
| | | | | Jewish | 0.047 | | |
| | | | | Mormon | −0.004** | | |
| | | | | Cancer deaths[e] 1976–80 | | | |
| | | | | Conservative Protestants | −0.001** | | |
| | | | | Moderate Protestants | −0.004** | | |
| | | | | Liberal Protestants | −0.002 | | |
| | | | | Catholic | −0.008* | | |
| | | | | Jewish | 0.067* | | |
| | | | | Mormon | −0.004** | | |

SMR = Standardized mortality ratio (comparison to US or State population).
MR = Mortality ratio (age-adjusted for comparison to selected group).
ns = Not significant.
[a]Note related study: Lemon and Kuzma (1969)
[b]Note related study: Fønnebø 1994
[c]95% confidence interval does not include 1.0
[d]Test for linear trend across categories: p < 0.001
[e]ICD code or codes not given
[f]Significance level not reported
*0.01 < p ≤ 0.05
**0.001 < p ≤ 0.01
***p ≤ 0.001

Table 17.2  Results of studies reporting all-cause and cause-specific mortality by individual differences in religiousness

| Study | Period of follow-up | Sample | Measure of religiousness | Cause of death / Religion measure | Results[a] Males | Results[a] Females | Authors' comment on mechanism of association |
|---|---|---|---|---|---|---|---|
| *US regional samples* | | | | | | | |
| House et al. (1982) | 1967–1979 12 years | Tecumseh Community Health Study (MI) Ages 35–69 N = 2,754 Deaths = 259 | Religious attendance More than once a week Not in last year | All-cause mortality More than once a week Not in last year | Multiple logistic coefficient −0.018 | Multiple logistic coefficient −0.134** | "Social relationships and activities have been considered beneficial to human health and well-being because they give people a sense of belonging and support, because they give people reasons for living that transcend their individual selves, and because they may in various ways influence people to engage in more preventive and therapeutic health behaviors." (pp. 139–140) |
| Schoenbach et al. (1986) | 1967–1980 13 years | Evans County Cardiovascular Epidemiologic Study (GA) Ages 15+ N = 2,059 1,013 deaths | Spends spare time in church activities (yes/no) | All-cause mortality Whites No church activities Church activities Blacks No church activities Church activities | Hazard ratio 1.5 (1.1–2.0) 1.0 0.9 (0.6–1.3) 1.0 | Hazard ratio 1.2 (0.8–1.2) 1.0 1.4 (0.9–2.1) 1.0 | "The specific social ties we studied may have different meanings and effects in a fast-growing, industrialized, urban population like Alameda County than in a comparatively stable, predominantly rural society in which individuals have deep roots and long associations with community, church, family, and land. Because of this stability and lower population density in Evans County, ordinary daily activities provide opportunities for social affirmation and support even for individuals who have few close friends and family." (p. 589) |
| Eaker et al. (1992) | 1965–1985 20 years | Framingham Study (MA) Ages 45–64 N = 749 females | Religious attendance: More than once a week 1–3 times per month Less than once a month Rarely | Myocardial infarction (incidence, fatal or nonfatal) and coronary mortality[g] More than once a week 1–3 times per month Less than once a month Rarely | No males in sample | No significant differences in multivariate analyses | "When all women were analyzed together, those who rarely attended religious services … were significantly more likely to develop definite coronary disease than women in the more positive categories of these variables." (p. 860) [But when physiological and behavioral risk factors were included, the association was no longer significant.] |

**Table 17.2** (continued)

| Study | Period of follow-up | Sample | Measure of religiousness | Cause of death / Religion measure | Results[a] Males | Females | Authors' comment on mechanism of association |
|---|---|---|---|---|---|---|---|
| Oman and Reed (1998) | 1990–1995 5 years | Marin County (CA) Ages 55+ N = 2,025 Deaths = 454 | Religious attendance: 3+ times per week / 1–2 times per week / 1–3 times per month / Less than 1 per month / Never | All-cause mortality Weekly / Occasional / Never | | Relative hazard 0.72 (0.55, 0.93) 0.80 (0.62, 1.03) 1.0 | "... attendance at religious services predicted lower mortality in an affluent elderly White population ... Even after controlling for 6 classes of potential confounding and intervening variables, we were unable to explain the protection against mortality offered by religious attendance." (p. 1474) |
| Oman et al. (2002)[b] | 1965–1996 31 years | Alameda County Study (CA) N = 6,545 Ages 21+ | Religious attendance: Never / Once or twice a year / Every month or so, Once or twice a month / Every week | All-cause mortality Less than weekly Weekly Circulatory disease ICD-9 390-459 Less than weekly Weekly | | Hazard ratio 1.21** 1.0 Hazard ratio 1.21* 1.0 | "The association of religious involvement with mortality reductions across many causes of death suggests the importance of continued study of how religious involvement affects health, and how knowledge of the underlying processes might inform individual and community-level health promotion and disease prevention efforts." (p. 84) |
| Lutgendorf et al. (2004) | 1982–1994 12 years | Iowa Established Populations for the Epidemiologic Studies of the Elderly (IA) Ages 65+ N = 557 Deaths = 111 | Religious attendance: Never / 1–2 times per year / Every few months / 1–2 times per month / Weekly / More than once a week | All-cause mortality Attendance -> IL-6 IL-6 -> Mortality | Structural equation model path coefficients −0.10* 0.19* | | "The data presented here are prospective and consistent with the interpretation that religious attendance is associated with lower IL-6 levels, which in turn may contribute to decreased pathogenic processes, resulting in enhanced survival." (p. 473) |

## 17 Religion and Adult Mortality

**Table 17.2** (continued)

| Study | Period of follow-up | Sample | Measure of religiousness | Cause of death / Religion measure | Results[a] Males | Results[a] Females | Authors' comment on mechanism of association |
|---|---|---|---|---|---|---|---|
| Bagiella et al. (2005) | 1981–1987 6 years | Established Populations for the Epidemiologic Studies of the Elderly (NC, CT, MA, IA) Age 65+ N = 14,456 Deaths = 4,499 | Religious attendance: Never 1–2 times per year Every few months Once a week More than once a week | All-cause mortality Once a week/ More than once a week 1–2 times per year/ Every few months Never | | Risk ratio 0.78 (0.70, 0.88) 0.92 (0.80, 1.04) 1.0 | "We speculate that remaining socially engaged in one's community is the operative factor in studies demonstrating relationships between religious attendance and mortality: religious attendance may represent one of the many different ways of remaining socially engaged and the degree to which it is expressed in relationship to mortality depends upon the opportunities for involvement in social activities available in different communities." (p. 450) |
| Hill et al. (2005) | 1993–2001 8 years | Hispanic Established Populations for the Epidemiologic Studies of the Elderly (TX, CA, NM, AZ, CO) Age 65+ N = 3,050 Deaths = 933 | Religious attendance: More than 1 per week Almost every week 1–2 times per month Several times a year Never | All-cause mortality More than 1 per week Almost every week 1–2 times per month Several times a year Never | | Hazard ratio 0.96 0.68** 0.80 0.86 1.0 | "We find that general social resources have no mediating influence. More specific measures of church-based social support might help to explain some of the association." (S108) |
| Dupre et al. (2006)[c] | 1986–1996 10 years | Piedmont Established Populations for Epidemiologic Studies of the Elderly (NC) Age 65+ N = 4,136 | Religious attendance: Never/almost never Once or twice a year Every few months Once or twice a month Once a week More than once a week | All-cause mortality Never Less than once a week Weekly or more | Log odds coefficients 0.35*** 0.22*** reference | Log odds coefficients 0.47*** 0.29*** reference | "Although the relationship between attendance and mortality is reduced after taking into account differences in health practices, the association remains robust for both men and women. As expected, the attenuation of the religion effect is greater for men (17%) than for women (10%)." (p. 159) |

**Table 17.2** (continued)

| Study | Period of follow-up | Sample | Measure of religiousness | Cause of death / Religion measure | Results[a] Males | Females | Authors' comment on mechanism of association |
|---|---|---|---|---|---|---|---|
| Østbye et al. (2006) | 1998–2005 7 years | Cache County Memory Study (UT) Ages 65+ N = 2,768 | Meditate Volunteer in religious organization Read scriptures Attend worship service Direct experience of God Visits from people at church | All-cause mortality Meditate Volunteer in religious organization Read scriptures Attend worship service Direct experience of God Visits from people at church | Relative rate (Cox models) ns 0.78 (0.61, 0.99) ns ns ns 1.43 (1.12, 1.81) | | "... volunteering is associated with enhanced survival, whereas having visits from church members increases with age and is predictive of mortality, which seems to indicate the increased aid and attention given by the church community to those who are the sickest." (p. 207) |

*US national samples*

| Rogers (1996)[d] | 1984–1991 7 years | National Health Interview Survey, Supplement on Aging (US) Ages 55+ N = 15,938 Deaths = 4,116 | Religious attendance in last 2 weeks | All-cause mortality Attended church or temple in last 2 weeks Did not attend church or temple | Logit coefficient −0.244*** reference | | No comment is made on findings concerning religious attendance. |
| Krause (1998) | 1992–1997 5 years | Medicare Beneficiary Eligibility Sample (US) Ages 65+ N = 819 Deaths = 173 | Organizational religiosity Nonorgani- zational religiosity Religious coping | All-cause mortality Organizational religiosity Nonorganizational religiosity Religious coping | Odds ratio 0.88 (0.79, 0.98) 0.99 (0.86, 1.14) 1.14 (1.02, 1.29) | | "... older adults who are more involved in the activities of formal religious institutions are less likely to die during the follow-up period than older adults with lower levels of organizational religiosity... However, greater use of religious coping responses increases the odds of dying..." (pp. 248, 250) |

**Table 17.2** (continued)

| Study | Period of follow-up | Sample | Measure of religiousness | Cause of death Religion measure | Results[a] Males | Females | Authors' comment on mechanism of association |
|---|---|---|---|---|---|---|---|
| Hummer et al. (1999)[e] | 1987–1995 8 years | National Health Interview Survey Cancer Risk Factor Supplement-Epidemiology Study (US) Ages 18–89 N = 21,204 2,016 deaths | Religious attendance: Never Less than once a week Once a week More than once a week | All-cause mortality Never Less than once a week Once a week More than once a week Circulatory disease ICD-9 390-459 Never Less than once a week Once a week More than once a week Cancer ICD-9 140-239 Never Less than once a week Once a week More than once a week | | Hazard ratio 1.50** 1.24* 1.21* 1.0 Hazard ratio 1.32+ 1.18 1.14 1.0 Hazard ratio 1.14 1.03 1.09 1.0 | "... religion, like socioeconomic status, might best be conceptualized as a 'fundamental cause' of mortality (Link and Phelan 1995). That is, a fundamental cause of mortality is multidimensional, allows for access to important resources, affects various health and cause-of-death outcomes, and may even maintain an association with health and mortality when intervening mechanisms change over time ..." (p. 283) |
| Eng et al. (2002) | 1988–1998 10 years | Health Professionals Follow-up Study (US) Ages 40–75 N = 28,369 males; 1,365 deaths | Religious attendance: Never/almost never Once per year or more | All-cause mortality Never/almost never Once per year or more Cardiovascular disease ICD-9 410-414, 798 Never/almost never Once per year or more | Relative risk 1.15 (1.02, 1.3) 1.0 Relative risk 1.21 (0.95, 1.53) 1.0 | No females in sample | "In addition, every additional [increase over baseline] religious service attendance per month was associated with a significant, although modest decline [in all-cause mortality] of 7 percent." (p. 706) |
| Musick et al. (2004) | 1986–1994 7.5 years | Americans' Changing Lives study (US) Ages 25+ N = 3,617 Deaths = 542 | Religious attendance Volunteer for church Subjectivity religiosity Private religious activity Negative justice Fatalism | All-cause mortality >1/Week 1/Week 1-3 times/month Never Volunteer for church Subjectivity religiosity Private activity Negative justice Fatalism | | Hazard ratio 0.65* 0.65* 0.69* Reference 1.01 1.09 1.07 1.04 1.02 | "Consistent with prior research, the analyses show that several indicators of health behaviors or lifestyle, notably physical activity, mediate perhaps 20–30 percent of the protective effect of church attendance, with social relationships and supports adding marginally to that mediation." (p. 208) |

**Table 17.2** (continued)

| Study | Period of follow-up | Sample | Measure of religiousness | Cause of death / Religion measure | Results[a] Males | Females | Authors' comment on mechanism of association |
|---|---|---|---|---|---|---|---|
| Gillum et al. (2008) | 1988–2000 12 years | National Health and Nutrition Examination Survey III (US) Ages 40+ N = 8,450 Deaths = 2,058 | Religious attendance: >Weekly Weekly <Weekly Never | All-cause mortality >Weekly Weekly <Weekly Never | | Hazard ratio 0.84 (0.69, 1.03) 0.92 (0.78, 1.08) 0.99 (0.84, 1.16) 1.0 | "... part of the apparent residual protective effect after controlling for confounders could be explained statistically by effects of religious practice on likely mediators including health behaviors, non-religious social support, blood pressure and inflammation." (p. 127) |
| *International samples* | | | | | | | |
| Abramson et al. (1982) | 1969/71–1976 5 years | Jerusalem male cohort Ages 60+ N = 387 | Unspecified "religiosity" | All-cause mortality | No significant differences at bivariate level | No females in sample | No comment on absence of association |
| Goldbourt et al. (1993) | 1963–1986 23 years | Israeli Ischaemic Heart Disease Study Ages 40+ N = 10,059 males; 3,473 deaths | Religious orthodoxy index 3 items, ≤ ranks for combined items: Education (religious or secular) Self-definition (orthodox, traditional, secular) Synagogue attendance (Never, High holidays only, all holidays and Sabbath, Daily) | All-cause mortality Most orthodox Orthodox Traditional Secular Nonbelievers CHD mortality[f] Most orthodox Orthodox Traditional Secular Nonbelievers | Age-adjusted rate 135[g] 162 162 166 168 Age-adjusted rate 38[g] 51 51 54 61 | No females in sample | "In comparing the upper (unadjusted) to the lower (adjusted) life table curves for these groups, it appeared that the difference between the above-mentioned most secular group and the more traditional (or less secular) groups is, in most part, accounted for by a more unfavorable CHD risk profile for the former. However, a statistically significant advantage of at least 20% reduced fatal CHD risk persisted for the 2,103 'most orthodox' (adjusted CHD mortality, 7.7%) over the years, as compared to the other groups (adjusted cumulative CHD mortality rates between 9.7 and 10.7%)." (p. 116) |

# 17 Religion and Adult Mortality

**Table 17.2** (continued)

| Study | Period of follow-up | Sample | Measure of religiousness | Cause of death / Religion measure | Results[a] Males | Results[a] Females | Authors' comment on mechanism of association |
|---|---|---|---|---|---|---|---|
| La Cour et al. (2006) | 1984–2004 20 years | Glostrup 1914 Cohort Study (Denmark) Age 70 $N = 734$ | Denomination Importance of religion Religious attendance TV or radio | All-cause mortality Importance of religion Religious attendance TV or radio | Hazard ratio 0.92 (0.68, 1.24) 0.92 (0.71, 1.18) 1.22 (0.96, 1.55) | Hazard ratio 0.79 (0.59, 1.07) 0.73 (0.55, 0.97) 0.86 (0.67, 1.13) | "In this Danish study, the mechanisms of effect seem to be slightly different.... we found church members significantly more overweight than non-attenders, with no difference in either smoking or drinking behaviour. The positively related variables of church attendance dealt with better social network: church attenders gave more help to others, they received more help from others and they had contact with friends, children or grandchildren more than once a week." (p. 163) |
| Yeager et al. (2006) | 1999–2003 4 years | Social Environment and Biomarkers of Aging Study (Taiwan) Ages 70+ $N = 3,800$ 14% died | Religious attendance Religious beliefs Religious practices | All-cause mortality Often Sometimes Rarely Never Religious beliefs Religious practices | Logit coefficient −0.477* −0.393* −0.054 Reference group 0.026+ −0.001 | | "On the one hand, religion may foster positive health behaviors and enhance social activity (i.e. mediation); on the other hand, people with better health behaviors and who are more socially active may be more likely to attend religious services, in which case pre-existing differences rather than religious practices could account for differences in health (i.e. selection)." (p. 2239) |

Note: The following studies were not included in the table because of the absence of health status measures at baseline: Comstock (1971), Comstock and Tonascia (1977), Jaffe et al. (2005), Krause (2006), Kraut et al. (2004) and Zhang (2008).
ns = Not significant.
[a] Results presented show the full models from each analysis, including all mediating and control variables.
[b] Note related Alameda County Study analyses: Reynolds and Kaplan (1990), Strawbridge et al. (1997, 2000).
[c] Note related Established Populations for Epidemiologic Study of the Elderly (EPESE) analyses: Helm et al. (2000) and Koenig et al. (1999).
[d] Note related Longitudinal Study of Aging (LSOA) analyses: Bryant and Rakowski (1992) and Goldman et al. (1995).
[e] Note related National Health Interview Survey (NHIS) Cancer Risk Factor Supplement analysis: Ellison et al. (2000).
[f] ICD code not given.
[g] Significance level not reported.
+ $p \leq 0.10$.
* $0.01 < p \leq 0.05$.
** $0.001 < p \leq 0.01$.
*** $p \leq 0.001$.

studies report results from multivariate analyses, usually in the form of hazard ratios. I include studies only if they are well-controlled, with measures of disability or diagnoses included to reduce selectivity by health status at baseline; this criterion eliminated a number of potentially interesting studies that are listed at the bottom of Table 17.2. To be included in Table 17.2, studies must have reported main effects for one or more measures of religiousness. The table reports main effects from models prior to the testing of interactions, but after all demographic variables, health status covariates, and mediating variables have been included. Both Tables 17.1 and 17.2 present the findings for all-cause mortality, and also, for comparative purposes, the findings for cause-specific cardiovascular and cancer mortality if they were reported in the study. Additional causes of death, if available, were not included due to space constraints. Version-specific ICD codes are reported as given in the publication.

## All-Cause Mortality of Distinctive Religious Groups

Studies in the first group compared the rates of all-cause and/or cause-specific mortality in one regional or state-based religious group to the rates in the surrounding general population. Table 17.1 shows a description of each study, including the period of follow-up, the study sample characteristics, the reference population, SMRs for all-cause mortality and cardiovascular and/or cancer mortality if available, and the authors' comments on causal mechanisms for the associations they report. Studies are grouped by religious affiliation and arranged chronologically within groups.

*Amish.* There is one such study for Amish populations in the major US Amish population centers of Pennsylvania, Ohio, and Indiana (Hamman et al. 1981). The study made comparisons with both regional and US populations, finding significantly lower all-cause and cardiovascular mortality for Amish adult males (aged 40–69 and 70+), but not for adult females. Compared with local populations, the all-cause SMR for middle-aged Amish men was 0.61, and compared with the United States as a whole, it was 0.55. For elderly men, and middle-aged women, there were no differences in all-cause deaths, and elderly Amish women had a significantly higher SMR (1.19) than the neighboring county population. The Amish are an ethnically homogeneous, endogamous, genetically distinct religious group with origins in sixteenth century Switzerland. Their way of life is rural, agricultural, and family-centered, and rejecting of modern conveniences to a greater or lesser extent; as such it involves hard physical labor and a diet of food "... produced at home, without commercial preservatives or additives" (Hamman et al. 1981: 846). Amish men do use tobacco, although cigarettes are taboo.

*Seventh-Day Adventists.* A series of studies of Seventh-Day Adventists (SDA) in Norway, the Netherlands, Denmark, Poland, and the United States have focused on their generally low rates of overall mortality (reviewed by Fraser 1999). In three studies of California Seventh-Day Adventists, Phillips et al. (1978, 1980) find a strong mortality advantage for SDA men, when compared with the population of California or participants in an American Cancer Society study; for example, SDA males have a 74% lower SMR from coronary heart disease at ages 35–64 and a 34% lower SMR for all-cause mortality at all ages. SMRs and life expectancy advantages for SDA females were similar but not as large, with a 12% lower overall SMR (Phillips et al. 1980). In the Netherlands, Berkel and de Waard (1983) report SMRs compared with the Dutch population for all-cause mortality of 0.45, cardiovascular disease 0.41, ischemic heart disease 0.43, cerebrovascular disease 0.54, and neoplasms 0.50. SMR results were not reported for males and females separately, but in the text the authors calculate SDA male life expectancy as 8.9 years longer than the Dutch population, and SDA female life expectancy as 3.6 years longer. A study in Poland showed higher survival probabilities for SDA members at every age from 30 to 89, for both males and females; surprisingly, male SDA survival probabilities were *higher* than SDA females' at the oldest ages, and almost identical at the younger ages, a finding at odds with the Polish comparison group and most other populations (Jedrychowski et al. 1985). Finally, Fønnebø (1992) reports a comparison of SDA church rosters in Norway with data on the European population. He found significantly lower all-cause SMRs for SDA men but not for women; the SMR for SDA men of all ages was 0.82, or 18% lower. Fønnebø's further analysis (1994) shows that the mortality risk reductions are found almost exclusively among SDA members who joined the church early in life; among those joining over the age of 35 there were no differences in SMR. He concludes, "The site mainly responsible for the low SMR in young converts was cardiovascular disease (men, 44; women, 52)" (Fønnebø 1992: 157).

Fraser (1999) and the authors of individual studies make it clear that the SDA population has been studied, both initially and in such detail, because of the SDA lifestyle, which includes strict adherence to prohibitions of smoking and alcohol use; moreover, one-third of SDA members adhere to a lacto-ovo-vegetarian diet, eating neither meat nor fish. Such differences in lifestyle made the SDA church a natural laboratory for investigating two of the most important risk factors first identified in the Framingham studies of the development of cardiovascular disease in healthy persons that began in 1948: smoking and dietary cholesterol. The Seventh-Day Adventist church is a Christian denomination begun in the northeastern United States in the mid-nineteenth century. It is an evangelical religion that grew through the inclusion of new members from other religions and denominations who were rapidly differentiated from their former communities by their adoption of a strict new lifestyle and by the identification of Saturday instead of Sunday as the Sabbath day of rest. The importance for health of strict adherence to their beliefs is shown in studies that have examined meat consumption *within* the SDA population; those following the strictest vegetarian diet had dramatically lower CHD risk than meat-consuming SDA members (Snowdon et al. 1984). Authors of the set of studies in Table 17.1 emphasize both the non-smoking and the vegetarianism of SDA members in explaining their lower cardiovascular and all-cause mortality rates.

*Mormons.* The next group of studies reports on cardiovascular disease deaths among Mormons, or the church of Jesus Christ of Latter-day Saints (LDS) in Utah, Canada, and California. In 1975 Enstrom calculated crude all-cause mortality rates per 1,000 for Utah and California Mormons and non-Mormons for the decades of the 1950s, 1960s, and 1970s, finding considerably lower rates for Mormons in every case; in the 1970s, for example, the rate was 8.4/1,000 for California non-Mormons, and 4.5/1,000 for Mormons (Enstrom 1975). Lyon et al. (1978) show SMRs for a set of heart-disease deaths including rheumatic heart disease, hypertensive heart disease, and ischemic heart disease (further divided into acute and chronic). The SMRs for Mormon men and women are significantly lower than they are for the comparison Utah non-Mormon white population, ranging from 0.54–0.73, with the exception of rheumatic heart disease, where Mormon male and female SMRs are approximately 50% *higher* (representing, however, just 4.8% of cardiovascular deaths) (Lyon et al. 1978). In this study the gender differences are inconsistent, with men having lower SMRs than women in some cases (hypertensive heart disease and chronic ischemic heart disease) and higher SMRs in others (acute ischemic heart disease). Overall, the Mormon rate of cardiovascular disease death was 35% lower than the rate for non-Mormons in Utah, whose rates are similar to those of US whites. A study of Mormons in Alberta, Canada, finds significantly lower SMRs for males for circulatory disease (0.72), ischemic heart disease (0.62), and cerebrovascular disease (0.71) deaths, but fewer deaths for females only for ischemic heart disease (0.71), when compared to the population of Alberta, Canada (Jarvis 1977). A third group of studies reports all-cause, cardiovascular, and cancer mortality among Mormons in California and Utah; the comparison group is US whites (Enstrom 1980, 1989; Enstrom and Breslow 2008). Ordinary and religiously active Mormon "high priests" and their wives were identified from church records. SMRs range from an astoundingly low 0.19 for smoking-related cancers among religiously active males, to 0.83 for non-smoking-related cancers for all Mormon females, but all SMRs are significantly lower than 1.0 and are lower for males than for females in every case.

The LDS (Mormon) church was founded in upstate New York by Joseph Smith in the 1820s; he and his followers migrated to Utah and other Western states in the 1840s. Today approximately 72% of the population of Utah is Mormon, creating an ethnically and culturally distinct society. The teachings of the Mormon church include abstention from all forms of tobacco, as well as abstention from the consumption of tea, coffee, and alcohol, but in other respects the Mormon diet is similar to that of US residents (Lyon et al. 1978). The effects of these uniform social conditions on disease and death rates in Utah were noted by health economist Victor Fuchs (1974) in his famous "A Tale of Two States," in which he compared the favorable health status in Utah with the much higher adult and infant mortality rates in the neighboring but very different social conditions of Nevada. Authors of the studies of the LDS church consistently identified the non-smoking status of Mormons as an important cause of their lower cardiovascular and all-cause mortality rates.

*Jews.* In an early study of lung-cancer deaths in Pittsburgh, Pennsylvania, Jewish males' age-adjusted death rate was lower than the rate for non-Jewish males', but Jewish females' rates were actually higher than the comparison population (Herman and Enterline 1970). A study in Israel found that residents of religious census districts had higher life expectancy than those from non-religious districts (Friedlander et al. 1995). In a second study from Israel, Kark et al. (1996) compare mortality from all causes and specific causes in twenty-two Israeli kibbutzim, religious and secular. Male residents of the secular, compared with religious, kibbutzim had significantly higher age-adjusted rates for all-cause mortality, as well as coronary heart disease, cancer, and external causes. Secular women's age-adjusted rate ratios were significantly greater for all-cause mortality but not for other causes of death, compared with those for women in religious kibbutzim. The authors note that demographic differences between the two types of kibbutzim are small, and there are uniformly high levels of social support and health services; however, smoking was more prevalent in secular kibbutzim. Thus, among Jews in both the United States and Israel, the effects of religious group membership appear to benefit men more than women.

*Clergy.* The next group of studies in Table 17.1 report SMRs from clergy and religious orders in the United States and Japan. Although the clergy do not constitute religious affiliation groups in the same way as do the groups examined in the other work, the structure of these studies was similar to that of the studies previously reviewed, as was the motivation for studying such a sample: the clergy were identified as one among a number of "populations at low risk of cancer" (King and Locke 1980). Taylor et al. (1959) found lower death rates for cardiovascular disease among the religious orders when compared with women from Massachusetts, but little difference for all-cause or cancer mortality. King et al. (1975), King and Locke (1980), and Locke and King (1980) find that Presbyterian, Baptist, and Lutheran clergy (virtually all males at the time) have SMRs for cardiovascular/renal diseases and all causes that are just 62–76% of those of US white males. In a study of priests of the Myoshinji Branch of the Rinzai Sect of Zen Buddhists, SMRs for all causes, cerebrovascular diseases, and hypertensive diseases were significantly lower than they were in the Japanese male population; however, the SMR for heart diseases was not different (Ogata et al. 1984). The authors also conducted a questionnaire survey of a sample of Zen priests, finding that they smoked somewhat less, did not drink coffee, ate less meat, fish, bread, and salty, pickled foods than comparable Japanese males, and lived in more rural, less polluted areas; however, their alcohol intake appeared to be similar to the rest of the Japanese population.

*Geographic Concentrations.* A final study at the group level compares US counties with concentrations of particular religious groups with concentrations of "noncommunicants"; it found lower cancer mortality rates in counties with many conservative Protestants or Mormons, and higher rates where there were liberal Protestants, Catholics, and Jews (Dwyer et al. 1990).

To summarize briefly, the religious groups chosen by researchers for study showed consistently lower rates for cardiovascular, cancer, and all-cause mortality than the comparison population in the region or nation from which they came. These differences were frequently greater for men than for women, and in several cases, women appeared to be at a disadvantage relative to the general population (we return to the issue of gender differences below). No consistent differences between the SMRs for all-cause, cardiovascular disease, and cancer were found when all were reported; cancer and cardiovascular deaths would make up the largest proportion of all deaths. It should be reiterated that the time period for the data in these studies is the 1950s, 1960s, and 1970s. This is important because the consensus identification of risk factors for cardiovascular disease was still beginning at that point; it is likely, then, that the behaviors were driven more purely by religious belief than they would be today when health risks are more widely understood. Moreover, these studies of homogeneous low-risk lifestyles themselves contributed to our current understanding, an understanding that has led to the decline in deaths that has taken place since the studies were conducted.

As a group, the religious affiliation studies in Table 17.1 have some important underlying similarities. At one level, we might argue that they have rather little to do with religion. As many of the introductions to these articles imply, the religious affiliation group in question is of interest because of one or more lifestyle characteristics that have known or suspected links to mortality—primarily smoking, alcohol use, and dietary sources of cholesterol. The spiritual beliefs or theology of the group are of interest only to the extent that they support the health-relevant behaviors. One might argue that these religious groups simply provided health researchers with "natural experiments" with which to efficiently identify the important primary prevention risk factors, in parallel with the more laborious study of representative populations, as in the Framingham Study. From the retrospective position of today's research on religion and health, we might say that these earlier researchers were more interested in the mediators than they were in the independent variable.

But the reason researchers in the 1970s and 1980s found such *substantially* lower mortality rates among Seventh-Day Adventists and Mormons was not that they had conveniently identified collections of people with relevant alternative lifestyles, but that they were studying something larger than the sum of the individual (behavioral) parts. They studied social institutions that had the power to compel individuals to deny themselves a rich diet, or the stimulation of caffeine or nicotine, or the pleasure of a glass of wine, over many years or an entire lifetime. Religious groups maintain effective social control through numerous mechanisms, including both sanctions for negative behavior and rewards for faithful adherence. They provide self-esteem, and an identity for individuals based on positive (insider) and negative (outsider) reference groups. Most importantly, these religious groups are historic, permanent institutions that control the behavior of individuals who remain within them throughout their life course; recall Fønnebø's (1992) finding that Norwegian SDA members who had joined the church prior to age 18 had the largest cardiovascular disease mortality reductions; those who joined after age 35 had rates that were not different from the comparison European population. In sum, these group-level studies provide an important insight, and it would be incorrect to exclude them as most of the recent reviews of research on religion and mortality have done.

## Differences in All-Cause Mortality by Individual Religious Observance

The second set of studies of religion and mortality has been conducted by more interdisciplinary teams of researchers, including sociologists and demographers, in addition to epidemiologists and physicians. These studies are mostly prospective cohort studies rather than retrospective comparisons of mortality rates, and they are also distinguished from the first set by their conceptualization and measurement of religion. Rather than focusing on a single religious affiliation group and its members, these analyses of data from representative samples of regional or national populations measure "religiousness" as a characteristic of individuals, regardless of the individual's religious affiliation or lack of it. Most often, the indicator of religiousness used is the behavioral indicator of attendance at religious services. Religious affiliation is often not available in the data at all and thus cannot be studied. It should be kept in mind that representative samples of regional populations in the United States and abroad would have very different profiles of religious groups, were they known. Summaries of the studies are displayed in Table 17.2, grouped by US regional, US national, and international data sources.

*US Regional Studies.* The ten US regional studies come from all parts of the country—east, south, midwest, and west. Their sample sizes range from 557 to 14,456, and follow-up periods range from 5 to 20 years. Most were secondary analyses conducted in the course of health assessments of populations of interest; religion was included as a dimension of social networks or indicator of social integration and was not a focus of the study. Several of these studies were framed as replications of the Alameda County study (Berkman and Syme 1979; Oman et al. 2002), in which religion is just one form of social network contact (House et al. 1982; Oman and Reed 1998; Schoenbach et al. 1986). A second set come from the related Established Populations for Epidemiologic Studies of the Elderly (EPESE) studies (Bagiella et al. 2005; Dupre et al. 2006; Hill et al. 2005; Lutgendorf et al. 2004). Adults of all ages are included; six of the ten studies focus on the over-65 population. With a single exception, only one dimension of religiousness is tested: attendance at religious services or activities. Nine of the ten studies report a significant reduction in the risk of mortality for more frequent participants in religious activities after all demographic, baseline health status, and mediating variables are included in the models. One reports significant associations for males but not females, one for females but not males, two for both tested separately, and the remaining five for pooled samples; one reports findings for whites but not blacks. Hazard ratios are not reported in all studies, but effect sizes range from a 50% higher hazard for those with "no church activities" compared with those with frequent activities (Schoenbach et al. 1986) to a 22% lower risk for those attending weekly compared with never attending (Bagiella et al. 2005).

Several of the studies had distinctive features worth noting. The analysis with no significant association is from the Framingham Study. In a study limited to female Framingham participants aged 25–64, Eaker et al. (1992) found that weekly or more frequent attendance at religious services was associated with lower risk of myocardial infarction and coronary death, but this effect was seen at the bivariate level only; when health-risk factors (blood pressure, cholesterol, diabetes, cigarette smoking, and body mass index) were adjusted, the association was no longer significant.

Few of the regional studies analyzed cause-specific mortality, but the Alameda County Study was analyzed for cause-specific results by Oman et al. (2002) after 31 years of follow-up. In this large sample from a county whose population was proportionally similar to the ethnic and racial make-up of the United States in 1965, attendance at religious services less than once per week is associated with a significant hazard ratio of 1.21 for all-cause mortality and also 1.21 for circulatory disease mortality, when adjusted for all health status, social connection, and health behavior variables and compared with attendance of once a week or more. Circulatory disease deaths were the only specific cause of death (among cancer, digestive, respiratory, external, and other causes) that remained significant after all confounding and mediating variables were adjusted.

Lutgendorf et al. (2004), with data from a subset of the Iowa EPESE sample, identify a physiological mediating pathway; they find that more frequent religious attendance is associated with lower levels of interleukin-6 (IL-6), and consequently with lower mortality. Higher levels of (IL-6), which become more common in old age, are implicated in coronary heart disease, osteoporosis, frailty and muscle wasting, functional disability, certain cancers, and in higher all-cause mortality.

A final study of particular note is by Østbye et al. (2006). This was the only regional study that reported on multiple dimensions of individual religiousness. It found no effect of lower mortality for once-a-week-or-more meditating, reading scriptures, attending worship services, or having a direct experience of God. However, participants who volunteered in religious organizations had a 22% lower hazard of mortality than those who did not. There was also a significantly *increased* hazard (43%) of mortality for those who received visits from "people at church," likely an indication of those respondents' declining health status.

In sum, the regional studies show little in the way of gender differences. Most had available only the single indicator of attendance at services. In general, there is a pattern of a protective effect of religious attendance on mortality. Most of the authors' discussions of causal mechanisms focus on the better health practices associated with religious attendance, and social support and integration, and there is a rare example of a biological mechanism.

*US National Studies.* There are six studies of US national data, from the National Health Interview Survey (NHIS) Supplements on Cancer and Aging (Hummer et al. 1999; Rogers 1996), the Medicare Beneficiary Eligibility sample (Krause 1998), the Health Professionals Follow-Up study (Eng et al. 2002), the Americans' Changing Lives study (Musick et al. 2004), and the third National Health and Nutrition Examination Survey (NHANES III; Gillum et al. 2008). Sample sizes range from 819 to 28,369, length of follow-up ranges from 5 to 12 years, and the studies include a range of ages. All have religious attendance as their measure of religiousness, and two report on other dimensions as well. One of the six finds no reduction in the risk of mortality for religious attenders after adjustment for covariates (Gillum et al. 2008). Of the others, one finds significant mortality reductions for males (females not included in study), and four find significant reductions for their sample as a whole. Significant effect sizes range from a 50% increase in the hazard of all-cause mortality for those who never attend compared with those who attend more than once a week (Hummer et al. 1999) to a 12% lower odds of mortality among those who attend, compared to those who do not (Krause 1998).

Hummer et al. (1999) and Eng et al. (2002) report on cause-specific as well as all-cause mortality; in both cases the findings are stronger for all-cause mortality. Eng et al. (2002) find no significantly reduced risk for cardiovascular mortality for attenders as there had been for all-cause mortality; Hummer et al. (1999) find a borderline reduction for circulatory disease deaths, and no significant reduction for cancer. Two studies include alternative dimensions of religiousness. Musick et al. (2004) measured volunteering for church, subjective religiosity, private devotional activity, negative justice, and fatalism, but none were associated with mortality. Krause (1998) measured nonorganizational religiosity (which had no association with mortality) and religious coping (which *increased* the odds of mortality).

Again the majority of these studies find a protective effect of religious participation on mortality risk. They also show little evidence of gender differences. Several of the authors note the important mediating role of health behaviors and lifestyle, and social support.

*International Studies.* The four international studies come from Israel (Abramson et al. 1982; Goldbourt et al. 1993), Denmark (La Cour et al. 2006), and Taiwan (Yeager et al. 2006). The participants in the Israeli studies were Jewish, the Danish participants mostly members of the Danish Folk church (Lutheran), and the Taiwanese a mixed group of Taoists, Buddhists, Christians, and the unaffiliated. Sample sizes range from 387 to 10,059, follow-ups range from 4 to 23 years, and the respondents in three of the four studies are aged 60 or older. Perhaps because of the international context, measures of religiousness are more varied and different from the US studies; one Israeli study creates a multi-indicator index of religious orthodoxy (Goldbourt et al. 1993), the Danish study includes listening to religious TV or radio (La Cour et al. 2006), and the importance of religion, along with religious attendance, and the Taiwanese study includes religious beliefs and practices along with attendance (Yeager et al. 2006). One of the four shows significant reductions in mortality risk for both males and females, one shows them for males only, one for females only, and one shows none. The single hazard ratio reported shows a 27% reduction in the hazard of all-cause mortality for Danish females who attend services frequently compared with those who do not attend.

Two of these studies are notable for the extensive physical examination and clinical data available for the participants. Goldbourt et al. (1993) report on a 23-year follow-up of the Israeli Ischemic Heart Disease Study ($N = 10{,}059$). The study had very little attrition, and an intensive medical, behavioral, and psychosocial examination at baseline; participants were interviewed for dietary habits, and underwent biochemical, electrocardiographic, and blood testing, to provide a state-of-the-art cardiovascular risk profile.

The 2,103 most orthodox study participants had an adjusted CHD mortality rate of 7.7%, compared with rates of 9.7–10.7% for the traditional, secular, and nonbelieving Israelis after adjustment for the full CHD risk profile (Goldbourt et al. 1993). Yeager et al. (2006) collected urine samples for cortisol, fasting blood samples for IL-6, physical examination, blood pressure, and anthropometric measures, as well as cognitive performance and self-reported functional ability measures on over 1,000 elderly men and women in Taiwan. In contrast to Lutgendorf et al. (2004), Yeager et al. (2006) found no association of religiousness with any biomarker, including IL-6.

Table 17.2 summarizes studies that span a 30-year period, in the United States, Denmark, Taiwan, and Israel. Rather than treating religion as a characteristic of groups, as did the studies in Table 17.1, these studies treat religion as a characteristic of individuals, expressed most often by the behavioral indicator of attendance at services. The religious affiliation of the respondents is not known in most of the US studies, or at least not featured in the analysis. Studies that reported both all-cause and cardiovascular mortality risks found that the results were stronger for all-cause mortality. There were few or no differences by gender. In most cases, the studies reported bivariate associations between religious attendance and mortality that were quite strong but which were then reduced or even eliminated with the addition of several sets of mediating variables; in other words, there were substantial indirect effects of religiousness through variables such as smoking and social support, a topic returned to below.

## Discussion

### *Social Regulation of Multiple Risk Factors*

The initial conclusion to be drawn from a comparison of Tables 17.1 and 17.2 is that the effects are generally stronger and more consistent when religious groups with distinctive lifestyle characteristics are compared with the general population, in Table 17.1, than when individual differences in religiousness are measured, as in Table 17.2. Table 17.2 also shows fewer discernible gender differences (albeit few by gender analyses).

Furthermore, Table 17.2 shows weaker effects for cardiovascular outcomes when compared with all-cause mortality in the same study, whereas the two were quite similar when both were reported in studies in Table 17.1. This pattern of findings might be somewhat surprising, especially in the US context where the comparison group of the population as a whole (in Table 17.1) is also relatively religiously observant, for example, where the comparison group for Mormons would, for example, include Seventh-Day Adventists, and vice versa. Comparison of the rates of entire groups also ignores individual differences within the group; for example, nonobservant SDA members contribute person-years for the analysis just as highly observant members do. For these reasons the estimated differences in Table 17.1 might be considered to minimize the effect of religiousness. Enstrom (1989) addresses this issue in his analysis of Mormon high priests; by selecting the most observant members of the California Mormon church, he minimizes the heterogeneity of the study sample.

## Mediators and Confounders

Thus, the studies in Table 17.2 would appear to have an advantage. Measuring religious observance as a characteristic of individuals would seem to be a more targeted, powerful study design for assessing the impact of religiousness on health. An important reason why the effects found in Table 17.2 studies are weaker is that the individual level of measurement allows the researcher to test directly the mechanisms of effect that can only be alluded to in the group-level analyses in Table 17.1. If the hypothesized causal mechanisms are operating, then we would expect to see initial strong bivariate, unadjusted associations between religious observance and health outcomes that are subsequently reduced by the introduction of mediating variables such as smoking. And in fact this is exactly what we see when we examine the studies in Table 17.2. Eaker et al. (1992) report a significantly higher incidence rate of 1.68 per 100 Framingham women for myocardial infarction/coronary death among those who attend services rarely, compared with 0.97 for those who attend more than once per week and 0.82 for those who attend 1–3 times per month. But when age, systolic blood pressure, ratio of total to HDL serum cholesterol, diabetes, cigarette smoking, and body mass index were entered, religious attendance was no longer associated with coronary death.

Hummer et al. (1999) report a hazard ratio of 1.67 ($p < 0.01$) for circulatory-disease death among those who never attend services, compared with those who attend more than once per week, when the model is adjusted only for demographic variables; when adjusted for demographic, health, socioeconomic, and behavioral variables (smoking, overweight, alcohol use), the hazard ratio drops to 1.43 ($p < 0.05$), and when social ties are added it drops further to 1.32 ($p < 0.10$) (this final model is the one reported in Table 17.2). Oman et al. (2002) find a hazard ratio for circulatory disease of 1.41 ($p < 0.0001$) when adjusted only for age and sex; when the model is adjusted for sociodemographic factors, social network connections, and health behaviors (current smoking, exercise, heavy alcohol consumption), the hazard ratio drops to 1.21 ($p < 0.05$) (the model I report). Eng et al. (2002) do not report unadjusted data for religious service attendance; however, with respect to their full social network index (which includes religious attendance) they comment, "... covariates related to health behavior and physical condition appeared to be the most influential confounders or, alternatively, to demonstrate the most potential as mediators between social networks and mortality" (706).

In this quote, Eng et al. (2002) raise the important issue of the classification of covariates as confounders (variables that co-vary with the independent variable and cause change in the dependent variable), versus mediators or intervening variables (variables that are caused by the independent variable and have a subsequent effect on the dependent variable) (Susser 1973). Eng et al. (2002) imply in the above-quoted sentence that the physical condition variables are confounders (i.e., poor health is associated with lower religious attendance and also causes mortality) and that the behavioral variables are influenced by religious attendance/social networks and help to explain their association with mortality. Hummer et al. (1999) refer to the same issue by differentiating between "selectivity" variables (health status measures that might prevent respondents from attending religious services at baseline) and "mediating" variables such as smoking, excessive use of alcohol, and overweight, which are known to be lower among religious attenders. As

Kark et al. articulated, "... diet, smoking, obesity, alcohol intake, exercise, and exposure to accidents ... may be viewed as potential intervening variables in a causal pathway rather than as confounders (i.e., *they are determined by religious practices*)" (1996: 345; emphasis added). This distinction has important implications for psychosocial health research in general, but particularly for research on religion, where so many important mediating variables are associated with religiousness. The more possible intervening pathways there are between an independent variable and its dependent variable, the more likely the initial effect is to be reduced or even eliminated, thus appearing to diminish the importance of the independent variable, when in fact its multiple intervening pathways should underscore its significance.

## Gender Differences

The presence of the mediating variables in analyses summarized in Table 17.2 may also explain the gender differences that are relatively strong in Table 17.1 but largely absent in Table 17.2. As noted earlier, the time period for studies in Table 17.1 that included women were the 1960s and 1970s. In 1965, there was a strong sex difference in US smoking rates; 51.2% of US men but just 33.7% of women were current smokers (National Center for Health Statistics 2003: 212). Since then (the Surgeon General's Report on the Health Effects of Smoking was published in 1964), smoking rates have declined for both men and women, and today they are much closer (24.7 and 20.8%, respectively). If one of the primary reasons for the lower cardiovascular and all-cause mortality among the religious groups in Table 17.1 was their lower smoking rates (as virtually all of the authors contend it was), then men's higher smoking rates in the general population would provide the basis for a stronger impact of religion than women's lower rates would. Evidence for this interpretation can be seen in Dupre et al. (2006), who observe that the attenuation of the religion effect is greater for men (17%) than for women (10%) when health practices are introduced into the model. This further underscores the importance of the behavioral proscriptions and normative constraints of the religious groups: they change men's behaviors more than they do women's.

## Selection

Another important force at work in multiple ways in these studies is the process of selection, which may prevent individuals in poor health from attending services, thereby confounding the association of attendance with mortality. In addition, however, there are much more inchoate, lifelong selection processes reflected in the studies in both Tables 17.1 and 17.2. Some individuals are selected into religious group membership through family relationships early in their lives, others may undergo conversion experiences and join as adults, whereas others may select themselves out of groups whose way of life they do not see as compatible with their own. Thus, it is important to see religious group affiliation, particularly in the United States where there is so much religious diversity, as a continuously enacted selection process, and the regulation and constraint of the social group as an influence that is at least to some extent acceded to by the individual. As Fuchs (1974) remarks about Nevada and Utah in "A Tale of Two States,"

> The populations of these two states are, to a considerable extent, self-selected extremes from the continuum of life-styles found in the United States. Nevadans, as has been shown, are predominantly recent immigrants from other areas, many of whom were attracted by the state's permissive mores. The inhabitants of Utah, on the other hand, are evidently willing to remain in a more restricted society. Persons born in Utah who do not find these restrictions acceptable tend to move out of the state (53–54).

## Future Research

There are many promising directions for future research on religion and health, and the results of this review lead directly to some specific recommendations.

*Endpoints.* All-cause mortality as an endpoint suggests that many other specific disease outcomes, including both mortality and morbidity, acute and chronic, could be examined. Indeed, the complete natural history of a disease, from primary prevention risk factors, to prodromal perceptions, to active symptoms, diagnosis, treatment, crises, recovery, and eventual death, could all be examined with respect to the integration and regulation functions of religiousness and spirituality. Dimensions of religiousness/spirituality that are particularly relevant at one stage in the natural history of a disease—such as behavioral regulation for smoking cessation—may be less effective in other stages, for example, at the end of life.

The approach of the studies in Table 17.1 also suggests that outcomes measured at the level of populations may be just as compelling as outcomes measured at the individual level. There is a long tradition in social health research for studying societal-level religion variables and suicide rates (Pescosolido and Georgianna 1989) and some work on cancer (Dwyer et al. 1990), but much more could be accomplished. From a health policy standpoint, the societal burden of poor health and the costs of health care are just as important as the individual outcomes are for clinical care.

*Measuring religion(s)*. Existing research has been largely concentrated in western nations where Judeo-Christian faiths predominate. Studies from Asia, Africa, and the Middle East where the majority of the population are Muslim, Hindu, or Buddhist would be welcome additions to the literature. Future research should also conceptualize religion as both an individual-level and a higher-order characteristic, of local communities, counties, states, or nations. Religion is a social institution whose fundamental units are congregations, social groups with a history and presence in the community that have functions and structures, and important differentiations between them (Cnaan 2002). With the wider availability of statistical packages for analyzing multilevel data, the capability for conceptualizing religion simultaneously as an individual-level characteristic, and as a characteristic of larger social bodies promises a great deal more power in understanding the nature of religion in health than either approach taken by itself.

*Mediators*. The size of the mediating effects of the health-risk variables introduced into the analyses in Table 17.2—analyses of individual-level data from religiously diverse, representative samples—suggests that further research on the relationship between religion and mortality risk factors should be pursued. Such research should again use multilevel approaches that could take account of the risks and resources characteristic of the whole communities under study. Mediating variables are variables that are caused by the independent variable, and are associated with the dependent variable in the analysis, and, when introduced into the model, reduce the effect of the independent variable. Once an association is established, the search for mediating variables usually becomes the primary strategy for research. In research on religion and cardiovascular disease, for example, the logical place to look for mediating variables is among the set of already well-defined proximal risk factors for cardiovascular mortality, still the leading cause of death in the United States.

A substantial literature exists showing an association between lower rates of cigarette smoking and religiousness. The dramatic religion-based differences in smoking rates mentioned by Fuchs in 1974 are just as strong today. Utah still has by far the lowest smoking rates in the United States (13.9%), the next lowest is Hawaii (18.6%), and Nevada has the highest (31.5%) (Centers for Disease Control 2004). Studies at the individual level consistently show lower smoking rates among those with high levels of religious involvement in elderly samples (Idler and Kasl 1997; Koenig et al. 1998; Williams et al. 2001), among adults (Strawbridge et al. 1997), and most importantly among adolescents and young adults (Nonnemaker et al. 2003; Whooley et al. 2002). But few of these studies detail the religious affiliation of their respondents, or characteristics of the community that facilitate or deter smoking.

It is especially important to consider alcohol use as an intervening variable because of the complex nature of the association; there is substantial evidence that moderate levels of alcohol consumption are protective against coronary heart disease and death (Beaglehole and Jackson 1992; Murray et al. 2002), as well as all-cause mortality (Ashley et al. 2000; Rehm et al. 2001) when compared with either higher or lower levels of consumption. For example, Mukamal et al. (2003) found, using the health professionals follow-up study, that men who consumed alcohol between three and seven times per week had lower risks for myocardial infarction than either men who drank less than three drinks or more than seven per week. This U-shaped function has perplexing implications for the study of religion; religious groups such as Mormons or Seventh-Day Adventists that require total abstinence from alcohol are *in*creasing their risk of poor cardiovascular outcomes, a factor that would have acted to minimize the differences we saw in Table 17.1.

On the other hand, religious teachings that discourage binge drinking but not moderate alcohol use could be protective.

Unlike cigarette smoking, which has been on a steady decline since the 1960s, hypertension rates continue to rise. Rates have climbed from 21.7% of all US adults in 1988–1994 to 25.6% in 1999–2000. Among adults aged 75 and older, 68.8% of men and 84.1% of women have a systolic blood pressure of at least 140 mmHg or diastolic pressure of at least 90 mmHg, or are taking hypertension medication (National Center for Health Statistics 2003: 227). Religiousness has been associated with fewer self-reported cases of hypertension (Krause et al. 2002), lower average pressures when measured in the clinic and in daily life (Hixson et al. 1998; Steffen et al. 2001), and lower lifetime blood pressures have been seen in specific religious groups such as the Amish (Jorgenson et al. 1972). Hypertension may play an important mediating role for a range of important health outcomes.

By comparison, there are rather few studies of religiousness and diabetes, some documenting higher rates among particular ethnic/religious groups (Simmons et al. 1992), and others highlighting the role of religion/spirituality in coping with the disease (Daaleman et al. 2001; Naeem 2003). But this disease, too, is increasing in prevalence, and as a cause of death it has been increasing rapidly since 1980 (National Center for Health Statistics 2003: 13).

A rather large body of research on cholesterol and religious affiliation and practices exists, much of it directed toward documenting levels of dietary fats in religious groups with specific dietary observances: Seventh-Day Adventists (Fraser et al. 1987), orthodox Jews (Friedlander et al. 1987), Muslims (Maislos et al. 1998), Old Order Mennonites (Glick et al. 1998), Buddhists (Pan et al. 1993), and others. Another study has recently documented religious affiliation differences in adherence rates for cholesterol screening and also higher rates of screening for those who were more observant (Benjamins and Brown 2004). Religiously motivated vegetarianism or fasting, which results in fewer dietary sources of cholesterol, and lower measured lipid levels in a number of these studies, is a potential mechanism for the effect of general religious observance on the specific outcome of cardiovascular mortality.

This brief survey of mediating variables suggests that there is reason to link religiousness and/or religious affiliation to several of the behavioral risk factors and comorbid conditions for cardiovascular disease and mortality. These factors deserve further research as mediating mechanisms not simply because they are statistically associated with religiousness in one or another form, but because the behaviors are themselves expressions of religious piety and group identity (Shatenstein and Ghadirian 1998). As Goldbourt et al. put it: to be an orthodox Jew is to preserve "... all the 'Mitzvot' (practical day-to-day religious rules), in particular those related to Kosher foods, prayers and the following to the letter of rules of the Sabbath" (1993: 119). This is what being *observant* means. To be sure, the "day-to-day rules" of one religious group differ from another, but there are substantial similarities in health-risk behaviors that cut across religious groups, and they have consistently shown mediating effects in the studies of all-cause mortality in general populations with the representative samples studied in Table 17.2. Moreover, the influence of religious observance works in the same direction for several of the mediating variables at once, in effect, joining and multiplying their effects. A single independent variable that is linked to several effective, proximal, mediating variables is a powerful independent variable.

In 1937, Charles Edward-Amory Winslow wrote, in the opening sentences of the entry for "Public Health" in the first *Encyclopedia of the Social Sciences*:

> The earliest examples of practices designed to promote the public health are to be found, among primitive peoples, inextricably mingled with the ritual of religion. When the Dyaks of Borneo in times of epidemic hung a string across the stream below their dwellings and fastened thereon red and white flags as a sign that no one might pass, they were practicing what was in part a quarantine measure and in part a religious tabu. When the Magi in ancient Persia required that not only dead bodies but even the clippings of hair and the parings of nails should be buried 'so that the hands of evil spirits might not make of them spears, arrows, or sling shots and so that these impurities might not generate vermin, lice, meal moths and clothes moths,' they were actuated by similar mixed motives. Disease was due to malign supernatural influences and must be warded off through the power of magic. When this magic was practiced as a tribal custom for protection on a community scale instead of being limited to the well being of a single individual, it may fairly be called public health practice—within the limits of existing knowledge (Winslow 1937: 646–647).

Winslow's linking of religious practices to the first public health practices is a prescient one from the point of view of debates about religion and health 70 years later. In addition to these practices in ancient Persia and Borneo, Winslow also mentions Biblical practices of isolation and quarantine for leprosy, and later, in medieval times, for bubonic plague. All of the practices Winslow describes are measures, possibly somewhat successful ones, taken against *infectious* diseases—the primary causes of death in ancient times, and in fact up until the early twentieth century. Today infectious disease is a minor cause of death in industrialized societies; the great majority of individuals die of chronic disease and especially diseases of the heart, for which there are complex causes, many of them depending on the lifelong behaviors of individuals. It is somewhat remarkable that religious observance, in the twenty-first century, should again be a force for health practices—effective, but entirely different health practices that are related to entirely different causes of death.

The lesson from Winslow's observation of the "public health" practices of early religious groups is that the mechanism for the effect of religion on behavior is directly related to the rituals and practices of the religious community that make it what it is. To be a member of a religious community is to stay within its literal or figurative boundaries, whether marked off for the purpose of quarantine or by keeping one's behavior within accepted limits. But no matter if it is ancient burial practices or modern injunctions against smoking, the mechanism for the effect of religion on health seems to be that religion provides an effective social control mechanism for compelling behaviors over the course of their lifetimes that may deny individuals freedom, pleasure, or stimulation, but which appear to promote survival.

**Acknowledgment** The author thanks Allan Horwitz, Richard Contrada, and Kirsten Song for their comments on the chapter.

# References

Abramson, J.H., R. Gofin, and E. Peritz. 1982. "Risk Markers for Mortality among Elderly Men—A Community Study in Jerusalem." *Journal of Chronic Disease* 35:565–72.

Ashley, M.J., J. Rehm, S. Bondy, E. Single, and J. Rankin. 2000. "Beyond Ischemic Heart Disease: Are There Other Health Benefits from Drinking Alcohol?" *Contemporary Drug Problems* 27:735–77.

Bagiella, E., V. Hong, and R. Sloan. 2005. "Religious Attendance as a Predictor of Survival in the EPESE Cohorts." *International Journal of Epidemiology* 34:443–51.

Beaglehole, R. and R. Jackson. 1992. "Alcohol, Cardiovascular Diseases and All Causes of Death: A Review of the Epidemiologic Evidence." *Drug and Alcohol Review* 11:275–90.

Benjamins, M.R. and C. Brown. 2004. "Religion and Preventative Health Care Utilization among the Elderly." *Social Science and Medicine* 58:109–18.

Berkel, J. and F. de Waard. 1983. "Mortality Pattern and Life Expectancy of Seventh-Day Adventists in the Netherlands." *International Journal of Epidemiology* 12:455–59.

Berkman, L.F. and S.L. Syme. 1979. "Social Networks, Host Resistance and Mortality: A Nine-Year Follow-Up Study of Alameda County Residents." *American Journal of Epidemiology* 109(2):186–204.

Bryant, S. and W. Rakowski. 1992. "Predictors of Mortality among Elderly African-Americans." *Research on Aging* 14:50–67.

Cnaan, R.A. 2002. *The Invisible Caring Hand: American Congregations and the Provision of Welfare*. New York, NY, New York University Press.

Comstock, G. 1971. "Fatal Arteriosclerotic Heart Disease, Water Hardness at Home, and Socioeconomic Characteristics." *American Journal of Epidemiology* 94:1–10.

Comstock, G. and K.B. Partridge. 1972. "Church Attendance and Health." *Journal of Chronic Disease* 25:665–72.

Comstock, G. and J.A. Tonascia. 1977. "Education and Mortality in Washington County, Maryland." *Journal of Health and Social Behavior* 18:54–61.

Daaleman, T.P., A.K. Cobb, and B.B. Frey. 2001. "Spirituality and Well-Being: An Exploratory Study of the Patient Perspective." *Social Science and Medicine* 52:1503–11.

Dupre, M.E., A.T. Franzese, and E.A. Parrado. 2006. "Religious Attendance and Mortality: Implications for the Black-White Mortality Crossover." *Demography* 43:141–64.

Durkheim, E. 1898 (1951). *Suicide*. New York, NY, The Free Press.

Dwyer, J.W., L.L. Clarke, and M.K. Miller. 1990. "The Effect of Religious Concentration and Affiliation on County Cancer Mortality Rates." *Journal of Health and Social Behavior* 31:185–202.

Eaker, E.D., J. Pinsky, and W.P. Castelli. 1992. "Myocardial Infarction and Coronary Death among Women: Psychosocial Predictors from a 20-year Follow-up of Women in the Framingham Study." *American Journal of Epidemiology* 135:854–64.

Ellison, C.G., R.A. Hummer, S. Cormier, and R.G. Rogers. 2000. "Religious Involvement and Mortality Risk among African American Adults." *Research on Aging* 22:630–67.

Eng, P.M., E.B. Rimm, G. Fitzmaurice, and I. Kawachi. 2002. "Social Ties and Change in Social Ties in Relation to Subsequent Total and Cause-Specific Mortality and Coronary Heart Disease Incidence in Men." *American Journal of Epidemiology* 155:700–9.

Enstrom, J.E. 1975. "Cancer Mortality among Mormons." *Cancer* 36:825–41.

Enstrom, J.E. 1980. "Cancer Mortality among Mormons in California During 1968–75." *Journal of the National Cancer Institute* 65:1073–82.

Enstrom, J.E. 1989. "Health Practices and Cancer Mortality among Active California Mormons." *Journal of the National Cancer Institute* 81:1807–14.

Enstrom, J.E. and L. Breslow. 2008. "Lifestyle and Reduced Mortality Among Active California Mormons, 1980–2004." *Preventive Medicine* 46:133–36.

Fønnebø, V. 1992. "Mortality in Norwegian Seventh-Day Adventists 1962–1986." *Journal of Clinical Epidemiology* 45:157–67.

Fønnebø, V. 1994. "The Healthy Seventh-Day Adventist Lifestyle: What is the Norwegian Experience?" *American Journal of Clinical Nutrition* 59(suppl):1124S–29S.

Fraser, G.E. 1986. *Preventive Cardiology*. New York, NY, Oxford University Press.

Fraser, G.E. 1999. "Diet as Primordial Prevention in Seventh-Day Adventists." *Preventive Medicine* 29:S18–S23.

Fraser, G.E., W. Dysinger, C. Best, and R. Chan. 1987. "Ischemic Heart Disease Risk Factors in Middle-Aged Seventh-Day Adventists Men and their Neighbors." *American Journal of Epidemiology* 126:638–46.

Friedlander, Y., J.D. Kark, and Y. Stein. 1987. "Religious Observance and Plasma Lipids and Lipoproteins among 17-Year-Old Jewish Residents of Jerusalem." *Preventive Medicine* 16:70–79.

Friedlander, D., J. Schellekens, and R.S. Cohen. 1995. "Old-age Mortality in Israel: Analysis of Variation and Change." *Health Transition Review* 5:59–83.

Fuchs, V. 1974. *Who Shall Live? Health, Economics, and Social Choice*. New York, NY, Basic Books.

Gillum, R.F., D.E. King, T.O. Obisesan, and H.G. Koenig. 2008. "Frequency of Attendance at Religious Services and Mortality in A US National Cohort." *Annals of Epidemiology* 18:124–29.

Glick, M., A.C. Michel, J. Dorn, M. Horwitz, T. Rosenthal, and M. Trevisan. 1998. "Dietary Cardiovascular Risk Factors and Serum Cholesterol in an Old Order Mennonite Community." *American Journal of Public Health* 88:1202–5.

Goldbourt, U., S. Yaari, and J.H. Medalie. 1993. "Factors Predictive of Long-Term Coronary Heart Disease Mortality among 10,059 Male Israeli Civil Servants and Municipal Employees." *Cardiology* 82:100–21.

Goldman, N., S. Korenman, and R. Weinstein. 1995. "Marital Status and Health among the Elderly." *Social Science and Medicine* 40:1717–30.

Hamman, R.F., J.I. Barancik, and A.M. Lilienfeld. 1981. "Patterns of Mortality in the Old Order Amish." *American Journal of Epidemiology* 114:845–61.

Helm, H.M., J.C. Hays, E.P. Flint, H.G. Koenig, and D. Blazer. 2000. "Does Private Religious Activity Prolong Survival? A Six-Year Follow-Up Study of 3,851 Older Adults." *Journal of Gerontology: Medical Sciences* 55A:M400–M05.

Herman, B. and P.E. Enterline. 1970. "Lung Cancer among the Jews and Non-Jews of Pittsburgh, Pennsylvania, 1953–1967: Mortality Rates and Cigarette Smoking Behavior." *American Journal of Epidemiology* 91:355–67.

Hill, T.D., J.L. Angel, C.G. Ellison, and R.J. Angel. 2005. "Religious Attendance and Mortality: An 8-Year Follow-Up of Older Mexican Americans." *Journal of Gerontology: Social Sciences* 60B:S102–S09.

Hixson, K.A., H.W. Gruchow, and D.W. Morgan. 1998. "The Relation between Religiosity, Selected Health Behaviors, and Blood Pressure Among Adult Females." *Preventive Medicine* 27:545–52.

House, J.S., C. Robbins, and H.L. Metzner. 1982. "The Association of Social Relationships and Activities with Mortality: Prospective Evidence from the Tecumseh Community Health Study." *American Journal of Epidemiology* 116:123–40.

Hummer, R.A., R.G. Rogers, C.B. Nam, and C.G. Ellison. 1999. "Religious Involvement and U.S. Adult Mortality." *Demography* 36:273–85.

Idler, E.L. and S.V. Kasl. 1997. "Religion among Disabled and Nondisabled Elderly Persons I: Cross-Sectional Patterns in Health Practices, Social Activities and Well-Being." *Journal of Gerontology: Social Sciences* 52B:S294–S305.

Jaffe, D.H., Z. Eisenbach, Y.D. Neumark, and O. Manor. 2005. "Does Living in a Religiously Affiliated Neighborhood Lower Mortality?" *Annals of Epidemiology* 15:804–10.

Jarvis, G.K. 1977. "Mormon Mortality Rates in Canada." *Social Biology* 24:294–302.

Jarvis, G.K. and H.C. Northcott. 1987. "Religion and Differences in Morbidity and Mortality." *Social Science and Medicine* 25:813–24.

Jedrychowski, E., B. Tobiasz-Adamczyk, A. Olma, and P. Gradzikiewicz. 1985. "Survival Rates among Seventh Day Adventists Compared with the General Population in Poland." *Scandinavian Journal of Social Medicine* 13:49–52.

Jorgenson, R.J., D.R. Bolling, O.C. Yoder, and E.A. Murphy. 1972. "Blood Pressure Studies in the Amish." *Hopkins Medical Journal* 131:329–50.

Kark, J.D., G. Shemi, Y. Friedlander, O. Martin, and S.H. Blondheim. 1996. "Does Religious Observance Promote Health? Mortality in Secular vs Religious Kibbutzim in Israel." *American Journal of Public Health* 86:341–46.

King, H. and F.B. Locke. 1980. "American White Protestant Clergy as a Low-Risk Population for Mortality Research." *Journal of the National Cancer Institute* 65:1115–24.

King, H., G. Zafros, and R. Hass. 1975. "Further Inquiry into Protestant Clerical Mortality Patterns." *Journal of Biosocial Science* 7:243–54.

Koenig, H.G., L.K. George, H.J. Cohen, J.C. Hays, D.B. Larson, and D.G. Blazer. 1998. The Relationship Between Religious Activities and Cigarette Smoking in Older Adults." *Journal of Gerontology: Medical Sciences* 53A:M426–M34.

Koenig, H.G., J.C. Hays, D.B. Larson, L.K. George, H.J. Cohen, M.E. McCullough, K.G. Meador, and D.G. Blazer. 1999. "Does Religious Attendance Prolong Survival? A Six-Year Follow-Up Study of 3,968 Older Adults." *Journal of Gerontology: Medical Sciences* 54A:M370–M76.

Koenig, H.G., M.E. McCullough, and D.B. Larson. 2001. *Handbook of Religion and Health*. New York, NY, Oxford University Press.

Krause, N. 1998. "Stressors in Highly Valued Roles, Religious Coping, and Mortality." *Psychology and Aging* 13:242–55.

Krause, N. 2001. "Aging and Social Support." In R.H. Binstock and L.K. George (eds.), *Handbook of Aging and the Social Sciences*, San Diego, CA, Academic Press.

Krause, N. 2006. "Church-Based Social Support and Mortality." *Journal of Gerontology: Social Sciences* 61B:S140–S46.

Krause, N., J. Liang, B.A. Shaw, H. Sugisawa, H.-K. Kim, and Y. Sugihara. 2002. "Religion, Death of a Loved One, and Hypertension among Older Adults in Japan." *Journal of Gerontology: Social Sciences* 57B:S96–S107.

Kraut, A., S. Melamed, D. Gofer, and P. Froom. 2004. "Association of Self-Reported Religiosity and Mortality in Industrial Employees: The CORDIS Study." *Social Science and Medicine* 58:595–602.

La Cour, P., K. Avlund, and K. Schultz-Larsen. 2006. "Religion and Survival in a Secular Region. A Twenty Year Follow-Up of 734 Danish Adults Born in 1914." *Social Science and Medicine* 62:157–64.

Laaksonen, M., R. Prattala, and E. Lahelma. 2003. "Sociodemographic Determinants of Multiple Unhealthy Behaviors." *Scandinavian Journal of Public Health* 31:37–43.

Lemon, F.R. and J.W. Kuzma. 1969. "A Biologic Cost of Smoking." *Archives of Environmental Health* 18:950–55.

Levin, J.S. and H.Y. Vanderpool. 1987. "Is Frequent Religious Attendance Really Conducive to Better Health? Toward an Epidemiology of Religion." *Social Science and Medicine* 24:589–600.

Locke, F.B. and H. King. 1980. "Mortality among Baptist Clergymen." *Journal of Chronic Disease* 33:581–90.

Lutgendorf, S.K., D. Russell, P. Ullrich, T.B. Harris, and R. Wallace. 2004. "Religious Participation, Interleukin-6, and Mortality in Older Adults." *Health Psychology* 23:465–75.

Lyon, J.L., H.P. Wetzler, J.W. Gardner, M.R. Klauber, and R.R. Williams. 1978. "Cardiovascular Mortality in Mormons and Non-Mormons in Utah, 1969–1971." *American Journal of Epidemiology* 108:357–66.

Maislos, M., Y. Abou-Rabiah, I. Auili, S. Iordash, and S. Shany. 1998. "Gorging and Plasma HDL-Cholesterol – The Ramadan Model." *European Journal of Clinical Nutrition* 52:127–30.

McCullough, M., W.T. Hoyt, D. Larson, H. Koenig, and C. Thoresen. 2000. "Religious Involvement and Mortality: A Meta-Analytic Review." *Health Psychology* 19:211–22.

Mukamal, K.J., K.M. Conigrave, M.A. Mittleman, C.A. Camargo, M.J. Stampfer, W.C. Willett, and E.B. Rimm. 2003. "Roles of Drinking Pattern and Type of Alcohol Consumed in Coronary Heart Disease in Men." *New England Journal of Medicine* 348:109–18.

Murray, R.P., J.E. Connett, S.L. Tyas, R. Bond, O. Ekuma, C.K. Silversides, and G.E. Barnes. 2002. "Alcohol Volume, Drinking Pattern, and Cardiovascular Disease Morbidity and Mortality: Is There a U-shaped Function?" *American Journal of Epidemiology* 155:242–48.

Musick, M.A., J.S. House, and D.R. Williams. 2004. "Attendance at Religious Services and Mortality in a National Sample." *Journal of Health and Social Behavior* 45:198–213.

Naeem, A.G. 2003. "The Role of Culture and Religion in the Management of Diabetes: A Study of Kashmiri Men in Leeds." *Journal of the Royal Society of Health* 123:110–16.

National Center for Health Statistics. 2003. *Health, United States, 2003.* Hyattsville, MD, National Center for Health Statistics.

Newell, C. 1988. *Methods and Models in Demography.* New York, NY, Guilford Press.

Nonnemaker, J.M., C.A. McNeely, and R.W. Blum. 2003. "Public and Private Domains of Religiosity and Adolescent Health Risk Behaviors: Evidence from the National Longitudinal Study of Adolescent Health." *Social Science and Medicine* 57:2049–54.

Ogata, M., M. Ikeda, and M. Kuratsune. 1984. "Mortality among Japanese Zen Priests." *Journal of Epidemiology and Community Health* 38:161–66.

Oman, D., J.H. Kurata, W.J. Strawbridge, and R.D. Cohen. 2002. "Religious Attendance and Cause of Death over 31 Years." *International Journal of Psychiatry in Medicine* 32:69–89.

Oman, D. and D. Reed. 1998. "Religion and Mortality among the Community-Dwelling Elderly." *American Journal of Public Health* 88:1496–75.

Østbye, T., K.M. Krause, M.C. Norton, J. Tschanz, L. Sanders, K. Hayden, C. Pieper, and K.A. Welsh-Bohmer. 2006. "Ten Dimensions of health and Their Relationships with Overall Self-Reported Health and Survival in a Predominately Religiously Active Elderly Population: The Cache County Memory Study." *Journal of the American Geriatrics Society* 54:199–209.

Pan, W.-H., C.-J. Chin, C.-T. Sheu, and M.-H. Lee. 1993. "Hemostatic Factors and Blood Lipids in Young Buddhist Vegetarians and Omnivores." *American Journal of Clinical Nutrition* 58:354–59.

Pescosolido, B. and S. Georgianna. 1989. "Durkheim, Suicide and Religion: Toward a Network Theory of Suicide." *American Sociological Review* 54:33–48.

Phillips, R.L., J.W. Kuzma, W.L. Beeson, and T. Lotz. 1980. "Influence of Selection versus Lifestyle on Risk of Fatal Cancer and Cardiovascular Disease among Seventh-Day Adventists." *American Journal of Epidemiology* 112:296–314.

Phillips, R.L., F.R. Lemon, W.L. Beeson, and J.W. Kuzma. 1978. "Coronary Heart Disease Mortality among Seventh-Day Adventists with Differing Dietary Habits: A Preliminary Report." *The American Journal of Clinical Nutrition* 31:S191–S98.

Powell, L., L. Shahabi, and C.E. Thoresen. 2003. "Religion and Spirituality: Linkages to Physical Health." *American Psychologist* 58:36–52.

Rehm, J., T.K. Greenfield, and J.D. Rogers. 2001. "Average Volume of Alcohol Consumption, Patterns of Drinking, and All-Cause Mortality: Results from the U.S. National Alcohol Survey." *American Journal of Epidemiology* 153:64–71.

Reynolds, P. and G.A. Kaplan. (Fall) 1990. "Social Connections and Risk for Cancer: Prospective Evidence from the Alameda County Study." *Behavioral Medicine* 16(3):101–10.

Rogers, R.G. 1996. "The Effects of Family Composition, Health, and Social Support Linkages on Mortality." *Journal of Health and Social Behavior* 37:326–38.

Schoenbach, V.J., B. Kaplan, L. Fredman, and D. Kleinbaum. 1986. "Social Ties and Mortality in Evans County, Georgia." *American Journal of Epidemiology* 123:577–91.

Shatenstein, B. and P. Ghadirian. 1998. "Influences on Diet, Health Behaviours and Their Outcome in Select Ethnocultural and Religious Groups." *Nutrition* 14:223–30.

Simmons, D., D.R. Williams, and M.J. Powell. 1992. "Prevalence of Diabetes in Different Regional and Religious South Asian Communities in Coventry." *Diabetic Medicine* 9:428–31.

Sloan, R.P. and E. Bagiella. 2001. "Spirituality and Medical Practice: A Look at the Evidence." *American Family Physician* 36:33–34.

Snowdon, D., R.L. Phillips, and G. Fraser. 1984. "Meat Consumption and Fatal Ischemic Heart Disease." *Preventive Medicine* 13:490–500.

Steffen, P.R., A.L. Hinderliter, J.A. Blumenthal, and A. Sherwood. 2001. "Religious Coping, Ethnicity, and Ambulatory Blood Pressure." *Psychosomatic Medicine* 63:523–30.

Strawbridge, W.J., R.D. Cohen, and S.J. Shema. 2000. "Comparative Strength of Association between Religious Attendance and Survival." *International Journal of Psychiatry in Medicine* 30:299–308.

Strawbridge, W.J., R.D. Cohen, S.J. Shema, and G.A. Kaplan. 1997. "Frequent Attendance at Religious Services and Mortality over 28 Years." *American Journal of Public Health* 87:957–61.

Susser, M. 1973. *Causal Thinking in the Health Sciences: Concepts and Strategies in Epidemiology*. New York, NY, Oxford University Press.

Taylor, R.S., B.E. Carroll, and J.W. Lloyd. 1959. "Mortality among Women in 3 Religious Orders with Special Reference to Cancer." *Cancer* 12:1207–25.

Umberson, D. 1987. "Family Status and Health Behaviors: Social Control as a Dimension of Social Integration." *Journal of Health and Social Behavior* 28:306–19.

Waite, L. and E.L. Lehrer. 2003. "The Benefits from Marriage and Religion in the United States: A Comparative Analysis." *Population and Development Review* 29: 255–75.

Whooley, M.A., A.L. Boyd, J.M. Gardin, and D.R. Williams. 2002. "Religious Involvement and Cigarette Smoking in Young Adults: The CARDIA Study (Coronary Artery Risk Development in Young Adults) Study." *Archives of Internal Medicine* 162:1604–10.

Williams, C.D., O. Lewis-Jack, K. Johnson, and L. Adams-Campbell. 2001. "Environmental Influences, Employment Status, and Religious Activity Predict Current Cigarette Smoking in the Elderly." *Addictive Behaviors* 26: 297–301.

Winslow, C.-E.A. 1937. "Public Health." In *Encyclopedia of the Social Sciences*, pp. 646–57. New York, NY, The MacMillan Company.

Yeager, D.M., D.A. Glei, M. Au, H.-S. Lin, R.P. Sloan, and M. Weinstein. 2006. "Religious Involvement and Health Outcomes among Older Persons in Taiwan." *Social Science and Medicine* 63:2228–41.

Zhang, W. 2008. "Religious Participation and Mortality Risk among the Oldest Old in China." *Journal of Gerontology: Social Sciences* 63B:S293–S97.

# Part III
# Biological Risk Factors

# Chapter 18
# Links Between Biomarkers and Mortality

Eileen M. Crimmins and Sarinnapha Vasunilashorn

## Introduction

### Biomarker Definition

A biomarker is an objectively measured indicator of a physiological state. Biomarkers include indicators of genotype, normal biological processes, pathogenic processes, and pharmacologic responses to a therapeutic intervention (Biomarkers Definitions Working Group 2001; National Heart Lung and Blood Institute 2007). Biomarkers can serve as objective indicators of health status within a sample, indicators of health change over time, and, with comparable measurement, indicators of differences across populations. They signal disease status, early physiological dysregulation preceding disease, or change in organ reserve or functioning. And they can clarify how the social, psychological, and behavioral factors traditionally examined in social science research get under the skin to influence biology and subsequent health outcomes (Crimmins and Seeman 2001, 2004; Crimmins et al. 2008a; Seeman and Crimmins 2001).

### Brief History

The identification and treatment of "risk factors" for cardiovascular events and mortality became widespread beginning in the 1950s (Black 1992). Community studies—such as the Framingham Study,

E.M. Crimmins (✉)
Department of Gerontology, Davis School of Gerontology, Andrus Gerontology Center, University of Southern California, Los Angeles, CA 90089, USA
e-mail: crimmin@usc.edu

which began in 1948, and the World Health Organization (WHO) Multinational Monitoring of Trends and Determinants in Cardiovascular Disease (MONICA) study, which began in 1980 in many countries of the world—were important sources of early linkage between a number of biomarkers and the risk of mortality and cardiovascular events (Dawber et al. 1957; Tunstall-Pedoe et al. 1994; WHO MONICA Project Principal Investigators 1988). The family of National Health and Nutrition Examination Surveys (NHANES) conducted by the National Center for Health Statistics has been the source of national data on indicators of biological risk in the United States for about 50 years (Crimmins et al. 2005; Kant and Graubard 2007; Muenning et al. 2007; Seeman et al. 2008).

As heart disease dominates mortality rates, biomarkers that indicate risk for cardiovascular events and mortality dominated early studies. High blood pressure, or what Janeway in 1913 called "hypertensive vascular disease" (Esunge 1991), has long been studied and known as a risk factor for several diseases that constitute the leading causes of death in the United States. In the mid-1960s, two landmark studies found that lowering hypertension was associated with a reduction in strokes (Hamilton and Thompson 1964; VA Cooperative Study Group 1967). Ancel Keys and J. Stamler promoted the idea of cholesterol as a risk factor for cardiovascular disease and stressed the role of diet and weight in raising cholesterol, leading to routine monitoring of the risk posed by elevated lipid levels (Keys et al. 1950; Stamler et al. 1986).

With rising obesity, much recent research has focused on the links among obesity, the metabolic syndrome, and mortality (Adams et al. 2006; Alberti et al. 2005; Després and Lemieux 2006). This has been accompanied by growing emphasis on multisystem effects and links. Markers of inflammation have been identified as indicators of risk for a variety of diseases and have sometimes been included in metabolic syndrome and linked to other cardiovascular risk factors (Dandona et al. 2005; Danesh et al. 1999; Yeh and Willerson 2003). In recent decades, treatment of chronic conditions has been increasingly related to the management of levels of biomarkers to delay disease progression and mortality. Recently, there has been much emphasis on the use of pharmaceuticals to control biomarkers and subsequent events (Grundy et al. 2004; Koenig et al. 2008; Neaton et al. 1993; Ridker et al. 2009).

As biomarkers became increasingly important as indicators of health in clinical practice, they have also become increasingly important indicators of population health in large demographic surveys. In the last decade, biomarkers have been added to self-reports of health in a number of national-level studies with a focus on population health (Lindau and McDade 2007; Weir 2007). These studies tend to be broad-based social science studies designed to address trends and differences in health in a multidisciplinary framework, and usually health is only one of many topics central to the study. This has led to the inclusion of biomarkers that predict a variety of major health outcomes in populations as well as biological indicators that might be affected by social, psychological, and economic circumstances.

Changes in technology have also contributed to the inclusion of biomarkers in population studies by allowing interviewers rather than medically trained personnel to collect samples in the field. For instance, the development of portable electronic measuring devices for blood pressure, cholesterol, anemia, and glucose has made field measurement of these markers possible. In addition, the diffusion of methods of collecting dried blood spots in field situations has also added to the ability to collect blood for later assay and include many more biomarkers in national surveys (McDade et al. 2007). Recent development of relatively noninvasive field methods for integrated collection and assays for many biomarkers allows new possibilities (Gootjes et al. 2009).

In recent years, biomarkers have been collected in the United States in a number of large nationally representative studies, including the Health and Retirement Survey (HRS), the National Social Life, Health and Aging Project (NSHAP), and the Adolescent Health Study (Add Health). Many other countries have also collected biomarkers in nationally representative studies, including the English Longitudinal Study of Aging (ELSA), the Taiwanese Social Environment and Biomarkers of Aging Study (SEBAS), the Chinese Health and Retirement Study (CHARLS), the Mexican Family Life Study (MxFLS), the Indonesian Family Life Study (IFLS), and the Costa Rican Study of Longevity and Healthy Aging (CRELES). The WHO has added collection of biomarkers to studies of aging (SAGE) in Mexico, China, Ghana, India, the Russian Federation, and South Africa (Crimmins et al. 2010b). The number of countries including biomarkers in national-level population studies increases every year, and the technology for collecting such indicators is improving very rapidly.

## Links Between Biomarkers in Population Studies and Mortality

Our discussion of biomarkers and mortality will be limited to biomarkers collected in large population surveys oriented toward the general population, not populations with specific conditions or diseases. Because the next chapter in this volume links genetic factors and biomarkers (Chapter 19 by Christensen and Vaupel, this volume), we do not include a discussion of genetic factors and mortality in this chapter. Our discussion of biomarkers and mortality is divided by physiological systems.

### *Cardiovascular System*

We begin with indicators of cardiovascular functioning, as heart disease is the leading cause of adult death in almost all countries.

*Blood pressure.* Blood pressure is one of the most commonly measured biomarkers because it can be an early indicator of cardiovascular dysregulation. High levels of either systolic blood pressure (SBP) or diastolic blood pressure (DBP) indicate hypertension. Hypertension is currently defined as SBP $\geq 140$ mm Hg or DBP $\geq 90$ mm Hg. Hypertension increases with age (Franklin et al. 1997) and varies by gender (Goldman et al. 2004; Kim et al. 2006; Price and Fowkes 1997), social and economic status (Colhoun et al. 1998), and race-ethnicity (Cornoni-Huntley et al. 1989), as well as across countries (Crimmins et al. 2008b; Wolf et al. 1997; Wolf-Maier et al. 2003). While much of the emphasis is on hypertension, rather than level of blood pressure, there is no evidence of a blood pressure threshold above which there is an adverse effect and below which there is no effect, as is sometimes implied by the rigid use of cutoffs for hypertension. There is a continuous and graded effect of increasing blood pressure down to 115/75 mm Hg; and persons age 40–69 experience a doubling of mortality risk from cardiovascular disease (CVD) with every 20 mm Hg increment in SBP or 10 mm Hg increase in DBP (Kannel et al. 2003). While low blood pressure has been associated with higher mortality among older persons, this is attributed to comorbid conditions rather than the direct effect of blood pressure and emphasizes the need to control for these conditions to determine the effect of blood pressure (Glynn et al. 1995).

Hypertension is regarded as a major cause of mortality. The WHO estimates that elevated blood pressure is the cause of 20.1% of attributable mortality for men and 23.9% for women (Figueras et al. 2008). Cohort studies have shown that SBP has stronger power to predict coronary heart disease (CHD) and life expectancy than does DBP (SHEP Cooperative Research Group 1991; Staessen et al. 1997; Stamler et al. 1989). Analysis of the Framingham sample with blood pressure measured in participants' at ages in their 40s showed that those with high SBP were only about half as likely to survive to age 85 as those without high SBP (20% versus 38%) (Terry et al. 2005). Framingham sample members with hypertension at age 50 lived about 5 years less than those with normal blood pressure levels (5.1 years for men and 4.9 years for women) (Franco et al. 2005). SBP values of 20 mm Hg lower almost halved the relative risk (RR) for mortality (0.57) (Terry et al. 2005). Similar results were found in the European cohorts of the Seven Countries Study, where the effect of having 20 mm Hg higher blood pressure at ages 40–59 on mortality up to 35 years later was substantial. It was largest (RR 1.41) in the first 10 years (after excluding the first 5 years after measurement), but still significant for the second (RR = 1.26) and third (RR = 1.11) 10-year periods. The effect on CVD deaths was even higher: 1.65, 2.33, and 1.22, respectively (Menotti et al. 2004).

Typically links between DBP and mortality are not as strong as those between SBP and mortality. Among the Framingham cohort, DBP at age 40 was not related to survival to age 85 (Terry et al. 2005), although DBP at ages 60 and over in the Framingham sample was inversely related to the risk of CHD (Franklin et al. 2001). However, some long-term cohort studies do find a link between high DBP at early ages and mortality; for instance, one using data from the Second National Health and Nutrition Examination Survey (1976–1980) finds that if DBP for those over age 35 had been controlled in 1990, men would have gained 1.1 years of life expectancy and women 0.4 years (Tsevat et al. 1991).

Treatment for hypertension is widespread and changes the link between hypertension and mortality (see also Chapter 28 by Bonneux, this volume). Estimates of the size of the effect depend on whether all or only cardiovascular mortality is examined. They also depend on the age and sex groups and time period examined. One estimate is that mortality within age–sex groups is reduced by 50% for every reduction of 20 mm Hg in SBP (Ford et al. 2000). Estimates of the effect of treatment in the elderly are somewhat smaller; a reduction of 26% was found in Celis et al. (2001) and 14% in the Europe (Syst-Eur) trial (Staessen et al. 1998).

While treatment greatly reduces the risk of mortality, treated hypertensives still had a RR of 1.5 for cardiovascular mortality relative to people who were never hypertensive. The higher mortality among treated individuals is due to the fact that for many, SBP is not controlled with treatment (Benetos et al. 2003). Only 60% of Americans aged 65 and over taking antihypertensives in 1999–2000 actually have measured SBP below the cutoff for hypertension (Crimmins et al. 2005).

Increasing use of antihypertensives to control blood pressure has been one of the major factors in the decrease in death rates from heart disease. In the United States, 20% of the decrease in mortality from CHD between 1980 and 2000 is said to be due to the control of SBP (Ford et al. 2007). Over time, treatment has occurred at lower levels of blood pressure and at older ages; this may result in diminishing returns to increasing treatment in the future.

*Pulse pressure.* Pulse pressure is an alternative measure of blood pressure based on the difference between SBP and DBP. Some researchers prefer to use pulse pressure as an indicator of blood pressure risk in the aged. During middle age, SBP and DBP tend to change similarly; but after age 60, DBP decreases and SBP continues to rise, resulting in larger increases in pulse pressure in older ages (Franklin et al. 2001). In some studies pulse pressure has been shown to be a more important determinant of CVD incidence and mortality than its components (Benetos et al. 1997; Celis et al. 2001; Kannel et al. 2003).

*Heart rate.* Most population studies also collect information on heart rate or pulse rate. At rest, the average adult pulse rate is 70 beats per minute (bpm) for males and 75 bpm for females; however, these rates may vary by age (Gillum et al. 1991; Limmer et al. 2005), sex (Gillum 1992), race and ethnicity (Gillum 1992), and exercise status (Bramwell and Ellis 1929). A pulse rate of 90 bpm or greater is considered high (Seccareccia et al. 2001) and is associated with increased risk of CHD, as well as all-cause mortality and both of its components, cardiovascular and noncardiovascular mortality (Gann et al. 1995; Gillum et al. 1991). Compared to a non-elevated pulse rate, a high pulse rate is associated with an increase in all-cause mortality at ages 45–74: RR = 1.95 for men and RR=1.27 for women (Gillum et al. 1991). Use of medication and changes in behavior, such as increases in physical activity, can decrease resting pulse rate and lower the risk of CVD and mortality (Andrews et al. 1993; Palatini et al. 1999; Sanchez-Delgado and Liechti 1999; Young et al. 1993).

## Metabolic Processes

The next set of markers is indicators of metabolic processes, several of which are included in measures of the metabolic syndrome (discussed in further detail below). These markers are related to both cardiovascular mortality and diabetes.

*Lipids.* Most population studies with nonfasting subjects measure total cholesterol and one subcomponent, high-density lipoprotein (HDL). Indicators of low-density lipoprotein (LDL) and triglycerides are often generated in fasting populations. Each lipid measure has a cutoff value, above which, or below which, in the case of HDL, a person is viewed as dyslipidemic. The WHO estimates that in developed countries, high cholesterol accounts for 14.5% of male and 17.6% of female attributable mortality (Figueras et al. 2008). At age 35 and older, control of total cholesterol to values of <200 mg/dL is estimated to add about ¾ of a year to life expectancy (Tsevat et al. 1991). Analysis of the Framingham Study data indicates that having elevated cholesterol at ages in the 40s reduced survival to age 85 from 35 to 30%; an increase of 40 mg/dL of serum cholesterol lowered a person's chances of surviving to 85 by about 11% (0.89 RR) (Terry et al. 2005). A study of three large long-term cohorts of American men estimated that those with favorable baseline serum-cholesterol levels had 3.8–6.7 years longer life expectancy than those with high cholesterol (Stamler et al. 2000).

Many studies emphasize the risk of high cholesterol, but a large meta-analysis has made clear that total cholesterol is related to CHD at all levels with no threshold (Prospective Studies Group 2007). The link between mortality in middle-aged populations and high total cholesterol level has long been established (Manolio et al. 1992). Recent evidence from prospective studies makes it clearer that high cholesterol is related to subsequent mortality across the age range (Prospective Studies Group 2007). Because at older ages the relationship between total cholesterol and mortality has sometimes been found to be U- or J-shaped, the question of whether high cholesterol poses the same risk at older ages has arisen (Anderson et al. 1987; Staessen et al. 1997). Because some people may experience a drop in cholesterol at the oldest ages, the age at which cholesterol is measured is important in determining its association with mortality. Lowered cholesterol at high ages may be an indicator of disease and impending death, suggesting that comorbidity needs to be considered at older ages in evaluating the effect of cholesterol on mortality (Ali and Alexander 2007).

A high level of LDL cholesterol, or bad cholesterol, has been shown to contribute to the development of coronary atherosclerosis and to increased risk of heart disease and mortality (Reed et al. 1986); again, studies limited to older persons report inconsistent findings on the relationship between LDL and health outcomes (Benfante et al. 1992; Fried et al. 1998; Frost et al. 1996; Jacobs et al. 1992; Karlamangla et al. 2004; Kronmal et al. 1993; Krumholz et al. 1994; Pekkanen et al. 1994; Raiha et al. 1997; Weverling-Rjinsburger et al. 1997). HDL is called the "good" cholesterol, and low levels (<40 mg/dL, although sometimes this level is sex-specific) have been related to increased risk for heart disease (Barter and Rye 1996; Barter et al. 2004; Gordon et al. 1989).

There has been a marked increase in many countries in the use of statins to reduce cholesterol (Crimmins et al. 2010a). In the United States, 24% of the decline in CHD death rates between 1980 and 2000 was due to control of cholesterol (Ford et al. 2007). (See Chapter 28 for further discussion of cholesterol.) In 2001–2006, one-third of the US population over age 70 used cholesterol-lowering drugs (Crimmins et al. 2010b). Statins appear useful in both primary and secondary treatment, although their use in the elderly for primary prevention is not clearly recommended (Ali and Alexander 2007; Nixon 2004). Observational studies indicate that statin use reduces mortality by 40–50%, but the estimates from randomly controlled trials are smaller (12%) (Shalev et al. 2009).

Sometimes the ratio of total cholesterol to HDL cholesterol is used as the indicator of risk. The prospective studies group has termed this ratio the most informative indicator of lipid regulation (Prospective Studies Group 2007). Studies of fasting populations may also include levels of triglycerides, which are an indicator of stored fat. High triglyceride levels have been associated with heart attack (Gaziano et al. 1997), CHD (Cullen 2000), and coronary artery disease (Linton and Fazio 2003), as well as cardiovascular and all-cause mortality (Shankar et al. 2007) relative to non-elevated triglyceride levels. In comparison to those in the lowest quartile, Australians in the highest quartile of triglycerides had a RR of 1.58 for cardiovascular mortality and 1.40 for all-cause mortality (Shankar et al. 2007).

*Glucose control.* Higher-than-normal fasting blood glucose can signal diabetes and pre-diabetes. Glucose intolerance in middle age markedly reduces the probability of survival to old age. Impaired fasting glucose and impaired glucose tolerance are strongly associated with increased risk of CVD and all-cause mortality (Barr et al. 2007). Members of the Framingham sample with glucose intolerance in their 40s were only 47% as likely to survive to age 85 as those without. Their survival was only 10%, while for others it was 35% (Terry et al. 2005).

Because it can be collected in a nonfasting sample, many population studies are collecting measures of glycosylated hemoglobin (HbA1c) as an alternative to fasting glucose. HbA1c indicates the average amount of sugar attached to red blood cells for the past 2–3 months and is an indicator of glucose control over that time. Glycosylated hemoglobin levels have been related to CVD and mortality among both diabetics and nondiabetics (Khaw et al. 2004). Among nondiabetics, a 1% increase in HbA1c was associated with an all-cause mortality RR of 1.24 in men and 1.28 in women. A very similar result was found among known diabetics (RR = 1.26).

*Weight and adiposity.* There are a number of indicators of weight and adiposity that can be collected in population surveys. These include self-reports or measurement of weight. If height is either self-reported or measured, the combination of height and weight can be used to calculate body mass index (BMI). Waist and hip circumference can be measured, and waist size or waist-to-hip ratio (WHR) can be used to indicate adiposity. Those with higher values of BMI, waist and hip circumferences, and WHR tend to be at higher risk for hypertension, adult-onset diabetes mellitus, heart disease, stroke, various forms of cancer, and mortality (see also Chapter 14 by Himes, this volume).

The WHO estimates that high BMI accounts for 9.6% of attributable mortality for men and 11.5% for women (Figueras et al. 2008). Reducing weight to ideal levels among 35-year olds is estimated to add 0.8 years to male life expectancy and 0.4 years to female life expectancy (Tsevat et al. 1991). Olshansky et al. (2005) have estimated that life expectancy would be one-third to three-quarters of a year higher in the US if obesity were eliminated.

Cohort studies estimate that the years of life lost because of obesity range from 5 to 25 years (Allison et al. 1999). For instance, in the Framingham study, male sample members who were obese at age 45 lived 6.0 years less than persons of normal weight and obese women lived 8.4 years less (Silva et al. 2006). The size of the effect varies with the length of follow-up, the age at baseline, the definition of obesity, and the treatment of short-term deaths. Studies that do not have long follow-up periods are subject to issues of reverse causation in linking weight and mortality, whereas studies that initially measure weight at ages 40–60 and follow people through ages 60–80 find a large effect of weight on mortality (Manson et al. 2007). Analysis of 57 prospective studies where the recruitment age averaged 46, and the first 5 years were eliminated to reduce the effect of reverse causation, found mortality lowest at a BMI of 22.5–25 kg/m$^2$. Above that group, mortality increased 30% for every 5 kg/m$^2$ increase in BMI. The effect of these differences was that people with Class 1 obesity, BMI 30–35 kg/m$^2$, had a life expectancy of

2–4 years shorter than those in the lowest-mortality BMI group, and those with Class III obesity, BMI 40–45 kg/m$^2$, had a life expectancy reduction of 8–10 years (Prospective Studies Collaboration et al. 2009).

The higher mortality at lower weights is often thought to be a confound of smoking, because smokers tend to weigh less. Some studies eliminate smokers to study the link between weight and mortality. For instance, a study of the very large NIH-AARP cohort, who were ages 50–71 at baseline and were then followed up to 10 years, found that those with the highest and lowest BMI had a higher risk of death. This study was limited to healthy never smokers, and the increase in mortality for overweight individuals was 20–40%; for the obese, it was 2–3 times greater (Adams et al. 2006). On the other hand, some studies analyze both smoking and weight. A study of Swedish military conscripts who were weighed in early adulthood (at about age 18) and followed for 38 years found that the effects of obesity and overweight on mortality were similar to those of engaging in heavy and light smoking, respectively (Neovius et al. 2009). Obesity and smoking were also similar in their effects on life expectancy in the Framingham study (Peeters et al. 2003).

Short-term studies examining mortality and BMI among the elderly may be especially problematic in terms of interpreting results. While no relationship between overweight and mortality, as well as elevated mortality below normal weights, is a common finding in studies of the elderly (Reynolds et al. 2005; Snih et al. 2007), these studies may underestimate the risks linked to higher weight for a number of reasons (Zamboni et al. 2005).

As the relationship between obesity and mortality continues to be debated, more attention has focused on other indicators of obesity and their associated risks. Comparing links between mortality and three indicators of adiposity (BMI, waist circumference, and WHR), Srikanthan et al. (2009) found that only WHR was associated with an increase in all-cause mortality in the MacArthur study of successful aging. This suggests that WHR may be a better indicator of the risk associated with adiposity.

*Height.* Height is frequently collected in population surveys and is one part of the BMI calculation; however, height is thought to represent an independent risk for mortality. Because height is determined at a young age and reflects both genetic and environmental conditions (Case and Paxson 2008) including both infection experience and nutrition, it reflects early life circumstances. Shorter height has been linked to higher mortality (Davey Smith et al. 2000; Song et al. 2003; see also Chapter 9 by Montez and Hayward, this volume).

## Inflammation, Immunity, and Infection

Inflammation is part of the body's immune response to tissue damage and infection. Past infections can both prime the immune system to respond to challenge and wear out the immune system, resulting in senescence.

*Inflammation.* The most commonly collected measured marker of inflammation is C-reactive protein (CRP). CRP is a protein produced in the liver that indicates general systemic levels of inflammation in response to infection or tissue damage or chronic disease (Pradhan et al. 2001; Ridker et al. 1997; Rifai and Ridker 2001). Chronically high levels of CRP (>3 and <10 mg/dL, omitting levels ≥10 mg/dL, which are assumed to represent current infection) are linked to higher mortality (Harris et al. 1999; Reuben et al. 2002), heart attack (Ridker et al. 1997), and stroke (Ridker et al. 2000) compared to those without chronically elevated CRP values. The effect of having high CRP (>3 mg/L) is a 3-year difference in life expectancy at age 70 (Jenny et al. 2007). While there is no prescribed treatment for high CRP, people with CRP ≥ 2 mg/L, but without elevated cholesterol, who take statins have been shown to have a reduction in major cardiovascular events (Ridker et al. 2008).

Cytokine levels also indicate an inflammatory response. Interleukin-6 (IL-6) is the cytokine most commonly measured in population surveys. IL-6 levels also rise with advancing age and are related to an increased risk of disability (Ferrucci et al. 1999; Reuben et al. 2002), cognitive decline (Weaver et al. 2002), and mortality (Harris et al. 1999; Reuben et al. 2002). Compared to older adults with no change or with decreases in IL-6, individuals with increased IL-6 were 2.4 times as likely to die over a 3-year period (Alley et al. 2007).

*Immunity and infection.* In most population studies, functioning of the immune system is indicated by the levels of common viruses. Most people are exposed to these viruses early in life, and their immune system continually works to keep the level of the virus in check. As the immune system wears out, levels of the virus rise. Cytomegalovirus (CMV) is a herpes virus that eventually infects almost everyone. In the United States, CMV infection prevalence is almost universal (91% in people ages 80 and over) (Staras et al. 2006). As age increases, the level of CMV increases, which may reflect an inability of the immune system to keep the virus under control. CMV seropositivity and high antibody levels have been associated with inflammation, CVD (Sorlie et al. 2000), endothelial dysfunction (Shen et al. 2004), frailty (Schmaltz et al. 2005), cognitive decline (Aiello et al. 2006), and mortality (Pawelec et al. 2009). Among adults with CHD, CMV seropositivity was shown to be associated with a doubling of risk for subsequent mortality after an average of 2.7 years follow-up (Hazard Ratio [HR] = 1.9) (Muhlestein et al. 2000).

There are many other indicators of exposure to infection that can indicate past and present challenges to the immune system. Many population studies have included indicators of the level of Epstein-Barr virus (EBV), another herpes virus to which almost all adults in the United States have been exposed. Levels of EBV also increase with age (Glaser et al. 1985), and EBV antibody level is used by some researchers as a marker of cell-mediated immunity (Glaser et al. 1991; Kiecolt-Glaser et al. 1999; McDade et al. 2000). At present no studies link EBV to mortality in the general population.

## Activity of the Hypothalamic-Pituitary Axis (HPA) and Sympathetic Nervous System (SNS)

*HPA axis.* Cortisol and its antagonist, dehydroepiandrosterone sulfate (DHEA-S), are indicators of HPA activity. Cortisol, a hormone produced in response to stress, is associated with negative health outcomes in old age, and consistently high levels may result from chronic physiological stress (Epel et al. 2000). However, in two samples of older adults, one in Taiwan and the MacArthur Study of Successful Aging in the US, cortisol was not related to mortality (Goldman et al. 2006; Seeman et al. 2004). On the other hand, in a case-control study of individuals with myocardial infarction, those who died exhibited higher baseline cortisol levels than survivors (Bain et al. 1992). The association between DHEA-S and mortality seems to differ by gender (Glei et al. 2004), with an inverse relationship for men (Barrett-Connor et al. 1986; Roth et al. 2002) and little or no relationship for women (Berr et al. 1996; Mazat et al. 2001; Trivedi and Khaw 2001). Among healthy men enrolled in the Baltimore Longitudinal Study of Aging, 25 years after initial examination only 20% of those with the highest distribution of DHEA-S had died; for men in the lowest distribution of DHEA-S, about 50% had died (Roth et al. 2002).

Insulin-like growth factor-1 (IGF-1) is a polypeptide protein hormone that affects neuronal structure and function across the lifespan. While high IGF-1 levels are associated with increased risk of prostate and breast cancer (Renehan et al. 2004), low IGF-1 levels have been linked to increased mortality (Cappola et al. 2003; Ekenstedt et al. 2006; Roubenoff et al. 2003) and coronary artery disease (Janssen et al. 1998). However, a recent study of a national US sample indicated no relationship between low IGF-1 and all-cause mortality or mortality from heart disease or cancer (Savdeh et al. 2007). A similar nonsignificant relationship between IGF-1 and mortality was found among Taiwanese older adults (OR = 0.99) (Goldman et al. 2006).

*Catecholamines.* Norepinephrine and epinephrine are catecholamines that are indicators of stress response. Norepinephrine is a neurotransmitter that mediates chemical communication in the sympathetic nervous system (SNS). Older persons have higher levels of norepinephrine because of a reduction in clearance (Christensen 1982; Wallin et al. 1981; Ziegler et al. 1976). High plasma norepinephrine is linked to higher mortality in the elderly (Semeraro et al. 1997), as are high levels of urinary catecholamine excretion (Reuben et al. 2000). In the MacArthur Study, the RR of 7-year mortality was 1.8 among people with high urinary norepinephrine excretion and 1.2 for those with high urinary epinephrine excretion compared to non-elevated levels (Reuben et al. 2000). No significant relationship was found among Taiwanese adults, where the OR linking high norepinephrine and mortality was 1.02 (Goldman et al. 2006).

The relationship between plasma epinephrine and adverse health outcomes seems varied (Christensen and Jensen 2006): high plasma epinephrine levels seem to have adverse effects on the cardiovascular system under certain conditions (e.g., among individuals with a previous myocardial infarction) (Goldstein 1984), whereas low-resting plasma epinephrine levels in a population study have been associated with increased cardiovascular mortality (Christensen and Schultz-Larsen 1994). Seeman and colleagues report a marginally significant association between higher urinary epinephrine and subsequent death in an older sample (Seeman et al. 2004). However, in a Taiwanese sample, Goldman et al. (2006) found no significant relationship between mortality and urinary epinephrine (OR = 0.82).

## Markers of Organ Function

*Kidney.* Creatinine is a chemical waste molecule excreted in the urine that indicates kidney function. It can be measured in either blood serum or urine. Reduced glomerular filtration rate (GFR), measured from serum creatinine, is associated with increased risk of CVD and death (Go et al. 2004). Studies have shown that creatinine clearance predicts stroke and cardiovascular mortality (Wannamethee et al. 1997). Individuals in the British Regional Heart Study in the highest tertile of serum creatinine had an all-cause mortality RR of 1.5 and a cardiovascular mortality RR of 1.8 (Wannamethee et al. 1997).

Cystatin C also provides an indicator of kidney function, perhaps a more sensitive one than serum creatinine (Dharnidharka et al. 2002). In contrast to serum creatinine, cystatin C levels are independent of age, sex, and lean muscle mass. Cystatin C predicts all-cause and cardiovascular mortality (Larsson et al. 2005; Shlipak et al. 2005, 2006a), risk of CVD (Sarnak et al. 2005), myocardial infarction (Shlipak et al. 2003), stroke (Shlipak et al. 2003), and chronic kidney disease (Shlipak et al. 2006b). In the health, aging, and body composition study, participants in the highest quintile of cystatin C were at greater risk of 6-year mortality for all causes of death compared to those in the lowest quintile of cystatin C (HR = 2.18) (Shlipak et al. 2006a). The results were similar for cardiovascular and other causes of mortality, except cancer mortality.

*Lung.* The peak flow rate (PEF) provides an indicator of functioning of the respiratory system. Normal PEF is 500–700 L/min for men and 380–500 L/min for women (Cross and Nelson 1991), but this varies with differences in height and weight (van Helden et al., 2001). Studies have shown that PEF is related to mortality; the RR of death increased 1.27 per 100 L/min decrease in PEF (Cook et al. 1991).

## Effects of Biomarkers on Mortality in Two Samples

Because it is difficult to ascertain the relative effect of the various biomarkers on mortality from so many different studies, many of which are clinical trials, it is useful to compare the effects of multiple biomarkers in the same sample and to examine the links between biomarkers and mortality in samples that are relatively representative of the population. Seeman and Crimmins and colleagues (Crimmins et al. 2008a; Seeman et al. 2004) have shown the links between a number of individual biomarkers and mortality in two US samples (Table 18.1): the MacArthur Study of Successful Aging (the first large-scale community-based study that collected an extensive number of biomarkers in a home-based setting) and the National Health and Nutrition Examination Survey (NHANES) III (1998–1994), a nationally representative sample of Americans. The MacArthur sample includes a wider range of biomarkers than NHANES. Logistic models were used in the MacArthur analysis and hazard models in the NHANES analysis to indicate the relative potential of each individual marker to explain the likelihood of dying among sample members. The NHANES III sample includes persons over age 40, while the MacArthur Study is limited to people ages 70–79 at baseline. In the MacArthur sample, deaths occurred in the 7.5 years after the measurement of the biomarkers, and in the NHANES sample up to 12 years after the interview. In each case, biomarkers are coded as high risk or not high risk, using either established clinical cutoffs or cutoffs used in previous research. Table 18.1 shows odds ratios (OR) indicating the relative likelihood associated with dying in years following the two surveys for each high-risk biomarker. Empty cells in Table 18.1 reflect unavailability of a given variable for that study.

In the NHANES sample, which spans the adult ages, many of the high-risk levels of the biomarkers are significantly associated with higher mortality, including SBP, pulse, glycosylated hemoglobin, fibrinogen,

**Table 18.1** Link between presence of risk levels of individual biomarkers and subsequent mortality[a]

|  | MacArthur—Age 70–79 7.5-year mortality ($N = 657$) | NHANES III—Age 40+ Mortality from interview to 2000 ($N = 7,417$) |
|---|---|---|
|  | Odds ratios for mortality | |
| Systolic blood pressure | 1.37 | 1.16* |
| Diastolic blood pressure | 1.40 | 1.01 |
| Pulse rate at 60 s | – | 1.26* |
| Total cholesterol (total cholesterol/HDL in MacArthur) | 0.87 | 0.98 |
| HDL cholesterol | 1.31 | 1.06 |
| Glycosylated hemoglobin | 1.34 | 1.31* |
| Body mass index (waist/hip ratio in MacArthur) | 1.27 | 0.90 |
| C-reactive protein | 1.67* | 1.00 |
| Il-6 | 1.41 | – |
| Fibrinogen | 1.28 | 1.29* |
| Albumin | 0.86 | 1.07 |
| Cortisol | 1.14 | – |
| DHEA-S | 1.39 | – |
| Norepinephrine | 1.49 | – |
| Epinephrine | 1.38* | – |
| Creatinine clearance | 2.22 | 1.31* |
| Peak flow | 2.18* | 1.40* |

Data Source: Seeman et al. (2004), calculated using logistic models. NHANES, calculated from data using hazard models.
Table reproduced from Crimmins et al. (2008a). HDL = high-density lipoprotein; IL-6 = interleukin-6; DHEA-S = dehydroepiandrosterone sulfate
[a] Age, gender, and education controlled.
*$p<0.01$.

creatinine clearance, and peak flow. The largest ORs are from markers linked to organ functioning, including creatinine clearance (OR = 1.31) and peak flow (OR = 1.40). In the older MacArthur sample, high-risk peak flow (OR = 2.18), CRP (OR=1.67), and epinephrine (OR = 1.38) were the only biological indicators associated with mortality. The results suggest the potential importance of some biomarkers not currently employed in clinical settings (e.g., epinephrine and markers of inflammation). Since only three biomarkers are significantly associated with mortality for ages 70–79 (as compared to six biomarkers for ages 40 and older), these results also suggest that some biomarkers may be more important in predicting mortality at younger ages than at older ages. Age may also influence the size of these relationships to mortality. At older ages, many risk factors are no longer significantly related to mortality, as those most susceptible to the risk would have died (Crimmins 2001).

Noreen Goldman and colleagues have examined the effect of multiple biomarkers on mortality in a national sample of older Taiwanese (Goldman et al. 2006, 2009; Turra et al. 2005). These studies also emphasize the importance of what would be considered nonclinical biomarkers, including markers of immunity and infection and neuroendocrine markers. Many of the more traditional biomarkers are not significantly related to mortality in this sample.

## Summary Measures of Biological Risk

Individual risk factors are interrelated, and multiple risk factors have been shown to increase mortality more than additively (Gruenewald et al. 2006; Seeman et al. 2001; Terry et al. 2005; Wang et al. 2006). For this reason, summary indicators of biological risk that include multiple factors have been developed. Some of the most commonly investigated summary measures include allostatic load, the Framingham score, syndrome X, and metabolic syndrome. These summary measures are better predictors of mortality than single measures (Seeman et al. 1997).

*Allostatic load.* Allostatic load is based on theories about the cumulative effects of physiological responses to stressors (McEwen 2000), and operational definitions reflect the body's stress response in multiple systems, including the cardiovascular, metabolic, HPA, SNS, and inflammatory/immune (Seeman et al. 1997, 2010). It is usually calculated as the number of high-risk markers out of ten or more. Higher allostatic load predicts increased risk of mortality (Karlamangla et al. 2006; Seeman et al. 1997). The risk of mortality increases with the score on allostatic load; increases in the RR over those with no high-risk markers are 1.67 for those with scores of 1–2, 2.45 for scores of 3–4, and 6.42 for those in the highest category of 7 or more (Seeman et al. 2001).

In an analysis of NHANES linking subsequent mortality to what they called "biological risk," because it included ten risk indicators included in allostatic load but not indicators of HPA and SNS processing, Crimmins et al. (2009) estimated that having three biological risk factors would reduce life expectancy at age 20 by 6–7 years.

*Framingham score.* The Framingham score was created using various known risk factors for CHD (Wilson et al. 1998). It includes behavioral as well as biological indicators. One point is given for each of seven risk factors: age (≥55 years for women, ≥45 years for men), hypertension, taking antihypertensive medication, smoking, diabetes, high total or LDL cholesterol, and low HDL cholesterol. This score is currently used in clinical practice to assess a patient's risk of developing heart disease over the next 10 years. It has been suggested, however, that the Framingham risk score is less predictive of adverse events, specifically of all-cause mortality, among older persons than among younger adults (Grundy et al. 2001).

*Metabolic syndrome or syndrome X.* In 2001, the term metabolic syndrome was defined by the National Expert Cholesterol Education Program (NCEP) and the Adult Treatment Panel III (ATPIII) to define a cluster of metabolic conditions characterized by obesity, hypertension, and dyslipidemia (Alberti et al. 2006). The most current definition includes high waist circumference and two of the following: high triglycerides, low HDL cholesterol, high SBP, or high fasting plasma glucose (Alberti et al. 2006). Individuals with metabolic syndrome have been shown to have a mortality risk from CVD that is twice as high as those without metabolic syndrome over a 7-year follow-up period (Isomaa et al. 2001).

Many of the metabolic syndrome or syndrome X markers overlap with those included in allostatic load. Seeman et al. (2001) have compared the links of allostatic load, syndrome X, and non-syndrome X biomarkers and shown the relative importance of some of the non-syndrome X markers, which include the catecholamines (norepinephrine and epinephrine), dihydroepiandrosterone sulfate, and urinary cortisol.

A number of researchers have used more sophisticated methods than a simple summation of the numbers of high-risk factors to examine the effect of multiple biomarkers on mortality. Karlamangla et al. (2006) used canonical correlation analysis to suggest that allostatic load was a better predictor of all-cause mortality risk than the Framingham risk score. Canonical correlation weights individual biomarkers differentially in creating a summary risk score (Karlamangla et al. 2002). It also allows inclusion of indicators of changes in biological indicators over time, as opposed to examining these indicators at a single-time-point.

Recursive partitioning uses multiple biological measures to partition individuals into low, intermediate, and high-allostatic load according to the outcome variable of interest. Applying this method to data from the MacArthur Study of Successful Aging, Gruenewald et al. (2006) demonstrated that multiple paths, composed of different combinations of biological markers, can lead to increased mortality risk. Another striking finding from recursive partitioning is the critical role that inflammatory markers play as mediators in older adult mortality. Recently Seeman et al. (2010) have used structural equation modeling to examine the value of estimating allostatic load as a metafactor.

## Future of Biomarkers in Studying Mortality

This chapter has briefly discussed how a number of biological indicators now included in some large-scale population studies are associated with mortality. We view many of these biomarkers as early signs of the process of dysregulation that can result in mortality (Crimmins, Kim, and Vasunilashorn 2010b). These biomarkers provide some clarification of the mechanisms by which more distal factors, including race/ethnicity, socioeconomic status, and health behaviors, affect mortality. It is also important to interpret these findings in their context, as some effects may be population or age specific, and some biomarkers may be more predictive of disability than of death.

The ability to collect and assay biologically relevant data in populations is changing very rapidly. Technological change is likely to continue at a rapid pace and to allow the collection of more markers using a variety of techniques. In addition, the ability to collect indicators of physiological status over some time period or in response to a challenge is likely to increase. For many studies biological markers are just beginning to be included and are taken at a single-time-point. Measures at multiple time points will improve upon our understanding of the relationship between biomarkers and mortality over a lifecycle. Finally, in the future, analysis of genetic factors, including expression, will be regularly incorporated into analysis of existing biomarkers and social and behavioral circumstances.

The real value of population surveys will be in incorporating the rich data on these social, economic, behavioral, and psychological factors along with biological data to explain health outcomes. Progress in the field is likely to come from understanding how the traditionally researched environmental and behavioral mechanisms work through or interact with biology to affect health outcomes.

**Acknowledgments** Support for this research was provided by NIH Grants P30 AG017265, T32 AG0037, and the USC Oakley Fellowship Fund.

## References

Adams, K.F., A. Schtzkin, T.B. Harris, V. Pipnis, T. Maouw, R. Ballard-Barbash, A. Hollenbeck, and M.F. Leitzmann. 2006. "Overweight, Obesity, and Mortality in a Large Prospective Cohort of Persons 50 to 71 Years Old." *New England Journal of Medicine* 355:763–78.

Aiello, A.E., M. Haan, L. Blythe, K. Moore, J.M. Gonzalez, and W. Jagust. 2006. "The Influence of Latent Viral Infection on Rate of Cognitive Decline Over 4 Years." *Journal of the American Geriatrics Society* 54:1046–54.

Alberti, K.G., P. Zimmet, and J. Shaw, for the IDF Epidemiology Task Force Consensus Group. 2005. "The Metabolic Syndrome—A New Worldwide Definition." *Lancet* 366:1059–62.

Alberti, K.G., P. Zimmet, and J. Shaw. 2006. "Metabolic Syndrome—A New Worldwide Definition. A Consensus Statement From the International Diabetes Federation." *Diabetes Medicine* 23:469–80.

Ali, R. and K.P. Alexander. 2007. "Statins for the Primary Prevention of Cardiovascular Events in Older Adults: A Review of the Evidence." *American Journal of Geriatric Pharmacotherapy* 5:52–63.

Alley, D.E., E. Crimmins, K. Bandeen-Roche, J. Guralnik, and L. Ferrucci. 2007. "Three Year Change in Inflammatory Markers in Elderly People and Mortality: The Invecchiare in Chianti Study." *Journal of the American Geriatrics Society* 55:1801–7.

Allison, D.B., K.R. Fontaine, J.E. Manson, J. Stevens, and T.B. VanItallie. 1999. "Annual Deaths Attributable to Obesity in the United States." *Journal of the American Medical Association* 282:1530–38.

Anderson, K.M., W.P. Castelli, and D. Levy. 1987. "Cholesterol and Mortality: 30 Years of Follow-Up From the Framingham Study." *Journal of the American Medical Association* 257:2176–80.

Andrews, T.C., T. Fenton, N. Toyosaki, S.P. Glasser, P.M. Young, G. MacCallum, R.S. Gibson, T.L. Shook, and P.H. Stone. 1993. "Subsets of Ambulatory Myocardial Ischemia Based on Heart Rate Activity. Circadian Distribution and Response to Anti-Ischemic Medication. The Angina and Silent Ischemia Study Group (ASIS)." *Circulation* 88: 92–100.

Bain, R.J., J.P. Fox, J. Jagger, M.K. Davies, W.A. Littler, and R.G. Murray. 1992. "Serum Cortisol Levels Predict Infarct Size and Patient Mortality." *International Journal of Cardiology* 37:145–50.

Barr, E.L.M., P.Z. Zimmet, T.A. Welborn, D. Jolley, D.J. Magliano, D.W. Dunstan, A.J. Cameron, T. Dwyer, H.R. Taylor, A.M. Tonkin, T.Y. Wong, J. McNeil, and J.E. Shaw. 2007. "Risk of Cardiovascular and All-Cause Mortality in Individuals With Diabetes Mellitus, Impaired Fasting Glucose, and Impaired Glucose Tolerance: The Australian Diabetes, Obesity, and Lifestyle Study (AusDiab)." *Circulation* 116:151–57.

Barrett-Connor, E., K.T. Khaw, and S.S.C. Yen. 1986. "A Prospective Study of Dehydroepiandrosterone Sulfate, Mortality, and Cardiovascular Disease." *New England Journal of Medicine* 315:1519–24.

Barter, P.J., S. Nicholls, K.A. Rye, G.M. Anantharamaiah, M. Navab, and A.M. Fogelman. 2004. "Anti-inflammatory Properties of HDL." *Circulation Research* 95: 764–72.

Barter, P.J. and K.A. Rye. 1996. "High Density Lipoproteins and Coronary Heart Disease." *Atherosclerosis* 121:1–12.

Benetos, A., M. Safar, A. Rudnichi, H. Smulyan, J.L. Richard, P. Ducimetièère, and L. Guize. 1997. "Pulse Pressure: A Predictor of Long-Term Cardiovascular Mortality in a French Male Population." *Hypertension* 30:1410–15.

Benetos, A., F. Thomas, K. Bean, and L. Guize. 2003. "Why Cardiovascular Mortality Is Higher in Treated Hypertensives Versus Subjects of the Same Age, in the General Population." *Journal of Hypertension* 21:1635–40.

Benfante, R., D. Reed, and J. Frank. 1992. "Do Coronary Heart Disease Risk Factors Measured in the Elderly Have the Same Predictive Roles as in the Middle Aged: Comparisons of

Relative and Attributable Risks." *Annals of Epidemiology* 2:273–82.
Berr, C., S. Lafont, B. Debuire, J.F. Dartigues, and E.E. Baulieau. 1986. "Relationships of Dehydroepiandrosterone Sulfate in the Elderly with Functional, Psychological, and Mental Status, and Short-Term Mortality: A French Community-Based Study." *Proceedings of the National Academy of Sciences USA* 93:13410–15.
Biomarkers Definitions Working Group. 2001. "Biomarkers and Surrogate Endpoints: Preferred Definitions and Conceptual Framework." *Clinical Pharmacoloy and Therapeutics* 69:89–95.
Black, H. 1992. "Cardiovascular Risk Factors." In B.L. Zaret, L.S. Cohen, and M. Moser (eds.), *The Yale University School of Medicine Heart Book 1992*, pp. 23–35. New York, NY, Hearst Books.
Bramwell, C. and R. Ellis. 1929. "Clinical Observations on Olympic Athletes." *European Journal of Applied Physiology* 2:51–60.
Cappola, A.R., Q.L. Xue, L. Ferrucci, J.M. Guralnik, S. Volpato, and L.P. Fried 2003. "Insulin-Like Growth Factor I and Interleukin-6 Contribute Synergistically to Disability and Mortality in Older Women." *Journal of Clinical Endocrinology Metabolism* 88:2019–25.
Case, A., and C. Paxson. 2008. "Stature and Status: Height, Ability, and Labor Market Outcomes." *Journal of Political Economy* 116:499–532.
Celis, H., R. Fagard, J. Staessen, and L. This. 2001. "Risk and Benefit of Treatment of Isolated Systolic Hypertension in the Elderly: Evidence from the Systolic Hypertension in Europe Trial." *Current Opinion in Cardiology* 6:342–48.
Christensen, N.J. 1982. "Sympathetic Nervous Activity and Age." *European Journal of Clinical Investigation* 12:91–92.
Christensen, N.J. and E.W. Jensen. 2006. "Sympathoadrenal Activity and Psychosocial Stress." *Annals of the New York Academy of Sciences* 771:640–47.
Christensen, N.J. and K. Schultz-Larsen. 1994. "Resting Venous Plasma Adrenalin in 70-Year-Old Men Correlated Positively to Survival in a Population Study: The Significance of the Physical Working Capacity." *Journal of Internal Medicine* 235:229–32.
Colhoun, H.M., H. Heminway, and N.R. Poulter. 1998. "Socio-Economic Status and Blood Pressure: An Overview Analysis." *Journal of Human Hypertension* 12:91–110.
Cook, N.R., D.A. Evans, P.A. Scherr, F.E. Speizer, J.O. Taylor, and C.H. Hennekens. 1991. "Peak Expiratory Flow Rate and 5-Year Mortality in an Elderly Population." *American Journal of Epidemiology* 133:784–94.
Cornoni-Huntley, J., A.Z. LaCroix, and R.J. Havlik. 1989. "Race and Sex Differentials in the Impact of Hypertension in the United States." *Archives of Internal Medicine* 149:780–88.
Crimmins, E.M. 2001. "Mortality and Health in Human Life Spans." *Experimental Gerontology* 36:885–97.
Crimmins, E.M., D. Alley, S.L. Reynolds, M. Johnston, A. Karlamangla, and T. Seeman. 2005. "Changes in Biological Markers of Health: Older Americans in the 1990s." *Journals of Gerontology A Biological Sciences Medical Sciences* 60:1409–13.
Crimmins, E.M., K. Garcia, and J.K. Kim 2010a. "Are International Differences in Life-Expectancy Similar to International Differences in Health?" In E.M. Crimmins, S.H. Preston, and B. Cohen, (Eds.), *International Differences in Mortality at Older Ages: Dimensions and Sources.* Panel on Understanding Divergent Trends in Longevity in High-Income Countries. Washington, DC, The National Academies Press.
Crimmins, E.M., J.K. Kim, and T. Seeman. 2009. "Poverty and Biological Risk: The Earlier 'Aging' of the Poor." *Journals of Gerontology A Biological Science Medical Science* 64: 286–92.
Crimmins, E.M., J.K. Kim, and S. Vasunilashorn. 2010b. "Biodemography: New Approaches to Understanding Trends and Differences in Population Health and Mortality." *Demography* 47:41–64.
Crimmins, E.M. and T. Seeman. 2001. "Integrating Biology into Demographic Research on Health and Aging (With a Focus on the MacArthur Study of Successful Aging)." In C. Finch and J. Vaupel. (eds.), *Cells and Surveys: Should Biological Measures Be Included in Social Science Research?* pp. 9–41. Washington, DC, National Academy Press.
Crimmins, E.M. and T. Seeman. 2004. "Integrating Biology into the Study of Health Disparities." *Population Development Review* 30:89–107.
Crimmins, E.M., S. Vasunilashorn, J.K. Kim, and D. Alley. 2008a. "Biomarkers Related to Aging in Human Populations." *Advances in Clinical Chemistry* 46:161–217.
Crimmins, E.M., S. Vasunilashorn, J.K. Kim, A. Hagedorn, and Y. Saito. 2008b. "A Comparison of Biological Risk Factors in Two Populations: The United States and Japan." *Population Development Review* 34:457–82.
Cross, D. and H.S. Nelson. 1991. "The Role of the Peak Flow Meter in the Diagnosis and Management of Asthma." *Journal of Allergy and Clinical Immunology* 87: 120–28.
Cullen, P. 2000. "Evidence That Triglycerides Are an Independent Coronary Heart Disease Risk Factor." *American Journal of Cardiology* 86:943–49.
Dandona, P., A. Aljada, A. Chaudhuri, P. Mohanty, and R. Garg. 2005. "Metabolic Syndrome. A Comprehensive Perspective Based on Interactions Between Obesity, Diabetes, and Inflammation." *Circulation* 111:1448–54.
Danesh, J., J. Muir, Y.K. Wong, M. Ward, J.R. Gallimore, and M.B. Pepys. 1999. "Risk Factors for Coronary Heart Disease and Acute-Phase Proteins. A Population-Based Study." *European Heart Journal* 20:954–59.
Davey Smith, G., C. Hart, M. Upton, D. Hole, C. Gillis, G. Watt, and V. Hawthorne. 2000. "Height and Risk of Death Among Men and Women: Aetiological Implications of Associations With Cardiorespiratory Disease and Cancer Mortality." *Journal of Epidemiology and Community Health* 54:97–103.
Dawber, T.R., F.E. Moore, and G.V. Mann. 1957. "Coronary Heart Disease in the Framingham Study." *American Journal of Public Health Nations Health* 47:424.
Després, J.-P. and I. Lemieux. 2006. "Abdominal Obesity and Metabolic Syndrome." *Nature* 444:881–87.
Dharnidharka, V.R., C. Kwon, and G. Stevens. 2002. "Serum Cystatin C Is Superior to Serum Creatinine as a Marker of Kidney Function: A Meta-Analysis." *American Journal of Kidney Diseases* 40:221–26.
Ekenstedt, K.J., W.E. Sonntag, R.F. Loeser, B.R. Lindgren, and C.S. Carlson. 2006. "Effects of Chronic Growth

Hormone and Insulin-Like Growth Factor 1 Deficiency on Osteoarthritis Severity in Rat Knee Joints." *Arthritis and Rheumatism* 54:3850–58.

Epel, E.S., B. McEwen, T. Seeman, K. Matthews, G. Castellazzo, K.D. Brownell, J. Bell, and J.R. Ickovics. 2000. "Stress and Body Shape: Stress-Induced Cortisol Secretion Is Consistently Greater Among Women With Central Fat." *Psychosomatic Medicine* 62:623–32.

Esunge, P.M. 1991. "From Blood Pressure to Hypertension: The History of Research." *Journal of the Royal Society of Medicine* 84:621.

Ferrucci, L., T.B. Harris, J.M. Guralnik, R.P. Tracy, M.C. Corti, H.J. Cohen, B. Penninx, M. Pahor, R. Wallace, and R.J. Havlik. 1999. "Serum IL-6 Level and the Development of Disability in Older Persons." *Journal of the American Geriatrics Society* 47:639–46.

Figueras, J., M. Mckee, S. Lessof, A. Duran, and N. Menabde. 2008. *Health Systems, Health, and Wealth: Assessing the Case for Investing in Health Systems*, pp. 1–80. Copenhagen, Denmark, WHO.

Ford, E.S., U.A. Ajani, J.B. Croft, J.A. Critchley, D.R. Labarthe, T.E. Kottke, W.H. Giles, and S. Capewell. 2007. "Explaining the Decrease in U.S. Deaths from Coronary Disease, 1980–2000." *New England Journal of Medicine* 356:2388–98.

Ford, E.S., W.H. Giles, and J.B. Croft. 2000. "Prevalence of Nonfatal Coronary Heart Disease Among American Adults." *American Heart Journal* 139:371–77.

Franco, O.H., A. Peeters, L. Bonneux, and C. de Laet. 2005. "Blood Pressure in Adulthood and Life Expectancy with Cardiovascular Disease in Men and Women." *Hypertension* 46:280–86.

Franklin, S.S., W. Gustin, IV, N.D. Wong, M.G. Larson, M.A. Weber, W.B. Kannel, and D. Levy. 1997. "Hemodynamic Patterns of Age-Related Changes in Blood Pressure: The Framingham Heart Study." *Circulation* 96:308–15.

Franklin, S.S., M.G. Larson, S.A. Kahn, N.D. Wong, E.P. Leip, W.B. Kannel, and D. Levy. 2001. "Does the Relation of Blood Pressure to Coronary Heart Disease Risk Change With Aging? The Framingham Heart Study." *Circulation* 103:1245–49.

Fried, L.P., R.A. Kronmal, A.B. Newman, D.E. Bild, M.B. Mittelmark, J.F. Polak, J.A. Robbins, and J.M. Gardin. 1998. "Risk Factors for 5-Year Mortality in Older Adults: The Cardiovascular Health Study." *Journal of the American Medical Association* 279:585–92.

Frost, P.H., B.R. Davis, A.J. Burlando, J.D. Curb, G.P. Guthrie, Jr., J.L. Isaacsohn, S. Wassertheil-Smoller, A.C. Wilson, and J. Stamler. 1996. "Serum Lipids and Incidence of Coronary Heart Disease. Findings from the Systolic Hypertension in the Elderly Program (SHEP)." *Circulation* 94:2381–82.

Gann, P.H., M.L. Daviglus, A.R. Dyer, and J. Stamler. 1995. "Heart Rate and Prostate Cancer Mortality: Results of a Prospective Analysis." *Cancer Epidemiology Biomarkers and Prevention* 4:611–16.

Gaziano, J.M., C.H. Hennekens, C.J. O'Donnell, J.L. Breslow, and J.E. Buring. 1997. "Fasting Triglycerides, High-Density Lipoprotein, and Risk of Myocardial Infarction." *Circulation* 96:2520–25.

Gillum, R.F. 1992. "Epidemiology of Resting Pulse Rate of Persons Age 25–74 – Data from NHANES 1971–1974." *Public Health Report* 107:193–201.

Gillum, R.F., D.M. Makuc, and J.J. Feldman. 1991. "Pulse Rate, Coronary Heart Disease and Death: The NHANES I Epidemiologic Follow-up Study." *American Heart Journal* 121:172–77.

Glaser, R., J.K. Kiecolt-Glaser, C.E. Speicher, and J.E. Holliday. 1985. "Stress, Loneliness, and Changes in Herpesvirus Latency." *Journal of Behavioral Medicine* 8:249–60.

Glaser, R., G.R. Pearson, J.F. Jones, J. Hillhouse, S. Kennedy, H.Y. Mao, and J.K. Kiecolt-Glaser. 1991. "Stress-Related Activation of Epstein-Barr Virus." *Brain, Behavior, and Immunity* 5:219–32.

Glei, D.A., N. Goldman, M. Weinstein, and I.W. Liu. 2004. "Dehydroepiandrosterone Sulfate (DHEAS) and Health: Does the Relationship Differ by Sex?" *Experimental Gerontology* 39:321–31.

Glynn, R.J., T.S. Fiedl, B. Rosner, P.R. Hebert, J.O. Taylor, and C.H. Hennekens. 1995. "Evidence for a Positive Linear Relation Between Blood Pressure and Mortality in Elderly People." *Lancet* 345:825–29.

Go, A.S., G.M. Chertow, D. Fan, C.E. McCulloch, and C.Y. Hsu. 2004. "Chronic Kidney Disease and the Risks of Death, Cardiovascular Events, and Hospitalization." *New England Journal of Medicine* 351:1296–305.

Goldman, N., D. Glei, Y.-H. Lin, and M. Weinstein. 2009. "Improving Mortality Prediction Using Biosocial Surveys." *American Journal of Epidemiology* 169:769–79.

Goldman, N., C. Turra, D. Glei, C. Seplaki, Y.-H. Lin, and M. Weinstein. 2006. "Predicting Mortality from Clinical and Nonclinical Biomarkers." *Journal of Gerontology: Medical Sciences* 61:1070–74.

Goldman, N., M. Weinstein, J. Cornman, B. Singer, T. Seeman, and M. Chang. 2004. "Sex Differentials in Biological Risk Factors for Chronic Disease: Estimates from Population-Based Surveys." *Journal of Women's Health* 13:393–403.

Goldstein, D.S. 1984. "Plasma Catecholamines in Clinical Studies of Cardiovascular Diseases." *Acta Physiologica Scandinavica Supplementum* 527:39–41.

Gootjes, J., R.M. Tel, F. Bergkamp, and J. Gorgols. 2009. "Laboratory Evaluation of a Novel Capillary Blood Sampling Device for Measuring 8 Clinical Chemistry Parameters and HbA1C." *Clinica Chimica Acta* 401:152–57.

Gordon, D.J., J.L. Probstfield, R.J. Garrison, J.D. Neaton, W.P. Castelli, J.D. Knoke, D.R. Jacobs, Jr., S. Bandiwala, and H.A. Tyroler. 1989. "High-Density Lipoprotein Cholesterol and Cardiovascular Disease. Four Prospective American Studies." *Circulation* 79:8–15.

Gruenewald, T.L., T. Seeman, C.D. Ryff, A.S. Karlamangla, and B.H. Singer. 2006. "Combinations of Biomarkers Predictive of Later Life Mortality." *Proceedings of the National Academy of Sciences of the United States of America* 103:14158–63.

Grundy, S.M., J.I. Cleeman, C.N. Merz, H.B. Brewer, Jr., L.T. Clark, D.B. Hunninghake, R.C. Pasternak, S.C. Smith, Jr., N.J. Stone, and Coordinating Committee of the National Cholesterol Education Program. 2004. "Implications of Recent Clinical Trials for the National Cholesterol Education Program Adult Treatment Panel Guidelines." *Circulation* 110:227–39.

Grundy, S.M., R.B. D'Agostino, L. Mosca, G.L. Burke, P.W. Wilson, D.J. Rader, J.I. Cleeman, E.J. Roccella, J.A. Cutler, and L.M. Friedman. 2001. "Cardiovascular Risk Assessment Based on US Cohort Studies: Findings From a National Heart, Lung, and Blood Institute Workshop." *Circulation* 104:491–96.

Hamilton, M. and E.N. Thompson. 1964. "The Role of Blood Pressure Control in Preventing Complications of Hypertension." *Lancet* 1:235–39.

Harris, T.B., L. Ferrucci, R.P. Tracy, M.C. Corti, S. Wacholder, W.H. Ettinger, Jr., H. Heimovitz, H.J. Cohen, and R. Wallace. 1999. "Associations of Elevated Interleukin-6 and C-Reactive Protein Levels with Mortality in the Elderly." *American Journal of Medicine* 106:506–12.

Isomaa, B., P. Almgren, T. Tuomi, B. Forsén, K. Lahti, M. Nissén, M.-R. Taskinen, and L. Groop. 2001. "Cardiovascular Morbidity and Mortality Associated with the Metabolic Syndrome." *Diabetes Care* 24:683–89.

Jacobs, D., H. Blackburn, M. Higgins, D. Reed, H. Iso, G. McMillan, J. Nelson, J. Potter, and B. Rifkind. 1992. "Report of the Conference on Low Blood Cholesterol: Mortality Associations." *Circulation* 86:1046–60.

Janssen, J.A., R.P. Stolk, H.A. Pols, D.E. Grobbee, and S.W. Lamberts. 1998. "Serum Total IGF-I, Free IGF-I, and IGFB-1 Levels in an Elderly Population: Relation to Cardiovascular Risk Factors and Disease." *Arteriosclerosis, Thrombosis, and Vascular Biology* 18:277–82.

Jenny, N., N. Yanez, B. Psaty, L. Kuller, C. Hirsch, and R. Tracy. 2007. "Inflammation Biomarkers and Near-Term Death in Older Men." *American Journal of Epidemiology* 165: 684–95.

Kannel, W., R. Vasan, and D. Levy. 2003. "Is the Relation of Systolic Blood Pressure to Risk of Cardiovascular Disease Continuous and Graded, or Are There Critical Values?" *Hypertension* 42:453–56.

Kant, A. and B.I. Graubard. 2007. "Secular Trends in the Association of Socio-Economic Position with Self-Reported Dietary Attributes and Biomarkers in the US Population: National Health and Nutrition Examination Survey (NHANES) 1971–1975 to NHANES 1999–2002." *Public Health Nutrition* 10:158–67.

Karlamangla, A.S., B.H. Singer, B.S. McEwen, J.W. Rowe, and T.E. Seeman. 2002. "Allostatic load as a predictor of functional decline MacArthur studies of successful aging." *Journal of Clinical Epidemiology* 55:696–710.

Karlamangla, A.S., B.H. Singer, D.B. Reuben, and T.E. Seeman. 2004. "Increases in Serum Non-High-Density Lipoprotein Cholesterol May Be Beneficial in Some High-Functioning Older Adults: MacArthur Studies of Successful Aging." *Journal of the American Geriatrics Society* 52:487–94.

Karlamangla, A.S., B.H. Singer, and T.E. Seeman. 2006. "Reduction in Allostatic Load in Older Adults Is Associated with Lower All-Cause Mortality Risk: MacArthur Studies of Successful Aging." *Psychosomatic Medicine* 68: 500–7.

Keys, A., O. Mickelsen, E.O. Miller, and C.B. Chapman. 1950. "The Relation in Man Between Cholesterol Levels in the Diet and in the Blood." *Science* 112:79–81.

Khaw, K.T., N. Wareham, S. Bingham, R. Luben, A. Welch, and N. Day. 2004. "Association of Hemoglobin A1c with Cardiovascular Disease and Mortality in Adults: The European Prospective Investigation Into Cancer in Norfolk." *Annals of Internal Medicine* 141:413–20.

Kiecolt-Glaser, J.K., M.W. Malarkey, J.T. Cacioppo, and R. Glaser. 1999. "Stressful Personal Relationships: Immune and Endocrine Function." In R.K. Glaser, *Handbook of Human Stress and Immunity*, pp. 321–39. San Diego, CA, Academic Press.

Kim, J.K., D. Alley, T. Seeman, A. Karlamangla, and E. Crimmins. 2006. "Recent Changes in Cardiovascular Risk Factors Among Women and Men." *Journal of Women's Health* 15:734–46.

Koenig, W., P. Libby, A.J. Lorenzatti, J.G. MacFadyen, B.G. Nordestgaard, J.Shepherd, J.T. Willerson, R.J. Glynn, and the JUPITER Trial Study Group. 2008. "Rosuvastin to Prevent Vascular Events in Men and Women with Elevated C-Reactive Protein." *New England Journal of Medicine* 359:2195–207.

Kronmal, R.A., K.C. Cain, Z. Ye, and G.S. Omenn. 1993. "Total Serum Cholesterol Levels and Mortality Risk as a Function of Age. A Report Based on the Framingham Data." *Archives of Internal Medicine* 153:1065–73.

Krumholz, H.M., T.E. Seeman, S.S. Merrill, C.F. Mendes de Leon, V. Vaccarino, D.I. Silverman, R. Tsukahara, A.M. Ostfeld, and L.F. Berkman. 1994. "Lack of Association Between Cholesterol and Coronary Heart Disease Mortality and Morbidity and All-Cause Mortality in Persons Older Than 70 years." *Journal of the American Medical Association* 272:1335–40.

Larsson, A., J. Helmersson, L.O. Hansson, and S. Basu. 2005. "Increased Serum Cystatin C is Associated with Increased Mortality in Elderly Men." *Scandinavian Journal of Clinical and Laboratory Investigation* 65:301–5.

Limmer, D., M. O'Keefe, J.D. Bergeron, B. Murray, H. Grant, and E. Dickinson. 2005. *Emergency Care AHA Update* (10th ed.) Upper Saddle River, NJ, Prentice Hall.

Lindau, S.T. and T.W. McDade. 2007. "Minimally Invasive and Innovative Methods for Biomeasurement in Population-Based Research." In M. Weinstein, J.W. Vaupel, and K.W. Wachter (eds.), *Biosocial Surveys 2007*, pp. 251–77. Washington, DC, National Academies Press.

Linton, M.F. and S. Fazio. 2003. "A Practical Approach to Risk Assessment to Prevent Coronary Artery Disease and Its Complications." *American Journal of Cardiology* 92: 19–26.

Manolio, T.A., T.A. Pearson, N.K. Wenger, E. Barrett-Connor, G.H. Payne, and W.R. Harlan. 1992. "Cholesterol and Heart Disease in Older Persons and Women. Review of an NHLBI Workshop." *Annals of Epidemiology* 2:161–76.

Manson, J.E., S.S. Bassuk, F.B. Hu, M.J. Stampfer, G.A. Colditz, and W.C. Willett. 2007. "Estimating the Number of Deaths Due to Obesity: Can the Divergent Findings Be Reconciled?" *Journal of Women's Health* 16:168–76.

Mazat, L., S. Lafont, C. Berr, B. Debuire, J.F. Tessier, J.F. Dartigues, and E.E. Baulieu. 2001. "Prospective Measurements of Dehyproepiandrosterone Sulfate in a Cohort of Elderly Subjects: Relationship to Gender, Subjective Health, Smoking Habits, and 10-Year Mortality." *Proceedings of the National Academy of Sciences USA* 98:8145–50.

McDade, T.W., J.F. Stallings, A. Angold, E.J. Costello, M. Burleson, J.T. Cacioppo, R. Glaser, and C.M. Worthman. 2000. "Epstein-Barr Virus Antibodies in Whole Blood Spots: A Minimally Invasive Method for Assessing an Aspect of Cell-Mediated Immunity." *Psychosomatic Medicine* 62: 560–67.

McDade, T.W., S. Williams, and J.J. Snodgrass. 2007. "What a Drop Can Do: Dried Blood Spots as a Minimally-Invasive Method for Integrating Biomarkers Into Population-Based Research." *Demography* 44:899–925.

McEwen, B.S. 2000. "Allostasis and Allostatic Load: Implications for Neuropsychopharmacology." *Neuropsychology* 22:108–24.

Menotti, A., M. Lanti, A. Kafatos, A. Nissinen, A. Donatas, S. Nedeljkovic, and D. Kromhout. 2004. "The Role of Baseline Causal Blood Pressure Measurement and of Blood Pressure Changes in Middle Age in Prediction of Cardiovascular and All-Cause Mortality Occurring Late in Life: A Cross-Cultural Comparison Among the European Cohorts of the Seven Countries Study." *Journal of Hypertension* 22:1683–90.

Muenning, P., N. Sohler, and B. Mahato. 2007. "Socioeconomic Status as an Independent Predictor of Physiological Biomarkers of Cardiovascular Disease: Evidence from NHANES." *Preventive Medicine* 45:35–40.

Muhlestein, J.B., B.D. Horne, J.F. Carlquist, T.E. Madsen, T.L. Bair, R.R. Pearson, and J.L. Anderson. 2000. "Cytomegalovirus Seropositivity and C-Reactive Protein Have Independent and Combined Predictive Value for Mortality in Patients with Angiographically Demonstrated Coronary Artery Disease." *Circulation* 102: 1917–23.

National Cholesterol Education Program and Adult Treatment Panel III. 2001. "Executive Summary of the Third National Cholesterol Education Program (NCEP) Expert Panel on Detection, Evaluation, and Treatment of High Blood Cholesterol in Adults (Adult Treatment Panel III)." *Journal of the American Medical Association* 285:2486–97.

National Heart Lung and Blood Institute. 2007. *Shaping the Future of Research: A Strategic Plan for the National Heart, Lung, and Blood Institute.* Available online at http://apps.nhlbi.nih.gov/strategicplan/StrategicPlan.pdf

Neaton, J.D., R.H. Grimm, Jr., R.J. Prineas, J. Stamler, G.A. Grandits, P.J. Elmer, J.A. Cutler, J.M. Flack, J.A. Schoenberger, R. McDonald, et al. 1993. "Treatment of Mild Hypertension Study." *Journal of the American Medical Association* 270:713–24.

Neovius, M., J. Sundstrom, and F. Rasmussen. 2009. "Combined Effects of Overweight and Smoking in Late Adolescence on Subsequent Mortality: Nationwide Cohort Study." *British Medical Journal* 338:b496.

Nixon, J. 2004. "Cholesterol Management and the Reduction of Cardiovascular Risk." *Preventive Cardiology* 7:34–39.

Olshansky, S.J., D. Passaro, R. Hershow, J. Leyden, B. Carnes, J. Brody, L. Hayflick, R. Butler, D. Allison, and D. Ludwig. 2005. "A Potential Decline in Life Expectancy in the US in the 21st Century." *New England Journal of Medicine* 352:1138–45.

Palatini, P., E. Casiglia, S. Julius, and A.C. Pessina. 1999. "High Heart Rate. A Risk Factor for Cardiovascular Death in Elderly Men." *Archives of Internal Medicine* 159:585–92.

Pardo Silva, M., C. De Laet, W.J. Nusselder, A.A. Mamun, and A. Peeters. 2006. "Adult Obesity and Number of Years Lived with and Without Cardiovascular Disease." *Obesity* 14:1264–73.

Pawelec, G., E. Derhovanessian, A. Larbi., J. Strindhall, and A. Wikby 2009. "Cytomegalovirus and Human Immunosenescence." *Reviews in Medical Virology* 19:47–56.

Peeters, A., J.J. Barendregt, F. Wilekens, J.P. Mackenbach, A.A. Mamun, and L. Bonneux, for NEDCOM, the Netherlands Epidemiology and Demography Compression of Morbidity Research Group. 2003. "Obesity in Adulthood and Its Consequences for Life Expectancy: A Life-Table Analysis." *Annals of Internal Medicine* 138:24–32.

Pekkanen, J., A. Nissinene, E. Vartiainen, J.T. Salonen, S. Punsar, and M.J. Karvonen. 1994. "Changes in Serum Cholesterol Level and Mortality: A 30-year Follow-Up. The Finnish Cohorts of the Seven Countries Study." *American Journal of Epidemiology* 139:155–65.

Pradhan, A.D., J.E. Manson, N. Rifai, J.E. Buring, and P.M. Ridker. 2001. "C-Reactive Protein, Interleukin 6, and Risk of Developing Type 2 Diabetes Mellitus." *Journal of the American Medical Association* 286:327–34.

Price, J. and F. Fowkes. 1997. "Risk Factors and the Sex Differential in Coronary Artery Disease." *Epidemiology* 8:584–91.

Prospective Studies Group. 2007. "Blood Cholesterol and Vascular Mortality by Age, Sex, and Blood Pressure: A Meta-Analysis of Individual Data from 61 Prospective Studies with 55,000 Vascular Deaths." *Lancet* 370: 1829–39.

Raiha, I., J. Marniemi, P. Puukka, T. Toikka, C. Ehnholm, and L. Sourander. 1997. "Effect of Serum Lipids, Lipoproteins, and Apolipoproteins on Vascular and Nonvascular Mortality in the Elderly." *Arteriosclerosis, Thrombosis, and Vascular Biology* 17:1224–32.

Reed, D., K. Yano, and A. Kagan. 1986. "Lipids and Lipoproteins as Predictors of Coronary Heart Disease, Stroke, and Cancer in the Honolulu Heart Program." *American Journal of Medicine* 80:871–78.

Renehan, A.G., M. Zwahlen, C. Minder, S.T. O'Dwyer, S.M. Shalet, and M. Egger. 2004. "Insulin-like Growth Factor (IGF)-I, IGF Binding Protein-3, and Cancer Risk: Systematic Review and Meta-Regression Analysis." *Lancet* 363: 1346–53.

Reuben, D.B., A.I. Cheh, T.B. Harris, L. Ferrucci, J.W. Rowe, R.P. Tracy, and T.E. Seeman. 2002. "Peripheral Blood Markers of Inflammation Predict Mortality and Functional Decline in High-Functioning Community-Dwelling Older Persons." *Journal of the American Geriatrics Society* 50:638–44.

Reuben, D.B., S.L. Talvi, J.W. Rowe, and T.E. Seeman. 2000. "High Urinary Catecholamine Excretion Predicts Mortality and Functional Decline in High-Functioning, Community-Dwelling Older Persons: MacArthur Studies of Successful Aging." *Journals of Gerontology A Biological Sciences and Medical Sciences* 55:618–24.

Reynolds, S.L., Y. Saito, and E. Crimmins. 2005. "The Impact of Obesity on Active Life Expectancy in Older American Men and Women." *The Gerontologist* 45:438–44.

Ridker, P.M., M. Cushman, M.J. Stampfer, R.P. Tracy, and C.H. Hennekens. 1997. "Inflammation, Aspirin, and the Risk of Cardiovascular Disease in Apparently Healthy Men." *New England Journal of Medicine* 336:973–79.

Ridker, P., E. Danielson, F.A.H. Fonesca, J. Genest, A.M. Gotto Jr, J.J.P. Kastelein, W., P. Libby, A.J. Lorenzatti,

J.G. MacFadyen, B.G. Nordestgaard, J. Shepherd, J.T. Willerson, R.J. Glynn, for the JUPITER Study Group. 2008. "Rosuvastatin to Prevent Vascular Events in Men Women with Elevated C-Reactive Protein." *New England Journal of Medicine* 359:2195–2207.

Ridker, P.M., E. Danielson, F.A.H. Fonseca, J. Genest, A.M. Gotto, Jr., J.J.P. Kastelein, W. Koenig, P. Libby, A.J. Lorenzatti, J.G. MacFadyen, B.G. Nordestgaard, J. Shepherd, J.T. Willerson, R.J. Glynn, and the JUPITER Trial Study Group. 2009. "Reduction in C-Reactive Protein and LDL Cholesterol and Cardiovascular Event Rates After Initiation of Rosuvastatin: A Prospective Study of the JUPITER Trial." *Lancet* 373:1175–82.

Ridker, P.M., C.H. Hennekens, J.E. Buring, and N. Rifai. 2000. "C-Reactive Protein and Other Markers of Inflammation in the Prediction of Cardiovascular Disease in Women." *New England Journal of Medicine* 342:836–43.

Rifai, N. and P.M. Ridker. 2001. "High-Sensitivity C-Reactive Protein: A Novel and Promising Marker of Coronary Heart Disease." *Clinical Chemistry* 47:403–11.

Roth, G.S., M.A. Lane, D.K. Ingram, J.A. Mattison, D. Elahi, J.D. Tobin, D. Muller, and E.J. Metter. 2002. "Biomarkers of Caloric Restriction May Predict Longevity in Humans." *Science* 297:811.

Roubenoff, R., H. Parise, H.A. Payette, L.W. Abad, R. D'Agostino, P.F. Jacques, P.W. Wilson, C.A. Dinarello, and T.B. Harris. 2003. "Cytokines, Insulin-Like Growth Factor 1, Sarcopenia, and Mortality in Very Old Community-Dwelling Men and Women: The Framingham Heart Study." *American Journal of Medicine* 115:429–35.

Sanchez-Delgado, E. and H. Liechti. 1999. "Lifetime Risk of Developing Coronary Heart Disease." *Lancet* 353:924–25.

Sarnak, M.J., R. Katz, C.O. Stehman-Breen, L.F. Fried, N.S. Jenny, B.M. Psaty, A.B. Newman, D. Siscovick, M.G. Shlipak, and Cardiovascular Health Study. 2005. "Cystatin C Concentration as a Risk Factor for Heart Failure in Older Adults." *Annals of Internal Medicine* 142:497–505.

Savdeh, S., B. Graubard, R. Ballard-Barbash, and D. Berrigan. 2007. "Insulin-Like Growth Factors and Subsequent Risk of Mortality in the United States." *American Journal of Epidemiology* 166:518–26.

Schmaltz, H.N., L.P. Fried, Q.L. Xue, J. Walston, S.X. Leng, and R.D. Semba. 2005. "Chronic Cytomegalovirus Infection and Inflammation Are Associated With Prevalent Frailty in Community-Dwelling Older Women." *Journal of the American Geriatrics Society* 53:747–54.

Seccareccia, F., F. Pañoso, F. Dima, A. Minoprio, A. Menditto, C. Noce, and S. Giampaoli. 2001. "Heart Rate as a Predictor of Mortality: The MATISS Project." *American Journal of Public Health* 91:1258–63.

Seeman, T.E. and E.M. Crimmins. 2001. "Social Environment Effects on Health and Aging: Integrating Epidemiologic and Demographic Approaches and Perspectives." *Annals of the New York Academies of Sciences* 954:88–117.

Seeman, T.E., E. Crimmins, M.H. Huang, B. Singer, A. Bucur, T. Gruenewald, L.F. Berkman, and D.B. Reuben. 2004. "Cumulative Biological Risk and Socio-Economic Differences in Mortality: MacArthur Studies of Successful Aging." *Social Sciences and Medicine* 58:1985–97.

Seeman, T.E., T. Gruenewald, A. Karlamangla, S. Sidney, K. Liu, B. McEwen, and J. Schwartz. 2010. "Modeling Multisystem Biological Risk in Young Adults: The Coronary Artery Risk Development in Young Adults Study." *American Journal of Human Biology* 22:463–472.

Seeman, T.E., B.S. McEwen, J.W. Rowe, and B.H. Singer. 2001. "Allostatic Load as a Marker of Cumulative Biological Risk: MacArthur Studies of Successful Aging." *Proceedings of the National Academy of Sciences of the United States of America* 98:4770–75.

Seeman, T.E., S.S. Merkin, E. Crimmins, B. Koretz, S. Charette, and A. Karlamangla. 2008. "Education, Income, and Ethnic Differences in Cumulative Biological Risk in a National Sample of US Adults: NHANES III (1988–1994)." *Social Science and Medicine* 66:72–87.

Seeman, T.E., B. Singer, J.W. Rowe, R. Horwitz, and B.S. McEwen. 1997. "Price of Adaptation – Allostatic Load and Its Health Consequences. MacArthur Studies of Successful Aging." *Archives of Internal Medicine* 157: 2259–68.

Semeraro, C., F. Marchini, P. Ferlenga, C. Masotto, G. Morazzoni, L. Pradella, and F. Pocchiari. 1997. "The Role of Dopaminergic Agonists in Congestive Heart Failure." *Clinical and Experimental Hypertension* 19:201–5.

Shalev, V., G. Chodick, H. Silber, E. Kokia, J. Jan, and A. Heymann. 2009. "Continuation of Statin Treatment and All-Cause Mortality." *Archives of Internal Medicine* 169: 260–68.

Shankar, A., P. Mitchell, E. Rochtchina, and J.J. Wang. 2007. "The Association Between Circulating White Blood Cell Count, Triglyceride Level and Cardiovascular and All-Cause Mortality: Population-Based Cohort Study." *Atherosclerosis* 192:177–83.

Shen, Y.H., B. Utama, J. Wang, M. Raveendran, D. Senthil, W.J. Waldman, J.D. Belcher, G. Vercellotti, D. Martin, B.M. Mitchelle, and X.L. Wang. 2004. "Human Cytomegalovirus Causes Endothelial Injury Through the Ataxia Telangiectasia Mutant and p53 DNA Damage Signaling Pathways." *Circulation Research* 94:1310–17.

SHEP Cooperative Research Group. 1991. "Prevention of Stroke by Antihypertensive Drug Treatment in Older Persons with Isolated Systolic Hypertension." *Journal of the American Medical Association* 265:3255–64.

Shlipak, M.G., L.F. Fried, C. Crump, A.J. Bleyer, T.A. Manolio, R.P. Tracy, C.D. Furberg, and B.M. Psaty. 2003. "Elevations of Inflammatory and Procoagulant Biomarkers in Elderly Persons with Renal Insufficiency." *Circulation* 107: 87–92.

Shlipak, M.G., C.L.F. Fyr, G.M. Chertow, T.B. Harris, S.B. Kritchevsky, F.A. Tylavsky, S. Satterfield, S.R. Cummings, A.B. Newman, and L.F. Fried. 2006a. "Cystatin C and Mortality Risk in the Elderly: The Health, Aging, and Body Composition Study." *Journal of the American Society of Nephrology* 17:254–61.

Shlipak, M.G., R. Katz, M.J. Sarnak, L.F. Fried, A.B. Newman, C. Stehman-Breen, S.L. Seliger, B. Kestenbaum, B. Psaty, R.P. Tracy, and D.S. Siscovick. 2006b. "Cystatin C and Prognosis for Cardiovascular and Kidney Outcomes in Elderly Persons Without Chronic Kidney Disease." *Annals of Internal Medicine* 145:237–46.

Shlipak, M.G., M.J. Sarnak, R. Katz, L.F. Fried, S.L. Seliger, A.B. Newman, D.S. Siscovick, and C. Stehman-Breen. 2005. "Cystatin C and the Risk of Death and Cardiovascular Events

Among Elderly Persons." *New England Journal of Medicine* 352:2049–60.
Snih, S., K. Ottenbacher, K. Markides, Y.F. Kuo, K. Eschbach, and J. Goodwin. 2007. "The Effect of Obesity on Disability Versus Mortality in Older Americans." *Archives of Internal Medicine* 167:774–80.
Song, Y.-M., G. Davey Smith, and J. Song. 2003. "Adult Height and Cause-Specific Mortality: A Large Prospective Study of South Korean Men." *American Journal of Epidemiology* 158:479–85.
Sorlie, P.D., F.J. Nieto, E. Adam, A.R. Folsom, E. Shahar, and M. Massing. 2000. "A Prospective Study of Cytomegalovirus, Herpes Simplex Virus 1, and Coronary Heart Disease: The Atherosclerosis Risk in Communities (ARIC) Study." *Archives of Internal Medicine* 160:2027–32.
Srikanthan, P., T. Seeman, and A. Karlamangla. 2009. "Waist-Hip-Ratio as a Predictor of All-Cause Mortality in High-Functioning Older Adults." *Annals of Epidemiology* 19: 724–31.
Staessen, J.A., R. Fagard, L. Thijs, H. Celis, G.G. Arabidze, W.H. Birkenhäger, C.J. Bulpitt, P.W. de Leeuw, C.T. Dollery, A.E. Fletcher, F. Forette, G. Leonetti, C. Nachev, E.T. O'Brien, J. Rosenfeld, J.L. Rodicio, J. Tuomilehto, and A. Zanchetti. 1997. "Randomized Double-Blind Comparison of Placebo and Active Treatment for Older Patients With Isolated Systolic Hypertension." *Lancet* 350:757–64.
Staessen, J., L. Thijs, J. Gasowski, H. Cells, and R. Fagard, for the Systolic Hypertension in Europe (Syst-Eur) Trial Investigators. 1998. "Treatment of Isolated Systolic Hypertension in the Elderly: Further Evidence from the Systolic Hypertension in Europe (Syst-Eur) Trial." *American Journal of Cardiology* 82:20–22.
Stamler, J., M. Davighus, D. Garside, A. Dyer, P. Greenland, and J. Neaton. 2000. "Relationship of Baseline Serum-Cholesterol Levels in 3 Large Cohorts of Younger Men to Long-Term Coronary, Cardiovascular, and All-Cause Mortality." *Journal of the American Medical Association* 19:311–18.
Stamler, J., J.D. Neaton, and D.N. Wentworth. 1989. "Blood Pressure (Systolic and Diastolic) and Risk of Fatal Coronary Heart Disease." *Hypertension* 13:2–12.
Stamler, J., D. Wentworth, and J.D. Neaton. 1986. "Is Relationship Between Serum Cholesterol and Risk of Premature Death From Coronary Heart Disease Continuous and Graded?" *Journal of the American Medical Association* 256:2823–28.
Staras, S.A., S.C. Dollard, K.W. Radford, W.D. Flanders, R.F. Pass, and M.J. Cannon. 2006. "Seroprevalence of Cytomegalovirus Infection in the United States, 1988–1994." *Clinical Infectious Diseases* 43:1143–51.
Terry, D.F., M. Pencina, R.Vasan, J. Murabiti, P. Wolf, M. Hayes, D. Levy, R. Agostino, and E. Benjamin. 2005. "Cardiovascular Risk Factors Predictive for Survival and Morbidity-Free Survival in the Oldest-Old Framingham Heart Study Participants." *Journals of the American Geriatrics Society* 53:1944–50.
Trivedi, D.P. and K.T. Khaw. 2001. "Dehyproepiandrosterone Sulfate and Mortality in Elderly Men and Women." *Journal of Clinical Endocrinology and Metabolism* 86:4171–77.
Tsevat, J., M. Weisstein, L. Williams, A. Tosteson, and L. Goldman. 1991. "Expected Gains in Life Expectancy from Various Coronary Heart Disease Risk Factor Modifications." *Circulation* 83:1194–201.
Tunstall-Pedoe, H., K. Kuulasmaa, P. Amouyel, D. Arveiler, A. Rajakangas, and A. Pajak, for the WHO MONICA Project. 1994. "Myocardial Infarction and Coronary Deaths in the World Health Organization MONICA Project: Registration Procedures, Event Rates, and Case-Fatality Rates in 38 Populations from 21 Countries in Four Continents." *Circulation* 90:583–612.
Turra, C.M., N. Goldman, C.L. Seplaki, D.A. Glei, Y. Lin, and M. Weinstein. 2005. "Determinants of Mortality of Older Ages: The Role of Biological Markers of Chronic Disease." *Population Development Review* 31:675–98.
VA Cooperative Study Group. 1967. "Effects of Treatment on Morbidity of Hypertension." *Journal of the American Medical Association* 202:1028–33.
Van Helden, S.N., E.G. Hoal-van Helden, and P.D. van Helden. 2001. "Factors Influencing Peak Expiratory Flow in Teenage Boys." *South African Medical Journal* 91: 996–1000.
Wallin, B.G., G. Sundlof, B.M. Eriksson, P. Dominiak, H. Grobecker, and L.E. Lindblad. 1981. "Plasma Noradrenaline Correlates to Sympathetic Muscle Nerve Activity in Normotensive Man." *Acta Physiologica Scandinavica* 111:69–73.
Wang, T.J., P. Gona, M.G. Larson, G.H. Tofler, D. Levy, C. Newton-Cheh, P.F. Jacques, N. Rifai, J. Selhub, S.J. Robins, E.J. Benjamin, R.B. D'Agostino, and R.S. Vasan. 2006. "Multiple Biomarkers for the Prediction of First Major Cardiovascular Events and Death." *New England Journal of Medicine* 355:2631–39.
Wannamethee, S.G., A.G. Shaper, and I.J. Perry. 1997. "Serum Creatinine Concentration and Risk of Cardiovascular Disease: A Possible Marker for Increased Risk of Stroke." *Stroke* 28:557–63.
Weaver, J.D., M.H. Huang, M. Albert, T. Harris, J.W. Rowe, and T.E. Seeman. 2002. "Interleukin-6 and Risk of Cognitive Decline: MacArthur Studies of Successful Aging." *Neurology* 59:371–78.
Weir, D. 2007. "Elastic Powers: The Integration of Biomarkers into the Health and Retirement Study." In M. Weinstein, J.W. Vaupel, and K.W. Wachter (eds.), *Biosocial Surveys 2007*, pp. 78–95. Washington, DC, National Academies Press.
Weverling-Rjinsburger, A.W., G.J. Blauw, A.M. Lagaay, D.L. Knook, A.E. Meinders, and R.G. Westendorp. 1997. "Total Cholesterol and Risk of Mortality in the Oldest Old." *Lancet* 350:1119–23.
Prospective Studies Collaboration, G. Whitlock, S. Lewington, P. Sherliker, R. Clarke, J. Emberson, J. Halsey, N. Qizilbash, R. Collins, and R. Peto. 2009. "Body-Mass Index and Cause-Specific Mortality in 900,000 Adults: Collaborative Analyses of 57 Prospective Studies." *Lancet* 28:1083–96.
WHO MONICA Project Principal Investigators. 1988. "The World Health Organization Monica Project (Monitoring Trends and Determinants in Cardiovascular Disease): A Major International Collaboration." *Journal of Clinical Epidemiology* 41:105–14.
Wilson, P.W.F., R.B. Do'Agostino, D. Levy, A.M. Belanger, H. Silbershatz, and W.B. Kannel. 1998. "Prediction of Coronary Heart Disease Using Risk Factor Categories." *Circulation* 97:1837–47.

Wolf, H.W., J. Tuomilehto, K. Kuulasmaa, S. Domarkiene, Z. Cepaitis, A. Molarius, S. Sans, A. Dobson, U. Keil, and S. Rywik. 1997. "Blood Pressure Levels in the 41 Populations of the WHO MONICA Project." *Journal of Human Hypertension* 11:733–42.

Wolf-Maier, K., R.S. Cooper, J.R. Banegas, S. Giampaoli, H.-W. Hense, M. Joffres, M. Kastarinen, N. Poulter, P. Primatesta, F. Rodríguez-Artalejo, B. Stegmayr, M. Thamm, J. Tuomilehto, D. Vanuzzo, and F. Vescio. 2003. "Hypertension Prevalence and Blood Pressure Levels in 6 European Countries, Canada, and the United States." *Journal of the American Medical Association* 289:2363–69.

Yeh, E.T.H. and J.T. Willerson. 2003. "Coming of Age of C-Reactive Protein. Using Inflammation Markers in Cardiology." *Circulation* 107:370–72.

Young, D.R., W.L. Haskell, D.E. Jatulis, and S.P. Fortmann. 1993. "Association Between Changes in Physical Activity and Risk Factors for Coronary Heart Disease in a Community-Based Sample of Men and Women: The Stanford Five-City Project." *American Journal of Epidemiology* 138:205–16.

Zamboni, M., G. Mazzali, E. Zoico, T. Harris, J. Meigs, V. Francesco, F. Fantin, L. Bissoli, and O. Bosello. 2005. "Health Consequences of Obesity in the Elderly: A Review of Four Unresolved Questions." *International Journal of Obesity* 29:1011–29.

Ziegler, M.G., C.R. Lake, and I.J. Kopin. 1976. "Plasma Noradrenaline Increases with Age." *Nature* 261:333–35.

# Chapter 19
# Genetic Factors and Adult Mortality

Kaare Christensen and James W. Vaupel

The introductory statement of this international handbook of adult mortality emphasizes that the remarkable gain in life expectancy stands out as one of the most important accomplishments of the twentieth century. More than 50% increase in life expectancy, also in populations characterized by little immigration, such as the Nordic countries, indicates that there is little room for genetic factors being of any importance for this development. In genetic evolutionary terms, a century is also a very short time period, and therefore changes in the gene pool are unlikely to have contributed significantly to the increase in lifespan in the twentieth century. This has lead to the widespread view that genetic factors are irrelevant for the study of adult mortality. However, when studying genetic factors influencing adult mortality, it is not the mean life expectancy or the average lifespan of a cohort that is of interest, but the variation within a given cohort in a given country at a specific time. For example, consider Swedish females born in year 1900 (Fig. 19.1): within this birth cohort in an egalitarian country there is still a large variation in lifespan. Why do some people die at age 60, most around age 80, and few after age 100? Clarifying to what extent this variation is related to genetic differences among individuals and understanding the roles of specific genetic factors is central to the understanding of adult human mortality.

The first section of this chapter deals with the evidence for familial clustering of adult mortality risk and lifespan, including sections on heritability and twin and adoption studies, whereas the second section of the chapter describes how adult mortality studies among relatives are a powerful tool to disentangle causal effect from selection processes in studies of both social and biological mortality risk factors.

## Familial Aggregation of Mortality Risk and Lifespan

Traditional family studies of parents, offspring, and siblings determine whether there is a familial resemblance for the phenotype being studied—here mortality or lifespan—but they do not indicate whether this resemblance is due to genetic or shared environmental factors (Christensen and Herskind 2006). Socioeconomic status (SES) is clearly associated with mortality and lifespan and often shared within families, but genetic factors are also shared within families, so the effects of genetic factors and rearing environment are confounded. Studies of relatives suggest that there is a within-family correlation in lifespan. But studies have generally found only small correlations in lifespan between parents and offspring (0.01–0.15) (Cohen 1964; Pearl 1931; Wyshak 1978), whereas correlations between siblings tend to be higher (0.15–0.35) (Cohen 1964; Wyshak 1978).

K. Christensen (✉)
The Danish Twin Registry and the Danish Aging Research Center, Institute of Public Health, University of Southern Denmark, Odense DK-5000, Denmark
e-mail: kchristensen@health.sdu.dk

**Fig. 19.1** Large variation in lifespan within a birth cohort. The distribution of age of death is shown for a twentieth century western population that did not experience any world wars—the Swedish female 1900 birth cohort. Data are taken from the Human Mortality Database

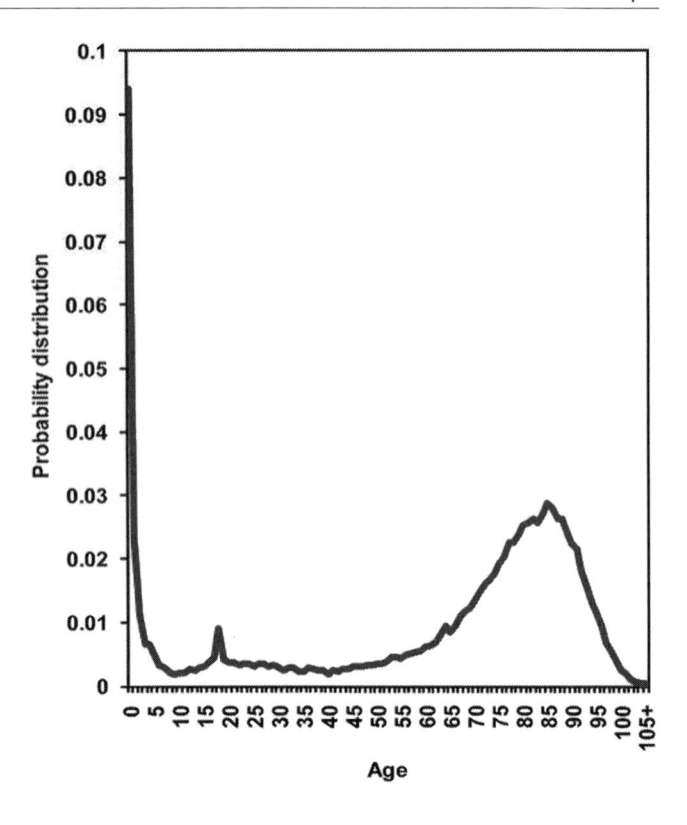

## Heritability of Lifespan

Heritability is defined as the proportion of the total variance in a population that is attributable to genetic differences between individuals. Hence, a high heritability for a trait indicates that a large proportion of the individual differences in the trait are caused by genetic differences, whereas a low heritability suggests that the reasons for the phenotypic differences are primarily to be sought in differences in environmental exposures or in stochastic processes. In this way, heritability estimates are useful in pointing toward the potentially most fruitful research directions.

But the heritability concept has a number of limitations. First, it is time- and population-specific and sensitive to changes in overall and environmental variances as well as to violations in underlying assumptions. For instance, if the environmental variance goes down, due to more homogeneous living conditions, and the genetic variance stays the same, then the total variance goes down, and heritability goes up, despite no change in the genetic variance. On the contrary, a dramatic increase in environmental variance (as would happen during a time of famine or epidemic) may overshadow the influence of genetic variance. Despite these limitations, a heritability estimate is very useful because it can suggest the potential for identifying specific genetic or environmental factors of importance for a trait in the population from which the heritability estimate was derived (Plomin et al. 2008).

Heritability estimates of lifespan based on regression analysis have been found to be in the range of 0.10–0.33 for parents and offspring and 0.33–0.41 for siblings, constant over a period of 300 years (Mayer 1991). But as indicated, these estimates comprise both genetic and shared environmental factors (Lee et al. 2004). Some family studies have found a stronger maternal than paternal effect (Abbott et al. 1974), but not all (Wyshak 1978). The lower correlation found for parents and offspring than for siblings suggests that genetic non-additivity (genetic effects due to gene interactions which are not passed from one generation to the next) is present, although it may also reflect a higher degree of shared environment among siblings than among parents and offspring, two generations who may live under very different conditions.

## Twin Studies of Lifespan

The fact that twinning is relatively common and that nationwide twin registries exist in several countries has made twin studies the most important tool for estimating the heritability of life duration in humans. Therefore, this section provides details about the model and the assumption behind the heritability estimates obtained in twin studies.

In humans, two types of twinning occur: monozygotic (MZ) twins share all their genetic material and dizygotic (DZ) twins, like ordinary siblings, share, on average, 50% of their genes. In a classical twin study, MZ and DZ correlations for a trait are compared. A significantly higher correlation in MZ than in DZ twins indicates that genetic factors play an etiological role, as the higher degree of similarity among MZ are ascribed to the higher degree of genetic similarity. Figure 19.2 is a path diagram showing the relationship between the different genetic and environmental components in an MZ twin pair and in a DZ twin pair. The double-headed arrows represent expected correlations between the latent variables in a pair of twins reared together. The single-headed paths express the extent to which genetic and environmental deviations cause phenotypic deviations. MZ twins are genetically identical and hence share all additive and non-additive genetic effects. Additive genetic effects are independent of other genetic variants, whereas the effect of non-additive genetic variants depends on other genetic variants, that is, genetic interaction. DZ twins are correlated but not identical: DZ twins share on average 1/2 of all additive effects and 1/4 of genetic dominance effects. Shared environment is assumed to be perfectly correlated within both MZ twin pairs and DZ twin pairs (Plomin et al. 2008). Based on these assumptions, heritability can be calculated for lifespan and longevity (Hjelmborg et al. 2006).

Twin studies are designed to separate the effects of additive and non-additive genetic factors as well as shared and non-shared environmental factors. But, most early twin studies had methodological problems due to left truncation of the cohorts, including selection bias, lack of zygosity diagnosis, or heavy right censoring. Carmelli and Andersen (1981) included a sample of 2,242 Mormon twin pairs born 1800–1899 in which

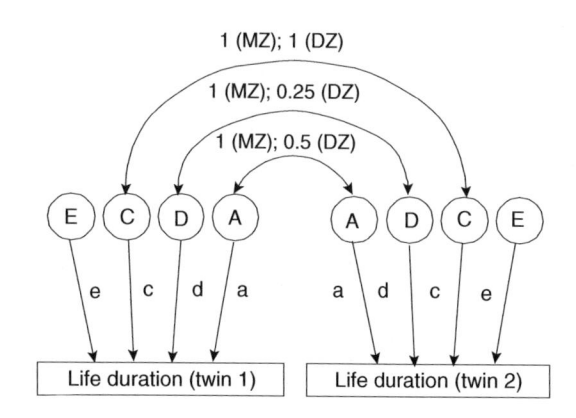

**Fig. 19.2** Path model. The figure illustrates a model for causes of longevity. Latent etiologic factors are divided into additive genetic factors (**a**), genetic dominance factors (**d**), shared (**c**), and non-shared (**e**) environment. Additive genetic factors and genetic dominance factors are both perfectly correlated in MZ twins, whereas in DZ twins, the correlation between additive genetic factors equals 1/2, and the correlation between genetic dominance factors equals 1/4. Shared environment is assumed to contribute equally to the correlation in MZ and DZ twins. The proportions of variance attributable to the latent factors are the square of the respective standardized path coefficients (e.g., the proportion of additive genetic variance equals $a^2$), which are estimated through maximum likelihood procedures. Heritability equals genetic variance divided by total phenotypic variance (modified after Herskind et al. 1996)

both co-twins had died, corresponding to 60% of the original sample. Wyshak (1978) followed 972 Mormon twin pairs, possibly included in the study of Carmelli and Andersen (1981), until death. Unfortunately, both studies lacked zygosity diagnosis, meaning heritability estimates could not be provided. However, similarity in length of life was found, and it was more pronounced for like-sexed twins (which include both MZ and like-sexed DZ twins) than for opposite-sexed twins (including only DZ twins), suggesting genetic influences on lifespan. Jarvik et al. (1960) followed a sample of 853 twin pairs for 12 years including only pairs with at least one of the twins surviving to the age of 60. At the end of the follow-up period, both co-twins had died in only 35% of the twin pairs. The mean intra-pair difference in lifespan was found to be higher in DZ than in MZ twins, suggesting genetic influences on lifespan. Hrubec and Neel (1981) followed a sample of 31,848 male twin veterans born 1917–1927 for 30 years to ages 51–61. Around 10%

were deceased at the time of analysis. To avoid censoring problems, longevity was analyzed as a categorical variable (dead/alive), and heritability of 'liability' to death was estimated to be 0.5.

The first non-censored and population-based twin study that could provide an estimate of the magnitude of genetic influences on lifespan was conducted by McGue et al. (1993). A total of 600 Danish twin pairs born 1870–1880 were included. Using path analysis, a heritability of 0.22 was found, with genetic influences being mainly non-additive. Later, Herskind et al. (1996) expanded this study to include more than 2,800 twin pairs with known zygosity born 1870-1900. These cohorts were followed from age 15 to death. This study confirmed that approximately a quarter of the variation in lifespan in this population could be attributed to non-additive genetic factors, whereas the remaining three-quarters were due to non-shared environmental factors (see Fig. 19.3). Ljungquist et al. (1998) studied the 1886–1900 Swedish twin cohorts and concluded that a maximum of around a third of the variance in longevity is attributable to genetic factors. Hence, it seems to be a rather consistent finding in the Nordic countries that approximately 25% of the variation in lifespan is caused by genetic differences. It is interesting that animal studies have revealed similar estimates for a number of species not living in the wild (Curtsinger et al. 1995; Finch and Tanzi 1997).

## Are Twins a Valid Model for Studies of Adult Mortality?

The representativeness of twin cohorts for aging and mortality studies has been tested extensively through studies of twin–singleton differences for a broad range of outcomes and phenotypes. There have been two main reasons for these studies. First, researchers wanted to test whether twins are a good population model for human aging: if there were major health and aging differences between twins and singletons, the results from twin studies might not be valid for the general population. Second, researchers set out to test the Fetal-Origins hypothesis (the Barker hypothesis), which states that impaired intrauterine growth "programs" later metabolism and increases the risk for cardiovascular diseases, diabetes, and early death. Birthweight for twins is on average about 2 pounds less than that of singletons, and twins are therefore an extreme example of growth impairment in the third trimester.

A series of Danish studies have convincingly shown no twin–singleton differences after the infancy period. The only study showing a modest but significant difference was a study of suicide in twins, where it was found that twins commit suicide less often than singletons (Tomassini et al. 2003). The studies have used very large samples with excellent power to detect even

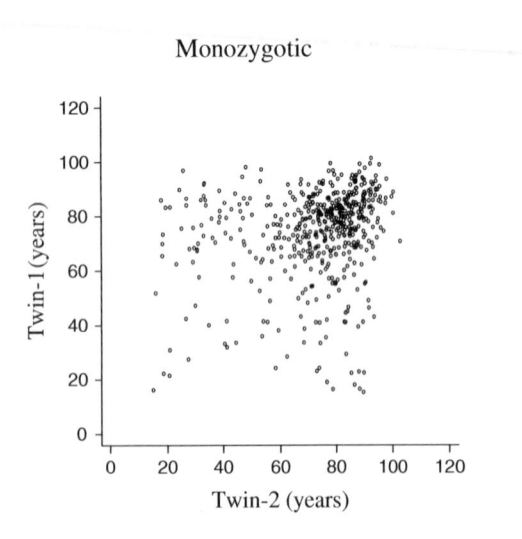

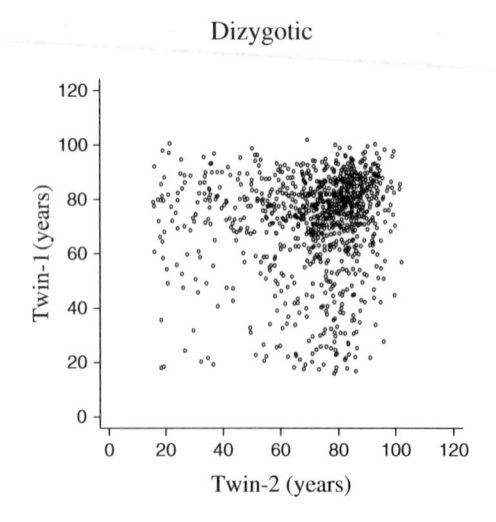

**Fig. 19.3** Twin lifespan. Similarity in lifespan for monozygotic and dizygotic Danish twins of the same sex from cohorts born 1870–1910 and who survived to at least age 6. Each dot in the graphs represents a twin pair. The pattern suggests that approximately one quarter of the variation in lifespan can be attributed to genetic factors (Herskind et al. 1996)

minimal differences. Among the key results are: (1) Danish twins born 1870–1900 have mortality rates similar to the background population from age 6 to 90 years (Christensen et al. 1995), (2) Danish twins born 1870–1910 have cardiovascular mortality rates similar to the background population (Christensen et al. 2001), (3) Danish twins have fecundability similar to singletons (Christensen et al. 1998), and (4) contemporary Danish adolescent twins have school test results similar to singletons (Christensen et al. 2006).

Based on this line of research and a number of similar findings using the Swedish Twin Registry (Vågerö and Leon 1994), which is the only other twin registry going back more than a century on a population level, it can be stated that twins are a good population model for health, aging, and mortality studies.

## Genetic Factors and Exceptional Longevity

There has been more than a century of scientific work on causes of variation in adult lifespan including traditional family studies, while valid studies of exceptional longevity have been mainly conducted within the last two decades. While large twin datasets have provided good estimates for heritability of overall variation in lifespan, generally about 25%, a key question remained: do genetic factors become less or more important as individuals reach progressively higher ages, or does the genetic influence remain stable?

A priori different scenarios could be envisioned. For instance, studying late deaths will remove early deaths from the analyses, which could reduce the genetic influence, because the influence of genetic diseases with high early mortality, such as familial hypercholesterolemia and cystic fibrosis, are removed. On the other hand, many violent deaths are excluded when considering only those who survived to older ages, and this could increase genetic influences, relatively speaking, by removing early 'random' deaths. Theoretical arguments could also be made for both scenarios: a prevailing assumption in gerontology is that the accumulation of unique environmental exposures during a long life is the key determinant of health at older ages and of lifespan (Harris et al. 1992). Alternatively, evolutionary biologists have argued that there is less selective pressure against deleterious genetic mutations first expressed late rather than early in life. This hypothesis predicts an increase in genetic variance among the oldest (Charlesworth 1990).

## Family Studies of Exceptional Survival

A moderate familial clustering of extreme longevity has been observed in the few studies published in this area. Perls et al. (1998) found that the chance of survival for siblings of centenarians versus siblings of people who died at the age of 73 was about four times better at ages 80–94. Kerber et al. (2001) also found, based on Mormon genealogies, an increased recurrence risk for siblings for surviving to extreme ages, although the estimate was somewhat lower than that reported by Perls et al. (1998). Gudmundsson and colleagues (2000), using the population-based genealogy in Iceland, found that the first-degree relatives of individuals who live to an extreme old age ($\geq 95$ percentile) are twice as likely as the controls to survive to the same age. Schoenmaker et al. (2006) studied nonagenarian sib pairs and their first-degree relatives (parents, brothers and sisters, offspring), as well as spouses of the nonagenarians in the Dutch Leiden Longevity Study. The longevity propensity of these families was illustrated by a 30% survival benefit for first-degree family members of nonagenarian sib-pair individuals, but not for the spouses of the nonagenarians, which indicates that genetic factors are of importance for the familial clustering of longevity.

## Twin Studies of Exceptional Survival

Data from the Swedish, Finnish, and Danish national twin registries were combined as part of the GenomEUtwin project (Hjelmborg et al. 2006). These jointly comprise the largest population-based sample of twins with almost complete lifespans ever studied. The study consisted of MZ and same sex DZ pairs from the Danish, Finnish, and Swedish twin cohorts born between 1870 and 1910, a total of 20,502 individuals. The cohort was followed through the 1st of July 2003, so the minimum age for a twin still alive at the end of the follow-up period was 92 years of age. As mentioned, traditional heritability analyses of the uncensored cohorts showed the previously obtained heritability estimate of 20–30%. Using the combined data set with substantially increased statistical power, it was possible to show that prior to age 60, there is no indication of similarity in a twin pair's age-at-death, and from age 60, a co-twin's age-at-death is significantly predictive of twin lifespan. For MZ twins, lifespan increases approximately 0.40 years in males and 0.35 years in females for every additional year of co-twin life from age 60 to at least age 85. For DZ twins, the increase in lifespan is approximately 0.20 years in males and 0.25 in females for every additional year of co-twin life from age 60 to at least age 85. These findings suggest that there are minimal genetic effects on lifespans less than 60 years, moderate genetic effects on lifespans greater than 60 years, and that the influence of genetic factors is likely to be most important at the highest ages (Hjelmborg et al. 2006). These findings provide support for the search for genes affecting longevity in humans, especially at advanced ages.

## Adoption Studies of Early-Adult Deaths

Adoption studies are much fewer and smaller than other kinds of family studies. Nevertheless, adoption studies have had a tremendous impact on the nature–nurture debate for a number of traits because these studies have produced remarkable results and their design is easily understood and interpreted. Adoption studies use the fact that adoptees share genes but not environment with their biological families, and environment but not genes with their adoptive families. But adoption studies are not without weaknesses. In particular, a bias can be introduced by selective placement of adoptees (i.e., the adoptees are preferably placed with adoptive parents who are similar to the birth parents in some ways). It can be shown that selective placement tends to overestimate the effect of both genetic and shared family environment (Plomin et al. 2008). Furthermore, similarity among offspring and biological parents may not only be due to genetic factors, but also to environmental factors during pregnancy or early childhood (if adoption took place later than right after birth).

There are no adoption studies on lifespan, but there is a series of studies on early adult mortality, all from the same adoption study population in Denmark. This study shows a correlation between Danish adoptees and their biological parents, especially for death due to infection and vascular causes. In contrast, death due to cancer appeared to be influenced by the family environment (Sørensen et al. 1988). However, longer follow-up of other cohorts of adoptees in Denmark were unable to confirm the initial findings (Petersen et al. 2002, 2005).

## Specific Genetic Factors Influencing Adult Mortality

A very large number of candidate genes have been investigated for putative associations with human aging and longevity (Christensen et al. 2006). Based on promising results from animal studies, genes from the insulin/IGF-1 pathway, stress response genes (heat and oxidative stress) and genes influencing mitochondrial functioning have been obvious candidates as have immune system regulating genes (e.g., interleukines), as the immune system is a biological system with a sufficiently broad spectrum of functions likely to be associated with aging and survival (Finch and Crimmins 2004; Francheschi et al. 2000). A distinct group of candidates are the genes for premature aging syndromes (Yu et al. 1996), where "leaky mutations" are considered, that is, the syndrome causing gene is investigated to test if "milder" common mutations could be associated with aging and survival more generally. Many initially positive findings have not been replicated, probably due to issues of study design and publication bias. Many studies compare the frequency of genetic variants in centenarians with younger, typically middle-aged, individuals. In the United States, such studies are vulnerable to the different ethnic composition of waves of immigrants into the United States, so genetic differences between the centenarians and the controls can be due to ethnic differences and not to genes related to exceptional longevity. Furthermore, due to technological improvements, a large number of genetic variants can be investigated, and if primarily positive findings are published, many of them will be false positive results (type I errors due to multiple testing) (Christensen et al. 2006). New findings of positive associations between gene variants and longevity usually do not replicate in subsequent studies, the exception being the association of genetic variation at the apoE (Gerdes et al. 2000) and the FOXO 3A locus (Flachsbart et al. 2009) that have provided consistent results.

ApoE, which is the only gene with common variants that have consistently been associated with longevity, plays an important role in regulating lipoproteins. The protein is found in three versions—ApoE-2, ApoE-3, and ApoE-4—which alter circulating levels of cholesterols in the blood. ApoE-4 has repeatedly been associated with a moderately increased risk of both cardiovascular and Alzheimer's disease, whereas ApoE-2 is protective (Corder et al. 1993; Lewis and Brunner 2004; Panza et al. 2004). Not only is ApoE-4 a risk factor for these diseases per se, but ApoE-4 carriers are also more susceptible to damage after some environmental exposures. For example, they have an increased risk of chronic brain injury after head trauma (Jordan et al. 1997). Furthermore, individuals with atherosclerosis, peripheral vascular disease, or diabetes mellitus have a substantially higher risk of cognitive decline if they also carry the ApoE-4 variant (Haan et al. 1999).

In contrast to other candidate genes, cross-sectional studies of ApoE allele frequency differences between age groups have been remarkably consistent. ApoE-4 frequency varies considerably between populations of younger adults (from about 25% among Finns, 17–20% among Danes, and about 10% among French, Italians, and Japanese), but in all these populations the frequency among centenarians is about half of these values. However, although these changes in ApoE allele frequency with age are substantial, they are compatible with a scenario in which ApoE-2 carriers have an estimated average mortality risk in adulthood that is 4–12% lower than for ApoE-3 carriers, and ApoE-4 carriers have a risk that is 10–14% higher than for ApoE-3 carriers throughout adulthood (Gerdes et al. 2000). This would make ApoE a "frailty-gene" that has a small influence on mortality at every age rather than a "longevity-gene" that "ensures" a long life.

Although there are many biologically plausible candidates for genes that influence human lifespan, only a few research findings have been replicated so far. Replications of positive findings are central in studies of genetic variants and longevity as thousands of genetic candidate variants can be determined for rather modest costs, and many false positive findings will therefore occur due to multiple tests for associations. Understanding the genetic basis for longevity is an extraordinarily difficult task, but it has the potential to provide insights into central mechanisms of aging, disease, and mortality (Christensen et al. 2006).

## Adult Mortality Studies Among Relatives: Research that Controls for Confounding due to Genetic Factors and Rearing Environment

The previous sections of this chapter have dealt with evidence for familial clustering of mortality patterns and the underlying causes for this clustering. Studies of relatives, including twin and adoption studies, suggest that genetic factors play a substantial role in adult mortality patterns, although few specific common genetic variants have yet been identified. This section will describe a completely different use of mortality studies among relatives, namely, how they can be used to control for confounding due to genetic factors and rearing environment. The principle is best described by MZ twins who share all their genes as well as rearing environment (except in the few cases where the twins were reared apart). This means that differences between MZ twins cannot be attributed to genetic factors or rearing environment, and therefore within twin comparisons control for these factors in the analyses. This tool can be applied in a very broad range of mortality risk factor studies to disentangle selection from causal effects. Here we give an example from social science (marital status and mortality) and one from molecular biology (telomere length and mortality).

### *The Marital Status–Mortality Association—Causal or Selection Effect?*

Living alone or being unmarried are well-known risk factors for poor health, and changes from being married to divorced or widowed is a strong predictor of mortality (Ben-Slohmo et al. 1993; Johnson et al. 2000; Joung et al. 1998; Lund et al. 2004). At least two possible mechanisms have been suggested to explain the association between marital status and health: marriage protection and health selection. The protection hypothesis focuses on the beneficial effects of marriage through, for example, better economic security, social integration, and health behaviors. The selection hypothesis assumes that persons with certain traits or behavior, influenced by their genotypes or early environments, are selected into marriage while some persons, such as people with health problems, are at a higher risk of never marrying, and if married, of divorcing (Johnson et al. 2000, 2004). It is difficult to distinguish the beneficial impact of marital status on health from the confounding effect of selection into the married state. However, as mentioned above, the study of twins provides an opportunity to isolate the effects of adult marital status from the genetic and social influences operating early in life. This can be done in an especially sophisticated way by including DZ twins (fraternal twins) in the study who, on average, share half their genes but all aspects of their childhood family environment (except in the few cases of twins reared apart). Thus, studies of twins who are discordant for current marital status offer a unique opportunity to determine whether the association of marital status with prospective health outcomes such as mortality is consistent with protection or selection effects.

We can make the following predictions in this co-twin design: if the association of adult marital status and mortality reflects selection effects only, then we do not expect health differences in MZ pairs discordant on adult marital status, because these twins are concordant on early rearing environmental and genetic factors. Alternatively, health outcome differences in DZ pairs but not MZ pairs discordant for adult marital status would suggest that genetic factors underlie selection effects, because DZ twins share the same rearing environment, but are imperfectly matched on genotype. Finally, a direct (causal) beneficial effect of marriage would be implicated by finding that both MZ and DZ twins discordant for marital status are also discordant on health and behavior outcomes. We are currently conducting such studies in Denmark to investigate whether differences in marital status influence the health and behavior of twins who share genetic constitution and rearing environment.

A few studies using this co-twin design have investigated the basis for the association between SES and health outcomes. A Danish analysis showed that for most health outcomes, the variability within twin pairs was related to zygosity (higher for DZ than for MZ), but not to occupational social class. Osler et al. (2007) concluded that the relationship between social class and health is due mainly to selection effects rather than being a causal effect of social class exposures on health and behavior. A similar US study found the opposite result which was that the relationship between social class and health is due mainly to direct causal effects (Krieger et al. 2005). It is unclear whether this contradictory result is due to the different settings (Denmark has a more egalitarian social system than the United States) or is a chance finding due to small sample size. The study is currently being replicated as a large-scale data-based registry study.

## The Telomere–Mortality Association—Causal or Genetic Confounding?

Each of our chromosomes, our genetic material, terminates in a "cap" which contains the number of repeats of the sequence TTAGGG that is needed to protect and enable the replication of the chromosome when the cell divides. At birth, each chromosome end is equipped with approximately 15,000 units of this telomere sequence, but this sequence is shortened during each cell division. In cell cultures, telomere shortening is associated with senescence, a phenomenon that has also been observed in normal adult tissues, indicating that telomere loss is associated with organismal aging. Furthermore, shortened telomere length has been observed in a host of aging-related diseases, including cardiovascular diseases (Benetos et al. 2001, 2004; Brouilette et al. 2003; Cawthon et al. 2003; Demissie et al. 2006; Fitzpatrick et al. 2007; Samani et al. 2001), dementia (Panossian et al. 2003; von Zglinicki et al. 2000), obesity and insulin resistance (Demissie et al. 2006; Fitzpatrick et al. 2007; Gardner et al. 2005; Valdes et al. 2005), cigarette smoking (Gardner et al. 2005; Nawrot et al. 2004), psychological stress (Epel et al. 2004), and low SES (Cherkas et al. 2006), all of which reduce the human lifespan. What is more, both lifespan and telomere length (Benetos et al. 2001; Fitzpatrick et al. 2007; Nawrot et al. 2004) are longer in women than men. This has lead to the speculation that there is a causal relation between telomere length and lifespan, that is, that the telomere is not only the cap of the chromosome, but also the cap of lifespan.

Telomere length varies greatly among individuals of the same age and, as mentioned above, it is influenced by many factors, including genetic factors: there is substantial heritability in telomere length (Bischoff et al. 2005; Slagboom et al. 1994). It is not yet clear whether telomere length is a causal factor affecting mortality risk or just a marker of past exposure and genetic constitution.

Therefore, we explored the association between leukocyte telomere parameters and mortality in 548 (274 pairs) Danish twins aged 73–94 years, of whom 255 twins died during an 8–9 year follow-up. Comparison within 185 twin pairs of the same sex (either male or female) eliminated confounding due to age and gender as well as genetic factors (100% for MZ and 50% for DZ). The intra-pair comparisons in same sex twins showed that the twin with the shorter telomere length died first in the majority of the twin pairs and that there was a "dose-response" pattern; that is, the bigger the difference in telomere length between the two twins in a pair, the greater the chance that the twin with the shortest telomere died first. As this "dose-response pattern" was also found among the MZ twins, it could be concluded that the telomere length–mortality association was not due to genetic confounding (Kimura et al. 2008).

These two examples, the SES-mortality study and the telomere length–mortality investigation, illustrate the broad potential that mortality studies among relatives provide for the disentangling of the complex etiology beneath these associations.

## Conclusion

There is no evidence that human populations are currently approaching a genetically determined upper limit for lifespan (Christensen et al. 2009; Oeppen and Vaupel 2002). The dramatic improvement we have experienced in mean life expectancy over the last century can only be attributed to environmental factors (such as living conditions and medical treatment) and not to genetic factors. Nevertheless, genetic factors are important for understanding variation in adult mortality risk and lifespan. Family studies suggest that about a quarter of the variance in adult lifespan in contemporary western populations can be explained by genetic factors, and that the influence of these factors is likely to be of larger importance for exceptionally long survival and generally of little importance for early adult death. In spite of this insight, we still know of very few specific common genetic variants that have a well-documented influence on adult survival. This scenario will most likely change considerably within the next years, because this is a very rapidly developing field of research. Many population studies now include analyses of specific candidate gene variants (SNPs) and their association with a range of outcomes, including mortality. Such studies are based on knowledge about genes and their functioning. Another approach made possible by the rapid development of gene technology is called genome-wide association studies (GWAS) in which hundreds of thousands or even one million genetic markers throughout the whole genome are measured. This approach can detect regions of the genome of importance for longevity if cases (e.g., long-lived individuals) are compared with controls (the background population from which the cases emerged). GWAS have only been successful in identifying genetic variants with strong effects for a few medical conditions, but have been very successful in identifying markers weakly but consistently associated with various diseases and conditions. Although it has been disappointing that the effect size and the predictive power of the variants identified through GWAS are usually very small, such studies are likely to provide insight into fundamental biological mechanisms (Christensen and Murray 2007).

Genetics are, however, useful in studies of adult mortality independently of progress on the molecular level: Adult mortality studies that focus on related individuals, and in particular on twins, is a powerful tool scientists can use to disentangle causal effect from selection processes in studies of both social and biological mortality risk factors. Together with molecular genetic studies of adult mortality, they can shed important light on what causes differences in adult mortality risks among individuals.

**Acknowledgment** This research was supported by a grant from the Danish National Research Foundation and the National Institute on Aging: P01-AG08761, U01 AG023712. The DARC is supported by the VELUX Foundation.

# References

Abbott, M.H., E.A. Murphy, D.R. Bolling, and H. Abbey. 1974. "The Familial Component in Longevity. A Study of Offspring of Nonagenarians. II. Preliminary Analysis of the Completed Study." *Johns Hopkins Medical Journal* 134(1):1–16.

Ben-Slohmo, Y., G. Davey Smithand, and M. Shipley. 1993. "Magnitude and Causes of Mortality Differences Between Married and Unmarried Men." *Journal of Epidemiology and Community Health* 47:200–5.

Benetos, A., K. Okuda, M. Lajemi, M. Kimura, F. Thomas, J. Skurnick C. Labat, K. Bean, and A. Aviv. 2001. "Telomere Length as an Indicator of Biological Aging: The Gender Effect and Relation with Pulse Pressure and Pulse Wave Velocity." *Hypertension* 37(2):381–5.

Benetos, A., J.P. Gardner, M. Zureik, C. Latab, L. Xiaobin, C. Adamopoulos, M. Tenmar, K.E. Bean, F. Thomas, and A. Aviv. 2004. "Short Telomeres are Associated with Increased Carotid Atherosclerosis in Hypertensive Subjects." *Hypertension* 43:182–5.

Bischoff, C., J. Graakjaer, H.C. Petersen, J.B. Hjelmborg, J.W. Vaupel, V. Bohr, S. Koelvraa, and K. Christensen. 2005. "The Heritability of Telomere Length Among the Elderly and Oldest-Old." *Twin Research and Human Genetics* 8(5):433–9.

Brouilette, S., R.K. Singh, J.R. Thompson, A.H. Goodall, and N.J. Samani 2003. "White Cell Telomere Length and Risk of Premature Myocardial Infarction." *Arteriosclerosis, Thrombosis, and Vascular Biology* 23:842–6.

Carmelli, D. and S. Andersen. 1981. "A Longevity Study of Twins in the Mormon Genealogy." *Progress in Clinical Biological Research* 69:187–200.

Cawthon, R.M., K.R. Smith, E. O'Brien, A. Sivatchenko, and R.A. Kerber. 2003. "Association Between Telomere Length in Blood and Mortality in People Aged 60 Years or Older." *Lancet* 361:393–5.

Charlesworth, B. 1990. "Mutation-Selection Balance and the Evolutionary Advantage of Sex and Recombination." *Genetics Research* 55(3):199–221.

Cherkas, L.F., A. Aviv, A.M. Valdes, J.L. Hunkin, J.P. Gardner, G.L. Surdulescu, M. Kimura, and T.D. Spector. 2006. "The Effects of Social Status on Biological Ageing as measured by White Cell Telomere Length." *Aging Cell* 5(5):361–65.

Christensen, K., J.W. Vaupel, N.V. Holm, and A.I. Yashin 1995. "Mortality Among Twins After Age 6: Fetal Origins Hypothesis Versus Twin Method." *British Medical Journal* 310:432–36. (PMCID: PMC2548817).

Christensen, K., O. Basso, K.O. Kyvik, S. Juul, J. Boldsen, J.W. Vaupel, and J. Olsen. 1998. "Fecundability of Female Twins." *Epidemiology* 9(2):189–92.

Christensen, K., A. Wienke, A. Skytthe, N.V. Holm, J.W. Vaupel, and A.I. Yashin. 2001. "Cardiovascular Mortality in Twins and the Fetal Origins Hypothesis." *Twin Research* 4(5):344–49.

Christensen, K., I. Petersen, A. Skytthe, A.M. Herskind, M. McGue, and P. Bingley 2006. "Comparison of Academic Performance of Twins and Singletons in Adolescence: Follow-up Study." *British Medical Journal* 333:1095. (PMCID: PMC1661694).

Christensen, K., T.E. Johnson, and J.W. Vaupel 2006. "The Quest for Genetic Determinants of Human Longevity: Challenges and Insights." *Nature Reviews Genetics* 7(6):436–48.

Christensen, K. and A.M. Herskind 2006. "Genetic Factors Associated with Individual Life Duration: Heritability." In J.M. Robine, E.M. Crimmins, S. Horiuchi, and S. Yi (eds.), *Human Longevity, Individual Life Duration, and the Growth of the Oldest-Old Population*, Vol. 4, pp. 237–50. Netherlands, Springer.

Christensen, K. and J.C. Murray. 2007. "What Genome-wide Association Studies can do for Medicine." *New England Journal of Medicine* 356(11):1094–97.

Christensen, K., G. Doblhammer, R. Rau, and J.W. Vaupel 2009. "Ageing Populations: The Challenges Ahead." *Lancet* 374:1196–208. (NIHMSID 164804).

Cohen, B. 1964. "Family Pattern of Mortality and Life-Span." *Quarterly Review of Biology* 39:130–81.

Corder E.H., A.M. Saunders, W.J. Strittmatter, D.E. Schmechel, P.C. Gaskell, G.W. Small, A.D. Roses, J.L. Haines, and M.A. Pericak-Vance. 1993. "Gene Dose of Apolipoprotein E Type 4 Allele and the Risk of Alzheimer's Disease in Late Onset Families." *Science* 261(5123):921–23.

Curtsinger, J.W., H.H. Fukui, A.A. Khazaeli, A. Kirscher, S.D. Pletcher, D.E. Promislow, and M. Tatar 1995. "Genetic Variation and Aging." *Annual Review of Genetics* 29:553–75.

Demissie S., D. Levy, E.J. Benjamin, L.A. Cupples, J.P. Gardner, A. Herbert, M. Kimura, M.G. Larson, J.B. Meigs, J.F. Keany, and A. Aviv. 2006. "Insulin Resistance, Oxidative Stress, Hypertension, and Leukocyte Telomere Length in Men from the Framingham Heart Study." *Aging Cell* 5:325–30.

Epel E.S., E.H. Blackburn J. Lin, F.S. Dhabhar, N.E. Adler, J.D. Morrow, and R.M. Cawthon. 2004. "Accelerated Telomere Shortening in Response to Life Stress." *Proceedings of the National Academy of Science* 101:17312–15.

Finch, C.E. and R.E. Tanzi. 1997. "Genetics of Aging." *Science* 278(5337):407–11.

Finch, C.E. and E.M. Crimmins. 2004. "Inflammatory Exposure and Historical Changes in Human Life-Spans." *Science* 305:1736–29.

Fitzpatrick, A.L., R.A. Kronmal, J.P. Gardner, B.M. Psaty, N.S. Jenny, R.P. Tracy, J. Walston, M. Kimura, and A. Aviv. 2007. "Leukocyte Telomere Length and Cardiovascular Disease in the Cardiovascular Health Study." *American Journal of Epidemiology* 165(1):14–21.

Flachsbart, F., A. Caliebe, R. Kleindorp, H. Blanché, H. von Eller-Eberstein, S. Nikolaus, S. Schreiber, and A. Nebel. 2009. "Association of FOXO3A Variation with Human Longevity Confirmed in German Centenarians." *Proceedings of the National Academy of Science* 106(8):2700–5.

Franceschi, C., M. Bonafe, S. Valensin, F. Olivieri, M. De Luca, E. Ottaviani, and G. de Benedictis. 2000. "Inflamm-Aging: An Evolutionary Perspective on Immunosenescence." *Annals of the New York Academy of Sciences* 908:244–54.

Gardner, J.P., S. Li, S.R. Srinivasan, W. Chen, M. Kimura, X. Lu, G.S. Berenson, and A. Aviv. 2005. "Rise in Insulin Resistance is Associated with Escalated Telomere Attrition." *Circulation* 111:2171–77.

Gerdes, L.U., B. Jeune, K.A. Ranberg, H. Nybo, and J.W. Vaupel. 2000. "Estimation of Apolipoprotein E

Genotype-Specific Relative Mortality Risks from the Distribution of Genotypes in Centenarians and Middle-Aged Men: Apolipoprotein E Gene is a 'Frailty Gene,' not a 'Longevity Gene'." *Genetic Epidemiology* 19:202–10.

Gudmundsson, H., D.F. Gudbjartsson, M. Frigge, J.R. Gulcher, and K. Stefansson. 2000. "Inheritance of Human Longevity in Iceland." *European Journal of Human Genetics* 8:743–49.

Haan, M.N., L. Shemanski, W.J. Jagust, T.A. Manolio, and L. Kuller. 1999. "The Role of APOE Epsilon4 in Modulating Effects of Other Risk Factors for Cognitive Decline in Elderly Persons." *Journal of the American Medical Association* 282:40–46.

Harris, J.R., N.L. Pedersen, G.E. McClearn, R. Plomin, and J.R. Nesselroade. 1992. "Age Differences in Genetic and Environmental Influences for Health from the Swedish Adoption/Twin Study of Aging." *Journal of Gerontology* 47(3):213–20.

Herskind, A.M., M. McGue, N.V. Holm, T.I. Sorensen, B. Harvald, and J.W. Vaupel. 1996. "The Heritability of Human Longevity: A Population-Based Study of 2872 Danish Twin Pairs Born 1870–1900." *Human Genetics* 97(3):319–23.

Hjelmborg J.V.B., I. Iachine, A. Skytthe, J.W. Vaupel, M. McGue, M. Koskenvuo, J. Kaprio, N.L. Pedersen, and K. Christensen 2006. "Genetic Influence on Human Lifespan and Longevity." *Human Genetics* 119(3):312–21.

Hrubec, Z. and J.V. Neel. 1981. "Familial Factors in Early Deaths: Twins Followed 30 Years to Ages 51–61 in 1978." *Human Genetics* 59(1):39–46.

Jarvik, L., A. Falek, F.J. Kallmann, and I. Lorge. 1960. "Survival Trends in a Senescent Twin Population." *American Journal of Human Genetics* 12:170–79.

Johnson, N.J, E. Backlund, P.D. Sorlie, and C.A. Loveless. 2000. "Marital Status and Mortality: The National Longitudinal Mortality Study." *Annals of Epidemiology* 10:224–38.

Johnson, W., M. McGue, P.F. Krueger, and T.J. Bouchard. 2004. "Marriage and Personality: A Genetic Analysis." *Journal of Personality and Social Psychology* 86:285–94.

Jordan, B.D., N.R. Relkin, L.D. Ravdin, A.R. Jacobs, A. Bennett, and S. Gandy 1997. "Apolipoprotein E Epsilon4 Associated with Chronic Traumatic Brain Injury in Boxing." *Journal of the American Medical Association* 278:136–40.

Joung, I.M., H.D. Van de Mheen, K. Stronks, F.W. Poppel, and J.P. Mackenbach. 1998. "A Longitudinal Study of Health Selection in Marial Transitions." *Social Science and Medicine* 46:425–35.

Kerber, R.A., E. O'Brien, K.R. Smith, and R.M. Cawthon. 2001. "Familial Excess Longevity in Utah Genealogies." *Journal of Gerontology Series A: Biological Sciences and Medical Sciences* 56(3):B130–B39.

Kimura, M., J.V.B. Hjelmborg, J.P. Gardner, L. Bathum, M. Brimacombe, X. Lu, L. Christiansen, J.W. Vaupel, A. Aviv, and K. Christensen. 2008. "Telomere Length and Mortality: A Study of Leukocytes in Elderly Danish Twins." *American Journal of Epidemiology* 167:799–806.

Krieger, N., J.T. Chen, B.A. Couli, and J.V. Selby. 2005. "Lifetime Socioeconomic Position and Twins' Health: An Analysis of 308 Pairs of United States Women Twins." *PLoS Medicine* 2:e162.

Lee, J.H., A. Flaquer, R. Costa, H. Andrews, P. Cross, R. Lantigua, N. Schupf, M.X. Tang, and R. Mayeux. 2004. "Genetic Influences on Life span and Survival Among Elderly African-Americans, Caribbean Hispanics, and Caucasians." *American Journal of Medical Genetics Part A* 128A(2):159–64.

Lewis, S.J. and E.J. Brunner. 2004. "Methodological Problems in Genetic Association Studies of Longevity: The Apolipoprotein E Gene as an Example." *International Journal of Epidemiology* 33:962–70.

Ljungquist, B., S. Berg, J. Lanke, G.E. McClearn, and N.L. Pedersen. 1998. "The Effect of Genetic Factors for Longevity: A Comparison of Identical and Fraternal Twins in the Swedish Twin Registry." *Journal of Gerontology Series A: Biological Sciences and Medical Sciences* 53(6):M441–M46.

Lund, R., B. Holstein, and M. Osler. 2004. "Marital History From age 15 to 40 Years and Subsequent 10-year Mortality: A Longitudinal Study of Danish Males Born in 1953." *International Journal of Epidemiology* 33:389–97.

Mayer, P.J. 1991. "Inheritance of Longevity Evinces No Secular Trend Among Members of Six New England Families Born 1650–1874." *American Journal of Human Biology* 3(1):49–58.

McGue, M., J.W. Vaupel, N. Holm, and B. Harvald. 1993. "Longevity is Moderately Heritable in a Sample of Danish Twins Born 1870–1880." *Journal of Gerontology* 48(6):B237–B44.

Nawrot, T.S., J.A. Staessen, J.P. Gardner, and A. Aviv. 2004. "Telomere Length and Possible Link to X Chromosome." *Lancet* 363:507–10.

Oeppen, J. and J.W. Vaupel. 2002. "Broken Limits to Life Expectancy." *Science* 296(5570):1029–31.

Osler M., M. McGue, and K. Christensen. 2007. "Socioeconomic Position and Twins' Health: A Life-Course Analysis of 1266 Pairs of Middle-Aged Danish Twins." *International Journal of Epidemiology* 36(1):77–83.

Panossian, L.A., V.R. Porter, H.F. Valenzuela, X. Zhu, E. Reback, D. Masterman, J.L. Cummings, and R.B. Effros. 2003. "Telomere Shortening in T Cells Correlates with Alzheimer's Disease Status." *Neurobiology of Aging* 24:77–84.

Panza, F., A. D'Introno, A.M. Colacicco, C. Capurso, S. Capurso, P.G. Kehoe, A. Capurso, and V. Solfrizzi. 2004. "Vascular Genetic Factors and Human Longevity." *Mechanisms of Ageing and Development* 125:169–78.

Pearl, R. 1931. "Studies on Human Longevity. IV: The Inheritance of Longevity." *Human Biology* 3:245–69.

Perls, T.T., E. Bubrick, C.G. Wager, J. Vijg, and L. Kruglyak 1998. "Siblings of Centenarians Live Longer." *Lancet* 351(9115):1560.

Petersen L., G.G. Nielsen, P.K. Anderson, and T.I.A. Sorensen. 2002. "Case-Control Study of Genetic Environmental Influences on Premature Death of Adult Adoptees." *Genetic Epidemiology* 23(2):123–32.

Petersen L., P.K. Andersen, and T.I. Sorensen. 2005. "Premature Death of Adult Adoptees: Analyses of a Case-Cohort Sample." *Genetic Epidemiology* 28(4):376–82.

Plomin, R., J.C. DeFries, G.E. McClearn, and P. McGuffin 2008. *Behavioral Genetics*, 5th ed. New York, NY, Worth Publisher.

Samani, N.J., R. Boultby, R. Butler, J.R. Thompson, and A.H. Goodall. 2001. "Telomere Shortening in Atherosclerosis." *Lancet* 358:472–73.

Schoenmaker, M., A.J. de Craen, P.H. de Meijer, M. Beekman, G.J. Blauw, P.E. Slagboom, and R.G. Westendorp. 2006. "Evidence of Genetic Enrichment for Exceptional Survival Using a Family Approach: The Leiden Longevity Study." *European Journal of Human Genetics* 14(1):79–84.

Slagboom, P.E., S. Droog, and D.I. Boomsma. 1994. "Genetic Determination of Telomere Size in Humans: A Twin Study of Three Age Groups." *American Journal of Human Genetics* 55:876–82.

Sørensen, T.I., G.G. Nielsen, P.K. Andersen, and T.W. Teasdale. 1988. "Genetic and Environmental Influences on Premature Death in Adult Adoptees." *New England Journal of Medicine* 318(12):727–32.

Tomassini, C., K. Juel, N.V. Holm, A. Skytthe, and K. Christensen 2003. "Risk of Suicide in Twins: 51 Year Follow up Study." *British Medical Journal* 327(7411):373–74. (PMCID: PMC261828).

Vågerö, D. and D. Leon. 1994. "Ischaemic Heart Disease and low Birth Weight: A Test of the Fetal-Origins Hypothesis from the Swedish Twin Registry." *Lancet* 343(8892):260–63.

Valdes, A.M., T. Andrew, J.P. Gardner, M. Kimura, E. Oelsner, L.F. Cherkas, A. Aviv, and M.D. Spector. 2005. "Obesity, Cigarette Smoking, and Telomere Length in Women." *Lancet* 366:662–64.

von Zglinicki T., V. Serra, M. Lorenz, G. Saretzki, R. Lenzen-Grobimlighaus, R. Gebner, A. Risch, and E. Steinhagen-Thiessen. 2000. "Short Telomeres in Patients with Vascular Dementia: An Indicator of Low Antioxidative Capacity and a Possible Risk Factor?" *Lab Invest* 80:1739–47.

Wyshak, G. 1978. "Fertility and Longevity in Twins, Sibs, and Parents of Twins." *Social Biology* 25(4):315–30.

Yu, C.E., J. Oshima, Y.H. Fu, E.M. Wijsman, F. Hisama, R. Alisch, S. Matthews, J. Nakura, T. Miki, S. Ouais, G.M. Martin, J. Mulligan, and G.D. Schellenberg. 1996. "Positional Cloning of the Werner's Syndrome Gene." *Science* 272:258–62.

# Part IV
# Contextual Effects on Mortality

# Chapter 20
# Neighborhood Effects on Mortality

Arijit Nandi and Ichiro Kawachi

## Introduction

John Donne's (1572–1631) epigram, "No man is an island, entire of itself," neatly encapsulates the rationale and motivation behind much of the research investigating the influences of neighborhood contexts on population health outcomes. As human beings, our lives are embedded in a series of social contexts through the life course, extending from the families we are raised in, the schools we attend as children, the places where we work, to the neighborhoods in which we reside. Accordingly, it is reasonable to hypothesize that our behaviors and actions are influenced by our social context, and moreover, that the nature of these social influences would be relevant to health outcomes. For example, if your neighbors don't like to buy low-fat dairy products, your local convenience store owner is less likely to stock them. Thus, even if you have a strong personal preference for consuming low-fat dairy products, your food choices may be constrained by the spillover effects of other people's preferences. The field of "neighborhood effects research" is concerned with empirically demonstrating the existence of these types of contextual influences on health. It is a burgeoning area of research with contributions from diverse disciplines ranging from demography, social epidemiology, geography, medical sociology, and economics (Kawachi and Berkman 2003b).

The aim of this chapter is threefold. In the first section, we discuss the plausibility of neighborhood effects on mortality, i.e., we discuss the potential mechanisms and processes by which exposure to different neighborhood contexts could produce variations in adult mortality outcomes. In the second section, we provide a systematic review of the empirical, multilevel studies documenting neighborhood contextual influences on all-cause and cause-specific mortality outcomes. In the third and final section, we outline the challenges in this field of research, particularly pertaining to the issue of causal inference.

## Mechanisms

It is almost a truism to say that depending on one's race/ethnicity and socioeconomic status (SES), people end up living in neighborhoods of markedly different quality. In turn, neighborhood quality is further conceptualized along three separate dimensions—the physical, service, and social environments. Neighborhood *physical environment* encompasses features such as local traffic patterns that expose residents to noise and air pollution, as well as concepts such as the "built environment" and "walkability" of neighborhoods, which has been studied in relation to the physical activity patterns of residents and their risk of developing obesity. Chapter 21 by Chris Browning, Eileen Bjornstrom, and Kathleen Cagney discusses some of these environmental effects. The *service environment* refers to features of neighborhoods such as accessibility of health services, the quality of schools, as well as the quality of the local food environment (e.g., the presence of supermarkets versus the presence

A. Nandi (✉)
Institute for Health and Social Policy & Department of Epidemiology, Biostatistics, and Occupational Health, McGill University, Montreal, QC Canada
e-mail: arijit.nandi@mcgill.ca

of fast food outlets). Finally, the neighborhood *social environment* refers to resources (e.g., social capital) as well as risks (e.g., exposure to violence and crime) arising out of social interactions between residents (Coutts and Kawachi 2006).

In the neighborhood effects literature, differential exposure to these neighborhood characteristics is assumed to lie at the root of the disparities that are often observed between the health of residents living in affluent areas compared to those living in socioeconomically deprived areas. For example, much work has focused in recent years on area-level explanations for the obesity epidemic. Even as the prevalence of obesity has risen markedly during the last two decades, the between-neighborhood variation in the prevalence of obesity has been equally striking. Neighborhoods that are socioeconomically disadvantaged and have high minority concentration consistently show higher prevalence of obesity compared to more affluent, predominantly white neighborhoods. The working hypothesis of neighborhood studies in the obesity field is that residential segregation (both by race and SES) produces unequal exposure of residents to "obesogenic" environments. That is, low and minority residents are more likely to reside in neighborhoods with lower quality food environment ("food deserts") as well as lower walkability (e.g., heavier traffic, fewer parks). The crucial distinction to be drawn here is that low-SES neighborhoods are hypothesized to have a higher prevalence of obesity not because of the characteristics of the *people* who tend to be clustered in these areas, but because of the characteristics of the neighborhood *environments*. The former refers to the *compositional* effect of neighborhoods, whereas the latter refers to *contextual* effects, and multilevel analysis is used to tease these effects apart.

## Caveats

As our systematic review in the next section will conclude, there is considerable evidence to suggest that living in socioeconomically disadvantaged neighborhoods is associated with a contextual excess risk of mortality for residents. That said, there are several disadvantages of using mortality as the health outcome to study neighborhood effects. The first issue is the problem of the lag time between exposure to a particular neighborhood environment and elevated risk of death. Unlike the case of studying obesity (where the average lag period between exposure to an obesogenic environment and weight gain could be as short as 1–2 years), the induction time for mortality is likely to be longer. In general, the longer the lag period, the higher the likelihood of misclassification because of residential mobility. A second problem is that mortality mixes together effects of disease incidence and prognosis. For example, suppose a study demonstrates a link between neighborhood deprivation and cardiovascular mortality; it is unclear whether the association is driven by an excess incidence (in turn, reflecting increased levels of risk factors for cardiovascular disease), worse prognosis in those with established disease (e.g., because of lack of access to high-quality hospitals offering interventional cardiology), or both. A third and related problem is the lack of specificity of an outcome measure such as all-cause mortality. In the example of research on neighborhood effects on obesity, there is a clear mechanism—or at least a plausible "storyline"—linking local food environment to weight gain. By contrast, the precise pathways and mechanisms linking neighborhood environments to mortality are harder to spell out (or at least, the "storyline" depends on a longer interconnected chain of causation). For all the foregoing reasons, empirical research has tended to shift away from all-cause mortality to cause-specific mortality, and whenever possible, to disease incidence. In the name of truth-in-advertising, the present chapter will not discuss studies of disease incidence (since this is a *Handbook of Adult Mortality*), but readers are referred to recent surveys of neighborhood effects on specific health outcomes, such as obesity (Feng et al. 2009).

## Empirical Evidence

### *Methods*

#### Selection Criteria

The sampling frame, for our empiric review included population-based studies that investigated the effect of a neighborhood-level exposure on an indicator of mortality and were published in the English language. There is substantial heterogeneity in the types of small-area units used to proxy "neighborhoods" as geographic areas with some a priori relevance to the health of their inhabitants. Although there is growing consensus that some geographic units (e.g., census tracts) may be more valid proxies of neighborhoods than others (e.g., zip codes), the definition of neighborhood is often specific to the research question being investigated. As such, our sampling frame included any study of an exposure measured at the level of small areas described as "neighborhoods." We excluded studies that explicitly used neighborhood exposures (e.g., median household income per neighborhood) as substitutes for missing individual-level measures (e.g., individual income) or adjusted for potentially confounding neighborhood-level variables to estimate the independent effect of an individual-level factor. Additionally, we excluded studies that were not multilevel, including ecologic studies.

## Search Strategy

We identified papers for our review using a four-step procedure. First we performed a systematic search of the peer-reviewed literature using the ISI Web of Knowledge database. We identified potential studies for inclusion by querying the topics field for the terms "neighborhood" and "mortality." Second, we analyzed abstracts for all studies identified and excluded papers that did not satisfy selection criteria. Third, we analyzed the full-text version of all remaining studies and excluded those that did not satisfy selection criteria. Fourth, we retrieved articles not identified by our literature review from the references of remaining papers, as well as other reviews of neighborhood effects on health (Kawachi and Berkman 2003a; Pickett and Pearl 2001) and excluded those that did not satisfy selection criteria. Our search concluded at the end of 2008.

## Search Results

Our search identified more than 500 papers, 37 of which satisfied selection criteria. Table 20.1 presents a summary of all findings alphabetically by type of mortality assessed (i.e., all-cause, cancer, cardiovascular, drug, HIV/AIDS, infant, injury). The table provides a summary of the citation, sample, and sample size in the first column, the timeframe in the second column, the geographic definition of "neighborhood" in the third column, neighborhood covariates in the fourth column, and main findings in the fifth column. In general, Table 20.1 presents the most conservative estimates from models with full adjustment for individual-level covariates. This table aims to highlight the most meaningful conclusions from the studies collected.

## Results

We identified 21 studies of all-cause mortality, 1 of cancer mortality, 6 of cardiovascular mortality, 3 of drug mortality, 2 of HIV/AIDS mortality, 3 of infant mortality, and 1 of injury mortality. Consistent with broader neighborhood effects research, our review shows that adverse socioeconomic circumstances measured at the neighborhood level are consistently associated with greater mortality and that these associations frequently vary or are moderated by individual-level race/ethnicity and socioeconomic characteristics.

## The Neighborhood Socioeconomic Environment and Mortality

*Consistency of findings.* The most consistently reported association was between neighborhood SES and mortality. Six studies assessed the influence of neighborhood SES, measured as residence in a federally designated poverty area or by the percent of residents below the federally designated poverty level, on all-cause mortality (Chen et al. 2006; Haan et al. 1987; Johnson et al. 2008; Kaplan 1996; Subramanian et al. 2005; Waitzman and Smith 1998). For example, Chen and colleagues (2006) found that the age-adjusted relative risk of mortality was 39% higher in Boston census tracts with at least 20% of residents in poverty, the federal threshold for a poverty area, compared to less than 5% in poverty (Chen et al. 2006). While the objective of this study was to monitor disparities in mortality across neighborhoods, lack of adjustment for the individual-level characteristics of neighborhood residents precludes inference about whether neighborhood environments have effects independently of "compositional effects" or residential selection mechanisms, topics discussed in further detail in Section "Causal

Table 20.1 Key studies assessing the relation between the neighborhood environment and mortality

| (Citation); Sample (n) | Timeframe | Geographic area | Neighborhood measures | Main findings |
|---|---|---|---|---|
| *All-cause mortality* | | | | |
| Anderson et al. (1997); US black and white adults (25–64) from the National Longitudinal Mortality Study, with follow-up using National Death Index; $n = 239,187$ | Ascertainment of deaths between 1979 and 1989 | Census tracts | Census tract median income categorized as low (<$16,200), medium ($16,200–22,900), or high (>$22,900) | • After adjusting for family-level income, the RRs for living in a low vs. high income census tract were 1.26 (95%CI 1.15, 1.38) and 1.16 (95%CI 1.04, 1.29) for white men and women, respectively; and 1.49 (95%CI 1.14, 1.95) and 1.30 (95%CI 0.91, 1.87) for black men and women, respectively |
| Bond Huie et al. (2002); US black, white, and Hispanic adults (18–64) from the National Health Interview Survey-National Death Index; $n = 561,023$ | Ascertainment of deaths between 1986 and 1997 | 9,433 very-small areas (VSAs) | % black, % Hispanic, % immigrant, % never married, % low income, % low-educational attainment, % high-unemployment status | • In a full model adjusted for individual- and family-level covariates (i.e., race/ethnicity, nativity, age, sex, employment status, family income, education, marital status, self-rated health, geographic region), living in a VSA that was ≥ 14% black vs. ≤4% (HR = 1.08), ≥ 8% Hispanic vs. ≤ 3% (HR = 1.11), ≥ 40% immigrant vs. ≤ 9% (HR = 0.96), ≥ 10% unemployed vs. < 10 (HR = 1.04), ≥ 50% low income vs. ≤ 9% (HR = 1.08), ≥ 50% low education vs. ≤ 9% (HR = 1.15), and ≥ 21% never married vs. ≤ 9% (HR = 1.09) was associated with mortality ($p \leq 0.05$ for all) |
| Bosma et al. (2001); Random sample of men and women aged 15–74 from Eindhoven, Netherlands; $n = 8,506$ | 1991–1996 | 86 administratively defined neighborhoods | % of respondents: with primary schooling only (educational level), who were unskilled manual workers (occupational status), unemployed or disabled (employment status), reporting severe financial problems (financial status) | • After adjusting for individual-level age, sex, baseline health, educational level, occupational level, employment status, and financial status, residing in a neighborhood in the worst-off quartile vs. the best-off quartile of educational, occupational, employment, and financial status was associated with ORs of 1.40 (95%CI 0.96, 1.20), 1.19 (95%CI 0.81, 1.73), 1.47 (95%CI 1.02, 2.11), and 1.22 (95%CI 0.88, 1.69), respectively |
| Chen et al. (2006); All reported premature deaths (death before age 75) in Boston; $n = 5,945$ | Ascertainment of deaths between 1999 and 2001 | 156 census tracts | % of persons below poverty level | • In age-adjusted models, the RR for premature mortality was 1.39 (95% credible interval 1.09, 1.78) comparing census tracts with ≥ 20% of persons in poverty compared to tracts with <5% in poverty |
| Ecob and Jones (1998); Random sample of adults aged 25–74 from England and Wales; $n = 287,787$ | Ascertainment of deaths between 1971 and 1985 | Electoral wards | Craig-Webber classification of neighborhoods into 36 types (e.g., modern high-status housing, older industrial settlements, rural areas with small holdings, urban local authority estates, clydeside inner areas, inner London, very-high status areas) | • In models adjusted for individual-level covariates including age, housing tenure, car ownership, social class, and economic activity, the odds ratios of mortality ranged from 0.87 to 1.38 among women and from 0.79 to 1.22 among men, depending on place |

**Table 20.1** (continued)

| (Citation); Sample (*n*) | Timeframe | Geographic area | Neighborhood measures | Main findings |
|---|---|---|---|---|
| Eschbach et al. (2004); Probability sample of elderly Mexican-Americans aged 65 or older from five southwestern states; *n* = 3,050 | Baseline in 1993–1994 with follow-up interviews in 1995–1996, 1998–1999, and 2000–2001 | 210 census tracts | Ethnic concentration of Mexican-Americans measured as the percentage of neighborhood residents who were Mexican-American, scaled 0–1 | • After adjusting for individual-level covariates (i.e., age, gender, marital status, educational attainment, household income, immigrant status, language of interview, baseline health status, and disability), living in a tract with 100% vs. 0% Mexican-Americans was associated with a 36% reduced risk of death [HR = 0.64 (95%CI 0.42, 0.96)] |
| Haan et al. (1987); Random sample of residents of Oakland, CA aged 35 or older; *n* = 1,811 | Ascertainment of deaths between 1965 and 1974 | Poverty areas (37 census tracts) | Residence in poverty area (about 41% of sample); criteria for federal poverty status included % low-income families, % substandard housing, % low education, % unskilled male laborer, % children in homes with single parent | • After adjusting for individual-level covariates (i.e., age, sex, race, baseline health status, socioeconomic factors, and health practices), the odds of mortality were 46–60% higher among those living in a poverty area relative to a non-poverty area |
| Jaffe et al. (2005b); Adults aged 45–89 from the Israel Longitudinal Mortality Study; *n* = 131,156 | Census records from 1983, with death ascertainment through 1992 | 880 statistical areas | Area-level socioeconomic status index based on demographic characteristics, financial resources, housing density and quality, home equipment (e.g., color television), mode of transportation, level of education, and employment status | • After adjusting for individual-level covariates (i.e., continent of origin, marital status, educational attainment, household amenities, number of rooms), living in the lowest tertile vs. highest tertile of socioeconomic status was associated with an increased odds of mortality for men aged 45–69 [OR=1.26 (95%CI 1.16, 1.36)] and women aged 45–69 [OR=1.17 (95%CI 1.09, 1.27)] |
| Jaffe et al. (2005a); Adults aged 45–89 from the Israel Longitudinal Mortality Study; *n* = 141,683 | Census records from 1983, with death ascertainment through 1992 | 882 statistical areas | Neighborhood religious affiliation based on the proportion adults in each statistical area who voted for any religious political party in the 1984 national elections, split into religiously affiliated (>30% of residents voted for religious parties) or non-affiliated | • After adjusting for individual-level covariates (i.e., continent of origin, marital status, educational attainment) and area socioeconomic status, living in a religiously affiliated vs. non-affiliated neighborhood was associated with a decreased odds of mortality for both men [OR = 0.75 (95%CI 0.67, 0.84)] and women [OR = 0.86 (95%CI 0.67, 0.96)] |
| Kaplan (1996); Random sample of residents of Oakland, CA aged 35 or older; *n* = 1,811 | Ascertainment of deaths between 1965 and 1974 | Poverty areas (37 census tracts) | Residence in a poverty area (about 41% of sample); criteria for federal poverty status included % low-income families, % substandard housing, % low education, % unskilled male laborer, % children in homes with single parent | • After adjusting for age, sex, and race, residence in a poverty area was associated with an increased odds of mortality [OR = 1.45 (95%CI 1.10, 1.92)] |

Table 20.1 (continued)

| (Citation); Sample ($n$) | Timeframe | Geographic area | Neighborhood measures | Main findings |
|---|---|---|---|---|
| LeClere et al. (1997); Representative sample of adults aged 18 and over from the National Health Interview Survey 1986–1990 with follow-up using the National Death Index; $n = 346{,}917$ | Ascertainment of deaths between 1986 and 1991 | 5,919 census tracts | Neighborhood racial segregation based on % African-American; highest (>17%) vs. lowest (0.5%) | • In models adjusted for individual-level covariates (i.e., race, age, income to needs ratio, education, marital status), living in a highly racially segregated neighborhood was associated with an increased risk of mortality for both men [risk ratio = 1.22 ($p \leq 0.05$)] and women [risk ratio = 1.17 ($p \leq 0.05$)]<br>• After adjusting for the degree of racial segregation per neighborhood the elevated relative risk of death for African-Americans relative to non-Hispanic whites was no longer significant |
| Naess et al. (2007): Adults aged 50–74 who lived in Oslo, Norway in 1992; $n = 105{,}359$ | Ascertainment of deaths between 1992 and 1998 | 468 administrative neighborhoods | Neighborhood air pollution based on concentrations of particulate matter pollutants ($PM_{2.5}$)<br>Neighborhood deprivation based on educational attainment, household income, status of ownership of dwelling, and household crowding | • Neighborhood measures of $PM_{2.5}$ and deprivation were significantly associated<br>• After adjusting for age, living in a neighborhood with a higher concentration of $PM_{2.5}$ was associated with an increased odds of all-cause mortality for both men [OR = 1.10 (95%CI 1.03, 1.18)] and women [OR = 1.11 (95%CI 1.04, 1.19)]<br>• Although attenuated, significant associations between neighborhood $PM_{2.5}$ and mortality persisted after adjusting for indicators of individual- and neighborhood-level deprivation |
| Roos et al. (2004); Adults residents of Manitoba and Nova Scotia, Canada aged 18–75; $n = 8{,}032$ from Manitoba and 2,116 from Nova Scotia | Respondents followed from 1996–2002 in Manitoba and 1990–1999 in Nova Scotia | Enumeration areas | Neighborhood characteristics included mean household income, mean dwelling value, % less than grade 9 education, unemployment rate, % single mothers | • Neighborhood characteristics were not significantly associated with mortality regardless of the individual-level covariates adjusted for |
| Sloggett and Joshi (1998); Random sample of non-institutionalized residents of England and Wales | Ascertainment of deaths between 1983 and 1992 | Approximately 9,000 electoral wards | Social deprivation index based on % unemployed, % without access to a car, % households not owner occupied, % employed men and women in two lowest social classes | • After adjusting for individual-level covariates (i.e., age, geographic region, employment status, being a housewife, social class, housing status, car ownership), the odds of premature mortality (death before age 70) increased by 2% (95%CI 1.00, 1.03) and 4% (95%CI 1.02, 1.06) per unit increase in the social deprivation score for men and women, respectively |

Table 20.1 (continued)

| (Citation); Sample (n) | Timeframe | Geographic area | Neighborhood measures | Main findings |
|---|---|---|---|---|
| Subramanian et al. (2005); All deaths among Massachusetts residents; n = 142,836 | Ascertainment of deaths from 1989 to 1991 | 5,532 block groups nested within 1,307 census tracts | Neighborhood poverty based on the % population living below the poverty line per census tract, with cutpoints at 5, 10, and 20% | • After adjusting for individual-level covariates (i.e., age, sex, race/ethnicity), living in a high vs. low (≥ 20% vs. <5%) poverty neighborhood was associated with an increased odds of mortality among whites [OR=1.42 (95%CI 1.33, 1.51) and blacks [OR=3.00 (95%CI 2.28, 3.94)]; neighborhood poverty accounted for a substantial proportion of variations in black excess mortality |
| Subramanian et al. (2008); Nationally representative sample of elderly couples aged 67–98; n = 200,000 couples | Ascertainment of deaths from 1993 to 2001 | 23,272 ZIP codes | Neighborhood poverty based on % population living in poverty. Neighborhood concentration of widowed individuals measure by % population who were widowed, % male population who were widowed, % female population who were widowed | • In models adjusted for time-trends, age, comorbidity, race, individual poverty status, and widowhood status, living in a high poverty neighborhood was associated with an OR of 1.06 (95%CI 1.04, 1.07) for men and 1.04 (1.02, 1.06) for women<br>• In models adjusted for time-trends, age, comorbidity, race, individual poverty status, and ZIP code-level poverty, male widowhood was associated with ORs of 1.22 (95%CI 1.18, 1.25) and 1.17 (95%CI 1.13, 1.19) in neighborhoods with low and high concentration of widowed individuals, respectively; for women, the ORs were 1.17 (95%CI 1.14, 1.20) and 1.15 (95%CI 1.12, 1.19) in neighborhoods of low and high concentrations of widowed individuals, respectively |
| Veugelers et al. (2001); Representative sample of adult non-institutionalized population aged 18–75 from Nova Scotia; n = 2,116 | Ascertainment of deaths from 1990 to 1999 | 1,442 enumeration areas | Neighborhood household income, average dwelling value, unemployment rate, neighborhood disadvantage (more than 15% of residents with education <9th grade or having >10% of families headed by single mothers) | • In models adjusted for individual-level age, gender, smoking status, BMI, and diabetes, none of the neighborhood-level contextual variables were associated with the odds of mortality<br>• After stratifying by level of neighborhood advantage, greater individual income and education were associated with a decreased odds of mortality in advantaged neighborhoods, but not disadvantaged neighborhoods |
| Waitzman and Smith (1998); Representative sample of black and white US adults aged 25–74 from the National Health and Nutrition Examination Survey conducted from 1971 to 1975; n=10161 | Ascertainment of deaths through 1987 | Census tracts | Residence in a federal poverty area, defined as contiguous census tracts that ranked in the bottom quartile based of several areal factors, including the proportions of families with low income, substandard housing, children in single-headed households, unskilled males in the labor force, and adults with low educational attainment | • In models adjusted for age, race, sex, marital status, household income as a percentage of the poverty line, formal education, alcohol consumption, BMI, smoking, exercise frequency, baseline health status, hypertension, and cholesterol level, living in a poverty area was associated with an increased risk of all-cause mortality among those aged 25–54 [RR = 1.78 (95%CI 1.33, 2.38)], but not among those aged 55–74 [RR = 0.87 (95%CI 0.74, 1.01)] |

Table 20.1 (continued)

| (Citation); Sample (n) | Timeframe | Geographic area | Neighborhood measures | Main findings |
|---|---|---|---|---|
| Wen and Christakis (2005); Elderly Medicare beneficiaries in Chicago newly diagnosed and hospitalized for the first time with one of five common serious diseases; $n = 10,557$ | Initial diagnosis in 1993 with follow-up until 1999 | 51 zip codes | Neighborhood socioeconomic status measured using an index based on % residents with household income ≥ $50,000, % households below federal poverty threshold, and % college graduates<br>Neighborhood social environment measured using an index based on self-reports of collective efficacy, social support, voluntary association, and perceived violence | • After adjusting for individual-level age, sex, race, diagnosis, baseline comorbidity, and individual poverty, a one standard deviation increase in neighborhood socioeconomic status and social environment index were associated with 4.3 and 3.4% lower risks of death, respectively ($p \leq 0.05$ for both)<br>• Interaction terms between neighborhood- and individual-level covariates showed that neighborhood SES was more beneficial for those not in poverty |
| Winkleby et al. (2006); Men and women aged 25–74 from four California cities; $n = 4,476$ women and 3,721 men | Surveys between 1979 and 1990 with ascertainment of deaths through 2002 | 82 neighborhoods | Neighborhood socioeconomic status defined using an index based on % aged 25 or older with less than high school education, median annual family income, % blue collar workers, % unemployed, median housing value; index split into thirds (low, moderate, and high SES) for analysis | • In models adjusted for individual-level covariates (i.e., age, and baseline obesity, smoking, hypertension, hypercholesterolemia, physical inactivity, and alcohol intake), the risk of mortality was highest for low-SES men and women living in high-SES neighborhoods |
| Yen and Kaplan (1999); Non-institutionalized adults aged 39–96 from 1983 subsample of Alameda County, California residents; $n = 1,129$ | Ascertainment of deaths between 1983 and 1994 | Census tracts | Neighborhood social environment score created using census tract per capita income, % white-collar employees, crowding, prevalence of commercial stores, population, area, % households renting, and % single-unit housing structures; dichotomized for analysis | • In models adjusting for individual-level age, sex, race/ethnicity, income, smoking, BMI, alcohol consumption, and perceived health status, living in a low-social environment neighborhood was associated with an increased odds of mortality [OR = 1.58 (95%CI 1.13, 2.24)] |
| *Cancer mortality* | | | | |
| Gomez et al. (2007); SEER-Medicare colorectal cancer patients diagnosed between 1992–1996 and aged 65 or older; $n = 41,901$ | Follow-up through 1999 | 82 neighborhoods defined using block groups or census tracts | Neighborhood socioeconomic status based on census tract poverty, education, and income, split into quartiles | • After adjusting for individual-level covariates (i.e., age, sex, year of diagnosis, cancer characteristics, treatment, SEER region, comorbidity), residence in a neighborhood in the lowest quartile of income was associated with cancer mortality among Filipinos [relative rate = 2.54 (95%CI 1.02, 6.33)], and residence in a neighborhood in the lowest quartile of education was associated with cancer mortality among non-Hispanic whites [relative rate = 1.14 (95%CI 1.04, 1.24)] |

Table 20.1 (continued)

| (Citation); Sample (n) | Timeframe | Geographic area | Neighborhood measures | Main findings |
|---|---|---|---|---|
| *Cardiovascular mortality* | | | | |
| Chaix et al. (2007b); Two cohorts (baseline in 1986 or 1996) of residents from Scania, Sweden aged 50–64 at baseline, assessed for ischemic heart disease mortality; ($n = 69,815$ for 1986 cohort; $n = 73,547$ for 1996 cohort) | Baseline in 1986 or 1996 with 7 years of follow-up | 627 neighborhood units | Neighborhood socioeconomic position based on income of neighborhood residents aged 50–89 at 1-year prior to baseline and split into quartiles | • After adjusting for individual-level covariates (i.e., sex, age, household structure, occupation, individual income), living in a neighborhood in the lowest quartile of socioeconomic position (vs. the highest quartile) was associated with a HR of 1.60 (95% credible interval 1.36, 1.89) in the 1986 cohort and 2.54 (95% credible interval 1.99, 3.21) in the 1996 cohort |
| Chaix et al. (2007a); Residents from Scania, Sweden aged 50–64 in 1996, assessed for ischemic heart disease mortality ($n = 52,084$) | Baseline in 1996 with 7 years of follow-up | 648 neighborhood units | Neighborhood socioeconomic position based on income of neighborhood residents aged 50–79 at 1-year prior to baseline and split into quartiles; residential stability based on the % of residents in each neighborhood who were living there 5 years before baseline and split into quartiles | • Low vs. high neighborhood socioeconomic position [HR=1.85 (95% credible interval 1.37, 2.72)] and low vs. high residential stability [HR=1.89 (95% credible interval 1.39, 2.52)] were both associated with ischemic heart disease mortality, independent of individual-level covariates (i.e., prior health conditions, sex, age, household structure, educational attainment, occupation, individual income)<br>• Low vs. high residential stability was associated with mortality after acute myocardial infarction [HR = 2.54 (95% credible interval 1.35, 5.07)], independent of individual-level covariates; results for neighborhood socioeconomic position were not significant |
| Franzini and Spears (2003); All reported heart disease deaths for individuals aged 25 or older in Texas during 1991; $n = 50,268$ | Ascertainment of deaths in 1991 | 247 counties, 3,788 census tracts, and 12,344 block groups in Texas | Educational attainment measured at the tract and county levels<br>Economic environment measured by block group median house value and county-level median income, poverty rate, and unemployment rate<br>Racial/ethnic composition measured by % black and % Hispanic at the tract and county levels<br>Income inequality measured by the 90/10 ratio and the Robin Hood index<br>Social capital measured by homeownership at the tract and county level and the crime index at the county level | • The proportion of total variance attributable to variances at the block, tract, and county levels was about 4%<br>• After adjusting for individual-level covariates (i.e., sex, race/ethnicity, educational attainment), fewer years of life lost to heart disease was associated with living in a block group with higher median house value, tract with higher own racial/ethnic group density (among blacks and Hispanics), and county with more social capital ($p < 0.05$ for all) |

**Table 20.1** (continued)

| (Citation); Sample (n) | Timeframe | Geographic area | Neighborhood measures | Main findings |
|---|---|---|---|---|
| Gerber et al. (2008); Adult residents of Olmsted County, MN who experienced an myocardial infarction; $n = 705$ | Enrollment and follow-up between 2002 and 2006 | 33 census tracts | Neighborhood median household income | • After adjusting for individual-level covariates (i.e., age, sex, race, education, cardiovascular risk factors, characteristics of myocardial infarction and comorbidity, treatment), neighborhood income was associated with mortality risk after myocardial infarction [HR=1.62 (95%CI 1.08, 2.45)] |
| LeClere et al. (1998); Representative sample of women aged 18–64 from the National Health Interview Survey 1986–1990 with follow-up using the National Death Index; $n = 199{,}221$ | Ascertainment of deaths between 1986 and 1991 | 5,921 census tracts | Neighborhood factors included % female-headed families, % black, median family income, % households receiving public assistance, % persons in deep poverty, % female-headed poor families, unemployment | • In models adjusted for individual-level covariates (age, ethnicity, BMI, pre-existing conditions, education, income, marital status, unemployment), living in a neighborhood with a high vs. low % of female-headed households (>24% vs. ≤9.9%) was associated with an increased risk for heart disease mortality for women <65 [risk ratio = 1.85 ($p \leq 0.01$)] and women ≥65 [risk ratio = 1.23 ($p \leq 0.05$)] |
| Winkleby et al. (2007); Total population of Sweden in 1995 who lived there since 1985; $n = 1.9$ million women and 1.8 million men | Ascertainment of deaths from 1996 to 2000 | 8,293 small-area market statistics | Neighborhood deprivation index based on education attainment, income, unemployment, and receipt of social welfare; categorized as low, moderate, or high | • After adjusting for individual-level covariates (i.e., age, marital status, family income, educational attainment, immigration status, mobility, and urban/rural status), living in a high vs. low deprivation neighborhood was associated with an increased odds of 1-year case fatality from CHD among women [OR = 1.33 (95%CI 1.08,1.65)] and men [OR = 1.36 (95%CI 1.22, 1.52)] |

*Drug mortality*

| | | | | |
|---|---|---|---|---|
| Galea et al. (2003); Reports on fatal accidents in adults aged 15–64 due to overdose (cases) and other causes (controls) collected from the Office of the Medical Examiner of NYC; $n = 725$ cases and 453 controls | Ascertainment of deaths in 1996 | 59 community districts | Neighborhood income inequality measured by the Gini coefficient | • After adjusting for individual-level covariates (i.e., age, race, sex) and neighborhood-level covariates (i.e., income, drug use, racial composition), the odds of death due to drug overdose was 1.63 (95%CI 1.06, 2.52) in neighborhoods in the least-equitable decile of income distribution compared with neighborhoods in the most-equitable decile |

**Table 20.1** (continued)

| (Citation); Sample (n) | Timeframe | Geographic area | Neighborhood measures | Main findings |
|---|---|---|---|---|
| Hembree et al. (2005); Reports on fatal accidents in adults aged 15–64 due to overdose (cases) and other causes (controls) collected from the Office of the Medical Examiner of NYC; n = 725 cases and 453 controls | Ascertainment of deaths in 1996 | 59 community districts | Neighborhood external-built environment based on number of structural fires; % buildings that were dilapidated, deteriorating, had external wall problems, window problems, and stairway problems; % acceptably clean streets and sidewalks<br><br>Neighborhood internal-built environment based on % households with toilet breakdowns, non-functioning kitchens, heating breakdowns, inadequate heat in winter, peeling plaster or paint, and internal water leakage | • After adjusting for neighborhood drug use, median household income, age, sex, and race, the % of buildings in dilapidated condition ($p < 0.001$), the % of buildings with window problems ($p = 0.04$), % of buildings with stairway problems ($p = 0.0004$), % of buildings in deteriorated condition ($p = 0.05$), number of structural fires ($p = 0.01$), and % of acceptably clean streets ($p = 0.04$) were associated with the likelihood of overdose mortality<br>• After adjusting for neighborhood drug use, median household income, age, sex, and race, the % of housing units with toilet breakdowns ($p=0.03$), % of households needing additional heat ($p < 0.001$), and % of housing units with peeling paint or plaster ($p = 0.04$) were associated with the likelihood of overdose mortality |
| Nandi et al. (2006); Reports on fatal accidents in adults aged 15–64 due to overdose (cases) and other causes (controls) collected from the Office of the Medical Examiner of NYC; n=725 cases and 453 controls | Ascertainment of deaths in 1996 | 59 community districts | Neighborhood income inequality measured by the Gini coefficient<br>Neighborhood environmental disorder measured using % of acceptably clean sidewalks<br>Neighborhood police activity measured using per capita misdemeanor arrests<br>Neighborhood built environment measured using % of buildings in dilapidated condition | • Compared to the midpoint of the lowest Gini decile, the relative odds of death due to drug overdose was 1.63 (95%CI = 1.06, 2.52) in neighborhoods in 95th percentile of the Gini distribution; after adjusting for the three mediator variables (i.e., neighborhood environmental disorder, police activity, built environment), the OR decreased to 1.12 (95% 0.67, 1.86)<br>• Path analyses showed that 64% of the association between the distribution of income and the rate of overdose death was explained by the three mediator variables |

*HIV/AIDS mortality*

| Joy et al. (2008); HIV positive adults aged 18 or older accessing or not accessing treatment in British Columbia; n=2,080 | Ascertainment of deaths between 1997 and 2004 | Census tracts | Neighborhood SES based on % residents with postsecondary education, % unemployed residents, % aboriginal residents, % residents living below the Canadian poverty line, median household income, urban vs. rural neighborhood | • After adjusting for individual-level covariates (i.e., age, baseline CD4 count, viral load, adherence, late access to treatment), HIV-related mortality was associated with residence in neighborhoods with lower levels of postsecondary education [HR = 0.80 (95%CI 0.71, 0.91) per 10% increase in education] and a high % of residents living below the poverty line [HR = 1.07 (95%CI 1.01, 1.13) per 10% increase in poverty] |

**Table 20.1** (continued)

| (Citation); Sample ($n$) | Timeframe | Geographic area | Neighborhood measures | Main findings |
|---|---|---|---|---|
| Katz et al. (1998); Residents of San Francisco, CA aged 13 or older who were diagnosed with AIDS between 1985 and 1995; $n = 18,167$ | Ascertainment of deaths through 1996 | Census block groups | Neighborhood socioeconomic status based on % population below the poverty line (split at 20%), % working class residents (split at 66%), and % residents who completed high school (split at 25%) | • In both unadjusted models and models adjusted for individual-level covariates (i.e., age, sex, ethnicity, AIDS risk group, site of AIDS diagnosis, time period of diagnosis, AIDS-indicator illness), neighborhood socioeconomic status was not significantly associated with mortality |
| *Infant mortality* | | | | |
| Johnson et al. (2008); Infants born to American-Indian women residing in a metropolitan area of Minnesota; $n = 4,751$ | Ascertainment of deaths between 1990 and 1999 | Census tracts | Neighborhood poverty based on the Federal poverty threshold and split into four categories | • After using propensity score matching (based on individual-level sociodemographic variables, maternal smoking, prenatal care utilization, number of prior maternal births and deaths, birth weight, number of children at birth), the endogenous-cause infant mortality rate for infants born into neighborhoods with moderately high poverty (20–39%) was higher than the rate for infants born into neighborhoods with <5% of residents in poverty [risk ratio = 4.0 (95%CI 1.8, 19.0)]; comparisons between other poverty categories were not significant |
| Luo et al. (2004); All births registered in British Columbia, 1985–2000; $n = 697,477$ | Ascertainment of deaths between 1985 and 2000 | Enumeration areas | Neighborhood income based on household size-adjusted income per single person; split into quintiles for analysis | • In models adjusted for individual-level covariates (i.e., infant sex, parity, plurality, ethnicity, maternal age, marital status, abortion history, mode of delivery, maternal illness, community size, distance to nearest hospital with obstetricians), living in an urban (but not rural) neighborhood in the poorest vs. richest quintile of income was associated with an increased odds of preterm birth (OR range from 1.11 to 1.26) and small for gestational age (OR range from 1.34 to 1.50); lower neighborhood income was associated with a nonsignificant increase in the odds of stillbirth, neonatal death, and postneonatal death |
| Pena et al. (2000); Children from a representative sample of women aged 15–49 in Leon, Nicaragua; $n = 7,073$ children | Ascertainment of deaths among all live births between 1988 and 1993 | 50 geographic clusters | Socioeconomic status of neighborhood based on unsatisfied basic needs (UBN) assessment, an index measuring housing quality, school enrollment, dependency ratio, and availability of sanitary services; UBN score split at median | • After adjusting for individual-level covariates (i.e., mother's age, education, parity, and infant's sex), the relative risk of infant mortality was higher for poor households in non-poor neighborhoods than for poor households in poor neighborhoods ($p < 0.01$); the relative risk for infant mortality comparing a poor household in a non-poor neighborhood to a non-poor household in a non-poor neighborhood was 1.74 (95%CI 1.12, 2.71) |

**Table 20.1** (continued)

| (Citation); Sample (n) | Timeframe | Geographic area | Neighborhood measures | Main findings |
|---|---|---|---|---|
| *Injury mortality*<br>Cubbin et al. (2000); Representative sample of adults aged 18–64 from the National Health Interview Survey 1987–1994 with follow-up using the National Death Index; $n = 472,364$ | Ascertainment of deaths (motor vehicle related, suicide, homicide, and all other external causes) between 1987 and 1995 | 6,179 census tracts | Neighborhood socioeconomic status measured by blue collar workers, family income, poverty, education, housing value, crowded housing split into four categories (low, mid-low, mid-high, high)<br>Residential and family stability measured by mobility, unemployment, vacant housing, female headship, divorced split into four categories<br>Racial concentration measured by proportion black or Hispanic split into four categories<br>Urbanization measured by multi-unit housing and urban residence split into four categories | • After adjusting for individual-level covariates (i.e., age, gender, race/ethnicity, marital status, income to needs, educational attainment employment/occupation status):<br>• Residence in neighborhoods with low incomes (HR = 2.66), high poverty (HR = 2.00), low educational attainment (HR = 2.73), low housing values (HR = 1.65), high proportions of crowded housing (HR = 1.70), high black racial concentration (HR = 2.16), high female headship (HR = 3.50), and high divorce rate HR = 2.61) was associated with an increased risk of homicide mortality ($p < 0.05$ for all)<br>• Residence in neighborhoods with mid-low income (HR = 1.46), mid-high poverty (HR = 1.44), mid-high racial concentration (HR = 1.43), and mid-high residential mobility (HR = 1.45) was associated with an increased risk of suicide mortality ($p < 0.05$ for all)<br>• Residence in neighborhoods with low incomes (HR = 1.73), high poverty (HR = 1.48), low-educational attainment (HR = 1.75), low-housing values (HR = 1.60), and with high proportions of blue collar workers (HR = 1.88) was associated with increased risk of motor vehicle-related mortality; residence in neighborhoods with high proportions of vacant housing (HR = 0.72), multi-unit housing (HR = 0.54), and urban residence (HR = 0.64) were at lower risk of motor vehicle-related mortality ($p < 0.05$ for all)<br>• Residence in neighborhood with high poverty (HR = 1.57) and high proportions of crowded housing (HR = 1.96) were at increased risk of death from other external causes ($p < 0.05$ for all) |

Notes: Numbers in parentheses denote 95%CI; RR = rate ratio; HR = hazard ratio; OR = odds ratio.

Inference in the Study of Neighborhood Effects on Mortality." However, other work using longitudinal population-based samples, including the Alameda County study, have shown that residence in poverty areas was associated with a greater than 40% increased odds of all-cause mortality independent of individual-level sex, race, health status, socioeconomic factors, and health behaviors (Haan et al. 1987; Kaplan 1996).

Other socioeconomic indicators or indices of socioeconomic deprivation have been used to assess the influence of neighborhood SES on mortality (Jaffe et al. 2005b; Roos et al. 2004; Sloggett and Joshi 1998; Veugelers et al. 2001; Wen and Christakis 2005; Winkleby et al. 2006). Slogett and Joshi (1998), for example, measured social deprivation per electoral ward in England and Wales using an index based on percent unemployment, percent without access to a car, percent of households not owner occupied, and percent of employed men and women in the two lowest social classes; premature mortality for men and women was positively associated with social deprivation scores (Sloggett and Joshi 1998). Similarly, Jaffe and colleagues (2005b) found that residence in statistical areas of lower SES, measured using an index comprised of sociodemographic characteristics, financial resources, housing density and quality, and mode of transportation, was associated with an increased odds of mortality among adults aged 45–69 in Israel (Jaffe et al. 2005b). However, two studies, both based on samples of adults from Canadian provinces, showed null associations between indicators of neighborhood SES, including median household income, mean housing values and levels of educational attainment, and all-cause mortality (Roos et al. 2004; Veugelers et al. 2001).

Following the earlier work of LeClere et al. (1997), a number of recent studies have investigated whether neighborhood socioeconomic circumstances are linked to mortality from cardiovascular diseases (LeClere et al. 1998). This work shows that neighborhood SES is linked to overall mortality from cardiovascular disease (Chaix et al. 2007a, b; Franzini and Spears 2003; LeClere et al. 1998). For example, using a measure of SES based on the income of neighborhood residents, Chaix and colleagues (2007a) found that living in a neighborhood in the lowest quartile of SES relative to the highest quartiles was associated with an 85% increased hazard of ischemic heart disease mortality among adults aged 50–64 in Scania,

Sweden (Chaix et al. 2007a). Neighborhood SES also seems to be related to survival after a cardiovascular event (Gerber et al. 2008). Winkleby et al. (2007), for example, found that neighborhood deprivation, based on an index comprised of educational attainment, income, unemployment, and receipt of social welfare, was positively associated with 1-year case fatality from coronary heart disease (Winkleby et al. 2007).

A sparse amount of work has investigated the association between neighborhood SES and cancer mortality (Gomez et al. 2007), HIV/AIDS mortality (Joy et al. 2008; Katz et al. 1998), infant mortality (Johnson et al. 2008; Luo et al. 2004; Pena et al. 2000), and injury-related mortality (Cubbin et al. 2000). With few exceptions (Katz et al. 1998), these results have shown that adverse neighborhood socioeconomic circumstances are associated with increased mortality; however, it is difficult to draw conclusions across studies, given a limited number of studies in each particular area.

*Cross-level interactions.* The influence of the neighborhood socioeconomic environment on mortality may differ by individual-level characteristics, including age (LeClere et al. 1998; Waitzman and Smith 1998), race/ethnicity (Anderson et al. 1997; Gomez et al. 2007; Subramanian et al. 2005), and SES (Pena et al. 2000; Wen and Christakis 2005; Winkleby et al. 2006).

Subramanian et al. (2005) showed that living in a Massachusetts block group with at least 20% of residents below the poverty level relative to less than 5% was associated with a 42% increased odds of mortality among whites compared to a 200% increased odds of mortality among blacks (Subramanian et al. 2005). These findings corroborate earlier work by Anderson et al. (1997) using data from the National Longitudinal Mortality Study with follow-up from the National Death Index, which showed that the relative risk of mortality associated with living in a high- versus low-income census tract was higher for black men and women than their white counterparts (Anderson et al. 1997). Together, this work suggests that the neighborhood socioeconomic environment may account for a greater proportion of excess mortality among blacks than whites (Anderson et al. 1997; Subramanian et al. 2005). We identified one study that assessed whether the association between the neighborhood socioeconomic environment and cancer mortality differed by race/ethnicity. In a study of survival after colorectal cancer diagnosis in the SEER-Medicare database, Gomez et al. (2007) found that residence in a neighborhood in the lowest quartiles of income and education was associated with cancer mortality among Filipinos and non-Hispanic whites, respectively, but not other racial/ethnic groups (Gomez et al. 2007).

Three studies examined whether neighborhood and individual-level SES interacted in producing excess mortality risk. For example, in a sample of adults from four California cities, Winkleby et al. (2006) found that the risk of mortality was greatest for men and women of lower SES who were living in high-SES neighborhoods (Winkleby et al. 2006). Similarly, in a representative sample of children and their mothers in Leon, Nicaragua, Pena et al. (2000) found that the relative risk of infant mortality was higher for poor households in non-poor neighborhoods than for poor households in poor neighborhoods Pena et al. (2000). These results suggest that poorer individuals residing in higher SES neighborhoods may be excluded from accessing the salutary resources in those neighborhoods, may suffer from social comparisons and the attendant psychosocial stressors hypothesized to link inequalities to health, or both.

## Social Environment

We identified two studies with the explicit objective of assessing the influence of the neighborhood social environment, as a construct distinct from neighborhood SES, on mortality. Wen assessed whether the neighborhood social environment, measured using an index based on self-reports of collective efficacy, social support, voluntary association, and perceived violence, were associated with all-cause mortality among elderly Medicare beneficiaries in Chicago who were newly diagnosed and hospitalized for the first time with one of five common diseases; after adjusting for individual-level characteristics, a one standard deviation increase in neighborhood social environment index was associated with a greater than 3% lower risk of death (Wen and Christakis 2005). Yen and Kaplan (1999) found that living in a neighborhood with a poorer social environment, measured using census tract income, percent white-collar employees, crowding, prevalence of commercial stores, and other indicators, was associated with an increased odds of mortality among adults in the Alameda County study (Yen and Kaplan 1999).

## Racial Composition

*Consistency of findings.* Although there is a more substantive literature on the impact of neighborhood racial composition and, more specifically, levels of racial segregation, or various indicators of population morbidity, we identified only two studies that focused on mortality outcomes. LeClere and colleagues (1997) found that living in more racially segregated neighborhoods, measured using the percent of black residents, was associated with an increased risk of mortality among US men and women; furthermore, levels of neighborhood racial segregation partially explained the excess risk of all-cause mortality among blacks relative to whites (LeClere et al. 1997). Using a similar approach and sample, Bond Huie et al. (2002) found that living in a neighborhood composed of at least 14% blacks, relative to less than 5%, was associated with an 8% increased hazard of all-cause mortality (Bond Huie et al. 2002).

*Cross-level interactions.* Two studies assessed the interaction between neighborhood and individual-level race/ethnicity. In a study of all reported heart disease deaths in Texas during 1991, Franzini and Spears (2003) assessed the interaction between neighborhood ethnic/racial composition and individual-level race/ethnicity, finding that blacks and Hispanics who lived in neighborhoods with higher densities of their own racial/ethnic groups experienced fewer years of life lost to heart disease (Franzini and Spears 2003). Assessing all-cause mortality, Eschbach et al. (2004) similarly found residence in a neighborhood with a higher proportion of Mexican-American residents had a protective effect among elderly Mexican-Americans from five southwestern states (Eschbach et al. 2004). Although more research is clearly necessary, these preliminary results suggest that residence in neighborhoods characterized by racial, ethnic, or immigrant enclaves may benefit the individual members of those groups, particularly for Hispanics.

## Physical Environment

Few studies have assessed the impact of physical or environmental characteristics of neighborhoods on mortality. Although indicators of housing quality were frequently used to create indices of neighborhood SES, only one study examined whether features of the physical environment were related to mortality. In that study, Hembree and colleagues (2005) found that New York City neighborhoods with more deteriorated external and internal built environments had higher rates of overdose mortality, even after adjusting for levels of neighborhood drug use, median household income, and other characteristics, Hembree et al. (2005). Naess et al. (2007) assessed whether neighborhood concentrations of particulate matter were associated with levels of mortality among adults aged 50–74 in Oslo, Norway; living in a neighborhood with a higher concentration of $PM_{2.5}$ was associated with an increased odds of all-cause mortality, even after adjusting for levels of neighborhood socioeconomic deprivation, which were positively associated with levels of pollution (Naess et al. 2007).

## Discussion: Stepping Outside the Boundaries of Neighborhood Research on Mortality

Since Haan published the first multilevel study of neighborhood effects on mortality in 1987, there has been an increasing interest in examining whether characteristics of the neighborhood environment influence risks of mortality. In judging how much closer we are to answering that question now than we were more than two decades ago, we comment in this section on how and in what directions the emerging literature has evolved since the seminal work of Haan.

In contrast to the relative diversity among studies interested in neighborhood effects on morbidity, studies of mortality demonstrate a clear "founder effect," such that the vast majority of published work shows little variation in its general makeup when compared to Haan's classic paper. Like the work of Haan, which investigated whether socioeconomic deprivation was associated with increased risk of all-cause mortality, most work has considered similar exposures (i.e., neighborhood SES or deprivation, commonly measured by levels of poverty), focused on the same mortality outcome (i.e., all-cause mortality), measured neighborhoods in the same way (i.e., using administrative boundaries, typically census tracts), measured neighborhood environments similarly (i.e., objectively, again using administrative data), and employed the same methods to adjust for threats to internal validity (i.e., adjustment for potentially confounding individual-level characteristics using traditional regression).

While pointing to this homogeneity is not a sufficient argument for change, the fact that studies of neighborhood effects on mortality are, in many ways, the same today as they were 20 years ago speaks to the strength of Haan's original work and also highlights areas where the literature should be improved upon if it is to inform policies aimed at reducing excess mortality associated with adverse neighborhood conditions. To step outside of the metaphorical boundaries of research concerning the impact of neighborhoods on mortality, we need to identify the most important challenges to extant work. In the following sections, we focus on two areas, measurement of neighborhoods and causal inference, where we envision substantial room for improvement.

## *Measurement*

The definition and measurement of neighborhood boundaries and neighborhood constructs reflects the integration of theories and methods across multiple disciplines, including sociology, geography, demography, public health, urban planning, and public policy. In this section we discuss how neighborhoods have been defined in principle, critically assess how they have been defined practically in research concerning neighborhood effects on mortality, and comment on alternative approaches that have emerged in the broader neighborhood effects literature.

### Theoretical Perspectives on Measuring Neighborhoods in Health Research

One of the fundamental premises of neighborhood effects research, that the environments we live in affect our health, can be traced back at least as far as the mid-nineteenth century, when William Farr explored area-level variability in mortality due to cholera in London. Although Farr initially used his observation that mortality varied with population density to bolster the miasmatic theory of disease, his work, along with the celebrated work of John Snow, implicated the water supply, an early indicator that our service environments matter to health (Susser and Adelstein 1975). Although Farr made no explicit mention of neighborhoods, his description of "healthy districts" is reminiscent of modern conceptualizations of neighborhoods as distinct areas with a priori relevance to the health of their residents (Whitehead 2000).

In parallel to the sanitary reforms in Europe was the Report of the Sanitary Commission of Massachusetts (1850), which became the basis for similar reforms in the United States after the Civil War. Lemuel Shattuk, the primary author of the report, recommended that "open space be reserved, in cities and villages, for public walks …. [that] would afford to the artizan [sic] and the poorer classes the advantages of fresh air and exercise," an early reference to how the built environment may influence socioeconomic disparities in health (Shattuck 1948). Around the turn of the twentieth century, the work of W.E.B. Dubois provided one of the earliest examples of incorporating census data, along with thousands of in-person interviews, into the study of small-area effects on health; his work comparing death and other rates in different Philadelphia wards demonstrated strong socioeconomic gradients that he linked, in part, to living conditions (Du Bois 1899).

The sociological origins for the study of neighborhoods are commonly attributed to Ernest Burgess and Robert Park, who spearheaded the program on urban sociology at the University of Chicago in the 1920s. Drawing on Darwinian theories of natural selection, Burgess and Park argued that individuals and social phenomena were not randomly distributed in cities, but rather, were shaped by ecological, cultural, economic, and political pressures, particularly the competition for land (Park 1915; Park et al. 1925). This resulted in the partition of urban space into "natural areas" or community subsets where individuals shared similar characteristics and conditions. Park and Burgess considered neighborhoods the smallest unit in the social and political organization of cities. While they did not explicitly investigate mortality, their work stimulated exploration of neighborhood-level social processes hypothesized to link neighborhood conditions to health.

Interest about how neighborhoods influence health is nascent. Although there is no established definition, commonly accepted properties of neighborhoods include that they: (1) are spatially defined geographic areas (in contrast to "communities") of limited size, (2) have a name and recognized identity and carry symbolic significance for their residents, and (3) are, with respect to characteristics theorized to be important to health, including physical (e.g., housing quality), social (e.g., social capital), and service (e.g., presence of fast food outlets) environments, like mosaics—a heterogeneous collection of relatively homogenous subunits (Chaskin 1997).

## Practical Definitions of Neighborhood Boundaries and Measures

In practice, the characterization of neighborhood boundaries and measurement of relevant constructs in the multilevel neighborhood effects literature has generally followed two main paths. The primary method for defining neighborhood boundaries is through the use of predefined boundaries (e.g., zip codes, counties, census tracts, census block groups), with few studies employing alternative methods, such as elicitation of residents' perceptions of the margins of their neighborhoods. Neighborhood-level constructs have been defined either objectively or subjectively. Objective measures, obtained by aggregating responses from the census or other survey or through the use of geographic information systems (GIS) and mapping, are independent of residents' perceptions. In contrast, subjective measures are typically obtained by aggregating individual-level assessments about perceptions of the neighborhood environment or through the systematic observation of neighborhood environments. Group-level measures may include derived measures, such as median household income, the unemployment rate, or the percent of streets with boarded-up housing, or integral variables without an individual-level analog, such as population density or the concentration of fast food establishments (Diez Roux 2002).

In neighborhood effects research in general, and research on mortality in particular, neighborhoods have been defined according to predetermined administrative boundaries, such as census tracts in the United States and electoral wards in the United Kingdom, and measured using objective indicators. From a practical standpoint, there are a number of advantages to this approach. Foremost, data on group-level indicators (e.g., median household income, percent poverty) that can be used to measure relevant constructs (e.g., relative deprivation, income inequality) are accessible from government sources such as the census, facilitating investigation of neighborhood effects in studies that may not have been designed for this purpose.

There are also a number of potential limitations to this approach. First, administrative boundaries are, to varying degrees, imperfect proxies for neighborhoods. Zip codes, for example, were defined by the US Postal Service for the efficacious delivery of mail (Krieger et al. 2002); however, most residents cannot identify the geographic boundaries of their zip code and these boundaries are unlikely to overlap with residents' perceptions of their neighborhoods. The misspecification of neighborhood boundaries is likely to result in an underestimation of the between-neighborhood variance in the health outcome of interest (Mujahid et al. 2007). Selecting boundaries that are consistent with the neighborhood mechanisms hypothesized to influence residents' health may reduce the misspecification of boundaries. For example, the use of police districts rather than commonly used census boundaries may be more appropriate for measuring exposure to neighborhood crime (Auger et al. 2008). Second, indices based on administrative data are only indirect measures for the underlying neighborhood attribute theorized as important to health; therefore, the use of objective indicators potentially introduces measurement errors that may bias effect estimates. Third, when compared to most biological and behavioral disease determinants, neighborhood environments are relatively static. However, the work of William Julius Wilson (Wilson 1987), among others, demonstrates that neighborhoods are influenced by macro-level political and economic processes and do change dramatically over time. Dependence on administratively collected data, which are often updated decennially, at longer time intervals, or not at all, makes it difficult to update neighborhood exposures without making strong assumptions about how they have changed during unascertained periods (e.g., linear extrapolation to derive intercensal estimates). This has important implications for causal inference, as discussed further below.

Although research on mortality outcomes has relied almost exclusively on administratively defined boundaries and objectively defined indicators of neighborhood SES, research concerning other neighborhood effects has incorporated alternative methods for measuring neighborhoods and neighborhood environments. One alternative is to use residents' own reports of neighborhood conditions, which are then aggregated to administrative units, such as census tracts (Moren-Cross et al. 2006; Wen and Christakis 2005; Wen et al. 2006; Xue et al. 2005). For example, in a study of older adults residing in Cook County, Illinois, Wen and colleagues (2006) found a significant association between respondents' perceptions of neighborhood physical, social, and service environments and their self-rated health, even after accounting for objective indicators of neighborhood SES (Wen et al. 2006). One of the advantages to assessing perceptions of neighborhood quality is that investigators can measure aspects of neighborhoods, such as access to salutary resources and facilities, for which administrative data are often sparse. However, an obvious limitation of relying on the subjective reports of neighborhood residents is the potential for same-source bias, where the predilection of participants with poorer health to report negatively about their neighborhood conditions may induce a spurious association between neighborhood exposures and health. The use of independent "informants" whose neighborhood perceptions are aggregated to the neighborhood level and linked to the study population of interest has been suggested as a means for minimizing same-source bias when neighborhood measures are based on subjective self-reports (Mujahid et al. 2007). Same-source bias is, of course, less of a concern for studies of mortality and biological markers of disease progression than for self-reported health events.

Whether objective or subjective measures of neighborhood constructs are more valid is a complex and unresolved issue, the answer to which likely depends on the particular hypotheses being tested. Some work suggests that residents' perceptions of the neighborhood environment may be less revealing than objective indicators of the neighborhood environment (Macintyre and Ellaway 2003). This may be more germane to investigations of contextual processes that may not be perceived by individual residents but still shape their health. For example, asking residents to rate the adequacy of services within their neighborhoods often results in misleadingly low levels of variation. Use of perceived characteristics also opens the door for misclassification of neighborhood exposures. As Amartya Sen (1992) has explained, the leveling of aspirations among destitute individuals is a natural protective mechanism against despair that may result in estimates of neighborhood effects that are biased toward the null. Few studies have assessed the independent effects of objectively and subjectively defined measures of the neighborhood environment on health. Consistent with the results of Wen et al. (2006), Weden and colleagues (2008) recently assessed the relation between objective and subjective measures of neighborhood conditions and self-rated health in a nationally representative sample of US adults and found that both types of measures were related to health when considered individually (Weden et al. 2008). Their findings suggest that perceived and objective assessments of the neighborhood environment may be linked but distinct constructs, with perceptions located more proximally than objective characteristics on the pathway between neighborhoods and health.

An increasingly popular alternative to asking residents about the quality of their neighborhoods is to have trained investigators who systematically observe each neighborhood and rate various domains of the neighborhood environment using standardized instruments (Laraia et al. 2006; Sampson and Raudenbush 1999; Weiss et al. 2007). In a study of Chicago neighborhoods, trained observers drove down the streets of Chicago neighborhoods and videotaped block faces while taking written accounts of their observations; these data were used to develop reliable scales of neighborhood disorder, physical characteristics, and social interactions (Sampson and Raudenbush 1999). In a study of neighborhood conditions and gonorrhea, Cohen et al. (2000) used a similar approach to characterize the physical structures of block groups in New Orleans (Cohen et al. 2000). More recently, Weiss and colleagues (2007) defined neighborhood boundaries by aggregating block groups (the smallest unit at which census data are available) based on land use and other data and then had a single individual assess neighborhood features using a pre-identified list of neighborhood characteristics (Weiss et al. 2007). Although more labor and resource intensive than the use of objective indicators, systematic observation offers several unique advantages to alternative modes of neighborhood measurement. For example, by directly observing streets or block faces, this method allows researchers to aggregate data to any level of analysis desired (e.g., block groups can be aggregated into larger neighborhood units) based on pre-specified criteria (e.g., walkability) that may be more consistent with the particular hypotheses being investigated. This approach takes advantage of available census data while potentially reducing the misspecification of neighborhood boundaries. These efforts have given rise to "ecometrics," a science of ecological assessment analogous to psychometric analysis of individual-level measures (Mujahid et al. 2007; Raudenbush and Sampson 1999).

While we have focused our discussion on the predominant method of defining neighborhood boundaries, namely by using administratively defined units, alternative approaches are worth mentioning. Consistent with the suggestion that individuals may define their neighborhoods in different ways (Chaskin 1997), Propper et al. (2005) assigned each participant in the British Household Panel Survey to a "bespoke" neighborhood by locating each individual within their enumeration district and then joining this district to adjacent districts until a population threshold of 500 individuals was reached; while still drawing on administrative boundaries and data for defining neighborhood constructs, this approach is unique in that each participant has his or her own neighborhood defined by the 500 or so nearest neighbors (Propper et al. 2005).

## Issues in the Conceptualization and Measurement of Neighborhoods

While the measurement of neighborhoods has evolved considerably, a number of questions remain largely unanswered. For example, few studies have considered the membership of individuals in multiple neighborhood environments, including the neighborhoods of residence and employment. It is plausible that individuals are more connected to the neighborhoods in which they work relative to their neighborhoods of residence. Mapping participants to their neighborhoods of residence may therefore result in the misclassification of neighborhood exposures. Some studies have attempted to account for this potential misclassification bias by restricting their samples to participants who spend a certain proportion of their time in their neighborhood of residence (Weiss et al. 2007). Exploration of innovative approaches, whether in the design (e.g., use of ecological momentary assessment to obtain real-time information on the contextual environments a participant is exposed over the course of follow-up (Cain et al. 2009; Shiffman et al. 2008)) or statistical analyses (e.g., analytic approaches that smooth effect estimates over multiple neighborhoods) is warranted.

## Causal Inference in the Study of Neighborhood Effects on Mortality

As highlighted by our review, a growing body of observational evidence suggests that neighborhood deprivation is consistently associated with mortality. Do these associations represent contextual influences and, if so, are they causal? Alternatively, do neighborhood associations reflect compositional variations between individuals residing in different neighborhoods? If so, are these compositional variations the result of the non-random residential selection of individuals into neighborhoods (i.e., social selection) or, conversely, the true etiologic effect of neighborhood-level processes (i.e., social causation)? Another distinct but related question is whether neighborhood contexts themselves are endogenous to individual-level characteristics. In Section "Identification of Neighborhood Effects," we attempt to parse these interconnected questions by informally defining average causal and neighborhood effects, identifying some of the most salient challenges to causal inference in neighborhood effects research, and commenting on analytic methods for addressing them. Directed acyclic graphs (DAGs) are a useful tool for conceptualizing bias in the design and analysis of epidemiologic studies and may be particularly apposite to neighborhood effects research. Our commentary is not intended to require prerequisite knowledge of DAGs; however, for excellent guides to their application, please see (Fleischer and Diez Roux 2008; Glymour 2006b).

### Identification of Neighborhood Effects

Within the potential outcomes framework that has guided causal inference in public-health research (Little and Rubin 2000), average causal effects are identifiable when two outcomes, one in which a treatment (or exposure) is given and another in which the same treatment is withheld, are simultaneously compared. Because only potential outcomes for the treatment actually received are observed in real-life settings, the other must be inferred. Randomized experiments, considered the gold standard for evaluating causal hypotheses in epidemiology and public health, allow estimation of the average causal effect of a treatment by comparing the outcomes of treatment and control groups that have comparable or "exchangeable" distributions of measured and unmeasured characteristics. Assuming successful randomization, no losses to follow-up, and complete adherence to treatment assignment, the effect estimate from a randomized experiment will approximate the true causal effect.

Estimates of the influence of neighborhood exposures on health are seldom characterized as causal, primarily because neighborhood exposures are not easily articulated with the potential outcomes model. Say, for example, that we are interested in estimating the effect of living in an impoverished neighborhood on individual-level mortality. Within the potential outcomes framework, this effect is only identifiable if we can compare the outcomes of residents of impoverished neighborhoods with those of another neighborhood in which all neighborhood and individual-level conditions are identical, with the exception of neighborhood poverty. Whether such a comparison is feasible given the inextricability of neighborhood exposures and shifting of neighborhood residents is questionable and challenges the notion of causal neighborhood effects. Other types of neighborhood exposures, such as features of the service environment (e.g., access to healthy foods), may be more easily harmonized with the potential outcomes model. However, it can still be argued that changing one feature of the service environment, through the introduction of a food store, for example, changes everything from neighborhood traffic patterns to the composition of residents. Further compounding criticism of neighborhood effects is the impracticality of manipulating neighborhood environments using randomized experiments. While debate continues concerning whether neighborhood contexts, as well as other social determinants, qualify as causes of morbidity and mortality, we suggest that it is constructive to underline the limitations of extant observational work and point toward new approaches and methodologies for approximating causal effects in neighborhood research.

As both epidemiologists and sociologists have noted, the selection issue (i.e., the non-random migration of individuals into particular neighborhoods based on individual-level characteristics that may be related to health) is the largest challenge to causal inference in observational studies of neighborhood effects (Diez

Roux 2004; Harding 2003). For example, unemployed individuals may choose to live in more socioeconomically deprived neighborhoods because of the availability of cheaper and more affordable housing. If unemployment were linked to mortality, then not accounting for individual employment status would render neighborhoods non-exchangeable and bias estimates of the effect of neighborhood socioeconomic deprivation on mortality. Similarly, individuals with a proclivity for fast food may selectively migrate into neighborhoods with more pre-existing fast food outlets. If these individuals are at greater risk for cardiovascular disease, then not accounting for preferences for fast food may bias associations between the concentration of fast food outlets and mortality from cardiovascular disease.

The extent to which residential selection engenders compositional differences between neighborhoods is arguable, with sides drawn along disciplinary lines. Economists, particularly from the rational choice school of thought, emphasize the role of residential preference in accounting for area-level variations in health. For example, poorer individuals and people of minority ethnic groups choose to move to low-income and racially segregated neighborhoods because of the availability of affordable housing and concentration of people of the same racial/ethnic background, respectively. In contrast, sociologists generally contend that people are constrained in their choices, suggesting that exogenous factors impact where we live. The recent housing crisis, for example, has showed us that the targeting of "subprime" or high-risk mortgages to low-income individuals and members of minority ethnic groups has influenced patterns of foreclosure and relocation, illustrating how the decisions of others can constrain individuals' choices about where to reside.

Of course, the dichotomy between individuals having either full autonomy or zero latitude when it comes to decisions about where they live is false. Neighborhoods are likely a mixture of individuals lying along a gradient of choice. Importantly, from a methodological perspective, compositional differences between neighborhoods that arise from either the rational choice of poorer individuals to move to socioeconomically deprived neighborhoods or the choices of others (e.g., predatory lending practices that have resulted in foreclosure and relocation) both threaten the exchangeability of neighborhoods, an issue that would not exist had we been able to experimentally randomize neighborhood-level treatments.

## Separating Context from Composition: Challenges to Causal Inference

How can we account for potential confounding due to compositional differences between neighborhoods? The modus operandi, and the general approach taken in every study included in our review, is to estimate the effect of a neighborhood-level construct on individual mortality after multivariable adjustment for individual-level sociodemographic characteristics (denoted *Covariates* in Fig. 20.1a), hereafter called individual-level covariates. For example, most studies in our review attempted to estimate the contextual effect of neighborhood deprivation on mortality by accounting for individual-level covariates (e.g., age, sex, race/ethnicity, income) using multivariable regression. While traditional regression or propensity score adjustment may account for some of the potential differences between neighborhoods, there are also limitations to this approach.

Through processes of social causation, the individual-level covariates frequently adjusted for in neighborhood effects studies may be time-varying confounders affected by prior exposure. For example, employment status may predict whether an individual lives in a relatively wealthier or poorer neighborhood; in turn, neighborhood poverty may influence future employment prospects and the probability of mortality. Therefore, time-varying individual-level covariates plausibly lie on the pathway between neighborhood poverty and mortality, suggesting they may act contemporaneously as mediators (denoted *Covariates*$_{t-1}$ in Fig. 20.1b) and confounders (denoted *Covariates*$_{t-2}$ in Fig. 20.1b) of the relation between neighborhood conditions and mortality.

Traditional adjustment for these characteristics may bias results in at least two ways. First, adjustment for certain individual-level characteristics may "over-control" for covariates on the pathway between neighborhood poverty and mortality, resulting in an underestimate of the overall neighborhood contextual effect. Second, if we introduce unmeasured characteristics into our example (denoted $U_{t-2}$ and $U_{t-1}$ in Fig. 20.1c) an additional challenge emerges.

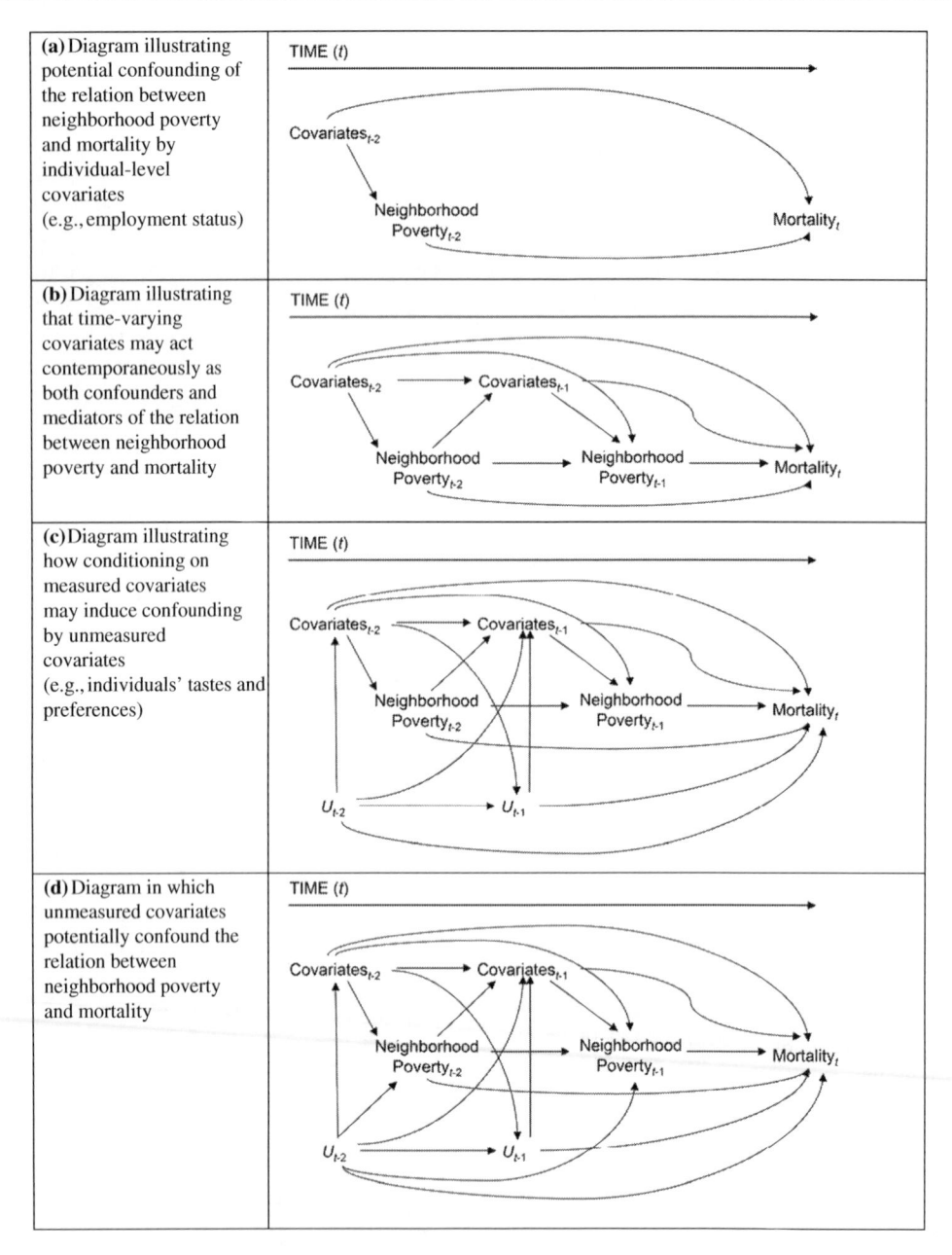

**Fig. 20.1** Causal diagram of the effect of neighborhood poverty on mortality, where "covariates" denote individual-level, time-varying, sociodemographic and health variables measured prior to neighborhood poverty (e.g., sex, race, educational attainment, income, employment status, health status), and 'U' denotes unmeasured characteristics

(a) Diagram illustrating potential confounding of the relation between neighborhood poverty and mortality by individual-level covariates (e.g., employment status)

(b) Diagram illustrating that time-varying covariates may act contemporaneously as both confounders and mediators of the relation between neighborhood poverty and mortality

(c) Diagram illustrating how conditioning on measured covariates may induce confounding by unmeasured covariates (e.g., individuals' tastes and preferences)

(d) Diagram in which unmeasured covariates potentially confound the relation between neighborhood poverty and mortality

Unmeasured characteristics may include individuals' tastes and preferences, which are generally not surveyed in most studies. If, as in Fig. 20.1c, these unmeasured covariates are assumed to have no causal effect on the level of neighborhood poverty one is exposed to, then they do not confound the relation between neighborhood poverty and mortality. However, if these unmeasured coviarates are linked to time-varying sociodemographic characteristics frequently adjusted for in neighborhood research, then adjusting for these covariates using traditional methods may induce collider-stratification bias (Greenland 2003).

## Emerging Methodologies for Estimating Causal Effects in Neighborhood Effects Research

The degree to which time-varying covariates act simultaneously as confounders and mediators of relations between neighborhood exposures and mortality can be empirically investigated using longitudinal data. If there is evidence of time-varying confounding affected by prior levels of exposure, then controlling for these covariates using standard methods may yield biased estimates of the total causal effect of a neighborhood exposure. Fortunately, alternative strategies for estimating neighborhood effects exist and are gradually being incorporated into the literature.

One method for handling such variables is to fit models using inverse probability weights (IPW). By assigning a weight that is proportional to the probability that each participant received her own treatment, IPW creates a "pseudo-population" in which the exposure or treatment is independent of measured covariates. As such, models fit using IPWs allows for the control of time-fixed and time-varying variables without conditioning on these variables (Cole et al. 2003; Hernan and Robins 2006a; Hernan et al. 2000; Robins et al. 2000), allowing investigators to estimate the contextual effect of a neighborhood exposure while accounting for potentially confounding measured characteristics. Although IPWs have been applied widely in the epidemiologic literature [see, e.g. (Cole et al. 2005; Hernan et al. 2008)], few studies have used IPWs to address potential confounding bias related to selection into neighborhoods (Nandi et al. 2010; Sampson et al. 2008). Importantly, models fit using IPWs, like traditional analyses of observational data, cannot account for unmeasured confounding. Under these circumstances other techniques are necessary.

An inverse probability weighted estimate of the effect of a neighborhood exposure on mortality may be biased if there are causal paths leading from unmeasured covariates into neighborhood poverty and mortality (Fig. 20.1d). The use of instrumental variable (IV) methods, although scarcely used in public-health research, has been suggested as an attractive approach for estimating average causal effects even in the presence of unmeasured confounding (Kawachi and Subramanian 2007). In the context of neighborhood effects research, IV analyses can be drawn on "natural experiments," in which a random factor influences the probability of exposure but is not under the control of the investigator, to estimate the effect of a neighborhood exposure on a particular health outcome. For example, the opening of a new supermarket within a neighborhood, or the implementation of a new transport policy within a metro area—*so long as they do not reflect the underlying preferences of residents* (e.g., lobbying by citizens to bring these resources into their neighborhoods)—could be studied as "natural experiments" to identify the causal effects of contextual environments on health-related behaviors and outcomes. Valid IV estimates, however, are contingent on the identification of a suitable instrument. In brief, a valid instrument must be associated with the neighborhood exposure of interest and all paths between the instrument and mortality outcome must pass through the neighborhood exposure. A valid IV estimate is also based on a number of strong assumptions, some of which are empirically unverifiable (Hernan and Robins 2006b). For a concise overview on the application of instrumental variables for studying social phenomena see Glymour (2006a).

## Conclusions

There is a sense that empirical studies of neighborhood effects on mortality have "hit a methodological wall" in terms of demonstrating causality. Comparatively little progress has been made during the past two decades, despite study after study replicating the initial finding of an excess risk of mortality among residents located in deprived neighborhoods. Mortality is a crude endpoint that is several steps removed from the causal processes of interest, because it mixes the potential influences of neighborhood environments on disease incidence with prognosis. One solution to this conundrum is to focus on more proximal (and shorter-term) endpoints, such as health behaviors and biomarkers. Reflecting this philosophy, there has been a recent explosion in studies focusing on the influence of residential environments on endpoints such as obesity. In turn, the literature on neighborhood effects on obesity (Black and Macinko 2008; Feng et al. 2009; Lovasi et al. 2009)—a topic that is beyond the scope of the present chapter—is motivated by (1) the presence of substantial between-area variations in child and adult obesity, and (2) the emerging consensus that individual-level behaviors such as eating healthy and exercising are embedded within (and partly driven by) broader social contexts. Needless to add, if the risk of obesity is truly influenced by the neighborhood context, then it would represent a partial "explanation" for why neighborhoods also matter for mortality (since obesity is a risk factor for excess mortality from various causes, including cardiovascular disease, diabetes, and cancer).

More careful theorizing would also be beneficial to the field in which investigators pre-specify the spatial units at which the "action" lies, and carefully conceptualize the relevant neighborhood "exposures," i.e., moving beyond summary measures of neighborhood deprivation. Again, an example of a fruitful direction of inquiry is represented by recent attempts to operationalize and to measure the "built environment" (e.g., GIS-based concepts of neighborhood "walkability") as well as the local food environment in relation to residents' risk of obesity.

Advances in the application of multilevel analysis during the past decades have also allowed investigators to tease out the compositional effects of neighborhoods from potential contextual effects. Here also, much work remains to be carried out in advancing causal inference (Oakes 2004). In other words, establishing the presence of contextual effects is just the beginning of causal inference. Even multilevel longitudinal study designs are insufficient to overcome problems of unobserved residential preferences and selective mobility. Innovative approaches to analysis, including utilization of natural experiments (instruments) and inverse probability weighting (to overcome time-varying confounding), represent promising directions for further research. These criticisms are not intended to take away the luster from what has been accomplished so far, but rather, they point toward the remaining challenges that need to be tackled in a field of research that is poised on the threshold of new discoveries through the application of rigorous theories and analytical methods.

## References

Anderson, R.T., P. Sorlie, E. Backlund, N. Johnson, and G.A. Kaplan. 1997. "Mortality Effects of Community Socioeconomic Status." *Epidemiology* 8(1):42–47.

Auger, N., M. Daniel, R.W. Platt, Y. Wu, Z.C. Luo, and R. Choiniere. 2008. "Association Between Perceived Security of the Neighbourhood and Small-for-Gestational-Age Birth." *Paediatric and Perinatal Epidemiology* 22(5):467–77.

Black, J.L. and J. Macinko. 2008. "Neighborhoods and Obesity." *Nutrition Reviews* 66(1):2–20.

Bond Huie, S.A., R.A. Hummer, and R.G. Rogers. 2002. "Individual and Contextual Risks of Death among Race and Ethnic Groups in the United States." *Journal of Health and Social Behavior* 43(3):359–81.

Bosma, H., H.D. van de Mheen, G.J. Borsboom, and J.P. Mackenbach. 2001. "Neighborhood Socioeconomic Status and All-Cause Mortality." *American Journal of Epidemiology* 153(4):363–71.

Cain, A.E., C.A. Depp, and D.V. Jeste. 2009. "Ecological Momentary Assessment in Aging Research: A Critical Review." *Journal of Psychiatric Research* 43(11):987–96.

Chaix, B., M. Rosvall, and J. Merlo. 2007a. "Neighborhood Socioeconomic Deprivation and Residential Instability: Effects on Incidence of Ischemic Heart Disease and Survival after Myocardial Infarction." *Epidemiology* 18(1):104–11.

Chaix, B., M. Rosvall, and J. Merlo. 2007b. "Recent Increase of Neighborhood Socioeconomic Effects on Ischemic Heart Disease Mortality: A Multilevel Survival Analysis of Two Large Swedish Cohorts." *American Journal of Epidemiology* 165(1):22–26.

Chaskin, R.J. 1997. "Perspectives on Neighborhood and Community: A Review of the Literature." *Social Science Review* 71(4):521–47.

Chen, J.T., D.H. Rehkopf, P.D. Waterman, S.V. Subramanian, B.A. Coull, B. Cohen, M. Ostrem, and N. Krieger. 2006. "Mapping and Measuring Social Disparities in Premature Mortality: The Impact of Census Tract Poverty within and across Boston Neighborhoods, 1999–2001." *Journal of Urban Health* 83(6):1063–84.

Cohen, D., S. Spear, R. Scribner, P. Kissinger, K. Mason, and J. Wildgen. 2000. "'Broken Windows' and the Risk of Gonorrhea." *American Journal of Public Health* 90(2):230–36.

Cole, S.R., M.A. Hernan, J.B. Margolick, M.H. Cohen, and J.M. Robins. 2005. "Marginal Structural Models for Estimating the Effect of Highly Active Antiretroviral Therapy Initiation on CD4 Cell Count." *American Journal of Epidemiology* 162(5):471–78.

Cole, S.R., M.A. Hernan, J.M. Robins, K. Anastos, J. Chmiel, R. Detels, C. Ervin, J. Feldman, R. Greenblatt, L. Kingsley, S. Lai, M. Young, M. Cohen, and A. Munoz. 2003. "Effect of Highly Active Antiretroviral Therapy on Time to Acquired Immunodeficiency Syndrome or Death Using Marginal Structural Models." *American Journal of Epidemiology* 158(7):687–94.

Coutts, A. and I. Kawachi. 2006. "The Urban Social Environment and Its Impact on Health." In N. Freudenberg, S. Galea, and D. Vlahov (eds.), *Cities and the Health of the Public*, pp. 49–60. Nashville, TN, Vanderbilt University Press.

Cubbin, C., F.B. LeClere, and G.S. Smith. 2000. "Socioeconomic Status and Injury Mortality: Individual and Neighbourhood Determinants." *Journal of Epidemiology and Community Health* 54(7):517–24.

Diez Roux, A.V. 2002. "A Glossary for Multilevel Analysis." *Journal of Epidemiology and Community Health* 56(8):588–94.

Diez Roux, A.V. 2004. "Estimating Neighborhood Health Effects: The Challenges of Causal Inference in a Complex World." *Social Science and Medicine* 58(10):1953–60.

Du Bois, W.E.B. 1899. *The Philadelphia Negro*. Philadelphia, PA, University of Pennsylvania Press.

Ecob, R. and K. Jones. 1998. "Mortality Variations in England and Wales Between Types of Place: An Analysis of the Ons Longitudinal Study. Office of National Statistics." *Social Science and Medicine* 47(12):2055–66.

Eschbach, K., G.V. Ostir, K.V. Patel, K.S. Markides, and J.S. Goodwin. 2004. "Neighborhood Context and Mortality Among Older Mexican Americans: Is There a Barrio Advantage?" *American Journal of Public Health* 94(10):1807–12.

Feng, J., T.A. Glass, F.C. Curriero, W.F. Stewart, and B.S. Schwartz 2009. "The Built Environment and Obesity: A Systematic Review of the Epidemiologic Evidence." *Health Place* 16(2):175–90.

Fleischer, N.L. and A.V. Diez Roux. 2008. "Using Directed Acyclic Graphs to Guide Analyses of Neighbourhood Health Effects: An Introduction." *Journal of Epidemiology and Community Health* 62(9):842–46.

Franzini, L. and W. Spears. 2003. "Contributions of Social Context to Inequalities in Years of Life Lost to Heart Disease in Texas, USA." *Social Science and Medicine* 57(10): 1847–61.

Galea, S., J. Ahern, D. Vlahov, P.O. Coffin, C. Fuller, A.C. Leon, and K. Tardiff. 2003. "Income Distribution and Risk of Fatal Drug Overdose in New York City Neighborhoods." *Drug and Alcohol Dependence* 70(2):139–48.

Gerber, Y., S.A. Weston, J.M. Killian, T.M. Therneau, S.J. Jacobsen, and V.L. Roger. 2008. "Neighborhood Income and Individual Education: Effect on Survival after Myocardial Infarction." *Mayo Clinic Proceedings* 83(6):663–69.

Glymour, M.M 2006a. "Natural Experiments and Instrumental Variable Analyses in Social Epidemiology." In J.M. Oakes and J.S. Kaufman (eds.), *Methods in Social Epidemiology*, pp. 429–60. San Francisco, CA, Jossey-Bass.

Glymour, M.M. 2006b. "Using Causal Diagrams to Understand Common Problems in Social Epidemiology." In J.M. Oakes and J.S. Kaufman (eds.), *Methods in Social Epidemiology*, pp. 393–428. San Francisco, CA, Jossey-Bass.

Gomez, S.L., C.D. O'Malley, A. Stroup, S.J. Shema, and W.A. Satariano. 2007. "Longitudinal, Population-Based Study of Racial/Ethnic Differences in Colorectal Cancer Survival: Impact of Neighborhood Socioeconomic Status, Treatment and Comorbidity." *BMC Cancer* 7:193.

Greenland, S. 2003. "Quantifying Biases in Causal Models: Classical Confounding Vs Collider-Stratification Bias." *Epidemiology* 14(3):300–6.

Haan, M., G.A. Kaplan, and T. Camacho. 1987. "Poverty and Health. Prospective Evidence from the Alameda County Study." *American Journal of Epidemiology* 125(6):989–98.

Harding, D.J. 2003. "Counterfactual Models of Neighborhood Effects: The Effect of Neighborhood Poverty on Dropping out and Teenage Pregnancy." *American Journal of Sociology* 109(3):676–719.

Hembree, C., S. Galea, J. Ahern, M. Tracy, T. Markham Piper, J. Miller, D. Vlahov, and K.J. Tardiff. 2005. "The Urban Built Environment and Overdose Mortality in New York City Neighborhoods." *Health Place* 11(2):147–56.

Hernan, M.A., A. Alonso, R. Logan, F. Grodstein, K.B. Michels, W.C. Willett, J.E. Manson, and J.M. Robins. 2008. "Observational Studies Analyzed Like Randomized Experiments: An Application to Postmenopausal Hormone Therapy and Coronary Heart Disease." *Epidemiology* 19(6):766–79.

Hernan, M.A., B. Brumback, and J.M. Robins. 2000. "Marginal Structural Models to Estimate the Causal Effect of Zidovudine on the Survival of HIV-Positive Men." *Epidemiology* 11(5):561–70.

Hernan, M.A. and J.M. Robins. 2006a. "Estimating Causal Effects from Epidemiological Data." *Journal of Epidemiology and Community Health* 60(7):578–86.

Hernan, M.A. and J.M. Robins 2006b. "Instruments for Causal Inference: An Epidemiologist's Dream?" *Epidemiology* 17(4):360–72.

Jaffe, D.H., Z. Eisenbach, Y.D. Neumark, and O. Manor 2005a. "Does Living in a Religiously Affiliated Neighborhood Lower Mortality?" *Annals of Epidemiology* 15(10): 804–10.

Jaffe, D.H., Z. Eisenbach, Y.D. Neumark, and O. Manor. 2005b. "Individual, Household and Neighborhood Socioeconomic Status and Mortality: A Study of Absolute and Relative Deprivation." *Social Science and Medicine* 60(5):989–97.

Johnson, P.J., J.M. Oakes, and D.L. Anderton 2008. "Neighborhood Poverty and American Indian Infant Death: Are the Effects Identifiable?" *Annals of Epidemiology* 18(7):552–59.

Joy, R., E.F. Druyts, E.K. Brandson, V.D. Lima, C.A. Rustad, W. Zhang, E. Wood, J.S. Montaner, and R.S. Hogg. 2008. "Impact of Neighborhood-Level Socioeconomic Status on HIV Disease Progression in a Universal Health Care Setting." *Journal of Acquired Immune Deficiency Syndromes* 47(4):500–5.

Kaplan, G.A. 1996. "People and Places: Contrasting Perspectives on the Association between Social Class and Health." *International Journal of Health Services* 26(3):507–19.

Katz, M.H., L. Hsu, M. Lingo, G. Woelffer, and S.K. Schwarcz. 1998. "Impact of Socioeconomic Status on Survival with Aids." *American Journal of Epidemiology* 148(3):282–91.

Kawachi, I. and L.F. Berkman. 2003a. "Introduction." In I. Kawachi and L.F. Berkman (eds.), *Neighborhoods and Health*, pp. 1–19. New York, NY, Oxford University Press.

Kawachi, I. and L.F. Berkman. 2003b. *Neighborhoods and Health*. New York, NY, Oxford University Press.

Kawachi, I. and S.V. Subramanian. 2007. "Neighbourhood Influences on Health." *Journal of Epidemiology and Community Health* 61(1):3–4.

Krieger, N., J.T. Chen, P.D. Waterman, M.J. Soobader, S.V. Subramanian, and R. Carson. 2002. "Geocoding and Monitoring of US Socioeconomic Inequalities in Mortality and Cancer Incidence: Does the Choice of Area-Based Measure and Geographic Level Matter? The Public Health Disparities Geocoding Project." *American Journal of Epidemiology* 156(5):471–82.

Laraia, B.A., L. Messer, J.S. Kaufman, N. Dole, M. Caughy, P. O'Campo, and D.A. Savitz. 2006. "Direct Observation of Neighborhood Attributes in an Urban Area of the US South: Characterizing the Social Context of the pregnancy." *International Journal of Health Geographics* 5:11.

LeClere, F.B., R.G. Rogers, and K. Peters. 1997. "Ethnicity and Mortality in the United States: Individual and Community Correlates." *Social Forces* 76:169–98.

LeClere, F.B., R.G. Rogers, and K. Peters. 1998. "Neighborhood Social Context and Racial Differences in Women's Heart Disease Mortality." *Journal of Health and Social Behavior* 39(2):91–107.

Little, R.J. and D.B. Rubin. 2000. "Causal Effects in Clinical and Epidemiological Studies Via Potential Outcomes: Concepts and Analytical Approaches." *Annual Review of Public Health* 21:121–45.

Lovasi, G.S., M.A. Hutson, M. Guerra, and K.M. Neckerman. 2009. "Built Environments and Obesity in Disadvantaged Populations." *Epidemiologic Reviews* 31:7–20.

Luo, Z.C., W.J. Kierans, R. Wilkins, R.M. Liston, J. Mohamed, and M.S. Kramer. 2004. "Disparities in Birth Outcomes by Neighborhood Income: Temporal Trends in Rural and Urban Areas, British Columbia." *Epidemiology* 15(6): 679–86.

Macintyre, S. and A. Ellaway 2003 "Neighborhoods and Health: An Overview." In I. Kawachi and L.F. Berkman (eds.), *Neighborhoods and Health*, pp. 20–42. New York, NY, Oxford University Press.

Moren-Cross, J.L., D.R. Wright, M. LaGory, and R.G. Lanzi. 2006. "Perceived Neighborhood Characteristics and Problem Behavior among Disadvantaged Children." *Child Psychiatry and Human Development* 36(3):273–94.

Mujahid, M.S., A.V. Diez Roux, J.D. Morenoff, and T. Raghunathan. 2007. "Assessing the Measurement Properties of Neighborhood Scales: From Psychometrics to Ecometrics." *American Journal of Epidemiology* 165(8):858–67.

Naess, O., F.N. Piro, P. Nafstad, G.D. Smith, and A.H. Leyland. 2007. "Air Pollution, Social Deprivation, and Mortality: A Multilevel Cohort Study." *Epidemiology* 18(6):686–94.

Nandi, A., S. Galea, J. Ahern, A. Bucciarelli, D. Vlahov, and K. Tardiff 2006. "What Explains the Association between Neighborhood-Level Income Inequality and the Risk of Fatal Overdose in New York City?" *Social Science and Medicine* 63(3):662–74.

Nandi, A., T.A. Glass, S.R. Cole, H. Chu, S. Galea, D.D. Celentano, G.D. Kirk, D. Vlahov, W.W. Latimer, and S.H. Mehta. 2010. "Neighborhood Poverty and Injection Cessation in a Sample of Injection Drug Users." *American Journal of Epidemiology* 171(4):391–98.

Oakes, J.M. 2004. "The (Mis)Estimation of Neighborhood Effects: Causal Inference for a Practicable Social Epidemiology." *Social Science and Medicine* 58(10):1929–52.

Park, R. 1915. "Suggestions for the Investigations of Human Behavior in the Urban Environment." *American Journal of Sociology* 20(5):577–612.

Park, R.E., E.W. Burgess, and R. McKenzie. 1925. *The City*. Chicago, IL, University of Chicago Press.

Pena, R., S. Wall, and L.A. Persson. 2000. "The Effect of Poverty, Social Inequity, and Maternal Education on Infant Mortality in Nicaragua, 1988–1993." *American Journal of Public Health* 90(1):64–69.

Pickett, K.E. and M. Pearl. 2001. "Multilevel Analyses of Neighbourhood Socioeconomic Context and Health Outcomes: A Critical Review." *Journal of Epidemiology and Community Health* 55(2):111–22.

Propper, C., K. Jones, A. Bolster, S. Burgess, R. Johnston, and R. Sarker. 2005. "Local Neighbourhood and Mental Health: Evidence from the UK." *Social Science and Medicine* 61(10):2065–83.

Raudenbush, S.W. and R.J. Sampson. 1999. "Ecometrics: Toward a Science of Assessing Ecological Settings, with Application to the Systematic Social Ovservation of Neighborhoods." *Sociological Methodology* 29:1–41.

Robins, J.M., M.A. Hernan, and B. Brumback. 2000. "Marginal Structural Models and Causal Inference in Epidemiology." *Epidemiology* 11(5):550–60.

Roos, L.L., J. Magoon, S. Gupta, D. Chateau, and P.J. Veugelers. 2004. "Socioeconomic Determinants of Mortality in Two Canadian Provinces: Multilevel Modelling and Neighborhood Context." *Social Science and Medicine* 59(7):1435–47.

Sampson, R.J. and S.W. Raudenbush. 1999. "Systematic Social Observation of Public Spaces: A New Look at Disorder in Urban Neighborhoods." *American Journal of Sociology* 105(3):603–51.

Sampson, R.J., P. Sharkey, and S.W. Raudenbush. 2008. "Durable Effects of Concentrated Disadvantage on Verbal Ability among African-American Children." *Proceedings of the National Academy of Sciences of the United States of America* 105(3):845–52.

Sen, A. 1992. *Inequality Re-Examined*. Cambridge, MA, Harvard University Press.

Shattuck, L. 1948. *Report on the Sanitary Commission of Massachusetts*. Cambridge, MA, Harvard University Press.

Shiffman, S., A.A. Stone, and M.R. Hufford. 2008. "Ecological Momentary Assessment." *Annual Review of Clinical Psychology* 4:1–32.

Sloggett, A. and H. Joshi. 1998. "Deprivation Indicators as Predictors of Life Events 1981–1992 Based on the UK ONS Longitudinal Study." *Journal of Epidemiology and Community Health* 52(4):228–33.

Subramanian, S.V., J.T. Chen, D.H. Rehkopf, P.D. Waterman, and N. Krieger. 2005. "Racial Disparities in Context: A Multilevel Analysis of Neighborhood Variations in Poverty and Excess Mortality among Black Populations in Massachusetts." *American Journal of Public Health* 95(2):260–65.

Subramanian, S.V., F. Elwert, and N. Christakis. 2008. "Widowhood and Mortality among the Elderly: The Modifying Role of Neighborhood Concentration of Widowed Individuals." *Social Science and Medicine* 66(4):873–84.

Susser, M. and A. Adelstein. 1975. "An Introduction to the Work of William Farr." *American Journal of Epidemiology* 101(6):469–76.

Veugelers, P.J., A.M. Yip, and G. Kephart. 2001. "Proximate and Contextual Socioeconomic Determinants of Mortality: Multilevel Approaches in a Setting with Universal Health Care Coverage." *American Journal of Epidemiology* 154(8):725–32.

Waitzman, N.J. and K.R. Smith. 1998. "Phantom of the Area: Poverty-Area Residence and Mortality in the United States." *American Journal of Public Health* 88(6):973–76.

Weden, M.M., R.M. Carpiano, and S.A. Robert. 2008. "Subjective and Objective Neighborhood Characteristics and Adult Health." *Social Science and Medicine* 66(6):1256–70.

Weiss, L., D. Ompad, S. Galea, and D. Vlahov. 2007. "Defining Neighborhood Boundaries for Urban Health Research." *American Journal of Preventive Medicine* 32(6 Suppl): S154–S59.

Wen, M. and N.A. Christakis. 2005. "Neighborhood Effects on Posthospitalization Mortality: A Population-Based Cohort Study of the Elderly in Chicago." *Health Services Research* 40(4):1108–27.

Wen, M., L.C. Hawkley, and J.T. Cacioppo. 2006. "Objective and Perceived Neighborhood Environment, Individual SES and Psychosocial Factors, and Self-Rated Health: An Analysis of Older Adults in Cook County, Illinois." *Social Science and Medicine* 63(10):2575–90.

Whitehead, M. 2000. "William Farr's Legacy to the Study of Inequalities in Health." *Bulletin of the World Health Organization* 78(1):86–87.

Wilson, W.J. 1987. *The Truly Disadvantaged*. Chicago, IL, University of Chicago Press.

Winkleby, M., C. Cubbin, and D. Ahn. 2006. "Effect of Cross-Level Interaction between Individual and Neighborhood Socioeconomic Status on Adult Mortality Rates." *American Journal of Public Health* 96(12): 2145–53.

Winkleby, M., K. Sundquist, and C. Cubbin. 2007. "Inequities in CHD Incidence and Case Fatality by Neighborhood Deprivation." *American Journal of Preventive Medicine* 32(2):97–106.

Xue, Y., T. Leventhal, J. Brooks-Gunn, and F.J. Earls. 2005. "Neighborhood Residence and Mental Health Problems of 5- to 11-Year-Olds." *Archives of General Psychiatry* 62(5): 554–63.

Yen, I.H. and G.A. Kaplan. 1999. "Neighborhood Social Environment and Risk of Death: Multilevel Evidence from the Alameda County Study." *American Journal of Epidemiology* 149(10):898–907.

# Chapter 21

# Health and Mortality Consequences of the Physical Environment

Christopher R. Browning, Eileen E.S. Bjornstrom, and Kathleen A. Cagney

## Introduction

The relationship between features of physical environments and health status has become a prominent focus of research on health and mortality. Recent innovation in theoretical approaches to the mechanisms linking environments with health, combined with more sophisticated methodological tools and data collection efforts, have spurred advances in the field of contextual effects research. Mounting interest in the origin of socioeconomic status (SES) and race/ethnic differences in health has also played an important role in directing attention to broader health-relevant characteristics of residential contexts as possible explanations for durable health disparities. This chapter reviews the current state of knowledge on the relationship between physical features of environments and adult mortality. We define the physical environment to include components of the built environment (including land use, housing, transportation, such amenities as food, activity options, and green space; and urban design and decline); climate and climate-related disasters; and air and water quality. Collectively, these aspects of the physical environment play a significant role in accounting for variability across space in patterns of adult mortality.

## Mortality Risk and the Physical Environment

Despite increased attention to the potential health consequences of the physical environment, empirical research that assesses the impact of specific features of the physical environment on health outcomes, particularly adult mortality, is limited. Thus, we proceed to review work on the physical environment with a wider lens, including morbidity and mortality outcomes in broad scope under the supposition that detrimental morbidity effects increase overall mortality risk.

Effects of the physical environment on health and mortality may take three forms. First, physical environment-induced mortality may be *socially unconditioned*, i.e., the result of direct exposure to environmental harm; the consequences of which are indiscriminate with respect to socioeconomic position. For instance, the catastrophic eruption of Mount Vesuvius in AD 79 completely destroyed the city of Pompeii, burying its residents under 60 feet of ash. The severity and immediacy of this disaster likely resulted in minimal impact of wealth or social position on the odds of survival. Second, *socially conditioned* environment-induced mortality arises from "natural" environmental harms that exhibit differential impact due to social position. Hurricane Katrina, striking Louisiana's coast in the year 2005, was among the deadliest natural disasters in US history, but its mortality consequences were differentially distributed across race and class (Picou and Marshall 2007). Finally, *socially produced* mortality consequences of the physical environment can be understood as environmental harms that follow from human actions. This chapter focuses on socially produced and conditioned health

C.R. Browning (✉)
Department of Sociology, The Ohio State University,
Columbus, OH 43210, USA
e-mail: browning.90@osu.edu

and mortality consequences of the physical environment with particular emphasis on effects of the built environment.

The organization of the chapter is as follows. First, we discuss key mediating and moderating factors that may combine with the physical environment to impact health and mortality. Second, we review socially produced health and mortality consequences of the physical environment, with a focus on the content and quality of the built environment and the consequences thereof, including toxins and crime. Third, we discuss socially conditioned mortality consequences of the physical environment, emphasizing the differential impact of "natural" disasters and climate on vulnerable subpopulations. Finally, we conclude with some directions for future research.

## Individual and Contextual Pathways that Mediate Effects of the Physical Environment on Health and Mortality

*Health-Related Behavior.* The physical environment can affect mortality risk by increasing the likelihood of engaging in either health compromising or health promoting behavior. Heath-related behaviors that have been linked to mortality risk include smoking, poor diet, excessive alcohol use, and lack of exercise (McGinnis and Foege 1993; Mokdad et al. 2004). Macintyre and Ellaway (2000) offer evidence of differences in both morbidity and associated health behaviors across spatial/environmental units of analysis (e.g., neighborhoods) that persist when controls for individual (compositional) characteristics are included. The authors argue that the physical environment, which residents share, may be an explanation of these differences.

*Stress.* Physical features of context may also affect mortality risk by influencing levels of environmentally induced stress. Stress leads to production of hormones such as epinephrine, norepinephrine, and cortisol via complex physiological pathways between the immune and central nervous systems (Glaser and Kiecolt-Glaser 2005). Work by McEwen (1998) also elaborates the link between stress, allostatic load, and serious health problems. Allostasis is a natural physiological response to stressful conditions, with by-products that include the aforementioned cortisol, epinephrine, and norepinephrine. When the body is forced to use this response more often than is "normal" (i.e., chronic stress), a price is paid resulting in symptoms such as hostility, demoralization, low energy, and irritability (McEwen 1998). Allostatic load, the term introduced to describe the sum of the effects the body experiences due to physiological adaptations to stress, is empirically associated with coronary heart disease, obesity, and hypertension, and compromised cognitive and physical function in older adults, independent of controls for individual characteristics (McEwen 1998; Seeman et al. 1997). Further, evidence suggests that both aging of the immune system and infectious disease onset and recurrence may be increased, and wound healing slowed, in response to chronic stress.

Individuals from lower socioeconomic backgrounds are more likely to be affected by stress, probably because they experience more chronic stressors (Almeida et al. 2005; Grzywacz et al. 2004). Notably, a synergistic effect may occur because behaviors such as smoking, sedentary lifestyle, poor nutrition, and alcohol misuse can lower immune function as well, and individuals who are stressed are more likely to engage in such behaviors (Glaser and Kiecolt-Glaser 2005).

*Social Relationships.* Social connection and isolation have been hypothesized and empirically demonstrated to influence health status in individuals at levels comparable to smoking and obesity (House et al. 1988). House et al. (1988) argue that isolation is associated with greater morbidity and mortality risk and hypothesize that this is due to the benefits of social relationships such as those with spouses, friends, and secondary group members, for reducing stress levels (House et al. 1988). For example, research has shown that diversity in type of social ties, such as spouse, children, neighbors, and coworkers, significantly affects the ability to respond to the cold virus, indicating a possible association between social ties and immune function (Cohen et al. 1997). Further, in a well-known study of 6,928 adults in Alameda County, California, mortality was found to be higher 9 years after the initial 1,965 data collection for those with lower social and community ties. This relationship held when controlling for smoking, alcohol, income, physical activity, prior self-reported health, and other influential individual characteristics (Berkman and Syme 1979). Moreover, social support is significantly related to the likelihood of exercising (Wilcox et al. 2000). Finally, Cacioppo and colleagues have extended this line of research in recent years by addressing the health consequences of loneliness (Cacioppo and Patrick 2008; Cacioppo et al. 2002). A sense of isolation and disconnection is associated with high blood pressure, and may amplify perceived and experienced stress (Hawkley and Cacioppo 2003; Hawkley et al. 2006).

*Social Capital.* Social capital and related constructs are increasingly shown to be beneficial for health and mortality. A general definition of social capital has been given by Putnam (1995) as "features of social life, such as networks, norms, and social trust that facilitate coordination and cooperation for mutual benefit." Krieger (2001) addresses the health benefits that social capital offers with the definition "population level psychosocial assets that shape population health by influencing norms and strengthening the bonds of civil society." The notion of "collective efficacy" extends the concept of social capital to incorporate the capacity to mobilize social resources on behalf of a common goal. Specifically, collective efficacy has been defined as the combination of mutual trust, group attachment, and the willingness of a collectivity to come together for the common good (Sampson et al. 1997). Originally designed to explain variation across communities in crime and delinquency, the concept has increasingly been applied to spatial variation in health and mortality outcomes (Browning and Cagney 2002; Browning et al. 2006).

Research has demonstrated the relevance of social capital for a variety of morbidity and mortality outcomes (see Chapter 20 by Nandi and Kawachi, this volume). State-level measures of social capital, such as levels of distrust, have been linked to self-rated health and firearm crime (Kawachi et al. 1999; Kennedy et al. 1998). Additionally, social capital has been linked to infectious disease and mortality due to heart disease and all-causes in local communities (Holtgrave and Crosby 2003; Lochner et al. 2003). Other work demonstrates that collective efficacy is associated with obesity, self-rated health, and asthma in individuals as well as all-cause, homicide, and cardiovascular mortality in those under 65 years of age (Browning and Cagney 2002; Cagney and Browning 2004; Cohen et al. 2003, 2006). Next we turn to a discussion of socially produced mortality consequences of the physical environment, incorporating these and other potential mediating and moderating effects into understanding the health–environment link.

## Socially Produced Health Consequences of the Physical Environment

### The Built Environment

The built environment is conceptually broad and encompasses anything that is built or modified by humans for the purpose of use by humans (Northridge et al. 2003). Physical construction is a component of the built environment, by definition, but in places where the natural and built environments converge, the definitional line is less clear. For example, any natural space in an urban area is likely modified by humans. Planned green space is an example of this. The built environment includes the design and characteristics of land use, transportation, housing, and options applicable to routine activities, including food and recreation (Frumkin 2005; Northridge et al. 2003).

Land use patterns and outcomes of other planning decisions at the city or neighborhood level, and conditions of the built environment within communities, can affect mortality risk indirectly by altering (1) the likelihood of engaging in various individual behaviors relevant to health and mortality, (2) exposure to stress, (3) individual social relationships, (4) community social capital, (5) exposure to toxins, and (6) exposure to accidents. These mechanisms are applicable to all residents, but have a special significance for those who are most vulnerable, as they may be more dependent on the local community and are less likely to be able to withstand environmental stressors without harm than others. Notably, vulnerability to the physical environment may be associated with age (Glass and Balfour 2003).

The following section begins with a brief overview of the historical context of public-health and urban-planning approaches to the built environment. We then discuss some of the major research foci regarding the ways the built environment is linked with increased morbidity and mortality risk. We focus first on the form of the built environment—i.e., physical design and land use patterns at the neighborhood and regional level. We then discuss the character of the physical environment, including the presence of particular commercial establishments, recreational facilities, and public transportation. A third section reviews the health consequences of variation in the quality of the built environment, considering the role of physical disorder, substandard housing, pollution related to the built environment, and links to crime. Finally, we conclude with a discussion of the health impact of the built environment on mortality risk for certain demographic subpopulations, particularly the elderly.

*History and Background.* Recent interest in the relationship between the built environment and health is the latest chapter in the long-scholarly relationship between urban planning and public health in which the two disciplines were collaborative in their early years, diverged, and are now converging again in some areas of research (Corburn 2004; Northridge et al. 2003; Perdue et al. 2003). Public health and urban planning evolved simultaneously with the latter initially focused on the reduction of (primarily) infectious disease. In the mid-nineteenth century, physicians and environmental health professionals advocated for the inception of city planning in order to have a formal enterprise that was focused on the well-being of those affected by the "urban health penalty" (Coburn 2004; Perdue et al. 2003). Public sewage systems can be counted among the successes resulting from this endeavor (Perdue et al. 2003). At the turn of the century, the fields of urban planning and public health maintained a cooperative relationship wherein both tried to remedy the effects of poor sanitation and substandard housing (Dearry 2004). In the 1920s, urban planners began to emphasize the importance of distinct uses of physical space primarily to separate residential and industrial space, and single-use zoning became more common (Corburn 2004). More recently, work rooted in the new urbanist perspective (Duany and Plater-Zyberk 1991; Fleming et al. 1985), and that draws from Jacobs (1961), focuses on community-centered design and incorporates elements often referred to using the umbrella term "walkable neighborhoods." Such neighborhoods contain complementary mixed uses as a fundamental component and promote pedestrian activity, the ability to carry-out routine activities locally with minimal driving, and informal social interaction among residents. Thus, single-use zoning has moved from being beneficial for populations exposed to harmful industrial pollution in earlier historical periods to being problematic in places that have transitioned to a post-industrial economy (Corburn 2004; Dearry 2004; Krieger and Higgins 2002; Perdue et al. 2003).

*The Design of the Built Environment.* One principal way that the built environment is postulated to affect adult mortality risk is through urban form and physical design features, such as land use patterns, street characteristics, and the presence of private and public recreation space (Kelly-Schwartz et al. 2004; Saelens et al. 2003 (hereafter Saelens et al. 2003a); Saelens et al. 2003b). Physical design can encourage or discourage health-related behaviors, particularly walking, and to the extent that residents are more likely to interact when they are out in the community, may increase social interaction, social capital, and informal social control (Jacobs 1961; Leyden 2003).

*Land Use.* Mixed-use zoning is a major component of walkable neighborhoods. Current thinking increasingly views single-use zoning as detrimental to public health, due primarily to the problematic outcomes associated with automobile dependence. In contrast to historical preferences regarding the benefits of separation of uses, mixed-use zoning is now encouraged at the neighborhood level (Jackson 2003a; Leyden 2003).

Work assessing the effects of mixed-use zoning (principally, combining residential and commercial uses) has examined links between land use patterns and utilitarian walking. For example, Frank and Engelke (2001) argue that community characteristics can either support and encourage, or oppose and discourage, physical activity based on non-motorized travel. Indeed, evidence suggests that individuals are more likely to walk for utilitarian purposes in the course of routine activities if their neighborhood contains a diverse mix of commercial activity (Saelens et al. 2003a). Despite the significant relationship between mixed uses and an increased likelihood of utilitarian walking, evidence is inconclusive as to whether this translates into a reduced likelihood of obesity among residents in the community. Frank et al. (2004) found the likelihood of obesity, as defined by a body mass index (BMI) over 30, was related to a diverse land use mix in the neighborhood and distance walked (as well as time in the car). Notably, relationships between land use and walking were stronger for whites than African-Americans. However, in a multilevel analysis with controls for individual income, Rutt and Coleman (2005) found that land use mix was associated with increased BMI in a low-income Latino community, a finding contrary to theoretical expectations. In sum, although evidence is mounting that shows mixed-use zoning increases walking for utilitarian purposes, this physical activity does not necessarily lead to lower obesity rates, and these relationships may vary across SES, race-ethnicity, and/or region.

Neighborhood walkability, promoted by mixed land use, may also promote social interaction and the emergence of community-based social capital (Jacobs 1961; Leyden 2003). Supporting this, Leyden (2003) created a neighborhood walkability variable based on responses to questions as to whether residents could walk to a variety of establishments, such as a store, church, park, school, or recreation center from their home if they so desired. Resident perceptions of walkability correlated with researcher characterizations and expectations, and mixed-use neighborhoods were found to have higher levels of social capital as defined by knowing neighbors, political engagement, trust, and social involvement. Thus, mixed land use may operate indirectly to benefit health by promoting social–capital–productive physical uses of neighborhood space.

*Street Layout.* A key aspect of the built environment that increases the likelihood of walking is the level of street connectivity, often measured by the number of intersections in an area. This results from both the prevalence of short blocks and the extent to which streets are designed on a grid. Jacobs (1961) famously advocated for street connectivity as a structural feature of neighborhood layout that would increase walking and social interaction. Also, incorporating attention to small blocks, Kelly-Schwartz et al. (2004) found, in a multilevel study of individuals in metropolitan areas, that residents of areas with more highly accessible streets on a grid have significantly higher self-rated health with controls for health-related individual characteristics, including social support, amount of walking, and BMI. Street characteristics were not important for physician-rated health. But among residents with chronic conditions, the significance of these relationships was reversed: street layout was significant for physician-reported health but not for self-rated health. Street layout was initially significant in predicting self-rated health among those with chronic disease, but the relationship was mediated by BMI. These measures were not significantly associated with time spent walking, BMI, or diagnosis of various chronic diseases. Hence, this work suggests that street characteristics are associated with perceived health—an important predictor of subsequent morbidity and mortality—but does not offer evidence that connectivity is associated with specific health conditions, such as obesity or chronic disease diagnosis.

Although several studies have found residents of walkable neighborhoods do indeed walk more, other research fails to find a link between features of walkability and time spent walking or vigorous exercise. Sallis et al. (1997) examined a neighborhood environment scale comprised of aesthetics, sidewalks, traffic, crime, whether the area was mixed or single use, and perceptions of safety, with a home environment measure that included the extent to which respondents had home gym equipment and found that only home environment mattered in predicting vigorous exercise. Walkable neighborhoods probably increase the likelihood of utilitarian walking and may increase walking for exercise, both of which may have implications for reduced isolation and increased social capital. But it is unclear whether walkable neighborhoods are sufficient to reduce the likelihood of obesity.

*Metropolitan Sprawl.* Research has increasingly focused on the relationship between metropolitan sprawl and public health. Indeed, at the metropolitan area level, the proportion of walkable neighborhoods can be seen in part as a function of the prevalence of sprawl. This literature centers around (1) the theoretical link between increased sprawl, time spent in automobiles, and obesity-related outcomes such as BMI and lower activity level (indirect effects); (2) the link between sprawl, automobile usage, and traffic-related mortality; and (3) the association between sprawl, pollution, and resultant health implications (direct effects).

*Definition and Measurement in Brief.* Sprawl is an ambiguous concept and as such, presents both conceptualization and measurement challenges (Lopez and Hynes 2003; Wolman et al. 2005). Hasse and Lathrop (2003: 159) define sprawl as "dispersed and inefficient urban growth." Generally, it is conceptualized by comparatively low-density (but not rural) levels of development, the presence of strip malls, "leapfrog" development along highways and major arterials, separation of uses, and street design that does not facilitate easy access to different spaces (Carruthers 2002; Ewing et al. 2003 (hereafter Ewing et al. 2003a); Ewing et al. 2003b; Lopez and Hynes 2003). The necessity of the automobile is also a key component of sprawl (Frumkin 2002). Ewing and colleagues use a county-level measure of sprawl that is easily available from census data comprised of gross population density, percent in low suburban density, percent in moderate to high density, percent urban land area, average block size, and percent of blocks that approximate average city block size (small blocks) (Ewing et al. 2003a, b). Thus, sprawl has been defined and operationalized in a variety of ways with a common emphasis on population density, sometimes in conjunction with variables that capture block size and other descriptive characteristics when data are available.

*Health Effects and Time Spent in Automobiles.* Research suggests there may be a link between sprawl, increased automobile usage, and obesity. Frank et al. (2004) found that features of sprawl that included land use mix, residential density, and intersection density were associated with time in the car for both African-Americans and whites, though to a lesser extent for African-American males. In turn, they found that time spent in the car is related to an increase in the likelihood of obesity with controls for influential individual characteristics. In another study, Lopez (2004) examined sprawl effects on obesity using a measure based on residential density at the metropolitan level. He found that sprawl increases the likelihood of being obese after controls for gender, age, income, education, and race-ethnicity are included. In another multilevel study, Ewing et al. (2003b) found that the relationship between features of sprawl and obesity (and other health outcomes) was inconsistent—although their findings indicate that county sprawl indices are associated with minutes walked, hypertension, and obesity, these associations were not replicated at the metropolitan level, calling into question the robustness of the sprawl–obesity link. Thus, evidence regarding the effect of sprawl on obesity is still emerging and remains inconclusive at this point.

*Traffic-Related Safety.* More and more, there appears to be an association between sprawl and both vehicle occupant and pedestrian fatalities. Frumkin (2002) summarizes why this might be the case. First, and quite simply, increases in sprawl are associated with increased driving and/or a greater percentage of the population that drives. Second, the types of streets that are more common in sprawling places, such as wide arterials that lack pedestrian friendly design, increase the likelihood of accidents. Lucy (2003) finds traffic fatalities are highest in exurban areas, where sprawl exists by definition. Trips leaving home for routine activities may require more miles in the car in sprawling areas than similar trips in communities with mixed-use zoning where residents can walk or drive shorter distances to accomplish many errands, thus increasing the likelihood of accidents. Similarly, Ewing et al. (2003a) tested the relationship between county-level sprawl as defined by low-residential density and lack of street accessibility, and both automobile and pedestrian–automobile mortality. Specifically, the authors included all types of traffic fatality (vehicles, trains, buses, taxis, bicycles, and pedestrians) and pedestrian specific mortality with an adjustment for time spent walking. They found that more densely populated counties had lower traffic and pedestrian specific fatality rates. Finally, Trowbridge, Burka and O'Conner (2009) found sprawl, measured with Ewing's index above, is associated with slower response time and a greater probability of delayed response by emergency personnel to the scene of traffic accidents involving at least one death. Thus, sprawl appears to be associated with traffic accidents and the ability to survive them.

*Exposure to Toxins.* Components and correlates of sprawl are associated with increased toxic exposure in air and water. For example, suburban development is linked to increases in polycyclic aromatic hydrocarbons in local surface water (Van Metre et al. 2000). These compounds result from vehicle use, as well as power plants, industry, and burning, and are classified as being reasonably expected to be carcinogenic in humans (Centers for Disease Control [CDC] 1996; Van Metre et al. 2000). Driving time is also associated with air pollution (Frumkin 2002). Although a major explanation of the relationship between the built environment and air pollution is via increased automobile usage and exposure to the associated emissions, planners face challenges when considering this relationship. While mixed-use zoning and more dense residential space tend to benefit residents by increasing walking and local socialization, there are conflicting outcomes with regard to air pollution from automobiles. Dense, mixed-use neighborhoods do reduce air pollution at the metropolitan level, but within these areas of the city, there is an increased exposure to vehicle emissions (Frank and Engelke 2005). Accessible and environmentally conscious public transportation may reduce this problem.

## The Character of the Built Environment

*Commercial Establishments.* The types of commercial establishments in local communities may influence resident propensity to consume certain health-relevant products, be they beneficial or detrimental. The prevalence of certain types of commercial activity, such as the ability to obtain healthy food or the concentration of fast food, may be tied to community affluence. The presence of commercial establishments in the neighborhood does not force residents to patronize those businesses, nor does the absence of establishments stop them from traveling to other neighborhoods to shop. But variability in the presence of a given health-relevant type of business in the immediate vicinity may influence the likelihood of patronage, thus affecting health behavior.

One line of research has used this reasoning to make connections between neighborhood availability of high- (or low-) quality food and disparities in obesity across race-ethnic and income groups. Large supermarkets are presumed to be especially important food sources because they provide a range of healthy food options. Morland et al. (2002) assessed spatial patterns in the location of supermarkets in cities, suburbs, and counties in Mississippi, North Carolina, Maryland, and Minnesota. Analyses of geocoded address data revealed that supermarkets are more likely to be located in white and affluent neighborhoods. Other work supports disparities in access to healthy food across neighborhood SES in the United States (Moore and Diez Roux 2006; Zenk et al. 2005) but disputes it in other wealthy nations, such as Canada and Australia (Apparicio et al. 2007; Winkler et al. 2006).

Additional research seeks to understand whether access to healthy food explains poor dietary choices. Moreland, Wing, and Roux (2002) found an association between eating more fruits and vegetables and the proximity of supermarkets for both blacks and whites in the United States. Finally, some evidence indicates that healthy food may be more expensive in less-affluent neighborhoods than it is in neighborhoods that are wealthier (Cummins and Macintyre 2002; Sooman et al. 1993).

Other types of businesses are postulated to be detrimental to health, and these may be distributed disproportionately in poor and/or minority neighborhoods. Fast food restaurants, liquor stores, and bars are examples of these types of establishments. Links between the economic and race-ethnic composition of neighborhoods and the prevalence of fast food restaurants have been examined, with some research finding more fast food restaurants in poor and/or minority neighborhoods in the United States and Europe. For example, Block et al. (2004) found that in New Orleans, the average number of fast food restaurants was over 60% higher in black neighborhoods than in white neighborhoods and that it was correlated with median household income. Work by Cummins et al. (2005) shows that the distribution of McDonalds in England and Scotland is correlated with community poverty levels, and in a study of Melbourne, Australia, Reidpath et al. (2002) found that fast food restaurants are more common in impoverished neighborhoods. But some contrary findings exist: Morland et al. (2002) found, in a study spanning four US states, that carry-out and fast food restaurants were more common in white and mixed race neighborhoods than in black ones. Similarly, fast food restaurants were more common in the lower-middle and middle-income communities than the poorest or wealthy areas. The prevalence of fast food restaurants has been linked to obesity (Morland and Evenson 2009). Specifically, respondents in Forsyth County, North Carolina, and Jackson, Mississippi, were more likely to be obese if one or more fast food restaurants were located in their census tract of residence, suggesting that proximity to poor quality food may have significant health consequences.

The prevalence of establishments selling alcohol has also been analyzed. LaVeist and Wallace (2000) examined the per capita distribution of liquor stores in Baltimore, Maryland, by racial composition and SES of neighborhoods. They found that there are significantly more liquor stores in less-affluent neighborhoods, and in neighborhoods with a higher percentage of black residents. They also tested the interaction between lower- and higher-income neighborhoods and percent black and found that low-income African-American neighborhoods have significantly more liquor stores than other neighborhoods. Similarly Morland et al. (2002) found fewer bars in higher than in lower-income neighborhoods.

*Public- and Private-Recreation Facilities.* The features of recreational facilities, both public and private, may affect adult health behaviors. The weight of the extant evidence indicates that access to facilities (proximity) is associated with physical activity (Humpel et al. 2002), and that access to facilities may vary by the SES of the local community, though more recently this has been called into question in the United Kingdom (Macintyre et al. 2008). It may be that different types of facilities are located in more deprived places than are found in more affluent ones. For example, in a study conducted in metropolitan Perth, Australia, Giles-Corti and Donovan (2002b) found that perceptions of access to recreation facilities vary by the SES of the neighborhood: lower-income residents reported lower levels of access to parks than did higher-income residents, but perceived higher access to sidewalks. Objective spatial access measures, however, found that access to some public and private facilities was greater in lower income neighborhoods (excepting golf courses, tennis courts, and the beach) but these residents were less likely to use them. This may be due to financial constraints in the case of private facilities or the perceived quality of the park space.

The presence of public-recreational space may increase the likelihood that residents will engage in physical activity (Black and Mancinko 2008; Duncan et al. 2005). Giles-Corti and Donovan (2002a) assessed the association between public spaces (such as parks, beaches, and streets), private gyms, and exercise. They found that the presence of recreation options is associated with increased likelihood of exercise. The association between proximity and use of facilities was more important for public places than private facilities. Importantly, the availability of facilities is also relevant in predicting exercise in older adults. Booth et al. (2000) found that access to a park and access to footpaths mattered in predicting more energetic exercise in a sample of Australian adults over age 60. Supporting this, work by Gordon-Larsen and colleagues (2006) shows access to recreational facilities is associated with the level of physical activity of residents and that disparities in availability (defined by proximity) exist across race-ethnicity and SES. Public-recreational facilities also appear to promote collective efficacy: Cohen et al. (2008) found the number of parks in a community was positively associated with collective efficacy, while controlling for factors such as disadvantage.

Social relationships may also interact with the built environment to encourage physical activity. Supportive social relationships may increase the likelihood that individuals will utilize the available built environment. In the aforementioned work by Giles-Corti and Donovan (2002a) conducted in Perth, Australia, public and private facilities were helpful in increasing the likelihood of exercising, but whether the respondents had another individual with whom they exercise was a more significant predictor of exercise. The authors concluded that a supportive physical environment is necessary but not sufficient to promote exercise. This finding offers insight into the complex way that the physical and social context of communities interacts to encourage positive health behaviors.

*Public Transportation.* Access to public transportation can improve public health indirectly by increasing access to care and other resources such as food and exercise facilities, thus increasing the likelihood of engaging in health improving behaviors, and directly by reducing traffic mortality and automobile pollution (Blankenship et al. 2000). Public transportation may be especially important for vulnerable populations, such as the elderly, who may not have family or friends to transport them to medical facilities or may not wish to impose on others. Rittner and Kirk (1995) find that public transportation is especially important for low-income elderly individuals in obtaining health care. In a sample of poor elderly people in Southern Florida, the authors found that availability of transportation was a significant factor as to whether the respondents sought medical care. Though some segments of the older population, particularly the poor, are more likely to need transportation assistance, they are less inclined to use public transportation in some cases because they may fear for their personal safety. The reasons for this are varied but include uncovered bus stops in bad weather, fear of missed or complicated transfers, and personal victimization. In many cases, these fears are valid (Rittner and Kirk 1995).

## The Quality of the Built Environment

*Substandard Housing.* The quality of housing stock has important implications for both morbidity and mortality. Substandard housing is associated with mortality risk directly through exposure to toxins and unsafe structural features. These conditions and their health implications have been reviewed extensively by Bashir

(2002), Krieger and Higgins (2002), and Northridge et al. (2003). Structural defects and old or substandard materials can lead to a variety of toxic exposures. Probably the most commonly known is exposure to lead. Lead is contained in some older types of paint and in pipes. Toxic paint can be inadvertently ingested (most commonly by young children), but lead can leach into drinking water as well (CDC 2007). Chronic exposure to lead over the life course may have long-lasting effects. For instance, lead exposure has been linked to compromised neurological and cardiovascular functioning in adulthood (Schwartz 1988). Additionally, defects in basement foundations, which are more prominent in older and lower income housing, may lead to radon exposure, which has been linked with lung cancer. Low-income housing is also more likely to expose inhabitants to carbon monoxide (Bashir 2002). Finally, some materials, such as older carpet, tile, and insulation contain asbestos, which is associated with lung cancer and asthma (Northridge et al. 2003).

Environmental conditions within substandard housing are also associated with respiratory illness. Dampness and cold foster growth of molds and possibly bacteria (Northridge et al. 2003). Mold and cold, damp conditions are linked to asthma and may cause other respiratory infections as well (Krieger and Higgins 2002; Northridge et al. 2003). These structures may also have poor ventilation, and exacerbate problematic conditions in the home. Collins (1986) found that cold housing is associated with worse health and an increase in the number of visits to the doctor in the elderly. Some substandard housing also has poor wastewater disposal and thus may be more inclined to encourage rat infestation and infectious disease (Krieger and Higgins 2002). The presence of rats and cockroaches, which is higher in lower income housing, is related to asthma as well because droppings are respiratory irritants (Cagney and Browning 2004; Perry et al. 2003; Sarpong et al. 1996).

*The Built Environment and Air Pollution.* Toxic pollution emissions result from a variety of sources related to the built environment that varies by location (Environmental Protection Agency [EPA] 2007, 2008). Air, soil, and water are all relevant vectors, but here we focus on air pollution and its relationship to the built environment as it directly increases mortality risk.

Motor vehicles have received a considerable amount of attention in regard to emissions, but industry and other sources are also contributors. Some of the core primary pollutants that vehicles, industrial facilities, fires, and firms that use solvents emit are carbon monoxide, nitrogen oxide, and volatile organic compounds (VOCs or hydrocarbons). These are not only problematic at or near the point of emission, but also lead to the formation of ozone, a secondary pollutant that is the major component of smog. Smog formation is a result of interactions between primary pollutants and sunlight, which is typically most problematic downwind of places where primary pollutants are produced (Houston et al. 2004). Hazardous ozone should not be confused with atmospheric ozone, which is beneficial. Another air pollutant of primary significance for public health is particulate matter (PM). This results from similar sources as those listed above but can also be formed from the reaction of carbon monoxide, nitrogen oxide, and VOCs. Though the number and type of vehicles in operation affects pollution levels (mobile sources), their spatial distribution (i.e., on major roadways) and the placement of non-mobile sources of pollution, such as power plants and industrial facilities, also influences concentrations of pollutants. Hence, primary pollutants from vehicles are more prevalent near major roads and interstates whereas pollutants from industrial and other polluters are more concentrated near the places those particular sources of pollution are located. Both are dispersed along natural air currents to additional sites.

Exposure to pollution based on the built environment varies with social vulnerability. Poor and minority individuals are more likely to live near heavy traffic (Gunier et al. 2003) and Houston et al. (2004) find that minority and poor communities in Southern California experience local traffic that is more than twice as heavy as the region experiences on average because these neighborhoods are closer to major roadways and freeways. But ozone may be more prevalent in suburban communities. Supporting this, Wilhelm et al. (2009) found that carbon monoxide and nitrogen oxide were more concentrated as disadvantage increased, but ozone was more concentrated in advantaged neighborhoods in Los Angeles, California.

These components of air pollution lead to a variety of respiratory and other related problems (EPA 2008). Evidence suggests that living near very heavy traffic or stationary sources of pollution (industry) is linked to cancers, including leukemia, as well as asthma and other respiratory illness (Houston et al. 2004). Notably, much work in this collection of studies focuses on children, but several assess adults.

Air pollution is associated with mortality in the short, middle, and long term (Brunekreef and Holgate 2002; Goodman et al. 2004). Goodman et al. (2004) find cardiovascular mortality risk was greater immediately following particulate matter exposure (within days), while respiratory mortality was more likely to occur over a longer period of time (weeks later). A reduction in fine particulate matter is associated with a decline in all-cause, cardiovascular, and lung cancer mortality risk (Laden et al. 2006). Further, Hong et al. (2002) found particulate matter, sulfur dioxide, carbon monoxide, nitrogen dioxide, and ozone were all associated with an increased likelihood of ischemic stroke mortality. Finally, ozone probably causes diminished lung function in individuals who reside in places with elevated levels of ozone for four or more years (Galizia and Kinney 1999).

## The Built Environment and Crime

*Theoretical Explanations.* Theories that explain how aspects of the built environment prevent or increase crime focus on the benefits derived from the production of informal social control and/or relationships among neighbors. These ideas have been articulated by Jacobs (1961) in her theory of street ecology and Newman (1972) in his theory of defensible space. Below we briefly consider these theories, review characteristics of the built environment that are applicable to them, including the decline of the built environment, and discuss how crime is associated with health.

*Physical Design and Crime.* Jacobs (1961) argues that design elements can promote surveillance and thus, informal social control, by increasing pedestrian traffic and other "eyes on the street." According to Jacobs, mixed land use containing multi- and single-family housing, different types of commercial establishments, old and new buildings, sidewalks, and connected streets will encourage more residents to walk when engaging in routine activities. Further, research shows aesthetics, defined by individual responses to survey questions regarding perceived pleasantness, attractiveness, and friendliness of the neighborhood, play a role in the likelihood that residents will walk in the community (Ball et al. 2001). Street activity, in turn, draws the interest and "eyes" of business owners and local residents who provide a natural source of monitoring and street control (Jacobs 1961). Hence, streets and parks that are visible from local residences and businesses will likely be more effectively monitored (Jacobs 1961).

Newman (1972) extends on Jacobs' ideas. According to the theory of defensible space, buildings can be designed in ways that increase the likelihood of informal surveillance, thus reducing crime. Based on work in housing projects, Newman (1972) argued that if public space and pedestrian areas are clearly defined and widely visible, it is more likely neighbors will intervene if a problem occurs, and the number of secluded places in which problematic behaviors can occur is limited. Taken together, these scholars advocate for community to be designed to encourage people to use the streets at all hours of the day, establish informal relationships through frequent interaction, and promote visual monitoring of local happenings by residents and business owners.

Fowler (1987) directly tested Jacobs' model by assessing how four aspects of physical diversity in neighborhoods were associated with neighboring, and how physical diversity and neighboring were associated with crime. Some support for her theory was found such that places with greater physical diversity had higher rates of acquaintanceship among neighbors and less juvenile delinquency. But physically diverse places with higher rates of neighboring did not have lower neighbor-reported crime. The author notes this could be because residents tend to know more about what occurs in these places.

The decline of the built environment, indicated by disorder, tends to occur in the absence of informal control. The term disorder generally refers to visible signs of physical and social decay, and is found largely in impoverished communities (Ross and Mirowsky 1999; Skogan 1990). The components of physical disorder include the presence of graffiti, vandalism, abandoned buildings, and residences or businesses that are not maintained (Ross and Mirowsky 1999; Skogan 1990).

Disorder may be consequential for health to the extent that it increases social isolation and stress, and encourages a spiral of neighborhood decay as residents withdraw from public space. Physical disorder is linked to distrust, probably due to fear of victimization (Ross and Jang 2000); if trust is eroded, social networks and cohesion are likely to be compromised.

Hence, and as theory would predict, interactions between neighbors are not typically as strong in communities containing disorder. Ross et al. (2001) found that urban residents, particularly those in areas of concentrated disadvantage, are more distrustful and that disorder may mediate this relationship. Therefore, disorder may have effects on health that are the result of a decrease in social capital/collective efficacy. Cohen et al. (2003) found disorder was associated with all-cause and cardiovascular mortality among individuals under 65 years of age, and that there was a significant interaction with collective efficacy such that collective efficacy was beneficial in low-disorder neighborhoods but not in high-disorder communities. Further, reductions in social control, and consequently, increased crime may result (Wilson and Kelling 1982). We briefly discuss the health and mortality implications of crime below.

*Crime and Health.* The level of violent crime in the local community directly and indirectly affects residents' health. First, violent crime—most obviously, homicide—has clear public-health implications. Second, residence in high-crime areas may cause health-consequential stress responses. Curry et al. (2008) analyzed a high-risk population of current and former drug users residing in block groups in Baltimore, Maryland. They found that subjects were at an increased risk of victimization in places with higher-crime rates. In addition, they found that victimization was associated with depressive symptoms and that the neighborhood crime rate also affected depression through perceptions of disorder. In another study assessing the relationship between crime and mental health, Clarke et al. (2008) found that exposure to violence among urban adult females is related to depressive symptoms and anxiety after controlling for individual characteristics. Thus, in addition to raising the possibility of violent victimization, high-crime rates may lead to stress and distress. Chronic stress may have physical-health consequences, such as a decline in cardiovascular functioning (Seeman et al. 1997).

Other studies support the link between neighborhood disadvantage, fear of crime, and health. Ross and Mirowsky (2001) found that residing in a disadvantaged neighborhood is associated with fear and accompanying stress, with implications for physical health. Similarly, Stafford et al. (2007) found that individuals with elevated fear of crime experience less-optimal lung function and slower walking speed (as proxies for physical functioning). This work also found individuals who fear crime are less likely to exercise, spend time on hobbies, or socialize.

## Implications of the Built Environment for Higher-Risk Subpopulations

*The Elderly and Functional Decline.* The local-built environment is especially important for the elderly because their routine activity space is typically more restricted when compared with younger adults. The viability of the neighborhood environment for physical activity may more directly affect exercise patterns and opportunities to avert functional decline (Jackson 2003b). Among older adults, functional decline is associated with increased risk of mortality. Major risk factors for functional decline in the elderly include depression, weight gain or loss, social isolation, and lack of exercise (Stuck et al. 1999; Unger et al. 1997). Thus, if community design allows for or encourages regular physical activity in the older population, functional decline might be slowed and mortality risk reduced. Supporting this idea, the quality of streets and sidewalks has been associated with level of disability in adults over age 45 (Clarke et al. 2008). The authors used data based on social observations of the quality of streets and sidewalks in local areas and found that, among those adults who are not physically impaired, disrepair was not problematic. Among adults with impaired movement, however, street disrepair was a significant predictor of severe mobility disability.

In another study, Berke et al. (2007) found that residents aged 65–97 were more likely to walk if commercial activity was nearby and was diverse across retail types. This supports work showing diversity in retail clusters increases walking and that proximity of grocery stores to residences is especially significant. However, the authors found that larger office buildings and educational facilities nearby may discourage walking, suggesting that useful and accessible destinations increase the likelihood of walking, but what could be perceived as an overwhelming level of commercial activity might decrease walking among older adults. Residents might perceive that larger structures could impede pedestrian safety. Although these variables predicted the number of days that older residents walked each week, this was not associated with BMI. Nevertheless, walking may safeguard against functional decline.

*Additional Considerations for Disadvantaged Populations.* Aspects of the built environment that are negatively associated either directly or indirectly with health are disproportionately located in poor and/or minority neighborhoods. Further, health-promoting amenities such as supermarkets and quality housing are less likely to be present in these communities. This, in conjunction with diminished access to individual resources, suggests that modifications to the built environment may be especially helpful for poor and minority individuals. Indeed, Lovasi et al. (2009) found, in an extensive review of the literature on obesity-promoting built environments, that quality food availability, safety, disorder/aesthetics, and local places to exercise were especially lacking in disadvantaged neighborhoods. Notably, in the case of amenities (as opposed to disorder and crime-related issues, which poor communities disproportionately shoulder), it may be that more financially affluent individuals use them to their advantage, while there is a not an effect on disadvantaged individuals (Lovasi et al. 2009).

Finally, there are implications of exposure in childhood to adverse features of the built environment, and physical environment more broadly, that may have long-lasting effects that are relevant for adult mortality (see Chapter 9 by Montez and Hayward, this volume). Hayward and Gorman (2004) have demonstrated that social conditions in childhood are significantly associated with life expectancy among adults aged 45–83. Likewise, children who are obese are more likely to be obese as adults, and some researchers have identified the built environment as a point of intervention (Dehghan et al. 2005). Further, children play, move about, and become adults within the physical context of their home, school, and neighborhood, which may expose them (or not expose them) to toxins and other asthma inducing substances, pedestrian and bike friendly streets, opportunities for recreation, and so forth, with lasting implications (Cummins and Jackson 2001).

*Summary.* In sum, there is an emerging interest in the ways that the built environment is linked to morbidity and mortality risk in post-industrial societies. To date, this research has focused primarily on the ways that land use mix, street characteristics, composition of commerce and public facilities, and amenities such as public transportation, are associated with the likelihood of obesity and some chronic diseases via indirect mechanisms. The mechanisms considered are health behaviors, social interaction, stress, and the production of social capital and related resources. Further, the quality of the built environment, as measured by adequate or substandard housing stock, level of air pollution, crime, and some land use characteristics, all have direct health implications due to exposure to toxins, criminal victimization, and likelihood of accidents. Pathways between the built environment and health have unique implications for vulnerable populations, such as the elderly and disabled, the economically disadvantaged, and children.

## Socially Conditioned Consequences of the Environment: Natural Disasters, Temperature, and Climate Change

### Natural Disasters

Natural hazards include drought, biological hazards, floods, hurricanes and other coastal storms, earthquakes, wildfires, extreme temperature, volcanic eruptions, and landslides (Wisner et al. 2004). Though all of these hazards are highly and directly relevant for adult mortality, we begin with a discussion of the most significant disasters in terms of loss of life that occurred between 1900 and 2010. We exclude epidemics and insect infestations because they are biological, rather than physical hazards. We then focus on a brief review of the socially conditioned nature of disaster-related mortality risk.

Table 21.1 lists the ten deadliest disasters and their mortality estimates from 1900 to January 2010 by country. Estimates are from the Centre for Research on the Epidemiology of Disasters International Disaster Database. We included earthquakes, extreme temperature, floods, storms, mass movements, volcanic eruptions, and wildfires in the search criteria, though only floods, storms, and earthquakes were deadly enough to make the list (CRED 2009). The most deadly natural disaster during this time period was a general flood in China (as opposed to a flash flood). About

**Table 21.1** Ten most deadly natural disasters by country, 1900–2010[a]

| Event | Country | Date | Estimated deaths[b] |
|---|---|---|---|
| General flood | China | July, 1931 | 3,700,000 |
| General flood | China | July, 1959 | 2,000,000 |
| General flood | China | July, 1939 | 500,000 |
| Tropical cyclone | Bangladesh | December 11, 1970 | 300,000 |
| Earthquake | China | July 27, 1976 | 242,000 |
| Earthquake | Haiti | January 12, 2010 | 222,570 |
| Earthquake | China | December 16, 1920 | 180,000 |
| Tsunami | Indonesia | December 26, 2004 | 165,708 |
| Earthquake | Japan | September 1, 1923 | 143,000 |
| General flood | China | 1935 | 142,000 |

[a]All estimates are from The Centre for Research on the Epidemiology of Disasters (CRED 2009 (www.emdat.be)). We use data from their disaster profiles database and include earthquakes, extreme temperature, floods, storms, mass movements, volcanic eruptions, and wildfires. We do not include the earthquake that occurred in the Peoples Republic of China on May 22, 1927 due to a large difference in mortality estimates between the OFDA/CRED and the United States Geological Survey (USGS 2009) (http://earthquake.usgs.gov/earthquakes/world/world_deaths.php).
[b]Mortality estimates reflect deaths directly and indirectly attributable to the event in question.

3.7 million people were killed when the Yangtze River flooded during the summer of 1931. China experienced additional devastating floods in 1959, 1939, and 1935. On December 11, 1970, a cyclone hit Bangladesh that resulted in about 300,000 causalities. Earthquakes and complications thereof round out the list. Two of the earthquakes occurred in China in 1976 and 1920 and killed an estimated 422,000 people combined. Haiti experienced a devastating earthquake on January 12, 2010 that resulted in an estimated 222,570 casualties. In December, 2004 a tsunami hit many countries in Southeast Asia as a consequence of an offshore earthquake and killed an estimated 165,708 residents of Indonesia. And an earthquake in Japan in 1923 killed approximately 143,000 people. Notably, we omitted droughts in order to observe the relevance of other types of disasters, as had we included them, they would have consumed eight of the ten events on the table. Notable droughts include those that occurred in China in 1928 and 1920 (3,000,000 and 500,000 estimated deaths, respectively), Bangladesh in 1943 (1,900,000 deaths), India in 1942, 1965, and 1900 (1,500,000, 1,500,000, and 1,250,000 estimated deaths), and the Soviet Union in 1921 (500,000 deaths) (CRED 2009).

Disasters cause death and serious injury from a variety of causes. For example, floods lead to mortality in a number of ways that include but are not limited to an increase in infectious disease, malnutrition, drowning, hypothermia, electrocution, and often lead to mental health problems that remain long after the event (Ohl and Tapsell 2000). For example, in the Yangtze River flood of 1931, deaths occurred from disease and starvation in addition to drowning (NOAA 1999). Further, mortality can occur as an immediate outcome of the disaster, or as a result of delay in rescue or lack of understanding of acute medical problems associated with unique disaster-related circumstances (Noji 1992). Moreover, the extent of personal loss, both human and material, has been linked to all-cause and heart disease mortality in the first 6 months following a disaster (e.g., the 1988 Armenian earthquake) and to onset of heart disease and other conditions (Armenian et al. 1988), illustrating that mortality risk remains a factor long after the incident. With this in mind, we discuss some of the ways disasters affect individual and community-level health.

*Individual Social Locations and Vulnerability.* Natural disasters, on first glance, may appear to affect all groups equally. There may be a relatively equal chance of being struck by disaster across groups, but a closer look into the nature of detrimental effects supports a gradient based on vulnerability, to which it is argued SES and other social locations are central (Wisner et al. 2004). Indeed, scholars have asserted, "There is no such thing as a natural disaster" (Hartman and Squires 2008)—i.e., a disaster with socially unconditioned consequences. Risk varies with the quality of the built environment, residence near components of the natural environment that elevate risk (such as proximity to the coast), and social vulnerability.

Wisner et al. (2004: 11) define vulnerability as it applies to natural disasters as "the characteristics of a person or group and their situation that influence their capacity to anticipate, cope with, resist, and recover from the impact of a natural hazard." Recent disasters have highlighted the vulnerability of those who live and work in coastal communities. Hurricane Katrina struck the Gulf Coast of Louisiana, Alabama, and Mississippi in August, 2005, and the 2004 Indian Ocean tsunami struck large areas of Southeast Asia. In the latter case, the destruction reached as far as the Somali coast. The vulnerability associated with the intersection of race, class, and age was seen during and following Hurricane Katrina in the southern United States (Louisiana Department of Health and Hospitals 2009; Picou and Marshall 2007), while mortality across social locations as a result of the tsunami on December 26, 2004 in southeast Asia has been associated with gender, occupation, and age (Doocy et al. 2007). Specifically, Doocy et al. (2007) studied mortality in the Aceh Province of Indonesia and, in addition to the risk associated with coastal proximity, found it to be highest in the elderly and among young children. The authors hypothesized that the more limited physical strength characterizing these groups resulted in greater exposure to risk during the tsunami. With respect to gender, some speculated that men were more likely to be out to sea fishing (where the ultimately dangerous tsunami waves rolled inconsequentially under their vessels) or farming in areas that were unaffected, while women remained home and were more likely to experience the tsunami (Oxfam 2005).

*Disasters, Distress, and Socioeconomic Status.* Distress following a disaster is common across all groups, but the severity and length of time distress is experienced appears to be differentially distributed across socioeconomic groups and possibly race-ethnicity. Poor people are more likely to experience stress after a disaster, in part because their financial losses are more devastating (Garrison 1985). In nations such as the United States, financial resources and race are closely tied. In work assessing distress resulting from Hurricane Katrina, Elliott and Pais (2006) found that blacks experienced more immediate and intense stress than whites with respect to both the short- and long-term future after Hurricane Katrina.

In some cases, distress may result in more severe negative outcomes. Krug et al. (1998) examined the extent to which suicide increases after disasters. The authors took a broad look, by defining disaster as anything declared by the United States government as such over a period of 7 years. Comparing pre- and post-disaster suicide rates they found that suicides were higher in the periods following earthquakes, floods, and hurricanes but did not differ following tornadoes or other severe storms.

Individual social networks are in danger of disruption after a disaster, which may have implications for stress. Bland et al. (1997) assessed working-class Italian men who were either relocated or not relocated following an earthquake. They found that those who were permanently relocated away from family and friends experienced increased long-term psychological distress by comparison with men who did not relocate. Those who returned to their communities experienced levels of distress similar to those who did not leave. In the aforementioned study of distress following Hurricane Katrina (Elliott and Pais 2006), it was found that personal networks were the resources most relied upon by residents to help them through disaster-related challenges. Network resources were especially important for blacks, who were more reliant on personal ties than whites.

Notably, there appears to be some variation by region as to the extent that distress is associated with SES. Frankenberg et al. (2008), in assessing outcomes resulting from the tsunami in Aceh and North Sumatra, Indonesia, found that post-traumatic stress disorder varied with residence in more damaged areas, exposure to trauma (such as hearing screams), as well as with age and gender, but not with SES.

*Preparation and Evacuation.* Disaster preparation may be anticipatory (insurance coverage) or reactionary (evacuation). It is likely more difficult for lower income residents to prepare for a disaster. For example, insurance is an added cost that residents may forgo (Fothergill and Peek 2004; Palm and Carroll 1998). Fothergill and Peek's review (2004) indicates that research is mixed in regard to evacuation responses across socioeconomic groups. Some work shows those with low education are also less likely to take warnings seriously because they may not be as likely to see it as legitimate, perhaps due to distrust (Perry 1987). Further, less-educated people may be more fatalistic and therefore, less prepared in the event of a crisis (Turner et al. 1986). If oriented in this way, preparation may not be viewed as worth the time, effort, or resources it requires. Others demonstrate the poor are less physically able to heed warnings due to material constraints, such as lack of transportation (Gladwin and Peacock 1997), and still others do not find an association with SES and evacuation behavior (Perry and Lindell 1991). Perhaps most self-evident, non-English speakers in the United States are at disadvantage in regard to receiving and/or understanding warnings (Fothergill and Peek 2004), a finding which probably extends to non-native speakers in other countries as well. Of course some events, such as earthquakes, occur without advance warning, and evacuation warnings are not relevant in the short term. When an earthquake occurs, the quality of building materials is important, and in more impoverished nations that cannot afford earthquake resistant structures, death tolls are greatly increased.

*Effects on Communities.* In addition to the myriad consequences for individuals that disasters produce, there are often consequences for communities as well. Local communities may be especially vulnerable to challenges in reconstruction and consequences thereof, a failure to repopulate, and an undoing of social cohesion.

Reconstruction of the built environment is a challenge in communities that have been victimized by natural disaster. For example, New Orleans, Louisiana, has been criticized for failing residents by not rebuilding schools, public transportation, and health-care facilities in a timely manner (Picou and Marshall 2007). A lack of reconstruction may appear as or precipitate disorder, which, as discussed previously, can lead to crime and social isolation. The decision to return by residents who relocated as a result of the disaster may be affected by the rate at which reconstruction is completed as well as social problems, such as increased crime, that are a consequence of physical disorder and disrupted social cohesion (Picou and Marshall 2007).

Not only can unanticipated disasters wreak havoc on health and mortality, and the built environment, they can have consequences for the social fabric of the community for years to come. This possibility is vividly illustrated by Erikson (1976) in his description of the social outcomes following the Buffalo Creek flood in West Virginia that occurred in 1972. A massive flood of mine waste flowed directly into Buffalo Creek from the mine high on the hill. Buffalo Creek was a highly cohesive community, though it was not affluent. Despite some research that indicates that people join together in solidarity after a disaster, this did not occur after this particular event. Instead, due to loss of life, displacement, and other aspects of change, the social cohesiveness of the community was disrupted. We refer to this event as an example of how disasters affect mortality risk immediately and directly, but also through indirect channels, such as through the loss of community social capital.

## *Temperature*

We now turn our attention to temperature. Extreme hot and cold temperatures pose health risks that vary both by place and by subpopulation within place. Urban areas have been labeled "urban heat islands" due to their comparatively high-ambient temperatures (Basu and Samet 2002; Frumkin 2002). This occurs because increasing urban land area is associated with much more concrete and asphalt and much less green space, which both raises ambient temperatures during the day and increases the propensity to retain heat at night (Basu and Samet 2002). Concrete radiates heat while greenery has a cooling effect, and as a result, urban areas can experience temperatures 6–8° (Fahrenheit) higher than nearby non-urbanized areas. Heat waves are known risk factors for increased mortality (Curriero et al. 2002), and several notable events of this type have occurred in recent years. Perhaps the most deadly was a lengthy and severe heat wave affecting Europe in August, 2003, that took approximately 35,000 lives (Stott et al. 2004).

Total heat exposure is central to mortality risk. Researchers typically use ambient temperature, dew point, or the heat index, which combines heat and humidity, to measure heat exposure (Basu and Samet 2002). Importantly, stress on the body from heat occurs as a result of cumulative exposure during the entire day (day and overnight). Thus, any exposure to air conditioning can reduce exposure threat, illustrating the relevance of the overnight cooling period. Excess mortality is typically measured compared to previous years during the same time period. Death most commonly occurs between 1 and 3 days following the critical point, though this varies. Those most likely to die due to heat exposure are those with preexisting cardiovascular, respiratory, or cerebrovascular diseases (Basu and Samet 2002).

Individual risk factors for mortality during heat waves include being elderly, poor, living alone, preexisting disease, and not having access to transportation. Protective factors include the presence of greenery around the residence, physical fitness, and access to air conditioning (Basu and Samet 2002). Recent research on the 1995 Chicago heat wave supports these characteristics as risk factors (Klinenberg 2003). The cooling process of the body is altered in the elderly, which results in increased physiological risk. With regard to heat exposure, these characteristics decrease the likelihood that individuals would have access to periods of time in cooler places. For example, those with higher SES may be employed in air-conditioned offices, while elderly, unemployed individuals who live alone, who do not have air conditioning and do not have immediate access to transportation are much less likely to have access to time in air-conditioned places. Some of the disparities in heat-related mortality across race-ethnicity and SES may be due to lack of air conditioning, which is correlated with income. In a study of heat-related mortality in Chicago, Detroit, Minneapolis, and Pittsburgh, O'Neill et al. (2003) found that whites were four times more likely to have air conditioning than blacks. In a study of the Chicago heat wave, older adults who resided in communities with higher quality commercial activity (i.e., limited presence of bars, liquor stores, and run-down commercial buildings) were at lower risk of heat-related mortality (Browning et al. 2006). This finding suggests that older adults who do not have (or, for economic reasons, are unwilling to use) air conditioning may benefit from nearby businesses that provide a source of relief during heat waves.

In August of 2003, a heat wave struck Europe. Some estimate that the summer of 2003 was the hottest in Europe since 1500 (Poumadere et al. 2005). In France, the most affected of all countries, there were about 15,000 excess deaths (55% higher than the expected count of all-cause mortality) (Fouillet et al. 2006; Poumadere et al. 2005). Social factors associated with the likelihood of death in France included age; being female; being single, widowed, or divorced (living alone); living in an urban area; and poverty (Fouillet et al. 2006; Poumadere et al. 2005). Those most at risk were women over 75 years of age (Pirard et al. 2005). Key direct causes of death due to the heat wave included dehydration, hypothermia, and heat stroke. Preexisting conditions such as cardiovascular and respiratory disease increased the likelihood of mortality (Fouillet et al. 2006; Poumadere et al. 2005). In other affected European counties, Italy saw an estimated 3,134 (15.2% higher) excess deaths in capital cities, and England and Wales experienced about 2,130 excess deaths (16% higher), also most commonly in urban dwellers over 75 years of age (Conti et al. 2005; Johnson et al. 2005). Switzerland's mortality was about 7% higher due to the heat wave (975 excess deaths) (Grize et al. 2005).

Elevated mortality due to temperature extremes varies by latitude (Curriero et al. 2002) and thresholds are based on local temperature norms. For example, in the United States, northern cities are more likely to experience excess mortality during a heat wave than are southern cities (Curriero et al. 2002). Conversely, Gouveia et al. (2003) found that mortality in Sao Paulo, Brazil, is more sensitive to extreme cold than extreme heat.

Elevated winter mortality is less pronounced than that of summer, and is probably not due to direct effects of cold temperatures. Rather, although some winter deaths may be due to lack of sufficient heat, most excess death is due to the influenza season (Reichert et al. 2004). But there may also be interactive effects as it is possible that cold weather influences the extent and severity of the influenza season (Reichert et al. 2004). Due to the relationship between ozone and other pollutant formation and heat, interactions are also potentially relevant for heat-related mortality. Scholars have examined the relationship between air pollution and temperature, but studies are inconsistent (Basu and Samet 2002). Some research finds no relationship, whereas other work either finds that pollution exacerbates heat effects on mortality, or explains them.

Finally, new research suggests that the season in which individuals are born may have a long-term impact on life expectancy. Doblhammer and Vaupel (2001) examined the association between season of birth and life expectancy among those 50 years of age and older in Denmark and Austria and found that those born in autumn have longer life expectancy than those born in the spring. Moreover, they found a similar pattern with a 6-month shift in Australia. Neither socioeconomic status nor seasonal distribution of death during year one accounted for the significant findings. In another study McEniry et al. (2008) examined season of birth, based on extent of overlap of the third trimester with the slack season in the Puerto Rican sugar cane industry (July–December; sugar cane is harvested January–June) among a rural population under the supposition that season of birth is a proxy for nutritional quality and exposure to infectious disease during late gestation and early infancy. Seasons were defined by full, some, or no overlap with the slack season in the third trimester of gestation. Results indicate that full exposure to the slack period in late gestation was associated with greater risk of heart disease later in life than either partial or no exposure. Findings on diabetes were less conclusive and interacted with indicators of family history of diabetes. Significant associations were only relevant for those who live in rural areas as a child. The authors conclude that season of birth may be a valid measure of exposure to poor nutrition in this rural population and that exposure to poor nutrition and infectious disease is an important predictor of heart disease later in life.

## *Climate Change and Health*

We conclude our review of the socially conditioned consequences of the environment with a brief discussion of climate change. Significant climate change is expected over the next century, and scientists believe that both average temperatures and climate variability will increase (McGeehin and Mirabelli 2001; McMichael et al. 2006). Therefore, there are implications for disaster and temperature-related mortality. Notably, temperature increase is expected to be greater at higher latitudes, where they are most harmful. Because both average temperature and temperature variability are expected to increase, European and US cities at higher latitudes can expect more, and more severe heat waves. The effects of these fundamental changes will be wide ranging. Although some outcomes will actually be beneficial, most will be detrimental for humans. In addition to other consequences discussed, climate change is expected to cause (and, in some cases, is already associated with) more floods and drought (which are especially problematic in developing countries), higher ozone levels, forests fires, and allergens (Haines and Patz 2004). Among the expected outcomes are an increase in mortality related to elevated temperature and natural disasters. Further, infectious disease is expected to rise due to warmer conditions, which will increase bacterial growth. Crops will be subject to these more extreme conditions and will likely suffer. Some of these effects may be conditionally beneficial in certain regions. For example, higher temperatures may lead to fewer deaths in the winter in colder climates. But the overall impact will increase the risk of mortality (McGeehin and Mirabelli 2001).

## Conclusions and Directions for Future Research

We have presented a framework organized around the distinction between socially unconditioned, socially conditioned, and socially produced effects of the physical environment, for describing extant knowledge on the link between environment and mortality risk in the adult population. We first discussed the built environment, drawing attention to the ways that land use, street characteristics, sprawl, and the content and quality of commerce and public places are associated with both direct and indirect mechanisms influencing health and mortality. The second section of this chapter outlined major components of the natural environment that affect mortality, with a focus on natural disasters and climate, and discussed how their effects are often not randomly distributed.

Throughout our discussion we have attempted to emphasize the complex nature of the relationship between the physical environment and mortality. The physical environment influences mortality at multiple levels of analysis, through numerous mechanisms, and in varying social contexts that may shape the nature of environment–mortality associations. Moreover, we have emphasized the potential for social location (e.g., SES, race/ethnicity, age, and social isolation) to condition the influence of the physical environment. In particular, we have highlighted the need to identify high-risk groups that may be uniquely vulnerable to the health consequences of risky environments.

With these concerns in mind, we note a number of potentially fruitful pathways for future research on links between the physical environment, health, and mortality. First, research on mortality, as opposed to morbidity or more general health outcomes, remains limited. While it is intuitive to assess mortality risk due to disasters and heat waves, or events proximate to mortality itself, it is more difficult to test effects of the built environment on mortality directly due to the greater lag between contextual characteristics of interest, the proposed intermediate mechanisms, and death. A significant complication concerns limited availability of data on the timing of individual exposures to contextual characteristics across the life course. Thus, quantification of the significance of the built environment on mortality risk is difficult. Research that focuses on those at greatest risk, such as the elderly, chronically ill, or disadvantaged, may best capture the relevance of the built environment on mortality risk. Attention at the research design phase to the potentially health-consequential exposures to varying physical environments will also yield more rigorous analyses of environmental effects on mortality.

The delineation of the mechanisms through which physical environment effects operate also remains as a vexing question from the standpoint of both theory and empirical investigation. Theories of built environment effects on health, for instance, should continue to refine models of the process by which such environments ultimately affect health and mortality. As this chapter has emphasized, physical environment influences on health range from direct and immediate to indirect and potentially quite distal. Moreover, the social embeddedness of physical environments cannot be ignored when assessing their health consequences—social factors, including social capital, collective efficacy, and social network dynamics may play an important role in conditioning the influence of physical environments.

Concerns about causality and selection are another significant challenge to research on physical environment effects on health. Although by no means unique to research on environmental effects on health, the problem of causal estimation—particularly of built environment effects on health outcomes—is especially intractable. The relatively pervasive reliance on cross-sectional data in research on the built environment has left the field open to the persistent criticism that individuals at higher risk of poor health and mortality may select into neighborhoods characterized by compromised physical environments. Longitudinal and quasi-experimental (e.g., the moving to opportunity demonstration [Kling et al. 2004]) studies are an important advance in this regard, but have not been a major focus of research on the physical environment.

At this juncture, with a continuing increase in urbanization throughout the world, climate change, and a focus on environmental quality, research on aspects of the built and broader physical environment on mortality risk should continue to offer important insights into the social determinants of health.

**Acknowledgment** We would like to thank Eileen Crimmins and Richard Rogers for their helpful comments.

## Suggested Internet Resources

### Land Use and Urban Planning

http://www.euro.who.int/en/what-we-do/health-topics/environmental-health/urban-health
http://icupph.wikidot.com/about-icupph
http://www.library.cornell.edu/Reps/DOCS/homepage.htm
http://planning-research.com/
http://www.smartcommunities.ncat.org/landuse/mixed.shtml

### Air Pollution

http://www.epa.gov/ebtpages/air.html
http://www.euro.who.int/air
http://www.hc-sc.gc.ca/ewh-semt/pubs/air/index-eng.php
http://www.nlm.nih.gov/medlineplus/airpollution.html
http://www.cdc.gov/nceh/airpollution/

### Disasters

http://www.bt.cdc.gov/disasters/
http://www.colorado.edu/hazards/

http://www.colorado.edu/hazards/resources/centers/
http://www.cred.be/
http://www.emdat.be/
http://www.who.int/topics/disasters/en/

## Weather and Climate Change

http://www.hc-sc.gc.ca/ewh-semt/pubs/climat/index-eng.php
www.noaa.org
http://www.who.int/topics/climate/en/

## References

Almeida, D.M., S.D. Neupert, S.R. Banks, and J. Serido 2005. "Do Daily Stress Processes Account for Socioeconomic Health Disparities?" *Journals of Gerontology Series B: Psychological Sciences and Social Sciences* 60(Special Issue 2):34–39.

Apparicio, P. M.S. Cloutier, and R. Shearmur 2007. "The Case of Montreal's Missing Food Deserts: Evaluation of Accessibility to Food Supermarkets." *International Journal of Health Geographics* 6(4). doi:10.1186/1476-072X-6-4, http://www.ijhealthgeographics.com/content/6/1/4

Armenian H.K., A.K. Melkonian, and A.P. Hovanesian. 1988. "Long Term Mortality and Morbidity Related to Degree of Damage Following the 1998 Earthquake in Armenia." *American Journal of Epidemiology* 148: 1077–84.

Ball, K., A. Bauman, E. Leslie, and N. Owen. 2001. "Perceived Environmental Aesthetics and Convenience and Company Are Associated with Walking for Exercise among Australian Adults." *Preventive Medicine* 33(5):434–40.

Bashir, S.A. 2002. "Home Is Where the Harm is: Inadequate Housing as a Public Health Crisis." *American Journal of Public Health* 92(5):733–38.

Basu, R. and J.M. Samet. 2002. "Relation between Elevated Ambient Temperature and Mortality: A Review of the Epidemiologic Evidence." *Epidemiologic Reviews* 24(2):190–202.

Berke, E.M., T.D. Koepsell, A.V. Moudon, R.E. Hoskins, and E.B. Larson. 2007. "Association of the Built Environment with Physical Activity and Obesity in Older Persons." *American Journal of Public Health* 97(3):486–92.

Berkman, L.F. and S.L. Syme. 1979. "Social Networks, Host Resistance, and Mortality: A Nine-Year Follow-up Study of Alameda County Residents." *American Journal of Epidemiology* 109(2):186–204.

Black, J.L. and J. Mancinko. 2008. "Neighborhoods and Obesity." *Nutrition Reviews* 66(1):2–20.

Bland S.H., E.S. O'Leary, E. Farinaro, F. Jossa, V. Krogh, J.M. Violanti, and M. Trevisan. 1997. "Social Network Disturbances and Psychological Distress Following Earthquake Evacuation." *Journal of Nervous and Mental Disease* 185:188–94.

Blankenship, K.M., S.J. Bray, and M.H. Merson. 2000. "Structural Interventions in Public Health." *AIDS* 14:S11.

Block, J.P., R.A. Scribner, and K.B. DeSalvo. 2004. "Fast Food, Race/Ethnicity, and Income: A Geographic Analysis." *American Journal of Preventive Medicine* 27(3):211–17.

Booth, M.L., N. Owen, A. Bauman, O. Clavisi, and E. Leslie. 2000. "Social-Cognitive and Perceived Environment Influences Associated with Physical Activity in Older Australians." *Preventive Medicine* 31(1):15–22.

Browning, C.R. and K.A. Cagney. 2002. "Neighborhood Structural Disadvantage, Collective Efficacy, and Self-Rated Physical Health in an Urban Setting." *Journal of Health and Social Behavior* 43(4):383–99.

Browning, C.R., D. Wallace, S.L. Feinberg, and K.A. Cagney. 2006. "Neighborhood Social Processes, Physical Conditions, and Disaster-Related Mortality: The Case of the 1995 Chicago Heat Wave." *American Sociological Review* 71(4):661–78.

Brunekreef, B. and S.T. Holgate. 2002. "Air Pollution and Health." *The Lancet* 360(9341):1233–42.

Cacioppo, J.T., L.C. Hawkley, L.E. Crawford, J.M. Ernst, M.H. Burleson, R.B. Kowalewski, W.B. Malarkey, E. Van Cauter, and G.G. Berntson. 2002. "Loneliness and Health: Potential Mechanisms." *Psychosomatic Medicine* 64(3):407.

Cacioppo, J.T. and W. Patrick. 2008. *Loneliness.* New York, NY, W.W. Norton.

Cagney, K.A. and C.R. Browning. 2004. "Exploring Neighborhood Level Variation in Asthma and Other Respiratory Disease." *Journal of General Internal Medicine* 19(3):229–36.

Carruthers, J.I. 2002. "Evaluating the Effectiveness of Regulatory Growth Management Programs: An Analytic Framework." *Journal of Planning Education and Research* 21(4):391–405.

Centers for Disease Control [CDC]. 1996. *ToxFAQs[TM] for Polycyclic Aromatic Hydrocarbons (PAHs).* http://www.atsdr.cdc.gov/tfacts69.html. Retrieved November, 2008.

Centers for Disease Control [CDC]. 2007. *ToxFAQs[TM] for Lead (Pb).* http://www.atsdr.cdc.gov/tfacts13.html. Retrieved November, 2008.

Centre for Research on the Epidemiology of Disasters. 2009. *EM-DAT: The OFDA/CRED International Disaster Database.* www.emdat.be, Université catholique de Louvain, Brussels, Belgium." Retrieved January, 2010.

Clarke, P., J.A. Ailshire, M. Bader, J.D. Morenoff, and J.S. House. 2008. "Mobility Disability and the Urban Built Environment." *American Journal of Epidemiology* 168(5):506–13.

Cohen, S., W.J. Doyle, D.P. Skoner, B.S. Rabin, and J.M. Gwaltney. 1997. "Social Ties and Susceptibility to the Common Cold." *JAMA* 277(24):1940–1944.

Cohen, D.A., T.A. Farley, and K. Mason. 2003. "Why is Poverty Unhealthy? Social and Physical Mediators." *Social Science and Medicine* 57(9):1631–41.

Cohen, D.A., B.K. Finch, A. Bower, and N. Sastry. 2006. "Collective Efficacy and Obesity: The Potential Influence of Social Factors on Health." *Social Science and Medicine* 62(3):769–78.

Cohen, D.A., S. Inagami, and B.K. Finch. 2008. "The Built Environment and Collective Efficacy." *Health and Place* 14(2):198–208.

Collins, K.J. 1986. "Low Indoor Temperatures and Morbidity in the Elderly." *Age and Ageing* 15(4):212–20.

Conti, S., P. Meli, G. Minelli, R. Solimini, V. Toccaceli, M. Vichi, C. Beltrano, and L. Perini. 2005. "Epidemiologic Study of Mortality during the Summer 2003 Heat Wave in Italy." *Environmental Research* 98(3):390–99.

Corburn, J. 2004. "Confronting the Challenges in Reconnecting Urban Planning and Public Health." *American Journal of Public Health* 94(4):541–46.

Cummins, S.K. and R.J. Jackson. 2001. "The Built Environment and Children's Health." *Pediaticr Clinics of North America.* 48:1241–52.

Cummins, S.C. and S. Macintyre. 2002. "A Systematic Study of an Urban Foodscape: The Price and Availability of Food in Great Glasgow." *Urban Studies* 39:2115.

Cummins, S.C., J.L. McKay, and S. Macintyre. 2005. "McDonald's Restaurants and Neighborhood Deprivation in Scotland and England." *American Journal of Preventive Medicine* 29(4):308–10.

Curriero, F.C., K.S. Heiner, J.M. Samet, S.L. Zeger, L. Strug, and J.A. Patz. 2002. "Temperature and Mortality in 11 Cities of the Eastern United States." *American Journal of Epidemiology* 155(1):80.

Curry, A., C. Latkin, and M. Davey-Rothwell. 2008. "Pathways to Depression: The Impact of Neighborhood Violent Crime on Inner-City Residents in Baltimore, Maryland, USA." *Social Science and Medicine* 67(1):23–30.

Dearry, A. 2004. "Editorial: Impacts of Our Built Environment on Public Health." *Environmental Health Perspectives* 112(11):A600.

Dehghan, M., N. Akhtar-Danesh, and A.T. Merchant. 2005. "Childhood Obesity, Prevalence and Prevention." *Nutrition Journal* 4:24–32.

Doblhammer, G. and J.W. Vaupel. 2001. "Lifespan Depends on Month of Birth." *Proceedings of the National Academy of Sciences of the USA* 98(5):2934.

Doosy, S., A. Rofi, C. Moodie, E. Spring, S. Bradley, G. Burnham, and C. Robinson. 2007. "Tsunami Mortality in Aceh Province, Indonesia." *Bulletin of the World Health Organization* 85(4):273–78.

Duany, A. and E. Plater-Zyberk. 1991. *Towns and Town-Making Principles.* New York, NY, Rizzoli.

Duncan, M.J., J.C. Spence, and W.K. Mummery. 2005. "Perceived Environment and Physical Activity: A Meta-Analysis of Selected Environmental Characteristics." *International Journal of Behavioral Nutrition and Physical Activity* 2:11.

Elliott, J.R. and J. Pais. 2006. "Race, Class, and Hurricane Katrina: Social Differences in Human Responses to Disaster." *Social Science Research* 35(2):295–321.

Environmental Protection Agency. 2007. *Mobile Source Emissions: Past, Present and Future.* Washington, DC. http://www.epa.gov/otaq/invntory/overview/index.htm. Retrieved November 2008.

Environmental Protection Agency. 2008. *Air Emissions Sources: Basic Information.* Washington, DC. http://www.epa.gov/air/emissions/basic.htm#dataloc. Retrieved November 2008.

Erikson, K. 1976. *Everything in its Path: The Destruction of a Community in the Buffalo Creek Mining Disaster.* New York, NY, Simon & Schuster.

Ewing, R., R.A. Schieber, and C.V. Zegeer. 2003a. "Urban Sprawl as a Risk Factor in Motor Vehicle Occupant and Pedestrian Fatalities." *American Journal of Public Health* 93(9):1541–45.

Ewing, R., T. Schmid, R. Killingsworth, A. Zlot, and S. Raudenbush. 2003b. "Relationship between Urban Sprawl and Physical Activity, Obesity, and Morbidity." *American Journal of Health Promotion* 18(1):47–57.

Fleming, R., A. Baum, and J.E. Singer 1985. "Social Support and the Physical Environment." In S. Cohen and S.L. Syme (eds.), *Social Support and Health*, pp. 327–345. Orlando, FL, Academic Press.

Fothergill, A. and L.A. Peek. 2004. "Poverty and Disasters in the United States: A Review of Recent Sociological Findings." *Natural Hazards* 32(1):89–110.

Fouillet, A., G. Rey, F. Laurent, G. Pavillon, S. Bellec, C. Guihenneuc-Jouyaux, J. Clavel, E. Jougla, and D. Hémon. 2006. "Excess Mortality Related to the August 2003 Heat Wave in France." *International Archives of Occupational and Environmental Health* 80(1):16–24.

Fowler, E.P. 1987. "Street Management and City Design." *Social Forces* 66(2):365–89.

Frank, L.D., M.A. Andresen, and T.L. Schmid. 2004. "Obesity Relationships with Community Design, Physical Activity, and Time Spent in Cars." *American Journal of Preventive Medicine* 27(2):87–96.

Frank, L.D. and P.O. Engelke. 2001. "The Built Environment and Human Activity Patterns: Exploring the Impacts of Urban Form on Public Health." *Journal of Planning Literature* 16(2):202–18.

Frank, L.D. and P.O. Engelke. 2005. "Multiple Impacts of the Built Environment on Public Health: Walkable Places and the Exposure to Air Pollution." *International Regional Science Review* 28(2):193–216.

Frankenberg, E., J. Friedman, T. Gillespie, N. Ingwersen, R. Pynoos, I.U. Rifai, B. Sikoki, A. Steinberg, C. Sumantri, and W. Suriastini. 2008. "Mental Health in Sumatra after the Tsunami." *American Journal of Public Health* 98(9):1671–77.

Frumkin, H. 2002. "Urban Sprawl and Public Health." *Public Health Reports* 117(3):201–18.

Frumkin, H. 2005. "Health, Equity, and the Built Environment." *Environmental Health Perspectives* 113(5):A290–A291.

Galizia, A. and P.L. Kinney 1999. "Long-Term Residence in Areas of High Ozone: Associations with Respiratory Health in a Nationwide Sample of Nonsmoking Young Adults." *Environmental Health Perspectives* 107(8):675–79.

Garrison, J.L. 1985. "Mental Health Implications of Disaster Relocation in the United States: A Review of the Literature." *International Journal of Mass Emergencies and Disasters* 3(2):49–65.

Giles-Corti, B. and R.J. Donovan 2002a. "The Relative Influence of Individual, Social and Physical Environment Determinants of Physical Activity." *Social Science and Medicine* 54(12):1793–812.

Giles-Corti, B. and R.J. Donovan. 2002b. "Socioeconomic Status Differences in Recreational Physical Activity Levels and Real and Perceived Access to a Supportive Physical Environment." *Preventive Medicine* 35(6):601–11.

Gladwin, H. and W.G. Peacock. 1997. "Warning and Evacuation: A Night for Hard Houses." In W.G. Peacock, B.H. Morrow, and H. Gladwin. (eds.), *Hurricane Andrew: Ethnicity, Gender, and the Sociology of Disasters*, pp 52–74. London, Routledge.

Glaser, R. and J.K. Kiecolt-Glaser. 2005. "Stress-Induced Immune Dysfunction: Implications for Health." *Nature Reviews Immunology* 5:243–51.

Glass, T.A. and J.L. Balfour 2003. "Neighborhoods, Aging, and Functional Limitations." In I. Kawachi and L.F. Berkman (eds.), *Neighborhoods and Health*, pp. 303–34. Oxford; New York, NY, Oxford University Press.

Goodman, P.G., D.W. Dockery, and L. Clancy. 2004. "Cause-Specific Mortality and the Extended Effects of Particulate Pollution and Temperature Exposure." *Environmental Health Perspectives* 112(2):179–85.

Gordon-Larsen, P., M.C. Nelson, P. Page, and B.M. Popkin. 2006. "Inequality in the Built Environment Underlies Key Health Disparities in Physical Activity and Obesity." *Pediatrics* 117(2):417–24.

Gouveia, N., S. Hajat, and B. Armstrong. 2003. "Socioeconomic Differentials in the Temperature-Mortality Relationship in Sao Paulo, Brazil." *International Journal of Epidemiology* 32(3):390.

Grize, L., A. Huss, O. Thommen, C. Schindler, and C. Braun-Fahrländer 2005. "Heat Wave 2003 and Mortality in Switzerland." *Schweizer Medizinische Wochenzeitschrift* 135:200–5.

Grzywacz, J.G., D.M. Almeida, S.D. Neupert, and S.L. Ettner. 2004. "Socioeconomic Status and Health: A Microlevel Analysis of Exposure and Vulnerability to Daily Stressors." *Journal of Health and Social Behavior* 45(1):1–16.

Gunier, R.B., A. Hertz, J. von Behren, and P. Reynolds. 2003. "Traffic Density in California: Socioeconomic and Ethnic Differences among Potentially Exposed Children." *Journal of Exposure Analysis and Environmental Epidemiology* 13:240–46.

Haines A. and J.A. Patz. 2004. "Health Effects of Climate Change." *JAMA* 291:99–103.

Hartman, C. and G.D. Squires. 2008. *There Is No Such Thing as a Natural Disaster: Race, Class, and Hurricane Katrina*. New York, NY, Routledge.

Hasse, J.E. and R.G. Lathrop. 2003. "Land Resource Impact Indicators of Urban Sprawl." *Applied Geography* 23(2–3):159–75.

Hawkley, L.C. and J.T. Cacioppo. 2003. "Loneliness and Pathways to Disease." *Brain, Behavior and Immunity* 17:S98–S105.

Hawkley, L.C., C.M. Masi, J.D. Berry, and J.T. Cacioppo. 2006. "Loneliness is a Unique Predictor of Age Related Differences in Systolic Blood Pressure." *Psychology and Aging* 21(1):152–64.

Hayward, M.D. and B.K. Gorman 2004. "Long Arm of Childhood: The Influence of Early-Life Social Conditions on Men's Mortality." *Demography* 41(1):87–107.

Holtgrave, D.R. and R.A. Crosby. 2003. "Social Capital, Poverty, and Income Inequality as Predictors of Gonorrhoea, Syphilis, Chlamydia and AIDS Case Rates in the United States." *Sexually Transmitted Infections* 79(1):62–64.

Hong, Y.C., J.T. Lee, H. Kim, and H.J. Kwon. 2002. "Air Pollution: A New Risk Factor in Ischemic Stroke Mortality." *Stroke* 33(9):2165–69.

House, J.S., K.R. Landis, and D. Umberson. 1988. "Social Relationships and Health." *Science* 241(4865):540–45.

Houston, D., J. Wu, P. Ong, and A. Winer. 2004. "Structural Disparities of Urban Traffic in Southern California: Implications for Vehicle-Related Air Pollution Exposure in Minority and Hh-Poverty Neighborhoods." *Journal of Urban Affairs* 26(5):565–92.

Humpel, N., N. Owen, and E. Leslie. 2002. "Environmental Factors Associated With Adults' Participation in Physical Activity: A Review." *American Journal of Preventive Medicine* 22(3):188–99.

Jackson, L.E. 2003a. "The Relationship of Urban Design to Human Health and Condition." *Landscape and Urban Planning* 64(4):191–200.

Jackson, L.E.2003b. "The Impact of the Built Environment on Health: An Emerging Field." *American Journal of Public Health* 93(9):1382–84.

Jacobs, J. 1961. *The Death and Life of Great American Cities*. New York, NY, Random House.

Johnson, H., R.S. Kovats, G. McGregor, J. Stedman, M. Gibbs, and H. Walton. 2005. "The Impact of the 2003 Heat Wave on Daily Mortality in England and Wales and the Use of Rapid Weekly Mortality Estimates." *Euro Surveill* 10(7):168–71.

Kawachi, I., B.P. Kennedy, and R. Glass. 1999. "Social Capital and Health: A Contextual Analysis." *American Journal of Public Health* 89(8):1187–93.

Kelly-Schwartz, A.C., J. Stockard, S. Doyle, and M. Schlossberg. 2004. "Is Sprawl Unhealthy? A Multilevel Analysis of the Relationship of Metropolitan Sprawl to the Health of Individuals." *Journal of Planning Education and Research* 24(2):184–96.

Kennedy, B.P., I. Kawachi, D. Prothrow-Stith, K. Lochner, and V. Gupta. 1998. "Social Capital, Income Inequality, and Firearm Violent Crime." *Social Science and Medicine* 47(1):7–17.

Klinenberg, E. 2003. *Heat Wave: A Social Autopsy of Disaster in Chicago*. Chicago, IL, University Of Chicago Press.

Kling, J.R., J.B. Liebman, L.F. Katz, and L. Sanbonmatsu. 2004. *Moving to Opportunity and Tranquility: Neighborhood Effects on Adult Economic Self-Sufficiency and Health from a Randomized Housing Voucher Experiment*. Working Papers 860, Princeton University, Department of Economics, Industrial Relations Section.

Krieger, N. 2001. "Theories for Social Epidemiology in the 21st Century: An Ecosocial Perspective." *International Journal of Epidemiology* 30(4):668–77.

Krieger, J. and D.L. Higgins. 2002. "Housing and Health: Time Again for Public Health Action." *American Journal of Public Health* 92(5):758–68.

Krug, E.G., M. Kresnow, J.P. Peddicord, L.L. Dahlberg, K.E. Powell, A.E. Crosby, and J.L. Annest. 1998. "Suicide after Natural Disasters." *New England Journal of Medicine* 338(6):373–78.

LaVeist, T.A. and J.M. Wallace. 2000. "Health Risk and Inequitable Distribution of Liquor Stores in African American Neighborhood." *Social Science and Medicine* 51(4):613–17.

Laden, F., J. Schwartz, F.E. Speizer, and D.W. Dockery. 2006. "Reduction in Fine Particulate Air Pollution and Mortality: Extended Follow-Up of the Harvard Six Cities Study." *American Journal of Respiratory and Critical Care Medicine* 173(6):667–72.

Leyden, K.M. 2003. "Social Capital and the Built Environment: The Importance of Walkable Neighborhoods." *American Journal of Public Health* 93(9):1546–51.

Lochner, K.A., I. Kawachi, R.T. Brennan, and S.L. Buka. 2003. "Social Capital and Neighborhood Mortality Rates in Chicago." *Social Science and Medicine* 56(8):1797–805.

Lopez, R. 2004. "Urban Sprawl and Risk for Being Overweight or Obese." *American Journal of Public Health* 94(9):1574–79.

Lopez, R. and H.P. Hynes. 2003. "Sprawl in the 1990s: Measurement, Distribution and Trends." *Urban Affairs Review* 38(3):325–55.

Louisiana Department of Health and Hospitals. 2009. *Reports on Deceased.* http://www.dhh.louisiana.gov/offices/page.asp?ID=303&Detail=7047. Accessed October, 2009.

Lovasi, G.S., M.A. Hutson, M. Guerra, and K.M. Neckerman. 2009. "Built Environments and Obesity in Disadvantaged Populations." *Epidemiologic Reviews* 31(1):7–20.

Lucy, W.H. 2003. "Mortality Risk Associated with Leaving Home: Recognizing the Relevance of the Built Environment." *American Journal of Public Health* 93(9):1564–69.

Macintyre, S. and A. Ellaway 2000. "Ecological Approaches: Rediscovering the Role of the Physical and Social Environment." In L. Berkman and I. Kawachi (eds.), *Social Epidemiology.* pp. 332–48. Oxford, Oxford University Press.

Macintyre, S., L. Macdonald, and A. Ellaway. 2008. "Do Poorer People Have Poorer Access to Local Resources and Facilities? The Distribution of Local Resources by Area Deprivation in Glasgow, Scotland." *Social Science and Medicine* 67(6):900–14.

McEniry, M., A. Palloni, A.L. Davila., and A.G. Gurucharri 2008. "Early Life Exposure to Poor Nutrition and Infectious Diseases and Its Effects on the Health of Older Puerto Rican Adults." *Journals of Gerontology Series B: Psychological Sciences and Social Sciences* 63(6):S337.

McEwen, B.S. 1998. "Stress, Adaptation, and Disease: Allostasis and Allostatic Load." *Annals of the New York Academy of Sciences* 840:33–44.

McGeehin, M.A. and M. Mirabelli. 2001. "The Potential Impacts of Climate Variability and Change on Temperature-Related Morbidity and Mortality in the United States." *Environmental Health Perspectives Supplements* 109(2):185–90.

McGinnis, J.M. and W.H. Foege. 1993. "Actual Causes of Death in the United States." *JAMA* 270(18):2207–12.

McMichael, A.J., R.E. Woodruff, and S. Hales. 2006. "Climate Change and Human Health: Present and Future Risks." *The Lancet* 367(9513):859–69.

Mokdad, A.H., J.S. Marks, D.F. Stroup, and J.L. Gerberding. 2004. "Actual Causes of Death in the United States, 2000." *JAMA* 291(10):1238–45.

Moore, L.V. and A.V. Diez-Roux. 2006. "Associations of Neighborhood Characteristics with the Location and Type of Food Stores." *American Journal of Public Health* 96:325–31.

Moreland, K.B. and K.R. Evenson. 2009. "Obesity Prevalence and the Local Food Environment." *Health and Place* 15(2):491–95.

Morland, K., S. Wing, and A. Diex Roux. 2002. "The Contextual Effect of the Local Food Environment on Residents' Diets: The Atherosclerosis Risk in Communities Study." *American Journal of Public Health* 92(11):1761–68

Morland, K., S. Wing, A. Diez Roux, and C. Poole. 2002. "Neighborhood Characteristics Associated with the Location of Food Stores and Food Service Places." *American Journal of Preventive Medicine* 22(1):23–29.

National Oceanic and Atmospheric Administration. 1999. *NOAA's Top Global Weather, Water and Climate Events of the 20th Century.* http://www.noaanews.noaa.gov/stories/s334b.htm . Retrieved January, 2010.

Newman, O. 1972. *Defensible Space: Crime Prevention Through Urban Design.* New York, NY, Macmillan.

Noji, E.K. 1992. "Acute Renal Failure in Natural Disasters." *Renal Failure* 14(3):245–49.

Northridge, M.E., E.D. Sclar, and P. Biswas. 2003. "Sorting Out the Connections Between the Built Environment and Health: A Conceptual Framework for Navigating Pathways and Planning Healthy Cities." *Journal of Urban Health: Bulletin of the New York Academy of Medicine* 80(4):556–68.

Ohl, C.A. and S. Tapsell. 2000. "Flooding and Human Health: The Dangers Posed Are Not Always Obvious." *British Medical Journal* 321(7270):1167–68.

Oxfam. 2005. "Gender and the Tsunami." *Oxfam Briefing Note.* www.oxfamamerica.org

O'Neill, M.S., A. Zanobetti, and J. Schwartz. 2003. "Modifiers of the Temperature and Mortality Association in Seven US Cities." *American Journal of Epidemiology* 157(12):1074–82.

Palm, R. and J. Carroll. 1998. *Illusions of Safety: Culture and Earthquake Hazard Response in California and Japan.* Boulder, CO, Westview Press.

Perdue, W.C., L.O. Gostin, and L.A. Stone. 2003. "Public Health and the Built Environment: Historical, Empirical, and Theoretical Foundations for an Expanded Role." *The Journal of Law, Medicine & Ethics* 31(4):557–66.

Perry, R.W. 1987. "Disaster preparedness and response among minority citizens." In: R.R Dynes, B. de Marchi, and C. Pelanda (eds.), *Sociology of Disasters: Contributions of Sociology to Disaster Research,* pp. 135–151. Milan, F Angeli Libri.

Perry, R.W. and M.K. Lindell. 1991. "The Effects of Ethnicity on Evacuation Decision-Making." *International Journal of Mass Emergencies and Disasters* 9(1):47–68.

Perry, T., E. Matsui, B. Merriman, T. Duong, and P. Eggleston. 2003. "The Prevalence of Rat Allergen in Inner-City Homes and Its Relationship to Sensitization and Asthma Morbidity." *The Journal of Allergy and Clinical Immunology* 112(2):346–52.

Picou, J.S. and B.K. Marshall. 2007. "Introduction: Katrina as a Paradigm Shift: Reflections on Disaster Research in the Twenty-First Century." In D.L. Brunsma, D. Overfelt, and J.S. Picou (eds.), *The Sociology of Katrina: Perspective on a*

*Modern Catastrophe*, pp. 1–22. Lanham, MD, Rowman and Littefield.

Pirard, P., S. Vandentorren, M. Pascal, K. Laaidi, A. Le Tertre, S. Cassadou, and M. Ledrans. 2005. "Summary of the Mortality Impact Assessment of the 2003 Heat Wave in France." *Euro Surveillance: Bulletin Europeen Sur Les Maladies Transmissibles = European Communicable Disease Bulletin* 10(7):153–56.

Poumadere, M., C. Mays, S. Le Mer, R. Blong, and N. Ryde. 2005. "The 2003 Heat Wave in France: Dangerous Climate Change Here and Now." *Risk Analysis* 25(6):1483–94.

Putnam, R.D. 1995. "Bowling Alone: America's Declining Social Capital." *Journal of Democracy* 6:65–78.

Reichert, T.A., L. Simonsen, A. Sharma, S.A. Pardo, D.S. Fedson, and M.A. Miller. 2004. "Influenza and the Winter Increase in Mortality in the United States, 1959–1999." *American Journal of Epidemiology* 160(5): 492–502.

Reidpath D, C. Burns, J. Garrand, M. Mahoney, and M. Townsend. 2002. "An Ecological Study of the Relationship between Social and Environmental Determinants of Obesity." *Health and Place* 8:141–45.

Rittner, B. and A.B. Kirk. 1995. "Health Care and Public Transportation Use by Poor and Frail Elderly People." *Social Work* 40(3):365–73.

Ross, C.E. and S.J. Jang. 2000. "Neighborhood Disorder, Fear, and Mistrust: The Buffering Role of Social Ties with Neighbors." *American Journal of Community Psychology* 28(4):401–20.

Ross, C.E. and J. Mirowsky. 2001. "Neighborhood Disadvantage, Disorder, and Health." *Journal of Health and Social Behavior* 42(3):258–76.

Ross, C.E. and J. Mirowsky. 1999. "Disorder and Decay: The Concept and Measurement of Perceived Neighborhood Disorder." *Urban Affairs Review* 34(3): 412–32.

Ross, C.E., J. Mirowsky, and S. Pribesh. 2001. "Powerlessness and the Amplification of Threat: Neighborhood Disadvantage, Disorder, and Mistrust." *American Sociological Review* 66(4):568–91.

Rutt, C.D. and K.J. Coleman. 2005. "Examining the Relationships among Built Environment, Physical Activity, and Body Mass Index in El Paso, TX." *Preventive Medicine* 40(6):831–41.

Saelens, B.E., J.F. Sallis, J.B. Black, and D. Chen. 2003a. "Neighborhood-Based Differences in Physical Activity: An Environment Scale Evaluation." *American Journal of Public Health* 93(9):1552–58.

Saelens, B.E., J.F. Sallis, and L.D. Frank. 2003b. "Environmental Correlates of Walking and Cycling: Findings from the Transportation, Urban Design, and Planning Literatures." *Annals of Behavioral Medicine* 25(2):80–91.

Sallis, J.F., M.F. Johnson, K.J. Calfas, S. Caparosa, and J.F. Nichols. 1997. "Assessing Perceived Physical Environmental Variables that may Influence Physical Activity." *Research Quarterly for Exercise and Sport* 68(4): 345–51.

Sampson, R.J., S.W. Raudenbush, and F. Earls. 1997. "Neighborhoods and Violent Crime: A Multilevel Study of Collective Efficacy." *Science* 277(5328):918–24.

Sarpong, S.B., R.G. Hamilton, P.A. Eggleston, and N.F. Adkinson. 1996. "Socioeconomic Status and Race as Risk Factors for Cockroach Allergen Exposure and Sensitization in Children with Asthma." *Journal of Allergy and Clinical Immunology* 97(6):1393–401.

Schwartz, J. 1988. "The Relationship between Blood Lead and Blood Pressure in the NHANES II Survey." *Environmental Health Perspectives* 78:15–22.

Seeman, T.E., B.H. Singer, J.W. Rowe, R.I. Horwitz, and B.S. McEwen. 1997. "Price of Adaptation–Allostatic Load and its Health Consequences. Macarthur Studies of Successful Aging." *Archives of Internal Medicine* 157(19): 2259–68.

Skogan, W.G. 1990. *Disorder and Decline: Crime and the Spiral of Decay in American Neighborhoods*. New York, NY, Free Press.

Sooman, A., S. Macintyre, and A. Anderson. 1993. "Scotland's Health: A More Difficult Challenge for Some? The Price and Availability of Healthy Foods in Socially Contrasting Localities in the West of Scotland." *Health Bulletin* 51(5):276–84.

Stafford, M., T. Chandola, and M. Marmot. 2007. "Association between Fear of Crime and Mental Health and Physical Functioning." *American Journal of Public Health* 97(11):2076–81.

Stott, P.A., D.A. Stone, and M.R. Allen 2004. "Human Contribution to the European Heatwave of 2003." *Nature* 432:610–14.

Stuck, A.E., J.M. Walthert, T. Nikolaus, C.J. Büla, C. Hohmann, and J.C. Beck. 1999. "Risk Factors for Functional Status Decline in Community-Living Elderly People: A Systematic Literature Review." *Social Science and Medicine* 48(4):445–69.

Trowbridge, M.J., M.J. Gurka, and R.E. O'Connor. 2009. "Urban Sprawl and Delayed Ambulance Arrival in the US." *American Journal of Preventive Medicine* 37(5): 428–32.

Turner, R.H., J.M. Nigg, and D.H. Paz. 1986. *Waiting for Disaster: Earthquake Watch in California*. Berkeley, CA, University of California Press.

Unger, J.B., C.A. Johnson, and G. Marks. 1997. "Functional Decline in the Elderly: Evidence for Direct and Stress-Buffering Protective Effects of Social Interactions and Physical Activity." *Annals of Behavioral Medicine* 19(2):152–60.

United States Geological Survey. 2009. *Earthquakes with 1,000 or More Deaths Since 1900*. http://earthquake.usgs.gov/earth quakes/world/world_deaths.php. Retrieved January, 2010.

Van Metre, P.C., B.J. Mahler, and E.T. Furlong. 2000. "Urban Sprawl Leaves Its PAH Signature." *Environmental Science & Technology* 34(19):4064–70.

Wilcox, S., C. Castro, A.C. King, R. Housemann, and R.C. Brownson. 2000. "Determinants of Leisure Time Physical Activity in Rural Compared with Urban Older and Ethnically Diverse Women in the United States." *Journal of Epidemiology and Community Health* 54(9): 667–72.

Wilhelm, M., L. Qian, and B. Ritz. 2009. "Outdoor Air Pollution, Family and Neighborhood Environment, and Asthma in LA FANS Children." *Health and Place* 15(1):25–36.

Wilson, J.Q. and G. Kelling. 1982. "The Police and Neighborhood Safety: Broken Windows." *Atlantic Monthly* 249(3):29–38.

Winkler, E., G. Turrell, and C. Patterson. 2006. "Does Living in a Disadvantaged Area Mean Fewer Opportunities to Purchase Fresh Fruit and Vegetables in the Area? Findings from the Brisbane Food Study." *Health and Place* 12(3):306–19.

Wisner, B., B. Wisner, and P.M. Blaikie. 2004. *At Risk: Natural Hazards, People's Vulnerability and Disasters*. New York, NY, Routledge.

Wolman, H., G. Galster, R. Hanson, M. Ratcliffe, K. Furdell, and A. Sarzynski. 2005. "The Fundamental Challenge in Measuring Sprawl: Which Land Should Be Considered?" *The Professional Geographer* 57(1): 94–105.

Zenk, S.N., A.J. Shultz, B.A. Isreal, S.A. James, S. Bao, and M.L. Wilson. 2005. "Neighborhood Racial Composition, Neighborhood Poverty, and the Spatial Accessibility of Supermarkets in Metropolitan Detroit." *American Journal of Public Health* 94:1549–54.

# Part V
# Classification of Causes of Death

# Chapter 22
# Coding and Classifying Causes of Death: Trends and International Differences

Robert N. Anderson

## Introduction

Knowing why and how people die is of critical importance in understanding the nature and magnitude of health problems in a population and in the planning, implementation, and evaluation of public-health strategies and programs (Byass 2007; Hill 2006; Mathers et al. 2005; Ruzicka and Lopez 1990; Sharma 2008; Woolsey 1978; World Health Organization [WHO] 2008). Data on causes of death are the most widely available and frequently used data for these purposes and are a staple of public-health statistics.

Developing and evaluating effective public-health interventions requires cause-of-death information that is accurate, comparable, and timely. Unfortunately, these criteria are not always met. The quality and availability of cause-of-death data vary widely from country to country. Problems are particularly evident in those countries with the highest burden of disease (Mathers et al. 2005; Murray et al. 2004; Sibai 2004). The majority of deaths occur in these countries, yet there are large gaps in our knowledge about the health and mortality of their populations. Even among countries where the completeness and coverage of the collection of cause-of-death information approach 100%, there is significant variation that may result in comparability problems. Differences exist in data collection methods, in the standards used for classifying and coding the cause of death, and in the tabulation and presentation of data.

An understanding of how cause-of-death data are collected, classified and coded, and presented is vital for individuals who conduct public-health research. One must understand the limitations of the existing data to effectively interpret research findings and apply these in the development of effective interventions and policy. Variations and changes in the way the cause-of-death is collected, classified, and coded can result in comparability problems that can dramatically affect the interpretation of national trends and international comparisons.

The purpose of this chapter is to provide an overview of the major issues related to the collection, classification, coding, and analysis of cause-specific mortality. The chapter is divided into four sections. The first section focuses on how and from whom cause-of-death data are collected and includes discussion of issues related to the accuracy of cause-of-death data. The second section describes the classification and coding of cause-of-death information, including the selection of the underlying cause of death. The third section summarizes some of the changes in cause-of-death classification over time and how these changes impact the analysis of trends. The fourth section presents some issues related to the tabulation and presentation of cause-specific mortality data, especially those affecting international comparisons. Finally, the chapter concludes with a summary of the key issues and a discussion of future developments.

R.N. Anderson (✉)
Mortality Statistics Branch, Division of Vital Statistics, National Center for Health Statistics, Centers for Disease Control and Prevention, Hyattsville, MD 20782, USA
e-mail: rca7@cdc.gov

## Collection of Cause-of-Death Information

### Civil Registration Systems

Cause-of-death information is most commonly derived from civil registration systems. The registration of vital events dates back to ancient times (e.g., Egypt, Greece, Rome, China) when births and deaths were recorded primarily for administrative purposes, such as taxation and military conscription (United Nations 1991). In medieval Europe, birth and death records were kept primarily for religious reasons. Over time, the purpose, especially for death records, expanded to include public health. In fifteenth century Italy, boards of health were organized to deal with the repeated epidemics of plague. Among other strategies, in an attempt to stay informed, these boards mandated the recording of cause of death (Hays 1998). In seventeenth century England, a similar strategy for containing the plague led to the development of the London Bills of Mortality, which included the cause of death (Graunt 1662). Eventually, these strategies evolved into modern civil death registration systems, making possible the continuous collection of information on each death, including both characteristics of the decedent and the circumstances surrounding the death, including the cause of death.

### The Death Certificate

Cause-of-death information derived from civil registration systems is typically collected on a death certificate or death notification form. The World Health Organization (WHO) has developed a standard format for the medical portion of the death certificate—the International Form of Medical Certificate of Cause of Death (Fig. 22.1; WHO 2004a, b). Causes of death include "all those diseases, morbid conditions or injuries which either resulted in or contributed to death and the circumstances of the accident or violence which produced these injuries" (WHO 2004b: 33). The medical certification of death is divided into two sections. In Part I, the certifier (usually a physician) is asked to provide the causal chain of morbid conditions that led to death, beginning with the condition most proximate to death on line (a) and working backward to the initiating condition. The lines (a) through (d) in Part I are connected by the phrase "due to, or as a consequence of." This format was designed to elicit a causally related sequence of medical conditions that resulted in death. Thus, the condition on line (a) should be due to the condition on line (b), which in turn should be a consequence of the condition on line (c), and so forth, until the full sequence is described back to the originating or initiating condition. If only one step in the chain of morbid events is recorded, a

**Fig. 22.1** International form of medical certificate of cause of death. Source: WHO. 2004b. *International Statistical Classification of Diseases and Related Health Problems, Vol. 2*

**Fig. 22.2** An example of proper cause-of-death certification

| | Cause of death | Approximate interval between onset and death |
|---|---|---|
| **I** Disease or condition directly leading to death* | (a) Rupture of left ventricle | Minutes |
| | due to (or as a consequence of) | |
| *Antecedent causes* Morbid conditions, if any, giving rise to the above cause, stating the underlying condition last | (b) Acute myocardial infarction | 2 days |
| | due to (or as a consequence of) | |
| | (c) Coronary atherosclerosis | 2 years |
| | due to (or as a consequence of) | |
| | (d) ............ | ............ |
| **II** Other significant conditions contributing to the death, but not related to the disease or condition causing it | Diabetes mellitus | Years |
| | Hypertension | Years |

*This does not mean the mode of dying, e.g. heart failure, respiratory failure. It means the disease, injury, or complication that caused death.

single entry on line (a) is adequate. Part I of the medical certification is designed to facilitate the selection of the underlying cause of death when two or more causes are recorded on the certificate. The underlying cause of death is defined as "(a) the disease or injury which initiated the train of morbid events leading directly to death, or (b) the circumstances of the accident or violence which produced the fatal injury" (WHO 2004b: 34) and is generally considered the most useful cause from a public-health standpoint. Part II solicits other conditions that the physician believed contributed to death, but were not in the causal chain. An example of a properly completed cause-of-death statement is shown in Fig. 22.2. The conditions shown are logically linked in terms of time, etiology, and pathology.

The primary purpose of the International Form is to provide a standardized mechanism for collecting the cause-of-death statement, thereby promoting comparability in international mortality statistics. While many countries use the International Form or some close variant, many other countries do not. Variation or changes in format can result in incomparable cause-of-death statistics and discontinuous trends (Hoyert et al. 2000; Johansson 2000; Jougla et al. 1998; Ohmi and Yamamoto 2000). Even small, seemingly innocuous changes can have an important impact. For example, in 1989, the United States changed the cause-of-death section of its standard death certificate to add an additional line to Part I, increasing from three lines to four, and added instructions and examples of proper cause-of-death certification (Hoyert et al. 2000). One important effect of this change was to increase the likelihood of diabetes being reported as the underlying cause of death. As a result, the death rate due to diabetes increased nearly 14% from 1988 to 1989, the largest change since 1949 (MacDorman and Hudson 1992).

## Cause-of-Death Certifiers

The cause-of-death section of the death certificate or notification form is most appropriately and most commonly completed by a physician. Physicians, more than other medical practitioners, have the clinical expertise and judgment needed to identify the underlying cause and any other conditions that may have contributed to death. In most countries with civil registration systems, when the manner of death is natural, the attending physician typically has responsibility for certifying the cause of death. When the death is unattended, due to injury or poisoning, or occurs under suspicious circumstances, certification of the cause of death is often the jurisdiction of a medicolegal officer (e.g., a medical examiner or coroner) or the police, who typically retain a physician to determine the cause of death. Most jurisdictions and countries require that the certifier be a physician. But in some jurisdictions and countries, someone other than a physician may certify the cause of death. For example, coroners in the United States, the United Kingdom, and Australia are not necessarily physicians. Also, nurse practitioners and hospice nurses are allowed to certify natural deaths in a few states in the United States and nurse midwives and dentists may certify some natural deaths in Korea and Japan. In places where physicians are scarce and the death is not attended by a physician, the cause of death may be reported by a community or tribal leader.

## *Other Strategies for Collecting Cause-of-Death Information*

Almost all countries have legislation mandating civil registrations systems, but many either are not functioning or do not cover the entire population (Mathers et al. 2005; Sibai 2004). In these cases, other strategies may be used to collect and compile cause-of-death statistics. These strategies address two major problems. First, if coverage of the civil registration system is incomplete, the system will undercount deaths due to all causes. Second, even if all deaths are registered, if a large proportion of deaths are not attended by medical practitioners, cause-of-death information will be missing or, at best, unreliable.

Sample registration systems, such as that currently used in China and India, can provide reasonable estimates of mortality for countries with poor coverage (Jha et al. 2006; Kumar et al. 2007; Mathers et al. 2005; Setel et al. 2006). Sample registration systems typically involve periodic (usually monthly) monitoring of a random selection of households for vital events—both births and deaths. Members of the household are then interviewed to obtain details about the event, including, in the case of deaths, the cause of death. Cause-of-death information obtained through sample registration systems is typically reported by household members with no medical training. The value of these data has, therefore, been suspect. Verbal autopsy is a tool used to improve the quality and utility of cause-of-death information collected by survey (Baiden et al. 2007; Chandramohan et al. 2005; Murray et al. 2007a; Soleman et al. 2006) and has been used effectively in combination with sample registration systems to estimate cause-specific mortality in both India and China (Jha et al. 2006; Setel et al. 2005). Work has also been done to validate and test methods in several African countries, including Tanzania, Ghana, and Ethiopia (King and Lu 2008; Quigley et al. 1999, 2000). While verbal autopsy techniques have been in use for several decades, there is substantial variation in methodology, including instrument design, methods for assigning an underlying cause, and cause-of-death lists (Murray et al. 2007a). More recently, a renewed interest in mortality data for developing countries has prompted the development of standards for verbal autopsy (Setel et al. 2006; WHO 2007). Work has also been done recently to estimate cause-specific mortality using data on in-hospital deaths, which are typically available even in the poorest countries (Murray et al. 2007b).

While verbal autopsy is a useful strategy for estimating cause-specific mortality in countries where there is no reliable cause-of-death reporting, it is at best only a crude substitute for proper medical certification of cause of death (Setel et al. 2005, 2006). Other chapters in this volume discuss more fully the issues related to estimating cause-specific mortality in Latin America (Chapter 5 by Palloni and Pinto-Aguirre), Asia (Chapter 6 by Zhao), and Africa (Chapter 7 by Reniers, Masquelier, and Gerland).

## *Accuracy of Cause-of-Death Statements*

A proper cause-of-death statement should represent the best medical opinion of the certifier as to the cause of and circumstances surrounding the death. Given the importance of cause-of-death statistics as a critical information source for health programs and policy, there is naturally much concern regarding the accuracy of cause-of-death statements on which these statistics are based.

There are at least four factors that may adversely affect the accuracy of cause-of-death statements. First, many certifiers do not understand the importance of the cause-of-death statement. Often, the death certificate is viewed as an administrative nuisance and may be delegated to less-experienced physicians with sometimes little or no clinical contact with the decedent (Kircher and Anderson 1987). Such an attitude leads to carelessness and often results in modes of dying, for example, cardiac or respiratory arrest, reported as the cause of death. Second, certifiers are rarely trained in formulating and writing proper cause-of-death statements. The result is often a cause-of-death sequence that does not make sense. In some cases, the certifier may simply copy the layout of the discharge diagnoses from the medical record directly onto the death certificate (Lu et al. 2006). Discharge diagnoses are intended to elicit the reason for admission and the severity of disease. The cause-of-death statement, in contrast, is intended to elicit the chain of events leading to death and the underlying cause of death. Third, clinical-autopsy rates have been declining worldwide (Burton and Underwood 2007; Chariot et al. 2000; Dalen 1997; Harrington and Sayre 2007; Peacock et al. 1988; Start et al. 1995; Wood and Guha 2001) for various reasons (Hanzlick and Baker 1998). The clinical autopsy is invaluable for educating physicians and improving clinical diagnosis and is particularly useful for determining the cause of death in cases where clinical information on the decedent is ambiguous or missing (Hanzlick 2001; Hanzlick and Baker 1998; Kircher et al. 1985; Kock et al. 2003; Shojiana and Burton 2004; Shojiana et al. 2002; Wood and Guha 2001). Fourth, the circumstances of some deaths are such that the cause of death is very difficult to determine. With autopsy rates declining, there is increasing potential for misdiagnosis and inaccurate certification, especially in these more difficult cases. In approximately 5% of autopsied deaths, the cause of death cannot be determined (Lahti and Penttilä 2001; Shojiana et al. 2002). Furthermore, it may be difficult to distinguish between the underlying cause of death and contributing causes for decedents suffering from multiple, concurrent chronic conditions (Gorina and Lentzner 2008; Hadley 1992; Moriyama 1989; Stallard 2002). This makes proper certification, i.e., choosing a primary sequence of events and an underlying cause, very difficult.

Given the potential for inaccuracies, it is unsurprising that much has been written regarding the accuracy of cause-of-death statements and the statistics on which they are based (D'Amico et al. 1999; Gittelsohn and Royston 1982; Jewell 2007; Kircher et al. 1985; Moriyama 1989; NCVHS 1989, 1991; Sehdev and Hutchins 2001; Sharp et al. 2001). Ironically, most of the criticism of the quality of cause-of-death statements is published by physicians—those who have primary responsibility for providing this information. Studies to determine the accuracy of cause-of-death statements generally rely on two standards for comparison: autopsy results (see, e.g., Kircher et al. 1985; Kock et al. 2003; Sington and Cottrell 2002) and clinical records (see Coady et al. 2001; Iribarren et al. 1998; Johansson and Westerling 2002; Muhlhauser et al. 2002; Percy et al. 1981). These studies have generally found varying degrees of accuracy overall and substantial variation by cause of death (Johansson et al. 2006; Laurenti et al. 2000; Moriyama 1989). Deaths due to neoplasms (e.g., cancer) tended to be most accurately diagnosed, and those involving circulatory or digestive diseases tended to be least accurate (Kircher et al. 1985; Percy et al. 1981). However, while it is logical that differences in the difficulty of diagnosis would result in variation by cause of death, contradictory results have been noted even for studies examining the same cause of death (Johansson et al. 2006). While these studies are informative and highlight the problems associated with cause-of-death certification, the lack of consistency in the results of these studies and differences in coverage and methodology make it difficult to draw definitive conclusions about the prevalence of these problems (Moriyama 1989; Rosenberg 1989; Sirken et al. 1987). That is, we do not really know the true extent of inaccuracies.

Even though autopsy is generally viewed as the "gold standard" in determining the cause of death, the findings of autopsy-based studies, while informative, tend to be less than representative, suffering from selection bias. Those deaths chosen for clinical autopsy tend to be the most difficult cases and, therefore, would tend to naturally have lower rates of accuracy (Moriyama 1989). As a result, these studies likely underestimate the accuracy of cause-of-death statements overall. In addition, autopsy-based studies typically compare autopsy results with physicians' initial cause-of-death diagnoses. When an autopsy is done, the results are often used to certify the final cause of death. Cause-of-death statistics, in these cases, would be based on the autopsy results and not on the initial diagnosis. Thus, what these studies are measuring is the difficulty of diagnosis without autopsy rather than the accuracy of cause-of-death statistics.

Studies based on review of clinical records typically employ a panel of physicians to retrospectively review clinical records for a sample of decedents and determine their causes of death. The panel's determination is then compared with that of the certifying physician. Because clinical records typically focus on treatment and patient care, the emphasis may be on the immediate cause of death (e.g., infections, pneumonia) or complications (e.g., heart failure, kidney failure) rather than the underlying cause of death (Johansson et al. 2006). In addition, the panels reviewing the clinical records do not always have all the information that is available to the certifier. Medical records may be incomplete and may omit some information to which the certifier is privy (Kircher and Anderson 1987; Moriyama 1989). Even if all of the information is available to the review panel, the more difficult cases (e.g., decedents suffering from multiple chronic conditions) may result in several possible valid opinions as to the cause of death, rendering the "true" cause of death impossible to determine (Kircher and Anderson 1987). Finally, these studies generally focus on what was written by the certifying physician and do not typically take into account the underlying cause of death registered by the agency in charge of mortality statistics (Johansson et al. 2006). Because errors may occur in completing the cause-of-death statement, a set of standardized rules are used to select the best underlying cause from the information provided by the certifier (see "Selection of the Underlying Cause of Death" in Section "The International Classification of Diseases"). Thus, although informative, evaluating cause-of-death statements does not necessarily provide a correct assessment of the quality of cause-of-death statistics (Johansson et al. 2006; Sirken et al. 1987).

While studies of the accuracy of cause-of-death statements must be interpreted with caution, the results of these studies, along with more objective measures of statistical quality, such as the percent of reported conditions that are ill-defined or non-specific (Mathers et al. 2005) or the percent of statements with invalid sequences (Lu et al. 2006), underscore the need for improvements. There are multiple strategies with the potential to improve cause-of-death statements and the statistics on which they are based. Foremost among these strategies is to train cause-of-death certifiers how to properly complete the cause-of-death statement. Despite strong recommendations for training curricula (e.g., NCVHS 1989, 1991), most physicians still receive little or no training in medical school or through continuing medical education programs. Materials, instructions, and tutorials are available in print and on the Internet (Eurostat 2008; Hanzlick 1994; ISTAT 2003; Kircher and Anderson 1987; NCHS 2004; NYC 2008; Pace et al. 2005), yet they do not seem to be widely disseminated among physicians. Such materials and training can be effective in improving cause-of-death statements (Jougla et al. 1998; Pace and Grippo 2006; Pavillon et al. 2000; Villar and Perez-Mendez 2007).

Cause-of-death querying, the process in which the agency responsible for compiling mortality statistics contacts the cause-of-death certifier for clarification or more information regarding the cause of death, can also be very effective in ensuring and improving the quality of cause-of-death statistics (Hanzlick 1996; Hopkins et al. 1989; Hoyert and Lima 2005; Lahti and Penttilä 2003; Lu and Huang 2002; NCHS 2007; Rosenberg 1989). Querying the certifier not only provides quality assurance, but also provides an effective way to educate the physician in proper cause-of-death certification (Rosenberg 1989).

## The International Classification of Diseases

### History

The International Classification of Diseases (ICD) is published by the WHO and provides standardized guidelines for reporting and coding causes of death. The stated purpose of the ICD is "to permit the systematic recording, analysis, interpretation and comparison of mortality and morbidity data collected in different countries or areas and at different times" (WHO 2004b: 3). Translation of the information reported by the certifier on death certificates into a set of standardized alphanumeric codes allows for the easy storage, retrieval, and analysis of the data. The ICD also facilitates the aggregation and tabulation of causes of death categories.

Attempts to develop systematic and comprehensive disease classifications date back to the eighteenth century (Cullen 1772; Sauvages de la Croix 1763). By the mid-nineteenth century, the importance of a uniform classification of causes of death for statistical purposes was widely recognized (Registrar General of England and Wales 1839; WHO 2004b). In 1893, Jacques Bertillon, Chief of Statistical Services of the City of Paris developed, at the request of the International Statistical Institute, a statistical classification of causes of death. The International List of Causes of Death, or the Bertillon Classification as it was typically called,

**Table 22.1** Ten revisions of the International Classification of Diseases (ICD)

| Revision of the ICD | Adopted |
|---|---|
| First | 1900 |
| Second | 1909 |
| Third | 1920 |
| Fourth | 1929 |
| Fifth | 1938 |
| Sixth | 1948 |
| Seventh | 1955 |
| Eighth | 1965 |
| Ninth | 1975 |
| Tenth | 1989 |

Source: History of the development of the ICD. 2004. In International Statistical Classification of Diseases and Related Health Problems, Tenth Revision, Volume 2, 2nd ed. pp. 147–59. Geneva, World Health Organization.

was adopted by several countries and was endorsed both by the International Statistical Institute and the American Public Health Association, which recommended adoption of the list and suggested that it be revised every 10 years (Institute of International Statistics 1900) to accommodate changes in terminology and advancements in medical knowledge. In August 1900, the first International Conference for the Revision of the Bertillon or International List of Causes of Death was convened in Paris and attended by delegates from 26 countries. The result is what is now referred to as the first revision of the ICD, a classification of causes of death consisting of 179 categories (US Bureau of the Census 1900). The ICD has been revised nine times since the first revision (Table 22.1). Over the years, the ICD has evolved from a simple list of causes of death into a much more detailed classification of diseases used widely for both mortality and morbidity statistics.

The growing need for a more extensive classification for morbidity prompted the United States to modify the eighth revision of the ICD. The eighth revision of the ICD, adapted for use in the United States (ICDA-8) was used for mortality and morbidity classification in both the US and Canada (National Center for Health Statistics 1968). ICDA-8 is generally consistent with ICD-8, but gives greater detail and specificity, especially for circulatory diseases.

The tenth revision of the ICD (ICD-10) is the most recent revision of the ICD. It was first published in 1992 and, by 2002 was being widely used by WHO member countries for cause-of-death classification (WHO 2004a). ICD-10 is published in three volumes. Volume 1 contains a tabular list of alphanumeric codes, a set of standard tabulation lists for the statistical presentation of mortality data, standard definitions (e.g., live birth, maternal death), and reporting requirements. Volume 2 is the instruction manual, which provides guidance on the use of Volume 1, including coding instructions, a standard format for collecting cause-of-death information, and a history of the ICD. Volume 3 is the alphabetical index.

The ICD has been revised roughly every 10 years until the most recent revision (WHO 2004a). Although there were 14 years between adoption of ICD-9 and ICD-10, it was actually a longer period between the time ICD-9 was published (WHO 1977) and the time ICD-10 was published and complete (the tabular list was first published in 1992, but the alphabetical index was not published until 1994). Because full and proper implementation of the ICD cannot take place without the alphabetical index, it was nearly 20 years before most member countries began to make the transition from ICD-9 to ICD-10. During this period, as in others, medical knowledge continued to advance and medical terminology continued to evolve. This period also saw the emergence of new diseases, most notably HIV. Without a mechanism to update the ICD over such a long period, ICD-9 became increasingly anachronistic. Member countries were left to develop their own methods for coding and tabulating emerging diseases, running the risk of decreased international comparability. For example, in 1987, the United States assigned codes 042–044 to HIV disease, although these codes were not officially part of ICD-9 (NCHS 1988). While some other member countries followed the lead of the United States, the WHO, and many other countries, did not. HIV disease did not officially become part of the ICD until the tenth revision. To avoid this lapse in the future, a mechanism was implemented with ICD-10 to allow for updates between revisions. Two separate bodies were established to manage the updating process: the Mortality Reference Group (MRG) and the Updating and Revision Committee (URC).

The eleventh revision (ICD-11) is currently under development by the WHO. Plans are for completion and adoption by the World Health Assembly in 2014 with implementation in WHO member states in the following years. It is likely that ICD-11 will be generally similar in structure and content to ICD-10.

## Cause-of-Death Coding

The attribution of a single cause of death to each decedent has long been recognized by statisticians as desirable. Doing so facilitates the statistical tabulation, presentation, and analysis of cause-of-death data. However, more than one-half of all deaths have more than two conditions reported. When more than one cause is reported by the certifier, as is often the case, which of the multiple causes does one choose? This was a major challenge for statisticians of earlier generations. In the US Bureau of the Census' publication of the first revision of the ICD, the author of the introduction states, "[t]his is one of the most annoying and difficult subjects ... that occurs in the practical compilation of mortality statistics" (US Bureau of the Census 1900: 12). Fortunately, some solutions have been developed, and these have evolved over time, culminating in the development of the concept of the underlying cause of death.

With publication of the first revision, the US Bureau of the Census developed a set of rules for dealing with "jointly reported causes of death" (US Bureau of the Census 1900). These rules would allow for the selection of a single cause from among two or more causes reported on the death certificate. For example, these rules indicate a preference for primary diseases over their complications and communicable diseases and injury (i.e., diseases with more rapid evolution) over chronic diseases, except in cases where the communicable disease or injury is considered trivial in comparison. In 1914, the United States produced a manual that refined and systematized these rules (US Bureau of the Census 1914). The *Manual of Joint Causes of Death* was not intended to be an authoritative manual, but rather "a temporary guide for those who are groping for help in making their assignments ..." (US Bureau of the Census 1925: 1). During the Fifth International Revision Conference (1938), the US Census Bureau was recognized for its efforts and tasked by the Conference to set up an international subcommittee to develop a standard methodology for selecting a single, underlying cause of death. The recommendations of this subcommittee were incorporated into the sixth revision of the ICD (WHO 1948), which presented for the first time the International Form of Medical Certificate of Cause of Death, the concept of the underlying cause of death, and a set of standardized rules for selecting the underlying cause.

## Selection of the Underlying Cause of Death

If the medical portion of the death certificate (or its equivalent) is properly completed, the disease or condition listed on the lowest line used in Part I is usually accepted as the underlying cause of death. This is an application of "The General Principle" (WHO 2004b: 39). The General Principle is applied unless it is highly improbable that the condition on the lowest line used could have given rise to all of the diseases or conditions listed above it. In some cases, the sequence of morbid events entered on the death certificate is not specified correctly. A variety of errors may occur in completing the medical certification of death. Common problems include the following: the causal chain may be listed in reverse order; the distinction between Parts I and II may have been ignored so that the causal sequence in Part I is simply extended unbroken into Part II; or the reported underlying cause is unlikely, in an etiological sense, to have caused the condition listed above it. In addition, sometimes the physician attributes the death to uninformative causes, such as cardiac arrest or pulmonary arrest. The rules for selecting the underlying cause of death were designed to resolve the problems of incorrect or implausible cause-of-death statements. The rules for the tenth revision as updated by the WHO since publication of ICD-10 are described in a National Center for Health Statistics (NCHS) instruction manual (NCHS 2008a). Coding rules beyond the "General Principle" are invoked if the cause-of-death section is completed incorrectly or if their application can improve the specificity and characterization of the cause of death in a manner consistent with the ICD. The rules are applied in two steps: selection of a tentative underlying cause of death, and modification of the tentative underlying cause in view of the other conditions reported on the certificate in either Part I or II. Modification involves several considerations by the medical coder: determining whether conditions in Part II could have given rise to the underlying cause, giving preference to specific terms over generalized terms, and creating linkages of conditions that are consistent with the terminology of the ICD.

## *Multiple Cause-of-Death Coding*

Although it is desirable from the standpoint of statistical presentation to select a single, underlying cause of death for each decedent, the other information reported by the certifier is also useful. Indeed, as the population ages and as the proportion of the population with multiple, concurrent chronic conditions grows, analysis based on a single, underlying cause becomes increasingly unsatisfactory, especially for the very old (Dorn and Moriyama 1964; Guralnick 1966; Israel et al. 1986; NCHS 1984; Tardon et al. 1995). All cause-of-death information reported on the death certificate can and should be coded. The result is what is commonly referred to as "multiple cause data." Multiple-cause data represent all conditions and diseases that were either present in the sequence leading from the underlying cause to the immediate cause (Part I) or contributed to death in some way (Part II) (Israel et al. 1986; NCHS 1984, 2008b).

Underlying cause coding, while complex, requires the codification of only one entity on the death certificate. Multiple-cause coding, on the other hand, requires the coder to code each individual entity reported and apply the appropriate coding rules. This can be time consuming and often requires additional personnel and resources. In addition, the WHO does not require multiple-cause data from member countries. As a result, there are still many countries that only code the underlying cause of death.

## *Automated Coding Systems*

To facilitate the coding of both multiple and underlying cause-of-death data, automated coding systems have been developed in several countries. In 1968, NCHS implemented the use of a computerized algorithm called ACME (automated classification of medical entities) for selection of the underlying cause of death according to the ICD rules (Glenn 1999; Israel 1990). Other software has since been developed to provide automated input to ACME. MICAR (mortality medical indexing, classification, and retrieval) and SuperMICAR (an enhancement of MICAR) allow for the input of the literal text as reported on death certificates by the certifier. An additional software program, TRANSAX (translation of axes) is used to process and produce multiple-cause codes suitable for analysis. Together these computer programs form the mortality medical data system (MMDS) (Glenn 1999).

Automated coding of mortality data has important advantages over manual coding. The computer algorithms allow for more consistent application of the ICD coding and selection rules, resulting in better comparability both nationally and internationally (McKenzie et al. 2001; Rooney 1999; Rosenberg 1999). With this in mind, NCHS organized the International Collaborative Effort (ICE) on Automating Mortality Statistics. The primary purpose of the ICE is to promote the international development and implementation of automated coding systems in order to improve the international comparability of mortality statistics (Rosenberg 1999). As a result of this effort, several countries in addition to the United States have been able to implement such automated coding systems.

English speaking countries, specifically the United Kingdom, Canada, and Australia, have been able to adapt (e.g., for differences in spelling) and use the MMDS (McKenzie et al. 2001; Rooney 1999; Rooney and Devis 1996). Although much of the system is language independent, SuperMICAR, in particular, is not, and efforts to translate to other languages have met with little success. A few countries, most notably Sweden, France, Brazil, Japan, and Mexico, have developed automated systems largely based on ACME (Johansson 2001a; Kimura et al. 2006; Laurenti 2006; Ortega Garcia 2006; Pavillon 2001). But these systems were developed only with considerable effort and expense, making it difficult for other countries with fewer resources or commitment to do likewise. In response to these challenges, the ICE on automation has fostered the development of a language-independent system based on MMDS. This system, called IRIS (not an acronym), was introduced at the most recent meeting of the ICE in May of 2008 (Miniño 2009). IRIS requires only that countries develop a dictionary of terms indexed to their language version of the ICD. IRIS then employs the language-independent components of MMDS resulting in the assignment of an underlying cause of death and a set of multiple-cause codes generally consistent with that produced by MMDS.

## Analyzing Trends Across Revisions of the ICD

With each revision of the ICD there are changes, sometimes substantial, in the coding structure and sometimes in the rules for selecting the underlying cause of death. Consequently, the introduction of a new revision of the ICD often results in comparability problems and major disruptions in cause-of-death trends over time. Major changes in the ICD over time are documented below. See Moriyama et al. (2011) for a more comprehensive description of ICD revisions.

## First-Five Revisions

Each revision of the International List of Causes of Death from the first to the fifth has resulted in some degree of discontinuity (Dunn and Shackley 1944; US Bureau of the Census 1945; Van Buren 1940). Comparability was primarily affected by changes in the international list, including additions, deletions, and renumbering of the list; changes in terminology; and reclassification of terms to different categories. Revision of the *Manual of Joint Causes of Death* also resulted in some comparability issues due to changes in the method for selection of the primary cause. Some specific examples of the effect of revision of the list and of the *Manual of Joint Causes of Death* can be found in Van Buren (1940). These changes were generally minor and discontinuities not particularly problematic for the analysis of cause-of-death trends, at least not for leading causes of death.

## Sixth Revision

The sixth revision of the ICD represented a much more substantial change than any of the previous revisions (Faust and Dolman 1963, 1964). Sixth revision categories were assigned three-digit codes with a fourth digit added as a decimal for subcategories. In addition, the revision involved considerable regrouping of causes of death as well as a major modification in the method for selecting the underlying cause of death. This resulted in serious discontinuities in mortality trends for several causes of death, most notably for diabetes mellitus. Other major causes for which trends were affected by the revision include: septicemia, heart disease, stroke, hypertension, pneumonia, chronic liver disease, and chronic nephritis (kidney disease).

## Seventh, Eighth, and Ninth Revisions

Few substantial changes were made with the seventh, eighth and ninth revisions of the ICD. With the seventh revision, the rules for selecting the underlying cause, introduced with the sixth revision, were recast and simplified, but only very minor revisions to the rules were made (Faust and Dolman 1965). As a result, mortality trends for major causes of death are largely unaffected by the implementation of the seventh revision.

With the eighth revision (both ICD-8 and ICDA-8), a new category was added for the classification of deaths where it was not possible for the certifier to determine whether injuries were accidentally or purposefully inflicted (Klebba and Dolman 1975). This had the impact of reducing deaths assigned to both accidents and suicide. Other major causes of death affected by the eighth revision include diseases of early infancy, arteriosclerosis, and nephritis and nephrosis (kidney disease).

The ninth revision introduced only a few changes in coding rules and only minor revision to the classification structure (Klebba and Scott 1980). Major causes of death affected were chronic obstructive pulmonary diseases (COPD), pneumonia, kidney failure, and diseases of early infancy (perinatal conditions).

## Tenth Revision

The tenth revision saw some substantial changes in both the classification structure and the rules for selecting the underlying cause of death (Anderson et al. 2001; Rooney et al. 2002). It is the most consequential revision of the ICD since the sixth revision. ICD-10 differs from ICD-9 in several respects. The tenth revision is far more detailed than the ninth and previous revisions, with about 8,000 categories compared with about 5,000 categories, and uses alphanumeric codes (a letter followed by two numbers, with a third number in decimal form for subcategories) rather than numeric codes. In addition, significant additions and modifications were made to the chapters in the ICD and to the rules for selecting the underlying cause of death. Major causes of death affected were pneumonia, stroke, septicemia, HIV disease (for those countries that added an HIV code in ICD-9), Alzheimer's disease, sudden infant death syndrome, and certain perinatal conditions.

## Bridge-Coding Studies

To study and assess the effect of an ICD revision on cause-of-death trends, it is necessary to create a bridge between the two revisions. Bridge-coding or comparability studies, as these are often called, allow for the quantification of discontinuities between revisions. To illustrate the need for bridge coding, Fig. 22.3 shows the trend in age-adjusted death rates for nephritis, nephrosis, and nephrotic syndrome (kidney disease) from 1968 to 2005, spanning three revisions of the ICD (eighth, ninth, and tenth). There are clear and substantial discontinuities in the trend corresponding with the implementation of the ninth revision in 1979 and the tenth revision in 1999.

Bridge-coding studies are accomplished by coding data according to both the previous and current revisions. The comparability ratio (CR) is a measure of the discontinuity and is calculated by tabulating deaths according to cause-of-death categories defined by both revisions. The CR for cause-of-death category $i$ is calculated as:

$$\text{CR}_i = \frac{D_i^{\text{Current ICD}}}{D_i^{\text{Previous ICD}}},$$

where $D_i$ is the number of deaths assigned to cause-of-death category $i$. A ratio of 1.0 indicates the same number of deaths assigned to a cause of death under both revisions and denotes that there is no net effect of the revision on that particular cause-of-death category. A ratio less (greater) than 1.0 indicates fewer (more) deaths allocated to cause $i$ in the current revision compared with the previous revision. For example, for the ICD-9 to ICD-10 transition, a ratio of 1.23 for kidney disease indicates that in ICD-10, there were 23% more underlying cause deaths allocated to kidney disease than were allocated to the same cause in ICD-9. Therefore, the effect of the implementation of the tenth revision on kidney disease mortality is to increase the number of underlying cause deaths by 23%. This should be taken into account when analyzing the trend in kidney disease mortality across the two ICD revisions.

Adjustment of trends using comparability ratios can be done by simply multiplying the observed data by

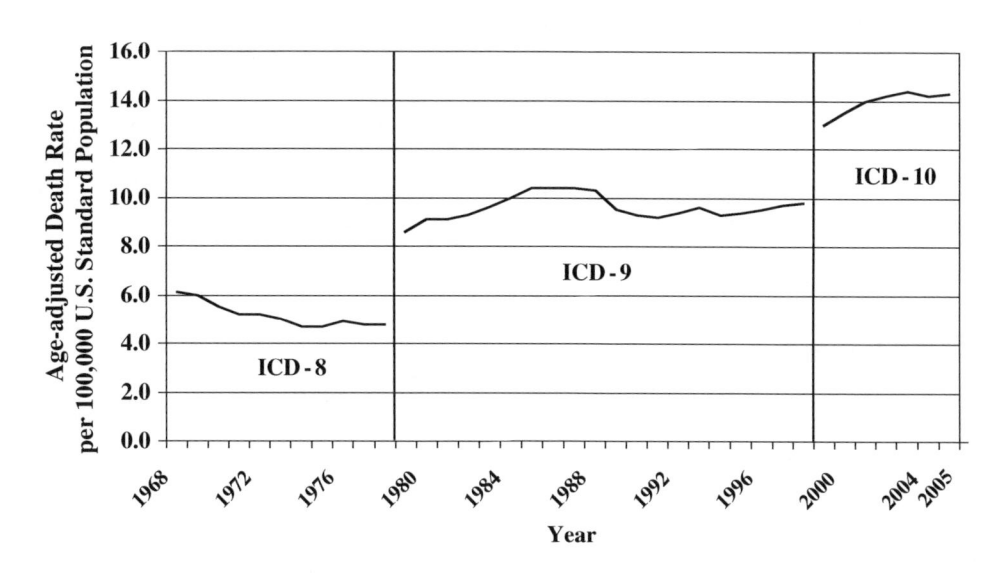

**Fig. 22.3** Age-adjusted death rates for nephritis, nephrotic syndrome, and nephrosis: United States, 1968–2005

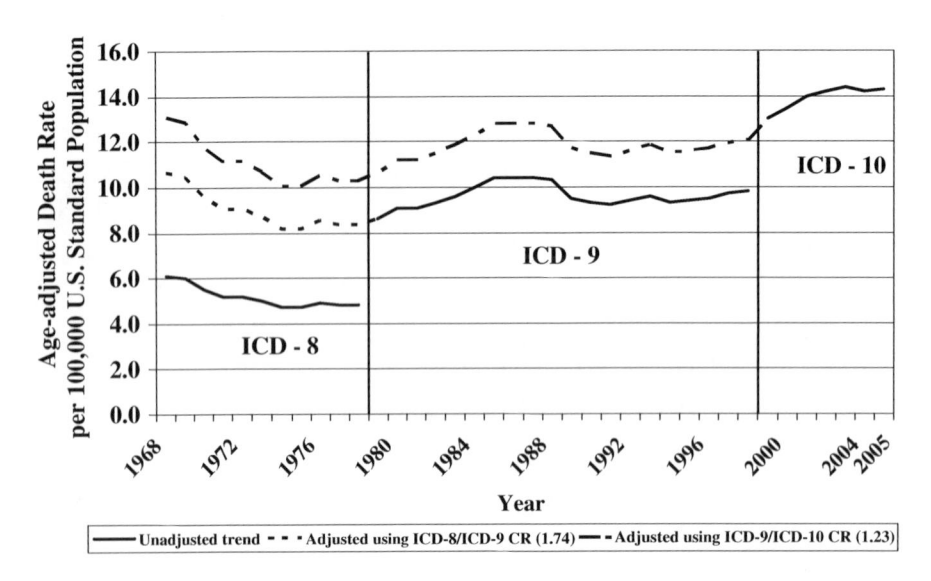

**Fig. 22.4** Age-adjusted death rates for nephritis, nephrotic syndrome, and nephrosis: United States, 1968–2005

the CR. Figure 22.4 shows the adjusted trend in age-adjusted death rates due to kidney disease from 1968 to 2005. Rates from 1968 to 1978 are multiplied by a CR of 1.74, which was derived from a US study bridging the eighth and ninth revisions (Klebba and Scott 1980). These adjusted rates, along with the observed rates for 1979–1998 are then multiplied by 1.23, which was derived from the US study bridging the ninth and tenth revisions (Anderson et al. 2001). The result is a trend of comparable rates without major discontinuities that is much more appropriate for analysis.

That said, one should apply comparability ratios with some caution. Comparability ratios are typically calculated based on the bridge coding of data for a single year. Bridge coding in different years may result in comparability ratios that are different due to changes in the composition of the cause-of-death categories and in certification practices over time. For example, in the US bridge-coding study (Anderson et al. 2001) based on data for 1996, the CR for HIV disease was 1.06. Re-estimation of the CR based on subsequent years (1997 and 1998) resulted in progressively higher ratios. Based on 1998 data, the CR was 1.14. The difference is largely due to changing certification practices (Grigg et al. 2001; Selik et al. 2003). Adjustment of previous data using the 1996 estimate would tend to underestimate mortality for 1997 and 1998, while adjustment using the 1998 estimate would tend to overestimate mortality for 1996 and prior years. Differences in cause-of-death composition and certification practices may also result in both demographic and geographic variation in comparability ratios (Anderson et al. 2001; Rooney et al. 2002).

Bridge-coding studies including comparability ratios have been conducted in the United States for every revision since the sixth revision (Anderson et al. 2001; Faust and Dolman 1964, 1965; Klebba and Dolman 1975; Klebba and Scott 1980). Studies between the ninth and tenth revisions have been done by several other countries, including England and Wales, Japan, Scotland, Sweden, France, Italy, Canada, and Australia (Australian Bureau of Statistics [ABS] 2000; Frova et al. 2010; Geran et al. 2005; Johansson 2001b; Ohmi and Yamamoto 2000; Pavillon et al. 2005; Registrar General of Scotland 2001; Rooney et al. 2002). These studies have generally produced similar results, although some differences are evident. The variation is due primarily to differences in the distribution of causes of death and differences in cause-of-death certification practices (Rooney et al. 2002).

# Tabulation and Presentation of Cause-of-Death Data

The presentation of mortality statistics is typically based on the underlying cause of death. While tables can (and should) also be constructed based on multiple-cause data, underlying-cause tabulations are simpler and more easily interpretable, the international format for the death certificate is oriented specifically to elicit an underlying cause of death, and many countries only code the underlying cause. Therefore, underlying-cause tabulations continue to be important, especially for international comparability.

The WHO publishes a set of standard cause-of-death tabulation lists according to which they publish underlying cause-of-death statistics for 193 member countries (WHO 2004a). These lists are intended to provide some standardization in the tabulation and presentation of international mortality statistics and are also used by the WHO as a reporting tool for countries that cannot or will not release individual-record data. Eurostat, the statistical agency of the European Union, has also developed a European shortlist to standardize the presentation of cause-of-death data for European countries.

Countries typically publish their own data according to a cause-of-death tabulation list that has been developed with their own needs in mind. A look at mortality reports for several countries shows some variation in the number and content of the cause-of-death lists (ABS 2008; Federal Health Reporting 2008; Heron et al. 2009; Korean National Statistical Office 2006; ONS 2008; Statistics Bureau 2009; Statistics Canada 2007; Statistics Norway 2008; Statistics Sweden 2008). Some use the European shortlist (e.g., Norway and Sweden). Others use some variation on the WHO lists. Cause-of-death categories, in many cases, are consistent, but in others are quite different.

The WHO lists rightly include a broad range of causes of death, including causes that may be common only regionally or in developing countries, some of which may be extremely rare or nonexistent in others. For national tabulations, these rare or nonexistent categories are often not needed, and other causes not shown in the WHO list may be relevant. For example, the European shortlist and standard tabulation lists for England and Wales, Japan, Canada, and the United States exclude many of the infectious diseases found in the WHO lists. These national lists also include some cause-of-death categories, for example, asthma, heart failure, renal failure, and external causes of undetermined intent, not shown in the WHO lists.

## Multiple-Cause Tabulations

The importance of multiple-cause data has been well-known for decades (Janssen 1940). A single, underlying cause of death does not always adequately describe deaths, particularly those due to chronic diseases that tend to coexist with a number of other chronic conditions (Dorn and Moriyama 1964; Guralnick 1966; Israel et al. 1986; NCHS 1984). In addition, underlying-cause statistics do not adequately describe the burden of mortality due to certain diseases and conditions that are often reported on the death certificate, but not selected as the underlying cause. In these cases, the presentation of multiple-cause data may make more sense. Table 22.2 shows multiple and underlying cause counts for selected causes of death in the United States. Some of these causes, for example, hypertension and diabetes, are commonly reported in Part II of the death certificate as contributing factors and are, thus, much more likely to be reported on the death certificate than to be selected as the underlying cause of death. Other causes, for instance, heart failure and renal failure, are more likely to be reported than selected as the underlying cause because they are often reported as complications of the underlying cause. In contrast, causes of death, such as those involving injury, HIV infection, and cancer, are least likely to be reported along with other existing conditions, are most likely to be selected as the underlying cause when they are reported, and are most likely to be the only causes reported.

Multiple-cause data are also useful in describing associations among medical conditions reported on the death certificate. These data provide some insight into the joint occurrence at death of multiple diseases and the competing and cooperating morbid processes leading to death (Israel et al. 1986; Manton and Stallard 1982; Stallard 2002, 2006). In addition, these data illustrate the difficulties inherent in selecting a single underlying cause of death (Stallard 2002).

In addition to describing diseases and other medical conditions, multiple-cause data also provide additional information about injury-related deaths, i.e., about the nature of the injury and body region affected, or, in the case of poisoning, about the substance involved (Israel et al. 1986; Miniño et al. 2002). Underlying cause data are limited to the external circumstances that resulted in the death, for example, accidental fall, intentional

**Table 22.2** Number of deaths from selected reported causes, number selected as the underlying cause, and ratio of reported causes to underlying cause: United States, 2005

| Cause of death (based on the *International Classification of Diseases, Tenth Revision*, 1992) | Total deaths with cause reported | Selected as underlying cause | Ratio of reported to underlying cause | Average number of causes per death | Percent only cause reported |
|---|---|---|---|---|---|
| Hypertension (I10,I12) | 276,368 | 24,902 | 11.1 | 4.2 | 0.5 |
| Complications of medical and surgical care (Y40–Y84,Y88) | 28,132 | 2,653 | 10.6 | 4.3 | 0.9 |
| Anemias (D50–D64) | 48,588 | 4,624 | 10.5 | 4.8 | 0.9 |
| Nutritional deficiencies (E40–E64) | 19,761 | 3,183 | 6.2 | 4.6 | 0.6 |
| Renal failure (N17–N19) | 219,037 | 42,868 | 5.1 | 4.0 | 3.6 |
| Heart failure (I50) | 292,180 | 58,933 | 5.0 | 3.7 | 6.5 |
| Atherosclerosis (I70) | 54,411 | 11,841 | 4.6 | 3.8 | 4.4 |
| Septicemia (A40–A41) | 152,706 | 34,136 | 4.5 | 3.8 | 4.1 |
| Pneumonia (J12–J18) | 209,638 | 61,189 | 3.4 | 3.5 | 7.4 |
| Diabetes mellitus (E10–E14) | 233,615 | 75,119 | 3.1 | 4.2 | 1.0 |
| Cerebrovascular diseases (I60–I69) | 242,346 | 143,579 | 1.7 | 3.3 | 14.5 |
| Congenital malformations (Q00–Q99) | 15,107 | 10,410 | 1.5 | 3.3 | 11.0 |
| Alzheimer's disease (G30) | 107,525 | 71,599 | 1.5 | 2.9 | 21.6 |
| Ischemic heart diseases (I20–I25) | 606,774 | 445,687 | 1.4 | 3.3 | 12.4 |
| Accidents (V01–X59,Y85–Y86) | 155,174 | 117,809 | 1.3 | 2.4 | 45.6 |
| Perinatal conditions (P00–P96) | 18,701 | 14,549 | 1.3 | 2.1 | 42.5 |
| Human immunodeficiency virus (HIV) disease (B20–B24) | 14,132 | 12,543 | 1.1 | 2.2 | 36.7 |
| Malignant neoplasms (cancer) (C00–C97) | 616,646 | 559,312 | 1.1 | 2.4 | 38.7 |
| Assault (homicide) (X85–Y09,Y87.1) | 18,283 | 18,124 | 1.0 | 1.1 | 91.5 |
| Intentional self-harm (suicide) (X60–X84,Y87.0) | 32,746 | 32,637 | 1.0 | 1.3 | 82.9 |

Source: US National Vital Statistics System.

self-poisoning, assault by blunt object. Multiple-cause data can provide valuable additional information about the medical effects of the trauma, for example, a fracture of the hip in the case of an accidental fall. In the case of deaths due to poisoning, the multiple-cause data are much more detailed in terms of the substance involved.

Both the tabulation and analysis of multiple-cause data is much more complex than that based on the underlying cause. There are several important issues to consider when tabulating and analyzing multiple-cause data. First, it is important to remember that the international format of the death certificate is not designed to elicit conditions or diseases that did not contribute to death. As a result, the multiple-cause information reported on the death certificate should not be taken to represent a comprehensive list of conditions and diseases that the decedent may have had. Multiple-cause data obtained from death certificates are not necessarily good for measuring the prevalence of decedents with a particular condition. A distinction, therefore, must be made between dying with and dying from a condition. For example, not all decedents with diabetes die from diabetes. As a result, one would not expect to see diabetes reported on a death certificate if the certifier did not think that diabetes was a cause of or contributed to death. This is very important to consider when interpreting multiple-cause tabulations.

Second, when tabulating multiple-cause data using hierarchical tabulation lists, caution should be taken not to count deaths more than once in higher-level categories. For example, a death certified due to an acute myocardial infarction due to atherosclerotic heart disease would be assigned multiple-cause codes (in ICD-10) I21.9 and I25.9, respectively. In the United States, ischemic heart disease (I20–I25) is divided into several subcategories, including acute myocardial infarction (I21–I22) and other forms of chronic ischemic heart disease (I20, I25). In a multiple-cause tabulation using these categories, the death in the example above would be assigned to both subcategories. Adding these categories up to the total ischemic heart disease would result in the death being counted twice. Therefore, to avoid a distorted picture of the burden of mortality, it is important to ensure that deaths in all of the categories in a tabulation list are counted only once (Israel et al. 1986).

Finally, one must make a decision on how to deal with uninformative medical information, such as modes of dying. Modes of dying, such as cardiac and respiratory arrest, are often reported as the immediate cause of death. Because all deaths involve the cessation of heart and lung activity, this is not useful information. In multiple-cause tabulations and analysis, particularly when examining associations between coexisting conditions, it is usually best to ignore modes of dying.

## Ranking Causes of Death

Ranking causes of death is a popular method of presenting mortality statistics. Leading causes of death derived from the ranking illustrate the relative burden of cause-specific mortality and are often used to make a case for funding and research to prevent and treat these diseases. Ranking is a useful tool, but must be used with a clear understanding of its inherent limitations (Rosenberg and Anderson 2004). The rank order of causes of death depends heavily on the list of causes from which the rankable causes are drawn and the determination of what constitutes a rankable cause (Becker et al. 2006; Griffiths et al. 2005; Heron 2007). As a result, changes or differences in cause lists can result in a lack of comparability over time and between countries.

Rankable cause-of-death categories are determined based on a few general methodological principles. Cause-of-death categories should be ranked according to the number of deaths assigned to the rankable causes. The number of deaths most accurately represents the frequency and burden of cause-specific mortality. While crude death rates also reflect the burden of mortality, they are less precise and therefore less than ideal. Age-standardized rates should never be used for ranking as the numerical value of the age-standardized rate depends on the population age distribution used as the standard. An older standard age distribution, for example, will tend to give more weight in the ranking to causes of death affecting the older population.

Choosing rankable cause-of-death categories should be done according to the following principles. Rankable causes should be medically meaningful and useful from a public-health perspective. Thus, ill-defined conditions, such as cardiac or respiratory arrest, and symptoms should not be rankable. Nonspecific and residual categories should be excluded as well. Rankable causes should also be mutually exclusive. For example, if the category "malignant neoplasms" is to be rankable, then its component subcategories (e.g., malignant neoplasm of trachea, bronchus, and lung, and malignant neoplasm of breast) should not be rankable.

International comparisons of leading causes of death are complicated by the fact that different countries often use different cause lists from which they select rankable causes. There is also a diversity of opinion as to which categories should be rankable. These differences necessarily arise because of variation in reporting practices, the prevalence of certain types of diseases, and health priorities. For example, in the United States, heart diseases are all combined for ranking because of the tendency for physicians to report heart disease without specifying the type of heart disease. Australia combines Alzheimer's disease with all dementias for the same reason. Less prevalent diseases are often relegated to non-rankable residual categories. For example, in the United States, cholera and diphtheria are not rankable causes of death (they are embedded in a residual category) because of their rarity. In developing countries, these diseases may be important in a list of rankable causes.

Table 22.3 shows leading causes of death for the world and three selected countries and illustrates the difficulty in making international comparisons of leading causes based on published data from each country and the WHO. Differences are apparent in the composition of the categories in the cause lists from which the rankable categories are derived. For example, both the United States and Korea combine all heart diseases, but use different sets of ICD codes to define this category. The United States ranks Alzheimer's disease separately; Australia combines it with vascular and other dementias. There are also differences in the choices made as to which categories should be rankable. For instance, the United States and Korea rank all malignant neoplasms; the WHO and Australia rank the malignant neoplasm subcategories. The United States and Korea rank all heart diseases; the WHO

**Table 22.3** Ten leading causes of death for the world and selected countries

Cause of death (based on the *International Classification of Diseases, Tenth Revision, 1992*)

| Rank | World (2004) | USA (2006) | Korea (2004) | Australia (2006) |
|---|---|---|---|---|
| 1 | Ischaemic heart disease (I20–I25) | Diseases of heart (I00–I09, I11, I13, I20–I51) | Malignant neoplasms (C00–C97) | Ischaemic heart diseases (I20–I25) |
| 2 | Cerebrovascular disease (I60–I69) | Malignant neoplasms (C00–C97) | Cerebrovascular diseases (I60–I69) | Strokes (I60–I69) |
| 3 | Lower-respiratory infections (J10–J18, J20–J22) | Cerebrovascular disease (I60–I69) | Heart diseases (I00–I09, I20–I51) | Trachea and lung cancer (C33–C34) |
| 4 | COPD (J40–J44) | Chronic lower-respiratory disease (J40–J47) | Intentional self-harm (X60–X84) | Dementia and Alzheimer's disease (F01–F03, G30) |
| 5 | Diarrhoeal diseases (A00, A01,A03,A04,A06–A09) | Accidents (V01–X59, Y85–Y86) | Diabetes mellitus (E10–E14) | Chronic lower-respiratory diseases (J40–J47) |
| 6 | HIV/AIDS (B20–B24) | Diabetes mellitus (E10–E14) | Transport accidents (V01–V99) | Colon and rectum cancer (C18–C21) |
| 7 | Tuberculosis (A15–A19, B90) | Alzheimer's disease (G30) | Chronic lower-respiratory diseases (J40–J47) | Blood and lymph cancer (including leukaemia) (C81–C96) |
| 8 | Trachea, bronchus, lung cancers (C33–C34) | Influenza and pneumonia (J10–J18) | Diseases of liver (K70–K76) | Diabetes (E10–E14) |
| 9 | Road traffic accidents (V01–V04,V06, V09–V80,V87,V89,V99)[a] | Nephritis, nephrotic syndrome, and nephrosis (N00–N07, N17–N19, N25–N27) | Hypertensive diseases (I10–I13) | Diseases of the kidney and urinary system (N00–N39) |
| 10 | Prematurity and low birth weight (P05, P07, P22, P27–P28) | Septicemia (A40–A41) | Pneumonia (J12–J18) | Prostate cancer (C61) |

Sources: World—WHO (2008); USA—Heron et al. (2009); Korea—Korean National Statistical Office (2006); Australia—Australian Bureau of Statistics (2008).

[a]For countries that code to the fourth-digit level, the list of codes is much more detailed. See WHO (2008, Table C3, footnote e, p. 125).

and Australia have chosen to rank the subcategories, including ischemic heart disease. Further illustration as to how the choice of different rankable categories can affect the leading causes can be found in Becker et al. (2006) and Griffiths et al. (2005). Recently, an attempt has been made to develop a standard cause list for ranking and to standardize ranking procedures for international comparisons (Becker et al. 2006).

## Conclusions

An understanding of the issues related to the collection, classification and coding, and presentation of cause-of-death data is crucial for public-health research and the development of effective interventions and policy. Such knowledge is especially important when making international comparisons and analyzing cause-of-death data over time. For some causes of death, changes over time coinciding with revisions of the ICD may be due to the revisions rather than to real changes in the risk of mortality. International variation may, in some cases, be due to differences in how the data are collected, coded, and tabulated rather than substantive differences in the risk of mortality.

## Counting Deaths Due to Common Risk Factors

Cause of death as discussed in this chapter refers specifically to the pathophysiological diseases or conditions identified at the time of death and not to the root causes or risk factors that gave rise to those conditions. Data collected at the time of death does not lend itself well to the collection of information on risk factors, for example, tobacco use, obesity, alcohol and drug use, and sexual behavior. The death certificate is not intended for or designed to collect such information, nor is it typically reported. One cannot survey the decedent as to their habits or behavior, and an extensive survey of medical records and the next of kin at the time of death is neither practical nor considerate.

Longitudinal data and linkage studies with mortality follow-up can be used to assess the impact of risk factors on mortality (see, e.g., Flegal et al. 2005; Liao et al. 2000; Shultz et al. 1991). Measures of relative risk from such studies can be used with prevalence estimates to calculate attributable fractions (Rückinger et al. 2009), which are then used to estimate the number of deaths attributable to the risk factor of interest (Allison et al. 1999; Centers for Disease Control and Prevention 2005; Danaei et al. 2009; Flegal et al. 2005; McGinnis and Foege 1993; Mokdad et al. 2004; Stevenson 2001).

Such estimates of attributable deaths are useful in illustrating the burden of disease and mortality due to risky behavior. However, estimating these deaths is not as straightforward as counting diseases or conditions reported on a death certificate. Lack of a standardized methodology is a problem. Differences in definition and methodology can result in substantially different and sometimes controversial estimates for the same risk factor (Allison et al. 1999; Couzin 2005; Flegal et al. 2005; Mokdad et al. 2004). Himes provides a more detailed discussion regarding the role of behavioral risk factors in disease and mortality in Chapter 14 of this volume.

## Future Directions

Much of the discussion in this chapter has been limited to developed countries, most of which have well-established vital registration systems that are able to register and collect information, including the cause of death, on virtually 100% of deaths. Unfortunately, death registration systems are either nonfunctioning or inadequate in most developing countries. Serious gaps exist in our knowledge of mortality patterns for these countries. Estimates, especially those for cause-specific mortality, are at best imprecise and may provide a misleading picture of the true risk due to disease and injury. While strategies such as sample registration and verbal autopsy can provide valid inferences where data do not currently exist, they have limits, especially with regard to producing data that are internationally comparable. The development and augmentation of vital registration systems where the cause of death is reported by a medically qualified person continues to be essential and should be promoted as the gold standard for the collection of cause-of-death data. Such systems provide the best opportunity for collecting high-quality cause-of-death information.

Among developed countries, despite high levels of coverage and completeness in the collection of cause-of-death data, there remains significant variation in the way cause-of-death data are collected, coded, and presented. Some efforts have been made, notably by the WHO through the ICD, to provide international standards. The ICD provides a standard format for collecting the cause of death, standard rules for classification, and coding and standard tabulation lists for presentation. But use of ICD and application of the coding rules is not necessarily uniform internationally. In addition, standards for the reporting of cause-of-death information by medical certifiers are lacking. Thus, much remains to be done, especially with regard to promoting standards for coding and improvements to the quality of cause-of-death reporting.

Automated coding systems provide important opportunities for improvements in the international comparability of cause-of-death data. While the ICD provides standard coding rules, these rules are quite complex and are often interpreted differently by human coders. Automated systems, in contrast, provide a standardized application of the ICD coding rules. In addition, automated systems facilitate the coding of multiple-cause data, making them more widely accessible internationally. Development and enhancement of automated coding systems continues through the International Collaborative Effort on Automating Mortality Statistics. However, automated systems are currently in place in only a few countries. Wider dissemination is needed if such systems are to be effective in promoting international comparability. Hopefully, the recent development of IRIS, which mitigates much of the difficulty in adapting automated coding for differences in language, will result in wider adoption of automated coding internationally.

Automated coding systems can have an important impact, but are not a panacea for providing accurate and comparable cause-of-death data. The coded output from automated systems is only as good as the input provided by medical certifiers. As discussed in this chapter, the quality of cause-of-death certification is a matter of concern. Certifiers often do not understand the importance of or how to write a proper cause-of-death statement. While training materials for medical certifiers are available in several countries, these materials tend not to be widely disseminated or easily accessible. Electronic death registration (EDR) systems, in which medical certifiers enter the cause of death directly into the system, have the potential to improve cause-of-death information in three ways. First, training materials can be made directly accessible in electronic format to the certifier as the cause of death is being reported. Second, EDR systems can be programmed to enhance cause-of-death querying. For example, if insufficient detail or an unsuitable underlying cause is reported, the certifier may be queried in real-time while the facts of the case are fresh. Third, the potential for error is reduced if the cause of death is entered directly by the certifier and not by data entry personnel. EDR systems additionally have the potential to provide more timely cause-of-death data that can be used for disease surveillance. Currently, such systems are in their infancy, under development in only a few countries, including the United States, France, and Australia.

Information about causes of death is vital. If we do not know why people die, we cannot devise effective programs and interventions to prevent death, improve health, and ultimately increase life expectancy. This information is lacking, of poor quality, or incomparable in too many countries around the world. This limits our ability to draw valid conclusions on a global scale. Much more needs to be done to close these information gaps and improve the availability, comparability, and quality of cause-of-death information globally.

# References

Allison, D.B., K.R. Fontaine, J.E. Manson, J. Stevens, and T.B. VanItallie. 1999. "Annual Deaths Attributable to Obesity in the United States." *Journal of the American Medical Association* 282:1530–38.

Anderson, R.N., A.M. Miniño, D.L. Hoyert, and H.M. Rosenberg. 2001. "Comparability of Cause of Death Between ICD-9 and ICD-10: Preliminary Estimates." *National Vital Statistics Reports* 49(2):1–32.

Australian Bureau of Statistics (ABS). 2000. *Causes of Death, Australia, 1999*. Available at http://www.abs.gov.au/ausstats/abs@.nsf/mf/3303.0

Australian Bureau of Statistics (ABS). 2008. *Causes of Death, Australia, 2006*. Available at http://www.abs.gov.au/ausstats/abs@.nsf/mf/3303.0

Baiden, F., A. Bawah, S. Biai, F. Binka, T. Boerma, P. Byass, D. Chandramohan, S. Chatterji, C. Engmann, D. Greet, R. Jakob, K. Kahn, O. Kunii, A.D. Lopez, C.J.L. Murray, B. Nahlen, C. Rao, O. Sankoh, P.W. Setel, K. Shibuya, N. Soleman, L. Wright, and G. Yang. 2007. "Setting International Standards for Verbal Autopsy." *Bulletin of the World Health Organization* 85:570–71.

Becker, R., J. Silvi, D. Ma Fat, A. L'Hours, and R. Laurenti. 2006. "A Method for Deriving Leading Causes of Death." *Bulletin of the World Health Organization* 84: 297–308.

Burton, J. and J. Underwood. 2007. "Clinical, Educational and Epidemiological Value of Autopsy." *The Lancet* 369: 1471–80.

Byass, P. 2007. "Who Needs Cause-of-Death Data?" *PLoS Medicine* 4:e333. doi:10.1371/journal.pmed.0040333.

Centers for Disease Control and Prevention. 2005. "Annual Smoking-Attributable Mortality, Years of Potential Life Lost, and Productivity Losses – United States, 1997—2001." *Morbidity and Mortality Weekly Report* 54:625–28.

Chandramohan, D., N. Soleman, K. Shibuya, and J. Porter. 2005. "Ethical Issues in the Application of Verbal Autopsies in Mortality Surveillance Systems." *Tropical Medicine and International Health* 10:1087–89.

Chariot, P., K. Witt, V. Pautot, R. Porcher, G. Thomas, E.S. Zafrani, and F. Lemaire. 2000. "Declining Autopsy Rate in a French Hospital: Physicians' Attitudes to the Autopsy and Use of Autopsy Material in Research Publications." *Archives of Pathology and Laboratory Medicine* 124: 739–45.

Coady, S.A., P.D. Sorlie, L.S. Cooper, A.R. Folsom, W.D. Rosamond, and D.E. Conwill. 2001. "Validation of Death Certificate Diagnosis for Coronary Heart Disease: The Atherosclerosis Risk in Communities (ARIC) Study." *Journal of Clinical Epidemiology* 54:40–50.

Couzin, J. 2005. "A Heavyweight Battle Over CDC's Obesity Forecasts." *Science* 308:770–71.

Cullen, W. 1772. *Synopsis Nosologiae Methodicae*. Edinburgh, Kincaid & Creech.

Dalen, J.E. 1997. "The Moribund Autopsy: DNR or CPR?" *Archives of Internal Medicine* 157:1633.

Danaei, G., E.L. Ding, D. Mozaffarian, B. Taylor, J. Rehm, C.J.L. Murray, and M. Ezzati. 2009. "The Preventable Causes of Death in the United States: Comparative Risk Assessment of Dietary, Lifestyle, and Metabolic Risk Factors." *PLoS Medicine* 6:e1000058.

Dorn, H.F. and I.M. Moriyama. 1964. "Uses and Significance of Multiple Cause Tabulations for Mortality Statistics." *American Journal of Public Health* 54:400–6.

Dunn, H.L. and W. Shackley. 1944. "Comparison of Cause of Death Assignments by the 1929 and 1939 Revisions of the International List: Deaths in the United States, 1940." *Vital Statistics – Special Reports* 19(14):153–277.

D'Amico, M., E. Agozzino, A. Biagino, A. Simonetti, and P. Marinelli. 1999. "Ill-defined and Multiple Causes on Death Certificates – A Study of Misclassification in Mortality Statistics." *European Journal of Epidemiology* 15: 141–48.

Eurostat. 2008. *E-learning Website for Death Certification (Online Tutorial).* Available at http://ec.europa.eu/eurostat/health/deathcert/

Faust, M.M. and A.B. Dolman. 1963. "Comparability of Mortality Statistics for the Fifth and Sixth Revisions: United States, 1950." *Vital Statistics – Special Reports* 51(2): 131–78.

Faust, M.M. and A.B. Dolman. 1964. "Comparability Ratios Based on Mortality Statistics for the Fifth and Sixth Revisions: United States, 1950." *Vital Statistics – Special Reports* 51(3):179–245.

Faust, M.M. and A.B. Dolman. 1965. "Comparability of Mortality Statistics for the Sixth and Seventh Revisions: United States, 1958." *Vital Statistics – Special Reports* 51(4):247–97.

Federal Health Reporting. 2008. *Health in Germany, 2006.* Berlin, Federal Statistical Office.

Flegal, K.M., B.L. Graubard, D.F. Williamson, and M.H. Gail. 2005. "Excess Deaths Associated with Underweight, Overweight, and Obesity." *Journal of the American Medical Association* 293:1861–67.

Frova, L., M. Pace, and M. Pappagallo. 2010. "Analisi del bridge coding Icd-9-Icd-10 per le statistiche di mortalità per causa in Italia." *Metodi e norme* (Forthcoming).

Geran, L., P. Tully, P. Wood, and B. Thomas. 2005. *Comparability of ICD-10 and ICD-9 for Mortality Statistics in Canada.* Ottawa, ON, Statistics Canada.

Gittelsohn, A. and P. Royston. 1982. "Annotated Bibliography of Cause-of-Death Validation Studies, 1958–80." *Vital and Health Statistics* 2(89):1–42.

Glenn, D. 1999. "Description of the National Center for Health Statistics Software Systems and Demonstrations." In K. Peters (ed.), *Proceedings of the International Collaborative Effort on Automating Mortality Statistics,* Volume 1, pp. 6-1–6-13. Hyattsville, MD, National Center for Health Statistics.

Gorina, Y. and H. Lentzner. 2008. "Multiple Causes of Death in Old Age." *Aging Trends* No. 9. Available at http://www.cdc.gov/nchs/data/ahcd/agingtrends/09causes.htm

Graunt, J. 1662. *Natural and Political Observations in a Following Index and Made Upon the Bills of Mortality.* London, Roycroft.

Griffiths, C., C. Rooney, and A. Brock. 2005. "Leading Causes of Death in England and Wales – How Would We Group Causes?" *Health Statistics Quarterly* 28:6–17.

Grigg, B., R.G. Brooks, S. Lieb, and M. Grigg. 2001. "Coding Changes and Apparent HIV/AIDS Mortality Trends in Florida, 1999." *Journal of the American Medical Association* 286:1839.

Guralnick, L. 1966. "Some Problems in the Use of Multiple Causes of Death." *Journal of Chronic Diseases* 19:979–90.

Hadley, E. 1992. "Cause of Death among the Oldest Old." In R.M. Suzman, D.P. Willis, and K.G. Manton (eds.), *The Oldest Old,* pp. 183–198. New York, NY, Oxford University Press.

Hanzlick, R. 1994. *The Medical Cause of Death Manual.* Northfield, IL, College of American Pathologists.

Hanzlick, R. 1996. "The Relevance of Queries and Coding Procedures to the Writing of Cause-of-Death Statements." *American Journal of Forensic Medicine and Pathology* 17:319–23.

Hanzlick, R. 2001. "The Autopsy, Medicine, and Mortality Statistics." *Vital and Health Statistics* 3(32):1–42.

Hanzlick, R. and P. Baker. 1998. "Institutional Autopsy Rates." *Archives of Internal Medicine* 158:1171–72.

Harrington, D.E. and E.A. Sayre. 2007. *Death of the Autopsy: Is Better Imaging Technology or Cost Cutting to Blame?* Social Science Research Network Working Paper. Available at http://ssrn.com/abstract=1264039

Hays, J.N. 1998. *The Burdens of Disease: Epidemics and Human Response in Western History.* New Brunswick, NJ, Rutgers University Press.

Heron, M.P. 2007. "Deaths: Leading Causes for 2004." *National Vital Statistics Reports* 56(5):1–96.

Heron, M.P., D.L. Hoyert, S.L. Murphy, J. Xu, K.D. Kochanek, and B. Tejada-Vera. 2009. "Deaths: Final Data for 2006." *National Vital Statistics Reports* 57(14):1–136.

Hill, K. 2006. "Making Deaths Count." *Bulletin of the World Health Organization* 84:161–256.

Hopkins, D.D., J.A. Grant-Worley, and T.L. Bollinger. 1989. "Survey of Cause-of-Death Query Criteria Used by State Vital Statistics Programs in the U.S. and the Efficacy of the Criteria Used by the Oregon Vital Statistics Program." *American Journal of Public Health* 79:570–74.

Hoyert, D.L. and A. Lima. 2005. "Querying of Death Certificates in the United States." *Public Health Reports* 120: 1–9.

Hoyert, D.L., H.M. Rosenberg, and M.F. MacDorman. 2000. "Effect of Changes in Death Certificate Format on Cause-Specific Mortality Trends, United States, 1979–92." In M.P. Coleman and P. Aylin (eds.), *Death Certification and Mortality Statistics: An International Perspective, Series Studies on Medical and Population Subjects No. 64,* pp. 47–58. London, The Stationary Office.

Institute of International Statistics. 1900. *Bulletin of the Institute of International Statistics* 12:280.

Iribarren, C., R.S. Crow, P.J. Hannan, D.R. Jacobs, and R.V. Luepker. 1998. "Validation of Death Certificate Diagnosis of Out-of-Hospital Sudden Cardiac Death." *American Journal of Cardiology* 82:50–53.

Israel, R.A. 1990. "Automation of Mortality Data Coding and Processing in the United States of America." *World Health Statistics Quarterly* 43:259–62.

Israel, R.A., H.M. Rosenberg, and L.R. Curtin. 1986. "Analytical Potential for Multiple Cause-of-Death Data." *American Journal of Epidemiology* 124:161–79.

Italian National Institute of Statistics (ISTAT). 2003. *Manual on Certification of Causes of Death in Europe.* Available at http://circa.europa.eu/Public/irc/dsis/health/library?l=/methodologiessandsdatasc/causessofsdeath/training_certification

Janssen, T.A. 1940. "Importance of Tabulating Multiple Causes of Death." *American Journal of Public Health* 30:871–79.

Jewell, D. 2007. "Death Certification." *British Journal of General Practice* 57:583.

Jha, P., V. Gajalakshmi, P.C. Gupta, R. Kumar, P. Mony, N. Dhingra, and R. Peto. 2006. "Prospective Study of One Million Deaths in India: Rationale, Design, and Validation Results." *PLoS Medicine* 3:e18. doi:10.1371/journal.pmed.0030018.

Johansson, L.A 2000. "Changes in Swedish Death Certification Practice – What Is the Cause?" In M.P. Coleman and

P. Aylin (eds.), *Death Certification and Mortality Statistics: An International Perspective, Series Studies on Medical and Population Subjects No. 64*, pp. 31–38. London, The Stationary Office.

Johansson, L.A. 2001a. "Swedish MIKADO Coding System." In A.M. Miniño and H.M. Rosenberg (eds.), *Proceedings of the International Collaborative Effort on Automating Mortality Statistics*, Volume 2, pp. 27–45. Hyattsville, MD, National Center for Health Statistics.

Johansson, L.A. 2001b. "Mortality Bridge Coding ICD-9/ICD-10: Preliminary Results from Statistics Sweden's Study." In A.M. Miniño and H.M. Rosenberg (eds.), *Proceedings of the International Collaborative Effort on Automating Mortality Statistics*, Volume 2, pp. 135–144. Hyattsville, MD, National Center for Health Statistics.

Johansson, L.A. and R. Westerling. 2002. "Comparing Hospital Discharge Records with Death Certificates: Can the Differences be Explained?" *Journal of Epidemiology and Community Health* 56:301–8.

Johansson, L.A., R. Westerling, and H.M. Rosenberg. 2006. "Methodology of Studies Evaluating Death Certificate Accuracy Were Flawed." *Journal of Clinical Epidemiology* 59:125–31.

Jougla E., G. Pavillon, F. Rossollin, M. De Smedt, and J. Bonte. 1998. "Improvement of the Quality and Comparability of Causes-of-Death Statistics Inside the European Community. EUROSTAT Task Force on Causes of Death Statistics." *Revue d'épidémiologie et de santé publique* 46:447–56.

Kimura, M., K. Takemura, H. Ueda, H. Takeuchi, R. Agematsu, and T. Tamura. 2006. "Automated Coding of Diagnostic Expressions and Selection of Underlying Cause of Death (ACSEL) System in Japan." In A.M. Miniño and H.M. Rosenberg (eds.), *Proceedings of the International Collaborative Effort on Automating Mortality Statistics*, Volume 3, pp. 18–19. Hyattsville, MD, National Center for Health Statistics.

King, G. and Y. Lu. 2008. "Verbal Autopsy Methods with Multiple Causes of Death." *Statistical Science* 23:78–91.

Kircher, T. and R.E. Anderson. 1987. "Cause of Death: Proper Completion of the Death Certificate." *Journal of the American Medical Association* 258:349–52.

Kircher, T., J. Nelson, and H. Burdo. 1985. "The Autopsy as a Measure of Accuracy of the Death Certificate." *New England Journal of Medicine* 313:1263–69.

Klebba, A.J. and A.B. Dolman. 1975. "Comparability of Mortality Statistics for the Seventh and Eighth Revisions of the International Classification of Diseases." *Vital and Health Statistics* 2(66):1–93.

Klebba, A.J. and J.H. Scott. 1980. "Estimates of Selected Comparability Ratios Based on Dual Coding of 1976 Death Certificates by the Eighth and Ninth Revisions of the International Classification of Diseases." *Monthly Vital Statistics Report* 28(11):1–19.

Kock, K.F., V. Vestergaard, M. Hardt-Madsen, and E. Garne. 2003. "Declining Autopsy Rates in Stillbirths and Infant Deaths: Results from Funen County, Denmark, 1986–96." *Journal of Maternal-Fetal and Neonatal Medicine* 13:403–7.

Korean National Statistical Office. 2006. *Annual Report on the Cause of Death Statistics*. Seoul, Korean National Statistical Office.

Kumar, A., D.K. Rout, P. Gupta, and U. Singh. 2007. *Mortality Statistics in India, 2006*. New Delhi, Central Bureau of Health Intelligence. Available online at http://www.cbhidghs.nic.in/

Lahti, R.A. and A. Penttilä. 2001. "The Validity of Death Certificates: Routine Validation of Death Certification and its Effects on Mortality Statistics." *Forensic Science International* 115:15–32.

Lahti, R.A. and A. Penttilä. 2003. "Cause-of-Death Query in Validation of Death Certification by Expert Panel; Effects on Mortality Statistics in Finland, 1995." *Forensic Science International* 131:113–24.

Laurenti, R. 2006. "Brazilian Diagnosis Coding System." In A.M. Miniño and H.M. Rosenberg (eds.), *Proceedings of the International Collaborative Effort on Automating Mortality Statistics*, Volume 3, pp. 16–17. Hyattsville, MD, National Center for Health Statistics.

Laurenti, R., P. Aylin, and M.P. Coleman. 2000. "Accuracy of Statements of the Cause of Death on Death Certificates and the International Comparability of Mortality Statistics." In M.P. Coleman and P. Aylin (eds.), *Death Certification and Mortality Statistics: An International Perspective, Series Studies on Medical and Population Subjects No. 64*, pp. 1–9. London, The Stationary Office.

Liao, Y., D.L. McGee, G. Cao, and R.S. Cooper. 2000. "Alcohol Mortality: Findings from the National Health Interview Survey (1998 and 1990)." *American Journal of Epidemiology* 151:651–59.

Lu, T.H., P.Y. Hsu, C. Bjorkenstam, and R.N. Anderson. 2006. "Certifying Diabetes-Related Cause-of-Death: A Comparison of Inappropriate Certification Statements in Sweden, Taiwan and the USA." *Diabetologia* 49:2878–81.

Lu, T.H. and S.M. Huang. 2002. "Querying the Ill-Defined Stroke Diagnoses on Death Certificates and Their Effects on Type-Specific Mortality in Taiwan." *Kaohsiung Journal of Medical Sciences* 18:182–90.

MacDorman, M.F. and B.L. Hudson. 1992. "Advance Report of Final Mortality Statistics, 1989." *Monthly Vital Statistics Report* 40(8):Supplement 2.

Manton, K.G. and E. Stallard. 1982. "Temporal Trends in U.S. Multiple Cause of Death Mortality Rates, 1968–1977." *Demography* 19:527–47.

Mathers, C.D., D. Ma Fat, M. Inoue, C. Rao, and A.D. Lopez. 2005. "Counting the Dead and What They Died from: An Assessment of the Global Status of Cause of Death Data." *Bulletin of the World Health Organization* 83:171–77.

McGinnis, J.M. and W.H. Foege. 1993. "Actual Causes of Death in the United States." *Journal of the American Medical Association* 270:2207–12.

McKenzie K., S. Walker, and S. Tong. 2001. "Assessment of the Impact of the Change from Manual to Automated Coding on Mortality Statistics in Australia." *Health Information Management Journal* 30(3). Available online at http://www.himaa.org.au/reviewed_papers/HIMJ303.htm

Miniño, A.M. (ed.). 2009. *Proceedings of the International Collaborative Effort on Automating Mortality Statistics*, Volume 4. Hyattsville, MD, National Center for Health Statistics.

Miniño, A.M., R.N. Anderson, L.A. Fingerhut, M.A. Boudreault, and M. Warner. 2002. "Deaths: Injuries, 2002." *National Vital Statistics Reports* 54(10):1–128.

Mokdad, A.H., J.S. Marks, D.F. Stroup, and J.L. Gerberding. 2004. "Actual Causes of Death in the United States, 2000." *Journal of the American Medical Association* 291: 1238–45.

Moriyama, I.M. 1989. "Problems in the Measurement of Accuracy of Cause-of-Death Statistics." *American Journal of Public Health* 79:1349–50.

Moriyama, I.M., R.M. Loy, and A.H.T. Robb-Smith. 2011. *History of the Statistical Classification of Diseases and Causes of Death*. Hyattsville, MD, National Center for Health Statistics (Forthcoming).

Muhlhauser, I., P.T. Sawicki, M. Blank, H. Overmann, B. Richter, and M. Berger. 2002. "Reliability of Causes of Death in Persons with Type I Diabetes." *Diabetologia* 45: 1490–97.

Murray, C.J.L., A.D. Lopez, J.T. Barofsky, C. Bryson-Cahn, and R. Lozano. 2007b. "Estimating Population Cause-Specific Mortality Fractions from In-Hospital Mortality: Validation of a New Method." *PLoS Medicine* 4:e326. doi:10.1371/journal.pmed.0040326.

Murray, C.J.L., A.D. Lopez, D.M. Feehan, S.T. Peter, and G. Yang. 2007a. "Validation of the Symptom Pattern Method for Analyzing Verbal Autopsy Data." *PLoS Medicine* 4:e327. doi:10.1371/journal.pmed.0040327.

Murray, C.J.L., A.D. Lopez, and S. Wibulpolprasert. 2004. "Monitoring Global Health: Time for New Solutions." *BMJ* 329:1096–100.

National Center for Health Statistics (NCHS). 1968. *Eighth Revision of the International Classification of Diseases, Adapted for Use in the United States*. Washington, DC, Public Health Service.

National Center for Health Statistics (NCHS). 1984. "Multiple Causes of Death in the United States." *Monthly Vital Statistics Report* 32(10):Supplement 2.

National Center for Health Statistics (NCHS). 1988. *Instruction Manual, Part 9: ICD-9 Underlying Cause-of-Death Lists for Tabulating Mortality Statistics, Notice of Change No. 5, March 1988*. Hyattsville, MD, National Center for Health Statistics.

National Center for Health Statistics (NCHS). 2004. *Physician's Handbook on Medical Certification of Death*. Hyattsville, MD, National Center for Health Statistics.

National Center for Health Statistics (NCHS). 2007. *Instruction Manual, Part 20: ICD-10 Cause-of-Death Querying, 2007*. Hyattsville, MD, National Center for Health Statistics.

National Center for Health Statistics (NCHS). 2008a. *Instruction Manual, Part 2a: Instructions for Classifying the Underlying Cause-of-Death, ICD-10, 2008*. Hyattsville, MD, National Center for Health Statistics.

National Center for Health Statistics (NCHS). 2008b. *Instruction Manual, Part 2b: Instructions for Classifying the Multiple Causes of Death, ICD-10, 2008*. Hyattsville, MD, National Center for Health Statistics.

National Committee on Vital and Health Statistics (NCVHS). 1989. *Report of the Workshop on Improving Cause-of-Death Statistics*. Hyattsville, MD, National Center for Health Statistics.

National Committee on Vital and Health Statistics (NCVHS). 1991. *Report of the Second Workshop on Improving Cause-of-Death Statistics*. Hyattsville, MD, National Center for Health Statistics.

New York City Department of Health and Mental Hygiene (NYC). 2008. *Improving Cause of Death Reporting (online tutorial)*. Available at http://www.nyc.gov/html/doh/media/video/icdr/

Office for National Statistics (ONS). 2008. *Mortality Statistics: Deaths Registered in 2007 (England and Wales)*. London, Office for National Statistics.

Ohmi, K. and A. Yamamoto. 2000. "Changes in Mortality Statistics in Japan, 1995: The Effects of Implementation of ICD-10 and Revision of the Death Certificate." In M.P. Coleman and P. Aylin. (eds.), *Death Certification and Mortality Statistics: An International Perspective, Series Studies on Medical and Population Subjects No. 64*, pp. 21–27. London, The Stationary Office.

Ortega Garcia, J.A. 2006. "Automation of Cause-of-Death Coding in Mexico." In A.M. Miniño and H.M. Rosenberg (eds.), *Proceedings of the International Collaborative Effort on Automating Mortality Statistics*, Volume 3, pp. 20–22. Hyattsville, MD, National Center for Health Statistics.

Pace, M., S. Bruzzone, S. Marchetti, F. Grippo, S. Cinque, G. di Fraia, M. Pappagallo, S. Pennazza, S. Sindoni, and L. Frova. 2005. "A Training Package on Certification of Causes of Death for European Professionals." *European Journal of Public Health* 15(Supplement 1):104–5.

Pace, M. and F. Grippo. 2006. "Quality in Causes of Death Certification is a Key Point for Better Mortality Data: The Italian Experience." *European Journal of Public Health* 16(Supplement 1):21.

Pavillon, G. 2001. "French Automated Coding System: Styx." In A.M. Miniño and H.M. Rosenberg (eds.), *Proceedings of the International Collaborative Effort on Automating Mortality Statistics*, Volume 2, pp. 50–56. Hyattsville, MD, National Center for Health Statistics.

Pavillon, G., J. Boileau, G. Renaud, H. Lefèvre, and E. Jougla. 2005. "Conséquences des changements de codage des causes médicales de décès sur les données nationales de mortalité en France à partir de l'année 2000." *Bulletin épidémiologique hebdomadaire* 4:13–16.

Pavillon, G., E. Jougla, L. Chérié-Challine, and F. Hatton. 2000. "Randomised Comparison of Death Certification with and Without Guidelines." In M.P. Coleman and P. Aylin (Eds.), *Death Certification and Mortality Statistics: An International Perspective, Series Studies on Medical and Population Subjects No. 64*, pp. 10–20. London, The Stationary Office.

Peacock, S.J., D. Machin, C.E.H. Duboulay, and N. Kirkham. 1988. "The Autopsy: A Useful Tool or an Old Relic?" *Journal of Pathology* 156:9–14.

Percy, C., E. Stanek, and L.C. Gloeckler. 1981. "Accuracy of Cancer Death Certificates and Its Effect on Cancer Mortality Statistics." *American Journal of Public Health* 71: 242–50.

Quigley M.A., D. Chandramohan, and L.C. Rodrigues. 1999. "Diagnostic Accuracy of Physician Review, Expert Algorithms, and Data-Derived Algorithms in Adult Verbal Autopsies." *International Journal of Epidemiology* 28: 1081–87.

Quigley, M.A., D. Chandramohan, P. Setel, F. Binka and L.C. Rodrigues. 2000. "Validity of Data-Derived Algorithms for Ascertaining Causes of Adult Death in Two African Sites

Using Verbal Autopsy." *Tropical Medicine and International Health* 5:33–39.

Registrar General of England and Wales. 1839. *First Annual Report of the Registrar General of Births, Deaths and Marriages in England*. London, The Stationary Office.

Registrar General of Scotland. 2001. "The Introduction of ICD10 for Cause of Death Coding in Scotland", Appendix 2. In *Annual Report of the Registrar General of Births, Deaths and Marriages for Scotland, 2000*, pp. 157–73. Edinburgh, General Register Office for Scotland.

Rooney, C. 1999. "Implementing Automated Coding in England and Wales: How it Affected Mortality Statistics." In K. Peters (ed.), *Proceedings of the International Collaborative Effort on Automating Mortality Statistics*, Volume 1, pp. 8-1–8-19. Hyattsville, MD, National Center for Health Statistics.

Rooney, C. and T. Devis. 1996. "Mortality Trends by Cause of Death in England and Wales 1980–94: The Impact of Introducing Automated Cause Coding and Related Changes in 1993." *Population Trends* 86:29–35.

Rooney, C., C. Griffiths, and L. Cook. 2002. "The Implementation of ICD-10 for Cause of Death Coding – Some Preliminary Results from the Bridge Coding Study." *Health Statistics Quarterly* 13:31–41.

Rosenberg, H.M. 1989. "Improving Cause-of-Death Statistics." *American Journal of Public Health* 79:563–64.

Rosenberg, H.M. 1999. "International Collaborative Effort on Automating Mortality Statistics: Background and Issues." In K. Peters (ed.), *Proceedings of the International Collaborative Effort on Automating Mortality Statistics*, Volume 1, pp. 1-1–1-16. Hyattsville, MD, National Center for Health Statistics.

Rosenberg, H.M. and R. Anderson. 2004. *Leading Causes of Death: A Tool for Health Assessment*. WHO Family of International Classifications Network Meeting, Iceland, October 2004. WHOFIC/04.088. Available at http://www.nordclass.uu.se

Ruzicka, L.T. and A.D. Lopez. 1990. "The Use of Cause of Death Statistics for Health Situation Assessment: National and International Experiences." *World Health Statistics Quarterly* 46:249–58.

Rückinger, S., R. von Kries, and A.M. Toschke. 2009. "An Illustration of and Programs Estimating Attributable Fractions in Large Scale Surveys Considering Multiple Risk Factors." *BMC Medical Research Methodology* 9:7.

Sauvages de la Croix, F.B. 1763. *Nosologia methodica sistens morborum classes, genera et species, Juxta' Sydenhami mentem et botanicorum ordinem*. Amsterdam, Sumptibus Fratrum de Tournes.

Sehdev, A.E.S. and G.M. Hutchins. 2001. "Problems with Proper Completion and Accuracy of the Cause-of-Death Statement." *Archives of Internal Medicine* 161:277–84.

Selik, R.M., R.N. Anderson, M.T. McKenna, and H.M. Rosenberg. 2003. "Increase in HIV Deaths Due to Changes in Rules for Selecting Underlying Cause of Death." *Journal of Acquired Immune Deficiency Syndromes* 32: 62–69.

Setel, P.W., C. Rao, Y. Hemed, D.R. Whiting, G. Yang, D. Chandramohan, K.G.M.M. Alberti, and A.D. Lopez. 2006. "Core Verbal Autopsy Procedures with Comparative Validation Results from Two Countries." *PLoS Medicine* 3:e268. doi:10.1371/journal.pmed.0030268.

Setel, P.W., O. Sankoh, C. Rao, V.A. Velkoff, C. Mathers, Y. Gonghuan, Y. Hemed, P. Jha., and A.D. Lopez. 2005. "Sample Registration of Vital Events with Verbal Autopsy: A Renewed Commitment to Measuring and Monitoring Vital Statistics." *Bulletin of the World Health Organization* 83:611–17.

Sharma, B.R. 2008. "Cause-of-Death Data in Public Health Planning – An Overview." *Journal of the Indian Academy of Forensic Medicine* 30:101–3.

Sharp, G.B., J.B. Cologne, T. Fukuhara, H. Itakura, M. Yamamoto, and S. Tokuoka. 2001. "Temporal Changes in Liver Cancer Incidence Rates in Japan: Accounting for Death Certificate Inaccuracies and Improving Diagnostic Techniques." *International Journal of Cancer* 93:751–58.

Shojiana, K.G. and E.C. Burton. 2004. "The Persistent Value of the Autopsy." *American Family Physician* 69:2540–42.

Shojiana K.G., E.C. Burton, K.M. McDonald, and L. Goldman. 2002. *The Autopsy as an Outcome and Performance Measure*. Rockville, MD, Agency for Healthcare Research and Quality.

Shultz, J.M., T.E. Novotny, D.P. Rice. 1991. "Quantifying the Disease Impact of Cigarette Smoking with SAMMEC II Software." *Public Health Reports* 106:326–33.

Sibai, A.M. 2004. "Mortality Certification and Cause of Death Reporting in Developing Countries." *Bulletin of the World Health Organization* 82:83.

Sington, J.D. and B.J. Cottrell. 2002. "Analysis of the Sensitivity of Death Certificates in 440 Hospital Deaths: A Comparison with Necropsy Findings." *Journal of Clinical Pathology* 55:499–502.

Sirken, M.G., H.M. Rosenberg, F.M. Chevarley, and L.R. Curtin. 1987. "The Quality of Cause-of-Death Statistics." *American Journal of Public Health* 77:137–39.

Soleman, N., D. Chandramohan, and K. Shibuya. 2006. "Verbal Autopsy: Current Practices and Challenges." *Bulletin of the World Health Organization* 84:239–45.

Stallard, E. 2002. "Underlying and Multiple Cause Mortality at Advanced Ages: United States 1980–1998." *North American Actuarial Journal* 6(3):64–87.

Stallard, E. 2006. "Disease Patterns in Multiple-Cause Data at Advanced Ages: United States 1980–1998." In A.M. Miniño and H.M. Rosenberg (eds.), *Proceedings of the International Collaborative Effort on Automating Mortality Statistics*, Volume 3, pp. 52–76. Hyattsville, MD, National Center for Health Statistics.

Start, R.D., J.A. Firth, F. Macgillivray, and S.S. Cross. 1995. "Have Declining Necropsy Rates Reduced the Contribution of Necropsy to Medical Research?" *Journal of Clinical Pathology* 48:402–4.

Statistics Bureau. 2009. *Japan Statistical Yearbook, 2009*. Tokyo, Statistics Bureau.

Statistics Canada. 2007. *Causes of Death*. Available at http://www.statcan.gc.ca/pub/84-208-x/84-208-x2007001-eng.htm

Statistics Norway. 2008. *Causes of Death, 2006*. Available at http://www.ssb.no/english/subjects/03/01/10/dodsarsak_en/

Stevenson, R.B. 2001. *The Quantification of Drug-Caused Mortality and Morbidity in Australia, 1998*. Canberra, Australian Institute of Health and Welfare.

Statistics Sweden. 2008. *Causes of Death, 2006*. Stockholm, Socialstyrelsen.

Tardon, A.G., J. Zaplana, R. Hernandez, and A. Cueto. 1995. "Usefulness of the Codification of Multiple Causes of Death in Mortality Statistics." *International Journal of Epidemiology* 24:1132–37.

U.S. Bureau of the Census. 1900. *Manual of International Classification of Causes of Death (ICD-1)*. Washington, DC, Government Printing Office.

U.S. Bureau of the Census. 1914. *Index of Joint Causes of Death*. Washington, DC, Government Printing Office.

U.S. Bureau of the Census. 1925. *Manual of Joint Causes of Death*. 2nd ed. Washington, DC, Government Printing Office.

U.S. Bureau of the Census. 1945. "Classifications of Terms and Comparability of Titles Through Five Revisions of the International List of Causes of Death." *Vital Statistics – Special Reports* 19(13):147–52.

United Nations. 1991. *Handbook of Vital Statistics Systems and Methods. Studies in Methods, Series F, No 35*. New York, NY, United Nations.

Van Buren, G.H. 1940. "Some Things You Can't Prove By Mortality Statistics." *Vital Statistics – Special Reports* 12:13.

Villar, J. and L. Perez-Mendez. 2007. "Evaluating an Educational Intervention to Improve the Accuracy of Death Certification among Trainees from Various Specialties." *BMC Health Services Research* 7:183.

Wood, M.J. and A.K. Guha. 2001. "Declining Clinical Autopsy Rates Versus Increasing Medicolegal Autopsy Rates in Halifax, Nova Scotia: Why the Difference? A Historical Perspective." *Archives of Pathological Laboratory Medicine* 125:924–30.

Woolsey, T.D. 1978. "Cause-of-Death Data." *Statistical Notes for Health Planners, No. 6*. Hyattsville, MD, National Center for Health Statistics.

World Health Organization (WHO). 1948. *Manual of the International Statistical Classification of Diseases, Injuries and Causes of Death, Sixth Revision*. Geneva, World Health Organization.

World Health Organization (WHO). 1977. *Manual of the International Statistical Classification of Diseases, Injuries and Causes of Death, Ninth Revision*. Geneva, World Health Organization.

World Health Organization (WHO). 2004a. *International Statistical Classification of Diseases and Related Health Problems, Tenth Revision*, Volume 1, 2nd Ed. Geneva, World Health Organization. Available at http://www.who.int/classifications/icd/en/

World Health Organization (WHO). 2004b. *International Statistical Classification of Diseases and Related Health Problems, Tenth Revision*, Volume 2, 2nd ed. Geneva, World Health Organization.

World Health Organization (WHO). 2007. *Verbal Autopsy Standards: Ascertaining and Attributing Causes of Death*. Geneva, World Health Organization.

World Health Organization (WHO). 2008. *The Global Burden of Disease: 2004 Update*. Geneva, World Health Organization.

# Chapter 23
# Avoidable Mortality

Hiram Beltrán-Sánchez

## Introduction

This chapter reviews the most relevant papers related to the concept of avoidable mortality since its origin in the late 1970s. However, for the presentation of empirical results, I concentrate on research published after 2005; for earlier years, there is a review of the literature by Nolte and McKee covering about 200 articles related to avoidable mortality. I searched PubMed and ISI-Web of Science for articles using key words such as avoidable mortality, avoidable causes, amenable mortality, and amenable causes. Additionally, I provide a summary table of avoidable conditions used by different authors at various times using the ninth international classification of diseases (ICD9).[1]

The chapter is divided into five sections. The first three describe the historical development of the concept of avoidable mortality in the late 1970s, 1980s, 1990s, and 2000s, followed by a section on recent empirical results from studies on avoidable mortality. Then, I conclude with a discussion of some limitations of the concept of avoidable mortality.

## Historical Development of the Concept of Avoidable Mortality

The concept of avoidable mortality derives from the work of Rutstein and colleagues, who wanted alternative measures of the quality of medical care "based on all unnecessary diseases, disabilities, and untimely deaths" (1976: 583). The authors viewed unnecessary and untimely deaths as cases in which death should not have occurred if everything had gone well in the medical care system, including the use of timely and effective medical care. The occurrence of these deaths "is a warning signal, a sentinel health event that the quality of care may need to be improved" (1976: 583). The medical care system being evaluated in this approach is broadly defined as "the application of all relevant medical knowledge, the basic and applied research ..., the services of all medical and allied health personnel, institutions and laboratories, the resources of governmental, voluntary, and social agencies, and the co-operative responsibilities of the individual himself" (1976: 582).

Rutstein and colleagues separated conditions into three main groups based on whether the condition was viewed as preventable and/or treatable. The authors stated that the list of conditions was derived with "the assistance of specialists in many fields of medicine" (1976: 583); that is, they provided no scientific evidence to support their choice of conditions. For each condition they distinguished among unnecessary disease, unnecessary disability, and unnecessary

H. Beltrán-Sánchez (✉)
Andrus Gerontology Center, University of Southern California, Los Angeles, CA 90089, USA
e-mail: beltrans@usc.edu

[1] ICD codes have been adopted by most of the countries in the world to classify causes of death. The version currently use in vital statistics agencies is ICD10 but I use ICD9 to summarize the conditions because this is the most common classification used in the literature. There are, however, some differences in cause codification between ICD classifications. For further details see Chapter 22 by Robert Anderson in this volume in which he describes these differences and their importance for mortality analysis when making comparison across ICD classifications. In addition, more details in cause-specific nomenclature in ICD codes are found at the World Health Organization website: www.who.int/classifications/icd/en

untimely death. The first group, "clear-cut" cases, corresponded to conditions in which each case of a disease, disability, or untimely death could be viewed as either preventable, treatable, or both. For example, all deaths from tuberculosis were considered unnecessary deaths that could have been treated. Thus, the occurrence of any condition in this group should have raised the question of "why did it happen?" The second group included conditions in which the presence of effective and timely medical care should have lowered incidence rates for that condition, even if not every case was preventable or treatable. For example, Hodgkin's disease was considered an unnecessary and untimely death that could be treated at lower stages of malignancy in young people. The last group comprised conditions that could have a serious effect on health but whose diagnosis, prevention, and treatment might not be very well-defined.

The authors identified some conditions as providing particularly clear warning signals. For example, deaths from asthma among people aged 50 or younger were considered sentinel health events reflecting the quality of medical care. The idea was that with good medical care, the number of these deaths should be very low.

The Rutstein group developed their initial list of conditions using the eighth ICD. They subsequently updated it for comparability with the ninth ICD revision, but, as in the first version, the authors provided no evidence to support their selection of causes (Rutstein et al. 1980: 583).

Rutstein's approach has been the basis for the concept and operationalization of avoidable mortality used in the literature. By 1990, there were about a dozen papers on avoidable mortality in which the categorization of causes of death was mainly derived from Rutstein's. Most of this work focused on European countries—Belgium (Humblet et al. 1987), England and Wales (Bauer and Charlton 1986; Carr-Hill et al. 1987; Charlton and Velez 1986; Charlton et al. 1983), the Netherlands (Mackenbach et al. 1988a, b; Mackenbach et al. 1990), and Finland (Poikolainen and Eskola 1986)—on the United States (Adler 1978); and on cross-country mortality comparisons (Holland 1986, 1988, 1991, 1993, 1997; Kunst et al. 1988; Poikolainen and Eskola 1988). However, the work by Charlton and colleagues, Holland and colleagues, Poikolainen and Eskola, and Mackenbach and colleagues modified the lists of conditions included in avoidable mortality to some extent, and these modifications became the basis for most studies after the 1990s. At this point, the focus on avoidable mortality shifted to selecting conditions based on the particular mechanism that was thought to be responsible for their prevention and/or treatment. Thus, conditions were generally classified as medical care indicators, and health policy indicators (Nolte and McKee 2003, 2004, 2008; Nolte et al. 2002; Simonato et al. 1998; Tobias and Jackson 2001; Tobias and Yeh 2007; Westerling 2003; Westerling et al. 1996).

## Conception of Avoidable Mortality in the 1980s

Charlton and colleagues (1983) studied variation in mortality from amenable causes in England and Wales, using a subset of conditions from Rutstein's list. Charlton and colleagues selected 14 causes of death from Rutstein's list, "conditions that were regarded as most amenable to medical intervention (excluding conditions whose control depends mainly on prevention such as lung cancer) and for which there were sufficient numbers of deaths to make a feasible analysis of the variation in mortality rates" (1983: 691). The main difference from Rutstein's work is that Charlton and colleagues focused on causes that were mainly treatable, which they called amenable conditions, excluding preventable conditions. That is, their concept of amenable mortality was a subset of the more general construct of avoidable mortality. Although they selected causes for which there were sufficient numbers of deaths to make analysis feasible, they excluded, without explanation, some causes with large numbers of deaths such as prostate, colon, and rectal cancers, epilepsy, and peptic ulcers (Table 23.1). Like Rutstein et al. (1976), Charlton et al. (1983) linked their concept of amenable mortality to certain ages, which varied somewhat by cause, but for most of the causes, the range comprised ages 5–64 years. A year later, Charlton et al. (1984) classified deaths from each cause as being indicative of failures in hospitals, general practice, or public health services. Neither of these studies, however, provided epidemiologic evidence to support the selection of causes as being avoidable causes of death.

In a subsequent analysis comparing mortality rates from avoidable causes in six countries, Charlton and

23 Avoidable Mortality  493

**Table 23.1** List of avoidable causes of death from relevant studies, 1983–2002

| Cause of death | ICD9 | (1)[a] 1983 | (2) 1986 | (3) 1988/91 | (4)[b] 1993 | (5) 1997 | (6)[a] 1986 | (7)[a] 1988 | (8)[b] 1988 | (9) 1993 | (10) 1996 | (11) 1998 | (12) PAM[c] | SAM | TAM | (13) 2002 |
|---|---|---|---|---|---|---|---|---|---|---|---|---|---|---|---|---|
| *Infectious diseases* | | | | | | | | | | | | | | | | |
| Typhoid | 002.0 | | | X | | | AM | AM | | | | Group 3 | 0.30 | 0.40 | 0.30 | MCI |
| Brucellosis | 023 | | | | X | | | AM | | | | Group 3 | 0.90 | 0.05 | 0.05 | |
| Diphtheria | 032 | | | | | | | AM | Group VII | | | Group 3 | 0.90 | 0.05 | 0.05 | MCI |
| Whooping cough | 033 | | | X | | | AM | AM | Group VII | | | Group 3 | 0.90 | 0.05 | 0.05 | MCI |
| Streptococcus | 034 | X | | | | | AM | AM | | | | Group 3 | 0.30 | 0.40 | 0.30 | |
| Meningococcal infection | 036 | | | | | | PAM | AM | | | | Group 3 | 0.30 | 0.40 | 0.30 | |
| Tetanus | 037 | | | X | | | AM | AM | Group VII | | | Group 3 | 0.90[1] | 0.050[1] | 0.050[1] | MCI |
| Septicemia | 038 | | | | | | | PAM | Group IV | | | Group 3 | | | | MCI |
| Poliomyelitis | 045 | | | | | | AM | AM | Group VII | | | Group 3 | 0.90 | 0.05 | 0.05 | MCI |
| Measles | 055 | | | X | | | AM | AM | | | | Group 3 | 0.90 | 0.05 | 0.05 | MCI |
| Rubella | 056 | | | | | | | PAM | | | | Group 3 | 0.90 | 0.05 | 0.05 | |
| Hepatitis | 070 | | | | | | | AM | | | | Group 3 | 0.70 | 0.10 | 0.20 | |
| Malaria | 084 | | | | | | | AM | | | | Group 3 | 0.30 | 0.40 | 0.30 | |
| Syphilis | 090–97 | | | | | | AM | AM | | | | Group 3 | 0.80[2] | 0.10[2] | 0.10[2] | |
| Osteomyelitis | 730 | X[3] | | X | | | AM | AM | | | | Group 3 | | | | MCI |
| Other infectious diseases – Part I[d] 001, 002.1–003, 004.0, 006, 008–9, 020, 022, 050, 060, 098, 126 | | | | | | | AM | AM | | | | Group 3 | | | | MCI[4] |
| Other infectious diseases – Part II[e] 030, 035, 087, 120,125, 127–28 | | | | | | | | AM | | | | Group 3 | 0.30[5] | 0.40[5] | 0.30[5] | |
| All other[f] 005, 007, 021, 024–27, 031, 040, 047–48, 051–54, 057, 061, 065–66, 071–72, 074–79, 085, 088, 099, 100–04, 110–11, 113–118, 130–36 | | | | | | | | PAM | | | | Group 3[6] | 0.30[7] | 0.40[7] | 0.30[7] | |
| Tuberculosis | 010–18, 137 | X | X | X | | X | AM | AM | Group IV | | | | 0.60 | 0.35 | 0.05 | MCI |
| HIV/AIDS | 042 | | | | | | | | | | HPI | | 0.90 | 0.05 | 0.05 | |
| *Malignant neoplasms of* | | | | | | | | | | | | | | | | |
| Lip | 140 | | | | | | | | Group X | | | Group 1 | 0.60 | 0.10 | 0.30 | |
| Buccal cavity and pharynx | 141–149 | | | | | | PAM | PAM | | | | Group 1 | 0.80 | 0.10 | 0.10 | |
| Esophagus | 150 | | | | | | | | | | | Group 1 | | | | |
| Stomach | 151 | | | | | | | | | | | | 0.40 | 0.20 | 0.40 | |

Table 23.1 (continued)

| Cause of death | ICD9 | (1)[a] 1983 | (2) 1986 | (3) 1988/91 | (4)[b] 1993 | (5) 1997 | (6)[a] 1986 | (7)[a] 1988 | (8)[b] 1988 | (9) 1993 | (10) 1996 | (11) 1998 | (12) PAM[c] | SAM | TAM | (13) 2002 |
|---|---|---|---|---|---|---|---|---|---|---|---|---|---|---|---|---|
| Large intestine, except rectum | 153 | | | | | | | | | MCI | MCI | | 0.40 | 0.50 | 0.10 | MCI |
| Rectum and rectosigmoid junction | 154 | | | | | | | | | MCI | MCI | | 0.40 | 0.50 | 0.10 | MCI |
| Liver | 155 | | | | | | PAM | | | | | Group 1 | 0.70 | 0.10 | 0.20 | PPI |
| Larynx | 161 | | | | | | | | | | | Group 2 | | | | |
| Trachea, bronchus, and lung | 162 | | | X | | | | | | HPI | HPI | Group 1 | 0.95 | 0.00 | 0.05 | MCI |
| Skin | 173 | | | | X | | PAM | PAM | Group X | | | Group 2[8] | 0.15 | 0.35 | 0.50 | MCI |
| Breast | 174 | | | | X | | | | | | OI | Group 2 | 0.30 | 0.50 | 0.20 | MCI |
| Cervix uteri | 180 | X | X | X | | X | AM | AM | Group X | MCI | MCI | Group 2 | 0.10 | 0.40 | 0.50 | MCI |
| Uterus | 179, 182 | | | X | | X | | | | | | Group 2 | 0.00 | 0.30 | 0.70 | |
| Testis | 186 | | | | X | | | | Group X | | | Group 3 | | | | |
| Bladder | 188 | | | | | | | | | | | Group 1 | 0.00 | 0.00 | 1.00 | |
| Kidney | 189 | | | | | | | | Group X | | | | 0.10 | 0.20 | 0.70 | |
| Eye | 190 | | | | | | | | | | | | | | | |
| Thyroid | 193 | | | | | | | | | | | | | | | |
| Hodgkin's disease | 201 | X | X | X | | X | | | Group X | | MCI | Group 3 | 0.00 | 0.10 | 0.90 | MCI |
| Leukemia | 204–208 | | | | X | | | | Group X | | | Group 3 | 0.05[9] | 0.05[9] | 0.90[9] | MCI |
| Benign neoplasm and unspec. | 210–29, 235–39 | | | | | | | PAM | | | | | 0.00[10] | 0.00[10] | 1.00[10] | |
| Goiter/thyrotoxicosis | 240–42 | | | | | | AM | AM | Group I | | | | 0.10[11] | 0.70[11] | 0.20[11] | MCI |
| Diabetes mellitus | 250 | | | | | | AM | AM | Group I | | MCI | | 0.30 | 0.50 | 0.10 | MCI |
| Other endocrine and metabolic disease | 245–46, 251–59, 270–78 | | | | | | | PAM | Group I[12] | | | | 0.00[13] | 0.80[13] | 0.20[13] | MCI[12] |
| Nutritional deficiencies | 260–69 | | | | | | AM | AM | Group I[14] | | | | 1.00 | 0.00 | 0.00 | |
| Deficiency anemias | 280–81 | X | | | | | | | Group I | | | | 1.00 | 0.00 | 0.00 | |
| Other anemia | Remainder of 281 | | | | | | | PAM | | | | | | | | |
| Other diseases of blood and blood-forming organs | 286–89 | | | | | | | | | | | | 0.90 | 0.00 | 0.10 | |
| Psychosis, alcoholism, alcoholism cardiomyopathy | 291, 303, 305.0, 425.5 | | | | | | PAM | PAM | | | | | | | | |
| Meningitis | 320–22 | X | | | | | | | | | MCI[15] | | 0.9[16] | 0.05[16] | 0.05[16] | |

**Table 23.1** (continued)

| Cause of death | ICD9 | (1)[a] 1983 | (2) 1986 | (3) 1988/91 | (4)[b] 1993 | (5) 1997 | (6)[a] 1986 | (7)[a] 1988 | (8)[b] 1988 | (9) 1993 | (10) 1996 | (11) 1998 | (12) PAM[c] | SAM | TAM | (13) 2002 |
|---|---|---|---|---|---|---|---|---|---|---|---|---|---|---|---|---|
| Epilepsy | 345 | | | | | | AM | AM | | | | | 0.00 | 0.90 | 0.10 | |
| Other diseases of nervous system and sense organs 323–25, 336, 341, 343–44, 346, 348, 350–59, 361–62, 367, 369, 371, 378–79, 384–89 | | | | | | | PAM | PAM | | | | | | | | |
| Inflammatory diseases of eye, cataract, glaucoma | 363–66, 370, 372–76 | | | | | | | AM | | | | | | | | |
| Otitis media and mastoiditis | 381–83 | X | | | | | AM | AM | | | | | 0.10 | 0.70 | 0.20 | |
| Active rheumatic fever | 390–92 | X | | | | | AM | AM | | | | | 0.30 | 0.60 | 0.10 | |
| Chronic rheumatic heart disease | 393–98 | X | X | X | | X | PAM | PAM | Group VI | | MCI | Group 3 | | | | MCI |
| Hypertensive disease | 401–04 | X | X | X | | X | AM | AM | Group IX | | MCI[17] | Group 3[17] | 0.30[18] | 0.65[18] | 0.05[18] | MCI[17] |
| Ischemic heart disease | 410–14 | | X | X | X[19] | X[19] | PAM | PAM[20] | | | MCI | | 0.50 | 0.25 | 0.25 | MCI/PPI |
| Cerebrovascular disease | 430–38 | | X | X | | X | AM | AM | Group IX | MCI | MCI | Group 1 | 0.30[21] | 0.50[21] | 0.20[21] | MCI |
| Venous thrombosis and embolism | 451–53 | | | | | | | AM | | | | | | | | |
| *All respiratory diseases* | | | | | | | | | | | | | | | | |
| Acute respiratory infections | 460–66 | X | | X | | | AM | AM | | | | Group 3 | 0.40 | 0.50 | 0.10 | MCI |
| Pneumonia | 480–86 | X | | X | | X | AM | AM | Group IV | MCI[22] | | Group 3 | 0.40 | 0.50 | 0.10 | MCI |
| Influenza | 487 | | | X | | X | AM | AM | Group IV | | | Group 3 | 0.40 | 0.50 | 0.10 | MCI |
| Bronchitis | 490 | X | | X | | X | AM | AM | | | | Group 3 | 0.80 | 0.10 | 0.10 | MCI |
| Chronic bronchitis/emphysema | 491–92 | | | X | | X | AM | AM | | MCI | MCI | Group 3 | 0.80[23] | 0.10[23] | 0.10[23] | MCI |
| Asthma | 493 | X | | X | | X | AM | AM | | MCI | MCI | Group 3 | 0.10 | 0.70 | 0.20 | MCI |
| Other diseases of respiratory system 470–73, 475–78, 494–96, 500–09, 511–12, 514–19 | | | | | | X | | PAM | | | | Group 3 | | | | MCI |
| Hypertrophy of tonsils; empyema, and abscess of lung | 474, 510, 513 | | | X | | X | | AM | | | | Group 3 | | | | MCI |
| Diseases of teeth and supporting structures | 520–25 | | | | | | | AM | | | | | | | | |
| Peptic ulcer | 531–34 | | | | X | X | AM | AM | Group II | MCI[24] | MCI[24] | Group 3 | 0.05 | 0.75 | 0.20 | MCI[25] |
| Gastritis and duodenitis | 535 | | | | | | AM | AM | | | | | 0.90[26] | 0.00[26] | 0.10[26] | |
| Appendicitis | 540–43 | X | X | X | | X | AM | AM | Group II | | MCI | Group 3 | 0.00 | 0.00 | 1.00 | MCI |

**Table 23.1** (continued)

| Cause of death | ICD9 | (1)[a] 1983 | (2) 1986 | (3) 1988/91 | (4)[b] 1993 | (5) 1997 | (6)[a] 1986 | (7)[a] 1988 | (8)[b] 1988 | (9) 1993 | (10) 1996 | (11) 1998 | (12) PAM[c] | SAM | TAM | (13) 2002 |
|---|---|---|---|---|---|---|---|---|---|---|---|---|---|---|---|---|
| Hernia or abdominal cavity | 550–53 | X | | | | X | AM | AM | Group II | | | Group 3 | 0.00 | 0.00 | 1.00 | MCI |
| Intestinal obstruction | 560 | | | X | | | AM | AM | Group II | | | | 0.00 | 0.00 | 1.00 | |
| Cholelithiasis and cholecystitis | 574–75 | X[27] | X | X | | X | AM | AM | Group II[28] | | | Group 3 | 0.20[29] | 0.00[29] | 0.80[29] | MCI |
| Other diseases of digestive system | 526–30, 534, 536–37, 555–58, 562–69, 572–73, 576–77 | | | | | | | PAM | | | | | | | | |
| Cirrhosis of liver | 571 | | | | | | | | | HPI | HPI | Group 1 | 0.90[30] | 0.00[30] | 0.10[30] | PPI |
| Nephritis and nephrosis | 580–589 | | | X | | | | AM[31] | Group VIII | | | | 0.10[32] | 0.20[32] | 0.70[32] | MCI |
| Diseases of genito-urinary system | 590, 592, 594, 600, 610–11 | | | | | | | AM | Group III[33] | | | | | | | MCI[33] |
| Other diseases of genito-urinary system | 591, 593, 595–99, 601–08, 614–29 | | | | | | | PAM | | | | | 0.80[34] | 0.10[34] | 0.10[34] | |
| Maternal deaths (all causes) | 630–76 | X | X | X | | X | AM | AM | Group III | | | Group 3 | 0.20 | 0.50 | 0.30 | MCI |
| Inflammatory conditions of skin/arthropathies/ rheumatism | 690–709, 710, 712–16, 725–29 | | | | | | | AM | | | | | | | | |
| Infections of skin, bone and joints | 680–86, 711, 730 | X | | | | | | | | | | | 0.20 | 0.50 | 0.30 | |
| Spondylopathies and acquired musculoskeletal deformities | 720, 734, 737–38 | | | | | | | AM | | | | | | | | |
| Other diseases of musculoskeletal system | 718–19, 731–33 | | | | | | | PAM | | | | | | | | |
| Congenital anomalies of brain and spinal cord | 740–742 | | | | | | | | | | | | 0.60 | 0.20 | 0.20 | |

23  Avoidable Mortality

**Table 23.1** (continued)

| Cause of death | ICD9 | Source (1)[a] 1983 | (2) 1986 | (3) 1988/91 | (4)[b] 1993 | (5) 1997 | (6)[a] 1986 | (7)[a] 1988 | (8)[b] 1988 | (9) 1993 | (10) 1996 | (11) 1998 | (12) PAM[c] | SAM | TAM | (13) 2002 |
|---|---|---|---|---|---|---|---|---|---|---|---|---|---|---|---|---|
| Congenital cardiovascular anomalies | 745–747 | | | | X | | | | Group V | MCI[35] | | | 0.10[36] | 0.20[36] | 0.70[36] | MCI |
| Cleft palate and cleft lip | 749 | | | | | | | AM | | MCI | | | 0.10 | 0.20 | 0.70 | |
| Congenital digestive anomalies | 750, 751 | | | | | | | | Group V | | | | 0.10[37] | 0.20[37] | 0.70[37] | |
| Certain causes of perinatal mortality | ICD 8: 760–778 | | | | | | | | | MCI | | | | | | |
| Diseases of the mother | 760 | | | | | | | | Group III | | | | | | | MCI |
| Conditions of placenta and cord | 762 | | | | | | AM | | Group III | | | | | | | MCI |
| Prematurity, low birthweight, respiratory disease from prematurity | 764–765, 770.7 | | | | | | | | | | | | 0.50[38] | 0.10[38] | 0.40[38] | MCI |
| Birth injury and difficult labor | 763, 767, 768.2–.9, 769 | | | | | | AM | AM | Group III[39] | | | | 0.10[40] | 0.40[40] | 0.50[40] | MCI |
| Hemolytic disease | 773.0–.2, 773.4 | | | | | | AM | AM | Group III | | | | | | | MCI |
| Anoxic and hypoxic conditions | 768.0–.1 | | | | | | AM | AM | | | | | | | | MCI |
| Other causes of perinatal morbidity and mortality | Remainder or 764–779 | | | | | | AM | | Group III | | | | 0.30[41] | 0.20[41] | 0.50[41] | MCI |
| Symptoms and other ill-defined conditions | 781, 785–88, 798–99 | | | | | | | PAM | | | | | 1.00[42] | 0.00[42] | 0.00[42] | |
| *Injury and poisoning* | | | | | | | | | | | | | | | | |
| Motor vehicle accidents | E810–825 | | | | | | | | | HPI | HPI | Group 1 | 0.60[43] | 0.00[43] | 0.40[43] | PPI |
| Poisoning | E850–869 | | | | | | | | | | | Group 1 | 0.60 | 0.00 | 0.40 | |
| Swimming pool falls and drownings | E883.0, E910.5, E910.6 | | | | | | | | | | | Group 1 | 0.80 | 0.00 | 0.20 | |
| Falls from playground equipment, sport injury | E884.0, E884.5, E886.0, EE917.0, E927 | | | | | | | | | | | Group 1 | 0.60 | 0.00 | 0.40 | |

**Table 23.1** (continued)

| Cause of death | ICD9 | Source (1)[a] 1983 | (2) 1986 | (3) 1988/91 | (4)[b] 1993 | (5) 1997 | (6)[a] 1986 | (7)[a] 1988 | (8)[b] 1988 | (9) 1993 | (10) 1996 | (11) 1998 | (12) PAM[c] | SAM | TAM | (13) 2002 |
|---|---|---|---|---|---|---|---|---|---|---|---|---|---|---|---|---|
| Burns and scalds | E890–899 | | | | | | | | | | | Group 1 | 0.80 | 0.00 | 0.20 | |
| Drowning | E910–910.4, E910.7–910.9, E984 | | | | | | | | | | | Group 1 | 0.80 | 0.00 | 0.20 | |
| Suicide | E950–959, E980–989 | | | | | | | | | | OI | Group 1 | 0.60 | 0.30 | 0.10 | |
| Complications of treatment | E870–879 | | | | | | | | | | | Group 1 | 0.00 | 0.20 | 0.80 | |
| Other injury and poisoning | remainder of E800–999 | | | | | | | | | | | Group 1 | | | | |

Note: AM stands for "amenable to medical care," PAM for "partly amenable," MCI stands for "medical care indicator," OI represents "other indicator (neither MCI nor HPI)," HPI corresponds to "health policy indicator," PPI stands for "primary prevention (national health policy) indicator," Group I corresponds to "specific medical therapies," Group II corresponds to "improvements in surgery/anesthesia," Group III corresponds to "improvements in antenatal and perinatal care," Group IV corresponds to "chemotherapeutics and antibiotics," Group V corresponds to "surgical repair of congenital anomalies," Group VI corresponds to "prophylaxies and heart valve surgery," Group VII correspond to "mass vaccinations," Group VIII corresponds to "hemodialysis," Group IX corresponds to "hypertension detection and treatment," Group X corresponds to "improvements in cancer treatment," Group XI corresponds to "mass screening," Group 1 corresponds to "avoidable causes through primary prevention," Group 2 are causes "avoidable through early detection and treatment," and Group 3 are "causes avoidable through improved treatment and medical care."

Source: (1) Charlton et al. (1983), (2) Charlton and Velez (1986), (3) Holland (1988), (4) Holland (1991), (5) Holland (1997), (6) Poikolainen and Eskola (1986), (7) Poikolainen and Eskola (1988), (8) Mackenbach et al. (1988b), (9) Westerling et al. (1993), (10) Westerling et al. (1996), (11) Simonato et al. (1998), (12) Tobias and Jackson (2001), and (13) Nolte et al. (2002).

[a] I assigned the disaggregated ICD9 codes.
[b] ICD-9 codes taken from Nolte and McKee (2004).
[c] PAM: Primary avoidable mortality; SAM: Secondary avoidable mortality; TAM: Tertiary avoidable mortality. Each number corresponds to the proportion of deaths for each cause considered to be avoidable.
[d] Cholera/paratyphoid fever and other salmonella infections/bacillary dysentery and amebiasis/enteritis and other diarrheal diseases/plague/anthrax/smallpox/yellow fever/gonococcal infections/ankylostomiasis.
[e] Leprosy/erysipelas/relapsing fever/schistosomiasis/filarial infection/other helminthiasis.
[f] Other bacterial/other viral/all other infective and parasitic diseases.

[1] Also includes tetanus neonatorum (ICD9 code 771.3).
[2] Also includes gonococcal infections, and other venereal diseases (ICD9 codes 098–99).
[3] Only includes dysentery (ICD9 code 004).
[4] Includes all intestinal infectious diseases except typhoid (ICD9 codes 001–009).
[5] Only includes leprosy and erysipelas (ICD9 codes 030, 035).
[6] Also includes late affects of poliomyelitis and of other infectious and parasitic diseases (ICD9 codes 138–39).
[7] Only includes glanders, melioidosis (ICD9 codes 024, 025).
[8] Also includes malignant melanoma of skin (ICD9 code 172).

**Table 23.1** (continued)

[9] Only includes lymphoid leukemia (ICD9 code 204).
[10] Also includes carcinoma in situ (ICD9 code 230–34), but it does not include cancers of uncertain behavior (ICD9 code 235–39).
[11] Also includes acquired hypothyroidism (ICD9 code 244).
[12] Only includes congenital hypothyroidism, acquired hypothyroidism, thyroiditis, and other disorders of the thyroid (ICD9 code 243–46).
[13] Only includes congenital hypothyroidism, adrenogenital disorders, phenylketonuria (PKU), galactosemia (ICD9 codes 243, 255.2, 270.1, 271.1).
[14] Only includes pernicious anemia (ICD9 code 281.0).
[15] Only includes bacterial meningitis (ICD9 code 320).
[16] Includes only hemophilus meningitis (ICD9 code 320.0).
[17] Includes secondary hypertension (ICD9 code 405).
[18] Also includes secondary hypertension and hypertensive encephalopathy (ICD9 codes 405, 437.2).
[19] Also includes unspecified cardiovascular disease (ICD9 code 429.2).
[20] Also includes other forms of heart disease (ICD9 code 420–29).
[21] Only includes intracerebral hemorrhage, occlusion and stenosis of precerebral arteries, occlusion of cerebral arteries, and acute but ill-defined cerebrovascular disease (ICD9 codes 431, 433–34, 436).
[22] Only includes pneumonia other than viral (ICD8 codes 481, 486).
[23] Also includes chronic airways obstruction, not elsewhere classified (ICD9 code 496).
[24] Only includes gastric and duodenal ulcers (ICD9 codes 531–32, 534).
[25] Does not include gastrojejunal ulcer (ICD9 code 534).
[26] Only includes alcoholic gastritis (ICD9 code 535.3).
[27] Only includes acute and other cholecystitis (ICD9 code 575.0–575.1).
[28] Also includes cholangitis (ICD9 code 576.1).
[29] Also includes other disorders of billiary tract (ICD9 code 576).
[30] Only includes alcoholic liver cirrhosis (ICD9 codes 571.0–0.5).
[31] Only includes acute nephritis (ICD9 code 584).
[32] Only includes acute renal failure (ICD9 code 584).
[33] Only includes benign prostatic hyperplasia (ICD9 code 600).
[34] Only includes inflammatory disease of ovary, fallopian tube, pelvic cellular tissue, and peritoneum (ICD9 codes 614.0–614.5, 614.7–616.9).
[35] Only includes congenital malformations of heart (ICD9 code 746).
[36] Only includes congenital anomalies of eye, ear, face, neck, bulbus cordis, cardiac septal closure, other congenital anomalies of heart, and other congenital anomalies of circulatory system (ICD9 codes 743–746.6, 746.8–747.9).
[37] Also includes congenital anomalies of genital organs, urinary system, musculoskeletal deformities, the integument, other congenital anomalies of limbs, other congenital musculoskeletal anomalies, chromosomal anomalies, and other and unspecified congenital anomalies (ICD9 codes 752–59).
[38] Also includes other complications of pregnancy and childbirth (ICD9 code 769).
[39] Also includes fetus or newborn affected by maternal complications of pregnancy (ICD9 code 761).
[40] Also includes meconium aspiration syndrome, fetal blood loss, and umbilical hemorrhage after birth (ICD9 codes 770.1, 772.0, 772.3).
[41] Only includes birth trauma, intra-uterine hypoxia and birth asphyxia, meconium aspiration syndrome, fetal blood loss, and umbilical hemorrhage after birth (ICD9 codes 767–768, 770.1, 772.0, 772.3).
[42] Only includes sudden infant death (ICD9 code 798.0).
[43] Also includes other road vehicle accidents (ICD9 codes E826–29).

Velez selected only 9 causes from their original list of 14, but added cerebrovascular disease as an amenable cause. The inclusion of cerebrovascular disease as amenable was based on empirical evidence from the "Hypertension Detection and Follow-up Program Cooperative Group (HDFP) study that shows that mortality from strokes may be reduced by half with intensive antihypertensive treatment" (1986: 296). However, the results from the randomized controlled trial of the HDFP study came from a "preliminary analysis of mortality ... [with] no tests for statistical significance for the specific causes of death" (Hypertension Detection Follow-up Program Cooperative Group 1979: 2567). Furthermore, the authors justified their exclusion of pneumonia–bronchitis and acute respiratory diseases from their list of amenable causes because "incidence and severity tend to fluctuate widely from year to year" (1986: 296), but gave no explanation of why they excluded important conditions such as infectious diseases, deficiency anemias, and respiratory diseases (Table 23.1).

Basing its work on Rutstein's and Charlton's lists of avoidable causes, the European Community Concerted Action Project on Health Services and "Avoidable Deaths" generated several reports in a 10-year period on avoidable mortality (Holland 1988, 1991, 1993, 1997) (Table 23.1). The first, an analysis of mortality variation in Europe in the 1980s, included 17 preventable and/or treatable conditions with identifiable effective interventions (Holland 1988). The project classified the conditions into two main groups: those that were considered to be indicators of the success of national health policy in primary prevention, including causes such as lung cancer, liver cirrhosis, and motor vehicle accident; and those that reflected adequacy of curative medical care and secondary prevention. The authors restricted the age range of avoidable mortality to people younger than 65. A second edition of this document, published in 1991, incorporated eight more conditions to reflect advances in medical knowledge, for example, congenital anomalies. Finally, a last revision published in the late 1990s listed 16 conditions (Holland 1997), selected from the initial 17 causes plus the 8 added in the second revision. It is interesting to note that in the final revision cerebrovascular and ischemic heart disease were included as avoidable causes, while prostate, colon, and rectal cancers were never included in the lists.

In the late 1980s, Poikolainen and Eskola (1986, 1988) studied the impact of health services on amenable mortality in Finland and in 25 developed nations, classifying conditions as amenable or partially amenable to medical care. Most of the causes of death used by Pokolainen and Eskola are taken from Rutstein's original list, with the exception of chronic nonspecific lung disease, which is not included in Rutstein's list. Although Rutstein's group and Charlton's group noted the potential factors that influenced mortality from each condition (e.g., primary care), it was Poikoilanen and Eskola who first began grouping conditions to represent the possible effect of health interventions (Table 23.1). This grouping of conditions was the main focus of the studies conducted after the 1990s. Poikoilanen and Eskola defined one group of causes as amenable by prevention or treatment (e.g., infectious diseases and hypertensive disease); a second group as not amenable to intervention by health services (e.g., anemias and mental disorders); a third group as partly amenable, including "other deaths from natural causes ... which could not be further subdivided into categories of amenable and non-amenable deaths" (Poikolainen and Eskola 1988: 87) (e.g., cancer of the skin and ischemic heart disease); and a fourth group as violent causes (e.g., accidents, suicides, and poisonings). Their 1986 list of about 25 causes was expanded in 1988 to include about 70 amenable conditions and about 20 partly amenable causes. For most of the conditions, Poikolainen and Eskola restricted the age range to 0–64 years.

The first attempt to justify the inclusion/exclusion of causes of death classified as avoidable by using epidemiological evidence was conducted by Mackenbach and colleagues (1988b) in their study of the contribution of medical care innovations to mortality changes during 1950–1984 in the Netherlands. Their list of conditions is derived with the intention "to cover all medical care innovations, for which the evidence on favorable incidence or case fatality effects is relatively undisputed" (p. 889). They omitted conditions "for which [they] were not able to find convincing evidence of significantly increasing effectiveness of medical care (p. 889)" (e.g., cancer of the thyroid). Thus, the Mackenbach group's list is not entirely derived from that of the Rutstein group. For example, they included congenital digestive anomalies, nephritis and nephrosis, and cancer of the testis, while the Rutstein group did not include any of these causes (Table 23.1). The

Mackenbach group's lists included 35 causes divided into 11 groups by source of improvement: specific medical therapies (Group I, e.g., diseases of the thyroid), improvements in surgery/anesthesia (Group II, e.g., appendicitis), improvements in antenatal and perinatal care (Group III, e.g., maternal and perinatal causes), chemotherapeutics and antibiotics (Group IV, e.g., tuberculosis), surgical repair of congenital anomalies (Group V, e.g., congenital anomalies), prophylaxis and heart valve surgery (Group VI, e.g., rheumatic heart disease), mass vaccinations (Group VII, e.g., tetanus), hemodialysis (Group VIII, e.g., nephritis and nephrosis), hypertension detection and treatment (Group IX, e.g., cerebrovascular disease), improvements in cancer treatment (Group X, e.g., leukemia), and mass screening (Group XI, e.g, cancer of the cervix). An important difference from previous studies is that Mackenbach and colleagues found no evidence that incidence or case fatalities were limited to certain age groups, and they did not restrict mortality to specific ages (except for diabetes mellitus, where improved survival was found to be effective only among people younger than 25, and cancer of the kidney and leukemia, for which more effective treatment occurs mainly in children younger than 15). Additionally, the Mackenbach list included only four kinds of cancers—lips and skin, kidney, testis, and cervix—excluding other important cancers such as breast, prostate, and colon.

## Avoidable Mortality in the 1990s and the 2000s

In the 1990s and early 2000s, research on avoidable mortality concentrated on distinguishing between causes amenable to medical care intervention (i.e., secondary prevention and treatment), and those amenable through public health policies (Nolte et al. 2002; Simonato et al. 1998; Tobias and Jackson 2001; Westerling 1993; Westerling et al. 1996). While the Rutstein and Holland groups had previously noted the different effects of medical care interventions on specific conditions, they did not include this dimension in their classification system (Table 23.1).

Westerling and colleagues (Westerling 1993; Westerling et al. 1996), for example, used the lists of causes from the Rutstein group (1976), Holland (1988, 1991, 1997), and the Mackenbach group (1988b) to classify conditions into medical care indicators (e.g., diabetes and asthma), health policy indicators (e.g., liver cirrhosis), and other indicators. Surprisingly, infectious diseases and maternal deaths were eliminated altogether from Westerling's list.

A few years later, Simonato and colleagues (1998) further disaggregated avoidable causes by level of prevention into those that are amenable to primary prevention through reduction of exposures (Group 1), secondary prevention through early detection and treatment (Group 2), and tertiary prevention through improved treatment and medical care (Group 3). They included most of the conditions from Rutstein's, Charlton's, and Holland's lists, with a focus mainly on cancers. For example, four out of seven conditions in Group 1 are cancers, and Group 2 comprises cancers only. They eliminated important diseases even within cancer types, such as cancer of the kidney, as well as diabetes mellitus, diseases of the thyroid, deficiency anemias, perinatal deaths, nephritis and nephrosis, and congenital anomalies.[2] Most of the epidemiological evidence provided to support their selection of conditions referred to cancer types only, mainly those related to smoking, and cancers of the breast, larynx, skin, and cervix.

In the early 2000s, Tobias and Jackson (2001) extended the arbitrary age range to include people up to 75, and subcategorized avoidable causes according to the level of intervention: primary avoidable (PAM), secondary avoidable (SAM), and tertiary avoidable (TAM) (Table 23.1). This classification was based on "expert consensus" (2001: 13). A proportion of deaths from each condition was assigned to each subcategorized avoidable group. These proportions (weights) were first derived by the authors "based on extensive review of the literature" (p. 13) and then "reviewed and refined by an expert panel comprising clinicians and epidemiologists" (2001: 13). Deaths from ischemic heart disease, for example, received relative weights of 0.5, 0.25, and 0.25 corresponding to its primary (PAM), secondary (SAM), and tertiary (TAM) preventability (see Table 23.1 for more details).

---

[2] Mackenbach et al. (1988) had provided evidence to justify the inclusion of these conditions as avoidable (Table 23.1).

A year later, Nolte and colleagues (2002) returned to the original idea of the Rutstein group by focusing on "amenable," or "treatable," and "preventable" conditions. The authors defined amenable or treatable conditions as indicating the impact of medical care in the form of secondary prevention or medical treatment, and preventable conditions as representing primary prevention through health policies. They further distinguished between causes responsive to medical care and those responsive to health policy, separating, for the first time, ischemic heart disease as a cause that could be both preventable and treatable. They argued that ischemic heart disease is a condition that can represent both medical care and primary prevention. Recently, Nolte and McKee (2008) maintained that half of deaths from ischemic heart disease can be considered amenable.

From this point forward, most of the research on avoidable mortality derives lists of causes from the papers previously described.

## Results of Studies on Avoidable Mortality

Concentrating on research published after 2005, I searched PubMed and ISI-Web of Science for articles using key words such as avoidable mortality, avoidable causes, amenable mortality, and amenable causes. I divided the papers found into four groups to cover broad regions of the world: North America, Europe, Asia, and Australia and New Zealand.

### North America

There are a few papers related to avoidable mortality in Canada (James et al. 2006, 2007), the United States (Macinko and Elo 2009), and both countries (Kunitz and Pesis-Katz 2005). Some of these studies classified causes as amenable to medical care, amenable to public health policy, and all other causes, with ischemic heart disease as a separate condition (James et al. 2006, 2007). Kunitz and Pesis-Katz (2005) classified deaths as avoidable through medical care without any further disaggregation, following the concept from Holland (1988, 1991, 1997). Macinko and Elo added HIV/AIDS as a separate condition because "[this condition] was initially sensitive only to policy/behaviour interventions before the advent of highly active antiretroviral therapy in the mid-1990s, and because of its sizable contribution to black–white mortality disparities" (2009: 715). Most of the studies restricted the analysis to people younger than 65, with the exception of James et al. (2007), who extended the age range to 75 years.

Results for Canada showed important changes in amenable mortality by regions and by urban neighborhoods between the 1970s and the 1990s. For example, declines in mortality rates were more pronounced for amenable causes than for nonamenable causes between 1975 and 1979 and between 1995 and 1999, with Ontario and British Columbia having lower mortality rates from injuries, lung cancer, and ischemic heart disease than the Atlantic region (Prince Edward Island, Newfoundland, Nova Scotia, and New Brunswick), Quebec, and the Prairies region (Manitoba, Saskatchewan, and Alberta) (James et al. 2006). While income disparities in mortality in urban neighborhoods from causes amenable to public health interventions increased between 1971 and 1996 (0.7% in men and 20% in women), reductions in mortality rates from causes amenable to medical care made the largest contribution to narrowing socioeconomic mortality disparities (60% for men and 78% for women) (James et al. 2007).

For the United States, the evidence shows that "all other" causes of death were the largest contributors to the decline in the black–white mortality gap among men and women, followed by causes amenable to medical care among women, and causes amenable to policy/behavior among men (Macinko and Elo 2009). For men, for example, the black–white difference in all-cause mortality increased between 1980 and 1989 because of a widening gap in mortality from ischemic heart disease and HIV/AIDS. After 1989, there was a narrowing in the black–white mortality gap, with mortality from causes amenable to policy/behavior making the second largest contribution from 1989 to 1998, and HIV/AIDS contributing to a further decline between 1998 and 2005. For women, conditions amenable to medical care were the second largest contributors to narrowing the racial mortality gap in the whole period, followed by ischemic heart disease. A comparison of white Americans and

Canadians showed that, despite important declines in mortality rates among Americans and Canadians between 1980 and 1999, Canadians experienced much lower mortality rates for most of the amenable conditions (except for breast cancer, all respiratory diseases in children, and peptic ulcer, for which the rates are very similar) (Kunitz and Pesis-Katz 2005). Among white Americans, for example, there was a more rapid increase in mortality from HIV/AIDS in the 1980s than among Canadians. While mortality from diabetes had been increasing in both countries during the period of study, white Americans showed a more pronounced increase.

## Europe

Most of the work on avoidable mortality has been conducted in Europe, principally in Spain (Duarte et al. 2009; Gispert et al. 2008), England and Wales (Wheller et al. 2007), Norway (Dahl et al. 2007), the Netherlands (Stirbu et al. 2006), and cross-country comparisons (Nolte and McKee 2008; Stirbu et al. 2009; Weisz et al. 2008).

The results for Spain show that between the late 1980s and early 2000s most of the mortality decline was due to nonavoidable causes (Duarte et al. 2009; Gispert et al. 2008). Gispert and colleagues (2008), for example, showed that nonavoidable causes accounted for about 80% of all deaths in each 5-year period between 1987–1991 and 1997–2001. The largest contribution to the increase in life expectancy in the period was due to nonavoidable causes for both men and women. The exception is people aged 20–34, for whom avoidable causes contributed the most to the gain in life expectancy at birth for both men and women.

Mortality from amenable causes of death declined faster than mortality from nonamenable conditions in England and Wales between 1993 and 2005 (Wheller et al. 2007). Mortality from amenable causes (mainly preventable) showed a considerable decline between 1993 and 2005, but this was not the case for nonavoidable causes. Ischemic heart disease was the leading cause of amenable mortality in every year in the period of study. Among preventable deaths, smoking- and alcohol-related diseases account for the majority of deaths for both men and women.

In Norway, the empirical evidence suggests that there was a very steep educational gradient in avoidable mortality for both men and women during the 1990s. Dahl et al. (2007) showed that, for both sexes, people with only basic education had higher mortality than those with college education, but this gradient was more pronounced for avoidable causes. This result is mainly due to higher mortality rates from ischemic heart disease and preventable deaths.

Mortality comparison between migrant populations and native Dutch showed that migrants experienced a higher mortality from all avoidable causes than did native Dutch (Stirbu et al. 2006). Migrants experienced lower risks of death from most cancers than did native Dutch, but they showed higher mortality from infectious diseases (about two times higher), diabetes, hypertension, and cerebrovascular disease. Sociodemographic factors were mainly responsible for the differences in mortality between the migrant groups and the native Dutch. Surinamese and Antillean/Aruban people had higher risks of death from avoidable causes than did native Dutch, while Turkish and Moroccan people tended to have lower risks of death than the native Dutch.

International comparisons in avoidable mortality have shown that the United States has higher mortality rates from amenable conditions than do other developed countries (Nolte and McKee 2008). In their study of avoidable mortality rates in the United States, Canada, Australia, New Zealand, Japan, and 14 European countries between 1997 and 2003, Nolte and McKee (2008) found that, even though mortality from amenable conditions declined in all the countries, the United States had the slowest decline for both men and women. In particular, there has been comparatively slow progress in reducing mortality from ischemic heart disease and other circulatory diseases in the United States. However, the United States experienced the largest decline in nonavoidable mortality in the whole period. The implications of the latter result were never described by the authors. In a study comparing mortality rates from amenable causes for Paris, London, and Manhattan, Weisz et al. (2008) found that Paris had the lowest all-cause mortality and the lowest mortality from amenable conditions, while inner London had the highest amenable mortality rate. Manhattan, on the other hand, had the largest decline in amenable mortality in the period of study. However, people living in the lowest-income neighborhoods in

Manhattan experienced a significantly higher mortality rate from avoidable causes than did those living in better-off neighborhoods. This is not the case for neighborhoods in London and Paris. Finally, Stirbu and colleagues studied educational inequalities in avoidable mortality in 16 European countries between 1990 and 2000 and found that there were large educational inequalities in mortality from infectious and from cardio-respiratory diseases in all European countries. In particular, people living in central eastern Europe and the Baltic experienced the largest educational inequalities in avoidable mortality, while people living in southern Europe had the lowest inequalities in mortality.

## Asia

A recent article published in Korea (Chung et al. 2008) described time trends in all-cause and avoidable mortality between 1983 and 2004 by sex. The authors classified conditions as avoidable through primary prevention, secondary prevention, and hygiene conditions and medical care. They added stomach and colorectal cancers to their list, but excluded perinatal deaths because of possible data errors (mainly underreporting of deaths). For most of the causes, they restricted the age range to ages 1–64 years. Their results showed continuous mortality decline over the period of study, with mortality avoidable through medical care showing the fastest decline. Although men had higher mortality from each avoidable cause, they benefited more than women from reductions in mortality avoidable through secondary prevention, whereas women benefited more from declines in mortality avoidable through primary prevention and medical care.

## Australia and New Zealand

Recent work in Australia and New Zealand has been carried out by Korda et al. (2007, 2006), Piers et al. (2007), and Tobias and Yeh (2007, 2009). Korda and colleagues classified conditions into two main groups, amenable to medical care and responsive to health policy but with no effective treatment once the condition has developed, with ischemic heart disease as a separate cause. The studies by Piers et al. (2007), and Tobias and Yeh (2007, 2009) used Tobias and Jackson's list of conditions in which causes of death are classified into PAM, SAM, and TAM (see Table 23.1 for more details). All these studies restricted the age range to people younger than 75 years.

The studies in Australia show that mortality from avoidable causes has declined faster than mortality from nonavoidable causes for both men and women since the late 1960s, but there remain important mortality differentials by socioeconomic groups (Korda and Butler 2006; Korda et al. 2007). Between 1968 and 2001 mortality from all avoidable causes experienced a yearly decline of about 3.5 and 3.9% in women and men, respectively, while the corresponding figures for nonavoidable causes were 1.1 and 0.95% (Korda and Butler 2006). For men, the decline in avoidable mortality can be attributed to reductions of about 57% in ischemic heart disease deaths, 32% in deaths from causes amenable to medical care, and 11% in deaths from conditions amenable to health policies. For women, the corresponding percentages are 45, 54, and 1%, respectively. Declines in avoidable mortality resulted in a rise in relative mortality inequality, with the lowest quintile of socioeconomic status (SES) having lower declines than the highest quintile (Korda et al. 2007). The relative inequality was larger for conditions amenable to public policy and ischemic heart disease but not for treatable conditions. In addition, there was a decrease in absolute inequality in avoidable mortality over time, but not in nonavoidable mortality. In a study in Victoria, Australia, Piers et al. (2007) showed that avoidable mortality declined about 5 and 3.6 times faster than nonavoidable mortality in men and women, respectively. In rural places, men had significantly higher avoidable mortality rates than females, whereas in metropolitan areas, the sex difference was almost negligible.

For New Zealand, the two recent studies focused on estimating trends in amenable causes by ethnic groups and SES (Tobias and Yeh 2007, 2009). Both studies restricted the age range to people younger than 75, but they cover different time periods, 2000–2002 (Tobias and Yeh 2007) and 1981–1984 to 2001–2004 (Tobias and Yeh 2009). The main difference between these studies is that the former uses small-area deprivation as a measure of SES, while the latter uses an adjusted household income based on household size and composition. The results of both studies are very similar, suggesting that amenable mortality made a higher contribution to the mortality decline among women than among men, a higher contribution for European/other, Maori, and Asian people than for Pacific people, and a higher contribution for low- and middle-SES groups than for those of high SES.

## Limitations of the Avoidable Mortality Approach

Critics have pointed to several limitations on the usefulness and accuracy of the avoidable mortality approach for assessing the contribution of health care to population health. Some authors argue that if avoidable mortality is an indicator of the effectiveness of medical treatment, then there should be a clear association between health care resources and avoidable mortality (Carr-Hill et al. 1987). The empirical evidence does not show such an association (Carr-Hill et al. 1987; Kunst et al. 1988; Mackenbach et al. 1988a). Nolte and McKee (2004) argue that the lack of association may be due to poor data quality (whether the "data reflect only what is measurable and not necessarily what is important" or "geographical level analysis may be insufficiently detailed to identify any real differences"), or to unspecified lags between changes in resources and changes in mortality.

In addition, as Table 23.1 shows, there is no clear rule for classifying conditions as avoidable. For example, even in their latest update of conditions, Nolte and McKee (2008) have failed to include prostate cancer as an avoidable cause, even though the 5-year survival rate from prostate cancer in the United States is close to 100% (above 99%) and the disease can be readily identified (Preston and Ho 2009). In the latest edition of the *European Community Atlas of Avoidable Mortality* in 1997, the authors did not include important causes of death associated with behavioral factors such as lung cancer (which are mostly due to smoking), cirrhosis of the liver (mostly due to drinking), homicides, and motor vehicle accidents. More importantly, HIV/AIDS has been excluded as an avoidable cause (except in Tobias and Jackson (2001)), even though mortality rates from this condition have had important impacts in changing life expectancy (see Chapter 8 by Bongaarts, Pelletier, and Gerland, this volume; Macinko and Elo 2009).

Additionally, the rule for deciding what proportion of deaths from each cause is considered amenable to medical care seems rather subjective. The weighting system developed by Tobias and Jackson (2001) and Nolte and McKee (2008) to define the proportions of deaths from each cause that are considered avoidable seems rather arbitrary. For instance, Nolte and McKee (2008) stated that half of deaths from ischemic heart disease can be considered amenable. As Preston and Ho (2009) note, "[the] rule of thumb is clearly a poor substitute for an effort to attribute international variation in mortality from ischemic heart disease to its various components, including health care systems and behavioral and social factors." This procedure is akin to measuring change of mass on a scale whose calibration depends on the mass being measured.

Moreover, the choice of conditions classified as avoidable can have an important influence on the relationships observed. French and Jones (2006) contrasted mortality results obtained from the set of avoidable conditions proposed by Charlton and colleagues (1983) and by Holland (1988). The main difference between the two definitions is the proportion of total deaths classified as avoidable. Using Charlton's approach, the authors found that avoidable mortality was higher for women than for men in Great Britain between 1981 and 1998, but the opposite was true when they used Holland's list. When they used Holland's list there was also a larger decline, on average, in avoidable mortality during the period of the study, particularly for the late 1980s and early 1990s among young people. The difference between Charlton's and Holland's definitions persists at the regional level. Holland's list shows higher standardized mortality ratios (SMRs) in the north of England and in Scotland, whereas Charlton's list shows low SMRs in this same region.

Furthermore, focusing on avoidable conditions has made most of the researchers pay little to no attention to conditions classified as nonavoidable. They assume that the health care system reduces mortality rates only for avoidable conditions, when it may have other indirect effects on nonavoidable causes. This is particularly relevant when important treatable conditions, such as prostate cancer, are lumped together as nonavoidable. For example, from Nolte and McKee's study, the United States is the only country whose male mortality from other causes is larger than that from amenable conditions, and its decline far exceeded the declines in amenable mortality in all the other countries in the period of study. There is a similar result in Spain (Gispert et al. 2008). Between 1987–1991 and 1997–2001, nonavoidable causes accounted for about 80% of all deaths in each 5-year period, and they showed the largest contribution to the increase in life expectancy in the period for both men and women. The authors of these studies, however, spent very little time describing the implications of these results.

Another important limitation of the avoidable mortality approach relates to comparability across time. As Nolte and McKee note, "a degree of caution is required [when interpreting trends in mortality] because of factors such as disease incidence, which may reflect changes in risk factors acting over prolonged periods." Additionally, the concept of avoidable mortality has been changing according to what is considered "amenable" to medical care or "treatable;" time trend analysis is difficult when a recent list of conditions is used to evaluate performance of a health system in the distant past. Several authors have proposed that the list of amenable conditions be tailored to each country (Gispert et al. 2006, 2007; Malta and Duarte 2007; Melchor et al. 2008; Page et al. 2006; Westerling 2001) to create a list of conditions similar to the European atlas of avoidable death proposed by Holland and colleagues in the late 1980s. Following this approach, however, will complicate international comparisons, as the list of causes is likely to be different.

Finally, as Table 23.1 shows, there is a need for a more consistent and systematic way of characterizing conditions as avoidable. In particular, it is important to recognize that avoidable mortality is a broader concept than amenable mortality. The former includes conditions whose fatality can be averted by treatment and/or prevention, whereas the latter focuses on deaths that could be averted mainly by treatment, excluding prevention. We should keep in mind that the initial concept of avoidable mortality proposed by the Rutstein group was intended to "serve as a stimulus to identify objective outcome indexes of the more subtle and personal aspects of health" (Rutstein et al. 1976: 583). Accordingly, in making cross-country comparisons we should use the concept of avoidable mortality with great caution, as only a crude indicator of the quality of medical care.

**Acknowledgment** The author thanks Eileen M. Crimmins and Richard G. Rogers for their valuable comments on this chapter. Financial support was provided by grants from the National Institute on Aging: T32AG000037.

## References

Adler, G.S. 1978. "Measuring Quality of Medical-Care." *New England Journal of Medicine* 298(10):574.
Bauer, R.L. and J.R.H. Charlton. 1986. "Area Variation in Mortality from Diseases Amenable to Medical Intervention: The Contribution of Differences in Morbidity." *International Journal of Epidemiology* 15(3):408–12.
Carr-Hill, R.A., G.F. Hardman, and I.T. Russell. 1987. "Variations in Avoidable Mortality and Variations in Health Care Resources." *The Lancet* 329(8536):789–92.
Charlton, J.R.H., R. Bauer, and A. Lakhani. 1984. "Outcome Measures for District and Regional Health Care Planners." *Journal of Public Health* 6(4):306–15.
Charlton, J.R.H., R. Silver, R.M. Hartley, and W.W. Holland. 1983. "Geographical Variation in Mortality from Conditions Amenable to Medical Intervention in England and Wales." *The Lancet* 321(8326):691–96.
Charlton, J.R. and R. Velez. 1986. "Some International Comparisons of Mortality Amenable to Medical Intervention." *British Medical Journal (Clin Res Ed)* 292(6516):295–301.
Chung, J.I., Y.-M. Song, J.S. Choi, and B.M. Kim. 2008. "Trends in Avoidable Death over 20 years in Korea." *Journal of Korean Medical Science* 23(6):975–81.
Dahl, E., D. Hofoss, and J.I. Elstad. 2007. "Educational Inequalities in Avoidable Deaths in Norway: A Population Based Study." *Health Sociology Review* 16(2):146–59.
Duarte, M.V., J. Benach, J.M. Martinez, M.B. Pujolras, and Y. Yasui. 2009. "Avoidable and Nonavoidable Mortality: Geographical Distribution in Small Areas in Spain (1990–2001)." *Gaceta Sanitaria* 23(1):16–22.
French, K.M. and K. Jones. 2006. "Impact of Definition on the Study of Avoidable Mortality: Geographical Trends in British Deaths 1981–1998 Using Charlton and Holland's Definitions." *Social Science and Medicine* 62(6):1443–56.
Gispert, R., M.d. Arán Barés, and A. Puig de fàbregas. 2006. "La Mortalidad Evitable: Lista de Consenso para la Actualización del Indicador en España." *Gaceta Sanitaria* 20:184–93.
Gispert, R., J. Gervas, J. Librero, and M. Bares. 2007. "Criteria to Define the List of Causes of Avoidable Mortality: An Unavoidable Discussion." *Gaceta Sanitaria* 21(2):177–78.
Gispert, R., I. Serra, M.A. Bares, X. Puig, A. Puigdefabregas, and A. Freitas. 2008. "The Impact of Avoidable Mortality on Life Expectancy at Birth in Spain: Changes between Three Periods, from 1987 to 2001." *Journal of Epidemiology and Community Health* 62(9):783–89.
Holland, W.W. 1986. "The 'Avoidable Death' Guide to Europe." *Health Policy* 6(2):115–17.
Holland W.W. (ed). 1988. *European Community atlas of 'avoidable death'*. Commission of the European Communities

Health Services Research Series No. 3. Oxford, Oxford University Press.

Holland W.W. (ed). 1991. *European Community atlas of 'avoidable death'*. 2nd edn., Vol. I. Commission of the European Communities Health Services Research Series No. 6. Oxford, Oxford University Press.

Holland W.W. (ed). 1993. *European Community atlas of 'avoidable death'*. 2nd edn., Vol. II. Commission of the European Communities Health Services Research Series No. 9. Oxford, Oxford University Press.

Holland, W.W. 1997. *European Community Atlas of 'Avoidable Death' 1985–89*. Oxford; New York, NY, Oxford University Press.

Humblet, P.C., R. Lagasse, G.F.G. Moens, E. Wollast, and H. van de Voorde. 1987. "La Mortalite Evitable en Belgique." *Social Science and Medicine* 25(5):485–93.

Hypertension Detection Follow-up Program Cooperative Group. 1979. "Five-Year Findings of the Hypertension Detection and Follow-up Program: I. Reduction in Mortality of Persons with High Blood Pressure, Including Mild Hypertension." *Journal of American Medical Association* 242(23):2562–71.

James, P., D. Manuel, and Y. Mao. 2006. "Avoidable Mortality across Canada from 1975 to 1999." *BMC Public Health* 6(1):137.

James, P.D., R. Wilkins, A.S. Detsky, P. Tugwell, and D.G. Manuel. 2007. "Avoidable Mortality by Neighbourhood Income in Canada: 25 years After the Establishment of Universal Health Insurance." *Journal of Epidemiology and Community Health* 61(4):287–96.

Korda, R.J. and J.R.G. Butler. 2006. "Effect of Health Care on Mortality: Trends in Avoidable Mortality in Australia and Comparisons with Western Europe." *Public Health* 120(2):95–105.

Korda, R.J., J.R. Butler, M.S. Clements, and S.J. Kunitz. 2007. "Differential Impacts of Health Care in Australia: Trend Analysis of Socioeconomic Inequalities in Avoidable Mortality." *International Journal of Epidemiology* 36(1):157–65.

Kunitz, S.J. and I. Pesis-Katz. 2005. "Mortality of White Americans, African Americans, and Canadians: The Causes and Consequences for Health of Welfare State Institutions and Policies." *The Milbank Quarterly* 83(1):5–39.

Kunst, A.E., C.W.N. Looman, and J.P. Mackenbach. 1988. "Medical Care and Regional Mortality Differences within the Countries of the European Community." *European Journal of Population/Revue européenne de Démographie* 4(3): 223–45.

Macinko, J. and I.T. Elo. 2009. "Black-White Differences in Avoidable Mortality in the USA, 1980–2005." *Journal of Epidemiology and Community Health* 63(9):715–21.

Mackenbach, J.P., M.H. Bouvier-Colle, and E. Jougla. 1990. "'Avoidable' Mortality and Health Services: A Review of Aggregate Data Studies." *Journal of Epidemiology and Community Health* 44(2):106–11.

Mackenbach, J., A. Kunst, C. Looman, J. Habbema, and P. van der Maas. 1988a. "Regional Differences in Mortality from Conditions Amenable to Medical Intervention in the Netherlands: A Comparison of Four Time Periods." *Journal of Epidemiology and Community Health* 42:325–32.

Mackenbach, J.P., C.W.N. Looman, A.E. Kunst, J.D.F. Habbema, and P.J. van der Maas. 1988b. "Post-1950 Mortality Trends and Medical Care: Gains in Life Expectancy due to Declines in Mortality from Conditions Amenable to Medical Intervention in the Netherlands." *Social Science and Medicine* 27(9):889–94.

Malta, D.C. and E.C. Duarte. 2007. "Causas de Mortes Evitáveis por Ações Efetivas dos Serviços de Saúde: Uma Revisão da Literatura." *Ciência and Saúde Coletiva* 12:765–76.

Melchor, I., A. Nolasco, C. García-Senchermes, P. Pereyra-Zamora, J.A. Pina, J. Moncho, P. Martínez, S. Valero, andÓ. Zurriaga. 2008. "La Mortalidad Evitable: ¿Cambios en el Nuevo Siglo?" *Gaceta Sanitaria* 22:200–9.

Nolte, E. and C.M. McKee. 2003. "Measuring the Health of Nations: Analysis of Mortality Amenable to Health Care." *British Medical Journal* 327(7424):1129–31.

Nolte, E. and C.M. McKee. 2004. *Does Health Care Save Lives? Avoidable Mortality Revisited*. London, The Nuffield Trust for Research and Policy Studies in Health Services.

Nolte, E. and C.M. McKee. 2008. "Measuring the Health of Nations: Updating an Earlier Analysis." *Health Affairs* 27(1):58–71.

Nolte, E., R. Scholz, V. Shkolnikov, and C.M. McKee. 2002. "The Contribution of Medical Care to Changing Life Expectancy in Germany and Poland." *Social Science and Medicine* 55(11):1905–21.

Page, A., M. Tobias, J. Glover, C. Wright, D. Hetzel, and E. Fisher. 2006. *Australian and New Zealand Atlas of Avoidable Mortality*. Adelaide, SA, Public Health Information Unit, University of Adelaide.

Piers, L.S., N.J. Carson, K. Brown, and Z. Ansari. 2007. "Avoidable Mortality in Victoria between 1979 and 2001." *Australian and New Zealand Journal of Public Health* 31(1):5–12.

Poikolainen, K. and J. Eskola. 1986. "The Effect of Health Services on Mortality: Decline in Death Rates From Amenable and Non-Amenable Causes in Finland, 1969–81." *The Lancet* 327(8474):199–202.

Poikolainen, K. and J. Eskola. 1988. "Health Services Resources and their Relation to Mortality from Causes Amenable to Health Care Intervention: A Cross-National Study." *International Journal of Epidemiology* 17(1): 86–89.

Preston, S.H. and J.Y. Ho. 2009. *Low Life Expectancy in the United States: Is the Health Care System at Fault?* PSC Working Paper Series. Philadelphia, PA, Population Studies Center, University of Pennsylvania.

Rutstein, D., W. Berenberg, T. Chalmers, C. Child, A. Fishman, and E. Perrin. 1976. "Measuring the Quality of Medical Care. A Clinical Method." *New England Journal of Medicine* 294:582–88.

Rutstein, D.D., W. Berenberg, T.C. Chalmers, A.P. Fishman, E.B. Perrin, and G.D. Zuidema. 1980. "Measuring the Quality of Medical-Care – 2nd Revision of Tables of Indexes." *New England Journal of Medicine* 302(20): 1146–46.

Simonato, L., T. Ballard, P. Bellini, and R. Winkelmann. 1998. "Avoidable Mortality in Europe 1955–1994: A Plea for Prevention." *Journal of Epidemiology and Community Health* 52(10):624–30.

Stirbu, I., A.E. Kunst, M. Bopp, M. Leinsalu, E. Regidor, S. Esnaola, G. Costa, P. Martikainen, C. Borrell, R. Kalediene, J. Rychtarikova, B. Artnik, P. Deboosere, and J.P. Mackenbach. 2009. "Educational Inequalities in Avoidable Mortality in Europe." *Journal of Epidemiology and Community Health* 64(10):913–20.

Stirbu, I., A. Kunst, V. Bos, and J. Mackenbach. 2006. "Differences in Avoidable Mortality Between Migrants and the Native Dutch in the Netherlands." *BMC Public Health* 6(1):78.

Tobias, M. and G. Jackson. 2001. "Avoidable Mortality in New Zealand, 1981–97." *Australian and New Zealand Journal of Public Health* 25:12–20.

Tobias, M. and L.-C. Yeh. 2007. "How much does Health Care Contribute to Health Inequality in New Zealand?" *Australian and New Zealand Journal of Public Health* 31(3):207–10.

Tobias, M. and L.-C. Yeh. 2009. "How much does Health Care Contribute to Health Gain and to Health Inequality? Trends in Amenable Mortality in New Zealand 1981–2004." *Australian and New Zealand Journal of Public Health* 33(1):70–78.

Weisz, D., M.K. Gusmano, V.G. Rodwin, and L.G. Neuberg. 2008. "Population Health and the Health System: A Comparative Analysis of Avoidable Mortality in Three Nations and their World Cities." *European Journal of Public Health* 18(2):166–72.

Westerling, R. 1993. "Indicators of 'Avoidable' Mortality in Health Administrative Areas in Sweden 1974–1985." *Scandinavian Journal of Social Medicine* 21(3):176–87.

Westerling, R. 2001. "Commentary: Evaluating Avoidable Mortality in Developing Countries – An Important Issue for Public Health." *International Journal of Epidemiology* 30(5):973–75.

Westerling, R. 2003. "Decreasing Gender Differences in 'Avoidable' Mortality in Sweden." *Scandinavian Journal of Public Health* 31(5):342–49.

Westerling, R., A. Gullberg, and M. Rosén. 1996. "Socioeconomic Differences in 'Avoidable' Mortality in Sweden 1986–1990." *International Journal of Epidemiology* 25(3):560–67.

Wheller, L., A. Baker, C. Griffiths, andC. Rooney. 2007. "Trends in Avoidable Mortality in England and Wales, 1993–2005." *Health Statistics Quarterly/Office for National Statistics* 34:6–25.

# Part VI
# Mathematical and Modeling Approaches to Mortality

# Chapter 24
# Model Schedules of Mortality

Patrick Heuveline and Samuel J. Clark

The observation of empirical regularities in mortality risks across many populations with reliable data (see Chapter 10 by Robine, this volume) led to the development of model schedules of mortality. These models are parsimonious representations of typical age and gender variations in the risk of death. These representations take one or a combination of two forms: mathematical and tabular. Mathematical representations incorporate empirical regularities in a parametric function linking each age to a mortality risk. Tabular representations incorporate these regularities in a set of tables showing mortality rates corresponding to different age groups. Each table is indexed by one or a few parameters. Hybrid representations combine both strategies by applying a parametric function to transform a "standard" table of age-specific mortality rates. Any parameter set thus yields a new table of age-specific mortality rates. In either mathematical, tabular, or hybrid form, a model mortality schedule requires only a few parameters to provide mortality risks over the life span that vary with age in a manner consistent with one of a few typical patterns observed in our massive extant mortality records. While accuracy of representation is always a major goal of model building, other considerations include the number of parameters (with more parameters placing higher demands on existing data) and their interpretability (to allow for possible extrapolations outside of the range of existing data).

Demographers have used these model schedules for a variety of analytical purposes (Preston et al. 2000); one the most common is the analysis of data quality. A set of reported age-specific mortality rates that cannot be reasonably well-described by any model representation is to be treated as "suspicious," unless unusual factors can explain the idiosyncrasies (e.g., war, famine, or a "new" disease not yet accounted for in earlier models, such as HIV/AIDS). A related purpose for using model schedules is to complete age-specific mortality rates that are only observed, or reliably observed, for a narrow range of the life span. For instance, childhood mortality rates may be known from data on children's survival provided by their parents, whereas adult mortality rates are unknown. In such cases, a model that adequately represents available mortality data would provide mortality rates at all ages. Model schedules can also be used for their parsimony in denoting differences in mortality over the life span for many populations or for a given population at many points in time. A case in point is the preparation of population projections by the common cohort-component method. A 50-year forward projection of a population by sex and 5-year age group requires 10 survival ratios (one for each 5-year projection interval) for each sex, and for each of the age groups—as many as 18 if the oldest, open-ended age interval is "85 years and over." Making separate assumptions for each of these age-specific survival ratios is not only cumbersome, but it may also result in inconsistencies across the life span. Selecting survival ratios derived from model representations involves selecting only a few parametric values in each projection interval and ensures that these ratios will be consistent with the extant record of mortality variations with age. The interpretability of the model

P. Heuveline (✉)
Department of Sociology and California Center for Population Research, University of California, Los Angeles, CA 90077, USA
e-mail: Heuveline@Soc.ucla.edu

**Fig. 24.1** Graunt's deaths by age and corresponding age-specific cohort mortality rates. Source: Authors' calculations from Graunt (1662) data, reproduced in Sutherland (1963)

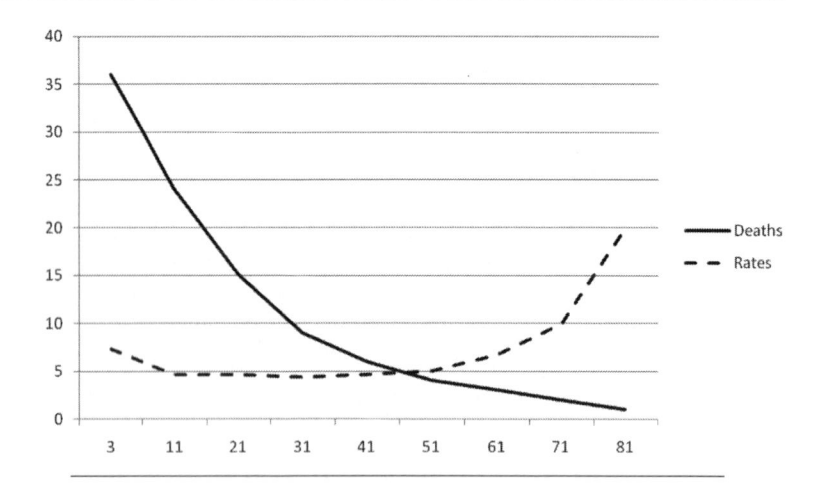

parameters matters here, as it facilitates the choice of reasonable future parameter values.

## Regularities in Age-Specific Mortality

The relationship between age and mortality varies from one population to another, but also exhibits some basic regularities. We do not discuss this relationship in any detail here because it was discussed extensively in Chapter 10. However, we consider some of the most basic regularities in the age-dependency of mortality, since such long-observed regularities have provided the impetus for the development of model mortality schedules.

John Graunt (1662), with the possible help of William Petty, is credited for producing the first life table from the mortality records for London. Graunt's data, however, were not tabulated by age—Caspar Neuman, a clergyman for the city of Breslau, might have been the first one to compile mortality data in that manner, to the benefit of Edmond Halley (1693). The production of the first life table thus required some amount of guesswork, and Graunt hypothesized that in a cohort of 100 births, 36 might die before age 6 and that the last survivor might die between ages 76 and 86. He reasoned that in each decade of age in between the number of deaths from a birth cohort should go down. Any decay process at a constant rate of attrition would produce similarly declining number of attritions (here deaths) over time (here age). However, the cohort mortality rates that we can estimate from his deaths by age number are *not* constant, but rather J-shaped, declining during early childhood and increasing at older ages (Fig. 24.1).

Although he did not seem to have any data on death by age at his disposal and did not document which underlying process he had in mind when picking his number of deaths by age, Graunt still appeared to have the correct intuition about age-specific mortality rates. Age-specific mortality data from many different populations since have shown most consistently that, when plotted against age, mortality rates indeed display a J-shaped pattern similar to that shown in Fig. 24.1. As a function of age, mortality rates decline rapidly after birth to a minimum in late childhood, after which they increase more slowly but steadily over the rest of life span.

In 1930, Ronald Fisher observed, "it is probably not without significance [...] that the death rate in Man takes a course generally inverse to the curve of the reproductive value" (1930: 29). This reproductive value function measures the contribution of individuals at a given age to the future ancestry of a population. In a stable population growing at rate $r$, with survival probabilities $p(x, y)$ from age $x$ to age $y$, and maternity rates $m(y)$ at age y, this function at age $x$ is the cumulative sum for all ages $y > x$ of the product $exp(r(x-y)) \times p(x, y) \times m(y)$. The cumulative sum of the maternity function is at its maximum from birth to the onset of reproduction and declines to zero at the end of the reproductive age span. The first two terms in the product discount the maternity function at pre-reproductive ages by conditioning reproduction to survival to the age of reproduction and the amount of population growth in the interval. In a stationary or

**Fig. 24.2** Death rates by age and sex: United States, 2005 (in natural logarithm). Source: Kung et al. (2008). Note: The upward inflection between the "80–84" and the "85 and over" age groups does not indicate an increase in death rates after age 85, because the last age group is open-ended and its median age is more than 5 years older than the median age of the previous age group (about 82.5 years)

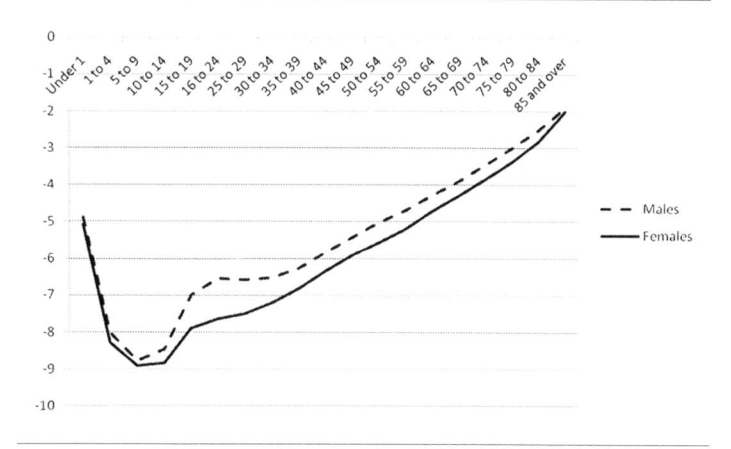

growing stable population, the reproductive value then reaches its maximum just at the outset of reproduction. The inverse relationship, Fischer reasoned, reflects that the reproductive value at a given age measures the effectiveness of genetic selection at that age.

In non-stable, age-structured, two-sex populations, measuring the effectiveness of selection as a function of age is more complex than the product of the first two terms in Fisher's formula (see Charlesworth 2000 for a review). Nonetheless, the basic idea remains that genes with a negative impact on survival early in the reproductive age span are more efficiently selected out than those with a negative impact later in life (Carnes et al. 1996). In fact, animal populations appear to display similar age patterns of mortality, to the extent that mortality risks also appear to be lowest at the outset of reproduction.

Figure 24.2 presents death rates by age and sex for the United States in 2005 (displayed on a logarithmic scale to increase the readability of the pattern at low-mortality ages). Beyond a common, general shape, most features of human mortality cannot be explained by genetic selection alone. In particular, natural selection cannot explain why or how fast mortality increases with age-past reproductive ages. Human mortality also depends on organizational features of human societies that may contribute to mortality in some societies and not in others, such as a survival advantage of boys over girls where parents have strong gender preferences, or a hump in adolescent mortality clearly visible for American males (Fig. 24.2). Recent work building on Fisher's intuition integrates genetic influences and the allocation of resources in human societies (Carey and Judge 2001; Chu and Lee 2006). From a pure-modeling perspective, these variations in age patterns of mortality imply that to model mortality over the whole age range will require more than just the few parameters already required to model the reproductive value function.

## Mathematical Models of Age-Specific Mortality

With data on mortality over the life span becoming more readily available, mathematicians began to seek functions of age that could approximate the age pattern of mortality. Besides the general J-shape, the most striking feature of the age patterns shown in Fig. 24.2 is the near-linear increase after age 35. Abraham de Moivre (1725) was perhaps the first to suggest a mathematical representation of mortality change with age as:

$$\mu(a) = \frac{1}{\omega - a}, \qquad (1)$$

where $\mu(a)$ is the mortality rate at age $a$ and $\omega$ represents an ultimate age at which mortality risk would be infinite (for which de Moivre suggested the value of 86 years). Over the next century, several other mathematical formulae were proposed (see Forfar 2004 for a review), but without exactly capturing the nature of mortality's age-dependency.

On the logarithmic scale used in Fig. 24.2, the linearity after age 35 reflects an exponential increase in adult mortality. Benjamin Gompertz first observed that a "law of geometric progression pervades, in an approximate degree, large portions of different life tables of mortality; during which portions the number of persons living at a series of age in arithmetical progression, will be nearly in geometric progression" (1825: 514). This geometric law is more frequently stated in demography in terms of mortality rates than in terms of survivors in a life table, that is,

$$\mu(a) = \beta \exp(\gamma a), \quad (2)$$

where $\mu(a)$ is again the mortality rate at age $a$. Although the Gompertz' formula is only used for adult ages, the coefficient $\beta$ represents the extrapolated value of the mortality rate at age 0, while $\gamma$ expresses the argument of the geometric progression (for each additional year of age, the mortality rate is multiplied by $exp(\gamma)$).

Makeham (1860) argued that mortality data always include deaths from causes that are intrinsically independent of age (of relatively constant occurrence over the life span, such as accidents), and that the estimation of Gompertz' two parameters could be improved by adding one parameter to capture that underlying level of mortality at all ages:

$$\mu(a) = \alpha + [\beta \exp(\gamma a)]. \quad (3)$$

The Gompertz–Makeham formula performs very well for a large spectrum of adult ages, and has been used to complete life tables when data are too incomplete or unreliable for some age groups (e.g., Horiuchi and Coale 1982). As more reliable data became available for older ages from countries with relatively accurate age reporting, Horiuchi and Coale (1990) found that the exponential rate of mortality change appeared to slow down after a certain age, 75 for females (the pattern for males is confounded by substantial cohort variations that may reflect World War I experiences). Extrapolations of the Gompertz–Makeham formula which hold this rate to be constant thus appear to overestimate mortality beyond age 90 or so (see for instance, Fig. 24.5 in Vaupel 1997: 1802). This deceleration of the pace of mortality increase with age might reflect population heterogeneity (Vaupel et al. 1979).

William Perks (1932) introduced the logistic curve to represent the sub-exponential growth of mortality rates at the oldest ages. Perks showed that if individual mortality risk indeed follows a Gompertz–Makeham curve but with individual-specific values of $\beta$ to represent individual heterogeneity, the population-level mortality rates differ from the individual-level formula because the distribution of $\beta$ among survivors changes with age. With a particular distribution of $\beta$ values at birth (gamma distribution), Perks shows that the population-level mortality rates follow:

$$\mu(a) = \frac{\{\alpha + [\beta \exp(\gamma a)]\}}{\{1 + [\delta \exp(\gamma a)]\}}. \quad (4)$$

At younger ages, when $a$ is small, this modified curve might be similar to a Gompertz–Makeham curve, but as $a$ increases, the mortality risk approaches a maximum value close to $(\beta/\delta)$. Actual ages might not get large enough for mortality rates to approach that asymptotic value, but the addition of the denominator suffices to reduce the exponential growth of mortality with age.

While actuaries mostly focused on adult mortality, demographers also tried to model declining mortality in the first part of the life span. Like Makeham, Bourgeois-Pichat (1946) began with a decomposition of infant mortality into two different sets of causes, those originating in the post-natal environment (e.g., infectious diseases, accidental injuries), and those associated with or even preceding birth (e.g., congenital, traumatic delivery). Between the end of the first month and the end of the first day of life, he showed that the cumulative proportion of deaths at age $n$ (in days) among a birth cohort appeared to fit the following function:

$$q(n) = \alpha + \{\beta[\ln(n+1)]^3\}. \quad (5)$$

The constant term $\alpha$ represents the level of endogenous mortality, independent from the post-natal environment, and only operating in the first month of life, whereas the coefficient of the cubic term, $\beta$, is associated with the exogenous, environmental component of mortality, which continues to operate throughout the first year of life. Bourgeois-Pichat was only able to fit this relationship to data from a few western countries. With data from a more diverse set of populations, historically and geographically, becoming available, however, researchers were able to show substantial variations in age pattern of infant mortality, which were likely linked to maternal breastfeeding and the timing of weaning (Knodel and Kintner 1977). In the last third of the twentieth century, medical care immediately after delivery also contributed to substantial declines in mortality in the first month of life in the most developed countries and challenged the distinction between endogenous and exogenous mortality based on the timing of infant deaths (Lantoine and Pressat 1984).

To model mortality over the whole life span, candidate mathematical functions should account for the two above-discussed features (decline after birth, and near-exponential increase after age 35), as well as, in some populations, the accident "hump" for young adults, males in particular, already noted in Fig. 24.2. Thiele (1872) proposed a seven-parameter function representing these three features as:

$$\mu(a) = [\alpha \exp(-\beta a)] + [\gamma \exp(-\delta\{a - \varepsilon\}^2)] \\ + [\zeta \exp(\eta a)]. \quad (6)$$

The last term represents the Gompertz' increase of mortality at older ages. The first term is similar, but as all parameters are positive, it is actually declining with age. The middle term is bell-shaped and centered on a maximum at age $\varepsilon$. As the function is additive, each term dominates in a different age range of the life span. Whole lifespan functions have been continuously elaborated since. Among those, the following nine-parameter function proposed by Heligman and Pollard (1980) continues to provide a very good fit to some of the most recent mortality data:

$$q(a) = \{\exp[\alpha(a+\beta)^\gamma]\} + \{\delta \exp[-\varepsilon \ln(a/\zeta)^2]\} \\ + \left\{\frac{[\eta \exp(\theta a)]}{[1 + \kappa \exp(\theta a)]}\right\}, \quad (7)$$

where $q(a)$ is the probability of dying at age $a$.

Such models are useful whenever accuracy is the main consideration, for instance in actuarial work, when good data is available for a population and the analyst needs to fine tune estimates of mortality at very precise ages. When good-quality data on mortality are scarce, however, simpler models may place more realistic demands on available data. In addition, if the objectives are more modest, for instance the estimation of an abridged life table with 18 5-year age groups, the use of a nine-parameter function then provides little benefits over the actual table. With the growing concerns over the world's population "explosion" in the second-half of the twentieth century, more and more demographers turned their attention to poor data quality and sought more parsimonious models.

## Model Life Tables of Typical Mortality Regimes

The interest in model life tables grew largely from the objective of deriving the best mortality estimates when little reliable data were available for the population of interest. Given the robust empirical regularities in mortality schedules discussed above, a natural approach to these data limitations is to extrapolate a mortality schedule for the population of interest from the schedules of other populations with good data.

For instance, if mortality in every population follows a Gompertz curve from age 35 on as shown in Eq. (2) above, then we can relate age-specific mortality in any two populations as:

$$\ln[\mu_1(a)] = \beta' + \{\gamma' \ln[\mu_2(a)]\}, \quad (8)$$

with $\gamma' = (\gamma_1/\gamma_2)$, that is, the ratio of the arguments in the geometric progression of mortality in the two populations, and $\beta' = \ln(\beta_1) - [\gamma'\ln(\beta_2)]$, where $\beta_1$ and $\beta_2$ are the constant terms in Eq.(2) for each of the two populations. If we have mortality estimates for a given population at a few different ages only, and a reliable age pattern of mortality for a second population, Eq. (8) can be used to estimate the coefficients $\beta'$ and $\gamma'$ and thus derive a full age pattern of mortality for the first population. This is, in essence, the rationale for the relational models that, chronologically, were developed after model life tables and to which we will return later.

Another look at the linear relationship in Eq. (8) also suggests that if we can express $\ln[\mu_2(a)]$ at any age $a$, as a polynomial (say, quadratic) relationship of $\ln[\mu_2(a_0)]$ where $a_0$ is an age of reference (say, 15), then the same type of polynomial relationship, with different coefficients, will prevail in the first population (that is, with $\mu_1$). The basic principle underlying the development of model life tables is the search for such relationships between mortality indicators at different ages, which can be estimated from the many populations for which good data are available, and then extended to populations with incomplete or unreliable data. We review below historical developments in model life table systems. Even though some early systems are little used nowadays, this review allows us to discuss the rationale for model life tables and their pros and cons more concretely.

The first model life tables were published by the United Nations (1955) from a set of 158 mortality tables available at the time. The relationship underlying this set is quadratic and relates consecutive survival probabilities in an abridged life table, starting with $_1q_0$, $_4q_1$, and then 5-year survival probabilities, $_5q_x$, as follows:

$$_5q_{x+5} = \alpha + (\beta \times {}_5q_x) + (\gamma [{}_5q_x]^2). \quad (9)$$

Once the three coefficients ($\alpha$, $\beta$, and $\gamma$) are estimated from the 158 extant tables, a new table (and one only) can be constructed from any value of the first survival probability, $_1q_0$. Tables that are entirely defined by a single parameter are referred to as "single-parameter" models. Forty initial tables were constructed from values of $_1q_0$ ranging from 20 to 330 per thousand, with corresponding life expectancies at birth between 19 and 72 years. For ease of use, new interpolated tables were then provided for life expectancies at birth by 2.5 years increments, starting with 20.

These tables had several limitations. First, closer examination showed that some of the 158 tables used to estimate the coefficients in Eq. (9) were not reliable. Second, Eq. (9) is intuitively appealing because the closest relationships between survival probabilities at different ages should be between those for adjacent age groups, but in the end any survival probability, regardless of age, is estimated from $_1q_0$. Gabriel and Ronen (1958) showed that this "chained" method compounds estimation errors for all intervening age groups, and that a better approach would, in fact, estimate any survival probability from $_1q_0$ directly. Third, single-parameter life tables in which the whole table derives from a single value of the parameter ($_1q_0$ here) essentially assume a single age pattern of mortality. As discussed with respect to Eq. (8), while there are reasons to expect the same functional relationship between mortality indicators for different age groups, the coefficients of that function may vary across populations. The whole process of deriving a life table for a population with poor mortality data from another population with good data should thus be questioned.

Indeed, age patterns of mortality reflect the respective importance of specific causes of deaths (Preston 1976), which tend to affect certain age groups more than others (e.g., childhood-infectious diseases, early-adulthood motor vehicle injuries, older-adult cancer, and degenerative diseases). The prevalence of these causes of death at each age in a population being influenced by its natural, cultural, and medical environments largely determines the age pattern of mortality, and, different populations with similar such environments often share relatively similar age patterns of mortality.

Ansley Coale and Paul Demeny (1966, with Barbara Vaughan 1983) undertook an extensive examination of mortality age patterns across populations. Their analyses were based on 326 male and 326 female life tables. The majority of these tables were from Europe (over 60%), and in nearly equal proportions from three periods: pre-World War I, between World Wars (1919–1945), and post-World War II. The main finding from their analyses was that the age patterns of mortality displayed in these life tables appeared to form four clusters and that the tables in each of these clusters corresponded to geographically close populations. This is consistent with the expectation that a given pattern corresponds to the relative prevalence of different causes of death in a given region, and is determined in part by a population's environment. For this reason, the four clusters or *mortality patterns* were labeled "West," "North," "South," and "East," referring to the region of Europe from which originated the majority of tables in the cluster.

The Coale and Demeny model life tables are probably the most widely used today, and to allow us to discuss their advantages and limitations, we shall first review their construction in some detail. The procedure used to uncover these four clusters was quite ingenious at a time when cluster analysis was not well-established in the social sciences. In a first step, original sex-specific life tables were "broken up" to yield 17 age-specific survival probabilities from each that were then rearranged into a large matrix of 326 × 17 probabilities, with probabilities sorted from their lowest to their highest value in each column (e.g., for each age-group). Each of the 326 rows in this matrix contains in effect a new, hypothetical life table: the first row constitutes the set of the lowest survival probabilities in each age interval. The next step was to compare each original table with one of these new tables with a similar overall mortality level. This comparison first provided a data-quality check that led to the elimination of tables displaying wild deviations from their comparison tables. In the end, only 125 of the original 326 tables could be used (and none of the tables for periods earlier than 1870).

Among the remaining tables, four main patterns of typical variations were established with respect to the specific age intervals for which the original probabilities were higher in the original table than in its comparison table. One of these patterns is characterized by higher mortality, relative to comparison tables, between ages 1 and 45 or 50 and lower mortality at other ages ("North" pattern). A second pattern ("East" pattern) is almost the opposite of this "North" pattern, exhibiting higher mortality before age 1 and after age 50. A third pattern ("South" pattern) is relatively close to this "East" pattern, except that high early mortality extends to age 5, while high mortality at older ages is only visible after age 65, and mortality between ages 40 and 60 is relatively low. The remaining tables exhibited mortality rates relatively close to those in their comparison tables at most ages and were grouped in a residual pattern ("West" pattern).

The construction of the final series of tables involved a couple of regressions for each sex and age group, estimated separately from each of the four groups of tables (i.e., belonging to one of the four patterns above). The two regressions were linear regressions of $_5q_x$ and of $\log(_5q_x)$ on life expectancy at age 10. For most values of life expectancy at age 10, the average value predicted by these two regressions was used. As values of life expectancy at age 10 become very low, however, the regression based on $\log(_5q_x)$ would eventually predict probabilities of death above 1, which is of course impossible, and for low values of life expectancy at age 10, only the regression of $_5q_x$ was used. Similarly, for high values of life expectancy at age 10, only the regression of $\log(_5q_x)$ was used as the other regression could predict negative probabilities.

For each of the four patterns, 24 values of female life expectancy at age 10 were then selected so that female life expectancy at birth would range from exactly 20 to 77.5 years by increments of 2.5 years. For each of these values, a full set of $_5q_x$'s were obtained and a full female life table constructed using the usual life table relationships. In the 1983 revision of these tables, a 25th level was added, increasing life expectancy at birth to a maximum of 80 years, and breaking up the open-ended age interval 80 years and over into fourty five-year age intervals and a new open-ended age interval 100 years and over. Each table corresponds to one of four patterns, and one of 25 levels. A corresponding male life table was also constructed by estimating the average sex differences in life expectancy at birth in the original tables.

Compared to the United Nations tables, the Coale and Demeny tables have two significant advantages. First, they are in effect two-parameter model tables (level, indexed by female life expectancy at birth, and "regional" pattern), which accommodates population-to-population variations in the age pattern of mortality. These variations are shown in Fig. 24.3.

**Fig. 24.3** Coale and Demeny's four female age patterns of mortality (probabilities of dying on age intervals from birth to age 65; in natural logarithm). Source: Author's calculations using the Match procedure in Mortpak 4.0 (United Nations 2003). Note: Each model was fit to match a value of 0.2 for the probability of dying between birth and age 5

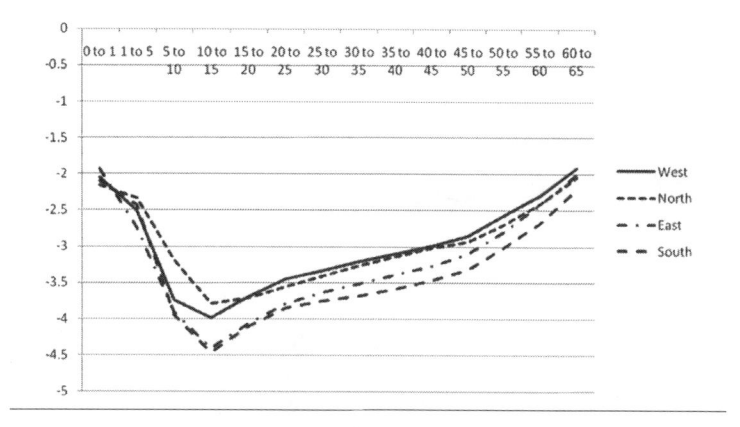

The four sets of probabilities shown in Fig. 24.3 correspond to a probability of dying between birth and age 5 of 0.2, yet important differences are visible over the life span. This illustrates the advantage of a two-parameter system over any single-parameter system. A second advantage of the Coale and Demeny tables over their predecessors is the data quality of the tables retained for constructing the final tables (less than half of the original set). Unfortunately, the limited availability of good-quality empirical data at the time required that they incorporate only a relatively narrow range of mortality experience. These model life tables were and still are used first and foremost to estimate demographic parameters in populations with little good-quality data (i.e., primarily non-European populations), whereas the empirical basis for the model tables is almost exclusively from European populations. Meanwhile some distinct, non-European patterns of deviations from the "Western" model were being documented contemporaneously (Preston 1976).

Two systems of model life tables attempted to remedy this limitation, with data originating from non-European populations only. The Development Center of the Organization for Economic Co-operation and Development (OECD) undertook the collection of a mortality database for populations from less-developed regions exclusively. The resulting tables (OECD 1980) represent four mortality patterns, simply labeled A, B, C, and D rather than referring to specific regions of origins. The OECD tables were also meant to improve on Coale and Demeny's tables by including both single- and double-parameter tables. This model life table feature had actually been introduced earlier by French demographer Sully Lederman. Lederman rightly pointed to a major discrepancy between the mode of production and the typical usage of model life tables. On the one hand, the regression analyses used in life table construction provide the life table values that best fit the empirical record on the basis of their relationship to another life table indicator, the parameter of the set of model life tables (say, life expectancy at birth). On the other hand, that very parameter might not be known to the user, who then chooses a life table among the model tables based on other available life table indicators. In such cases, the user "enters" (picks) a life table, for a life table value itself estimated empirically from another life table value. In Fig. 24.2 for instance, we represent values of the probabilities of dying based on a common value of $_5q_0$, which might more commonly be available than life expectancy at birth. These values, however, are not necessarily those that would have been obtained if we had predicted them directly from $_5q_0$—an issue related to the compounding of errors discussed above with respect to "chained" estimation. Multiple single- and double-parameter models are thus produced by estimating their life table indicators based on several bivariate or multiple regressions of the following form:

$$\ln(_5q_x) = \alpha_x + [\beta_x \ln(Q_1)] + [\gamma_x \ln(Q_2)], \qquad (10)$$

with $\{Q_1, Q_2\}$ one of several parameter sets (with the convention $Q_2 = 1$ for single-parameter tables). Lederman's tables (1969) included seven single- and three double-parameters sets of model life tables, among which one could choose based on data availability.

Also, of interest in these life tables is that Lederman approached the determination of how many and which parameters were necessary to provide a good model of mortality age patterns in the most general terms. The investigation started with a set of 157 life tables referring to periods between 1900 and 1950, each one treated as a multidimensional observation (or vector) of 38 indicators: 18 age-specific probabilities of dying and life expectancy at birth for each sex (Lederman and Breas 1959). Principal component analysis then helped determine how many components were necessary to adequately represent the variance across these observations. This method provides the most efficient way to summarize this variance, here variations in age patterns of mortality across life tables, with only a few "principal components" as opposed to the original dimension of the vectors (38). These principal components are linear combinations of the original 38 indicators, and a potential shortcoming of the method is that the principal components may not be easily interpreted. In this case, however, the first primary component turned up to be a linear combination of the age-specific probabilities of dying, with positive coefficients at all ages, and highest values between ages 10 and 35 for males and between ages 5 and 45 for females. Readily interpreted as an indicator of overall mortality level, this component alone explains 77% of the total variance. Explaining, respectively, 10 and 6.5% of the total variance, the next two components are determined primarily by mortality after age 40 and 70, respectively. These analyses thus provide support for choosing life expectancy at birth or at age 10 as the parameter to predict age-specific probabilities of dying using a single parameter. They also show that the models can be improved by adding a second or a third dimension corresponding to mortality at or above specific ages, but in practice, model life tables are used precisely when mortality indicators at different ages are hard to come by. Linking the second dimension to the geographical origins of the tables used to construct the model, "regional" model life tables has been much more popular because they are easier to choose from. Less compelling theoretically, the choice of regional model is still justified, as mentioned above, by the fact that age patterns of mortality are determined in part by the disease environment and living conditions of the population.

The second attempt to produce better model life tables for non-European populations (United Nations 1982) actually combined the principal component and the regional approach. First, the OECD database was subjected to data-quality checks that resulted in the elimination of all but 72 of the original 286 life tables (these 72 tables originating in only 22 of the original 67 countries). Second, the remaining tables were arranged into clusters using one graphical and two statistical procedures. The graphical procedure consisted in plotting at each age the ratio of the probability of dying to the corresponding probability in Coale and Demeny's West model table with the same life expectancy at age 10. The three procedures produced essentially the same results: four clear clusters and a residual group that did not fit in either one of the four clusters. The four clusters consisted of tables from (1) Latin American countries, plus the Philippines, Sri Lanka, and Thailand, (2) Chile, (3) south Asian countries, plus Iran and Tunisia, and (4) far eastern countries, plus Guyana and Trinidad and Tobago.

The final tables were produced for each gender and life expectancy at birth ranging from 35 to 75 years in 1-year increments. The General pattern is an average of the four other patterns, each of those corresponding to one of the above clusters. The Latin American pattern is characterized by high mortality (relative to Coale and Demeny's West model table with the same life expectancy at age 10) during infancy, childhood, and into early adulthood, but low mortality at older ages. The Chilean pattern characterized by very-high infant mortality thought to reflect the high incidence of respiratory diseases. The South Asian pattern displays high-mortality rates both at younger ages and at the oldest ages, and lower mortality during adulthood. The Far Eastern pattern presents high mortality at the oldest ages, which has been linked to the prevalence of tuberculosis. These variations are shown in Fig. 24.4.

The last model of typical mortality regimes we will review here is Brass' transformational model, which actually combines the mathematical and tabular approaches in a powerful way. To allow both for the empirical regularities found in all regular-mortality age patterns and for the deviations in age-specific mortality across populations, Brass (1971) originally proposed to derive each life table as a mathematical transformation of a specific, unique model life table, the "standard" life table. Specifically, Brass' model relates linearly the logit of the probability of dying

**Fig. 24.4** United Nations' five female age patterns of mortality (probabilities of dying on age intervals from birth to age 65; in natural logarithm). Source: Author's calculations using the Match procedure in Mortpak 4.0 (United Nations 2003). Note: Each model was fit to match a value of 0.2 for the probability of dying between birth and age 5

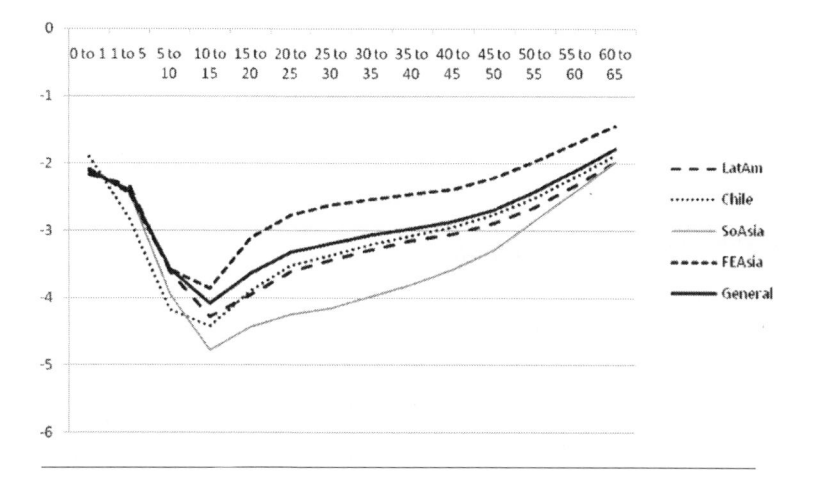

**Fig. 24.5** Logit of the cumulative probabilities of dying up to a certain age (ages 1–65), values from a North, an East, and a South Coale–Demeny model life table plotted against those from a West Coale–Demeny model life table. Source: Author's calculations using the Match procedure in Mortpak 4.0 (United Nations 2003). The four model life tables are the same as those shown in Fig. 24.3

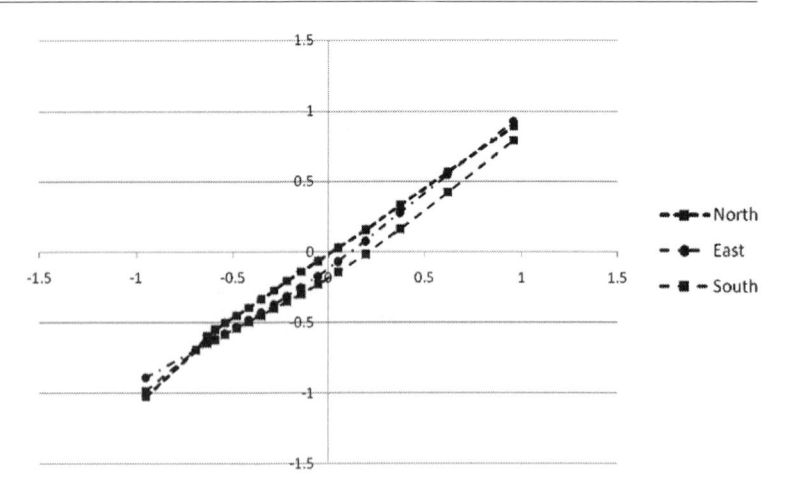

between ages 0 and $x$ in the standard table to any other life table as follows:

$$\text{logit}(_xq_0) = \alpha + [\beta \text{logit}(_xq_o^s)]. \quad (11)$$

With $\text{logit}(_xq_0) = \frac{1}{2} \ln(_xq_0/[1-_xq_0])$ and $_xq_o^s$ denoting the probabilities of dying in the standard life table.

Figure 24.5 plots the values of $\text{logit}(_xq_0)$ for the four Coale and Demeny's model life tables previously shown in Fig. 24.3. Although these mortality pattern are clearly different, the relationship between the $\text{logit}(_xq_0)$ from the different models still display a very nearly linear relationship across the different age groups.

The general applicability of this relatively simple linear transformation and the motivation for suggesting this particular transformation might be surprising at first. This particular transformation originates in dose response theory which was popular at the time of Brass' writing. Dose response refers to the binary outcome of an exposure that can be graded continuously, such as the survival to a certain "dose" of a potentially toxic element. Individual tolerance (the maximum dose that can be tolerated without failure) varies in the population, and assuming it follows a logistic distribution, the cumulative proportion of individuals that would not tolerate a given dose $D$ can be expressed as $\exp[2f(D)]/\{1+\exp[2f(D)]\}$, where $f(D)$ is a linear function of $D$ with parameters related to those of the logistic distribution of individual tolerance. The logit of $p$, the proportion of individual failure is then linearly related to the dose. In a particular experiment, individual tolerance to a given dose may not be logistically distributed, but considering the relationship between $\text{logit}(p)$ and the dose, it is always possible to find a transformation of the dose, $\varphi(D)$, for which the relationship between $\text{logit}(p)$ and $\varphi(D)$, is linear.

The analogy with the analysis of age-specific mortality is straightforward, considering exposure as aging, dose being measured as a function of age, $\varphi(a)$, and death as failure. Taking the cumulative proportion dying, $_xq_0$, there is a function $\varphi(a)$, such that $\text{logit}(_xq_0)$ is a linear function of $\varphi(a)$. If the parameters of the linear relationship vary across populations, but the transformation $\varphi(a)$ remains the same, then the values of $\text{logit}(_xq_0)$ in two different populations are also linearly related, which is expressed above in Eq. (11).

Brass' model has two parameters that can be readily interpreted. With respect to parameter $\alpha$, we can observe first that the value of $\text{logit}(_xq_0)$ increases from negative to positive with age, reaching zero at the median age at death in the population. Turning to Eq. (11), a positive value of the parameter $\alpha$ then indicates that $\text{logit}(_xq_0)$ is positive at the median age at death in the standard life table. The median age at death in the standard life table is thus older than the median age at death in the population, indicating that cumulative mortality by age in that population is higher than in the standard population. The parameter $\alpha$ can thus be taken as an indicator of the mortality level, comparable to life expectancy at birth within a set of model life tables, except that higher values are here indicative of higher mortality.

On the contrary, increasing the value of the parameter $\beta$ only raises the values of $\text{logit}(_xq_0)$ relative to those of $\text{logit}(_xq_o^s)$ when the latter is positive, that is, at ages beyond the median age of death in the standard life table. This second parameter thus allows the model to account for the different age patterns of mortality, with higher values of $\beta$ decreasing cumulative probabilities of dying up to the median age at death in the standard life table and increasing these probabilities at older ages. Selecting the value of this parameter is thus comparable to the choice of a regional pattern in model life table sets, but the parameter can now take continuous rather than discrete values.

By varying the values of the two parameters, Brass' model can thus adjust the standard life table to fit a wide variety of different age patterns of mortality. Varying the value of $\beta$ raises mortality at some ages and lowers it at other ages, whereas varying the value of $\alpha$ adjusts mortality in the same direction at all ages. A combination of the two forms of adjustment can thus accommodate many deviations from the standard age pattern of mortality. Brass developed his model in part to address issues he observed while working on mortality data from Africa, where the age pattern of mortality seemed to differ from the standard mostly at younger ages, before the median age at death. His first "standard" pattern was thus an "African" standard, although he later introduced a second, more general "standard."

The choice of a standard can be seen as a third parameter in Brass' model of age-specific mortality patterns, although the results are not very sensitive to the choice of a particular standard. There have been several extensions of Brass' original representation aiming at increasing the flexibility of Brass' transformation. Ewbank et al. (1983), for instance, proposed a four-parameter model linearly relating the logit of the probability of surviving to any age $x$, $l_x$, to a transform of $l_x$. The first-two parameters are the coefficients of the linear relationship, whereas the third and fourth parameters affect the transformation of $l_x$, one before, and the other after the median age at death in the standard life table. When the values of the third and fourth parameters approach zero, the transformation of $l_x$ approaches logit($l_x$) and the model is then similar to the original Brass model. This model has more flexibility since varying only the third or fourth parameter yields variations from the standard only at younger or at older ages, respectively. Using a different functional form, Zaba (1979) achieves the same objective by introducing a new standard as the sum of three terms, the original standard, a deviation at younger ages, and one at older ages, and two additional parameters as weights of the two deviations.

## Models of Atypical Mortality Regimes

The "classic" model life tables of Coale and Demeny and of the United Nations have been widely used in demographic analysis, in particular for the estimation of demographic parameters and in population projections. For many users, these tables represent a good compromise between empirically sound life table construction and ease of use, requiring only a few interpretable parameters to select a model table.

However, there remain a few important instances for which these models provide a poor representation of mortality patterns. These misrepresentations can arise from two types of discrepancies—in mortality *level* and in cause-of-death *prevalence*—between the empirical dataset from which the model tables were constructed and the actual mortality experience being modeled. *Prevalence* discrepancies may emerge when a cause-of-death is important enough in the population of interest to influence the overall age pattern of mortality, but that particular cause is not salient in any of the populations included in the empirical dataset. Sometimes, the age pattern of the cause of death in the population of interest might be close enough to the age pattern of another cause of death in the empirical dataset to render acceptable the use of a model life table. Such age-pattern similarities across causes explain, for instance, why the North model of the Coale and Demeny life table system, based mostly on the record from Scandinavian countries in the early twentieth century, when tuberculosis was prevalent, has often been used to represent mortality patterns in African countries, where mortality is also dominated by infectious diseases. We describe later in this section situations where, on the contrary, the age pattern of an important cause-of-death does not share enough similarities with the age pattern of causes represented in the empirical dataset. First, however, we discuss discrepancies in *level*, when the actual-life expectancy in the population of interest is substantially higher or substantially lower than in the empirical dataset from which the model life tables were constructed. In Coale and Demeny (1966) model life tables, for instance, the actual range of life expectancies at birth among the life tables that satisfied the data-quality checks for inclusion in the empirical dataset was narrower than the range of the final tables (20–80 years for female tables). Later examinations showed the extrapolation from the actual range toward the bounds of the final range to be problematic.

This issue has received extensive attention as mortality kept declining at older ages during the second-half of the twentieth century in a manner that would have been hard to predict from earlier declines. The 1983 revision of Coale and Demeny model life tables extended the range of life expectancies to age 100 instead of the previous age 80 by fitting a Gompertz curve to mortality rates at older ages. As discussed above, this curve has been shown to overestimate mortality at the oldest ages. Coale and Guo (1989) then published a new set of model life tables for higher values of life expectancy at birth (beyond 80 years) that relied on an alternative method of calculating rates at the oldest age. In the new tables, the exponential rate of mortality change is no longer constant, as in Eqs. (2) and (3), but instead a declining function of age $a$, for ages 80 and older. Specifically,

$$k(a) = k(80) - [R(a - 80)], \qquad (12)$$

where $k(a) = \ln(_5m_a/_5m_{a-5})$. Unlike with the Gompertz curve, closing the life table then requires a value of the coefficient $R$. This value can be derived from a value of $_5m_{105}$ and while the choice of this value is somewhat arbitrary (lacking reliable data on mortality at these ages), Coale and Kisker (1990) showed that this method is actually relatively robust to the choice of $_5m_{105}$. Compared to the previous mortality rates based on the Gompertz curve from age 80 on, these new estimates were found closer to recorded rates in 8 out of 12 populations at ages 85–89, 10 out of 12 at ages 90–94, and in all 12 at ages 95–99.

Himes et al. (1994) took a different approach to extending life tables to higher values of life expectancy at birth, using a hybrid or relational model. The authors used the results of consistency tests based on the intercensal cohort method comparing population age distributions and death registration data for 18 low-mortality countries from 1950 to 1985 (Condran et al. 1991). Mortality rates in empirical life tables were retained only up to the ages for which data were sufficiently consistent. The authors then derived a "standard" set of 1-year age-specific mortality rates from age 45 to 99 years. The standard exhibits a peak in the rate at which mortality increases with age between 70 and 80, as observed in empirical data by Horiuchi and Coale (1990). As their standard was based on relatively few observations from age 95 to age 99 and none beyond age 99, the authors fitted a linear equation to the standard pattern to both smooth and extend the pattern to older ages. Specifically, they fitted the relationship as follows:

$$\text{logit}(_1m_a) = \alpha + (\beta a), \qquad (13)$$

with age $a$. Eq. (13) can be rewritten to mirror the third and last term in Heligman and Pollard's (1980) Eq. (7), with the difference that this one is expressed in terms of mortality rates as opposed to Heligman and Pollard's, which is expressed in terms of probability of dying.

The importance of modeling age patterns of mortality accurately as mortality declines further explains why much work has focused on this issue. The extrapolation from common-mortality experiences to situations with very-high mortality has received less attention, but it remains important in the study of historical populations. Although Coale and Demeny (1983) for instance provide tables with life expectancy at birth as low as 20 years, these tables seem to extrapolate poorly toward very-low life expectancies (Bhat 1987). Some of the best records from a very-high mortality regime document the experience of African-Americans resettling in Liberia between 1820 and 1843 (McDaniel 1995). Their high mortality was likely due to high incidence of infectious diseases, most importantly malaria, to which the settlers had not been exposed, and thus had not acquired any immunity, prior to reaching the Liberian shores. Based on the relatively good records of the settlers' mortality, Preston et al. (1993) derived a set of high-mortality model life tables, with very-low levels of life expectancies and likely applicable to many populations in which high mortality is driven by infectious diseases.

With respect to the other type of discrepancy, linked instead to cause-of-death *prevalence*, two causes typically absent from common-mortality life tables but relatively common historically are famine and conflict. Although no specific age pattern of mortality has been constructed to represent such situations, high mortality driven by famine mortality has been studied extensively and shown to exhibit several regularities (Dyson and Gráda 2002). Extant data suggest that famine increases mortality rates most at extreme ages, among the very young and old. To the extent that the age pattern of famine mortality is thus J-shaped as are typical mortality patterns, albeit with a more substantial

## 24 Model Schedules of Mortality

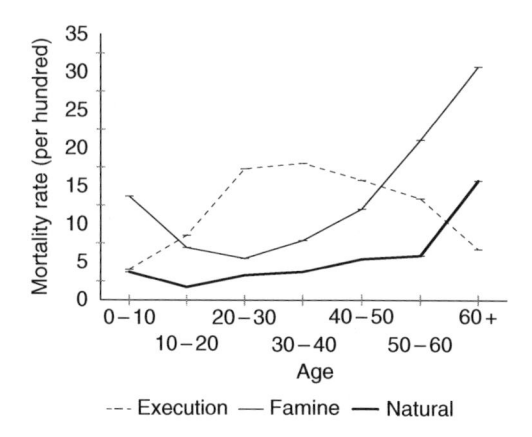

**Fig. 24.6** Age pattern of mortality from execution, famine, and natural causes in Cambodia, 1970s. Source: Heuveline (2001) from data in Sliwinsky (1995)

decrease with age at younger ages and faster increase with age at older ones, famine mortality might be approached by regular-mortality models at low levels of life expectancy.

This is not the case for conflict-related mortality. For illustrative purposes, Fig. 24.6 presents male age patterns of mortality from two types of exceptional mortality in Cambodia during the 1970s, (1) war-related and executions and (2) famine-related, and from (3) other, "natural" causes. As mentioned above, famine-related and other causes of death share a general J-shape age pattern, but on the contrary, the age pattern of death due to conflict (both war-related and executions) exhibits a "bell shape," peaking among young and middle-aged adults. In fact, these age patterns are so distinct that the contribution of war-related causes to overall mortality can be indirectly estimated from the age pattern of overall mortality (Heuveline 1998). A bell-shaped age pattern is probably typical of conflict-related mortality, but the sex ratio and age range of those directly involved in a particular conflict determine the age- and sex-specific mortality rates that increase most. The overall age and sex pattern of mortality also depends on the extent to which the general population is affected by the conflict. This makes it unlikely that a model pattern could be produced that would readily apply to all populations experiencing conflict-related mortality.

Since the 1990s, the HIV/AIDS pandemic has created a unique and significant deviation from the standard age pattern of mortality. The Human Immunodeficiency Virus (HIV) has complex effects on mortality that depend on the predominant modes of transmission and overall prevalence of the virus in a population. Large increases in mortality associated with HIV/AIDS are observed in countries where prevalence in the general population is greater than about 1%. A stationary population with an expectation of life of 10 years, similar to the HIV-positive population, has a crude death rate of $1/10 = 0.1$ or 100 per 1,000. A population containing 1% HIV-positive people will therefore add about 1 additional death per 1,000 to the crude death rate. Consequently, for populations with baseline (non-HIV) crude death rates of 10 per 1,000, an HIV prevalence of 1% corresponds to a significant 10% increase in the overall crude death rate. The greatest concentration of populations in that prevalence range are located in eastern and southern Africa, where HIV prevalence in the general population can reach 20–30% (UNAIDS 2008).

The HIV virus attacks a person's immune system, gradually wearing it down until it cannot control infections, or even itself. The result is a long period of infection and gradually worsening illness ending in death. Because of the long lag time between infection and death, the effect of HIV on mortality is observed several years after infection. In the absence of antiretroviral treatment, the time between infection and death for children is between 5 and 10 years (Marston et al. 2005) and for adults about 10 years (Jaffar et al. 2004; Morgan et al. 2002). The age pattern of the effect of HIV on mortality is determined by the age pattern of transmission and whether or not there is widespread use of antiretroviral drug therapy (highly active anti-retroviral therapy, HAART) in the population. The common modes of transmission in high-prevalence populations are heterosexual sexual intercourse and mother-to-child transmission at birth or during breastfeeding. Consequently infections occur at or shortly after birth and at ages when people are most sexually active. Those ages vary from population to population but generally span the late teens through older adulthood, with peaks sometime in the twenties or thirties. Layered on top of this is individual variation in sexual activity that effectively protects a fraction of the population and creates a gradient of risk in the remaining fraction. The net result in a mature HIV epidemic in a population without widespread treatment is that the bulk of the at-risk portion of the population is infected soon after becoming sexually active, and as a consequence the effect of HIV on mortality is relatively concentrated at the youngest possible ages, about 10 years after the average age at infection. Finally, because women typically pair with slightly older men, the average age at infection for women is usually several years younger than men, and hence the mortality effect of HIV is slightly younger for women compared to men. In general this leads to an age-profile of HIV-related mortality that affects infants and young children, women roughly aged 25–50, and men roughly aged 30–60. Although there is a lot of variation in this general pattern, depending on the specifics of HIV transmission and whether or not HAART is available, this general sex–age pattern of HIV mortality is commonly observed in populations with high prevalence.

Data to describe all-age mortality in populations with high-HIV prevalence are rare, and hence most age patterns of mortality published for those populations are based on modeled results of one kind or another. Some of the good data that are available come from demographic surveillance system sites that intensively monitor small populations for long periods of time. The examples of HIV-affected mortality shown in Figs. 24.7 and 24.8 come from one such study in the rural northeast of South Africa, where the HIV-prevalence rate is about 12% in the general population (South Africa National Department of Health 2009). Figure 24.7 displays age-specific all-cause mortality in various periods during which the HIV epidemic was growing in this population. There is an obvious increase in mortality over time for infants and young children less than 5 years old, which is seen more clearly in Fig. 24.8. Concurrently, there is a dramatic increase in mortality for men age 20–65 and a slightly smaller but no less dramatic increase for women age 15–55. The only other cause of death that has a comparable impact on adult mortality is armed conflict, as described above. In both cases, mortality during the middle years of life is elevated severalfold above normal; with HIV, the effect typically peaks at slightly older ages and covers a wider range of ages, especially older ages.

These examples of atypical mortality patterns reveal the limitations and weaknesses of our existing mortality models. It is common now to observe age patterns of mortality that produce life expectancies that exceed the majority of those used to create the commonly used Coale and Demeny and United Nations model life tables, and in some rare cases significantly lower life expectancies have also been observed. These are examples of unusual *levels* of mortality that fall outside the

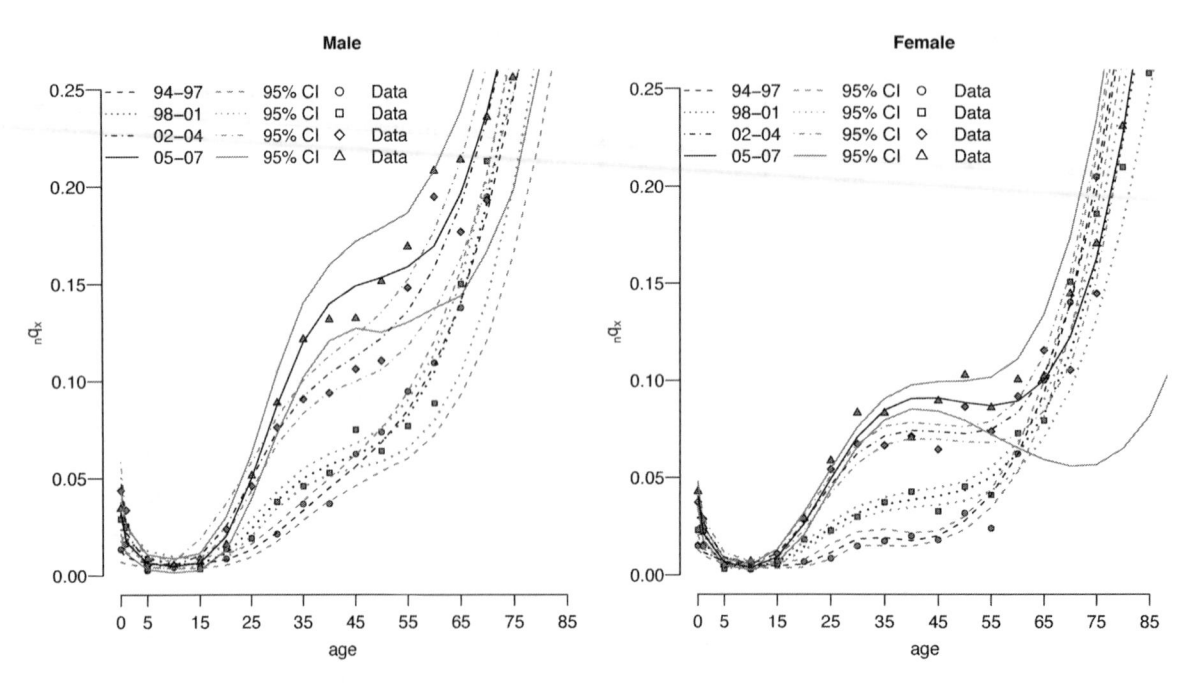

**Fig. 24.7** Age pattern of all-cause mortality from the Agincourt study population in the rural northeast of South Africa, probability of dying and 95% credible intervals in 5-year age groups, 1992–2007. Source: Sharrow and Clark (2010)

**Fig. 24.8** Age pattern of all-cause child mortality from the Agincourt study population in the rural northeast of South Africa, probability of dying in 1-month age groups, 1992–2007. Source: Sharrow and Clark (2010)

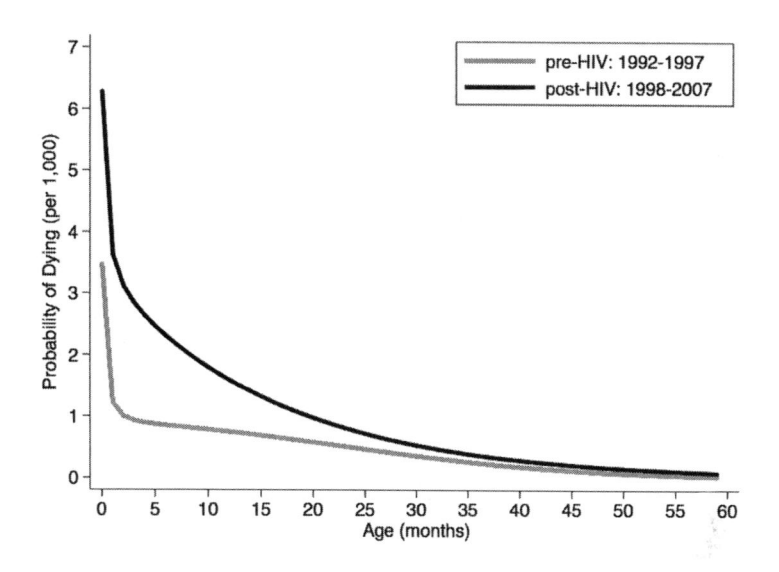

range that our models in their usual form can easily handle. In addition, there are specific conditions that dramatically increase the *prevalence* of a given cause of death to a level at which it has an important effect on the overall age pattern of mortality. Armed conflict and especially HIV-related causes are significant examples of this category of atypical mortality age profiles, and the most commonly used mortality models are unable to adequately handle either of these situations. Current work on mortality models is aimed at solving these and other emerging challenges.

## New Developments in Mortality Models

### New Theory-Based Frailty and Vitality Models

Briefly alluded to above is the seminal work of Vaupel et al. (1979) that formalized the notion of "frailty" to explain the deceleration in the increase in the risk of dying at the oldest ages in humans, that is, the empirical fact that the risk of dying begins to "flatten out" rather than continue to increase as age advances to the very oldest ages lived by human beings (and some other organisms as well). As used in this modeling framework, "frailty" is a term that describes the distribution of the risk of dying in a population. The idea is that members of a given cohort are each born with a "frailty" value that remains unchanged throughout their life. As the cohort ages, the distribution of this frailty value among the members of the cohort changes as those with high frailty die and are removed from the cohort. As time progresses, the distribution is skewed to contain increasingly less-frail individuals who as a group are less likely to die, and this change in the distribution of frailty becomes important and has a significant impact when a substantial fraction of the cohort has died; the result being the steady deceleration in the risk of dying observed at the oldest ages. The two central ideas in the frailty model are that a cohort is heterogeneous with respect to frailty from the start, and that frailty affects the risk of dying, which leads to a gradual change in the distribution of frailty (and the "average" risk of dying) as the cohort ages and more frail members die, leaving a group who are on average more robust, leading to a slowing of the rate of increase in the risk of dying at the oldest ages. The mathematics underlying the frailty model are too involved to summarize adequately here, but for interested readers, good discussions of this model can be found by Steinsaltz and Wachter (2006) and Vaupel et al. (1979).

Closely related to frailty models, but different in critical ways, are the first passage time or "vitality" models. These models originate in work in ecology to describe the survival patterns of various non-human organisms and even mechanical mechanisms. Like the frailty models, the mathematics of these models will not be described here, but nice discussions can be found by Anderson et al. (2008), Li and Anderson (2009), and Steinsaltz and Evans (2004, 2007). In contrast to the somewhat abstract relationship between frailty and mortality contained in the frailty models, the vitality models aim to more closely mirror the physiological and contextual mechanisms that are likely to contribute to the risk of dying, albeit still in relatively abstract ways. Vitality models are based on the notion that each organism is born with a given "vitality" that is continuously depleted over the course of its lifetime. The age at death is determined by the age when vitality has been depleted completely. Vitality can be thought of as a combination of an endowment at birth and an accumulation of use, abuse, or small failures that gradually wear down the initial vitality until it is gone, at which point death occurs. In this way, vitality relates to life sustaining processes *intrinsic* to the individual organism. Like the frailty models, vitality models also assume heterogeneity in vitality among members of a cohort, and the same gradual culling out also operates on a cohort with heterogeneous vitality, with results similar to those predicted by frailty models. However, some vitality models (see Li and Anderson 2009) have another important component that differentiates them from frailty models. This is a stochastic challenge process that is independent from vitality and creates challenges with random magnitude to each organism at random times during their lives. Each challenge temporarily and reversibly depletes vitality, so that if the magnitude of a challenge is equal to or greater than the current store of vitality possessed by an individual, the individual dies; otherwise the challenges are harmless in the long term and leave vitality to deplete as it would have without any challenges. These challenges have an obvious interpretation as accidents or harm from sources *extrinsic* to the organism.

Vitality models that include random challenges have the attractive property of containing few parameters that can be interpreted in terms of intrinsic and extrinsic processes affecting individuals. Because the initial distribution of vitality, the vitality decrement process, and the random challenge process are independent in vitality models, it is possible to estimate parameters that describe each net of the effects of the others. In particular, the way in which vitality decreases, *net of heterogeneity and random challenges*, determines the average age at death in a cohort, sometimes termed longevity. So, in addition to being able to represent and explain the deceleration in the increase in the risk of dying at old ages, vitality models are also able to provide information about the typical lifespan of an organism. This is particularly interesting in the context of the ongoing debate regarding the future longevity of humans: is there a natural limit to the lifespan of human beings? The application of vitality models to human populations is still at the very forefront of work in this area, so no definitive results are available. However, anecdotal evidence emerging from the work of Li and Anderson (2009) applying a vitality-with-challenges model to long-time series of mortality data from Sweden, Japan, and Switzerland suggests a long and uninterrupted improvement in the senescence parameter, and no indication that we are approaching a fundamental limit on that parameter.

## *New Empirically Based Models for Mortality Age Patterns*

Advances in mortality modeling are being driven by a combination of growing access to better quality data, continuing development of statistical and related methods, and an increasing desire to incorporate biological or physiological knowledge into models of mortality. The Human Mortality Database is a relatively new repository of high-quality life tables describing the history of mortality in a number of populations around the world. Having all of those data in one easily accessible place is enabling a range of innovative new work on mortality. Likewise in the developing world, the INDEPTH Network (2010) of demographic surveillance sites is gradually making high-quality mortality data from Africa and Asia available for study, which for the first time allows useful models of mortality to be created for populations living in those areas. Advances in Bayesian statistical estimation techniques are addressing some of the challenges inherent in estimating and/or fitting complex mortality models to data and simultaneously providing a better means through which to understand the uncertainty in the outputs of such models. Finally, borrowing ideas and techniques from biology and ecology, demographers are coming back to the idea of making mortality models more mechanistic so that they include parameters that can be interpreted either biologically or physiologically.

Working with data from the Human Mortality Database, John Wilmoth and colleagues propose a new model of mortality that serves the same purpose as the traditional model life tables constructed by Coale and Demeny and the United Nations and others (see above), but does so in a fundamentally different way (Wilmoth et al. 2009). Wilmoth recognized that one of the most common and consequential uses of model life tables is to extrapolate mortality at ages older than 5 years from a measure of child mortality, typically the probability that a newborn dies before reaching its fifth birthday, $_5q_0$ in the terminology of life tables. This is done routinely to estimate all-age mortality in developing world settings—Africa in particular—where empirical measures of mortality at all ages are not available. In addition to this practical motivation, it has been recognized for some time that there is a strong and regular relationship between child and adult mortality. Instead of looking for empirical regularities on which to build the typical "families" within a model life table system, Wilmoth and his coworkers decided to use the relationship between adult and child mortality as the fundamental empirical regularity in their model. After experimenting with several specifications, they propose the following equation to describe the relationship between child and adult mortality:

$$\log(m_x) = a_x + b_x h + c_x h^2 + v_x k$$

where:

$$h = \log(_5q_0)$$

This equation describes the log of mortality at age $x$ (on the left) with a quadratic curve in units of $\log(_5q_0)$ (on the right) plus an extra term $v_x k$. The quadratic component describes the fundamental underlying relationship between mortality at ages older (and younger) than five to mortality between ages zero and five, and the extra $v_x k$ term allows some age-specific modification to that fundamental relationship. The $v_x k$ term is necessary because of the empirical observation that there is sometimes a slight age-specific deviation from the strong underlying shape of this relationship; the age schedule of $v_x$ defines the general shape of this deviation with age, and $k$ modulates the magnitude of the deviation. The exact form of the basic relationship is set by the values of the $a_x$, $b_x$, and $c_x$ coefficients, and the exact nature of the age-specific deviation is defined by $v_x$. For this model to describe mortality at all ages, each age group needs a set of values for $a$, $b$, $c$, and $v$. Wilmoth et al. (2009) derived the age-specific values for $a$, $b$, and $c$ by estimating a regression defined by Eq. (14) for each age group using the approximately 1,800 life tables in the Human Mortality Database. Age-specific values for $v$ were derived by summarizing the regular age pattern observed in the residuals from those regressions. With this full set of empirically derived values for $a_x$, $b_x$, $c_x$, and $v_x$, it is possible to generate a very-wide range of mortality age patterns by providing different values for $_5q_0$. Wilmoth and colleagues validate their model by "fitting" it to a large variety of life tables that are not part of the Human Mortality Database, and in all but two specific cases, the model performs very well. The two cases where it does not perform well are when the age pattern of mortality reflects severe armed conflict, such as the two world wars, and when HIV/AIDS is a significant cause of death. In both of these cases, there is a very unusual "bulge" in the mortality age pattern for young to middle-aged adults, see above.

Addressing the need for model life tables that embody the experience of people living in the developing world today, especially in places where HIV/AIDS is a significant cause contributing to mortality, Clark and colleagues (2009) have developed a new component model of mortality and clustering algorithm that enables "empirical regularities" in mortality age patterns to be identified and used to generate model age patterns of mortality in a general and reproducible way. Underpinning this method is a component model of mortality based on the simple notion that it is possible to represent the arbitrary "shape" of a specific age pattern of mortality with a linear combination of a small number of age-based components. On the left in Eq. (15) (below) is the mortality age pattern, **M**, as a column vector of age-specific mortality rates, *m*, and on the right is a weighted sum (linear combination) of age-specific mortality components, **S**, represented as column vectors, each multiplied by its weight, *b*. Finally on the right there is a constant, **C**, added to the weighted sum as a column vector with only one value, *c*, repeated for all ages, and finally a column vector of residuals, **R**, that contains whatever is left over. To use this model to generate mortality age patterns, **R** is ignored (**R** is only necessary when using the model to fit an existing age pattern) and the weights $b$ and constant **C** are varied to generate an arbitrary **M**, limited only by the variation encoded in the set of components **S** that are used in the model.

$$\begin{bmatrix} m_1 \\ m_2 \\ \vdots \\ m_{19} \end{bmatrix} = b_1 \begin{bmatrix} s_{1,1} \\ s_{2,1} \\ \vdots \\ s_{19,1} \end{bmatrix} + b_2 \begin{bmatrix} s_{1,2} \\ s_{2,2} \\ \vdots \\ s_{19,2} \end{bmatrix} + \cdots \\ + b_n \begin{bmatrix} s_{1,n} \\ s_{2,n} \\ \vdots \\ s_{19,n} \end{bmatrix} + \begin{bmatrix} c \\ c \\ \vdots \\ c \end{bmatrix} + \begin{bmatrix} r_1 \\ r_2 \\ \vdots \\ r_{19} \end{bmatrix} \quad (15)$$

The components must be chosen such that together they contain all of the information necessary to represent a wide range of possible age patterns of mortality. This can be easily accomplished if one has a relatively large and diverse set of empirical age patterns of mortality available. A principal components analysis of the matrix of empirical mortality schedules yields a small number of score vectors that are shaped like mortality schedules, or typical deviations in mortality schedules, and together contain the vast majority of the information in the empirical data set, and these are precisely the components necessary for this model of mortality.

This component model of mortality is being used to identify empirical regularities in the mortality age patterns contained in the Human Mortality Database and the data contributed by the INDEPTH Network of demographic surveillance system sites in the developing world (Clark et al. 2009; INDEPTH Network (Prepared by S.J. Clark) 2002). For this purpose, the component model is estimated for each empirical mortality age pattern by regressing the empirical age pattern on the first few components resulting from a principal components analysis of the full collection of empirical age patterns. The resulting $b$'s and $c$'s are a very compact representation of the empirical dataset and can be fed into any of a number of clustering algorithms to identify a small number of "clusters" of very similar age patterns of mortality. Within each cluster, the $b$'s and $c$'s can be summarized by averaging or taking the median to yield a characteristic age pattern for each cluster. The characteristic age pattern within each cluster can then be used as the basis for a "family" of similar age patterns at various levels of mortality within a system of model life tables, each cluster being the basis of a family. The only remaining task is to generate age patterns at different levels within each family, and this can be accomplished by describing the characteristic age-dependent way in which mortality moves from generally low to high within each empirical cluster. This too can be parsimoniously encoded in a set of $b$'s and $c$'s, making it possible to represent any arbitrary level of mortality within each family in a simple and compact way using the component model of mortality and one extra parameter to specify the level. The result is effectively a two-parameter system of model life tables, one parameter to specify the family, and one parameter for the level or mortality within each family—very similar to the Coale and Demeny (1983) and United Nations (1982) model life table systems described earlier. Advantages of the procedure outlined here are that it is fully automated and thus reproducible because it does not require *judgment* on the part of the analyst at any stage, and because the model age patterns are generated through the linear component model of mortality, it is possible to manipulate them formally in many ways, including creating combinations of two or more families. For example, one could calculate a mortality age pattern from a combination of one-half family A and one-quarter each of families B and C, at whatever level desired in each family.

Another area of innovation involves the methodological treatment of some of the older models presented earlier in this chapter. Recent developments in statistics make it possible to more carefully quantify the uncertainty associated with models of many types, including the deterministic models typically applied to mortality. Uncertainty arises in several forms: uncertainty about which model is best, uncertainty associated with the parameters used or estimated by the model, and uncertainty in the outputs of the model. "Uncertainty" in these circumstances describes a situation in which information is imperfect and exact values are unknown. Another way to think about this is in terms of precision, which is inversely related to uncertainty. In all cases, the objective is to quantify uncertainty or precision so that we are in a better position to say what we know and what we do not know, and this is usually expressed by creating a probability distribution of the quantity of interest.

Recent work by Sharrow and Clark (2010) applies some of these new methods to the eight-parameter Heligman and Pollard (1980) model described above. A common application of this model involves fitting it to some empirical data either to smooth those data or to obtain parameter values that can be interpreted on their own or in comparison to similar values derived from fitting the model to another set of data. In the past, several researchers have noted that standard fitting procedures involving least squares and maximum likelihood methods do not perform well with this model (Congdon 1993; Dellaportas et al., 2001; Rogers 1986). Additionally, neither of those methods provides a robust measure of uncertainty in the values of the parameters that appear to fit the data best nor in the outputs of the model, i.e., the mortality age patterns that it generates with the best fitting sets of parameter values. Finally, it is hard if not impossible to constrain either the parameters or the model output using these traditional techniques. A Bayesian statistical technique known as *Bayesian Melding* (Poole and Raftery 2000; Raftery and Bao 2010) addresses these and other shortcomings by allowing the analyst to define prior distributions of the parameter values and the model outputs and then explore the joint set of parameter values and model outputs that satisfy those constraints to find combinations of parameter values and model outputs that maximize the likelihood of observing a given set of data. The resulting joint posterior distribution can be integrated to yield conditional posterior distributions for each parameter and the model outputs, each of which describes the probability associated with various values of the parameters and the model outputs. A typical result of applying this method is a sample from this posterior distribution consisting of a set of parameter-value vectors and corresponding model outputs. Summarizing this sample with respect to each parameter and the model outputs provides the distribution of inputs and outputs most consistent with the data. A significant advantage of this Bayesian technique is that it does not require the parameters and model outputs to be "well-behaved" in the common sense of sharing approximately Normal (approximately elliptical) relationships with each other, a set of assumptions that is rarely met with complex deterministic models of the type that are interesting in practice.

Sharrow and Clark have applied this method to mortality data coming from the Agincourt demographic surveillance site in South Africa to produce a set of

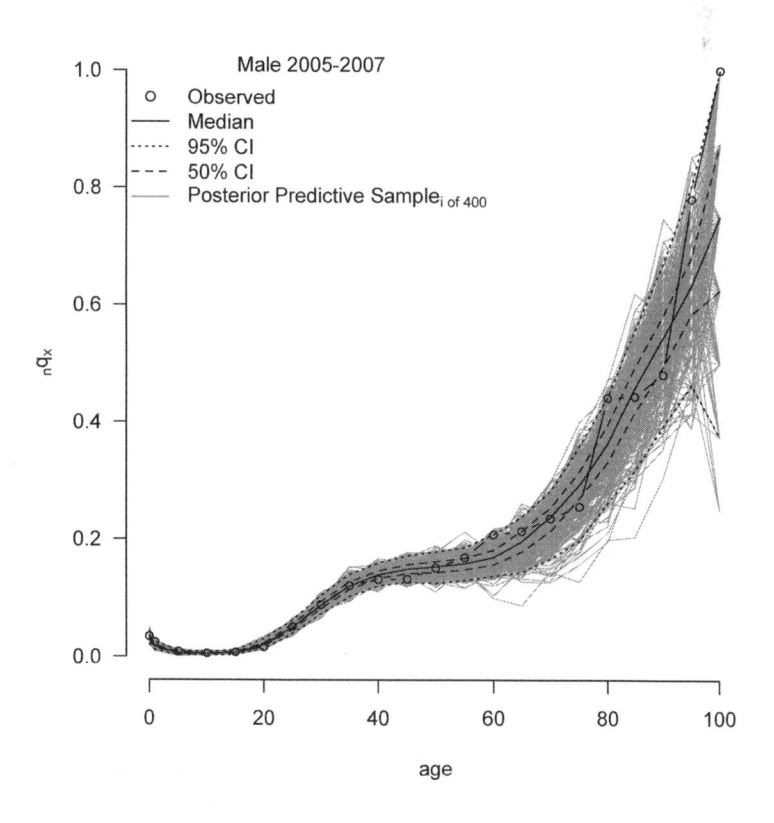

**Fig. 24.9** Result of applying Bayesian melding model estimation technique to Heligman and Pollard model of mortality, male mortality, 2005–2007 in the Agincourt study population, northeast South Africa. Source: Sharrow and Clark (2010). The dotted line represents the actual data, the family of light *curves* are the sample from the posterior distribution of model outputs, the *solid line* is the median of the sample, the *dotted lines* define the 50% and 95% credible intervals around the median. This mortality age pattern demonstrates the severe impact of HIV discussed earlier

robust parameter estimates from mortality age patterns associated with various stages of the HIV epidemic in that population. An example plot from this work is displayed in Fig. 24.9 in which one can see the family of model output curves corresponding to the sample from the posterior distribution. These clearly communicate the precision with which the data define the probability of dying in each age group. Similar distributions exist for each of the eight parameters in the model. And after fitting the model in this manner to mortality age patterns from several different periods, it is possible to compare parameter values across multiple periods and quantify with precision how the various components of this model have changed as the prevalence of HIV rose. As expected, the overall level of child and adult mortality increased dramatically, and the intensity of the accident "hump" defined by this model increased dramatically to accommodate the adult-age bulge in the age pattern of mortality created by HIV.

These new developments illustrate that while the construction of model mortality schedules has been one of the primary endeavors of formal demography at its outset, this endeavor has remained central to the discipline to this date. The availability of large mortality database and regression analysis software today makes it relatively easy for the analyst to construct her own "model" based on extant tables that are expected to reflect a cause-of-death environment shared with the population of interest. This recent ease in the construction of new, even ad hoc models has decreased the need to rely on the classic systems such as the Coale and Demeny (1983) or the United Nations (1982) model life tables, but leaves intact the reliance on mortality schedules in demographic analysis and forecasting.

Looking forward, there will remain an urgent need to continue refining and creating model mortality schedules to reflect continuing changes in the level and age patterns of mortality. Population projections and forecasts are perhaps the most widely used "products" of demography, and both make extensive use of model mortality schedules. To function well in those applications, model mortality schedules need to be able to accurately reflect what has happened in the past (the estimation part of constructing a forecast) and also provide a reasonable set of possible futures for mortality. Particularly in terms of predicting future mortality, ongoing and future work will seek to better understand and represent senescent mortality or longevity independent of other causes because the long-term future of mortality is tied to the trend in senescent mortality. It is for this reason that frailty and vitality models have and are receiving so much attention. Future work will also lead to models that are better able to handle atypical mortality schedules such as those created by HIV-related causes of death. This work is of crucial importance to Africa and other parts of the developing world where vital registration systems function poorly or not at all, resulting in missing or incomplete data to describe mortality. In those situations, model mortality schedules are used extensively to smooth, interpolate, extrapolate, or make *indirect* estimates of mortality that serve in the place of vital registration. The challenge is that the populations for which indirect estimates are necessary are often those whose mortality schedules are atypical and not well-represented by existing models. Last, recent advances in statistical methodology are providing opportunities to re-conceptualize existing models and formulate new models in novel ways. It is likely that the next generation of model mortality schedules will use significantly different methods that more fully account for uncertainty, and more robust fitting and estimation procedures.

Promising areas for future research and modeling of mortality schedules include better understanding and modeling of: mortality at the oldest ages, senescent mortality and the long-term trend in senescent mortality, and atypical causes of death and how they affect age patterns of mortality. With respect to atypical causes resulting from disease (like HIV), it will be important to *link* model mortality schedules with epidemiological models that describe the transmission or development of the disease. Together, these can then be used to better understand the population-level effects of the disease and perhaps help illuminate how best to disrupt or affect the disease to bring about a desired change in the population-level effects. In areas where mortality data are incomplete or missing, it will be important to continue thinking about measurement: how to replace direct measures of age-specific mortality with indirect measures, modeled measures, and measures derived from cutting-edge sampling techniques such as adaptive sampling or respondent-driven sampling or new sampling methods not yet conceived. The aim in each case is to increase the accuracy and representativeness of the data while simultaneously keeping the measurement system cheap and logistically feasible. It is likely that model mortality schedules will be an integral part of designing and testing sophisticated sampling strategies of these types.

## References

Anderson, J.J., M.C. Gildea, D.W. Williams, and T. Li.. 2008. "Linking Growth, Survival, and Heterogeneity Through Vitality." *The American Naturalist* 171:E20–E43.

Bhat, P.N.B.. 1987. *Mortality in India: Levels, Trends and Patterns*. Ph.D. Dissertation. Philadelphia, PA, University of Pennsylvania.

Bourgeois-Pichat, J. 1946. De la Mesure de la Mortalité Infantile. *Population* 1(1):53–68.

Brass, W. 1971. On the Scale of Mortality. In W. Brass (ed.), *Biological Aspects of Demography*, pp. 69–110. London, Taylor and Francis Ltd; New York, NY, Barnes and Noble Inc.

Carey, J.R. and D. Judge. 2001. "Life Span Extension in Humans Is Self-Reinforcing: A General Theory of Longevity." *Population and Development Review* 27(3):411–36.

Carnes, B.A., S.J. Olshansky, and D. Grahn. 1996. "The Search for a Law of Mortality." *Population and Development Review* 22(2):231–64.

Charlesworth, B.. 2000. "Fisher, Medawar, Hamilton and the Evolution of Aging." *Genetics* 156(3):927–31.

Chu, C.Y. and R.D. Lee.. 2006. "The Co-evolution of Intergenerational Transfers and Longevity: An Optimal Life History Approach." *Theoretical Population Biology* 69(2):193–201.

Clark, S.J., M. Jasseh, A.A. Bawah, and O. Sankoh. 2009. *INDEPTH Model Life Tables 2.0*. Annual Meeting of the Population Association of America. Detroit, MI, Population Association of America.

Coale, A.J. and P. Demeny. 1966. *Regional Model Life Tables and Stable Populations*. Princeton, Princeton University Press.

Coale, A.J. and P. Demeny, B. Vaughan. 1983. *Regional Model Life Tables and Stable Populations*. New York, NY, Academic Press.

Coale, A.J. and G. Guo. 1989. "Revised Regional Model Life Tables at Very Low Levels of Mortality." *Population Studies* 55(4):613–43.

Coale, A.J. and E.E. Kisker. 1990. "Defects in Data on Old-Age Mortality in the United States: New Procedures for Calculating Schedules and Life Tables at the Highest Ages." *Asian and Pacific Population Forum* 4(1):1–31.

Condran, G.A., C. Himes, and S.H. Preston.. 1991. "Old Age Mortality Patterns in Low-Mortality Countries: An Evaluation of Population and Death Data at Advanced Ages, 1950 to the Present." *Population Bulletin of the United Nations* 30:23–60.

Congdon, P. 1993. "Statistical Graduation in Local Demographic Analysis and Projection." *Journal of the Royal Statistical Society. Series A (Statistics in Society)* 156(2):237–70.

Dellaportas, P., A.F.M. Smith, and P. Stavropoulos. 2001. "Bayesian Analysis of Mortality Data." *Journal of the Royal Statistical Society. Series A (Statistics in Society)* 164(2):275–91.

de Moivre, A. 1725. *Annuities on Lives*. London, W. Pearson.

Dyson, T. and C.Ó. Gráda. 2002. *Famine Demography: Perspectives from the Past and Present*. Oxford; New York, NY, Oxford University Press.

Ewbank, D.C., J.C. Gomex de Leon, and M.A. Stoto. 1983. "A Reducible Four-Parameter System of Model Life Tables." *Population Studies* 37(1):105–27.

Fisher, R.A.. 1930. *The Genetical Theory of Natural Selection*. Oxford, Clarendon Press.

Forfar, D.O. 2004. "Mortality Laws." In J.L. Teugels and B. Sundt (eds.), *Encyclopedia of Actuarial Science*, vol. 2, pp. 1139–44. Hoboken, NJ, Wiley.

Gabriel, K.R. and I. Ronen. 1958. "Estimates of Mortality from Infant Mortality Rates." *Population Studies* 12(2):164–69.

Gompertz, B. 1825. "On the Nature of the Function Expressive of the Law of Mortality, and a New Mode of Determining the Value of Life Contingencies." *Philosophical Transactions of Royal Society of London* 115(Series A):513–83.

Graunt, J. 1662. *Natural and Political Observations Mentioned in a Following Index, and Made Upon the Bills of Mortality*. London, John Martyn.

Halley, E. 1693. "An Estimate of the Degrees of Mortality of the Manking." *Philosophical Transactions* 196:596–610, 654–56.

Heligman, L. and J.H. Pollard. 1980. "The Age Pattern of Mortality." *Journal of the Institute of Actuaries* 107 Part 1(434):49–80.

Heuveline, P. 1998. "'Between One and Three Million': Towards the Demographic Reconstruction of a Decade of Cambodian History (1970–1979)." *Population Studies* 52(1):49–65.

Heuveline, P. 2001. "The Demographic Analysis of Mortality Crises: The Case of Cambodia." In H. Reed and C. Kelley (eds.), *Forced Migration and Mortality*, pp. 102–29. Washington, DC, National Academy Press.

Himes, C., S.H. Preston, and G.A. Condran. 1994. "A Relational Model of Mortality at Older Ages in Low Mortality Countries." *Population Studies* 48(2):269–91.

Horiuchi, S. and A.J. Coale. 1982. "A Simple Equation for Estimating the Expectation of Life at Old Ages." *Population Studies* 36(2):317–26.

Horiuchi, S. and A.J. Coale. 1990. "Age Patterns of Mortality for Older Women: An Analysis Using the Age-Specific Rate of Mortality Change with Age." *Mathematical Population Studies* 2(4):25–67.

Human Mortality Database. University of California, Berkeley (USA) and Max Planck Institute for Demographic Research (Gernmany). Available at www.mortality.org

INDEPTH Network (Prepared by S.J. Clark). 2002. "*INDEPTH Mortality Patterns for Africa*." In *INDEPTH* (ed.), *Population, Health, and Survival at INDEPTH Sites*, vol. 1. Population and Health in Developing Countries. Ottawa, IDRC Press.

INDEPTH Network. 2010. *An International Network of Field Sites with Continuous Demographic Evaluation of Populations and Their Health in Developing Countries –*

INDEPTH. www.indepth-network.net; www.indepth-network.org

Jaffar, S., A.D. Grant, J. Whitworth, P.G. Smith, and H. Whittle. 2004. "The Natural History of HIV-1 and HIV-2 Infections in Adults in Africa: A Literature Review." *Bulletin of the World Health Organization* 82:462–69.

Knodel, J. and H. Kintner. 1977. "The Impact of Breast Feeding Patterns on the Biometric Analysis of Infant Mortality." *Demography* 14(4):391–409.

Kung, H.C., D.L. Hoyert, J. Xu, and S.L. Murphy. 2008. "Deaths: Final Data for 2005." *National Vital Statistics Reports* 56:10.

Lantoine, C. and R. Pressat. 1984. "Nouveaux Aspects de la Mortalité Infantile." *Population* 39(2):253–64.

Lederman, S. 1969. *Nouvelles Tables-Types de Mortalité*, INED Travaux et Documents, Cahiers 53. Paris, Presses Universitaires de France.

Lederman, S. and J. Breas. 1959. "Les Dimensions de la Mortalité." *Population* 14(4):637–82.

Li, T. and J.J. Anderson. 2009. "The Vitality Model: A Way to Understand Population Survival and Demographic Heterogeneity." *Theoretical Population Biology* 76:118–31.

Makeham, W.M. 1860. "On the Law of Mortality and the Construction of Annuity Tables." *The Assurance Magazine and Journal of the Institute of Actuaries* 8:301–10.

Marston, M., B. Zaba, J.A. Salomon, H. Brahmbhatt, and D. Bagenda. 2005. "Estimating the Net Effect of HIV on Child Mortality in African Populations Affected by Generalized HIV Epidemics." *JAIDS Journal of Acquired Immune Deficiency Syndromes* 38(2):219.

McDaniel, A. 1995. *Swing Low, Sweet Chariot: The Mortality Cost of Colonizing Liberia in the Nineteenth Century*. Chicago and London, The University of Chicago.

Morgan, D., C. Mahe, B. Mayanja, J.M. Okongo, R. Lubega, and J.A.G. Whitworth. 2002. "HIV-1 Infection in Rural Africa: Is There a Difference in Median Time to AIDS and Survival Compared with that in Industrialized Countries?" *Aids* 16(4):597.

OECD. 1980. *Mortality in Developing Countries*, vol. 3. Paris, France, Organization for Economic Cooperation and Development.

Perks, W. 1932. "On Some Experiments in the Graduation of Mortality Statistics." *Journal of the Institute of Actuaries* 63:12–57.

Poole, D. and A.E. Raftery. 2000. "Inference for Deterministic Simulation Models: The Bayesian Melding Approach." *Journal of the American Statistical Association* 95:452.

Preston, S.H. 1976. *Mortality Patterns in National Populations*. New York, NY, Academic Press.

Preston, S.H.; Heuveline, P., and M. Guillot. 2000. *Demography: Measuring and Modeling Population Processes*. Oxford, UK; Malder, MA, Blackwell Publishers.

Preston, S.H., A. McDaniel, and C. Grushka. 1993. "New Model Life Tables for High-Mortality Populations." *Historical Methods* 26(4):149–59.

Raftery, A.E. and L. Bao. 2010. "Estimating and Projecting Trends in HIV/AIDS Generalized Epidemics Using Incremental Mixture Importance Sampling." *Biometrics* 9999:9999.

Rogers, A. 1986. "Parameterized Multistate Population Dynamics and Projections." *Journal of the American Statistical Association* 81(393):48–61.

Sharrow, D.J. and S.J. Clark. 2010. "A Parametric Investigation of Mortality at All Ages in a Rural, South African Population." In *Annual Meeting of the Population Association of America*. Dallas, TX, Population Association of America.

Sliwinsky, M. 1995. *Le Génocide Khmer Rouge: Une Analyse Démographique*. Paris, L'Harmattan.

South Africa National Department of Health. 2009. *2008 National Antenatal Sentinel HIV & Syphilis Prevalence Survey South Africa*. Report available at http://www.doh.gov.za/docs/nassps-f.html.

Steinsaltz, D. and S.N. Evans. 2004. "Markov Mortality Models: Implications of Quasistationarity and Varying Initial Distributions." *Theoretical Population Biology* 65(4): 319–37.

Steinsaltz, D. and S.N. Evans. 2007. "Quasistationary Distributions for One-Dimensional Diffusions with Killing." *Transactions of the American Mathematical Society* 359(3):1285.

Steinsaltz, D.R. and K.W. Wachter. 2006. "Understanding Mortality Rate Deceleration and Heterogeneity." *Mathematical Population Studies* 13(1):19–37.

Sutherland, I. 1963. "John Graunt: A Tercentenary Tribute." *Journal of the Royal Statistical Society* 126(Series A):537–56.

Thiele, T.N. 1872. "On a Mathematical Formula to Express the Rate of Mortality Throughout the Whole Life." *Journal of the Institute of Actuaries and Assurance Magazine* 16: 313–29.

UNAIDS. 2008. *2008 Report on the Global AIDS Epidemic*. Report, UNAIDS, Gevena. www.unaids.org/en/KnowledgeCentre/HIVData/GlobalReport/2008/2008_Global_report.asp

United Nations. 1955. *Age and Sex Patterns of Mortality: Model Life Tables for Underdeveloped Countries*. Population Studies 22. New York, NY, United Nations.

United Nations. 1982. *Model Life Tables for Developing Countries*. Population Studies 77. New York, NY, United Nations.

United Nations. 2003. *Mortpak for Windows, Version 4.0*. New York, NY, United Nations.

Vaupel, J.W. 1997. "The Remarkable Improvement of Survival at Old Ages." *Philosophical Transactions of the Royal Society of London* 352(1363, Series B): 1799–804.

Vaupel, J.W., K.G. Manton, and E. Stallard. 1979. "The Impact of Heterogeneity in Individual Frailty on the Dynamics of Mortality." *Demography* 16(3):439–54.

Wilmoth, J.R., V. Canudas-Romo, S. Zureick, and C.C. Sawyer. 2009. *A Flexible Two-Dimensional Mortality Model for Use in Indirect Estimation*. Annual Meeting of the Population Association of America. Detroit, MI, Population Association of America.

Zaba, B. 1979. "The Four-Parameter Logit Life Table System." *Population Studies* 33(1):79–100.

# Chapter 25
# Period Versus Cohort Life Expectancy

Michel Guillot

## Introduction

Mortality can be analyzed according to two main frameworks: the cohort framework, which takes into account mortality risks as they unfold along the actual life cycle of a group of individuals born during the same period of time, and the period framework, which takes into account risks experienced by different cohorts during a single period of time. These frameworks provide two alternative ways for studying life expectancy. Analysis of time trends in life expectancy will differ depending on whether it is calculated by period or cohort.

The purpose of this chapter is to contrast these two approaches and their respective interpretations. In particular, I examine the extent to which period and cohort life expectancies can be interpreted in terms of underlying health *conditions* for the corresponding periods and cohorts. Finally, I discuss a third and intermediate approach, the cross-sectional cohort approach, which offers some additional insights about the dynamics of mortality.

## Definitions

### Cohort Life Expectancy

Cohort life expectancy summarizes the mortality experience of an actual birth cohort of individuals as they

M. Guillot (✉)
Department of Sociology and Population Studies Center,
University of Pennsylvania, Philadelphia, PA 19104, USA
e-mail: miguillo@sas.upenn.edu

age over time, from birth until the cohort becomes extinct through the death of the last survivor. By nature, individuals gain 1 year of age every year. Thus, this mortality experience will be spread over a period of time that is as long as the age at which the cohort's last survivor dies. In a matrix of mortality rates indexed by age $x$ and time $t$ ($\mu(x,t)$), the mortality rates experienced by a cohort born at time $t$ will be located along the age and time coordinates $(x, t + x)$.

Cohort life expectancy at birth for the cohort born at time $t$ is defined as follows:

$$e_0^c(t) = \int_0^\infty p_c(x,t)dx, \qquad (1)$$

where $p_c(x,t)$ is the probability of surviving from birth to age $x$ for the cohort born at time $t$. This cohort survival probability is related to age- and time-specific mortality rates as follows:

$$p_c(x,t) = e^{-\int_0^x \mu(a,t+a)da}. \qquad (2)$$

Ignoring migration, cohort life expectancy at birth corresponds to the mean age at death for that cohort.

### Period Life Expectancy

Period life expectancy, by contrast, summarizes the mortality risks experienced by different cohorts (or, equivalently, at different ages) during one period of time. When calculating period life expectancy at birth at time $t$, risks experienced during the first year of life (age 0) during year $t$ will be combined with risks experienced at age 1, at age 2, and so forth, during the same year $t$. Period life expectancy is calculated by resorting to the concept of synthetic (or fictitious) cohorts. Unlike real cohorts, synthetic cohorts do not gain 1 year of age every year; they hypothetically spend their entire life during one period of time. Period life expectancy at birth can thus be interpreted as the mean age at death that would be experienced by a synthetic cohort hypothetically exposed to the age-specific mortality rates of one period. Equivalently, period life expectancy at birth can be interpreted as the mean age at death that would be experienced by a real cohort under the hypothetical scenario that age-specific mortality rates observed during one period remain constant in the future. In a matrix of mortality rates by age and time, the mortality experience of the synthetic cohort born at time $t$ will be located along the age and time coordinates (x,t).

Period life expectancy at birth for period $t$ is defined as follows:

$$e_0^P(t) = \int_0^\infty p(x,t)dx, \quad (3)$$

where $p(x,t)$ is the probability of surviving from birth to age $x$ for the synthetic cohort born at time $t$ and exposed to the age-specific mortality rates of time $t$. This surviving probability is derived from period rates as follows:

$$p(x,t) = e^{-\int_0^x \mu(a,t)da}. \quad (4)$$

## Practical Considerations Regarding the Computation of Cohort Versus Period Life Expectancy

Cohort life expectancy at birth ($e_0^c$) is not as commonly calculated as period life expectancy because it requires the availability of mortality data spanning about a century. Furthermore, $e_0^c$ can be calculated with certainty only for cohorts that are now extinct or near extinct. This means that in practice, even when historical mortality data are available, the most recent cohorts for which $e_0^c$ can be estimated were born about 90–100 years ago. Thus, $e_0^c$ will refer to mortality experienced in the past and will ignore a large amount of more recent mortality information.

Period life expectancy at birth ($e_0^P$), by contrast, involves only mortality information for one period. No

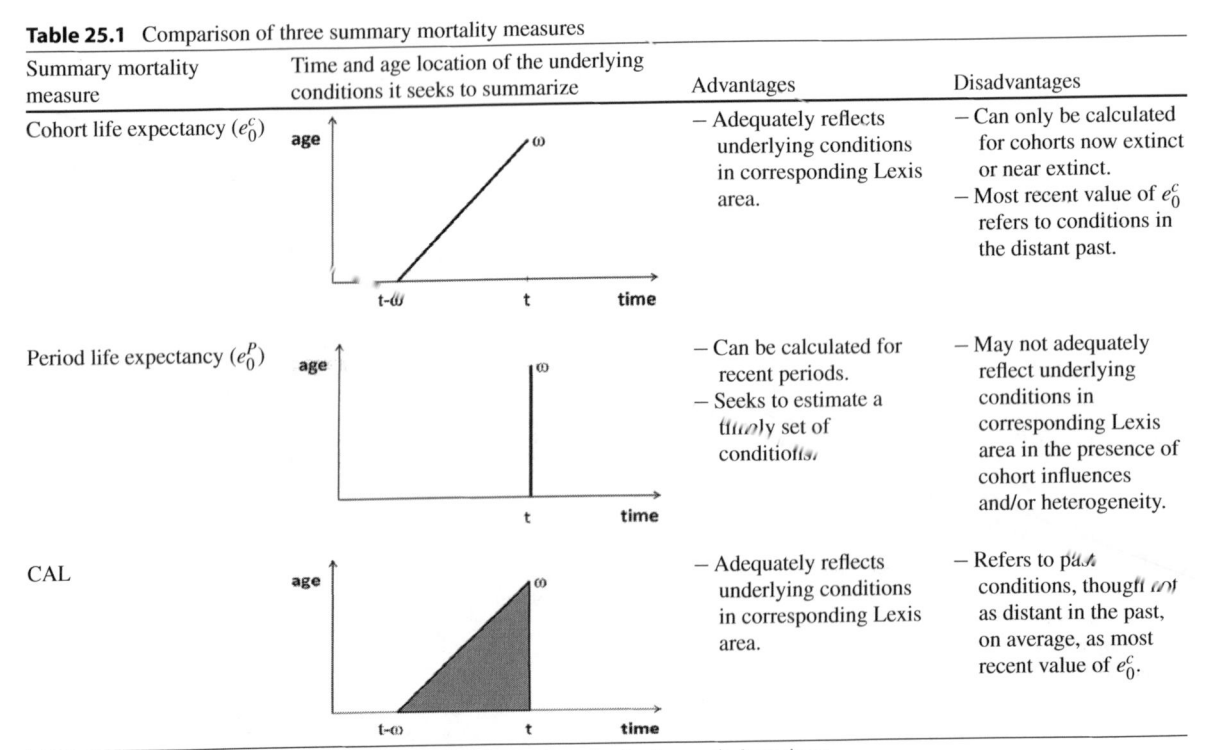

**Table 25.1** Comparison of three summary mortality measures

| Summary mortality measure | Time and age location of the underlying conditions it seeks to summarize | Advantages | Disadvantages |
|---|---|---|---|
| Cohort life expectancy ($e_0^c$) | | – Adequately reflects underlying conditions in corresponding Lexis area. | – Can only be calculated for cohorts now extinct or near extinct.<br>– Most recent value of $e_0^c$ refers to conditions in the distant past. |
| Period life expectancy ($e_0^P$) | | – Can be calculated for recent periods.<br>– Seeks to estimate a timely set of conditions. | – May not adequately reflect underlying conditions in corresponding Lexis area in the presence of cohort influences and/or heterogeneity. |
| CAL | | – Adequately reflects underlying conditions in corresponding Lexis area. | – Refers to past conditions, though not as distant in the past, on average, as most recent value of $e_0^c$. |

Note: $\omega$ is the age at which there remains a negligible number of cohort or period survivors.

## 25 Period Versus Cohort Life Expectancy

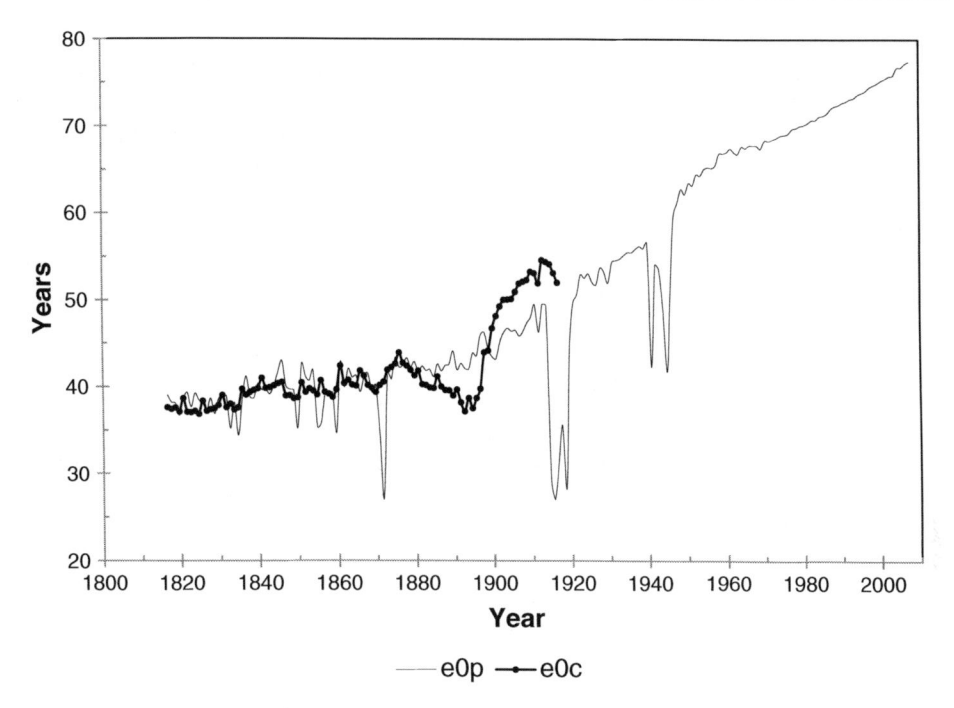

**Fig. 25.1** Period versus cohort life expectancy at birth, French males, 1816–2007 (period), and 1816–1916 (cohort). Source: Human mortality database

historical data are needed for calculating today's $e_0^P$. $e_0^P$ involves current as opposed to past mortality rates, and in this sense, it is more "timely." For these reasons, $e_0^P$ is more often calculated than $e_0^c$. Most discussions of mortality trends or international mortality comparisons rely on the period approach. Less-developed countries, in particular, rely almost exclusively on period mortality measures.

The Lexis diagrams in the first two rows of Table 25.1 contrast the time location of the mortality rates involved in the calculation of $e_0^c$ versus $e_0^P$. Given the availability of age-specific mortality rates up to time $t$, and if we define $\omega$ as the age at which the number of cohort or period survivors is negligible, the most recent cohort for which $e_0^c$ can be estimated is the cohort born at time $t-\omega$ (top row of Table 25.1). $e_0^P$, however, can be calculated for time $t$ (middle row of Table 25.1).

Figure 25.1 presents trends in $e_0^c$ versus $e_0^P$, using data for French males as an example. This figure illustrates the difference in the range of years for which $e_0^c$ versus $e_0^P$ can be calculated. With annual age-specific mortality rates available between 1816 and 2007, $e_0^P$ can be calculated annually between 1816 and 2007, whereas $e_0^c$ can be calculated from 1816 until 1916, i.e., the most recent cohort for which $e_0^c$ can be reliably calculated. This figure also illustrates differences in levels and trends between these two indicators. The interpretation of these levels and trends is developed in the next section.

## Interpretations

### Cohort Life Expectancy

Cohort life expectancy varies over time and place. For example, among Swedish females, $e_0^c$ increased from 35.81 years for the cohort born in 1751 to 70.44 years for the cohort born in 1916. Among French males (shown in Fig. 25.1), it increased from 37.62 years for the 1816 cohort to 51.99 for the 1916 cohort. (These two populations are chosen for purely illustrative purposes.)

The overall order of magnitude of these life expectancies (i.e., the fact that the above values are measured in years and not, say, in days) reflects the underlying biological vulnerability of humans and how it evolves with age. This underlying theoretical influence of age on mortality, also called theoretical biological aging (Wilmoth et al. 1990) explains why humans live longer on average than, say, fruit flies. It also explains why, in spite of the wide range of variation in human experience over time and place, newborns tend to face higher mortality risks than, say, 10-year olds; and 90-year olds tend to face higher mortality risks than, say, 30-year olds. Patterns of theoretical biological aging are thought to be species-specific. By nature, these patterns may change only slowly over time and thus may not explain historical improvements in life expectancy in a country like Sweden over the past 250 years.

Theoretical biological aging takes place within specific historical conditions that may have powerful impacts on survival. By contrast to biological aging, these conditions may change rapidly over time. Factors that can be invoked for explaining improvements in life expectancy include improvements in nutrition and housing conditions, advances in medical technology, public health measures, and improvements in personal health behaviors (Riley 2001). For the relatively low values of life expectancy among certain cohorts of French males shown in Fig. 25.1, especially those born toward the end of the nineteenth century, the impact of World Wars I and II can also be invoked.

In view of these various time-specific influences, cohort life expectancy is perhaps best understood by examining the time location of these factors and their impact on age-specific mortality. These influences can be broadly divided into two main categories: (1) health conditions that a cohort faces at a given time and that have an *immediate* impact on the cohort's mortality, and (2) health conditions that a cohort faces at a given time and that have a *delayed* impact on the cohort's mortality. These influences operate in combination with theoretical biological aging.

The Lexis diagram in Fig. 25.2 illustrates these two types of influences. This figure represents the life course of a birth cohort as it passes through different calendar years. Year after year, the cohort faces a set of potentially changing conditions. Certain foods may become more abundant. A new drug may become available. The quality of drinking water may improve. Smoking may become fashionable or fall out of fashion. A war may break out or end. Some of these changes may have an immediate impact on the cohort's mortality. For example, a cohort's mortality may increase during a war as result of the immediate impact of combat and bombardments. Some of these changes in conditions, however, may have a delayed impact on a cohort's mortality. For example, in addition to causing immediate deaths, combat may cause injuries that can lead to increased mortality long after the war has ended. Overall, the unique set of health conditions that a cohort faces at different ages may leave a specific imprint on that cohort and have an impact on the cohort's subsequent mortality.

In Fig. 25.2, the origin of the arrows identifies the time location of the health conditions or factors having an impact on mortality. The destination point of the arrows locates the time location of mortality rates that are affected by these factors. Conditions or factors that have an immediate impact on a cohort's mortality are represented with vertical arrows. These conditions are referred to in this chapter as "period influences." Conditions or factors that have a delayed impact on

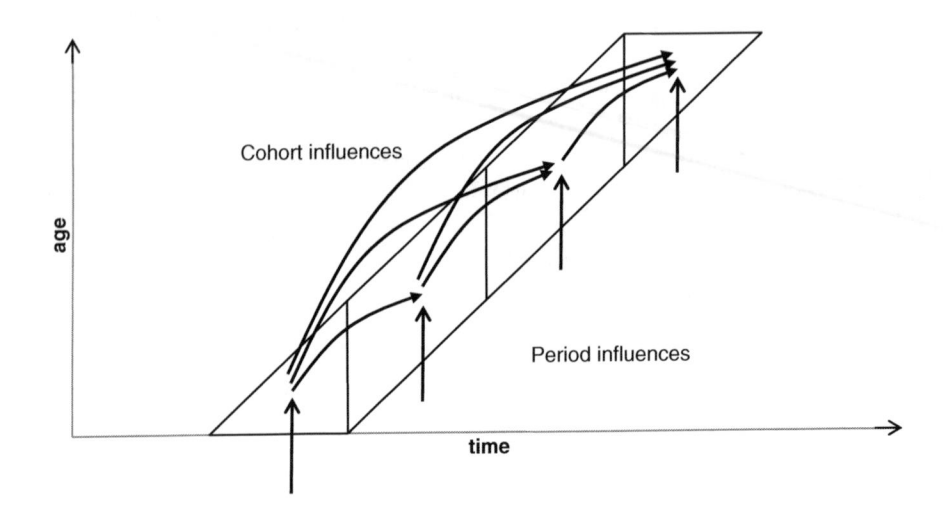

**Fig. 25.2** Period versus cohort influences on age-specific mortality rates

mortality are represented with diagonal arrows. These conditions are referred to in this chapter as "cohort influences." (The distinction between immediate and delayed impacts is somewhat arbitrary. Except perhaps in the case of some external causes, such as certain accidents, homicides, and suicides, causal processes leading to increased mortality require some time to unfold. Since mortality rates are typically calculated over discrete time intervals, immediate influences can be thought of as situations in which the cause and effect both take place during the same time interval over which mortality rates are calculated, such as a calendar year. Note also that in Fig. 25.2 the origin of the arrows indicates the time at which health conditions are present in the population, not the time at which they first appeared. For example, a drug that treats a disease common in old age may become available when a cohort is still young. This medical advance would have an impact on the cohort's mortality only once the cohort reaches old age. Such an influence would not be represented with diagonal arrows in the diagram, but with a vertical one. It is the availability of that drug when the cohort reaches old age that has an impact on the cohort's mortality. The availability of the drug when the cohort is young is irrelevant—at that point it is not part of the cohort's experience.)

In the demographic literature, factors that have an immediate impact on mortality are often referred to as "period effects," whereas factors that have a delayed impact on mortality are often called "cohort effects." Period and cohort effects operate in combination with theoretical biological aging, often referred to as "age effects." The precise definition of these period, cohort, and age effects varies from author to author, in part due to differences in methodological approaches designed for the estimation of these processes. Sometimes a clear connection is established between a health condition or factor and its immediate versus later mortality effects, in relation to the age at which this condition is experienced (see Chapter 9 by Montez and Hayward, this volume; see also Elo and Preston 1992; Preston and Wang 2006; Preston et al. 1998). Sometimes period versus cohort effects (or full age-period-cohort [APC] models) are evaluated by examining correlations among age-specific death rates (Caselli and Capocaccia 1989; Crimmins and Finch 2006; Hobcraft et al. 1982; Myrskylä 2010; Wilmoth et al. 1990). The purpose of this chapter is not to review or evaluate age-period-cohort procedures, but rather to illustrate the time-specific connection between health conditions and age-specific mortality, and the implication of this connection for interpreting levels and trends in life expectancy. (To emphasize the fact that we refer to the time-specific connection between health conditions and age-specific mortality, rather than to some other type of connection, we use the term period versus cohort "influences" in this chapter, rather than the more common and general term period versus cohort "effects.")

Classic examples of conditions that have immediate effects on age-specific mortality include wars, epidemics, famines, and such natural disasters as earthquakes, storms, floods, and heat waves. (For more information about environmental effects, see Chapter 21 by Browning, Bjornstrom, and Cagney, this volume.) These extreme conditions are easy to detect because their occurrence is typically well-defined in time, and because they have obvious short-term causal effects on mortality. For example, in Fig. 25.1, the effects on mortality of the Franco-Prussian war and the Paris commune (1870–1871), World War I and the Spanish Influenza epidemic (1914–1918), and World War II (1940–1945), appear clearly in the trend in period life expectancy. However, many conditions with period influences may evolve more gradually over time and may appear less clearly in trajectories of age-specific death rates or life expectancy.

Conditions that are often cited as having delayed effects on mortality include exposure to infectious diseases, dietary patterns, exposure to non-infectious inflammogens, smoking, and alcohol consumption (Chapter 9 by Montez and Hayward, this volume; Crimmins and Finch 2006; Elo and Preston 1992). Such effects are usually difficult to detect in trajectories of age-specific mortality rates, because they often involve factors that may change more gradually over time and affect mortality over a broad range of ages. Nonetheless, in a number of cases, there are clear causal, biological mechanisms that support the existence of these effects. Perhaps the clearest example of a health condition with delayed impacts on mortality is respiratory tuberculosis (TB) (Frost 1939; Mason and Smith 1985). This disease can have a long period of latency, and therefore many adult deaths from respiratory TB result from childhood exposures. Another important health condition that has long-lasting impacts on mortality is cigarette smoking (Doll et al. 2004; Preston and Wang 2006). Exposure to asbestos is another example of a condition that has delayed impacts on mortality (Peto et al. 1982).

A number of complications to this simple distinction between immediate versus delayed influences can be introduced. First, some health conditions may have both immediate and delayed impacts. Exposure to infections and inflammation in childhood, for example, may increase mortality rates both at childhood ages and at older ages (Crimmins and Finch 2006; see also Chapter 9 by Montez and Hayward, this volume). Another example is alcohol consumption, which can have both immediate impacts (with deaths from alcohol poisoning) and delayed impacts (with deaths from liver cirrhosis). In some cases, the delayed versus immediate impacts may operate in opposite directions. For example, high exposure to diseases for which life-long immunity can be acquired may generate both high childhood mortality and low later life mortality from these diseases (Preston et al. 1998). Second, for most if not all mortality factors (except perhaps some extreme natural disasters), the impact (immediate and/or delayed) depends on the age at which these factors are experienced. For example, it is believed that exposure to infections and/or malnutrition is particularly consequential when experienced at childhood ages (or even in utero), rather than at adult ages (Barker 2007; Forsdahl 1977). Similarly, wars involving mostly military combat will impact mortality primarily within the draft age range. Third, factors affecting mortality may interact with one another in complex ways (Chapter 9 by Montez and Hayward, this volume). (This discussion of immediate versus delayed influences focuses on physiological processes affecting the risk of death at the individual level. We will see in the next section that, when examining mortality rates at the aggregate level, another mechanism through which health conditions can have a delayed influence on mortality rates is mortality selection.)

The life expectancy of a cohort summarizes these two kinds of influences, period and cohort, on age-specific mortality. Exposed to a specific set of period conditions, which they experience at specific ages, the cohort's mortality responds immediately (period influences) or with some delay (cohort influences). These conditions may interact with one another in complex ways. The cohort's set of age-specific death rates reflect this unique combination of circumstances. Changes in cohort life expectancy can thus be directly interpreted in terms of changes in the underlying mortality conditions experienced by successive cohorts. Even though the exact nature of the underlying causes and mechanisms is often unclear, an increase in $e_0^c$ from one cohort to the next implies that the second cohort has been exposed to a more favorable combination of mortality conditions. (This interpretation ignores possible intergenerational influences, i.e., the fact that a mother's past exposure to specific conditions may also influence her children's risk of mortality throughout their life course. One example of such mechanism is the possibility that persons exposed to radiation (for example, Japanese atomic survivors) may suffer genetic defects that will influence the mortality of their yet-to-be born children. While this particular example is unsupported by data (Neel and Schull 1991), the existence of such a mechanism would imply that two birth cohorts exposed to identical mortality conditions may still exhibit different survival, depending on their parents' past experience. In other words, cohort life expectancy may not only reflect mortality conditions; it may also be affected to some extent by the underlying characteristics at birth of the cohort exposed to these conditions. The scale of intergenerational influences is difficult to establish, and thus these influences are often ignored in the literature on period versus cohort influences. If we include in utero exposures as part of a cohort's exposure to period conditions, a number of influences that are sometimes considered as intergenerational influences, such as pre-natal malnutrition or mother–child HIV transmission, would be excluded from this mechanism and would not undermine the interpretation of the cohort life expectancy as an index summarizing the cohort's unique set of time-specific circumstances.)

## Period Life Expectancy

Interpreting levels and trends in period life expectancy in terms of underlying health conditions is not as straightforward as in the case of cohort life expectancy. Strictly speaking, period life expectancy summarizes period mortality *rates*. However, it is often taken as summary of the mortality *conditions* operating during that year (Vaupel 2002). The implicit assumption is that if mortality conditions (i.e., all factors affecting age-specific mortality besides theoretical biological aging, such as environmental, behavioral, and technological factors) were to remain constant from time $t$ onward, the cohort born at time $t$ would experience age-specific mortality rates that would be equal to those observed at time $t$, and thus would experience a mean age at death equal to the observed period life expectancy at time $t$. This interpretation is subject to a number of biases. Three main types of biases have been discussed in the literature: (1) cohort influences, (2) heterogeneity, and (3) tempo effects.

*Cohort influences.* As we saw in the previous section, the existence of health conditions with delayed influences on mortality generates a situation in which the mortality rate observed at age $x$ at time $t$ is in part due to the past experience of the cohort born at time $t-x$. To the extent that the cohort's past experience differs from the conditions experienced at time $t$ in the population, the mortality rate at age $x$ at time $t$ will not perfectly reflect current conditions. For example, under the hypothesis that a cohort's exposure to infections at infant ages has an impact on its mortality at age 80, the current mortality rate at age 80 would reflect in part the level of exposure to infections 80 years ago. This past exposure would in turn affect current life expectancy. This would not be a problem if mortality conditions, including infant exposure to infections, had not changed over time. Indeed, if mortality conditions were constant, period and cohort life expectancy would be equal to one another, and period life expectancy would adequately reflect current mortality conditions, even in the presence of cohort influences. But whenever health conditions change, cohort influences create a situation in which current period life expectancy does not perfectly reflect current mortality conditions. This means that, if underlying mortality conditions were to stay constant in the future, there is no guarantee that the level of life expectancy for today's birth cohort would be equal to today's period life expectancy.

The magnitude and direction of this bias is difficult to evaluate. It depends on: (1) the prevalence of health conditions with delayed versus immediate influences, (2) the size and direction of the effect for conditions with delayed versus immediate influences, (3) the length of the delay for conditions with delayed influences, (4) the speed of change in the prevalence of conditions with delayed influences, and (5) the magnitude of interactions among health conditions.

While there is a large literature on identifying factors that have long-term effects on survival or on the relative importance of period versus cohort influences in mortality, few studies have quantified the impact of cohort influences on period life table measures. In one such study, Preston and Wang (2006) examine the impact of past cohort smoking patterns on current mortality rates. They compare actual period life table measures with those predicted with current smoking behavior (rather than with actual smoking histories). They predict that the period probability of surviving from age 50 to 85 under current smoking behavior would be 0.384 for men and 0.479 for women in 2003, compared with values of 0.302 and 0.464, respectively, in the US life table for 2003. The discrepancies illustrate the impact of changing conditions on current mortality in the presence of cohort influences. Since the prevalence of smoking has declined over time, and since smoking has a delayed, detrimental impact on mortality, current survival probabilities underestimate the probabilities that would be observed under current conditions. Obviously smoking is only one of many conditions that have changed over time and may have delayed effects on mortality. Whereas smoking may bias current mortality rates upward, other changes may bias current rates downward. The total impact of cohort influences on period life expectancy is difficult to assess. In the context of overall improvements in health conditions, though, it is likely that current mortality rates are biased upward. Overall, if detrimental exposures and behaviors with lagged effects on mortality have been replaced with more favorable ones, current life expectancy would be biased downward as an indicator of current exposures and behaviors.

*Heterogeneity.* When reaching age $x$ at time $t$, members of a cohort do not all face the same mortality risks. Individuals possess different underlying characteristics that influence their risk of mortality. Such characteristics may be observed (for example, socioeconomic status, race/ethnicity, health status, DNA markers), or they may be unobserved. They may be fixed at birth (for example, race/ethnicity) or may vary with age (for example, health status). As a result of this heterogeneity, the observed "average" mortality rate at age $x$ at time $t$ in a population can be viewed as a product of two components: (1) individual-level risks of mortality, and (2) distribution of the population aged $x$ according to individual-level characteristics that influence mortality. As the cohort reaches age $x + n$, this distribution will have changed. For characteristics that are fixed at birth, the proportion of individuals possessing characteristics associated with higher mortality will have decreased, since attrition among these individuals will be greater. This process is often referred to as selection (Vaupel et al. 1979). For characteristics that can change over the life course, distributional changes will depend on both differential mortality and individual-level changes in background characteristics. The implication of these mechanisms is that a cohort's current average mortality rate is not only affected by processes that are currently occurring, but also by processes that occurred in the past (Vaupel 2002).

When constructing a classic cohort or period life table, the implicit assumption is that there is no heterogeneity in mortality risks, or, equivalently, that the population is homogenous with respect to the risk of mortality: at each age, all survivors have the same risk of dying.

In a cohort life table, the homogeneity assumption does not bias the estimate of the cohort's life expectancy or mean age at death. This is because the series of cohort age-specific mortality rates is consistent with the cohort's distributional changes over the life course. These rates simply summarize how average mortality risks evolve as the cohort ages, reflecting both individual-level mortality risks over the life course, and corresponding distributional changes. The resulting cohort life expectancy accurately summarizes these average age-specific mortality risks (which nonetheless should not be interpreted in terms of individual risks).

In a period life table, however, there is no guarantee that the observed cross-sectional series of age-specific mortality rates is consistent with the distributional changes that would be observed in a synthetic cohort hypothetically exposed to current mortality conditions. The current population could have higher or lower proportions of individuals with characteristics associated with higher mortality than the current synthetic cohort. As a result, period life expectancy under the homogeneity assumption may differ from a period life expectancy that would take heterogeneity into account (Vaupel 2002).

The impact of the homogeneity assumption appears clearly when results from an increment–decrement (multistate) life table are compared with those of a single decrement life table based on the same data (see, Chapter 26 by Jagger and Robine, this volume). A multistate life table takes into account some heterogeneity in the population by assuming that the age-specific risk of mortality varies according to a particular status variable. For example, in a multistate system that takes disability into account, the risk of death at age $x$ at time $t$ is assumed to vary depending on whether individuals are disabled or not at time $t$. Once these differences are taken into account, along with the current incidence of and recovery from disability, the system-wide life expectancy will likely differ from a life expectancy calculated using the same data but without taking disability status into account (i.e., merging disabled and disability-free individuals and using a single decrement life table approach). This is due to the fact that the current distribution of the population by disability status, which results from the past dynamics of mortality and disability, is often different from that of the synthetic cohort exposed to current transition rates.

Lievre et al. (2003) showed that the current prevalence of disability in the United States is higher than the one that would be experienced by a synthetic cohort exposed to current state-specific transition and mortality rates. As a result, the homogeneity assumption in the classic period life table calculation biases life expectancy downward. In their illustration, however, the difference is not large (0.1 year of difference in life expectancy at age 70). Crimmins et al. (1994) make a similar point, though in their example the bias works in the other direction.

In a classic article, Vaupel et al. (1979) define frailty as an individual-level variable that is fixed at birth and makes an individual's risk of death higher or lower, by a constant factor, relative to that of a "standard" individual. Since this variable is fixed for an individual at birth, the proportion of frail individuals will decrease as the cohort ages. In the context of declining mortality rates for the "standard" individual, the current population tends to be more robust than the synthetic cohort exposed to current rates of frailty-specific mortality. As a result, current mortality rates that do not take heterogeneity into account will be underestimated, and current life expectancy will be overestimated. Using various assumptions about the distribution of frailty among individuals at birth, they find that, for Swedish females in 1975, the official value of life expectancy at birth (78.15 years) may be overestimated by 0.34–1.79 years (Vaupel et al. 1979; see also Vaupel 2002). (Note that if frailty-specific mortality is constant over time, along with the frailty distribution at birth, current life expectancy at birth would be unbiased.)

Cohort influences and heterogeneity both generate a situation in which a cohort's past history affects

...it average mortality rate and consequently ...rmine the interpretation of period life expectancy as an indicator reflecting current mortality conditions. Although these two concepts are usually treated separately in the literature, they have many overlaps. If an individual's level of frailty is allowed to vary over time in response to exposure to a series of period health conditions, then we obtain a mechanism which explains why an individual's current risk of death may be related to earlier exposures. Together with the process of mortality selection, these variations in individual frailty generate relationships at the aggregate level between current average mortality and earlier health conditions. If, however, an individual's level of frailty is assumed to be fixed at birth, then we obtain a situation in which there is no delayed impact of earlier exposures on the current risk of death at the individual level. These earlier exposures would still influence current mortality at the aggregate level through the process of mortality selection. In other words, cohort influences, both at the individual and aggregate level, can be interpreted in terms of heterogeneity. Heterogeneity, however, may affect current mortality rates even in the absence of cohort influences at the individual level.

*Tempo effects.* This third mechanism examines bias in period life expectancy from a different angle. It assumes that, as mortality conditions improve in a population during a given year, cohort deaths from all age groups are postponed by a certain amount of time. Because this postponement of deaths happens for all cohorts at the same time, there is a decrease in the number of deaths occurring during the year when new mortality conditions appear, producing a decrease in period age-specific death rates. However, as a result of the way averted deaths are assumed to be distributed over time, these postponements later generate an *increase* in period age-specific death rates. Tempo effects refer to the discrepancy between that later mortality level and the level observed during the year when deaths start being postponed.

The concept of mortality tempo has been proposed by Bongaarts and Feeney (2002, 2003). Building on the well-known concept of fertility tempo, they argue that period life expectancy is biased whenever mortality conditions are changing. In particular, in the context of steady improvements in mortality conditions, they argue that period life expectancy is biased upward as a measure reflecting current mortality conditions. One implication of this model is that if mortality conditions stopped improving, period life expectancy would actually go down. This decline contrasts with the conventional interpretation of period life expectancy, which expects period life expectancy to remain constant if mortality conditions stop changing.

Bongaarts and Feeney's (BF) model rests on assumptions about what happens to postponed deaths once new mortality conditions appear. Indeed, whenever mortality conditions improve, some deaths are averted and postponed to future years. While both the conventional and BF models can be interpreted in terms of delays in ages at death, the two frameworks make different assumptions about the pattern of these delays. Figure 25.3 contrasts these two frameworks, using a simple example in which everyone dies by the time they reach their fourth birthday. The Lexis diagram, Panel (a) shows the distribution of cohort life table deaths (assuming a radix of 10,000) under a baseline scenario of no change in mortality conditions. Panels (b) and (c) contrast the conventional versus BF models of mortality change in the case where new mortality conditions appear during the second calendar year and remain constant thereafter. In both scenarios, 100 deaths are averted during year 2 as a result of improved conditions during that year, but these averted deaths are redistributed differently in the two models. The conventional model assumes that the averted deaths will be redistributed according to the new set of age-specific mortality rates observed during year 2. As a result, these averted deaths are redistributed to different years, as far as year 5. In BF's model, however, the 100 averted deaths are *all* postponed to year 3. Since new mortality conditions remain constant in the future, postponements also occur among deaths that would have occurred during years 3, 4, and 5 in the baseline model. For example, some of the 5,000 deaths that would have occurred during year 3 in the baseline scenario are postponed into the future. Here also the two models differ. In the conventional framework, the 500 averted deaths are redistributed into years 4 and 5. In BF's model, they are all redistributed into year 4.

Figure 25.3 also illustrates why mortality rates are eventually higher in the BF scenario, compared to the conventional scenario. While both scenarios involve the same number of individuals at risk at the beginning of year 3 ($10,000 - 2,000 - 900 = 7,100$), the number of deaths occurring during year 3 is larger in BF's scenario ($4,500 + 100$) than under the conventional

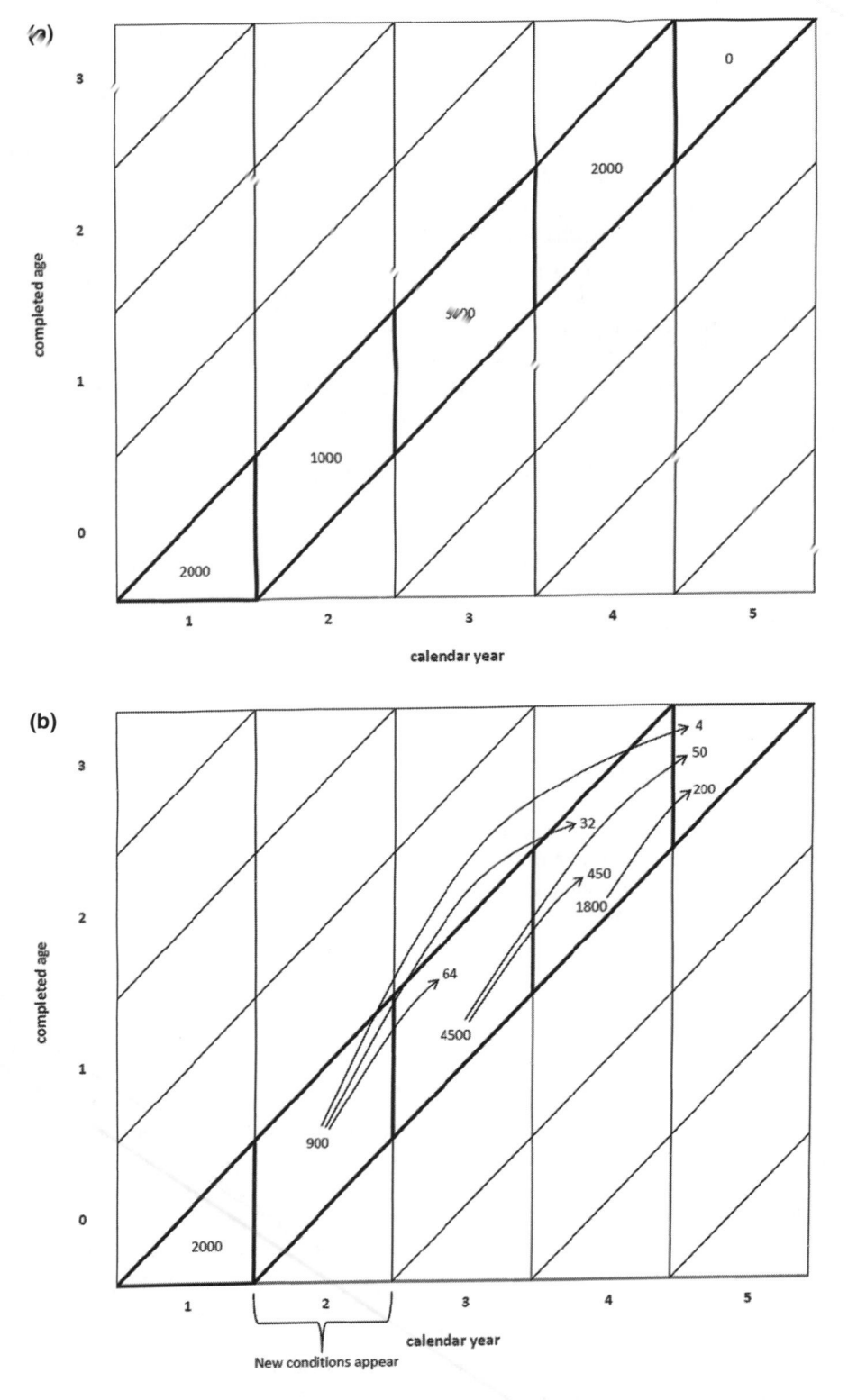

**Fig. 25.3** Lexis diagram comparing the conventional versus Bongaarts and Feeney's scenarios of mortality change. (**a**) Baseline scenario (no mortality change). (**b**) Conventional scenario of mortality change. (**c**) Bongaarts and Feeney's scenario of mortality change. Note: Adapted from Guillot (2006) and Luy and Wegner (2009)

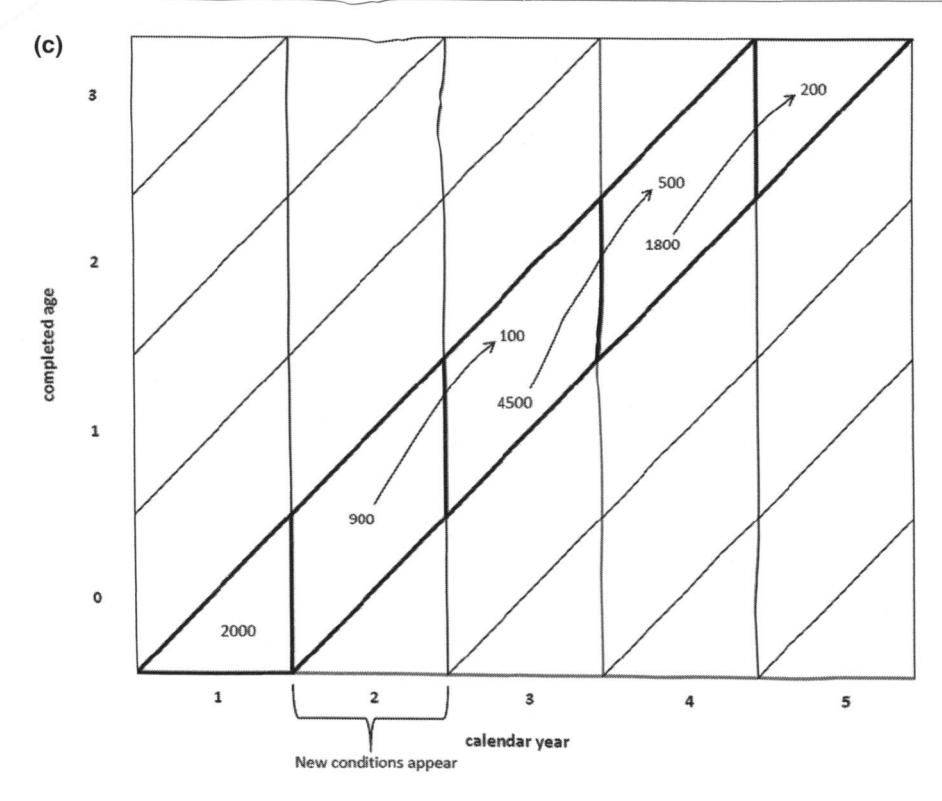

**Fig. 25.3** (continued)

scenario (4,500 + 64). Expanding these two scenarios of mortality change to all cohorts, age-specific mortality rates will be higher during year 3, 4, and 5 under BF's scenario. Bongaarts and Feeney believe that the age-specific mortality rates observed starting at year 3 in the delay model better represent the new mortality regime, whereas the risks observed during year 2 underestimate the underlying mortality conditions. Therefore, according to BF's model of mortality change, life expectancy under new mortality conditions will eventually stabilize at a level lower than the one observed during the year at which the new conditions appeared. This is why BF believes that, under their model of mortality change, current period life expectancy overestimates the underlying level implied by current mortality conditions. In the conventional model, however, mortality rates will stay constant at the level observed during the year when the new mortality conditions appear.

Consistent with their model of mortality change, Bongaarts and Feeney propose a method for correcting period life expectancy, which they believe produces a value that better reflects underlying mortality conditions. They estimate that, as a result of tempo effects, period life expectancy at age 30 among females as conventionally calculated is overestimated by 2.4 years in France and 1.6 years in the United States and Sweden.

It is difficult to empirically determine the amount of time by which cohort deaths are delayed as a result of new mortality conditions, such as a medical innovation (a new drug is invented) or a behavioral change (individuals stop smoking). Mortality conditions change year after year, producing cumulative changes in the distribution of cohort deaths. As a result, the impact of one year's worth of changes in health conditions cannot easily be isolated. This is why observing a shifting distribution of cohort deaths in actual populations does not provide evidence for a delay model of mortality change.

A similar criticism can be raised for the classic model. As we saw in the earlier section, due to the existence of cohort influences and heterogeneity, the new set of mortality rates reflecting the new conditions, and the corresponding distribution of future cohort deaths, are unknown.

In spite of its weaknesses, the conventional approach offers a more realistic framework for understanding changes in mortality conditions than BF's delay model, for the following reasons. First, in BF's model, all deaths that would have occurred at age $x$ under the old regime are postponed by the same amount under the new regime. By contrast, the conventional framework offers a range of new ages at death to the survivors, even in homogenous populations. This seems a more realistic framework, because individuals whose death is averted due to changing mortality conditions are likely to experience various amounts of additional life. (BF's assumption about shifts in the age distribution of deaths refers to the population level rather than the individual level. There may exist situations in which fixed shifts at the population level are produced by varying delays at the individual level. BF's approach would still apply to such situations. However, it is not clear what pattern of varying individual delays would produce such shifts at the population level.)

Second, in BF's model, the cumulative amount of change in conditions during a period of time can never generate delays greater than that period of time. For example, one year's worth of changes in health conditions can never generate delays greater than 1 year. Otherwise, there would be zero death during that year, which is theoretically impossible in large populations. In BF's tempo model, an averted death can never be postponed very far into the future. This constraint does not exist in the conventional framework, which allows some deaths to be postponed far into the future, and can accommodate rapid improvements or deterioration in mortality conditions while never generating zero period mortality.

Bongaarts and Feeney (2008) believe that the conventional model is a framework that applies primarily to certain causes of deaths (such as infections, accidents, and violence) occurring more or less at random and predominating in childhood and young adulthood. Indeed, a young child whose death from an infectious disease is averted thanks to a medical intervention may survive, say, another 70 years. By contrast, they claim that their delay model applies primarily to causes of death resulting from senescence, which predominate at older ages and for which interventions may only provide a few months of additional life. This is why Bongaarts and Feeney apply tempo corrections to ages 30 and above only. However, even if we restrict the analysis to ages 30 and above, BF's delay model remains theoretical and lacks empirical evidence about the impact of interventions on ages at death. trasts with cohort influences and heterogeneity, sources of bias that are known to occur in reality. In sum, period life expectancy may not accurately reflect current conditions, but this appears more likely due to cohort influences and heterogeneity than to tempo effects.

## Relationship Between Period and Cohort Life Expectancy

As discussed earlier, the life expectancy at birth of a cohort provides a clear measure of the set of mortality conditions to which a cohort has been exposed. However, it can be calculated with certainty only for cohorts that are now extinct. For more timely information, demographers calculate period life expectancy, resorting to synthetic cohorts.

Although synthetic cohorts are simulations rather than actual depictions of the reality (no actual cohort spends its entire life course in one calendar year), the life expectancy of a synthetic cohort can often be related to the life expectancy of an actual cohort. In particular, whenever mortality has been steadily declining, period life expectancy corresponds to the life expectancy of a cohort born some years earlier. Also, in the context of steady mortality decline, period life expectancy underestimates cohort life expectancy by a certain amount.

A set of empirical and analytical relationships between period and cohort life expectancy has been proposed by Goldstein and Wachter (2006), who thus extended to mortality Ryder's classic analysis of period-cohort translation (Ryder 1964; see also Eng 1980). They define lags as the number of years one must move back before time $t$ to find a cohort that has a life expectancy equal to the period life expectancy at time $t$, and gaps as the discrepancy between the period life expectancy at time $t$ and the life expectancy for the cohort born at time $t$. Analyzing observed and forecast mortality data from Sweden and the United States, they find that during the twentieth century, lags have increased from about 20 years in 1900 to about 50 years in 2000. In both countries, cohort life expectancy is consistently above period life expectancy during the twentieth century, due to mortality decline. In the

States, gaps have been decreasing from about years in 1900 to about 6 years in 1960.

Using mortality models and approximations, they find that lags are a function of the mean age at which mortality improvement is occurring. The recent increase in lags in the United States and Sweden is thus largely explained by the fact that mortality improvements are taking place at older ages. They also find that gaps are to a large extent explained by the pace of mortality decline. The faster the decline in age-specific death rates, the greater the gain in life expectancy for the cohort born at time $t$, relative to period life expectancy at time $t$. In this sense, the recent decrease in the gap in the United States indicates a flattening of the pace of change in period mortality. Similar conclusions are reached by Canudas-Romo and Schoen (2005).

While the analysis of the period-cohort correspondence does not resolve the interpretation of period life expectancy as an indicator of current mortality conditions, it does show that whenever mortality is steadily changing, period life expectancy can be considered as a lagged indicator of cohort life expectancy. This is justified by the fact that age-specific mortality rates are ultimately experienced by actual cohorts, even if period life table construction organizes these rates by period.

## A Third Dimension: Cross-Sectional Cohort Mortality Indexes

Cohorts that are not extinct at time $t$ do not have a known life expectancy, since their survival history is truncated. However, they do have a known survival probability, from birth until the age they reach at time $t$. These truncated cohort survival histories contain useful mortality information, which is ignored in both cohort life expectancy calculations (which deal only with non-truncated mortality histories) and period life expectancy calculations (which ignore cohort survivorship altogether).

One mortality indicator, the cross-sectional average length of life (CAL), takes advantage of this information, and combines it in a way that has some useful interpretations. This index was first proposed by Brouard (1986) and then further developed by Guillot (2003).

Formally, CAL is defined as follows:

$$\text{CAL}(t) = \int_0^\infty p_c(x, t-x) dx, \qquad (5)$$

where $p_c(x, t-x)$ is the probability of surviving from birth to age $x$ for the cohort born at time $t-x$. (In a population, $p_c(x, t-x)$ corresponds to the proportion of cohort survivors for the cohort aged $x$ at time $t$.) Simply put, CAL is the cross-sectional sum of proportions of cohort survivors at a given time. CAL is clearly not a cohort indicator, because it involves information from many different cohorts. It is not a period indicator either, because it uses past mortality information and does not involve synthetic cohorts. CAL thus involves a third perspective in mortality analysis. Schoen (2006) termed it the "wedge-period" perspective. The time and age location of the age-specific death rates involved in the calculation of CAL is illustrated in the Lexis diagram in the bottom row of Table 25.1.

CAL has a number of interpretations:

1. CAL is a mortality measure that summarizes the mortality history of all the cohorts present in a population at a given time (Guillot 2003). Since cohorts present in a population at time $t$ have been exposed to past mortality levels that are typically higher than at time $t$, CAL$(t)$ will typically be lower than period life expectancy at time $t$.

2. CAL corresponds to the size of a model population in which a unit number of births each year is exposed to actual, changing mortality. In that sense, CAL shows how mortality change directly influences population size. (One implication of the population interpretation of CAL is that the discrepancy between $e_0^P$ and CAL during a given year can be interpreted in terms of population momentum [Guillot 2005].)

The first two interpretations do not involve any particular assumption about the age pattern of mortality and its change over time. Introducing assumptions about the age–time pattern of mortality, CAL has the following additional interpretations:

3. Under Bongaarts and Feeney's proportionality assumption (Bongaarts and Feeney 2003), CAL is approximately equal to a weighted average of past levels of period life expectancy (Wachter 2005). This interpretation is consistent with the first

interpretation and also predicts CAL levels that are lower than period life expectancy levels whenever mortality has been steadily declining.

4. Under Bongaarts and Feeney's proportionality assumption, CAL corresponds to the observed mean age at death in the CAL model population described above. This interpretation also predicts that CAL will be lower than period life expectancy, because a CAL population that has experienced steady mortality decline in the past is younger at time $t$ than the stationary-equivalent population at time $t$.

5. Under a linear shift pattern of mortality (which is a special case of BF's proportionality assumption), CAL corresponds exactly to the cohort life expectancy for the cohort born CAL years earlier (CAL$(t) = e_0^c(t\text{-CAL}(t))$) (Goldstein 2006; Guillot and Kim 2010; Wilmoth 2005; Rodriguez 2006). This correspondence also holds approximately under a Gompertz mortality model with log-linear decline. In that sense, CAL can be considered as a lagged indicator of cohort life expectancy.

6. If changes in period mortality conditions generate fixed delays in future cohort deaths, as proposed by Bongaarts and Feeney, CAL immediately adjusts to the level of life expectancy under the new mortality regime and may thus better reflect underlying period mortality conditions than period life expectancy during that year. This last interpretation of CAL is controversial, because, as explained above, it requires strong assumptions about the way changes in mortality conditions produce changes in the timing of future cohort deaths.

Figure 25.4 shows the trend in CAL among French males, together with period and cohort life expectancy at birth. As expected, CAL is typically lower than $e_0^P$, except during the World Wars I and II. Figure 25.4 also shows that CAL reacts more gradually than $e_0^P$ to abrupt changes in period mortality.

Since CAL involves cohort survival probabilities, it has a stronger connection with cohort life expectancy than with period life expectancy. This connection is illustrated by the fact that, under certain patterns of mortality change, CAL is equal to the cohort life expectancy for the cohort born CAL years ago. However, CAL is also related to period life expectancy in the sense that the relative position of $e_0^P$ with respect to CAL will influence how CAL will change.

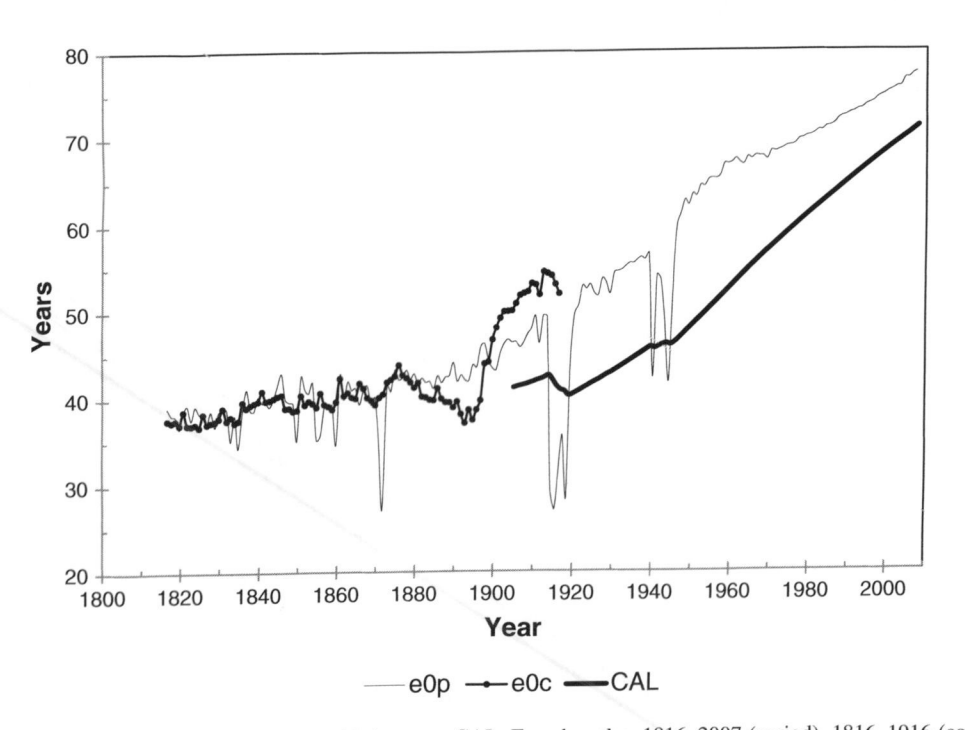

**Fig. 25.4** Period versus cohort life expectancy at birth versus CAL, French males, 1816–2007 (period), 1816–1916 (cohort), and 1905–2007 (CAL). Source: Human mortality database

In particular, CAL tends to increase when $e_0^P$ is above its value, and it tends to decrease when $e_0^P$ is below (Guillot 2003; 2006: 17). This mechanism appears on Fig. 25.4.

The ultimate goal of a summary mortality measure is to give an indication of a population's underlying mortality conditions and how it evolves over time. As we discussed earlier, cohort life expectancy adequately summarizes the specific set of conditions to which one cohort has been exposed. By contrast, period life expectancy, which seeks to summarize the conditions of one period, is affected by a number of biases. How does CAL perform under that criterion? The basic component of CAL is the truncated survival history of a cohort present at time $t$ in the population. This survival history of that particular cohort, although truncated, adequately reflects the set of conditions to which the cohort has been exposed up to time $t$, even in the presence of cohort influences and heterogeneity. Combining this information for all cohorts present in the population at time $t$, it can be said that CAL adequately summarizes the average conditions to which cohorts have been exposed to. This implies that increases in CAL do not only reflect improvements in cohort mortality *rates*, but they also reflect improvements in cohort mortality *conditions*. Perhaps the most blatant sign that mortality conditions are improving in a population is the fact that these improvements generate population growth: more people are surviving. This is precisely what CAL seeks to measure. Similarly, if CAL is higher in population A than in population B, this reflects the fact that cohorts in population A have experienced more favorable mortality *conditions*, on average, than in population B. As we saw earlier, similar statements cannot be made with period life expectancy.

While a link can be made between CAL and underlying mortality conditions, one needs to keep in mind that the time and age location of the conditions that CAL seeks to summarize is unusual. With $\omega$ defined as the age at which the number of cohort survivors is negligible, the age and time-specific conditions summarized by CAL($t$) are located in the Lexis triangle defined by the age and time coordinates $(0, t-\omega)$, $(0,t)$, $(\omega,t)$. (See the bottom row of Table 25.1 for a graphical representation of this area in a Lexis diagram.) Thus, these conditions refer to the past, even though they refer to a more recent past, on average, than the conditions reflected in the most recent cohort life expectancy that can be calculated at time $t$. (This contrasts with BF's interpretation of CAL as a measure reflecting current conditions. As we saw earlier, this interpretation remains controversial.)

# Conclusion

Life expectancy is perhaps the most important summary measure of mortality. For a cohort, it summarizes the unique set of conditions experienced by the cohort at various ages. For a period, however, the connection with underlying current conditions remains elusive. This chapter examined mechanisms that make it difficult to interpret variations in period life expectancy over time and place in terms of variations in underlying health conditions. As a result, small differences in period life expectancy between countries should not be automatically interpreted in terms of differences in conditions, as these differences may reflect differences in past rather than current behaviors. Similarly, short-term variations (or lack thereof) in period life expectancy should be interpreted with caution. This chapter also discussed CAL, an alternative summary index of mortality that offers useful insight about mortality change in relation to changes in mortality conditions.

These three mortality measures, along with their advantages and disadvantages, are compared in Table 25.1. Cohort life expectancy and CAL are two summary measures that adequately reflect the mortality conditions they seek to capture, without any further corrections or adjustments. Therefore, much can be gained by using these indicators as a basis for studies of mortality levels and trends. Their main drawback, however, is that they refer to conditions of the past. For many purposes, especially in the area of health policy, it remains important to capture conditions of the present.

Because period life expectancy is an imperfect reflection of current conditions, appropriate corrections need to be implemented. Two main approaches have been outlined in this chapter. The first approach focuses on cohort influences and consists of establishing relationships between past health conditions and their impact on current mortality rates. Once these relationships are established, information on historical changes in health conditions allows us to purge current mortality rates of the lagged effect of past conditions. An example of this approach is the study by Preston and Wang (2006) discussed earlier. The second approach focuses on heterogeneity and recognizes that the imprint left on an individual as a result of past exposures should in theory be observable as part of the individual's current characteristics. This approach thus consists of studying current characteristics associated with mortality at the individual level and how they vary in response to current conditions. If one could find a set of variables that adequately identifies these underlying characteristics, and study how they interact with the current conditions to produce current mortality patterns, period life expectancy could be corrected through the use of synthetic cohorts that take this heterogeneity into account. The multistate life table approach outlined above is one example of such an attempt (Crimmins et al. 1994; Lievre et al. 2003). The advantage of this approach, compared to the first approach, is that it is based only on current information and thus does not require information about past health conditions. However, this approach poses important methodological challenges, because it requires the identification of the correct individual characteristics summarizing an individual's current level of frailty, and also necessitates data from longitudinal surveys which are complex to carry out.

Nonetheless, these two approaches show that corrections of period life expectancy are theoretically grounded and empirically possible, even if incomplete. Future research should seek to develop and systematize ways to improve the measurement of current mortality conditions, net of past influences. While life unfolds on a cohort basis, health policy operates on a period basis. Thus, health policy would be better guided by indicators that correctly reflect current conditions.

**Acknowledgments** I am grateful to John Bongaarts, Douglas Ewbank, Samuel Preston, and the editors of this volume for their comments and suggestions.

## References

Barker, D.J.P. 2007. "The Origins of the Developmental Origins Theory." *Journal of Internal Medicine* 621:412–17.
Bongaarts, J. and G. Feeney. 2002. "How Long Do We Live?" *Population and Development Review* 28(1):13–29.
Bongaarts, J. and G. Feeney. 2003. "Estimating Mean Lifetime." *Proceedings of the National Academy of Sciences* 100(23):13127–33.
Bongaarts, J. and G. Feeney. 2008. In E. Barbi, J. Bongaarts, and J.W. Vaupel (eds.), *How Long Do We Live? Demographic Models and Reflexions on Tempo Effects*, pp. 263–69. Hiedelberg, Germany, Springer.
Brouard, N. 1986. "Structure et Dynamique des Populations. La Pyramide des Années à Vivre, Aspects Nationaux et Exemples Régionaux." *Espace, Populations, Sociétés* 2 (14–15):157–68.
Canudas-Romo, V. and R. Schoen. 2005. "Age-Specific Contributions to Changes in the Period and Cohort Life Expectancy." *Demographic Research* 13:63–82.
Caselli, G. and R. Capocaccia. 1989. "Age, Period, Cohort and Early Mortality: An Analysis of Adult Mortality in Italy." *Population Studies* 43:133–53.
Crimmins, E.M. and C.E. Finch. 2006. "Infection, Inflammation, Height, and Longevity." *PNAS* 103(2):498–503.
Crimmins, E.M., M.D. Hayward, and Y. Saito. 1994. "Changing Mortality and Morbidity Rates and the Health Status and Life Expectancy of the Older Population." *Demography* 31(1):159–75.
Doll, R., R. Peto, J. Boreham, and I. Sutherland. 2004. "Mortality in Relation to Smoking: 50 years' Observations on Male British Doctors." *British Medical Journal* 328:1519–28.
Elo, I.T. and S.H. Preston. 1992. "Effects of Early-Life Conditions on Adult Mortality: A Review." *Population Index* 58(2):186–212.
Eng, J.P. 1980. "A Mathematical Model Relating Cohort and Period Mortality." *Demography* 17(1):115–27.
Forsdahl, A. 1977. "Are Poor Living Conditions in Childhood and Adolescence an Important Risk Factor for Arteriosclerotic Heart Disease?" *British Journal of Preventive and Social Medicine* 31:91–95.
Frost, W.H. 1939. "The Age Selection of Mortality from Tuberculosis in Successive Decades." *American Journal of Hygiene* 30(3):91–96.
Goldstein, J. 2006. "Found in Translation." *Demographic Research* 14(5):71–84.
Goldstein, J. and K. Wachter. 2006. "Relationships Between Period and Cohort Life Expectancy: Gaps and Lags." *Population Studies* 60(3):257–69.
Guillot, M. 2003. "The Cross-Sectional Average Length of Life (CAL): A Cross-Sectional Mortality Measure that Reflects the Experience of Cohorts." *Population Studies* 57(1):41–54.
Guillot, M. 2005. "The Momentum of Mortality Decline." *Population Studies* 59(3):283–94.
Guillot, M. 2006. "Tempo Effects in Mortality: An Appraisal." *Demographic Research* 14(1):1–26.
Guillot, M. and H.S. Kim. 2010. *On the Correspondence between CAL and Lagged Cohort Life Expectancy*. Paper Presented at the 2010 PAA Meetings.
Hobcraft, J., J. Menken, and S. Preston. 1982. "Age, Period, and Cohort Effects in Demography: A Review." *Population Index* 48(1):4–43.
Lièvre, A., N. Brouard, and C. Heathcote. 2003. "The Estimation of Health Expectancies from Cross-Longitudinal Surveys." *Mathematical Population Studies* 10:211–48.
Luy, M. and C. Wegner. 2009. "Conventional Versus Tempo-Adjusted Life Expectancy—Which Is the More Appropriate Measure for Period Mortality?" *Genus* 65(2):1–28.

Mason, W.M. and H.L. Smith. 1985. "Age-Period-Cohort Analysis and the Study of Deaths from Pulmonary Tuberculosis." In W.M. Mason and S.E. Feinberg (eds.), *Cohort Analysis in Social Research*, pp. 151–227. New York, NY, Springer.

Myrskylä, M. 2010. "The Effects of Shocks in Early Life Mortality on Later Life Expectancy and Mortality Compression: A Cohort Analysis." *Demographic Research* 22(12):289–320.

Neel, J.V. and W.J. Schull. (eds.). 1991. *The Children of Atomic Bomb Survivors: A Genetic Study*. Washington, DC, National Academy Press.

Peto, J., H. Seidman, and I.J. Selikoff. 1982. "Mesothelioma Mortality in Asbestos Workers: Implications for Models of Carcinogenesis and Risk Assessment." *British Journal of Cancer* 45(1):124–35.

Preston, S.H., M.E. Hill, and G.L. Drevenstedt. 1998. "Childhood Conditions that Predict Survival to Advanced Ages among African-Americans." *Social Science and Medicine* 47(9):1231–46.

Preston, S.H. and H. Wang. 2006. "Sex Mortality Differences in the United States: The Role of Cohort Smoking Patterns." *Demography* 43(4):631–46.

Riley, J.C. 2001. *Rising Life Expectancy: A Global History*. Cambridge, Cambridge University Press.

Rodriguez, G. 2006. "Demographic Translation and Tempo Effects: An Accelerated Failure Time Perspective." *Demographic Research* 14(6):85–110.

Ryder, N.B. 1964. "The Process of Demographic Translation." *Demography* 1(1):74–82.

Schoen, R. 2006. *Dynamic Population Models*. New York, NY, Springer.

Vaupel, J.W. 2002. "Life Expectancy at Current Rates vs. Current Conditions: A Reflexion Stimulated by Bongaarts and Feeney's 'How Long Do We Live?'" *Demographic Research* 7(8):365–78.

Vaupel, J.W, K.G. Manton, and E. Stallard. 1979. "The Impact of Heterogeneity in Individual Frailty on the Dynamics of Mortality." *Demography* 16(3):439–54.

Wachter, K. 2005. "Tempo and Its Tribulation." *Demographic Research* 13(9):201–22.

Wilmoth, J.R. 2005. "On the Relationship Between Period and Cohort Mortality." *Demographic Research* 13(1):231–80.

Wilmoth, J., J. Vallin, and G. Caselli. 1990. "When Does a Cohort's Mortality Differ from What We Might Expect?" *Population: An English Selection* 2:93–126.

# Chapter 26
# Healthy Life Expectancy

Carol Jagger and Jean-Marie Robine

## Historical Development

Historically, mortality data have been used to monitor the health of populations, because they are relatively easily collected and comparable across countries. Thus, decreasing mortality rates have been seen as reflecting improving population health. While this was a reasonable assumption when the burden of ill-health was due to acute, infectious diseases, the substantial increases in life expectancy that have taken place over the previous century, but particularly in the last 30 or 40 years, have seen a shift to more long-standing, chronic diseases, such as heart disease, stroke, and dementia, as our populations age. So mortality rates no longer correlate as well with the burden of ill-health in the population, necessitating new measures, such as health expectancies, that capture the quality rather than or as well as the quantity of life.

During the 1970s, a number of theories began to emerge on the relationship between the quantity and quality of remaining life. Kramer (Kramer 1980) reasoned that the increases in life expectancy were a result of medical technology prolonging the life of the frail and sick who would previously have died, resulting in an expansion of morbidity. Fries (1980, 2000), on the other hand, proposed that there was a natural limit to life and that prevention could delay the onset of disease and disability to minimize the gap between the morbidity and mortality curves (Fig. 26.1). The consensus is that there is no evidence thus far to suggest that a natural limit exists, since in most countries life expectancy gains are not slowing down. A third, intermediate scenario was later put forward that suggested that although morbidity/disability might increase, its severity on average would be reduced (Manton 1982).

## Definition of Health Expectancy

Health expectancies divide life expectancy into years lived in different health states. They are a natural extension of life expectancies and were developed in response to exploring which of the "aging scenarios" was true. Life expectancies are the average number of years of life remaining at a particular age, considering current mortality. For example, in 2006 the female life expectancy at birth in the United Kingdom was 81.6 years, so a baby girl born in 2006 could expect to live to age 82, assuming that the conditions of 2006 prevailed over her whole life. By considering not only mortality, but also ill-health at particular ages, we can divide this remaining number of years into years spent in good and bad health; these are then health expectancies. The notion of health expectancy was first introduced in 1964 by Sanders, and 5 years later Sullivan (1971) documented its calculation.

One can question what extra information is brought by health expectancies, since the amount of ill-health in a population is often measured by the prevalence alone. However, because our populations are getting older, with more people surviving to the oldest age

---

C. Jagger (✉)
Institute for Ageing and Health, Newcastle University, Newcastle upon Tyne, UK
e-mail: carol.jagger@ncl.ac.uk

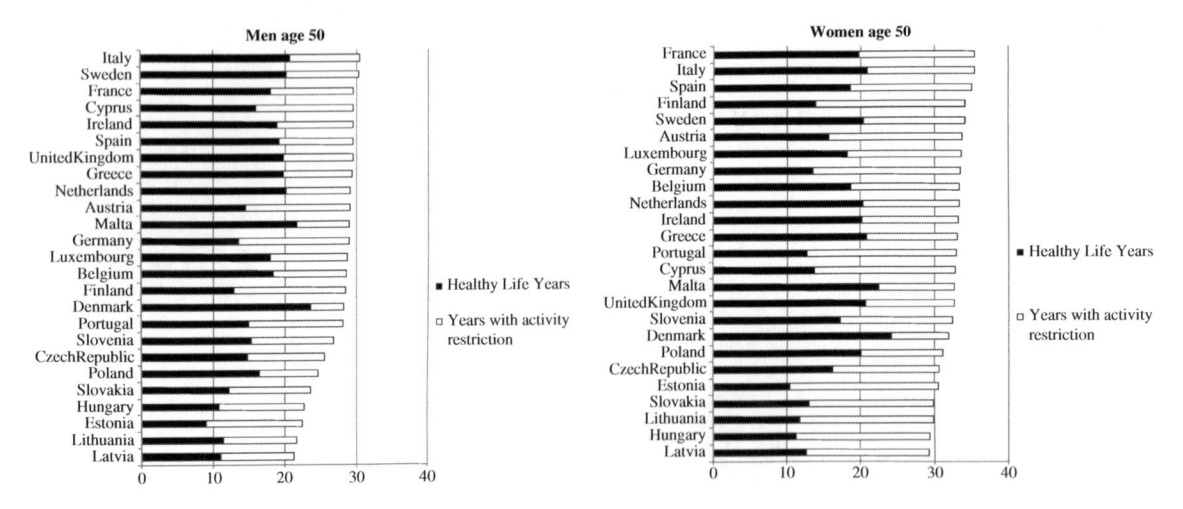

**Fig. 26.1** Healthy life years at age 50 for EU countries. Source: EU-SILC 2005

groups, and older people are more likely to suffer from disability and multiple comorbidities, overall prevalence may increase in a population without individuals being more at risk of ill-health than previously. Health expectancies take into account both the changes in living with ill-health and the changes in mortality, which are responsible for the increase in life expectancy. Therefore, improving population health in an aging population leads to an increase in the part of life expectancy spent in good health despite an increase in the overall prevalence of ill-health due to more people being at risk. Health expectancy is therefore a potent tool to identify the interaction among health, ill-health, and mortality.

The scenarios of compression and expansion of morbidity and dynamic equilibrium have now been more clearly defined in terms of health expectancies by further concepts of absolute and relative compression/expansion (Nusselder 2003; Robine and Mathers 1993). *Absolute* compression of morbidity (or disability) occurs if the total years spent with morbidity decrease, whereas a *relative* compression of morbidity occurs when the years lived with morbidity decrease as a proportion of total life expectancy. An absolute compression of morbidity generally coincides with a relative compression, but an absolute expansion of morbidity can coincide with a relative expansion, equilibrium, or compression of morbidity, depending on how total life expectancy and life expectancy free of morbidity are increasing relative to each other. We explore this later in the chapter with examples from different countries.

## Types of Health Expectancy

As health expectancies combine mortality with a health measure, there are as many health expectancies as health measures. The most popular indicator is disability-free life expectancy (DFLE), but it is also possible to construct many other indicators that might measure healthy life. A number of countries routinely monitor life expectancy "in good perceived health" (often known as healthy life expectancy) (Bronnum-Hansen 2005; White 2009). However, a limited number of "disease-free" life expectancies have also been estimated, for example, dementia-free life expectancy (Perenboom et al. 1996; Ritchie et al. 1994; Roelands et al. 1994; Sauvaget et al. 1997), life expectancy free of cognitive impairment (Dubois and Hebert 2006; Lievre et al. 2008; Matthews et al. 2009; Sauvaget et al. 2001; Suthers et al. 2003), life expectancy without diabetes (Jonker et al. 2006; Laditka and Laditka 2006), and life expectancy without cardiovascular disease (Crimmins et al. 2008; De Laet et al. 2003; Franco et al. 2005, 2007; Mamun et al. 2004; Pardo Silva et al. 2006).

## Calculation Methods

Health expectancy calculation broadly follows life expectancy calculation, with the numbers of individuals in each age interval of the life table partitioned according to the age-specific probabilities of being in each of the health states under consideration. In life expectancy, the age-specific probabilities of dying are derived from the registered number of deaths and are thus *flow* data collected over a defined period. The age-specific probabilities of being in each of the health states for the health expectancy should be derived similarly, which means from the incidence rates of entry into and exit from the health state. Practically, this is difficult, since data on transitions in and out of health states, unlike data on mortality, are not collected regularly. As a consequence, direct calculation of the incidence rates is often difficult, and the "period prevalence" associated with the states under study is estimated as the proportion of the population in the state over a specific period of time. Three main methods for calculating health expectancy exist, and these correspond to the different approaches to estimate the transition rates or "period prevalence:" cross-sectional or observed prevalence life table methods (the Sullivan method); increment–decrement or multistate life table methods; and multiple-decrement life table methods.

## Cross-Sectional Methods

The Sullivan method remains the most popular method of calculating health expectancies, since the only data required are the prevalence of ill-health within age groups (usually 5- or 10-year age groups) and by gender from a cross-sectional survey of the population, and a period life table for the population for the same time period as the survey. The prevalence of ill-health is then applied to the person-years lived ($L_x$) to produce the years lived in bad health. The life table is then constituted in the usual way, although the end product is now life expectancy in bad health. Life expectancy in good health is formed from the total life expectancy at a particular age minus the life expectancy in bad health. The period prevalence has been estimated therefore by the observed prevalence, providing an approximation of true period conditions. This has been shown to be a reasonable approximation provided that the health transition under study is stable over time or evolves regularly (Mathers and Robine 1997). More recent research has provided a statistical underpinning to the method and shown that the Sullivan estimator of DFLE is unbiased and consistent under the less stringent assumptions of stationarity (Imai and Soneji 2007). Further details of the Sullivan method, together with a training manual (Jagger 1999) and Excel spreadsheets for the calculation, can be found online at www.ehemu.eu. A Bayesian formulation of the Sullivan method has also been developed (Lynch and Brown 2005).

Health expectancies are usually formed with two states—for instance, with and without disability—but more levels of severity may be included and indeed are necessary to address the dynamic equilibrium scenario. Although health expectancy calculation apportions only a binary weighting (zero or one) to the health or disability state, it is possible to include a weighting system based on severity levels, similar to that of quality adjusted life years (QALYs), thus obtaining a disability-adjusted life expectancy (DALE) or health-adjusted life expectancy (HALE), such as disability-adjusted life years (DALY) (Murray and Lopez 1997b).

Health expectancies using the Sullivan method have now been calculated for over 50 countries (Robine et al. 1999), many by members of the International Network on Health Expectancy and the Disability Process (REVES) (www.reves.net). The obvious benefits of the Sullivan method are the relative availability of data, its requirements being only a population life table and the prevalence of ill-health from a cross-sectional survey. It is also the preferred method for assessing trends in health expectancies, information that is essential for determining whether countries are undergoing compression or expansion of morbidity. Though more and more countries have national health surveys conducted regularly, relatively fewer countries have good time series on health expectancies (Robine et al. 2003). We summarize these later in this chapter, but it is worth noting here the key elements necessary to compare health expectancies either between or within countries over time as follows:

- The *general design of the surveys* used to derive prevalence should be identical, as estimates of the prevalence of ill-health can be sensitive to the method by which the data are collected (e.g., face-to-face interview, telephone interview, postal questionnaire) as well as to any change in the questionnaire itself (Cambois et al. 2007).
- The *definition of health* used in the calculation of prevalence of health should be identical, since differences between health expectancies calculated for different countries have been explained by differences in the measurement instruments used

to collect the prevalence data (Buratta and Egidi 2003).
- If possible, health expectancies should be compared on *total populations*. Life tables generally include total populations, but surveys from which the prevalence of the health states are derived often exclude people in institutions. Omitting these may produce bias, particularly for older populations and for certain health conditions associated with admission to institutional care, such as dementia (Ritchie 1994). It is therefore preferable that either the prevalence survey include those in institutions or a separate survey of those in institutional care be undertaken to estimate prevalence and be combined with the prevalence outside institutions by weighting. If these requirements are impossible to meet, then with knowledge of the size of the population in institutions, assumptions can be made about the prevalence, and these can then be combined using appropriate weighting.
- The *final age group in the life table* should be the same when the Sullivan method is used, since the age distribution of this group may be substantially different between surveys, also affecting the comparability of health expectancies.

## Multistate Methods

While prevalence reflects past and present incidence and survival, and therefore the Sullivan (1971) method implicitly includes past transitions to and from ill-health, multistate life tables explicitly apply incidence, recovery, and mortality rates to a population to estimate the years spent in good or bad health by age. The essential component for multistate life tables is longitudinal data, and this has been the reason why these methods are less well-used than the Sullivan method and have been increasing in popularity only over the last two decades, alongside the increase in large-scale longitudinal studies (Crimmins et al. 1994; Rogers et al. 1989).

Though theoretically a person can make multiple movements in and out of states within a time period (Schoen 1988), and the incidence rates reflect this fact, the nature of longitudinal surveys, with relatively long intervals between interviews, means that states are observable only at the ends of intervals, and multiple movements between these states are unobserved. It is generally assumed, therefore, that individuals make only one transition between interviews; hence the method underestimates the number of transitions, and this may be particularly acute at older ages (Laditka and Hayward 2003; Wolf and Gill 2009).

Multistate life tables have two major advantages over the Sullivan method. First, health expectancies allow comparison of the evolution of health status between different subpopulations, often defined by region, gender, education, or race. The Sullivan method is limited since such analyses require life tables to be available for subgroups, and for many countries only regional life tables are easily accessible. Multistate methods, on the other hand, can more readily incorporate covariates to define subpopulations for comparison. Second, since the incidence rates to and from ill-health and to death are explicitly estimated, their relative contributions to the prevalence of ill-health can be ascertained, and this can be important in explaining differences between subpopulations (Jagger et al. 2007b).

One disadvantage of longitudinal data is that they are often subject to attrition between survey waves and, in some cases, the intervals between survey waves are unequal. Microsimulation techniques have been developed in software such as interpolated Markov chain (IMaCH) (Lievre et al. 2003), and these have been key in the analysis of irregularly spaced data, a particular feature of the Medical Research Council Cognitive Function and Ageing Study (MRC CFAS) (Jagger et al. 2007a, b; Peres et al. 2008). Programs for multistate life tables have been written for STATA (see http://www.ssc.wisc.edu/~mweden/), for SAS (Cai et al. 2006), and using Bayesian techniques (van den Hout and Matthews 2009). A further issue is that if the interval between waves is long, then transitions may be missed, though intervals of 1–2 years are thought to be sufficient to accurately estimate active and disabled life expectancy (Gill et al. 2005).

## Multiple-Decrement Methods

Multiple-decrement life tables are a special case of multistate life tables that include transitions to ill-health and death but not the return to the initial state (that is, recovery of health). The probabilities of survival by age in the initial (active) state can be estimated from two waves of data collection, and these are then applied, age by age, to a hypothetical cohort to obtain the active life table of the survey population. Katz et al. (1983) used a multiple-decrement life table to calculate active life expectancy using longitudinal data, but this method is of particular interest for states (often disease states) where recovery is impossible, for instance stroke-free or dementia-free life expectancy. In certain instances, for example, cognitive impairment, transitions to improved states are assumed to be impossible, though educational bias (and learning or practice effects) with cognitive measurement scales may result in apparent improvement. Recent advances in statistical modeling have dealt with these by assuming that such transitions are misclassification errors (van den Hout and Matthews 2008).

## Relevance of Health Expectancies

This section reviews how health expectancies have been used to identify inequalities between spatial groupings (country, region) and social groupings within populations defined by gender, race, and social disadvantage (education, social class, income, deprivation). Though these analyses may go some way to address the important issue of compression of morbidity by identifying whether the extra years lived by one group are years of healthy life, definitive answers can come only from comparable time trends within countries. We review the few countries that have these data. Finally, we detail how health expectancies, in particular disability-free life expectancy, have allowed a fuller exploration of the public health impact of both fatal and nonfatal disease.

## Spatial Comparisons

*Global estimates of health expectancy.* Estimations of health expectancies (disease-free, disability-free, or healthy life expectancy) were available for 67 countries in the REVES database (available at www.reves.net) as of April 2009 (see Table 26.1). These were predominantly European (29) and Asian (15) countries,

**Table 26.1** List of the 67 countries for which at least one estimation of health expectancy was available in the REVES database by April 2009

| Africa (9) | Asia (15) | Europe (29) | Europe (contd.) |
|---|---|---|---|
| Botswana* | Burma* | Austria | Slovak Rep. |
| Egypt* | Cambodia | Belgium | Slovenia |
| Ethiopia* | China (mainland) | Bulgaria | Spain |
| Ghana | India | Cyprus* | Sweden |
| Mali* | Indonesia | Czech Republic | Switzerland |
| Mauritius* | Japan | Denmark | United Kingdom |
| South Africa | Korea (North)* | Estonia* | |
| Sudan | Korea (South)* | Finland | *Oceania (2)* |
| Tunisia | Malaysia* | France | Australia |
| | Pakistan* | Germany | New Zealand |
| *America, North (2)* | Philippines | Greece* | |
| Canada | Singapore | Hungary | |
| USA | Sri Lanka* | Ireland | |
| | Taiwan | Italy | |
| *America, Central (4)* | Thailand | Latvia* | |
| Mexico | | Lithuania* | |
| Antilles (Nether.) | *Middle East (4)* | Luxemburg* | |
| Cuba | Bahrain* | Netherlands (the) | |
| Trinidad and Tobago* | Israel* | Norway | |
| | Jordan* | Malta* | |
| *America, South (2)* | Kuwait* | Poland | |
| Brazil | | Portugal | |
| Venezuela* | | Russian Fed. | |

*Indicates countries part of international studies not having independent national published values or studies.

but there are also estimates for almost all the countries of North and Central America, as well as Oceania. Indeed, the REVES bibliography database contained, by April 2009, 207 studies for the United States, 74 for Canada, 73 for the United Kingdom, 72 for the Netherlands, 65 for France, 51 for Japan, 42 for Spain, 36 for Denmark, 32 for Australia, 29 for China, 27 for Belgium, 25 for Italy, 11 for Taiwan, and 6 for Brazil.

Setting aside China, Taiwan, and Brazil, most studies report values for the most advanced western and Japanese economies. However, the REVES database contains health expectancy estimates for some less-developed and developing countries, for instance Cambodia, Cuba, Ghana (including working life expectancy), India, Indonesia, Philippines, the Russian Federation, Singapore, South Africa, Sudan, Thailand, Tunisia, the Caribbean in general, and the Netherlands Antilles. In total, the database contains estimates from independent national published values or studies for 43 countries (4 in Africa, 2 in North America, 3 in Central America, 1 in South America, 9 in Asia, 22 in Europe, and 2 in Oceania). In addition, estimates of health expectancies have been produced in ten developing countries in the context of international studies: for Bahrain, Egypt, Jordan, and Kuwait in a study of the elderly in eastern Mediterranean countries (Lamb et al. 1994); for Bahrain, Egypt, Ethiopia, Mali, and Pakistan in a study of aging and disability in the third world (Romieu and Robine 1994); for Botswana, Mauritius, Trinidad and Tobago, and Venezuela in a study by the United Nations (Haber and Dowd 1994); for five Asian countries (Burma, Malaysia, North Korea, South Korea, and Sri Lanka) in the framework of an international training on health expectancy calculation organized by Asia-REVES (Saito et al. 2003); for Israel in the framework of a European study (Minicuci et al. 2004); and for seven European countries (Cyprus, Estonia, Greece, Latvia, Lithuania, Luxemburg, and Malta) by Eurostat and the European Health Expectancy Monitoring Unit (EHEMU) (Jagger et al. 2008).

As the majority of these estimates were computed independently, they are poorly comparable, mainly because of differing methods of calculation, health measures, survey design, year, and starting age for the health expectancies. Even the few studies conducted internationally rarely provide satisfactory comparison among the countries studied because they use preexisting data collected separately within each of the countries involved.

Harmonization of national health surveys is very difficult to achieve, but considerable progress has been made within Europe with the advent of healthy life years (HLY), a new European Union (EU) structural indicator. HLY is a disability-free life expectancy based on a global measure of activity restriction, known as the GALI (Robine et al. 2003), and is calculated using the Statistics of Income and Living Conditions (SILC) survey conducted in all 25 EU countries. The range in HLY at age 50 (HLY50) in 2005 was 14.5 years for men, from 9.1 years (Estonia) to 23.6 years (Denmark), and 13.7 years for women, from 10.4 years (Estonia) to 24.1 years (Denmark), wider than the range in total remaining years of life at age 50, which was 9.1 years for men and 6.1 years for women (Jagger et al. 2008) (Fig. 26.1). Figure 26.1 also clearly shows that countries with the highest life expectancies at age 50 were not necessarily those with the highest HLY, and rankings of countries according to life expectancy at age 50 were not the same as rankings for HLY. Furthermore, differences between the new EU10 countries (predominantly eastern European countries) and the existing EU15 countries were particularly marked. Metaregression techniques demonstrated that some of the variation among the 25 countries could be ascribed to differences in other structural indicators reflecting wealth, employment, and education (Jagger et al. 2008); for example, the gross domestic product (GDP) in Estonia was 63, half that of Denmark (GDP in 2005 = 126.8). Though this is the most comparable data to date for European countries, harmonization of the underlying activity limitation measure was suboptimal, particularly for Denmark.

*Subregional estimates of health expectancy.* Countries that have regularly estimated health expectancies at the regional level, often to assist internal resource allocation, include Canada, England and Wales, France, and Spain. As a concise summary of findings to 2003 has been produced by Bebbington and Bajekal (2003), we include here only results published after this. In Italy, DFLE and life expectancy in good perceived health have been regularly computed by region, with a gradient of longer DFLE in the northern and central regions than in the south (Burgio et al. 2009). In Mexico, older people in regions with the longest life expectancy tended to spend a lower proportion of remaining life active (Reyes-Beaman et al. 2005), suggesting that social, economic, technological, and medical developments have focused on extending the lives of older people who are already dependent, echoing the "pandemic" scenario of Kramer (1980). Similar results have also been found in Spain (Gispert et al. 2007). Although the Netherlands appears a relatively small, homogeneous country, substantial regional differences have been found in healthy life expectancy (Groenewegen et al. 2003).

A study of five centers in the United Kingdom found that only for healthy life expectancy (self-perceived health) did the centers rank similarly to the way they ranked for life expectancy, while the centers ranked differently for DFLE and life expectancy free of cognitive impairment, confirming the existence of considerable differences in life experience across regions beyond basic life expectancy (Matthews et al. 2006a). Smaller area analyses for England, at the level of health authority and local authority, have been undertaken using 1991 and 2001 census data. In 1991, there was considerable variation in both LE and DFLE at birth at regional (local and health authority) levels across England, with greater variation in DFLE (men: 6.5 years men; women: 5 years) than in LE (men: 3 years; women: 2.5 years) (Bone et al. 1995). Almost all the variation in 1991 was explained by a small set of factors: unemployment rate, low social class, population sparsity (as a surrogate for access to services), retirement migration, and the size of ethnic minorities. Whynes (2009) has analyzed differences in HLE (based on self-rated health) between local authorities in 2001 using a more limited set of explanatory factors and found that the HLE observed in the most deprived areas was less than the regression model predicted. More recent studies in other countries have further confirmed the role of socioeconomic indicators in explaining regional variations, concluding that more favorable socioeconomic conditions lead to longer life expectancy, more years free of disability, and fewer years with disability (Kurimori et al. 2006; Van Oyen et al. 2005).

Although useful for resource allocation, such subregional analyses are not without methodological problems. For instance, the geographic areas need to be large enough to have the power to detect differences; Bebbington and Bajekal (Bebbington and Bajekal 2003) calculate that if two areas have a sample size of 1,000, then the difference in health expectancy required to qualify as significantly different at a 5% level of significance would be 5 years. A further issue is that subregional estimates are strongly affected by migration. Thus, differences between subregions may result from migration of certain subgroups of the population, e.g., into retirement areas, rather than the general "healthiness" of the area.

## *Temporal Comparisons Within Countries*

In total, 16 countries have recently published at least one chronological series of health expectancies, including 4 countries outside Europe (China, Japan, Thailand, and the United States). There are no recent published series for Australia and Canada. Table 26.2 lists these series by country, indicating for each series the period concerned, the number of health expectancy estimations over time (*n*), the health domain under consideration, the method of calculation, and the main references for each study. The health domains used have been collated into seven categories: self-perceived health (SPH), chronic morbidity or long-standing illness (LSI), impairment (IMP), functional limitation (FL), activity limitation including basic and instrumental daily activities (AL), happiness (HAP), and well-being (W). Long-standing illness and disability have been combined in recent health expectancy calculations for the United Kingdom, forming a new category labeled LSI&D (Table 26.2). The methods of calculation used are the Sullivan method (Sullivan) or the multistate life table (multistate), though the majority have used the Sullivan method, demonstrating the difficulty of obtaining chronological series from longitudinal data.

Out of the 16 countries having a least one chronological series of health expectancies, 12 have series based on self-perceived health, 6 have series based on activity limitation, and 4 countries have series based on chronic or long-standing illness, other health dimensions being rarely used. General self-perceived health is a popular question available in almost all health surveys, following past recommendations of the World Health Organization for national health survey harmonization. Although often considered as more important for assessing the compression of morbidity and/or disability, data on long-standing illness and disability are less frequently available.

**Table 26.2** Chronological series of health expectancies published since 2000

| Country | Period | N | Domain | Method | References |
|---|---|---|---|---|---|
| Austria | 1978–1998 | 4 | SPH | Sullivan | Doblhammer and Kytir (2001) |
| Belgium | 1997–2004 | 3 | SPH, LSI, AL | Sullivan | Van Oyen et al. (2008) |
| China | 1987–2006 | 2 | IMP | Sullivan | Liu et al. (2009) |
|  | 1987–2006 | 2 | IMP | Sullivan | Lai (2009) |
| Czech Rep. | 1993–2002 | 4 | SPH | Sullivan | Hrkal (2004) |
| Denmark | 1987–2000 | 4 | SPH, LSI, FL | Sullivan | Bronnum-Hansen (2005) |
|  | 1987–2005 | 5 | SPH, LSI, FL | Sullivan | Jeune and Bronnum-Hansen (2008) |
| France | 1980–2003 | 3 | AL | Sullivan | Cambois et al. (2006) and Cambois et al. (2008a) |
| Germany | 1984–1998 | 2 | SPH, AL | Sullivan | Kroll et al. (2008) |
| Italy | 1991–2000 | 3 | SPH, AL | Sullivan | Burgio et al. (2009) |
|  | 1994–2005 | 3 | SPH, AL | Sullivan | Egidi et al. (2009) |
| Japan | 1986–2004 | 7 | SPH | Sullivan | Yong and Saito (2009) |
| Lithuania | 1997–2004 | 2 | SPH | Sullivan | Kalédiené and Petrauskiené (2004) |
| Netherlands | 1981–2007 | 27 | SPH, LSI, FL | Sullivan | Bruggink et al. (2009) |
|  | 1989–2000 | 12 | LSI, AL, W | Sullivan | Perenboom et al. (2004a, b, 2005) |
| Spain | 1986–1999 | 2 | AL | Sullivan | Sagardui-Villamor et al. (2005) |
|  | 1987–2003 | 4 | SPH | Sullivan | Gomez Redondo et al. (2006) |
| Switzerland | 1992–2002 | 2 | SPH | Sullivan | Guilley (2005) |
| Thailand | 1986–1995 | 2 | SPH | Sullivan | Jitapunkul and Chayovan (2000) |
| USA | 1970–1990 | 3 | AL | Sullivan | Crimmins and Saito (2001) |
|  | 1982–1999 | 5 | AL | Sullivan | Manton et al. (2006) |
|  | 1992–2003 | 2 | AL | Multistate | Cai and Lubitz (2007) |
|  | 1982–1999 | 5 | AL | Sullivan | Manton (2008) |
|  | 1982–2004 | 6 | AL | Sullivan | Manton et al. (2008) |
|  | 1970–2000 | 4 | HAP | Sullivan | Yang (2008) |
|  | 1984–2000 | 6 | AL | Multistate | Crimmins et al. (2009) |
| United Kingdom | 1980–1996 | 17 | SPH, LSI | Sullivan | Kelly et al. (2000) |
|  | 1981–2002 | 22 | SPH, LSI&D | Sullivan | Office for National Statistics (2006) |
|  | 2004–2006 | 2 | SPH, LSI&D | Sullivan | Smith et al. (2008) |
|  | 2000–2006 | 7 | SPH, LSI&D | Sullivan | Office for National Statistics (2008) |

Several countries have computed a set of health expectancies to better describe the changes in the health status of their population, for instance Belgium, Denmark, Italy, the Netherlands, and the United Kingdom. These analyses are based on the premise that the main health domains (i.e., morbidity, functioning, and perceived health) may evolve differently.

Out of the 16 countries, 11 now have series made of three or more estimates over the studied period. The ranges of the series span 26 years in the United Kingdom and the Netherlands, 23 years in France, 22 years in the United States, 20 years in Austria, 19 years in China, 18 years in Denmark and Japan, and 16 years in Spain. However, forecasts of health expectancy values are still an exception (Manton et al. 2006).

Jagger et al. (2011) have computed a comparable series of health expectancies across 13 EU member states over the time period 1995–2001 using the European Community Household Panel (ECHP). They found consistent increases in life expectancy at ages 16 and 65 in all 13 countries over the period 1995–2001, but in the majority of countries this was not accompanied by a compression of disability. Only two countries (Austria and Italy) had strong evidence of compression of disability, while three countries (the Netherlands, Germany, and the United Kingdom) showed strong evidence of expansion of disability in the majority of age and gender groups, although these expansions were not accompanied by increases in years with severe disability, suggesting dynamic equilibrium. In contrast, in Greece there was a significant increase in the number of years with severe disability in all the age and gender groups (Table 26.3). There are a number of potential explanations for the fact that the majority of countries experienced an expansion of disability.

**Table 26.3** Evidence for absolute and relative compression/expansion and dynamic equilibrium for men and women at ages 16 and 65

| | Age 16 | | | Age 65 | | |
|---|---|---|---|---|---|---|
| | Absolute compression/expansion | Relative compression/expansion | Dynamic equilibrium | Absolute compression/expansion | Relative compression/expansion | Dynamic equilibrium |
| **Men** | | | | | | |
| Austria | Compression* | Compression* | | Compression** | Compression** | |
| Belgium | Compression** | Compression** | | Compression** | Compression** | |
| Denmark | Expansion* | Expansion* | Yes | Expansion** | Expansion** | Yes |
| Finland | Compression** | Compression** | | Expansion** | Compression** | |
| France | Expansion** | Expansion** | | Expansion** | Compression** | Yes |
| Germany | Expansion** | Compression** | | Expansion* | Expansion** | |
| Greece | Expansion** | Expansion** | | Expansion** | Expansion** | Yes |
| Ireland | Expansion* | Expansion* | Yes | Expansion* | Expansion** | |
| Italy | Compression* | Compression* | | Compression** | Compression* | |
| Netherlands | Expansion* | Expansion* | Yes | Expansion* | Expansion* | Yes |
| Portugal | Expansion* | Expansion** | Yes | Expansion** | Expansion** | |
| Spain | Compression** | Compression** | | Compression** | Compression** | |
| UK | Expansion* | Expansion* | Yes | Expansion* | Expansion* | Yes |
| **Women** | | | | | | |
| Austria | Compression* | Compression* | | Compression** | Compression** | |
| Belgium | Compression** | Compression** | | Compression** | Compression** | |
| Denmark | Expansion** | Expansion** | | Compression** | Compression** | |
| Finland | Expansion* | Expansion* | Yes | Expansion* | Expansion** | Yes |
| France | Expansion** | Expansion** | | Compression** | Compression** | |
| Germany | Expansion** | Expansion** | Yes | Expansion* | Expansion* | Yes |
| Greece | Expansion** | Expansion** | | Expansion** | Expansion** | |
| Ireland | Expansion** | Expansion** | | Expansion** | Expansion** | |
| Italy | Compression* | Compression* | | Compression* | Compression* | |
| Netherlands | Expansion* | Expansion* | | Expansion* | Expansion* | Yes |
| Portugal | Expansion** | Expansion** | | Expansion* | Expansion** | Yes |
| Spain | Compression** | Compression** | | Compression** | Compression** | |
| UK | Expansion* | Expansion* | Yes | Expansion* | Expansion** | |

*Increase/decrease at 5% level.
**Nonsignificant increase/decrease.

Limitations of the data may be part of this: the ECHP, which provided the disability prevalence, did experience a falling response rate over time, although representativeness did not seem to have been adversely affected (Watson 2003); the underlying disability question in the ECHP was not optimally harmonized across countries, though this is less of a problem in comparing trends over time; and the ECHP included only the noninstitutionalized population, so an apparent expansion of disability might result from changes in the care systems, allowing more older dependent people to remain at home rather than being admitted to a care home. If the expansions of disability are real, they confirm Kramer's (1980) hypothesis that medical and technological advances are keeping alive frail older people who previously would have died.

## Social Inequalities in Health Expectancy

One of the major uses of health expectancy calculations has been to identify inequalities in the quality, not simply the quantity, of life between subgroups within the population. The subgroups explored by most countries are gender and socioeconomic status (defined by education, occupation, income, level of deprivation, or ethnicity). Although here we review each of these socioeconomic indicators separately, it should be remembered that they are not interchangeable, and they indicate inequity at varied points throughout the life course. Crimmins and Cambois (2003) have reviewed studies comparing socioeconomic groups up to 2003, so here we concentrate on more recent studies.

*Gender.* As life tables are generally available separately for men and women, most health expectancies are calculated by gender. Almost all studies, using either Sullivan or multistate methods, show that women live longer in total than men and have more years free of disability or ill-health, but that these latter years are a smaller proportion of remaining life expectancy. Thus, in general women live longer but spend a greater proportion of remaining life with disability or ill-health. This has been shown to be true even at the oldest ages in Denmark (Bronnum-Hansen et al. 2009), although recent findings from one city in Brazil suggest that from age 75 women spent a shorter proportion of remaining life with ill-health than did men (Camargos et al. 2008).

*Education.* As a measure of social inequity in health particularly at older ages, education has the advantage that it has been completed early in life and therefore is less likely to suffer from reverse causation than measures such as income or occupation. Comparisons of the absolute size of differentials between educational groups from different studies are difficult because both levels of education and the health measures are rarely the same. However, the consensus is that the highest education group has even more advantage over the lowest for healthy life than for total life. Thus, those in the lowest education group live shorter lives, have more years of ill-health, and enjoy fewer healthy years than those with the highest levels of education (Crimmins and Cambois 2003), although for life expectancy with cognitive impairment the burden for the highly educated is similar to that for the less educated (Matthews et al. 2009). Whether gaps between education groups have increased or decreased over time is debatable. In the Netherlands, between 1989 and 2000 educational differentials in morbidity-free life expectancy decreased by 2.5 years for men and 0.7 years for women, perhaps because of earlier diagnosis of chronic diseases in the less educated (Perenboom et al. 2005). However, for two countries, Denmark and the United States, the gaps between the educationally advantaged and disadvantaged have widened over time. Over the two decades beginning in 1970, the most educated in the United States experienced a compression of morbidity while the least educated continued to experience an expansion, so that the gaps between them widened (Crimmins and Saito 2001). In Denmark, the gaps in healthy life expectancy (based on self-rated health) and DFLE between the most and least educated increased between 1994 and 2005, despite the decrease in numbers of people with the lowest level of education (Bronnum-Hansen and Baadsgaard 2008).

In some countries, such as the United Kingdom, Sullivan's method cannot be used to generate health expectancies by educational status since life tables are not routinely available by education. Educational differentials in life expectancy free of mobility disability at age 65 have been estimated (Jagger et al. 2007b) from the Medical Research Council Cognitive Function and Ageing Study (see www.cfas.ac.uk), a large-scale longitudinal study of aging conducted at five centers in the United Kingdom. Differences in life expectancy between the least educated individuals

**Fig. 26.2** DFLE at ages 65 and 85. Source: MRC CFAS

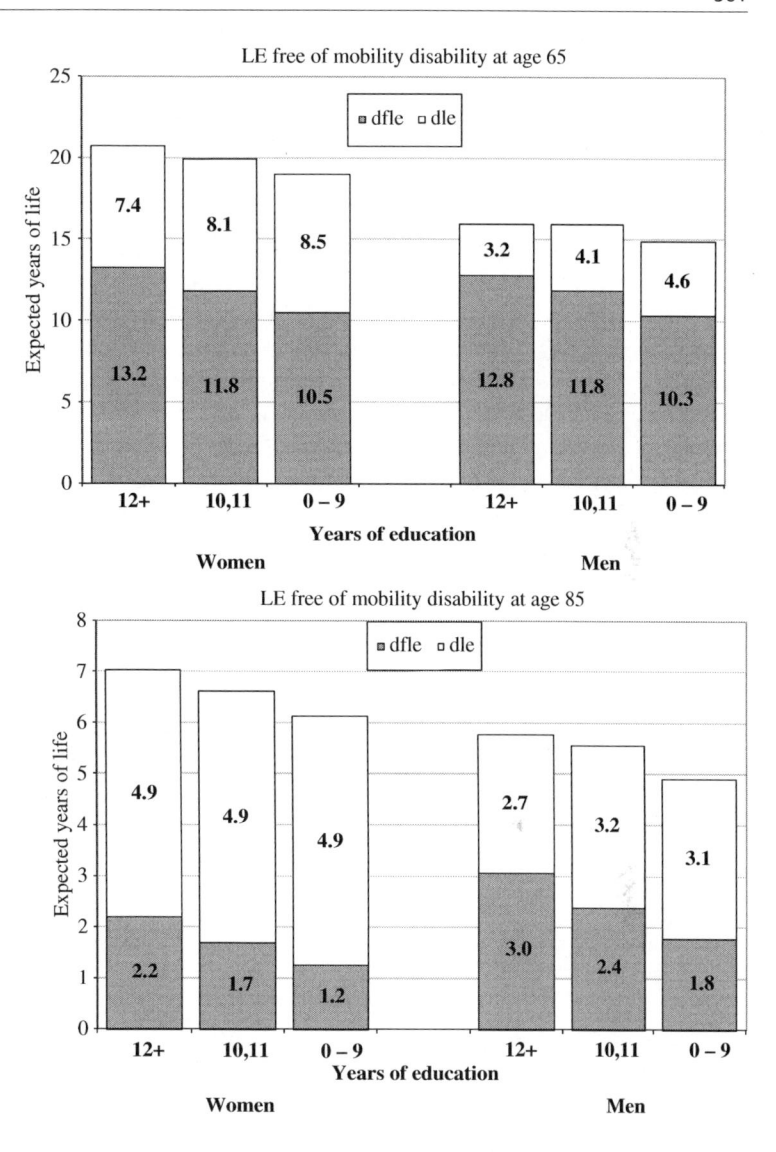

(0–9 years of education) and the most educated (12 or more years) were 1.7 years for women and 1.1 years for men at age 65, while differences in life expectancy free of mobility disability were considerably larger at 2.8 years for women and 2.4 years for men, and these persisted to age 85 years (Fig. 26.2). Despite the societal differences in China, similar gaps in active life expectancy (based on activities of daily living) have been found from a longitudinal study in Beijing (Kaneda et al. 2005). The United Kingdom differences appeared to arise from the least educated experiencing a significantly higher incidence of disability and lower rate of recovery, even after adjustment for the presence of comorbid conditions (Jagger et al. 2007b). Others have looked more specifically at the part that diseases and conditions play, finding that nonfatal conditions (arthritis, back complaints, and asthma/chronic obstructive pulmonary disease) explain a substantial part of differences in DFLE by education in Belgium (Nusselder et al. 2005), as do musculoskeletal diseases in Denmark (Bronnum-Hansen and Davidsen 2006; Bronnum-Hansen et al. 2006), since these diseases have a much greater impact on DFLE than on life expectancy.

*Occupation.* Occupation is often viewed as a measure of inequity in middle rather than early or late life. Health expectancies by occupation have been estimated for Finland (Kaprio et al. 1996), France (Cambois et al. 2008b; Cambois et al. 2001), Great Britain (Bebbington 1993; Matthews et al. 2006b;

Melzer et al. 2000), Sweden (Pettersson 1995), Italy (Spadea et al. 2005), and China (Kaneda et al. 2005). The majority of researchers use Sullivan's method and, as for education, all consistently find that those with the lowest occupational status live shorter lives, with more years of disability and fewer years disability-free.

*Income and deprivation.* Income and deprivation are more current measures of inequity. Social inequalities in health expectancies have been measured through income alone in Canada (Wilkins and Adams 1983), the United States (Katz et al. 1983), England (Matthews et al. 2006b), and China (Kaneda et al. 2005), and all studies again show that those with lower incomes have shorter lives with more disability. As with occupation, care must be taken since disability earlier in life might itself result in lower occupational status, more periods of unemployment and reduced incomes.

Deprivation is measured through area-level variables and is a common indicator for resource allocation in the United Kingdom. In the 1990s, those in the most deprived areas in the United Kingdom spent twice as many years in poor health as did those in the least deprived areas, and between 1994 and 1999 these gaps did not decrease (Bajekal 2005). An interesting analysis of the 2001 census in the United Kingdom demonstrated not only the unsurprising result that gaps between the most and least deprived areas were greater for healthy life expectancy (13.4 years for men and 11.8 for women at birth) and DFLE (14.1 years for men and 12.8 years for women at birth) than for life expectancy (7.6 years for men and 4.8 years for women at birth), but also "that for approximately equivalent levels of deprivation, the gap in health expectancies between the most and least deprived areas was widest in the northern regions and Wales and smallest in the East of England, London and the South West" (Rasulo et al. 2007). Significant reductions in DFLE and life expectancy in the most deprived areas compared to the least were found to persist in men, though not in women, at age 75 years (Matthews et al. 2006b).

*Race/ethnicity.* Comparisons of health expectancies by ethnic group are almost entirely confined to the United States, where racial differences (between white and African-Americans) in health expectancy are greater than those in life expectancy (Crimmins and Saito 2001; Crimmins et al. 1989), though gaps are age dependent (Crimmins et al. 1996; Guralnik et al. 1993). Ethnic inequalities in healthy life expectancy are, however, insignificant in highly educated groups and up to 6 years in those with the least education (Crimmins and Saito 2001). When ethnicity is further differentiated, the picture becomes more complex. Asian-Americans live longer and have relatively fewer years of disability than white Americans. African-Americans and Hispanics live shorter lives, but Hispanics have fewer years of disability (Hayward and Heron 1999). Two other countries, the United Kingdom and New Zealand, have estimated the impact of ethnicity on variations in healthy life expectancy. In New Zealand Maoris live shorter lives with more years of disability than Europeans, even within the same levels of deprivation (Tobias and Cheung 2003), while in the United Kingdom the proportion of ethnic minorities was found to contribute significantly to the variation in healthy life expectancy between local authorities (Bone et al. 1995).

## Measuring the Burden of Disease by Disability-Free Life Expectancy

Most models of the disablement process place disease at the start of the process (Verbrugge and Jette 1994). A number of studies have estimated the impact on DFLE of individual diseases or conditions, such as depression (Peres et al. 2008; Reynolds et al. 2008) or diabetes (Jagger et al. 2003; Laditka and Laditka 2006), one of the benefits of health expectancies being that they provide the same metric for comparison of both fatal and nonfatal diseases. The original approach, and still the most common method, for comparing the impact of disease on DFLE has been through cause-deleted life tables. This method was first proposed in the 1980s (Colvez and Blanchet 1983), but other studies have followed (Bone et al. 1995; Mathers 1999; Nusselder et al. 1996), including the Global Burden of Disease study (Murray and Lopez 1997a). These studies have highlighted that elimination of such fatal diseases as cancer and cardiovascular disease not only increases DFLE, but also increases years with disability. Elimination of such nonfatal diseases as arthritis and psychiatric diseases increases DFLE and reduces years with disability.

Cause-elimination methods based on the Sullivan method rely on cause-of-death data. Nonfatal diseases, particularly dementia, are known to be

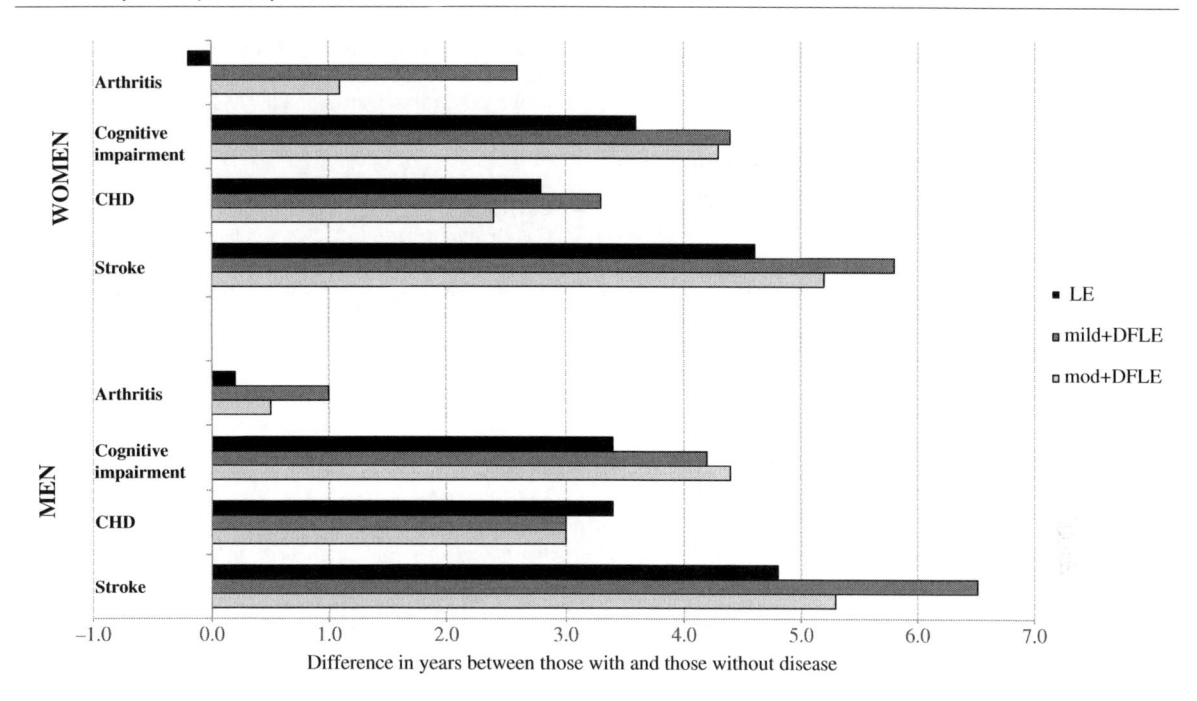

**Fig. 26.3** Difference in years of life expectancy, free of any disability (Mild+) and free of moderate or severe disability at age 65 in participants with and without diseases at baseline. Source: MRC CFAS

underrepresented on death certificates, and for the oldest old, comorbidity is common, so it can be difficult to ascertain the main cause of disability. Multistate methods do not suffer from this problem, though disease in longitudinal studies is often self-reported, and a large study size is needed to assess the impact of less prevalent diseases such as diabetes. Only the MRC Cognitive Function and Ageing Study had sufficient size to compare a range of fatal and nonfatal diseases (Jagger et al. 2007a). The number of disability-free years gained in persons free of stroke, cognitive impairment, and arthritis at baseline was greater than the years gained in total life expectancy (Fig. 26.3) suggesting that eliminating these conditions would compress disability, in contrast to coronary heart disease (CHD), where, at least for men, the years gained in life expectancy exceeded those gained in DFLE.

## Directions for Future Research

Future research in health expectancies is required both on harmonization of health measures and on methodology. Though considerable progress has been made within Europe in achieving comparability in disability measures with the healthy life years indicator, it is still impossible to compare national estimates of DFLE or trends among Europe, the United States, and Japan. A key concern for Europe is to ascertain whether different social groups within Europe are experiencing compression or expansion of disability, which requires life tables by social group. Methodological advances will focus on further extending methods to explain the variability in health expectancies between and within countries. Three ways are being pursued at present. Metaregression has begun to be used (Jagger et al. 2008), but more might be gained through the advances that have already been made in meta-analysis. Work is ongoing within the European Health and Life Expectancy Information System (EHLEIS) project (see www.ehemu.eu) on decomposition methods (Nusselder and Looman 2004). Finally, current software programs for longitudinal data, for example, IMaCH (Lievre et al. 2003) and SPACE (Cai et al. 2006), allow a very limited set of covariates, and further developments are required to allow adjustment for potential confounding factors—for instance, to better ascertain educational differences in healthy life expectancy after adjustment for comorbidity.

## Conclusion

Since the development of health expectancy measures in the late 1960s, the use of these indicators to monitor population health and to identify health inequalities has burgeoned. The growth in the number of longitudinal studies of aging in both the developed and developing worlds affords greater possibilities for multistate methods to explore inequalities in health expectancies between social groups and discover which transitions and diseases contribute to inequalities. Moreover, the last 5 years have seen a real acceptance of the political importance of health expectancies within the EU with the addition of healthy life years (HLY), a DFLE, to the set of EU structural indicators.

## References

Bajekal, M. 2005. "Healthy Life Expectancy by Area Deprivation: Magnitude and Trends in England, 1994–1999." *Health Stat Q* 25:18–27.

Bebbington, A.C. 1993. "Regional and Social Variations in Disability-Free Life Expectancy in Great Britain." In J.-M. Robine, C.D. Mathers, M.R. Bone, and I. Romieu. (eds.), *Calculation of Health Expectancies: Harmonization, Consensus Achieved and Future Perspectives/Calcul des espérances de vie en santé: harmonisation, acquis et perspectives*, pp. 175–191. Montrouge, John Libbey Eurotext.

Bebbington, A.C. and Bajekal, M. 2003. "Sub-National Variations in Health Expectancy." In J.-M. Robine, C. Jagger, C.D. Mathers, E.M. Crimmins, and R.M. Suzman. (eds.), *Determining Health Expectancies*, pp. 127–148. Chichester, Wiley.

Bone, M.R., A.C. Bebbington, C. Jagger, K. Morgan, and G. Nicolaas. 1995. *Health Expectancy and its Uses*. London, Department of Health.

Bronnum-Hansen, H. 2005. "Health Expectancy in Denmark, 1987–2000." *European Journal of Public Health* 15(1):20–25.

Bronnum-Hansen, H. and M. Baadsgaard. 2008. "Increase in Social Inequality in Health Expectancy in Denmark." *Scandinavian Journal of Public Health* 36(1):44–51.

Bronnum-Hansen, H. and M. Davidsen. 2006. "Social Differences in the Burden Of Long-Standing Illness in Denmark." *Sozial-und Praventivmedizin* 51(4):221–31.

Bronnum-Hansen, H., K. Duel, and M. Davidsen. 2006. "The Burden of Selected Diseases Among Older People in Denmark." *Journal of Aging and Health* 18(4):491–506.

Bronnum-Hansen, H., I. Petersen, B. Jeune, and K. Christensen. 2009. "Lifetime According to Health Status Among the Oldest Olds in Denmark." *Age and Ageing* 38(1):47–51.

Bruggink, J.-W., B.J.H. Lodder, and M. Kardal. 2009. "Healthy Life Expectancy Higher/Gezonde levensverwachting neemt toe." Accessed 23 March 2009. Available from: http://www.cbs.nl/en-GB/menu/themas/gezondheid-welzijn/publicaties/artikelen/archief/2009/2009-2679-wm.htm?Languageswitch=on

Buratta, V. and V. Egidi. 2003. "Data Collection Methods and Comparability Issues." In J.-M. Robine, C. Jagger, C.D. Mathers, E.M. Crimmins, and R.M. Suzman (eds.), *Determining Health Expectancies*, pp. 187–202. Chichester, Wiley.

Burgio, A., L. Murianni, and P. Folino-Gallo. 2009. "Differences in Life Expectancy and Disability Free Life Expectancy in Italy. A Challenge to Health Systems." *Social Indicators Research* 92(1):1–11.

Cai, L. and J. Lubitz. 2007. "Was There Compression of Disability for Older Americans from 1992 to 2003?" *Demography* 44(3):479–95.

Cai, L.M., N. Schenker, and J. Lubitz. 2006. "Analysis of Functional Status Transitions by Using a Semi-Markov Process Model in the Presence of Left-Censored Spells." *Journal of the Royal Statistical Society Series C-Applied Statistics* 55:477–91.

Camargos, M.C.S., C.J. Machado, and R.N. Rodrigues. 2008. "Sex Differences in Healthy Life Expectancy from Self-Perceived Assessments of Health in the City of Sao Paulo, Brazil." *Ageing and Society* 28:35–48.

Cambois, E., A. Clavel, and J.-M. Robine. 2006. "L'espérance de vie sans incapacité continue d'augmenter." *Solidarité Santé* 2:7–21.

Cambois, E., A. Clavel, I. Romieu, and J.M. Robine. 2008a. "Trends in Disability-Free Life Expectancy at Age 65 in France: Consistent and Diverging Patterns According to the Underlying Disability Measure." *European Journal of Ageing* 5(4):287–98.

Cambois, E., C. Laborde, and J.-M. Robine. 2008b. "A Double Disadvantage for Manual Workers: More Years of Disability and a Shorter Life Expectancy." *Population et Sociétés* 441, Ined, January 2008.

Cambois, E., J.M. Robine, and M.D. Hayward. 2001. "Social Inequalities in Disability-Free Life Expectancy in the French Male Population, 1980–1991." *Demography* 38(4):513–24.

Cambois, E., J.-M. Robine, and P. Mormiche. 2007. "Did the Prevalence of Disability in France Really Fall in the 1990s? A Discussion of Questions Asked in the French Health Survey." *Population-E* 62(2):315–37.

Colvez, A. and M. Blanchet. 1983. "Potential Gains in Life Expectancy Free of Disability – A Tool for Health-Planning." *International Journal of Epidemiology* 12(2):224–29.

Crimmins, E.M. and E. Cambois. 2003. "Social Inequalities in Health Expectancy." In J.-M. Robine, C. Jagger, C.D. Mathers, E.M. Crimmins, and R.M. Suzman. (eds.), *Determining Health Expectancies*, pp. 111–26. Chichester, Wiley.

Crimmins, E.M., M.D. Hayward, A. Hagedorn, Y. Saito, and N. Brouard. 2009. "Change in Disability-Free Life Expectancy for Americans 70 Years Old and Older" *Demography* 46(3):627–46.

Crimmins, E.M., M.D. Hayward, and Y. Saito. 1994. "Changing Mortality and Morbidity Rates and the Health Status and Life Expectancy of the Older Population." *Demography* 31(1):159–75.

Crimmins, E.M., M.D. Hayward, and Y. Saito. 1996. "Differentials in Active Life Expectancy in the Older Population of the United States." *Journals of Gerontology Series B-Psychological Sciences and Social Sciences* 51(3):S111–S20.

Crimmins, E.M., M.D. Hayward, H. Ueda, Y. Saito, and J.K. Kim. 2008. "Life with and Without Heart Disease Among Women and Men Over 50." *Journal of Women & Aging* 20(1–2):5–19.

Crimmins, E.M. and Y. Saito. 2001. "Trends in Healthy Life Expectancy in the United States, 1970–1990: Gender, Racial, and Educational Differences." *Social Science and Medicine* 52(11):1629–41.

Crimmins, E.M., Y. Saito, and D. Ingegneri. 1989. "Changes in Life Expectancy and Disability-Free Life Expectancy in the United-States." *Population and Development Review* 15(2):235–67.

De Laet, C.E., A. Peeters, A. Mamun, and L. Bonneux. 2003. "Normal Blood Pressure at Age 40 Extends Life Expectancy and Life Expectancy Free of Cardiovascular Disease in Both Men and Women." *Circulation* 108(17):3447.

Doblhammer, G. and J. Kytir. 2001. "Compression or Expansion of Morbidity? Trends in Healthy-Life Expectancy in the Elderly Austrian Population Between 1978 and 1998." *Social Science and Medicine* 52(3):385–91.

Dubois, M.F. and R. Hebert. 2006. "Cognitive-Impairment-Free Life Expectancy for Canadian Seniors." *Dementia and Geriatric Cognitive Disorders* 22(4):327–33.

Egidi, V., S. Salvini, D. Spizzichino, and D. Vignoli. 2009. "Capitolo 2: Salute e qualità della sopravvivenza [Health and Quality of Life]." In F. Onagro and S. Salvini (eds.), *Rapporto sulla popolazione – Salute e sopravvivenza*, pp. 33–49. Bologna, Il Mulino.

Franco, O.H., A. Peeters, L. Bonneux, and C. de Laet. 2005. "Blood Pressure in Adulthood and Life Expectancy with Cardiovascular Disease in Men and Women: Life Course Analysis" *Hypertension* 46(2):280–86.

Franco, O.H., E.W. Steyerberg, F.B. Hu, J. Mackenbach, and W. Nusselder. 2007. "Associations of Diabetes Mellitus with Total Life Expectancy and Life Expectancy with and without Cardiovascular Disease." *Archives of Internal Medicine* 167(11):1145–51.

Fries, J.F. 1980. "Aging, Natural Death, and the Compression of Morbidity." *New England Journal of Medicine* 303(3):130–35.

Fries, J.F. 2000. "Compression of Morbidity in the Elderly." *Vaccine* 18(16):1584–89.

Gill, T.M., H. Allore, S.E. Hardy, T.R. Holford, and L. Han. 2005. "Estimates of Active and Disabled Life Expectancy Based on Different Assessment Intervals." *Journals of Gerontology Series a-Biological Sciences and Medical Sciences* 60(8):1013–16.

Gispert, R., M. Ruiz-Ramos, M.A. Bares, F. Viciana, and G. Clot-Razquin. 2007. "Differences in Disability-Free Life Expectancy by Gender and Autonomous Regions in Spain [Differences in Disability-Free Life Expectancy by Gender and Autonomous Regions in Spain]." *Revista Espanola De Salud Publica* 81(2):155–65.

Gomez Redondo, R., R. Genova Maleras, and E. Robles. 2006. "Mortality Compression and Equilibrium Trend in Health: The Spanish Case." In Institut des Sciences de la Santé (ed.), *Living Longer But Healthier Lives: How to Achieve Health Gains in the Elderly in the European Union. Europe Blanche XXVI, Budapest, 25–26 November 2005*, pp. 65–82. Paris, ISS.

Groenewegen, P.P., G.P. Westert, and H.C. Boshuizen. 2003. "Regional Differences in Healthy Life Expectancy in the Netherlands." *Public Health* 117(6):424–29.

Guilley, E. 2005. "Longévité et santé." In P. Wanner, C. Sauvain-Dugerdil, E. Guilley, and C. Hussy (eds.), *Ages et générations: La vie après 50 ans en Suisse*, pp. 55–71. Neuchâtel, Office Fédéral de la Statistique.

Guralnik, J.M., K.C. Land, D. Blazer, G.G. Fillenbaum, and L.G. Branch. 1993. "Educational Status and Active Life Expectancy Among Older Blacks and Whites." *New England Journal of Medicine* 329(2):110–16.

Haber, L.D. and J.E. Dowd. 1994. *A Human Development Agenda for Disability: Statistical Considerations*." Prepared for the United Nations, Statistical Division.

Hayward, M.D. and M. Heron. 1999. "Racial Inequality in Active Life Among Adult Americans." *Demography* 36(1):77–91.

Hrkal, J. 2004. "Střední délka zdravého života [Healthy Life Expectancy Based on Limitation of Usual Activities]." In J. Kříž. (ed.), *Zdravotní stav populace ČR. Jak jsme na tom se zdravím? [Health status of the Czech population. How healthy are we?]*, pp. 24–25. Praha:SZÚ.

Imai, K. and S. Soneji. 2007. "On the Estimation Of Disability-Free Life Expectancy: Sullivan's Method and its Extension." *Journal of the American Statistical Association* 102(480):1199–211.

Jagger, C. 1999. "Health Expectancy Calculation by the Sullivan Method: A Practical Guide." NUPRI Research Paper Series no. 68. Tokyo, Nihon University.

Jagger, C., E. Cambois, H. Van Oyen, W. Nusselder, J.-M. Robine, and EHLEIS. 2011. Trends in Disability-Free Life Expectancy at Age 16 and Age 65 in the European Union 1995–2001: A Comparison of 13 EU Countries. *Forthcoming in the European Journal of Public Health*.

Jagger, C., C. Gillies, F. Mascone, E. Cambois, H. Van Oyen, W.J. Nusselder, J.-M. Robine., and EHLEIS Team. 2008. "Inequalities in Healthy Life Years in the 25 Countries of the European Union in 2005: A Cross-National Meta-Regression Analysis." *The Lancet* 372(9656):2124–31.

Jagger, C., E. Goyder, M. Clarke, N. Brouard, and A. Arthur. 2003. "Active Life Expectancy in People with and Without Diabetes." *Journal of Public Health Medicine* 25(1):42–46.

Jagger, C., R. Matthews, F. Matthews, T. Robinson, J.M. Robine, and C. Brayne. 2007a. "The Burden of Diseases on Disability-Free Life Expectancy in Later Life." *Journals of Gerontology Series a-Biological Sciences and Medical Sciences* 62(4):408–14.

Jagger, C., R. Matthews, D. Melzer, F. Matthews, and C. Brayne. 2007b. "Educational Differences in the Dynamics of Disability Incidence, Recovery and Mortality: Findings from the MRC Cognitive Function and Ageing Study (MRC CFAS)." *International Journal of Epidemiology* 36:358–65.

Jeune, B. and H. Bronnum-Hansen. 2008. "Trends in Health Expectancy at Age 65 for Various Health Indicators, 1987–2005, Denmark." *European Journal of Ageing* 5(4):279–85.

Jitapunkul, S. and N. Chayovan. 2000. "Healthy Life Expectancy of Thai Elderly: Did it Improve During the Soap-Bubble Economic Period?" *Journal of the Medical Association of Thailand* 83(8):861–64.

Jonker, J., C. De Laet, O. Franco, A. Peeters, J. Mackenbach, and W. Nusselder. 2006. "Physical Activity and Life Expectancy with and without Diabetes: Life Table Analysis of the Framingham Heart Study." *Diabetes Care* 29(1):38–43.

Kalédiené, R. and J. Petrauskiené. 2004. "Healthy Life Expectancy – An Important Indicator for Health Policy Development in Lithuania." *Medicina (Kaunas)* 40(6): 582–88.

Kaneda, T., Z. Zimmer, and Z. Tang. 2005. "Socioeconomic Status Differentials in Life and Active Life Expectancy Among Older Adults in Beijing." *Disability and Rehabilitation* 27(5):241–51.

Kaprio, J., S. Sarna, M. Fogelholm, and M. Koskenvuo. 1996. "Total and Occupationally Active Life Expectancies in Relation to Social Class and Marital Status in Men Classified as Healthy at 20 in Finland." *Journal of Epidemiology and Community Health* 50(6):653–60.

Katz, S., H. Aguerro-Torres, L. Fratiglioni, S. Gadeyne, Z. Guo, M. Viitanen, E.V. Strauss, B. Winblad, R. Wilkins, L.G. Branch, M.H. Branson, J.A. Papsidero, J.C. Beck, and D.S. Greer. 1983. "Active Life Expectancy." *New England Journal of Medicine* 309:1218–24.

Kelly, S., A. Baker, and S. Gupta. 2000. "Healthy Life Expectancy in Great Britain, 1980–96, and its Use as Indicator in United Kingdom Government Strategies." *Health Statistics Quarterly* 7:32–37.

Kramer, M. 1980. "The Rising Pandemic of Mental Disorders and Associated Chronic Diseases and Disabilities." *Acta Psychiatrica Scandinavica* 62(Suppl 285):382–97.

Krollm, L.E., T. Lampert, C. Lange, and T. Ziese. 2008. *Entwicklung und Einflussgrößen der gesunden Lebenserwartung/Trends and Determinants of Healthy Life Expectancy*. Veröffentlichungsreihe der Forschungsgruppe Public Health, Schwerpunkt Bildung, Arbeit und Lebenschancen. Wissenschaftszentrum Berlin für Sozialforschung (WZB).

Kurimori, S., Y. Fukuda, K. Nakamura, M. Watanabe, and T. Takano. 2006. "Calculation of Prefectural Disability-Adjusted Life Expectancy (DALE) Using Long-Term Care Prevalence and its Socioeconomic Correlates in Japan." *Health Policy* 76(3):346–58.

Laditka, S.B. and M.D. Hayward. 2003. "The Evolution of Demographic Methods to Calculate Health Expectancies." In J.-M. Robine, C. Jagger, C.D. Mathers, E.M. Crimmins, and R.M. Suzman. (eds.), *Determining Health Expectancies*, pp. 221–234. Chichester, Wiley.

Laditka, J.N. and S. Laditka. 2006. "Effects of Diabetes on Healthy Life Expectancy: Shorter Lives with More Disability for Both Men and Women." In Z. Yi, E.M. Crimmins, Y. Carrière, and J.-M. Robine. (eds.), *Longer Life and Healthy Aging*, pp. 71–90. Dordrecht, Springer.

Lai, D.J. 2009. "A Comparative Study of Handicap-Free Life Expectancy of China in 1987 and 2006." *Social Indicators Research* 90(2):257–65.

Lamb, V.L., G.C. Myers, and G.R. Andrews. 1994. "Healthy Life Expectancy of the Elderly in Eastern Mediterranean Countries." In C.D. Mathers, J. McCallum, and J.-M. Robine (eds.), *Advances in Health Expectancies*, pp. 383–391. Canberra, Australian Institute of Health and Welfare.

Lievre, A., D. Alley, and E.M. Crimmins. 2008. "Educational Differentials in Life Expectancy with Cognitive Impairment Among the Elderly in the United States." *Journal of Aging and Health* 20(4):456–77.

Lievre, A., N. Brouard, and C.R. Heathcote. 2003. "The Estimation of Health Expectancies from Cross-Longitudinal Surveys." *Mathematical Population Studies* 10:211–48.

Liu, J.F., G. Chen, X.M. Song, I. Chi, and X.Y. Zheng. 2009. "Trends in Disability-Free Life Expectancy Among Chinese Older Adults." *Journal of Aging and Health* 21(2): 266–85.

Lynch, S.M. and J.S. Brown. 2005. "A New Approach to Estimating Life Tables with Covariates and Constructing Interval Estimates of Life Table Quantities." *Sociological Methodology* 35:189–237.

Mamun, A., A. Peeters, J. Barendregt, F. Willekens, W. Nusselder, and L. Bonneux. 2004. "Smoking Decreases the Duration of Life Lived with and Without Cardiovascular Disease: A Life Course Analysis of the Framingham Heart Study." *European Heart Journal* 25(5):409–15.

Manton, K.G. 1982. "Changing Concepts of Morbidity and Mortality in the Elderly Population." *Milbank Memorial Fund Q Health Society* 60:183–244.

Manton, K.G. 2008. "Recent Declines in Chronic Disability in the Elderly US Population. Risk Factors and Future Dynamics." *Annual Review of Public Health* 29:91–113.

Manton, K.G., X.L. Gu, and V.L. Lamb. 2006. "Long-Term Trends in Life Expectancy and Active Life Expectancy in the United States." *Population and Development Review* 32(1):81–106.

Manton, K.G., X.L. Gu, and G.R. Lowrimore. 2008. "Cohort Changes in Active Life Expectancy in the US Elderly Population: Experience from the 1982–2004 National Long-Term Care Survey." *Journals of Gerontology Series B-Psychological Sciences and Social Sciences* 63(5):S269–S81.

Mathers, C.D. 1999. "Gains in Health Expectancy from the Elimination of Diseases among Older People." In *Disability and Rehabilitation*, 21(5–6):211–21.

Mathers, C.D. and J.-M. Robine. 1997. "How Good is Sullivan's Method for Monitoring Changes in Population Health Expectancies? Reply." *Journal of Epidemiology and Community Health* 51:578–79.

Matthews, R.J., C. Jagger, and R.M. Hancock. 2006b. "Does Socio-Econornic Advantage Lead to a Longer, Healthier Old Age?" *Social Science and Medicine* 62(10):2489–99.

Matthews, F.E., C. Jagger, L.L. Miller, and C. Brayne. 2009. "Education Differences in Life Expectancy with Cognitive Impairment." *Journals of Gerontology Series B-Psychological Sciences and Social Sciences* 64(1):125–31.

Matthews, F.E., L.L. Miller, C. Brayne, and C. Jagger. 2006a. "Regional Differences in Multidimensional Aspects of Health: Findings from the MRC Cognitive Function and Ageing Study." *BMC Public Health* 6:Art. no 90.

Melzer, D., B. McWilliams, C. Brayne, T. Johnson, and J. Bond. 2000. "Socioeconomic Status and the Expectation of Disability in Old Age: Estimates for England." *Journal of Epidemiology and Community Health* 54(4): 286–92.

Minicuci, N., M. Noale, S.M.F. Pluijm, M.V. Zunzunegui, T. Blumstein, D.J.H. Deeg, C. Bardage, M. Jylhä, and CLESA Working Group. 2004. "Disability-Free Life Expectancy: A Cross-National Comparison of Six Longitudinal Studies on Aging. The CLESA Project." *European Journal of Ageing* 1(1):37–44.

Murray, C.J.L. and A.D. Lopez. 1997a. "Alternative Projections of Mortality and Disability by Cause 1990–2020: Global Burden of Disease Study." *Lancet* 349(9064):1498–504.

Murray, C.J.L. and A.D. Lopez. 1997b. "Regional Patterns of Disability-Free Life Expectancy and Disability-Adjusted Life Expectancy: Global Burden of Disease Study." *Lancet* 349:1347–52.

Nusselder, W.J. 2003. "Compression of Morbidity." In J.-M. Robine, C. Jagger, C.D. Mathers, E.M. Crimmins, and R.M. Suzman (eds.), *Determining Health Expectancies*, pp. 35–58. Chichester, Wiley.

Nusselder, W.J. and C.W.N. Looman. 2004. "Decomposition of Differences in Health Expectancy by Cause." *Demography* 41(2):315–34.

Nusselder, W.J., C.W.N. Looman, J.P. Mackenbach, M. Huisman, H. van Oyen, P. Deboosere, S. Gadeyne, and A.E. Kunst. 2005. "The Contribution of Specific Diseases to Educational Disparities in Disability-Free Life Expectancy." *American Journal of Public Health* 95(11):2035–41.

Nusselder, W.J., K. VanderVelden, J.L.A. VanSonsbeek, M.E. Lenior, and G.A.M. vandenBos. 1996. "The Elimination of Selected Chronic Diseases in a Population: The Compression and Expansion of Morbidity." *American Journal of Public Health* 86(2):187–94.

Office for National Statistics. 2006. "Health Expectancies in the UK, 2002." *Health Statistics Quarterly* 29:59–62.

Office for National Statistics. 2008. "Health Expectancies in the UK, 2004." *Health Statistics Quarterly* 37:48–51.

Pardo Silva, M., C. De Laet, W. Nusselder, A. Mamun, and A. Peeters. 2006. "Adult Obesity and Number of Years Lived with and without Cardiovascular Disease." *Obesity* 14(7):1264–73.

Perenboom, R.J.M., H.C. Boshuizen, M.M.B. Breteler, A. Ott, and H.P.A. Van de Water. 1996. "Dementia-Free Life Expectancy (DemFLE) in the Netherlands." *Social Science and Medicine* 43(12):1703–7.

Perenboom, R.J.M., L.M. Van Herten, H.C. Boshuizen, and G.A.M. Van den Bos. 2004b. "Trends in Life Expectancy in Wellbeing." *Social Indicators Research* 65(2):227–44.

Perenboom, R.J.M., L.M. van Herten, H.C. Boshuizen, and G.A.M. Van den Bos. 2004a. "Trends in Disability-Free Life Expectancy." *Disability and Rehabilitation* 26(7):377–86.

Perenboom, R.J.M., L.M. van Herten, H.C. Boshuizen, and G.A.M. van den Bos. 2005. "Life Expectancy Without Chronic Morbidity: Trends in Gender and Socioeconomic Disparities." *Public Health Reports* 120(1):46–54.

Peres, K., C. Jagger, and F.E. Matthews. 2008. "Impact of Late-Life Self-Reported Emotional Problems on Disability-Free Life Expectancy: Results from the MRC Cognitive Function and Ageing Study." *International Journal of Geriatric Psychiatry* 23(6):643–49.

Pettersson, H. 1995. *Trends in Health Expectancy for Socio-Economic Groups in Sweden*. In 8th Work-Group Meeting REVES, International Research Network for Interpretation of Observed Values of Healthy Life Expectancy, Chicago.

Rasulo, D., M. Bajekal, and M. Yar. 2007. "Inequalities in Health Expectancies in England and Wales – Small Area Analysis from the 2001 Census." *Health Statistics Quarterly* 34:35–45.

Reyes-Beaman, S., C. Jagger, C. Garcia-Peña, O. Munz, P. Beaman, and B. Stafford. 2005. "Active Life Expectancy of Older People in Mexico." *Disability and Rehabilitation* 27(5):213–19.

Reynolds, S.L., W.E. Haley, and N. Kozlenko. 2008. "The Impact of Depressive Symptoms and Chronic Diseases on Active Life Expectancy in Older Americans." *American Journal of Geriatric Psychiatry* 16(5):425–32.

Ritchie, K. 1994. "International Comparisons of Dementia-Free Life Expectancy: A Critical Review of the Results Obtained." In C.D. Mathers, J. McCallum, and J.-M. Robine (eds.), *Advances in Health Expectancies*, pp. 271–79. Canberra, Australian Institute of Health and Welfare.

Ritchie, K., C.D. Mathers, and A.F. Jorm. 1994. "Dementia-Free Life Expectancy in Australia." *Australian Journal of Public Health* 18(2):149–52.

Robine, J.-M., C. Jagger., and Euro-REVES Group. 2003. "Creating a Coherent Set of Indicators to Monitor Health Across Europe: The Euro-Reves 2 Project." *European Journal of Public Health* 13(3):6–14.

Robine, J.M. and C.D. Mathers. 1993. "Measuring the Compression or Expansion of Morbidity Through Changes in Health Expectancy." In J.M. Robine, C.D. Mathers, M.R. Bone, and I. Romieu (eds.), *Calculation of Health Expectancies; Harmonization, Consensus Achieved and Future Perspective*, pp. 269–86. Montrouge, John Libbey Eurotext.

Robine, J.-M., I. Romieu, and E. Cambois. 1999. "Health Expectancy Indicators." *Bulletin of the World Health Organization* 77(2):181–85.

Robine, J.-M., I. Romieu, and J.-P. Michel. 2003. "Trends in Health Expectancies." In J.-M. Robine, C. Jagger, C.D. Mathers, E.M. Crimmins, and R.M. Suzman. (eds.), *Determining Health Expectancies*, pp. 75–104. Chichester, Wiley.

Roelands, M., H. Van Oyen, and F. Baro. 1994. "Dementia-Free Life Expectancy in Belgium." *European Journal of Public Health* 4(1):33–37.

Rogers, A., R.G. Rogers, L.G. Branch, A. Rogers, R.G. Rogers, and L.G. Branch. 1989. "A Multistate Analysis of Active Life Expectancy." *Public Health Reports* 104(3):222–26.

Romieu, I., J.-M. Robine, J-M. 1994. "World atlas on health expectancy calculations." In C.D. Mathers, J. McCallum, and J.-M. Robine (eds.), Advances in Health Expectancies, pp. 59–69. Canberra, Institute of Health and Welfare.

Sagardui-Villamor, J., P. Guallar-Castillon, M. Garcia-Ferruelo, J.R. Banegas, and F. Rodriguez-Artalejo. 2005. "Trends in Disability and Disability-Free Life Expectancy Among Elderly People in Spain: 1986–1999." *Journals of Gerontology Series A – Biological Sciences and Medical Sciences* 60(8):1028–34.

Saito, Y., Z.-K. Qiao, and S. Jitapunkul. 2003. "Health Expectancy in Asian Countries." In J.-M. Robine, C. Jagger, C.D. Mathers, E.M. Crimmins, and R.M. Suzman (eds.), *Determining Health Expectancies*, pp. 289–318. Chichester, Wiley.

Sauvaget, C., C. Jagger, and A.J. Arthur. 2001. "Active and Cognitive Impairment-Free Life Expectancies: Results from the Melton Mowbray 75+ Health Checks." *Age Ageing* 30:509–15.

Sauvaget, C., I. Tsuji, Y. Minami, A. Kukao, S. Hisamichi, and M. Sato. 1997. "Dementia-Free Life Expectancy Among Elderly Japanese." *Gerontology* 43:168–75.

Schoen, R. 1988. "Practical Uses of Multistate Population-Models." *Annual Review of Sociology* 14:341–61.

Smith, M., G. Edgar, and G. Groom. 2008. "Health Expectancies in the United Kingdom, 2004–2006." *Health Statistics Quarterly* 40:77–80.

Spadea, T., D. Quarta, M. Demaria, C. Marinacci, and G. Costa. 2005. "Healthy Life Expectancy in the Occupied Segment of the Turin Population." *Medicina del Lavoro* 96: S28–S38.

Suthers, K., J.K. Kim, and E.M. Crimmins. 2003. "Life Expectancy with Cognitive Impairment in the Older Population of the United States." *Journal of Gerontology: Social Sciences* 58B(3):S179–S86.

Tobias, M.I. and J. Cheung. 2003. "Monitoring Health Inequalities: Life Expectancy and Small Area Deprivation in New Zealand." *Population Health Metrics* 1:2.

Van Oyen, H., N. Bossuyt, P. Deboosere, S. Gadeyne, E. Abatih, and S. Demarest. 2005. "Differential Inequity in Health Expectancy by Region in Belgium." *Sozial und Präventivmedizin* 50(5):301–10.

Van Oyen, H., B. Cox, S. Demarest, P. Deboosere, and V. Lorant. 2008. "Trends in Health Expectancy Indicators in the Older Adult Population in Belgium Between 1997 and 2004." *European Journal of Ageing* 5(2):137–46.

Van den Hout, A. and F.E. Matthews. 2008. "Multi-State Analysis of Cognitive Ability Data: A Piecewise-Constant Model and a Weibull Model." *Statistics in Medicine* 27(26):5440–55.

Van den Hout, A. and F.E. Matthews. 2009. "Estimating Dementia-Free Life Expectancy for Parkinson's Patients Using Bayesian Inference and Microsimulation." *Biostatistics* 10(4):729–43.

Verbrugge, L.M. and A.M. Jette. 1994. "The Disablement Process." *Social Science and Medicine* 38(1):1–14.

Watson, D. 2003. "Sample Attrition Between Waves 1 and 5 in the European Community Household Panel." *European Sociological Review* 19(4):361–78.

White, C. 2009. "Health Expectancies in the UK, 2004." *Health Statistics Quarterly* 37:48–51.

Whynes, D.K. 2009. "Deprivation and Self-Reported Health: Are There 'Scottish Effects' in England and Wales?" *Journal of Public Health* 31:147–53.

Wilkins, R. and O.B. Adams. 1983. "Health Expectancy in Canada, Late 1970s: Demographic, Regional, and Social Dimensions." *American Journal of Public Health* 73: 1073–80.

Wolf, D.A. and T.M. Gill. 2009. "Modeling Transition Rates Using Panel Current-Status Data: How Serious Is the Bias?" *Demography* 46(2):371–86.

Yang, Y. 2008. "Long and Happy Living: Trends and Patterns of Happy Life Expectancy in the US, 1970–2000." *Social Science Research* 37(4):1235–52.

Yong, V. and Y. Saito. 2009. "Trends in Healthy Life Expectancy in Japan: 1986–2004." *Demographic Research* 20:467–94.

# Part VII
# Government Policies Designed to Affect Mortality

# Chapter 27
# Public Policies Intended to Influence Adult Mortality

S. Jay Olshansky and Leonard Hayflick

## Introduction

Life expectancy at birth (an actuarial measure of the duration of life for a population) rose by several decades in many developed nations in the twentieth century, with notable increases also occurring in most developing countries in the last few decades (Vaupel 2010). The increase in the duration of life of individuals (referred to as "lifespan") and the rise in the life expectancy of populations are achievements of the modern era that are unrivaled in history. The consensus among scientists is that the first longevity revolution was caused by a combination of advances in public health and technological and behavioral innovations (Omran 1971). Examples include reductions in communicable diseases, the introduction of refrigeration, temperature-controlled indoor living and working environments, availability of clean drinking water, indoor plumbing, antibiotics, vaccines, understanding and application of the germ theory of disease, and advances in medical technology. Reductions in adult mortality occurred at varying levels in most nations throughout this first longevity revolution, with notable gains occurring in the last quarter of the twentieth century (Riley 2001).

S.J. Olshansky (✉)
Division of Epidemiology and Biostatistics, School of Public Health, University of Illinois, Chicago, IL 60612, USA
e-mail: sjayo@uic.edu

## Public Policy and Mortality

Although most reductions in adult mortality have been due, in part, to the extraordinary work of public health experts and scientists who worked hard to convince politicians of the merits of implementing the products of their work, federal and local government policies contributed to reductions in adult mortality in a variety of ways. These include mandates for clean drinking water, the construction of waste removal facilities, health education and more recently, the creation of the National Institutes of Health and its predecessor organizations. A detailed description of how government policies influence adult mortality is interesting, but this history has already been published (Riley 2001). We will focus instead on the historical and contemporary discussion of whether the federal government should be engaging in activities designed to further influence adult mortality as a means to extend the lifespan of our species.

At first blush this might seem like a rhetorical question since it would be easy to justify almost all facets of modern medicine as a public good, but the science behind life extension has now entered new territory where the ability to manipulate our fundamental biology has already arrived, and these technologies will occur at an ever accelerating pace in the coming decades (Butler et al. 2008; Miller 2009). On one hand, it is uncertain whether humanity is ready to comprehend the implications of profoundly altering our own biology, but then again, never before have such unique opportunities to save and extend human life presented itself (President's Council on Bioethics 2003). The discussion presented here will not fall so much within the realm of philosophy, but rather, within the context of how these emerging technologies might influence adult health and longevity in the near-term.

## *Pursuing Life Extension*

The question of whether governments should be in the life extension business, or allow themselves to be influenced by scientists who have found the means to increase the duration of life is, ironically, the exact question that brought the first author of this chapter into the field of aging to begin with. In a 1979 graduate course on human aging at the University of Chicago, Dr. Bernice Neugarten from the Department of Human Development posed a question to the class that she and her colleagues had addressed in a recently published book (Neugarten and Havighurst 1977). This chapter's senior author wrote the lead article for that 1977 publication. Leaving aside the importance of ongoing debates about prolonging the life of an individual patient, the authors of the Neugarten/Havighurst book chapters were asked whether it is appropriate to focus government resources on a concerted effort to use our expanding knowledge of basic biology to extend the longevity of the human species. This question was posed at a unique time in American history—just when the National Institute on Aging had arisen. The answer to this question had then, and currently has, important ethical, economic, and public policy implications.

Neugarten and her co-authors identified two ways in which life extension could be accomplished: through continuing efforts to conquer disease (referred to as "disease control"), and through an effort to "identify the intrinsic biological processes that are thought to underlie aging and that proceed independently from disease processes—that is, to discover the genetic and biochemical secrets of aging, then to alter the biological clock that is presumably programmed into the human species" (p. 4) (referred to as "rate control"). It has since been discovered that there is no biological clock that directly governs the rate of aging or timing of death (Kirkwood 2005), but in the late 1970s that was a popular view.

The authors of the 1977 book co-edited by Neugarten and Havighurst used both biological and philosophical arguments to support their positions. For example, Hayflick (1977) was one of the first scientists to discuss how the elimination of specific diseases would have only a marginal effect on life expectancy (see, Keyfitz 1977 for the first discussion of this issue by a demographer), and that if increases in duration of life like those observed in the twentieth century were to occur again, it would be necessary to slow the fundamental biology of aging itself. A similar conclusion was arrived at some 13 years later by scientists speculating on the upper limits to human longevity (Olshansky et al. 1990). Hayflick predicted that under-funded gerontologists would not fully solve the aging puzzle and also fail to develop treatments that would dramatically increase life expectancy within the next 25 years (by 2002), but he did suggest that the time was ripe (back in 1977) for research efforts of this kind to be aggressively pursued. Hayflick's rationale was simple, "It is easier to affect a biological rate than it would be to prevent its occurrence" (p. 5). No one listened.

Hayflick also emphasized the importance of addressing aging disparities, especially in the United States. Using unambiguous language, Hayflick stated, "It is doubtless true that to be old in America is unpleasant, to be old and poor in America is a tragedy, but to be old, poor, and a member of an ethnic minority in America is devastating" (p. 9). It was at this point that Hayflick recommended specific government policies to address some of these issues, only some of which are now—some 34 years later—being contemplated (Olshansky et al. 2011; Rowe et al. 2010). Examples included revamping society's attitudes toward the aged; the abolishment of retirement based on chronological age; and a concerted effort to extend the healthy years of life (not necessarily life expectancy itself) as a result of efforts to slow the biological clock of aging. Although Hayflick supported government efforts to slow aging, his views were tempered by the belief that it was at least possible that society is not yet ready for the dramatic changes in our social, political, and economic institutions that such achievements would bring.

Havighurst and Sacher (1977) focused their attention on the importance of clarifying the distinction between interventions that modulate the rate of aging and those that increase vigor. According to Fig. 27.1, *a* represents a standard survival curve that is a product of a mortality rate doubling time (MRDT) of approximately 8 years. The *c* curve would be realized if mean lifespan is extended by slowing the rate of aging—which is characterized by an increase in MRDT from 8 to 16 years and an increase in life expectancy of about

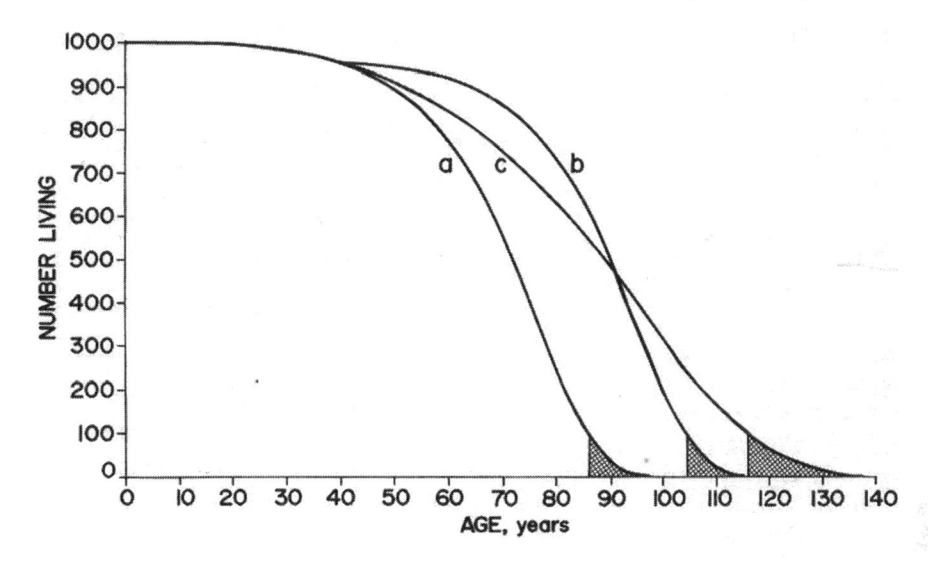

**Fig. 27.1** Survivorship curves based on various patterns of mortality. (**a**) Adult US population, 1970. (**b**) If "vigor" were improved. (**c**) If the "rate of aging" were slowed. Source: Havighurst and Sacher (1977: 15)

15–20 years (with a notable extension of maximum lifespan as well). The *b* survival curve would occur only if "vigor" was actively improved, and it was vigor or healthy life that these authors believed should be the goal of research in this area. In the example provided, *b* would result from a reduction in the death rate to one-fifth its value (in 1977) after age 40, with a resulting increase in life expectancy of about 18 years and a modest increase in maximum lifespan. Havighurst and Sacher favored public policies that would encourage the realization of the *b* survival curve because it would lead to a compression of morbidity and disability and save more lives between ages 40 and 90. Policies that favor the *c* survival curve were considered less than optimal because they would save more lives at ages 90 and older—a phase in the lifespan when aging has already played itself out and frailty and disability are at extremely high levels. Importantly, Havighurst and Sacher argued that *b* could best be achieved by a combination of policies that encourage healthy behaviors (e.g., reduction in smoking, better medical care, and cholesterol reduction) *and* those that encourage the development of pharmacological agents with anti-aging properties that have a systemic positive affect on bodily vigor.

Goddard (1977) contemplated what would be required to set and achieve the extension of lifespan as a national goal. Drawing on the scientific literature that existed at that time, experimental evidence suggested that life extension could be achieved by one of the following methods: cooling of body temperature; reducing infection by manipulating the immune system; caloric restriction; introduction of antioxidants; and manipulation of a "biological clock" that was believed at the time to regulate the rate of aging. Which method eventually proved fruitful was irrelevant to Goddard—a combination of experimental evidence that lifespan can be manipulated in other animals, and a series of affirmative comments from leading gerontologists that it could be done, was sufficient to justify setting lifespan extension as a national goal for the year 2000.

It is worth emphasizing at this point what gerontologists in the 1970s believed could be achieved in the way of lifespan extension in order to provide perspective on contemporary views. Hayflick stated in 1974, "The goal that appears to be not only more desirable, but indeed more attainable, is not the extension of longevity per se, but the extension of our most vigorous and productive years" (in Goddard 1977: 21). This view was echoed by Nathan Shock in 1975, "We are not interested in our laboratory in increasing the lifespan. I don't buy that as a legitimate goal. I'd rather make the years that we have into good years" (in Goddard 1977: 21). These admonitions aside, Dr. Ivan Asimov suggested in 1975 that by the year 2000 men and women would routinely live up to and perhaps beyond 100, and Dr. Alex Comfort boldly predicted that by 1990 we will know of an experimental way of slowing down age changes that would increase lifespan by 20% (in Goddard 1977: 21–22). Bold predictions about how science will dramatically extend the human lifespan have been part of folklore for centuries (Gruman 1966; Olshansky and Carnes 2001).

According to Goddard (1977), establishing life extension as a national goal "requires a coalition of outstanding leadership, strong political support, the presence of strong vested interests, a constellation of pressures which combine to cause substantial public support, the economic wherewithal, and in those few instances which have involved science, the existence of a capability which can reasonably be expected to lead to a successful outcome" (p. 22). Examples of accelerated US national efforts of this kind include legislation to address wastewater as early as the mid-nineteenth century (Burian et al. 2000), the creation of the transcontinental railroad in the 1860s, municipal water treatment legislation in 1914 (EPA 2000), the building of the national highway system in the 1920s, the Manhattan project in the 1940s to develop an atomic weapon, the declaration by President Kennedy in 1961 that the United States would land a man on the moon by the end of the decade, and President Nixon's declaration of war on cancer in 1977. It is interesting to note that in most of these examples, the technical means to accomplish these national goals were not known at the time they were initiated, and in some cases the benefits of the stated goals had not yet been fully established by science. Yet, in each instance a political leader or leaders led the charge by establishing a vision, marshalling the resources, and rallying the populace—often in direct response to persuasive arguments made by scientists (e.g., Einstein's letter to President Roosevelt regarding atomic fission.) Goddard suggested that a similar set of conditions would be required to set life extension as a national goal for the United States.

Not everyone agreed with Goddard's proposal. Wick (1977) suggested that setting a national goal to extend life "is exactly what we do not need . . ." (p. 45), and his reasoning was straightforward. According to Wick, the life extension we have already witnessed has led to considerable increases in the number of people requiring care in nursing care facilities, and the further extension of life might very well increase the number and proportion of people requiring this undesirable scenario. A nearly identical argument was set forth in the same year by Greunberg (1977) who coined the phrase "the failures of success" as a way of describing how life extension can inadvertently increase the prevalence of conditions of frailty, disability, and morbidity. Both Wick and Greunberg were prophetic—the prevalence of these undesirable conditions has risen dramatically in the last quarter century, although recent research demonstrates that in some parts of the world people are living longer lives in a healthy state (see Chapter 26 by Jagger and Robine, this volume). However, not everyone considers morbidity undesirable; Vaupel (2010) has suggested, "to the extent that the unhealthy state is better than death, greater prevalence of morbidity among the elderly may be a positive development" (p. 538). Wick also argued that the responsibility that comes with acquiring the ability to modify our own biology seems, at least so far, to be well beyond our current comprehension. In short, Wick suggested that humanity is not yet ready to wield the power of a demigod (which is how he viewed manipulating our biology for the sole purpose of life extension) because we do not yet fully understand the consequences of our actions, nor are we going to be able to undo this process once it has begun.

Sacher had a significantly different and somewhat counterintuitive view than anyone else (in Englehardt 1977). He suggested that extending life by slowing aging would have the opposite effect as that intended; it would result in a disproportionate increase in the number of person-years of disease and disability for the 10% of the population living the longest. This would occur because such interventions as caloric restriction and reducing body temperature (which at the time were the only methods thought to delay aging) resulted in an extension of the senescent phase of life (i.e., such interventions were thought to make us older longer). Sacher argued,

> Biologists frequently say that their goal is to decrease the rate of aging, and they have tried to approach this goal by several chemical therapies—for example, by administering antioxidants or procaine (temperature-lowering and caloric restrictions are separate cases [*that Sacher argued did reduce the rate of aging, but which also had the curious effect of extending years, not all of which could be expected to be healthy*]). However, all of the pharmacological methods, although they are used and proposed as anti-aging agents, do not, in fact, reduce the rate of aging. Insofar as they are effective, they reduce the *vulnerability* to disease. In other words, they have the kind of consequence that I said would be more favorable—i.e., deferring the senescent phase rather than stretching it out. However, the researchers are getting a wrong result so far as their original hypothesis is concerned. (p. 50)

Sacher's main argument was that the only intervention programs that should be pursued should be those that reduce our vulnerability to disease without altering the rate of aging, the result of which would be a *decrease* in the prevalence of disabled in the population and concomitant reductions in the relative costs of debility and medical care. Since the authors expressed their opinion on this topic in 1977, scientists have subsequently shown that animals that are likely to experience an experimental delay in their biological aging are also likely to experience both a reduction in vulnerability to disease and a compression of disability (Bartke and Brown-Borg 2004; Clements et al. 2008; Flurkey et al. 2001; Miller et al. 2005). Using Sacher's own criteria for intervention programs that should be pursued, it is reasonable to conclude that even those that slow aging would meet with his approval.

The question of whether efforts to slow human aging should be pursued has been the subject of a number of papers both before and after the edited volume by Neugarten and Havighurst. For example, McKay et al. (1956) suggested that successful life extension already achieved in laboratory animals justified the experimental manipulation of lifespan in humans. Strehler (1975) invented the term "gerontogeny" to describe the hoped-for development of interventions that extend healthy life, and suggested that societies are generally unprepared for scientific windfalls like the one that would result from delayed aging. He went on to argue that society has not yet pursued this golden era because public policy makers are themselves ensnared in time's net where they experience a form of societal senescence. Miller (2002) identified eight obstacles to applied gerontology: (1) the presence of hucksters selling phony anti-aging interventions cast a negative shadow on real scientists with the potential to make scientific breakthroughs; (2) there are strong political lobbies for major diseases but no lobby to attack aging; (3) experiments on mammals take too long, thus discouraging new scientists to work in this area; (4) young scientists are seduced to learn new technologies rather than conduct simple experiments; (5) pharmaceutical companies could make money selling phony anti-aging nostrums, so why should they bother investing in trying to discover something that actually works; (6) pharmaceutical companies cannot afford to wait for research on mammals to be completed; (7) the absence of a well-validated method to measure biological age; and (8) the biochemical pathways that influence the rate of aging have yet to be elucidated. Add to this list the illogical argument set forth by many that slowing aging is undesirable because it will make us older longer (Kass 2004), and Miller has outlined a series of obstacles that will be difficult to overcome.

## *Pursuing Immortality*

Several approaches have surfaced in recent years to address Goddard's 1977 proposal that life extension serve as a national goal. One of the more flamboyant among them goes well beyond the mere pursuit of life extension to the demand that humanity should set nothing short of immortality as the target. British advocate for radical life extension—Aubrey de Grey—contends that the only enemy we should have in our sights is death itself, because anything short of immortality would eventually lead us right back to where we are now: unsatisfied with the fate that appears to await us all, even if life is lived longer. Indeed, as the reasoning goes, anything short of immortality is not worth pursuing (de Grey and Rae 2007; Kurzweil and Grossman 2005).

## *Immortalists*

The immortalists as we refer to them contend that physical immortality is on the horizon (where it has been since recorded history 3,500 years ago—see Gruman 1966), and that some people alive today will literally drink from a fountain of youth. For example, de Grey maintains that the preferred solution to aging according to gerontologists is to disrupt the cellular and molecular processes that give rise to it (i.e., their focus is on cleaning up the business of being alive so the side effects are lessened). An engineer's approach to aging would be entirely different according to de Grey. An engineer would let the damage happen unhindered, but instead all of their attention would be focused on repairing it, indefinitely and perfectly. If repaired to perfection like that of an automobile or house that is constantly monitored, de Grey believes we could perpetually maintain ourselves in a youthful state (i.e., a 20-year-old could eternally remain in that physical state)—achieving immortality along the way. Since humans are made up of nothing more than "cells and the stuff between cells" (de Grey

2004: 254), simply repair everything he declares (de Grey identifies only seven molecular and cellular differences between people who are young and old), and by ignoring the second law of thermodynamics, poof, we become immortal (de Grey et al. 2002).

Kurzweil and Grossman (2005) claim that humanity is on the verge of immortality because of technological bridges to life extension that are forthcoming. Bridge One technologies are composed of a combination of nutritional supplements, changes in lifestyle, and extensive health care screening which, taken together, will (according to the authors) allow people to live an additional 20 years beyond the life expectancies that prevail today. These interventions are already available to the public (in part because the authors themselves created an online longevity store where they sell Bridge One supplements), and if used, would enable people to live long enough to benefit from Bridge Two technologies 20 years hence. Bridge Two technologies are anticipated forthcoming advances in biomedicine such as stem cell therapy, genetic engineering, and "rejuvenation technologies" thought to be on the very near horizon. Once people live into the window of time when Bridge Two technologies prevail, according to Kurzweil and Grossman, the survivors will then inevitably live long enough to benefit from nanotechnology (the Bridge Three technology they say will come into existence within the next 50 years). It is Bridge Three technologies that these authors claim will lead to immortality, which is the basis for Kurzweil's standard credo "live long enough to live forever." Driving this particular line of reasoning is the underlying premise that if information technology continues to rise at an ever faster exponential rate, then human immortality is sure to follow (Kurzweil 2006).

In both the de Grey and Kurzweil scenarios, physical immortality would be achieved for all of humanity sometime by the middle of the twenty-first century. Both authors suggest that accompanying physical immortality would be eternal youth, which means that the centenarians they envision occupying the future will be no different than people at younger and middle ages today. In effect, old age as we know it would cease to exist and only those who are physically healthy and mentally vibrant would populate the world.

The immortalist line of reasoning suffers from a host of problems, not the least of which is that it is entirely dependent on the creation of something that does not exist: life-extending technologies that yield eternal life. de Grey (2003) stated that in the past few years it has become possible to enumerate a comprehensive panel of technically feasible interventions that would represent real anti-aging interventions, but *enumerating a plan* is not the same as developing one that is scientifically verified to actually work by at least proof of principle. Thus, De Grey's concept of "technically feasible" is considered spurious by many of the scientists currently involved in this research (Warner et al. 2005). The line of reasoning formulated by Kurzweil is equally problematic. First, there is no evidence to support the position that 20 years could be added to life expectancy by purchasing anything from their longevity store, and second, the basis for the bridges to immortality is the unsupported linkage between exponential increases in information technology and life expectancy. The modern painters and engineers of this hypothetical immortal world act more like advocates or self-proclaimed prophets rather than scientists (Olshansky 2011; Warner et al. 2005). The immortalist's operate, as they have done for centuries, almost exclusively on a vision without science.

Promises of immortality and indefinite youth and vigor have been made by longevity prophets of every era dating back thousands of years (Gruman 1966). For now at least, there is no science to back up boastful claims that humanity is headed toward a genuine elixir that will yield eternal life. In fact, even the partial or complete elimination of the major fatal diseases that kill three of every four people in developed nations (heart disease, cancer, and stroke) would yield life expectancies of less than 100 (Olshansky et al. 1990), so it is evident that radical life extension can only be accomplished by the development of technologies that do not exist. And yet, having now levied the greatest of all insults to immortalists, it is worth remembering a point we made earlier about Manhattan-type projects of the past—the technical means to accomplish them were often unknown at the time they were initiated, and the benefits and unintended consequences were sometimes not fully established in advance by science.

## *The Language of Life Extension*

Strehler (1975) once said that humanity is not ready for scientific windfalls of the magnitude we speak regarding the extension of life. We agree. As such, equal attention must be paid to *how* the message of life extension is presented to public policy makers and the general public as much as the science that supports it. This view about being careful regarding the content of the message has surfaced regularly in the scientific literature—perhaps none more clearly stated than Miller's (2002) description of "gerontologiphobia" as "... an irrational public predisposition to regard research on specific late-life diseases as marvelous but to regard research on aging, and thus on all late-life diseases together, as a public menace bound to produce a world filled with nonproductive, chronically disabled, unhappy senior citizens consuming more resources than they produce" (p. 170). It is safe to say that no one in the field of gerontology, past or present, is in favor of using science to extend the period of old age and its accompanying undesirable health consequences. Hayflick (1977) articulated this idea best when he distinguished between being old and being aged; the focus of research designed to slow aging should be on helping us get older without becoming aged. There is also no disagreement on the fact that too little money is being spent on the fundamental biology of aging and longevity determinants (Hayflick 2007). Aside from these two points of agreement, it is here that two distinct camps have formed that are taking radically different approaches to the common goal of enabling us to age without growing old.

The immortalists have not just ignored the admonition proffered by many about the importance of the content of the message; they have intentionally chosen language that we believe is destructive to their cause. By setting immortality as the only goal that is reasonable and achievable, a number of political problems arise that may very well decrease the chances that formal efforts to slow aging will ensue. For example, the first tactic used by the immortalists is to label aging as a disease (de Grey 2003). This is done, in part, because the general public and policy makers view disease in the traditional sense as something that can be cured by medical intervention. If aging is labeled a disease, then as the reasoning goes, perhaps lobbies will form, funds can be marshaled, and the Food and Drug Administration will approve of interventions to combat it. As appealing and logical as this might seem, scientists tend to shy away from creating labels for political reasons, especially when the evidence suggests that aging is not a disease (Carnes et al. 2008), any more so than puberty, menopause, or childbirth are diseases. This issue has been discussed extensively in the scientific literature for many years, with reasonable arguments on both sides (Butler 2000; Carnes et al. 2008; Hayflick 1998, 2004; Holliday 2004), so it is pointless to reiterate the arguments here. Nevertheless, Hayflick (2007) has given six reasons why aging is not a disease. Suffice it to say that if we did successfully manage to label aging as a disease, it is questionable whether this would be sufficient to garner the financial resources necessary to combat it.

The problem created by the immortalists is that their chosen goal—anything less than immortality is considered shortsighted. This view presents several problems. The worst among them is that it will be impossible to use methods of science to demonstrate that the goal has been approached or achieved. The reason is that it would take forever to test the hypothesis that a specific intervention makes any animal live forever. Wick (1977) suggested that trying to gain political and popular support for a crash program to bring us indefinite life would backfire because "... it will raise the same old question in the public mind, 'What have you done for us this year?'" (p. 57). Setting a goal that cannot be measured by the tools of science, especially over short periods of time, makes it impossible to demonstrate progress, and without such a demonstration, there is no reason for politicians (or scientists and health care practitioners for that matter) to commit to it. As such, because of a stubborn all-or-nothing mentality that is perhaps the most effective brake to scientific research imaginable, the immortalists have chosen a strategy that may very well guarantee their own demise.

## The Longevity Dividend

An alternative new approach to setting decelerated aging as a national goal for health research has coalesced under the umbrella of what has come to be known as the Longevity Dividend. The line of reasoning goes something like this. Governments across the globe have already committed trillions of dollars in the last 50 years combating the fatal and disabling diseases that accompany old age, but most of these funds were intended to treat diseases rather than determine their etiology. The rationale used to attack disease is straightforward—cancer, heart disease, stroke, sensory impairments, Alzheimer's, and a host of other ailments are not just lethal or disabling when they occur—they are frightening—and it is fear of both disease and death that have driven our collective decision to engage in an ongoing battle against diseases. However, instead of trying to fit a square peg into a round hole by transforming aging into a disease like the immortalists, advocates of the Longevity Dividend suggest that decelerated aging will accomplish what we already understand and are already trying to do when we attack diseases with new detection devices, surgical procedures, drugs, chemicals, and radiation, but without the high cost and often painful extension of frailty, disability, side effects, and even old age.

Our modern world has already made the psychological commitment to extend life—that battle has been fought and won. In fact, it was an easy sell since advances in medicine and science quickly lead to interventions designed to postpone the onset of major fatal and disabling diseases, or more effectively treat them once they occur.

The premise of the modern version of the Longevity Dividend is fivefold as follows: (1) convince the medical and scientific community and public policy makers that biological aging is the greatest risk factor for most of what goes wrong with us as we grow older; (2) the current medical model that treats one disease at a time, independent of all others, may eventually lead to the very thing we fear most—an extension of old age; (3) a successful effort to slow aging, even by a small margin, would be a monumental achievement that would yield the benefits we already pursue aggressively by attacking diseases, but with much greater efficiency; (4) a modest deceleration in the rate of aging would yield dramatic health, social, and economic dividends for individuals and the countries in which they live that will pay off in the short-term and for all future generations; and (5) the cost to create the Longevity Dividend is estimated to be about 1% of the current Medicare budget annually, but the savings to health care would more than pay this back. A successful effort to slow aging would create scientific, medical, and economic windfalls that would be roughly equivalent in impact to the discovery of antibiotics in the middle of the twentieth century.

The underlying rationale behind the Longevity Dividend is not new—elements of the idea were mentioned in one form or another by numerous authors in the past (see Goddard 1977; Hayflick 1977; Holliday 1984; Strehler 1975). Other scientists have since documented the economic benefits associated with rising life expectancy (Bloom and Canning 2000; Bloom et al. 2004; Murphy and Topel 2006; Nordhaus 1998) and discussed the prospects of success in slowing aging and the various benefits that would accrue to society as a result (Miller 2009; Rattan 2005; Sierra et al. 2008).

The modern version of the Longevity Dividend first appeared in Olshansky et al. (2006), and the logic actually has not strayed too far from the original proposal set forth by Goddard (1977). However, the science has progressed so far beyond what was known 30 years ago that some find it reasonable to conclude that the technical means to slow aging in people is a plausible goal. Butler et al. (2008) also dispel the old belief still held by some that aging is an immutable process that was genetically programmed by evolution. This is now known to be wrong. Indeed, because there can be no aging or death genes that arose under the direct force of evolution (Kirkwood 2005; Hayflick 2007), interventions designed to slow aging in people would have no genetic barriers to success.

Goddard suggested decades ago that setting life extension as a national goal required not just the science, but the political will to make it happen and a champion in the world of politics to carry the vision forward in Congress and to the public. To address this issue, the executive director of the Alliance for Aging Research (Daniel Perry) arranged a Capital Hill Symposium on the Longevity Dividend in September 2006 (http://www.agingresearch.org/content/calendar/detail/1096/). Attending the symposium were the authors of the Longevity Dividend, a number of scientists working in the field of aging, several US Senators, their staff, and representatives from interest groups involving health, economics, and longevity. During a subsequent meeting that day between the authors of the Longevity Dividend and US Senator, Tom Harkin, it was established that Congress cannot specifically direct the National Institutes of Health (NIH) to support research on a single topic, but they can include language in the appropriations bill that guides the funding agency to channel money to scientists working in a particular area. The following language was provided to Senator Harkin, and eventually included in the 2008 appropriations bill:

> The Committee commends the (National Institute on Aging) for work it has done to improve understanding of the biological factors that regulate the processes of aging. These new discoveries have led many scientists to believe that it may become possible to postpone the onset of a wide range of fatal and disabling diseases, in a coordinated fashion, by retardation of the aging process.

It is widely understood that chronic illness is a powerful driver of medical costs, which in the United States are expected to reach $16 billion annually by 2030. To alleviate this financial burden and to develop interventions that can extend health and longevity, the Committee urges the NIH to increase dramatically its annual investment in the biological basis of aging.

At the briefing in Washington, DC the authors of the Longevity Dividend discussed how to move forward. It was determined that a successful effort to obtain funding for this idea required the understanding and support from the medical community, in addition to scientists. To help achieve this goal, an outline for a second manuscript was devised. The result of that effort was an article authored by numerous well-known scientists and physicians, including two former directors of the National Institute on Aging, and published in the *British Medical Journal* (Butler et al. 2008). The argument contained in the *BMJ* article was straightforward: if the amelioration of disease is the goal of modern medicine and public health, then one of the best ways to ensure success in the coming decades is to attack the major risk factor for all fatal and disabling diseases expressed throughout the life course—aging. This view echoes in nearly identical language the argument made more than three decades ago by Hayflick (1977). Indeed, the authors went so far as to suggest that a new model of health promotion and disease prevention for the twenty-first century should include at its foundation efforts to slow down the biological processes of aging. By getting physicians to understand and appreciate the value of aging research, the authors of the Longevity Dividend believe that the next critical step in achieving this goal would have been taken. The Alliance for Aging Research is continuing their effort to promote the Longevity Dividend by organizing conferences that include scientists involved in research on aging and politicians responsible for controlling research funds.

## Conclusions

In developed nations, the three main causes of adult mortality are heart disease, cancer, and stroke. Interventions that diagnose these conditions earlier, extend the lives of people with these diseases (i.e., declining case fatality rates), or that treat their complications more effectively (e.g., through the use of new and more effective pharmaceuticals, chemotherapy, and radiation), represent the primary way in which adult mortality has been influenced in the past. The battle against these diseases will continue, but there is reason to believe the benefits of this medical model based on attacking individual diseases independent of each other, will diminish as the survivors eventually succumb to currently immutable biological processes of aging (Butler et al. 2008). In fact, it has already been established that the complete resolution of these diseases would yield relatively small increases in life expectancy (Hayflick 1977, 2007; Olshansky et al. 1990), and it is possible that successful efforts to curtail fatal diseases could have the unintended effect of extending the period of old age as biological aging would remain uninfluenced by these efforts. A new weapon in the ongoing battle to extend the period of healthy life has presented itself—an attack on biological processes of aging.

When Neugarten and Havighurst posed the question to a group of scientists in 1977 as to whether it is appropriate to focus government resources on extending the longevity of the human species, they set in motion a debate about the future of human longevity that continues to this day. In fact, the question is more relevant now because some scientists believe that we have already achieved life extension in the laboratory for a broad range of species (e.g., fruit flies, round worms, yeast, mice, primates)—leading them to believe that at least some measure of increase in human longevity is plausible by slowing biological aging (Miller 2009; Sierra et al. 2008). Immortalists suggest that radical life extension (on the order of thousands of years, or immortality itself) should be the target for research in this area, while others claim that more modest and measurable goals are the only way to move from theory to practical interventions.

In spite of substantial differences in how to approach the extension of healthy life by slowing aging, one critical view shared by everyone with a voice in this debate is that the end result should be an extension of the period of healthy life and the avoidance of an extension of old age and its accompanying frailty and disability. Precisely how this will be achieved is as yet unknown, which means the question posed by Neugarten and Havighurst more than 30 years ago is more relevant now than it has ever been.

# References

Bartke, A. and H. Brown-Borg. 2004. "Life Extension in the Dwarf Mouse." *Current Topics in Developmental Biology* 63:189–225.

Bloom, D. and D. Canning. 2000. "The Health and Wealth of Nations." *Science* 287:1207–9.

Bloom, D.E., D.M. Canning, and J. Michael. 2004. "The Effect of Improvements in Health and Longevity on Optimal Retirement and Saving." NBER Working Paper Series w10919.

Burian, S.J., S.J. Nix, R.E. Pitt, and S.R. Durrans. 2000. "Urban Wastewater Management in the United States: Past, Present, and Future." *Journal of Urban Technology* 7(3):33–62.

Butler, R.N. 2000. "Turning Back the Clock. Has Aging Become a 'Disease' Again – To be Prevented, Treated, and Even Cured?" *Geriatrics* 55(7):11.

Butler, R.N., R.A. Miller, D. Perry, B.A. Carnes, T.F. Williams, C. Cassel, J. Brody, M.A. Bernard, L. Partridge, T. Kirkwood, G.M. Martin, and S.J. Olshansky. 2008. "New Model of Health Promotion and Disease Prevention for the 21st Century." *British Medical Journal* 337:149–50.

Carnes, B.A., D.O. Staats, W.E. Sonntag. 2008. "Does Senescence Give Rise to Disease?" *Mechanisms of Ageing and Development* 129(12):693–99.

Clements, M., et al. 2008. "Evidence for Lifespan Extension and Delayed Age-Related Biomarkers in Insulin Receptor Substrate 1 Null Mice." *Faseb Journal* 22:807–18.

de Grey, A. 2003. "The Foreseeability of Real Anti-Aging Medicine: Focusing the Debate." *Experimental Gerontology* 38(9):927–34.

de Grey, A. 2004. An Engineer's Approach to Developing Real Anti-aging Medicine. In S.G. Post and R.H. Binstock (eds.) Oxford University Press: New York, *The Fountain of Youth*, pp. 249–67.

de Grey, A. and M. Rae. 2007. *Ending Aging*. New York, NY, St. Martin's Griffin.

de Grey, A., B.N. Ames, J.K. Anderson, A. Bartke, J. Campisi C.B. Heward, R.J.M. McCarter, and G. Stock. 2002. "Time to Talk SENS: Critiquing the Immutability of Human Aging." *Annals of the New York Academy of Sciences* 959(1): 452–62.

EPA. 2000. *The History of Drinking Water Treatment*. Environmental Protection Agency, Office of Water (4606), Fact Sheet EPA-816-F-00-006, United States.

Englehardt, H.T. 1977. "Discussion." In Neugarten and Havighurst (co-eds.), Extending the Human Life Span: Social Policy and Social Ethics. National Science Foundation NSF/RA 770123, pp. 53.

Flurkey, K., J. Papaconstantinou, R.A. Miller, and D.E. Harrison. 2001. "Lifespan Extension and Delayed Immune and Collagen Aging in Mutant Mice with Defects in Growth Hormone Production." *Proceedings of the National Academy of Sciences USA* 98:6736–41.

Goddard, J.L. 1977. "Extension of the Lifespan: A National Goal?" In Neugarten and Havighurst (co-eds.), Extending the Human Life Span: Social Policy and Social Ethics. National Science Foundation NSF/RA 770123, pp. 19–26.

Greunberg, E.M. 1977. "The Failures of Success." *The Milbank Memorial Fund Quarterly* 55(1):3–24.

Gruman, G.J. 1966. "A History of Ideas About the Prolongation of Life: The Evolution of Prolongevity Hypotheses to 1800." *Transactions of the American Philosophical Society* 56(9): 1–102.

Havighurst, R.J. and G.A. Sacher. 1977. "Prospects of Lengthening Life and Vigor." In Neugarten and Havighurst (co-eds.), Extending the Human Life Span: Social Policy and Social Ethics. National Science Foundation NSF/RA 770123, pp. 13–18.

Hayflick, L. 1977. "Perspectives on Human Longevity." In Neugarten and Havighurst (co-eds.), Extending the Human Life Span: Social Policy and Social Ethics. National Science Foundation NSF/RA 770123, pp. 1–12.

Hayflick, L. 1998. "Aging is Not a Disease." *Aging* 2:146.

Hayflick, L. 2004. "Debates: The Not-So-Close Relationship Between Biological Aging and Age-Associated Pathologies in Humans." *Journal of Gerontology: Biological Sciences* 59(6):B547–B50.

Holliday, R. 1984. "The Ageing Process is a Key Problem in Biomedical Research." *Lancet* 2:1386–87.

Holliday, R. 2004. "The Close Relationship Between Biological Aging and Age-Associated Pathologies in Humans." *Journal of Gerontology: Biological Sciences* 59(6):B543–B46.

Kass, L.R. 2004. "L'Chaim and Its Limits: Why Not Immortality?" In S.G. Post and R.H. Binstock (eds.), *The Fountain of Youth: Cultural, Scientific, and Ethical Perspectives on a Biomedical Goal*, pp. 249–267. New York, NY, Oxford University Press.

Keyfitz, N. 1977. "What Difference Would it Make if Cancer Were Eradicated? An Examination of the Taeuber Paradox." *Demography* 14(4):411–18.

Kirkwood, T.B.L. 2005. "Understanding the Odd Science of Aging." *Cell* 120(4):437–47.

Kurzweil, R. 2006. *The Singularity is Near: When Humans Transcend Biology*. New York, NY, Viking.

Kurzweil, R. and T. Grossman. 2005. *Fantastic Voyage: Live Long Enough to Live Forever*. New York, NY, Plume.

McKay, C.M., F. Pope, and W. Lunsford. 1956. "Experimental Prolongation of the Life Span." *Bulletin of the New York Academy of Medicine* 32(2):91–101.

Miller, R.A. 2002. "Extending Life: Scientific Prospects and Political Obstacles." *The Milbank Quarterly* 80(1):155–74.

Miller, R.A. 2009. "'Dividends' from Research on Aging—Can Biogerontologists, at Long Last, Find Something Useful to Do?" *Journal of Gerontology: Biological Sciences, Medical Sciences* 64:157–60.

Miller, R.A., G. Buehner, Y. Chang, J.M. Harper, R. Sigler, and M. Smith-Wheelock. 2005. "Methionine-deficient Diet Extends Mouse lifespan, Slows Immune and Lens Aging, Alters Glucose, T4, IGF-I and Insulin Levels, and Increases Hepatocyte MIF Levels and Stress Resistance." *Aging Cell* 4:119–25.

Murphy, K.M. and R.H. Topel. 2006. "The Value of Health and Longevity." *Journal of Political Economy* 114(5);871–904.

Neugarten, B.L. and R.J. Havighurst. 1977. *Extending the Human Life Span: Social Policy and Social Ethics*. National Science Foundation NSF/RA 770123.

Nordhaus, W.D. 1998. *The Health of Nations: Irving Fisher and the Contribution of Improved Longevity to Living Standards*. Cowles Foundation Discussion Papers 1200, Cowles Foundation, Yale University.

Olshansky, S.J. et al. 2011. "The Global Agenda Council on the Ageing Society: Policy Principles." *Global Policy* 2(1): 97–105.

Olshansky, S.J. and B.A. Carnes. 2001. *The Quest for Immortality: Science at the Frontiers of Aging*. New York, NY, Norton.

Olshansky, S.J., B.A. Carnes, and C. Cassel. 1990. "In Search of Methuselah: Estimating the Upper Limits to Human Longevity." *Science* 250:634–40.

Olshansky, S.J., D. Perry, R.A. Miller, and R.N. Butler. 2006. "In Pursuit of the Longevity Dividend." *The Scientist* 20(3): 28–36.

Omran, A. 1971. "The Epidemiologic Transition: A Theory of the Epidemiology of Population Change." *Milbank Memorial Fund Quarterly* 49(4):509–38.

President's Council on Bioethics. 2003. *Beyond Therapy: Biotechnology and the Pursuit of Happiness*. www.bioethics.gov

Rattan, S.I.S. 2005. "Anti-ageing Strategies: Prevention or Therapy?" *EMBO Reports* 6:S25–S29.

Riley, J.C. 2001. *Rising Life Expectancy*: A Global History. Cambridge, Cambridge University Press.

Rowe, J.W., et al. 2010. "Policies and Politics of Aging for an Aging America." *Contexts* 8(4):16–21.

Sierra, F., E. Hadley, R. Suzman, and R. Hodes. 2008. "Prospects for Life Span Extension." *Annual Review of Medicine* 60:457–69.

Strehler, B. 1975. "Implications of Aging Research for Society." *Federation Proceedings* 34(1):5–8.

Vaupel, J. 2010. "Biodemography of Human Ageing." *Nature* 464:536–42.

Warner, H., J. Anderson, S. Austad, et al. 2005. "Science Fact and the SENS Agenda." *EMBO Reports* 6(11): 1106–8.

Wick, W.A. 1977. "The Aging Society and the Promise of Human Life." In Neugarten and Havighurst (co-eds.), Extending the Human Life Span: Social Policy and Social Ethics. National Science Foundation NSF/RA 770123, pp. 41–45.

# Chapter 28

# Mortality Affected by Health Care and Public Health Policy Interventions

Luc Bonneux

## Introduction

Interestingly, in the 1950s and 1960s, when medical care became truly effective, social historians tried to downplay the role of medicine in the mortality decline. These theses became particularly popular by Thomas McKeown, physician and demographic historian (McKeown 1976; McKeown and Brown 1955). He claimed that the so-called epidemiologic (or health) transition from approximately 1700 to the present had little to do with public health and medical interventions, but was prompted by social and economic changes. Relatively uncontroversial is the thesis that therapeutic care had little substantive effect on the declining mortality rates in the nineteenth and early twentieth century. There were few effective interventions available. The first antibiotics, sulfa drugs, appear only during the 1930s. McKeown contended that the improvements in population health from 1700 to 1950 were due to improvements in overall standards of living, especially diet and nutritional status, resulting from better economic conditions. This is certainly an acceptable viewpoint. But he also called into question the effectiveness of all public health, including sanitary reforms and vaccinations.

Health is embedded in a complex system, even more so public health (Szreter 2003). In a complex system, many forces can operate simultaneously, reinforcing or ameliorating each other. In the age of Enlightenment, many societal processes changed at the same time. One primary social determinant of health is empowerment of the people. The most important factor for improving population health in the nineteenth century was the growing political voice of the urban masses in Europe, who gained power and began to defend their interests (Szreter 2003). Population health in the early nineteenth century was miserable, particularly in the cities. Rising standards of living masked a great number of social and political conditions, all affecting and being affected by public health reform.

In the twentieth century, along with declining mortality from communicable diseases and maternal and perinatal mortality, mortality from "man-made, degenerative and stress related" diseases increased. This is known as "the third demographic transition" (Omran 1971, 1977). The concepts "stress-related" and "man-made" suggest a rather romantic view of history as much of the late eighteenth and early nineteenth century string of epidemics and famines can be explained by the painful transition to a liberalized market and an industrial society. Small farms and cottage industries were destroyed by early industrialization and the penniless flocked to the cities, desperately searching for employment (Szreter 2003). Stress was most likely increased by the epidemics, famines, and dreadful sewers and disgusting water supply of early nineteenth-century London.

Certainly, changes in lifestyle were important in the increase of degenerative diseases, with more sedentary occupations and increasing food for some (against a background of fetal malnutrition) (Roseboom et al. 2006; Sparen et al. 2004). By the end of World War II, there was an amazing gender difference in life expectancy in Europe and the United States. Life expectancy of women is commonly higher than that

L. Bonneux (✉)
Netherlands Interdisciplinary Demographic Institute,
The Hague, The Netherlands
e-mail: bonneux@nidi.nl

of men, but after the war, the gender gap in Europe increased rapidly. Remarkably, in women cardiovascular mortality continued to decline, while for men mortality reached a nadir in the developed countries at the end of the 1960s. In all Western European countries, life expectancy stagnated or even declined in the third quarter of the twentieth century. In the last quarter of the century, cardiovascular mortality began to decrease, first slowly, then with accelerating speed in the 1980s, and the decline continues until today in many countries. This has been called "the age of delayed degenerative disease" (Olshansky and Ault 1986), which was a slightly myopic characterization. It could be called "the age of delayed cardiovascular disease, of continuing struggle against tobacco and of impressive progress in road safety." The next sections discuss delayed cardiovascular mortality and the other avoidable causes of death.

## The Age of Delayed Cardiovascular Disease

Cardiovascular diseases (CVD) are the main cause of death in the European Union (EU), and other developed countries (Huisman et al. 2009; Mathers and Loncar 2006). They account for 42% of all deaths in the EU. Diseases of the circulatory system are more common at advanced ages: 81% of male deaths and 94% of female deaths due to this disease are older than 65 years. Deaths from ischemic heart and from cerebrovascular diseases make up two thirds of all cardiovascular deaths. Other heart diseases are often related to ischemic disease and lethal peripheral vascular diseases, such as aortic aneurysms and renal vascular disease, and share the same causes. The human species is vulnerable in the make-up of blood vessels, and many causes of death and disease share degenerative atherosclerotic changes of the blood vessel wall as their main cause.

There is little doubt that a sedentary lifestyle and diets rich in animal fats and calories are an important factor in the causation of atherosclerotic disease. Coronary heart disease, the most important cause of fatal circulatory disease, was rare in traditional agricultural societies where diets rich in animal fats are less available and food is won by hard manual labor. As a medical doctor in tropical rural Africa, I witnessed many strokes but never saw one case of angina pectoris or ischemic heart disease (IHD). While Hippocrates described stroke as a disease 2,400 years ago, the first report of angina pectoris, describing 20 cases, was published more than 2,000 years later by William Heberden in 1772 in the Transactions of the Royal College. Data and theories explaining these apparent historic disparities between stroke and acute coronary heart disease in developing countries are rare, as is all etiological research of non-communicable diseases in low-income countries (Feigin et al. 2009). The incidence of coronary heart disease is increasing sharply and moving up to the second position as cause of death in lower income countries, with stroke mortality being fifth according to the World Health Organization (WHO; http://www.who.int/mediacentre/factsheets/fs310_2008.pdf). These WHO estimates, while based on expert consensus, may be biased by disease advocacy. A careful systematic review showed that stroke mortality, while declining in high-income countries, is increasing dramatically in low- and middle-income countries (Feigin et al. 2009). Lower population income has been shown to be the best predictor of higher population stroke mortality, better than the prevalence rates of traditional risk factors, except for blood pressure (Johnston et al. 2009). The relationship between high blood pressure and stroke is stronger in lower income than higher income countries (Eastern Stroke and Coronary Heart Disease Collaborative Research Group 1998; Kisjanto et al. 2005). In low-income countries, over- and under-nutrition coexist, and both high and low body mass indexes (BMI) are risk factors for stroke (Johnston et al. 2009). Weaker healthcare systems play an important role in explaining high stroke mortality in low-income countries. Case fatality is higher in lower income countries where diabetes and hypertension are more poorly managed (Feigin et al. 2009).

Socioeconomic factors such as a less education, lower income, and unemployment also contribute significantly to the risk of vascular mortality (Brunner 1997). Gender is also related in that women reach a given level of disease at an older age than men. The reasons for the relatively lower risks of women are many, including gender differences in physiology. As indicated above, the mortality gap between genders increased in the twentieth century; differential tobacco use by men and women explained part of that increasing gap (Peto et al. 1992). The male disadvantage in mortality is particularly high in the former socialist economies of Europe, with life expectancy differences by gender of 10 years and more (Huisman et al. 2009). Most of these differences can be explained by differences in tobacco use (high lung cancer mortality), alcohol use (high alcohol-related mortality and alcohol associated chronic liver disease, high injury, and road traffic accident mortality), and hopelessness (high levels of suicide) (Huisman et al. 2009). Part of the explanation is that men seem more vulnerable to social disruption, unemployment, and lack of perspective (Brunner 1997).

Mortality from IHD has decreased spectacularly in the Western world beginning in the fourth quarter of the previous century and is even more rapid in the recent period. In the United States, coronary heart disease mortality halved in the period 1980–2000 (Ford et al. 2007). The reasons for these declines are many and the relative contributions are arguable (see Table 28.1), but the general picture is one of shared progress, both in prevention and therapy with a growing contribution from evidence-based medical therapies. Lifestyle changes were also important explanations of this decline, predominantly smoking cessation and the switch to diets with less saturated fat. Obviously, the obesity epidemic is now counteracting these changes. However, significant gain has been accomplished in managing cardiovascular risk.

Understanding this mortality decline requires knowledge of multiple concurrent trends. Societal changes lowered heart disease risk as advances were made in reducing the smoking epidemic. Cardiovascular risk management through drug usage targeted the remaining risks, with increasing effectiveness. Antihypertensives were used to reduce blood pressure and statins to reduce cholesterol levels. Aspirin usage also increased. The originally poor prognosis for acute myocardial infarctions, by far the most important cause of cardiovascular death and the most important of all causes of death, improved tremendously through new treatment approaches. The long-term prognosis improved through new drugs and increasingly effective smoking cessation in heart disease patients. Prognosis in congestive heart failure, the common endpoint of most heart disease, improved considerably by employing evidence-based treatments. Heart health booked successes at all stages: primary, secondary, and tertiary prevention as well as sharply lowering case fatality.

Explaining the mortality decline involves understanding the roles of many societal institutions. Epidemiological research discovered the major determinants of IHD, the primary drivers of the cardiovascular disease epidemic. Public health professionals started health promotion campaigns. Although the effectiveness of these campaigns has been questioned, smoking among men dropped steeply in the 1970s, followed a decade later by dropping lung cancer rates and concomitant decreases in IHD. Pharmaceutical research manufactured safe and effective drugs to

**Table 28.1** Quantified causes of the coronary heart disease mortality decline in the United States between 1980 and 2000

| | | |
|---|---|---|
| All risk factors: over all change explained | | +44% |
| Reductions in mortality by risk factor change | | +61% |
| – Total cholesterol (partly related to cholesterol-lowering therapies) | 24% | |
| – Systolic blood pressure (partly related to blood pressure lowering therapies) | 20% | |
| – Smoking prevalence (modest contribution of smoking cessation therapies) | 12% | |
| – Physical inactivity | 5% | |
| Increases in mortality by risk factor change | | −17% |
| + Increases in BMI | 8% | |
| + Increases in diabetes mellitus | 10% | |
| Therapeutic innovation: all change explained | | +47% |
| – Secondary preventive therapies in clinical heart disease, including drugs, percutaneous and surgical interventions | 16% | |
| – Initial treatment of acute coronary events by drugs or interventions | 11% | |
| – Treatment for heart failure | 9% | |
| – Diverse other therapies | 12% | |

Source: Ford et al. (2007).

manage CVD risks. First blood pressure lowering therapies became increasingly widely used and later statins, the cholesterol-lowering drugs that were most effective in lowering CVD mortality of thrombotic origins. Aspirin, β-blockers, and, increasingly, surgical and procedural interventions improved prognosis for patients with clinical heart disease. Case-fatality rates of acute myocardial infarctions were high, but therapeutic advances in the treatment of acute and chronic coronary heart disease lowered the mortality risks (Briffa et al. 2009). Societal changes pushed the powerful tobacco industry slowly but relentlessly into a defensive mode.

Table 28.1 summarizes causes attributed to reductions in coronary heart disease (CHD) mortality in the United States. It should be noted that changes in risk factors are partly due to medical innovation and partly to lifestyle changes, including smoking cessation. The same risk factor changes also decreased the risk of stroke; while therapeutic progress in stroke has remained limited. In the non-Western world, cardiovascular heart disease mortality in general, and CHD in particular, is increasing for the same reasons as mortality increased historically in the West: increased smoking and an increasingly sedentary lifestyle with diets rich in calories and animal fats (Joshi et al. 2007; Mathers and Loncar 2006).

## Lowering Cardiovascular Risk

Numerous factors increase cardiovascular risk; and some reduce risk. But more than 90% of all population attributable risk for acute myocardial infarction can be accounted for by a limited set of easy-to-measure risk factors (Yusuf et al. 2004). These risk factors are ranked according to their importance using the results of the landmark INTERHEART study. Although a case-control study, its results were comparable to many prospective studies and it covered at least 52 countries, offering a worldwide vista of cardiovascular risk.

1. Raised ApoB/ApoA1 ratio (blood apolipoproteins; odds ratio (OR) 3.25 for top versus lowest quintile, population attributable risk (PAR) 49.2% for top four quintiles versus lowest quintile). ApoB/ApoA1 ratios perform better at predicting cardiovascular risk than traditional cholesterol measures. This is true at all ages, for both sexes, and among all ethnic groups (McQueen et al. 2008).
2. Smoking (OR 2.87 for current versus never smokers, PAR 35.7% for current and former versus never). For these calculations current smoking was defined as any tobacco use in the previous 12 months. Former smokers were defined as those who had quit more than a year earlier.
3. Psychosocial factors (OR 2.67, PAR 32.5%). These included depression, locus of control, perceived stress, and adverse major life events (Rosengren et al. 2004). Stress was indexed by questions about feeling irritable, being filled with anxiety, or having sleeping difficulties as a result of conditions at work or at home. Major life events were defined as marital separation or divorce, loss of job or retirement, loss of crop or business failure, violence, major conflicts, injury, illness or death of the person or a close family member.
4. Abdominal obesity (OR 1.12 for top versus lowest tertile and 1.62 for middle versus lowest tertile, PAR 20.1% for top two tertiles versus lowest tertile). BMI is related to risk of myocardial infarction, but this relation is weaker than that of abdominal obesity (waist/hip ratio), and becomes non-significant after controlling for abdominal obesity.
5. History of hypertension (1.91, PAR 17.9%). Only self-reported history of hypertension was used in this analysis. This may be an underestimate of the role of hypertension.
6. Diabetes (2.37, PAR 9.9%), also indicated by self report.
7. Regular alcohol consumption (0.91, PAR 6.7%), defined as alcohol consumption at least three times a week.
8. Regular physical activity (0.86, PAR 12.2%). Individuals were judged to be physically active if they were regularly involved in moderate (walking, cycling, or gardening) or strenuous (jogging, football, and vigorous swimming) exercise for 4 hours or more a week.

These associations were noted in men and women, old and young, and in all regions of the world. Collectively, these nine risk factors accounted for 90% of the PAR for acute myocardial infarction in men and 94% in women.

## Hypertension

Persistent hypertension is one of the main risk factors for strokes, heart attacks, heart failure, arterial aneurysms, and renal failure. Even moderate elevation of arterial pressure leads to shortened life expectancy.

Factors increasing the risk of hypertension include age, salt sensitivity, and obesity. More than 85% of all cases of hypertension occur in overweight individuals (or those with a BMI of 25 or more). The risk is five times higher in the obese as compared to those of normal weight and up to two thirds of cases can be attributed to excess weight (Haslam and James 2005). Approximately one third of the essential hypertensive population is responsive to sodium intake (Frost et al. 1991; Law et al. 1991). The increased sodium stimulates individuals to increase their water intake and the kidneys into retaining water, thereby augmenting volume and pressure.

The relationship between high blood pressure and cardiovascular complications is clear and unambiguous: increasing blood pressure increases risk. This risk increases at all levels, without a threshold. The main complication of hypertension in middle-aged European and American people is CHD, whereas in Asian and older people it is stroke (Staessen et al. 2003). Black individuals tend to have higher blood pressure and hypertension-related mortality rates than other individuals. There is no doubt that lowering high blood pressure levels is good for your health. Every millimeter of lowered blood pressure for those with high blood pressure results in equal health benefit, whether the reduction results from drug or lifestyle change (Staessen et al. 2001).

Behavioral interventions affecting hypertension include increasing physical activity, a calorie restricted diet rich in fruit and vegetables and moderately restricted in salt (strict salt restriction is not sustainable). However, blood pressure lowering drugs are the most effective means of reducing hypertension in those with high blood pressure. Stroke mortality has been declining for some time. However, when calculated quantitatively, the portion of the decline explained by antihypertensive treatment was modest (Bonita and Beaglehole 1989; Niessen et al. 1993; Tuomilehto et al. 1991), yet tangible and important. The best estimates suggest that one third of the mortality decline could be explained by lowered prevalence rates of smoking and increased uptake of antihypertensive medications. A smaller part might be explained by improving case-fatality rates. These are hard to interpret as improved case detection diagnosed more benign cases of strokes, which previously remained hidden, but that carry a better prognosis. Specific treatment options remained limited, but the overall effect of aspecific, general improvements in knowledge and care was crucial (Niessen et al. 1993; Peeters et al. 2003b).

Mean blood pressure and the prevalence of hypertension has been declining since the 1950s (Antikainen et al. 2006; Burt et al. 1995). While this is attributed to increasing awareness and treatment, evidence to document this is lacking. Healthier foods, salt reduction, improved preservation practices, and generally better living conditions all may have contributed. Given the strong correlation between BMI and hypertension, increases in blood pressure and incidence of hypertension likely will follow increasing trends in BMI (Fields et al. 2004; Hajjar and Kotchen 2003).

## Cholesterol and the Lipoproteins

Although the role of hypertension on CVD is clear, researchers have debated the risk for CVD related to cholesterol over the last 50 years. A platform summarizing the evidence against the cholesterol hypothesis is the *International Network of Cholesterol Skeptics* (www.thincs.org/). To summarize the debate: total cholesterol levels have an exponential relationship with CHD, but a U-shaped relationship with all-cause mortality. At lower levels of cholesterol, all-cause mortality increases. The proponents of the cholesterol hypothesis declare the exponential relationship with heart disease causal and the U-shaped relationship spurious, a consequence of declining cholesterol levels because of disease. The skeptics believe that the increased mortality at lower levels of cholesterol is causal, but the increased mortality at higher levels of cholesterol spurious, a consequence of cholesterol as a marker not a determinant of risk. There is no debate that CHD risks go up with increasing cholesterol levels. The question relates to interventions: does lowering cholesterol reduce CHD mortality and all-cause mortality? What is the evidence that cholesterol-lowering diets and drugs lower heart disease?

In familial hypercholesterolemia, genetic variants cause increased cholesterol levels and increased levels of heart disease. A systematic review found no evidence that a cholesterol-lowering diet is effective at lowering cholesterol and reducing IHD (Poustie and Rutherford 2001). The dietary improvements recommended center on the reduction of salt and fat intake and an increase in the intake of fruit, vegetables, and fiber. A review that evaluated the effectiveness of dietary advice in reducing cholesterol (Brunner et al. 2007) found 38 trials in which healthy adults were randomly assigned to receive dietary advice or no dietary advice. Modest improvements were shown in the treatment groups in cardiovascular risk factors, such as blood pressure and total and LDL-cholesterol levels. The trials did not last long enough to answer the question of whether the beneficial changes in cardiovascular risk factors resulted in a reduced incidence of heart disease, stroke, or heart attack. Diets that reduced modified dietary fat for prevention of heart disease found a small but potentially important reduction in cardiovascular risk in trials lasting longer than 2 years; however, they found no effect on all-cause mortality (Hooper et al. 2001). Cholesterol-lowering trials with diet or drugs other than statins showed modest and poorly understood increases in injury mortality (suicide and accidents) (Hooper et al. 2001; Muldoon et al. 2001). A "meta-meta-analysis" that reviewed all meta-analyses published on cholesterol reduction before 1995 found that the results of a meta-analysis depend on the inclusion criteria of the study and the "characteristics of the investigator" (Katerndahl and Lawler 1999). Overall, the meta-meta-analysis satisfied both parties in the cholesterol wars: cholesterol reduction was most strongly related to decreased non-fatal CVD event rates, modestly related to decreased mortality from all cardiovascular causes and not related to decreased all-cause mortality (Katerndahl and Lawler 1999).

## Statins

The cholesterol wars became history with the appearance of statin drugs in the late 1980s and the early 1990s. The first publications indicating the effects of statins date from 1976 (Endo 2008; Endo et al. 1976). In 1980, the therapeutic effect in patients with familial hypercholesterolemia was demonstrated (Yamamoto et al. 1980). The "4 S trial" showed that statin use was safe and highly effective in patients with clinical heart disease and high cholesterol levels (Scandinavian Simvastatin Survival Study (4S) 1994; Strandberg et al. 2004). Evidence-based medicine became linked to evidence-based marketing as the market of wealthy persons with moderate hypercholesterolemia is enormous. The weapons used to conquer the hearts and minds of first cardiologists, then all medical doctors, were randomized controlled trials. There is substantial evidence and little debate that statins work and are safe. They are effective in people with CHD (LaRosa et al. 1999), stroke (Amarenco et al. 2004), and diabetes (Kearney et al. 2008), and in the elderly (Roberts et al. 2007); they are effective as primary prevention in healthy people (Mills et al. 2008). They seem to improve bone mineral density (Uzzan et al. 2007), may prevent melanoma (Dellavalle et al. 2005), and although not yet clinically demonstrated, may lower the risk of dementia (Hoglund and Blennow 2007).

After statins became available, active treatment of hypercholesterolemia became (almost) universally considered to be good medical practice. Statins not only revolutionized cardiovascular risk management, but they also revolutionized the traditional cholesterol hypothesis. Statins reduced cardiovascular event rates within weeks after initiation of therapy, long before any LDL reduction could have reduced the atheromas in the vessel wall and reduced disease. Statins did show minor effects on atheromas, the accumulation of fat in debris in the vessel wall. The cholesterol skeptics were quick to point out that statins worked not because but in spite of lowering cholesterol levels. In addition, the unexpected side effects of statins were positive. Statins have beneficial effects on inflammation, thrombosis, platelet aggregation, immunomodulation, and endothelial function (Shaw et al. 2009).

Statins have proven to be highly effective in reducing all CVD event rates with thrombotic origin. The fear of increased cancer risks did not materialize, and the known adverse side effects (cognitive changes and muscle weakness in the elderly) are either minor or hard to prove. Statins lower all-cause mortality as expected from reductions in cardiovascular mortality. In contrast to other cholesterol-lowering interventions, this suggests that the hazard of death from non-cardiovascular mortality should remain unchanged. In primary prevention, all-cause mortality is lowered by 8%, which is still marginally insignificant (Mills et al.

2008). As the absolute risk of death is rather low in primary prevention, statistical significance does not equate with clinical significance.

## *Mass Chemoprofylaxis of Heart Disease*

Statins are very effective for large portions of the population. In the short and medium term, in middle-aged populations, they have few side effects that are generally easily managed. This success has raised the idea of mass treatment for the entire population with the "risk pill" that lowers CVD risk. This idea was extended to extremes with the "poly pill," a pill combining a statin, three blood pressure lowering drugs (a diuretic, a beta blocker, and an angiotensin converting enzyme inhibitor), each at half standard dose; folic acid (0.8 mg); and aspirin (75 mg) (Wald and Law 2003). The authors conveniently assumed multiplicative interactions of all benefits of all these drugs and no harmful effects. However, three blood pressure lowering medications and aspirin for healthy persons at low risk might mean that the benefits of a polypill are unlikely to supersede the harm. The idea of "more than 80% reduction of cardiovascular mortality," however, captured the imagination. We responded in a special issue of the *British Medical Journal* that publishes papers with the intent "to make you think, to make you laugh, to make you think again." Our satire, only partly in jest, about the "polydiet," mixed many dietary compounds and multiplied the effects in a multiplicative model resulting in the elimination of cardiovascular mortality (Franco et al. 2004).

Management of risk based on 10-year absolute risk for CVD events or death has become the cornerstone of diagnosing need for treatment (Califf et al. 1996; Graham et al. 2007; Haq et al. 1995; Standing Medical Advisory Committee 1997). People at the highest risks have enjoyed the greatest benefits. But in a life course, reduction of the risk of death means postponing not averting death. Postponing age-related disorders, or increasing the age at which they occur, has more or less the same effect, regardless of prior risk. If effects persist lifelong, nonsmokers save more life years than smokers, but at older ages (Bonneux 2000). For any combination of risk factors such as lipid and blood pressure levels, diabetes, smoking or a family history, absolute risk level can be determined and related to age. Those at high risk reach a given risk level at an early age; those at low risk reach that risk level at a later age. There are few ethical objections to this. The problem arises from the added healthcare costs, and the tradeoffs between treating the healthy against the consequences of progressing age and caring for the disabled and treating the diseased who are at high risk of death. Statins in primary prevention reduce all-cause mortality rates by 7% (Mills et al. 2008). Applying this reduction to the Dutch life table of 2008, 30 years of treatment (from age 50 until 80) would increase life expectancy by 5 months for men and 4 months for women. This is not a minor effect. The interesting ethics question is then, do we wish to reduce risk by pills or by healthier lifestyles, such as smoking cessation, better diets, and increased physical activity? Furthermore, in social welfare systems, who pays for risk intervention?

## Smoking

Smoking dwarfs all other risky behaviors in compromising health and increasing the risk of death (Table 28.2). The US Surgeon General concludes that smoking affects nearly all human non-communicable diseases (US Department of Health and Human Services 2004). Smoking works as a general "aging agent," harming every organ. It is particularly deleterious for what German researchers in the Third Reich called "the Rauchstrasse," the smoking street (mouth, pharynx, larynx, and lung). German researchers under the Third Reich were the first to discover and collect evidence demonstrating the disastrous health consequences of smoking. But after World War II, the sad and terrible heritage of public health under the Nazis overshadowed the value of any scientific research (Proctor 1996, 2001).

This adverse effect of smoking is related to the amount of tobacco smoked daily and to the duration of smoking. The best measure of tobacco exposure is "pack-years," packages per day smoked during past years. The effects of smoking on CVD interact synergistically with other CVD risk factors such as age, gender, arterial hypertension, and diabetes (Graham et al. 2007).

There are many ways to calculate smoking attributable mortality. Formally, you need the population

**Table 28.2** Diseases considered to be caused by smoking by the U.S. Surgeon General

| Cancer | Cardiovascular diseases | Respiratory diseases | Reproductive effects | Other |
|---|---|---|---|---|
| Bladder | Atherosclerosis | Chronic obstructive lung disease | Fetal death and stillbirth | Low bone density and hip fractures |
| Cervix uteri | Abdominal aortic aneurysm | Pneumonia | Fertility | Cataract |
| Esophagus | Stroke | | Low birth weight | Peptic ulcer disease |
| Kidney | Coronary heart disease | | | |
| Larynx | | | | |
| Leukemia | | | | |
| Lung | | | | |
| Mouth and pharynx | | | | |
| Pancreas | | | | |
| Stomach | | | | |

Source: US Department of Health and Human Services (2004).

structure, age-specific mortality by cause of death, age-specific relative risks, and prevalence rates of smoking-related diseases. But current prevalence is not the best estimate of smoking exposure. Time lags between smoking and the various target diseases vary. For IHD, these time lags are short, but for lung cancer and chronic obstructive lung disease, the time lags are long and may go back decades. Further, the effects vary by intensity. Women may run lower risks than men because they are less addicted, smoke less, and quit for pregnancies.

The elegant method developed by Peto et al. (1992) does not require information on historical smoking prevalence as lung cancer mortality in developed nations is a proxy for smoking intensity. In developed countries, nearly all lung cancer is smoking-related. Lung cancer as a cause of death is reliably recorded. The ratio between the observed lung cancer mortality and the expected lung cancer mortality in non-exposed smokers, calculated from very large epidemiological studies, replaces smoking prevalence as a more reliable proxy of the historical smoking exposition leading to clinical disease. Based on the relative risks for all other smoking-related diseases, from the same studies, the numbers of deaths from all other smoking-related causes are then attributed to the excess numbers of lung cancer deaths.

On average smoking is said to kill one out of two smokers. If smokers had not smoked, their mortality would be halved. A 50% reduction in all-cause mortality of non-communicable degenerative disorders would be linked to a life expectancy 5 years longer. Some studies show even more loss of life: smoking kills more often at middle age when the relative risks are higher than 2 (Doll et al. 1994; Peto 1994). In the Framingham Heart Study, persistent smokers lived 8.7 years (men) and 7.6 years (women) less than nonsmokers (Mamun et al. 2004; Peeters et al. 2003a). It is also true that people who took up smoking after the 1970s were well aware of the risks of smoking and they may also share other risky lifestyles that could explain their 1–2 year greater reduction in life expectancy (Peto et al. 1992). Mr. David Goerlitz, a former model who had appeared in ads for the R.J. Reynolds Tobacco Company, asked Reynolds executives at a session "Don't any of you smoke?" One of them shook his head. "Are you kidding? We reserve that right for the poor, the young, the black and the stupid" (Herbert 1993). Poor, black, and less-educated persons are known to have shorter life expectancies, even after adjusting for smoking, obesity, and other known risky lifestyles (Mackenbach et al. 2008).

By far the best behavioral intervention for reducing CVD is stopping smoking. Quitting smoking is even more important as age and smoking history increase. The cumulative risk of lung cancer among nonsmokers is very low, lower than 0.5% (Peto et al. 2000). The cumulative risk of death from lung cancer by age 75 was 16% at 1990 rates in male cigarette smokers, and 10% in female cigarette smokers (generally because women smokers smoke less). For men who stopped at ages 60, 50, 40, and 30, the cumulative risks of lung cancer by age 75 were 10, 6, 3, and 2% (Peto et al. 2000). If we extrapolate the lung cancer risks to all-cause mortality, this would correspond to savings of 3, 4, 5 and 6 years of life expectancy. Quitting smoking confers health benefits even among the oldest old through immediate effects of tobacco smoking on CVD mortality, mediated by nicotine and carbon monoxide (CO).

## Anti-tobacco Strategies

Because of the important effect of tobacco smoking on health, all strategies that are effective in reducing tobacco use have a large health impact. Originally, anti tobacco activity was motivated by moral principles. The powerful public health campaigns of Nazi Germany against tobacco smoking were based on sound medical and epidemiological observations, but added racist and nationalist hygiene arguments. The Aryan race had a duty to be healthy: the men for fighting, the women for breeding. While smoking was frowned upon, the cigarette remained a trusted friend of the soldier in harsh conditions and Hitler did not try to eliminate smoking in the army. But while the racist hygiene arguments were immoral, they saved many German young women from smoking. Lung cancer rates in the German female cohorts born around the 1930s are amongst the lowest in Europe (Proctor 1999).

After World War II, the movement to reduce tobacco use increased in strength through the accumulating knowledge of the health risks posed by tobacco use. Despite overwhelming evidence of the adverse health consequences of smoking, the norm of male smoking in the United States and Europe has receded slowly, in part because of the continued promotion of smoking by tobacco companies that work synergistically with tobacco-addicted smokers who do not want to believe their addiction is lethal (US Surgeon General 2000). However, it is important to note that, even in the face of the stepped up propaganda from the tobacco industry, the prevalence of smoking started decreasing in the 1960s, a decrease that sped up in the 1970s, largely as an effect of health education. Male smokers became a minority and health advocates focused on the prevention of harm to nonsmokers, particularly of children (US Surgeon General 2006).

While smoking is an individual choice, inhaling environmental tobacco smoke is not. Norms have changed and smoking is increasingly becoming socially unacceptable, regarded as annoying and harmful to others. The epidemiology of passive smoking is less convincing than often suggested, a consequence of the impossibility of discerning small relative risks against a large background of noise, associated with poverty, education, occupational class, and other risk factors (Bonneux and Coebergh 2004). However, there is ample evidence that environmental tobacco smoke contains many carcinogens, that active smoking increases all cancer risks threefold, and that people exposed to environmental tobacco smoke have nicotine metabolites in their blood. There is no need for more evidence: EU laws regulating health at the workplace impose regulation of occupational exposures using a perspective of "ALARA (as low as reasonably achievable)." ALARA of environmental tobacco smoke is obviously a smoke-free environment. Strict laws prohibiting smoking in the workplace and in public places affect smoking prevalence rates and assist people in deciding to quit or not to start. The economically powerful tobacco industry used multiple means to fight against many laws and regulations, but lost many crucial cases.

Given the tremendous health consequences of smoking, nearly all strategies that succeed in effectively lowering smoking are cost-effective if they are not terribly expensive. Efforts at reducing smoking fall in two categories: lowering uptake of smoking in the young and helping smokers quit. As in tuberculosis treatment or HIV-AIDS prevention, where single drugs promote resistance and are not very effective, single programs are less effective than multiple approaches. The statements below summarize the findings presented in the report of the US Surgeon General on reducing tobacco use (US Surgeon General 2000).

## Lowering Uptake of Smoking

Educational strategies, conducted in conjunction with community- and media-based activities, can postpone or prevent smoking onset in 20–40% of adolescents. More effective school programs are part of the standard curriculum and cooperate with parents, mass media, and other community resources to lower the attractiveness of smoking, promoted by the industry (US Surgeon General 2000).

Regulatory efforts have been less effective, partly because they have been less well enforced. Because most people take up smoking in adolescence, a minor's access to tobacco should be reduced as much as possible. Successful measures include enforcing minimum age laws and requiring licensure of tobacco retailers. Licensure provides an incentive to obey the law when revocation of the license is a consequence of selling tobacco to minors.

The price of tobacco has an important influence on the demand for tobacco products, particularly among young people who are not yet addicted. Increasing the "sin taxes" on cigarettes would have a considerable impact on the prevalence of smoking and, in the long term, reduce the adverse health effects caused by tobacco. However, higher taxes may increase poverty in addicted smokers. The money gained from "sin taxes" should be used to finance smoking cessation programs.

Numerous attempts to regulate advertising and promotion of tobacco products have had only modest success, often because the advertising departments of the tobacco industry were more creative in subverting these efforts. All tobacco advertising and sponsorship on television has been banned within the EU since 1991, but this leads to very successful—from the point of view of the tobacco industry—sponsoring of attractive sports and cultural events directed at the young. Bans on sponsoring these events lead to widespread protests (and more unwelcome publicity), and because of massive increases in budgets, these events had become largely dependent on tobacco sponsorship and needed to downsize after the ban. Sports that were largely sponsored by tobacco industries included Formula 1 racing, NASCAR races, snooker, golf, tennis, and darts. Snooker, Formula 1, and golf tournaments needed a dispensation to be able to adapt to the sponsorship ban (http://en.wikipedia.org/wiki/Tobacco_advertising, accessed 05 February 2009) (Fig. 28.1).

EU legislation and most national legislations now foresee a blanket ban on all future promotion, publicity, and sponsoring. In 2009 US legislation prohibited radio ads, television commercials, event sponsoring, promotional giveaways, and other types of brand advertising, as well as in-store product displays. Product placement promoting "light" or "ultra light" tobacco products is forbidden in the EU, as it fools consumers into believing that these are safer.

Clean indoor regulations are only effective if they foresee a smoking ban. While they protect nonsmokers from environmental tobacco smoke, they protect smokers even more, by reducing intensity of smoking and promoting cessation efforts.

In the long term, tobacco production must be reduced. Economic investments in programs that help tobacco farmers to diversify and change to healthier crops are effective in reducing tobacco production and minimizing economic pressure.

## Alcohol Use

Alcohol consumption is both harmful and protective of mortality. Although drinking prevalence rates are relatively high in most more developed countries, some religions prohibit their members from drinking both because it is considered wrong and because of the dreadful consequences of alcoholism. Indeed, the traditional puritan heritage led to prohibition and later to strict alcohol laws in the United States.

In observational studies, alcohol lowers CVD and all-cause mortality (Klatsky and Udaltsova 2007). The now common U-shaped (or J-shaped) relationship, demonstrating increased mortality among heavy alcohol use and abstainers, was first identified by Pearl in 1926. Most scientific associations recommend mild alcohol use (http://www.health.gov/dietaryguidelines/dga2005/document/html/chapter9.htm), but do not recommend starting drinking to improve health. However, alcohol use has not been subjected to randomized clinical trials and light and moderate drinkers often engage in healthier lifestyles, in addition to their moderate alcohol consumption. Further, abstainers also include people with past or current histories of alcoholism. Ecologically, there is a close correlation between the amount of alcohol consumed and alcohol-related harm and alcohol dependence. Nevertheless, light to moderate alcohol use is associated with reduced CHD; it also causes pleasure and enjoyment. Prohibition in the United States and the failed War on Drugs show that unbalanced anti-alcohol policies or drug enforcements have large hidden costs, rarely taken into account in cost-effectiveness analyses.

**Fig. 28.1** Publicity for Marlboro at Formula 1 races. Source: From Wikipedia (public domain)

The lower mortality risk associated with lighter drinking is attributable to lower risk of CHD and other atherothrombotic vascular conditions. Substantial evidence exists for several plausible biological mechanisms for protection by alcohol against CHD (Klatsky and Udaltsova 2007). Lower CHD mortality is even observed in heavy drinkers, which argues against confounding. The size of the relative protection alcohol confers against CHD makes the effect of alcohol use dependent on CHD epidemiology. If CHD mortality is higher, the relative positive effect due to alcohol use will be larger. In developed countries, the effects of alcohol consumption on CHD will be greatest in middle and old ages.

While some deaths are attributed to alcohol use (e.g., alcohol poisoning), most alcohol-related mortality is linked to other causes of death. Using an elegant case-control design, Zaridze et al. (2009) estimated the relative risks of alcohol-related mortality in Russian cities among heavy drinkers (equivalent to three or more bottles of vodka per week), compared to mild drinkers (less than half a bottle vodka a week). Fewer women were heavy drinkers, but those who were had extremely high risks of death from alcohol-related causes. The highest risks were found for alcohol poisoning (RR 27.1 for men, 75.2 for women) and accidents and violence (5.9 for men, 9.3 for women), although many other causes were elevated including road traffic accidents, homicide, suicides and falls, tuberculosis, pneumonia, pancreas, and liver disease (Zaridze et al. 2009). As in other studies, cancers most notably linked to alcohol use were in the liver (2.1 and 1.6) and the upper aerodigestive tract (3.5 and 2.2). Cancers often attributed to alcohol use (breast cancer and colorectal cancer) are likely caused by the excess calorie intake induced by alcohol, and not directly related to alcohol (in this study, the effect of alcohol use was predominantly protective). Mortality from acute IHD showed relative risks of 3.0 among men and 9.3 among women. In the three Russian cities, more than half of all the deaths between ages 15 and 54 were caused by alcohol use.

In the EU comparisons between new member states (nearly all former socialist economies before the fall of the Berlin Wall) and the EU-15 (the "old" European Union, mostly market economies since World War II), the difference in life expectancy was 6 years for men and 4 years for women (Huisman et al. 2009). Among men, 0.8 years of the difference was explained by smoking-related cancers and respiratory disease, 1.4 years by accident- and alcohol-related mortality, and 3.8 years by CVD. Among women, only cardiovascular mortality appeared different, accounting for a loss of life expectancy of 3.9 years.

Alcohol addiction has a stronger effect on persons in the younger ages and the poor (Rehm et al. 2009). In poorer populations, heavy episodic or binge drinking is more common and very harmful (Anderson et al. 2009). In low- and middle-income countries where CHD mortality is lower, the protective effect of alcohol is lower too. Direct morbidity and mortality from alcohol use are compounded by severe indirect morbidity from family disruptions and from the high economic costs due to lost productivity (Rehm et al. 2009).

## *Effectiveness of Policies to Reduce the Harm Caused by Alcohol*

Box 28.1. summarizes the effectiveness of alcohol control programs (Anderson et al. 2009). There is good evidence that policies regulating the marketing of alcohol, its price and availability, are effective in reducing alcohol-related harm. Most effective in reducing the harm of road traffic accidents are enforced legislative measures to reduce drink driving. Individually directed measures to at-risk drinkers are effective too.

### Box 28.1. Overview of effective policies limiting the harm of alcohol use

- Education and information
    - School-based education showed some positive effects of increased knowledge, but no sustained effect on behavior change.
    - Parenting programs showed reductions of alcohol use in six out of 14 programs.
    - Social marketing programs showed some significant effects in the short term (up to 12 months).
    - Health warnings noted some effects on intentions to change drinking behavior, but no effect on actual behavior change.

- Health sector response
    - Brief advice noted a positive effect on alcohol consumption and many alcohol-related endpoints.
    - Cognitive behavioral therapies for alcohol dependence are effective
    - Benzodiazepines, glutamate inhibitors and opiate antagonists for the treatment of withdrawal or dependence are effective.

- Community programs
    - Evidence is limited.

- Drink driving policies
    - Introduction and/or reduction of alcohol concentration in the blood while driving decreases alcohol-related fatal traffic accidents.
    - Sobriety checkpoints and random breath testing decreases alcohol-related fatal traffic accidents.
    - Restrictions on young and inexperienced drivers (e.g., lower concentrations of alcohol in blood of novice drivers) are moderately effective.
    - Mandatory treatment for alcohol dependence reduced recurrence of drunk-driving offences and reduced alcohol-related accidents.
    - Alcohol locks were moderately effective in reducing recurrence of alcohol-related offences, but only while present.

- Addressing the availability
    - Government policies are effective in reducing the availability of alcohol.
    - Minimum purchase age is effective in reducing youth drinking and alcohol-related harms, particularly road traffic accidents.
    - Reductions in hours of sale reduce consumption and harm.

> - Addressing the marketing of alcoholic beverages
>   o Advertising increases youth initiation and alcohol consumption among current users (evidence of harm). Self-regulation is not effective and does not prevent types of marketing that can affect young people.
>   o Alcohol taxation is effective.
>
> Source: Anderson et al. (2009).

## Avoidable Mortality

Causes of avoidable mortality highlight those causes of death that are considered amenable to medical or policy interventions (see also Chapter 23 by Beltrán-Sánchez, this volume). The idea was pioneered by Rutstein (Rutstein et al. 1976) for use as an indicator of the performance of health care. Some causes of death are partly avoidable through medical interventions, others are not. Lists of avoidable mortality contain a level of medical consensus but vary somewhat by author, indicating possible variance in interpretations about what is avoidable and, if avoidable, by how much. Effective medicine will lower but not eliminate the risk of most avoidable causes of death. The Global Burden of Disease Project (GBD) shows the variance in major causes of death over the world (Lopez et al. 2006) and highlights the most important avoidable causes of death. GBD data are not based on actual data, but generated by formalized expert consensus and give the best overview of the state of world health for two periods—1990 and 2001.

The GBD makes the distinction between three classes of causes of death in two parts of the world. The three classes are communicable disorders with maternal and perinatal causes and nutritional deficiencies, non-communicable causes and external causes (injury, suicide and homicide). The two parts of the world are low- and middle-income versus high-income countries. The low- and middle-income part is rather big and heterogeneous; however, life expectancies in Latin America, Asia (except South Asia), and North Africa are increasing and converging, whereas Sub-Saharan Africa (SSA) is falling further behind. Life expectancy in South Asia (predominantly India, Pakistan, Sri Lanka, and Bangladesh) is increasing, but not as fast as in the rest of the middle- and low-income countries. In 2001, these low- and middle-income countries (LMIC) accounted for 85% of world population and 97% of deaths. The age-standardized death rate (with the young World Population Standard) was 1.14% in the LMIC and 0.5% in the high-income countries (HIC), indicating a hazard of death more than double in LMIC.

## Causes of Death Related to Infectious Disease, Pregnancy, Birth, and Malnutrition

In the high-income countries, this category of causes of death accounted for 7.0% of mortality, in the LMIC, this was 36.4% of mortality, in SSA 69% in 2001, according to the GBD (Lopez et al. 2006). In SSA (11% of the world population), 237,000 women died during childbirth, of whom 223,000 were between ages 15 and 24. In the rest of the LMIC (74% of the world population), 270,000 young mothers died; in the high-income countries, 15% of the world population, there were 1,000 deaths to young mothers. Of the half million mothers dying each year, close to 80% die of bleeding, sepsis, hypertensive disorders of pregnancy, or of obstructed labor or abortion (causing 66,000 deaths per year). Maternal mortality is therefore a good indicator of the quality and performance of primary health care, including the two basic levels of care: the first line and the secondary hospital of reference. A decent maternity service in the referral secondary hospital with a performing primary healthcare system will reduce maternal mortality to low levels.

It is common knowledge that infectious diseases have been nearly eradicated in high-income countries by vaccinations, antibiotics, and effective health care. However, as noted before, in the case of measles, infectious diseases have a very different outcome in healthy and well-nourished children living in salubrious housing than in malnourished children living in crowded conditions. This argument has been put forth in explaining the history of tuberculosis decline by McKeown (1976). He rightly noted that tuberculosis in the United Kingdom was already reduced to very low levels in the late 1940s, when the first antibiotic for treatment of tuberculosis, streptomycin, was introduced (BCG, the vaccine, was introduced 10 years before, but it did not work very well).

In the high-income countries, of the 7% dying of infectious disease, two thirds (4.4%) die of lower respiratory infections, and of these, 90% die at ages 70 and older. This is caused by waning immunity at the end of life, and is one reason pneumonia is known as the "old man's best friend." The same holds for malnutrition, which is limited to old age, often associated with cognitive decline. Additional infectious diseases that cause 8% of the deaths from infectious disease include HIV, tuberculosis, and hepatitis B and C. In high-income countries, these are often prevalent in minority groups: men who have sex with men, migrants from Sub-Saharan Africa, the homeless, alcoholics, and other substance abusers, often with co-occurring mental illness (Huisman et al. 2009; Lopez et al. 2006). Hepatitis C is a frequent problem among blood transfusion recipients.

In LMIC, infectious diseases are still an important cause of death, claiming 14.2 million deaths (nearly 30%). An added 2.5 million deaths are caused by perinatal deaths, 700,000 during traumatic deliveries. The most important causes of death are, in order of magnitude, lower respiratory infections, HIV-AIDS, diarrheal diseases, tuberculosis, malaria, measles, pertussis, tetanus, meningitis, and syphilis. Pertussis, tetanus, and measles are vaccinable diseases; lower respiratory infections, meningitis, syphilis, tuberculosis, and malaria are treatable and curable. Mortality may be hard to eradicate completely, but can be pushed back to very low levels.

Except in African populations, HIV-AIDS has not spread widely in the general heterosexual population (Hamers et al. 2003). Rates of partner change and multiple concurrent partnerships were too low to increase the basic reproductive rate ("R 0" is the probability that an infected person will infect another person. If this is under 1.0, no epidemic can be maintained) (May and Anderson 1987). In Africa (and African populations outside Africa), HIV-AIDS spread into the general population for reasons not always well understood.

HIV-AIDS remains a difficult challenge, as highly active antiretroviral treatments (HAART) effectively lower mortality but will not eliminate the virus and cure the disease. RNA viruses are labile, fast-mutating viruses that easily acquire resistance to existing drugs, which makes the long-term outlook for even successfully treated patients uncertain. The lack of development of HIV-vaccines is one of the most notable failures of medical research in recent decades (Robb 2008).

Although behavioral campaigns have been highly promoted, evidence of their success is scant, absent in high-risk African populations, and plagued by ideology and religion. Right-winged religions sabotage information campaigns about healthy sexual behaviors, considering these to be pornographic and promoting promiscuous and immoral behaviors. In high-income countries, such campaigns against sexual education have little effect, but in low-income countries where religion offers dignity and hope to impoverished people, these radical campaigns against contraception and safe sexual behaviors have been very damaging (Bonneux 1994; Mashta 2008).

On the other side, left-wing, nongovernmental organizations overestimated the effectiveness of condoms and deliberately ignored the high risks of multiple concurrent partnerships (Epstein 2008). Condoms are efficacious at reducing the risk of transmission in laboratory conditions and effective in the hands of professional sex workers, but they appear less successful in community settings particularly among young and inexperienced partners (Weller 1993; Weller and Davis 2002). In randomized trials in Africa, condom use increased the risk of HIV transmission, likely as a consequence of risk compensation (people engaging in unsafe sex, who have but do not use condoms) (Hearst and Chen 2004; Kajubi et al. 2005). The ABC campaigns of Uganda seemed to be the only ones that were effective in the real-life conditions of Africa (Murphy et al. 2006; Potts et al. 2008; Shelton 2007). A stood for Abstinence (targeted to youngsters: think and talk before you start having sex), B for Be faithful (concurrent partnerships are the HIV highways through sexual networks), and C for condom use (when experimenting with new relations outside marriage, use condoms). There is a general consensus that behavioral HIV campaigns should be multifactorial and a growing consensus of the health dangers of concurrent sexual partnerships (Coates et al. 2008; Merson et al. 2008a, b; Potts et al. 2008; Shelton 2007).

## Cancers

By far the most important amenable causes of cancer are affected by health policy interventions: those cancers that are related to and caused by tobacco smoking, alcohol, obesity, and occupational exposure. The most important contribution of a well-organized and funded healthcare sector to the decline of cancer mortality is a timely diagnosis, lowered complication rates from the extensive surgical treatment often needed, and increasing effectiveness and appropriateness of radiotherapy and chemotherapy. These all add up to a sizeable but hard-to-define improving prognosis for cancer. In the most common chronic cancers (breast, colorectal, and prostate cancer), such therapeutic progress has improved prognosis considerably.

The foundation of the progress in cancer treatments was the development of evidence-based medicine, and the organization of carefully designed multicenter treatment trials recruiting large numbers of eligible patients. Progress was real but limited and piecemeal. Survival of most cancers improved. However, early detection and population screening of populations at low risk make these figures hard to interpret. Active case detection will preferentially detect those cancers that are longstanding with a more benign disease course. The "cancer epidemic" is usually an epidemic of cancer incidence, not of mortality, and is largely iatrogenic. It is a difficult public health choice between improved prognosis through early diagnosis and increased overdiagnosis of essentially benign lesions.

For all specific cancers, with the exception of lung cancer in smokers, the probability of dying of the specific cancer is small, compared to competing mortality risks. The effect on population life expectancy of targeting these cancers is therefore limited, if measurable at all. The important cancer causes of death are lung cancer (discussed with smoking-related cancers), colorectal cancer, breast cancer (among women), and stomach cancer.

**Stomach Cancer**

Stomach cancer used to be the most important cancer causing death in Europe, before it was overtaken by lung cancer, previously a rare disorder. Stomach cancer is retreating fast to low levels in developed countries (Boyle and Ferlay 2005). The decline is hypothesized to be linked to improved diets allowed by better preservation practices. Refrigerators and freezers have likely been more important than medical care in reducing stomach cancer. The recognition and treatment of Helicobacter pylori (H pylori) as an infectious cause of stomach ulcers along with reducing transmission of the condition through less crowded living conditions helped.

**Breast Cancer**

Breast cancer is a true scourge of women in middle age. In the EU, it is the most important cause of lost-life years among women. While most diseases show negative correlations with socioeconomic status (SES), breast cancer is more prevalent among the wealthy, tall, and well-nourished populations, and breast cancer incidence in a country tends to increase with economic development (Linos et al. 2008; Silva Idos et al. 2008). The most important risk factor is reproductive behavior (Collaborative Group on Hormonal Factors in Breast Cancer and Breastfeeding 2002). There is ancillary evidence that hormone regulating therapy is harmful too. Hormone replacement therapy (HRT), very popular in the 1980s and early 1990s and widely promoted by the medical industry for its "cardiovascular prevention potential" might have increased breast cancer (Beral 2003; Kumle 2008). After HRT was linked to cardiovascular risk rather than prevention, the usage of HRT dropped sharply (Chlebowski et al. 2009; Roberts 2009; Writing Group for the Women's Health Initiative Investigators 2002). The best primary prevention for breast cancer is having many children early in life and breastfeeding them for a prolonged period (Collaborative Group on Hormonal Factors in Breast Cancer and Breastfeeding 2002). Health is set in complex social and physiological systems: what is good for one system may be bad for another. A "healthy breast choice" may conflict with women's preferences, and the social consequences of low levels of education and low income later in life resulting from early and frequent childbearing could be far more detrimental than the prevented breast cancer. Breast cancer screening is of limited effectiveness in reducing breast cancer mortality and of dubious effectiveness in lowering all-cause mortality (Black et al. 2002; Gotzsche and Nielsen 2006). Decline in breast cancer mortality, against an increasingly unfavorable reproductive lifestyle, has been attributed, except for the discontinuation of HRT, to increasingly effective treatment of cancer patients by chemotherapy and tamoxifen (a hormonal treatment) (Early Breast Cancer Trialists' Collaborative Group 2005; Yerushalmi and Gelmon 2008).

In colorectal cancer, high-quality care reduces mortality. There are large differences in the EU in prognosis, after adjusting for surgery and stage at diagnosis (Boyle and Ferlay 2005; Verdecchia et al. 2007). As mentioned in the introduction, increased case detection may increase incidence, prevalence and survival of colorectal cancer, but will not necessarily lower mortality. Active screening tends to detect more benign lesions, by the typical screening bias "length time": rapid, highly malignant cancer growth is missed by periodic screening, the slower and the less malignant a cancerous lesion is, the more likely it will be detected (Black and Welch 1993). However, colorectal cancer screening is more complex, as during colonoscopy, precancerous lesions are removed, which may decrease colorectal cancer incidence (Pignone et al. 2002). The US Preventive Services Task Force finds that there is fair to good evidence to recommend screening for colorectal cancer using fecal occult blood testing, sigmoidoscopy, or colonoscopy in adults, beginning at age 50 years and continuing until age 75 years. There was a 25% risk reduction of colorectal cancer mortality (RR 0.75, 95% CI 0.66–0.84) for those attending at least one round of screening using the FOBT (Hewitson et al. 2008). This implies that the reduction of the absolute risk of colorectal cancer mortality is relatively limited.

Childhood cancers are less frequent, but young children dying of cancer not only lose many life years, but also spoil many life years for their kin and parents. While most childhood cancers were considered incurable until the early 1970s, 5-year survival from all childhood cancers for children diagnosed in the early 1980s was 65%. In the early 1990s it was 75% (Gatta et al. 2005). Progress in lymphoid leukemia (one-quarter of all childhood cancers) was tremendous, reaching 5-year survival rates of 83% in children diagnosed in the early 1990s. For Hodgkin's disease, 5-year survival is now more than 95% (Gatta et al. 2005). This was again a victory for evidence-based medicine, with oncologists cooperating in large multicenter trials testing increasingly effective but ever more aggressive multi-drug therapies, mastering the complications of these highly aggressive treatments and, last but not least, developing and adhering to progressively more specified and standardized treatment guidelines and protocols. The same evolution was observed for testis cancer, where 5-year survival is now more than 95% (Verdecchia et al. 2007).

Cervical cancer is caused by a sexually transmitted wart virus, Human papillomavirus (HPV). A healthy sexual lifestyle is therefore important for prevention. Having unprotected sex, especially at a young age, and having many sexual partners increases the risk of HPV infection. Women who have many sexual partners or who have sex with men who have had many partners have a greater chance of getting HPV. However, most women with HPV infection do not develop cervical cancer and other risk factors must come into play. Cervical cancer screening with PAP smears has been highly effective in reducing incidence and mortality of invasive cervical cancer. But to be cost-effective, well-organized cancer screening programs have to actively target women at high risk of cervical cancer, while limiting the adverse effects of over-screening and over-treating women at low risk. In the future, this may change, as HPV vaccination will seriously decrease cervical cancer incidence (Koutsky et al. 2002). This may cause new dilemmas for public health. Cervical cancer screening will still be effective, but to be cost-effective, screening programs will have to be revised in vaccinated women, particularly if at very low risk of sexually transmitted diseases (Kim and Goldie 2008).

## Surgical Disorders

Most surgical disorders fall under the heading of gastrointestinal surgery. These used to be important causes of death that were nearly eliminated by safer anesthesia and competent surgery, although late diagnosis and low quality of care can increase rates of complications and still claim lives. In most lists of avoidable mortality, peptic ulcer, appendicitis, abdominal hernia, gallstones, and gallbladder infections are included.

Appendicitis incidence is related to economic development with a strong inverted U-relationship. Appendicitis used to be rare in developing countries, peaked in developed countries in the early twentieth century, and then declined in incidence with greater decline in mortality (Bickler and DeMaio 2008; Kang et al. 2003). The surgical intervention was developed at the end of the nineteenth century. Untreated, mortality from appendicitis is high as the inflamed and infected appendicitis perforates and can cause a generalized peritonitis. The incidence of appendicitis is increasing as developing countries modernize. The reasons are poorly understood but is generally attributed to changes in diet and hygiene (Bickler and DeMaio 2008; Walker and Segal 1995).

Peptic ulcer disease also has an interesting history, showing the interaction between medicine, society, and fashionable paradigms. Peptic ulcer was thought to be caused by stress, diet, smoking, alcohol, and drugs (most analgesic drugs may cause gastritis). In the 1960s and 1970s, mental stress was considered to be the most important determinant of peptic ulcer. In World War II, peptic ulcer peaked extraordinarily high in London during the period of the frequent bombings. But in the 1980s H pylori was discovered to be an infectious cause of gastritis. This changed the theory so that ulcers once assumed to be caused by stress were then seen as caused by infections. However, because infection with H pylori is extraordinarily prevalent, and most infected people do not develop gastritis and ulcers, the "postmodern" consensus blames an interaction of factors. H pylori is important, but so are stress, smoking, and analgesic drugs (Raiha et al. 1998). Genetic factors, which can predispose a person to more harmful consequences of H pylori, are of only modest importance (Raiha et al. 1998).

The prevalence of gallstones in a population is also positively correlated with development, through increases in cholesterol levels in the bile, increases in weight, diabetes, and high fat low fiber diets. Until the age of abdominal surgery, there was no generally effective treatment for gallstones. Gallstone patients faced a high death rate with crippling abdominal pains. The first surgical removal of the gallbladder was carried out in 1882 by Carl von Langenbuch (Tait and Little 1995). The safety and success of this operation was soon established and together with safe anesthesia, analgesia, and antibiotics has changed this risk forever.

## *Injuries*

In the EU, important causes of loss of adult life are injuries, particularly road traffic accidents and suicide among the young and fatal falls among the elderly. In the EU 6.9% and 3.5% of all deaths respectively among men and women were caused by injuries. In Europe, 22% of all fatal injuries were caused by transport accidents, primarily road traffic accidents; three-quarters of the victims were male (Huisman et al. 2009). Worldwide, road traffic accidents are an increasing health problem, ranked tenth in importance as cause of death in 2002 and eighth in the projections for 2030 (Mathers and Loncar 2006). In African countries, the death toll per number of cars is highest. In Zambia, a country plagued by AIDS and malaria, road traffic accidents are now the third leading cause of mortality (Schatz 2008). Mortality at young and adult age from accidents, drugs, alcohol, and suicide share common characteristics, suggesting a continuum of self-destructive tendencies (Neeleman et al. 1998).

Ten percent of all injury deaths are caused by accidental falls, where half of all victims are women. Other unintentional causes of fatal injuries are poisoning, drowning, and burns. One in four of all injury victims committed suicide, three-quarters being male. Homicide is a relatively rare cause of death in the EU, but frequent in the United States, accounting for 2.5% of all injury mortality or 1.3 per 1,000 deaths. Two thirds were men. Except for accidental falls, men dominate injury mortality. Among European men, injuries are the most prominent cause of potential years of life lost (PYLL) before age 65, causing no less than 27.8% of all PYLL, nearly 10 percentage points more than cardiovascular diseases (Huisman et al. 2009). Women are less affected, but injuries still cause 15.2% of all PYLL, still more than circulatory diseases. Only cancer causes more PYLL. As accidental falls are predominantly a cause of death among the elderly, the causes of PYLL are dominated by suicide and traffic accidents.

Low income is one of the determinants of the risk of injury. This holds for countries and individual people. Injuries are linked to poverty and inequality in many ways (Sethi et al. 2006). Poor individuals and families live riskier lives in more risky environments and have less access to high-quality emergency medical and rehabilitative services. They are financially more vulnerable, and once injured, the healthcare costs and lost income increase poverty. In the United Kingdom, children from lower social classes are three–four times more likely to die from injuries than those of higher classes (Edwards et al. 2006; Roberts and Power 1996). Childhood traffic accident deaths are strongly associated with poverty, single parenthood, low maternal education, low maternal age at birth, poor housing, large family size, and parental alcohol or drug abuse (Sethi et al. 2006). Suicide rates are higher for people experiencing unemployment. Alcohol and drugs, related to lower SES too, further increase risks for all unintentional injuries and violence. In general, reducing inequalities of wealth between nations and people will most likely lead to decreases in injuries and violence.

**Road Safety**

The main risk factors for fatal accidents are speed and alcohol, exposing vulnerable road users to motorized traffic, poor visibility, and not using such protective equipment as seat belts (Sethi et al. 2006). Road safety policies have been highly effective in reducing accident mortality. Peaking in the early 1970s, the numbers of road traffic accidents have been declining tremendously, although this decline is stagnating. In the Netherlands for example, the rate of traffic accident mortality declined nearly sixfold, from 25.6 in 1970 to 4.4 per 100,000 in 2008. In that period, the population was increasing, but the large fraction of young and inexperienced drivers in the post-World War II baby boom were instrumental in these high death rates. In recent years in the established market economies of the EU, the road has been dominated by experienced drivers from the baby boom. This might change in the future, as the elderly are at increased risk of traffic accidents.

In most European countries, the problems of drinking, driving, and speeding are quite prominent. Particularly in the former socialist economies, high alcohol-related mortality is linked to very high accident mortality, and related to a certain societal acceptance of alcoholism and drunk driving (Mackenbach et al. 2008). But even in the Netherlands where alcohol-related mortality is relatively limited, one-quarter of all accidental deaths in the twenty-first century have been caused by drunk driving (http://www.swov.nl/uk/). Most European countries have created public campaigns that underscore the social unacceptability of drunk driving, including criminalizing such behavior.

Because higher speeds contribute to the risk of severe injury and fatal crashes, speed management is one of the most important cornerstones of road safety. Speeding is related to personality characteristics, road layout and environment, the vehicle, and enforcement by control. Speed management intervenes at all these levels. Acceptable and sustainable speed limits must be determined (and depend partly on societal choice), road users have to know the local speed limit, and local infrastructural measures such as speed bumps and roundabouts enforce a safe speed. Future developments are active speed control depending on traffic density, and increasingly information provided to the car on prevailing speed limits and realized speed by global positioning systems (GPS). Strict police control remains essential for those who deliberately drive too fast.

Individual passive safety is best served by safety belt use (Cohen and Einav 2003; Sethi et al. 2006). The relation between safety belt use and mortality is more complex than generally presented and tends to be overestimated, as safety belt users tend to be more risk averse and more prudent drivers with or without safety belts. More erratic users may show compensating behavior and drive more recklessly when wearing a seat belt (Cohen and Einav 2003). Still, seat belt use does decrease overall traffic fatalities, and the presence of seat belt reminders that warn car drivers if the seat belt is not fastened significantly increases the proportion of motorists wearing a belt.

**Occupational Safety**

Occupational safety increased tremendously, which drastically reduced the numbers of victims, as the most hazardous industries, such as mining and steel manufacturing, were phased out or moved to developing countries where labor force is cheaper (Centers for Disease Control 1998). People face a variety of hazards, including chemicals and biological agents. These may produce a wide range of fatal events, including injuries, cancer, and respiratory disease. Only the workers employed in the jobs with specific risks are affected, causing high risk in the concerned group. For example, healthcare workers are at high risk of transmission of HIV and Hepatitis B virus (HBV) through needle stick injuries, but they rarely constitute more than 1% of the population, limiting the total health burden in the population. Policies to standardize needle usage, increased HBV immunization coverage, and post-exposure antiretroviral profylaxis seriously decreased the risks.

Most fatal occupational injuries occur among industrial and agricultural workers. The highest risks are among fishermen and pilots. Work-related falls, motor vehicle injuries, and contact with machinery still result in nearly 1,000 occupational deaths every day throughout the world (World Health Report 2002, http://www.who.int/whr/2002/en/whr02_ch4.pdf).

Many of the 150 chemical or biological agents classified as carcinogens are encountered in occupational settings. Worldwide, occupational exposures to lung carcinogens, including asbestos, arsenic, beryllium, cadmium, chromium, diesel exhaust, nickel, and silica account for about 10.3% of cancer of the lung, trachea and bronchus, which is the most frequent occupational cancer (World Health Report 2002, http://www.who.int/whr/2002/en/whr02_ch4.pdf). And worldwide 2.4% of leukemia is attributable to occupational exposures. Microscopic airborne particles of silica, asbestos, and coal dust may not only cause cancer of the lung, but also the non-malignant but often fatal fibrotic lung disease pneumoconiosis ("dusty lung"). In practice, these exposures are often controllable, and are increasingly controlled.

## Suicide

Self-inflicted injuries and suicide are the most frequent cause of death from injury in Europe. Suicide rates are high among young people, but increase with age until the age of 80 and over. At all ages, men are much more likely to take their own lives than women. In the EU, men lose 3.4 more life years from suicide than women, in spite of their shorter life expectancy.

Risk factors for suicidal behavior are numerous. Apart from age and gender, the most important factors are psychological and social. Many people who commit suicide have demonstrated depression and hopelessness (Bernal et al. 2007). Drugs and alcohol use also play an important part; a quarter of suicides involve alcohol abuse (Bernal et al. 2007). Among the elderly, suicide may also be the consequence of severe, painful, or disabling diseases, often in combination with social isolation. Rates of suicide are higher in rural than in urban areas, presumably due to social isolation. Religious affiliation is one of the determinants that protects against suicide, by religious prohibitions and by strengthening the social network (Neeleman and Lewis 1999). Suicide rates increase during periods of economic recession and unemployment (Gunnell et al. 1999; Stuckler et al. 2009).

In the EU, national identity is a determinant of suicide risks. Borders separate regions with a common history but with now tremendously different risks of suicide. In the Benelux (the Netherlands, Belgium, and Luxemburg) countries that shared a common history until the sixteenth century, and which share a common language in the Netherlands and Flanders, suicide mortality is 2.5 times lower in the Netherlands than in Flanders (Bonneux and Huisman 2008). In Slovenia, the suicide mortality rate is four times higher than across the Italian border, in the neighboring North Eastern Italian region.

Efficient primary health care may identify and treat mental disorders in a timely manner, resulting in a decrease in suicidal behavior and suicide rates. Control and treatment of alcohol and substance abuse are important in lowering suicide rates. Social interventions include restricting access to dangerous substances used in suicide, removal of carbon monoxide from domestic gas, and handgun control.

## The Future

Foreseeable change in population mortality ought to be based on existing technology with proven evidence. It is unlikely that the population at large will benefit from not yet existing technologies within the next 20 years. In very low mortality populations, people die of such distal causes of death as CVD, cancer, respiratory disease, Alzheimer's disease, and other debilitating disorders at the end of life. Old age cannot be listed as the primary cause of death on official documents: people are not allowed to die of old age. The rationality of this practice is arguable. In medical practice, the reduction of the elderly patient to a set of distinct diseases treated in an uncoordinated manner has led to poor geriatric care (Fialova and Onder 2009). Indeed, advancing both the length and the quality of life at old age will require a clear focus on the aging process, which is the proximal cause of death. Other proximal causes of the disease process are the usual suspects: smoking, obesity, lack of physical activity, and lack of high-quality care at old age.

With delayed cardiovascular mortality, cancer is becoming the most important cause of death before the age of 75 in developed countries. Spectacular advances in cancer treatment are comparable to similar advances in nuclear fusion: many technologies are promising, but progress is piecemeal and limited in impact. To have a real population impact, the disease has to be frequent. Cancers from infectious origins, such as cervical cancer, are rather rare, for example: HPV vaccination is an important asset for public health, but its impact on all-cause mortality is small in most developed countries, with low cervical cancer mortality. Efficient cervical cancer screening, done in well-organized population screening programs, is as effective as vaccination. Where sexual behavior has been changing as a consequence of successful HIV prevention, this is again as effective. Other cancer vaccines have been studied for decades, to little benefit. Dendritic cell vaccines are more popular among cancer quacks than in clinical medicine. After 15 years of development, such dendritic cell vaccines are an experimental therapy only in melanoma treatment (Lesterhuis et al. 2008). Anti-angiogenic treatments that fight cancer by inhibiting the genesis of new blood vessels that feed the tumor have been studied for years, but clinical benefits have not yet been ascertained. Evidence from animal studies suggests that such drugs may actually accelerate the spread of cancer (Hayden 2009). The most promising new technologies are monoclonal antibodies that interfere with systems promoting cancer growth. An example is trastuzumab (Herceptin), which interferes with the HER2/neu receptor. The HER proteins regulate cell growth. In some breast cancers, HER2 is stuck in the "on" position, and causes breast cells to reproduce uncontrollably, causing breast cancer. For individuals with specific cancers, the benefits of continuing progress in cancer treatments are large, but as their numbers are limited, the potential for lowering population mortality by therapeutic progress will remain limited within the next 20 years.

Cancer screening policies would be effective if cancer followed a linear growth model. It does not: cancer follows an evolutionary model of random mutation and selection for aggression. Advancing diagnosis to an earlier but detectable stage therefore comes at the price of considerable overdiagnosis: fatal tumors have been small, but small tumors will not necessarily be fatal. The mortality reduction remains small, as metastasis may easily occur before any detectable phase (Gotzsche and Nielsen 2006; Humphrey et al. 2002). To avoid one cancer death, the average screening program needs at least 10,000 person-years of follow-up. The false promises of cancer screening come under increasing scrutiny (Editorial 2009; Esserman et al. 2009; Godlee 2009; Gotzsche et al. 2009; Welch 2009; Woloshin and Schwartz 2009), and the reduction of these programs seems a more rational expectation than further expansion.

Major reductions in cancer incidence and mortality can be achieved through reducing smoking prevalence. Inhibiting smoking uptake by anti-tobacco policies that successfully can stop the addiction of youth can be quite effective. Obesity is a less important cause of cancer mortality (Renehan et al. 2008), but its population impact still may soon outweigh any therapeutic progress.

Cardiovascular mortality used to be the major cause of death in developed nations, but rates have declined tremendously since the 1960s (in the United States) and the 1970s (in Europe). But these rates can go down still further. Cardiovascular mortality at older ages is dominated by thrombotic events and their consequences for hearts (myocardial infarctions), brains (thrombotic stroke), and peripheral arteries. Case-fatality rates from acute myocardial infarctions dropped tremendously, but are still high enough to be vulnerable to effective therapeutic policies. The dominant paradigm is still "time is muscle." The sooner the clotted blood vessel can be reopened, the better. Most promising are rapid interventions with direct ambulatory thrombolysis before arrival in the hospital.

Stroke treatment, the second cause of death in CVD, is now following acute myocardial infarction therapy, first with thrombolysis and recently also with stent procedures. The difficulties are greater, but progress is undeniable. Stroke units have improved prognosis further by treating and preventing disability.

For population mortality, cardiovascular risk management of high-risk population is in competition with mass chemoprofylaxis of the entire population. Two low-dose antihypertensives and one generic statin have the theoretical potential of halving residual cardiovascular mortality, or reducing all-cause mortality by 10–15%. Randomized controlled trials have been started, and beneficial results are expected. The complications of these very well known drugs are minor and the costs are small and decreasing. It is likely that such mass profylaxis will spread in the future.

Rising BMI in populations may reduce life expectancy gains from reduced cardiovascular mortality (Stewart et al. 2009). Until now, health policy has had remarkably little effect on the "growing masses" in western populations, but many feel that obesity ought not to be a difficult target for drug therapy. However, promising drug therapies have consistently failed to this point because of high rates of complications. Obesity becomes more lethal at BMIs over 33 and is comparable to smoking at BMI over 40 (Reuser et al. 2009; Whitlock et al. 2009). If no treatments become available, health policy remains as ineffective as it is today, and BMI continues rising, the impact on mortality and life expectancy may be considerable (Stewart et al. 2009).

At old age, individual causes of death are eclipsed and replaced by senescence and multi-organ failure. Can we fight aging? Dreams of the Fountain of Youth are as old as humanity, so only the future will tell (Olshansky et al. 2002). Nevertheless, current Japanese life expectancy of 86 for women and 2–3 years lower for men indicates that a total population life expectancy of 85 years is easily attainable with the technology of today.

# References

Amarenco, P., J. Labreuche, P. Lavallee, and P.J. Touboul. 2004. "Statins in Stroke Prevention and Carotid Atherosclerosis: Systematic Review and Up-to-Date Meta-Analysis." *Stroke* 35(12):2902–9.

Anderson, P., D. Chisholm, and D.C. Fuhr. 2009. "Effectiveness and Cost-Effectiveness of Policies and Programmes to Reduce the Harm Caused by Alcohol." *Lancet* 373(9682):2234–46.

Antikainen, R.L., V.A. Moltchanov, C. Chukwuma, Sr., K.A. Kuulasmaa, P.M. Marques-Vidal, S. Sans, L. Wilhelmsen, and J.O. Tuomilehto. 2006. "Trends in the Prevalence, Awareness, Treatment and Control of Hypertension: The WHO MONICA Project." *European Journal of Cardiovascular Prevention and Rehabilitation* 13(1):13–29.

Beral, V. 2003. "Breast Cancer and Hormone-Replacement Therapy in the Million Women Study." *Lancet* 362(9382):419–27.

Bernal, M., J.M. Haro, S. Bernert, T. Brugha, R. de Graaf, R. Bruffaerts, J.P. Lepine, G. de Girolamo, G. Vilagut, I. Gasquet, J.V. Torres, V. Kovess, D. Heider, J. Neeleman, R. Kessler, and J. Alonso. 2007. "Risk Factors for Suicidality in Europe: Results From the ESEMED Study." *Journal Affective Disorders* 101(1–3):27–34.

Bickler, S.W. and A. DeMaio. 2008. "Western Diseases: Current Concepts and Implications for Pediatric Surgery Research and Practice." *Pediatric Surgery International* 24(3):251–55.

Black, W.C., D.A. Haggstrom, and H. Welch. 2002. "All Cause Mortality in Randomized Trials of Cancer Screening." *Journal of National Cancer Institute* 94:167–73.

Black, W.C. and H.G. Welch. 1993. "Advances in Diagnostic Imaging and Overestimations of Disease Prevalence and the Benefits of Therapy." *New England Journal of Medicine* 328(17):1237–43.

Bonita, R. and R. Beaglehole. 1989. "Increased Treatment of Hypertension Does Not Explain the Decline in Stroke Mortality in the United States, 1970–1980." *Hypertension* 13(5 Suppl):I69–I73.

Bonneux, L. 1994. "Rwanda: A Case of Demographic Entrapment." *Lancet* 344(8938):1689–90.

Bonneux, L. 2000. "Cholesterol-Lowering Therapy for Smokers and Non-Smokers: A Life-Table Analysis." *Lancet* 356(9246):2004–6.

Bonneux, L.G. and J.W. Coebergh. 2004. "Passive Smoking: An Environmental Health Risk." *Nederlands Tijdschrift Geneeskunde* 148(14):647–50.

Bonneux, L. and C. Huisman. 2008. "Borders Determine Mortality, Differences Between Flanders and the Netherlands [in Dutch]." *DEMOS* 24(6):1–4.

Boyle, P. and J. Ferlay. 2005. "Cancer Incidence and Mortality in Europe, 2004." *Annals of Oncology* 16(3):481–88.

Briffa, T., S. Hickling, M. Knuiman, M. Hobbs, J. Hung, F.M. Sanfilippo, K. Jamrozik, and P.L. Thompson. 2009. "Long Term Survival After Evidence Based Treatment of Acute Myocardial Infarction and Revascularisation: Follow-Up of Population Based Perth MONICA Cohort, 1984–2005." *British Medical Journal* 338(Jan26_2):b36.

Brunner, E. 1997. "Socioeconomic Determinants of Health: Stress and the Biology of Inequality." *British Medical Journal* 314(7092):1472–1476.

Brunner, E.J., K. Rees, K. Ward, M. Burke, and M. Thorogood. 2007. "Dietary Advice for Reducing Cardiovascular Risk." *Cochrane Database Systematic Reviews* (4): CD002128.

Burt, V.L., J.A. Cutler, M. Higgins, M.J. Horan, D. Labarthe, P. Whelton, C. Brown, and E.J. Roccella. 1995. "Trends in the Prevalence, Awareness, Treatment, and Control of Hypertension in the Adult US Population. Data from the health examination surveys, 1960 to 1991." *Hypertension* 26(1):60–69.

Califf, R.M., P.W. Armstrong, J.R. Carver, R.B. D'Agostino, and W.E. Strauss. 1996. "27th Bethesda Conference: Matching the Intensity of Risk Factor Management with the Hazard for Coronary Disease Events. Task Force 5. Stratification of Patients into High, Medium and Low Risk Subgroups for Purposes of Risk Factor Management." *Journal of American College of Cardiology* 27(5):1007–19.

Centers for Disease Control. 1998. "Fatal Occupational Injuries – United States, 1980–1994." *Morbidity and Mortality Weekly Report* 47(15):297–302.

Chlebowski, R.T., L.H. Kuller, R.L. Prentice, M.L. Stefanick, J.E. Manson, M. Gass, A.K. Aragaki, J.K. Ockene, D.S. Lane, G.E. Sarto, A. Rajkovic, R. Schenken, S.L. Hendrix, P.M. Ravdin, T.E. Rohan, S. Yasmeen, and G. Anderson. 2009. "Breast Cancer after Use of Estrogen plus Progestin in Postmenopausal Women." *New England Journal of Medicine* 360(6):573–87.

Coates, T.J., L. Richter, and C. Caceres. 2008. "Behavioural Strategies to Reduce HIV Transmission: How to Make Them Work Better." *Lancet* 372(9639):669–84.

Cohen, A. and L. Einav. 2003. "The Effects of Mandatory Seat Belt Laws on Driving Behavior and Traffic Fatalities." *Review of Economics and Statistics* 85(4):828–43.

Collaborative Group on Hormonal Factors in Breast Cancer and Breastfeeding. 2002. "Breast Cancer and Breastfeeding: Collaborative Reanalysis of Individual Data From 47 Epidemiological Studies in 30 Countries, Including 50,302 Women with Breast Cancer and 96,973 Women Without the Disease." *Lancet* 360(9328):187–95.

Dellavalle, R.P., A. Drake, M. Graber, L.F. Heilig, E.J. Hester, K.R. Johnson, K. McNealy, and L. Schilling. 2005. "Statins and Fibrates for Preventing Melanoma." *Cochrane Database Systematic Review* (4):CD003697.

Doll, R., R. Peto, K. Wheatley, R. Gray, and I. Sutherland. 1994. "Mortality in Relation to Smoking: 40 years' Observations on Male British Doctors." *British Medical Journal* 309(6959):901–11.

Early Breast Cancer Trialists' Collaborative Group. 2005. "Effects of Chemotherapy and Hormonal Therapy for Early Breast Cancer on Recurrence and 15-Year Survival: An Overview of the Randomised Trials." *Lancet* 365(9472):1687–717.

Eastern Stroke and Coronary Heart Disease Collaborative Research Group. 1998. "Blood Pressure, Cholesterol, and Stroke in Eastern Asia." *Lancet* 352(9143):1801–7.

Editorial. 2009. "The Trouble with Screening." *Lancet* 373(9671):1223.

Edwards, P., I. Roberts, J. Green, and S. Lutchmun. 2006. "Deaths from Injury in Children and Employment Status in Family: Analysis of Trends in Class Specific Death Rates." *British Medical Journal* 333(7559):119.

Endo, A. 2008. "A Gift from Nature: The Birth of the Statins." *Nature Medicine* 14(10):1050–52.

Endo, A., M. Kuroda, and Y. Tsujita. 1976. "ML-236A, ML-236B, and ML-236C, New Inhibitors of Cholesterogenesis Produced by Penicillium Citrinium." *Journal Antibiot (Tokyo)* 29(12):1346–48.

Epstein, H. 2008. "AIDS and the Irrational." *British Medical Journal* 337:a2638.

Esserman, L., Y. Shieh, and I. Thompson. 2009. "Rethinking Screening for Breast Cancer and Prostate Cancer." *Journal of the American Medical Association* 302(15):1685–92.

Feigin, V.L., C.M. Lawes, D.A. Bennett, S.L. Barker-Collo, and V. Parag. 2009. "Worldwide Stroke Incidence and Early Case Fatality Reported in 56 Population-Based Studies: A Systematic Review." *Lancet Neurol* 8(4):355–69.

Fialova, D. and G. Onder. 2009. "Medication Errors in Elderly People: Contributing Factors and Future Perspectives." *British Journal of Clinical Pharmacology* 67(6):641–45.

Fields, L.E., V.L. Burt, J.A. Cutler, J. Hughes, E.J. Roccella, and P. Sorlie. 2004. "The Burden of Adult Hypertension in the United States 1999 to 2000: A Rising Tide." *Hypertension* 44(4):398–404.

Ford, E.S., U.A. Ajani, J.B. Croft, J.A. Critchley, D.R. Labarthe, T.E. Kottke, W.H. Giles, and S. Capewell. 2007. "Explaining the Decrease in U.S. Deaths from Coronary Disease, 1980–2000." *New England Journal of Medicine* 356(23):2388–98.

Franco, O.H., L. Bonneux, C. de Laet, A. Peeters, E.W. Steyerberg, and J.P. Mackenbach. 2004. "The Polymeal: A More Natural, Safer, and Probably Tastier (Than the Polypill) Strategy to Reduce Cardiovascular Disease by More Than 75%." *British Medical Journal* 329(7480):1447–50.

Frost, C.D., M.R. Law, and N.J. Wald. 1991. "By How Much Does Dietary Salt Reduction Lower Blood Pressure? II – Analysis of Observational Data Within Populations." *British Medical Journal* 302(6780):815–18.

Gatta, G., R. Capocaccia, C. Stiller, P. Kaatsch, F. Berrino, and M. Terenziani. 2005. "Childhood Cancer Survival Trends in Europe: A EUROCARE Working Group Study." *Journal of Clinical Oncology* 23(16):3742–51.

Godlee, F. 2009. "Less Medicine is More." *British Medical Journal* 338(Jun25_1):b2561.

Gotzsche, P.C., O.J. Hartling, M. Nielsen, J. Brodersen, and K.J. Jorgensen. 2009. "Breast Screening: The Facts – Or Maybe Not." *British Medical Journal* 338:b86.

Gotzsche, P.C. and M. Nielsen. 2006. "Screening for Breast Cancer With Mammography." *Cochrane Database Systematic Review* (4):CD001877.

Graham, I., D. Atar, K. Borch-Johnsen, G. Boysen, G. Burell, R. Cifkova, J. Dallongeville, G. De Backer, S. Ebrahim, B. Gjelsvik, C. Herrmann-Lingen, A. Hoes, S. Humphries, M. Knapton, J. Perk, S.G. Priori, K. Pyorala, Z. Reiner, L. Ruilope, S. Sans-Menendez, W. Scholte op Reimer, P. Weissberg, D. Wood, J. Yarnell, J.L. Zamorano, E. Walma, T. Fitzgerald, M.T. Cooney, A. Dudina, A. Vahanian, J. Camm, R. De Caterina, V. Dean, K. Dickstein, C. Funck-Brentano, G. Filippatos, I. Hellemans, S.D. Kristensen, K. McGregor, U. Sechtem, S. Silber, M. Tendera, P. Widimsky, J.L. Zamorano, I. Hellemans, A. Altiner, E. Bonora, P.N. Durrington, R. Fagard, S. Giampaoli, H. Hemingway, J. Hakansson, S.E. Kjeldsen, M.L. Larsen, G. Mancia, A.J. Manolis, K. Orth-Gomer, T. Pedersen, M. Rayner, L. Ryden, M. Sammut, N. Schneiderman, A.F. Stalenhoef, L. Tokgozoglu, O. Wiklund, and A. Zampelas. 2007. "European Guidelines on Cardiovascular Disease Prevention in Clinical Practice: Executive Summary." *European Heart Journal* 28(19):2375–414.

Gunnell, D., A. Lopatatzidis, D. Dorling, H. Wehner, H. Southall, and S. Frankel. 1999. "Suicide and Unemployment in Young People. Analysis of Trends in England and Wales, 1921–1995." *British Journal of Psychiatry* 175:263–70.

Hajjar, I. and T.A. Kotchen. 2003. "Trends in Prevalence, Awareness, Treatment, and Control of Hypertension in the United States, 1988–2000." *Journal of the American Medical Association* 290(2):199–206.

Hamers, F.F., A. Infuso, J. Alix, and A.M. Downs. 2003. "Current Situation and Regional Perspective on HIV/AIDS Surveillance in Europe." *JAIDS Journal of Acquired Immune Deficiency Syndromes* 32(1):S39–S48.

Haq, I.U., P.R. Jackson, W.W. Yeo, and L.E. Ramsay. 1995. "Sheffield Risk and Treatment Table for Cholesterol Lowering for Primary Prevention of Coronary Heart Disease." *Lancet* 346(8988):1467–71.

Haslam, D.W. and W.P. James. 2005. "Obesity." *Lancet* 366(9492):1197–209.

Hayden, E.C. 2009. "Cutting off Cancer's Supply Lines." *Nature* 458(7239):686–87.

Hearst, N. and S. Chen. 2004. "Condom Promotion for AIDS Prevention in the Developing World: Is it Working?" *Studies in Family Planning* 35(1):39–47.

Herbert, B. 1993. "In America: Tobacco Dollars." *New York Times*. November, 28:http://query.nytimes.com/gst/fullpage.html?res=9F0CE7D8113FF8193BA15752C15751A96595 8260

Hewitson, P., P. Glasziou, E. Watson, B. Towler, and L. Irwig. 2008. "Cochrane Systematic Review of Colorectal Cancer Screening Using the Fecal Occult Blood Test (Hemoccult): An Update." *American Journal of Gastroenterology* 103(6):1541–49.

Hoglund, K. and K. Blennow. 2007. "Effect of HMG-CoA Reductase Inhibitors on Beta-Amyloid Peptide Levels: Implications for Alzheimer's Disease." *CNS Drugs* 21(6):449–62.

Hooper, L., C.D. Summerbell, J.P. Higgins, R.L. Thompson, G. Clements, N. Capps, S. Davey, R.A. Riemersma, and S. Ebrahim. 2001. "Reduced or Modified Dietary Fat for Preventing Cardiovascular Disease." *Cochrane Database System Review* (3):CD002137.

Huisman, C., L. Bonneux, and J. De Beer. 2009. *Atlas on Mortality in the European Union: Data 2002–04.* Luxembourg, Office for Official Publications of the European Communities. Available at http://epp.eurostat.ec.europa.eu/portal/page/portal/product_details/publication?p_product_code=KS-30-08-357

Humphrey, L.L., M. Helfand, B.K.S. Chan, and S.H. Woolf. 2002. "Breast Cancer Screening: A Summary of the Evidence for the U.S. Preventive Services Task Force." *Annals of Internal Medicine* 137(5_Part_1):347–60.

Johnston, S.C., S. Mendis, and C.D. Mathers. 2009. "Global Variation in Stroke Burden and Mortality: Estimates From Monitoring, Surveillance, and Modelling." *Lancet Neurology* 8(4):345–54.

Joshi, P., S. Islam, P. Pais, S. Reddy, P. Dorairaj, K. Kazmi, M.R. Pandey, S. Haque, S. Mendis, S. Rangarajan, and S. Yusuf. 2007. "Risk Factors for Early Myocardial Infarction in South Asians Compared With Individuals in Other Countries." *Journal of the American Medical Association* 297(3):286–94.

Kajubi, P., M.R. Kamya, S. Kamya, S. Chen, W. McFarland, and N. Hearst. 2005. "Increasing Condom Use Without Reducing HIV Risk: Results of a Controlled Community Trial in Uganda." *Journal of Acquired Immune Deficiency Syndrome* 40(1):77–82.

Kang, J.Y., J. Hoare, A. Majeed, R.C. Williamson, and J.D. Maxwell. 2003. "Decline in Admission Rates for Acute Appendicitis in England." *British Journal of Surgery* 90(12):1586–92.

Katerndahl, D.A. and W.R. Lawler. 1999. "Variability in Meta-Analytic Results Concerning the Value of Cholesterol Reduction in Coronary Heart Disease: A Meta-Meta-Analysis." *American Journal of Epidemiology* 149(5):429–41.

Kearney, P.M., L. Blackwell, R. Collins, A. Keech, J. Simes, R. Peto, J. Armitage, and C. Baigent. 2008. "Efficacy of Cholesterol-Lowering Therapy in 18,686 People with Diabetes in 14 Randomised Trials of Statins: A Meta-Analysis." *Lancet* 371(9607):117–25.

Kim, J.J. and S.J. Goldie. 2008. "Health and Economic Implications of HPV Vaccination in the United States." *New England Journal of Medicine* 359(8):821–32.

Kisjanto, J., L. Bonneux, J. Prihartono, T.A. Ranakusuma, and D.E. Grobbee. 2005. "Risk Factors for Stroke Among Urbanised Indonesian Women of Reproductive Age: A Hospital-Based Case-Control Study." *Cerebrovascular Diseases* 19(1):18–22.

Klatsky, A.L. and N. Udaltsova. 2007. "Alcohol Drinking and Total Mortality Risk." *Annals of Epidemiology* 17(5, Suppl 1):S63–S67.

Koutsky, L.A., K.A. Ault, C.M. Wheeler, D.R. Brown, E. Barr, F.B. Alvarez, L.M. Chiacchierini, and K.U. Jansen. 2002. "A Controlled Trial of a Human Papillomavirus Type 16 Vaccine." *New England Journal of Medicine* 347(21):1645–51.

Kumle, M. 2008. "Declining Breast Cancer Incidence and Decreased HRT Use." *Lancet* 372(9639):608–10.

LaRosa, J.C., J. He, and S. Vupputuri. 1999. "Effect of Statins on Risk of Coronary Disease: A Meta-Analysis of Randomized Controlled Trials." *Journal of the American Medical Association* 282(24):2340–46.

Law, M.R., C.D. Frost, and N.J. Wald. 1991. "By How Much Does Dietary Salt Reduction Lower Blood Pressure? I – Analysis of Observational Data Among Populations." *British Medical Journal* 302(6780):811–15.

Lesterhuis, W.J., E.H. Aarntzen, I.J. De Vries, D.H. Schuurhuis, C.G. Figdor, G.J. Adema, and C.J. Punt. 2008. "Dendritic Cell Vaccines in Melanoma: From Promise to Proof?" *Critical Review in Oncology/Hematology* 66(2):118–34.

Linos, E., D. Spanos, B.A. Rosner, K. Linos, T. Hesketh, J.D. Qu, Y.T. Gao, W. Zheng, and G.A. Colditz. 2008. "Effects of Reproductive and Demographic Changes on Breast Cancer Incidence in China: A Modeling Analysis." *Journal of National Cancer Institute* 100(19):1352–60.

Lopez, A.D., C.D. Mathers, M. Ezzati, D.T. Jamison, and C.J. Murray. 2006. *Global Burden of Disease and Risk Factors.* New York, NY, World Bank Publications.

Mackenbach, J.P., I. Stirbu, A.J. Roskam, M.M. Schaap, G. Menvielle, M. Leinsalu, and A.E. Kunst. 2008. "Socioeconomic Inequalities in Health in 22 European Countries." *New England Journal of Medicine* 358(23):2468–81.

Mamun, A.A., A. Peeters, J. Barendregt, F. Willekens, W. Nusselder, and L. Bonneux. 2004. "Smoking Decreases the Duration of Life Lived with and Without Cardiovascular Disease: A Life Course Analysis of the Framingham Heart Study." *European Heart Journal* 25(5):409–15.

Mashta, O. 2008. "Government Strategy on HIV and AIDS in Developing Countries Lacks Detail, Say MPs." *British Medical Journal* 337:a2832.

Mathers, C.D. and D. Loncar. 2006. "Projections of Global Mortality and Burden of Disease from 2002 to 2030." *PLoS Medicine* 3(11):e442.

May, R.M. and R.M. Anderson. 1987. "Transmission Dynamics of HIV Infection." *Nature* 326(6109):137–42.

McKeown, T. 1976. *The Role of Medicine: Dream, Mirage, or Nemesis.* In Classic Texts in Health Care, L. Mackay, K. Soothill, K. Melia (eds). Butterworth-Heinemann Ltd., Oxford: pp. 31–34.

McKeown, T. and R.G. Brown. 1955. "Medical Evidence Related to English Population Changes in the Eighteenth Century." *Population Studies* 9(2):119–41.

McQueen, M.J., S. Hawken, X. Wang, S. Ounpuu, A. Sniderman, J. Probstfield, K. Steyn, J.E. Sanderson, M. Hasani, E. Volkova, K. Kazmi, and S. Yusuf. 2008. "Lipids, Lipoproteins, and Apolipoproteins as Risk Markers of

Myocardial Infarction in 52 Countries (the INTERHEART Study): A Case-Control Study." *Lancet* 372(9634):224–33.

Merson, M.H., J. O'Malley, D. Serwadda, and C. Apisuk. 2008b. "The History and Challenge of HIV Prevention." *Lancet* 372(9637):475–88.

Merson, M., N. Padian, T.J. Coates, G.R. Gupta, S.M. Bertozzi, P. Piot, P. Mane, M. Bartos, and H.I.V.P.S.A. Lancet. 2008a. "Combination HIV Prevention." *Lancet* 372(9652):1805–6.

Mills, E.J., B. Rachlis, P. Wu, P.J. Devereaux, P. Arora, and D. Perri. 2008. "Primary Prevention of Cardiovascular Mortality and Events with Statin Treatments: A Network Meta-Analysis Involving More Than 65,000 Patients." *Journal of the American College of Cardiology* 52(22):1769–81.

Muldoon, M.F., S.B. Manuck, A.B. Mendelsohn, J.R. Kaplan, and S.H. Belle. 2001. "Cholesterol Reduction and Non-Illness Mortality: Meta-Analysis of Randomised Clinical Trials." *British Medical Journal* 322(7277):11–15.

Murphy, E.M., M.E. Greene, A. Mihailovic, and P. Olupot-Olupot. 2006. "Was the 'ABC' Approach (Abstinence, Being Faithful, Using Condoms) Responsible for Uganda's Decline in HIV?" *PLoS Med* 3(9):e379.

Neeleman, J. and G. Lewis. 1999. "Suicide, Religion, and Socioeconomic Conditions. An Ecological Study in 26 Countries, 1990." *Journal Epidemiology and Community Health* 53(4):204–10.

Neeleman, J., S. Wessely, and M. Wadsworth. 1998. "Predictors of Suicide, Accidental Death, and Premature Natural Death in a General-Population Birth Cohort." *Lancet* 351(9096):93–97.

Niessen, L.W., J.J. Barendregt, L. Bonneux, and P.J. Koudstaal. 1993. "Stroke Trends in an Aging Population. The Technology Assessment Methods Project Team." *Stroke* 24(7):931–39.

Olshansky, S.J. and A.B. Ault. 1986. "The Fourth Stage of the Epidemiologic Transition: The Age of Delayed Degenerative Diseases." *Milbank Quarterly* 64(3):355–91.

Olshansky, S.J., L. Hayflick, and D.A. Carnes. 2002. "No Truth to the Fountain of Youth." *Scientific American* 286(6):92–95.

Omran, A.R. 1971. "The Epidemiologic Transition. A Theory of the Epidemiology of Population Change." *Milbank Memorial Fund Quarterly* 49(4):509–38.

Omran, A.R. 1977. "Epidemiologic Transition in the United States: The Health Factor in Population Change." *Population Bulletin* 32(2):1–42.

Peeters, A., J.J. Barendregt, F. Willekens, J.P. Mackenbach, A. Al Mamun, and L. Bonneux. 2003a. "Obesity in Adulthood and its Consequences for Life Expectancy: A Life-Table Analysis." *Annals of Internal Medicine* 138(1):24–32.

Peeters, A., L. Bonneux, J.J. Barendregt, and J.P. Mackenbach. 2003b. "Improvements in Treatment of Coronary Heart Disease and Cessation of Stroke Mortality Rate Decline." *Stroke* 34(7):1610–14.

Peto, R. 1994. "Smoking and Death: The Past 40 Years and the Next 40." *British Medical Journal* 309:937–39.

Peto, R., S. Darby, H. Deo, P. Silcocks, E. Whitley, and R. Doll. 2000. "Smoking, Smoking Cessation, and Lung Cancer in the UK Since 1950: Combination of National Statistics with Two Case-Control Studies." *British Medical Journal* 321(7257):323–29.

Peto, R., A.D. Lopez, J. Boreham, M. Thun, and C. Heath. 1992. "Mortality from Tobacco in Developed Countries: Indirect Estimation from Vital Statistics." *Lancet* 339:1268–78.

Pignone, M., M. Rich, S.M. Teutsch, A.O. Berg, and K.N. Lohr. 2002. "Screening for Colorectal Cancer in Adults at Average Risk: A Summary of the Evidence for the US Preventive Services Task Force." *Annals of Internal Medicine* 137(2):132.

Potts, M., D.T. Halperin, D. Kirby, A. Swidler, E. Marseille, J.D. Klausner, N. Hearst, R.G. Wamai, J.G. Kahn, and J. Walsh. 2008. "Public Health. Reassessing HIV Prevention." *Science* 320(5877):749–50.

Poustie, V.J. and P. Rutherford. 2001. "Dietary Treatment for Familial Hypercholesterolaemia." *Cochrane Database Systematic Review* (2):CD001918.

Proctor, R.N. 1996. "The Anti-Tobacco Campaign of the Nazis: A Little Known Aspect of Public Health in Germany, 1933–45." *British Medical Journal* 313(7070):1450–53.

Proctor, R. 1999. *The Nazi War on Cancer*. Princeton, NJ, Princeton University Press.

Proctor, R.N. 2001. "Commentary: Schairer and Schoniger's Forgotten Tobacco Epidemiology and the Nazi Quest for Racial Purity." *International Journal of Epidemiol* 30(1):31–34.

Raiha, I., H. Kemppainen, J. Kaprio, M. Koskenvuo, and L. Sourander. 1998. "Lifestyle, Stress, and Genes in Peptic Ulcer Disease: A Nationwide Twin Cohort Study." *Archives of Internal Medicine* 158(7):698–704.

Rehm, J., C. Mathers, S. Popova, M. Thavorncharoensap, Y. Teerawattananon, and J. Patra. 2009. "Global Burden of Disease and Injury and Economic Cost Attributable to Alcohol Use and Alcohol-Use Disorders." *Lancet* 373(9682):2223–33.

Renehan, A.G., M. Tyson, M. Egger, R.F. Heller, and M. Zwahlen. 2008. "Body-Mass Index and Incidence of Cancer: A Systematic Review and Meta-Analysis of Prospective Observational Studies." *Lancet* 371(9612):569–78.

Reuser, M., L.G. Bonneux, and F.J. Willekens. 2009. "Smoking Kills, Obesity Disables: A Multistate Approach of the US Health and Retirement Survey." *Obesity (Silver Spring)* 17(4):783–89.

Robb, M.L. 2008. "Failure of the Merck HIV Vaccine: An Uncertain Step Forward." *Lancet* 372(9653):1857–58.

Roberts, H. 2009. "Reduced Use of Hormones and the Drop in Breast Cancer." *British Medical Journal* 338:b2116.

Roberts, C.G., E. Guallar, and A. Rodriguez. 2007. "Efficacy and Safety of Statin Monotherapy in Older Adults: A Meta-Analysis." *Journals of Gerontology: Series A, Biological Sciences and Medical Sciences* 62(8):879–87.

Roberts, I. and C. Power. 1996. "Does the Decline in Child Injury Mortality Vary by Social Class? A Comparison of Class Specific Mortality in 1981 and 1991." *British Medical Journal* 313(7060):784–86.

Roseboom, T., S. de Rooij, and R. Painter. 2006. "The Dutch Famine and its Long-Term Consequences for Adult Health." *Early Human Development* 82(8):485–91.

Rosengren, A., S. Hawken, S. Ounpuu, K. Sliwa, M. Zubaid, W.A. Almahmeed, K.N. Blackett, C. Sitthi-amorn, H. Sato, and S. Yusuf. 2004. "Association of Psychosocial Risk Factors with Risk of Acute Myocardial Infarction in 11119 Cases and 13648 Controls from 52 Countries (the INTERHEART Study): Case-Control Study." *Lancet* 364(9438):953–62.

Rutstein, D.D., W. Berenberg, T.C. Chalmers, C.G. Child, III, A.P. Fishman, and E.B. Perrin. 1976. "Measuring the Quality of Medical Care. A Clinical Method." *New England Journal of Medicine* 294(11):582–88.

Scandinavian Simvastatin Survival Study (4S). 1994. "Randomised Trial of Cholesterol Lowering in 4444 Patients with Coronary Heart Disease: The Scandinavian Simvastatin Survival Study (4S)." *Lancet* 344(8934):1383–89.

Schatz, J. 2008. "On the Road in Zambia." *Lancet* 372(9637):435–36.

Sethi, D., F. Racioppi, I. Baumgarten, and P. Vida. 2006. *Injuries and Violence in Europe. Why They Matter and What Can be Done.* Edited by W.R.O.F. Europe, Copenhagen.

Shaw, S.M., J.E. Fildes, N. Yonan, and S.G. Williams. 2009. "Pleiotropic Effects and Cholesterol-Lowering Therapy." *Cardiology* 112(1):4–12.

Shelton, J.D. 2007. "Ten Myths and One Truth About Generalised HIV Epidemics." *Lancet* 370(9602):1809–11.

Silva Idos, S., B. De Stavola, and V. McCormack. 2008. "Birth Size and Breast Cancer Risk: Re-Analysis of Individual Participant Data from 32 Studies." *PLoS Medicine* 5(9):e193.

Sparen, P., D. Vagero, D.B. Shestov, S. Plavinskaja, N. Parfenova, V. Hoptiar, D. Paturot, and M.R. Galanti. 2004. "Long Term Mortality After Severe Starvation During the Siege of Leningrad: Prospective Cohort Study." *British Medical Journal* 328(7430):11.

Staessen, J.A., J. Wang, G. Bianchi, and W.H. Birkenhager. 2003. "Essential Hypertension." *Lancet* 361(9369):1629–41.

Staessen, J.A., J.G. Wang, and L. Thijs. 2001. "Cardiovascular Protection and Blood Pressure Reduction: A Meta-Analysis." *Lancet* 358(9290):1305–15.

Standing Medical Advisory Committee. 1997. *The Use of Statins.* London, Department of Health.

Stewart, S.T., D.M. Cutler, and A.B. Rosen. 2009. "Forecasting the Effects of Obesity and Smoking on U.S. Life Expectancy." *New England Journal of Medicine* 361(23):2252–60.

Strandberg, T.E., K. Pyorala, T.J. Cook, L. Wilhelmsen, O. Faergeman, G. Thorgeirsson, T.R. Pedersen, and J. Kjekshus. 2004. "Mortality and Incidence of Cancer During 10-year Follow-Up of the Scandinavian Simvastatin Survival Study (4S)." *Lancet* 364(9436):771–77.

Stuckler, D., S. Basu, M. Suhrcke, A. Coutts, and M. McKee. 2009. "The Public Health Effect of Economic Crises and Alternative Policy Responses in Europe: An Empirical Analysis." *Lancet* 374(9686):315–23.

Szreter, S. 2003. "The Population Health Approach in Historical Perspective." *American Journal of Public Health* 93(3):421–31.

Tait, N. and J.M. Little. 1995. "The Treatment of Gall Stones." *British Medical Journal* 311(6997):99–105.

Tuomilehto, J., R. Bonita, A. Stewart, A. Nissinen, and J.T. Salonen. 1991. "Hypertension, Cigarette Smoking, and the Decline in Stroke Incidence in Eastern Finland." *Stroke* 22(1):7–11.

US Department of Health and Human Services. 2004. *The Health Consequences of Smoking: A Report of the Surgeon General.* Washington, DC. www.surgeongeneral.gov/library/smokingconsequences/

US Surgeon General. 2000. *Reducing Tobacco Use. A Report of the Surgeon General.* Atlanta, GA, Centers for Disease Control and Prevention.

US Surgeon General. 2006. *The Health Consequences of Involuntary Exposure to Tobacco Smoke, A Report of the Surgeon General.* Atlanta, GA, US Department of Health and Human Services, Centres for Disease Control and Prevention.

Uzzan, B., R. Cohen, P. Nicolas, M. Cucherat, and G.Y. Perret. 2007. "Effects of Statins on Bone Mineral Density: A Meta-Analysis of Clinical Studies." *Bone* 40(6):1581–87.

Verdecchia, A., S. Francisci, H. Brenner, G. Gatta, A. Micheli, L. Mangone, and I. Kunkler. 2007. "Recent Cancer Survival in Europe: A 2000–02 Period Analysis of EUROCARE-4 Data." *Lancet Oncology* 8(9):784–96.

Wald, N.J. and M.R. Law. 2003. "A Strategy to Reduce Cardiovascular Disease by More Than 80%." *British Medical Journal* 326(7404):1419.

Walker, A.R. and I. Segal. 1995. "Appendicitis: An African Perspective." *Journal of the Royal Society of Medicine* 88(11):616–19.

Welch, H.G. 2009. "Overdiagnosis and Mammography Screening." *British Medical Journal* 339:b1425.

Weller, S.C. 1993. "A Meta-Analysis of Condom Effectiveness in Reducing Sexually Transmitted HIV." *Social Science and Medicine* 36(12):1635–44.

Weller, S. and K. Davis. 2002. "Condom Effectiveness in Reducing Heterosexual HIV Transmission." *Cochrane Database Systematic Review* (1):CD003255.

Whitlock, G., S. Lewington, P. Sherliker, R. Clarke, J. Emberson, J. Halsey, N. Qizilbash, R. Collins, and R. Peto. 2009. "Body-Mass Index and Cause-Specific Mortality in 900 000 Adults: Collaborative Analyses of 57 Prospective Studies." *Lancet* 373(9669):1083–96.

Woloshin, S. and L.M. Schwartz. 2009. "Numbers Needed to Decide." *Journal of National Cancer Institute* 101(17):1163–65.

Writing Group for the Women's Health Initiative Investigators. 2002. "Risks and Benefits of Estrogen Plus Progestin in Healthy Postmenopausal Women: Principal Results From the Women's Health Initiative Randomized Controlled Trial." *Journal of the American Medical Association* 288:321–33.

Yamamoto, A., H. Sudo, and A. Endo. 1980. "Therapeutic Effects of ML-236B in Primary Hypercholesterolemia." *Atherosclerosis* 35(3):259–66.

Yerushalmi, R. and K. Gelmon. 2008. "Chemotherapy for Oestrogen-Receptor-Negative Breast Cancer." *Lancet* 371(9606):4–5.

Yusuf, S., S. Hawken, S. Ounpuu, T. Dans, A. Avezum, F. Lanas, M. McQueen, A. Budaj, P. Pais, J. Varigos, and L. Lisheng. 2004. "Effect of Potentially Modifiable Risk Factors Associated With Myocardial Infarction in 52 Countries (the INTERHEART Study): Case-Control Study." *Lancet* 364(9438):937–52.

Zaridze, D., P. Brennan, J. Boreham, A. Boroda, R. Karpov, A. Lazarev, I. Konobeevskaya, V. Igitov, T. Terechova, P. Boffetta, and R. Peto. 2009. "Alcohol and Cause-Specific Mortality in Russia: A Retrospective Case-Control Study of 48,557 Adult Deaths." *Lancet* 373(9682):2201–14.

# Conclusion

Richard G. Rogers and Eileen M. Crimmins

This handbook has presented information on mortality trends and patterns over time, over geographic area, and by social, demographic, behavioral, and psychological factors. These chapters have presented new and important techniques and data sets for the examination of mortality, "set the stage" for our current understanding of adult mortality, and identified promising new areas of research.

As environmental factors decrease in importance, socioeconomic status (SES) and health behaviors increase in relative importance in affecting the risk of death. We have learned much about how to behave to avoid death. The impact of smoking on mortality for a population is affected by current and past prevalence rates, the length of time smoking, as well as the age and sex distributions. Meslé and Vallin (Chapter 2) point out that compared to other MDCs, including France and Japan, the United States has relatively low life expectancies. But compared to many other populations, the United States has also had a long history of smoking, including exceptionally heavy smoking, especially among males, but more recently among females. Thus, future country-specific trends in life expectancy may be sensitive to long-term trends in smoking (Pampel 2002; Preston et al. 2010) as well as other health behaviors, including diet, exercise, and alcohol consumption.

There are many opportunities for additional data, especially with the tremendous growth in the number of longitudinal data sets, including harmonizing data, integrating data sets, expanding the variables used, providing more detail in the variables used, linking to additional administrative data, and expanding additional data for mortality analysis, including developing additional longitudinal data collection efforts that can assess changes over time. Some countries (including China and India) rely on sample registration systems, whereas others rely on verbal autopsies (Anderson, Chapter 22). As vital registration systems increase worldwide, we can expect better overall and cause-specific mortality data that will contribute to better international comparisons. Extant data sets can be further strengthened with additional links to other data sources, including multilevel data that includes information about contextual effects of crime, housing, schooling, employment, health behaviors and conditions, and natural hazards and disasters (see Chapters 20 and 21).

SES is strongly associated with mortality (see Chapters 9, 12, and 13). Use of detailed questions about SES collected in longitudinal sample surveys—including questions about employment, job characteristics, income, wealth, assets, and debt—provides ways to better understand how SES disparities in mortality arise. Although educational attainment is strongly associated with mortality, it is important to consider additional dimensions of education, including IQ, informal training, degrees, certification, quality and status of the educational institution, and time to completion of degrees.

Jylhä (Chapter 16) demonstrated the continued association of self-rated health and mortality, even net of a host of different and extensive variables. This relationship may warrant additional data collection efforts to identify and collect information on such important but heretofore unmeasured or underused variables as,

R.G. Rogers (✉)
Department of Sociology and Population Program, IBS, University of Colorado, Boulder, CO 80309-0483, USA
e-mail: richard.rogers@colorado.edu

say, genetic factors, stress, Vitamin D, depression, and cognitive impairment. Further research is also merited to examine the cumulative effects of such adverse and traumatic social and economic stressors as exposure to daily hassles, physical threats and assaults, rape, muggings and thefts, divorce, death of a loved one, witness to an assault or death, job loss, widowhood, and natural disasters and their potential coping mechanisms on subsequent mortality (see Jackson and colleagues, Chapter 15).

There is increasing interest in comparing health across countries. For example, much interest arose over the research by Banks et al. (2006), which found that compared to the United Kingdom, individuals in the United States generally report worse health status. There have also been innovative collaborative ventures to collect similar data between Canada and the United States, including the Joint Canada/United States Survey of Health (see www.cdc.gov/nchs/nhis/sjcush.htm). Many international groups are working on the harmonization of data sets, which should add significant resources for future study of mortality. Several data sets have been harmonized to the US Health and Retirement Study: in Europe, the English Longitudinal Study of Ageing (ELSA) and the Survey of Health, Ageing and Retirement in Europe (SHARE); and in Asia, the Chinese Health and Retirement Study (CHARLS), the Korean Longitudinal Study of Aging (KLOSA), and the Japanese Study of Aging and Retirement (STARS).

Much research has examined causes of death (see Chapters 7, 22, and 23). Future research could further examine detailed causes of death, including diabetes, Alzheimer's disease, external causes, and HIV/AIDS. Because HIV/AIDS has a major impact on mortality worldwide, and because of current HIV prevalence rates, it is of paramount importance to better document and understand HIV/AIDS morbidity and mortality (see Bongaarts, Pelletier, and Gerland, Chapter 8). As many chronic and degenerative diseases are controlled, MDCs and LCDs are experiencing large and sometimes increasing risks of death from external causes. Currently, Russia demonstrates exceptionally high mortality among males aged 25–44 for traffic accidents, suicides, and homicides (Meslé and Vallin, Chapter 2). As Meslé and Vallin observe, although the United States has homicide rates below Russia, it still suffers from unacceptably high levels of violence. Researchers should answer the challenge to reduce the risk of violence and of homicide mortality throughout the world. Further research could examine the overall effects of Alzheimer's disease—which is increasing in many countries—on mortality and on country-specific life expectancies, especially at older ages.

Researchers and policymakers need to be clear about what data are needed and how they will be used to better understand mortality trends and to reduce the risk of death. Importantly, Anderson (Chapter 22) distinguishes between individuals "dying with and dying from a condition." Death certificates ascertain whether an individual died from a condition; many researchers are interested in whether a decedent died with a condition. For example, diabetic individuals who die from other causes may not have diabetes listed on their death certificate. Such nuances suggest that even if the prevalence of diabetes increases, which has occurred in many countries around the world, and even if diabetes contributes to increased morbidity risks, the risk of death due to diabetes will not necessarily increase. Such variations warrant additional research to better understand and prevent specific causes of death, including diabetes.

One benefit of this handbook is the application and discussion of multiple mortality methods and techniques. Indeed, various chapters discussed single- and multistate life tables, hazard models, and various forms of direct and indirect estimation (see especially Chapters 24, 25 and 26). For example, Heuveline and Clark (Chapter 24) apply a Bayesian Melding technique to improve model schedules of mortality with data from the Agincourt demographic surveillance site in South Africa. They also demonstrate that frailty models and vitality-with-challenges models represent ways to better understand mortality patterns, especially at older ages.

Over the next several decades, some countries may see substantial increases in life expectancy while others may see stagnant or even declining life expectancies. Many countries around the world have experienced substantial mortality improvements by combating infectious diseases and improving treatment of such degenerative diseases as cancer and heart disease. Many LDCs have borrowed and implemented health care technologies of MDCs and improved their public health and medical infrastructure to produce life expectancy gains. But many countries have experienced mortality reversals due to HIV/AIDS mortality, famine, political and military conflict, economic crises, and declines in health care (Reniers, Masquelier, and Gerland, Chapter 7). We are regularly reminded of the potential threats from armed conflict, including terrorist attacks, executions, and war-related deaths (Heuveline and Clark, Chapter 24). Some of these negative forces persist for long periods of time, and may also produce lagged effects. For example, the war in Afghanistan has contributed to the country's exceptionally low life expectancy, and even when the war ends, there may be slow gains in life expectancy due to slow social and economic recovery.

And many individuals cope with stress and continue to engage in such risky behaviors as reckless driving, excessive drinking, drug abuse, tobacco consumption, overeating, and inactivity. For instance, even though cigarette smoking prevalence rates have declined in the United States, one fifth of the adult population continues to smoke. And the prevalence of overweight and obesity is increasing in many countries around the world. While we can hope for remarkable mortality declines that could result from genetic and medical breakthroughs (see Chapters 19 and 27), more likely mortality reductions may be realized through consistent and prolonged engagement of healthy behaviors.

Japanese males and females enjoy the highest life expectancy at birth in the world, due to healthy diets, exercise, support and respect for the elderly, good average incomes with low-income inequality and unemployment, and strong social support, including support for family members. But this high Japanese life expectancy is a recent accomplishment. From the mid-nineteenth century through the mid-twentieth century New Zealand (non-Maori) enjoyed one of the highest life expectancies in the world (Meslé and Vallin Chapter 2; Oeppen and Vaupel 2002), in part owing to high European migration, which selected healthy individuals (Meslé and Vallin, Chapter 2). Thus, there are interesting contrasts between the early healthy migrant effects among New Zealanders and the beneficial effects of low migration and ethnic homogeneity among the Japanese. Future research should further explore the effects of migration on mortality among the migrants (see Chapter 11) and on country-specific life expectancies. Furthermore, researchers should examine how long the Japanese can hold their number one position in life expectancy as they still experience demanding jobs with high levels of stress, relatively large sex inequality, increasing unemployment, and increasing rates of smoking, and whether another country is poised to claim the top spot of highest life expectancy in the world.

Great gains in many countries in life expectancy have resulted from increased road and occupational safety, increased knowledge about healthy behaviors, and improved drug therapies (including antihypertensive drugs and statins). But such gains in life expectancy may also delay the age of death, contribute the population aging, and change the cause-of-death structure. More individuals will die at older ages and from such chronic and degenerative diseases as cancer, heart disease, stroke, and Alzheimer's disease. For example, as Bonneux (Chapter 28) points out, reductions in cardiovascular mortality may increase the risk of death from cancer. Although there have been some remarkable gains in cancer survival, they come at some costs. For example, cancer screening reduces cancer mortality, but requires additional screening and follow-up.

Based on expected future changes in health behaviors, medical technology, public health, and SES, we expect future life expectancies to continue to increase on average, but potentially at a decreasing rate. Some new medical technologies may provide life-saving benefits, but to select populations with rare diseases; some medical interventions may increase life at the oldest ages by modest amounts, which can improve the life of the oldest old, but may have modest impacts on overall life expectancy. And although new technologies may be available, their use may be restricted to those who are wealthy and who have health insurance. Thus, even with heroic new medical treatment, financial considerations, inequality, and lack of health insurance may limit the ability of new treatments to vastly increase population life expectancies.

Although we have the potential to make great gains in years of life, higher life expectancy is not always the ultimate goal. Some individuals place greater value on perceived higher quality rather than quantity of life, or the benefits of engaging in risky avocations (e.g., rock climbing, downhill skiing, skydiving, hang gliding, and scuba diving), dangerous occupations (e.g., fire fighters, test pilots, oil-rig workers, deep-sea fishers, and deep-sea divers), or, say, indulging in rich foods, alcohol consumption, recreational drug use, and thrill-seeking behavior. Some individuals may actually extend their lives by risking their lives (Lyng 1990).

This handbook—which documents past, present, and future trends in life expectancy—provides a solid resource for academics, government workers, policymakers, researchers, graduate students, and others interested in understanding and potentially increasing population life expectancy. We hope that this handbook contributes to reduced risk of death throughout the world; to reduced disparities by age, sex, race/ethnicity, SES, and geographic area; and ultimately to long, healthy, happy lives.

## References

Banks, J., M. Marmot, Z. Oldfield, and J.P. Smith. 2006. "Disease and Disadvantage in the United States and in England." *Journal of the American Medical Association* 295(17):2037–45.

Lyng, S. 1990. "Edgework: A Social Psychological Analysis of Voluntary Risk Taking." *American Journal of Sociology* 95(4):851–86.

Oeppen, J. and J.W. Vaupel. 2002. "Broken Limits to Life Expectancy." *Science* 296:1029–30.

Pampel, F. 2002. "Cigarette Use and the Narrowing Sex Differential in Mortality." *Population and Development Review* 28(1):77–104.

Preston, S., D.A. Glei, and J.R. Wilmoth. 2010. "Contribution of Smoking to International Differences in Life Expectancy." In E. Crimmins, S. Preston, and B. Cohen (eds.), *International Differences in Mortality at Older Ages: Dimensions and Sources*. Washington, DC, The National Academies Press.

# Index

**A**

Accidents and suicides mortality rates, LAC countries, 120
ACME (automated classification of medical entities), 475
Activity limitation including basic and instrumental daily activities, 557
Adult mortality
    between age 15 and 59 ($_{45}q_{15}$), probabilities of, 136
    estimates by United Nations Agencies, 158
    *See also Adult mortality in individual countries*
Adults—young (25–44), mortality among, 31–35
    decrease in total mortality, nineteenth century, 31
    focus on productive and reproductive activity, 31
    maternal mortality, reduction, 31
    ratio of 5-year age probabilities of death, 32
    standardized death rate, 34
    trends in probability of death, 32
Africa, adult mortality in, 151
    adult mortality estimates by UN Agencies, 158
    approaches for estimating, 152–154, 158
    causes of death, 158–160
    cause-specific mortality rates in adults, 159
    comparison of female $_5q_0$ and $_{45}q_{15}$, 156
    data for estimating mortality, 152
    estimates of $_{45}q_{15}$
        by country and sex, sibling histories, 165
    long-term trends in $_{45}q_{15}$, 162
        by country and sex, 163–164
    reconciling adult mortality estimates, 154–158
    sibling survival data as source, 160–162
    sibling survival estimates, 157
    trends in, 162–167
Age-/cause-specific death rates
    to female life-expectancy, 16
    impact on mortality changes, 26
    to male life-expectancy in Poland, 24
    to male life-expectancy in Russia/France, 23
Age of delayed cardiovascular disease (CVD)
    blood pressure lowering therapies, 586
    cardiovascular risk management through drug usage, 585
    case-fatality rates, 586
    causes of coronary heart disease mortality decline in US, 585
    cholesterol and lipoproteins, 587–588
    genetic variants, 588
    meta-meta-analysis, 588
    CVD and drug usage, 585
    hypertension, 587
        behavioral interventions, 587
        persistent, 587
    lifestyle changes, 585
    lowering cardiovascular risk, 586
        abdominal obesity, 586
        diabetes, 586
        factors, 586
        history of hypertension, 586
        psychosocial factors, 586
        raised ApoB/ApoA1 ratio, 586
        regular alcohol consumption, 586
        regular physical activity, 586
        smoking, 586
    male disadvantage, 584–585
    mass chemoprofylaxis of heart disease, 589
        poly pill/polydiet, 589
    mortality from IHD, 585
    sedentary lifestyle, 584
    statins, 588–589
    4 S trial, 588
Age of delayed degenerative disease, 584
Age patterns in adult mortality, 207–224
    adult longevity revolution, 213–217
    distribution of deaths by age, 212
    emergence of oldest old population, 217–218
        nonagenarians, 222
    historical development, 208
        Lexis's distribution of ages at death, 210–213
        number of deaths diminishes with age, 208–209
        number of deaths remains constant with age, 209–210
    increase in modal length of life
        since 1751, 214
        since 1947, 215–216
        since 1947, females, 218
    increase in the number of centenarians
        in 14 European countries, 219
        in France since 1816, by sex, 220
    Lexis's normal life duration, 213
    mortality according to age, 223
    mortality datasets by age, 211

Age patterns in adult mortality (cont.)
　mortality trajectory by age, 210
　number of centenarians, 219–222
　　Centenarian rate, 222
　　in European countries, sex-ratio, 221
　　in Japan and European countries, 221
　number of deaths by age, 210
　survival curve
　　by age, 210
　　drawn by Christiaan Huygens, 209
Ages, different stories for different: adult mortality, 28
　countries, age groups and, 28
　mortality among middle-aged adults (45–64), 35–39
　mortality among young adults (25–44), 31–35
　mortality among youth (15–24), 29–31
　　WWI and WWII, 29
　mortality at very old ages (80 and above), 43–44
　mortality in old age (65–79), 39–43
Age-specific death rates
　calculations, 49–50
　　exceptions, 50
　decline in, Austria/Sweden, 15
　　cause of, 16
AIDS mortality, global trends in, 171–182
　AIDS deaths, 176–178
　　by age, 178–179
　AIDS vs. No-AIDS scenarios, 181
　data, 171–172
　death rates in ages 15–59, 175
　　by HIV prevalence levels among adults aged 15–49, 175
　dynamics of HIV infections and AIDS deaths, 174–176
　estimated and projected deaths due to
　　by broad age group, 178
　　by region, 177
　evolution, 172–174
　life expectancy at age 15, 179–181
　percentage of deaths due to AIDS in age group 15–59, 179
Air pollution, websites on, 458
Alcohol consumption, 301–304, 592–595
　and mortality, 3
　recorded per capita, 302
All-cause mortality, 416–425
　of distinctive religious groups, 364–367
　rates, 313
　South Africa, age pattern of, 524–525
Alliance for Aging Research, 578–579
Allostatic load, 390
Amenable mortality, 492
Amish (religious groups), 364
ApoE (gene), 405
Asia, adult mortality in, 133–134
　changes in, 138–139
　　life expectancies at age 15, 137
　changes since 1950, 135–139
　major causes of death, 142–146
　　by major causes of death in selected WHO regions, 145
　mortality data collection in, 134–135
　population distribution by life expectancy at birth and sex ratio of, 142
　sex differentials in, 139–142

　sex ratios of (1990 and 2007), 141
　standardized mortality rates, 144
　transition, 146–148
Atypical mortality patterns, 524
Autopsy, 471
Avoidable mortality, 5
　causes of death, 1983–2002, 493–499
　concept development, 491–492
　　in 1980s, 492–501
　　in 1990s and 2000s, 501–502
　limitations, 505–506
　results of studies
　　Australia and New Zealand, 504–505
　　Europe, 503–504
　　North America, 502–503

B
Biological clock, manipulation of, 573
Biomarkers and mortality, 381–391
　activity of HPA axis and SNS, 387–388
　biomarkers in studying mortality, 390–391
　brief history, 381–382
　cardiovascular system, 382–384
　definition, 381
　effects of biomarkers on mortality, samples, 388–389
　inflammation, immunity, and infection, 386–387
　markers of organ function, 388
　　kidney, 388
　　lung, 388
　measures of biological risk, 389–390
　metabolic process, 384–386
　risk levels of individual biomarkers and subsequent mortality, 389
Black Americans, discrimination, chronic stress, and mortality among, 311–312
　age of onset of diabetes, arthritis, and menopause, 322
　Black:white ratios
　　all-cause mortality rates, 313
　　of endocrine, nutritional, and metabolic diseases mortality rates, 314
　　of linked birth/infant mortality rates, 312
　documenting shifting pattern of mortality rates, 312
　exploring mortality crossover, 321–324
　gestation and early life mortality crossover, 312–317
　negative life events by age and race, 319
　percent of adults who experienced traumatic event, 320
　recovery from traumatic events by race, 321
　stressors and stress effects over life course, 317–318
　　differential exposure to stress, 318–319
　　stress and coping, 319–320
　　stress and health, 320–321
Blood pressure, 382–383
Body mass index (BMI), 4
Brass model, 519–521
Bridge-coding studies, 477–478
Built environment, 443–446
　and air pollution, 449–450
　character of, 447–448
　　commercial establishments, 447
　　public- and private-recreation facilities, 447–448
　　public transportation, 448

Index

and crime, 450–451
    and health, 451
    physical design, 450
    theoretical explanations, 450
design of, 444
exposure to toxins, 446
health effects and time spent in automobiles, 446
history and background, 444
implications for higher-risk subpopulations, 451–452
    additional considerations for disadvantaged populations, 452
    elderly and functional decline, 451–452
land use, 444–445
metropolitan sprawl, 445
quality of, 448–450
    substandard housing, 448–449
street layout, 445
traffic-related safety, 446

## C

Calculation methods, health expectancies, 552–555
    cross-sectional methods, 553–554
        disability-adjusted life expectancy (DALE), 553
        disability-adjusted life years (DALY), 553
        health-adjusted life expectancy (HALE), 553
        Health Expectancy and the Disability Process (REVES), 553
        key elements, comparison, 553–554
        quality adjusted life years (QALYs), 553
    increment–decrement or multistate life table methods, 553
    multiple-decrement methods, 554–555
        life tables, 554
        stroke-free or dementia-free life expectancy, 555
    multistate methods, 554
        interpolated Markov chain (IMaCH), 554
        longitudinal data, disadvantage of, 554
        Medical Research Council Cognitive Function and Ageing Study (MRCCFAS), 554
        multistate life tables, advantages, 554
    period prevalence, 553
Cambodia, age pattern of mortality, 523
Cancer mortality, 420
Cardiovascular diseases (CVD)
    age of delayed
        blood pressure lowering therapies, 586
        cardiovascular risk management through drug usage, 585
        case-fatality rates, 586
        causes of coronary heart disease mortality decline in US, 585
        cholesterol and lipoproteins, 587–588
        hypertension, 587
        lifestyle changes, 585
        lowering cardiovascular risk, 586
        male disadvantage, 584
        mass chemoprofylaxis of heart disease, 589
        mortality from IHD, 585
        sedentary lifestyle, 584
        statins, 588–589
        4 S trial, 588
    communist countries, failure to prevent, 24

    and female life-expectancy trends, 28
    through drug usage, 585
Cardiovascular mortality, 37, 43, 421–422
    role of, 21–24
        beginning of convergence in, 23
        Russia, affected by, 22
        third age of epidemiologic transition, 21
Cardiovascular revolution, 12
    fourth stage of epidemiologic transition, 12
Cardiovascular system, 382–384
    biomarkers and mortality, 382–384
    blood pressure, 382
    glucose metabolism, 385
    heart rate, 384
    hypertension, 383
    pulse pressure, 383
Catecholamines, 387
Cause-of-death trends, 40
Cause-specific death rates, *see* Age-/cause-specific death rates
Cells and stuff between cells, 575–576
Cerebrovascular mortality, female, 40
Childhood and adulthood conditions, 200
    by gender and race/ethnicity, 199
Chile
    circulatory disease mortality, 37
    digestive diseases, 34
    enumerated to expected population in, 111
    infectious mortality, 30, 35
    male standardized death rates
        causes (ages 45–64), 38
    male standardized death rates by external causes at ages 25–44, 36
    mortality from traffic accidents, 35
    standardized death rate, 34
    suicide, 35
    trends in infectious diseases/digestive diseases/external causes, 35
    youth (15–24), mortality among, 29
Chronic morbidity or long-standing illness (LSI), 557
Circulatory disease
    categories, 40
    as cause of divergence, 41
    mortality, 37, 40, 43
        decline of, 23
        LAC countries, 118
Civil registration systems, 468
Clergy (religious groups), 354
Coale and Demeny model table, 517, 519–520
    values of logit($_x q_0$), 580
Coding and classifying causes of death, 467
    collection of cause-of-death information
        accuracy of, 470–472
        cause of death certifiers, 469–470
        civil registration systems, 468
        death certificate, 468–469
        strategies for, 470
    counting deaths due to common risk factors, 482–483
    international classification of diseases, 472–473
        analyzing trends across revisions of ICD, 476
        automated coding systems, 475–476
        bridge-coding studies, 477–478

Coding and classifying causes of death (*cont.*)
    cause-of-death coding, 474
        first five revisions of ICD, 476
        multiple cause-of-death coding, 475
        selection of underlying cause of death, 474–475
        seventh, eighth and ninth revisions of ICD, 476
    multiple-cause tabulations, 479–481
    ranking causes of death, 481–482
    tabulation and presentation of cause-of-death data, 478–479
Cohort life expectancy, 533–548
    age effects, 537
    cohort influences, 537
    complications, immediate *vs.* delayed influences, 538
    delayed effects on mortality, 537
    extreme conditions, 537
    "period effects," 537
    period life expectancy, relationship between, 544–545
    period *vs.* cohort influences on age-specific mortality rates, 536
    theoretical biological aging, 536
    time-specific influences, 536
Communist countries, failure to prevent cardiovascular diseases, 24
Compression/expansion of morbidity and dynamic equilibrium, 552
Continuous life-expectancy improvements, 15
    industrialized countries, 15
    Japan, Meiji era, 15
    New Zealand, "non-Maori" population, 15
    nineteenth century, 15–16
Conventional *vs.* tempo-adjusted life expectancy at age 15, 74
Convergence, idea of, 12
Coronary heart disease (CHD) mortality, 586
C-reactive protein (CRP), 386, 389
Creatinine, 332, 388, 389
Cross-sectional cohort mortality indexes, 545–547
    CAL and underlying mortality conditions, 547
    cross-sectional average length of life (CAL), 545
        interpretations, 545–546
Cumulative country populations/life expectancy
    1950–1955, 10
    1975–1980, 10
    2005–2010, 10
Czechoslovakia, changes in life expectancy at age 15, 69
Czech Republic
    death rates from ages 15 to 100 for 1981–1985/1961–1965, 62
    life expectancy, 21

## D

Death, coding and classifying causes of, 467
    age-adjusted death rates for nephritis, nephrotic syndrome, and nephrosis, 477–478
    autopsy, 471
    collection of cause-of-death information
        accuracy of, 470–472
        cause of death certifiers, 469–470
        civil registration systems, 468
        death certificate, 468–469
        strategies for, 470
    counting deaths due to common risk factors, 482–483
    Comparability ratio (CR) for cause-of-death category, 477
    international classification of diseases, 472–473
        analyzing trends across revisions of ICD, 476
        automated coding systems, 475–476
        bridge-coding studies, 477–478
        cause-of-death coding, 474
        first five revisions of ICD, 475
        multiple cause-of-death coding, 475
        selection of underlying cause of death, 474–475
        seventh, eighth and ninth revisions of ICD, 476
    multiple-cause tabulations, 479–481
    ranking causes of death, 481–483
    tabulation and presentation of cause-of-death data, 478–479
    ten leading causes of death for world and selected countries, 482
Death rates from ages 15 to 100, 62
Degenerative and man-made diseases, age of, 11, 20–21
Demographic and Health Surveys (DHS)
    mortality at ages 35–39, 32
    Niger, AIDS mortality, 30
    Zimbabwe, 31–32
Denmark, life expectancy
    male/female comparison, 25
    male life expectancy, 26
Diabetes mortality rates, LAC countries, 119
Diet
    exercise, 4
    nutritionally balanced, 3
    nutrition and, 295
        carbohydrates, 296–297
        fat, 295–296
        fruits and vegetables, 296
        special diets, 297
Disability-adjusted life expectancy (DALE), 553
Disability-adjusted life years (DALY), 553
Disability-free life expectancy (DFLE), 552
Disasters
    most deadly natural, 453
    websites on, 458
Divergence/convergence process, 13
    circulatory disease, as cause of, 41–42
    divergence
        cancers and other diseases, 43
        causes of death, 40
        since 1980s, France/Japan/US, 40
    first wave: pandemic receding, 13–14
    new phase of divergence among MDCs, 21
    second wave: cardiovascular revolution, 20–21
    Sub-Saharan Africa divergence, 19
    third wave, 24–28
    between western and eastern countries, 24
Dizygotic (MZ) twins, 401–402
Drug mortality, 422–423

## E

Early life conditions, mortality and
    challenges and directions for future research, 202–203
        key conceptual and analytical challenges, 202
    childhood/adult conditions
        by gender and race/ethnicity, 199

with risk of death, 197–198
    with risk of death, results, 198–201
frameworks linking early life conditions with adult mortality risks, 192
and later life mortality, 187–188
    imprint and pathway linkages between, 193
physical exposures in childhood and adulthood mortality risks
    infectious diseases as imprint process, 196–197
    infectious diseases as pathway process, 197
    nutrition as imprint process, 195–196
    nutrition as pathway process, 196
    ratios of death for each childhood and adulthood condition
        by gender among non-Hispanic white adults, 201
        by gender and race/ethnicity, 200
shape adult mortality risks, 187–188
social exposures in childhood and adulthood mortality risks, 192
    family environment as imprint process, 194
    family environment as pathway process, 194–195
    socioeconomic environment as imprint process, 192–193
    socioeconomic environment as pathway process, 193–195
theoretical frameworks, 189
    biological imprint/pathway, 191
    pathway frameworks, 190–191
Economic and social events, 4
Educational attainment and adult mortality, 241–242
    changes in educational differences in mortality over time, 254–255
    conceptual framework
        association between, 243–244
        measuring education, 242–243
        mechanisms, 244–246
    educational differences in US life expectancy at age 25, 254
    international comparisons, 255–256
    life expectancy differences, 253–254
    policy implications, 256–257
    risk among US adults aged 25–84, 247–251
    US adult mortality
        cause-specific adult mortality, 248
        differences by age and sex, 251–252
        differences by race/ethnicity, 252–253
        for females, stratified by age and race/ethnicity, 249
        hazard ratios for association between, 247
        for males, stratified by age and race/ethnicity, 250
        patterns of relative risk, 246–247
        stratified by age and sex, 248
Employment status and overall mortality, 265
Epidemiologic transition, theory of, 11–13
    AIDS – fifth transition, 13
    fourth stage of, 12
    sixth age, 13
    three ages, 11
Europe, adult mortality in, 49–51
    conventional *vs.* tempo-adjusted life expectancy at age 15, 75
    countries of, 49
    country-specific levels and trend, 56–60
    general trends and regional disparities, 51–56

length of life inequality, 63–65
life expectancy (conventional)/tempo-adjusted life expectancy at age 15
    females, 72
    males, 73
life inequality for adults, 1955–2005, 64
male and female life expectancy trends since 1950, 57–58
tempo-adjusted life expectancy in period 2001–2005, 71–75
trends in age-specific, 60–63
trends in cause-specific, 65–71
*European Community Atlas of Avoidable Mortality*, 505
European Community Concerted Action Project on Health Services and Avoidable Deaths, 500
European Community Household Panel (ECHP), 558
Eurostat and the European Health Expectancy Monitoring Unit (EHEMU), 556
Eurostat Population Database, 49
Exercise and diet, 4

**F**
Family environment
    as imprint process, 194
    as pathway process, 194–195
Female adult mortality estimates, Zimbabwe, 154
Female life-expectancy trends
    cardiovascular diseases and, 28
    contributions of decline, 19
    for selected developing countries, 18
    *vs.* male life expectancy, 25
Female standardized death rates, 41
Frailty models, 525–526
Framingham score, 390
France
    age-/cause-specific death rates to male life-expectancy in, 23
    cerebrovascular diseases, 27
    circulatory diseases, 37
    female mortality *vs.* male mortality, 31
    French female survival curve, 10
    homicide, 35
    infectious mortality, 35
    life expectancy at age 80 in, 44
    male mortality *vs.* female mortality, nineteenth century, 35
    male standardized death rates
        causes (ages 45–64), 38
        by external causes at ages 25–44, 36
    mental disorders at very old ages, 28
    standardized death rate, 34
    suicide, 35
    trends in female standardized death rates by causes at ages 80, 44
    youth (15-24), mortality among, 29
        mortality from external causes, 30
Functional limitation, 557

**G**
Genetic factors and adult mortality, 399
    adoption studies of early-adult deaths, 404
    adult mortality studies among relatives, 405
    exceptional longevity, 403
    familial aggregation of mortality risk and lifespan, 399
    family studies of exceptional survival, 403

Genetic factors and adult mortality (*cont.*)
  heritability of lifespan, 400
  large variation in lifespan within birth cohort, 400
  marital status–mortality association, 405–406
  path model, 401
  specific genetic factors influencing adult mortality, 404–405
  telomere–mortality association, 406–407
  twin studies of exceptional survival, 403–405
  twin studies of lifespan, 401–402
    twin lifespan, 402
    validity, 402–403
Genome-wide association studies (GWAS), 407
Geographic Concentrations (religious groups), 355
Glucose metabolism, 385

## H
Happiness, 557
Hayflick's rationale, 572
Health
  definition, 330
  evaluation, process, 330
  quantitative empirical research, 334
Health-adjusted life expectancy (HALE), 553
Health and mortality consequences of physical environment, 442
  built environment, 443–446
    character of, 447–448
    and crime, 450–451
    implications for higher-risk subpopulations, 451–452
    quality of, 448–450
  individual and contextual pathways mediating effects of, 442–443
    health-related behavior, 442
    social capital, 443
    social relationships, 442–443
    stress, 442
  mortality risk and physical environment, 442–443
  socially conditioned consequences of environment
    climate change and health, 457
    natural disasters, 452–455
    temperature, 455–457
Health behaviors, health, and mortality, relationships among, 289–290
  alcohol consumption, 301–304
    recorded per capita, 303
  measurement issues, 290–291
  nutrition and diet, 295
    carbohydrates, 296–297
    fat, 295–296
    fruits and vegetables, 296
    special diets, 297
  obesity, 299–301
    prevalence in adults, 301
  physical activity, 297–299
  tobacco use, 291–295
    tobacco use among adults, 293
Health domains, categories
  activity limitation including basic and instrumental daily activities, 557
  chronic morbidity or long-standing illness, 557
  functional limitation, 557
  happiness, 557
  impairment, 557
  self-perceived health (SPH), 557
  well-being, 557
Health expectancies, relevance of, 555–563
  measuring burden of disease by disability-free life expectancy, 562–563
    cause-elimination methods, 562–563
  social inequalities in health expectancy, 560–562
    DFLE at ages 65 and 85, 561
    education, 560–561
    gender, 560
    income and deprivation, 562
    occupation, 561–562
    race/ethnicity, 562
  spatial comparisons, 555–557
    GALI, 556
    global estimates of health expectancy, 555–556
    metaregression techniques, 556
    statistics of income and living conditions, 556
    subregional estimates of health expectancy, 556–557
  temporal comparisons within countries, 557–560
    chronological series of health expectancies published since 2000, 558
    health domains, categories, 557
Health policy indicators, 492
Health transition, 13
  first stage in, 19
    role of infectious diseases, 31
  levels, 13
Healthy life expectancy
  calculation methods, 552–555
    cross-sectional methods, 553–554
    multiple-decrement methods, 554–555
    multistate methods, 554
  definition, 551–552
    compression/expansion of morbidity and dynamic equilibrium, 552
  directions for future research, 563
  healthy life years at age 50 for EU countries, 552
  relevance of health expectancies, 555–563
    burden of disease by disability-free life expectancy, 562–563
    social inequalities in health expectancy, 560–562
    spatial comparisons, 555–557
    temporal comparisons within countries, 557–560
  types of health expectancy, 552
    dementia-free life expectancy, 552
    disability-free life expectancy (DFLE), 552
    disease-free life expectancies, 552
Healthy living practices, 3
Heart disease mortality, female, 40
Heart rate, 382
Heritability, 400
Heterogeneity, 50
Highly active anti-retroviral therapy (HAART), 523–524
Hispanic Paradox, 3
  adjusting misclassification of ethnicity, 229
  in adult mortality in US, 227
  age-specific/age-standardized death rates, 230
  background to, 227–228

biological risk profiles, 234–235
convergence to native levels in US, Canada, and Australia, 236
Hispanic neighborhoods, 233–234
migration data from Mexico, 235–236
mortality at young ages, 231–233
recent evidence, 228–229
Salmon Bias hypothesis revisited, 229–231
SES gradient, 231
HIV/AIDS, 502–503, 523–524
change in life expectancy at age 15 due to AIDS, 181
death rates in ages 15–59, 175
by HIV prevalence levels among adults aged 15–49, 175
dynamics of, 174–176
*See also* AIDS mortality, global trends in
estimated and projected prevalence of, 173
incidence rate in population 15–49, 175
life expectancy at age 15 with and without, 180
lower life expectancy due to, 2
countries hit by, 20
mortality, 423–424
prevalence in 2007 among adults aged 15–49, 172
Human Life Table Database, 49
Human Mortality Database, 49, 526–527
Hypertension, 383
Hypertension Detection and Follow-up Program Cooperative Group, 500
"Hypertensive vascular disease," 381
Hypothalamic-Pituitary axis (HPA), 387–388

## I

Ill-defined diseases mortality rates, LAC countries, 120
Immortalists
anti-aging interventions, 576
rejuvenation technologies, 576
Immunity and infection, 386–387
Impairment, 557
Income
individual and family income and income portfolios, 268
inequality, 280–281
and material resources, 268–269
INDEPTH Network, 526
Industrial countries, male life-expectancy trends in, 22
Infant mortality, 424–426
Infectious diseases, 35, 493–498
as cause of death, protection against, 14
pioneers, 14–15
in first stage of health transition, role of, 31
as imprint process, 196–197
mortality rates, LAC countries, 117
as pathway process, 197
role in mortality, 16
Inflammation, 386
Injury mortality, 425, 599
Insulin-like growth factor-1 (IGF-1), 387
"Integrating" functions, 345
INTERHEART, 586
International classification of diseases (ICD), 472–473
analyzing trends across revisions of ICD, 476
automated coding systems, 475–476
bridge-coding studies, 477–478
cause-of-death coding, 474
first five revisions of ICD, 476
multiple cause-of-death coding, 475
selection of underlying cause of death, 474–475
seventh, eighth and ninth revisions of ICD, 476
International studies, 369
Interpolated Markov chain (IMaCH), 554
IRIS, 475
Ischemic heart disease (IHD), 584
Italy
causes of death, changes in life expectancy at age 15, 68
death rates from ages 15 to 100 for 1981–1985/1961–1965, 62

## J

Japan
cerebrovascular diseases, 27
divergence, 21
health transition, following Western countries, 24
homicide, 35
infectious mortality, 35
life expectancy, 2
life expectancy at age 80 in, 44
male standardized death rates
causes (ages 45–64), 38
by external causes at ages 25–44, 36
mortality decline after WWII, 35
mortality from traffic accidents, 35
standardized death rate, 34
suicide, 35
trends in female standardized death rates by causes at ages 80, 44
youth (15–24), mortality among, 29–31
Jews (religious groups), 366
Job-strain model and the hypothesized impact on mortality, 271

## L

Labor relationships and mortality, 279
LAC, adult mortality in, 101–102
absolute change in life expectancy and lagged causes of death, 117
accidents and suicides mortality rates, 120
changes in life expectancies at age 5, 122–124
contribution of causes of death, 117
to increases in life expectancies, 121
trends in mortality by causes of death, 117–121
countries and data sets used in estimation exercise, 106
determinants of mortality trends: 1950–2000, 121–125
decomposition of effects, 126–129
nature of models, 125–126
nature of variables, 125
results, 126
diabetes mortality rates, 119
enumerated to expected population in Chile and Uruguay, 111
estimation during 1900–2000
age misstatement, 104–105
completeness of census enumeration, 103–104
completeness of death registration, 103
methods for adjustment of observed death rates, 105
state of vital statistics in region, 103

LAC, adult mortality in (*cont.*)
  evaluation of estimates, 105
    global assessment: alternative estimates, 105–109
    local assessments: age patterns, 109–114
    mortality trends, 114–117
  female life expectancies
    at age 5, 116
    at age 60, 130
  ill-defined diseases mortality rates, 120
  infectious disease mortality rates, 119
  life expectancy at age 5
    attributable to changes in variables and parameters, 128
    and cause of death, 129
    and socioeconomic determinants, 127
    unmeasured conditions, 127
  life expectation at ages 5 and 60, 107–108
    differences between observed and expected, 110
  mortality at old ages, 129–130
  mortality statistics in, 102–103
  Neoplasm Mortality Rates, 118
  old-age mortality rates in, 112–113
LAC countries, *see* Latin American and the Caribbean (LAC) countries
Land use and urban planning, websites on, 458
Latin American and the Caribbean (LAC) countries, 2
Latter-day Saints (LDS), *see* Mormons (religious groups)
LDC, *see* Less developed countries (LDC)
Leaky mutations, 404
Length of life inequality, 50
Length of life project, database of, 49
Less developed countries (LDC), 1
  expanding diversity among, 17
  individual and family level
    measurement issues, 278–279
    occupations, 277
    work and employment, 276–277
Lexis's distribution of ages at death, 210–213
Lexis's normal life duration, 213
Life-expectancy
  at age 15
    in Europe in 1961–1965 and 1981–1985, 53–54
    male and female trends in European countries since 1950, 57–58
  changes, industrialized world, 21
  conventional *vs.* tempo-adjusted (at age 15), 74
  gains in, 1
  in Russia and United States, by sex, 88
  trajectories, LDCs, 17–18
Life-expectancy at birth, trends in, 9–13
  expanding diversity among LDCs, 17
  female, 14
  first divergence/convergence: pandemic receding, 13–14
  large convergence, 17–18
  LDCs, 11
  MDCs, 11
  in most advanced industrial countries, 25
  new phase of divergence among MDCs, 21
  number of obstacles, 19–20
  role of cardiovascular mortality, 21–24
  second wave of divergence–convergence: cardiovascular revolution, 20–21
  successful MDC story, 14–17
  Third Wave, 24–28
  trends in highest and lowest, 12
Life extension
  language of, 576–577
  pursuing, 572–575
    creation of transcontinental in 1860s, 574
    declaration of war on cancer in 1977, 574
    disease control, 572
    extension of lifespan national goal, 573
    gerontogeny, 575
    Goddard's proposal, 574
    Hayflick's rationale, 572
    manipulation of a "biological clock," 573
    mortality rate doubling time (MRDT), 572
    rate control, 572
    survivorship curves, 573
Life inequality for Adults of European Populations, 1955–2005, 64
Longevity dividend, 577–579
  fivefold, 578
  modern version, 578
  rationale, 578
Lung cancer (males and females), death rates from, 39

**M**
Macroeconomic growth and unemployment, 279–280
Male life-expectancy trends
  in industrial countries, 22
  *vs.* female life expectancy, 25
Man-made diseases, 11
Maternal mortality
  steps in reduction, 31
  trends since 1950, 36
MDC, *see* More developed countries (MDC)
Medical care indicators, 492
Medical care system, 491
Medical Research Council Cognitive Function and Ageing Study, 560
Mediterranean diet, 4, 297, 302
Metabolic syndrome or syndrome X, 390
Metropolitan sprawl, 445
Middle-aged adults (45–64), mortality among, 35–39
  cardiovascular mortality, 37
  lung cancer (males and females), death rates from, 39
  main features, 35
  stomach cancer (males), death rates from, 39
  trends in probability of death from age 45 to 65, 37
Monozygotic (MZ) twins, 401–402
Morbidity and dynamic equilibrium, compression/expansion of absolute/relative compression, 552
More developed countries (MDC)
  individual and family level
    income and related material resources, 275–276
    occupations and occupational status, 273–275
    work and employment, 271–273
  life expectancy at old age, 43
  life expectancy, 2–3
  successful MDC story, 14–17
Mormons (religious groups), 355

Mortality
   patterns, 516
   study of, 1
   varied by regions, 2
Mortality affected by health care and public health policy interventions
   age of delayed cardiovascular disease, 584–589
   alcohol use, 592–595
   avoidable mortality, 595–601
   smoking, 589–592
   the age of delayed degenerative disease, 584
Mortality age pattern models, empirically based, 526–531
   adult and child mortality equation, 527
   Heligman and Pollard model, 529
   Human Mortality Database, 526–527
   INDEPTH Network, 153, 155–156, 526, 528
   uncertainty, 528–529
Mortality crossover, 321
   exploring, 321–324
   gestation and early life, 312–317
Mortality model schedules
   age-specific cohort mortality rates, 512
   death rates by age and sex, 513
   mathematical models of age-specific, 513–515
   model life tables, 515–521
   mortality regimes, 521–525
   new developments in
      frailty and vitality models, theory based, 525–526
      mortality age pattern models, empirically based, 526–531
   regularities in age-specific, 512–513
Mortality rate doubling time (MRDT), 572
Mortality regime models, 521–525
   Coale and Demeny/United Nations life tables, 521
   discrepancies, 521–522
   famine and conflict, 522
   HIV/AIDS, 523
   hybrid or relational model, 522

## N

National Death Index, 5
National Health and Nutrition Examination Surveys (NHANES), 381
National Institute on Aging, 572
National Institutes of Health (NIH), 571, 578
*Natural and Political Observations on the Bills of Mortality*, 208, 211
Natural disasters, 452–455
   deadly, 453
   disasters, distress, and socioeconomic status, 454
   effects on communities, 455
   individual social locations and vulnerability, 453
   preparation and evacuation, 454–455
Natural experiments, 345
Natural hazards, 5
   *See also* Natural disasters
Neighborhood effects on mortality, 413
   assessing relation between, 416–425
   boundaries of neighborhood research on mortality, 428
      conceptualization/measurement of neighborhoods, 431
      measurement, 428
   causal inference, 432–435
      identification of neighborhood effects, 432–433
      separating context from composition, 433–434
   caveats, 414
   effect of neighborhood poverty, 434
   emerging methodologies for estimating causal effects, 435
   empirical evidence, 414–415
      results, 415
      search results, 415
      search strategy, 415
      selection criteria, 414–415
   measuring neighborhoods in health research, 428–429
   mechanisms, 413–414
   neighborhood boundaries and measures, definitions, 429–431
   neighborhood socioeconomic environment and mortality, 415–427
      cross-level interactions, 426
   physical environment, 427–428
   racial composition, 427
      consistency of findings, 427
      cross-level interactions, 427
   social environment, 427
Netherlands, life expectancy, 25–26
Ninth international classification of diseases (ICD9), 491
Norepinephrine, 387
Nutrition
   and diet, 295
      carbohydrates, 296–297
      fat, 295–296
      fruits and vegetables, 296
      special diets, 297
   as imprint process, 195–196
   as pathway process, 196

## O

Obesity, 299–301
   and overweight, 4
   prevalence in adults, 301
Occupational status, 265–268
Occupation scores and overall mortality, 266
Old age (65–79), mortality in, 39–43
   reduction, females, 39–40
   reduction post-WWII, males, 40
   trends in probability of death, 40
Organization for Economic Co-operation and Development (OECD), 518
   tables, 518

## P

Pandemic of mental disorders and disabilities, 28
Pasteur era, 14
*Pathocenosis*, 13
Period life expectancy, 533–534, 538–544
   Bongaarts and Feeney's (BF) model, 541–547
   and cohort life expectancy, relationship between, 544–545
   heterogeneity, 539–541
   impact of the homogeneity assumption, 540
   Lexis diagram comparing conventional *vs.* Bongaarts and Feeney's scenarios of mortality change, 542–543
   tempo effects, 541

Period *vs.* cohort life expectancy
  at birth, 535
  cohort life expectancy, 533, 535–538
    age effects, 537
    cohort influences, 537
    complications, immediate *vs.* delayed influences, 538
    delayed effects on mortality, 537
    extreme conditions, 537
    influences on age-specific mortality rates, 536
    period effects, 537
    theoretical biological aging, 535
    time-specific influences, 536
  comparison of three summary mortality measures, 534
  computation of cohort *vs.* period life expectancy, 534–535
  definitions, 533–535
  interpretations, 535–544
  period and cohort life expectancy, relationship between, 544–545
    analysis of period-cohort correspondence, 545
    empirical and analytical relationships, 544
  period life expectancy, 533–534, 538–544
    BF's delay model, 544
    heterogeneity, 539–541
    impact of the homogeneity assumption, 540
    Lexis diagram comparing conventional *vs.* Bongaarts and Feeney's scenarios of mortality change, 542–543
    tempo effects, 541
  third dimension, cross-sectional cohort mortality indexes, 545–547
    CAL and underlying mortality conditions, 547
    cross-sectional average length of life (CAL), 545–547
Period *vs.* cohort life expectancy at birth, 535
Pestilence and famine, age of, 11
Physical activity, 297–299
Physical environment
  mortality research, 5
  neighborhood, 413
  neighborhood effects on mortality, 427–428
Physical environment, health and mortality consequences of, 442
  built environment, 443–446
    character of, 446–448
    and crime, 450–451
    implications for higher-risk subpopulations, 451–452
    quality of, 448–450
  individual and contextual pathways mediating effects of, 442–443
  mortality risk and physical environment, 441–442
  socially conditioned consequences of environment
    climate change and health, 457
    natural disasters, 452–455
    temperature, 455–457
Physical exposures in childhood and adulthood mortality risks
  infectious diseases as imprint process, 196–197
  infectious diseases as pathway process, 197
  nutrition as imprint process, 195–196
  nutrition as pathway process, 196
Poisoning, 497
Poland
  life-expectancy in, 23
    age-/cause-specific death rates to male, 24

Population attributable risk (PAR), 586
Prevalence discrepancies, 521
Preventable mortality, 492
Primary avoidable mortality (PAM), 501
Public policy and mortality
  immortalists, 575–576
    anti-aging interventions, 576
    rejuvenation technologies, 576
  language of life extension, 576–577
  longevity dividend, 577–579
    fivefold, 578
    modern version, 578
    rationale, 578
  pursuing immortality, 575
  pursuing life extension, 572–575
    creation of transcontinental railroad in 1860s, 574
    declaration of war on cancer in 1977, 574
    disease control, 572
    extension of lifespan national goal, 573
    Goddard's proposal, 574
    Hayflick's rationale, 572
    manipulation of a biological clock, 573
    mortality rate doubling time (MRDT), 572
    rate control, 572
    survivorship curves, 573
Pulse pressure, 383

**Q**

$_{45}q_{15}$, *see* Adult mortality, between age 15 and 59 ($_{45}q_{15}$), probabilities of
Quality adjusted life years (QALYs), 553

**R**

Racial composition, neighborhood effects on mortality, 427–428
Racial residential segregation, 315
The Rauchstrasse, 589
Receding pandemics, age of, 11
Rejuvenation technologies, 576
Religion and adult mortality, 345–374
  all-cause/cause-specific mortality
    by individual differences in religiousness, 357–363
    of specific religious groups, 345–356
  all-cause mortality of distinctive religious groups, 364–367
  differences in all-cause mortality by individual religious observance, 367–369
  measuring religion(s), 372
  mediators, 372
  methods, 346–364
  social regulation of multiple risk factors, 369–370
    gender differences, 371
    mediators and confounders, 370–371
    selection, 371
Residential segregation, 319
Respiratory diseases, role in mortality, 16, 22, 25, 43, 495–497
Russia
  age-/cause-specific death rates to male life-expectancy in, 23
  age-standardized cause-specific death rates ages 25–64, 92–93
  age standardized mortality rates by age and sex, 89
  alcoholism, 22
  causes of death, changes in life expectancy at age 13, 69

circulatory disease mortality, 37
death rates from ages 15 to 100 for 1981–1985/1961–1965, 61
health transition second stage, failure to enter, 35
injury and poisoning deaths, 22
life expectancy at age 20, 90
life expectancy at birth by sex, 84
male standardized death rates
    causes (ages 45–64), 38
male standardized death rates by external causes at ages 25–44, 36
mortality, middle aged adults, 35
mortality from circulatory diseases, 34
Omran's third age, 22
ratio of age-standardized mortality rates by age and sex, 90
standardized death rate, 34
unfavorable mortality trends, adults, 31
youth (15–24), mortality among, 29
Russian mortality patterns, 88–91
  *See also* Soviet Union (former), adult mortality in

## S

Salmon Bias hypothesis revisited, 229–231
Secondary avoidable mortality (SAM), 501
Self-perceived health (SPH), 557
Self-rated health (SRH), 4, 329, 332
    comparability, 335–340
    measure of "true health," 334–335
    mortality, 329–330
    predict mortality, 332–333
    process of evaluation, 330–332
    subjective probability of survival and, 339–340
    subjective probability of survival as predictor of mortality, 337–339
    and subjective survival probabilities as predictors of mortality, 329
    use of different question versions in empirical research, 337
Senegal, $_{45}q_{15}$, 155
Service environment, neighborhood, 413
SES gradient, 231
Seventh-Day Adventists (religious groups), 364
Shape adult mortality risks, 187–189
Smoking, 3, 589–591
    aging agent, 589
    anti-tobacco strategies, 591
        ALARA (as low as reasonably achievable), 591
        campaigns of Nazi Germany, 591
    diseases to be caused by smoking, 590
    lowering uptake of smoking
        advertisements and bans, 592
        clean indoor regulations, 592
        EU legislation, 592
        licensure, 592
        price of tobacco, 592
    lung cancer mortality, 590
    multiplicative interaction of smoking with cholesterol levels and blood pressure, 589
    publicity for Marlboro at Formula 1 races, 593
    quitting, 591
Social environment
    neighborhood, 414
    neighborhood effects on mortality, 426
Social exposures in childhood and adulthood mortality risks, 192
    family environment as imprint process, 192
    family environment as pathway process, 194–195
    socioeconomic environment as imprint process, 192–193
    socioeconomic environment as pathway process, 193–194
Socially conditioned consequences of environment
    climate change and health, 457
    natural disasters, 452–455
    temperature, 455–457
Social regulation of multiple risk factors
    religion and adult mortality, 369–370
        gender differences, 371
        mediators and confounders, 370–371
        selection, 371
Socioeconomic environment
    as imprint process, 192–193
    and mortality, neighborhood, 415–427
    as pathway process, 193–194
Socioeconomic inequalities (SES), 3, 315, 399
South Africa, age pattern of all-cause mortality, 524–525
Soviet Union (former), adult mortality in, 83–84
    causes of death in, 91
    data quality and availability, 86–88
    excess mortality associated with recent Russian mortality patterns, 88–91
    explanations for observed patterns, 91
        alcohol, 94–95
        artifact, 94
        diet and nutrition, 95
        health services, 95
        smoking, 95
        stress and living conditions, 95–96
    historical background, 84–86
    life expectancy at age 20, 87
    life expectancy at birth by sex from 1950–1955 to 2000–2005, 84
    population of countries of FSU in 2008, 85
    probability of survival from age 20–65, 85
Standardized mortality ratios (SMRs), 505
Stomach cancer (males), death rates from, 39
Stress, 442
    and discrimination, 4
Stressors and stress effects over life course, 317–318
    differential exposure to stress, 318–319
    stress and coping, 319–320
Stress-related and manmade concepts, 583
Subjective probability of survival, 337
    as predictor of mortality, 337–339
    and self-rated health, 339–340
Sub-Saharan Africa
    AIDS epidemic, 19
    divergence, types, 19
    health transition, first stage, 19
    obstacles, in life expectancy, 19
    types of trends in female life expectancy, 20
Suicides mortality rates, LAC countries, 120
Sweden, life expectancy at age 20, 90
Sympathetic Nervous System (SNS), 387

## T

Telomere–mortality association, 406–407
Tempo-adjusted life expectancy, 50
    conventional *vs.* (at age 15) for European countries, 75
        females, 72
        males, 73
Tertiary avoidable mortality (TAM), 498
Tobacco use, 291–295
    tobacco use among adults, 293
    *See also* Smoking
Trends in mortality, 9
    different stories for different ages: adult mortality, 28
        mortality among middle-aged adults (45–64), 35–39
        mortality among young adults (25–44): period of reproduction and production, 31–35
        mortality among youth (15–24), 29–31
        mortality at very old ages (80 and above), 43–44
        mortality in old age (65–79), 39–43
    trends in life expectancy at birth, 9–13
        expanding diversity among LDCs, 17
        first divergence/convergence: pandemic receding, 13–14
        large convergence, 17–18
        new phase of divergence among MDCs, 21
        number of obstacles, 19–20
        role of cardiovascular mortality, 21–24
        second wave of divergence–convergence: cardiovascular revolution, 20–21
        successful MDC story, 14–17
        Third Wave, 24–28
Twins
    dizygotic (MZ), 401–402
    monozygotic (MZ), 401–402
    studies of lifespan, 401–402
        twin lifespan, 404
        validity, 402–403

## U

Unemployment, macroeconomic growth and, 279–280
United Nations' five female age patterns of mortality, 519
Uruguay, enumerated to expected population in, 111
USA
    adult mortality, educational attainment
        cause-specific adult mortality, 248
        differences by age and sex, 251–252
        differences by race/ethnicity, 252
        for females, stratified by age and race/ethnicity, 249
        hazard ratios for association between, 247
        for males, stratified by age and race/ethnicity, 250
        patterns of relative risk, 246–247
        risk among adults aged 25–84, 247–251
        stratified by age and sex, 248
    circulatory disease mortality, 37
    Hispanic paradox in adult mortality in, 227
        adjusting for misclassification of ethnicity on death certificates, 229
        background to, 227–228
        biological risk profiles, 234–235
        convergence to native levels in US, Canada, and Australia, 236
        Hispanic neighborhoods, 233–234
        migration data from Mexico, 235–236
        mortality at young ages, 231–233
        recent evidence, 228–229
        Salmon Bias hypothesis revisited, 229–231
        SES gradient, 231
    homicide, 35
    infectious mortality, 35
    life expectancy at age 80 in, 44
    life expectancy at birth by sex, 84
    male standardized death rates
        causes (ages 45–64), 38
    male standardized death rates by external causes at ages 25–44, 36
    standardized death rate, 34
    suicide, 35
    trends in female standardized death rates by causes at ages 80, 44
US national studies, 368
US regional studies, 367

## V

Very old ages (80 and above), mortality at, 43–44
    France, Japan, and United States, 43–44
Vitality models, 523–524

## W

Well-being, 557
WHO Multinational Monitoring of Trends and Determinants in Cardiovascular Disease (MONICA) study, 381
Work, occupation, income, and mortality, 263–264
    aggregate and comparative research
        global labor relationships and mortality, 279
        income inequality, 280–281
        macroeconomic growth and unemployment, 279–280
    causal, reciprocal, and spurious relationships, 269–270
        methodological concerns, 270
    empirical relationships, 264–265
    employment status, 265
    income and material resources, 268–269
    individual and family income and income portfolios, 268
    individual and family level: LDCs
        measurement issues, 278–279
        occupations, 277
        work and employment, 276–277
    individual and family level: MDCs
        income and related material resources, 275–276
        occupations and occupational status, 273–275
        work and employment, 271–273
    job-strain model and the hypothesized impact on mortality, 271
    occupational status, 265–268
    PMR for white aged 15 and older for selected occupations, 267
    relationship between employment status and overall mortality, 265
    relationship between standardized occupation scores and overall mortality, 266

## Y

Young ages, mortality decline at, 18
Youth (15–24), mortality among, 29–31

cause-of-death data, before WWII, 30
France, 29
Japan, 29
male standardized death rates from infectious diseases, 30
Russia, 29
standardized death rates, causes, 31
trends in probability of death, 29
wars, sensitivity, 29
WWI and WWII, 29

## Z

Zimbabwe
changes in 5-year death rates among adults in, 33
female adult mortality estimates, 154
mortality explosion, adults, 31

# International Handbooks of Population

# Volume 2

**Series Editor**

Dudley L. Poston, Jr.
Professor of Sociology, George T. & Gladys H. Abell Professor of Liberal Arts
Director, Asian Studies Program
Texas A&M University
ACAD Bldg. 425B (office)
College Station, Texas 77843-4351, USA

The *International Handbooks of Population* offer up-to-date scholarly summaries and sources of information on the major subject areas and issues of demography and population. Each handbook examines its particular subject area in depth, providing timely, accessible coverage of its full scale and scope, discusses substantive contributions for deeper understanding, and provides reliable guidance on the direction of future developments.

Volumes will explore topics of vital interest: Population Aging, Poverty, Mortality, Family Demography, Migration, Race and Ethnic Demography and more. Each volume will provide a state-of-the-art treatment of its respective area. The series will quickly prove useful to a broad audience including demographers, practitioners and scholars across a range of disciplines.

For further volumes:
http://www.springer.com/series/8111

# International Handbook of Adult Mortality